PRENTICE HALL
LITERATURE

TEACHER'S EDITION • THE AMERICAN EXPERIENCE, VOLUME 1

COMMON CORE EDITION ©

Copyright © 2012 by Pearson Education, Inc., or its affiliates. All Rights Reserved. Printed in the United States of America. This publication is protected by copyright, and permission should be obtained from the publisher prior to any prohibited reproduction, storage in a retrieval system, or transmission in any form or by any means, electronic, mechanical, photocopying, recording, or likewise. For information regarding permission(s), write to Rights Management & Contracts, One Lake Street, Upper Saddle River, New Jersey 07458.

Pearson® and **Prentice Hall®** are trademarks, in the U.S. and/or in other countries, of Pearson Education, Inc., or its affiliates.

"Understanding by Design" is registered as a trademark with the United States Patent and Trademark Office by the Association for Supervision of Curriculum Development (ASCD). ASCD claims exclusive trademark rights in the terms "Understanding by Design" and the abbreviation "UbD".

Pearson Education has incorporated the concepts of the Understanding by Design methodology into this text in consultation with contributing author Grant Wiggins, one of the creators of the Understanding by Design methodology. The Association for Supervision of Curriculum Development (ASCD), publisher of the "Understanding by Design Handbook" co-authored by Grant Wiggins, has not authorized, approved, or sponsored this work and is in no way affiliated with Pearson or its products.

Common Core State Standards: Copyright 2010. National Governors Association Center for Best Practices and Council of Chief State School Officers. All rights reserved.

ISBN-13: 978-0-13-319628-3
ISBN-10: 0-13-319628-3
5 6 7 8 9 10 V011 15 14 13 12

ALWAYS LEARNING   PEARSON

Preparing Students for College and Career

Literature opens minds. It should also open doors to a student's future. *Prentice Hall Literature Common Core Edition* is a comprehensive literacy program that teaches the new standards and helps students become better readers, better writers, and better thinkers so they're better prepared for college, careers, and beyond. You can be confident that what you are teaching meets the Common Core framework.

Common Core in *Prentice Hall Literature*

- Leveled support and scaffolding for understanding increasingly complex texts
- Informational texts across content areas
- Emphasis on writing argumentative, informative/explanatory, and narrative texts
- Critical thinking and higher-order thinking skills presented in instruction
- Traditional and performance-based assessments
- Best-in-class digital resources
- Teacher training to implement the new standards

Builds Better Readers

Prentice Hall Literature provides a scaffolded approach to rigorous instruction, enabling students to build a solid literary foundation that is necessary for success in college and careers.

Exposure to rich literature selections with increasing text complexity across genres builds students' literary and cultural knowledge, so they become comfortable reading different text structures and understanding the elements that appear in the selections.

Leveled Selection Pairs in the Student Edition let you choose the right text without skipping essential skills.

Text Complexity Rubrics guide you in choosing the selection that's appropriate for your students' abilities.

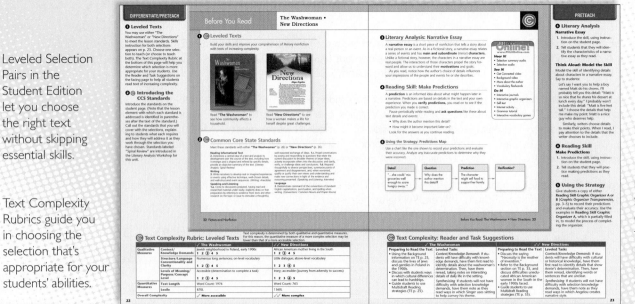

Reader and Task Suggestions offer support to ensure all readers meet achievable challenges.

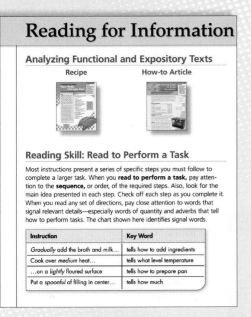

Informational texts provide context for learning and allow for the application of knowledge across science, social studies, and math.

Wide and deep independent readings of increasing complexity challenge learners. Support for reading complex texts is aligned to the Common Core.

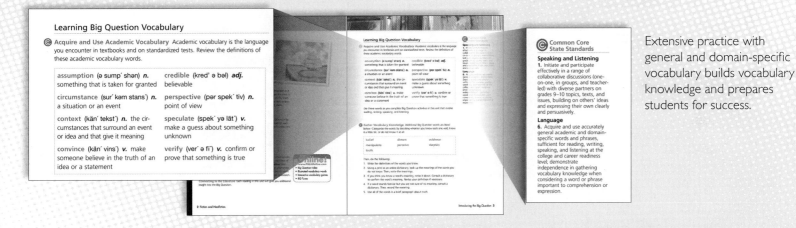

Extensive practice with general and domain-specific vocabulary builds vocabulary knowledge and prepares students for success.

Digital Resources Target Practice with Customized Instruction

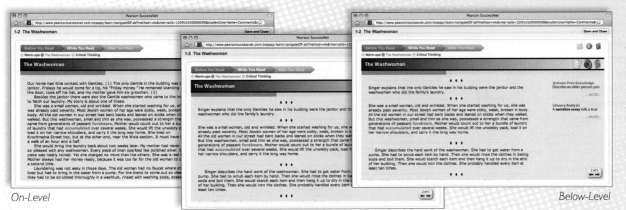

Online instruction instantly responds to students' needs with precise practice and scaffolding. PHLitOnline automatically assigns learner levels based on Diagnostic Test results.

On-Level

English Learner

Below-Level

Better Writers, Better Thinkers

Writing, speaking, and listening are integrated throughout *Prentice Hall Literature* with rigorous, robust skill instruction that takes students to the next level of mastery.

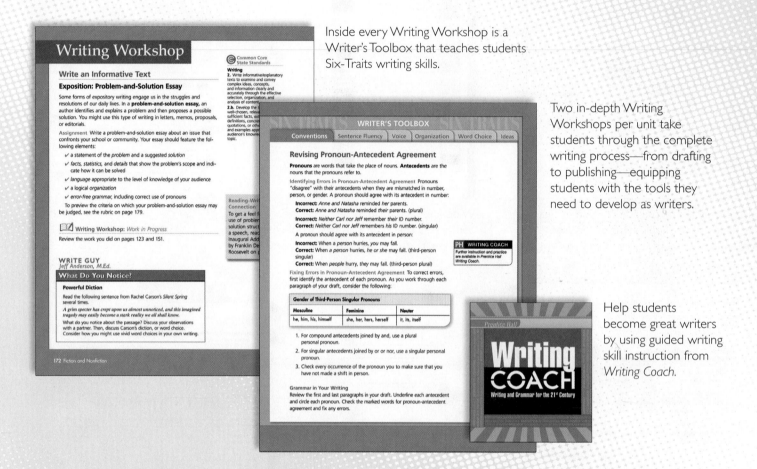

Inside every Writing Workshop is a Writer's Toolbox that teaches students Six-Traits writing skills.

Two in-depth Writing Workshops per unit take students through the complete writing process—from drafting to publishing—equipping students with the tools they need to develop as writers.

Help students become great writers by using guided writing skill instruction from *Writing Coach*.

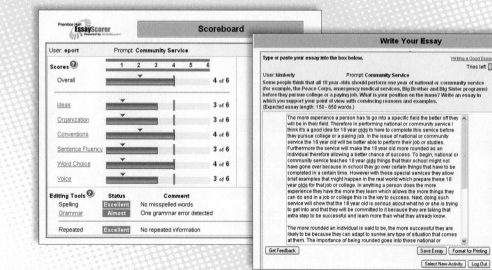

EssayScorer saves you hundreds of hours grading papers by providing students instant feedback on their writing.

Vocabulary Workshop

Using a Dictionary and Thesaurus

Common Core
State Standards

A **dictionary** is a resource that provides different kinds of information to help readers, writers, and speakers use words correctly. Consult a dictionary to find how to pronounce a word, its part of speech, and its history, or etymology. Look at this dictionary entry for the word *poet*.

Language
4.c. Consult general and specialized reference materials both print and digital, to find the pronunciation of a word or determine or clarify its precise meaning, its part of speech, or its etymology.

Dictionary

poet (pō′ət) *n.* [ME < OFr. *poete* < L *poeta* < Gr *poietes*, one who makes, poet < *poiein*, to make: see POEM] **1.** a person who writes poems or verses **2.** a person who displays imaginative power and beauty of thought, language, etc.

The pronunciation uses letters, symbols, and accents to show how the word is pronounced. A key to these letters appears at the bottom of the dictionary page or in the dictionary. The key includes a common word to show how pronounced.

A **thesaurus** is a book of synonyms. Use it to find your meaning and to vary word selection to avoid re

Thesaurus

teaching *n.* teaching, education, schooling, instruction, tuition, coaching, tutoring *v.* teach, educate, instruct, give information, give lessons in, school, edify

Many types of dictionaries can be found in the reference section of your library. Also look for them online and on CD-ROMs and DVDs.

180 Fiction and Nonfiction

Vocabulary and Communications Workshops build essential college and career-ready skills. Practical, valuable applications are used to help students become more fluent in these skills.

SPEAKING AND LISTENING
Communications Workshop

Giving and Following Oral Instructions

Common Core
State Standards

You can give and follow oral directions to perform specific tasks, answer questions, solve problems, and complete processes.

Speaking and Listening
4. Present information, findings, and supporting evidence such that listeners can follow the line of reasoning and the organization, development, and style are appropriate to task, purpose, and audience.

Learn the Skills
Use the strategies to complete the activity on page 185.

Present information. When you give instructions, explain complex processes in easy-to-follow steps. Ask questions to be sure that your audience understands.

Listen attentively. When you follow instructions, listen carefully. Repeat the steps to the instructor to show that you understand. If you are confused, ask the instructor to explain.

Use instructions for different purposes. Give and follow complex oral directions for each of the following purposes. Work with a partner to complete these practice exercises.

- **Perform specific tasks.** Draw a design using only straight lines. Do not let your partner see your drawing. Then, give your partner step-by-step instructions for drawing the design. Finally, compare your drawings to see how well the instructions were given and followed.

- **Answer questions.** Ask your partner how to get from school to a place he or she knows well. Follow your partner's instructions by tracing the route on a map.

- **Solve problems.** Name a problem you face, such as staying organized or managing your time. Ask your partner for instructions that will help you solve this problem. Report back to your partner after you have followed the instructions.

- **Complete processes.** Give instructions for completing a process you have learned in school, such as solving an equation.

182 Fiction and Nonfiction

Speaking and Listening are emphasized to help students develop the career-ready skills they need for life and work.

Critical Thinking

1. **Key Ideas and Details (a)** Which job does the washwoman perform for Singer's family? **(b) Connect:** Which laborious obstacles to doing the job well does Singer describe?

2. **Key Ideas and Details (a)** What prevents the washwoman from returning to the family for several months? **(b) Draw Conclusions:** What does the washwoman's eventual return tell you about her character? Explain.

3. **Craft and Structure (a)** What specific information about the washwoman's personal life does the author include? **(b) Speculate:** What other kinds of information about the washwoman might the author have chosen to include but left out? **(c) Assess:** Based on this essay, explain why an author might choose to include some details and leave others out.

4. **Integration of Knowledge and Ideas (a)** How would you describe the character of the washwoman at the beginning of the story and then at the end? **(b)** How do her relationships grow? *[Connect to the Big Question: Can Truth Change?]*

32 Fiction and Nonfiction

Critical Thinking questions build learning skills by helping students apply their reading.

PERFORMANCE TASKS
Integrated Language Skills

The Washwoman • New Directions

Conventions:
Common Nouns and Proper Nouns

A **common noun** names any one of a class of people, places, or things. A **proper noun** names a specific person, place, or thing and begins with a capital letter.

Type	Common Noun	Proper Noun
person	student	Deana Johnson
place	city	Raleigh-Durham
thing	novel	A Separate Peace

Some nouns can be either common or proper, depending on how they are used. Look at these examples:

My **mom** made us brownies for dessert.
May I please have another brownie, **Mom**?

The **president** must sign a bill before it becomes a law.
The bill was signed by **President** Roosevelt.

Practice A Copy each of the following sentences. Draw one line under each common noun and two lines under each proper noun.

1. "The Washwoman" is a story by Isaac

Practice B Rewrite each of the se replacing one common noun with in each.

1. The woman in the story starte

40 Fiction and Nonfiction

Integrated Language Skills offer full coverage of grammar, writing, speaking and listening, and research.

After You Read
from **The Giant's House • Desiderata**

1. **Key Ideas and Details** How does the **setting** of *The Giant's House* affect James's problem? Explain.

2. **Key Ideas and Details Generalize:** What is McCracken's **main purpose** for writing "Desiderata"? Explain.

3. **Key Ideas and Details** Identify one possible **theme** expressed in the excerpt from *The Giant's House*. Note details from the selection that support your answer.

4. **Key Ideas and Details (a)** Identify the key idea in each paragraph of "Desiderata." **(b)** Consider the relationships among the individual key ideas. Then, write a general statement in which you state the central idea of the entire work.

5. **Craft and Structure (a)** In the excerpt from *The Giant's House*, note two points at which the narrator, Peggy, refers to her training as a librarian. **(b) Analyze:** Do Peggy's efforts for James meet her criteria for being a good librarian? Explain.

6. **Craft and Structure (a)** In "Desiderata," what frustrations does McCracken experience in "meeting" people through family papers? **(b) Speculate:** Based on this essay, why do you think McCracken became a writer of fiction? Explain.

7. **Integration of Knowledge and Ideas (a)** Complete a chart like the one shown to list research sources, including those found on the Internet and in a library, that James could use to learn about his condition today.

Research Question	Possible Source

(b) Collaboration: Discuss your chart with a classmate to identify the most valuable resource.

Every selection is followed by critical thinking questions aligned to the organizational structure of the Common Core Reading Domain.

Ensure Mastery

The new standards require new assessments. *Prentice Hall Literature* provides traditional assessments along with new performance-based assessments as called for by the Common Core. Students are given opportunities to apply critical thinking to demonstrate mastery of the standards.

COMMON CORE
Assessment Workshop: Fiction and Nonfiction

Performance Tasks

Directions: *Follow the instructions to complete the tasks below as required by your teacher.*

As you work on each task, incorporate both general academic vocabulary and literary terms you learned in this unit.

> **Common Core State Standards**
> RL.9-10.2, RL.9-10.3, RL.9-10.5, RL.9-10.6; RI.9-10.2, RI.9-10.4; SL.9-10.4, SL.9-10.5; L.9-10.2
> [For full wording of the standards, see the standards chart in the front of your textbook.]

Writing

Task 1: Literature [RL.9-10.2; L.9-10.2]
Analyze the Development of Theme

Write an essay in which you compare and contrast the themes of two stories in this unit.

- Analyze the development of the theme in each story and discuss similarities and differences in the message each author expresses.
- Note specific strategies each author uses to introduce and develop the theme.
- Discuss specific details that contribute to the development of each theme. Explain what each detail adds.
- To ensure that readers understand your analysis, include an objective summary of each story.
- Capitalize proper nouns, including characters' and authors' names, correctly.

Task 2: Literature [RL.9-10.5]
Analyze the Effects of Structure in a Story

Write an essay in which you explain how the structure of a story in this unit leads to a specific emotional effect, such as tension or suspense.

- Identify the story's main conflict and summarize the narrative.
- Describe specific structural choices the writer makes. For example, discuss how much exposition the author provides and how he or she introduces the conflict. Also describe any use of plot devices, such as foreshadowing.
- Finally, explain how the story affects you as a reader and how the author's choices regarding structure contribute to that effect.
- Cite textual evidence to support your assertions.

Task 3: Informational Text [RI.9-10.2]
Analyze the Development of a Central Idea

Write an essay in which you analyze the development of the central idea in a work of literary nonfiction in this unit.

- Clearly explain the central idea of the work and discuss how it emerges or is introduced by the author.
- Identify specific details that shape and refine the central idea. Consider various types of evidence and explain what each adds to the development of the central idea.
- To ensure that readers understand your analysis, include an objective summary of the work.

Task 4: Informational Text [RI.9-10.6]
Analyze an Author's Purpose and Use of Rhetoric

Write an essay in which you determine an author's purpose and point of view and analyze his or her uses of rhetoric in a work of nonfiction in this unit.

- Explain the topic of the work and determine both the author's general and specific purposes for writing.
- Analyze the author's perspective or point of view on the topic. For example, explain whether the author has a positive or negative perspective or expresses a particular attitude toward the topic.
- Note specific examples of the author's uses of rhetoric. For example, identify examples of parallel structure or repetition. Then, explain how those uses of rhetoric work to advance the author's purpose and point of view.

Speaking and Listening

Task 5: Literature [RL.9-10.3; SL.9-10.4]
Analyze the Development of a Complex Character

Deliver an oral presentation in which you analyze a complex character from a story in this unit.

- Explain why you chose the character. Discuss the traits that make the character complex, or round, and dynamic, rather than static.
- Explain strategies the writer uses to portray the character's complexity. Note specific details that add to the character's portrayal as the story develops.
- Describe how the character's complexity, including his or her emotions, motivations, actions, and reactions, advances the plot and contributes to the story's theme.
- Present your analysis and evidence logically so that listeners can follow your line of reasoning. Make sure your overall approach, including both content and style, is appropriate for a classroom presentation on an academic topic.

Task 6: Literature [RL.9-10.6; SL.9-10.5]
Analyze a Cultural Perspective

Present a visual essay in which you analyze a cultural perspective reflected in a story in this unit.

- A visual essay combines images and text to explain an idea. The visual part of your essay may take the form of a slideshow, poster, or other format.
- Choose a story from this unit that reflects a cultural perspective from outside the United States. Explain how that cultural perspective is reflected in the setting and events as well as in characters' thoughts, emotions, actions, and reactions.

- Using the story as an example, discuss the kinds of factual information a work of fiction can provide. Explain what you learned about another culture by reading this story.
- Share your work with the class in an informal presentation. After you have delivered your presentation, answer questions from classmates.

Task 7: Informational Text [RL.9-10.4; SL.9-10.5]
Analyze the Effect of Word Choice on Tone

Write and present an essay in which you analyze the cumulative effect of word choice on tone in a work of literary nonfiction in this unit.

- Choose a work of literary nonfiction from this unit that offers a clear and distinct tone. Explain your choice.
- Identify specific word choices that contribute to the creation of that tone.
- Illustrate your analysis by creating a graphic organizer or chart that captures your ideas visually.
- Present your essay, including charts or graphic organizers, to the class. Use technology to display graphics, or distribute them as handouts.

> **Can truth change?**
> At the beginning of Unit 1, you participated in a discussion about the Big Question. Now that you have completed the unit, write a response to the question. Discuss how your initial ideas have either changed or been reinforced. Cite specific examples from the literature in this unit, from other subject areas, and from your own life to support your ideas. Use Big Question vocabulary words (see page 3) in your response.

Performance Tasks in the unit Assessment Workshops call for the application of higher-level thinking skills.

Students are assessed across the key Common Core domains of reading, writing, speaking and listening, and language.

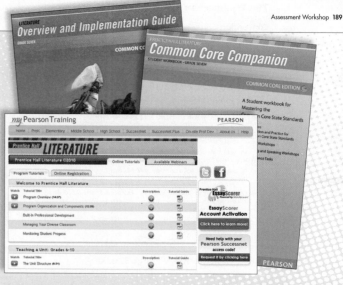

Prentice Hall Literature offers additional resources to ensure a successful implementation.

Cumulative Review

Common Core State Standards

RL.9-10.2, RL.9-10.3, RL.9-10.5; L.9-10.4.a
[For the full wording of the standards, see the standards chart in the front of your textbook.]

I. Reading Literature

Directions: *Read the passage. Then, answer each question that follows.*

I was born in Brooklyn, New York and lived there until I was eleven. I had never really been outside the city. Sure, I had been to Long Island for beach days with my family, but I had never been to the country. My mother got a job Upstate, and suddenly my parents were planning the move. They said that living in the country would be a great experience for all of us, but I was miserable. In August, as we drove the long winding country roads to our new home, I barely said a word.

Many things were lacking in the country. There was no basketball game to pick up. There was no Thai food. There was no skateboarding. There was no sitting on the stoop. Most importantly, there were no old friends. I was so lonely—and bored. It was just my mom, my dad, and me. We were in the middle of nowhere with the closest neighbor over a mile away. Life as I had known it came to an end that August day.

Dad tried to get me to go fishing, but I thought the whole idea was disgusting. Mom tried to get me to walk in the woods, but I didn't like all the bugs, and the brambles scratched my legs. I wanted to go back to Brooklyn in the worst way. All of that would soon change.

I was petrified when I walked into my homeroom. Everyone there knew everyone else, and I did not know anyone. I was set apart from all the other boys by my pale skin and long hair. I sat in the back, and no one said anything to me. The teacher came in and introduced herself.

"Class, we have two new students with us this year." My ears perked up at the word *two*, and I scanned the room for another outsider.

"First, I want to introduce Dave from Brooklyn." The teacher pointed to me. My face flushed as I said "Hi."

"Next, meet Alexis from Washington, D.C."

"Call me Al," she said to the class, looking as lost as I felt.

I had been staring at the back of her head. Her hair was as short as mine was long. I knew immediately that this was not only the year of the Big Move, but it was also the year of the New Best Friend.

1. From which **point of view** is this story told?

  A. first person
  B. second person
  C. third-person limited
  D. third-person omniscient

2. Which element from the passage helped you determine the **point of view**?

  A. The narrator directly addresses his audience, the reader.
  B. The narrator refers to himself as *I* and *me*.
  C. The narrator knows only one person's thoughts.
  D. The narrator has insight into all the people's thoughts.

3. Which word best describes the **author's voice**?

  A. formal
  B. casual
  C. friendly
  D. sarcastic

4. Which of the following sentences is an example of **foreshadowing**?

  A. All of that would soon change.
  B. I had never really been outside of the city.
  C. I wanted to go back to Brooklyn in the worst way.
  D. The teacher pointed to me.

5. Which event occurs during the **rising action** of the narrative?

  A. Dave is born in Brooklyn.
  B. Dave makes a new friend.
  C. Dave's mom gets a job Upstate.
  D. Dave meets Alexis.

6. Which event is the turning point, or **climax,** of the narrative?

  A. Dave moves in August.
  B. Dave wants to move back to Brooklyn.
  C. Dave refuses to go fishing.
  D. Dave hears the teacher say "two."

7. Vocabulary Which word is closest in meaning to the underlined word *petrified*?

  A. angry
  B. terrified
  C. annoyed
  D. disturbed

8. How is the conflict in the story resolved?

  A. Dave makes a new friend in the city.
  B. Dave wants to return to Brooklyn.
  C. Dave's mom does not like her job.
  D. Dave goes fishing with his dad.

9. In what way does the choice of narrator affect the description of the country in paragraph 2?

  A. Life in the country seems frightening.
  B. The country appears to offer lots of fun activities.
  C. Moving to the country sounds like a good idea.
  D. The country seems to lack a lot of things that life in the city has to offer.

⏱ Timed Writing

10. In a well-developed essay, **identify** the conflict in this story. **Explain** how the author of the text establishes the conflict. Cite evidence from the text to support your analysis. [20 minutes]

GO ON →

Traditional Cumulative Review prepares students for high-stakes testing.

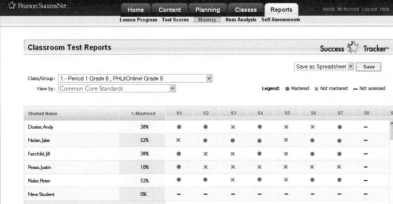

SuccessTracker® includes reporting tools to make progress monitoring easier.

Research Bibliography

▶ Reading and Concept-Driven Instruction

Alexander, Patricia A., and Tamara Jetton. "Learning from Text: A Multidimensional and Developmental Perspective." *Handbook of Reading Research*, vol. 3. Ed. M. L. Kamil, P. B. Mosenthal, P. D. Pearson, and R. Barr, 285–310. Mahwah, NJ: Lawrence Erlbaum Associates, 2000.

Blau, Sheridan. *The Literature Workshop: Teaching Texts and Their Readers*. Portsmouth: Heinemann Press, 2003.

Buehl, Doug, Judith L. Irvin, and Ronald M. Klemp. *Reading and the High School Student: Strategies to Enhance Literacy*. Boston: Allyn and Bacon, 2007.

Buehl, Doug, Judith L. Irvin, and Barbara J. Radcliffe. *Strategies to Enhance Literacy and Learning in Middle School Content Area Classrooms*. Boston: Allyn and Bacon, 2007.

Daniels, Harvey. *Literature Circles: Voice and Choice in Book Clubs and Reading Groups*. Portland: Stenhouse Publishers, 2002.

———*Mini-Lessons for Literature Circles*. Portsmouth: Heinemann Press, 2005.

Gallagher, Kelly. *Reading Reasons: Motivational Mini-Lessons for the Middle and High School*. Portland: Stenhouse Publishers, 2003.

Guthrie, John T. and Allan Wigfield. "Engagement and Motivation in Reading." *Handbook of Reading Research*, vol. 3, eds. M. L. Kamil, P. B. Mosenthal, P. D. Pearson, and R. Barr, 403–422. Mahwah: Lawrence Erlbaum Associates, 2000.

Harvey, Stephanie, and Anne Goudvis. "Determining Importance in Text: The Nonfiction Connection." *Strategies That Work: Teaching Comprehension to Enhance Understanding*. Portland: Stenhouse Publishers, 2000.

Langer, Judith. "Beating the Odds: Teaching Middle and High School Students to Read and Write Well," 1999. Center on English Learning and Achievement. May 2003.<http://cela.albany.edu/eie2/main.html>

National Reading Panel. *Teaching Children to Read: An Evidence-Based Assessment of the Scientific Research on Reading and Its Implications for Reading Instruction*. NIH Publication 00–4769. Bethesda: U.S. Department of Health and Human Services, 2000.

Pressley, Michael. "What Should Comprehension Instruction Be the Instruction Of?" *Handbook of Reading Research*, vol. 3, eds. M. L. Kamil, P. B. Mosenthal, P. D. Pearson, and R. Barr, 545–562. Mahwah: Lawrence Erlbaum Associates, 2000.

Scieszka, Jon. *Guys Write for Guys Read*. New York: Penguin Group, 2005.

Wiggins, Grant P., and Jay McTighe. *Understanding by Design*. Alexandria: Association for Supervision and Curriculum Development, 2006.

▶ Vocabulary, Writing, and Grammar

Anderson, Jeff. *Mechanically Inclined: Building Grammar, Usage, and Style into Writer's Workshop*. Portland: Stenhouse Publishers, 2005.

Baumann, J. F., and E. J. Kame'enui. *Vocabulary Instruction: From Research to Practice*. New York: Guilford Press, 2004.

Blachowicz, Camille, and Peter Fisher. *Teaching Vocabulary in All Classrooms*, Second Edition. Upper Saddle River: Merrill, 2002.

Feber, Jane. *Creative Book Reports: Fun Projects With Rubrics for Fiction and Nonfiction*. Gainesville: Maupin House Publishing, Inc., 2004.

———*Active Word Play*. Gainesville: Maupin House Publishing, Inc., 2008.

Kinsella, Kate. "Strategies to Teach Academic Vocabulary." *Strategies to Promote Academic Literacy for Second Language Learners Within the English Language Arts Classroom*. 2005.

Kinsella, Kate and Kevin Feldman. *Narrowing the Language Gap: The Case for Explicit Vocabulary Instruction*. New York: Scholastic, 2005.

Marzano, Robert J. "The Developing Vision of Vocabulary Instruction." In Baumann and Kame'enui, *Vocabulary Instruction: From Research to Practice*. New York: Guilford Press, 2004.

▶ Differentiated Instruction for Universal Access

Allington, Richard L. *What Really Matters for Struggling Readers: Designing Research Based Programs*. New York: Longman, 2001.

Armbruster, Bonnie, and Thomas H. Anderson. "On Selecting 'Considerate' Content Area Textbooks." *Remedial and Special Education*, 9.1 (1988): 47–52.

Balderrama, María V., and Lynne T. Díaz-Rico. *Teacher Performance Expectations for Educating English Learners*. Boston: Allyn and Bacon, 2006.

Ball, Arnetha F. and Ted Lardner. *African American Literacies Unleashed: Vernacular English and the Composition Classroom*. Carbondale: Southern Illinois University Press, 2005.

Carnie, Douglas, Jerry Silbert, and Edward J. Kame'enui. *Direct Instruction Reading*. 3rd ed. Upper Saddle River: Prentice Hall, 1997.

Deshler, Donald D., Keith B. Lenz, and Brenda R. Kissam. *Teaching Content to All: Evidence-Based Inclusive Practices in Middle and Secondary Schools*. Boston: Allyn and Bacon, 2004.

Francis, David, Mabel Rivera, Nonie Lesaux, Michael Kieffer, and Hector Rivera. *Practical Guidelines for the Education of English Language Learners*. Portsmouth: RMC Research Corporation, Center on Instruction, 2006.

Vaughn, Sharon, Candace S. Bos, and Jeanne Shay Schumm. *Teaching Exceptional, Diverse, and At-Risk Students in the General Education Classroom*. Boston: Allyn and Bacon, 2002.

Pearson Prentice Hall Literature:
A Rich Tradition of Learning Success

▶ The Research Process

Since 1988, *Pearson Prentice Hall Literature* has been at the forefront of language arts instruction, providing teachers and their students with quality instruction and assessment tools to ensure success. Each successive edition builds on the strong heritage of the program. Our research comprised these three design stages:

1. EXPLORATORY NEEDS ASSESSMENT

In conjunction with Pearson Prentice Hall authors, we conducted research proven to explore educational reading methodologies. This research was incorporated into our instructional strategy and pedagogy to create a more effective literature program. This stage included:

- reading research
- review of state standards
- teacher interviews

2. FORMATIVE RESEARCH, DEVELOPMENT, AND FIELD-TESTING

During this phase of the research, we developed and field-tested prototype material with students and teachers. Results informed revisions to the final design and pedagogy. Formative research included:

- field-testing of prototypes in classroom pilots
- classroom observations
- teacher reviews
- supervisor reviews
- educator advisory panels

3. SUMMATIVE RESEARCH AND VALIDATION RESEARCH

Finally, we have conducted and will continue to conduct longer-term research under actual classroom conditions. Research at this phase includes:

- pilot-testing
- prepublication learner verification research
- postpublication validation studies, including validation of test questions
- evaluation of results on standardized tests

Harvey Daniels
Voice and Choice

Excerpts from "Using Leveled Selections" and "Leveled Reading Selections, A Key to Differentiation" by Harvey Daniels

"With leveled texts, all students can understand their selection—and no one is left behind."

Harvey Daniels is known for his passionate work on literacy and student-led book clubs. He is the author of *Literature Circles: Voice and Choice in Book Clubs and Reading Groups* and *Mini-lessons for Literature Circles,* he has been a classroom teacher, writing project director, author, and university professor.

Read the full text of Harvey Daniels's articles at PHLitOnline.

We have all watched it unfold.

You select a wonderful book or article for your class to read. You hand it out to the students and what happens? The text is way too hard for some kids, far too easy for others, and "boring" to still others. Not a good feeling.

Using Leveled Readings.
Happily, research on differentiated instruction shows us a better way: leveled selections. **Prentice Hall Literature** offers two levels of text. All students can understand and enjoy their selection and still learn same required skills—and no one is left behind.

Why are leveled selections so important?

- If we expect kids to grow as readers, they must spend part of each day reading *text they can read.* As the Common Core State Standards put it: "Students need opportunities to stretch their reading abilities but also to experience the satisfaction and pleasure of easy, fluent reading, both of which the Standards allow for."
- A *choice* of texts means that more students will have the background knowledge to understand and enjoy the chosen selection.
- All students need to read increasingly challenging text as the school year unfolds, but every student does not need to read the same texts. As the Common Core standards explain: "Teachers who have had success using particular texts that are easier than those required for a given grade band should feel free to continue to use them, so long as the general movement during a given school year is toward texts of higher levels of complexity."

These are the reasons **Prentice Hall Literature** offers two leveled selections for almost every lesson—one more accessible and one more challenging. Every student can be challenged at his or her own level, from lesson to lesson, throughout the school year.

"When we make accommodations like leveled selections, we often find that such accommodations make learning work better for everyone."

Grant Wiggins
Better Big Questions

Excerpts from "Teaching Literature by Design: Introducing the Big Questions" by Grant Wiggins

> " . . . our methods have to foster that questioning and meaning-making."

Grant Wiggins is the co-author of *Understanding By Design*,* published by ASCD. He is also the president of Authentic Education in Hopewell, New Jersey. He consults with schools, districts, and state education departments on a variety of reform issues. His work has been supported by the Pew Charitable Trusts, the Geraldine R. Dodge Foundation, and the National Science Foundation.

Read the full text of Grant Wiggins's article at PHLitOnline.

*The Association for Supervision of Curriculum Development (ASCD), publisher of the "Understanding by Design Handbook" co-authored by Grant Wiggins and registered owner of the trademark "Understanding by Design," has not authorized, approved, or sponsored this work and is in no way affiliated with Pearson or its products.

A Big Question is different from many of the questions teachers typically ask students in class.

A Big Question is more of a *why?* or a *so what?* question rather than a *what?* or a *where?* question. We are not looking for an answer, really; we are inviting inquiry and reflection. The Big Questions awaken curiosity and thus provide a purpose for reading.

What Makes a Question "Big"?

"Big" connotes "substantial"—occupying a considerable amount of space and time. A question is "big" or "weighty" if it has significant depth and breadth—occupying a good deal of our psychic space, such as our thoughts and feelings. Another aspect of "bigness" is the time it consumes. Vital issues and inquiries remain alive over days, months, and years, unlike simple or superficial queries. Important questions recur over and through time, as we rethink and reflect on our present and past experiences. **Prentice Hall Literature** provides Big Questions that meet the criteria in ways that others do not.

- The questions cannot be answered with a list or a single answer.
- The questions are designed to allow answers to change to accommodate new information or experience.
- The questions are designed to encourage answers that change over time.

Why Ask Big Questions?

The teacher has a different intent when asking a "big" as opposed to an "academic" question. If we want students to end up asking Big Questions on their own, then our courses have to be designed "backward" from that goal. If we want students to learn from their reading, our methods have to foster that questioning and meaning-making.

> " Important questions occur over and through time."

CC 13

Kelly Gallagher
Multidraft Reading

Excerpts from "The Value of Second Draft Reading" and "Powerful, Purposeful Reading" by Kelly Gallagher

> " In our classrooms, we are the 'tour guides.'"

Kelly Gallagher is a full-time English teacher at Magnolia High School in Anaheim, California, where he has taught for twenty-two years. He is the author of several books:

- *Reading Reasons: Motivational Mini-Lessons for the Middle and High School*
- *Deeper Reading: Comprehending Challenging Texts*
- *Teaching Adolescent Writers*
- *Readicide*

Read the full text of Kelly Gallagher's article at PHLitOnline.

Where do adolescents get the idea that they can read complex text one time and get it? More importantly, how can we help our students to understand that much of our deepest thinking comes when we reread? How can we teach our students to recognize the value of second-draft reading?

The Importance of Rereading
The principal strategy that good readers employ when confronted by difficult text is to reread it. If the text is particularly difficult, you might have students read the text first with the sole purpose of monitoring where they were confused. Use the blue dots in the student edition of **Prentice Hall Literature** to help students "chunk" the text into passages with logical pause points to stop, reread, and clarify.

Multi-Lens Reading
Students often read difficult text better when they have been provided a purpose for their reading. In our classrooms, we are the "tour guides." We create student tours by first determining the purpose for each reading. Providing students with a specific purpose gives them a more focused, meaningful reading experience.

Prentice Hall Literature provides the tools for multiple reading purposes.

When students read with a purpose in mind, their anxiety is lowered, their comprehension deepens, and they are given the confidence to approach works they might have otherwise shunned.

> " Providing students with a specific purpose gives them a more focused, meaningful reading experience."

Elfrieda H. Hiebert
What Is Text Complexity?

> " . . . greater focus on text complexity will help . . . prepare students for the increasing demands of required reading in college and the workplace."

Dr. Elfrieda "Freddy" H. Hiebert is the President and CEO of TextProject, Inc. Her model of accessible texts for beginning and struggling readers—TExT—has been used to develop several reading programs. Most recently, Dr. Hiebert served on the Common Core State Standards development team focused on text complexity. Dr. Hiebert has published more than 130 research articles, chapters in edited volumes, and books. In particular, Hiebert's interests lie in how fluency, vocabulary, and knowledge can be fostered through appropriate texts.

The Common Core State Standards cite research that shows that the difficulty of texts used in elementary and secondary classrooms in the United States has decreased over the past 50 years, while the difficulty of college texts has not. As a result, students entering post-secondary education are not prepared for the level of text complexity required to be successful.

To address this issue, the Standards have identified text complexity grade bands (K–1, 2–3, 4–5, 6–8, 9–10, 11–12), in which students read increasingly complex texts within a defined spectrum. Ultimately, greater focus on text complexity will help close the gap that exists between secondary and post-secondary education and prepare students for the increasing demands of required reading in college and the workplace.

The Common Core State Standards identify a three-part model for measuring a text's complexity. This model, as detailed below, includes quantitative and qualitative measures as well as variables of individual readers.

Quantitative Dimensions

Quantitative dimensions are aspects of text complexity that can be measured with traditional readability formulas, such as the Lexile measure. These formulas measure such aspects of a text as word length and frequency, total number of words, average sentence length, and text cohesion.

Qualitative Dimensions

Qualitative dimensions consist of "those aspects of text complexity best measured or only measurable by an attentive human reader." Qualitative measures include categories such as a student's familiarity with a text's structure, levels of meaning, language clarity and conventionality, and knowledge demands, or what the reader needs to know to access the text.

Reader and Task Considerations

Reader and task considerations include an evaluation of student variables, such as the reader's motivation, background knowledge, experience, and cognitive abilities. Evaluating text complexity is best done by the classroom teacher, who brings to bear professional judgments concerning subject matter and individual students.

> " . . . students read increasingly complex texts . . ."

Text Complexity: Building Capacity for All Students

To better gauge a text's difficulty, Dr. Elfrieda Hiebert has created a Text Complexity Multi-Index. In this model, four comprehensive measures and considerations are taken into account to determine a text's appropriateness for a student or group of students.

The four parts of Dr. Hiebert's model expand upon the Common Core State Standards' three-part model for measuring text complexity. A critical component of both models is that qualitative measures and reader-task considerations are balanced with quantitative measures to achieve an overall text complexity recommendation. By measuring text complexity, both quantitative and qualitative, teachers can challenge students to read more complex texts as they move toward college and career readiness.

In Dr. Hiebert's Multi-Index, quantitative measures consist of Overall Text Difficulty and Specifics of Text Difficulty. Qualitative Measures include Themes and Knowledge Demands. Reader and Task in the Common Core aligns with Purpose and Task in Dr. Hiebert's index. These four parts of Dr. Hiebert's Text Complexity Multi-Index are explained below.

Text Complexity Multi-Index

❶ Themes and Knowledge Demands

- The reader's familiarity with the theme of a text and the concept presented must be considered as part of the assessment of text complexity.

- Knowledge demands are based on the background knowledge students need to bring to a given text. Teachers can assess background knowledge through informal classroom discussions.

❷ Specifics of Text Difficulty

- Readability scores are based on quantitative variables, such as average sentence length and overall word frequency.

- Sentence length is determined by averaging the number of words in each sentence in a selection. Formulaically speaking, shorter sentences should mean easier reading. However, teachers must consider conceptual and thematic complexity of a selection to accurately assess a text's difficulty.

- Word frequency refers to how often the same words appear in a text. A low score indicates that the text most likely has words that students may not have encountered. This is especially true when dealing with informational texts that may address unfamiliar content and concepts.

❸ Overall Quantitative Text Difficulty

- Overall quantitative text difficulty can be determined by a readability formula. Frequently used readability formulas include Lexile, Dale-Chall, and Spache.

❹ Purpose and Task

- Purpose and task refer to the why and what of reading—questions such as "Why am I reading this text?" and "What tasks are involved before, during, and after reading to build knowledge?"

- To address purpose and task, teachers use professional judgment to assess reader and task compatibility.

The Text Complexity Rubric in *Prentice Hall Literature*

The following is a sample from the Grade 11, Unit 1 book. The leveled texts "Speech in the Virginia Convention" and "Speech in the Convention" are featured in Unit 1 of this grade level. The leveling of these selections relies on many factors as depicted in the measures outlined here.

Analyze the Qualitative and Quantitative measures to determine the complexity of these texts.

© Text Complexity Rubric

		Speech in the Virginia Convention	Speech in the Convention
①	**Qualitative Measures**		
	Context/ Knowledge Demands	Historical knowledge demands (speech) 1 2 ③ 4 5	Historical knowledge demands (speech) 1 2 ③ 4 5
	Structure/Language Conventionality and Clarity	Eighteenth-century vocabulary; complicated sentence structure 1 2 3 ④ 5	Eighteenth-century vocabulary; complicated sentence structure 1 2 3 ④ 5
	Levels of Meaning/ Purpose/Concept Level	Challenging concept (argues against negotiation in favor of armed rebellion) 1 2 3 ④ 5	Challenging concept (complex reasoning; urges acceptance of Constitution) 1 2 3 ④ 5
②	**Quantitative Measures**		
	Lexile/Text Length	980L / 1,212 words	1490L / 656 words
③	**Overall Complexity**	**More complex**	**More complex**

① Themes and Knowledge Demands

Context/Knowledge Demands: The accessibility of texts is dependent in part on the range of students' experiences and their background knowledge.

Structure/Language Conventionality and Clarity: Conventional and unconventional structures as well as domain-specific language and vocabulary all affect the ability of students to access text.

Levels of Meaning/Purpose/Concept Level: An author's use of either single or multiple levels of meaning impacts the accessibility of a text's concepts.

② Specifics of Text Difficulty

Pearson has provided two quantitative measures of text complexity—text length and Lexile score. Use these measures in tandem with qualitative measures to make informed choices.

③ Overall Quantitative Text Difficulty

Based on the criteria cited above for Themes and Knowledge Demands and Specifics of Text Difficulty, texts can be deemed either more accessible or more complex.

© Text Complexity: Reader and Task Suggestions

	Speech in the Virginia Convention		Speech in the Convention	
④	**Preparing to Read the Text**	**Leveled Tasks**	**Preparing to Read the Text**	**Leveled Tasks**
	• Using the Background information on TE p. 99, discuss Henry as a firebrand in the years before the American Revolution. • Ask students what kind of language they might use to persuade an uncertain audience. • Guide students to use Multidraft Reading strategies (TE p. 99).	*Structure/Language* If students will have difficulty with structure, have them skim the selection, looking for the persuasive questions that Henry asks. As students reread, have them find an answer for each question. *Analyzing* If students will not have difficulty with structure, have them give an example of parallel language. Discuss how the parallelism reinforces Henry's persuasive appeal.	• Using the information on TE pp. 104–105, discuss Franklin's role after the American Revolution. • Ask students how they would prepare if they knew their speech might be historic. • Guide students to use Multidraft Reading strategies to deepen their comprehension (TE p. 99).	*Structure/Language* If students will have difficulty with syntax, guide them in paraphrasing a few sentences. Encourage students to continue paraphrasing as they reread, focusing on what Franklin suggests about the serious nature of this moment in history. *Evaluating* If students will not have difficulty with syntax, ask them if they think that the speech would have been more persuasive (or more historic) had Franklin not voiced his initial doubts.

④ Purpose and Task

Specific pre-reading suggestions are given in "Preparing to Read the Text." These are followed by "Leveled Tasks" that will help you guide students' comprehension as they analyze, synthesize, or evaluate the concept development of selections. Teachers may adapt the leveled tasks, as needed, to suit the needs of their students.

Jim Cummins
Second Language Learning

Excerpts from "The Challenge of Learning Academic English" by Jim Cummins

> **"** Students who gain a sense of control over language will want to use it for powerful purposes. **"**

Jim Cummins's research focuses on literacy development in multilingual school contexts as well as English Language Learners' academic trajectories. He has been a recipient of the International Reading Association's Albert J. Harris award, and has published in *Educational Researcher, International Education Journal, NABE Journal, and TESOL Quarterly.*

Read the full text of Jim Cummins's article at PHLitOnline.

Learning difficulties faced by struggling readers can derive from a variety of sources.
This is true regardless of whether their home language is English or a language other than English. Intervention should address the specific difficulties they are experiencing.

Scaffold Instruction
We can promote literacy engagement among ELL students and struggling readers by using "scaffolds" or supports to make the input more comprehensible (e.g., through graphic organizers, demonstrations, etc.). It is also important to scaffold students' use of language.

Build Background
Effective instruction for ELL students and struggling readers will also activate students' prior knowledge and build background knowledge as needed. Learning can be defined as the integration of new knowledge or skills with the knowledge or skills we already possess. Therefore, it is crucial to activate ELL students' preexisting knowledge so that they can relate new information to what they already know.

Validate Culture
Identity affirmation is also crucial for literacy engagement. Students who feel their culture and identity validated in the classroom are much more likely to engage with literacy than those who perceive their culture and identity ignored or devalued.

Literacy engagement among ELL students and struggling readers also requires that teachers across the curriculum explain how language works and stimulate students' curiosity about language. Students who gain a sense of control over language will want to use it for powerful purposes.

> **"** Students who feel their culture and identity validated in the classroom are much more likely to engage with literacy. . . . **"**

Sharroky Hollie
Culturally Responsive Instruction

Excerpts from "Expanding Academic Home Language" and "Navigating Cultural Discourse Styles" by Sharroky Hollie

Students entering the classroom bring with them a variety of experiences, traditions, interpretive frameworks, and learning styles. Culturally responsive instruction begins when a teacher acknowledges this variety as a positive resource for education. By capitalizing on the student's own resources, a teacher ensures success.

What is Culturally Responsive Instruction?
To make academic progress, a student must build on one success to another. How do we ensure that we are teaching to and through students' personal and cultural strengths and prior accomplishments?

- Build bridges from what students already know or have experienced to new knowledge and skills.
- Create a cooperative learning environment rich in affirmations of students' heritages.
- Build not just on individual strengths, but on the new strength that emerges when individuals join together in a community that respects their diversity.

" By capitalizing on the student's own resources, a teacher ensures success."

Sharroky Hollie is the Executive Director of the Center for Culturally Responsive Teaching and Learning. He is an assistant professor at California State University and a visiting professor at Webster University in St. Louis. His work focuses on African American education and on second language methodology. In addition to his university teaching, Dr. Hollie also teaches professional development courses, and he is the co-founding director of the Culture and Language Academy of Success, an independent charter school in Los Angeles.

Read the complete texts of Sharroky Hollie's articles on PHLitOnline.

Building on Strength
A key premise for culturally responsive pedagogy is that education proceeds from students' strengths and not students' weaknesses. **Prentice Hall Literature** consistently supports culturally responsive instruction with each selection in the anthology. Integrated throughout each lesson plan are the strategies for using what students bring with them into the classroom to enrich learning and foster success.

" . . . education proceeds from students' strengths and not students' weaknesses."

William G. Brozo
Response to Intervention

" Within RTI, the frontline of prevention is Tier 1, or the general education classroom, where every student regardless of ability is to receive high-quality instruction. What's revolutionary about these new standards is that they situate literacy and language development squarely within the content areas....Common core proponents assert that prevailing literacy curriculum needs to shift from a focus on developing reading skills and building fluency with simple narratives toward reading and writing to gain knowledge and express new understandings with informational text."

William G. Brozo, "The Role of Content Literacy in an Effective RTI Program,"
The Reading Teacher, (64)2, pp. 147–150

Donald J. Leu
21st-Century Solutions

" The good news about the Common Core State Standards is that we are going to increasingly support higher-level thinking, reasoning, and comprehension. Locating, evaluating, integrating, and communicating information – all these skills are essential to students' success in the future. We need to help students think in deeper, more complex ways as they read a wider variety of texts, both print and digital."

Karen K. Wixson
The Goal: College and Career Readiness

" The ELA Common Core State Standards are meant to be read as an integrated English Language Arts program beginning with College and Career Readiness Anchor Standards. It is absolutely essential that teachers and administrators look first at the anchor standards, next the appendices, and lastly at the grade-level standards."

Expanded essays by these authors are available at PHLitOnline.com.

Master Teacher Board **v**

Student Edition Pages

Contributing Authors

The contributing authors guided the direction and philosophy of Pearson Prentice Hall Literature. Working with the development team, they helped to build the pedagogical integrity of the program and to ensure its relevance for today's teachers and students.

 **Grant Wiggins, Ed.D.,** is the President of Authentic Education in Hopewell, New Jersey. He earned his Ed.D. from Harvard University and his B.A. from St. John's College in Annapolis. Grant consults with schools, districts, and state education departments on a variety of reform matters; organizes conferences and workshops; and develops print materials and Web resources on curricular change. He is the coauthor, with Jay McTighe, of Understanding by Design and The Understanding by Design Handbook, the award-winning and highly successful materials on curriculum published by ASCD. His work has been supported by the Pew Charitable Trusts, the Geraldine R. Dodge Foundation, and the National Science Foundation. *The Association for Supervision of Curriculum Development (ASCD), publisher of the "Understanding by Design Handbook" co-authored by Grant Wiggins and registered owner of the trademark "Understanding by Design", has not authorized, approved, or sponsored this work and is in no way affiliated with Pearson or its products.*

Jeff Anderson has worked with  struggling writers and readers for almost 20 years. Anderson's specialty is the integration of grammar and editing instruction into the processes of reading and writing. He has published two books, *Mechanically Inclined: Building Grammar, Usage, and Style into Writer's Workshop,* and *Everyday Editing: Inviting Students to Develop Skill and Craft in Writer's Workshop,* as well as a DVD, *The Craft of Grammar.* Anderson's work has appeared in *English Journal.* Anderson won the NCTE Paul and Kate Farmer Award for his *English Journal* article on teaching grammar in context.

Arnetha F. Ball, Ph.D., is a  Professor at Stanford University. Her areas of expertise include language and literacy studies of diverse student populations, research on writing instruction, and teacher preparation for working with diverse populations. She is the author of *African American Literacies Unleashed* with Dr. Ted Lardner, and *Multicultural Strategies for Education and Social Change.*

Sheridan Blau is Professor of Education and English at the University of California, Santa Barbara, where he directs the South Coast Writing Project and the Literature Institute for Teachers. He has served in senior advisory roles for such groups as the National Board for Professional Teaching Standards, the College Board, and the American Board for Teacher Education. Blau served for twenty years on the National Writing Project Advisory Board and Task Force, and is a former president of NCTE. Blau is the author of *The Literature Workshop: Teaching Texts and Their Readers,* which was named by the Conference on English Education as the 2004 Richard Meade Award winner for outstanding research in English education.

 **William G. Brozo, Ph.D.,** is a Professor of Literacy at George Mason University in Fairfax, Virginia. He has taught reading and language arts in junior and senior high school and is the author of numerous texts on literacy development. Dr. Brozo'z work focuses on building capacity among teacher leaders, enriching the literate culture of schools, enhancing the literate lives of boys, and making teaching more responsive to the needs of all students. His recent publications include *Bright Beginnings for Boys: Engaging Young Boys in Active Literacy* and the *Adolescent Literacy Inventory.*

Doug Buehl is a teacher, author, and national literacy consultant. He is the author of *Classroom Strategies for Interactive Learning* and coauthor of *Reading and the High School Student: Strategies to Enhance Literacy;* and *Strategies to Enhance Literacy and Learning in Middle School Content Area Classrooms.*

Jim Cummins, Ph.D, is a professor  in the Modern Language Centre at the University of Toronto. He is the author of numerous publications, including *Negotiating Identities: Education for Empowerment in a Diverse Society.* Cummins coined the acronyms BICS and CAPT to help differentiate the type of language ability students need for success.

Harvey Daniels, Ph.D., has been  a classroom teacher, writing project director, author, and university professor. "Smokey" serves as an international consultant to schools, districts, and educational agencies. He is known for his work on student-led book clubs, as recounted in *Literature Circles: Voice and Choice in Book Clubs & Reading Groups* and *Mini Lessons for Literature Circles.* Recent works include *Subjects Matter: Every Teacher's Guide to Content-Area Reading* and *Content Area Writing: Every Teacher's Guide.*

Student Edition Pages

Jane Feber taught language arts in  Jacksonville, Florida, for 36 years. Her innovative approach to instruction has earned her several awards, including the NMSA Distinguished Educator Award, the NCTE Edwin A. Hoey Award, the Gladys Prior Award for Teaching Excellence, and the Florida Council of Teachers of English Teacher of the Year Award. She is a National Board Certified Teacher, past president of the Florida Council of Teachers of English, and is the author of *Creative Book Reports* and *Active Word Play*.

Danling Fu, Ph.D., is Professor of Language and Culture in the College of Education at the University of Florida. She researches and provides inservice to public schools nationally, focusing on literacy instruction for new immigrant students. Fu's books include *My Trouble is My English* and *An Island of English* addressing English language learners in the secondary schools. She has authored chapters in the *Handbook of Adolescent Literacy Research* and in *Adolescent Literacy: Turning Promise to Practice*.

Kelly Gallagher is a full-time English  teacher at Magnolia High School in Anaheim, California. He is the former co-director of the South Basin Writing Project at California State University, Long Beach. Gallagher wrote *Reading Reasons: Motivational Mini-Lessons for the Middle and High School, Deeper Reading: Comprehending Challenging Texts 4-12*, and *Teaching Adolescent Writers*. Gallagher won the Secondary Award of Classroom Excellence from the California Association of Teachers of English—the state's top English teacher honor.

Sharroky Hollie, Ph.D., is an  assistant professor at California State University, Dominguez Hills, and an urban literacy visiting professor at Webster University, St. Louis. Hollie's work focuses on professional development, African American education, and second language methodology. He is a contributing author in two texts on culturally and linguistically responsive teaching. He is the Executive Director of the Center for Culturally Responsive Teaching and Learning and the co-founding director of the Culture and Language Academy of Success, an independent charter school in Los Angeles.

Dr. Donald J. Leu, Ph.D., teaches  at the University of Connecticut and holds a joint appointment in Curriculum and Instruction and in Educational Psychology. He directs the New Literacies Research Lab and is a member of the Board of Directors of the International Reading Association. Leu studies the skills required to read, write, and learn with Internet technologies. His research has been funded by groups including the U.S. Department of Education, the National Science Foundation, and the Bill & Melinda Gates Foundation.

Jon Scieszka founded GUYS READ, a nonprofit literacy initiative for boys, to call attention to the problem of getting boys connected with reading. In 2008, he was named the first U.S. National Ambassador for Young People's Literature by the Library of Congress. Scieszka taught from first grade to eighth grade for ten years in New York City, drawing inspiration from his students to write *The True Story of the 3 Little Pigs!, The Stinky Cheese Man*, the *Time Warp Trio* series of chapter books, and the *Trucktown* series of books for beginning readers.

Sharon Vaughn, Ph.D., teaches  at the University of Texas at Austin. She is the previous Editor-in-Chief of the *Journal of Learning Disabilities* and the co-editor of *Learning Disabilities Research and Practice*. She is the recipient of the American Education Research Association SIG Award for Outstanding Researcher. Vaughn's work focuses on effective practices for enhancing reading outcomes for students with reading difficulties. She is the author of more than 100 articles, and numerous books designed to improve research-based practices in the classroom.

Karen K. Wixson is Dean of the  School of Education at the University of North Carolina, Greensboro. She has published widely in the areas of literacy curriculum, instruction, and assessment. Wixson has been an advisor to the National Research Council and helped develop the National Assessment of Educational Progress (NAEP) reading tests. She is a past member of the IRA Board of Directors and co-chair of the IRA Commission on RTI. Recently, Wixson served on the English Language Arts Work Team that was part of the Common Core State Standards Initiative.

The selections in this book are presented through the lens of three Essential Questions:

What makes American literature American?

What is the relationship between literature and place?

How does literature shape or reflect society?

Student Edition Pages

Six units explore literature from consecutive periods in American history. Program pacing allows for 3-, 6-, or 9-week intervals.

A Gathering of Voices

Literature of Early America (Beginnings to 1800)

x Contents

✻ INFORMATIONAL TEXT HIGHLIGHTED

Student Edition Pages

PART THREE: **A NATION IS BORN**

Exemplar texts appear throughout the program.

Extended Studies provide in-depth exploration of important authors, genres, or themes in history.

Skills workshops provide practice with key language arts skills.

Student Edition Pages

A Growing Nation
Literature of the American Renaissance (1800 to 1870)

 www.PHLitOnline.com — Interactive resources provide personalized instruction and activities online.

Each unit includes an introduction to the historical context and literature of the period.

Each unit develops literary and reading skills, teaching them to mastery.

Contents **xiii**

A robust mix of literary and informational t provides a wide range of readin

Literary History features presen information ab prominent auth genres, and the within the historical contex of each period.

Reading for Information features in each unit present nonfiction forms such as manuals, newspaper articles, Web sites, and other real-life readings.

xiv Contents

Student Edition Pages

PART FOUR: **AMERICAN MASTERS**

Featured unit authors present professional models of writing strategies.

Division, Reconciliation, and Expansion
Literature of the Civil War and the Frontier (1850 to 1914)

xvi Contents

Vocabulary, Writing, and Grammar activities link to selection content.

PHLit
Online!
www.PHLitOnline.com

Interactive resources provide personalized instruction and activities online.

Contents **xvii**

Assessment Workshops prepare students for questions and formats they will encounter on the SAT and ACT tests.

Disillusion, Defiance, and Discontent

Literature of the Modern Age (1914 to 1945)

Essential Questions drive instruction, shaping selection groupings around critical issues.

Primary Sources documents enhance students' research skills and understanding of literature.

Contents **xix**

PART TWO: **FROM EVERY CORNER OF THE LAND**

ⓒ **Extended Study:** Short Stories

Extended Study features provide in-depth studies of the elements of major genres.

Interactive resources provide personalized instruction and activities online.

Student Edition Pages

PART THREE: **THE HARLEM RENAISSANCE**

Comparing Literary Works features support the study of literary and stylistic elements across selections.

PHLit Online!
www.PHLitOnline.com

All program resources are available online for classroom presentation or individual study.

Interactive resources provide personalized instruction and activities online.

Contents **xxi**

Independent Reading suggestions of opportunities students to re complex texts independently

Student Edition Pages

Prosperity and Protest
Literature of the Post-War Era (1945 to 1970)

> Snapshot of the Period features present historical information graphically.

Contents **xxiii**

World Literature Connections focus on authors, themes, and genres across world cultures.

Performance Tasks, modeled on those in the Common Core framework, enable students to go beyond multiple-choice assessments.

Interactive resources provide personalized instruction and activities online.

www.PHLitOnline.com

Contents **xxv**

New Voices, New Frontiers
Literature of the Contemporary Period (1970 to Present)

© **Multiple Perspectives on the Era**

Student Edition Pages

PART THREE: **CONTEMPORARY NONFICTION**

Primary Sources documents enhance students' research skills and understanding of literature.

Writing Workshops provide instruction to guide students through each step of the writing process.

Literature

▶ Stories

Adventure Stories

Allegories

Graphic Novels

Humor/Satire

Myths

Realistic Fiction

Science Fiction/Fantasy/Gothic

▶ Drama

Multi-Act Plays

Screenplays

▶ Poetry

Ballads

Student Edition Pages

Contents **xxix**

Informational Text—Literary Nonfiction

Contents **xxxi**

Student Edition Pages

Informational Text—Literary Nonfiction

▶ Historical and Literary Background

▶ The American Experience— Reading in the Humanities

▶ Literature in Context—Reading in the Content Areas

▶ Literary History

▶ World Literature Connections

▶ Writing Workshops

▶ Vocabulary Workshops

▶ Test-Taking Practice

▶ Communications Workshops

Contents **xxxv**

Introductory Unit

Common Core
State Standards

Reading Literature 2, 10
Reading Informational Text 2, 4, 5, 6, 8
Writing 1.a, 1.b, 1.e, 9, 9.b
Language 6

xlvii

Building Academic Vocabulary

Academic vocabulary is the language used in school, on standardized tests, and—often—in the business world. Academic terms are more formal and specific than the informal vocabulary most people use among friends and family members. Success in school and later in work requires a clear understanding of different types of academic language. The Common Core State Standards require that you acquire and use grade-appropriate academic words and phrases.

Technical Domain-Specific Academic Vocabulary The literary concepts you will learn throughout this book are one type of academic language. These words are specific to the content area—the subject or discipline—of literature. Other disciplines, such as social studies, the sciences, mathematics, and the arts, have their own academic vocabularies. Some content-area words cross disciplines, or have different meanings when applied to different areas of study.

Technical words are an even more specialized type of domain-specific academic vocabulary. These are words and phrases, such as the following, that identify a precise element in the content area and usually do not appear in other disciplines:

Science: pipette; genome
Music: clef; libretto

Critical Reading and Thinking Terms Many academic terms define modes of thinking, discussing, or writing about ideas. In this book, these words appear in the Critical Reading questions at the ends of the selections. Such academic terms also appear in instructions and writing prompts.

A Note on Etymology

Etymology is the branch of linguistics that deals with word origins and the development of languages. Etymologists trace the history of a word in its own language, and then to even earlier sources in other, more ancient languages. Knowledge of a word's etymology will contribute to your understanding of its meaning and help you determine the meaning of other words that share its history. Etymological information for content-area words appears in the charts on the following pages.

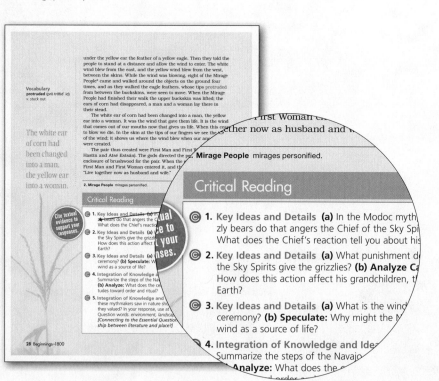

xlviii Building Academic Vocabulary

Student Edition Pages

Technical Domain-Specific Academic Vocabulary

Knowledge of technical content-area academic words, and the roots and affixes that compose them, will help you in all of your school courses. As you review the charts below, recognize words that apply to content areas other than those specified here.

Technical Domain-Specific Academic Vocabulary: Science

Term	Meaning	Root/Affix
Accelerate	v. increase speed	Latin root -celer- = swift Words with the same root: accelerator n.; celerity n.
Catalyst	n. something that acts to bring about a result	Latin root -cata- = down; away Words with the same root: cataclysm n.; catapult n.
Chlorophyll	n. green pigment found in plant cells	Greek root -chloro- = green Words with the same root: chlorine n.; chlorosis n.
Chromosome	n. strand of proteins that carries the genes of a living creature	Greek prefix chromo- = color; pigment Words with the same prefix: chromatic adj.; chromate n.
Cytoplasm	n. colorless substance of a cell; outside the nucleus	Greek suffix -plasm = molded; formed Words with the same suffix: bioplasm n.; protoplasm n.
Entropy	n. lack of order that increases over time in a system	Greek root -tropos- = turning; deviation Words with the same root: tropical adj.; trophy n.; heliotrope n.
Enzyme	n. chemical substance produced by living cells that causes changes in other chemicals	Greek suffix -zyme = leavening (an agent that causes fermentation) Words with the same suffix: vitazyme n.; microzyme n.
Mitosis	n. method of cell division	Greek suffix -osis = action; process Words with the same suffix: prognosis n.; psychosis n.
Thermometer	n. instrument for measuring temperature	Greek root -therme- = hot Words with the same root: thermonuclear adj.; thermostat n.
Viscous	adj. having a thick and sticky fluid consistency	Latin prefix visco- = sticky Words with the same prefix: viscometer n.; viscosity n.

Ordinary Language: Ice cubes placed in water will begin to **break down**.

Academic Language: Ice cubes placed in water will begin the process of **entropy**.

Exploring Academic Vocabulary: Science

The word *thermometer* combines the Greek roots -*therme*-, which means "heat," and -*metr*-, which means "measure." Using this knowledge, determine the meaning of the following words derived from the same roots:

dynameter   **odometer**   **hypothermia**   **thermography**

Then, use a dictionary to confirm the definitions you proposed. If a general dictionary is not sufficient, consult a specialized science dictionary to find the information you need. Explain how the meaning of each word relates to those of its Greek origins.

Technical Domain-Specific Academic Vocabulary: Mathematics

Term	Meaning	Root/Affix
Correlate	*v.* show mutual relationship between items	Latin prefix *cor-* = together; with Words with the same prefix: correspond *v.*; corrosion *n.*
Exponent	*n.* symbol placed above and to the right of a number or letter to show how many times that quantity is to be multiplied by itself	Latin suffix *-ponent* = to put; place; set Words with the same suffix: component *n.*; proponent *n.*
Inflection	*n.* change of a curve or arc from convex to concave or the reverse	Latin root *-flectere-* = to bend Words with the same root: reflection *n.*; deflect *v.*
Logarithm	*n.* power to which a base must be raised to produce a given number	Greek prefix *logos-* = word; speech; reason Words with the same prefix: logic *n.*; logotype *n.*
Statistics	*n.* numerical facts or data	Latin root *-stat-* = condition; position; state Words with the same root: statistical *adj.*; static *adj.*
Permutation	*n.* one of the ways in which a set of things can be arranged or ordered	Latin root *-mutare-* = change Words with the same root: mutable *adj.*; mutation *n.*
Estimate	*v.* calculate approximately	Middle French root *-estimer-* = value; appraise Words with the same root: estimation *n.*; esteem *v.*
Graphic	*adj.* relating to the use of diagrams, graphs, curves	Greek root *-graph-* = writing; drawing Words with the same root: telegraph *n.*; biography *n.*; autograph *n.*
Configure	*v.* construct; arrange	Latin root *-figura-* = shape; form; figure Words with the same root: disfigure *v.*; effigy *n.*

Ordinary Language: We arranged the **numerical information** in different charts.

Academic Language: We incorporated **statistical data** into charts.

Exploring Academic Vocabulary: Mathematics

The word *correlate* is built on the Latin prefix *cor-* (also *com-* or *con-*), which means "with" or "together." Using this knowledge, determine the meaning of the following words derived from the same prefix:

correspond   **concert**   **compress**   **congruent**

Then, use an online or print dictionary to confirm the definitions you proposed. Explain how the meaning of each word relates to that of its Latin ancestor.

| Building Academic Vocabulary

Technical Domain-Specific Academic Vocabulary: Social Studies

Term	Meaning	Root/Affix
Corporation	*n.* organization of many people authorized to act as a single person	Latin root -*corpus*- = body Words with the same root: corporeal *adj.*; incorporate *v.*
Demography	*n.* study of human populations	Greek prefix *demos*- = people Words with the same prefix: demographic *n.*; democracy *n.*
Economy	*n.* system by which a country's money and goods are used and produced	Greek suffix -*nomy* = law; received knowledge Words with the same suffix: economy *n.*; taxonomy *n.*
Invest	*v.* give money to a company in order to receive a profit	Latin root -*vestire*- = dress; clothe Words with the same root: vestment *n.*; investigation *n.*
Admiral	*n.* high-ranking Naval officer	Arabic root -*amir*- = leader Words with the same root: emirate *n.*; admiralship *n.*
Curfew	*n.* law requiring a population to stay indoors at a stated hour	Old French root -*covrir*- = to cover Words with the same root: covert *adj.*; coverlet *n.*
Lieutenant	*n.* someone who substitutes for another person of greater authority	Old French root -*lieu*- = place Word with the same root: milieu *n.*
Absolutism	*n.* system of government in which a ruler has unlimited power	Latin prefix *ab*- = away; from Words with the same prefix: absolve *v.*
Civic	*adj.* of a city, citizens, or citizenship	Latin root -*civ*- = citizen Words with the same root: civilian *n.*; civilization *n.*

Ordinary Language:
The government urges citizens to **put money into** local businesses.

Academic Language:
The government urges citizens to **invest in** local businesses.

Exploring Academic Vocabulary: Social Studies

The word *economy* is built on the Greek suffix –*nomy*, which means "law; body of received knowledge." Using this knowledge, determine the meaning of the following words derived from the same suffix:

taxonomy   **autonomy**   **astronomy**   **gastronomy**

Then, use an online or print dictionary to confirm the definitions you proposed. Explain how the meaning of each word relates to that of its Greek ancestor.

Technical Domain-Specific Academic Vocabulary: Technology

Term	Meaning	Root/Affix
Gigabyte	*n.* unit of storage capacity in a computer system, equal to 1,073,741,824 bytes	Greek prefix *giga-* = giant Words with the same prefix: gigahertz *n.*; gigantic *adj.*
Macro	*n.* single computer instruction that represents a sequence of operations	Greek prefix *macro-* = long, tall, deep, large Words with the same prefix: macrobiotic *adj.*; macrocosm *n.*
Pixel	*n.* smallest unit of an image on a television or computer screen	Old French suffix *-el* = small one Words with the same suffix: satchel *n.*; model *n.*
Processor	*n.* central part of a computer that does the calculations needed to deal with the information it is given	from Latin root *-cedere-* = to go Words with the same root: proceed *v.*; recede *v.*
Simulation	*n.* situation that produces conditions that are not real but appear real	Latin root *-sim-* = like derived through Indo-European base *sem-/som-* = same; as one Words with the same root: ensemble *v.*; simultaneous *adj.*
Streaming	*n.* method of transmitting data so that it can be delivered and received in a steady stream	German root *-strom-* = current; river Words with the same root: mainstream *n.*; streamline *v.*
Transmitter	*n.* equipment that sends out radio or television signals	Latin prefix *trans-* = across Words with the same prefix: transportation *n.*; transcontinental *adj.*
Debug	*v.* find and correct defects	Latin prefix *de-* = down; from Words with the same prefix: defuse *v.*; defrost *v.*
Export	*v.* in computers, to save data in a format usable by another program	Latin root *-portare-* = to carry Words with the same root: import *v.*; airport *n.*
Binary	*adj.* made up of two parts or things; twofold	Latin root *-bin-* = together; double Words with the same root: binocular *n.*; binomial *n.*

> **Ordinary Language:**
> I asked the technician to **remove the defects from** my computer.
>
> **Academic Language:**
> I asked the technician to **debug** my operating system.

Exploring Academic Vocabulary: Technology

The word *simulation* comes from the Latin root *-sim-,* which means "like." This Latin root derives from the Indo-European base *sem-/som-,* which means "same; as one." Using your knowledge of these origins, determine the meaning of the following words derived from the same roots:

resemble   **facsimile**   **verisimilitude**   **semblance**

Then, use a dictionary to confirm the definitions you proposed. Explain how the meaning of each word relates to that of its Indo-European base.

Technical Domain-Specific Academic Vocabulary: The Arts

Term	Meaning	Root/Affix
Allegro	*adv.* faster than allegretto but not so fast as presto	Latin root *-alacer-/-alacris-* = lively; brisk Words with the same root: allegretto *adj.*; *adv.*; alacrity *n.*
Alignment	*n.* arrangement in a straight line	Old French root *-lignier-* = to line Words with the same root: align *v.*; realign *v.*
Craftmanship	*n.* skill used in making handmade objects	Middle English suffix *-schipe*; derived through Anglian suffix *-scip* = state; condition; quality Words with the same suffix: friendship *n.*; dictatorship *n.*
Decrescendo	*n.* gradual decrease in volume	Old French *creissant*; derived through Latin root *-crescere-* = come forth; spring up; grow; thrive Words with the same root: crescent *n.*; increase *v.*
Baritone	*n.* male singing voice lower than a tenor and higher than a bass	Latin root *-tonus-* = sound; tone Words with the same root: monotone *n.*; intonation *n.*
Medium	*n.* material or technique used in art	Latin root *-medius-* = middle Words with the same root: media *n.*; mediate *v.*; median *adj.*
Musicality	*n.* sensitivity to, knowledge of, or talent for music	Latin suffix *-ity* = quality; state; degree Words with the same suffix: normality *n.*; publicity *n.*
Technique	*n.* method or procedure in rendering an artistic work	Indo-European prefix *tek-* = shape; make Words with the same prefix: technical *adj.*; technician *n.*
Tempo	*n.* speed at which a composition is performed	Latin root *-tempus-* = time Words with the same root: temporal *adj.*; temporary *adj.*

> **Ordinary Language:**
> The dancers moved in a perfectly **straight line.**
>
> **Academic Language:**
> The dancers moved in perfect **alignment** on stage.

Exploring Academic Vocabulary: The Arts

The word *craftsmanship* is built on the Anglian suffix *-scip*, which means "state, condition, quality." Using this knowledge, determine the meaning of the following words derived from the same suffix:

musicianship   readership   friendship   partnership

Then, use an online or print dictionary to confirm the definitions you proposed. Explain how the meaning of each word relates to that of its Anglian ancestor.

Vocabulary Across Content Areas

You might recognize words that apply to content areas other than those specified in the charts on the previous pages. For example, notice how the word *accelerator* relates to two different content areas:

Science: accelerator *n.* nerve or muscle that speeds up a body function

Automotive Technology: accelerator *n.* device, such as the foot throttle of an automobile, for increasing the speed of a machine.

While the objects referred to in each definition are different, both of their functions relate to the Latin root *-celer-,* meaning "swift." As you read texts for school, recognize similarities in roots or affixes among words in different content areas. This will help you better understand specific terms and make meaningful connections among topics.

Academic Vocabulary: Critical Thinking Terms

Throughout this book, you will encounter academic vocabulary related to the process of critical thinking. Unlike content-area vocabulary, these words apply equally in all school studies. Being familiar with these academic vocabulary words will be useful as you approach high-stakes standardized tests such as the SAT and ACT. Academic vocabulary will also aid you as you encounter business materials in the workplace.

Term (verb form)	Meaning	Root/Affix
Advocate	Speak or write in support of	Latin root *-voc-* = speak; call Related words: advocate *n.*; advocacy *n.*
Anticipate	Prepare for or signal something	Latin prefix *ante-* = before Related words: anticipatory *adj.*; anticipation *n.*
Arrange	Put into order or sequence	Old French root *-rang-* = rank Related words: arrangement *n.*
Assess	Determine importance, size, or value	Latin root *-sed-/-sess-* = sit Related words: assessment *n.*
Categorize	Place in related groups	Greek prefix *kata-/cata-* = down; against Related words: category *n.*; categorical *adj.*
Compare	Examine in order to discover similarities	Latin root *-par-* = equal Related words: comparison *n.*; comparable *adj.*
Conclude	Determine through logical reasoning	Latin root *-clud-* = shut Related words: conclusion *n.*; conclusive *adj.*
Contrast	Examine in order to discover differences	Latin prefix *con-/com-* = with; together Related words: contrastable *adj.*
Debate	Discuss opposing reasons; argue	French root *-batre-* = to beat Related words: debatable *adj.*
Deduce	Infer from a general principle	Latin root *-duc-* = to lead Related words: deduction *n.*; deductive *adj.*
Defend	Maintain or support in the face of argument	Latin root *-fend-* = to strike; push Related words: defense *n.*; defendant *n.*

liv Building Academic Vocabulary

Term (verb form)	Meaning	Root/Affix
Describe	Represent in words	Latin root -scrib- = to write Related words: description n.; descriptive adj.
Design	Create; fashion or construct according to plan	Latin root -sign- = to mark Related words: design n.; designer n.
Devise	Form in the mind by new combinations of ideas; invent	Latin root -vid- = to separate Related words: devisable adj.
Differentiate	Recognize a difference	Latin suffix -ate = act Related words: different adj.; differentiation n.
Evaluate	Determine significance, worth, or condition through careful study	Old French root -val- = worth; value Related words: evaluation n.; evaluative adj.
Format	Arrange according to a design or plan	Latin root -form- = form, shape Related words: format n.; formation n.
Generalize	Draw a larger principle from details	Latin root -genus- = stock; kind Related words: generalization n.
Hypothesize	Develop a theory about	Greek prefix hypo- = under, beneath Related words: hypothesis n.; hypothetically adv.
Illustrate	Give examples that support an idea	Latin root -lus- = brighten; illuminate Related words: illustration n.; illustrative adj.
Interpret	Explain the meaning of	Latin root -inter- = between Related words: interpretation n.; interpreter n.
Investigate	Make a systematic examination	French root -vestige- = mark; trace; sign Related words: investigation n.; investigative adj.
Paraphrase	Express in one's own words what another person has said or written	Greek prefix para- = beside Related words: paraphraser n.
Predict	Foretell on the basis of observation, experience, or reason	Latin root -dic- = speak, tell, say Related words: prediction n.; predictable adj.
Refute	Prove an argument or statement false or wrong	Latin root -fut- = beat Related words: refutable adj.; refutably adv.
Sort	Put in place according to kind, class, or nature	Old French root -sortir- = allot; assort Related words: sorter n.
Speculate	Use evidence to guess what might happen	Latin root -spec- = look at; view Related words: speculation n.; speculative adj.
Structure	Create a general plot or outline	Latin root -struct- = to build; assemble Related words: structure n.; structural adj.
Validate	Prove to be factual or effective	Latin root -val- = be strong Related words: valid adj.; validity n.

Ordinary Language:
She **explained the meaning of** the story's symbols.

Academic Language:
She **interpreted** the meaning of the story's symbols.

Building Academic Vocabulary **lv**

Writing an Objective Summary

The ability to write objective summaries is important in college course work and in many careers, such as journalism, business, law, and research work. Writing an effective objective summary involves recording the key ideas of a text as well as demonstrating your understanding.

Characteristics of an Objective Summary

An effective objective summary is a concise overview of a text. Following are important elements of an objective summary:

- It is **focused,** relaying the main theme or central idea of a text. It includes specific, relevant details that support that theme or central idea, and it leaves out unnecessary supporting details.

- It is **brief,** although the writer must be careful to balance brevity and thoroughness and not misrepresent the text by eliminating important parts.

- It is **accurate** and captures the essence of the longer text it is describing.

- It is **objective.** The writer should refrain from inserting his or her own opinions, reactions, or personal reflections into the summary.

Remember that an objective summary is *not* a collection of sentences or paragraphs copied from the original source. It is *not* a long retelling of every event, detail, or point in the original text. Finally, a good summary does *not* include evaluative comments, such as the reader's overall opinion of or reaction to the selection.

Checklist for Writing an Objective Summary

Before writing an objective summary, be sure you are well acquainted with the text.

- **Understand the entire passage.** You must clearly understand the text's meaning, including any advanced or technical terminology. In your summary, refer to details from the beginning, middle, and end of the text.

- **Prioritize ideas and details.** Determine the main or central ideas of a text and identify the key supporting details. Make sure you recognize which details are less important so that you do not include them in your objective summary.

- **Identify the author's audience and purpose.** Knowing what the author intended to accomplish in the text as well as what audience it was designed to reach will help you summarize accurately.

lvi Introductory Unit

Common Core
State Standards

Reading Informational Text
2. Determine two or more central ideas of a text and analyze their development over the course of the text, including how they interact and build on one another to provide a complex analysis; provide an objective summary of the text.

Reading Literature
2. Determine two or more themes or central ideas of a text and analyze their development over the course of the text, including how they interact and build on one another to produce a complex account; provide an objective summary of the text.

Student Edition Pages

INFORMATIONAL TEXT

Model Objective Summary

Note the key elements of an effective objective summary, called out in the sidenotes. Then, write an objective summary of a text you have recently read. Review your summary, and delete any unnecessary details, opinions, or evaluations.

Summary of "The Open Window"

"The Open Window," by Saki, ~~the pen name of H.H. Munro~~, is a short story about a nervous man by the name of Framton Nuttel. Set in rural England during the Victorian-Edwardian period, the story tells of a visit that Mr. Nuttel makes to a neighboring estate.

Mr. Framton Nuttel, who has been ordered by his physicians to rest and avoid excitement, has gone to the country for a "nerve cure." His sister has given him letters of introduction to various acquaintances of hers. Framton reluctantly takes his sister's suggestion and calls on the Sappletons.

When Framton arrives at the Sappleton estate, he is met by Mrs. Sappleton's fifteen-year-old niece, Vera. ~~She is quite a character.~~ Vera points to an open window and relates a tragic tale. She tells Framton that exactly three years ago, Mr. Sappleton, Mrs. Sappleton's two younger brothers, and their spaniel went out to hunt, leaving through that very window, and met their death in the bog. Their bodies have never been recovered. The niece explains that her aunt keeps the window open because she expects her husband and brothers to return some day.

Soon thereafter, Mrs. Sappleton enters the room and begins to speak of the hunters. Alarmed, Framton tries to change the topic. He rambles on about his health, noticing that Mrs. Sappleton keeps glancing out of the open window. Suddenly, Mrs. Sappleton exclaims, "Here they are at last!" Framton sees a look of horror in Vera's eyes. Then he turns and sees the figures of three men and a dog approaching. He frantically gathers his belongings and runs away.

As Mr. Sappleton enters through the window, he greets his wife and inquires about the man he spotted running away. Mrs. Sappleton responds that Framton Nuttel was a strange man who dashed off as if he had seen a ghost.

Then Vera mentions that Mr. Nuttel was most likely frightened by the dog. She says that he confided in her that he was once terrified by a pack of wild dogs.

The story ends with this sentence: "Romance at short notice was her specialty."

Eliminate unnecessary details.

A one-sentence synopsis highlighting the theme or central idea of the story can be an effective start to a summary.

This sentence states the writer's opinion and should not be included in an objective summary.

Relating the development of the text in chronological order makes a summary easy to follow.

The writer quotes the final sentence of the story because it is the key to understanding the plot.

Comprehending Complex Texts

Common Core State Standards

Reading Literature 10. By the end of grade 11, read and comprehend literature, including stories, dramas, and poems, in the grades 11-CCR text complexity band proficiently, with scaffolding as needed at the high end of the range.

During the final years of high school, you will be required to read increasingly complex texts in preparation for college and the workplace. A complex text features one or more of the following qualities:

- challenging vocabulary
- long, complex sentences
- figurative language
- multiple levels of meaning
- unfamiliar settings and situations

The selections in this textbook provide you with a range of readings in many genres. Some of these texts will fall within your comfort zone, but others will be, and should be, more challenging. In order to comprehend and interpret complex texts, practice the reading strategies described here.

Strategy 1: Multi-draft Reading

Good readers develop the habit of rereading texts in order to comprehend them completely. To fully understand a text, try this multi-draft reading strategy:

1st Reading

The first time you read a text, read to gain its basic meaning. If you are reading a narrative text, look for the basics of the plot: what is happening, and to whom. If the text is nonfiction, look for central ideas and key supporting details. If you are reading poetry, read first to get a sense of who the speaker is. Also take note of the setting and situation.

2nd Reading

During your second reading of a text, focus on the artistry or effectiveness of the writing. Also take note of text structures and organizational patterns. Think about why the author made those choices and the effects they created. Then, examine the author's creative uses of language and the effects of that language. For example, has the author used rhyme, figurative language, or words with negative connotations? If so, to what effect?

3rd Reading

After your third reading, compare and contrast the text with others of its kind you have read. For example, you might compare poems from a certain time period or compare poems written by a single author. Evaluate the text's overall effectiveness and its central idea or theme.

Independent Practice

As you read this sonnet by William Shakespeare, practice the multi-draft reading strategy by completing a chart like the one below.

Sonnet 27

Weary with toil, I haste me to my bed,

The dear repose for limbs with travel tired;

But then begins a journey in my head

To work my mind, when body's work's expired:

For then my thoughts—from far where I abide—

Intend a zealous pilgrimage to thee,

And keep my drooping eyelids open wide,

Looking on darkness which the blind do see:

Save that my soul's imaginary sight

Presents thy shadow to my sightless view,

Which, like a jewel hung in ghastly night,

Makes black night beauteous, and her old face new.

 Lo! thus, by day my limbs, by night my mind,

 For thee, and for myself, no quiet find.

Multi-Draft Reading Chart

	My Understanding
1st Reading Look for key ideas and details that unlock basic meaning.	
2nd Reading Read for deeper meanings. Look for ways in which the author used text structures and language to create effects.	
3rd Reading Read to integrate your knowledge and ideas. Connect the text to others of its kind and to your own experience.	

Strategy 2: Close Read the Text

Complex texts require close reading, a careful analysis of word choices, phrases, and sentences. An awareness of literary techniques and elements, such as allusion, symbolism, analogy, and text structure, contributes to a deep understanding of a complex text. However, a starting point for close reading is comprehension, which is the foundation for interpretation and analysis. Use the following tips to comprehend the text:

<table>
<tr><td>

Tips for Close Reading

1. Break down long sentences into parts. Look for the subject of the sentence and its verb. Then identify which parts of the sentence modify, or give more information about, its subject.

</td></tr>
<tr><td>

2. Reread passages. When reading complex texts, be sure to reread passages to confirm that you understand their meaning.

</td></tr>
<tr><td>

3. Look for context clues. There are several types of context clues, such as the following:

   a. Restatement of an idea. For example, in the example sentence, "to help . . . understand" restates the verb *clarify*.

     The sportscaster tried to **clarify** the offsides violation <u>to help</u> the spectators <u>understand</u> the referee's call.

   b. Definition of sophisticated words. In this sentence, the words *goes beyond* define the verb *transcends*.

     The watercolor painting **transcends,** or <u>goes beyond</u>, the expectations of the viewers.

   c. Examples of concepts and topics.

     The menu listed <u>green beans, corn, and okra</u> as side dishes.

   d. Contrasts of ideas and topics. In the following sentence, the examples help you understand the meaning of *claustrophobia*.

     Adam is **claustrophobic;** he is <u>terrified of elevators</u> and <u>cannot tolerate being cooped up in small spaces.</u>

</td></tr>
<tr><td>

4. Identify pronoun antecedents. If long sentences contain pronouns, reread the text to make sure you know to what the pronouns refer. The pronoun *its* in the following sentence refers to Yosemite National Park, not to the U.S. government.

Yosemite National Park was set aside by the U.S. government for people to enjoy for **its** natural beauty.

</td></tr>
<tr><td>

5. Look for conjunctions, such as *and, or, yet,* and *however,* to understand relationships between ideas.

</td></tr>
<tr><td>

6. Paraphrase, or restate in your own words, passages of difficult text in order to check your understanding. Remember that a paraphrase is essentially a word-for-word restatement of an original text; it is not a summary.

</td></tr>
</table>

Common Core State Standards

Reading Informational Text
4. Determine the meaning of words and phrases as they are used in a text, including figurative, connotative, and technical meanings; analyze how an author uses and refines the meaning of a key term or terms over the course of a text (e.g., how Madison defines *faction* in *Federalist* No. 10).

INFORMATIONAL TEXT

Close-Read Model

As you read this document, take note of the sidenotes that model ways to unlock meaning in the text.

from "The Perils of Indifference" by Elie Weisel

What is indifference? Etymologically, the word means "no difference." A strange and unnatural state in which the lines blur between light and darkness, dusk and dawn, crime and punishment, cruelty and compassion, good and evil.

> This list of contrasts helps you to know that "compassion" is the opposite of "cruelty."

What are its courses and inescapable consequences? Is it a philosophy? Is there a philosophy of indifference conceivable? Can one possibly view indifference as a virtue? Is it necessary at times to practice it simply to keep one's sanity, live normally, enjoy a fine meal and a glass of wine, as the world around us experiences harrowing upheavals?

> Look for antecedents. The abstract noun *indifference* is referred to by the pronouns *its* and *it*.

Of course, indifference can be tempting—more than that, seductive. It is so much easier to look away from victims. It is so much easier to avoid such rude interruptions to our work, our dreams, our hopes. It is, after all, awkward, troublesome, to be involved in another person's pain and despair. Yet, for the person who is indifferent, his or her neighbors are of no consequence. And, therefore, their lives are meaningless. Their hidden or even visible anguish is of no interest. Indifference reduces the other to an abstraction. . . .

> Search for context clues. The words in blue are context clues that help you infer the meaning of the word that appears in yellow.

In a way, to be indifferent to that suffering is what makes the human being inhuman. Indifference, after all, is more dangerous than anger and hatred. Anger can at times be creative. One writes a great poem, a great symphony, one does something special for the sake of humanity because one is angry at the injustice that one witnesses. But indifference is never creative. Even hatred at times may elicit a response. You fight it. You denounce it. You disarm it. Indifference elicits no response. Indifference is not a response.

> Break down this long sentence into parts. The text highlighted in yellow conveys the basic meaning of the sentence. The text highlighted in blue provides additional information.

Indifference is not a beginning, it is an end. And, therefore, indifference is always the friend of the enemy, for it benefits the aggressor—never his victim, whose pain is magnified when he or she feels forgotten. The political prisoner in his cell, the hungry children, the homeless refugees—not to respond to their plight, not to relieve their solitude by offering them a spark of hope is to exile them from human memory. And in denying their humanity we betray our own.

> The examples highlighted in pink help you understand that the word *plight* means "bad situation."

Indifference, then, is not only a sin, it is a punishment. And this is one of the most important lessons of this outgoing century's wide-ranging experiments in good and evil. . . .

Comprehending Complex Texts **lxi**

Strategy 3: Ask Questions

Be an attentive reader by asking questions as you read. Throughout this text, we have provided questions for you following each selection. Those questions are sorted into three basic categories that build in sophistication and lead you to a deeper understanding of the texts you read. Here is an example from this text:

Some questions are about **Key Ideas and Details** in the text. To answer these questions, you will need to locate and cite explicit information in the text or draw inferences from what you have read.

Some questions are about **Craft and Structure** in the text. To answer these questions, you will need to analyze how the author developed and structured the text. You will also look for ways in which the author artfully used language and how those word choices impacted the meaning and tone of the work.

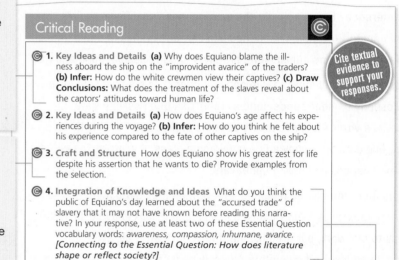

Critical Reading

1. **Key Ideas and Details (a)** Why does Equiano blame the illness aboard the ship on the "improvident avarice" of the traders? **(b) Infer:** How do the white crewmen view their captives? **(c) Draw Conclusions:** What does the treatment of the slaves reveal about the captors' attitudes toward human life?

2. **Key Ideas and Details (a)** How does Equiano's age affect his experiences during the voyage? **(b) Infer:** How do you think he felt about his experience compared to the fate of other captives on the ship?

3. **Craft and Structure** How does Equiano show his great zest for life despite his assertion that he wants to die? Provide examples from the selection.

4. **Integration of Knowledge and Ideas** What do you think the public of Equiano's day learned about the "accursed trade" of slavery that it may not have known before reading this narrative? In your response, use at least two of these Essential Question vocabulary words: *awareness, compassion, inhumane, avarice.* *[Connecting to the Essential Question: How does literature shape or reflect society?]*

Cite textual evidence to support your responses.

Some questions are about the **Integration of Knowledge and Ideas** in the text. These questions ask you to evaluate a text in many different ways, such as comparing texts, analyzing arguments in the text, and using many other methods of thinking critically about a text's ideas.

Preparing to Read Complex Texts

Reading for College and Career In both college and the workplace, readers must analyze texts independently, draw connections among works that offer varied perspectives, and develop their own ideas and informed opinions. The questions shown below, and others that you generate on your own, will help you more effectively read and analyze complex college-level texts.

Common Core State Standards

Reading Literature/Informational Text
10. By the end of grade 11, read and comprehend literature, including stories, dramas, and poems, and literary nonfiction, in the grades 11-CCR text complexity band proficiently, with scaffolding as needed at the high end of the range.

When reading analytically, ask yourself...

- What idea, experience, or story seems to have compelled the author to write? Has the author presented that idea, experience, or story in a way that I, too, find compelling?
- How might the author's era, social status, belief system, or personal experiences have affected the point of view he or she expresses in the text?
- How do my circumstances affect what I understand and feel about this text?
- What key idea does the author state explicitly? What key idea does he or she suggest or imply? Which details in the text help me to perceive implied ideas?
- Do I find multiple layers of meaning in the text? If so, what relationships do I see among these layers of meaning?
- Do I find the text believable and convincing? Why or why not?

Key Ideas and Details

- What patterns of organization or sequences do I find in the text? Do these patterns help me understand the ideas better? If so, how?
- What do I notice about the author's style, including his or her diction, uses of imagery and figurative language, and syntax?

As you read independently, ask similar types of questions to ensure that you fully enjoy and comprehend texts you read for school and for pleasure. Look for and use the sets of questions provided for Independent Reading at the end of each unit.

© EXEMPLAR TEXT

Model

Following is an example of a complex text. The call-out boxes show sample questions that an attentive reader might ask while reading.

Sample questions:

from *1776* by David McCullough

On January 14, two weeks into the new year, George Washington wrote one of the most forlorn, despairing letters of his life. He had been suffering sleepless nights in the big house by the Charles. "The reflection upon my situation and that of this army produces many an uneasy hour when all around me are wrapped in sleep," he told the absent Joseph Reed. "Few people know the predicament we are in."

Filling page after page, he enumerated the same troubles and woes he had been reporting persistently to Congress for so long, and that he would report still again to John Hancock that same day. There was too little powder, still no money. . . . So many of the troops had given up and gone home had, against orders, carried off muskets that were not their own that the supply of arms was depleted to the point where there were not enough for the new recruits.

Key Ideas and Details What central idea is revealed in this passage?

Craft and Structure Why does David McCullough use a direct quotation? What image does Washington create with the words "wrapped in sleep"?

Integration of Knowledge and Ideas What insight does this passage give you about Washington as a general? What insight do you gain about the Revolutionary War?

INFORMATIONAL TEXT

Independent Practice

Write three to five questions you might ask yourself as you read this passage from a speech delivered by James Bryant Conant, president of Harvard University, in 1940.

from "What Are We Arming to Defend?" by James Bryant Conant

. . . The history of this republic has been unique. And the uniqueness of our way of life rests not so much on constitutional democracy as on our social system—a system which is the embodiment of the golden mean of which I speak. I believe that fundamentally it is this unique form of society that we are really arming to defend. I believe that the ambition of every thoughtful citizen of this republic is to assist in keeping inviolate the free way of life which has developed on this continent in the last two hundred years.

. . . Let me examine for a moment the phrase "social mobility," for this is the heart of my argument. If large numbers of young people can develop their own capacities irrespective of the economic status of their parents, then social mobility is high. . . . Such is the American ideal.

Comprehending Complex Texts **lxiii**

Analyzing Arguments

The ability to evaluate an argument, as well as to make one, is a critical skill for success in college and in the workplace.

What Is an Argument?

An *argument* is a presentation of a controversial or debatable issue. In a formal, written argument, the writer logically supports a particular belief, conclusion, or point of view. A good argument is supported with sufficient and valid reasoning and evidence.

Purposes of Argument

There are three main purposes for writing a formal argument:

- to change the reader's mind about an issue
- to convince the reader to accept what is written
- to motivate the reader to take action, based on what is written

Elements of Argument

Claim (assertion)—what the writer is trying to prove
Example: Students should wear uniforms to public high schools.

Grounds (evidence)—the support used to convince the reader
Example: Students will focus less on what they and others are wearing and more on learning.

Justification—the link between the grounds and the claim; why the grounds are credible
Example: The purpose of school is to learn.

Evaluating Claims

When reading or listening to an argument, critically assess the claims that are made. Analyze the argument to identify claims that are based on fact or that can be proved true. Also evaluate evidence that supports the claims. If there is little or no reasoning or evidence provided to support the claims, the argument may not be sound or valid.

Analyzing and Evaluating Structures

As you read an argument, look for ways in which the writer uses structures. For example, the organizational structure, or order in which the writer presents claims and evidence, focuses and shapes the argument. Stylistic structural choices such as repetition and parallel structure can lend emotional power to an argument. Evaluate whether those structures strengthen or detract from the argument's effectiveness.

Student Edition Pages

Common Core
State Standards

Language 6. Acquire and use accurately general academic and domain-specific words and phrases, sufficient for reading, writing, speaking, and listening at the college and career readiness level; demonstrate independence in gathering vocabulary knowledge when considering a word or phrase important to comprehension or expression.
Reading Informational Text
5. Analyze and evaluate the effectiveness of the structure an author uses in his or her exposition or argument, including whether the structure makes points clear, convincing, and engaging.
6. Determine an author's point of view or purpose in a text in which the rhetoric is particularly effective, analyzing how style and content contribute to the power, persuasiveness, or beauty of the text.

Model Argument

from *The American Forests* by John Muir

The forests of America, however slighted by man, must have been a great delight to God; for they were the best he ever planted. The whole continent was a garden, and from the beginning it seemed to be favored above all the other wild parks and gardens of the globe . . .

. . . In the settlement and civilization of the country, bread more than timber or beauty was wanted; and in the blindness of hunger, the early settlers . . . regarded God's trees as only a larger kind of pernicious weeds, extremely hard to get rid of. Accordingly, with no eye to the future, these pious destroyers waged interminable forest wars; chips flew thick and fast; trees in their beauty fell crashing by millions, smashed to confusion, and the smoke of their burning has been rising to heaven more than two hundred years. . . . Thence still westward the invading horde of destroyers called settlers made its fiery way over the broad Rocky Mountains, felling and burning more fiercely than ever, until at last it has reached the wild side of the continent, and entered the last of the great aboriginal forests on the shores of the Pacific . . . Clearing has surely now gone far enough; soon timber will be scarce, and not a grove will be left to rest in or pray in. . . .

Every other civilized nation in the world has been compelled to care for its forests, and so must we if waste and destruction are not to go on to the bitter end . . .

[T]he forest plays an important part in human progress, and that the advance in civilization only makes it more indispensable . . . But the state woodlands are not allowed to lie idle. On the contrary, they are made to produce as much timber as is possible without spoiling them. In the administration of its forests, the state righteously considers itself bound to treat them as a trust for the nation as a whole, and to keep in view the common good of the people for all time . . .

Notwithstanding all the waste and use which have been going on unchecked like a storm for more than two centuries, it is not yet too late, though it is high time, for the government to begin a rational administration of its forests. . . .

In their natural condition, or under wise management, keeping out destructive sheep, preventing fires, selecting the trees that should be cut for lumber, and preserving the young ones and the shrubs and sod of herbaceous vegetation, these forests would be a never failing fountain of wealth and beauty . . .

The outcries we hear against forest reservations come mostly from thieves who are wealthy and steal timber by wholesale. They have so long been allowed to steal and destroy in peace that any impediment to forest robbery is denounced as a cruel and irreligious interference with "vested rights" . . .

The introduction shows Muir's fondness for the forests of America.

As evidence, Muir describes the millions of trees that have been destroyed over the past 200 years.

Muir draws the logical conclusion for the audience that the trees will be gone if they continue to be cut down at the current rate.

Muir cites other civilized nations' actions as evidence that we must do the same.

Justification: Sustainable and productive forests are a national resource kept for the common good of the people.

Claim: It is time for the governments to begin a rational administration of the forests.

The opposition is addressed and refuted.

The Art of Argument: Rhetorical Devices and Persuasive Techniques

Rhetorical Devices

Rhetoric is the art of using language in order to make a point or to persuade listeners. Rhetorical devices such as the ones listed below are accepted elements of argument. Their use does not invalidate or weaken an argument. Rather, the use of rhetorical devices is regarded as a key part of an effective argument.

Examples of Rhetorical Devices	
Repetition The repeated use of certain words, phrases, or sentences	We are compelled to fight the **injustice** of low wages, the **injustice** of long hours, and the **injustice** of child labor.
Parallelism The repeated use of similar grammatical structures	Children should spend their time **playing active games, reading good books,** and **writing imaginative stories.**
Rhetorical Question Calling attention to the issue by implying an obvious answer	Aren't all people created equal?
Sound Devices The use of alliteration, assonance, rhyme, or rhythm	The savage settlers sowed only the seeds of greed to replace the trees they destroyed.
Simile and Metaphor Comparing two seemingly unlike things or asserting that one thing *is* another	Is **America** a **melting pot** or a **tossed salad**?

Persuasive Techniques

Persuasive techniques are often found in advertisements and in other forms of informal persuasion. Although techniques like the ones below are sometimes found in formal arguments, they should not be regarded as valid evidence.

Persuasive Techniques	
Bandwagon Approach/Anti-Bandwagon Approach Appeals to a person's desire to belong; Encourages or celebrates individuality	Our clothes are as unique as you are.
Emotional Appeal Evokes people's fear, anger, or desire	Soon, all you will see will be strip malls and parking lots.
Endorsement/Testimony Employs a well-known person to promote a product or idea	"I support this just cause. You should too!"
Loaded Language The use of words that are charged with emotion	The child laborers are slaves; their childhoods are owned by the factories.
"Plain Folks" Appeal Shows a connection to everyday, ordinary people	"My parents immigrated to this great land and started a new life."
Hyperbole Exaggerates to make a point	All the money in the world wouldn't solve the problem.

INFORMATIONAL TEXT

Model Speech

The excerpted speech below includes examples of rhetorical devices and persuasive techniques.

from *Strike Against War* by Helen Keller

. . . I think the workers are the most unselfish of the children of men; they toil and live and die for other people's country, other people's sentiments, other people's liberties and other people's happiness! The workers have no liberties of their own; they are not free when they are compelled to work twelve or ten or eight hours a day. They are not free when they are ill paid for their exhausting toil. They are not free when their children must labor in mines, mills and factories or starve, and when their women may be driven by poverty to lives of shame. They are not free when they are clubbed and imprisoned because they go on strike for a raise of wages and for the elemental justice that is their right as human beings . . .

As civilization has grown more complex the workers have become more and more enslaved, until today they are little more than parts of the machines they operate. Daily they face the dangers of railroad, bridge, skyscraper, freight train, stokehold, stockyard, lumber raft and mine. Panting and training at the docks, on the railroads and underground and on the seas, they move the traffic and pass from land to land the precious commodities that make it possible for us to live. And what is their reward? A scanty wage, often poverty, rents, taxes, tributes and war indemnities . . .

It is your duty to insist upon still more radical measure. It is your business to see that no child is employed in an industrial establishment or mine or store, and that no worker is needlessly exposed to accident or disease. It is your business to make them give you clean cities, free from smoke, dirt and congestion. It is your business to make them pay you a living wage. It is your business to see that this kind of preparedness is carried into every department on the nation, until everyone has a chance to be well born, well nourished, rightly educated, intelligent and serviceable to the country at all times.

Strike against all ordinances and laws and institutions that continue the slaughter of peace and the butcheries of war. Strike against war, for without you no battles can be fought. Strike against manufacturing shrapnel and gas bombs and all other tools of murder. Strike against preparedness that means death and misery to millions of human being. Be not dumb, obedient slaves in an army of destruction. Be heroes in an army of construction.

Helen Keller uses parallelism to emphasize her point.

The continued use of repetition gives the speech rhythm and emphasizes her points.

The metaphor compares the workers to the machine parts.

The alliteration gives variety to the speech.

Helen Keller answers the rhetorical question to drive home the irony of the word *reward*.

The continued parallelism and repetition shows the increasing passion of her argument.

The repetition in the conclusion calls the audience to action; Keller is now using commands.

The emotional appeal and loaded words add intensity to the argument.

Analyzing Legal Meanings and Reasoning

Reading historical and legal texts requires careful analysis of both the vocabulary and the logical flow of ideas that support a conclusion.

Understanding Legal Meanings

The language of historical and legal documents is formal, precise, and technical. Many words in these texts have specific meanings that you need to understand in order to follow the flow of ideas. For example, the first amendment to the U.S. Constitution states that "Congress shall make no law respecting an establishment of religion, or prohibiting the free exercise thereof; or abridging the freedom of speech, or of the press...." To understand this amendment, it is important to know that in this context *exercise* means "practice," *abridging* means "limiting," and *press* means "media." To understand legal meanings:

- Use your knowledge of word roots to help you understand unfamiliar words. Many legal terms use familiar Greek or Latin roots, prefixes, or suffixes.

- Don't assume that you know a word's legal meaning: use a dictionary to check the meanings of key words to ensure that you are applying the correct meaning.

- Replace difficult words with synonyms to help you follow the logic of the argument.

Delineating Legal Reasoning

Works of public advocacy, such as court decisions, political proclamations, proposed laws, and constitutional amendments, use careful reasoning to support conclusions. These strategies can help outline the basic meanings of these texts:

- State the **purpose** of the document in your own words to help you focus on the writer's primary goal.

- Look for the line of reasoning that supports the **arguments** presented. To be valid and persuasive, key arguments should be backed up by clearly stated logical analysis. Be aware of persuasive techniques, such as citing facts and statistics, referring to expert testimonials, and using emotional language with strong connotations.

- Identify the **premises,** or evidence, upon which a decision rests. In legal texts, premises often include **precedents,** which are earlier examples that must be followed or else specifically overturned. Legal reasoning is usually based on the decisions of earlier trials. Be sure you understand precedents in order to identify how the court arrived at the current decision.

Writing about Legal Meanings

After reading the selection on the next page, write a detailed analysis of the meanings of the words *waive* and *waiver* in the *Miranda v. Arizona* decision. Explain the definitions of the terms as they are used in this context and provide an example that illustrates a situation in which a suspect "waives effectuation" of the rights outlined by this Supreme Court decision.

lxviii Introductory Unit

Common Core State Standards

Reading Informational Text

4. Determine the meaning of words and phrases as they are used in a text, including figurative, connotative, and technical meanings; analyze how an author uses and refines the meaning of a key term or terms over the course of a text.

8. Delineate and evaluate the reasoning in seminal U.S. texts, including the application of constitutional principles and use of legal reasoning and the premises, purposes, and arguments in works of public advocacy.

Writing

9. Draw evidence from literary or informational texts to support analysis, reflection, and research.

9.b. Apply grades 11–12 Reading standards to literary nonfiction.

INFORMATIONAL TEXT

Model Court Decision

Note the strategies used to evaluate legal meanings and reasoning in this Supreme Court decision from 1966 regarding the rights of criminal suspects. The court addressed the admissibility of information obtained by police.

from *Miranda v. Arizona,* Opinion of the Supreme Court

We dealt with certain phases of this problem recently in *Escobedo v. Illinois.* There . . . law enforcement officials took the defendant into custody and interrogated him in a police station for the purpose of obtaining a confession. The police did not effectively advise him of his right to remain silent or of his right to consult with his attorney. Rather, they confronted him with an alleged accomplice who accused him of having perpetrated a murder. When the defendant denied the accusation . . . they handcuffed him and took him to an interrogation room. There, while handcuffed and standing, he was questioned for four hours until he confessed. During this interrogation, the police denied his request to speak to his attorney, and they prevented his retained attorney, who had come to the police station, from consulting with him. At his trial, the State, over his objection, introduced the confession against him. We held that the statements thus made were constitutionally inadmissible. . . .

> The court cites and describes a **precedent**—an earlier court decision in which a suspect's confession was found inadmissible.

. . . Our holding will be spelled out with some specificity in the pages which follow, but, briefly stated, it is this: the prosecution may not use statements, whether exculpatory or inculpatory, stemming from custodial interrogation of the defendant unless it demonstrates the use of procedural safeguards effective to secure the privilege against self-incrimination. By custodial interrogation, we mean questioning initiated by law enforcement officers after a person has been taken into custody or otherwise deprived of his freedom of action in any significant way. As for the procedural safeguards to be employed, unless other fully effective means are devised to inform accused persons of their right of silence and to assure a continuous opportunity to exercise it, the following measures are required. Prior to any questioning, the person must be warned that he has a right to remain silent, that any statement he does make may be used as evidence against him, and that he has a right to the presence of an attorney, either retained or appointed. The defendant may waive effectuation of these rights, provided the waiver is made voluntarily, knowingly and intelligently. If, however, he indicates in any manner and at any stage of the process that he wishes to consult with an attorney before speaking, there can be no questioning. Likewise, if the individual is alone and indicates in any manner that he does not wish to be interrogated, the police may not question him. The mere fact that he may have answered some questions or volunteered some statements on his own does not deprive him of the right to refrain from answering any further inquiries until he has consulted with an attorney and thereafter consents to be questioned.

> The word root *culp-* means "guilt," as in *culpable.* Context and prefixes combine to show that *exculpatory* means "proving innocence" and *inculpatory* means "proving guilt."

> The **purpose** of the decision is stated: to guarantee that a suspect's statements are made in accordance with the rights granted by the U.S. Constitution. This **argument** is detailed and supported in the court decision. The context of the argument is the case summarized in the first paragraph.

Analyzing Legal Meanings and Reasoning **lxix**

Composing an Argument

Choosing a Topic

As you prepare to write an argument, choose a topic that interests you. The topic should be debatable or controversial to some degree.

Then, check to be sure you can make an arguable claim. Ask yourself:

1. What am I trying to prove? What ideas do I need to get across?
2. Are there people who would disagree with my claim? What counterclaims would they make?
3. Do I have evidence to support my claim? Is my evidence sufficient and relevant?

If you are able to put into words what you want to prove and answered "yes" to questions 2 and 3, you have an arguable claim.

Introducing the Claim and Establishing Its Significance

Before you begin writing, determine how much your audience already knows about your chosen topic. Then, provide only as much background information as necessary. If there are issues surrounding your topic, you will need to clarify them for your audience and narrow the focus to your specific claim. Remember that you are not writing a summary of the issue—you are crafting an argument. Once you have provided context for your argument, you should clearly state your claim, or thesis.

Developing Your Claim with Reasoning and Evidence

Now that you have made your claim, support it with evidence, or grounds, and reasons for your claim. A valid argument should have multiple pieces of evidence to support the claim. Evidence can range from personal experience to researched data or expert opinion. Knowing your audience's knowledge level, concerns, values, and possible biases can help you decide what kind of evidence will have the strongest impact. Make sure your evidence is up to date and comes from a credible source. Be sure to credit your sources.

You should also address the opposing counterclaim within the body of your argument. Consider points you have made or evidence you have provided that a person might challenge. Decide how best to refute these counterclaims. One technique for defusing an opponent's claims is to agree with selected parts of them.

Writing a Concluding Statement or Section

Restate your claim in the conclusion of your argument, and summarize your main points. The goal of a concluding section is to provide a sense of closure and completeness to an argument. Make your concluding statement strong enough to be memorable and to leave the reader thinking.

Common Core State Standards

Writing

1.a. Introduce precise, knowledgeable claim(s), establish the significance of the claim(s), distinguish the claim(s) from alternate or opposing claims, and create an organization that logically sequences claim(s), counterclaims, reasons, and evidence.

1.b. Develop claim(s) and counterclaims fairly and thoroughly, supplying the most relevant evidence for each while pointing out the strengths and limitations of both in a manner that anticipates the audience's knowledge level, concerns, values, and possible biases.

1.e. Provide a concluding statement or section that follows from and supports the argument presented.

Student Edition Pages

Practice

Exploring both sides of an issue can be a good way to start planning an argument.
Complete a chart like the one below to help you plan your own argument.

Topic:	
Issue: _____	
_____	

Claim:	**Counterclaim:**
Grounds (Evidence):	**Grounds (Evidence):**
1. _____	1. _____
2. _____	2. _____
3. _____	3. _____
Justification:	**Justification:**
1. _____	1. _____
2. _____	2. _____
3. _____	3. _____

When you have completed the chart and developed your own precise claim,
consider the following questions:

1. Who is your audience? What type of evidence can you use to best convince
   those who do not agree with your claim?

2. Is your evidence strong and difficult to dispute? If not, how can you strengthen
   it or find better evidence?

3. How will you refute the counterclaim? Are there any parts of the counterclaim
   you agree with?

Composing an Argument **lxxi**

Correlation to Prentice Hall Literature © 2012

The following correlation shows points at which focused, sustained instruction is provided in the Student Edition. The standards are spiraled and revisited throughout the program, and the Teacher's Edition provides further opportunity to address standards.

Key
SE/TE: Student Edition/Teacher's Edition
CCC: Common Core Companion

		Grade 11 Reading Standards for Literature	Prentice Hall Literature © 2012, Grade 11
Key Ideas and Details	RL.1	Cite strong and thorough textual evidence to support analysis of what the text says explicitly as well as inferences drawn from the text, including determining where the text leaves matters uncertain.	**SE/TE:** 270, 291, 728, 756, 764, 784, 814, 982, 1010, 1239, 1334, 1346, 1356 **CCC:** 2, 3, 9
	RL.2	Determine two or more themes or central ideas of a text and analyze their development over the course of the text, including how they interact and build on one another to produce a complex account; provide an objective summary of the text.	**SE/TE:** xlvii, 18, 334, 798, 901, 913, 1026, 1334 **CCC:** 15, 16, 22
	RL.3	Analyze the impact of the author's choices regarding how to develop and relate elements of a story or drama (e.g., where a story is set, how the action is ordered, how the characters are introduced and developed).	**SE/TE:** 226, 291, 323, 478, 506, 594, 640, 650, 728, 814. 832, 846, 1010, 1026, 1080, 1123, 1160, 1186, 1216, 1296, 1310 **CCC:** 28, 29, 35
Craft and Structure	RL.4	Determine the meaning of words and phrases as they are used in the text, including figurative and connotative meanings; analyze the impact of specific word choices on meaning and tone, including words with multiple meanings or language that is particularly fresh, engaging, or beautiful. (Include Shakespeare as well as other authors.)	**SE/TE:** 407, 424, 530, 706, 718, 756, 772, 778, 784, 798, 866, 908, 913, 1040, 1050, 1056, 1062, 1070, 1324, 1346, 1364 **CCC:** 41, 42, 48
	RL.5	Analyze how an author's choices concerning how to structure specific parts of a text (e.g., the choice of where to begin or end a story, the choice to provide a comedic or tragic resolution) contribute to its overall structure and meaning as well as its aesthetic impact.	**SE/TE:** 74, 80, 122, 256, 407, 424, 478, 530, 634, 706, 772, 778, 832, 846, 866, 872, 922, 1026, 1056, 1062, 1070, 1080, 1123, 1160, 1296, 1324, 1356 **CCC:** 54, 55
	RL.6	Analyze a case in which grasping point of view requires distinguishing what is directly stated in a text from what is really meant (e.g., satire, sarcasm, irony, or understatement).	**SE/TE:** 407, 569, 594, 626, 756, 772, 1186, 1216, 1356 **CCC:** 61, 62
Integration of Knowledge and Ideas	RL.7	Analyze multiple interpretations of a story, drama, or poem (e.g., recorded or live production of a play or recorded novel or poetry), evaluating how each version interprets the source text. (Include at least one play by Shakespeare and one play by an American dramatist.)	**SE/TE:** 676, 1160 **CCC:** 68, 69
	RL.8	(Not applicable to literature)	
	RL.9	Demonstrate knowledge of eighteenth-, nineteenth-, and early-twentieth-century foundational works of American literature, including how two or more texts from the same period treat similar themes or topics.	**SE/TE:** 122, 226, 291, 424, 506, 569, 640, 706, 718, 728, 784, 798, 872, 901, 922 **CCC:** 75, 76
Range of Reading and Level of Text Complexity	RL.10	By the end of grade 11, read and comprehend literature, including stories, dramas, and poems, in the grades 11–CCR text complexity band proficiently, with scaffolding as needed at the high end of the range.	**SE/TE:** xlvii, 207, 459, 687, 1467 **CCC:** 82, 83

Grade 11 Reading Standards for Informational Texts			Prentice Hall Literature © 2012, Grade 11
Key Ideas and Details	RI.1	Cite strong and thorough textual evidence to support analysis of what the text says explicitly as well as inferences drawn from the text, including determining where the text leaves matters uncertain.	**SE/TE:** 40, 376, 492, 614, 764, 982, 1398, 1408 **CCC:** 90, 91, 97
	RI.2	Determine two or more central ideas of a text and analyze their development over the course of the text, including how they interact and build on one another to provide a complex analysis; provide an objective summary of the text.	**SE/TE:** xlvii, 168, 1102, 1408 **CCC:** 103, 104, 110
	RI.3	Analyze a complex set of ideas or sequence of events and explain how specific individuals, ideas, or events interact and develop over the course of the text.	**SE/TE:** 139, 157, 858, 1094, 1376, 1392 **CCC:** 116, 117
Craft and Structure	RI.4	Determine the meaning of words and phrases as they are used in a text, including figurative, connotative, and technical meanings; analyze how an author uses and refines the meaning of a key term or terms over the course of a text (e.g., how Madison defines *faction* in *Federalist No. 10*).	**SE/TE:** 110, 364, 376, 569, 587, 858, 928, 1376, 1442 **CCC:** 123, 124, 130
	RI.5	Analyze and evaluate the effectiveness of the structure an author uses in his or her exposition or argument, including whether the structure makes points clear, convincing, and engaging.	**SE/TE:** 46, 128, 1000, 1094, 1102, 1250, 1382, 1392, 1408 **CCC:** 136, 137
	RI.6	Determine an author's point of view or purpose in a text in which the rhetoric is particularly effective, analyzing how style and content contribute to the power, persuasiveness, or beauty of the text.	**SE/TE:** 40, 56, 84, 98, 492, 518, 552, 928, 1382, 1424 **CCC:** 143, 144, 150
Integration of Knowledge and Ideas	RI.7	Integrate and evaluate multiple sources of information presented in different media or formats (e.g., visually, quantitatively) as well as in words in order to address a question or solve a problem.	**SE/TE:** 16, 224, 392, 476, 704, 980, 1000, 1292, 1456 **CCC:** 156, 157
	RI.8	Delineate and evaluate the reasoning in seminal U.S. texts, including the application of constitutional principles and use of legal reasoning (e.g., in U.S. Supreme Court majority opinions and dissents) and the premises, purposes, and arguments in works of public advocacy (e.g., *The Federalist,* presidential addresses).	**SE/TE:** xlvii, 110 **CCC:** 163, 164
	RI.9	Analyze seventeenth-, eighteenth-, and nineteenth-century foundational U.S. documents of historical and literary significance (including the Declaration of Independence, the Preamble to the Constitution, the Bill of Rights, and Lincoln's Second Inaugural Address) for their themes, purposes, and rhetorical features.	**SE/TE:** 98, 110, 139, 168, 178, 242, 492, 518, 536, 614 **CCC:** 170, 171
Range of Reading and Level of Text Complexity	RI.10	By the end of grade 11, read and comprehend literary nonfiction in the grades 11–CCR text complexity band proficiently, with scaffolding as needed at the high end of the range.	**SE/TE:** 207, 459, 687, 1467 **CCC:** 177, 178

	Grade 11 Writing Standards		Prentice Hall Literature © 2012, Grade 11
Text Types and Purposes	W.1	Write arguments to support claims in an analysis of substantive topics or texts, using valid reasoning and relevant and sufficient evidence.	**SE/TE:** 92, 120, 127, 133, 356, 390, 397, 448, 611, 639, 662, 714, 830, 886, 1113, 1182, 1214, 1255, 1256, 1321, 1363, 1390, 1406, 1447 **CCC:** 185, 186, 187, 188, 189, 190, 191, 192, 193, 194, 195
	W.1.a	Introduce precise, knowledgeable claim(s), establish the significance of the claim(s), distinguish the claim(s) from alternate or opposing claims, and create an organization that logically sequences claim(s), counterclaims, reasons, and evidence.	**SE/TE:** xlvii, 356, 397, 562, 1214, 1256, 1258, 1390 **CCC:** 185, 186, 187, 188, 189, 190, 191, 192, 193, 194, 195
	W.1.b	Develop claim(s) and counterclaims fairly and thoroughly, supplying the most relevant evidence for each while pointing out the strengths and limitations of both in a manner that anticipates the audience's knowledge level, concerns, values, and possible biases.	**SE/TE:** xlvii, 1214, 1258, 1260 **CCC:** 185, 186, 187, 188, 189, 190, 191, 192, 193, 194, 195
	W.1.c	Use words, phrases, and clauses as well as varied syntax to link the major sections of the text, create cohesion, and clarify the relationships between claim(s) and reasons, between reasons and evidence, and between claim(s) and counterclaims.	**SE/TE:** 1260, 1390 **CCC:** 185, 186, 187, 188, 189, 190, 191, 192, 193, 194, 195
	W.1.d	Establish and maintain a formal style and objective tone while attending to the norms and conventions of the discipline in which they are writing.	**SE/TE:** 1113, 1258 **CCC:** 185, 186, 187, 188, 189, 190, 191, 192, 193, 194, 195
	W.1.e	Provide a concluding statement or section that follows from and supports the argument presented.	**SE/TE:** xlvii, 1214, 1258 **CCC:** 185, 186, 187, 188, 189, 190, 191, 192, 193, 194, 195
	W.2	Write informative/explanatory texts to examine and convey complex ideas, concepts, and information clearly and accurately through the effective selection, organization, and analysis of content.	**SE/TE:** 79, 83, 108, 268, 372, 420, 440, 490, 514, 528, 543, 557, 584, 593, 664, 676, 726, 753, 762, 776, 783, 793, 807, 865, 871, 910, 919, 927, 998, 1024, 1055, 1068, 1101, 1158, 1236, 1249, 1332, 1344, 1355, 1369, 1381, 1397, 1421 **CCC:** 196, 197, 198, 199, 200, 201, 202, 203, 204, 205, 206, 207
	W.2.a	Introduce a topic; organize complex ideas, concepts, and information so that each new element builds on that which precedes it to create a unified whole; include formatting (e.g., headings), graphics (e.g., figures, tables), and multimedia when useful to aiding comprehension.	**SE/TE:** 108, 154, 442, 514, 528, 557, 584, 666, 946, 1038, 1101, 1158, 1236 **CCC:** 196, 197, 198, 199, 200, 201, 202, 203, 204, 205, 206, 207
	W.2.b	Develop the topic thoroughly by selecting the most significant and relevant facts, extended definitions, concrete details, quotations, or other information and examples appropriate to the audience's knowledge of the topic.	**SE/TE:** 285, 372, 420, 440, 442, 490, 528, 557, 584, 593, 666, 726, 753, 762, 776, 783, 807, 865, 871, 927, 944, 998, 1024, 1038, 1068, 1158, 1236 **CCC:** 196, 197, 198, 199, 200, 201, 202, 203, 204, 205, 206, 207
	W.2.c	Use appropriate and varied transitions and syntax to link the major sections of the text, create cohesion, and clarify the relationships among complex ideas and concepts.	**SE/TE:** 154, 285, 320, 528, 543, 726, 762, 948, 1024, 1344 **CCC:** 196, 197, 198, 199, 200, 201, 202, 203, 204, 205, 206, 207
	W.2.d	Use precise language, domain-specific vocabulary, and techniques such as metaphor, simile, and analogy to manage the complexity of the topic.	**SE/TE:** 55, 83, 444, 668, 910, 1421 **CCC:** 196, 197, 198, 199, 200, 201, 202, 203, 204, 205, 206, 207

Grade 11 Writing Standards			Prentice Hall Literature © 2012, Grade 11
	W.2.e	Establish and maintain a formal style and objective tone while attending to the norms and conventions of the discipline in which they are writing.	**SE/TE:** 444, 557, 1158, 1397 **CCC:** 196, 197, 198, 199, 200, 201, 202, 203, 204, 205, 206, 207
	W.2.f	Provide a concluding statement or section that follows from and supports the information or explanation presented (e.g., articulating implications or the significance of the topic).	**SE/TE:** 154, 584, 776, 865, 998, 1024, 1101, 1236 **CCC:** 196, 197, 198, 199, 200, 201, 202, 203, 204, 205, 206, 207
	W.3	Write narratives to develop real or imagined experiences or events, using effective technique, well-chosen details, and well-structured event sequences.	**SE/TE:** 29, 188, 240, 633, 648, 844, 857, 937, 1091, 1308, 1360, 1439, 1448 **CCC:** 208, 209, 210, 211, 212, 213, 214, 215, 216, 217, 218
	W.3.a	Engage and orient the reader by setting out a problem, situation, or observation and its significance, establishing one or multiple point(s) of view, and introducing a narrator and/or characters; create a smooth progression of experiences or events.	**SE/TE:** 188, 857, 937, 1448, 1450 **CCC:** 208, 209, 210, 211, 212, 213, 214, 215, 216, 217, 218
	W.3.b	Use narrative techniques, such as dialogue, pacing, description, reflection, and multiple plot lines, to develop experiences, events, and/or characters.	**SE/TE:** 190, 844, 937, 1091, 1308, 1448, 1450, 1452 **CCC:** 208, 209, 210, 211, 212, 213, 214, 215, 216, 217, 218
	W.3.c	Use a variety of techniques to sequence events so that they build on one another to create a coherent whole and build toward a particular tone and outcome (e.g., a sense of mystery, suspense, growth, or resolution).	**SE/TE:** 190, 633, 1308, 1448 **CCC:** 208, 209, 210, 211, 212, 213, 214, 215, 216, 217, 218
	W.3.d	Use precise words and phrases, telling details, and sensory language to convey a vivid picture of the experiences, events, setting, and/or characters.	**SE/TE:** 192, 240, 438, 844, 1091, 1308, 1439, 1450, 1452 **CCC:** 208, 209, 210, 211, 212, 213, 214, 215, 216, 217, 218
	W.3.e	Provide a conclusion that follows from and reflects on what is experienced, observed, or resolved over the course of the narrative.	**SE/TE:** 190, 937, 1360 **CCC:** 208, 209, 210, 211, 212, 213, 214, 215, 216, 217, 218
Production and Distribution of Writing	W.4	Produce clear and coherent writing in which the development, organization, and style are appropriate to task, purpose, and audience.	**SE/TE:** 438, 668, 714, 946, 1045, 1263 **CCC:** 219, 220
	W.5	Develop and strengthen writing as needed by planning, revising, editing, rewriting, or trying a new approach, focusing on addressing what is most significant for a specific purpose and audience.	**SE/TE:** 188, 444, 447, 662, 668, 675, 948, 951, 1077, 1263, 1321, 1452, 1455 **CCC:** 226, 227
	W.6	Use technology, including the Internet, to produce, publish, and update individual or shared writing products in response to ongoing feedback, including new arguments or information.	**SE/TE:** 535, 944, 951, 1007, 1077 **CCC:** 233, 234
Research to Build and Present Knowledge	W.7	Conduct short as well as more sustained research projects to answer a question (including a self-generated question) or solve a problem; narrow or broaden the inquiry when appropriate; synthesize multiple sources on the subject, demonstrating understanding of the subject under investigation.	**SE/TE:** 66, 176, 186, 254, 504, 623, 664, 762, 770, 944, 1007, 1256, 1381, 1406 **CCC:** 240, 241, 244
	W.8	Gather relevant information from multiple authoritative print and digital sources, using advanced searches effectively; assess the strengths and limitations of each source in terms of the task, purpose, and audience; integrate information into the text selectively to maintain the flow of ideas, avoiding plagiarism and overreliance on any one source and following a standard format for citation.	**SE/TE:** 186, 254, 504, 558, 623, 666, 668, 670, 770, 938, 944, 1007, 1406 **CCC:** 247, 248, 249, 251, 253, 254, 255, 256, 257, 258, 259, 260

Ⓒ Grade 11 Writing Standards			Prentice Hall Literature © 2012, Grade 11
Research to Build and Present Knowledge	W.9	Draw evidence from literary or informational texts to support analysis, reflection, and research.	**SE/TE:** 165, 593, 770, 919 **CCC:** 261, 262, 265, 266
	W.9.a	Apply *grades 11–12 Reading standards* to literature (e.g., "Demonstrate knowledge of eighteenth-, nineteenth-, and early-twentieth-century foundational works of American literature, including how two or more texts from the same period treat similar themes or topics").	**SE/TE:** 320, 333, 490, 593, 793, 871, 908, 1236, 1332, 1355, 1369 **CCC:** 261, 262, 265, 266
	W.9.b	Apply *grades 11–12 Reading standards* to literary nonfiction (e.g., "Delineate and evaluate the reasoning in seminal U.S. texts, including the application of constitutional principles and use of legal reasoning [e.g., in U.S. Supreme Court Case majority opinions and dissents] and the premises, purposes, and arguments in works of public advocacy [e.g., *The Federalist,* presidential addresses]").	**SE/TE:** lxviii, 684, 1464 **CCC:** 261, 262, 265, 266
Range of Writing	W.10	Write routinely over extended time frames (time for research, reflection, and revision) and shorter time frames (a single sitting or a day or two) for a range of tasks, purposes, and audiences.	**SE/TE:** 133, 165, 333, 397, 919, 943, 1249, 1255, 1447 **CCC:** 269, 270, 271, 272, 273, 274, 275, 276

Ⓒ Grade 11 Speaking and Listening Standards			Prentice Hall Literature © 2012, Grade 11
Comprehension and Collaboration	SL.1	Initiate and participate effectively in a range of collaborative discussions (one-on-one, in groups, and teacher-led) with diverse partners on *grades 11–12 topics, texts, and issues,* building on others' ideas and expressing their own clearly and persuasively.	**SE/TE:** 952, 1292, 1456 **CCC:** 278, 279, 280, 281, 282, 283, 284, 285
	SL.1.a	Come to discussions prepared, having read and researched material under study; explicitly draw on that preparation by referring to evidence from texts and other research on the topic or issue to stimulate a thoughtful, well-reasoned exchange of ideas.	**SE/TE:** 565, 901, 980, 1292,1456 **CCC:** 278, 279, 280, 281, 282, 283, 284, 285
	SL.1.b	Work with peers to promote civil, democratic discussions and decision-making, set clear goals and deadlines, and establish individual roles as needed.	**SE/TE:** 16, 565, 901, 1292 **CCC:** 278, 279, 280, 281, 282, 283, 284, 285
	SL.1.c	Propel conversations by posing and responding to questions that probe reasoning and evidence; ensure a hearing for a full range of positions on a topic or issue; clarify, verify, or challenge ideas and conclusions; and promote divergent and creative perspectives.	**SE/TE:** 565, 901, 980, 1292 **CCC:** 278, 279, 280, 281, 282, 283, 284, 285
	SL.1.d	Respond thoughtfully to diverse perspectives; synthesize comments, claims, and evidence made on all sides of an issue; resolve contradictions when possible; and determine what additional information or research is required to deepen the investigation or complete the task.	**SE/TE:** 565, 901, 1160 **CCC:** 278, 279, 280, 281, 282, 283, 284, 285
	SL.2	Integrate multiple sources of information presented in diverse formats and media (e.g., visually, quantitatively, orally) in order to make informed decisions and solve problems, evaluating the credibility and accuracy of each source and noting any discrepancies among the data.	**SE/TE:** 948, 1264, 1456 **CCC:** 286, 287
	SL.3	Evaluate a speaker's point of view, reasoning, and use of evidence and rhetoric, assessing the stance, premises, links among ideas, word choice, points of emphasis, and tone used.	**SE/TE:**196, 448, 676 **CCC:** 290, 291, 294

Ⓒ Grade 11 Speaking and Listening Standards			Prentice Hall Literature © 2012, Grade 11
Presentation of Knowledge and Ideas	SL.4	Present information, findings, and supporting evidence, conveying a clear and distinct perspective, such that listeners can follow the line of reasoning, alternative or opposing perspectives are addressed, and the organization, development, substance, and style are appropriate to purpose, audience, and a range of formal and informal tasks.	**SE/TE:** 676, 770, 1263 **CCC:** 297, 298, 301
	SL.5	Make strategic use of digital media (e.g., textual, graphical, audio, visual, and interactive elements) in presentations to enhance understanding of findings, reasoning, and evidence and to add interest.	**SE/TE:** 476, 704, 910, 944, 1363 **CCC:** 304, 305
	SL.6	Adapt speech to a variety of contexts and tasks, demonstrating a command of formal English when indicated or appropriate.	**SE/TE:** 66, 195, 224, 448 **CCC:** 306, 307, 310

Ⓒ Grade 11 Language Standards			Prentice Hall Literature © 2012, Grade 11
Conventions of Standard English	L.1	Demonstrate command of the conventions of standard English grammar and usage when writing or speaking.	**SE/TE:** 285, 320, 447, 584, 611, 753, 951, 952, 1091, 1264, 1321 **CCC:** 314, 315, 316, 317
	L.1.a	Apply the understanding that usage is a matter of convention, can change over time, and is sometimes contested.	**SE/TE:** 450, 1452 **CCC:** 314, 315
	L.1.b	Resolve issues of complex or contested usage, consulting references (e.g., *Merriam-Webster's Dictionary of English Usage, Garner's Modern American Usage*) as needed.	**CCC:** 198, 316, 317
	L.2	Demonstrate command of the conventions of standard English capitalization, punctuation, and spelling when writing.	**SE/TE:** 675, 676, 1452, 1455 **CCC:** 318, 319, 320, 321
	L.2.a	Observe hyphenation conventions.	**SE/TE:** 240 **CCC:** 318, 319
	L.2.b	Spell correctly.	**SE/TE:** 195, 447, 675, 951, 1263, 1455 **CCC:** 320, 321
Knowledge of Language	L.3	Apply knowledge of language to understand how language functions in different contexts, to make effective choices for meaning or style, and to comprehend more fully when reading or listening.	**SE/TE:** 490, 714, 1061, 1113, 1421 **CCC:** 322, 323
	L.3.a	Vary syntax for effect, consulting references (e.g., Tufte's *Artful Sentences*) for guidance as needed; apply an understanding of syntax to the study of complex texts when reading.	**SE/TE:** 29, 74, 92, 154, 192, 285, 444, 778, 798, 1094, 1260, 1439 **CCC:** 322, 323
Vocabulary Acquisition and Use	L.4	Determine or clarify the meaning of unknown and multiple-meaning words and phrases based on *grades 11–12 reading and content,* choosing flexibly from a range of strategies.	**SE/TE:** 84, 438, 582, 662, 807, 1038, 1045, 1055, 1068, 1234, 1266, 1332, 1369, 1397, 1458 **CCC:** 324, 325, 326, 327, 328, 329, 330, 331
	L.4.a	Use context (e.g., the overall meaning of a sentence, paragraph, or text; a word's position or function in a sentence) as a clue to the meaning of a word or phrase.	**SE/TE:** 29, 45, 84, 198, 450, 678, 807, 857, 865, 1024, 1038, 1068, 1101, 1182, 1266, 1308, 1381, 1442, 1458 **CCC:** 324, 325
	L.4.b	Identify and correctly use patterns of word changes that indicate different meanings or parts of speech (e.g., *conceive, conception, conceivable*).	**SE/TE:** 66, 120, 152, 390, 514, 528, 582, 611, 623, 648, 726, 776, 793, 830, 844, 886, 908, 1024, 1038, 1077, 1091, 1113, 1255, 1158, 1182, 1321, 1344, 1360, 1390, 1421, 1439 **CCC:** 326, 327

		Grade 11 Language Standards	Prentice Hall Literature © 2012, Grade 11
Vocabulary Acquisition and Use	L.4.c	Consult general and specialized reference materials (e.g., dictionaries, glossaries, thesauruses), both print and digital, to find the pronunciation of a word or determine or clarify its precise meaning, its part of speech, its etymology, or its standard usage.	**SE/TE:** 198, 318, 323, 450, 504, 582, 587, 954, 998, 1007, 1234, 1239, 1308, 1406 **CCC:** 328, 329
	L.4.d	Verify the preliminary determination of the meaning of a word or phrase (e.g., by checking the inferred meaning in context or in a dictionary).	**SE/TE:** 176, 438, 528, 611, 793, 844, 943, 1091, 1255, 1439 **CCC:** 330, 331
	L.5	Demonstrate understanding of figurative language, word relationships, and nuances in word meanings.	**SE/TE:** 55, 79, 92, 108, 152, 268, 285, 372, 390, 535, 582, 611, 639, 678, 762, 783, 830, 886, 908, 927, 1040, 1050, 1068, 1077, 1091, 1113, 1214, 1234, 1266, 1308, 1321, 1355, 1360, 1406, 1458 **CCC:** 332, 333, 334, 335
	L.5.a	Interpret figures of speech (e.g., hyperbole, paradox) in context and analyze their role in the text.	**SE/TE:** 364, 376, 420, 424, 569, 587, 676, 784, 858, 866, 927, 1040, 1050 **CCC:** 332, 333
	L.5.b	Analyze nuances in the meaning of words with similar denotations.	**SE/TE:** 198, 582, 676, 714, 908, 1355 **CCC:** 334, 335
	L.6	Acquire and use accurately general academic and domain-specific words and phrases, sufficient for reading, writing, speaking, and listening at the college and career readiness level; demonstrate independence in gathering vocabulary knowledge when considering a word or phrase important to comprehension or expression.	**SE/TE:** xlvii, 157, 186, 224, 450, 662, 678, 770, 954, 998, 1007, 1214, 1406, 1442 **CCC:** 336, 337

The following skills are particularly likely to require continued attention in higher grades as they are applied to increasingly sophisticated writing and speaking.

© Grade 11 Language Progressive Skills		Prentice Hall Literature © 2012, Grade 11
Conventions of Standard English	L.9–10.1.a	Use parallel structure.	449, 1068, 1423
	L.6.1.c	Recognize and correct inappropriate shifts in pronoun number and person.	755, 911
	L.7.1.c	Place phrases and clauses within a sentence, recognizing and correcting misplaced and dangling modifiers.	585, 675
	L.5.1.d	Recognize and correct inappropriate shifts in verb tenses.	755, 1093
	L.6.1.d	Recognize and correct vague pronouns (i.e., ones with unclear or ambiguous antecedents).	755, 911
	L.8.1.d	Recognize and correct inappropriate shifts in verb voice and mood.	1115
	L.6.1.e	Recognize variations from standard English in their own and others' writing and speaking, and identify and use strategies to improve expression in conventional language.	445, 448
	L.3.1.f	Ensure subject-verb and pronoun-antecedent agreement.	753, 911
	L.4.1.f	Produce complete sentences, recognizing and correcting inappropriate fragments and run-ons.	447, 1236
	L.4.1.g	Correctly use frequently confused words (e.g., *to/too/ two; there/their*).	R60-R61
	L.6.2.a	Use punctuation (commas, parentheses, dashes) to set off nonrestrictive/parenthetical elements.	31, 287
	L.3.3.a	Choose words and phrases for effect.	193, 668
	L.7.3.a	Choose language that expresses ideas precisely and concisely, recognizing and eliminating wordiness and redundancy.	193, 1452
	L.4.3.b	Choose punctuation for effect.	1453, 1455
	L.6.3.b	Maintain consistency in style and tone.	67, 445
	L.4.1.g	Correctly use frequently confused words (e.g., to/too/ two; there/their).	R60-R61
	L.6.2.a	Use punctuation (commas, parentheses, dashes) to set off nonrestrictive/parenthetical elements.	31, 287
Knowledge of Language	L.3.3.a	Choose words and phrases for effect.	193, 668
	L.7.3.a	Choose language that expresses ideas precisely and concisely, recognizing and eliminating wordiness and redundancy.	193, 1452
	L.4.3.b	Choose punctuation for effect.	1453, 1455
	L.6.3.b	Maintain consistency in style and tone.	67, 445

Unit	Scholarship and Commentary	Focus on Literary Forms	Literary History	Contemporary Connection
1. A Gathering of Voices: Literature of Early America (Beginnings–1800)	William L. Andrews, America Begins with a Promise and a Paradox pp. 14–15; "Museum Indians" pp. 32–39; William L. Andrews Introduces *The Interesting Narrative of the Life of Olaudah Equiano* pp. 166–167	Speeches pp. 96–97	All the News That's Fit to Print pp. 134–135	Exploration Past and Present pp. 68–72
2. A Growing Nation: Literature of the American Renaissance (1800–1870)	Gretel Ehrlich, Inspired by Nature pp. 222–223; Charles Johnson on Ralph Waldo Emerson pp. 362–363; Gretel Ehrlich Introduces *Walden* pp. 374–375	Poetry pp. 402–403	Transcendentalism: The Seekers pp. 360–361	Individualism Past and Present pp. 398–400
3. Division, Reconciliation, and Expansion: Literature of the Civil War and the Frontier (1850–1914)	Nell Irvin Painter, Defining an Era pp. 474–475; Nell Irvin Painter Introduces *An Account of an Experience with Discrimination* pp. 550–551	Narrative Nonfiction pp. 516–517	Mark Twain: The American Bard pp. 564–565; "School" of American Humor p. 586	Civil War Writings Past and Present p. 544
4. Disillusion, Defiance, and Discontent: Literature of the Modern Age (1914–1945)	Tim O'Brien, Literature as a Magic Carpet pp. 702–703; Tim O'Brien Introduces "Ambush" pp. 808–809	Short Stories pp. 796–797	The Harlem Renaissance pp. 896–897	Cartooning as Literature pp. 888–894
5. Prosperity and Protest: Literature of the Postwar Era (1945–1970)	Arthur Miller, The Purpose of Theater pp. 978–979; The Words of Arthur Miller on The Crucible pp. 1120–1121	Drama pp. 1116–1117	Twentieth-Century Drama: America Takes the Stage pp. 1184–1185	Tallahassee Bus Boycott p. 971; Jack Kerouac: King of the Road Trip p. 972; Artistic Upstarts Past and Present pp. 1046–1049
6. New Voices, New Frontiers: Literature of the Contemporary Period (1970–Present)	Julia Alvarez, All-American Writer pp. 1290–1291; Julia Alvarez Introduces "Antojos" pp. 1294–1295	Essays pp. 1374–1375	The Poets Laureate pp. 1362–1363	Poetry with Rhythm pp. 1370–1372

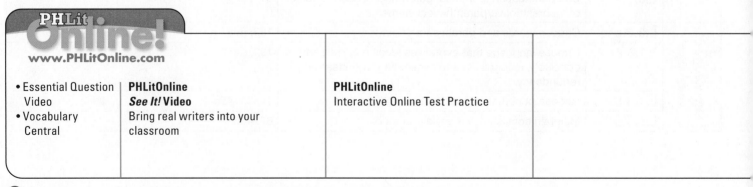

PHLit Online!
www.PHLitOnline.com

- Essential Question Video
- Vocabulary Central

PHLitOnline
See It! Video
Bring real writers into your classroom

PHLitOnline
Interactive Online Test Practice

Ⓒ Common Core State Standards appear in red throughout the Skills Navigator.

Informational Materials	Writing Workshop	Communications Workshop	Vocabulary Workshop	Test–Taking Practice
Real-Life Reading pp. 128–133; **Primary Sources** pp. 178–187	**Narration: Autobiographical Narrative** pp. 188–195	**Evaluate Persuasive Speech** pp. 196–197	**Using a Dictionary and Thesaurus** p. 198	**Reading Test: Social Science Passages** pp. 200–203 **Performance Tasks** pp. 204–205 SAT PREP ACT
Primary Sources pp. 242–255; **Real-Life Reading** pp. 392–397	**Narration: Reflective Essay** pp. 440–447	**Write and Deliver a Persuasive Speech** pp. 448–449	**Etymology: Political Science/History Terms** p. 450	**Reading Test: Paired Passages** pp. 452–455 **Performance Tasks** pp. 456–457 SAT PREP ACT
Real-Life Reading pp. 558–562; **Primary Sources** pp. 492–505, 614–624	**Research: Historical Investigation Report** pp. 664–675	**Oral Interpretation of a Literary Work** pp. 676–677	**Words from Mythology and Religious Traditions** p. 678	**Reading Test: Humanities Passage** pp. 680–683 **Performance Tasks** pp. 684–685 SAT PREP ACT
Primary Sources pp. 764–771; **Real-Life Reading** pp. 938–943	**Research: Multimedia Presentation** pp. 944–951	**Analyze a Nonprint Political Advertisement** pp. 952–953	**Etymology: Scientific, Medical, and Mathematical Terms** p. 954	**Critical Reading Test: Long Reading Passage** pp. 956–969 **Performance Tasks** pp. 960–961 SAT PREP ACT
Primary Sources pp. 1000–1008; **Real-Life Reading** pp. 1250–1255	**Persuasion: Persuasive Essay** pp. 1256–1263	**Analyze and Evaluate Entertainment Media** pp. 1264–1265	**Idioms and Idiomatic Expressions** p. 1266	**Reading Test: Prose Fiction** pp. 1268–1271 **Performance Tasks** pp. 1272–1273 SAT PREP ACT
Primary Sources pp. 1392–1401; **Real-Life Reading** pp. 1442–1447	**Narration: Short Story** pp. 1448–1455	**Compare Print News Coverage** pp. 1456–1457	**Cognates** p. 1458	**Critical Reading: Short Reading Passage** pp. 1460–1463 **Performance Tasks** pp. 1464–1465 SAT PREP ACT

PHLitOnline
EssayScorer: Score essays in seconds

PHLitOnline
Vocabulary Central:
• Games   • Audio
• Flash cards   • Images

Unit 1: A Gathering of Voices

	Selection	Reading Strategy	Literary Analysis
PART 1	"The Earth on Turtle's Back" (MA), SE, p. 20; "When Grizzlies Walked Upright" (MA), SE, p. 24; from *The Navajo Origin Legend* (MA), SE, p. 27	Reading Warm-ups A and B, *UR1,* pp. 17–18; Establish a Purpose for Reading, SE, p. 18; *UR1,* p. 20	Origin Myths, SE, p. 18; *UR1,* p. 19 **RL.2**
	from *The Iroquois Constitution* (A), SE, p. 41	Reading Warm-ups A and B, *UR1,* pp. 36–37; *UR1,* p. 39; Analyze Philosophical Assumptions and Beliefs, SE, p. 40 **RI.6**	*UR1,* p. 38; Political Document, SE, p. 40
	"A Journey Through Texas" (A), Alvar Núñez Cabeza de Vaca, SE, p. 48; "Boulders Taller Than the Great Tower of Seville" (A), García López de Cárdenas, SE, p. 52	Recognize Signal Words, SE, p. 46; Reading Warm-ups A and B, *UR1,* pp. 54–55; *UR1,* p. 57 **RI.6**	Exploration Narratives, SE, p. 46; *UR1,* p. 56
	from *Of Plymouth Plantation* (MC), William Bradford, SE, p. 57	Breaking Down Long Sentences, SE, p. 56; Reading Warm-ups A and B, *UR1,* pp. 72–73; *UR1,* p. 75 **RI.6**	Author's Purpose, SE, p. 56; *UR1,* p. 74
PART 2	"To My Dear and Loving Husband" (A), Anne Bradstreet, SE, p. 76	Reading Warm-ups A and B, *UR1,* pp. 90–91; Paraphrase, SE, p. 74; *UR1,* p. 93 **RL.5**	*UR1,* p. 92; Puritan Plain Style, SE, p. 74
	"Huswifery" (MC), SE, p. 82	Adjust Your Reading Rate, SE, p. 80; Reading Warm-ups A and B, *UR1,* pp. 108–109; *UR1,* p. 111 **RL.5**	Metaphor, SE, p. 80; *UR1,* p. 110
	from *Sinners in the Hands of an Angry God* (MC), Jonathan Edwards, SE, p.86	Context Clues, SE, pp. 84; Reading Warm-ups A and B, *UR1,* pp. 90–91; *UR1,* p. 93 **RI.6**	Sermon, SE, pp. 84; *UR1,* p. 92
PART 3	Speech in the Virginia Convention (MC), Patrick Henry, SE, p. 100; Speech in the Convention (MC), Benjamin Franklin, SE, p. 104	Critique Their Appeal to Friendly and Hostile Audiences, SE, p. 98; Reading Warm-ups A and B, *UR1,* pp. 108–109 **RI.6, RI.9**	Rhetorical Devices, SE, p. 98 **RI.9** Spiral Review, p. 102
	The Declaration of Independence (MC), Thomas Jefferson, SE, p. 112; from *The American Crisis, Number 1* (A), Thomas Paine, SE, p. 117 ©	Analyze Word Choice, SE, p. 110; *UR1,* p. 111 **RI.4, RI.9**	Persuasion, SE, p. 110; *UR1,* p. 110 **RI.9**
	"To His Excellency, General Washington" (MC), Phillis Wheatley SE, p. 125	Reread, SE, p. 122	Heroic Couplets, SE, p. 122 **RL.5**
	from *The Autobiography* (MC), Benjamin Franklin, SE, p. 140; from *Poor Richard's Almanack* (MA), Benjamin Franklin, SE, p. 148	*UR1,* p. 135; Analyze Cause and Effect, SE, p. 139; Reading Warm-ups A and B, *UR1,* pp. 151–152; *UR1,* p. 154 **RI.3**	Autobiography, SE, p. 139; *UR1,* p. 153 Spiral Review, p. 146
	"Straw into Gold: The Metamorphosis of the Everyday," Sandra Cisneros, SE, p. 159	Autobiographical Writing, SE, p. 157 **RI.3**	

Key: *UR:* *Unit Resources*   **A:** Average   **MA:** More Accessible   **MC:** More Challenging   © Indicates an Exemplar Text

Vocabulary	Grammar/Writing	Assessment
Vocab Warm-up List and Practice, *UR1*, pp. 15–16; **Vocabulary, SE**, p. 18: unconscious, depths, ancestors, protruded; **Vocabulary Builder**, *UR1*, p. 21; **Latin Root** *-trud- / -trus-*, **SE** p. 30; **Context Clues, SE**, p. 30 **L.4.a**	*UR1*, p. 22; **Coordinating Conjunctions, SE**, p. 31; *WG*, Ch.17, Section 4; **Connecting to the Essential Question, SE**, p. 18; *UR1*, p. 23; **Writing Lesson: Play, SE**, p. 30 **W.3, L.3.a**	**Critical Reading, SE**, pp. 23, 28; **Selection Tests A and B**, *UR1*, pp. 28–33
Vocab Warm-up List and Practice, *UR1*, pp. 34–35; **Vocabulary Builder**, *UR1*, p. 40; **Vocabulary, SE**, p. 40: disposition, constitute, tempered, deliberation, oblivion	*UR1*, p. 41; **Writing: Found Poem, SE**, p. 45	**Thinking About the Commentary, SE**, p. 33; **Critical Reading, SE**, pp. 39, 44; **Selection Tests A and B**, *UR1*, pp. 46–51
Vocabulary, SE, p. 46: entreated, feigned, subsisted, successive, advantageous, traversed; **Vocab Warm-up List and Practice**, *UR1*, pp. 52–53; **Use New Words Correctly, SE**, p. 55; **Vocabulary Builder**, *UR1*, pp. 52–53, 58	*UR1*, p. 59	**Selection Tests A and B**, *UR1*, pp. 64–69; **Critical Reading, SE**, p. 54
Vocabulary, SE, p. 56: peril, habitation, subject to, adversity, calamity, relent; **Vocab Warm-up List and Practice**, *UR1*, pp. 70–71; **Vocabulary Builder, Related Forms of *peril*, SE**, p. 67; **Antonyms or Synonyms, SE**, p. 67 **L.4.b**	**Writing Lesson: Explorer's Journal Entry, SE**, p. 55; **Writing Lesson: Speaker Introduction, SE**, p. 67 **W.6, W.7**	**Selection Tests A and B**, *UR1*, pp. 82–87; **Critical Reading, SE**, p. 65
Vocab Warm-up List and Practice, *UR1*, pp. 88–89; **Vocabulary, SE**, p. 74: quench, recompense, manifold, persevere; **Vocabulary Builder**, *UR1*, p. 94	*UR1*, p. 95; **Writing: Interpretive Essay, SE**, p. 79 **W.2**	**Critical Reading, SE**, p. 77; **Selection Tests A and B**, *UR1*, pp. 100–105
Vocab Warm-up List and Practice, *UR1*, pp. 106–107; **Vocabulary, SE**, p. 80: affections, ordinances, judgment, apparel; **Vocabulary Builder**, *UR1*, p. 112	**Writing: Reflective Essay, SE**, p. 83; *UR1*, p. 113 **W.2, W.2.d**	**Critical Reading, SE**, p. 82; **Selection Tests A and B**, *UR1*, pp. 118–123
Vocabulary, SE, p. 84: constitution, prudence, omnipotent, mediator, induce; **Word Analysis: Latin Prefix *omni-*, SE**, p. 93; **Analogies, SE** p. 93; **Vocabulary Builder**, *UR1*, p. 94 **L.4, L.4.a, L.3.a, L.5**	**Correlative Conjunctions, SE**, p. 94; *WG*, Ch.17, Section 4 ; **Writing Lesson: Evaluation of Persuasion, SE**, p. 93; *UR1*, p. 95 **W.1, L.3.a**	**Critical Reading, SE**, p. 91
Vocabulary, SE, p. 98: insidious, privileges, vigilant, despotism, salutary, unanimity; **Vocab Warm-up List and** *UR1*, pp. 106–107; **Relate New Vocabulary to Familiar Words, SE**, p. 109; **Antonyms, SE**, p. 109 **L.5**	**Writing Lesson: Compare-and-Contrast Essay, SE**, p. 109 **W.2, W.2.a**	**Selection Tests A and B**, *UR1*, pp. 100–105; **Critical Reading, SE**, pp. 103, 107
Vocabulary, SE, p. 110: candid, assent, harass, tyranny, redress, acquiesce, rectitude, prudent; **Vocabulary Builder**, *UR1*, p. 112; **Word Analysis: Latin Word Parts** *-rect-* and *-tude-*, **SE**, p. 121 **L.4.b**	110; *UR1*, p. 113; **Writing Lesson: Persuasive Editorial, SE**, p. 121 **W.1**	**Critical Reading, SE**, pp. 115, 119; **Selection Tests A and B**, *UR1*, pp. 118–123
Vocabulary, SE, p. 122: propitious, tempest, martial, implore, pensive, lament; **Sentence Completions**, p. 127	**Writing: Persuasive Memorandum, SE**, p. 127 **W1**	**Critical Reading, SE**, p. 126; **Test Practice: Reading, SE**, p. 133
Vocabulary, SE, p. 139: arduous, avarice, vigilance, incorrigible, posterity, squander; **Vocab Warm-up List and Practice**, *UR1*, pp. 149–150; **Word Analysis: Patterns of Word Changes, SE**, p. 153; **Analogies, SE**, p. 153; **Vocabulary Building**, *UR1*, p. 155 **L.4, L.5**	*UR1*, p. 137; **Subordinating Conjunctions, SE**, p. 155; *WG*, Ch.17, Section 4; **Writing Lesson: Essay Analyzing Cause and Effect, SE**, p. 154; *UR1*, p. 156 **W.2.a, W.2.c, W.2.f**	**Critical Reading, SE**, p. 150
Vocabulary, SE, p. 157: intuitively, capable, taboo, nostalgia, flourished **L.6**	**Writing to Compare Literary Works, SE**, p. 165 **W.9, W.10**	**Selection Tests A and B**, *UR1*, pp. 161–166; **Critical Reading, SE**, p. 164

All selections are supported in the *Reader's Notebooks*.

Unit 1: A Gathering of Voices *(continued)*

	Selection	Reading Strategy	Literary Analysis
PART 3 *(continued)*	from *The Interesting Narrative of the Life of Olaudah Equiano* (A), Olaudah Equiano, SE, p. 170 ©	Summarizing to Identify the Main Idea or Essential Message, SE, p. 168; **Reading Warm-ups A and B,** *UR1,* pp. 169–170; *UR1,* p. 172 RI.2	Slave Narrative, SE, p. 168; *UR1,* p. 171
	Primary Sources, SE, p. 178; Letter From the President's House (A), John Adams, SE, p. 181; Letter to Her Daughter From the New White House (A), Abigail Adams, SE, p. 182; Floor Plan of the President's House (A), Benjamin Henry Latrobe, SE, p. 184	Analyzing a Writer's Perspective, SE, p. 178; Reading Warm-ups A and B, *UR1,* pp. 187–188; *UR1,* p. 190 RI.9	Letters, SE, p. 178; *UR1,* p. 189

Unit 2: A Growing Nation

	Selection	Reading Strategy	Literary Analysis
PART 1	"The Devil and Tom Walker" (A), Washington Irving, SE, p. 227	Evaluate the Influences of the Historical Period, SE, p. 226	Characterization, SE, p. 226 RL.3
	"Commission of Meriwether Lewis" (A), Thomas Jefferson, SE p. 245; "Crossing the Great Divide" (A), Meriwether Lewis, SE, p. 250	Identify the Writer's Purpose, SE, p. 242 RI.9	Commission, SE, p. 242
	from "The Song of Hiawatha" (A), Henry Wadsworth Longfellow, SE, p. 258; "The Tide Rises, The Tide Falls" (MA), Henry Wadsworth Longfellow, SE, p. 260; "Thanatopsis" (MC), William Cullen Bryant, SE, p. 262; "Old Ironsides" (A), Oliver Wendell Holmes, SE, p. 266	Summarize, SE, p. 256 RL.1	Meter, SE, p. 256
PART 2	"The Minister's Black Veil" (MC), Nathaniel Hawthorne, SE, p. 272	Drawing Inferences, SE, p. 270 RL.5	Parable and Symbol, SE, p. 270 Spiral Review, p. 284
	"The Fall of the House of Usher" (MC), Edgar Allan Poe, SE, p. 293; "The Raven" (A), Edgar Allan Poe, SE, p. 312	Break Down Long Sentences, SE, p. 291	Gothic Literature, SE, p. 291 RL.1, RL.3, RL.9
	"Where Is Here?" SE, Joyce Carol Oates, p. 325	Comparing Gothic Literature Past and Present, SE, p. 323	Modern Gothic Literature, SE, p. RL.3 Spiral Review, p. 331

Key: *UR: Unit Resources*   **A:** Average   **MA:** More Accessible   **MC:** More Challenging   © Indicates an Exemplar Text

Vocabulary	Grammar/Writing	Assessment
Vocab Warm-up List and Practice, *UR1,* pp. 167–168; **Vocabulary, SE,** p. 168: copious, wretched, dejected, inseparable, heightened, pacify; **Vocabulary Builder,** *UR1,* p. 173; **Word Analysis: Latin Root** *-ject-,* **SE,** p. 177; **Categorize Key Vocabulary, SE,** 177; **Vocabulary, SE,** p. 179: account, commissioners, inspection, unabated, interspersed, scale, establishment, contract, procure, recourse **L.4**	**Response to Literature, SE,** p. 165; *UR1,* p. 174; **Writing Lesson: Museum Placard, SE,** p. 177 **W.7**	**Critical Reading, SE,** p. 175; **Selection Tests A and B,** *UR1,* pp. 179–184
Vocab Warm-up List and Practice, *UR1,* pp. 185–186; **Vocabulary Builder,** *UR1,* p. 191 **L.6**	**Research Task, Topic: Changing the White House,** p. 187; *UR1,* p. 192 **W.7, W.8**	**Critical Reading, SE,** p. 185; **Test Practice: Reading, SE,** p. 187

Vocabulary	Grammar/Writing	Assessment
Vocabulary, SE, p. 226: prevalent, discord, treacherous, extort, ostentation, parsimony; **Word Analysis: Latin Prefix** *ex-,* **SE,** p. 241; **Sentence Completions, SE,** p. 241	**Writing Lesson: Modern Retelling of a Story, SE,** p. 241 **W.3, W.3d, L.2.a**	**Critical Reading, SE,** p. 239; **Selection Tests A and B,** *UR2,* pp. 22–24
Vocabulary, SE, p. 243: celestial, practicable, latitude, longitude, membranes, conciliatory, discretion, dispatched, prospect, conspicuous **L.4.c**	**Research Task, Topic: The Life of Sacagawea,** p. 255 **W.7, W.8**	**Critical Reading, SE,** p. 253; **Test Practice: Reading, SE,** p. 255
Vocabulary, SE, p. 256: efface, eloquence, pensive, venerable; **Antonyms, SE,** p. 268 **L.5**	**Writing: Comparing Literary Works, SE,** p. 268 **W.2**	**Critical Reading, SE,** pp. 259, 264, 267; **Selection Tests A and B,** *UR2,* pp. 41–46
Vocabulary, SE, p. 270: inanimate, venerable, pathos, impertinent, obstinacy, imperceptible; **Word Analysis: Greek Root** *-path-,* **SE,** p. 286; **Word/Phrase Relationships, SE,** p. 286 **L.5**	**Adjective and Adverb Clauses, SE,** p. 287; **Grammar in Your Writing, SE,** p. 287; *WG,* **Ch. 19, Section 3; Connecting to the Essential Question, SE,** p. 270; **Writing Lesson: Interpretive Essay About Ambiguity, SE,** p. 286 **W.2.b, W.2.c, L.1, L.3.a**	**Critical Reading, SE,** pp. 284; **Selection Tests A and B,** *UR2,* pp. 60–65
Vocabulary, SE, p. 291: importunate, munificent, equivocal, specious, anomalous, sentience; **Latin Root** *-voc-,* **SE,** p. 319; **True or False? SE,** p. 319; **Gothic Style: Words for a Character in Torment, SE,** p. 319: agitation, feeble, futile, leaden, tremulous, trepidancy **L.4.c**	**Comparative and Superlative Adjectives and Adverbs, SE,** p. 321; **Grammar in Your Writing, SE,** p. 321; *WG,* **Ch. 24, Section 2; Connecting to the Essential Question, SE,** p. 291; **Writing Lesson: Essay Evaluating Differing Critical Views, SE,** p. 320	**Critical Reading, SE,** pp. 310, 317; **Selection Tests A and B,** *UR2,* pp. 81–86
Vocabulary, SE, p. 323: stealthily, exasperation, impulsively, fastidious, cavernous **L.4.c**	**Writing to Compare Literary Works, SE,** p. 333 **W.9, W.10**	**Critical Reading, SE,** pp. 332; **Selection Tests A and B,** *UR2,* pp. 90–91

All selections are supported in the *Reader's Notebooks.*

Unit 2: A Growing Nation (*continued*)

	Selection	Reading Strategy	Literary Analysis
PART 2	from *Moby-Dick* (MC), Herman Melville, SE, p. 336	Identify Relevant Details to Determine the Essential Message, SE, p. 334	Symbol and Theme, SE, p. 334 RL.2
PART 3	from *Nature* (A), Ralph Waldo Emerson, SE, p. 366; from *Self-Reliance* (A), Ralph Waldo Emerson, SE, p. 369; "Concord Hymn" (A), Ralph Waldo Emerson, SE, p. 371	Challenging or Questioning the Text, SE, p. 364	Figurative Language, SE, p. 364 RI.4
	from *Walden* (MC), Henry David Thoreau, SE, p. 378; from *Civil Disobedience* (A), Henry David Thoreau, SE, p. 388 ©	Analyze the Author's Implicit and Explicit Philosophical Assumptions, SE, p. 376 RL.1	Author's Style, Figurative Expressions, Metaphor, and Analogy, SE, p. 376 RL.4 Spiral Review, p. 388
PART 4	Emily Dickinson's Poetry (MC, A, MC, MC, MC, A, A, A), Emily Dickinson, SE, p. 408 ©	Reread, SE, p. 407;	Exact and Slant Rhyme, SE, p. 407 RL.4, RL.5, RL.6
	Walt Whitman's Poetry (MC, A, MA, A, A, MA), Walt Whitman, SE, p. 426 ©	Adjust Your Reading Rate, SE, p. 425	Epic Poetry, SE, p. 424 RL.4, RL.5

Unit 3: Division, Reconciliation, and Expansion

	Selection	Reading Strategy	Literary Analysis
PART 1	"An Occurrence at Owl Creek Bridge" (A), Ambrose Bierce, SE, p. 480	Analyzing the Story's Pattern of Organization, SE, p. 478 Spiral Review, p. 483	Point of View, SE, p. 478
	from *Mary Chesnut's Civil War,* Mary Chesnut, p. 495; "Recollections of a Private," Warren Lee Goss, p. 500; "A Confederate Account of the Battle of Gettysburg," Randolph McKim, p. 502	Generating Questions, SE, p. 492 RI.1, RI.6, RI.9	Diaries and Journals, SE, p. 492
	"An Episode of War" (A), Stephen Crane, SE, p. 508	Apply Background Knowledge, SE, p. 506; Strategies for Reading Narrative Accounts, SE, p. 517	Naturalism, SE, p. 506 RL.3, RL.9
	from *My Bondage and My Freedom* (MC), Frederick Douglass, SE, p. 520	Setting a Purpose, SE, p. 518	Autobiography, Author's Purpose, SE, p. 518 RI.6, RI.9
	"Go Down, Moses" (A), SE, p. 532; "Swing Low, Sweet Chariot" (MA), SE, p. 534	Listening, SE, p. 530	Spirituals, Biblical Allusions, Allegory, SE, p. 530 RL.4, RL.5
	"The Gettysburg Address" (A), Abraham Lincoln, SE, p. 538; "Letter to His Son" (MC), Robert E. Lee, SE, p. 541	Use Your Background Knowledge, SE, p. 536	Diction, SE, p. 536 RI.9
	"An Account of an Experience with Discrimination" (MA), Sojourner Truth, SE, p. 554	Identify Relevant Facts and Details, SE, p. 552	Author's General Purpose for Writing, SE, p. 552 RI.6

Key: *UR: Unit Resources*   **A:** Average   **MA:** More Accessible   **MC:** More Challenging   © Indicates an Exemplar Text

Vocabulary	Grammar/Writing	Assessment
Vocabulary, SE, p. 334: pedestrian, impulsive, inarticulate, inscrutable, maledictions, prescient; **Latin Prefix *mal-*, SE**, p. 357; **Synonyms, SE**, p. 357	**Participles, Gerunds, and Infinitives (Verbals), SE**, p. 358; **Grammar in Your Writing, SE**, p. 358; **WG**, Ch. 19, Section 2; **Connecting to the Essential Question, SE**, p. 334; **Writing Lesson: Character Study, SE**, p. 357 **W.1, W.1.a**	**Critical Reading, SE**, pp. 355; **Selection Tests A and B**, *UR2*, pp. 105–110
Vocabulary, SE, p. 364: perpetual, decorum, tranquil, conviction, chaos, aversion, absolve; **Latin Prefix *ab-*, SE**, p. 373; **Categorize Vocabulary, SE**, p. 373 **L.5**	**Writing Lesson: Evaluation of a Philosophical Essay, SE**, p. 373 **W.2, W.2.b**	**Thinking About the Commentary, SE**, p. 363; **Critical Reading, SE**, pp. 368, 370, 371; **Selection Tests A and B**, *UR2*, pp. 123–128
Vocabulary, SE, p. 376: dilapidated, sublime, superfluous, magnanimity, expedient, alacrity; **Latin Root *-flu-*, SE**, p. 391; **Synonyms, SE**, p. 391 **L.4.c, L.5**	**Writing Lesson: Editorial, SE**, p. 391 **W.1**	**Thinking About the Commentary, SE**, p. 375; **Critical Reading, SE**, pp. 387, 389; **Selection Tests A and B**, *UR2*, pp. 143–148
Vocabulary, SE, p. 407: surmised, eternity, interposed, affliction, ample, finite, infinity; **Latin Root *-fin-*, SE**, p. 421; **Antonyms, SE**, p. 421 **L.5.a, L.4.c, L.5**	**Writing Lesson: Blog Entry About Poetry, SE**, p. 421 **W.2, W.2.b**	**Critical Reading, SE**, pp. 409, 411, 414, 417; **Selection Tests A and B**, *UR2*, pp. 162–172
Vocabulary, SE, p. 425: stirring, abeyance, effuse, bequeath, stealthily, robust; **Multiple Meaning Words, SE**, p. 439; **Denotations, SE**, p. 439; **L.4, L.4.d**	**Writing Lesson: Free Verse Poem in Honor of Whitman, SE**, p. 439 **W.3.d**	**Critical Reading, SE**, pp. 427, 431, 433, 436; **Selection Tests A and B**, *UR2*, pp. 185–190

Vocabulary	Grammar/Writing	Assessment
Vocabulary, SE, p. 478: etiquette, deference, dictum, summarily, apprised, ineffable; **Latin Root *-dict-*, SE**, p. 491; **Vocabulary: Revising Sentences for Logic, SE**, p. 491 **L.3, L.9.a**	**Writing Lesson: Critical Essay on a Stylistic Device, SE**, p. 491 **W.2, W.2.b**	**Critical Reading, SE**, p. 489; **Selection Tests A and B**, *UR3*, pp. 19–24
Vocabulary, SE, p. 493: adjourned, convention, intercepted, obstinate, recruits, fluctuation, spectator, offensive, brigade, entrenchments **L.4.c**	**Research Task, Topic: Women and the Civil War, SE**, p. 505 **W.7, W.8**	**Critical Reading, SE**, pp. 499, 501, 503; **Test Practice: Reading, SE**, p. 505; **Selection Tests A and B**, *UR3*, pp. 27–28
Vocabulary, SE, p. 506: precipitate, aggregation, commotion, disdainfully, sinister; **Latin Root *-greg-*, SE**, p. 515; **Vocabulary: Analogies, SE**, p. 515 **L.4.b**	**Writing Lesson: Essay in Response to Criticism, SE**, p. 515 **W.2, W.2.a**	**Critical Reading, SE**, p. 513; **Selection Tests A and B**, *UR3*, pp. 41–46
Vocabulary, SE, p. 518: benevolent, deficient, fervent, opposition, consternation, intolerable; **Latin Root *-bene-*, SE**, p. 529; **Vocabulary: Sentence Completions, SE**, p. 529 **L.4.b, L.4.d**	**Writing Lesson: College Application Essay, SE**, p. 529 **W.2, W.2.a, W.2.b, W.2.c**	**Critical Reading, SE**, p. 527; **Selection Tests A and B**, *UR3*, pp. 59–62
Vocabulary, SE, p. 530: oppressed, smite; **Vocabulary: Antonyms, SE**, p. 535 **L.4**	**Writing: Electronic Slide Presentation, SE**, p. 535 **W.6**	**Critical Reading, SE**, p. 534; **Selection Tests A and B**, *UR3*, pp. 77–82
Vocabulary, SE, p. 536: consecrate, hallow, virtuous, anarchy; **Vocabulary: Use New Words in Sentences, SE**, p. 543	**Writing: Compare-and-Contrast Essay, SE**, p. 543 **W.2, W.2.c**	**Critical Reading, SE**, p. 542; **Selection Tests A and B**, *UR3*, pp. 104–109
Vocabulary, SE, p. 552: ascended, assault; **Vocabulary: True or False, SE**, p. 557	**Writing: Newspaper Article, SE**, p. 557 **W.2, W.2.a, W.2.b, L.2.e**	**Thinking About the Commentary, SE**, p. 551; **Critical Reading, SE**, p. 556; **Selection Tests A and B**, *UR3*, pp. 124–129

All selections are supported in the *Reader's Notebooks*.

Unit 3: Division, Reconciliation, and Expansion (*continued*

	Selection	Reading Strategy	Literary Analysis
PART 2	"The Boy's Ambition" from *Life on the Mississippi* (A), Mark Twain, SE, p. 570; "The Notorious Jumping Frog of Calaveras County" (MC), Mark Twain, SE, p. 576	Clarify and Interpret, SE, p. 569	Humor, SE, p. 569 RL.6, RL.9, RI.4 Spiral Review, p. 573
	from *The Life and Times of the Thunderbolt Kid*, Bill Bryson, SE, p. 589		Comparing American Humor Past and Present, SE p. 587 RI.4
	"To Build a Fire" (A), Jack London, SE, p. 596	Predict, SE, p. 594	Conflict, SE, p. 594 R.L.3, RL.6 Spiral Review, p. 599
	"Heading West" (MA), Miriam Davis Colt, SE, p. 617; "I Will Fight No More Forever" (MA), Chief Joseph, SE, p. 622	Analyzing an Author's Implicit and Explicit Philosophical Assumptions and Beliefs, SE, p. 614 RI.1, RI.9	Personal History, SE, p. 614
PART 3	"The Story of an Hour" (A), Kate Chopin, SE, p. 628	Analyze the Philosophical Argument, SE, p. 626	Irony, SE, p. 626 RL.6
	"Douglass" (A), Paul Laurence Dunbar, SE, p. 636; "We Wear the Mask" (A), Paul Laurence Dunbar, SE, p. 638	Analyze the Effect of the Historical Period, SE, p. 634	Rhyme Scheme, SE, p. 634 RL.5
	"Luke Havergal" (A), Edwin Arlington Robinson, SE, p. 642; "Richard Cory" (A), Edwin Arlington Robinson, SE, p. 644; "Lucinda Matlock" (A), Edgar Lee Masters, SE, p. 646; "Richard Bone" (A), Edgar Lee Masters, SE, p. 647	Comparing and Contrasting, SE, p. 640	Narrative Poetry, SE, p. 640 RL.3, RL.9
	"A Wagner Matinée" (MC), Willa Cather, SE, p. 652	Ask Questions to Clarify Meaning, SE, p. 650	Characterization, SE, p. 650 RL.3

Unit 4: Disillusion, Defiance, and Discontent

	Selection	Reading Strategy	Literary Analysis
PART 1	"The Love Song of J. Alfred Prufrock" (MC), T. S. Eliot, SE, p. 708	Adjust Your Reading Rate, SE, p. 706	Dramatic Monologue, Allusions, SE, p. 706 RL.4, RL.5
	The Imagist Poets (MC, A), SE, p. 719	Engaging Your Senses, SE, p. 718	Imagism, SE, p. 718 RL.4, RL.9
	"Winter Dreams" (MC), F. Scott Fitzgerald, SE, p. 730	Draw Inferences About Characters, SE, p. 728 RL.1, RL.3	Characters, SE, p. 728 Spiral Review, p. 744, 748

Key: *UR: Unit Resources* **A:** Average **MA:** More Accessible **MC:** More Challenging © Indicates an Exemplar Text

Vocabulary	Grammar/Writing	Assessment
Vocabulary, SE, p. 569: transient, prodigious, eminence, garrulous, conjectured, monotonous, interminable; **Greek Prefix mono-, SE**, p. 583; **Vocabulary: Antonyms, SE**, p. 583; **Using Resources to Build Vocabulary, SE**, p. 583 **L.4, L.4.b, L.4.c, L. 5, L.5.b**	**Fixing Misplaced and Dangling Modifiers, SE**, p. 585; **WG, Ch. 17, Section 4; Connecting to the Essential Question, SE**, p. 569; **Writing Lesson: Analytical Essay, SE**, p. 584; **Grammar in Your Writing, SE**, p. 585 **W.2, W.2.a, W.2.b, W.2.f, L.1**	**Critical Reading, SE**, pp. 574, 581; **Selection Tests A and B, UR3**, pp. 144–149
Vocabulary, SE, p. 587: embark, dubious; **Vocabulary: Logical Word Use, SE**, p. 593 **L.4.c, L.5.a**	**Compare-and-Contrast Essay, SE**, p. 593 **W.2, W.2.b**	**Critical Reading, SE**, p. 592; **Selection Tests A and B, UR3**, pp. 153–154
Vocabulary, SE, p. 594: conjectural, unwonted, appendage, conflagration, peremptorily; **Word Analysis: Latin Root –pend-, SE**, p. 612; **Vocabulary: Word/Phrase Relationships, SE**, p. 612 **L.4.b**	**Introductory Phrases and Clauses, SE**, p. 613; **WG, Ch. 19, Sections 1–3; Connecting to the Essential Question, SE**, p. 594; **Writing Lesson: Literary Criticism, SE**, p. 612; **Grammar in Your Writing, SE**, p. 613 **W.1, L.1**	**Critical Reading, SE**, p. 610; **Selection Tests A and B, UR3**, pp. 168–173
Vocabulary, SE, p. 615: shares, pervading, levee, emigrants, profusion, foothold, prairie, forded, ravine **L.4.b**	**Research Task, Topic: Westward Expansion, SE**, p. 624 **W.7, W.8**	**Critical Reading, SE**, pp. 621, 622; **Test Practice: Reading, SE**, p. 624; **Selection Tests A and B, UR3**, pp. 176–177
Vocabulary, SE, p. 626: forestall, repression, elusive, tumultuously; **Vocabulary: Synonyms, SE**, p. 633	**Writing: Reflective Essay, SE**, p. 633 **W.3, W.3.c**	**Critical Reading, SE**, p. 632; **Selection Tests A and B, UR3**, pp. 190–195
Vocabulary, SE, p. 634: salient, dissension, stark, guile, myriad; **Vocabulary: Antonyms, SE**, p. 639 **L.5**	**Writing: Report on Literary History, SE**, p. 639 **W.1**	**Critical Reading, SE**, p. 638; **Selection Tests A and B, UR3**, pp. 208–213
Vocabulary, SE, p. 640: repose, degenerate, epitaph, chronicles; **Word Analysis: Latin Root -genus-, SE**, p. 649; **Vocabulary: Evaluating Logic, SE**, p. 649 **L.4**	**Writing Lesson: Outline for a Short Story, SE**, p. 649 **W.3**	**Critical Reading, SE**, pp. 644, 647; **Selection Tests A and B, UR3**, pp. 226–231
Vocabulary, SE, p. 650: reverential, tremulously, inert, prelude, jocularity; **Multiple Meaning Words from Music, SE**, p. 663; **Vocabulary: Word Meanings, SE**, p. 663 **L.4, L.6**	**Writing Lesson: Editorial, SE**, p. 663 **RL.3, RL.9, W.1, W.5**	**Critical Reading, SE**, p. 661; **Selection Tests A and B, UR3**, pp. 244–249

Vocabulary	Grammar/Writing	Assessment
Vocabulary, SE, p. 706: tedious, insidious, digress, malingers, meticulous, obtuse; **Word Analysis: Greek Prefix di-, SE**, p. 715; **Vocabulary: Synonyms, SE**, p. 715	**Writing Lesson: Character Analysis, SE**, p. 715 **W.2, W.2.b, W.2.d**	**Critical Reading, SE**, p. 712; **Selection Tests A and B, UR4**, pp. 19–24
Vocabulary, SE, p. 718; voluminous, dogma, apparition; **Word Analysis: Forms of appear, SE**, p. 727; **Vocabulary: True or False, SE**, p. 727 **L.4.b**	**Writing Lesson: An Editor's Review of a Manuscript, SE**, p. 727 **W.2, W.2.b**	**Critical Reading, SE**, pp. 721, 722, 724, 725; **Selection Tests A and B, UR4**, pp. 37–42
Vocabulary, SE, p. 728; fallowness, fortuitous, sinuous, mundane, poignant, sediment; **Word Analysis: Latin Root -sed-, SE**, p. 754; **Context, SE**, p. 754 **L.4.a, L.4.b**	**Subject-Verb Agreement, SE**, p. 755; **WG, Chapter 21, Section 1; Connecting to the Essential Question, SE**, p. 728; **Writing Lesson: Literary Criticism, SE**, p. 754 **W.2, W.2.b, L.1**	**Critical Reading, SE**, p. 752; **Selection Tests A and B, UR4**, pp. 56–61

All selections are supported in the *Reader's Notebooks*.

Unit 4: Disillusion, Defiance, and Discontent (*continued*)

	Selection	Reading Strategy	Literary Analysis
PART 1 (*continued*)	"The Turtle" from *The Grapes of Wrath* (A), John Steinbeck, SE, p. 758	Analyze Patterns of Symbolism, SE, p. 756	Allegory, SE, p. 756 RL.1, RL.4, RL.6
	"Migrant Mother," Dorothea Lange, SE, p. 767; "Dust Bowl Blues," Woody Guthrie, SE, p. 768	Drawing Inferences, p. 764 RL.1, RI.1	
	"The Unknown Citizen" (A), W. H. Auden, SE, p. 774	Evaluate Structure as It Relates to Meaning, SE, p. 772	Satire, Tone, SE, p. 772
	"old age sticks" (MC), E. E. Cummings, SE, p. 780; "anyone lived in a pretty how town" (MC), E.E. Cummings, SE, p. 781	Paraphrase, SE, p. 778	Author's Style, SE, p. 778 RL.4, RL.5
	"Of Modern Poetry" (MC), Wallace Stevens, SE, p. 786; "Ars Poetica" (MC), Archibald MacLeish, SE, p. 789; "Poetry" (MC), Marianne Moore, SE, p. 791	Analyze Philosophical Arguments, SE p. 784 RL.1	Poetic Devices, SE, p. 784 RL.4
PART 2	"In Another Country" (A), Ernest Hemingway, SE, p. 800	Strategies for Reading Short Stories, SE p. 797; Identifying with Characters, SE, p. 798	Author's Style, SE, p. 798 RL.2, RL.4 Spiral Review, p. 804
	"A Rose for Emily" (A), William Faulkner, SE, p. 816; Nobel Prize Acceptance Speech (A), William Faulkner, SE, p. 828	Clarify Ambiguity, SE, p. 814	Resolution, SE p. 814 RL.1, RL.3 Spiral Review, p. 819
	"The Jilting of Granny Weatherall" (A), Katherine Anne Porter, SE, p. 834	Clarify the Sequence of Events, SE, p. 832	Stream of Consciousness, SE, p. 832 RL.3, RL.5
	"A Worn Path" (MC), Eudora Welty, SE, p. 848	Generate Questions, Then Make Predictions, SE, p. 846	Archetype, SE, p. 846 RL.3, RL.5
	"The Night the Ghost Got In" (A), James Thurber, SE, p. 860	Analyzing Cause and Effect, SE, p. 858	Humorous Essay, SE, p. 858 RI.3, RI.4
	"Chicago" (MA), Carl Sandburg, SE, p. 868; "Grass" (A), Carl Sandburg, SE, p. 870	Evaluate the Effects of Repetition, SE, p. 866	Apostrophe, SE, p. 866 RL.4, RL.5
	Robert Frost's Poetry (A, A, A, MA, A, MC), SE, p. 874	Read Poetry in Sentences, SE, p. 872	Blank Verse, SE, p. 872 RL.5, RL.9
PART 3	"The Negro Speaks of Rivers" (MC), Langston Hughes, SE, p. 902; "I, Too" (A), Langston Hughes, SE, p. 904; "Dream Variations" (MC), Langston Hughes, SE, p. 906; "Refugee in America" (A), Langston Hughes, SE, p. 907	Apply a Critical Perspective, SE, p. 901	Speaker, SE, p. 901 RL.2, RL.9
	"Study the Masters," Lucille Clifton, SE, p. 915; "For My Children," Colleen McElroy, SE, p. 916	Comparing Poetry of Cultural Identity, SE, p. 913 RL.2, RL.4	Poetry of Cultural Identity, SE, p. 913
	"The Tropics in New York" (MC), Claude McKay, SE, p. 923; "A Black Man Talks of Reaping" (MC), Arna Bontemps, SE, p. 924; "From the Dark Tower" (A), Countee Cullen, SE, p. 926	Applying a Political Approach to Literary Criticism, SE, p. 922	Stanza, SE, p. 922 RL.5, RL.9
	from *Dust Tracks on a Road* (A), Zora Neale Hurston, SE, p. 930	Analyze the Effect of the Author's Purpose, SE, p. 928; Evaluate Validity and Reliability, SE, p. 938 RI.4, RI.6	Autobiography, SE, p. 928 Spiral Review, p. 932

Key: *UR: Unit Resources*   **A:** Average   **MA:** More Accessible   **MC:** More Challenging   © Indicates an Exemplar Text

Vocabulary	Grammar/Writing	Assessment
Vocabulary, SE, p. 756: dispersal, plodding, embankment, frantic; **Word Analysis: Latin Prefix** *pro-*, **SE**, p. 763; **Word/Phrase Relationships, SE**, p. 763; **L.5**	**Connecting to the Essential Question, SE**, p. 756; **Writing Lesson: Essay About Historical Context, SE**, p. 763 **W.2, W.2.b, W.2.c, W.7**	**Critical Reading, SE**, p. 761; **Selection Tests A and B**, *UR4*, pp. 74–79
Vocabulary, SE, p. 765: migrant, exposures, huddled, stout		**Critical Reading, SE**, p. 769; **Selection Tests A and B**, *UR4*, pp. 82–83
Vocabulary, SE, p. 772: conduct, psychology, sensible; **Word Analysis: Greek Root** *-psych-*, **SE**, p. 777; **Vocabulary: Assessing Logic, SE**, p. 777; **L.4.b**	**Writing Lesson: Political Approach to Literary Criticism, SE**, p. 777 **W.2, W.2.b, W.2.f**	**Critical Reading, SE**, p. 776; **Selection Tests A and B**, *UR4*, pp. 96–101
Vocabulary, SE, p. 778: sowed, reaped; **Vocabulary: Analogies, SE**, p. 783 **L.5**	**Connecting to the Essential Question, SE**, p. 778; **Writing: Poet's Introduction, SE**, p. 783 **W.2, W.2.b**	**Critical Reading, SE**, p. 782; **Selection Tests A and B**, *UR4*, pp. 141–146
Vocabulary, SE, p. 784: suffice, insatiable, palpable, derivative; **Word Analysis: Latin Root** *-satis-*, **SE**, p. 794; **Vocabulary: Use New Words, SE**, p. 794; **W.4.b, W.4.d**	**Connecting to the Essential Question, SE**, p. 784; **Writing Lesson: Comparison-and-Contrast Essay, SE**, p. 794 **W.2, W.9.a**	**Critical Reading, SE**, pp. 787, 790, 792; **Selection Tests A and B**, *UR4*, pp. 161–166
Vocabulary, SE, p. 798: detached, disgrace, resign; **Vocabulary: Use New Words, SE**, p. 807 **W.4, W.4.a**	**Connecting to the Essential Question, SE**, p. 798; **Writing: Critical Essay on Style, SE**, p. 807 **W.2, W.2.b**	**Critical Reading, SE**, pp. 806, 813; **Selection Tests A and B**, *UR4*, pp. 179–184
Vocabulary, SE, p. 814: encroached, vanquished, vindicated, circumvent, virulent, inextricable; **Word Analysis: Latin Prefix** *-in-*, **SE**, p. 831; **Vocabulary: Analogies, SE**, p. 831; **L.4.b, L.5**	**Connecting to the Essential Question, SE**, p. 814; **Writing Lesson: Critical Review, SE**, p. 831 **W.1**	**Critical Reading, SE**, pp. 827, 829; **Selection Tests A and B**, *UR4*, pp. 191–202
Vocabulary, SE, p. 832: tactful, piety, dyspepsia; **Word Analysis: Greek Prefix** *dys-*, **SE**, p. 845; **Vocabulary: Sentence Completion, SE**, p. 845; **L.4.b, L.4.d**	**Connecting to the Essential Question, SE**, p. 832; **Writing Lesson: Stream-of-Consciousness Monologue, SE**, p. 845 **W.3, W.3.b, W.3.d**	**Critical Reading, SE**, p. 843; **Selection Tests A and B**, *UR4*, pp. 215–220
Vocabulary, SE, p. 846: grave, persistent, limber, obstinate; **Vocabulary: Yes or No?, SE**, p. 857 **L.4.a**	**Connecting to the Essential Question, SE**, p. 846; **Writing: Sequel, SE**, p. 857 **W.3, W.3.a**	**Critical Reading, SE**, p. 856; **Selection Tests A and B**, *UR4*, pp. 233–238
Vocabulary, SE, p. 858: despondent, intervene, reluctant, blaspheming; **Vocabulary: Context Clues, SE**, p. 865 **L.4.a, L.5.a**	**Connecting to the Essential Question, SE**, p. 858; **Writing: Analytical Essay on Humor, SE**, p. 865 **W.2, W.2.b, W.2.f**	**Critical Reading, SE**, p. 864; **Selection Tests A and B**, *UR4*, pp. 257–262
Vocabulary, SE, p. 866: brutal, wanton, cunning; **Vocabulary: Sentence Completions, SE**, p. 871 **L.2.b, L.5.a**	**Connecting to the Essential Question, SE**, p. 866; **Writing: Analytical Essay, SE**, p. 871 **W.2, W.2.b, W.9.a**	**Critical Reading, SE**, pp. 869, 870; **Selection Tests A and B**, *UR4*, pp. 275–280
Vocabulary, SE, p. 872: poise, rueful, luminary; **Word Root: Latin Root** *-lum-*, **SE**, p. 887; **Vocabulary: Analogies, SE**, p. 887 **L.4.b, L.5**	**Connecting to the Essential Question, SE**, p. 872; **Writing Lesson: Critical Essay, SE**, p. 887 **W.1**	**Critical Reading, SE**, pp. 876, 879, 881, 885; **Selection Tests A and B**, *UR4*, pp. 295–300
Vocabulary, SE, p. 901: lulled, dusky, liberty; **Word Analysis: Latin Root** *-liber-*, **SE**, p. 909; **Vocabulary: Analogies, SE**, p. 909; **Connotation and Denotation: Words for Freedom, SE**, p. 909	**Grammar and Style Lesson: Pronoun-Antecedent Agreement, SE**, p. 911; *WG*, Chapter 21, Section 2; **Connecting to the Essential Question, SE**, p. 901; **Writing Lesson: Multi-Genre Response to Literature, SE**, p. 910 **W.2, W.2.d, W.5, L.1**	**Critical Reading, SE**, pp. 905, 907; **Selection Tests A and B**, *UR4*, pp. 295–300
Vocabulary, SE, p. 913: handiwork, heritage, rituals, effigies	**Writing to Compare Literary Works, SE**, p. 919 **W.2, W.9**	**Critical Reading, SE**, p. 918; **Selection Tests A and B**, *UR4*, pp. 304–305
Vocabulary, SE, p. 922: benediction, increment, countenance, beguile; **Antonyms, SE**, p. 927 **L.5, L.5.a**	**Connecting to the Essential Question, SE**, p. 922; **Writing: Compare-and-Contrast Essay, SE**, p. 927 **W.2, W.2b**	**Critical Reading, SE**, pp. 925, 926; **Selection Tests A and B**, *UR4*, pp. 318–323
Vocabulary, SE, p. 928: brazenness, caper, duration, exalted; **Vocabulary: Use New Words, SE**, p. 937	**Connecting to the Essential Question, SE**, p. 928; **Writing: Reflective Essay, SE**, p. 937 **W.2, W.2.a, W.2.b, W.2.e**	**Critical Reading, SE**, p. 936; **Selection Tests A and B**, *UR4*, pp. 336–341

All selections are supported in the *Reader's Notebooks*.

Unit 5: Prosperity and Protest

	Selection	Reading Strategy	Literary Analysis
PART 1	from *Hiroshima* (MC), John Hersey, SE, p. 984; "The Death of the Ball Turret Gunner" (MA), Randall Jarrell, SE, p. 997	Analyzing the Writers' Political Assumptions, SE, p. 982	Implied Theme, SE, p. 982 RL.1 Spiral Review, p. 989
	Junk Rally, SE, p. 1003; "The Battle of the Easy Chair," Dr. Seuss, SE, p. 1004; "Backing the Attack," Editors of *The New York Times*, p. 1005	Evaluate the Persuasive Use of Symbols, SE, p. 1000 RI.5, RI.7	Editorial, SE, p. 1000
PART 2	"The Life You Save May Be Your Own" (A), Flannery O'Connor, SE, p. 1012	Draw Conclusions, SE, p. 1010	Grotesque Characters and Characterization, SE, p. 1010 RL.1, RL.3 Spiral Review, p. 1016
	"The First Seven Years" (A), Bernard Malamud, SE, p. 1028	Summarize, SE, p. 1026 RL.2	Plot, SE, p. 1026 RL.3, RL.4 Spiral Review, p. 1033
	"Constantly Risking Absurdity" (A), Lawrence Ferlinghetti, SE, p. 1042	Visualizing or Picturing the Action, SE, p. 1040	Extended Metaphor, SE, p. 1040 RL.4
	"Mirror" (A), Sylvia Plath, SE, p. 1052; "Courage" (MC), Anne Sexton, SE, p. 1053	Interpreting the Connotations, SE, p. 1050	Figurative Language, SE, p. 1050 RL.4
	"Cuttings" (A), Theodore Roethke, SE, p. 1059; "Cuttings (later)" (A), Theodore Roethke, SE, p. 1060	Using Background Knowledge, SE, p. 1056	Sound Devices, SE, p. 1056 RL.4, RL.5
	"The Explorer" (MC), Gwendolyn Brooks, SE, p. 1064; "Frederick Douglass" (MA), Robert Hayden, SE, p. 1066	Read the Poems Aloud, SE, p. 1062	Repetition and Parallelism, SE, p. 1062 RL.4, RL.5
	"One Art" (A), Elizabeth Bishop, SE, p. 1072; "Filling Station" (A), Elizabeth Bishop, SE, p. 1075	Read According to Punctuation, SE, p. 1070	Diction and Rhetorical Devices, SE, p. 1070 RL.4, RL.5
PART 3	"The Rockpile" (A), James Baldwin, SE, p. 1082	Identify Cause-and-Effect Relationships, SE, p. 1080 RL.5	Setting and Symbol, SE, p. 1080 RL.3
	"Life in His Language" (MC), Toni Morrison, SE, p. 1096	Analyze Patterns of Organization, SE, p. 1094 RI.3, RI.5	Eulogy, SE, p. 1094

Key: *UR:* *Unit Resources*   **A:** Average   **MA:** More Accessible   **MC:** More Challenging   © Indicates an Exemplar Text

Vocabulary	Grammar/Writing	Assessment
Vocabulary, SE, p. 982: evacuated, volition, rendezvous, incessant, convivial; **Military Words From Other Languages, SE,** p. 999; **Sentence Completions, SE,** p. 999 **L.6**	**Writing Lesson: Compare-and-Contrast Essay on Theme, SE,** p. 999 **W.2, W.2.b, W.2.f**	**Critical Reading, SE,** pp. 995, 997; **Selection Tests A and B,** *UR5,* pp. 19–24
Vocabulary, SE, p. 1001: civilian, license, undertaking, canvass, collective, expenditures, estimates, receipts **L.4.c, L.6**	**Research Task, Topic: Society and Culture in the Media, SE,** p. 1008 **W.6, W.7, W.8**	**Critical Reading, SE,** p. 1006; **Test Practice: Reading, SE,** p. 1008; **Selection Tests A and B,** *UR5,* pp. 22–24
Vocabulary, SE, p. 1010: desolate, listed, ominous, ravenous, morose; **Word Analysis: Latin Root -*sol-*, SE,** p. 1025; **Vocabulary: Context Clues, SE,** p. 1025 **L.4.a, L.4.b**	**Writing Lesson: Essay of Interpretation, SE,** p. 1025 **W.2, W.2.b, W.2.c, W.2.f**	**Critical Reading, SE,** p. 1023; **Selection Tests A and B,** *UR5,* pp. 41–46
Vocabulary, SE, p. 1026: diligence, illiterate, unscrupulous, repugnant, discern; **Word Analysis: Latin Root -*litera-*, SE,** p. 1039; **Vocabulary: Context Clues, SE,** p. 1039 **L.4.a, L.4.b**	**Writing Lesson: Personality Profile, SE,** p. 1039 **W.2.a, W.2.b**	**Critical Reading, SE,** p. 1037; **Selection Tests A and B,** *UR5,* pp. 59–64
Vocabulary, SE, p. 1040: absurdity, realist, taut; **Use New Words, SE,** p. 1045 **L.4**	**Writing: Poem Using an Extended Metaphor, SE,** p. 1045 **W.4**	**Critical Reading, SE,** p. 1043, 1049; **Selection Tests A and B,** *UR5,* pp. 77–82
Vocabulary, SE, p. 1050: preconceptions, endured, transfusion, transformed; **Sentence Completions, SE,** p. 1055 **L.4**	**Writing: Analytical Essay, SE,** p. 1055 **W.2**	**Critical Reading, SE,** p. 1054; **Selection Tests A and B,** *UR5,* pp. 55–100
Vocabulary, SE, p. 1056: intricate, seeping, quail; **Revise to Improve Logic, SE,** p. 1061	**Writing: Essay Comparing Science to Poetry, SE,** p. 1061 **L.3**	**Critical Reading, SE,** p. 1060; **Selection Tests A and B,** *UR5,* pp. 113–118
Vocabulary, SE, p. 1062: frayed, wily, gaudy; **Word/Phrase Relationships, SE,** p. 1069; **Assessing Logic, SE,** p. 1069 **L.4, L.4.a, L.5**	**Writing Lesson: Literary Criticism, SE,** p. 1069 **W.2, W.2.b**	**Critical Reading, SE,** p. 1064, 1067; **Selection Tests A and B,** *UR5,* pp. 131–136
Vocabulary, SE, p. 1070: master, intent, permeated, extraneous; **Latin Word *extra*, SE,** p. 1078; **Synonyms, SE,** p. 1078 **L.4.b, L.5**	**Writing Lesson: Multi-Genre Response to Poetry, SE,** p. 1078 **W.5, W.6**	**Critical Reading, SE,** p. 1076; **Selection Tests A and B,** *UR5,* pp. 155–160
Vocabulary, SE, p. 1080: latent, engrossed, jubilant, superficial, perdition; **Word Analysis: Latin Prefix *super-*, SE,** p. 1092; **Categorizing Vocabulary, SE,** p. 1092 **L.4.b, L.5**	**Avoiding Shifts in Verb Tense, SE,** p. 1093; **Grammar in Your Writing, SE,** p. 1093; *WG,* **Chapter 21, Section 2; Connecting to the Essential Question, SE,** pp. 1080; **Writing Lesson: Radio Play, SE,** p. 1092 **W.3, W.3.b, L.1**	**Critical Reading, SE,** pp. 1090; **Selection Tests A and B,** *UR5,* pp. 174–179
Vocabulary, SE, p. 1094: summation, scenario, platitudes, appropriate; **Vocabulary: Sentence Completions, SE,** p. 1101 **L.4.a**	**Writing Lesson: Essay of Tribute, SE,** p. 1101 **W.2, W.2.a**	**Critical Reading, SE,** p. 1100; **Selection Tests A and B,** *UR5,* pp. 192–197

All selections are supported in the *Reader's Notebooks.*

Unit 5: Prosperity and Protest (*continued*)

	Selection	Reading Strategy	Literary Analysis
PART 3 (continued)	*Inaugural Address* (A), John Fitzgerald Kennedy, SE, p. 1104; from "Letter from Birmingham City Jail" (A), Martin Luther King, Jr., SE, p. 1109	Identify Main Ideas and Supporting Details, SE, p. 1102	Rhetorical Devices, SE, p. 1102 RI.5
	The Crucible, Act I (A), Arthur Miller, SE, p. 1124	Identify the Text Structures, SE, p. 1123 RL.5	Plot and Dramatic Exposition, SE, p. 1123 RL.3 Spiral Review, p. 1140
	The Crucible, Act II (A), Arthur Miller, SE, p. 1161	Making Predictions, SE, p. 1160	Conflict and Biblical Allusions, SE, p. 1160 RL.3, RL.5, RL.7 Spiral Review, p. 1167
	The Crucible, Act III (A), Arthur Miller, SE, p. 1187	Evaluate Arguments, SE, p. 1186	Characterization and Irony, SE, p. 1186 RL.3, RL.6 Spiral Review, p. 1205
	The Crucible, Act IV (A), Arthur Miller, SE, p. 1217	Evaluate the Influences of the Historical Period, SE, p. 1216	Tragedy and Allegory, SE, p. 1216 RL.2, RL.3, RL.6 Spiral Review, p. 1232
	from *Good Night, and Good Luck,* George Clooney and Grant Heslov SE, p. 1239	Comparing Political Drama Past and Present, SE, p. 1239 RL.1	

Unit 6: New Voices, New Frontiers

	Selection	Reading Strategy	Literary Analysis
PART 1	"Antojos" (MA), Julia Alvarez, SE, p. 1298	Making Predictions, SE, p. 1296	In Medias Res, SE, p. 1296 RL.3, RL.5 Spiral Review, p. 1303
	"Everyday Use" (A), Alice Walker, SE, p. 1312	Comparing and Contrasting Characters, SE, p. 1310	Characterization, SE, p. 1310 RL.3
PART 2	"Everything Stuck to Him" (A), Raymond Carver, SE, p. 1326	Asking Questions, SE, p. 1324 RL.5	Author's Style, SE, p. 1324 RL.4
	"Traveling Through the Dark" (A), William Stafford, SE, p. 1336; "The Secret" (A), Denise Levertov, SE, p. 1339; "The Gift" (A), Li-Young Lee, SE, p. 1342	Interpreting, SE, p. 1334 RL.1	Lyric Poem, SE, p. 1334

Key: *UR: Unit Resources*   **A:** Average   **MA:** More Accessible   **MC:** More Challenging   © Indicates an Exemplar Text

...bulary	Grammar/Writing	Assessment
...lary, SE, p. 1102: alliance, invective, adversary, eradicate, ...t, profundity; **Word Analysis: Latin Root -vert- or -vers-, SE,** ... Synonyms, SE, p. 1114 L.5	**Using Active, Not Passive, Voice, SE, p. 1115; Grammar in Your Writing, SE, p. 1115; WG, Chapter 21, Section 4; Connecting to the Essential Question, SE, p. 1102; Writing Lesson: Letter to the Editor, SE, p. 1114** W.1, W.1.d, L.3	**Critical Reading, SE, p. 1107, 1112; Selection Tests A and B, UR5,** pp. 211–216
...lary, SE, p. 1123: predilection, ingratiating, dissembling, ...y, inculcation, propitiation, evade; **Word Analysis: Latin ...rat-, SE, p. 1159; Sentence Completions, SE, p. 1159**	**Writing Lesson: Newspaper Article, SE, p. 1159** W.2, W.2.a, W.2.b, W.2.e	**Thinking About the Commentary, SE,** p. 1121; **Critical Reading, SE, p. 1157; Selection Tests A and B, UR5,** pp. 232–237
...lary, SE, p. 1160: pallor, ameliorate, avidly, base, deference, ...y; **Word Analysis: Greek Suffix -logy, SE, p. 1183; True or** ...SE, p. 1183 L.4.b	**Writing Lesson: Persuasive Letter, SE, p. 1183** W.1	**Critical Reading, SE, p. 1181; Selection Tests A and B, UR5, pp. 250–255**
...lary, SE, p. 1186: contentious, deposition, imperceptible, ...nity, effrontery, incredulously; **Word Analysis: Legal Terms,** ...215; **Synonyms and Antonyms, SE, p. 1215** 6	**Writing Lesson: Workplace Document/Legal Brief, SE, p. 1215** W.1, W.1.a, W.1.b, W.1.e	**Critical Reading, SE, p. 1213; Selection Tests A and B, UR5, pp. 268–273**
...lary, SE, p. 1216: conciliatory, beguile, retaliation, adamant, ...tantalized; **Word Analysis: Words from Myths, SE, p. 1235;** ...ms, SE, p. 1235; **Using Resources to Build Vocabulary,** ...235 4.c, L.5	**Avoiding Sentence Fragments and Run-ons, SE, p. 1237; Grammar in Your Writing, SE, p. 1237; WG, Chapter 14, Section 4; Writing Lesson: Literary Criticism on Universal Theme, SE, p. 1236** W.2, W.2.a, W.2.b, W.2.f	**Critical Reading, SE, p. 1233; Selection Tests A and B, UR5, pp. 287–292**
...lary, SE, p. 1239: vulnerability, acknowledges, statute, ...rd	**Writing to Compare Literary Works, SE, p. 1249** W.2, W.10	**Critical Reading, SE, p. 1248; Selection Tests A and B, UR5, pp. 296–297**

...bulary	Grammar/Writing	Assessment
...lary, SE, p. 1296: dissuade, maneuver, appease, machetes, ...n, docile; **Words from Other Languages: Spanish, SE, p. 1309;** ...lary: **Synonyms or Antonyms, SE, p. 1309** L.5	**Writing Lesson: Same Story, Different Point of View, SE, p. 1309** W.3, W.3.b, W.3.c, W.3.d	**Thinking About the Commentary, SE,** p. 1295; **Critical Reading, SE, p. 1307; Selection Tests A and B, UR6,** pp. 21–26
...lary, SE, p. 1310: homely, furtive, cowering, doctrines; ...nalysis: **Latin Root -doc- / -doct-, SE, p. 1322; Vocabulary:** ...ies, SE, p. 1322 5	**Grammar and Style Lesson: Using Transitional Expressions, SE, p. 1323; WG, Chapter 27, Section 3; Connecting to the Essential Question, SE, p. 1310; Writing Lesson: Critical Review, SE, p. 1322; Grammar in Your Writing, SE, p. 1323** W.1, W.5, L.1	**Critical Reading, SE, p. 1320; Selection Tests A and B, UR6, pp. 40–45**
...lary, SE, p. 1324: coincide, ambitions, striking, fitfully; ...lary: **Use New Words, SE, p. 1332**	**Writing: Analytical Essay on the Ending, SE, p. 1332** W.2	**Critical Reading, SE, p. 1331; Selection Tests A and B, UR6, pp. 58–63**
...lary, SE, p. 1334: swerve, exhaust, shard; **Related Words:** ...t, SE, p. 1345; **Vocabulary: Repairing Logic, SE, p. 1345**	**Writing Lesson: Compare and Contrast Essay, SE, p. 1345**	**Critical Reading, SE, pp. 1340, 1343; Selection Tests A and B, UR6,** pp. 76–81

All selections are supported in the *Reader's Notebooks*.

Unit 6: New Voices, New Frontiers (*continued*)

	Selection	Reading Strategy	Literary Analysis
PART 2 *(continued)*	"Who Burns for the Perfection of Paper" (MA), Martin Espada, SE, p. 1348; "Camouflaging the Chimera" (MC), Yusef Komunyakaa, SE, p. 1350; "Streets" (MC), Naomi Shihab Nye, SE, p. 1353	Drawing Inferences About the Poet's Beliefs, SE, p. 1346 RL.1	Voice, SE, p. 1346 RL.4
	"Halley's Comet" (A), Stanley Kunitz, SE, p. 1358	Identify Key Details, SE, p. 1356 RL.1	Free Verse, SE, p. 1356 RL.5, RL.6
	"The Latin Deli: An Ars Poetica" (A), Judith Ortiz Cofer, SE, p. 1366	Analyze Sensory Details, SE, p. 1364	Imagery, SE, p. 1364 RL.4
	"Onomatopoeia" (MA), William Safire, SE, p. 1378	Paraphrase, SE, p. 1376	Expository Essay, SE, p. 1376 RI.3, RI.4
	"Coyote v. Acme" (A), Ian Frazier, SE, p. 1384	Analyze Cause and Effect, SE, p. 1382 RI.5	Parody and Satire, SE, p. 1382 RI.6 Spiral Review, p. 1387
PART 3	"One Day, Now Broken in Two" (A), Anna Quindlen, SE, p. 1392	Relate the Literary Work to Primary Sources, SE, p. 1392	Comparison-and-Contrast Essay, SE, p. 1394 RI.5
	"Urban Renewal" (A), Sean Ramsay, SE, p. 1401; "Playing for the Fighting Sixty-Ninth" (A), William Harvey, SE, p. 1403	Apply Background Knowledge, SE, p. 1398 RI.1	Oral History and E-mail, SE, p. 1398
	"Mother Tongue" (A), Amy Tan, SE, p. 1410; "For the Love of Books" (MA), Rita Dove, SE, p. 1417	Outline, SE, p. 1408 RI.1, RI.2	Reflective Essay, SE, p. 1408 Spiral Review, p. 1415
	from *The Woman Warrior* (A), Maxine Hong Kingston, SE, p. 1426; from *The Names* (A), N. Scott Momaday, SE, p. 1434	Relate [Memoirs] to Your Own Experience, SE, p. 1424	Memoirs, SE, p. 1424 RI.6

Key: *UR: Unit Resources*   **A:** Average   **MA:** More Accessible   **MC:** More Challenging   © Indicates an Exemplar Text

Vocabulary	Grammar/Writing	Assessment
Vocabulary, SE, p. 1346: crevices, terrain, refuge; **Vocabulary: Synonyms, SE**, p. 1355 L.5, L.5.b	**Analytical Essay on Theme, SE**, p. 1355 W.2	**Critical Reading, SE**, p. 1354; **Selection Tests A and B**, *UR6*, pp. 94–99
Vocabulary, SE, p. 1356: proclaiming, repent, steal; **Word Analysis: Latin Prefix *pro-*, SE**, p. 1361; **Vocabulary: Word Mapping, SE**, p. 1361 L.4.c, L.5	**Writing Lesson: Reflective Essay, SE**, p. 1361 W.3, W.3.e	**Critical Reading, SE**, p. 1359; **Selection Tests A and B**, *UR6*, pp. 112–117
Vocabulary, SE, p. 1364: heady, ample, divine; **Vocabulary: Sentence Completions, SE**, p. 1369 L.4	**Writing: Interpretive Essay, SE**, p. 1369 W.2	**Critical Reading, SE**, pp. 1368, 1372; **Selection Tests A and B**, *UR6*, pp. 130–135
Vocabulary, SE, p. 1376: synonymous, derive, speculation, coinage; **Vocabulary: Sentence Completions, SE**, p. 1381 L.4.A	**Writing: Research Paper on Word Origins, SE**, p. 1381 W.2, W.7	**Critical Reading, SE**, p. 1380; **Selection Tests A and B**, *UR6*, pp. 154–159
Vocabulary, SE, p. 1382: contiguous, incorporated, vigorously, systemic, emit, punitive; **Word Analysis: Latin Root *-corpus-*, SE**, p. 1391: **Vocabulary: Definitions, SE**, p. 1391 4.B	**Writing Lesson: Parody of an Opening Statement, SE**, p. 1391 W.1, W.1.A, W.1.C	**Critical Reading, SE**, p. 1389; **Selection Tests A and B**, *UR6*, pp. 172–177
Vocabulary, SE, p. 1402: mundane, induce, savagery, revelations, prosperity; **Vocabulary: Use New Words, SE**, p. 1397 L.4	**Writing: Letter to the Author, SE**, p. 1397 W.2, W.2.e	**Critical Reading, SE**, p. 1396; **Selection Tests A and B**, *UR6*, pp. 194–199
Vocabulary, SE, p. 1399: memorials, homages, intently, fatigues, intonation, regiment, casualties, cadence L.4.c, L.5, L.6	**Research Task: The Value and Values of Memorials, SE** p. 1407 W.1, W.7, W.8	**Critical Reading, SE**, p. 1405; **Selection Tests A and B**, *UR6*, pp. 180–181
Vocabulary, SE, p. 1408: transcribed, benign, ecstasy, daunting, aspirations; **Word Analysis: Latin Root *-scrib-*, *-script-*, SE**, p. 1422; **Vocabulary: Sentence Completions, SE**, p. 1422 L.3, L.4.b	**Writing Lesson: Letter to the Author, SE**, p. 1422; **Grammar in Your Writing, SE**, p. 1423 W.2, W.2.d	**Critical Reading, SE entire**, p. 1416, 1420; **Selection Tests A and B**, *UR6*, pp. 213–218
Vocabulary, SE, p. 1424: inaudibly, gravity, oblivious, pastoral, supple; **Word Analysis: Latin Root *-aud-*, SE**, p. 1440; **Vocabulary: Sentence Completions, SE**, p. 1440 L.3.a, L.4.b	**Writing Lesson: Memoir, SE**, p. 1440; **Grammar in Your Writing, SE**, p. 1441 W.3, W.3.d	**Critical Reading, SE**, p. 1432, 1438; **Selection Tests A and B**, *UR6*, pp. 232–237

All selections are supported in the *Reader's Notebooks*.

1 Where Do I Start?

Right here! These pages will guide you through the program's unique organization and describe the many resources that will enrich your teaching.

2 How Do I Introduce the Essential Questions?

The literature in this book is presented through the lens of three key Essential Questions. Use the **Introduction to the Essential Questions** to give students a framework for understanding the overarching ideas that will guide their reading.

3 How Do I Introduce the Unit?

Each unit in this book presents the literature of a specific time period. Use the unit **Introduction** to examine multiple perspectives on an era and to develop students' understanding and appreciation for literature in its broader context.

The **Snapshot of the Period** at the beginning of every unit presents key information graphically.

Recent Scholarship features provide students with college-level analyses of the time period and related topics or themes.

A **Historical Background** provides students with a deeper understanding of the historical context.

The **Integrate and Evaluate Information** pages provide both critical-thinking and extension activities.

4 What Should I Use to Plan and Prepare?

Start your planning with the **Time and Resource Manager** that precedes every selection or grouping of texts. This guide provides

- a detailed lesson plan.
- a list of the standards covered in the lesson.
- suggestions for incorporating program resources into your instruction.

For an at-a-glance look at selection resources, see the **Visual Guide to Featured Selection Resources** that precedes each selection or grouping.

Lesson Pacing Guide
Suggested pacing information

Meeting Common Core State Standards
Standard-coverage information

Resources
Suggested resources for differentiated instruction

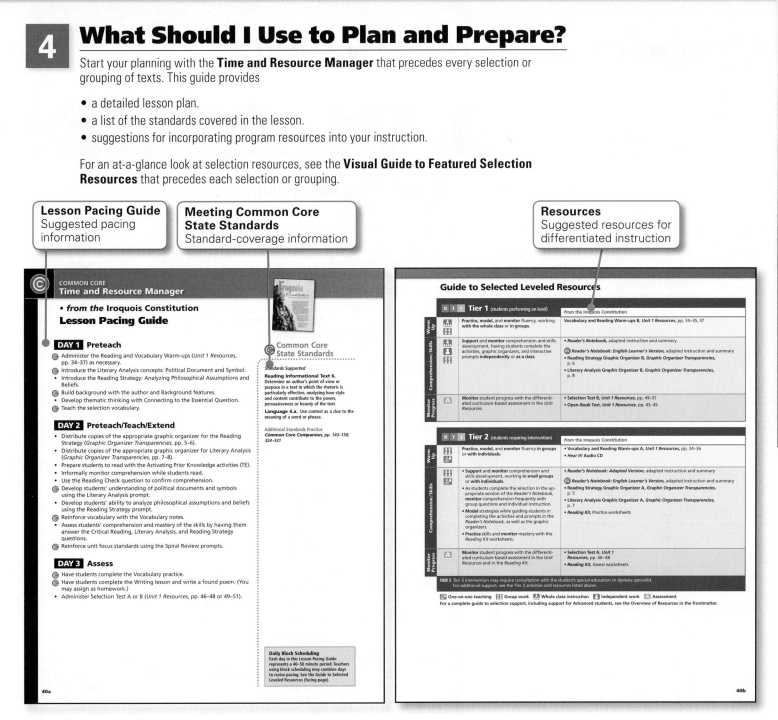

COMMON CORE
Time and Resource Manager

- *from the* **Iroquois Constitution**
Lesson Pacing Guide

DAY 1 Preteach

- Administer the Reading and Vocabulary Warm-ups (*Unit 1 Resources*, pp. 34–37) as necessary.
- Introduce the Literary Analysis concepts: Political Document and Symbol.
- Introduce the Reading Strategy: Analyzing Philosophical Assumptions and Beliefs.
- Build background with the author and Background features.
- Develop thematic thinking with Connecting to the Essential Question.
- Teach the selection vocabulary.

DAY 2 Preteach/Teach/Extend

- Distribute copies of the appropriate graphic organizer for the Reading Strategy (*Graphic Organizer Transparencies*, pp. 5–6).
- Distribute copies of the appropriate graphic organizer for Literary Analysis (*Graphic Organizer Transparencies*, pp. 7–8).
- Prepare students to read with the Activating Prior Knowledge activities (TE).
- Informally monitor comprehension while students read.
- Use the Reading Check question to confirm comprehension.
- Develop students' understanding of political documents and symbols using the Literary Analysis prompt.
- Develop students' ability to analyze philosophical assumptions and beliefs using the Reading Strategy prompt.
- Reinforce vocabulary with the Vocabulary notes.
- Assess students' comprehension and mastery of the skills by having them answer the Critical Reading, Literary Analysis, and Reading Strategy questions.
- Reinforce unit focus standards using the Spiral Review prompts.

DAY 3 Assess

- Have students complete the Vocabulary practice.
- Have students complete the Writing lesson and write a found poem. (You may assign as homework.)
- Administer Selection Test A or B (*Unit 1 Resources*, pp. 46–48 or 49–51).

Common Core State Standards

Standards Supported

Reading Informational Text 6. Determine an author's point of view or purpose in a text in which the rhetoric is particularly effective, analyzing how style and content contribute to the power, persuasiveness or beauty of the text.
Language 4.a. Use context as a clue to the meaning of a word or phrase.

Additional Standards Practice
Common Core Companion, pp. 143–150; 324–331

Daily Block Scheduling
Each day in this Lesson Pacing Guide represents a 40–50 minute period. Teachers using block scheduling may combine days to revise pacing. See the Guide to Selected Leveled Resources (facing page).

40a

Guide to Selected Leveled Resources

R T I **Tier 1** (students performing on level)	*from* the Iroquois Constitution
Warm Up	Practice, model, and monitor fluency, working with the whole class or in groups.	Vocabulary and Reading Warm-ups B, *Unit 1 Resources*, pp. 34–35, 37
Comprehension/Skills	Support and monitor comprehension and skills development, having students complete the activities, graphic organizers, and interactive prompts **independently** or **as a class**.	• *Reader's Notebook*, adapted instruction and summary • *Reader's Notebook: English Learner's Version*, adapted instruction and summary, p. 6 • Reading Strategy Graphic Organizer B, *Graphic Organizer Transparencies*, p. 8 • Literary Analysis Graphic Organizer B, *Graphic Organizer Transparencies*, p. 8
Monitor Progress	Monitor student progress with the differentiated curriculum-based assessment in the *Unit Resources*.	• Selection Test B, *Unit 1 Resources*, pp. 49–51 • Open-Book Test, *Unit 1 Resources*, pp. 43–45

R T I **Tier 2** (students requiring intervention)	*from* the Iroquois Constitution
Warm Up	Practice, model, and monitor fluency in groups or with individuals.	• Vocabulary and Reading Warm-ups A, *Unit 1 Resources*, pp. 34–36 • *Hear It!* Audio CD
Comprehension/Skills	• **Support** and **monitor** comprehension and skills development, working **in small groups** or **with individuals**. • As students complete the selection in the appropriate version of the *Reader's Notebook*, **monitor** comprehension frequently with group questions and individual instruction. • **Model** strategies while guiding students in completing the activities and prompts in the *Reader's Notebook*, as well as the graphic organizers. • **Practice** skills and **monitor** mastery with the *Reading Kit* worksheets.	• *Reader's Notebook: Adapted Version*, adapted instruction and summary • *Reader's Notebook: English Learner's Version*, adapted instruction and summary • Reading Strategy Graphic Organizer A, *Graphic Organizer Transparencies*, p. 5 • Literary Analysis Graphic Organizer A, *Graphic Organizer Transparencies*, p. 7 • *Reading Kit*, Practice worksheets
Monitor Progress	Monitor student progress with the differentiated curriculum-based assessment in the *Unit Resources* and in the *Reading Kit*.	• Selection Test A, *Unit 1 Resources*, pp. 46–48 • *Reading Kit*, Assess worksheets

TIER 3 Tier 3 intervention may require consultation with the student's special-education or dyslexia specialist. For additional support, see the Tier 2 activities and resources listed above.

One-on-one teaching   Group work   Whole class instruction   Independent work   Assessment
For a complete guide to selection support, including support for Advanced students, see the Overview of Resources in the frontmatter.

40b

5 How Does the Program Help Me with Pacing?

The program is organized into three-week instructional blocks, with each block focusing on core skills and standards. This consistent organization ensures thorough skills coverage presented in manageable chunks. A benchmark test is provided at the middle and end of each unit, allowing you to administer assessment at three-, six-, or nine-week intervals. This systematic, logical organization with built-in progress monitoring allows you to make sound instructional choices for your class without skipping or missing any skills or standards.

6 # How Do I Use Each Feature in a Unit?

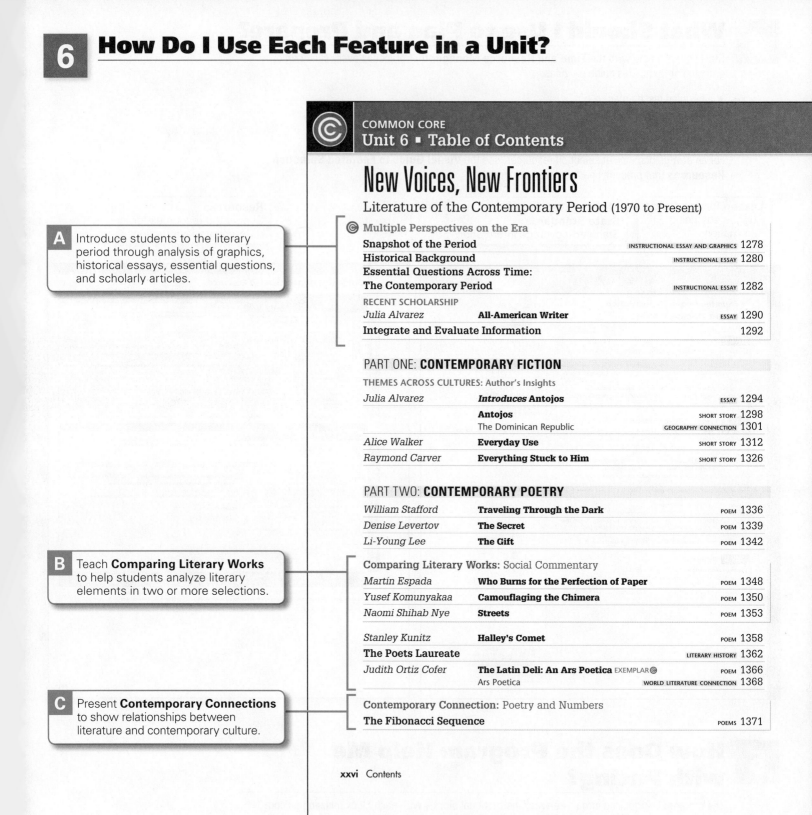

COMMON CORE
Unit 6 ▪ Table of Contents

New Voices, New Frontiers
Literature of the Contemporary Period (1970 to Present)

UNIT **6**

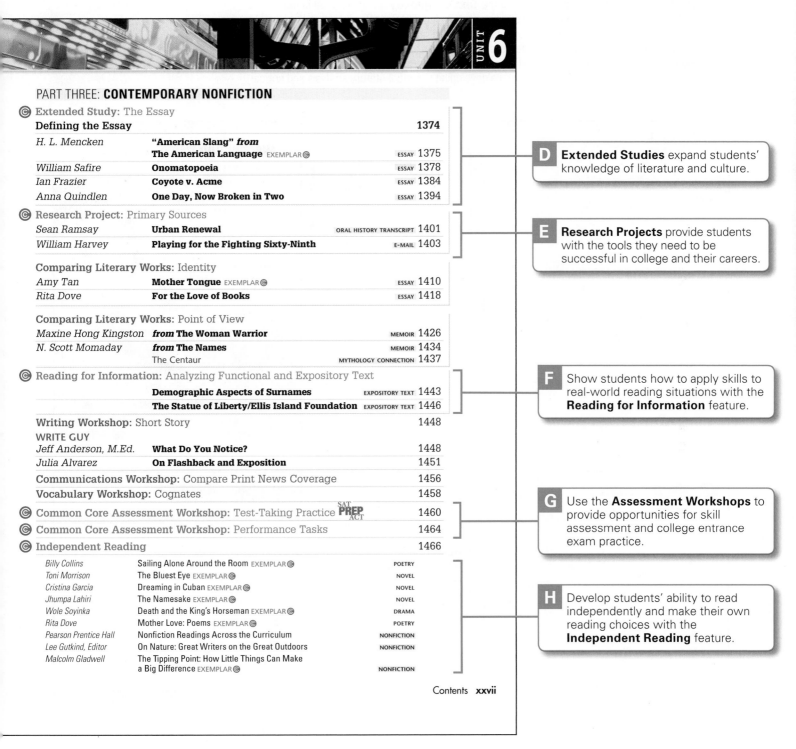

D **Extended Studies** expand students' knowledge of literature and culture.

E **Research Projects** provide students with the tools they need to be successful in college and their careers.

F Show students how to apply skills to real-world reading situations with the **Reading for Information** feature.

G Use the **Assessment Workshops** to provide opportunities for skill assessment and college entrance exam practice.

H Develop students' ability to read independently and make their own reading choices with the **Independent Reading** feature.

Contents **xxvii**

7 How Do I Teach a Selection?

Prentice Hall Literature addresses the challenges of today's mixed-ability classrooms through its unique combination of differentiated instruction, online activities, and skills support. When planning lessons for a diverse group of students, look for the **Text Complexity** rubric provided in the Teacher's Edition at the beginning of each selection or grouping. The Text Complexity rubrics provide a snapshot of each text's relative complexity. The Reader and Task suggestions on the following page provide suggestions for ensuring students' comprehension and success. The instruction for each selection or grouping follows a consistent pattern. This approach allows you and your students to appreciate significant works of literature while developing essential literary analysis and critical reading skills.

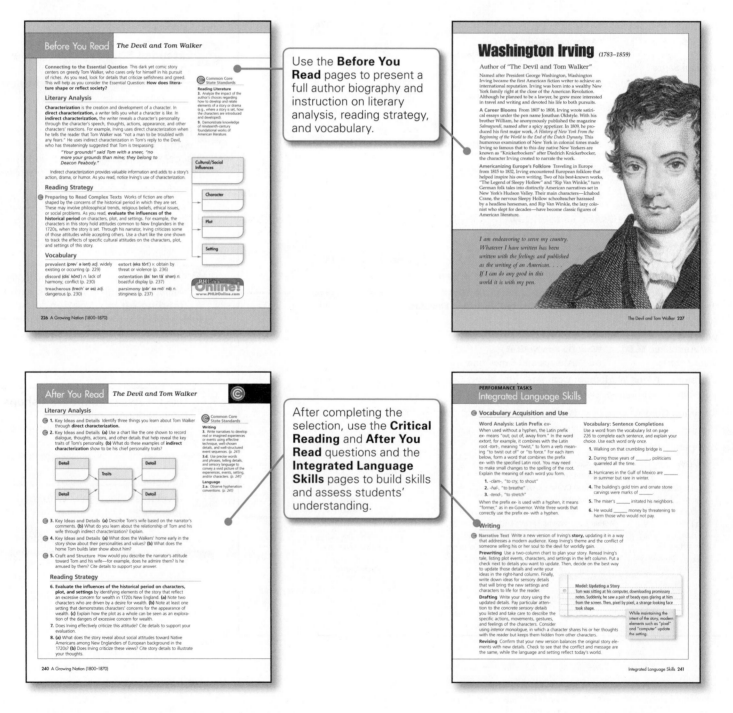

8 How Do I Differentiate Instruction?

Prentice Hall Literature provides unprecedented opportunities for differentiated instruction:

- **Teacher's Edition:** Use the strategies and techniques geared toward different reading levels and learning styles.

- **Reader's Notebooks:** Customize instruction with reading support for struggling readers and English learners.

- **Leveled Vocabulary and Reading Warm-ups:** For each selection, build background, fluency, and vocabulary.

- **Graphic Organizers:** Give struggling readers additional support with completed versions of all organizers in the Student Edition.

Differentiated Instruction for Universal Access

Background for Special-Needs Students
Point out that author Amy Tan uses nonstandard English for the mother's dialogue. Explain that this type of "broken" English is not intended to be derogatory; it represents the communication of a person whose first language is not English and who has not had much instruction in English. The author uses nonstandard English to make the character seem real to readers. Help students identify the nonstandard elements in the mother's speech, adding missing words to complete the thoughts in standard English.

EL Strategy for English Learners
Students may have difficulty understanding the descriptions in the story because of the use of unfamiliar phrases. Help students by using gestures and body language to communicate the meaning of descriptive phrases such as "pursing her lips" (p. 261) and "performed listlessly" (p. 263). Tell students to record these phrases as they read further and to take time to reread and visualize them or act them out.

PHLitOnline provides a customized learning experience for students. Learner levels are assigned to students based on Diagnostic Test results. All selections and support provided are based on that level, creating a truly personalized learning experience!

9 How Do I Monitor Student Progress?

Prentice Hall Literature makes progress monitoring easy with frequent opportunities to evaluate student progress and to reteach material. For more information on the program's assessments, see the Assessment Roadmap in PHLitOnline under Resources & Downloads.

Use the electronic test generator to customize assessment.

- The **Beginning-of-Year Benchmark Test** assesses students' skills and deficiencies at the onset of the year. Test results allow you to tailor your instruction to individual classes or students.

- Use the **Diagnostic Tests** at the beginning of the school year to determine readiness. You will find frequent **reading checks** and suggestions in the Teacher's Edition for monitoring student progress during reading. If taken online, learner levels are assigned automatically based on test results.

- After reading selections, use the **Open Book Tests** and leveled **Selection Tests** to assess comprehension and mastery of the literary, reading, and vocabulary skills.

- As you teach the unit, use the **Assessment Workshop** pages in standardized SAT and ACT test formats to give students practice in applying core skills and in writing for assessment under test-taking conditions. The Performance Task pages provide project-based activities for standards assessment.

- Use the **Benchmark Tests** to monitor progress at regular, frequent intervals. For your convenience, both mid-unit and end-of-unit tests are provided. If taken online, remediation for skills missed is assigned automatically!

- **Mid-Year** and **End-of-Year Summative Tests** provide a measure of student achievement over a longer period of time.

10 When Do I Teach Writing?

This program incorporates opportunities in every unit for both process writing and writing for assessment.

Process Writing: In each unit, a **Writing Workshop** with step-by-step instruction guides students to develop their ideas into full-length compositions, addressing these key stages in the writing process:

- Prewriting
- Drafting
- Revising
- Editing and Proofreading
- Publishing and Presenting

Timed Writing: To address the call for writing in the Common Core State Standards, the program provides numerous opportunities for students to practice writing for assessment. Each **Reading for Information** and **Comparing Literary Works** feature concludes with an annotated timed writing prompt that includes a step-by-step planner to help students complete the assignment. In addition, each Assessment Workshop includes a Timed Writing component.

The **Research Tasks** and **Communications Workshops** in each unit offer additional opportunities for students to engage in ambitious writing, research, and communications projects.

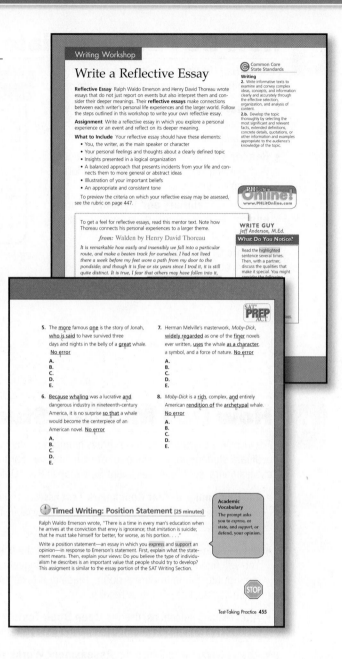

EssayScorer Prentice Hall
Powered by WriteToLearn™

Score student essays in seconds.

Finally, to facilitate your teaching of writing, the **Prentice Hall EssayScorer** provides instant scoring and feedback, plus tips for revision. You save time, and your students become better writers!

11 How Can I Use Technology in My Classroom?

PHLitOnline allows you to teach the entire program without using the print products. It contains all of the components of the program in one central location: all of the print and activity-based materials, PLUS integrated videos, animations, interactive practice activities, songs, and audio. You will navigate through the program by using the Table of Contents, exactly as you would in the textbook.

You can choose to use PHLitOnline only, or you may choose to use it in conjunction with the print program. Supporting resources such as videos, audio, online assessments, lesson planning, and reporting are just what you need to teach literature to your 21st-Century students!

All tests are scored automatically in PHLitOnline!

Enriched Online Student Edition
- Full narration of selections
- Interactive graphic organizers
- Linked Get Connected and Background videos
- All worksheets and other student resources

Professional Development
- The Professional Development Guidebook online
- Additional professional development essays by program authors

Planning, Assigning, and Monitoring
- Software for online assignment of work to students, individually or to the whole class
- A system for tracking and grading student work

12 How Can the Online Resource Help Me in the Classroom?

PHLitOnline Teacher Center has digital and print tools you can use to reach your students, manage your teaching resources, and meet the Common Core State Standards. You can:

- provide personal diagnosis, instruction, and remediation to all students.
- tailor instruction for the right level of support for each student's specific needs.
- create customized assignments.
- view Common Core State Standards from within lessons.
- plan with easy-to-use tools.
- access all print resources online.

PHLitOnline Student Center allows students to access the complete printed program while at their computers in the classroom or at home. In addition to all print and activity-based materials, PHLitOnline Student Center offers videos, animations, interactive practice activities, "sticky" notes, songs, and audio features.

13 How Can PHLitOnline Help Me Personalize Instruction?

PHLitOnline provides personalized differentiated support with **Diagnostic** and **Benchmark** tests. The digital product can assess, diagnose, and auto-assign reading materials and practice at each student's level. Students are assigned a learner level—On-Level, Below-Level, or English Learner. Selections, audio, graphic organizers, and other support served up to students is based on this level. And since you know your students better than anyone, you have the flexibility to change the learner level as needed!

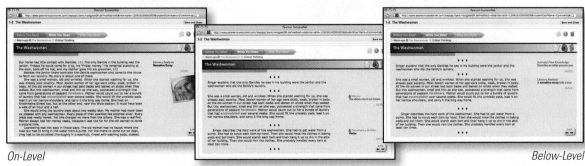

On-Level

English Learner

Below-Level

Full-size versions of these Media Literacy Handbook pages can be found in the Student Edition.

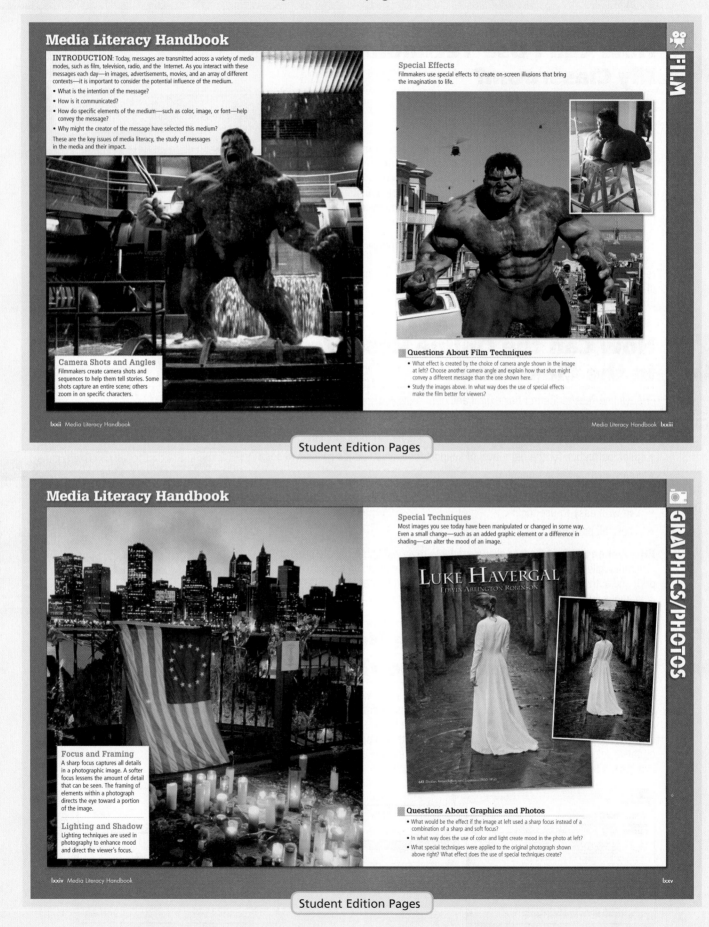

Media Literacy Handbook

INTRODUCTION: Today, messages are transmitted across a variety of media modes, such as film, television, radio, and the Internet. As you interact with these messages each day—in images, advertisements, movies, and an array of different contexts—it is important to consider the potential influence of the medium.

• What is the intention of the message?

• How is it communicated?

• How do specific elements of the medium—such as color, image, or font—help convey the message?

• Why might the creator of the message have selected this medium?

These are the key issues of media literacy, the study of messages in the media and their impact.

Camera Shots and Angles
Filmmakers create camera shots and sequences to help them tell stories. Some shots capture an entire scene; others zoom in on specific characters.

FILM

Special Effects
Filmmakers use special effects to create on-screen illusions that bring the imagination to life.

Questions About Film Techniques

• What effect is created by the choice of camera angle shown in the image at left? Choose another camera angle and explain how that shot might convey a different message than the one shown here.

• Study the images above. In what way does the use of special effects make the film better for viewers?

lxxii Media Literacy Handbook

Media Literacy Handbook lxxiii

Student Edition Pages

Media Literacy Handbook

Focus and Framing
A sharp focus captures all details in a photographic image. A softer focus lessens the amount of detail that can be seen. The framing of elements within a photograph directs the eye toward a portion of the image.

Lighting and Shadow
Lighting techniques are used in photography to enhance mood and direct the viewer's focus.

GRAPHICS/PHOTOS

Special Techniques
Most images you see today have been manipulated or changed in some way. Even a small change—such as an added graphic element or a difference in shading—can alter the mood of an image.

LUKE HAVERGAL
EDWIN ARLINGTON ROBINSON

Questions About Graphics and Photos

• What would be the effect if the image at left used a sharp focus instead of a combination of a sharp and soft focus?

• In what way does the use of color and light create mood in the photo at left?

• What special techniques were applied to the original photograph shown above right? What effect does the use of special techniques create?

lxxiv Media Literacy Handbook

lxxv

Student Edition Pages

Persuasive Techniques
Advertisements use carefully selected visual elements and specific language to appeal to the viewer's emotions.

Text and Graphics
Newspaper and magazine layouts are constructed to capture the eye and quickly convey the important ideas of a story. The use of type fonts, images, and page space direct the eye to portions of the printed page.

Questions About Print Media

- What image or graphic dominates the advertisement at left? In what way does the use of language in the ad enhance its message?
- Which of the above grabs your attention: the image or the graphic on the magazine cover? Explain.
- What do you notice first on the newspaper's front page? What overall effect does the use of type size and fonts create?

Student Edition Pages

How is this book organized?

- There are six chronological units, starting with Native American beginnings and extending to the present.
- Each unit has an introduction that offers multiple perspectives on the history, culture, and literature of the time period.

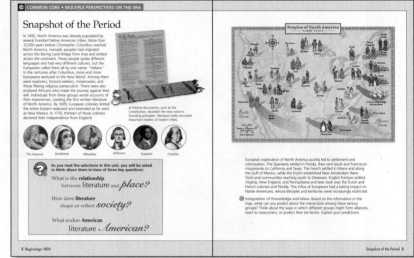

A **"Snapshot"** shows you key people, places, and innovations. ▶

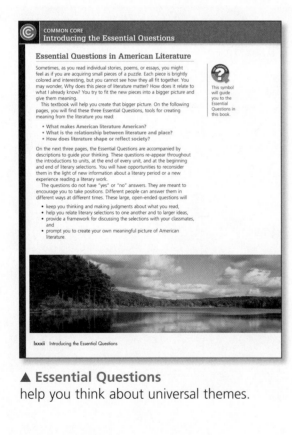

▲ **Essential Questions** help you think about universal themes.

Historical Background summarizes key events of the era. ▼

Student Edition Pages

Contemporary Connections links the classics to today. ▶

◀ **Primary Sources** features real documents that made history and supports in-depth research projects.

◀ **Reading for Information** features nonfiction texts you will encounter in daily life.

Comparing Literature Past and Present shows the continuity of ideas, themes, and styles. ▶

How to Use This Book **lxxxi**

Essential Questions in American Literature

Sometimes, as you read individual stories, poems, or essays, you might feel as if you are acquiring small pieces of a puzzle. Each piece is brightly colored and interesting, but you cannot see how they all fit together. You may wonder, Why does this piece of literature matter? How does it relate to what I already know? You try to fit the new pieces into a bigger picture and give them meaning.

This textbook will help you create that bigger picture. On the following pages, you will find these three Essential Questions, tools for creating meaning from the literature you read:

This symbol will guide you to the Essential Questions in this book.

- **What makes American literature American?**
- **What is the relationship between literature and place?**
- **How does literature shape or reflect society?**

On the next three pages, the Essential Questions are accompanied by descriptions to guide your thinking. These questions re-appear throughout the introductions to units, at the end of every unit, and at the beginning and end of literary selections. You will have opportunities to reconsider them in the light of new information about a literary period or a new experience reading a literary work.

The questions do not have "yes" or "no" answers. They are meant to encourage you to take positions. Different people can answer them in different ways at different times. These large, open-ended questions will

- keep you thinking and making judgments about what you read,
- help you relate literary selections to one another and to larger ideas,
- provide a framework for discussing the selections with your classmates, and
- prompt you to create your own meaningful picture of American literature.

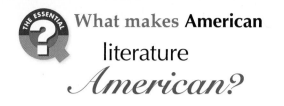

What makes **American** literature *American?*

In one sense, anything written in America is American. But in a deeper way, literature is "American" because it says something fundamental about our identity as Americans. In fact, literature may be the most powerful creative expression of our national and cultural identity.

The selections in this book will spread before you styles, images, expressions, characters, themes, and stories that are uniquely American. By addressing this Essential Question in different ways throughout the book, you will find yourself getting to the heart of American literature.

As you read, keep in mind what it means to be "American." After all, it is American literature that enables us to tell ourselves who we are.

Thematic Vocabulary
To help as you explore this Essential Question, use words like these:

beliefs	**heritage**	**liberty**
diversity	**immigration**	**self-reliance**
freedom	**individualism**	

"What then is the American, this new man?"

—Michel-Guillaume Jean de Crèvecoeur

What is the **relationship** between *literature* and *place?*

Europeans imagined America before they knew it. Columbus envisioned a fabled land of gold and spices. Ponce de León dreamt that Florida was the home of a Fountain of Youth. Puritans escaping persecution planned to build a City on a Hill where freedom would reign. Meanwhile, Native Americans told stories inspired by the natural world in which they dwelled.

To dwell in a place is to live in it fully, to merge its real life with the imaginative life you live there. As Emily Dickinson wrote, "I dwell in Possibility." How do Americans shape and reflect all the possibilities of their dwelling place on the earth? How does geography help make literature? Do Americans respond to nature in a unique way?

As you read the selections in this book, consider what it means to live—and to create literature—in a particular place at a particular time.

Thematic Vocabulary
To help as you explore this Essential Question, use words like these:

environment	natural	resources	urban
frontier	range	rural	wilderness
landscape	region		

"...offer thanks to the earth where men dwell..."

—The Iroquois Constitution

Student Edition Pages

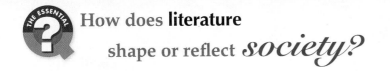

How does **literature** shape or reflect *society?*

Literature is a product of the society from which it springs, reflecting the values, concerns, and spirit of a people. However, literature can be more than a passive mirror. It can act as a force that changes or shapes a society. Novels, stories, plays, poems, and literary nonfiction made by writers can entertain, inform, persuade, challenge, and move readers, both singly and in great numbers. Writers are the entertainers who amuse, the critics who confront, the teachers who share wisdom, and—sometimes—the visionaries who lead the way to the future. Every day, writers celebrate America, define it, defy it, and tell its story. As you read this textbook and keep asking this Essential Question, you will become aware of the defining interactions between American society and its literature.

Thematic Vocabulary

To help as you explore this Essential Question, use words like these:

humorist	**regionalism**	**storytelling**
myth	**satire**	**vernacular**
persona	**social critic**	**visionary**

"In bombers named for girls, we burned The cities we had learned about in school—"

—Randall Jarrell

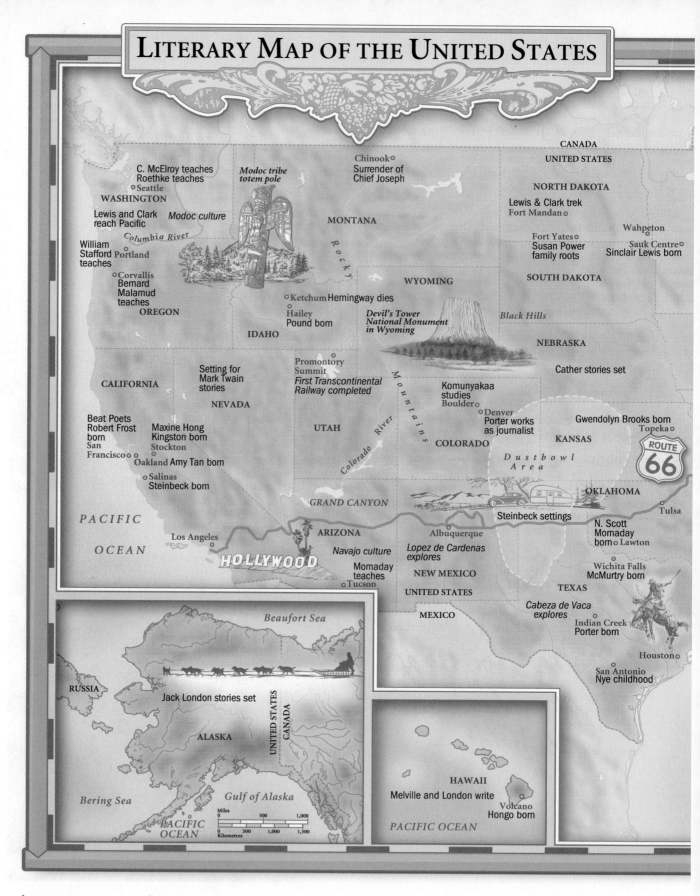

LITERARY MAP OF THE UNITED STATES

C. McElroy teaches
Roethke teaches
○ Seattle
WASHINGTON

Modoc tribe totem pole

CANADA
UNITED STATES

Chinook ○
Surrender of
Chief Joseph

NORTH DAKOTA

Lewis & Clark trek
Fort Mandan ○

Wahpeton ○

Lewis and Clark
reach Pacific

Modoc culture

MONTANA

Fort Yates ○
Susan Power
family roots

Sauk Centre ○
Sinclair Lewis born

William
Stafford Portland
teaches

Columbia River

SOUTH DAKOTA

○ Corvallis
Bernard
Malamud
teaches

WYOMING

OREGON

○ Ketchum Hemingway dies
○ Hailey
Pound born

Devil's Tower
National Monument
in Wyoming

Black Hills

IDAHO

Rocky

NEBRASKA

Promontory
Summit
First Transcontinental
Railway completed

Setting for
Mark Twain
stories

Cather stories set

CALIFORNIA

NEVADA

Komunyakaa
studies
Boulder ○
○ Denver
Porter works
as journalist

Gwendolyn Brooks born
Topeka ○

Beat Poets
Robert Frost
born
San
Francisco ○ ○
○ Oakland Amy Tan born

Maxine Hong
Kingston born
○ Stockton

UTAH

Mountains

Colorado River

COLORADO

KANSAS

ROUTE 66

○ Salinas
Steinbeck born

Dustbowl
Area

PACIFIC

OCEAN

GRAND CANYON

Los Angeles ○

HOLLYWOOD

ARIZONA

Navajo culture

Momaday
teaches
○ Tucson

Albuquerque ○

Lopez de Cardenas
explores

Steinbeck settings

OKLAHOMA

Tulsa ○

N. Scott
Momaday
born ○ Lawton

Wichita Falls ○
McMurtry born

NEW MEXICO

UNITED STATES

MEXICO

Cabeza de Vaca
explores

TEXAS

Indian Creek ○
Porter born

Houston ○

San Antonio ○
Nye childhood

Beaufort Sea

RUSSIA

Jack London stories set

ALASKA

UNITED STATES
CANADA

Bering Sea

Gulf of Alaska

PACIFIC
OCEAN

Miles
0   500   1,000
0 500 1,000 1,500
Kilometres

HAWAII
Melville and London write
Volcano
Hongo born

PACIFIC OCEAN

Literature of the United States: A Continuing Story

This map illustrates the richness and variety of American literature, from Native American creation myths to contemporary fiction. In an important sense, all these varied authors and their works are part of a single ongoing narrative, the story of American literature.

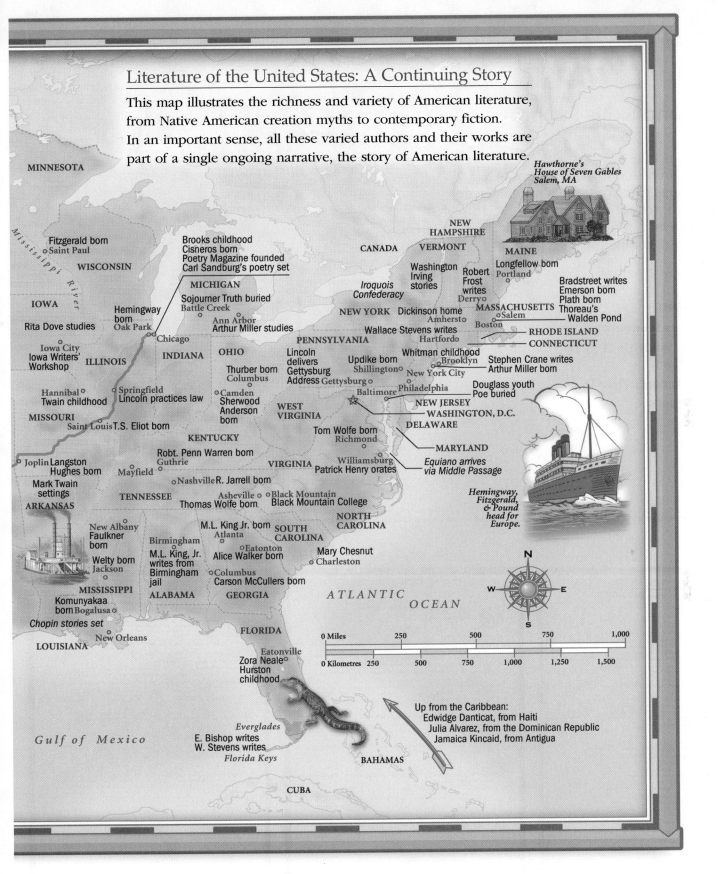

Hawthorne's House of Seven Gables Salem, MA

MINNESOTA

Fitzgerald born
Saint Paul

WISCONSIN

Mississippi River

IOWA

Rita Dove studies

Hemingway born
Oak Park

Iowa City
Iowa Writers' Workshop

ILLINOIS

Hannibal
Twain childhood

MISSOURI

Saint Louis T.S. Eliot born

Joplin Langston Hughes born

Mark Twain settings

ARKANSAS

New Albany
Faulkner born

Welty born
Jackson

MISSISSIPPI

Komunyakaa born Bogalusa

Chopin stories set

New Orleans

LOUISIANA

Brooks childhood
Cisneros born
Poetry Magazine founded
Carl Sandburg's poetry set

MICHIGAN

Sojourner Truth buried
Battle Creek

Ann Arbor
Arthur Miller studies

Chicago

INDIANA   OHIO

Thurber born
Columbus

Springfield
Lincoln practices law

Camden
Sherwood Anderson born

WEST VIRGINIA

KENTUCKY

Robt. Penn Warren born
Guthrie

Mayfield

Nashville R. Jarrell born

TENNESSEE

Asheville   Black Mountain
Thomas Wolfe born   Black Mountain College

M.L. King Jr. born   SOUTH
Atlanta   CAROLINA

Birmingham

M.L. King, Jr.   Eatonton
writes from   Alice Walker born
Birmingham
jail   Columbus
Carson McCullers born

ALABAMA   GEORGIA

FLORIDA

Eatonville
Zora Neale
Hurston
childhood

Everglades
E. Bishop writes
W. Stevens writes
Florida Keys

Gulf of Mexico

BAHAMAS

CUBA

CANADA   VERMONT

NEW HAMPSHIRE

MAINE

Washington
Irving
stories

Robert
Frost
writes
Derry

Longfellow born
Portland

Bradstreet writes
Emerson born
Plath born
Thoreau's
Walden Pond

Iroquois
Confederacy

NEW YORK   Dickinson home
Amherst

MASSACHUSETTS
Salem

Boston   RHODE ISLAND

Wallace Stevens writes
Hartford   CONNECTICUT

PENNSYLVANIA

Lincoln
delivers
Gettysburg
Address   Updike born
Shillington

Whitman childhood
Brooklyn

New York City

Stephen Crane writes
Arthur Miller born

Gettysburg   Philadelphia

Baltimore   NEW JERSEY

Douglass youth
Poe buried

WASHINGTON, D.C.

DELAWARE

Tom Wolfe born
Richmond

MARYLAND

Equiano arrives
via Middle Passage

VIRGINIA   Williamsburg
Patrick Henry orates

NORTH
CAROLINA

Mary Chesnut
Charleston

ATLANTIC   OCEAN

Hemingway,
Fitzgerald,
& Pound
head for
Europe.

N
W   E
S

0 Miles   250   500   750   1,000

0 Kilometres   250   500   750   1,000   1,250   1,500

Up from the Caribbean:
Edwidge Danticat, from Haiti
Julia Alvarez, from the Dominican Republic
Jamaica Kincaid, from Antigua

Selection and Skills Support

Every selection is fully supported with worksheets in *Unit Resources*, differentiated for various groups of learners. The Visual Guide to Selected Resources preceding each leveled selection pair gives a sample of the worksheets available. The full complement is presented on these pages.

RESOURCES FOR:

L1 Special-Needs Students
L2 Below-Level Students (Tier 2)
L3 On-Level (Tier 1)
L4 Advanced Students (Tier 1)
EL English Learners
All All Students

Prentice Hall **LITERATURE**
Unit Two Resources

Key Features
- All your teaching support for the unit in one easy-to-use booklet
- Diagnostic and Benchmark Tests
- Leveled tests for every selection or grouping of selections
- Leveled Reading and Vocabulary Warm-Ups
- Worksheets
- Answer Keys

Differentiated Instruction for Universal Access   THE AMERICAN EXPERIENCE

EL L1 L2 Vocabulary Warm-ups A and B

vocabulary and reading practice for lower-level students and English learners

All Writing About the Big Question

thematic vocabulary and thought-provoking activities centered around the unit Big Question

All Reading

a full page of support for the Reading Skill taught with the selection

All teacher resources
are available online at
www.PHLitOnline.com

"The Most Dangerous Game" by Richard Connell
Literary Analysis: Conflict

Conflict is a struggle between opposing forces. There are two types of conflict: internal and external.

- In **internal conflict**, a character struggles with his or her own opposing feelings, beliefs, needs, or desires.
- In **external conflict**, a character struggles against an outside force, such as another character, society, or nature.

Conflict and the search for a solution are the mainspring of a story's plot. The solution, which usually occurs near the end of a story, is called the **resolution**. In some stories, the conflict is not truly resolved. Instead, the main character experiences an **epiphany**, or sudden flash of insight. Although the conflict is not resolved, the character's thoughts about it change.

A. DIRECTIONS: *"The Most Dangerous Game" contains a number of conflicts. On the following lines, briefly describe the story situations surrounding each conflict.*

1. Rainsford vs. nature _____

2. General Zaroff vs. the "visitors" to his island _____

3. Rainsford vs. General Zaroff _____

4. Rainsford within himself _____

B. DIRECTIONS: *On the following lines, briefly discuss the story's ending. Does the ending contain a resolution that solves the story's main conflict? Have Rainsford's experiences changed his views about hunting? Explain your answer by citing details from the story.*

Unit 2 Resources: Short Stories

All Literary Analysis
a full page of support for the Literary Analysis concept taught with the selection

---

"The Most Dangerous Game" by Richard Connell
Vocabulary Builder

Word List

bizarre   futile   grotesque   indolently   naive   palpable   scruples

A. DIRECTIONS: *In each of the following items, think about the meaning of the italicized word, and then answer the question.*

1. What is the danger if you approach a research paper assignment *indolently*?

2. How are you feeling if you have *scruples* about doing something?

3. How would you feel if you make a long and *futile* journey?

4. If the tension during the final two minutes of a game is *palpable*, do you think the spectators feel suspense or not? Explain.

5. What is another word that can be used to describe something that is *grotesque*?

6. Is it easy to fool someone who is *naive*? Explain.

7. If an event is *bizarre*, is it likely surprising? Explain.

B. WORD STUDY: *The Latin suffix -esque means "in the style or manner of." Use the context of the sentences and what you know about the **Latin suffix -esque** to explain your answer to each question.*

1. Who directly influenced *Romanesque* architecture?

2. Is calling someone statuesque a compliment? Explain.

Unit 2 Resources: Short Stories

All Vocabulary Builder
selection vocabulary and Word Study skill practice

"The Most Dangerous Game" by Richard Connell
Enrichment: Dealing With Competition

General Zaroff develops his gruesome variation on hunting because he says that hunting animals is no longer a challenge for him. He is driven by competition: His need for ever-greater challenges spins out of control.

Competition can be a positive quality in life as a whole, and specifically in the environment of the workplace. However, competition can also be troublesome if carried to an extreme.

Role Play Imagine that you are a friend of General Zaroff's, perhaps a fellow officer or a hunting companion. Zaroff confides his feelings to you long before he starts to hunt human beings. With a partner playing General Zaroff, role-play a conversation in which you give him advice about how he might channel his competitive spirit into other pursuits.

Apply In each of the following everyday situations, a competitive situation causes problems. What advice would you give to the people in each situation? Write your advice on the lines provided.

1. Jose and his younger brother Miguel play one-on-one basketball every night. Jose is older and taller than Miguel and always wins. Miguel insists on playing, however, and he insists on keeping score.

2. Competition among teams in a softball club has grown fierce. The players care only about the standings. No one seems to be enjoying the game itself anymore.

3. Marian has the best voice in the school chorus. During tryouts, she always wins the solos for the choral concerts. The other singers are feeling left out and are thinking of quitting the chorus.

4. In science class, one student dominates the discussions and interrupts other students who attempt to express ideas. No one wants to be in class with this student anymore.

5. You and a friend are working part time at the same business. You would like to work together, but your friend is continually trying to outdo you in every task. You are afraid that this will make you look bad and you will be fired.

Unit 2 Resources: Short Stories

L4 Enrichment
a selection-related challenge for advanced learners

"American History" by Judith Ortiz Cofer
"The Most Dangerous Game" by Richard Connell
Integrated Language Skills: Grammar

Regular Verbs

A verb has four principal parts: the present, the present participle, the past, and the past participle. Most verbs in English are regular. **Regular verbs** form the past and the past participle by adding *-ed* or *-d* to the present form.

The past and past participle of regular verbs have the same form. In the following chart of principal parts, *has* is in parentheses in front of the past participle to remind you that this verb form is a past participle only if it is used with a helping verb.

Notice that the final consonant is sometimes doubled to form the present participle (*tapping* as well as the past and the past participle (*tapped*). Notice also that the final *e* may be dropped in forming the present participle (*wiping*).

Principal Parts of Regular Verbs

Present	Present Participle	Past	Past Participle
play	(is) playing	played	(has) played
tap	(is) tapping	tapped	(has) tapped
wipe	(is) wiping	wiped	(has) wiped

A. PRACTICE: *Write the answer(s) to each of the following questions on the lines provided.*

1. Give the four principal parts of the following verbs:
    walk: _____
    hunt: _____
    place: _____
    rip: _____

2. What do you add to form the past tense of regular verbs?

B. Writing Application: *Read the following sentences and notice the verb in italics. If the verb is used correctly, write Correct in the space provided. If the verb is not used correctly, rewrite the sentence using the correct form of the verb.*

1. In Paterson, New Jersey, Elena *lived* in El Building with her family.

2. After school started, Elena *looking* for Eugene in all her classes.

3. Mr. DePalma has *ask* us to line up in front of him.

4. Rainsford was exhausted when he *arrive* on the island.

Unit 2 Resources: Short Stories

L3 L4 Grammar
more practice with the grammar skill taught with the selection

---

"American History" by Judith Ortiz Cofer
"The Most Dangerous Game" by Richard Connell
Integrated Language Skills:
Support for Writing an Alternative Ending

For your alternative ending, use the following lines to jot down notes under each heading.

New ending grows out of earlier sequence of events: "American History"
Elena's life at school → Elena's attraction to Eugene → Mother's warnings → Study date with Eugene → Assassination of President Kennedy →

New ending grows out of earlier sequence of events: "The Most Dangerous Game"
Rainsford falls off yacht and lands on island → Rainsford meets General Zaroff and learns of Zaroff's "game" → Rainsford is forced to become the "huntee" → Rainsford confronts Zaroff in the general's bedroom →

New ending is consistent with portrayal of characters: "American History"
Elena's character traits: _____
Personality of Elena's mother: _____
Eugene's character traits: _____
Personality of Eugene's mother: _____
New ending is consistent with portrayal of characters: "The Most Dangerous Game"
Rainsford's character traits: _____
Zaroff's character traits: _____
New ending provides a resolution to the conflict:

Now, use your notes to write an alternative ending. Write your ending on a separate piece of paper. Be sure that your new ending resolves the main conflict in the story.

Unit 2 Resources: Short Stories

L3 L4 Writing
support for the Writing activity accompanying the selection

"American History" by Judith Ortiz Cofer
"The Most Dangerous Game" by Richard Connell
Integrated Language Skills: Support for Extend Your Learning

Research and Technology and Listening and Speaking
Use the following lines to identify a topic for your photo essay and to make plans for your photo essay.

1. **Day of national significance and reasons for significance:** _____

2. **Ideas for photos:** _____

3. **Sources for photos:** _____

4. **Captions for photos:** _____

Use the following to construct your photo essay.
Audience: _____   **Purpose:** _____
Organization: _____

Use the following lines to identify a topic for your photo essay and to conduct research on this topic.

1. **Choice of big-game species:** _____

2. **Ideas for photos:** _____

3. **Sources for photos:** _____

4. **Captions for photos:** _____

Use the following to construct your photo essay.
Audience: _____   **Purpose:** _____
Organization: _____

Unit 2 Resources: Short Stories

L3 L4 Extend Your Learning
customized support for the Listening and Speaking or Research and Technology activity related to the selection

CC 125

Selection Support

Graphic Organizer Transparencies

Prentice Hall LITERATURE

Key Features
- Teaching transparencies for every Reading Skill and Literary Analysis graphic organizer from the Student Edition
- Features two versions, one partially filled in and one blank, for differentiated instruction and effective teacher modeling
- Answer key for teachers
- Great for struggling readers and students with special needs

VOLUME 1
Differentiated Instruction for Universal Access
THE AMERICAN EXPERIENCE

EL L1 L2 Reading Graphic Organizer A

a partially filled-in graphic organizer to model or scaffold the use of the organizer

L3 Reading Graphic Organizer B

the blank version of the organizer

EL L1 L2 Literary Analysis Graphic Organizer A

a partially filled-in graphic organizer to model or scaffold the use of the organizer

L3 Literary Analysis Organizer B

the blank version of the organizer

Assessment

Prentice Hall LITERATURE

Unit Two Resources

Key Features
- All your teaching support for the unit in one easy-to-use booklet
- Diagnostic and Benchmark Tests
- Leveled tests for every selection or grouping of selections
- Leveled Reading and Vocabulary Warm-Ups
- Worksheets
- Answer Keys

Differentiated Instruction for Universal Access
THE AMERICAN EXPERIENCE

EL L1 L2 Selection Test A

selection test with complete skills coverage, adapted for lower-level students and English learners

L3 L4 Selection Test B

selection test with complete skills coverage, including multiple choice and essay items

L3 L4 Open-Book Test

an alternative assessment format for on-level and advanced students

Common Core Companion

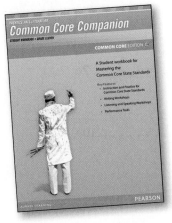

The Common Core Companion student workbook provides instruction and practice for all Common Core State Standards. Here is a closer look at this workbook.

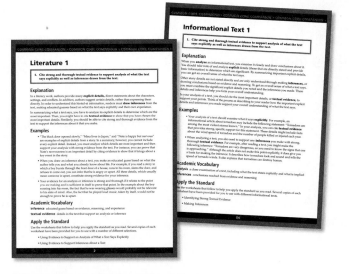

All **Literature and Informational Text**

Direct instruction and practice for each Common Core State Standard. Standards requiring writing or presentation outcomes are supported through process workshops.

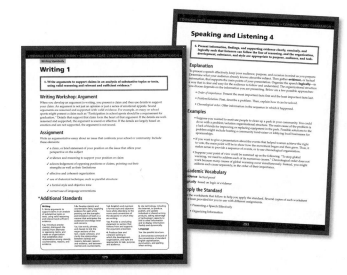

All **Writing and Speaking and Listening**

Full writing process workshops are supported with direct instruction and worksheets. Writing process standards are integrated with Speaking and Listening activities.

All **Language**

Explicit instruction supports each Language standard. Practice worksheets and graphic organizers provide additional opportunities for mastery.

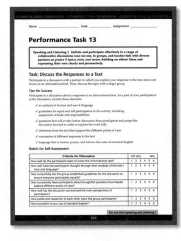

All **Performance Tasks**

Assessment opportunities are provided for each reading standard, along with tips for success and rubrics.

Classroom Strategies

Each unit in this Teacher's Edition begins with a professional development essay by a program author. For more professional development essays, visit www.PHLitOnline.com.

www.PHLitOnline.com

Log on as a teacher at www.PHLitOnline.com to access a library of all Professional Development articles by the Contributing Authors of *Pearson Prentice Hall Literature.*

PROFESSIONAL DEVELOPMENT   **Doug Buehl**

▼ APPLY THE STRATEGY

"Who Would Say It?" Model "Who would say it?" application with *infallibility* on p.105. When Franklin says "many private Persons think almost as highly of their own *infallibility*," he refers to people who strongly feel that their beliefs are the truth. Who else would say "*infallibility*"? A scientist might say: "The *infallibility* of this process is clear; if followed exactly, the desired results will always be obtained."

Partners should select two of the vocabulary words and brainstorm "who would say" them. Then they create statements using each of the words as they might be put "in play" by individuals they predict would say it. Then, partners share with the class.

For more of Doug Buehl's strategies, see his Professional Development essay, pp. 2a–2b

Authors give concrete applications for the strategies they discuss in their essays at point of use in the Teacher's Edition.

PRENTICE HALL
LITERATURE
GRADE 11

COMMON CORE EDITION ©

Upper Saddle River, New Jersey

Boston, Massachusetts

Chandler, Arizona

Glenview, Illinois

 \VAYS LEARNING

PEARSON

Student Edition Pages

Acknowledgments

Grateful acknowledgment is made to the following for copyrighted material:

Advancement Project "10 Things Every Florida Poll Worker Should Know" from *http://www.advancementproject.org*. Used by permission.

Archaeology Magazine "A Community's Roots" by Samir S. Patel from *http://www.archaeology.org*. Copyright © 2006 by The Archaeological Institute of America. Used by permission.

Arte Publico Press "The Latin Deli: An Ars Poetica" by Judith Ortiz Cofer from *The Latin Deli*. Used with permission from the publisher of "The Americas Review" (Copyright © 1992 Arte Publico Press-University of Houston).

The James Baldwin Estate "The Rockpile" is collected in *Going to Meet the Man*, © 1965 by James Baldwin. Copyright renewed. Published by Vintage Books. Used by arrangement with the James Baldwin Estate.

Susan Bergholz Literary Services "Antojos" by Julia Alvarez from *Antojos*. Copyright © 1991 by Julia Alvarez. Later published in slightly different form in *How the Garcia Girls Lost Their Accents*, Copyright © 1991 by Julia Alvarez. Published by Plume, an imprint of Dutton Signet, a division of Penguin USA, Inc., and originally in hardcover by Algonquin Books of Chapel Hill. "Straw into Gold: The Metamorphosis of the Everyday" by Sandra Cisneros from *The Texas Observer*. Copyright © 1987 by Sandra Cisneros. First published in *The Texas Observer*, September 1987. Used by permission of Susan Bergholz Literary Services, New York, NY and Lamy, NM. All rights reserved.

BOA Editions Limited "The Gift" by Li-Young Lee from Rose. Copyright © 1986 by Li-Young Lee. All rights reserved. "Study the Masters" by Lucille Clifton from *Blessing the Boats: New and Selected Poems 1988–2000*. Copyright © 2000 by Lucille Clifton. Used with the permission of BOA Editions, Ltd. www.boaeditions.org.

Brooks Permissions "The Explorer" by Gwendolyn Brooks from *Blacks*. Used by permission of Brooks Permissions. Copyright © 1991 by Gwendolyn Brooks, published by Third World Press, Chicago.

The California Council for the Humanities "California Council for the Humanities/Our Mission/Our History" from *http://www.calhum.org*. Courtesy of the California Council for the Humanities and its California Stories Initiative. Copyright © 2007 by The California Council for the Humanities. Used by permission.

California Department of Water Resources "California Water Plan Highlights" from *Department of Water Resources Bulletin 160-05*. Copyright © 2005 California Department of Water Resources.

California Secretary of State "Poll Worker Advertisement" from *www.sos.ca.gov/elections/outreach/posters/pollworker.pdf*. Used by permission.

Sandra Dijkstra Literary Agency "Mother Tongue" by Amy Tan from The Joy Luck Club. Copyright © 1989 by Amy Tan. Used by permission of the author and the Sandra Dijkstra Literary Agency. Copyright © 1989 by Amy-Tan. First appeared in *Threepenny Review*.

Doubleday "Cuttings (later)" by Theodore Roethke from Collected Poems of Theodore Roethke. "Cuttings" by Theodore Roethke from *The Collected Poems of Theodore Roethke. The Collected Poems of Theodore Roethke* by Theodore Roethke, copyright © 1946 by Editorial Publications, Inc. Used by permission of Doubleday, a division of Bantam Doubleday Dell Publishing Group.

Richard Erdoes "When Grizzlies Walked Upright" by Modoc Indians from *American History Customized Reader*. Used by permission.

Faber and Faber Limited "Mirror" by Sylvia Plath from *Crossing the Water*. Copyright © 1963 by Ted Hughes. Used by permission.

Farrar, Straus & Giroux, LLC "Losses" by Randall Jarrell from *The Complete Poems by Randall Jarrell*. Copyright © 1969, renewed 1997 by Mary von S. Jarrell. "The Death of the Ball Turret Gunner" by Randall Jarrell from *The Complete Poems of Randall Jarrell*. Copyright © 1969, renewed 1997 by Mary von S. Jarrell. "The First Seven Years" by Bernard Malamud from *The Magic Barrel*. Copyright © 1950, 1958 and copyright renewed 1977, 1986 by Bernard Malamud. "Coyote v. Acme" by Ian Frazier from *Coyote v. Acme*. Copyright © 1996 by Ian Frazier. "One Art" by Elizabeth Bishop from *Geography III*. Copyright © 1979, 1983 by Alice Helen Methfessel. "Filling Station" by Elizabeth Bishop from *The Complete Poems 1927–1979* by Elizabeth Bishop. Copyright © 1979, 1983 by Alice Helen Methfessel. Used by permission of Farrar, Straus and Giroux, LLC.

Florida Master Site File from *http://www.flheritage.com*. Used by permission.

Fulcrum Publishing "The Earth on Turtle's Back" by Joseph Bruchac and Michael J. Caduto from *Keepers of the Earth: Native American Stories and Environmental Activities for Children*, © 1998. Used by permission of Fulcrum Publishing, Inc.

Georgia State University "Georgia State University's Web Accessibility Policy," copyright © 2006 is used with permission from the University System of Georgia by and on behalf of Georgia State University.

Graywolf Press "Traveling Through the Dark" by William Stafford from *Stories That Could be True: New and Collected Poems*. Copyright 1962, 1998 by the Estate of William Stafford. Used from *The Way It Is: New and Selected Poems* with the permission of Graywolf Press, Saint Paul, Minnesota.

Harcourt, Inc. "Chicago" by Carl Sandburg from *Chicago Poems*, copyright © 1916 by Holt, Rinehart and Winston and renewed 1944 by Carl Sandburg. "Grass" by Carl Sandburg from *Chicago Poems*. Copyright © 1916 BY Holt, Rinehart and Winston and renewed 1944 by Carl Sandburg. "Everyday Use" by Alice Walker from *In Love & Trouble: Stories of Black Women*, copyright © 1973 by Alice Walker. "The Jilting of Granny Weatherall" by Katherine Anne Porter from *Flowering Judas and Other Stories*, copyright © 1930 and renewed 1958 by Katherine Anne Porter. "The Life You Save May Be Your Own" by Flannery O'Connor from *A Good Man is Hard to Find and Other Stories*, copyright © 1953 by Flannery O'Connor and renewed 1981 by Regina O'Connor. "A Worn Path" by Eudora Welty from *A Curtain of Green and Other Stories*, copyright 1941 and renewed in 1969 by Eudora Welty. Used by permission of Harcourt, Inc. This material may not be reproduced in any form or by any means without the prior written permission of the publisher.

HarperCollins Publishers, Inc. From "Dust Tracks on a Road" by Zora N. Hurston. Copyright © 1942 by Zora Neale Hurston; renewed © 1970 by John C. Hurston. "Mirror" by Sylvia Plath from *Crossing the Water*. Copyright © 1963 by Ted Hughes. Originally appeared in The New Yorker. "Where Is Here?" by Joyce Carol Oates. Copyright © 1992 by The Ontario Review, Inc. Used by permission of HarperCollins Publishers. Excerpt from *Black Boy* by Richard Wright. Copyright © 1944, 1945 by Richard Wright.

Harvard University Press "Because I could not stop for Death (#712)", "I heard a Fly buzz—when I died (#465)", "My life closed twice before its close— (#1732)", "The Soul selects her own Society (#303)", "There a certain Slant of light (#258)", "There is a solitude of space (#1695)", by Emily Dickinson from *The Poems of Emily Dickinson*. Used by permission of the publishers and the Trustees of Amherst College from *The Poems of Emily Dickinson*, Thomas H. Johnson, ed., Cambridge, Mass.: The Belknap Press of Harvard University Press, Copyright (c) 1951, 1955, 1979 by the Presidents and Fellows of Harvard College.

Acknowledgments continue on page R80, which constitutes an extension of this copyright page.

ISBN-13: 978-0-13-319557-6
ISBN-10:   0-13-319557-0

2 3 4 5 6 7 8 9 10   15 14 13 12 11

Student Edition Pages

PRENTICE HALL
LITERATURE

TEACHER'S EDITION • THE AMERICAN EXPERIENCE, VOLUME 1

COMMON CORE EDITION ©

PEARSON

A Gathering of Voices

Literature of Early America

I come again to greet and thank the League;
> I come again to greet and thank the kindred;
I come again to greet and thank the warriors;
> I come again to greet and thank the women.
My forefathers—what they established—
> My forefathers—hearken to them!

- Iroquois Hymn

PHLit Online!
www.PHLitOnline.com

Teaching From Technology

Enriched Online Student Edition
- full narration of selections
- interactive graphic organizers
- linked **Get Connected** and **Background** videos
- all work sheets and other student resources

Professional Development
- the *Professional Development Guidebook* online
- additional professional-development essays by program authors

Planning, Assigning, and Monitoring
- software for online assignment of work to students, individually or to the whole class
- a system for tracking and grading student work

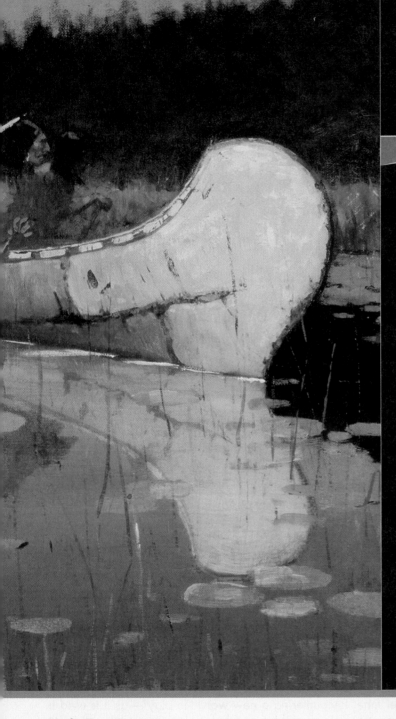

Beginnings to 1800

Unit 1

www.PHLitOnline.com

Hear It!
- Selection summary audio
- Selection audio

See It!
- Author videos
- Essential Question video
- Get Connected videos
- Background videos
- More about the authors
- Illustrated vocabulary words
- Vocabulary flashcards

Do It!
- Interactive journals
- Interactive graphic organizers
- Grammar tutorials
- Interactive vocabulary games
- Test practice

1

Introduce Unit 1

1. Direct students' attention to the title of the unit, including the time period covered. Have a volunteer read the quotation. **Ask:** What does the quotation suggest about the attitudes of the period? **Possible response:** The quotation suggests that the Iroquois acknowledged and honored their heritage, an appropriate introduction to a unit that explores the beginnings of American literature.

2. Discuss the artwork, *Radisson and Groseilliers,* 1905, by Frederic Remington. Point out that the painting shows two early explorers of the American interior. **Ask:** How does the painting suggest cooperative effort? **Possible response:** The painting shows both Europeans and Native Americans engaged in a common enterprise.

3. Have students speculate about the literature of the period, given the quotation and the art. **Possible response:** The literature of the period may focus on cross-cultural engagement and wilderness encounters.

Unit Resources

Unit 1 Resources includes these pages:

▶ **Benchmark Tests** assess and monitor student progress.

▶ **Vocabulary and Reading Warm-ups** provide additional vocabulary support, based on Lexile rankings, for each selection. "A" **Warm-ups** are for students reading two grades below level. "B" **Warm-ups** are for students reading one grade below level.

▶ **Selection Support**
- **Reading Skill**
- **Literary Analysis**
- **Vocabulary Builder**
- **Support for Writing**
- **Enrichment**

Unit Features

Unit Author
William L. Andrews helps introduce the period in the unit introduction, provides an Author's Insights on literature in the Unit, and offers insight in the Writing Workshop.

Extended Studies
Students explore in depth the works of Benjamin Franklin, presented with links to contemporary culture, a Critical Commentary, and a Comparing Literary Works feature.

Comparing Literary Works
Students compare classic and contemporary literary works.

Primary Sources
Students engage the documents that recorded history as it was made.

Informational Texts
Students learn to use and evaluate various types of informational text.

Themes Across Centuries
Students discover links between canonical literature and the contemporary world.

PHLit Online!
All worksheets and other student resources are also available online at www.PHLitOnline.com.

1

> "Knowing" a word represents a sophisticated array of knowledge in multiple dimensions (Nagy & Scott, 2000). A definition is only one facet of knowledge about a word.

What does it mean to *know* a word? Typically, vocabulary study emphasizes mastery of narrow, often single-word definitions, and use of the word in a sentence. Difficult words are identified from a text and students establish their "meanings" during vocabulary activities that happen independently of discussion of the text. Vocabulary lessons are treated as something extra, rather than integral to the exploration of a literary work. As a consequence, new vocabulary may rarely be integrated into the classroom. A more organic approach incorporates word study into the discourse of speaking and writing about literary works, and expects that students tackle new words as language-users.

Rich Contexts for Vocabulary Study

"Knowing" a word represents a sophisticated array of knowledge in multiple dimensions (Nagy & Scott, 2000). A definition is only one facet of knowledge about a word. In addition, we need to consider the following:

• How and where such a word might be used
• How the word works grammatically within a sentence
• Meaningful word parts
• Connotations
• Related words like antonyms and synonyms.

Vocabulary learning depends on "interrelatedness," which means that new words must be studied in context with the words with which they commonly occur, and must be connected to concepts with which learners are already familiar.

Facets of Word Knowledge

Predicting Words "in Play" Because there are many dimensions of vocabulary knowledge, students gradually develop insight about a word over time. Encountering a new word "in play"—as it is used in different contexts—is crucial for vocabulary learning. One activity that encourages students to consider their current knowledge of words and to anticipate how such words might be used in conjunction with each other is "Connect Two" (Bachowicz, 1986). Select a core of about a dozen key words used by an author (for example: *peril, sustain, loath, endure, distress, sundry, feigned*). Students work with partners to pair words they predict could be used together by an author. Encourage students to rely on hunches about unfamiliar words, and to elaborate on why a pair of words could be connected. For example, some students might pair *peril* and *distress* with the reasoning that someone in distress might feel his life is in peril. Other students might connect *peril* with *sustain* because you would be in peril if you did not have food to sustain you. As they read the selection, students discover how the author put these words "in play." This activity engages students in exploring relationships between words rather than focusing on isolated definitions.

Knowledge Mapping Ask students to create a variation of concept maps to track their growing knowledge of new words. A knowledge map provides a visual way to inventory understanding of a word. For example, facets of *feign* might be "to pretend something," "you do this to mislead," "to give a false impression," "the point is to deceive," and "usually regarded as a negative act, but not always." Examples, such as "she feigned illness to avoid work," and "he feigned interest in his grandmother's story," are also integrated into knowledge maps. Record knowledge maps in a section devoted to vocabulary learning in a class notebook.

Who Would Say It? Frequently, sentences created by students using new words turn out to be odd, awkward, or even nonsensical, because students tend to over-generalize synonyms and fixate only on one facet of a word—a definition (Scott, Jamieson-Noel, Asselin, 2003). Quite frankly, many new words penned into sentences are words students "would not say" without being asked to by a teacher! But who *would* use such words? As students explore vocabulary encountered in written texts, challenge them to speculate on other contexts a word might appear. "Who would say *feign?*" Students might speculate a prosecutor might say, "the defendant is feigning innocence." Or a biologist, might say, "opossums feign death to trick predators." Through this activity, students learn to place new words in meaningful contexts rather than in contrived sentences.

Pragmatic Practice: Wiring Vocabulary into the Language of Learning

Talking the Talk Intentionally weave new vocabulary into classroom discussions of selections. For example, ask students to elaborate ways the Plymouth settlers were in *peril* during the period described by William Bradford. Or speculate why some settlers might *feign* conditions in the colony in letters written home. Students gain practice experimenting with vocabulary modeled by the teacher while they talk about their understanding of a literary work. In addition, they begin to appreciate precision in word choice and why certain words more clearly communicate an author's message.

Integrating Vocabulary Assessment Instead of separate evaluations of vocabulary, embed a vocabulary layer into classroom activities and in particular, into the language of assessment measures. Ask students to demonstrate their knowledge of new vocabulary as they explain their understandings of author ideas, behavior of characters, or elements of author's craft. For example, ask students to comment on Ben Franklin's conception of virtue by meaningfully discussing the following terms: *avarice, frugality, vigilance, felicity,* and *resolution.*

Modeled Strategy
See p. 105 for a point-of-use note modeling these strategies.

Teacher Resources
- *Professional Development Guidebook*
- *Classroom Strategies and Teaching Routines cards*

Log on as a teacher at **www.PHLitOnline.com** to access a library of all Professional Development articles by the Contributing Authors of Pearson Prentice Hall *Literature*.

Doug Buehl

Doug Buehl is a teacher, author, and national literacy consultant. His 33 years with the Madison Metropolitan School District, Madison, WI, included experiences as a reading teacher and district adolescent literacy support teacher.

Supporting Research

Blachowicz, C. (1986). Making connections: Alternative to the vocabulary notebook. *The Journal of Reading.* Vol. 29, No. 7, pp. 643–649.

Nagy, W. & Scott, J. (2000). Vocabulary processes. In Kamil, M., Mosenthal, P., Pearson, P. D., and Barr, R. Edited. *Handbook of reading research, Volume III.* Mahway, NJ: Lawrence Erlbaum Associates, 269–284.

Scott, J. Jamieson-Noel, D., Asselin, M. (2003) Vocabulary instruction throughout the day in twenty-three canadian upper-elementary classrooms. *The Elementary School Journal,* Vol. 103, No. 3 (Jan.), pp. 269–286

Reading the Unit Introduction

A Gathering of Voices

Explain to students that this unit covers literature in America from before the arrival of Columbus to 1800, a period during which Europeans discovered the Americas and their original inhabitants. The Unit Introduction includes these components:

—a **Snapshot** offering a quick glimpse at the period

—a **Historical Background** section discussing major events

—a **Timeline** that covers the period from 1490 to 1800 over a span of eight pages

—a **Unit Essay** examining the literature of the period through the lens of three Essential Questions

—**Following-Through** activities

—a **Contemporary Commentary**

Introducing the Essential Questions

1. Introduce each of the Essential Questions on the student page.

2. Show the **Essential Question** video on the *See It!* **DVD**. Help students relate to the Essential Questions by asking the following:
   Literature and Place Would you ever consider leaving Earth to spend time on a space station or in a colony on another planet? Why or why not? What qualities do you think are needed to be a pioneer or explorer?
   Literature and Society Make a list of three famous Americans who strongly influence you. Your list can include television personalities, writers, movie directors or actors, athletes, politicians, and so on. Why is each person on your list?
   American Literature Choose one item in your home that most represents America to you. What does that item say about America?

3. Explain to students that the ideas they have considered in answering these questions also apply to the history of early America. Have them read the Unit Introduction, telling them to look for ideas related to their answers.

2

Snapshot of the Period

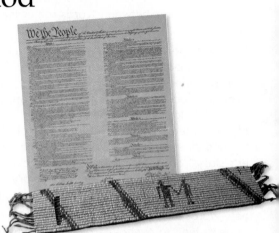

In 1492, North America was already populated by several hundred Native American tribes. More than 12,000 years before Christopher Columbus reached North America, nomadic peoples had migrated across the Bering Land Bridge from Asia and settled across the continent. These people spoke different languages and had very different cultures, but the Europeans called them all by one name: "Indians." In the centuries after Columbus, more and more Europeans ventured to the New World. Among them were explorers, fortune-seekers, missionaries, and those fleeing religious persecution. There were also enslaved Africans who made the journey against their will. Individuals from these groups wrote accounts of their experiences, creating the first written literature of North America. By 1699, European colonies dotted the entire Eastern seaboard and extended as far west as New Mexico. In 1776, thirteen of those colonies declared their independence from England.

▲ Political documents, such as the Constitution, recorded the new nation's founding principles. Wampum belts recorded important treaties of Eastern tribes.

The Iroquois   Bradstreet   Wheatley   Jefferson   Equiano   Franklin

As you read the selections in this unit, you will be asked to think about them in view of three key questions:

What is the **relationship** between literature and *place?*

How does **literature** shape or reflect *society?*

What makes **American** literature *American?*

2 Beginnings–1800

Teaching Resources

The following resources can be used to support, enrich, or extend the instruction for the Unit 1 Introduction.

Unit 1 Resources

 Names and Terms to Know, p. 11
 Essential Question, pp. 8–10
 Listening and Viewing, p. 14
 Follow-Through Activities, p. 12

Common Core Companion, pp. 10–16; 33–38

 Professional Development Guidebook
 Cross-Curricular Enrichment, pp. 223, 228, 230, 238

See It! DVD
 Essential Question Video: Unit 1
 Susan Power, Segment 1

PHLit Online! All resources are available at **www.PHLitOnline.com**

Peoples of North America
« 1490–1750 »

European exploration of North America quickly led to settlement and colonization. The Spaniards settled in Florida, then sent Jesuit and Franciscan missionaries to California and Texas. The French settled in Maine and along the Gulf of Mexico, while the Dutch established New Amsterdam (New York) and communities reaching south to Delaware. English Puritans settled Virginia, New England, and Pennsylvania and later took over the Dutch and French colonies and Florida. This influx of Europeans had a lasting impact on Native Americans, whose lifestyles and territories were increasingly restricted.

Ⓒ Integration of Knowledge and Ideas Based on the information in this map, what can you predict about the interactions among these various groups? Think about the ways in which different groups might form alliances, react to newcomers, or protect their territories. Explain your predictions.

Background
History

Tell students that although no original Native American written texts exist, archaeologists have deduced a great deal from artifacts, and folklorists have recorded a rich variety of oral Native American songs, legends, and myths. Native Americans usually—but not always—greeted the earliest European settlers as friends. They instructed the newcomers in their methods of agriculture and woodcraft and introduced them to maize (corn), beans, squash, maple sugar, snowshoes, toboggans, and birch-bark canoes. If it had not been for the help of these first Americans, even more Europeans would have succumbed to the bitter northeastern winters.

Critical Viewing
Interpreting Illustrations

Draw students' attention to the map. **Ask** the question on the student page: Based on the information in this map, what can you predict about the interactions among the various groups represented?
Possible response: There will probably be more hostility among rival European groups than between the Native Americans and any one group of Europeans. Native Americans may form alliances with rival European groups settling near each other, such as the French and English in the northeast. There may be greater harmony in the southwest, since the Spanish are unchallenged by other Europeans. In the northwest, with no Europeans, rivalries could exist between Native American nations.

Show or assign the **Essential Question** video for Unit 1 online at **www.PHLitOnline.com.**

3

Teaching the Historical Background

The Historical Background section discusses the most significant events of this period: the development and spread of the Native American culture in the Western Hemisphere over several millennia, the arrival of the European settlers in the 1500s, the settlement of the eastern coast of America by English colonists in the 1600s, the impact of Enlightenment thinking, the conflicts that spurred the American Revolution, and the founding of the new nation.

1. Point out that the story of this period is a story of people driven by ideals and ideas to face nearly impossible challenges.

2. Have students read the Background. Then, **ask** them to identify the challenges Americans faced in each of the following developments: the establishment of Jamestown, the founding of Plymouth, the Stamp Act, the battles of the Revolutionary War, the Constitution.
Possible response: Those who arrived in Jamestown had faced a long ocean voyage and also confronted a strange new land; those who settled Plymouth faced the same challenges, as well as harsher winters; the Stamp Act brought colonists into conflict with their mother country and each other; the Revolution pitted colonists against a superior military; in writing the Constitution they had to overcome differences with each other.

Background
Science

Europeans in America encountered many plants and animals that were previously unknown to them. Among the new types of trees were the locust, the live oak, and the hickory. The colonists adopted the Native American names for some animals, such as the skunk and opossum. They made up their own names for others, such as the bullfrog and garter snake.

Teaching the Timeline

Tell students that the Timeline from 1490 to 1800 appears on pages 4–13. Each portion identifies major events in the Americas and in the world.

Historical Background

Early America (Beginnings to 1800)

The First Americans

No one knows when or how the first Americans arrived in what is now the United States. It was probably between 12,000 and 70,000 years ago. The rich cultural presence of Native American tribes spanned the continent, and Native American oral literature—myths, legends, songs—begins our American literary heritage.

Colonists from Europe did not reach the North American continent until the late 1500s. The Europeans who settled at St. Augustine, Florida, in 1565 and at Jamestown, Virginia, in 1607 learned agriculture and woodcraft from the Native Americans. They learned about maize and squash and bark canoes. These men and women were tough and hardy, but without the help of those who knew the wilderness intimately, they would probably not have survived.

Puritans, Pilgrims, Planters

After a terrifying ocean voyage, the *Mayflower* sailed into harbor at Plymouth, Massachusetts, in 1620. Its passengers were religious reformers who had tried to "purify" the Church of England but thought they had a better chance in the New World. These Puritans, now called Pilgrims, gave every ounce of energy—and often their lives—to build a "city upon a hill," a model community based on the Bible.

Puritanism gradually declined, but around 1720 a revival called the Great Awakening brought some new converts. Genuine old-fashioned Puritanism never reawakened, although the "Puritan ethic" of hard work and self-discipline remained a basic American value.

The Southern Colonies differed from New England in climate, crops, social organization, and religion. Large plantations, not small farms, were the core of the economy, and slaves, who had been first brought to Virginia in 1619, were the core of the plantations. Planters thought of themselves as hardworking but aristocratic, and their way of life was more sociable and elegant than that of the Puritans.

TIMELINE

1490

1492: Christopher Columbus lands in the Bahamas. ▶

▲ **1499: England** 20,000 die in London Plague.

4 Beginnings–1800

Enrichment: Investigating Geography

Migration from Asia to America

Scholars now believe the term *Native American* may be misleading because the people we call "Native Americans" actually were native to Asia. Thousands of years ago, these peoples crossed to the Americas by way of a land bridge that once existed across the Bering Strait between northeastern Russia and Alaska. Later, they migrated southward and eastward, eventually spreading over all of North, Central, and South America. The different phases of this migration account for the different linguistic and cultural groups now identified as Native American.

Activity: Geography Report Have students use the **Investigating Geography** worksheet, *Professional Development Guidebook,* p. 228, to help them trace the journey of the peoples from northeastern Asia to the Americas. Ask students to use the map on page 3 and scaled maps to estimate the number of miles the following peoples traveled from the Bering Strait to what became their American homelands: the Chinook, the Pawnee, the Creek, and the Seminoles. Then, ask students to report their findings to the class.

The Age of Reason

The Enlightenment shocked Puritan beliefs. Inspired by brilliant scientists such as Galileo and Newton, and philosophers such as Voltaire and Rousseau, the thinkers of this time valued science, logic, and reason over faith. They believed that people are good by nature and capable of building a better society. They spoke of a "social contract" that forms the basis of government, an idea that laid the groundwork for the American Revolution.

The Birth of the Nation

Taxes, taxes, and more taxes imposed by Britain kept beating down American colonists. The Stamp Act, the Townshend Acts, the Tea Act, the Coercive Acts—by 1774 the colonists had had enough. They met in Philadelphia for the First Continental Congress, and in 1775, minutemen at Lexington and Concord fired "the shot heard 'round the world."

Six long years of bloodshed followed. At Bunker Hill, Saratoga, and many other sites, colonists fought alongside French and African American soldiers, until the British finally surrendered at Yorktown in 1781. Even then, the "united" states disagreed fiercely among themselves until the Constitution and Bill of Rights were ratified.

Heroes of the Revolution—Washington and Adams—became the first two presidents. Thomas Jefferson, a hero of the Enlightenment, became the third. By 1800, the United States of America had firmly established its political identity. It would soon establish its cultural identity as well.

Key Historical Theme: Creating a Nation

- Europeans came to America to create a "city upon a hill," an ideal community founded on moral and religious values.
- Colonists, with the help of Native Americans, learned to make the wilderness productive, on both small farms and large plantations.
- The United States arose from Enlightenment ideas—that people are basically good and can use reason to create a better society.

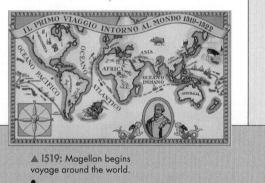

1508: Italy Michelangelo begins painting ceiling of Sistine Chapel. ▼

1513: Juan Ponce de León lands on the Florida peninsula.

▲ **1519:** Magellan begins voyage around the world.

1555

1513: Vasco Nuñez de Balboa reaches the Pacific Ocean.

1519: Spain Chocolate introduced to Europe.

1521: Mexico Cortés conquers the Aztecs.

Historical Background **5**

5

As students read this unit, they will examine its information through the lens of three Essential Questions. Each Essential Question is broken down into stepping-stone questions. Work through each stepping-stone question with the class. Then, have students pose answers to each Essential Question as it applies to the period.

What is the relationship between literature and place?

1. Before they read this section of the essay, tell students that the early settlers' view of the land was quite different from that of the Native Americans. To the settlers, the new land was a developing and often frightening mystery. To the Native Americans, the land was beloved and well known.

2. Have students read this section of the essay. Then, pose the first stepping-stone question. **Ask:** *What was the New World's natural environment?*
   Sample answer: The New World's environment included long shorelines, rocky coasts, sandy beaches, and inland mountains and valleys inhabited by a variety of plants and animals. To the colonists, everything was vast and unfamiliar. The Native Americans knew the land well and were accustomed to living on it.

3. Then, **ask** the second stepping-stone question: *What were the colonists' attitudes toward the New World environment?*
   Sample answer: The colonists believed the land belonged to the people—especially to their European monarchs. The religious colonists viewed the land as both an idealized dream (the Puritans' "city on a hill") and a frightening reality in which disease, animals, harsh weather, and starvation posed mortal dangers. As time went on, the colonists learned to survive in the New World and adapt it to their culture, building towns, roads, schools, and churches.

(continued on p. 8)

Essential Questions Across Time

Early America (Beginnings to 1800)

 What is the **relationship** between **literature** and *place?*

What was the New World's natural environment?
About one century before the colonists arrived in North America, many people thought that crossing the Atlantic Ocean meant sailing off the edge of the earth. Instead, the first European colonists found a continent more magnificent, strange, and dangerous than any of them had ever imagined.

Place of Wonder The colonists discovered long shores and sandy beaches backed by vast forests. They found ranges of mountains and fertile valleys and an astounding variety of plants, fish, birds, and animals. Nature in America was built on an immense scale. The wilderness looked endless. Nevertheless, for all its intimidating size and wild variety, this new place had one overwhelmingly satisfying quality: It was not Europe.

At One with the Place From the beginning, then, America was a place apart—but it was not so in the eyes of the Native Americans. In fact, for most Native American cultures, the people belonged to the land. The deep forests and wide plains were simply to be used and cared for by the human beings who lived in them temporarily. The lands and waters were life-giving environments, and the animals were part of the community. The facts of nature could be harsh, but they were also to be celebrated in myths, rituals, and songs. Nature was not to be feared as an enemy or overcome as an obstacle, but honored as the source of life.

TIMELINE

1555

1558: England Elizabeth I inherits throne.

1565: St. Augustine, Florida First permanent settlement in U.S., founded by Pedro Menendez.

1570: Iroquois Confederacy established to stop warfare among the Five Nations.

▲ **1587:** English colony at Roanoke Island disappears; known as the Lost Colony.

Enrichment: Understanding Anthropology

African American Culture
African Americans made up the majority of the population of South Carolina and Georgia. They generally had contact with only a few English colonists. As a result, African Americans were able to exercise greater control over their day-to-day lives than those enslaved in other colonies. Thus, they managed to preserve more of their African cultural traditions. Many still practiced the crafts of their homeland, such as basket weaving and pottery. In some cases, they maintained aspects of their native languages.

The best-known example is Gullah, a combination of English and African languages. As late as the 1940s, speakers of Gullah were using 4,000 words from over twenty separate West African languages.

Activity: Glossary Have students use the Internet to make a glossary of Gullah terms, such as *gumbo* (a kind of stew or soup). Invite them to record research in the **Investigating Culture** worksheet, *Professional Development Guidebook,* page 223.

What were the colonists' attitudes toward the New World environment?

For the colonists, the people did not belong to the land. Quite the opposite: Land belonged to people, and this land was to be claimed by Britain, France, and Spain. It was measured, divided, bought, sold, and governed as the property of European kings and trading companies. The Puritans, filled with religious zeal, may have wanted to build a "city upon a hill," but the hill would still belong to the King of England.

Dream vs. Reality During the seventeenth century, the colonists' attitude toward the American environment was a blend of dream and reality. The dream was to create a theocracy, an earthly community governed by religious principles. The reality was to avoid starving to death or falling prey to cold, disease, or animals. The colonists saw the continent's raw beauty, rich resources, and awe-inspiring possibilities. They also felt every day the hard facts of staying alive.

Independent Place and People By the eighteenth century, Europeans had gained a more secure foothold in America. Tree by tree, they had tamed a portion of the wilderness and built towns, roads, schools, and churches. They began to worry less about survival and more about self-government. They began to ask, "We live in an independent place, so why aren't we an independent people?" The effects of the Enlightenment began to set in, and people realized that they could belong to themselves rather than to a monarch. The spirit of self-reliance that had faced down the wilderness was the same spirit that would face down European kings. The place itself had taught Americans how to be Americans.

The American EXPERIENCE

A LIVING TRADITION

Anne Bradstreet and John Berryman

In the 1950s, American poet John Berryman responded powerfully to the life and work of Puritan poet Anne Bradstreet, who had lived 300 years earlier. In his long poem of praise called "Homage to Mistress Bradstreet," he reveals his understanding of her struggle to survive and to be a writer in seventeenth-century America. He imagines her winter ordeals and asserts that he is more sympathetic to her poetry than was her busy husband, Simon.

from "Homage to Mistress Bradstreet"
*Outside the New World winters in grand dark
white air lashing high thro' the virgin stands*

*foxes down foxholes sigh,
surely the English heart quails, stunned.
I doubt if Simon than this blast, that sea,
spares from his rigor for your poetry
more. We are on each other's hands
who care. Both of our worlds unhanded us.
    Lie stark,*

*thy eyes look to me mild. Out of maize & air
your body's made, and moves. I summon, see,
from the centuries it. . .*

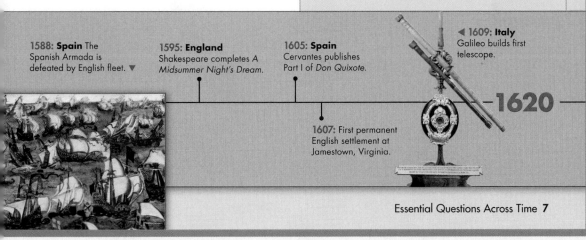

1588: Spain The Spanish Armada is defeated by English fleet. ▼

1595: England Shakespeare completes *A Midsummer Night's Dream*.

1605: Spain Cervantes publishes Part I of *Don Quixote*.

◄ **1609: Italy** Galileo builds first telescope.

1620

1607: First permanent English settlement at Jamestown, Virginia.

Essential Questions Across Time **7**

The American Experience
A Living Tradition

1. Have students read the sidebar feature about two poets, John Berryman (1914–1972) and Anne Bradstreet (1612–1672).

2. Explain that Berryman identifies with the Puritan Bradstreet, who wrote *The Tenth Muse Lately Sprung Up in America*, which was the first book of poetry published by an American woman. (See Bradstreet's "To My Dear and Loving Husband," p. 76.)

3. Tell students that Berryman sympathizes with the difficulties of Bradstreet's physical life in New England and her emotional life with her husband, Simon.

4. **Ask** students to tell which lines in Berryman's poem show his sympathy for Bradstreet's physical hardships and which show his sympathy for her emotional life. Have them list the key words that helped them identify these lines. **Possible answer:** Physical life: lines 1–4; key words: winters, lashing, sigh; Emotional life: lines 4–9; key words: heart quails, stunned, doubt, blast, rigor, unhanded, stark

Critical Viewing
Connect

1. Direct students to the Timeline illustration on page 6 of the statue of Pedro Menendez (1519–1574), the naval commander who founded the Spanish colony of St. Augustine in what was then called La Florida.

2. **Ask** students what details in the statue suggest the social position and character of Menendez. **Sample answer:** Menendez is wearing a fashionable high collar and the elaborate armor and high boots of a sixteenth-century Spanish military leader. He is watchful and alert, but not aggressive. He holds his helmet and has his sword poised to defend himself if necessary.

7

Teaching the Essential Question

(cont.)

4. **Ask** the third and final stepping-stone question: *How did attitudes toward nature show up in American literature?*

Sample answer: The Native American songs and legends showed the connection between people and nature. Cabeza de Vaca and William Bradford wrote journals describing the wonders of the New World. Religious figures, such as the Mather family, portrayed the wilderness as an evil place. Enlightenment thinking influenced American writers to celebrate their fresh New World and its superiority to Europe.

Applying the Essential Question

1. Summarize the class discussion of the three stepping-stone questions on pages 6–8.

2. Then, **ask** students: Are our contemporary attitudes toward the land more like those of the colonists or those of the Native Americans?

Possible response: Today, our attitudes toward the land combine elements of both attitudes. Many people today share the Native Americans' feeling that the people belong to the land and should cherish it. At the same time, our society is based on the view that land is property, and technology has given us incredible power over nature.

Critical Viewing

Draw Conclusions

1. Draw students' attention to the Timeline illustration of the Pilgrims' ship on this page.

2. **Ask** students: What impression of seventeenth-century ocean travel does the illustration of the ship suggest? What impression of the Pilgrims' voyage does it create?

Possible response: The ship's sails dominate the illustration, since they are the ship's main source of power. The illustration makes the ship appear safe and stable, coming to the end of a successful voyage.

How did attitudes toward nature show up in literature?

The close relationship between Native Americans and nature showed up in myths and legends. In these stories, people communicate with mountains and rivers. People and animals talk with each other and sometimes even change into each other. Human beings and nature live in harmony.

When the earliest explorers searched the continent, their responses to the land appeared in their journals and in the reports and letters they sent back home. Cabeza de Vaca recorded the natural wonders of the New World. William Bradford's *Of Plymouth Plantation*, the finest written work of the first European Americans, is filled with detailed descriptions of creating a colony in a place so delightful and so dangerous.

"Errand into the Wilderness" America's first literary family—Richard, Increase, and Cotton Mather—saw the environment from a religious point of view. Their writings describe a mission to combat evil in an "uncivilized" place. In time, this idea of the wilderness as a dark place of evil profoundly affected other writers. Forests and wild places play a large role, physically and symbolically, in the writings of American writers who would come later, including Washington Irving, James Fenimore Cooper, Nathaniel Hawthorne, and Mark Twain.

Place and Nation As the colonies developed, the power of reason began to make the continent a more hospitable place. Technology improved and agriculture flourished. In *Letters from an American Farmer*, Jean de Crèvecoeur even used the imagery of growing plants to emphasize the important idea that living in this particular place turned Europeans into Americans: "In Europe they were as so many useless plants … they withered and were mowed down by want, hunger, and war; but now by the power of transplantation, like all other plants they have taken root and flourished!" The very name of the new nation reveals the influence of place: The "United States of America" is made of separate distinct places (states) united into one—a federal republic.

ESSENTIAL QUESTION VOCABULARY

These Essential Question words will help you think and write about literature and place:

magnificent (mag nif´ə sənt) *adj.* grandly beautiful; impressive

obstacle (äb´stə kəl) *n.* something that impedes progress

resources (rē´ sôrs əs) *n.* natural sources of wealth, such as land or minerals

---

TIMELINE

1620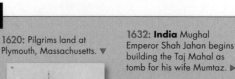

1620: Pilgrims land at Plymouth, Massachusetts. ▼

1632: India Mughal Emperor Shah Jahan begins building the Taj Mahal as tomb for his wife Mumtaz. ▶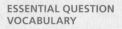

1639: First printing press in English-speaking North America arrives in Massachusetts.

"For we must consider that we shall be a city upon a hill. The eyes of all people are upon us." —John Winthrop, Governor of the Massachusetts Bay Colony from 1629–1649

1640: *Bay Psalm Book* published; first book printed in the colonies.

8 Beginnings–1800

Vocabulary Development

Essential Question Vocabulary

Students will use Essential Question Vocabulary (introduced on pp. 8, 10, and 13) when they discuss the Essential Questions in the unit. Introduce the vocabulary as students complete each section of this Unit introduction. Then, have students complete sentence starters like the following to help them internalize this vocabulary.

The new environment challenged the early settlers with **obstacles** such as _____.
(**Sample answer:** cold and disease)

The hope and **optimism** of the early Americans is seen in their _____. (**Sample answer:** political ideas)

The Declaration of Independence makes a **rational**, reasoned argument for independence by _____. (**Sample answer:** proving that King George III has broken his contract with his American subjects)

What makes American literature *American?*

American literature, naturally, shares the basic characteristics of all literature—characters, plots, settings, images, and themes. However, American literature is much more than literary works written by Americans. It also embodies certain ideas, evokes certain places, and tells stories of certain kinds of characters. There are qualities that distinguish American literature and make it a unique cultural expression.

What is a theme, and how does it find expression in literature?

A theme is the central idea, message, or insight that a literary work reveals. A theme is not the subject of a work, but rather the insight that the work reveals about the subject. A work reveals its themes through characters' words and actions, through details of setting and plot, through imagery, and even through language and style.

What were early American themes?

Three themes dominate early American writing:

Wilderness Writers revealed insights into the nature and meaning of the wilderness by the details they used to describe it and by the stories they told of their physical, political, and spiritual struggles with it.

The American EXPERIENCE

DEVELOPING AMERICAN ENGLISH

Our Native American Heritage
by Richard Lederer

If you had been a settler in North America, you would have found many things in your new environment unknown to you. The handiest way of filling voids in your vocabulary would have been to ask local Native Americans what words they used. Colonists began borrowing words from Native Americans almost from the moment of their first contact, and many of those shared words have remained in our everyday language. They are part of what makes American literature American.

Anglicizing Pronouncing many of the Native American words was difficult for the colonists, so they often shortened or simplified the words. For example, *askútasquash* became "squash," *otchock* became "woodchuck," *rahaugcum* turned into "raccoon," and the smelly *segankw* transformed into "skunk." The North American menagerie brought more new words into the English language, including *caribou* (Micmac), *chipmunk* (Ojibwa), *moose* (Algonquian), and *muskrat* (Abenaki).

The Poetry of Place Names Some of our loveliest place names—*Susquehanna, Shenandoah, Rappahannock*—began life as Native American words. Such names are the stuff of poetry. Colonists freely used words of Indian origin to name states (half of all of them), cities, towns, mountains, lakes, rivers, and ponds.

Teaching the Essential Question

What makes American literature American?

1. Before they read this section, explain to students that the literature created during this period is characterized by great variety. It includes Native American songs and legends, Puritan sermons and poems, journals by colonists and explorers, and political writings.

2. Have students read this section of the essay. Then **ask** the first stepping-stone question: *What is a theme, and how does it find expression in literature?*
   Possible answer: A theme is the central idea or insight in a literary work. Theme is revealed through the words and actions of characters; setting and plot details; and imagery, language, and style.

3. Then **ask** the second stepping-stone question: *What early American themes?*
   Answer: Three themes dominated early-American literature: wilderness, community, and individualism. Writers described people's struggle with their untamed new land and discussed their society's special blend of community and independence. Writers of all sorts focused on self-reliance as a basic American value.

(continued on p. 10)

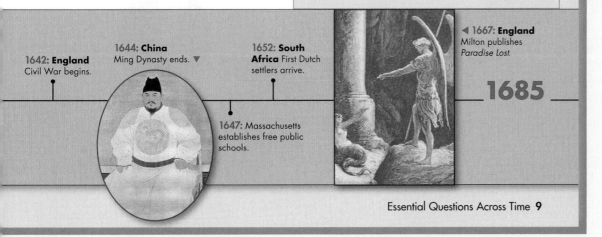

1642: England Civil War begins.

1644: China Ming Dynasty ends. ▼

1647: Massachusetts establishes free public schools.

1652: South Africa First Dutch settlers arrive.

◄ **1667: England** Milton publishes *Paradise Lost.*

1685

The American Experience

Developing American English

1. Tell students to think about Native American place names they already know, including those of states.

2. Then **ask** students to work together to come up with the complete list of states with Native American names.
   Answer: The following states have Native American names: Alabama, Alaska, Arizona, Arkansas, Connecticut, Hawaii, Idaho, Illinois, Iowa, Kansas, Kentucky, Massachusetts, Michigan, Minnesota, Mississippi, Missouri, Nebraska, New Mexico, North Dakota, Ohio, Oklahoma, Oregon, South Dakota, Tennessee, Texas, Utah, Wisconsin, Wyoming.

3. Then have students divide up the list of names in order to research their origin. Explain that different sources may give different translations or origins for Native American terms. If students have trouble finding sources, suggest that they use an almanac or the state's Web site.

4. Ask the third stepping-stone question, on this student page: *What was uniquely American about those themes?*

Sample answer: Americans realized the unique features of their physical environment. It was mysterious, promising and frightening, good and evil. Americans realized that much of traditional European writing did not apply to their experience. Still, it took a while before American writers found their own voices, rather than imitating European ones. The basic American themes stressed independence, inventiveness, self-reliance, youth, optimism, risk-taking, and originality.

Applying the Essential Question

1. Summarize discussion of the three stepping-stone questions on pages 8–10.

2. Then **ask** students what uniquely American themes they would choose for the early twenty-first century, and why.
Possible answer: Community might become more important as a theme in our time. Our society is more complex and varied than that of the colonists, and our actions have far-reaching consequences. Originality and inventiveness are still part of the American heart.

Critical Viewing

Draw Conclusions

1. Call students' attention to the image in the Timeline of the Salem witchcraft trials. Explain that Salem, a town in Massachusetts, was gripped by a strange phenomenon in 1692. Several young girls accused villagers of bewitching them. For several months, local authorities jailed ordinary men and women, nineteen of whom were hanged, and one died by having stones pressed on his chest. A few months later, most of the girls admitted that they had lied.

2. **Ask:** What can you tell about the witch trials from the illustration?
Answer: The judges and observers were mostly men; the accusers were all female, and ordinary

10

Community In public writing such as pamphlets and newspapers, colonists and patriots conveyed the central message that America was a unique combination of community and independence.

Individualism In history and memoir, and in everything from laws to lyric poems, writers made clear that self-reliance and individualism are fundamental American values.

What is uniquely American about those themes?

The Place Americans recognized that they were in a unique place, a New World, only a small part of which they had even seen. Nothing in their European experience had prepared them for the splendors and the terrors of the American wilderness. Sometimes, America seemed to be the Garden of Eden, a newly created place of natural wealth. Sometimes, it seemed to be an enemy, a punishment, or a source of fear and death. These themes entered into the American literary imagination.

The Past When Americans wrote, they were aware of the many traditional European subjects and themes that were now of no importance to them. After all, there had been no Middle Ages or Renaissance in America. Europeans had medieval romances that told tales of knights and chivalry; Americans did not. Europeans had Shakespeare's tragedies of kings and princes; Americans did not. Europeans had a heritage of elegant and witty writing; Americans had a plain, straightforward way of writing. Americans did have histories and journals, prayers and sermons, speeches and essays. They even had some poems, but all of these imitated European styles. With the turn of the nineteenth century, American writers would begin to forge unique ways of expressing their unique experience.

The Vision The themes of independence and self-reliance are at the heart of Americans' vision of themselves as a new and unique people. They knew they were creating not only a new nation but a new kind of nation. That sense of newness marked Americans as a people of youth, innocence, optimism, risk-taking, and boundless originality.

> **ESSENTIAL QUESTION VOCABULARY**
>
> These Essential Question words will help you think and write about American literature:
>
> **independence** (in´dē pen´ dəns) *n.* freedom from the control of others
>
> **straightforward** (strāt for´ wərd) *adj.* direct; clear-cut
>
> **optimism** (äp´ tə miz´ əm) *n.* hopefulness; a tendency to anticipate the best

TIMELINE

1685

1690: India Calcutta founded by the British.

1692: Salem witchcraft trials result in the execution of twenty people. ▼

▲ **1721: Germany** Bach composes *The Brandenburg Concertos.*

1726: England Jonathan Swift publishes *Gulliver's Travels.* ▼

men as well as women were accused. The woman who is pointing forcefully may be accusing the man with the raised arm of witchcraft, or she might be defending herself against someone else's accusation.

How does literature shape or reflect *society*?

What social and political forces affected early American literature?

Puritanism From the first, Puritanism influenced just about every aspect of colonial life. The impulse to escape to a New World and build a reformed and uncorrupted society shaped Puritan lawmaking, social relations, and daily life. Belief in predestination—John Calvin's doctrine that God has already decided who will be saved—made Puritans search every thought, action, and word for signs of grace. In hymns, sermons, histories, journals, and autobiographies, they aimed only for self-examination and spiritual insight.

The Enlightenment By the eighteenth century, the power of reason asserted itself in America. In speeches, pamphlets, essays, and newspaper articles, the spirit of the times called for debate, clear thinking, and reorganization of the political situation. The Declaration of Independence, for example, is not an outcry or an anarchic demand. It is a reasoned document, a controlled statement of the rational argument for independence.

Native Americans and African Americans Relations with Native Americans and the continued enslavement of African Americans left deep marks in American literature. In histories and captivity narratives, we have some record of relationships between colonists and Native

The American EXPERIENCE
CLOSE-UP ON HISTORY

African Americans and Women in the Revolution

In 1776, more than half a million African Americans lived in the colonies. At first, the Continental Congress did not permit enslaved or free African Americans to join the American army. However, when the British offered to free any male slave who fought for the king, George Washington changed American policy and allowed free African Americans to enlist. About 5,000 African Americans fought against the British. As this eyewitness account demonstrates, they fought with great courage:

Three times in succession, [African American soldiers] were attacked . . . by well-disciplined and veteran British troops, and three times did they successfully repel the assault, and thus preserve our army from capture.

Women also helped in the struggle for independence from Great Britain. When men went off to war, the women took on added work. They planted and harvested crops, and they made shoes and blankets and uniforms. Many followed their husbands and brothers to the front, where they washed, cooked, and cared for the wounded. Some even took part in battle, including a brave woman named Mary Hays, who carried water on the battle lines and became known as Molly Pitcher.

1727: Brazil First coffee plants cultivated. ▼

1735: John Peter Zenger acquitted of libel, furthering freedom of the press.

1741: Great Awakening, a series of religious revivals, begins to sweep the colonies.

▲ **1741:** Jonathan Edwards first delivers his sermon "Sinners in the Hands of an Angry God."

1748: France Montesquieu publishes *The Spirit of the Laws*, which later influences the U.S. Constitution.

1750

Essential Questions Across Time **11**

?THE ESSENTIAL Teaching the Essential Question

How does literature shape or reflect society?

1. Before they read this section, explain to students that during this time, the eastern and southeastern parts of America underwent the greatest change, as they were being colonized by the English.

2. Have students read this section of the essay. Then, **ask** the first stepping-stone question: *What social and political forces affected early- American literature?*
   Possible answer: The Puritans' laws reflected their zeal for purifying both the individual and society. As seen in the Declaration of Independence, the spirit of the Enlightenment encouraged Americans to engage in reasonable discourse, even as they rebelled against their mother country. Relations with Native Americans and the enslavement of Africans affected the American spirit. In particular, the writings of slaves and slaveholders show the wounds made by slavery.

(continued on p. 13)

The American Experience
Close-up on History

1. Tell students the names of several African Americans who served the Revolutionary cause: Crispus Attucks, James Amistead Lafayette, Prince Whipple, and James Forten.

2. Ask students to work together in groups to learn more about one of these men. They can search the names on the Internet.

3. Then, have each group report briefly on the information they found.

Enrichment: Investigating Popular Culture

The *New England Primer*

First published in 1690, the *New England Primer* became a staple of American education in the eighteenth and nineteenth centuries. The *Primer* combined instruction in such basics as the ABCs with moralizing. For example, the *Primer* taught the letter *A* with the little rhyme "A: In Adam's Fall/We sinned all." (However, some of the rhymes were less religious: "C: The Cat doth play/And after slay.") The *Primer* included numerous prayers to learn, but it also taught reading and writing. It taught vocabulary words of varying levels, grouped by number of

syllables and listed alphabetically (the first of the six-syllable words is *Abomination*). At one time, over 5 million children regularly used the *New England Primer* in school.

Activity: Research Have students make a list of research topics relating to the *New England Primer,* using the **Enrichment: Analyzing Popular Culture** worksheet from the *Professional Development Guidebook,* page 238, to guide them.

11

The American Experience

Contemporary Connection

1. Before students read the feature about Thomas Paine (1737–1809), tell them that Paine, born in England, seemed to have had revolution in his blood. When he served in the English army, he led a revolt for salary raises. He moved to America in 1774. His famous call to arms, *Common Sense,* told Americans that reason left them no choice but to rebel against England. Paine soon put his money where his mouth was, joining the Continental Army in 1776. George Washington was so inspired by Paine's powerful essay *The American Crisis* that he ordered it read to his troops before his famous crossing of the Delaware River in 1776. Paine's unconventional ideas were far ahead of his time. (For example, he advocated a system of guaranteed income that resembles our modern-day Social Security.) Eventually, Paine's unconventionality made him unpopular. When he died in New York City in 1809, only a few people attended his funeral.

2. **Ask** what issues Thomas Paine might sound off about if he were writing a blog on the Internet today.

   Answer: Paine would probably be concerned with economic issues, such as the distribution of income. He might also write about the seemingly unreasonable behavior of some political leaders.

The American EXPERIENCE

CONTEMPORARY CONNECTION

Thomas Paine: Essayist, Hero of the Revolution...Father of the Internet?

Thomas Paine believed that knowledge is power and that it belongs to all people, not just the wealthy or privileged. He believed that through knowledge, ordinary people could guarantee their own freedoms. Even at a time when the printed word was slow to publish and distribute, Paine's fiery words brought change, fueling both the American and the French revolutions.

While this pamphleteer and passionate advocate of communication is often seen as a pioneer of investigative journalism, perhaps his true legacy is the Internet. Writing in *Wired News* (issue 3.05– May 1995), journalist Jon Katz observed that regarding the Internet, Paine's "ideas about communications, media ethics, the universal connections between people, and the free flow of honest opinion are all relevant again, visible every time one modem shakes hands with another."

Paine once said, "Such is the irresistible nature of truth that all it asks, and all it wants, is the liberty of appearing." When the Internet is used in its best and highest forms, truth becomes available to anyone with a computer. Thomas Paine, advocate of "all mankind," might recognize the Internet as the true product of his own ideals.

TIMELINE

1750

◀ **1755: England** Samuel Johnson publishes *Dictionary of the English Language.*

1754: French and Indian War begins.

1773: Parliament's Tea Act prompts Boston Tea Party. ▼

▲ **1775:** American Revolution begins.

12 Beginnings–1800

Enrichment: Analyzing a Historic Event

The Lost Colony of Roanoke

In 1586, a group of English colonists had attempted to settle the island of Roanoke, off the coast of what is now North Carolina. When Sir Francis Drake stopped at Roanoke several months after the settlers had landed, the colonists boarded his ship and returned to England. Soon after, in 1587, English colonists made another attempt to settle the island. After leaving them at Roanoke, their captain, John White, sailed back to England, expecting to return with supplies in a few months. However, his return was delayed until 1590 by England's war with Spain. When White landed on Roanoke, he found only the remains of a campfire and two words carved on trees: "Croatan" and "Cro." Historians have speculated for centuries about what had happened.

Activity: Research Have students list research topics relating to the Lost Colony of Roanoke, using the **Enrichment: Analyzing a Historical Event** worksheet from the *Professional Development Guidebook*, page 230.

Americans, relationships that ranged from trust to distrust, from friendship to hatred. In narratives left by both slaves and slaveholders, we find heartrending stories of individuals, families, and communities scarred by slavery.

What were the major roles of early American writers?

Writers not only reflect the social and political forces of their societies, they also influence those forces. They are not just the mirrors of their cultures and their communities; they can also be the fires that make those communities burn with hope, anger, love, idealism, and creativity.

Writer as Oral Poet and Historian Native American oral poets held places of vital importance for their tribes. They told each community's story, related its history, and honored its heroes. Those European Americans who wrote journals and histories fulfilled a similar role—recording the social and political events that gave meaning to their community's experience. The narratives of de Cárdenas and Cabeza de Vaca, as well as William Bradford's *Of Plymouth Plantation,* give us perspective on our own heritage.

Writer as Preacher and Lawmaker The writers of hymns and sermons believed that their role was to articulate the will of God. Cotton Mather and Jonathan Edwards explained for their communities the working of divine Providence in the wilderness, and they did their utmost to instill the fear of God into every member of their trembling audiences. The writers of America's laws and political documents had a different role—to articulate the will of the people. Thomas Paine's pamphlets, Patrick Henry's speeches, and Thomas Jefferson's multifaceted writing survive today not only as a part of history but also as literature.

Writer as Autobiographer The autobiographer's role goes beyond answering the basic question, "What did I do and why did I do it?" The autobiographer also asks, "Why should you be interested in my life? What did I learn from it? What can you learn from it?" The slave narrative of Olaudah Equiano helped Americans face their own history and ultimately do something about it. Benjamin Franklin's *Autobiography* combined a fascinating life story with explorations of essential American values.

> **ESSENTIAL QUESTION VOCABULARY**
>
> These Essential Question words will help you think and write about literature and society:
>
> **rational** (rash´ən əl) *adj.* based on reason, not emotion
>
> **articulate** (är tik´ yōō lāt) *v.* express in words
>
> **idealism** (i dē´ əl iz´ əm) *n.* belief that one should live according to one's ideals, or high principles

1776: Second Continental Congress adopts Declaration of Independence.

"Any people that would give up liberty for a little temporary safety deserves neither liberty nor safety."
—Benjamin Franklin

1786: Austria Wolfgang Amadeus Mozart creates the comic opera *The Marriage of Figaro.* ▶

1787: Constitutional Convention meets in Philadelphia to draft the Constitution.

1800

▲ **1789:** George Washington elected first President of the United States.

Essential Questions Across Time **13**

Differentiated Instruction   for Universal Access

Strategies for Special-Needs Students
These students may benefit from creating their own Graphic Organizer to help master this unit's treatment of three Essential Questions. The organizer should be very simple: It can consist of three boxes, with the Essential Question written at the top of each, and each stepping-stone question listed under the Essential Question, with space left to write in any boldfaced terms included in the discussion of each stepping-stone question. Students might work in groups of three, with each student creating a box for one of the three Essential Questions.

Enrichment for Gifted/Talented Students
Have musically talented students put together a kind of "sound essay"—a mix of music and sound effects that suggests the times, events, and cultures referred to in this Unit Introduction. Sounds could include Native American chants; ocean and boat sounds for the voyagers; the sounds of the various European languages—Spanish, French, Dutch, and English; construction sounds that represent settlements being built; "Yankee Doodle" and other Revolutionary-era music; and the sounds of war for the Revolution.

? **Teaching the Essential Question**
   (cont.)

3. Have students read this section of the essay. Then, **ask** the second stepping-stone question: *What were the major roles of early American writers?*

Possible answer: Writers both reflected and influenced their times. Native American oral poets kept the tribe's history alive and celebrated its heroes. Similarly, European journal writers like de Cárdenas, Cabeza de Vaca, and William Bradford preserved their time in descriptions of social and political events. Writers were also preachers (Cotton Mather and Jonathan Edwards) who provided spiritual guidance to large numbers of people. Great political writing helped to inspire the Revolution (the speeches of Patrick Henry, the pamphlets of Thomas Paine, the writing of Thomas Jefferson). Finally, writers recorded their own lives (Olaudah Equiano, Benjamin Franklin) in order to offer insights to others.

Applying the Essential Question

1. Summarize the class discussions of the two stepping-stone questions on pages 11 and 13.

2. Then **ask** students to match up one type of contemporary writer or artist with one of the types of writers discussed in connection with the Essential Question: the oral poets of the Native Americans, the journal writers, the spiritual leaders, the revolutionary writers, or the autobiographers. Have them support their answers with examples from the Unit Introduction.

Possible answer: Political commentators on television could be the contemporary equivalent of a widely circulated writer like Thomas Paine or an influential orator like Patrick Henry.

13

Recent Scholarship

Introduce William L. Andrews

1. William L. Andrews, an author, editor, and professor, introduces the unit and provides insights into early American autobiographies, several examples of which are included in the unit.

2. Have students read the Meet the Author feature about William L. Andrews. Tell students that the anthologies Andrews has coedited are three of the primary academic resources on African American literature.

3. After students read Andrews's first paragraph, repeat the last sentence aloud to the class: "Autobiography and America were made for each other." **Ask** students why they think autobiography became such a popular literary form in early America. **Possible response:** Students may say that early Americans were in a quest of their own, distinctive identity, so they looked to the lives of other Americans for models and definitions.

Recent Scholarship

America Begins with a Promise and a Paradox

William L. Andrews

It's not just a coincidence that America's earliest literature is highly autobiographical. Nor is it by accident that autobiography emerged as a literary form about the same time that the United States became a new nation. Autobiography and America were made for each other.

The Promise: A New Person and a New Country

The revolution in the United States created a new person, as well as a new country. At least that's what the great spokesmen and propagandists of the Revolution, especially Thomas Jefferson, Patrick Henry, and Benjamin Franklin, claimed. Franklin, who wore a coonskin cap to the royal courts of Europe, became famous for inventing everything from streetlights to eyeglasses. But we read him today because his greatest invention was himself. Franklin gave the new nation (which he also helped to invent) its first literary classic. *The Autobiography of Benjamin Franklin* is the first great American success story: a tale of a poor boy who made good.

About the Author

William L. Andrews is an award-winning scholar and teacher whose work focuses on the historical links between white and black writers in the formation of American literature. In addition to his many scholarly publications, he has co-edited three major literature anthologies: *The Norton Anthology of African American Literature, The Oxford Companion to African American Literature,* and *The Literature of the American South: A Norton Anthology.* Andrews is currently the E. Maynard Adams Professor of English at the University of North Carolina, Chapel Hill.

All video resources are available online at www.PHLitOnline.com.

The Paradox: Freedom and Slavery

In 1789 Franklin, head of Pennsylvania's largest antislavery society, signed a petition to Congress advocating an end to slavery. In the same year, a pioneering African American autobiography, *The Interesting Narrative of the Life of Olaudah Equiano,* adapted the success story to antislavery purposes. Before the American Revolution got under way, Phillis Wheatley, an African-born slave in Boston, published a book of poetry, written in the learned and ornate style of the day to show that the enslaved were just as intelligent and capable as their so-called masters. Yet when the revolutionary orator Patrick Henry demanded in 1775, "Give me liberty or give me death!" no one asked whether the slaves he held on his Virginia plantation deserved the same freedom he so passionately proclaimed.

When I was in the sixth grade in a public school not far from Patrick Henry's plantation, I studied Virginia history, a mandatory subject at the time. I remember learning then that my home state was "the mother of presidents." My teacher didn't mention that all of Virginia's great heroes, including Washington and Jefferson, were

▲ **Critical Viewing** What image of the founding fathers—Franklin, Adams, and Jefferson—does this painting create? Which details support your response? **[Analyze]**

slaveholders as well. No one, not even the framers of the U.S. Constitution in 1787, had found a way to justify the presence of slavery in a land supposedly dedicated to freedom. Eventually the only solution to America's political paradox was civil war.

America's Destiny and a Persistent Question

Ever since the founding of the United States, Americans have trumpeted the new country's special destiny: to create a new form of government, democracy, that would reform humankind itself. The transplanted Frenchman Jean de Crèvecoeur believed that democracy would inspire in all who had immigrated to America an "original genius" that would bind them together in a shared national identity. America's dedication to human rights, particularly "life, liberty, and the pursuit of happiness," would give the new people of America a grand ideal and mission. The most important writers of the early Republic extolled the nation's founding ideals but often questioned the national commitment to them. Then as now we ask of ourselves: Has America become what Jefferson and Crèvecoeur imagined?

©Speaking and Listening: Collaboration

William L. Andrews raises an important question at the end of his essay: Has the United States become the country early citizens imagined? Conduct a **full-class discussion** about this issue. Work together to achieve the following goals:

- Determine the ideals held by Jefferson and his contemporaries.
- Come to a consensus about whether modern America has fulfilled these ideals.

As you conduct your discussion, work to engage everyone equally. Respond thoughtfully to different opinions and perspectives and resolve any contradictions. Cite specific examples from multiple relevant sources to support your opinions.

Recent Scholarship **15**

Speaking and Listening: Collaboration

1. Begin the class discussion by having students name ideals that America was founded upon, based upon their background knowledge and Andrews's essay. Have a volunteer write all responses on the board.
   Possible responses: Ideals include religious tolerance, individual liberty, and political equality.

2. Using this list, ask students to offer specific examples of how Jefferson and his contemporaries embodied these ideals. Then, ask for examples of behaviors of early American leaders that did not support these ideals.
   Possible responses: Students may point to the risks undertaken by leaders of the Revolution such as Patrick Henry as proof of their intense commitment to their ideals. They may point to these leaders' slaveholding as inconsistent with their ideals of liberty and equality.

3. Have students offer ideas or judgments about the main question: Has the United States become the country early citizens imagined? Encourage them to cite specific examples from their own knowledge to support their opinions.
   Possible response: Answers will vary, but students should support their responses with specific examples and reasoned arguments.

4. To help conduct the discussion, use the Discussion Guide in the *Professional Development Guidebook,* page 65.

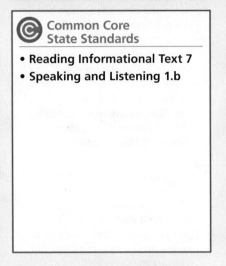

© **Common Core State Standards**

- **Reading Informational Text 7**
- **Speaking and Listening 1.b**

Integrate and Evaluate Information

1. Review the chart assignment with the class. Then, ask students to use the Activity A chart in the Follow-Through worksheet (p. 12 in *Unit 1 Resources*) to complete this activity.

   Possible response: *Literature and Place: Key Concept*—close relationship to nature; *Group*—Native Americans; *Literature and Society: Key Concept*—grace and salvation; *Group*—Puritans

2. **Possible response:** The illustration of the Roanoke colony on p. 6 adds to an understanding of the European colonists' desire for land and the conflict with Native Americans over the land.

3. **Possible response:** The themes of community, independence, and self-reliance reflect a similar view of human nature as being essentially rational and cooperative. The Puritans' belief in predestination and the continued enslavement of African Americans were in conflict with this belief.

4. **Possible response:** The "new person" is an inventive, self-reliant individualist who values democracy. This idea, although not always put into practice, still informs American identity today. For example, some candidates for public office try to project this identity in order to persuade voters that they are the "best American" for the job.

Integrate and Evaluate Information

1. Use a chart like the one shown to determine the key ideas expressed in the Essential Question essays on pages 6–13. Fill in two ideas related to each Essential Question, and note the groups most closely associated with each concept. One example has been done for you.

Essential Question	Key Concept	Group
Literature and Place		
American Literature	Self-determination	Revolutionaries like Thomas Jefferson
Literature and Society		

2. How do the visual sources in this section—illustrations, photographs, and maps—add to your understanding of the ideas expressed in words? Cite specific examples.

3. The Enlightenment belief in human goodness fueled the politics and literature of the American Revolution. How do other Revolutionary themes reflect a similar view of human nature? What conflicts with this optimism do you find in Puritan attitudes or other aspects of early colonial life? In your answer, cite evidence from the multiple sources presented on pages 4–15.

© 4. **Address a Question** William L. Andrews states that the American Revolution created "a new person, as well as a new country." What do you think "a new person" means? Does this idea still inform American identity? Integrate information from this textbook and other sources to support your ideas.

Speaking and Listening: Oral Presentation

The spoken word had great power in early America. With a small group, research one of the early American spoken forms listed below. Then, develop an **oral presentation** in which you perform an example of the form.

- Native American oral histories
- Puritan sermons or hymns
- Early American speeches
- Revolutionary War songs

© **Solve a Research Problem:** This assignment requires you to locate texts from the oral tradition, many of which predate recording devices. Formulate a plan to meet this research challenge. Identify print and media sources that provide reliable information about the content and style of forms in the oral tradition. Consider primary sources, such as journals, newspapers, and illustrations from the colonial era. Also consider secondary sources, such as writings by historians, interviews with scholars, and modern recordings, plays, or other dramatic interpretations. As part of your presentation, explain the process you used to identify information and solve the research problem.

© **Common Core State Standards**

Reading Informational Text 7. Integrate and evaluate multiple sources of information presented in different media or formats as well as in words in order to address a question or solve a problem.

Speaking and Listening 1.b. Work with peers to promote civil, democratic discussions and decision-making, set clear goals and deadlines, and establish individual roles as needed. *(p. 15)*

ESSENTIAL QUESTION VOCABULARY

Use these words in your responses:

Place and Literature
wilderness
splendor
terrors

American Literature
independence
optimism
community

Literature and Society
govern
doctrine
heritage

For definitions and pronunciations, see the Glossary, pp. R1–R7.

Speaking and Listening

1. Clarify that students are to create a research plan.

2. Have students identify the activity's key terms: *oral tradition, spoken form, primary and secondary sources.*

3. Then, have students complete Activity B in the **Follow-Through** worksheet (p. 12) in *Unit 1 Resources*.

4. Have students who chose the same spoken form work together to list likely research resources.

Meeting of Cultures

Selection Planning Guide

This section introduces students to the cultural groups that claimed a place in the early American wilderness. The origin myths and the Iroquois Constitution offer a closer look at the culture of several Native American nations. The focus then shifts to encounters experienced by European settlers in what was for them a new world. Two narratives of Spanish exploration of the Southwest are followed by an account of the arrival of Pilgrim settlers in the Northeast.

Humanities

Kee-o-kuk The Watchful Fox, Chief of the Tribe, 1835, George Catlin

Keokuk led the Sac and Fox peoples as the United States frontier edged westward. Despite the militant bearing he displays in this portrait, Keokuk chose to avoid war with the United States, eventually ceding lands to our government in the region that is now composed of Illinois, Missouri, and Wisconsin.

George Catlin gave up the practice of law to pursue his fascination with "the dignity and nobility of the Native Americans." His hundreds of closely observed paintings amount to an essential history of Native American peoples. Use these questions for discussion:

1. What impression of Keokuk do you form from this painting?
   Possible response: Students may say that he projects an air of leadership, power, and great dignity.

2. What details in the painting contribute to this overall impression?
   Possible response: Students may cite such details as his pose, straight posture, serious expression, and ceremonial weapons.

Monitoring Progress

Before students read the selections in Part 1, administer the **Diagnostic Test 1** (*Unit 1 Resources,* pp. 1–6). This test will determine students' level of readiness for the reading and vocabulary skills.

© Text Complexity: At a Glance

This chart gives a general text complexity rating for the selections in this part of the unit to help guide instruction. For additional text complexity support, see the Text Complexity Rubric at point of use.

The Earth on Turtle's Back	**More Accessible**	A Journey Through Texas	**More Complex**
When Grizzlies Walked Upright	**More Accessible**	Boulders Taller Than the Great Towers of Seville	**More Complex**
from The Navajo Origin Legend	**More Accessible**	*from* Of Plymouth Plantation	**More Complex**
from The Iroquois Constitution	**More Accessible**		

- **The Earth on Turtle's Back**
- **When The Grizzlies Walked Upright**
- *from* **The Navajo Origin Legend**

Lesson Pacing Guide

© **Common Core
State Standards**

DAY 1 Preteach

© Administer the Reading and Vocabulary Warm-ups (*Unit 1 Resources*, pp. 15–18) as necessary.

© Introduce the Literary Analysis concepts: Origin Myths and Archetypes.

- Introduce the Reading Strategy: Purpose for Reading: Cultural Characteristics.
- Build background with the author and Background features.
- Develop thematic thinking with Connecting to the Essential Question.

© Teach the selection vocabulary.

DAYS 2–3 Preteach/Teach/Assess

- Distribute copies of the appropriate graphic organizer for the Reading Strategy (*Graphic Organizer Transparencies*, pp. 1–2).
- Distribute copies of the appropriate graphic organizer for Literary Analysis (*Graphic Organizer Transparencies*, pp. 3–4).
- Prepare students to read with the Activating Prior Knowledge activities (TE).
- Informally monitor comprehension while students read.
- Use the Reading Check questions to confirm comprehension.

© Develop students' understanding of origin myths and archetypes using the Literary Analysis prompts.

- Develop students' ability to set a purpose for reading using the Reading Strategy prompts.

© Reinforce vocabulary with the Vocabulary notes.

- Assess students' comprehension and mastery of the skills by having them answer the Critical Reading, Literary Analysis, and Reading Strategy questions.
- Have students complete the Vocabulary Lesson.

DAY 4 Extend/Assess

© Have students complete the Conventions and Style Lesson.

© Have students complete the Writing Lesson and write a play. (You may assign as homework.)

- Administer Selection Test A or B (*Unit 1 Resources*, pp. 28–30 or 31–33).

Reading Literature 2. Determine two or more themes or central ideas of a text and analyze their development over the course of the text, including how they interact and build on one another to produce a complex account.

Writing 3. Write narratives to develop real or imagined experiences or events using effective technique, well-chosen details, and well-structured event sequences.

Language 3.a. Vary syntax for effect.
4.a. Use context as a clue to the meaning of a word or phrase.

Additional Standards Practice
Common Core Companion, pp. 15–22; 208–218; 322–323; 324–331

Daily Block Scheduling
Each day in this Lesson Pacing Guide represents a 40–50 minute period. Teachers using block scheduling may combine days to revise pacing. In addition, teachers may differentiate and support core instruction by integrating components for extended and intensive support as students require. See the Guide to Selected Leveled Resources (facing page).

Guide to Selected Leveled Resources

R T I Tier 1 (students performing on level)

The Earth on Turtle's Back • When Grizzlies Walked Upright *from* The Navajo Origin Legend

Warm Up	**Practice, model,** and **monitor** fluency, working **with the whole class** or **in groups**.	**Vocabulary and Reading Warm-ups B,** *Unit 1 Resources,* pp. 15–16, 18
Comprehension/Skills	**Support** and **monitor** comprehension and skills development, having students complete the activities, graphic organizers, and interactive prompts **independently** or **as a class**.	• *Reader's Notebook,* adapted instruction and summary EL *Reader's Notebook: English Learner's Version,* adapted instruction and summary • **Reading Strategy Graphic Organizer B,** *Graphic Organizer Transparencies,* p. 2 • **Literary Analysis Graphic Organizer B,** *Graphic Organizer Transparencies,* p. 4
Monitor Progress A	**Monitor** student progress with the differentiated curriculum-based assessment in the *Unit Resources.*	• **Selection Test B,** *Unit 1 Resources,* pp. 31–33 • **Open-Book Test,** *Unit 1 Resources,* pp. 25–27

R T I Tier 2 (students requiring intervention)

The Earth on Turtle's Back • When Grizzlies Walked Upright *from* The Navajo Origin Legend

Warm Up	**Practice, model,** and **monitor** fluency **in groups** or **with individuals**.	• **Vocabulary and Reading Warm-ups A,** *Unit 1 Resources,* pp. 15–17 • *Hear It!* Audio CD
Comprehension/Skills	• **Support** and **monitor** comprehension and skills development, working **in small groups** or **with individuals**. • As students complete the selection in the appropriate version of the *Reader's Notebook,* **monitor** comprehension frequently with group questions and individual instruction. • **Model** strategies while guiding students in completing the activities and prompts in the *Reader's Notebook,* as well as the graphic organizers. • **Practice** skills and **monitor** mastery with the *Reading Kit* worksheets.	• *Reader's Notebook: Adapted Version,* adapted instruction and summary EL *Reader's Notebook: English Learner's Version,* adapted instruction and summary • **Reading Strategy Graphic Organizer A,** *Graphic Organizer Transparencies,* p. 1 • **Literary Analysis Graphic Organizer A,** *Graphic Organizer Transparencies,* p. 3 • *Reading Kit,* Practice worksheets
Monitor Progress A	**Monitor** student progress with the differentiated curriculum-based assessment in the *Unit Resources* and in the *Reading Kit.*	• **Selection Test A,** *Unit 1 Resources,* pp. 28–30 • *Reading Kit,* Assess worksheets

TIER 3 Tier 3 intervention may require consultation with the student's special education or dyslexia specialist
For additional support, see the Tier 2 activities and resources listed above.

One-on-one teaching **Group work** **Whole-class instruction** **Independent work** A **Assessment**
For a complete guide to selection support, including support for Advanced students, see the Overview of Resources in the frontmatter.

- # The Earth on Turtles's Back
- # When Grizzlies Walked Upright
- # *from* The Navajo Origin Legend

RESOURCES FOR:

- **L1** Special-Needs Students
- **L2** Below-Level Students (Tier 2)
- **L3** On-Level Students (Tier 1)
- **L4** Advanced Students (Tier 1)
- **EL** English Learners
- **All** All Students

Vocabulary/Fluency/Prior Knowledge

Native American Origin Myths from the Onondaga, Modoc, and Navajo
Vocabulary Warm-up Word Lists

Study these words from the selections. Then, complete the activities.

Word List A

budge [BUJ] *v.* to move or change the position of something
The suitcase was so heavy that it was hard to budge it.

enclosure [en KLOH zher] *n.* area that is fenced in or surrounded
The animals in the enclosure could not stray onto the road.

grasp [GRASP] *v.* to take hold of something
The injury made it difficult for him to grasp a pen.

protruded [proh TROOD ed] *v.* stuck out; extended
I scratched myself on a nail that protruded from the wood.

repetition [rep uh TISH uhn] *n.* an event or action that occurs over and over
The repetition of the high, shrill noise was driving everyone crazy.

surface [SER fis] *n.* the part of the Earth, sea, or other water where it meets the air
The high winds caused the surface of the lake to be covered with waves.

swift [SWIFT] *adj.* speedy; fast; rapid
She was such a swift runner that college coaches tried to recruit her.

webbed [WEBD] *adj.* joined by membranes, often of skin
The ducks can swim rapidly because they have webbed feet.

Word List B

brushwood [BRUHSH wood] *n.* a heavy undergrowth of small trees and bushes
In fire season, it is important to keep your yard free of brushwood.

glittering [GLI ter ing] *adj.* sparkling; gleaming
From the windows of the airplane, we can see the glittering lights below.

mound [MOWND] *n.* a pile of earth, stones, or some other material
The hikers used a mound of stones to mark the path for the others to take.

scattered [SCAT terd] *v.* spread around; sprinkled
She scattered chocolate chips on top of the cake.

scrubby [SKRUHB ee] *adj.* covered with low or undersized trees
The lot they had purchased turned out to be a plot of scrubby land.

timber [TIM ber] *n.* standing trees or their wood
The land was covered with timber as far as the eye could see.

tremble [TREM buh] *adj.* to shake or vibrate
She was so frightened by the movie that she began to tremble.

uprooted [uhp ROOT id] *v.* torn up by the roots; removed
He uprooted himself because of the war and moved to a new country.

Unit 1 Resources: A Gathering of Voices
© Pearson Education, Inc. All rights reserved.
13

EL **L1** **L2** **Vocabulary Warm-ups A and B,**
pp. 15–16

Also available for these selections:
EL **L1** **L2** **Reading Warm-ups A and B,**
pp. 17–18
All **Vocabulary Builder,** p. 21

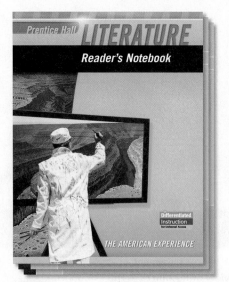

Reader's Notebooks

Pre- and postreading pages for these selections appear in an interactive format in the *Reader's Notebooks*. Each *Notebook* is differentiated for a different group of learners. The selections in the Adapted and English Learner's versions are abridged.

L2 **L3** *Reader's Notebook*
L1 *Reader's Notebook: Adapted Version*
EL *Reader's Notebook: English Learner's Version*
EL *Reader's Notebook: Spanish Version*

© *Common Core Companion*

Additional instruction and practice for each Common Core State Standard

Selection Support

"The Earth on Turtle's Back" (Onondaga)
"When Grizzlies Walked Upright" (Modoc)
from *The Navajo Origin Legend* (Navajo)

Before You Read A: Identifying Cultural Details

	Detail	Cultural Characteristic
Onondaga	• Chief tells wife her dream has power.	• Onondaga believe dreams convey messages.
Modoc		
Navajo		

EL L1 L2 Reading: Graphic Organizer A (partially filled in), p. 1

Also available for these selections:

EL L3 Reading: Graphic Organizer B, p. 2

EL L1 L2 Literary Analysis: Graphic Organizer A (partially filled in), p. 3

EL L3 Literary Analysis: Graphic Organizer B p. 4

Skills Development/Extension

Name _____ Date _____

"The Earth on Turtle's Back" (Onondaga)
"When Grizzlies Walked Upright" (Modoc)
from The Navajo Origin Legend (Navajo)

Grammar and Style: Coordinating Conjunctions

Coordinating conjunctions join words, phrases, and sentences. The main coordinating conjunctions are *and, but, or, so,* and *for.* Read these examples:

The Sky Chief and his young wife were expecting a child.

The Chief's young wife was expecting a child, and one night she dreamed that she saw the Great Tree uprooted.

In the first example, the coordinating conjunction *and* joins two phrases—*Sky Chief* with *his young wife.* In the second example, the coordinating conjunction *and* joins two complete sentences—*The Chief's young wife was expecting a child* with *one night she dreamed that she saw the Great Tree uprooted.*

A. Practice: *Write on the line any coordinating conjunction you see in each item. Then, identify what the conjunction is joining—words, phrases, or two complete sentences.*

1. The birds and animals looked up as the woman fell from the sky.

2. The water birds dove down, but they could not reach the woman.

3. The Sky Chief yelled, "You have wronged me, so from this moment you will walk on four feet."

4. The Sky Chief's daughter and a grizzly bear made the first Indians.

5. The Sky Chief punished the grizzlies, for he was angry.

B. Writing Application: *Use the coordinating conjunction in parentheses to combine each pair of sentences into a longer sentence. Write each new sentence on the lines provided.*

1. The grizzlies looked as they do today. They walked on two feet. (use *but*)

2. The daughter looked for the ocean. She fell out of the mountain. (use *and*)

3. The little girl could die. The grizzlies could save her. (use *or*)

EL L3 L4 Grammar and Style, p. 22

Also available for these selections:

All Literary Analysis: Origin Myths and Archetypes, p. 19

All Reading: Recognize Cultural Details, p. 20

EL L3 L4 Support for Writing, p. 23

L4 Enrichment, p. 24

Assessment

Name _____ Date _____

"The Earth on Turtle's Back" (Onondaga)
"When Grizzlies Walked Upright" (Modoc)
from The Navajo Origin Legend (Navajo)

Selection Test A

Critical Reading *Identify the letter of the choice that best answers the question.*

_____ 1. "The Earth on Turtle's Back," "When Grizzlies Walked Upright," and *The Navajo Origin Legend* are origin myths. What are origin myths?
A. stories about talking animals
B. stories about ancient people
C. stories that explain how life began
D. stories that explain the present day

_____ 2. "The Earth on Turtle's Back" tells how something came to exist. What is it that grew on Turtle's back?
A. the sky
B. the Earth
C. the sea
D. the woman

_____ 3. From reading "The Earth on Turtle's Back," you can tell that the Onondaga value certain things in their culture. Which two of these items do they value?
I. animals
II. clouds
III. riches
IV. dreams
A. I and III
B. II and IV
C. II and III
D. I and IV

_____ 4. Think about the animal characters in "The Earth on Turtle's Back." Which one is the archetype of the hero or heroine who is determined to succeed, even though the character is not as strong as the others?
A. the turtle
B. the loon
C. the muskrat
D. the young wife

EL L1 L2 Selection Test A, pp. 28–30

Also available for these selections:

L3 L4 Open-Book Test, pp. 25–27

EL L3 L4 Selection Test B, pp. 31–33

PHLit Online!
www.PHLitOnline.com

Online Resources: All print materials are also available online.

• complete narrated selection text
• a thematically related video with writing prompt
• an interactive graphic organizer
• highlighting feature
• access to all student print resources, adapted to individual student needs
• Spanish and English summaries
• adapted selection translations in Spanish

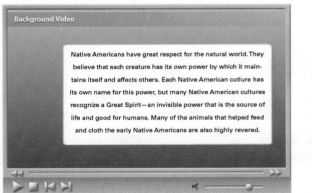

Background Video

Native Americans have great respect for the natural world. They believe that each creature has its own power by which it maintains itself and affects others. Each Native American culture has its own name for this power, but many Native American cultures recognize a Great Spirit—an invisible power that is the source of life and good for humans. Many of the animals that helped feed and cloth the early Native Americans are also highly revered.

Background Video

Also available:

Get Connected! (thematic video with writing prompt)
All videos are available in Spanish.

Vocabulary Central

Vocabulary Central (tools and activities for studying vocabulary)

Also available:

Writer's Journal (with graphics feature)

❶ 🔎 Connecting to the Essential Question

1. Review the assignment with the class.

2. **Ask** students how people today show respect and disrespect for the natural world. Then have them complete the assignment.

3. As students read, have them notice the qualities attributed to all natural elements.

❷ Literary Analysis

Introduce the skill.

Think Aloud: Model the Skill

Say to students:

To identify archetypes in literature, I look for familiar situations and character types as I read. As I read, I try to think of stories from my own culture in which a character faces a similar situation. When I recognize a common plot in stories I know, I can identify it as an archetype—a pattern that repeats across cultures.

❸ Reading Strategy

1. Introduce the strategy.

2. Give students a copy of **Reading Strategy Graphic Organizer B**, page 2 in *Graphic Organizer Transparencies*, to fill out as they read.

❹ Vocabulary

Pronounce each word, giving its definition, and have students say it aloud. For more guidance, see the *Classroom Strategies and Teaching Routines* card for introducing vocabulary.

Before You Read

The Earth on Turtle's Back •
When Grizzlies Walked Upright •
from *The Navajo Origin Legend*

❶ **Connecting to the Essential Question** These myths reveal the deep connections Native Americans saw between human society and the natural world. As you read, notice the qualities attributed to natural elements. Doing so will help as you consider the Essential Question: **What is the relationship between literature and place?**

❷ Literary Analysis

An **origin myth** is a traditional story that explains how life began. Often, origin myths also explain how a feature of the world was formed or how a specific social custom began. As part of the *oral tradition*, myths were shared by generations of storytellers before being written down.

Like other stories, myths express **themes,** insights about life or the human condition. Because they have many layers of meaning, myths may even convey multiple themes. Often, myths from different places and times express similar themes. Such universal messages may be conveyed in **archetypes**—symbols, patterns, or character types that repeat across cultures. For example, these myths place archetypal significance on the cardinal directions:

> *Then they told the people to stand at a distance and allow the wind to enter. The white wind blew from the east, and the yellow wind blew from the west.*

Comparing Literary Works As you read these myths, look for patterns of events, images, or character types that might be *archetypes*. Compare and contrast the themes these archetypes carry in each myth.

❸ Reading Strategy

© **Preparing to Read Complex Texts** When you **establish a purpose for reading,** you determine the main reason for which you are reading a particular work—to learn, to be entertained, and so on. One purpose for reading these myths would be to learn about the *cultural characteristics* of Native American peoples. As you read, look for details that show how the people of each culture live, think, or worship. Use a chart like the one shown to record your observations.

❹ Vocabulary

unconscious (un kän′ shəs) *adj.* having temporarily lost awareness; in a faint (p. 23)

depths (depths) *n.* the deepest areas (p. 23)

ancestors (an′ ses′ tərz) *n.* people from whom other people descend (p. 26)

protruded (prō troo′ did) *v.* stuck out (p. 28)

Common Core State Standards

Reading Literature
2. Determine two or more themes or central ideas of a text and analyze their development over the course of the text, including how they interact and build on one another to produce a complex account.

Details	Cultural Characteristics
Chief says wife's dream has power.	Onondaga believe dreams convey messages.

www.PHLitOnline.com

Vocabulary Development

Vocabulary Knowledge Rating

Create a **Vocabulary Knowledge Rating Chart** (*Professional Development Guidebook*, p. 33) for the vocabulary words on the student page. Give each student a copy of the chart with the words on it. Read the words aloud and have students mark their rating in the Before Reading column. Urge students to attend to these words as they read and discuss the selections.

In order to gauge how much instruction you need to provide, tally how many students are confident in their knowledge of each word. As students read, point out the words and their context.

PHLit **Online!** **Vocabulary Central,** featuring tools and activities for studying vocabulary, is available online at **www.PHLitOnline.com.**

⑤ ONONDAGA Tellers of "The Earth on Turtle's Back"

The Onondaga were key members of the Five Nations, or Iroquois Confederacy, in what is now upstate New York. Like other Iroquois, they lived in villages of wood-and-bark long houses occupied by related families. After siding with the British during the American Revolution, some Onondaga left for Canada after the British defeat. However, the majority returned to their ancestral valley in central New York state, near the lake that bears their name.

MODOC Tellers of "When Grizzlies Walked Upright"

The Modoc traditionally lived in what is now southern Oregon and northern California. There they farmed, fished, hunted, and became famous for their weaving. In the mid-nineteenth century, when the government tried to force the Modoc onto a reservation, they fought the resettlement under a leader known as Captain Jack. After several years of hostilities with United States troops, Captain Jack and his followers were forced to relocate to Oklahoma, although some were later able to return to Oregon.

NAVAJO Tellers of "The Navajo Origin Legend"

The largest Native American nation in the United States, the Navajo settled in the Southwest about a thousand years ago. Fierce warriors and hunters, they learned weaving and farming from the nearby Pueblo peoples, with whom they intermarried. Today, many Navajo live on a reservation that covers 24,000 square miles in Arizona, Utah, and New Mexico. Many Navajo still carry on their ancient customs, living in cone-shaped structures called hogans and practicing their tribal religion.

Native American Origin Myths **19**

🔔 Daily Bellringer

For each class during which you will teach these selections, have students complete one of the five activities for the appropriate week in the *Daily Bellringer Activities* booklet.

▌ Multidraft Reading

To assist struggling readers and to enhance reading for all, assign the text in chunks as warranted by length and apply multidraft reading protocols. For each reading, have students set the purpose indicated:

- **First reading**—identifying key ideas and details and answering any Reading Checks.
- **Second reading**—analyzing craft and structure and responding to the side-column prompts.
- **Third reading**—integrating knowledge and ideas, connecting to other texts and the world, and answering the end-of-selection questions.

For more guidance, refer to the *Classroom Strategies and Teaching Routines* card on multidraft reading.

⑤ Background
More About the Authors

Joseph Bruchac, one of the retellers of the first myth, is a novelist, poet, and storyteller of Abenaki descent. He lives in the foothills of New York's Adirondack Mountains, where his ancestors also lived.

The Modoc tale "When Grizzlies Walked Upright" was selected by Richard Erdoes and Alfonso Ortiz along with 165 other tales to appear in their anthology, *American Indian Myths and Legends*.

Around 1300, the Navajo, who created the third tale, migrated from northern areas in North America to what is now the southwestern United States.

PHLit Online!
www.PHLitOnline.com
Teaching From Technology

Go to in class or in a lab and display the slide show for these selections. Have the class brainstorm for responses to the slide show writing prompt, entering ideas in the interactive journal. Then have students complete their written responses individually in a lab or as homework.

To build background, display the Background and More About the Authors features.

Go to and display the As the class reads the selections or listens to the narration, record answers to side-column prompts using the graphic organizers accessible on the interactive page. Alternatively, have students use the online edition individually, answering the prompts as they read.

❶ About the Selection

This myth from the Onondaga people relates a story about the creation of the world. In this version, Earth grows, with the help of animals, between the water and a place called Skyland.

❷ Activating Prior Knowledge

Tell students that the three Native American selections all offer explanations of where the people who inhabit Earth came from. Ask students what other sources they know that take on the challenge of explaining this phenomenon. Students may mention sacred texts such as the Bible as well as the secular work of geneticists and molecular biologists. Inquire as to how students think they will respond to the Native American selections.

Concept Connector ➡

Tell students that they will return to their responses after reading the myths.

❸ Critical Viewing

Possible response: A long time ago, a turtle hitched a ride on the back of a large bird. When the bird accidentally dropped the turtle, it landed on the ground and cracked its shell. Since then, all turtles have had marks on their shells.

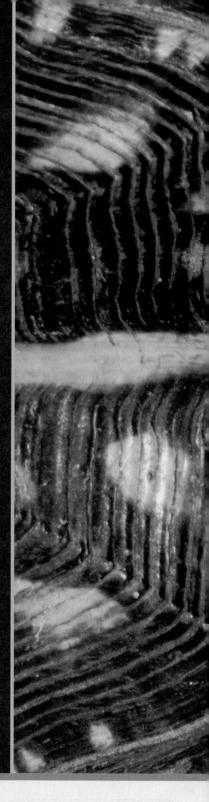

① THE EARTH ON ② TURTLE'S BACK

ONONDAGA-NORTHEAST WOODLANDS
RETOLD BY MICHAEL CADUTO
& JOSEPH BRUCHAC

BACKGROUND Native Americans have great respect for the natural world. They believe that each living thing possesses a unique power that sustains it and affects others. This power is part of a greater power, which many Native American cultures recognize as a Great Spirit—the source of all life. These beliefs are reflected in Native American myths, such as the stories that follow.

⑤ Before this Earth existed, there was only water. It stretched as far as one could see, and in that water there were birds and animals swimming around. Far above, in the clouds, there was a Skyland. In that Skyland there was a great and beautiful tree.

③ ▶ **Critical Viewing**
What story could you tell to explain the markings on the turtle shell in this picture? **[Apply]**

20 Beginnings–1800

© Text Complexity Rubric

	The Earth on Turtle's Back	When Grizzlies Walked Upright	*from* The Navajo Origin Legend
Qualitative Measures			
Context/ Knowledge Demands	Cultural knowledge demands 1 2 ③ 4 5	Cultural knowledge demands (myth) 1 2 ③ 4 5	Cultural knowledge demands (myth) 1 2 ③ 4 5
Structure/Language Conventionality and Clarity	Accessible vocabulary; some dialogue 1 ② 3 4 5	Accessible vocabulary 1 ② 3 4 5	Some difficult vocabulary; complicated sentences 1 2 ③ 4 5
Levels of Meaning/ Purpose/Concept Level	Accessible (simple plot) 1 ② 3 4 5	Challenging (complicated plot) 1 2 ③ 4 5	Abstract (religious ceremony) 1 2 ③ 4 5
Quantitative Measures			
Lexile/Text Length	730L / 843 words	1060L / 1087 words	940L / 384 words
Overall Complexity	**More accessible**	**More accessible**	**More accessible**

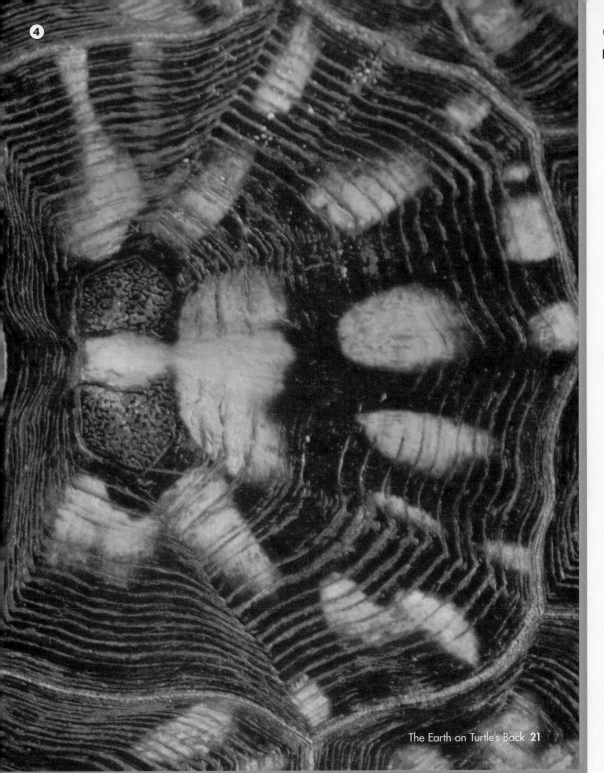

The Earth on Turtle's Back **21**

Individual Activity

1. Discuss the image of the turtle shell. **Ask** students to name its distinctive characteristics. **Possible response:** The ridges on the shell and the splotches of orange make graceful but irregular patterns.

2. Have students write a brief paragraph explaining what characteristics Native Americans might attribute to turtles based on this image of a turtle shell.

PHLit Online!

This selection is available in interactive format in the **Enriched Online Student Edition,** at www.PHLitOnline.com.

© Text Complexity: Reader and Task Suggestions

Preparing to Read the Texts	The Earth on Turtle's Back	When Grizzlies Walked Upright	*from* The Navajo Origin Legend
• Using the information on SE p. 19, compare and contrast the history of these Native American groups. • Ask students why they think that people in a given culture would want an explanation of their creation. • Guide students to use Multidraft Reading strategies to deepen their comprehension (TE p. 19).	**Leveled Tasks** *Knowledge Demands* If students will have difficulty with knowledge demands, have them begin by focusing on Sky Woman. As they reread, have them note the role of the animals and the Great Tree in Earth's creation. *Synthesizing* If students will not have difficulty with knowledge demands, have them retell the creation myth in a way that would engage a young child.	**Leveled Tasks** *Levels of Meaning* If students will have difficulty with the complexity of the plot, have them place key events on a timeline. Then, have them reread to fill in details and summarize the Modoc's creation beliefs. *Analyzing* If students will not have difficulty with the complexity of the plot, discuss how the relationships among the Chief, his daughter, and her children affected the creation of the world.	**Leveled Tasks** *Structure/Language* If students will have difficulty with vocabulary, have them first read to identify and define unfamiliar words related to the creation ceremony. Then, have them read the text aloud. *Evaluating* If students will not have difficulty with vocabulary, have them summarize the Navajo view of what gave the created humans life. Discuss why they agree or disagree with this view.

❺ Literary Analysis

Origin Myths

1. Explain to students that origin myths can be seen as a mixture of science and religion. Their purpose is to explain how the world and the things in it came to be.

2. Read the story's first sentence (p. 20) aloud with students.

3. Then, **ask** them the first Literary Analysis question: How do the opening words of this story identify it as an origin myth?
Answer: The first sentence describes what existed before the creation of Earth.

❻ Reading Strategy

Purpose for Reading: Cultural Characteristics

1. Remind students that one purpose for reading the Native American myths is to learn about Native American cultures.

2. Go on to remind students that the way to understand cultures is to pay attention to details of how the people live, think, and worship.

3. Then, **ask** students the Reading Strategy question: What does the chief's reaction to his wife's dream tell you about Onondaga beliefs?
Answer: The Onondaga believe that dreams are powerful, influential messages that must be obeyed.

❼ Literary Analysis

Origin Myths

1. Read aloud with students the paragraphs in which various animals dive down in the ocean.

2. Invite students to identify the unusual aspect of the animals' names. If necessary, draw students' attention to the generic quality of each name.

3. **Ask** students the Literary Analysis question: Why might characters in creation myths have generic names like "the Duck" and "the Beaver"?
Answer: Often, characters in oral literature are symbolic or archetypal figures that embody important cultural ideas rather than characters who present complex or individualized personalities.

22

---

❺

Literary Analysis
Origin Myths
How do the opening words of this story identify it as an origin myth?

❻

Reading Strategy
Purpose for Reading: Cultural Characteristics
What does the chief's reaction to his wife's dream tell you about Onondaga beliefs?

Literary Analysis
Origin Myths **❼**
Why might characters in creation myths have generic names like "the Duck" or "the Beaver"?

---

❺ It had four white roots which stretched to each of the sacred directions,[1] and from its branches all kinds of fruits and flowers grew.

There was an ancient chief in the Skyland. His young wife was expecting a child, and one night she dreamed that she saw the Great Tree uprooted. The next day she told her husband the story.

❻ He nodded as she finished telling her dream. "My wife," he said, "I am sad that you had this dream. It is clearly a dream of great power and, as is our way, when one has such a powerful dream we must do all we can to make it true. The Great Tree must be uprooted."

Then the Ancient Chief called the young men together and told them that they must pull up the tree. But the roots of the tree were so deep, so strong, that they could not budge it. At last the Ancient Chief himself came to the tree. He wrapped his arms around it, bent his knees and strained. At last, with one great effort, he uprooted the tree and placed it on its side. Where the tree's roots had gone deep into the Skyland there was now a big hole. The wife of the chief came close and leaned over to look down, grasping the tip of one of the Great Tree's branches to steady her. It seemed as if she saw something down there, far below, glittering like water. She leaned out further to look and, as she leaned, she lost her balance and fell into the hole. Her grasp slipped off the tip of the branch, leaving her with only a handful of seeds as she fell, down, down, down, down.

Far below, in the waters, some of the birds and animals looked up.

"Someone is falling toward us from the sky," said one of the birds.

"We must do something to help her," said another. Then two Swans flew up. They caught the Woman From The Sky between their wide wings. Slowly, they began to bring her down toward the water, where the birds and animals were watching.

"She is not like us," said one of the animals. "Look, she doesn't have webbed feet. I don't think she can live in the water."

"What shall we do, then?" said another of the water animals.

"I know," said one of the water birds. "I have heard that there is Earth far below the waters. If we dive down and bring up Earth, then she will have a place to stand."

So the birds and animals decided that someone would have to bring up Earth. One by one they tried.

❼ The Duck dove first, some say. He swam down and down, far beneath the surface, but could not reach the bottom and floated back up. Then the Beaver tried. He went even deeper, so deep that it all was dark, but he could not reach the bottom, either. The Loon tried, swimming with his strong wings. He was gone a long long time, but he, too, failed to bring up Earth. Soon it seemed that all had tried and all had failed. Then a small voice spoke.

"I will bring up Earth or die trying."

---

1. the sacred directions North, South, East, and West.

Think Aloud

Literary Analysis: Origin Myths
To model the process of looking for archetypes in origin myths, use the following "think aloud." Say to students:

I know that origin myths have archetypes, or patterns. One such archetype is the significance of the cardinal directions. I'm challenging myself as I read to look for something else in this myth that might show up in other origin myths and, therefore, qualify as an archetype. In the middle of this page, one of the birds announces that someone is falling out of the sky and toward the waters. Immediately, two swans set out to help the chief's wife. I think this is an extraordinary act. The animals have never before seen a person, and here they are offering to help rather than hiding in fear or deciding to attack. Maybe the kindness of animals toward the first humans shows up in other origin myths as an archetype.

They looked to see who it was. It was the tiny Muskrat. She dove down and swam and swam. She was not as strong or as swift as the others, but she was determined. She went so deep that it was all dark, and still she swam deeper. She swam so deep that her lungs felt ready to burst, but she swam deeper still. At last, just as she was becoming unconscious, she reached out one small paw and grasped at the bottom, barely touching it before she floated up, almost dead.

When the other animals saw her break the surface they thought she had failed. Then they saw her right paw was held tightly shut.

"She has the Earth," they said. "Now where can we put it?"

"Place it on my back," said a deep voice. It was the Great Turtle, who had come up from the depths.

They brought the Muskrat over to the Great Turtle and placed her paw against his back. To this day there are marks at the back of the Turtle's shell which were made by the Muskrat's paw. The tiny bit of Earth fell on the back of the Turtle. Almost immediately, it began to grow larger and larger and larger until it became the whole world.

Then the two Swans brought the Sky Woman down. She stepped onto the new Earth and opened her hand, letting the seeds fall onto the bare soil. From those seeds the trees and the grass sprang up. Life on Earth had begun.

Vocabulary

unconscious (un kän′ shəs) *adj.* temporarily lost awareness; in a faint

depths (depths) *n.* the deepest areas

...THE TREES AND THE GRASS SPRANG UP. LIFE ON EARTH HAD BEGUN.

Critical Reading

1. Key Ideas and Details (a) What happens to the young wife after the chief uproots the Great Tree? **(b) Interpret:** Why does this event generate concern among the animals?

2. Key Ideas and Details (a) What actions do the animals take when they realize the wife of the chief cannot live in water? **(b) Generalize:** How do these actions exhibit the best aspects of human nature?

3. Craft and Structure (a) What does the description of the Muskrat stress about her physical qualities? **(b) Interpret:** What message about human achievement is conveyed by the success of the Muskrat after the other creatures could not accomplish the same task?

4. Integration of Knowledge and Ideas (a) How would you characterize the Muskrat's swim and her decision to make it? **(b) Apply:** How does society benefit from actions like those of the Muskrat?

Cite textual evidence to support your responses.

The Earth on Turtle's Back **23**

⑧ About the Selection

This Modoc legend tells the story of the origin of all Native American people. After creating the world, the Chief of the Sky Spirits makes his home inside a mountain. At one point, his daughter disobeys him and is stranded on the mountainside. Adopted and brought up by the grizzly-bear people, who walk and talk, the spirit girl eventually marries a grizzly bear. When her father discovers her whereabouts, he curses the bears to walk on all fours and takes away their power of speech. The daughter's children fathered by her grizzly husband are the ancestors of the Native American people.

⑨ Background

Largest Living Land Animal

Modoc origin myths go back hundreds and perhaps thousands of years. Therefore it should come as no surprise that according to this myth the biggest animal that walked the earth was the grizzly bear. Indeed, in that part of the world and in the postdinosaur era, the grizzly bear merited that description. Today we know that the largest living land animal is the African elephant.

⑧ *When Grizzlies Walked Upright*

Modoc

Retold by
Richard Erdoes
and Alfonso Ortiz

*B*efore there were people on earth, the Chief of the Sky Spirits grew tired of his home in the Above World, because the air was always brittle with an icy cold. So he carved a hole in the sky with a stone and pushed all the snow and ice down below until he made a great mound that reached from the earth almost to the sky. Today it is known as Mount Shasta.

Then the Sky Spirit took his walking stick, stepped from a cloud to the peak, and walked down the mountain. When he was about halfway to the valley below, he began to put his finger to the ground here and there, here and there. Wherever his finger touched, a tree grew. The snow melted in his footsteps, and the water ran down in rivers.

The Sky Spirit broke off the small end of his giant stick and threw the pieces into the rivers. The longer pieces turned into beaver and otter; the smaller pieces became fish. When the leaves dropped from the trees, he picked them up, blew upon them, and so made the birds. Then he took the big end of his giant stick and made all the animals that walked on the earth, the biggest of which were ⑨ the grizzly bears.

Now when they were first made, the bears were covered with hair and had sharp claws, just as they do today, but they walked on two feet and could talk like people. They looked so fierce that the Sky Spirit sent them away from him to live in the forest at the base of the mountain.

Enrichment: Investigating Geography

Volcanic Mountains

While describing the origin of the world and its people, myths explain the existence of distinct geographic phenomena. Mount Shasta, a volcano mentioned in the first paragraph, is one such phenomenon. Dormant today, the volcano has a history that involves eruptions, and the Modoc needed to find a reason for its genesis—hence, "When Grizzlies Walked Upright."

Activity: Map Have students collect data on the location of Mount Shasta, routes to the summit, surrounding terrain, or nearby places of interest. Suggest that they record information in the **Enrichment: Investigating Geography** work sheet, in *Professional Development Guidebook,* page 228. With the results of their research, students can generate maps and keys showing how to travel to Mount Shasta from their hometown, which trail on Mount Shasta they would like to tackle, or what to do on a stay near Mount Shasta.

Pleased with what he'd done, the Chief of the Sky Spirits decided to bring his family down and live on earth himself. The mountains of snow and ice became their lodge. He made a big fire in the center of the mountain and a hole in the top so that the smoke and sparks could fly out. When he put a big log on the fire, sparks would fly up and the earth would tremble.

Late one spring while the Sky Spirit and his family were sitting round the fire, the Wind Spirit sent a great storm that shook the top of the mountain. It blew and blew and roared and roared. Smoke blown back into the lodge hurt their eyes, and finally the Sky Spirit said to his youngest daughter, "Climb up to the smoke hole and ask the Wind Spirit to blow more gently. Tell him I'm afraid he will blow the mountain over."

As his daughter started up, her father said, "But be careful not to stick your head out at the top. If you do, the wind may catch you by the hair and blow you away."

The girl hurried to the top of the mountain and stayed well inside the smoke hole as she spoke to the Wind Spirit. As she was about to climb back down, she remembered that her father had once said you could see the ocean from the top of their lodge. His daughter wondered what the ocean looked like, and her curiosity got the better of her. She poked her head out of the hole and turned toward the west, but before she could see anything, the Wind Spirit caught her long hair, pulled her out of the mountain, and blew her down over the snow and ice. She landed among the scrubby fir trees at the edge of the timber and snow line, her long red hair trailing over the snow.

There a grizzly bear found the little girl when he was out hunting food for his family. He carried her home with him, and his wife brought her up with their family of cubs. The little red-haired girl and the cubs ate together, played together, and grew up together.

When she became a young woman, she and the eldest son of the grizzly bears were married. In the years that followed they had many children, who were not as hairy as the grizzlies, yet did not look exactly like their spirit mother, either.

All the grizzly bears throughout the forests were so proud of these new creatures that they made a lodge for the red-haired mother and her children. They placed the lodge near Mount Shasta—it is called Little Mount Shasta today.

After many years had passed, the mother grizzly bear knew that she would soon die. Fearing that she should ask of the Chief of the Sky Spirits to forgive her for keeping his daughter, she gathered all the grizzlies at the lodge they had built. Then she sent her eldest grandson in a cloud to the top of Mount Shasta, to tell the Spirit Chief where he could find his long-lost daughter.

Literary Analysis
Origin Myths
What natural feature of the world does the Sky Spirit create in this passage?

"But be careful not to stick your head out at the top. If you do, the wind may catch you by the hair and blow you away."

11 ☑ Reading Check

Who finds the red-haired daughter of the Sky Spirit?

10 Literary Analysis
Origin Myths

1. Explain to students that origin myths not only provided explanations for the formation of the natural world but also provided entertainment.

2. Read aloud with students the story's opening paragraph. Then, review the bracketed passage.

3. **Ask** students the Literary Analysis question: What natural feature of the world does the Sky Spirit create in this passage?
   Answer: This passage explains the origin of the volcano. Mount Shasta is a volcanic peak about fifty miles south of the Oregon border in present-day California.

▶ **Monitor Progress Ask** students to link descriptions in the passage to features of the volcano.
   Answer: The hole in the top of the lodge is the volcano's vent. The sparks and smoke that fly out the hole are the effects of the volcano's eruption.

▶ **Reteach:** If students have difficulty understanding the connection between natural phenomena and origin myths, have them reread the explanation of origin myths on page 18. Help students recognize that Mount Shasta was so much a part of the Modoc people's everyday lives that the story arose to explain its origin.

11 Reading Check

Answer: A grizzly bear finds the girl and takes her home to his wife, the mother grizzly bear.

Differentiated Instruction for Universal Access

Strategy for Special-Needs Students
Use the Venn Diagram in the *Graphic Organizer Transparencies,* page 349, to help students contrast the way creation is presented in this Modoc myth and in the Onondaga myth (p. 20). Help students understand that the Onondaga believe that existing animals were instrumental in creating Earth, whereas the Modoc believe that the Sky Spirit created both Earth and its creatures.

Enrichment for Gifted/Talented Students
Ask students to relate this story to other stories in which people are rescued or raised by caring animals. Urge students to do research in order to collect two or three other examples of this narrative detail. (Examples may include stories about Tarzan and Mowgli as well as various other folktales.) Students might make brief oral presentations in which they compare and contrast these tales and hypothesize about why this theme appears now and then in literature.

This selection is available in interactive format in the **Enriched Online Student Edition**, at **www. PHLitOnline.com** which includes a thematically related video with a writing prompt and an interactive graphic organizer.

Purpose for Reading: Cultural Characteristics

1. Remind students that reading Native American myths can teach them about the values of the cultures that created the myths.

2. Stress paying attention to written details of how the people in the culture live, think, and worship.

3. Then, **ask** students the Reading Strategy question: What does the Sky Spirit's reaction to his daughter and grandchildren suggest about Modoc attitudes toward obedience?
   Possible answer: The Sky Spirit's hostility toward his grandchildren and physical removal of his daughter suggest he could not forgive the daughter's disobedience to his long-ago instruction: ". . . be careful not to stick your head out at the top"(p. 25). Obeying a parent must have been a prime value of the Modoc.

4. Point out that in addition to the value Sky Spirit places on obedience, his reaction demonstrates his hubris: He is enraged to learn of the creation of a "new race" (part spirit, part animal) without *his* involvement. This observation tells us that the Modoc must have had strict guidelines about where power resides and who must follow its dictates.

⓭ Engaging the Essential Question

1. Remind students of the Essential Question—What is the relationship between literature and place? Point out that animals in this tale are an integral part of the natural world where the story takes place.

2. **Ask** students whether or not they are surprised by how the Chief of the Sky Spirits treats the grizzlies, given the respect with which Native Americans viewed so many animals.
   Possible response: Some students may be surprised at the chief's harshness, given the kindness of the grizzlies toward his daughter. In light of other Modoc values explored above—regarding obedience and power—other students will not be surprised by the chief's harshness.

Reading Strategy
Purpose for Reading: Cultural Characteristics
What does the Sky Spirit's reaction to his daughter and grandchildren suggest about Modoc attitudes toward obedience?

Vocabulary
ancestors (an´ ses´ tərz) *n.* people from whom other people descend

---

When the father got this news he was so glad that he came down the mountainside in giant strides, melting the snow and tearing up the land under his feet. Even today his tracks can be seen in the rocky path on the south side of Mount Shasta.

As he neared the lodge, he called out, "Is this where my little daughter lives?"

He expected his child to look exactly as she had when he saw her last. When he found a grown woman instead, and learned that the strange creatures she was taking care of were his grandchildren, he became very angry. A new race had been created that was not of his making! He frowned on the old grandmother so sternly that she promptly fell dead. Then he cursed all the grizzlies:

⓬
⓭ "Get down on your hands and knees. You have wronged me, and from this moment all of you will walk on four feet and never talk again."

He drove his grandchildren out of the lodge, put his daughter over his shoulder, and climbed back up the mountain. Never again did he come to the forest. Some say that he put out the fire in the center of his lodge and took his daughter back up to the sky to live.

Those strange creatures, his grandchildren, scattered and wandered over the earth. They were the first Indians, the ancestors of all the Indian tribes.

That's why the Indians living around Mount Shasta would never kill a grizzly bear. Whenever a grizzly killed an Indian, his body was burned on the spot. And for many years all who passed that way cast a stone there until a great pile of stones marked the place of his death.

> "Get down on your hands and knees. You have wronged me, and from this moment all of you will walk on four feet and never talk again."

Vocabulary Development

Vocabulary Knowledge Rating
When students have completed reading and discussing these selections, have them take out their **Vocabulary Knowledge Rating** charts for the selections. Read the words aloud and have students rate their knowledge of the words again in the After Reading column. Clarify any words that are still problematic. Have students write their own definitions and example or sentence in the appropriate column. Then, have students complete the Vocabulary Lesson at the end of the selections. Encourage students to use the words in further discussion and written work about the selections. Remind them that they will be accountable for these words on the **Selection Test,** *Unit 1 Resources,* pages 28–30 or 31–33.

from The Navajo ORIGIN LEGEND

Retold by Washington Matthews

On the morning of the twelfth day the people washed themselves well. The women dried themselves with yellow cornmeal; the men with white cornmeal. Soon after the ablutions were completed they heard the distant call of the approaching gods.[1] It was shouted, as before, four times—nearer and louder at each repetition—and, after the fourth call, the gods appeared. Blue Body and Black Body each carried a sacred buckskin. White Body carried two ears of corn, one yellow, one white, each covered at the end completely with grains.

The gods laid one buckskin on the ground with the head to the west; on this they placed the two ears of corn, with their tips to the east, and over the corn they spread the other buckskin with its head to the east; under the white ear they put the feather of a white eagle,

---

1. **the approaching gods** the four Navajo gods: White Body, Blue Body, Yellow Body, and Black Body.

from The Navajo Origin Legend **27**

Origin Myths

1. Read aloud with students the story's next-to-last paragraph.

2. **Ask** students why the Navajo viewed the wind as the source of life.
   Answer: The wind is a major climatic force that, like breath, moves air, and since breath sustains human and animal life, comparing wind to breath makes sense.

ASSESS

Answers

Before students respond, you may wish to have them write a brief objective summary of the selection. As they answer the questions below, remind them to support their answers with evidence from the text.

1. (a) They take in his daughter and marry her to their son. (b) He is proud as creator of the Earth and does not want to share power.

2. (a) He forbids them to talk or to walk upright. (b) He causes his grandchildren, the first Indians, to wander over the Earth.

3. (a) The wind makes the ears humans. (b) Human breath is similar to wind: It moves air.

4. (a) 1. The spirit people cleanse themselves. 2. Gods place corn and feathers on buckskin. 3. Mirage people circle skins; wind transforms corn. (b) The Navajo value order and ritual.

5. ❓ **Possible answer:** The Onondaga thought of animals in their <u>environment</u> as helpful, so they respected animals; the Modoc lived in a <u>landscape</u> with a volcano, so they felt awe; the Navajo traced human beings to corn, so they went on to <u>cultivate</u> this crop.

---

under the yellow ear the feather of a yellow eagle. Then they told the people to stand at a distance and allow the wind to enter. The white wind blew from the east, and the yellow wind blew from the west, between the skins. While the wind was blowing, eight of the Mirage People[2] came and walked around the objects on the ground four times, and as they walked the eagle feathers, whose tips protruded from between the buckskins, were seen to move. When the Mirage People had finished their walk the upper buckskin was lifted; the ears of corn had disappeared, a man and a woman lay there in their stead.

The white ear of corn had been changed into a man, the yellow ear into a woman. It was the wind that gave them life. It is the wind that comes out of our mouths now that gives us life. When this ceases to blow we die. In the skin at the tips of our fingers we see the trail of the wind; it shows us where the wind blew when our ancestors were created.

The pair thus created were First Man and First Woman (Atsé Hastin and Atsé Estsán). The gods directed the people to build an enclosure of brushwood for the pair. When the enclosure was finished, First Man and First Woman entered it, and the gods said to them: "Live together now as husband and wife."

Vocabulary
protruded (prō trood´ id)
v. stuck out

> The white ear ⑯
> of corn had
> been changed
> into a man,
> the yellow ear
> into a woman.

2. **Mirage People** mirages personified.

Critical Reading

Cite textual evidence to support your responses.

© 1. **Key Ideas and Details (a)** In the Modoc myth, what do the grizzly bears do that angers the Chief of the Sky Spirits? **(b) Analyze:** What does the Chief's reaction tell you about his character?

© 2. **Key Ideas and Details (a)** What punishment does the Chief of the Sky Spirits give the grizzlies? **(b) Analyze Cause and Effect:** How does this action affect his grandchildren, the people of the Earth?

© 3. **Key Ideas and Details (a)** What is the wind's role in the Navajo ceremony? **(b) Speculate:** Why might the Navajo have viewed the wind as a source of life?

© 4. **Integration of Knowledge and Ideas (a) Summarize:** Summarize the steps of the Navajo creation ceremony. **(b) Analyze:** What does the ceremony show about Navajo attitudes toward order and ritual?

© 5. **Integration of Knowledge and Ideas** What do the qualities these mythmakers saw in nature show about the human traits they valued? In your response, use at least two of these Essential Question words: *environment, landscape, profound, cultivate.* *[Connecting to the Essential Question: What is the relationship between literature and place?]*

Concept Connector

Reading Strategy Graphic Organizer
Ask students to review the graphic organizers in which they have noted details and indicated the cultural attitudes reflected by these details. Then have students share their organizers and compare the details and cultural characteristics that they listed.

Activating Prior Knowledge
Remind students of their responses to the Activating Prior Knowledge question that asked them to predict their responses to the myths. Ask them to explain whether their predictions were right or not.

❓ **Connecting to the Essential Question**
Have students compare the responses they gave to the prompt before reading the myths with their thoughts after reading. Have them work individually or in groups, writing or discussing their thoughts, to formulate their new responses. Then lead a class discussion, probing for what students have learned that confirms or invalidates their initial thoughts. Encourage students to cite specific textual details to support their responses.

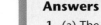
Literary Analysis

© 1. **Key Ideas and Details (a)** In which **origin myth** is the creation of the Earth unintentional, or almost an accident? **(b)** In which myth is the world's creation the result of a deliberate series of actions? Explain your answers.

© 2. **Key Ideas and Details (a)** In addition to the origins of life on Earth, what features of the land does the Modoc myth explain? **(b)** What social customs does the myth explain? **(c)** What does this suggest about the ways members of the Modoc tribe may have felt about the place in which they lived?

© 3. **Key Ideas and Details (a)** Which of the myths portrays the spirits or gods as generous and kind? **(b)** Which sees them as vengeful? Support your answers with details from the text.

© 4. **Key Ideas and Details (a)** In which myth is the world's creation the result of cooperation? **(b)** In which myth is it the result of aggression? **(c)** Do you think these differences suggest different views of life? Explain.

5. **Comparing Literary Works (a)** Using a chart like the one shown, note patterns, symbols, or character types that are similar in all three myths. **(b)** What common **themes** do these **archetypes** help express? Explain your thinking.

Details	Turtle's Back	Grizzlies	Navajo
Patterns			
Symbols			
Characters			

Reading Strategy

6. Assume that your **purpose for reading** these myths was to learn about the Native American cultures that produced them. **(a)** Identify at least two *cultural characteristics* that you learned from each myth. **(b)** What does each characteristic reveal about the general attitudes of the culture that produced it?

7. What similarities and differences do you see in the cultural attitudes expressed in these three myths? Explain your answers, citing details from the selections.

8. What are two other purposes you might have for reading these myths? Explain your answers.

9. Do the stories we tell today through film, TV, or books say something about who we are as a people? Explain your answer.

Native American Origin Myths **29**

© **Common Core State Standards**

Writing
3. Write narratives to develop real or imagined experiences or events using effective technique, well-chosen details, and well-structured event sequences. *(p. 30)*

Language
3.a. Vary syntax for effect. *(p. 31)*
4.a. Use context as a clue to the meaning of a word or phrase. *(p. 30)*

Answers

1. (a) The Onondaga tell that Earth resulted when someone fell from the sky. (b) The Navajo recount steps that made human beings.

2. (a) The myth explains Mount Shasta. (b) **Possible response:** The myth explains the Modoc's respect for grizzlies.
(c) **Possible response:** The Modoc valued but feared the region.

3. (a) The Navajo portray spirits and gods as generous. (b) The Modoc illustrate the chief's revenge—punishing the bears by rendering them mute and forcing them to go on all fours.

4. (a) The Onondaga show cooperation among animals. The Navajo show cooperation between gods and the Mirage People. (b) The Modoc show conflict between the Sky Spirit and the bears. (c) Perhaps the Onondaga and Navajo felt comfortable in their home, while the Modoc felt conflict between the laws imposed by the Sky Spirit and the prospect of happiness.

5. **Possible responses:**
(a) *Patterns:* All show animals or gods and spirits making human beings; *Symbols:* Turtle markings go back to the creation of Earth, the grizzlies' walking on four legs symbolizes the cost of overreaching, and the Navajo show corn bringing forth human life; *Characters:* All three include a female and supernatural forces.
(b) All three tell of animals, vegetation, and the supernatural, so these elements seem to be archetypes.

6. **Possible responses:**
(a) "Turtle's Back": respect for animals; the power of determination; "Grizzlies": importance of listening to parents; respect for grizzlies; Navajo: respect for wind, corn, deer; the sacred husband-wife relationship. (b) Each reveals a need to understand the world.

7. **Possible responses:** All acknowledge the supernatural; only the Modoc show anger.

8. **Possible response:** One might read myths for entertainment or to study their lessons.

9. **Possible response:** Many of today's stories show that we have not learned to make peace last.

Assessment Practice

Summarizing Written Texts (For more practice, see *All-in-One Workbook*.)

Students will need to recognize accurate summaries on tests. Use this sample item to help them practice:

The need to explain the origin of life and other great mysteries gave birth to myths, which are traditional stories, often about immortal beings, that are passed down from generation to generation. Myths often explain other phenomena, including customs, institutions, and religious rites.

Which of the following is the best summary?
  A Myths are created to help explain things that cannot be otherwise understood.
  B Myths are created to explain religion.
  C Myths explain how life begins.
  D Myths are passed through generations.
Choices **B**, **C**, and **D** have accurate but incomplete information. Choice **A** is best.

Vocabulary Acquisition and Use

1. Introduce the skill.
2. Have students complete the Word Analysis activity and the Vocabulary practice.

Word Analysis

1. *Intruder* means "one who forces himself into a place where he does not belong"; *intruder* derives from the prefix meaning "in" and *-trud-,* meaning "push."
2. *Extruded* means "to push out"; *extruded* derives from the prefix meaning "out" and *-trud-,* meaning "push."
3. *Obtrusive* means "calling attention to oneself"; *obtrusive* derives from the prefix meaning "to" or "before," *-trud-,* meaning "push," and *-ive,* meaning "inclined."
4. *Intrusive* means "forcing oneself where one does not belong"; *intrusive* derives from the prefix meaning "in," *-trud-,* meaning "push," and *-ive,* meaning "inclined" or "tending."

Vocabulary

1. If Lola were <u>unconscious,</u> "not conscious," I would give her smelling salts to rouse her.
2. A fish that lives far *below* the surface—not *on* the surface—of the sea lives in the <u>depths</u> of the sea.
3. <u>Ancestors</u> came before people now living; ancestors cannot inherit money from people now living.
4. If toes <u>protruded</u> from a shoe, you would see them.

Writing

1. Give students the Support for Writing page (*Unit 1 Resources,* p. 23).
2. Remind students that their plays should include stage directions.
3. If students have trouble starting, help them divide the myth into scenes.
4. Use the **Rubrics for Generic (Holistic) Writing,** in the *Professional Development Guidebook,* pages 282–283, to evaluate work.

30

Ⓔ Vocabulary Acquisition and Use

Word Analysis: Latin Root -trud- / -trus-

The Latin root *-trud-,* also spelled *-trus-,* means "push" or "thrust." Something that *protruded* was pushed out from where it was supposed to be. Use the context clues and your knowledge of the root *-trud- / -trus-* to explain the meaning of each italicized word below. Then, explain how the word's meaning reflects the meaning of the root.

1. Last night an *intruder* broke into the warehouse and robbed it.
2. The pastry bag *extruded* icing when the baker squeezed it.
3. In the quiet library, a noisy child is *obtrusive.*
4. Some uninvited guests are welcome, but others are simply *intrusive.*

Vocabulary: Context Clues

Answer each question. Then, explain how the context clues, or surrounding words and phrases, helped you determine your answer.

1. If Lola were *unconscious,* would you give her smelling salts or ask her to smile?
2. Which lives in the *depths* of the sea, an insect on the surface or a fish far below it?
3. Do people's *ancestors* usually inherit their money?
4. If a person's toes *protruded* from a sandal, could you see them, or would they be hidden?

Writing

Ⓔ **Narrative Text** Choose one of the three myths and turn it into a **play** that a group of classmates can perform for an audience.

Prewriting Reread the myth, listing each character and noting details about his or her appearance and personality. Also, list the various settings and jot down the actions that take place in each one. Then, decide if you will include a narrator who provides the audience with background information and transitions between scenes, or if you will rely solely on dialogue to tell the story.

Drafting List the characters. Then, organize the action into separate scenes that take place in each setting. Turn character's remarks or thoughts into dialogue. Use capital letters for the character names. Set stage directions that describe characters' behavior, tone, or actions in parentheses or brackets. Use italics to distinguish stage directions from dialogue.

> **Model: Setting Dialogue and Stage Directions**
>
> **SPIRIT CHIEF** [*angrily, stamping his feet*]: You have wronged me! You will now walk on all fours for eternity! [*The "bears" sink to their hands and knees and walk around the stage growling.*]

The use of italics and brackets clearly separates stage directions from dialogue.

Revising Read your draft aloud. If you find that some of the dialogue is hard to say, rewrite those sections so they sound more natural.

Assessment Resources

Unit 1 Resources

L1 L2 EL **Selection Test A,** pp. 28–30. Administer Test A to less advanced students and English learners.

L3 L4 EL **Selection Test B,** pp. 31–33. Administer Test B to on-level and more advanced students.

L3 L4 **Open-Book Test,** pp. 25–27. As an alternative, give the Open-Book Test.

All **Customizable Test Bank**

All **Self-tests**
Students may prepare for the **Selection Test** by taking the **Self-test** online.

PHLit Online! All assessment resources are available at www.PHLitOnline.com.

Conventions and Style: Coordinating Conjunctions

Include compound sentences in your writing by using **coordinating conjunctions** to combine short, choppy sentences. Coordinating conjunctions are words like *and, but, for, so,* and *yet* that connect words, phrases, or clauses of equal rank. Each coordinating conjunction shows a different relationship. For example, *and* shows addition or similarity, *but* and *yet* indicate contrast, and *or* and *nor* indicate a choice. *For* and *so* show a result.

Combining Sentences with Coordinating Conjunctions

Choppy: There was a great tree in Skyland. There was an ancient chief there, too.
Combined: There was a great tree *and* an ancient chief in Skyland.

Choppy: Several animals tried to swim the water's depths. The Muskrat succeeded.
Combined: Several animals tried to swim the water's depths, *but* the Muskrat succeeded.

Choppy: The Chief of the Sky Spirits must be strong. This being is in a position of power.
Combined: The Chief of the Sky Spirits must be strong, *for* he is in a position of power.

Punctuation Tip: If you use a coordinating conjunction to join two independent clauses, *place a comma before the coordinating conjunction.*

Practice In items 1–5, identify each coordinating conjunction and the words it connects. In items 6–10, combine the two sentences using a coordinating conjunction.

1. The Iroquois were five different tribes, yet they united to form one Indian nation.
2. The Sky Woman carries the seeds and allows them to fall.
3. The grizzlies were not supposed to act independently or challenge the chief.
4. Settlers conquered the Indians, but some tribes have survived.
5. Did the Modoc live in New York state or in Oregon?
6. The Chief of the Sky Spirits pledges to make the dream true. The Chief of the Sky Spirits is saddened by this pledge.
7. The chief has great power. He also has great responsibilities.
8. In one myth, an uprooted tree forms a hole in the sky. In another, a stone forms a hole.
9. They wanted potential allies to see the fire. They kept it burning constantly.
10. The woman gives her thanks to the swans. The woman gives her thanks to the turtle.

© **Writing and Speaking Conventions**

A. Writing For each word pair listed below, write a sentence in which you link the two words or word groups using a coordinating conjunction. Then, tell what relationship is indicated by the conjunction.

1. swans—muskrat
2. under the sky—below the waters
3. the roots spread in all directions—they support the world

   Example: swans—muskrat
   Sentence: The swans and the muskrat display strength in different ways.
   Relationship: similarity

B. Speaking Write and present a list of rules for your class. Use three different coordinating conjunctions. If you combine two independent clauses, remember to use a comma before the coordinating conjunction.

PH WRITING COACH
Further instruction and practice are available in *Prentice Hall Writing Coach.*

Integrated Language Skills **31**

Extend the Lesson

Sentence Modeling
Choose one of these sentences taken from the selections:

He wrapped his arms around the tree, bent his knees and strained. ("The Earth on Turtle's Back")
He drove his grandchildren out of the lodge, put his daughter over his shoulder, and climbed back up the mountain. ("When Grizzlies Walked Upright")

Ask students how the coordinating conjunction in this sentence differs from the one in items 1–5. (This conjunction joins three things, not only two as in items 1–5). Ask what they notice about commas. (In the sentence from "Turtle's Back," a comma comes after the first verb phrase but not after the second; in the sentence from "Grizzlies," a comma comes after the first verb phrase and the second. Either style is acceptable.)

Have students imitate the sentence on a topic they choose, matching the grammatical and stylistic features discussed.

Themes Across Centuries

Susan Power

1. Point out the brief biography of Susan Power. Explain that Power, the daughter of a Native American activist, is a graduate of Harvard Law School. Power was editor of the *University of Chicago Law Review* before leaving to write full time. Have students reread Power's introduction to Unit 1 on pages 15–16 if necessary.

2. Show students Segment 2 on Susan Power on the *See It!* DVD to provide insight into the sources of "Museum Indians."

3. **Ask:** How does "Museum Indians," an essay, differ from a story?
   Possible response: "Museum Indians" differs from a story because it is about the author's actual experiences. However, writing an essay involves the kind of shaping readers might associate more closely with fiction.

Bringing the Spark of Your Own Imagination

1. Explain to students Power's point that the origin myths they have read in Unit 1 have been transmitted orally from generation to generation.

2. **Ask:** How, according to Power, does being a part of the oral tradition shape these stories?
   Possible response: Power says that the stories are meant to be flexible, because they change and evolve with each telling. The listener plays an active role in bringing the stories to life.

Exposed to Two Cultures

1. Point out to students that, to a large extent, Power characterizes the differing worlds of traditional Native American culture and mainstream American culture in terms of their literary expression.

2. **Ask** students to describe the connections Power suggests between her two cultures.
   Possible response: Power's memorization and reciting of Shakespearean dialogue recalls the storytelling of her Native American culture.

Susan Power Introduces

MUSEUM INDIANS

Bringing the Spark of Your Own Imagination The origin myths of the Onondaga, Modoc, and Navajo tribes, recounted on pages 20–28 of this textbook, are examples of the oral tradition, stories repeated within a community, passed down from one generation to the next, keeping them alive. These spoken stories are meant to be performed, acted out with great drama before a circle of avid listeners of all ages. Each retelling of the story changes it a little, the performer emphasizing one episode over another, choosing slightly different words each time. These stories are meant to be flexible, interactive—modified according to the present audience's mood and tastes.

So as you read these tales, try to imagine them being acted out. Try to hear the storyteller's voice changing as different characters speak, rising with excitement, falling to a whisper. Your imaginative spark is needed to bring these stories fully to life.

Exposed to Two Cultures I am a grateful listener, eager to hear a gripping yarn, but I myself am not a traditional storyteller. I was very shy as a child and found it difficult to stand before people and speak aloud either a story or an idea. I was silent in my classes, unless called upon, and preferred committing my words to quiet paper rather than the storm of conversation. I was raised to be both Native (Yanktonnai Dakota) and American, and so I was exposed not only to traditional Native American stories, songs, ceremonies, and dances, but also to the culture of mainstream America and the wider world.

Meet the Author

Susan Power is a member of the Standing Rock Sioux Tribe of Fort Yates, North Dakota. Her novel, *The Grass Dancer,* won the PEN/Hemingway Award for First Fiction. She has also written a book of stories and autobiographical essays entitled *Roofwalker.*

Teaching Resources

See It! DVD
Susan Power, Segment 2

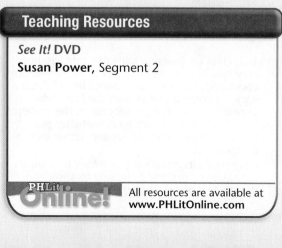

All resources are available at
www.PHLitOnline.com

I loved reading and graduated from pop-up books and comics to the Nancy Drew mystery series and the *Chronicles of Narnia*. When I was about twelve, I began listening to recordings made of the plays of William Shakespeare and would memorize long passages that I delighted in performing privately, with no one but my mother and our cats to overhear. I didn't understand much of what was being spoken in the famous plays, but I was fascinated with the rhythmic poetry of the words, the dramatic plot lines, and thought to myself that Shakespeare would have felt at home in the Native world, dramatic as our oral literature can be.

Looking for My Own Experience I began writing my own poems, stories, essays, and political songs when I was very young—five or six years old. Perhaps I needed to write because, although I heard traditional stories of the people who came before me and inhabited this continent prior to European contact, and although I read dozens of books that taught me what it was like to live everywhere else in the world, I never found myself, my own experience, in either of these literatures: the oral tradition or the novels of the world. Where were the stories of little girls who attended church as well as a Native ceremony in the deep Wisconsin woods? Where were the books that told of a child who could perform a variety of traditional dances at an intertribal pow-wow and also excel in her ballet classes? I could not find myself on the literary map, and so I had to develop my own literature, plot my own place in this world.

But is my writing more Native than American? In my fiction and essays, Native American themes are emphasized—my characters believe, as I do, that everything is potentially alive, a creature of spirit, whether it be a person, an animal, a family car, a stone. But the language I use is English, the paintbrush of words I wield to draw you a picture of what I see with my eyes.

Oral Literature and Print The essay that follows, "Museum Indians," is a brief examination of my childhood in cultural terms—specifically, what it was like to be Native American in the city of Chicago. Notice that even though I have *written* several scenes describing adventures I shared with my mother, employing narrative strategies familiar to any reader of books, my mother is constantly *telling* me stories within the piece—instances of our own family oral tradition still in practice today. So I have captured the oral literature with my printed words.

Critical Reading

1. **Key Ideas and Details (a)** What reason does Power give to explain why she is not a traditional storyteller? **(b) Connect:** What life experiences do you think contributed to Power's decision to become a writer?

2. **Key Ideas and Details (a)** How does Power solve the problem of not finding her own experience in the literature she read as a child? **(b) Interpret:** According to Power, how do the dual influences of her childhood show up in her writing?

As You Read "Museum Indians" . . .

3. **Integration of Knowledge and Ideas** Look for details in the essay that show the contrast between the "Native" and the "American" that Power describes here.

4. **Integration of Knowledge and Ideas** Consider the ways in which Power is like her mother and the ways in which she is different.

Looking for My Own Experience

1. Be sure students understand that in the first paragraph of this section, Power is searching for the reason she began to write. **Ask:** How did her relationship to her two cultures influence her? **Possible response:** Power suggests that as part of two cultures, her experience belonged to neither. She felt a need to create her own literary tradition using elements of both cultures.

2. Power asks: "But is my writing more Native than American?" Encourage students to keep this question in mind as they read.

Oral Literature and Print

1. Explain to students that Power is describing one way she tries to unite the Native American oral tradition and the mainstream American written tradition: by including her mother's storytelling in this written essay.

2. Instruct students to watch for moments of storytelling as they read "Museum Indians."

ASSESS
Answers

Critical Reading

Before students respond, you may wish to have them write a brief objective summary of the selection. As they answer the questions below, remind them to support their answers with evidence from the text.

1. (a) As a child, she was too shy to stand and tell stories. (b) Her experiences of shyness and her being part of two cultures may have led her to become a writer.

2. (a) She became a writer and tried to create a tradition that could include her experience. (b) She writes about Native American themes and characters, but her language is English.

3. Students are likely to point to her mother's old and new hair, as well as the contrast between Native culture as displayed in the museum and as lived by Power and her mother.

4. Students might note that Power seems both more conscious of her Native culture and less fully a part of it than her mother, who can cut her hair short without affecting her identity.

❶ About the Selection

In this personal essay, Susan Power describes aspects of the relationship she and her mother had when Power was a child. Her mother, a Dakota woman, is an inspiring figure—tall, fearless, and outspoken. She shows Power many aspects of Chicago, giving her daughter a sense of owning the city. Power focuses on the museums they visited together and on the stories the exhibits inspired her mother to tell. Through bits of her stories, we learn that Power's mother is so connected to her Native American heritage that she can never be as at home as her daughter is in Chicago.

❷ Activating Prior Knowledge

Much of "Museum Indians" unfolds in various museums in Chicago. Ask students about their own childhood experiences with museums. What kinds of museums did they most enjoy? What was their favorite museum exhibit or feature? Did museum visits have any lasting influence on their curiosity and imaginations? After discussion, tell students to read to discover how Power was affected by her museum experiences.

❸ Critical Viewing

Possible response: The woman in the painting, like Power's mother, stands tall and proud. However, Power's mother no longer has long hair and probably does not dress in traditional Native American clothing in everyday life.

34 Beginnings–1800

MUSEUM INDIANS ❶ ❷
Susan Power

She is so tall, a true

DAKOTA WOMAN;

she rises against the sun like a

SKYSCRAPER,

and when I draw her picture in my notebook, she takes up the

ENTIRE PAGE.

❸ ◀ Critical Viewing
How is the portrayal of the woman in this painting similar to and different from the author's description of her mother? **[Compare and Contrast]**

A snake coils in my mother's dresser drawer; it is thick and black, glossy as sequins. My mother cut her hair several years ago, before I was born, but she kept one heavy braid. It is the three-foot snake I lift from its nest and handle as if it were alive.

"Mom, why did you cut your hair?" I ask. I am a little girl lifting a sleek black river into the light that streams through the kitchen window. Mom turns to me.

"It gave me headaches. Now put that away and wash your hands for lunch."

"You won't cut my hair, will you?" I'm sure this is a whine.

"No, just a little trim now and then to even the ends."

I return the dark snake to its nest among my mother's slips, arranging it so that its thin tail hides beneath the wide mouth sheared by scissors. My mother keeps her promise and lets my hair grow long, but I am only half of her; my thin brown braids will reach the middle of my back, and in maturity will look like tiny garden snakes.

My mother tells me stories every day: while she cleans, while she cooks, on our way to the library, standing in the checkout line at the supermarket. I like to share her stories with other people, and chatter like a monkey when I am able to command adult attention.

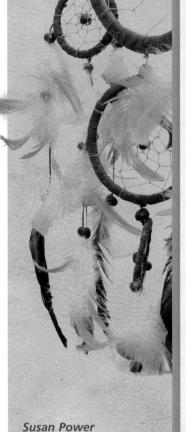

Susan Power
Author's Insight
I compare my mother's braid to my own—hers is a "sleek black river," mine are "tiny garden snakes"—to underscore my childhood impression that I was so much smaller and weaker, a diluted version.

 ⑤ ☑ **Reading Check**

What does the author's mother do every day?

Museum Indians **35**

④ Author's Insight

1. Discuss the first six paragraphs of "Museum Indians" and point out that Power is establishing a sense of the relationship she and her mother had when she was a young girl.

2. **Ask:** Why does Power describe her hair as "tiny garden snakes"? **Possible response:** She is comparing it to her mother's old braid, which she has described as "the three-foot snake."

3. Call students' attention to the Author's Insight note. Explain that Power describes her hair as she does to emphasize how much bigger and stronger than herself her mother seemed to be.

4. Have students identify other instances in the essay's first seven paragraphs in which Power compares herself to her mother. **Possible response:** Her mother tells stories, but when Power tries to repeat the stories, she only "chatters like a monkey." Furthermore, her mother is outspoken and politically active, but Power can "rage only on paper."

⑤ Reading Check

Answer: She tells her daughter stories.

Differentiated Instruction for Universal Access

Support for Less Proficient Readers
Review the Author's Insight notes on pages 35 and 36 with students. Point out that as a writer, Power wants to show that her mother was a "towering force" in comparison to her "diluted version." Then have students find and write down the details Power uses to describe her mother. Discuss these details with students, guiding them to recognize that they depict a powerful woman through the eyes of an awe-struck young girl.

EL Enrichment for English Learners
These students might feel a personal connection to Power's description of simultaneously being part of two different cultures. In discussion, encourage students to compare their own connections to their native cultures and American culture to those of Power. Students who were born in the United States to immigrant parents, or who moved here while very young, may have the most in common with Power.

This selection is available in interactive format in the **Enriched Online Student Edition**, at **www. PHLitOnline.com** which includes a thematically related video with a writing prompt and an interactive graphic organizer.

35

1. Have students read the bracketed passage. **Ask** them to describe the image of Power's mother the passage creates.
   Possible response: Power presents her mother as a woman of enormous scale and power, capable of virtually anything.

2. Call students' attention to the Author's Insight note near the bracketed passage. **Ask:** Does Power's use of this simile achieve the purpose she has in mind?
   Possible answer: The simile makes Power's mother seem huge because, like a skyscraper, she fills up her daughter's entire range of vision.

Susan Power
Author's Insight
I describe my mother as a "skyscraper" so the reader will have a visual image of my child's-eye view of her as a towering force.

Vocabulary ❻
integral (in′ tə grəl)
adj. essential

petrified (pe′ trə fid′) *adj.*
paralyzed as with fear

shrouded (shroud′ əd)
v. wrapped

intrigues (in′ trēgz′)
n. secrets

"She left the reservation when she was sixteen years old," I tell my audience. Sixteen sounds very old to me, but I always state the number because it seems integral to my recitation. "She had never been on a train before, or used a telephone. She left Standing Rock to take a job in Chicago so she could help out the family during the war. She was petrified of all the strange people and new surroundings; she stayed in her seat all the way from McLaughlin, South Dakota, to Chicago, Illinois, and didn't move once."

I usually laugh after saying this, because I cannot imagine my mother being afraid of anything. She is so tall, a true Dakota woman; she rises against the sun like a skyscraper, and when I draw her picture in my notebook, she takes up the entire page. She talks politics and attends sit-ins, wrestles with the Chicago police and says what's on her mind.

I am her small shadow and witness. I am the timid daughter who can rage only on paper.

We don't have much money, but Mom takes me from one end of the city to the other on foot, on buses. I will grow up believing that Chicago belongs to me, because it was given to me by my mother. Nearly every week we tour the Historical Society, and Mom makes a point of complaining about the statue that depicts an Indian man about to kill a white woman and her children: "This is the only monument to the history of Indians in this area that you have on exhibit. It's a shame because it is completely one-sided. Children who see this will think this is what Indians are all about."

My mother lectures the guides and their bosses, until eventually that statue disappears.

Some days we haunt the Art Institute, and my mother pauses before a Picasso.

"He did this during his blue period," she tells me.

I squint at the blue man holding a blue guitar. "Was he very sad?" I ask.

"Yes, I think he was." My mother takes my hand and looks away from the painting. I can see a story developing behind her eyes, and I tug on her arm to release the words. She will tell me why Picasso was blue, what his thoughts were as he painted this canvas. She relates anecdotes I will never find in books, never see footnoted in a biography of the master artist. I don't even bother to check these references because I like my mother's version best.

When Mom is down, we go to see the mummies at the Field Museum of Natural History. The Egyptian dead sleep in the basement, most of them still shrouded in their wrappings.

"These were people like us," my mother whispers. She pulls me into her waist. "They had dreams and intrigues and problems with their teeth. They thought their one particular life was of the utmost significance. And now, just look at them." My mother never fails to brighten. "So what's the use of worrying too hard or too long? Might as well be cheerful."

36 Beginnings–1800

Enrichment: Investigating Career Connections

Chicago's Museums

Chicago is home to many fine museums. The Chicago History Museum (formerly known as the Chicago Historical Society), where Power's mother disliked the negative representation of Native Americans, has a highly regarded collection focusing on Abraham Lincoln and the American Civil War.

The Art Institute of Chicago houses art from all over the world. It is especially famous for its collections of nineteenth-century Impressionist paintings and of modern art. Picasso's *The Old Guitarist* is only one of the many masterworks housed in the Art Institute.

The Field Museum is one of the world's most important natural history museums. It boasts a collection of more than 19 million items and conducts scientific research and education.

Activity: Research a Career Have students choose one type of job that might be found in a museum and research its potential as a career. Suggest that they record their findings in the **Enrichment: Investigating Career Connections** worksheet, *Professional Development Guidebook*, page 221.

The Old Guitarist, Pablo Picasso, 1903 (reproduction), The Art Institute of Chicago, ©2004 Estate of Pablo Picasso/Artists Rights Society (ARS), New York

Before we leave this place, we always visit my great-grandmother's buckskin dress. We mount the stairs and walk through the museum's main hall—past the dinosaur bones all strung together, and the stuffed elephants lifting their trunks in a mute trumpet.

The clothed figures are disconcerting because they have no heads. I think of them as dead Indians. We reach the traditional outfits of the Sioux in the Plains Indian section, and there is the dress, as magnificent as I remembered. The yoke is completely beaded—I know the garment must be heavy to wear. My great-grandmother used blue

8 ◄ Critical Viewing
Compare and contrast the effect of the color blue in this painting and in the dress on page 38.
[Compare and Contrast]

Vocabulary
disconcerting (dis′ kən surt′ iŋ) adj. upsetting

9 **Reading Check**

What do the author and her mother always do before leaving the museum?

Museum Indians **37**

❼ Humanities

The Old Guitarist, 1903, Pablo Picasso

Pablo Picasso (1881–1973) is one of the most important and famous artists of the twentieth century. Picasso was born in Spain and studied art in La Coruña and Barcelona. By the time he was a teenager, he was producing exceptionally advanced work.

Picasso emerged as a truly original artist in 1901, when he entered what is known as his "blue period." For a few years, his palette was dominated by shades of blue. The paintings from this period focused on poor and downtrodden people. *The Old Guitarist* is among the best-known paintings from this stage of Picasso's career. The sorrow and misery radiating from the elderly guitar player epitomizes the mood of the period.

Use these questions for discussion:

1. What details in this painting suggest that Picasso was "very sad," as Power imagines, when he painted it?
   Possible response: The guitar player is emaciated, and his clothes are ragged, suggesting poverty. His head is bowed, and his face has a sorrowful expression. These details suggest sadness.

2. Why might this painting attract Power and her mother?
   Possible response: It is a famous image of exceptional beauty, and its sorrowful mood might attract their attention when Power's mother is feeling sad.

❽ Critical Viewing

Possible response: The color blue in the Picasso painting evokes a feeling of sadness, while the blue in the Native American dress evokes the uplifting feeling that might be caused by a bright blue sky.

❾ Reading Check

Answer: They visit the author's great-grandmother's buckskin dress, which is on display in the museum.

❿ Author's Insight

1. Have students pause before reading the marked passage. Explain that Power and her mother are gazing at a beaded Native dress—apparently made by Power's great-grandmother—in a display case.

2. Call students' attention to the image of the beaded dress on this page. **Ask** them to describe the dress in their own words. What similarities and differences do they see between this dress and the one Power describes?
Possible response: Although the dress on this page does not have the geometric patterns of the dress Power describes, it has the same azure blue and heaviness.

3. Have students read the marked passage. Then, call their attention to the Author's Insight note. Explain that Power is linking the Native art represented by the dress and the art of Picasso.

4. Ask students what the connection Power makes between the dress and the Picasso painting suggests about the cultural traditions from which each comes.
Possible response: Power feels that she belongs to two cultures, her mother's Native culture and the mainstream culture of America and the world. By connecting the Native dress to the Picasso painting, she shows that she values both cultures equally and sees both from the same perspective—her own.

Susan Power ❿
Author's Insight
"Was this her blue period?" my character asks, to draw a connection between Picasso's art (one phase of Picasso's painting is called his "blue period") and the exquisite beadwork of Native American women.

⓫ ↓

38 Beginnings–1800

beads as a background for the geometrical design, and I point to the azure[1] expanse.

"Was this her blue period?" I ask my mother. She hushes me unexpectedly, she will not play the game. I come to understand that this is a solemn call, and we stand before the glass case as we would before a grave.

"I don't know how this got out of the family," Mom murmurs. I feel helpless beside her, wishing I could reach through the glass to disrobe the headless mannequin. My mother belongs in a grand buckskin dress such as this, even though her hair is now too short to braid and has been trained to curl at the edges in a saucy flip.

We leave our fingerprints on the glass, two sets of hands at different heights pressing against the barrier. Mom is sad to leave.

"I hope she knows we visit her dress," my mother says.

There is a little buffalo across the hall, stuffed and staring. Mom

---

1. azure (azh´ ər) *adj.* sky blue.

Enrichment: Investigating Daily Life

The Sioux People

In "Museum Indians," Susan Power's great-grandmother's buckskin dress is housed in an exhibit on the Sioux people of America's Great Plains. The Sioux were an alliance of several tribes that dominated the plains from the mid-1700s until the late 1800s. The Sioux resisted the encroachment of the United States, ultimately losing their battles and most of their territory.

Sioux culture was centered around the buffalo herds that populated the plains. They used the buffalo for food and to make tools, housing, and clothing. Clothing was decorated with dyes and beadwork, often using geometric designs. Power's great-grandmother's dress is an example of this kind of clothing.

Activity: Presentation Have students research the daily life of the Sioux. Suggest that they record their findings in the **Enrichment: Investigating Daily Life** worksheet, *Professional Development Guidebook,* page 224, and present their findings.

doesn't always have the heart to greet him. Some days we slip out of the museum without finding his stall.

"You don't belong here," Mom tells him on those rare occasions when she feels she must pay her respects. "We honor you," she continues, "because you are a creature of great endurance and great generosity. You provided us with so many things that helped us to survive. It makes me angry to see you like this."

Few things can make my mother cry; the buffalo is one of them.

"I am just like you," she whispers. "I don't belong here either. We should be in the Dakotas, somewhere a little bit east of the Missouri River. This crazy city is not a fit home for buffalo or Dakotas."

I take my mother's hand to hold her in place. I am a city child, nervous around livestock and lonely on the plains.

I am afraid of a sky without light pollution—I never knew there could be so many stars. I lead my mother from the museum so she will forget the sense of loss. From the marble steps we can see Lake Shore Drive spill ahead of us, and I sweep my arm to the side as if I were responsible for this view. I introduce my mother to the city she gave me. I call her home.

"THIS CRAZY CITY IS NOT A FIT HOME FOR BUFFALO OR DAKOTAS."

Cite textual evidence to support your responses.

Critical Reading

1. **Key Ideas and Details (a)** What is the snake in Power's mother's dresser drawer? **(b) Interpret:** Why does she keep it there?

2. **Key Ideas and Details (a)** What complaint does Power's mother make about the statue at the Historical Society? **(b) Analyze:** What is the effect of her complaints? **(c) Contrast:** How does the statue contrast with the exhibit at the Art Institute?

3. **Key Ideas and Details (a)** What is unique about Power's relationship to the buckskin dress at the Art Institute? **(b) Interpret:** What is her mother's attitude toward seeing the dress there?

4. **Integration of Knowledge and Ideas (a)** In what ways does her mother identify with the buffalo? **(b) Contrast:** How is Power different from her mother? **(c) Generalize:** What does the final paragraph tell you about the relationship between the writer and her mother and their relationship with the city? Explain.

5. **Integration of Knowledge and Ideas** How do you think Power's mother influenced her as a writer? Base your answer on this essay.

Museum Indians **39**

⓫ **Critical Thinking**

Make a Judgment

1. Discuss the bracketed passage. Be sure students recognize that Power's mother thinks that neither she nor the buffalo belongs in a city like Chicago.

2. **Ask** students if the mother's tears make her a less brave figure than described by her daughter. **Possible response:** Her tears show us that even the bravest of people have their own sorrows.

ASSESS

Answers

1. (a) The snake in the dresser drawer is a long, heavy braid of Power's mother's hair. (b) Power's mother no longer wears her hair long. She may keep the braid as a reminder of her roots or as a memento of her tradition.

2. (a) She complains that the statue presents a one-sided and very negative picture of Native Americans. (b) Because she makes clear, well-reasoned complaints over and over, the statue is eventually removed. (c) The statue is very negative, representing an inflammatory stereotype of Native Americans. The exhibit at the Art Institute is much more respectful, paying honor to the beauty of Native culture.

3. (a) The buckskin dress was made by her great-grandmother. (b) She is moved but saddened that it is no longer in the possession of her family.

4. (a) She feels that she and the buffalo are out of place and that they should both be in the open land of the Dakotas. (b) Unlike her mother, Power feels she is a part of the city. (c) Although she lives in Chicago, Power's mother is fully a part of Native culture. Power, however, feels that Chicago is her city. She loves her mother and connects to her Native culture, but she is also fully a part of the mainstream world.

5. Power's mother is a storyteller, and her stories move Power and inspire her imagination. By becoming a writer, perhaps she found a way to tell her mother's stories, and her own as well.

39

• *from the* Iroquois Constitution
Lesson Pacing Guide

DAY 1 Preteach

ⓒ Administer the Reading and Vocabulary Warm-ups (*Unit 1 Resources*, pp. 34–37) as necessary.

ⓒ Introduce the Literary Analysis concepts: Political Document and Symbol.

• Introduce the Reading Strategy: Analyzing Philosophical Assumptions and Beliefs.

ⓒ Build background with the author and Background features.

• Develop thematic thinking with Connecting to the Essential Question.

ⓒ Teach the selection vocabulary.

DAY 2 Preteach/Teach/Extend

• Distribute copies of the appropriate graphic organizer for the Reading Strategy (*Graphic Organizer Transparencies*, pp. 5–6).

• Distribute copies of the appropriate graphic organizer for Literary Analysis (*Graphic Organizer Transparencies*, pp. 7–8).

• Prepare students to read with the Activating Prior Knowledge activities (TE).

• Informally monitor comprehension while students read.

• Use the Reading Check question to confirm comprehension.

ⓒ Develop students' understanding of political documents and symbols using the Literary Analysis prompt.

• Develop students' ability to analyze philosophical assumptions and beliefs using the Reading Strategy prompt.

ⓒ Reinforce vocabulary with the Vocabulary notes.

• Assess students' comprehension and mastery of the skills by having them answer the Critical Reading, Literary Analysis, and Reading Strategy questions.

DAY 3 Assess

ⓒ Have students complete the Vocabulary practice.

ⓒ Have students complete the Writing lesson and write a found poem. (You may assign as homework.)

• Administer Selection Test A or B (*Unit 1 Resources*, pp. 46–48 or 49–51).

ⓒ Common Core State Standards

Reading Informational Text 1. Cite strong and thorough textual evidence to support analysis of what the text says explicitly as well as inferences drawn from the text.
6. Determine an author's point of view or purpose in a text in which the rhetoric is particularly effective, analyzing how style and content contribute to the power, persuasiveness or beauty of the text.

Language 4.a. Use context as a clue to the meaning of a word or phrase.

Additional Standards Practice
***Common Core Companion**, pp. 143–150; 324–331*

Daily Block Scheduling
Each day in this Lesson Pacing Guide represents a 40–50 minute period. Teachers using block scheduling may combine days to revise pacing. In addition, teachers may differentiate and support core instruction by integrating components for extended and intensive support as students require. See the Guide to Selected Leveled Resources (facing page).

Guide to Selected Leveled Resources

R T I Tier 1 (students performing on level)

from the Iroquois Constitution

Warm Up	**Practice, model,** and **monitor** fluency, working **with the whole class** or **in groups**.	Vocabulary and Reading Warm-ups B, *Unit 1 Resources,* pp. 34–35, 37
Comprehension/Skills	**Support** and **monitor** comprehension and skills development, having students complete the activities, graphic organizers, and interactive prompts **independently** or **as a class**.	• *Reader's Notebook,* adapted instruction and summary **EL** *Reader's Notebook: English Learner's Version,* adapted instruction and summary • Reading Strategy Graphic Organizer B, *Graphic Organizer Transparencies,* p. 6 • Literary Analysis Graphic Organizer B, *Graphic Organizer Transparencies,* p. 8
Monitor Progress **A**	**Monitor** student progress with the differentiated curriculum-based assessment in the *Unit Resources*.	• Selection Test B, *Unit 1 Resources,* pp. 49–51 • Open-Book Test, *Unit 1 Resources,* pp. 43–45

R T I Tier 2 (students requiring intervention)

from the Iroquois Constitution

Warm Up	**Practice, model,** and **monitor** fluency **in groups** or **with individuals**.	• Vocabulary and Reading Warm-ups A, *Unit 1 Resources,* pp. 34–36 • *Hear It!* Audio CD
Comprehension/Skills	• **Support** and **monitor** comprehension and skills development, working **in small groups** or **with individuals**. • As students complete the selection in the appropriate version of the *Reader's Notebook,* **monitor** comprehension frequently with group questions and individual instruction. • **Model** strategies while guiding students in completing the activities and prompts in the *Reader's Notebook,* as well as the graphic organizers. • **Practice** skills and **monitor** mastery with the *Reading Kit* worksheets.	• *Reader's Notebook: Adapted Version,* adapted instruction and summary **EL** *Reader's Notebook: English Learner's Version,* adapted instruction and summary • Reading Strategy Graphic Organizer A, *Graphic Organizer Transparencies,* p. 5 • Literary Analysis Graphic Organizer A, *Graphic Organizer Transparencies,* p. 7 • *Reading Kit,* Practice worksheets
Monitor Progress **A**	**Monitor** student progress with the differentiated curriculum-based assessment in the *Unit Resources* and in the *Reading Kit*.	• Selection Test A, *Unit 1 Resources,* pp. 46–48 • *Reading Kit,* Assess worksheets

TIER 3 Tier 3 intervention may require consultation with the student's special-education or dyslexia specialist. For additional support, see the Tier 2 activities and resources listed above.

One-on-one teaching   Group work   Whole class instruction   Independent work   **A** Assessment
For a complete guide to selection support, including support for Advanced students, see the Overview of Resources in the frontmatter.

• *from the* Iroquois Constitution

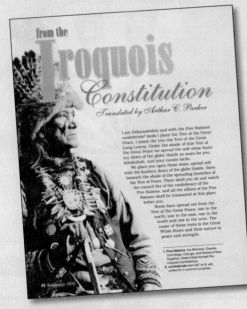

RESOURCES FOR:

L1 Special-Needs Students

L2 Below-Level Students (Tier 2)

L3 On-Level Students (Tier 1)

L4 Advanced Students (Tier 1)

EL English Learners

All All Students

Vocabulary/Fluency/Prior Knowledge

EL L1 L2 Reading Warm-ups A and B, pp. 36–37

Also available for these selections:

EL L1 L2 Vocabulary Warm-ups A and B, pp. 34–35

All Vocabulary Builder, p. 40

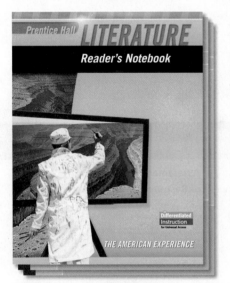

Reader's Notebooks

Pre- and postreading pages for this selection, as well as an excerpt from the *Iroquois Constitution*, appear in an interactive format in the *Reader's Notebooks*. Each *Notebook* is differentiated for a different group of learners. The selections in the Adapted and English Learner's versions are abridged.

L2 L3 *Reader's Notebook*

L1 *Reader's Notebook: Adapted Version*

EL *Reader's Notebook: English Learner's Version*

EL *Reader's Notebook: Spanish Version*

© *Common Core Companion*

Additional instruction and practice for each Common Core State Standard

Selection Support

from The Iroquois Constitution (Iroquois)

Before You Read B: Identify Philosophical Assumptions and Beliefs

	The Iroquois Constitution
Step One: Look for words that express negative or positive attitudes, such as *just, unfair, goodness,* or *evil.*	
Step Two: Look for statements that stem from a particular idea of right or wrong.	
Step Three: Look for details, including symbols, that suggest a point of view that someone else could argue against.	

EL L3 Reading: Graphic Organizer B, p. 6

Also available for these selections:

EL L1 L2 Reading: Graphic Organizer A, (partially filled in), p. 5

EL L1 L2 Literary Analysis: Graphic Organizer A, (partially filled in), p. 7

EL L3 Literary Analysis: Graphic Organizer B, p. 8

Skills Development/Extension

Name _____ Date _____

from The Iroquois Constitution
Literary Analysis: Political Document and Symbols

A **political document** describes the structure of a political organization and the responsibilities of its members. For example, the Constitution of the United States sets out the duties and responsibilities of the three branches of the U.S. government. The division of the government into three branches was a major **symbol** for the framers. The three branches symbolized, or stood for, a government that would provide restrictions on the ability of any one branch to gain too much power. This was a rejection of the absolute power held by the monarchy of England, from which many of the colonists came.

DIRECTIONS: *Read the passages from* The Iroquois Constitution. *Then, answer the questions about the document and the symbols within it.*

I am Dekanawidah and with the Five Nations confederate lords I plant the Tree of the Great Peace. . . . Under the shade of this Tree of the Great Peace . . . There shall you sit and watch the council fire of the confederacy of the Five Nations, and all the affairs of the Five Nations shall be transacted at this place before you.

1. How many peoples, or nations, are represented in the document known as *The Iroquois Constitution?*

2. What does the Tree of the Great Peace symbolize?

When a candidate lord is to be installed he shall furnish four strings of shells (or wampum) . . . . Such will constitute the evidence of his pledge to the confederate lords that he will live according to the constitution of the Great Peace and exercise justice in all affairs.

3. What behavior does the constitution demand of a lord of the Iroquois confederacy?

4. What do the four strings of wampum symbolize for a candidate lord?

We place at the top of the Tree of the Long Leaves an eagle who is able to see afar. If he sees in the distance any evil approaching or any danger threatening he will at once warn the people of the confederacy.

5. What does the eagle symbolize to the Iroquois people?

6. How does the symbol of the eagle represent what the confederacy really used to warn them of approaching danger?

All Literary Analysis: Political Document and Symbol, p. 38

Also available for these selections:

All Reading Analyze Author's Assumptions and Beliefs, p. 39

EL L3 L4 Support for Writing, p. 41

L4 Enrichment, p. 42

Assessment

Name _____ Date _____

from The Iroquois Constitution
Selection Test B

MULTIPLE CHOICE

Critical Reading *Identify the letter of the choice that best answers the question.*

___ 1. In terms of a governmental body, what do the roots of the Tree of Peace in *The Iroquois Constitution* symbolize to the Iroquois confederacy?
  A. strength from unity
  B. differences among people
  C. hidden secrets of rulers
  D. sources of food

___ 2. According to the author of *The Iroquois Constitution,* what is the mission of the Five Nations?
  A. to include anyone who agrees to the Constitution
  B. to be always on the watch for danger
  C. to divide the nations against one another
  D. to exclude anyone not in one of the nations

___ 3. To what other political organizations could you compare the Iroquois confederation and the Five Nations?
  A. the city council and the voters
  B. the federal government and the states
  C. a kingdom and its army
  D. a school district and its teachers

___ 4. With which American institution could you compare the council of the Five Nations?
  A. the Supreme Court
  B. the Chamber of Commerce
  C. the Treasury Department
  D. the Congress

___ 5. In *The Iroquois Constitution,* what is the task of the eagle that sits at the top of the Tree of Long Leaves?
  A. to hunt food for the people
  B. to defend the people from evil
  C. to warn the people of danger
  D. to fly and give news to people

___ 6. Who is meant to see the smoke of the confederacy council fire as it ascends to the sky?
  A. Iroquois allies
  B. Iroquois enemies
  C. all of the natural world
  D. lost travelers

___ 7. Why do the lords of the Five Nations give thanks to the earth before they begin deliberations?
  A. out of respect
  B. out of fear
  C. out of obedience
  D. out of comfort

EL L1 L2 Selection Test B, pp. 49–51

Also available for these selections:

L3 L4 Open-Book Test, pp. 43–45

EL L3 L4 Selection Test A, pp. 46–48

PHLit Online!
www.PHLitOnline.com

Online Resources: All print materials are also available online.

- complete narrated selection text
- a thematically related video with writing prompt
- an interactive graphic organizer
- highlighting feature
- access to all student print resources, adapted to individual student needs
- Spanish and English summaries
- adapted selection translations in Spanish

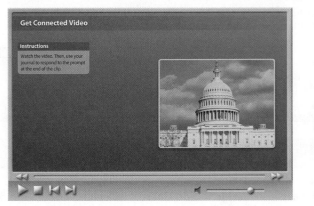

Get Connected!

Also available:

Background Video (thematic video with writing prompt)
All videos are available in Spanish.

Writer's Journal (with graphics feature)

Also available:

Vocabulary Central (tools and activities for studying vocabulary)

❶ Connecting to the Essential Question

1. Review the assignment with the class.

2. Point out that the natural world offers many examples of cooperative behavior. Animals in flocks or herds, for example, often interact for protection. Have students complete the assignment. As students read, have them look for examples in nature that model how human societies might work.

❷ Literary Analysis

Introduce the skill, using the instruction on the student page.

Think Aloud: Model the Skill

Say to students:

I notice that the Iroquois Constitution refers to an eagle, which I know is commonly used as a symbol of a nation's power, especially in war. Roman armies, for example, carried eagle symbols into battle. Eagles also represent vision and vigilance; a soaring eagle represents freedom. As I read, I am curious to know what the eagle symbolizes to the Iroquois.

❸ Reading Strategy

1. Introduce the strategy, using the instruction on the student page.

2. Give students a copy of **Reading Strategy Graphic Organizer B,** page 6 in *Graphic Organizer Transparencies,* to fill out as they read.

❹ Vocabulary

1. Pronounce each word, giving its definition, and have students say it aloud.

2. For more guidance, see the *Classroom Strategies and Teaching Routines* card for introducing vocabulary.

Before You Read — from the *Iroquois Constitution*

❶ **Connecting to the Essential Question** The makers of this document use natural imagery to describe society and government. As you read, find details related to the forces of nature and consider whether nature provides a sound model for human society. This will help as you consider the Essential Question: **What is the relationship between literature and place?**

❷ **Literary Analysis**

The Iroquois Constitution is a **political document** that defines the structure and practices of a political organization—the Iroquois Confederacy. One of the document's prominent features is its use of symbols. A **symbol** is a person, place, animal, or object that represents something else, often an abstraction. For example, in the Iroquois Constitution, a tree symbolizes the peace established among the uniting tribes:

> I am Dekanawidah and with the Five Nations' confederate lords I plant the Tree of the Great Peace.

Some symbols have a fixed meaning, representing the same thing in every context. A national flag is such a symbol. Other symbols have meanings that change depending on their context. Often, symbols have emotional associations that affect people more than the abstract ideas alone. As you read the Iroquois Constitution, think about the abstract ideas the symbols convey and how they intensify the emotional impact of the text.

❸ **Reading Strategy**

© **Preparing to Read Complex Texts** Political documents may express *explicit philosophical assumptions and beliefs*. These are statements in which the author directly states his or her point of view. A document may also express the writer's *implicit philosophical assumptions and beliefs,* or points of view that are suggested but not stated. To **analyze philosophical assumptions and beliefs,** follow the steps in the chart shown here.

❹ **Vocabulary**

disposition (dis′ pə zish′ ən) *n.* inclination; tendency (p. 43)

constitute (kän′ stə tōōt) *v.* serve as the parts or basis of; form; comprise (p. 43)

tempered (tem′ pərd) *v.* treated to achieve just the right strength or balance (p. 44)

deliberation (di lib′ ər ā′ shən) *n.* careful consideration (p. 44)

oblivion (ə bliv′ ē ən) *n.* the condition of being completely forgotten (p. 44)

40 Beginnings–1800

© **Common Core State Standards**

Reading Informational Text
1. Cite strong and thorough textual evidence to support analysis of what the text says explicitly as well as inferences drawn from the text.

6. Determine an author's point of view or purpose in a text in which the rhetoric is particularly effective, analyzing how style and content contribute to the power, persuasiveness or beauty of the text.

Step One

Look for words that are negative or positive, such as *just, goodness,* or *evil.*

Step Two

Find statements that show specific ideas of right and wrong.

Step Three

Look for ideas that someone could argue against.

www.PHLitOnline.com

Vocabulary Development

Vocabulary Knowledge Rating

Create a **Vocabulary Knowledge Rating Chart** (in *Professional Development Guidebook,* p. 33) for the vocabulary words on the student page. Give each student a copy of the chart with the words on it. Read the words aloud and have students mark their rating of each in the Before Reading column. When students have completed reading and discussing the selection, have them take out their **Vocabulary Knowledge Rating** charts. Read the words aloud and have students rate their knowledge again in the After Reading column. Clarify any words that are still problematic. Then, have students complete the vocabulary practice at the end of the selection.

PHLit Online! **Vocabulary Central,** featuring tools and activities for studying vocabulary, is available online at **www.PHLitOnline.com.**

The Iroquois

Authors of the **Iroquois Constitution**

The Iroquois are a group of Native American tribes with closely related languages and cultural traditions. They often call themselves the People of the Long House, a reference to the long communal homes in which they traditionally lived. The Iroquois united in the sixteenth century or perhaps earlier, when—according to legend—a mystic and prophet named Dekanawidah traveled from village to village in what is now upstate New York, urging the tribes to stop fighting and band together. The result was a confederacy, or united group, often called the Five Nations. The confederacy initially included the Seneca, Cayuga, Onondaga, Oneida, and Mohawk tribes. In 1722 a sixth tribe, the Tuscarora, joined the group, which became known as the Six Nations.

A Colonial Power Even though their numbers were relatively small, unification made the Iroquois a powerful force in the colonial era. They gained control over many other Native American tribes and kept the Dutch and British from spreading much beyond New York's Hudson River. They often fought the French, who had allied with their enemies, the Algonquins and Hurons. The Iroquois, in turn, allied with the British, helping them win the French and Indian War (1754–1763). The American Revolution divided the Iroquois. While most tribes remained loyal to the British, the Oneida and some Tuscarora supported the colonists. After the war, some Iroquois resettled in Canada, and many Oneida moved to Wisconsin.

The Great Binding Law The agreement that united the Iroquois established a framework of laws and practices that helped make them the most highly organized Native American political body in colonial North America. Known as the Great Binding Law or Great Law of Peace, it was passed down orally for generations and recorded in shell beads called wampum that served as a memory device for oral recitation. The current version, now often called the Iroquois Constitution, was written down in the nineteenth century.

from the Iroquois Constitution **41**

41

❶ About the Selection

The Iroquois Constitution tells how and why representatives of the Iroquois nation should hold formal councils to discuss and decide issues of concern to all. When Dekanawidah presented his *Kaianerekowa,* or Great Law of Peace, much of the Iroquois world was beset by persecution, disease, and power struggles. His plan established an alliance of mutual respect, cooperation, and ritual.

❷ Activating Prior Knowledge

Tell students that most organizations, from nations to school clubs, need guidelines that enable them to function effectively. Ask students to think of their own experiences in an organization and about its rules. What benefits do these rules have for the members of the group? Ask them to read to find out how the Iroquois benefited from their constitution.

❸ Literary Analysis

Political Document and Symbol

1. Read the first three paragraphs aloud.

2. Point out that the passage refers in detail to the branches and the roots of the Tree of Great Peace.

3. **Ask** students what political meanings are symbolized by branches and roots.
   Possible response: The branches are linked to shade, symbolizing protection. The roots, spreading in four directions, symbolize connection and strength. The passage explicitly links roots to "peace and strength."

from the Iroquois ❶ ❷ Constitution

Translated by Arthur C. Parker

I am Dekanawidah and with the Five Nations[1] confederate[2] lords I plant the Tree of the Great Peace. I name the tree the Tree of the Great Long Leaves. Under the shade of this Tree of the Great Peace we spread the soft white feathery down of the globe thistle as seats for you, Adodarhoh, and your cousin lords.

We place you upon those seats, spread soft with the feathery down of the globe thistle, there beneath the shade of the spreading branches of the Tree of Peace. There shall you sit and watch the council fire of the confederacy of the Five Nations, and all the affairs of the Five Nations shall be transacted at this place before you.

Roots have spread out from the Tree of the Great Peace, one to the north, one to the east, one to the south and one to the west. The name of these roots is the Great White Roots and their nature is peace and strength.

---

1. **Five Nations** the Mohawk, Oneida, Onondaga, Cayuga, and Seneca tribes. Together, these tribes formed the Iroquois Confederacy.
2. **confederate** (kən fed´ ər it) *adj.* united for a common purpose.

Ⓒ Text Complexity Rubric

Reader and Leveled Tasks

from **The Iroquois Constitution**	
Qualitative Measures	
Context/Knowledge Demands	Historical knowledge demands (document) 1 2 ③ 4 5
Structure/ Conventionality and Clarity	Formal, complicated sentences; average vocabulary 1 2 3 ④ 5
Levels of Meaning/ Purpose/Concept Level	Abstract (organization of government) 1 2 ③ 4 5
Quantitative Measures	
Lexile 1510L	**Text Length** Word Count: 887
Overall Complexity	**More complex**

Preparing to Read the Text
- Using the Background information on TE p. 41, discuss the founding of the Five Nations.
- Discuss the value of having groups cooperate to achieve a common goal. Ask students why guidelines might make cooperation easier to attain.
- Guide students to use Multidraft Reading strategies to deepen their comprehension (TE p. 41).

Leveled Tasks

Structure/Language If students will have difficulty with the structure, have them write a one-sentence summary of each section's guidelines. Have students reread to check their understanding.

Evaluating If students will not have difficulty with the structure, have them give an example of a clear guideline for being a leader in the confederacy.

If any man or any nation outside the Five Nations shall obey the laws of the Great Peace and make known their disposition to the lords of the confederacy, they may trace the roots to the tree and if their minds are clean and they are obedient and promise to obey the wishes of the confederate council, they shall be welcomed to take shelter beneath the Tree of the Long Leaves.

We place at the top of the Tree of the Long Leaves an eagle who is able to see afar. If he sees in the distance any evil approaching or any danger threatening he will at once warn the people of the confederacy.

The smoke of the confederate council fire shall ever ascend and pierce the sky so that other nations who may be allies may see the council fire of the Great Peace . . .

Whenever the confederate lords shall assemble for the purpose of holding a council, the Onondaga lords shall open it by expressing their gratitude to their cousin lords and greeting them, and they shall make an address and offer thanks to the earth where men dwell, to the streams of water, the pools, the springs and the lakes, to the maize and the fruits, to the medicinal herbs and trees, to the forest trees for their usefulness, to the animals that serve as food and give their pelts for clothing, to the great winds and the lesser winds, to the thunderers, to the sun, the mighty warrior, to the moon, to the messengers of the Creator who reveal his wishes and to the Great Creator who dwells in the heavens above, who gives all the things useful to men, and who is the source and the ruler of health and life.

Then shall the Onondaga lords declare the council open . . .

All lords of the Five Nations' Confederacy must be honest in all things . . . It shall be a serious wrong for anyone to lead a lord into trivial affairs, for the people must ever hold their lords high in estimation out of respect to their honorable positions.

When a candidate lord is to be installed he shall furnish four strings of shells (or wampum)[3] one span in length bound together at one end. Such will constitute the evidence of his pledge to the confederate lords that he will live according to the constitution of the Great Peace and exercise justice in all affairs.

When the pledge is furnished the speaker of the council must hold the shell strings in his hand and address the opposite side of the council fire and he shall commence his address saying: "Now behold him. He has now become a confederate lord. See how splendid he looks." An address may then follow.

_____

3. **wampum** (wäm′ pəm) *n.* small beads made of shells.

from the Iroquois Constitution **43**

Political Document and Symbol

1. Be sure students understand what wampum is, referring to the footnote on the preceding page if necessary.

2. **Ask** the Literary Analysis question: What agreement do the strings of shells, or wampum, symbolize?
   Answer: The strings symbolize the agreement among the council members.

ASSESS

Answers

Before students respond, you may wish to have them write a brief objective summary of the selection. As they answer the questions below, remind them to support their answers with evidence from the text.

1. (a) They plant the Tree of the Great Peace. (b) The roots symbolize strength and peace.

2. (a) They must thank one another and then "offer thanks to the earth where men dwell." (b) They respect each other and their environment and are conscious of their dependence on nature and its Great Creator.

3. (a) Lords must be honest in all things, slow to anger, and full of peace, good will, and a desire for the welfare of their people. A lord's actions should always exhibit farsightedness, deliberation, and compassion. (b) Some students may find the Iroquois leadership model apt for the modern world; others may say that modern leaders need to act with more practicality.

4. Students should support their responses. For example, they may agree that cooperation between independent groups can produce peace and strength.

5. 🔍 **Possible response:** Practically, the Iroquois <u>cultivate</u> nature for food, clothing, medicine, and shelter. Spiritually, they rely on nature as a connection to the Creator, the source and ruler of life. In both a practical and a <u>sacred</u> sense, Iroquois <u>civilization</u> is rooted in the natural world.

What agreement do the strings of shells, or wampum, symbolize?

Vocabulary

tempered (tem´ pərd) *v.* treated to achieve just the right strength or balance

deliberation (di lib´ ər ā´ shən) *n.* careful consideration

oblivion (ə bliv´ ē ən) *n.* the condition of being completely forgotten

---

❻ At the end of it he shall send the bunch of shell strings to the opposite side and they shall be received as evidence of the pledge. Then shall the opposite side say:

"We now do crown you with the sacred emblem of the deer's antlers, the emblem of your lordship. You shall now become a mentor of the people of the Five Nations. The thickness of your skin shall be seven spans—which is to say that you shall be proof against anger, offensive actions and criticism. Your heart shall be filled with peace and good will and your mind filled with a yearning for the welfare of the people of the confederacy. With endless patience you shall carry out your duty and your firmness shall be **tempered** with tenderness for your people. Neither anger nor fury shall find lodgement in your mind and all your words and actions shall be marked with calm **deliberation**. In all of your deliberations in the confederate council, in your efforts at law making, in all your official acts, self-interest shall be cast into **oblivion**. Cast not over your shoulder behind you the warnings of the nephews and nieces should they chide you for any error or wrong you may do, but return to the way of the Great Law which is just and right. Look and listen for the welfare of the whole people and have always in view not only the present but also the coming generations, even those whose faces are yet beneath the surface of the ground—the unborn of the future nation."

Critical Reading

> **Cite textual evidence to support your responses.**

1. **Key Ideas and Details (a)** What do the lords plant to commemorate their meeting? **(b) Analyze:** What do the roots of this plant symbolize?

2. **Integration of Knowledge and Ideas (a)** According to the Iroquois Constitution, what must confederate lords do to open a council meeting? **(b) Infer:** What does this decree suggest about the Iroquois?

3. **Integration of Knowledge and Ideas (a) Summarize:** Summarize the qualities and conduct required of council lords by the Iroquois Constitution. **(b) Synthesize:** How well do these qualities apply to leaders in the modern world?

4. **Integration of Knowledge and Ideas** Do you agree with and support the ideas presented in the Iroquois Constitution? Why or why not?

5. **Integration of Knowledge and Ideas** In what ways, both practical and spiritual, do the Iroquois rely on the natural world? Use these Essential Question words in your response: *cultivate, civilization, sacred.* *[Connecting to the Essential Question: What is the relationship between literature and place?]*

Assessment Practice

Summarizing Written Text (For more practice, see *All-in-One Workbook*.)

Students will need to recognize accurate summaries on tests. Use this sample test item to help students practice.

> Was the Iroquois confederacy a model for American government? Some scholars believe so, pointing out that Benjamin Franklin, a great fan of the confederacy, was also a framer of the United States Constitution. However, most scholars await more direct proof of Iroquois influence on American politics.

Which is the best summary of the passage?

A Franklin was interested in the Iroquois.

B Scholars believe that the Iroquois confederacy is a model for America.

C Franklin helped shape the Constitution.

D Scholars are not sure about the influence of the Iroquois on American government.

Choices **A** and **C** are details; choice **B** is inaccurate. **D** is the best answer.

Literary Analysis

1. **Key Ideas and Details** **(a)** Note one way in which this **political document** creates a structure for Iroquois society. **(b)** Note one way in which this document determines how the Iroquois will react to external threats.

2. **Craft and Structure** **(a)** Use a chart like the one shown to list three **symbols** in the document and explain the abstract idea each one represents. **(b)** Which of these symbols has fixed meanings sometimes found outside of Iroquois culture? Cite examples to support your answer.

Symbol	Abstract Idea

Reading Strategy

3. **(a)** Analyze explicit **philosophical assumptions and beliefs** in this document by explaining how the Iroquois see the ideal relationship between a lord and his people. **(b)** Analyze implicit **philosophical assumptions and beliefs** by explaining the views of nature that underlie many of the statements.

4. Based on the details in the last paragraph, what philosophical beliefs did the Iroquois hold about the qualities that make one a good leader?

PERFORMANCE TASKS
Integrated Language Skills

Vocabulary Acquisition and Use

Sentence Completions Use the context clues, or surrounding words and phrases, to choose a word from the vocabulary list on page 40 that best completes each sentence. Explain your choices. Use each word only once.

1. Oil and vinegar _____ the main ingredients of that salad dressing.
2. To make a good decision, emotion must be _____ with reason.
3. I came to my conclusion after careful _____.
4. Someone with amnesia may live in a continuous state of _____.
5. Clio has a lazy _____, while her brother is inclined to work hard.

Writing

Found Poem A found poem is a poem created from writing or speech not intended to be poetry. Choose a passage from the Iroquois Constitution that you think is especially strong or beautiful. Turn it into a poem by rewriting it with line breaks like those of poetry. Organize the stanzas and place the line breaks where you feel they create the most impact. Read your poem aloud to verify your choices; revise them if necessary.

Common Core State Standards

Language
4.a. Use context as a clue to the meaning of a word or phrase.

Assessment Resources

Unit 1 Resources

L1 L2 EL **Selection Test A,** pp. 46–48. Administer Test A to less advanced students.

L3 L4 EL **Selection Test B,** pp. 49–51. Administer Test B to on-level and more advanced students.

L3 L4 **Open-Book Test,** pp. 43–45. As an alternative, give the Open-Book Test.

All **Customizable Test Bank**

All **Self-tests**
Students may prepare for the **Selection Test** by taking the **Self-test** online.

PHLit Online! All assessment resources are available at **www.PHLitOnline.com**.

Answers

1. (a) **Possible response:** The document sets membership qualifications: to join, an individual or a nation must promise to obey the wishes of the council. (b) The eagle in the treetop indicates that member nations will warn each other of coming danger.

2. (a) **Sample answer:** Symbol: deer antlers; Abstract Idea: lordship or authority. (b) The deer antlers function as a crown, a symbol of leadership and authority in many cultures.

3. (a) The leader is to selflessly seek the long-term welfare of the people and future generations. The people must respect their leaders. They are allowed to share their views—the leader must "look and listen"—but the leader must not react with emotion but should follow the Great Law. (b) The Iroquois viewed nature as a system of interconnection and provision that provides life to humans. Students may say that this philosophical assumption provides a model for the interconnectedness of leaders and their people.

4. The Iroquois believed that good leaders are calm, objective, honest and selfless as they act on behalf of their people. The underlying assumption is that some gifted individuals possess these virtues and skills.

Vocabulary Acquisition and Use

1. constitute; Oil and vinegar are the basis of a salad dressing.

2. tempered; A balance of traits produces a good decision.

3. deliberation; A conclusion requires careful consideration.

4. oblivion; Amnesia is a condition of forgetfulness.

5. disposition; A lazy tendency is the opposite of one to work hard.

Writing

Sample answer:

Roots
have spread out
from the Tree of Great Peace,
One to the north,
one to the east,
one to the south,
and one to the west.

• A Journey Through Texas
• Boulders Taller Than the Great Tower of Seville
Lesson Pacing Guide

DAY 1 Preteach

- Administer the Reading and Vocabulary Warm-ups (*Unit 1 Resources*, pp. 52–55) as necessary.
- Introduce the Literary Analysis concept: Exploration Narratives.
- Introduce the Reading Strategy: Recognizing Signal Words.
- Build background with the author and Background features.
- Develop thematic thinking with Connecting to the Essential Question.
- Teach the selection vocabulary.

DAYS 2–3 Preteach/Teach/Assess

- Distribute copies of the appropriate graphic organizer for the Reading Strategy (*Graphic Organizer Transparencies*, pp. 11–12).
- Distribute copies of the appropriate graphic organizer for Literary Analysis (*Graphic Organizer Transparencies*, pp. 9–10).
- Prepare students to read with the Activating Prior Knowledge activities (TE).
- Informally monitor comprehension while students read.
- Use the Reading Check questions to confirm comprehension.
- Develop students' understanding of exploration narratives using the Literary Analysis prompts.
- Develop students' ability to recognize signal words using the Reading Strategy prompts.
- Reinforce vocabulary with the Vocabulary notes.
- Assess students' comprehension and mastery of the skills by having them answer the Critical Reading, Literary Analysis, and Reading Strategy questions.
- Have students complete the Vocabulary Lesson.

DAY 4 Extend/Assess

- Have students complete the Writing Lesson and write an explorer's journal entry. (You may assign as homework.)
- Administer Selection Test A or B (*Unit 1 Resources*, pp. 64–66 or 67–69).

Common Core State Standards

Reading Informational Text
5. Analyze and evaluate the effectiveness of the structure an author uses in his or her exposition or argument, including whether the structure makes points clear, convincing, and engaging.

Writing 2.d. Use precise language.

Language 5. Demonstrate understanding of figurative language, word relationships, and nuances in word meanings.

Additional Standards Practice
Common Core Companion, pp. 136–137; 196–207; 332–335

Daily Block Scheduling
Each day in this Lesson Pacing Guide represents a 40–50 minute period. Teachers using block scheduling may combine days to revise pacing. In addition, teachers may differentiate and support core instruction by integrating components for extended and intensive support as students require. See the Guide to Selected Leveled Resources (facing page).

Guide to Selected Leveled Resources

Tier 1 (students performing on level)

**A Journey Through Texas •
Boulders Taller Than the Great Tower of Seville**

Warm Up	**Practice, model,** and **monitor** fluency, working **with the whole class** or **in groups**.	Vocabulary and Reading Warm-ups B, *Unit 1 Resources,* pp. 52–53, 55
Comprehension/Skills	**Support** and **monitor** comprehension and skills development, having students complete the activities, graphic organizers, and interactive prompts **independently** or **as a class**.	• *Reader's Notebook,* adapted instruction and summary **EL** *Reader's Notebook: English Learner's Version,* adapted instruction and summary • Reading Strategy Graphic Organizer B, *Graphic Organizer Transparencies,* p. 12 • Literary Analysis Graphic Organizer B, *Graphic Organizer Transparencies,* p. 10
Monitor Progress **A**	**Monitor** student progress with the differentiated curriculum-based assessment in the *Unit Resources.*	• Selection Test B, *Unit 1 Resources,* pp. 67–69 • Open-Book Test, *Unit 1 Resources,* pp. 61–63

Tier 2 (students requiring intervention)

**A Journey Through Texas •
Boulders Taller Than the Great Tower of Seville**

Warm Up	**Practice, model,** and **monitor** fluency **in groups** or **with individuals**.	• Vocabulary and Reading Warm-ups A, *Unit 1 Resources,* pp. 52–54 • *Hear It!* Audio CD
Comprehension/Skills	• **Support** and **monitor** comprehension and skills development, working **in small groups** or **with individuals**. • As students complete the selection in the appropriate version of the *Reader's Notebook,* **monitor** comprehension frequently with group questions and individual instruction. • **Model** strategies while guiding students in completing the activities and prompts in the *Reader's Notebook,* as well as the graphic organizers. • **Practice** skills and **monitor** mastery with the *Reading Kit* worksheets.	• *Reader's Notebook: Adapted Version,* adapted instruction and summary **EL** *Reader's Notebook: English Learner's Version,* adapted instruction and summary • Reading Strategy Graphic Organizer A, *Graphic Organizer Transparencies,* p. 11 • Literary Analysis Graphic Organizer A, *Graphic Organizer Transparencies,* p. 9 • *Reading Kit,* Practice worksheets
Monitor Progress **A**	**Monitor** student progress with the differentiated curriculum-based assessment in the *Unit Resources* and in the *Reading Kit.*	• Selection Test A, *Unit 1 Resources,* pp. 64–66 • *Reading Kit,* Assess worksheets

TIER 3 Tier 3 intervention may require consultation with the student's special education or dyslexia specialist For additional support, see the Tier 2 activities and resources listed above.

One-on-one teaching Group work Whole-class instruction Independent work **A** Assessment

For a complete guide to selection support, including support for Advanced students, see the Overview of Resources in the frontmatter.

• A Journey Through Texas
• Boulders Taller Than The Great Tower of Seville

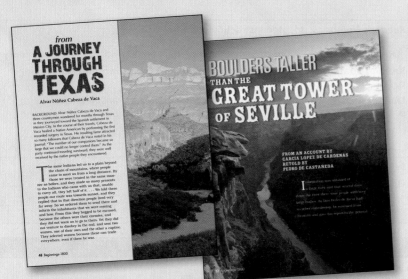

RESOURCES FOR:

L1 Special-Needs Students

L2 Below-Level Students (Tier 2)

L3 On-Level Students (Tier 1)

L4 Advanced Students (Tier 1)

EL English Learners

All All Students

Vocabulary/Fluency/Prior Knowledge

All **Vocabulary Builder,** p. 58

Also available for these selections:

EL **L1** **L2** **Vocabulary Warm-ups A and B,** pp. 52–53

EL **L1** **L2** **Reading Warm-ups A and B,** pp. 54–55

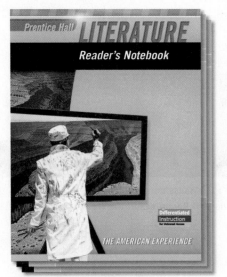

Reader's Notebooks

Pre- and postreading pages for these selections appear in an interactive format in the *Reader's Notebooks*. Each *Notebook* is differentiated for a different group of learners. The selections in the Adapted and English Learner's versions are abridged.

L2 **L3** *Reader's Notebook*

L1 *Reader's Notebook: Adapted Version*

EL *Reader's Notebook: English Learner's Version*

EL *Reader's Notebook: Spanish Version*

©️ *Common Core Companion*

Additional instruction and practice for each Common Core State Standard

Selection Support

Graphic Organizer Transparencies

EL L1 L2 Reading: Graphic Organizer A (partially filled in), p. 11

Also available for these selections:

EL L1 L2 Literary Analysis: Graphic Organizer A, (partially filled in) p. 9

EL L3 Literary Analysis: Graphic Organizer B, p. 10

EL L3 Reading: Graphic Organizer B p. 12

Skills Development/Extension

Unit 1 Resources

EL L3 L4 Support for Writing, p. 59

Also available for these selections:

All Literary Analysis: Exploration Narratives/Chronological Text Structure, p. 56

All Reading: Recognize Signal Words for Time, p. 57

Enrichment, p. 60

Assessment

L3 L4 Open-Book Test, pp. 39–41, 60–62

Also available for these selections:

EL L1 L2 Selection Test A, pp. 64–66

EL L3 L4 Selection Test B, pp. 67–69

PHLit Online!
www.PHLitOnline.com

Online Resources: All print materials are also available online.

- complete narrated selection text
- a thematically related video with writing prompt
- an interactive graphic organizer
- highlighting feature
- access to all student print resources, adapted to individual student needs
- Spanish and English summaries
- adapted selection translations in Spanish

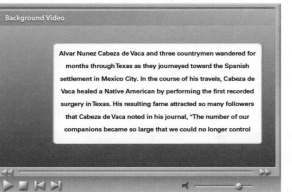

Background Video

Alvar Nunez Cabeza de Vaca and three countrymen wandered for months through Texas as they journeyed toward the Spanish settlement in Mexico City. In the course of his travels, Cabeza de Vaca healed a Native American by performing the first recorded surgery in Texas. His resulting fame attracted so many followers that Cabeza de Vaca noted in his journal, "The number of our companions became so large that we could no longer control

Background Video

Also available:

Get Connected! (thematic video with writing prompt)
All videos are available in Spanish.

Essay
Select one of the images to write about. Drag the image to the page.

Writer's Journal (with graphics feature)

Also available:

Vocabulary Central (tools and activities for studying vocabulary)

❶  **Connecting to the Essential Question**

1. Review the assignment with the class.

2. Suggest that the students think about their own encounters with other cultures. Then, have them complete the assignment.

3. Ask students to look for examples of the explorers' and the native peoples' reactions to each other.

❷ Literary Analysis

1. Introduce the skill, using the instruction on the student page.

2. Give students **Literary Analysis Graphic Organizer B,** page 10 in *Graphic Organizer Transparencies,* to fill out as they read.

Think Aloud: Model the Skill

Say to students:

Good exploration stories make me feel as though I am walking beside the adventurers. I can enhance this feeling by thinking through challenges the explorers face. When an explorer faces a problem, I pause in my reading to think how it might be resolved. Then, I read further to find out how the explorer's solution matched my own.

❸ Reading Strategy

Introduce the strategy.

❹ Vocabulary

1. Pronounce each word, giving its definition, and have students say it aloud.

2. For more guidance, see the *Classroom Strategies and Teaching Routines* card for introducing vocabulary.

Before You Read

from *A Journey Through Texas • Boulders Taller Than the Great Tower of Seville*

❶ Connecting to the Essential Question These accounts describe early meetings between Europeans and Native Americans. As you read, find details that show how the explorers and the native peoples react to each other. Doing so will help as you think about the Essential Question: **What is the relationship between literature and place?**

❷ Literary Analysis

The Europeans who first came to the Americas related their experiences in **exploration narratives**—firsthand accounts of their travels. These accounts generally provide information in **chronological order,** describing events in the order in which they occurred. By creating a clear sequence of events, the explorers allowed readers back home in Europe to follow their journeys, step by step.

Comparing Literary Works Every journey presents conflicts and problems. As you read, use a chart like the one shown to *compare and contrast the problems* each explorer faced and the solutions he found.

❸ Reading Strategy

ⓒ Preparing to Read Complex Texts When reading narrative accounts, analyze and evaluate the structure by making sure you are clear about the sequence in which events occur and the ways in which each event changes a situation. Pause and try to state events in order. To help, **recognize signal words** that clarify relationships of time and sequence, reason, or contrast.

> **Time:** *After five days,* they had not *yet* returned.
>
> **Sequence:** . . . and so we endured these seventeen days, *at the end of which* we crossed the river. . . .
>
> **Contrast:** . . . *although* this was the warm season, no one could live in the canyon because of the cold.

❹ Vocabulary

entreated (en trēt′ əd) *v.* begged; implored (p. 49)

feigned (fānd) *v.* pretended (p. 49)

subsisted (səb sist′ əd) *v.* remained alive; were sustained (p. 50)

successive (sək ses′ iv) *adj.* following one after another (p. 50)

advantageous (ad′ van tā ′ jəs) *adj.* favorable; beneficial (p. 51)

traversed (trə vʉrst′) *v.* moved over, across, or through (p. 51)

ⓒ Common Core State Standards

Reading Informational Text
5. Analyze and evaluate the effectiveness of the structure an author uses in his or her exposition or argument, including whether the structure makes points clear, convincing, and engaging.

De Vaca — Problems → Solutions

De Cárdenas — Problems → Solutions

www.PHLitOnline.com

46 Beginnings–1800

Vocabulary Development

Vocabulary Knowledge Rating
Create a **Vocabulary Knowledge Rating Chart** (in *Professional Development Guidebook,* p. 33) for the vocabulary words on the student page. Give each student a copy of the chart with the words on it. Read the words aloud and have students mark their rating of each in the Before Reading column. When students have completed reading and discussing the selec- tions, have them take out their **Vocabulary Knowledge Rating** charts. Read the words aloud and have students rate their knowledge again in the After Reading column. Clarify any words that are still problematic. Then, have students complete the vocabulary practice at the end of the selection.

PHLit Online! **Vocabulary Central,** featuring tools and activities for studying vocabulary, is available online at **www.PHLitOnline.com.**

❺ Alvar Núñez Cabeza de Vaca
(1490?–1557?)
Author of *A Journey Through Texas*

In 1528, Pánfilo de Narváez and 400 Spanish soldiers landed near Tampa Bay and set out to explore Florida's west coast. Alvar Núñez Cabeza de Vaca (äl´ bär nōōn´ yes kä bā´ sä dā bä´ kä) was second in command. Beset by hostile natives, illness, and the prospect of starvation, Narváez and his men then set sail for Mexico in five flimsy boats, but he and most of the men drowned. Cabeza de Vaca and a party of about sixty survived and reached the Texas shore near present-day Galveston.

Shipwrecked without supplies, only fifteen of the group lived through the winter. In the end, Cabeza de Vaca and three others survived. They were captured by natives and spent the next several years in captivity. During that time, Cabeza de Vaca gained a reputation as a medicine man and trader. The four Spaniards finally escaped and wandered for eighteen months across the Texas plains. In 1536, the survivors finally reached Mexico City.

Invitation to Others Cabeza de Vaca's adventures and his reports on the richness of Texas sparked exploration of the region. In "A Journey Through Texas," he speaks of Estevanico, the first African to set foot in Texas.

In 1541, Cabeza de Vaca also led a 1,000-mile expedition through the south of present day Brazil to Asunción, the capital of Río de la Plata. He was appointed governor of the Río de la Plata region (now Paraguay), but he was ousted two years later as a result of revolt.

Through his journals, Cabeza de Vaca encouraged others, including Francisco Vásquez de Coronado, to explore America.

García López de Cárdenas
(c. 1540)
Author of *Boulders Taller Than the Great Tower of Seville*

García López de Cárdenas (gär sē´ ä lō´ pes dā kär´ dä näs) is best remembered as the first European to visit the Grand Canyon. As a leader of Francisco Vásquez de Coronado's expedition to New Mexico (1540–1542), Cárdenas was dispatched from Cibola (Zuni) in western New Mexico to see a river that the Moqui Native Americans of northeastern Arizona had described to one of Coronado's captains. The river was the Colorado. López de Cárdenas departed on August 25, 1540, reaching the Grand Canyon after a westward journey of about twenty days. He became the first European to view the canyon and its river, which from the vantage of the canyon's rim appeared to be a stream merely six feet wide! Unable to descend to the river, they took back to Europe descriptions that attempted to record the magnitude of the sight. López de Cárdenas reported that boulders in the Grand Canyon were taller than the 300-foot high Great Tower of Seville, one of the world's tallest cathedrals.

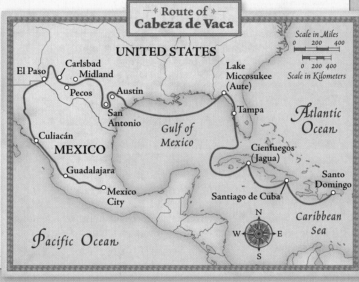

from A Journey Through Texas • Boulders Taller Than the Great Tower of Seville **47**

Teaching From Technology

Preparing to Read
Go to **www.PHLitOnline.com** in class or in a lab and display the **Get Connected!** slide show for this grouping. Have the class brainstorm for responses to the slide show writing prompt, entering ideas in the interactive journal. Then, have students complete their written responses individually in a lab or as homework.

To build background, display the Background and More About the Authors features.

Using the Interactive Text
Go to **www.PHLitOnline.com** and display the Enriched Online Student Edition. As the class reads the selections or listens to the narration, record answers to side-column prompts using the graphic organizers accessible on the interactive page. Alternatively, have students use the online edition individually, answering the prompts as they read.

◗ Multidraft Reading

To assist struggling readers and to enhance reading for all, assign the text in chunks as warranted by length and apply multidraft reading protocols. For each reading, have students set the purpose indicated:

- **First reading**—identifying key ideas and details and answering any Reading Checks.
- **Second reading**—analyzing craft and structure and responding to the side-column prompts.
- **Third reading**—integrating knowledge and ideas, connecting to other texts and the world, and answering the end-of-selection questions.

For more guidance, refer to the *Classroom Strategies and Teaching Routines* card on multidraft reading.

❺ Background
More About the Authors

Alvar Núñez Cabeza de Vaca came to North America as treasurer of the Narváez expedition, the goal of which was to colonize lands north of Mexico. Cabeza de Vaca was shipwrecked on an island in the Gulf of Mexico with two other Spaniards and an African, Estevanico. In a unique role reversal, the four became captive servants to the Cahoques people for about eight years. During this time, Cabeza de Vaca grew to understand the Native Americans as no other Spaniard had.

Cabeza de Vaca and his companions are also known for adding to the legend of the Seven Cities of Cibola. Their descriptions of fabulous golden cities spurred explorers such as Francisco Vázquez de Coronado to roam the American Southwest. It was his participation in Coronado's quest for gold that led García López de Cárdenas to the rim of the Grand Canyon.

❶ About the Selection

Cabeza de Vaca was a Spanish adventurer whose views and beliefs were dramatically altered by his extraordinary experiences living with Native Americans. This narrative describes his journey into what is now the state of Texas as he attempts to reach the Spanish settlements in Mexico City. Cabeza de Vaca came (albeit reluctantly) to understand and appreciate something of the people whose land he traveled through.

❷ Activating Prior Knowledge

Invite students to imagine that they are in a strange land among people whose language and customs are unknown to them. Have them jot down their thoughts about these questions: What if they had no way of sending for help and no way of knowing how to get back home? How would it feel to spend several years in this land with no apparent hope of returning home? To whom could they turn for help? Emphasize that Cabeza de Vaca and his followers spent eight years—many of them in enforced captivity—in just such a situation. Students may also benefit from referring to the map on page 47. Have them use the map to orient themselves to Cabeza de Vaca's route from Santo Domingo to Mexico City.

Concept Connector ➡

Tell students they will return to their responses after reading the selection.

❶
❷

from A JOURNEY THROUGH TEXAS

Alvar Núñez Cabeza de Vaca

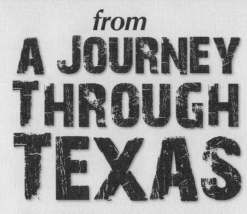

BACKGROUND Alvar Núñez Cabeza de Vaca and three countrymen wandered for months through Texas as they journeyed toward the Spanish settlement in Mexico City. In the course of their travels, Cabeza de Vaca healed a Native American by performing the first recorded surgery in Texas. His resulting fame attracted so many followers that Cabeza de Vaca noted in his journal: "The number of our companions became so large that we could no longer control them." As the party continued traveling westward, they were well received by the native people they encountered.

The same Indians led us to a plain beyond the chain of mountains, where people came to meet us from a long distance. By those we were treated in the same manner as before, and they made so many presents to the Indians who came with us that, unable to carry all, they left half of it. . . . We told these people our route was towards sunset, and they replied that in that direction people lived very far away. So we ordered them to send there and inform the inhabitants that we were coming and how. From this they begged to be excused, because the others were their enemies, and they did not want us to go to them. Yet they did not venture to disobey in the end, and sent two women, one of their own and the other a captive. They selected women because these can trade everywhere, even if there be war.

48 Beginnings–1800

ⓒ Text Complexity Rubric

from A Journey Through Texas, Boulders Taller . . . Seville	
Qualitative Measures	
Context/Knowledge Demands	Historical knowledge demands (journals) 1 2 ③ 4 5
Structure/Language Conventionality and Clarity	Long sentences; some archaic vocabulary 1 2 3 ④ 5
Levels of Meaning/ Purpose/Concept Level	Accessible (cultural perspective) 1 2 ③ 4 5
Quantitative Measures	
Lexile	1400L; 1270L	Text Length	Word Count: 1710; 569
Overall Complexity	**More complex**

Reader and Task Suggestions

Preparing to Read the Text

• Using the Background information on TE p. 47, discuss the expeditions of Cabeza de Vaca and Cárdenas.

• Ask students why it might be valuable to read an eyewitness history, even if the writer's style is unfamiliar to us.

• Guide students to use Multidraft Reading strategies to deepen their comprehension (TE p. 47).

Leveled Tasks

Structure/Language If students will have difficulty with the vocabulary in these accounts, have them look at the definitions in the sidenotes and footnotes before they read.

Analyzing If students will not have difficulty with vocabulary, have them compare the mood of the two accounts.

We followed the women to a place where it had been agreed we should wait for them. After five days they had not yet returned, and the Indians explained that it might be because they had not found anybody. So we told them to take us north, and they repeated that there were no people, except very far away, and neither food nor water. Nevertheless we insisted, saying that we wanted to go there, and they still excused themselves as best they could, until at last we became angry.

One night I went away to sleep out in the field apart from them; but they soon came to where I was, and remained awake all night in great alarm, talking to me, saying how frightened they were. They entreated us not to be angry any longer, because, even if it was their death, they would take us where we chose. We feigned to be angry still, so as to keep them in suspense, and then a singular[1] thing happened.

On that same day many fell sick, and on the next day eight of them died! All over the country, where it was known, they became so afraid that it seemed as if the mere sight of us would kill them. They besought[2] us not to be angry nor to procure the death of any more of their number, for they were convinced that we killed them by merely thinking of it. In truth, we were very much concerned about it, for, seeing the great mortality, we dreaded that all of them might die or forsake us in their terror, while those further on, upon learning of it, would get out of our way hereafter. We prayed to God our Lord to assist us, and the sick began to get well. Then we saw something that astonished us very much, and it was that, while the parents, brothers and wives of the dead had shown deep grief at their illness, from the moment they died the survivors made no demonstration whatsoever, and showed not the slightest feeling; nor did they dare to go near the bodies until we ordered their burial. . . .

The sick being on the way of recovery, when we had been there already three days, the women whom we had sent out returned, saying that they had met very few people, nearly all having gone after the cows, as it was the season. So we ordered those who had been sick to remain, and those who were well to accompany us, and that, two days' travel from there, the same women should go with us and get people to come to meet us on the trail for our reception.

The next morning all those who were strong enough came along, and at the end of three journeys we halted. Alonso del Castillo and Estevanico,[3] the negro, left with the women as guides, and the woman who was a captive took them to a river that flows between mountains, where there was a village, in which her father lived, and these were the first abodes we saw that were like unto real houses.

---

1. **singular** *adj.* strange.
2. **besought** (be sôt′) *v.* pleaded with.
3. **Estevanico** (es′ tä vä nē′ kō) Of Moorish extraction, Estevanico was the first African man to set foot in Texas.

from A Journey Through Texas **49**

---

3 ◀ **Critical Viewing**
In what ways might a landscape like the one in the photograph on the facing page pose difficulties for an expedition? **[Interpret]**

Vocabulary
entreated (en trēt′ əd) *v.* begged; pleaded
feigned (fānd) *v.* pretended

Reading Strategy
Recognizing Signal Words
Which words in this paragraph signal time and sequence relationships?

6 Reading Check
Why do the Indians fear going on ahead?

---

3 **Critical Viewing**
Answer: Students may note that the landscape appears to be hot, sunny, and very dry. Such terrain would probably supply little food or water, and travelers might easily starve, dehydrate, or suffer heatstroke.

4 **Reading Strategy**
Recognizing Signal Words
1. Ask students to explain the function of signal words. Then, have students review the bracketed passage.
2. **Ask** students the Reading Strategy question: Which words in this paragraph signal time and sequence relationships?
Answer: Students may cite "On that same day," "next day," and "then."

5 **Literary Analysis**
Exploration Narratives
1. Have students silently reread the bracketed paragraph at the bottom of this page.
2. Then, **ask** them to list, in chronological order, the actions taken by Castillo and Estevanico.
Answer: They leave with the women, go to a river and then a village, hold a parley at the village, and return to the expedition. Castillo reports their findings.
3. Have students explain the primary purpose of the Europeans' exploration narratives.
Answer: Students should specify that these exploration narratives were intended to provide detailed information about places and experiences to the people back home.

6 **Reading Check**
Answer: Their enemies live there.

Differentiated
Instruction   **for Universal Access**

Support for Special-Needs Students
Have students complete the **Before You Read** and the **Making Connections** pages for these selections in the *Reader's Notebook: Adapted Version.* These pages provide an abbreviated skills instruction, a selection summary, the Before You Read, and a **Note-taking Guide**.

Support for Less Proficient Readers
Have students complete the **Before You Read** and the **Making Connections** pages for these selections in the *Reader's Notebook.* These pages provide an abbreviated presentation of reading and literary skills instruction, a selection summary, the Before You Read, and a **Note-taking Guide**.

EL **Support for English Learners**
Have students complete the **Before You Read** and the **Making Connections** pages for these selections in the *Reader's Notebook: English Learner's Version.* These pages provide additional vocabulary, vocabulary skills, and vocabulary practice, along with a **Getting Ready to Read** activity.

This selection is available in interactive format in the **Enriched Online Student Edition**, at **www. PHLitOnline.com**, which includes a thematically related video with a writing prompt and an interactive graphic organizer.

50

❼ Humanities

Cabeza de Vaca, Esteban, and Their Companions, Tom Mirrat

This work portrays the encounter between the Spanish explorers and the sick Native Americans, as described in Cabeza de Vaca's journal. Use these questions for discussion:

1. How can you distinguish the Spaniards from the Native Americans?
   Answer: Students may say that the Spaniards are the ones with beards. Three Spaniards kneel beside sick Native Americans.

2. What are the people in the picture doing?
   Answer: Students may say that the Spaniards are praying over the victims or offering sympathy or medical help, while some frightened and worried Native Americans stand aside looking on.

❽ Critical Viewing

Answer: Students may respond that the Native Americans seem respectful or even slightly in awe of the Spaniards. They bring their sick to the Spaniards, then give them room to work their healing.

❾ Literary Analysis

Exploration Narratives

1. Read the bracketed text aloud to the students.

2. **Ask** them the following question: What were the Native American people afraid of?
   Answer: They were afraid of losing their crops.

3. **Ask** students the Literary Analysis question: What information about the region and its people do you learn from this paragraph?
   Answer: The area is settled by a lot of people. It has not rained in two years, so the people have not planted maize. The people pray to heaven for rain. Maize is plentiful in the country to the west.

❼

❽ ▲ **Critical Viewing**
What does this drawing suggest about the relationship between Cabeza de Vaca's party and the Native Americans? **[Interpret]**

Vocabulary
subsisted (səb sist′ əd)
v. remained alive; were sustained

successive (sək ses′ iv)
adj. one after another, in sequence

Literary Analysis
Exploration Narratives
What information about the region and its people do you learn from this paragraph?

❾

Castillo and Estevanico went to these and, after holding parley[4] with the Indians, at the end of three days Castillo returned to where he had left us, bringing with him five or six of the Indians. He told how he had found permanent houses, inhabited, the people of which ate beans and squashes, and that he had also seen maize.

Of all things upon earth this caused us the greatest pleasure, and we gave endless thanks to our Lord for this news. Castillo also said that the negro was coming to meet us on the way, near by, with all the people of the houses. For that reason we started, and after going a league and a half met the negro and the people that came to receive us, who gave us beans and many squashes to eat, gourds to carry water in, robes of cowhide, and other things. As those people and the Indians of our company were enemies, and did not understand each other, we took leave of the latter, leaving them all that had been given to us, while we went on with the former and, six leagues beyond, when night was already approaching, reached their houses, where they received us with great ceremonies. Here we remained one day, and left on the next, taking them with us to other permanent houses, where they subsisted on the same food also, and thence on we found a new custom.

The people who heard of our approach did not, as before, come out to meet us on the way, but we found them at their homes, and they had other houses ready for us. . . . There was nothing they would not give us. They are the best formed people we have seen, the liveliest and most capable; who best understood us and answered our questions. We called them "of the cows," because most of the cows die near there, and because for more than fifty leagues up that stream they go to kill many of them. Those people go completely naked, after the manner of the first we met. The women are covered with deerskins, also some men, especially the old ones, who are of no use any more in war.

The country is well settled. We asked them why they did not raise maize, and they replied that they were afraid of losing the crops, since for two successive years it had not rained, and the seasons were so dry that the moles had eaten the corn, so that they did not dare to plant any more until it should have rained very hard. And they also begged us to ask Heaven for rain, which we promised to do. We also wanted to know from where they brought their maize, and they said it came from where the sun sets, and that it was found all over that country, and the shortest way to it was in that direction.

---

4. **holding parley** (pär′ lē) conferring.

PROFESSIONAL DEVELOPMENT | Doug Buehl

▼ **APPLY THE STRATEGY**

Tier 2 Vocabulary Before students read the narrative, present two columns of Tier 2 words from the selection: Column A lists selection vocabulary *(entreated, feigned, subsisted, traversed)* and Column B lists other academic vocabulary *(inhabitants, venture, captive, endured, accompany, maize)*. Students work with partners to make four sets of possible connections between the two columns using what they currently know as well hunches. Partners then share paired terms with the class and

explain their speculation. For example, students might pair *traversed* from A with *accompany* from B, reasoning that *traversed* concerns travel, so you might *accompany* a person on a journey. After making predictions, students read the narrative and observe how the author put these terms "in play."

For more of Doug Buehl's strategies, see his Professional Development essay, pp. 2a–2b.

We asked them to tell us how to go, as they did not want to go themselves, to tell us about the way.

They said we should travel up the river towards the north, on which trail for seventeen days we would not find a thing to eat, except a fruit called *chacan*, which they grind between stones; but even then it cannot be eaten, being so coarse and dry; and so it was, for they showed it to us and we could not eat it. But they also said that, going upstream, we could always travel among people who were their enemies, although speaking the same language, and who could give us no food, but would receive us very willingly, and give us many cotton blankets, hides and other things; but that it seemed to them that we ought not to take that road.

In doubt as to what should be done, and which was the best and most advantageous road to take, we remained with them for two days. They gave us beans, squashes, and calabashes.[5] Their way of cooking them is so new and strange that I felt like describing it here, in order to show how different and queer are the devices and industries of human beings. They have no pots. In order to cook their food they fill a middle-sized gourd with water, and place into a fire such stones as easily become heated, and when they are hot to scorch they take them out with wooden tongs, thrusting them into the water of the gourd, until it boils. As soon as it boils they put into it what they want to cook, always taking out the stones as they cool off and throwing in hot ones to keep the water steadily boiling. This is their way of cooking.

After two days were past we determined to go in search of maize, and not to follow the road to the cows, since the latter carried us to the north, which meant a very great circuit, as we held it always certain that by going towards sunset we should reach the goal of our wishes.

So we went on our way and traversed the whole country to the South Sea,[6] and our resolution was not shaken by the fear of great starvation, which the Indians said we should suffer (and indeed suffered) during the first seventeen days of travel. All along the river, and in the course of these seventeen days we received plenty of cowhides, and did not eat of their famous fruit (*chacan*), but our food consisted (for each day) of a handful of deer-tallow, which for that purpose we always sought to keep, and so endured these seventeen days, at the end of which we crossed the river and marched for seventeen days more. At sunset, on a plain between very high mountains, we met people who, for one-third of the year, eat but powdered straw, and as we went by just at that time, had to eat it also, until, at the end of that journey we found some permanent houses, with plenty of harvested maize, of which and of its meal they gave us great quantities, also squashes and beans, and blankets of cotton. . . .

---

5. calabashes (kal′ ə bash′ əz) *n.* dried, hollow shells of gourds used to hold food or beverages.
6. the South Sea the Gulf of Mexico.

from A Journey Through Texas **51**

Vocabulary

advantageous (ad′ van tā′jəs) *adj.* favorable, profitable

traversed (trə vurst′) *v.* moved over, across, or through

Literary Analysis
Exploration Narratives
What might readers back in Europe have thought about the group's determination to find maize?

11 ☑ Reading Check

With what information does Castilo return?

---

⑩ Literary Analysis
Exploration Narratives

1. Have students take turns reading the selection's final paragraphs aloud. Ask students to be alert for references to maize.

2. **Ask** students the Literary Analysis question: What might readers back in Europe have thought about the group's determination to find maize?
   Answer: Students may say that these readers would have believed the explorers thought maize was a valuable crop.

⑪ Reading Check

Answer: Castillo returns with the information that he has seen permanent houses inhabited by people who eat beans and squash; he has also seen maize.

Strategy for Special-Needs Students
Encourage students to create a graphic organizer that helps them distinguish among the various Native American peoples mentioned by Cabeza de Vaca. Students might create a cluster diagram for each group, using words and phrases from the text to characterize each. The author alludes to five groups. Ensure that students record details about each group and their relationships with other groups and with the explorers.

Enrichment for Advanced Readers
Between 1492 and 1540, exploration and expansion fever spread through western Europe. By the time Cabeza de Vaca landed in Texas, the Spanish had gained a solid foothold in the Caribbean basin and in Mexico; Ponce de León had explored the coasts of what is now Florida; Verrazano had been up the Atlantic coast to Newfoundland; and Magellan's ships had rounded South America and crossed the Pacific Ocean. Invite interested students to prepare a research report on one or more of these explorers.

⓬ About the Selection

By the time of Coronado's expedition in 1540, the Spanish knew there was gold and silver in the Americas. Although Coronado's search for the Seven Cities of Cibola led only to impoverished villages in what is now New Mexico, the group he dispatched northward led to the European discovery of the Grand Canyon. García López de Cárdenas, with the help of Hopi guides from nearby mesas, became the first European to see this natural wonder. Unable to find water or cross the canyon, López de Cárdenas eventually left in frustration.

⓬ BOULDERS TALLER THAN THE GREAT TOWER OF SEVILLE

FROM AN ACCOUNT BY
GARCÍA LÓPEZ DE CÁRDENAS
RETOLD BY
PEDRO DE CASTAÑEDA

Information was obtained of a large river and that several days down the river there were people with very large bodies. As Don Pedro de Tovar had no other commission, he returned from Tusayán and gave his report to the general.

Think Aloud

Reading Strategy: Recognize Signal Words
Say to the students:

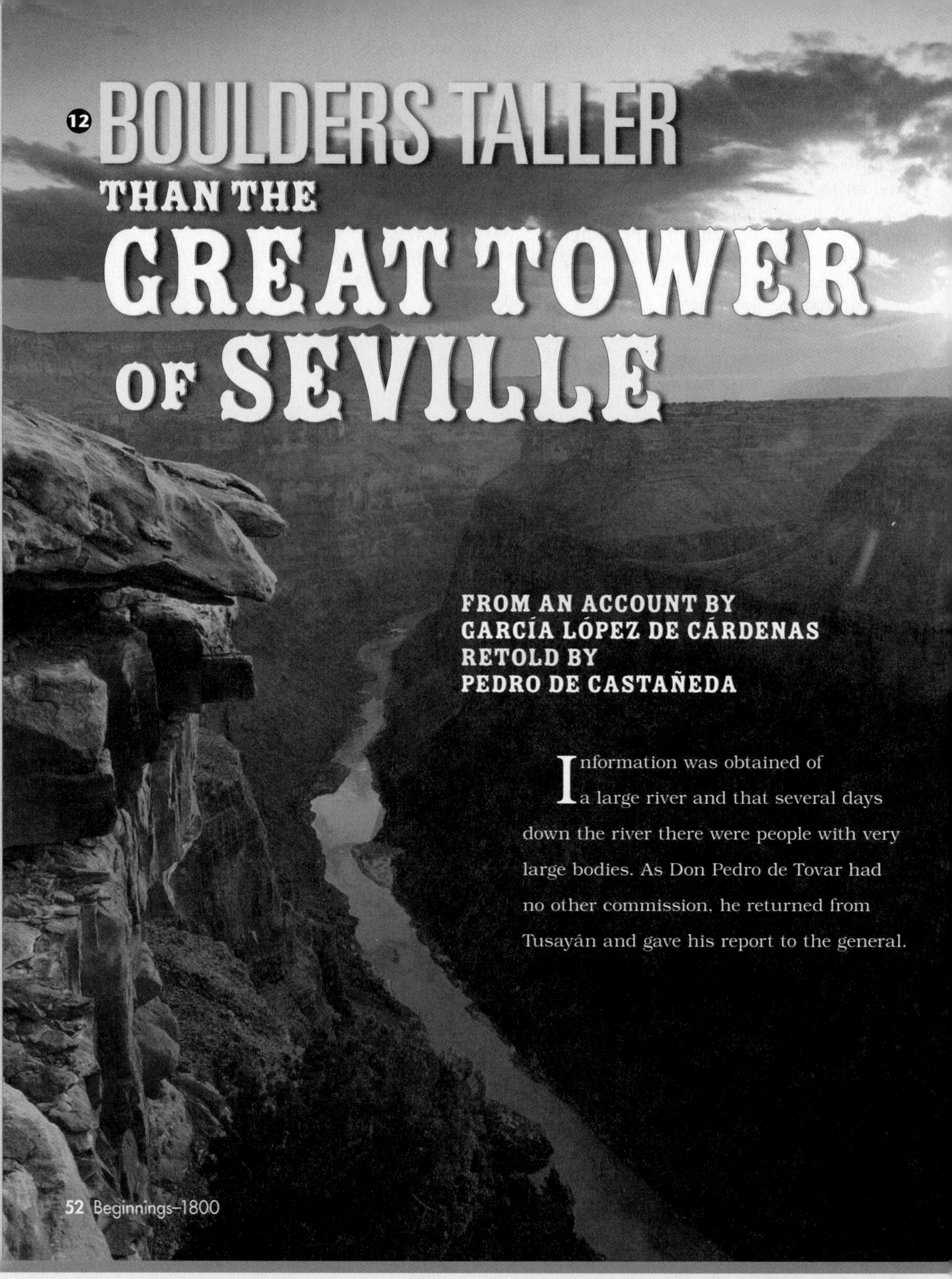

On page 53 García López de Cárdenas's men learn the width of the river. They do so by first sending two men to get a better view. Signal words show that it took "three days" to find a good approach to the river. The men who stayed above watched the explorers descend "until they lost sight of them." The explorers returned at "about four o'clock in the afternoon." Then, López de Cárdenas goes back to the hours before four o'clock to tell what the explorers learned while they were out of sight. The signal words indicate that López de Cárdenas is telling the story from his own point of view—he doesn't reveal the explorers' report until he hears it himself. With other signal words he might have told the explorers' story "as it happened," ending with their return at four o'clock. This illustrates just one of the many choices faced by anyone writing a narrative.

The latter at once dispatched Don García López de Cárdenas there with about twelve men to explore this river. When he reached Tusayán he was well received and lodged by the natives. They provided him with guides to proceed on his journey. They set out from there laden with provisions, because they had to travel over some uninhabited land before coming to settlements, which the Indians said were more than twenty days away. Accordingly when they had marched for twenty days they came to gorges of the river, from the edge of which it looked as if the opposite side must have been more than three or four leagues[1] away by air. This region was high and covered with low and twisted pine trees; it was extremely cold, being open to the north, so that, although this was the warm season, no one could live in this canyon because of the cold.

The men spent three days looking for a way down to the river; from the top it looked as if the water were a fathom[2] across. But, according to the information supplied by the Indians, it must have been half a league wide. The descent was almost impossible, but, after these three days, at a place which seemed less difficult, Captain Melgosa, a certain Juan Galeras, and another companion, being the most agile, began to go down. They continued descending within view of those on top until they lost sight of them, as they could not be seen from the top. They returned about four o'clock in the afternoon, as they could not reach the bottom because of the many obstacles they met, for what from the top seemed easy, was not so, on the contrary, it was rough and difficult. They said that they had gone down one-third of the distance and that, from the point they had reached, the river seemed very large, and that, from what they saw, the width given by the Indians was correct. From the top they could make out, apart from the canyon, some small boulders which seemed to be as high as a man. Those who went

FROM THE TOP THEY COULD MAKE OUT, APART FROM THE CANYON, SOME SMALL BOULDERS WHICH SEEMED TO BE AS HIGH AS A MAN.

🔟5 **Reading Check**

Who is dispatched to explore the river?

---

1. **leagues** (lēgz) *n.* units of measurement of approximately three miles.
2. **fathom** (fath′ əm) *n.* a unit of measurement equal to six feet.

🔟4 ▲ **Critical Viewing** Do the photographs on these two pages help you understand the explorers' confusion about the scale of the Grand Canyon? Explain. **[Connect]**

🔟3 **Literary Analysis**
Exploration Narratives

1. Review with students the purpose a writer has in creating an exploration narrative: to convey information about a travel expedition to an audience.

2. Point out to students that some exploration narratives may be thought of as reports to an employer.

3. **Ask** students the following question: What impression of the group's efforts is López de Cárdenas trying to convey in his narrative?
   Answer: By including details relating to the harsh landscape and the Spaniards' sober determination to explore it, the writer seems to wish to convey an impression of the group's physical and mental hardiness.

🔟4 **Critical Viewing**

Possible answer: Yes. The canyon is so massive and so unlike anything they had ever seen before, that it is understandable that they would have underestimated the size and scale of the canyon and river.

🔟5 **Reading Check**

Answer: Don García López de Cárdenas and approximately twelve other men are dispatched to explore the river.

Differentiated Instruction *for Universal Access*

Strategy for Less Proficient Readers
Point out to students that López de Cárdenas tries to show how big a new object is by comparing it to something his readers might know. We do this today, for example, when we say something is "as big as the Grand Canyon." Ask students how they would use this comparison process to describe an object bigger than a school desk. Bigger than a classroom? Bigger than a house? Bigger than a school? Work as a class to make useful size comparisons.

Enrichment for Gifted/Talented Students
Within the boundaries of Grand Canyon National Park are about 2,000 sites once inhabited by the Anasazi—the Native American peoples who lived in settlements throughout the plateau country of the Southwest. Encourage students to read further in the library or on the Internet about the Anasazi people. Have students write a poem or a drama about the Anasazi, focusing on what they might have thought upon seeing the European explorers gazing across the Grand Canyon.

This selection is available in interactive format in the **Enriched Online Student Edition**, at **www. PHLitOnline.com**, which includes a thematically related video with a writing prompt and an interactive graphic organizer.

53

Recognizing Signal Words

1. Read the bracketed sentence with students.

2. **Ask** students the Reading Strategy question: What change do the words "up to that time" signal?
Answer: They signal a change in the course of the journey.

▶ **Monitor Progress:** Ask a student volunteer to explain common types of relationships between ideas that are indicated by signal words.
Answer: Signal words most commonly indicate time relationships, spatial relationships, causality, and contrasts.

ASSESS

Answers

Before students respond, you may wish to have them write a brief objective summary of the selection. As they answer the questions below, remind them to support their answers with evidence from the text.

1. (a) The Native Americans resist the explorers' orders to lead them north. (b) The Native Americans believe that the explorers can kill them just by thinking.

2. (a) It had not rained for two years, so they did not want to chance losing a crop by planting before there had been sufficient rain. (b) They beg them to ask heaven to send rain. (c) **Possible response:** It suggests that they view the Spaniards as godlike.

3. (a) The Grand Canyon. (b) They are probably seeking gold, silver, or other valuables.

4. (a) The river and boulders are a great deal larger than they appear from the top of the gorge. (b) The explorers learn that the Native Americans' perspective was correct.

5. **Possible response:** The Europeans faced the hardships of exploration and the challenge of understanding populations that were new to them. The Europeans used their literature to explore their changing <u>perspective</u> on this new place, revealing their <u>values</u>.

54

Reading Strategy
Recognizing Signal Words
What change do the words "up to that time" signal? **16**

THOSE WHO
WENT DOWN
AND WHO
REACHED THEM
SWORE THAT
THEY WERE
TALLER THAN
THE GREAT
TOWER OF
SEVILLE.

---

down and who reached them swore that they were taller than the great tower of Seville.[3]

The party did not continue farther up the canyon of the river because of the lack of water. Up to that time they had gone one or two leagues inland in search of water every afternoon. When they had traveled four additional days the guides said that it was impossible to go on because no water would be found for three or four days, that when they themselves traveled through that land they took along women who brought water in gourds, that in those trips they buried the gourds of water for the return trip, and that they traveled in one day a distance that took us two days.

This was the Tizón river, much closer to its source than where Melchior Díaz and his men had crossed it. These Indians were of the same type, as it appeared later. From there Cárdenas and his men turned back, as that trip brought no other results.

---

3. **great tower of Seville** The Giralda, the tower on the Cathedral of Seville in Spain, rises above the cathedral more than twice its height.

Critical Reading

Cite textual evidence to support your responses.

© 1. **Key Ideas and Details (a)** In the Cabeza de Vaca narrative, what conflict in the party occurs immediately before the Native Americans begin to fall ill? **(b) Draw Conclusions:** What do the Native Americans believe is the cause of their sickness? Explain.

© 2. **Key Ideas and Details (a)** Why do the native people in the settled areas no longer plant corn? **(b)** What do they ask the Spaniards to do to fix this problem? **(c) Interpret:** What does this request suggest about the Native Americans' view of the Spaniards?

© 3. **Key Ideas and Details (a)** In the Cárdenas narrative, what natural feature are Cárdenas and his men sent to explore? **(b) Infer:** Why do you think Coronado sends the group on this mission? Explain.

© 4. **Key Ideas and Details (a) Compare and Contrast:** How does the appearance of the river and the boulders from the top of the gorge differ from the reality close up? **(b) Identify Cause and Effect:** In what ways do these differences in perspective affect the explorers?

© 5. **Integration of Knowledge and Ideas** Judging from these accounts, what are some of the challenges Europeans faced in exploring—and understanding—the Americas? In your response, use at least two of these Essential Question words: *perspective, values, respect, alter.* [Connecting to the Essential Question: *What is the relationship between literature and place?*]

54 Beginnings–1800

Concept Connector

Literary Analysis Graphic Organizer
Ask students to review the graphic organizers with which they have monitored their comprehension of problems and solutions in the two selections. Then have students share their organizers and compare their conclusions about the poet's meaning.

Activating Prior Knowledge
Have students return to their responses to the Activating Prior Knowledge activity. Ask them to explain whether their thoughts have changed and if so, how.

Connecting to the Essential Question
Have students compare the responses they gave to the prompt before reading the selections with their thoughts afterwards. Have them work individually or in groups, writing or discussing their thoughts, to define their new responses. Then lead a class discussion, probing for what students have learned that confirms or invalidates their initial thoughts. Encourage students to cite specific textual details to support their responses.

Literary Analysis

© **1. Key Ideas and Details** Which details in these **exploration narratives** suggest how the Native Americans viewed the Europeans? Explain your choices.

© **2. Integration of Knowledge and Ideas** **(a)** Why do you think the explorers in the Cárdenas party compare the boulders to the great tower of Seville? **(b)** What does this suggest about the ways in which people understand new experiences?

© **3. Craft and Structure** **(a)** Use a chart like this one to list four events from each account in **chronological order. (b)** Why might each explorer have felt a responsibility to create a clear sequence of events for his readers?

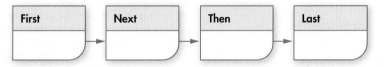

First	Next	Then	Last

4. Comparing Literary Works (a) Note two problems each explorer faced and the solutions each found. **(b)** How were they similar and different?

Reading Strategy

5. What type of relationship (time, sequence, reason, or contrast) is indicated by each of the italicized **signal words** in this passage? "*Nevertheless* we insisted, saying that we wanted to go there, and they *still* excused themselves as best they could, *until* at last we became angry."

PERFORMANCE TASKS
Integrated Language Skills

© Vocabulary Acquisition and Use

Use New Words Use the following word pairs correctly in sentences:

1. entreated/danger
2. feigned/surprise
3. advantageous/win
4. traversed/journey
5. successive/days
6. subsisted/food

Writing

© **Explanatory Text** Imagine that you are exploring a new territory. Write an **explorer's journal entry** that provides precise details about your discoveries. Choose a specific location and, if necessary, gather details through research so that your description is authentic. Share your draft with a partner. If your reader cannot "see" your description, replace weak words with vivid choices.
   Weak word choice: The river *was* ten miles from end to end.
   Strong word choice: The river *cut through* the mountains for ten miles.

from A Journey Through Texas • Boulders Taller Than the Great Tower of Seville **55**

Common Core State Standards

Writing
2.d. Use precise language.

Language
5. Demonstrate understanding of figurative language, word relationships, and nuances in word meanings.

Answers

1. The Native Americans gave Cabeza de Vaca's party numerous gifts, welcoming them.

2. **Possible response:** (a) Readers in Spain will be familiar with the great tower, so the comparison will make the scale of the canyon understandable. (b) People understand new experiences by comparing them to things with which they are familiar.

3. (a) **Sample answer:** First: Many Native Americans become sick. Next: Several die. Then: The Europeans pray for and minister to the sick. Last: Many of the sick begin to recover. (b) They wanted readers to understand the expedition.

4. (a) **Sample answer:** The Native Americans were afraid to take Cabeza de Vaca to an area where they had enemies. The solution was to send women, who could lead them without posing a threat. The López de Cárdenas party had difficulty finding a way down to the river. The solution was to search for several days to find a passable trail. (b) The problem faced by the Cabeza de Vaca party had to do with human fears. The problem faced by the López de Cárdenas party was caused by the terrain.

5. *Nevertheless,* contrast; *Still,* sequence; *Until,* sequence

Vocabulary Acquisition and Use
Sample responses:

1. He <u>entreated</u> me to take a road that would avoid <u>danger</u>.

2. She <u>feigned</u> <u>surprise</u> so that no one would know she had peeked at the gift.

3. An <u>advantageous</u> wind enabled our sailboat to <u>win</u>.

4. On our <u>journey,</u> we <u>traversed</u> several western states.

5. It rained for four <u>successive</u> <u>days.</u>

6. The lost hikers could not have <u>subsisted</u> without <u>food</u>.

Writing
Evaluate students' journal entries using the **Rubrics for Autobiographical Writing**, in *Professional Development Guidebook*, pages 248–249.

Assessment Resources

Unit 1 Resources

L1 L2 EL **Selection Test A,** pp. 64–66. Administer Test A to less-advanced students.

L3 L4 EL **Selection Test B,** pp. 67–69. Administer Test B to on-level and more-advanced students.

L3 L4 **Open-Book Test,** pp. 61–63. As an alternative, give the Open-Book Test.

All **Customizable Test Bank**

All **Self-tests**
Students may prepare for the **Selection Test** by taking the **Self-test** online.

 All assessment resources are available at **www.PHLitOnline.com.**

• *from* Of Plymouth Plantation
Lesson Pacing Guide

DAY 1 Preteach

- Ⓒ Administer the Reading and Vocabulary Warm-ups (*Unit 1 Resources*, pp. 70–73) as necessary.
- Ⓒ Introduce the Literary Analysis concept: Author's Purpose.
- • Introduce the Reading Strategy: Breaking Down Long Sentences.
- Ⓒ Build background with the author and Background features.
- • Develop thematic thinking with Connecting to the Essential Question.
- Ⓒ Teach the selection vocabulary.

DAYS 2–3 Preteach/Teach/Assess

- • Distribute copies of the appropriate graphic organizer for the Reading Strategy (*Graphic Organizer Transparencies*, pp. 13–14).
- • Distribute copies of the appropriate graphic organizer for Literary Analysis (*Graphic Organizer Transparencies*, pp. 15–16).
- • Prepare students to read with the Activating Prior Knowledge activities (TE).
- • Informally monitor comprehension while students read.
- • Use the Reading Check questions to confirm comprehension.
- Ⓒ Develop students' understanding of author's purpose using the Literary Analysis prompts.
- • Develop students' ability to break down long sentences using the Reading Strategy prompt.
- Ⓒ Reinforce vocabulary with the Vocabulary notes.
- • Assess students' comprehension and mastery of the skills by having them answer the Critical Reading, Literary Analysis, and Reading Strategy questions.
- Ⓒ Have students complete the Vocabulary Lesson.

DAY 4 Extend/Assess

- Ⓒ Have students complete the Writing Lesson and write an introduction to a speaker. (You may assign as homework.)
- • Administer Selection Test A or B (*Unit 1 Resources*, pp. 82–84 or 85–87).

Ⓒ **Common Core State Standards**

Reading Informational Text
6. Determine an author's point of view or purpose in a text in which the rhetoric is particularly effective, analyzing how style and content contribute to the power, persuasiveness, or beauty of the text.

Language 4.b. Identify and correctly use patterns of word changes that indicate different meanings or parts of speech.

Writing 7. Conduct short as well as more sustained research projects to answer a question or solve a problem; narrow or broaden the inquiry when appropriate; synthesize multiple sources on the subject, demonstrating understanding of the subject under investigation.

Speaking and Listening 6. Adapt speech to a variety of contexts and tasks, demonstrating a command of formal English when indicated or appropriate.

Additional Standards Practice
Common Core Companion, pp. 143–150; 240–244; 306–310; 324–331

Daily Block Scheduling
Each day in this Lesson Pacing Guide represents a 40–50 minute period. Teachers using block scheduling may combine days to revise pacing. In addition, teachers may differentiate and support core instruction by integrating components for extended and intensive support as students require. See the Guide to Selected Leveled Resources (facing page).

Guide to Selected Leveled Resources

R T I Tier 1 (students performing on level)

		from Of Plymouth Plantation
Warm Up	**Practice, model,** and **monitor** fluency, working **with the whole class** or **in groups.**	Vocabulary and Reading Warm-ups B, *Unit 1 Resources,* pp. 70–71, 73
Comprehension/Skills	**Support** and **monitor** comprehension and skills development, having students complete the activities, graphic organizers, and interactive prompts **independently** or **as a class.**	• *Reader's Notebook,* adapted instruction and summary **EL** *Reader's Notebook: English Learner's Version,* adapted instruction and summary • Reading Strategy Graphic Organizer B, *Graphic Organizer Transparencies,* p. 14 • Literary Analysis Graphic Organizer B, *Graphic Organizer Transparencies,* p. 16
Monitor Progress **A**	**Monitor** student progress with the differentiated curriculum-based assessment in the *Unit Resources.*	• **Selection Test B,** *Unit 1 Resources,* pp. 85–87 • **Open-Book Test,** *Unit 1 Resources,* pp. 79–81

R T I Tier 2 (students requiring intervention)

		from Of Plymouth Plantation
Warm Up	**Practice, model,** and **monitor** fluency **in groups** or **with individuals.**	• Vocabulary and Reading Warm-ups A, *Unit 1 Resources,* pp. 72–73 • *Hear It!* Audio CD
Comprehension/Skills	• **Support** and **monitor** comprehension and skills development, working **in small groups** or **with individuals.** • As students complete the selection in the appropriate version of the *Reader's Notebook,* **monitor** comprehension frequently with group questions and individual instruction. • **Model** strategies while guiding students in completing the activities and prompts in the *Reader's Notebook,* as well as the graphic organizers. • **Practice** skills and **monitor** mastery with the *Reading Kit* worksheets.	• *Reader's Notebook: Adapted Version,* adapted instruction and summary **EL** *Reader's Notebook: English Learner's Version,* adapted instruction and summary • Reading Strategy Graphic Organizer A, *Graphic Organizer Transparencies,* p. 13 • Literary Analysis Graphic Organizer A, *Graphic Organizer Transparencies,* p. 15 • *Reading Kit,* Practice worksheets
Monitor Progress **A**	**Monitor** student progress with the differentiated curriculum-based assessment in the *Unit Resources* and in the *Reading Kit.*	• **Selection Test A,** *Unit 1 Resources,* pp. 82–84 • *Reading Kit,* Assess worksheets

TIER 3 Tier 3 intervention may require consultation with the student's special-education or dyslexia specialist. For additional support, see the Tier 2 activities and resources listed above.

One-on-one teaching　　Group work　　Whole class instruction　　Independent work　　**A** Assessment

For a complete guide to selection support, including support for Advanced students, see the Overview of Resources in the frontmatter.

• *from* Of Plymouth Plantation

RESOURCES FOR:

L1 Special-Needs Students

L2 Below-Level Students (Tier 2)

L3 On-Level Students (Tier 1)

L4 Advanced Students (Tier 1)

EL English Learners

All All Students

Vocabulary/Fluency/Prior Knowledge

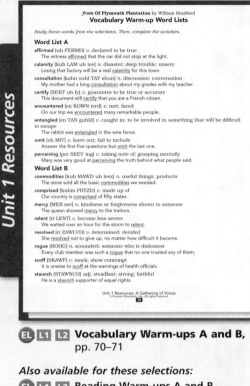

from Of Plymouth Plantation by William Bradford
Vocabulary Warm-up Word Lists

Study these words from the selections. Then, complete the activities.

Word List A

affirmed [uh FERMD] *v.* declared to be true
The witness affirmed that the car did not stop at the light.

calamity [kuh LAM uh tee] *n.* disaster; deep trouble; misery
Losing that factory will be a real calamity for this town.

consultation [kahn suhl TAY shun] *n.* discussion; conversation
My mother had a long consultation about my grades with my teacher.

certify [SERT uh fy] *v.* guarantee to be true or accurate
This document will certify that you are a French citizen.

encountered [en KOWN terd] *v.* met; faced
On our trip we encountered many remarkable people.

entangled [en TAN guhld] *v.* caught in; to be involved in something that will be difficult to escape
The rabbit was entangled in the wire fence.

omit [oh MIT] *v.* leave out; fail to include
Answer the first five questions but omit the last one.

perceiving [per SEEV ing] *v.* taking note of; grasping mentally
Mary was very good at perceiving the truth behind what people said.

Word List B

commodities [kuh MAWD uh teez] *n.* useful things; products
The store sold all the basic commodities we needed.

comprised [kuhm PRYZD] *v.* made up of
Our country is comprised of fifty states.

mercy [MER see] *n.* kindness or forgiveness shown to someone
The queen showed mercy to the traitors.

relent [ri LENT] *v.* become less severe
We waited over an hour for the storm to relent.

resolved [ri ZAWLVD] *v.* determined; decided
She resolved not to give up, no matter how difficult it became.

rogue [ROHG] *n.* scoundrel; someone who is dishonest
Every club member was such a rogue that no one trusted any of them.

scoff [SKAWF] *v.* mock; show contempt
It is unwise to scoff at the warnings of health officials.

staunch [STAWNCH] *adj.* steadfast; strong; faithful
He is a staunch supporter of equal rights.

Unit 1 Resources: A Gathering of Voices
© Pearson Education, Inc. All rights reserved.
70

Unit 1 Resources

EL L1 L2 **Vocabulary Warm-ups A and B,** pp. 70–71

Also available for these selections:

EL L1 L2 **Reading Warm-ups A and B,** pp. 72–73

All **Vocabulary Builder,** p. 76

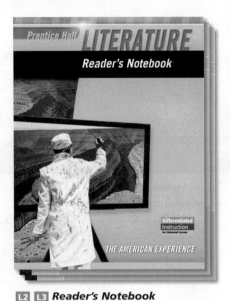

Reader's Notebooks

Pre- and postreading pages for this selections appear in an interactive format in the *Reader's Notebooks*. Each *Notebook* is differentiated for a different group of learners.
The selections in the Adapted and English Learner's versions are abridged.

L2 L3 *Reader's Notebook*

L1 *Reader's Notebook: Adapted Version*

EL *Reader's Notebook: English Learner's Version*

EL *Reader's Notebook: Spanish Version*

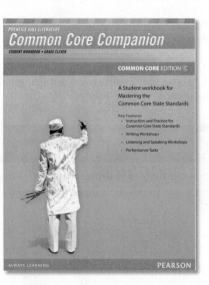

© *Common Core Companion*

Additional instruction and practice for each Common Core State Standard

Selection Support

Graphic Organizer Transparencies

EL L3 Literary Analysis: Graphic Organizer B, p. 16

Also available for these selections:

EL L1 L2 Reading: Graphic Organizer A, (partially filled in) p. 13

EL L3 Reading: Graphic Organizer B, p. 14

EL L1 L2 Literary Analysis: Graphic Organizer A (partially filled in), p. 15

Skills Development/Extension

Unit 1 Resources

L4 Enrichment, p. 78

Also available for these selections:

All Literary Analysis: Author's Purpose and Audience, p. 74

All Reading: Breaking Down Long Sentences, p. 75

EL L3 L4 Support for Writing, p. 77

Assessment

EL L1 L2 Selection Test A, pp. 82–84

Also available for these selections:

L3 L4 Open-Book Test, pp. 79–81

EL L3 L4 Selection Test B, pp. 85–87

PHLit Online!
www.PHLitOnline.com

Online Resources: All print materials are also available online.

- complete narrated selection text
- a thematically related video with writing prompt
- an interactive graphic organizer
- highlighting feature
- access to all student print resources, adapted to individual student needs
- Spanish and English summaries
- adapted selection translations in Spanish

Get Connected!

Also available:

Background Video (thematic video with writing prompt)
All videos are available in Spanish.

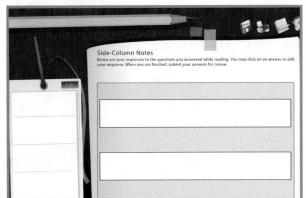

Writer's Journal (with graphics feature)

Also available:

Vocabulary Central (tools and activities for studying vocabulary)

❶ 🔍 **Connecting to the Essential Question**

1. Review the assignment. Ask students to focus on how they dealt with challenge. Have students complete the assignment.

2. Have students look for ways the settlers overcame challenges.

❷ Literary Analysis

Introduce the skill, using the instruction on the student page.

Think Aloud: Model the Skill

Say to students:

Determining an author's purpose can help me find my way through difficult writing. For example, I realize that Bradford's purpose is to persuade a new generation to hold to Puritan values. Keeping that purpose in mind, I have an easier time understanding the sentences in which he praises Puritan virtues—I will understand what he is getting at even if the ideas seem obscure.

❸ Reading Strategy

1. Introduce the strategy.

2. Give students a copy of **Reading Strategy Graphic Organizer B**, page 14, in *Graphic Organizer Transparencies.*

❹ Vocabulary

1. Pronounce each word, giving its definition; have students say it aloud.

2. Also see the *Classroom Strategies and Teaching Routines* card for vocabulary.

Before You Read | from *Of Plymouth Plantation*

❶ Connecting to the Essential Question William Bradford's account reveals courage and perseverance in the face of harsh circumstances. As you read, find details that show how the Pilgrims face and overcome challenges. Doing so will help as you consider the Essential Question: **What makes American literature American?**

❷ Literary Analysis

An **author's purpose** is his or her reason for writing. General purposes for writing are *to inform, to entertain,* and *to persuade.* Authors also have specific purposes that vary with the topic and **audience,** or readers. For example, Bradford wrote for an audience that included the children and grandchildren of the first settlers. He felt that young people were straying from the Pilgrims' faith. He wrote this account for two specific purposes:

- **To inform:** Bradford sought to tell the new generation about the Pilgrims' history.
- **To persuade:** Bradford sought to inspire the new generation to uphold Puritan values.

As you read, consider how the language, style, and content of the text help to advance Bradford's purposes for writing.

❸ Reading Strategy

© **Preparing to Read Complex Texts** Bradford wrote in *Puritan Plain Style,* which is relatively straightforward, but his writing can be challenging to modern readers. As you read, *monitor your understanding.* If you find you are not completely sure of the sequence of events or Bradford's insights, clarify the meaning by **breaking down long sentences.** To do so, separate a complex sentence into its essential parts—the subject (who or what) and the verb (action). This will help you isolate the main idea. As you read, use a chart like the one shown to analyze and interpret the meaning of complex sentences.

❹ Vocabulary

peril (per′ əl) *n.* danger (p. 59)

habitation (hab′ i tā′ shen) *n.* place to live; group of homes or dwellings (p. 60)

subject to (sub′ jikt too′) *adj.* likely to be affected by something (p. 61)

adversity (ad vʉr′ sə tē) *n.* hardship; difficulty (p. 61)

calamity (kə lam′ ə tē) *n.* disaster; catastrophe (p. 62)

relent (ri lent′) *v.* become less harsh; be more merciful (p. 62)

© **Common Core State Standards**

Reading Informational Text
6. Determine an author's point of view or purpose in a text in which the rhetoric is particularly effective, analyzing how style and content contribute to the power, persuasiveness, or beauty of the text.

Whole Sentence

Who	What

Central Point

56 Beginnings–1800

Vocabulary Development

Vocabulary Knowledge Rating
Create a **Vocabulary Knowledge Rating Chart** (in *Professional Development Guidebook,* p. 33) for the vocabulary words on the student page. Give each student a copy of the chart with the words on it. Read the words aloud and have students mark their rating in the Before Reading column. Urge students to attend to these words as they read and discuss the selection.

In order to gauge how much instruction is needed, tally how many students are confident in their knowledge of each word. As they read, point out the words and their context.

 **Vocabulary Central,** featuring tools and activities for vocabulary, is available at **www.PHLitOnline.com.**

⑤ William Bradford (1590–1657)

Author, *Of Plymouth Plantation*

Survival in North America was a matter of endurance, intelligence, and courage. William Bradford had all three qualities. Thirteen years after the first permanent English settlement was established in Jamestown, Virginia, Bradford helped lead the Pilgrims to what is now Massachusetts.

Seeking Freedom Bradford, who was born in Yorkshire, England, joined a group of Puritans who believed that the Church of England was corrupt. This group wished to separate from the church. In the face of stiff persecution, they eventually fled to Holland and from there sailed to North America. In *Of Plymouth Plantation,* Bradford provides an account of the experiences of these early settlers. Historians consider this account to be accurate.

A Long Leadership After the death of the colony's first leader, the Pilgrims elected Bradford governor. He was reelected thirty times. During his tenure, he organized the repayment of debts to financial backers, encouraged new immigration, and established good relations with the Native Americans, without whose help the colony never would have survived. He also instituted the town meeting within the colonies, a democratic process that continues to take place in state government today. Bradford was largely responsible for leading the infant colony through many hardships to success.

In 1630, Bradford began writing *Of Plymouth Plantation,* a firsthand account of the Pilgrims' struggle to endure, sustained only by courage and unbending faith. The work, written in the simple language known as Puritan Plain Style, was not published until 1856.

Our fathers were Englishmen which came over this great ocean, and were ready to perish in this wilderness.

from Of Plymouth Plantation **57**

from Of Plymouth Plantation

① ②

William Bradford

❶ About the Selection

William Bradford presents a firsthand description of the initial experiences of the Massachusetts settlers known to us as the Pilgrims. Historians consider this to be a factually accurate account. Bradford relates how this community of families, united in their goals and religious beliefs, begins the task of building a new settlement in the harsh wilderness. His account reflects religious faith, which he credits for the settlers' peaceful and beneficial relationship with their Native American neighbors.

❷ Activating Prior Knowledge

As students begin to read Bradford's narrative, have them form pairs to discuss the issues that potentially hostile neighbors must work out to survive when living near one another. Encourage students to consider the difficulties each party will face in such a situation.

Concept Connector ➜

Tell students they will return to their responses after reading the selection.

BACKGROUND In September of 1620, the tiny ship *Mayflower* set sail from Plymouth, England, bound for the Jamestown settlement in Virginia. The ship carried 102 Pilgrims, many of them members of a separatist religious congregation. During the stormy Atlantic crossing, the ship was blown off course, which forced it to miss its intended destination. The boat finally set anchor near Cape Cod, Massachusetts, in mid-November.

58 Beginnings–1800

© Text Complexity Rubric

from Of Plymouth Plantation

Qualitative Measures	
Context/Knowledge Demands	Historical knowledge demands (narrative) 1 2 3 ④ 5
Structure/Language Conventionality and Clarity	Seventeenth-century sentence structure and vocabulary (Puritan Plain Style) 1 2 3 ④ 5
Levels of Meaning/ Purpose/Concept Level	Accessible (description of settlement development) 1 2 ③ 4 5
Quantitative Measures	
Lexile	1440L	Text Length	Word Count: 2,482
Overall Complexity	More complex		

Reader and Task Suggestions

Preparing to Read the Text
- Using the information on SE p. 57, discuss why the Pilgrims came to America.
- Review with students the fact that the Pilgrims' faith extended to every area of their lives. Discuss how such faith would help Pilgrims cope with hardships.
- Guide students to use Multidraft Reading strategies (TE p. 57).

Leveled Tasks

Knowledge Demands If students will have difficulty with the context, have them first read to identify details that relate to matters of faith and then to focus on the concept of hardship.

Analyzing If students will not have difficulty with the context, have them read analyze how Bradford's conversational style makes his faith easier to understand.

from Chapter 9

Of Their Voyage and How They Passed the Sea; and of Their Safe Arrival at Cape Cod

[1620] SEPTEMBER 6 . . . After they[1] had enjoyed fair winds and weather for a season, they were encountered many times with cross-winds, and met with many fierce storms, with which the ship was shrewdly[2] shaken, and her upper works made very leaky; and one of the main beams in the mid ships was bowed and cracked, which put them in some fear that the ship could not be able to perform the voyage. So some of the chief of the company, perceiving the mariners to fear the sufficiency of the ship, as appeared by their mutterings, they entered into serious consultation with the master and other officers of the ship, to consider in time of the danger; and rather to return than to cast themselves into a desperate and inevitable peril. And truly there was great distraction and difference of opinion amongst the mariners themselves; fain[3] would they do what could be done for their wages' sake (being now half the seas over), and on the other hand they were loath to hazard their lives too desperately. But in examining of all opinions, the master and others affirmed they knew the ship to be strong and firm under water; and for the buckling of the main beam, there was a great iron screw the passengers brought out of Holland, which would raise the beam into his place; the which being done, the carpenter and master affirmed that with a post under it, set firm in the lower deck, and other ways bound, he would make it sufficient. And as for the decks and upper works, they would caulk them as well as they could, and though with the working of the ship they would not long keep staunch,[4] yet there would otherwise be no great danger, if they did not over-press her with sails. So they committed themselves to the will of God, and resolved to proceed.

In sundry of these storms the winds were so fierce, and the seas so high, as they could not bear a knot of sail, but were forced to hull,[5] for diverse day together. And in one of them, as they thus lay at hull, in a mighty storm, a lusty[6] young man (called John Howland) coming upon some occasion above the gratings, was, with a seele[7] of the ship thrown into [the sea]; but it pleased God that he caught hold of the topsail halyards,[8] which hung overboard, and ran out at length; yet he held his hold (though he was sundry

◄ Critical Viewing
How does this photograph of a *Mayflower* replica help you better understand the Pilgrims' experience? **[Connect]**

Vocabulary
peril (per´ əl) *n.* danger

Reading Check
How is the ship damaged in the storm?

---

1. **they** Even though Bradford is one of the Pilgrims, he refers to them in the third person.
2. **shrewdly** (shrōōd´ lē) *adv.* severely.
3. **fain** (fān) *adv.* gladly.
4. **staunch** (stônch) *adj.* watertight.
5. **hull** *v.* drift with the wind.
6. **lusty** *adj.* strong; hearty.
7. **seele** *n.* rolling; pitching to one side.
8. **halyards** (hal´ yərdz) *n.* ropes for raising or lowering sails.

from Of Plymouth Plantation **59**

---

❸ Reading Strategy
Breaking Down Long Sentences

1. Point out to students that Bradford's style is notable for its clarity—despite the considerable length and apparent complexity of some sentences.

2. Help students break down the first sentence into sections. Draw students' attention to signal words (such as *after, and,* and *which*) that indicate relationships among ideas and events.

❹ Critical Viewing

Answer: The ship's bow, which is not exceptionally large (we see only five figures at the bow), is not too distant from its stern. In other words, this is a small vessel. Given mention of "the stormy Atlantic crossing," the smallness of the ship probably made for a rough voyage.

❺ Reading Check

Answer: The ship is shaken and damaged by the wind and seas: in addition to leaks, the ship sustains a crack in a main beam amidships.

This selection is available in interactive format in the **Enriched Online Student Edition,** at **www.PHLitOnline.com**, which includes a thematically related video with a writing prompt and an interactive graphic organizer.

❻ The American Experience

History Connection

Historians have been unable to locate any detailed description of the original *Mayflower*. The dimensions given in The American Experience note represent their best estimate.

Connect to the Literature

Have students read The American Experience feature; next, share the fact given above. Then, **ask** the Connect to the Literature questions: What details in *Of Plymouth Plantation* suggest the kinds of challenges the travelers faced on the journey? What other challenges do you think travelers might face on a ship this size?

Possible answers: Bradford mentions crosswinds and fierce storms that threatened to destroy the ship and caused some passengers to fall overboard. On a ship this size, the travelers might have faced problems of disease or hunger.

❼ Reading Strategy

Breaking Down Long Sentences

1. Remind students that long sentences can be broken down to their two essential parts: (1) Who or What; (2) Action.

2. Direct students' attention to the sentence that begins with "Being thus arrived." Working with **Reading Strategy Graphic Organizer B**, page 14 in *Graphic Organizer Transparencies,* help students see that Who/What is *they* (the Pilgrims) and that the Action is *fell* (upon their knees) *and blessed* (the God of heaven).

3. You may want to acknowledge that the sentence contains another subject, *who,* and other verbs, *had brought . . . and delivered.* They, however, are subordinate—that is, less important—because they are the subject and verbs of the subordinate (or dependent) clause that describes *the God of heaven.* The main subject and verbs are those of the main clause, examined above.

---

❻ The *American* EXPERIENCE

HISTORY CONNECTION

The *Mayflower* was the British ship on which 102 Pilgrims sailed from Southampton, England, to North America during September, October, and November of 1620. In November, the Pilgrims disembarked at the tip of Cape Cod. Shortly before Christmas, they moved to the more protected site of Plymouth, Massachusetts. According to historians' estimates, the square-rigged *Mayflower* probably measured about 90 feet long and weighed 180 tons.

Connect to the Literature

What details in *Of Plymouth Plantation* suggest the kinds of challenges the travelers faced on the journey? What other challenges do you think travelers might face on a ship this size?

Vocabulary
habitation (hab´ i tā´ shen) *n.* place to live; group of homes or dwellings

---

fathoms under water) till he was held up by the same rope to the brim of the water, and then with a boat hook and other means got into the ship again, and his life saved; and though he was something ill with it, yet he lived many years after, and became a profitable member both in church and commonwealth. In all this voyage there died but one of the passengers, which was William Butten, a youth, servant to Samuel Fuller, when they drew near the coast.

But to omit other things (that I may be brief), after long beating at sea they fell with that land which is called Cape Cod; the which being made and certainly known to be it, they were not a little joyful. After some deliberation had amongst themselves and with the master of the ship, they tacked about[9] and resolved to stand for the southward (the wind and weather being fair) to find some place about Hudson's River for their habitation. But after they had sailed that course about half the day, they fell amongst dangerous shoals[10] and roaring breakers, and they were so far entangled therewith as they conceived themselves in great danger; and the wind shrinking upon them withal,[11] they resolved to bear up again for the Cape, and thought themselves happy to get out of those dangers before night overtook them, as by God's providence they did. And the next day they got into the Cape harbor,[12] where they rid in safety. . . .

Being thus arrived in a good harbor and brought safe to land, they fell upon their knees and blessed the God of heaven, who had brought them over the vast and furious ocean, and delivered them from all the perils and miseries thereof, again to set their feet on the firm and stable earth, their proper element. . . .

But here I cannot but stay and make a pause, and stand half amazed at this poor people's present condition; and so I think will the reader too, when he well considers the same. Being thus passed the vast ocean, and a sea of troubles before in their preparation (as may be remembered by that which went before), they had now no friends to welcome them, nor inns to entertain or refresh their weather-beaten bodies, no houses or much less towns to repair to, to seek for succor.[13] It is recorded in Scripture[14] as a mercy to the apostle and his shipwrecked company, that the barbarians

9. **tacked about** sailed back and forth so the wind would hit the sails at the best angles.
10. **shoals** (shōlz) *n.* sandbars or shallow areas that are dangerous to navigate.
11. **withal** (with ôl´) *adv.* also.
12. **Cape harbor** now called Provincetown Harbor.
13. **succor** (suk´ ər) *n.* help; relief.
14. **Scripture** In Acts 27–28, when the Apostle Paul and a group of other Christians are shipwrecked on the island of Malta, they are treated kindly by the "barbarians" who live there.

Enrichment: Building Context

Immigrants in America
Discuss the idea that some of today's immigrants to the United States also face hardships—similar to and different from those faced by the immigrants to Plymouth.

Activity: Comparison and Contrast First, have students conduct research into obstacles immigrants face today—say, learning the language, finding housing, finding employment, and dealing with earlier settlers in the area. If students record findings in the **Enrichment: Building**

Context worksheet, *Professional Development Guidebook,* page 222, they will have a place to note the insights their research gives into the Bradford excerpt.

Second, have students devise ways to present comparisons and contrasts between today's immigrants and those of 1620. Students may use words, visuals, or a combination of both in their comparison-and-contrast projects.

showed them no small kindness in refreshing them, but these savage barbarians, when they met with them (as after will appear) were readier to fill their sides full of arrows then otherwise. And for the season it was winter, and they that know the winters of that country know them to be sharp and violent, and *subject to* cruel and fierce storms, dangerous to travel to known places, much more to search an unknown coast. Besides, what could they see but a hideous and desolate wilderness, full of wild beasts and wild men? And what multitudes there might be of them they knew not. . . . What could now sustain them but the spirit of God and his grace? May not and ought not the children of these fathers rightly say: *Our fathers were Englishmen which came over this great ocean, and were ready to perish in this wilderness;*[15] *but they cried unto the Lord, and He heard their voice, and looked on their* adversity, *etc.*[16] *Let them therefore praise the Lord, because He is good, and His mercies endure forever.* . . .

from Book 2[17]

[1620] In these hard and difficult beginnings, they found some discontents and murmurings arise amongst some, and mutinous speeches and carriages in others; but they were soon quelled and overcome by the wisdom, patience, and just and equal carriage of things by the Governor[18] and better part, which cleaved faithfully together in the main. But that which was most sad and lamentable was that in two or three months' time, half of their company died, especially in January and February, being the depth of winter, and wanting houses and other comforts; being infected with the scurvy[19] and other diseases, which this long voyage and their inaccommodate[20] condition had brought upon them; so as there died sometimes two or three of a day, in the foresaid time; that of one hundred and odd persons, scarce fifty remained.

And of these in the time of most distress, there was but six or seven sound persons, who, to their great commendations be it spoken, spared no pains, night nor day, but with abundance of toil and hazard of their own health, fetched them wood, made them fires, dressed them meat, made their beds, washed their loathsome clothes, clothed and unclothed them; in a word, did all the homely[21] and necessary offices for them which dainty and queasy stomachs

Vocabulary
subject to (sub´ jikt t$\overline{oo}$) *adj.* likely to be affected by something

adversity (ad vɝr´ si tē) *n.* hardship; difficulty

Reading Check

What season was it when the Pilgrims arrived in Cape Cod?

---

15. **wilderness** Bradford is comparing the Pilgrims to the ancient Hebrews, who wandered in the desert after fleeing Egypt and before reaching the Promised Land.
16. **they cried . . . etc.** Bradford is paraphrasing a passage from the Hebrew Bible (Deuteronomy 26:7).
17. **Book 2** Here Bradford switches from chapter divisions to book divisions.
18. **Governor** John Carver (c. 1576–1621) was the first governor of Plymouth Colony but died during his first year of office. Bradford succeeded him as governor.
19. **scurvy** (skɝr´ vē) *n.* disease cause by a vitamin C deficiency.
20. **inaccommodate** (in´ ə käm´ ə dāt´) *adj.* unfit.
21. **homely** *adj.* domestic.

from Of Plymouth Plantation **61**

❓ Engaging the Essential Question

1. Remind students of the Essential Question—What makes American literature American?—and help them apply that question to this passage.

2. **Ask** why Bradford invokes "the Lord" when reporting the health of some men while so many others fell ill.
Possible response: Bradford has no other way of explaining the health of some people during the calamity, so in this piece he does not hesitate to refer to his faith time and time again, in effect stamping early-American literature with a religious accent.

⑪ Literary Analysis

Author's Purpose

1. Remind students of Bradford's general and specific purposes, defined on page 56.

2. Then **ask** the Literary Analysis question: Why do you think Bradford describes in such detail the different reactions of the crew and the Pilgrims to the illness?
Possible answer: Bradford wants to show that the Pilgrims' faith and values produce a sharp difference between their behavior and that of the crew. Bradford clinches this point when he quotes the boatswain: "O! you, I now see, show your love like Christians . . . but we let one another lie and die like dogs."

Vocabulary
calamity (kə lam′ ə tē) *n.* disaster; catastrophe

⑩

Literary Analysis
Author's Purpose
Why do you think Bradford describes in such detail the different reactions of the crew and the Pilgrims to the illness?

⑪

Vocabulary
relent (ri lent′) *v.* become less harsh; be more merciful

⑧ cannot endure to hear named; and all this willingly and cheerfully, without any grudging in the least, showing herein their true love unto their friends and brethren. A rare example and worthy to be remembered. Two of these seven were Mr. William Brewster,[22] their reverend Elder, and Myles Standish,[23] their Captain and military commander, unto whom myself, and many others were much beholden in our low and sick condition. And yet the Lord so upheld these persons, as in this general calamity they were not at all infected either with sickness, or lameness. And what I have said of these, I may say of many others who died in this general visitation,[24] and others yet living, that whilst they had health, yea, or any strength continuing, they were not wanting to any that had need of them. And I doubt not but their recompense is with the Lord.

But I may not here pass by another remarkable passage not to be forgotten. As this calamity fell among the passengers that were to be left here to plant, and were hasted ashore and made to drink water, that the seamen might have the more beer, and one[25] in his sickness desiring but a small can of beer, it was answered that if he were their own father he should have none; the disease began to fall amongst them also, so as almost half of their company died before they went away, and many of their officers and lustiest men, as the boatswain, gunner, three quartermasters, the cook, and others. At which the master was something stricken and sent to the sick ashore and told the Governor he should send for beer for them that had need of it, though he drunk water homeward bound.

But now amongst his company there was far another kind of carriage[26] in this misery then amongst the passengers; for they that had been boon[27] companions in drinking and jollity in the time of their health and welfare began now to desert one another in this calamity, saying they would not hazard their lives for them, they should be infected by coming to help them in their cabins, and so, after they came to die by it, would do little or nothing for them, but if they died let them die. But such of the passengers as were yet aboard showed them what mercy they could, which made some of their hearts relent, as the boatswain (and some others), who was a proud young man, and would often curse and scoff at the passengers; but when he grew weak, they had compassion on

22. **William Brewster** (1567–1644) one of the Pilgrim leaders.
23. **Myles Standish** (c. 1584–1656) professional soldier hired by the Pilgrims to be their military advisor. He was not originally a Puritan but later became a member of the congregation.
24. **visitation** *n.* affliction.
25. **one** Bradford is referring to himself.
26. **carriage** *n.* behavior.
27. **boon** *adj.* close.

Think Aloud

Vocabulary: Using Context
Point out the word *hazard* in the last paragraph on this page. Use the following "think aloud" to model the skill of using context to infer the meaning of the word. Say to students:
I may not immediately know the meaning of *hazard,* but because it's in the phrase *would not hazard,* I know it's a verb. What I have to figure out is whether *they would not hazard their lives* means that they are self-interested—that "they would not endanger their lives" for their companions—or means the opposite, that they are unselfish—that "they would not hesitate to risk their lives." Given the earlier remark that the companions "now began to desert one another in this calamity," I conclude that *they would not hazard their lives* means "they would not risk their lives" and that the verb *hazard* itself must mean something like "to expose to danger."

Jennie Brownscombe (1850–1936) was an American illustrator known for her detailed, nostalgic images. In fact, she has been called a kind of Norman Rockwell (1894–1978) for her time. From a young age, Brownscombe earned a living creating illustrations for books, magazines, Christmas cards, and calendars. Her skillful presentation of images won her awards, and her work has been exhibited around the world.

This famous symbolic painting is known for providing an emotional image of what people across the United States have come to know as Thanksgiving. Use this question for discussion:

> How does this painting echo Bradford's narrative?
> **Answer:** It shows the colonists at Plymouth as a community, and it portrays a peaceful gathering with Native Americans. The scene also appears to be very solemn, religious, and low-key—the same mood Bradford creates in his narrative.

him and helped him; then he confessed he did not deserve it at their hands, he had abused them in word and deed. O! saith he, you, I now see, show your love like Christians indeed one to another, but we let one another lie and die like dogs. . . .

All this while the Indians came skulking about them, and would sometimes show themselves aloof of, but when any approached near them, they would run away. And once they stole away their tools where they had been at work, and were gone to dinner. But about the 16th of March a certain Indian came boldly amongst them, and spoke to them in broken English, which they could well understand, but marveled at it. At length they understood by discourse with him that he was not of these parts, but belonged to the eastern parts, where some English ships came to fish, with whom he was acquainted, and could name sundry of them by their names, amongst whom he had got his language. He became profitable to them in acquainting them with many things concerning the state of the country in the east parts where he lived, which was afterwards profitable unto them; as also of the people here, of their names, number, and strength; of their situation and distance from this place, and who was chief amongst them. His name was Samoset;[28] he told them also of another Indian whose name was Squanto,[29] a native of this place, who had been

---

28. **Samoset** (sam´ə set´) (d. 1655) a Pemaquid tribal chief from Maine.
29. **Squanto** (skwän´tō) (d. 1622) a member of the Pawtuxet tribe who in 1614 had been kidnapped by an English sea captain and taken to Spain to be sold as a slave. He escaped and eventually returned to Massachusetts in 1619, only to find that his home village had been destroyed by plague.

▲ Critical Viewing
Do you think this picture is an accurate representation of the first Thanksgiving? Why or why not? **[Judge; Support]**

Reading Check

Who is Samoset, and how do the Pilgrims meet him?

from Of Plymouth Plantation **63**

⓭ Critical Viewing

Possible answer: Students may say that most of the items in the painting seem historically accurate, but the log cabin and the Native Americans' head feathers may be inaccurate.

⓮ Reading Check

Answer: Samoset is a Native American from lands east of Plymouth. He learned basic English while living in the vicinity of English fishing parties. The Pilgrims meet Samoset after he approaches their settlement and addresses them.

Differentiated
Instruction for Universal Access

Culturally Responsive Instruction

Culture Focus Bradford describes Samoset's speech as "broken English." Challenge students to find a good label to describe one's ability to learn English as a second language—perhaps *elementary English, emerging English,* or *developing English.* The goal is to create appreciation for the effort required to gain fluency in a second language after the age of twelve or so.

In her essay "Mother Tongue," Amy Tan warns against the terms *broken* or *fractured* or *limited English.* Even though her Chinese mother never spoke perfect English, she was fully capable of reading, listening to, and understanding sophisticated financial reports in English.

1. Remind students that all sentences contain two parts—(1) Who or What; (2) Action.

2. **Ask** the Reading Strategy question: What is the essential action described in the sentence beginning "Being, after some time"?
   Answer: The action is Samoset's revisit, return of tools, and preparation for a visit by Massasoit.

▶ **Monitor Progress Ask** who the sentence beginning with "Being" on the first line of page 64 is about.
   Answer: The subject is Samoset.

▶ **Reteach:** If students have trouble finding the subject and verb of each main clause, write the complete sentence on the board; then cross out everything but the subjects (underlined once) and the verbs (underlined twice). This process may reteach students to look always for the Who/What and the Action.

~~Being, after some time of entertainment and gifts, dismissed,~~ ~~a while after~~ <u>he</u> <u>came</u> ~~again,~~ ~~and 5 more with him, and~~ <u>they</u> <u>brought</u> ~~again all the tools~~ ~~that were stolen away before,~~ <u>and made way</u> ~~for the coming~~ ~~of their great sachem, called~~ ~~Massasoit, who, about four or~~ ~~five days after, came with the~~ ~~chief of his friends, and other~~ ~~attendance, with the aforesaid~~ ~~Squanto.~~

⓰ Literary Analysis

Author's Purpose

1. Remind students that authors have a general purpose—such as to inform—and a more specific one—such as to tell the new generation about the Pilgrims' history.

2. **Ask** the Literary Analysis question: Why do you think Bradford refers to Squanto as a "special instrument"?
   Possible answer: He is reminding his audience that the Pilgrims' belief in God is an active, benevolent presence in everyday life.

Reading Strategy
Breaking Down Long Sentences What is the essential action described in the sentence beginning "Being, after some time..."? **⓯**

Literary Analysis
Author's Purpose Why do you think Bradford refers to Squanto as a "special instrument"? **⓰**

in England and could speak better English then himself. Being, after some time of entertainment and gifts, dismissed, a while after he came again, and 5 more with him, and they brought again all the tools that were stolen away before, and made way for the coming of their great sachem,[30] called Massasoit,[31] who, about four or five days after, came with the chief of his friends, and other attendance, with the aforesaid Squanto. With whom, after friendly entertainment, and some gifts given him, they made a peace with him (which hath now continued this 24 years)[32] in these terms:

1. That neither he nor any of his should injure or do hurt to any of their people.
2. That if any of his did any hurt to any of theirs, he should send the offender, that they might punish him.
3. That if anything were taken away from any of theirs, he should cause it to be restored; and they should do the like to his.
4. If any did unjustly war against him, they would aid him; if any did war against them, he should aid them.
5. He should send to his neighbors confederates, to certify them of this, that they might not wrong them, but might be likewise comprised in the conditions of peace.
6. That when their men came to them, they should leave their bows and arrows behind them.

After these things he returned to his place called Sowams,[33] some 40 mile from this place, but Squanto continued with them and was their interpreter, and was a special instrument sent of God for their good beyond their expectation. He directed them how to set their corn, where to take fish and to procure other commodities, and was also their pilot to bring them to unknown places for their profit, and never left them till he died. He was a native of this place, and scarce any left alive besides himself. He was carried away with diverse others by one Hunt,[34] a master of a ship, who thought to sell them for slaves in Spain; but he got away for England and was entertained by a merchant in London and employed to Newfoundland and other parts, and lastly brought hither into these parts. . . .

---

30. **sachem** (sā´ chəm) chief.
31. **Massasoit** (mas´ ə soit´) (c. 1580–1661) the supreme sachem (chief) of the Wampanoag peoples.
32. **now . . . 24 years** The treaty actually lasted until King Philip's War began in 1675.
33. **Sowams** (sō´ ämz) present site of Warren, Rhode Island.
34. **Hunt** Thomas Hunt was captain of one of the ships in John Smith's expedition to Virginia.

Vocabulary Development

Vocabulary Knowledge Rating

When students have completed reading and discussing the selection, have them take out their **Vocabulary Knowledge Rating** charts for the selection. Read the words aloud and have students rate their knowledge of the words again in the After Reading column. Clarify any words that are still problematic. Have students write their own definitions and example or sentence in the appropriate column. Then have students complete the Vocabulary Lesson at the end of the selection. Encourage students to use the words in further discussion and written work about the selection. Remind them that they will be accountable for these words on the **Selection Test,** *Unit 1 Resources,* pages 82–84 or 85–87.

[1621] . . . They began now to gather in the small harvest they had,[35] and to fit up their houses and dwellings against winter, being all well recovered in health and strength, and had all things in good plenty; for as some were thus employed in affairs abroad, others were exercised in fishing, about cod and bass and other fish, of which they took good store, of which every family had their portion. All the summer there was no want. And now began to come in store of fowl, as winter approached, of which this place did abound when they came first (but afterward decreased by degrees). And besides water fowl, there was great store of wild turkeys, of which they took many, besides venison, etc. Besides they had about a peck of meal a week to a person, or now since harvest, Indian corn to that proportion. Which made many afterwards write so largely of their plenty here to their friends in England, which were not feigned, but true reports.

35. **They . . . had** This section of Bradford's narrative is often titled "The First Thanksgiving."

Critical Reading

1. **Key Ideas and Details (a)** What were some of the hardships the Pilgrims faced during their trip across the Atlantic and their first winter at Plymouth? **(b) Interpret:** What do their troubles tell you about the climate and landscape of Plymouth?

2. **Key Ideas and Details (a) Draw Conclusions:** What message do you think Bradford is trying to convey in this narrative? **(b) Apply:** How might the message have meaning for people today?

3. **Integration of Knowledge and Ideas Hypothesize:** In what ways might this account have been different if the Pilgrims had settled farther south?

4. **Integration of Knowledge and Ideas Evaluate:** Has this account changed your impression of the Pilgrims? Explain your answer.

5. **Integration of Knowledge and Ideas** How are the Pilgrims' values and beliefs evident in the ways they respond to problems? In your response, use at least two of these Essential Question words: *just, commitment, gratitude, conviction. [Connecting to the Essential Question: What makes American literature American?]*

Cite textual evidence to support your responses.

from Of Plymouth Plantation **65**

Concept Connector

Reading Strategy Graphic Organizer
Ask to see the graphic organizers in which students broke down long sentences into their essential parts and then stated their central points. Have students share their organizers and compare them.

Activating Prior Knowledge
Return to responses in the Activating Prior Knowledge activity. Ask students to explain whether their thoughts have changed and if so, how.

Connecting to the Essential Question
Have students compare the responses they gave to the prompt before they completed the work with their thoughts after. Have them work alone or in groups, writing or discussing their thoughts, to formulate new responses. Then probe for what students have learned that confirms or invalidates their initial thoughts. Encourage students to cite specific textual details to support their responses.

Answers

1. **Possible response:** Bradford wrote to convey the difficulties the Pilgrims faced. He wrote for a generation born in America.

2. **Sample detail:** The damage to the ship illustrates the travelers' fears; it underscores their bravery; it contributes to Bradford's depiction of their virtues.

3. (a) Bradford sees religious meaning in the decision to continue onward; the recovery of Howland ("it pleased God"); the ship's arrival at a good harbor; sparing some Pilgrims to care for others; the boatswain's repentance; the help from Squanto. (b) Seeing these incidents as religious underscores Bradford's purpose—to make the new generation appreciate the first.

4. Students should explain the reasons they think that Bradford did or did not fulfill his purpose.

5. **Sample similarity:** Both audiences forget sacrifices by preceding generations. **Sample difference:** Modern readers may need multimedia—not just words—to focus.

6. Some modern readers may emphasize morality and religion as centrally as earlier ones.

7. (a) The first audience might have seen Native Americans as inferior. (b) Today's readers know about the suffering that Europeans caused them.

8. **Sample response:** (a) "And now began to come in store of fowl, as winter approached, of which this place did abound when they came first (but afterward decreased by degrees)." (b) The subject is "store of fowl"; the verb is "began (to come in)." (c) As winter approached, so grew the supply of fowl, which were abundant in the area but later decreased.

9. **Sample response:** (a) "He should send to his neighbors confederates to certify them of this, that they might not wrong them, but might be likewise comprised in the conditions of peace." (b) He would get word to other Native Americans of the peace, a peace that they too must honor.

Literary Analysis

1. **Craft and Structure** Complete these sentences to describe Bradford's **purpose** for writing and the **audience** he wanted to reach:
   • Bradford wrote *Of Plymouth Plantation* in order to _____.
   • He wrote this historical account for an audience that included _____.

2. **Craft and Structure** Use a chart like the one shown to explore how specific details in Bradford's account help him achieve his purpose for writing. **(a)** Choose four details, descriptions, or incidents that you think are especially important to Bradford's narrative. **(b)** For each one, explain why you think Bradford chose to include it and how it helped him achieve his overall purpose for writing.

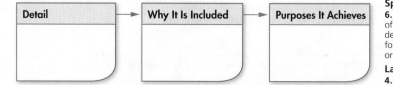

3. **Key Ideas and Details (a)** At what points does Bradford see religious or spiritual meaning in incidents that happen to the Pilgrims as a whole or to individuals? **(b)** In what ways does this both reflect his beliefs and support one of his purposes for writing?

4. **Integration of Knowledge and Ideas** Do you think Bradford succeeded in writing a document that fulfilled his original purpose? Explain why or why not.

5. **Integration of Knowledge and Ideas** In what ways are modern readers both similar to and different from Bradford's original audience?

6. **Integration of Knowledge and Ideas** Do you think that modern readers respond in the same way to Bradford's moral and religious goals as did his original readers? Explain.

7. **Integration of Knowledge and Ideas (a)** How might Bradford's first audience have responded to his depiction of Native Americans? **(b)** In what ways do today's readers bring a different perspective to this element of his narrative?

Reading Strategy

8. **(a)** Choose three sentences from the narrative that you find particularly challenging to understand. **(b) Break down the long sentences** into their essential parts—the subject and the verb. **(c)** Write the meaning of each sentence as you understand it.

9. **(a)** Choose a complex sentence and read it aloud at least twice, using punctuation to guide where to pause. **(b)** Then, restate the meaning of the sentence in simplified form.

Common Core State Standards

Writing
7. Conduct short as well as more sustained research projects to answer a question or solve a problem; narrow or broaden the inquiry when appropriate; synthesize multiple sources on the subject, demonstrating understanding of the subject under investigation. *(p. 67)*

Speaking and Listening
6. Adapt speech to a variety of contexts and tasks, demonstrating a command of formal English when indicated or appropriate. *(p. 67)*

Language
4.b. Identify and correctly use patterns of word changes that indicate different meanings or parts of speech. *(p. 67)*

Assessment Practice

Supporting Details (For more practice, see *All-in-One Workbook*.)

Students should recognize which details are important to the main idea and which not. Present the following sample item; the text is from *The General History of Virginia*:

> With this lodging and diet, our extreme toil in bearing and planting palisades so strained and bruised us and our continual labor in the extremity of the heat had so weakened us, as were cause sufficient to have made us so miserable in our native country or any other place in the world.

Which of the following does *not* support the main idea that early Virginians were miserable?
A They were weak from planting.
B They had little food.
C The heat was extreme.
D They were in conflict with the local Native Americans.

All of these support the main idea *except* choice D.

Integrated Language Skills

© Vocabulary Acquisition and Use

Word Analysis: Related Forms of *peril*

The word *peril* comes from the Latin word *periculum*, which means "danger." Using your knowledge of the base word, fill in each blank with the word that best completes the sentence.

  a. perilous **b.** perilously **c.** imperiled

1. Undertaking the risky voyage _____ the Pilgrims' lives.
2. The ship tossed _____ in the waves.
3. Building a new home in the wilderness was a _____ undertaking.

Vocabulary: Antonyms or Synonyms

Antonyms are words that have opposite meanings. Synonyms are words that have similar meanings. Decide whether the words in each of the following pairs are antonyms or synonyms. Then, explain your reasoning.

1. calamity, misfortune
2. relent, intensify
3. subject to, prone
4. adversity, ease
5. peril, safety
6. habitation, dwelling

Writing

© **Explanatory Text** Imagine that time travel is possible and William Bradford is coming to speak at your school. Write the opening **speech** that will be used to introduce him to the assembly. Include information about his life and achievements, and explain why his perspective will be valuable to the audience.

Prewriting Reread the biography of Bradford on page 57 and the excerpt from his narrative. In a chart like the one shown, record questions you still have about Bradford. Then, use both print and electronic sources to find answers to these questions. Document answers and sources in your chart.

Using Clear Research Questions

Research Question	Answer	Source
1.		
2.		
3.		

Drafting As you draft, strike a tone that is informative and respectful, but friendly. Avoid using words that are either too complicated or too casual. Use appropriate formal English, but try to sound natural and fresh, rather than stiff or overly proper. To check your tone, pause to read your work aloud to yourself.

Revising Reread your introduction and make sure that all of the facts you have included are accurate. Double-check specific details and correct them as needed. Finally, read your work aloud as though you are delivering it for an audience. Replace words or sections that sound artificial or forced.

Vocabulary Acquisition and Use

1. Introduce the skill, using the instruction on the student page.
2. Have students complete the Word Analysis activity and the Vocabulary practice.

Word Analysis
1. c. imperiled
2. b. perilously
3. a. perilous

Vocabulary
1. synonyms: Both *calamity* and *misfortune* are negative experiences.
2. antonyms: *Relent* means "to become less"; *intensify* means the opposite.
3. synonyms: Both *subject to* and *prone* deal with likelihood or tendency.
4. antonyms: *Adversity* means "difficulty," which is the opposite of *ease.*
5. antonyms: *Peril* means "danger," which is the opposite of *safety.*
6. synonyms: A *habitation* is a *dwelling* and vice versa.

Writing
1. To guide students in writing this introduction, give them the **Support for Writing** page (*Unit 1 Resources,* p. 77).
2. Remind students that their introduction should contain accurate information and should sound respectful but friendly, not stiff or formal.
3. If students have trouble coming up with research questions, suggest that they ask why Bradford did not stay in Holland.
4. Use the **Rubrics for Summary** or the **Rubrics for Biography** in the *Professional Development Guidebook,* pages 272–273 or pages 278–279, to evaluate students' work.

Assessment Resources

Unit 1 Resources
- **L1 L2 EL Selection Test A,** pp. 82–84. Administer Test A to less advanced students and English learners.
- **L3 L4 EL Selection Test B,** pp. 85–87. Administer Test B to on-level or more advanced students.
- **L3 L4 Open-Book Test,** pp. 79–81. As an alternative, give the Open-Book Test.

- **All Customizable Test Bank**
- **All Self-tests** Students may prepare for the **Selection Test** by taking the **Self-test** online.

PHLit Online! All assessment resources are available at **www.PHLitOnline.com**.

Contemporary Connection

"Mission Update" reproduces information first published in a blog on the Internet. Depending on access, you may wish to use a computer in the classroom to present the latest information about the Mars Exploration Rover project and to demonstrate the use of blogs.

Exploration Past and Present

1. Since it is a relatively recent NASA project, many students may be familiar with the Mars Exploration Rover venture. Ask volunteers to share what they know. Students may explain, for example, that the MER project is an ingeniously frugal space program. The Mars rovers are glorified remote-controlled cars. Rather than use expensive retro-rockets, the project deployed airbags to bounce the rovers to a safe landing on Mars.

2. The text invites a comparison between the Lopez de Cárdenas expedition to the Grand Canyon and the MER landing on Mars. **Ask** students to compare and contrast the two expeditions. **Possible response:** Students may note that both expeditions discovered new and wondrous vistas, but Lopez de Cárdenas was physically present to see the Grand Canyon, while NASA explorers view Mars through televised images.

Steve Squyres

1. Review the information on Steven Squyres with students.

2. **Ask:** When did Squyres discover his true passion? **Answer:** As a graduate student in geology, Squyres became enthralled by photographs of the Viking space exploration missions.

Exploration Past and Present

When producer Gene Roddenberry pitched a classic adventure drama to the NBC television network, his mission was to get the money he needed to explore new worlds on television. His series *Star Trek* debuted in 1966, and its opening phrase, "to boldly go where no man has gone before," became instantly memorable.

If space was a final frontier in twentieth-century science fiction, then Mars is "where no man has gone before" in twenty-first-century science fact. Just as the North American continent lured European explorers in the sixteenth century, the planet Mars lures scientists like Steve Squyres, the chief investigator for NASA's Mars Exploration Rover (MER) Project.

The rovers *Spirit* and *Opportunity* are twin robots that were launched toward Mars in 2003 to search for answers about the history of water on the Red Planet. From the moment they landed in early 2004, they began to send back amazing pictures, allowing people on Earth to see such Martian wonders as the floor of Victoria Crater: "We're still feeling a little awestruck," Squyres reports in his September 28, 2006, blog entry. López de Cárdenas probably felt the same when he first gazed upon the Grand Canyon.

Steve Squyres Scientist / Blogger

Steve Squyres became a geologist because he liked science and loved to climb mountains. However, he discovered his true passion when he was a graduate student at Cornell University. Looking for a subject for a term paper, he found a "room where they kept all the pictures from the *Viking* missions." Intending to look at these images of Mars explorations for a few minutes, Squyres says, "I was in that room for four hours." For the man who is now a professor at Cornell and also oversees the science operations of both Mars rovers and a team of 170 researchers at NASA's Jet Propulsion Laboratory, the Mars mission to seek "evidence concerning whether or not it once had liquid water and a habitable environment" was a success. However, Squyres is still not satisfied, saying he wants to "bring back samples." And that will require another mission, at least.

MISSION UPDATE

MARS BLOG BY STEVE SQUYRES

SEPTEMBER 28, 2006

Wow.

The last couple of days have been among the most exciting of the entire mission. The only other events I can compare this to are the two landings and the arrival of *Opportunity* at Endurance Crater. And in terms of sheer visual impact, this beats those.

Opportunity has arrived at Victoria Crater. As we expected, we came upon the view quite abruptly . . . it went from just the very tops of distant cliffs to a full-blown vista of the crater floor in just a handful of sols. And now we are perched just back from the lip of the crater at Duck Bay, with the whole thing laid out below us.

BLOG CONTINUES >>>

Mission Update **69**

Mission Update

1. Discuss with students their knowledge of blogs. Most students may already know that *blog* is derived from *Web log,* and refers to a Web site in which entries are displayed in reverse chronological order, most recent first. Though blogs originated as online diaries or journals, they have evolved to serve many purposes: as forums for news, commentary, politics, pursuit of hobbies, and other interests, using text, images, video, and other media. Most blogs offer a home page where the blogger's entries appear, links to other sites, an archive of past entries, and a comment section for feedback and dialogue. According to some estimates, there are more than 100 million blogs on the Internet.

2. Tell students that the text on these pages was posted on Squyres's blog September 28, 2006, and describes the situation and his reactions of that same day. **Ask:** What advantages does Squyres have in presenting his information on a blog rather than publishing it in a newspaper or magazine?

   Possible response: Squyres can reach a highly targeted audience—those interested enough in the Mars mission to seek out his blog—by simply typing and posting his thoughts. This approach avoids the delay and complication of placing an article in a printed publication for a general audience. His "news" is fresher and more immediate in a blog than in a newspaper.

Mission Update

1. As students read Squyres's blog entry, ask students to note his tone and the way he presents information to his readers. **Ask:** Is Squyres addressing scientific colleagues or a general audience? Explain.

   Possible response: Students may say that Squyres is addressing a general audience, noting the informal, enthusiastic tone and the absence of technical jargon. When he uses a term such as *superior conjunction,* he explains it. Squyres does seem to assume readers have read earlier entries and are familiar with the rovers and their locations.

2. Review the bulleted information on Mars on this page, and note that it took the rovers seven months to travel from Earth to Mars. **Ask:** What implication do these details have for possible human travel to Mars?

   Possible response: Humans would need huge amounts of supplies and apparatus to assure food, water, air, and power for more than a year in space, including the return trip to Earth. They would need a protective environment while on Mars. During months-long dust storms, they would probably be unable to explore the planet.

Our first order of business here, obviously, is going to be to take a very big Pancam panorama. We'll be starting on that very shortly, though of course it will take quite a while to get it all back to Earth. After that has been shot, we're heading for our next location . . . Cape Verde. We were considering both Cape Verde and Cabo Frio, and when we looked at all the factors together, Cape Verde won out. Wherever we stop next is where the rover will spend "superior conjunction"—the upcoming period when Mars will be out of sight behind the Sun, making communications impossible for a short while. Conjunction is coming soon, so we want to get to our conjunction spot quickly, and Cape Verde looked like an easier drive than Cabo Frio. Another factor is that we want to be parked on rock over conjunction, so that we can do some work on rock with the IDD. There seems to be good exposure of rock

BLOG CONTINUES >>>

- The distance between Earth and Mars varies from 33,900,000 to 249,000,000 miles because the two planets are orbiting the Sun at different speeds.

- Mars, named for the Roman war god, has two little moons: Phobos (fear) and Deimos (panic).

- Winds on Mars can blow up to 80 miles per hour, and dust storms sometimes blanket the planet for months.

- The gravity on Mars is only 38% as strong as the gravity on Earth.

- The temperature on Mars can be as warm as 80° Fahrenheit or as cold as -199° Fahrenheit.

- A Martian day is called a sol and lasts 24 hours, 39 minutes, and 35 seconds. A Martian year lasts 686.98 earth days.

Enrichment: Investigating Science

Humans in Deep Space

The success of the Mars rover project raises an issue about the need for humans to travel in space. One problem is distance: some space voyages would last decades and human lifetimes. Another problem is neediness: the human body needs water, food, oxygen, warmth, and gravity, for starters. The "simple" solution would be to create a mini-Earth, with gravity, atmosphere, and sustainable systems for air, food, and energy—and then to propel this object across the universe at close to the speed of light. Such a solution, of course, is more science fiction than science.

Activity: Research Ask students to investigate how scientists are addressing the complications of deep-space travel for humans. Students may use the **Investigating Science** worksheet, *Professional Development Guidebook*, page 241, as they do their research. Encourage students to report their findings to the class.

MARS ROVER

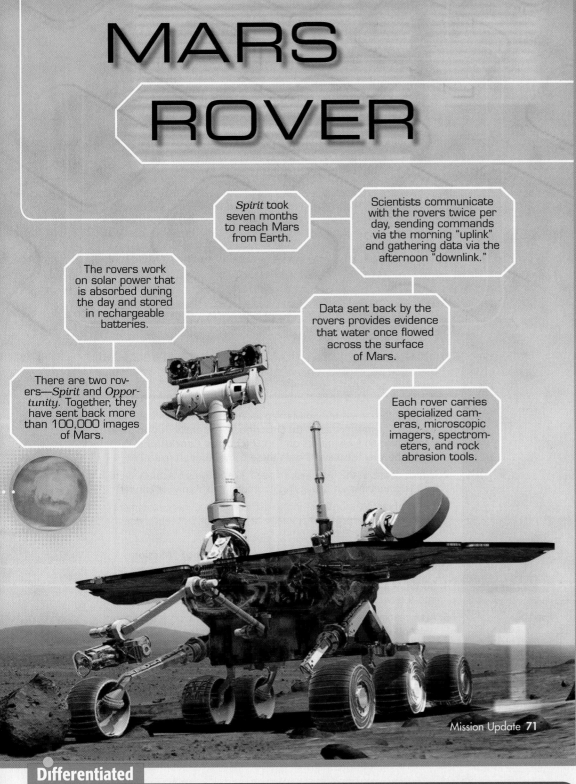

Spirit took seven months to reach Mars from Earth.

Scientists communicate with the rovers twice per day, sending commands via the morning "uplink" and gathering data via the afternoon "downlink."

The rovers work on solar power that is absorbed during the day and stored in rechargeable batteries.

Data sent back by the rovers provides evidence that water once flowed across the surface of Mars.

There are two rovers—*Spirit* and *Opportunity*. Together, they have sent back more than 100,000 images of Mars.

Each rover carries specialized cameras, microscopic imagers, spectrometers, and rock abrasion tools.

Mission Update **71**

1. Go over details of the rover shown on the page. Encourage volunteers to supply additional information about the vehicle that they may know, such as:

   • The hinged arm at the front of the rover contains research instruments.

   • The T-shaped device at the front is the Pancam mast, containing the Pancam optical system for capturing images of the Martian landscape as well as navigational cameras.

   • The vertical rod and the disc toward the back of the rover are antennas.

   • The flat deck of the rover is the solar array, which converts light into electricity that recharges the batteries that power all the rover's systems.

   • Including the mast, the rover is about five feet high, five feet long, and more than seven feet wide; it weighs 384 pounds.

2. Point out that the rovers are designed to be disposable, to be abandoned on Mars when they no longer function.

3. Discuss with students the issue of sending human explorers versus sending robots. **Ask:** Which is the better way to explore deep space: with human explorers or with robots like the rover?
   Possible response: Some students may say humans are essential to making on-the-spot decisions that no robot could make. Humans are essential to colonization, if establishing life beyond Earth is a goal. Other students may say that the huge risks and expenses of human space travel are unnecessary when robots can gather information at a fraction of the cost and with no risk to human life.

Differentiated
Instruction   for Universal Access

Support for Less Proficient Readers
Students may need help to understand some of the technical details Squyres mentions. To clarify "superior conjunction," draw a diagram on the board showing Mars and Earth, with the much-larger Sun between them. Point out that the Sun is blocking the straight line between the two planets. Because radio signals cannot bend around the Sun, there can be no communication between Mars and Earth in this position.

Enrichment for Gifted/Talented Students
Challenge students to develop materials that will teach elementary-age pupils about the Mars rover project. They might build a life-size replica of a rover, diagram the orbits of Earth and Mars to plot the rocket journey to Mars, or create a flowchart to show the communication process between the rovers on Mars and the controllers on Earth.

1. (a) Squyres mentions Endurance Crater, Victoria Crater, Duck Bay, Cape Verde, Cabo Frio. (b) Students may note that craters, capes, and bays are also names on Earth. (c) **Possible response:** These names may have associations with places or people on Earth.

2. Squyres writes in a casual, knowledgeable way about Martian features and uses the first-person point of view ("we came upon the view," and "we are perched").

3. (a) Word choice and punctuation convey Squyres's excitement. He begins his entry with "Wow," describes recent days as "most exciting," and admits to feeling "awestruck." He ends one sentence with an exclamation point sandwiched between two question marks. (b) **Possible response:** Students may say that the blog seems to break the stereotypes of scientists as objective and detached and science as a clinical discipline. Squyres and his colleagues show wonder and enthusiasm about their work, giving science an aura of excitement and adventure.

4. (a) The risks include physical danger to human explorers and catastrophic financial loss. The airless environments of space and oceans present huge complications for modern explorers. (b) **Possible response:** Some students may say that a significant increase in human knowledge is worth the risk; others may say that practical results—products or resources—are needed to justify the risks. These students may point out that most exploration and colonization in America has a profit motive.

5. **Possible response:** Students may say that modern explorers seem more scientific and intent on gathering knowledge in contrast to earlier explorers, who were seeking treasure, trade, and territory. Students may say that explorers past and present share the same curiosity and urge to see over the horizon—whether it be the rim of the Grand Canyon or the edge of a Martian crater.

72

---

at Cape Verde, but little or none of it at Cabo Frio. So Cape Verde it is. And how about that view?!? We're still feeling a little awestruck. The analytical part of my brain looks at that and is already doing science analysis and planning. The rest of me, though, just wants to sit back for a little while and take in the scenery.

This doesn't mean that we're going to traverse clockwise around the crater . . . we won't make that decision for quite a while yet. And it also doesn't mean we'll never go to Cabo Frio. And, to be honest, we can't even say for sure that we'll make it all the way to Cape Verde before conjunction . . . you have to be very careful when driving near cliffs this big! So we'll be driving slowly and cautiously. But Cape Verde is the next thing we're going to head off toward after we finish shooting the pan.

Critical Reading

1. **(a)** Note the names of two Martian locations or geographical features Squyres mentions. **(b) Describe:** What similarities do these names have to place names on Earth? **(c) Draw Conclusions:** Why might the scientists have chosen these names for each place?

2. Which details in the blog make it seem like Squyres is actually there on the planet instead of viewing it remotely? Explain your answer.

3. **(a) Analyze:** Which details in the text convey Squyres's excitement? Explain. **(b) Interpret:** What image of science and scientists does this blog convey? Explain.

Use these questions to hold a group discussion of "Mission Update":

4. **(a)** What are the risks of modern exploration—whether into space or into the deep sea? **(b)** Are the results worth the risks? Explain.

5. After reading this excerpt from Squyres's blog, how do you think our concepts of exploration and explorers have changed since Europeans first traveled in the Americas? In what way have those concepts remained the same as they once were?

The Puritan Influence

PART 2

Selection Planning Guide

This section explores the Puritan influence on America's emerging literary identity. The poetry of Anne Bradstreet and Edward Taylor exemplifies the Puritan "plain style," though Bradstreet's "To My Dear and Loving Husband" is unusual for its treatment of marital, rather than religious, love. Like the Puritans who first heard it, students are likely to find Jonathan Edwards's fiery sermon to be a compelling aspect of Puritan belief.

Humanities

Pilgrims Going to Church (detail), George Henry Boughton

George Henry Boughton (1833–1905) was born in Norwich, England. He lived for a time in New York, concentrating on landscape painting. Throughout his career, Boughton's work was exhibited in both England and the United States. He is primarily known as a painter of "subject pictures" such as *Pilgrims Going To Church*.

Use these questions for discussion:

1. Based on details in the painting, what seems to be the state of mind of the people going to church?
   Possible response: Most people in the painting seem serious and focused. The girl glancing to the side seems wary or distracted.

2. What does the situation in the painting—the weather, the setting, the colors, the posture of the people—suggest about life in the early days of the Puritan settlement?
   Possible response: The wintry landscape, the darkness at the edges of the painting, the stark colors, and the watchfulness of the people all suggest a somewhat bleak and difficult existence.

Monitoring Progress

Before students read the selections in Part 2, administer the **Diagnostic Test 1** (*Unit 1 Resources*, pp. 1–6). This test will determine students' level of readiness for the reading and vocabulary skills.

© Text Complexity: At a Glance

This chart gives a general text complexity rating for the selections in this part of the unit to help guide instruction. For additional text complexity support, see the Text Complexity Rubric at point of use.

To My Dear and Loving Husband	**More Accessible**	*from* Sinners in the Hands of an Angry God	**More Complex**
Huswifery	**More Complex**		

• To My Dear and Loving Husband
Lesson Pacing Guide

DAY 1 Preteach

- Ⓒ Administer the Reading and Vocabulary Warm-ups (*Unit 1 Resources*, pp. 88–91) as necessary.
- Ⓒ Introduce the Literary Analysis concept: The Puritan Plain Style.
- • Introduce the Reading Strategy: Paraphrasing.
- • Build background with the author and Background features.
- • Develop thematic thinking with Connecting to the Essential Question.
- Ⓒ Teach the selection vocabulary.

DAY 2 Preteach/Teach/Extend

- • Distribute copies of the appropriate graphic organizer for Literary Analysis (*Graphic Organizer Transparencies*, pp. 19–20).
- • Distribute copies of the appropriate graphic organizer for the Reading Strategy (*Graphic Organizer Transparencies*, pp. 17–18).
- • Prepare students to read with the Activating Prior Knowledge activities (TE).
- • Informally monitor comprehension while students read.
- • Develop students' ability to paraphrase using the Reading Strategy prompt.
- Ⓒ Reinforce vocabulary with the Vocabulary notes.
- • Assess students' comprehension and mastery of the skills by having them answer the Critical Reading, Literary Analysis, and Reading Strategy questions.
- Ⓒ Have students complete the Vocabulary Lesson.

DAY 3 Assess

- Ⓒ Have students complete the Writing Lesson and write an interpretive essay. (You may assign as homework.)
- • Administer Selection Test A or B (*Unit 1 Resources*, pp. 100–102 or 103–105).

Ⓒ Common Core
State Standards

Reading Literature 5. Analyze how an author's choices concerning how to structure specific parts of a text contribute to its overall structure and meaning as well as its aesthetic impact.

Writing 2. Write informative/explanatory texts to examine and convey complex ideas, concepts, and information clearly and accurately through the effective selection, organization, and analysis of content.

Language 5. Demonstrate understanding of figurative language, word relationships, and nuances in word meanings.

Additional Standards Practice
Common Core Companion, pp. 54–55; 196–207; 322–323; 332–335

Daily Block Scheduling
Each day in this Lesson Pacing Guide represents a 40–50 minute period. Teachers using block scheduling may combine days to revise pacing. In addition, teachers may differentiate and support core instruction by integrating components for extended and intensive support as students require. See the Guide to Selected Leveled Resources (facing page).

Guide to Selected Leveled Resources

R T I Tier 1 (students performing on level)

To My Dear and Loving Husband

Warm Up	**Practice, model,** and **monitor** fluency, working **with the whole class** or **in groups**.	Vocabulary and Reading Warm-ups B, *Unit 1 Resources,* pp. 88–89, 91
Comprehension/Skills	**Support** and **monitor** comprehension and skills development, having students complete the activities, graphic organizers, and interactive prompts **independently** or **as a class**.	• *Reader's Notebook,* adapted instruction and summary **EL** *Reader's Notebook: English Learner's Version,* adapted instruction and summary • **Reading Strategy Graphic Organizer B,** *Graphic Organizer Transparencies,* p. 18 • **Literary Analysis Graphic Organizer B,** *Graphic Organizer Transparencies,* p. 20
Monitor Progress	**Monitor** student progress with the differentiated curriculum-based assessment in the *Unit Resources.*	• **Selection Test B,** *Unit 1 Resources,* pp. 103–105 • **Open-Book Test,** *Unit 1 Resources,* pp. 97–99

R T I Tier 2 (students requiring intervention)

To My Dear and Loving Husband

Warm Up	**Practice, model,** and **monitor** fluency **in groups** or **with individuals**.	• **Vocabulary and Reading Warm-ups A,** *Unit 1 Resources,* pp. 88–90 • *Hear It!* Audio CD
Comprehension/Skills	• **Support** and **monitor** comprehension and skills development, working **in small groups** or **with individuals**. • As students complete the selection in the appropriate version of the *Reader's Notebook,* **monitor** comprehension frequently with group questions and individual instruction. • **Model** strategies while guiding students in completing the activities and prompts in the *Reader's Notebook,* as well as the graphic organizers. • **Practice** skills and **monitor** mastery with the *Reading Kit* worksheets.	• *Reader's Notebook: Adapted Version,* adapted instruction and summary **EL** *Reader's Notebook: English Learner's Version,* adapted instruction and summary • **Reading Strategy Graphic Organizer A,** *Graphic Organizer Transparencies,* p. 17 • **Literary Analysis Graphic Organizer A,** *Graphic Organizer Transparencies,* p. 19 • *Reading Kit,* Practice worksheets
Monitor Progress	**Monitor** student progress with the differentiated curriculum-based assessment in the *Unit Resources* and in the *Reading Kit.*	• **Selection Test A,** *Unit 1 Resources,* pp. 100–102 • *Reading Kit,* Assess worksheets

TIER 3 Tier 3 intervention may require consultation with the student's special-education or dyslexia specialist. For additional support, see the Tier 2 activities and resources listed above.

One-on-one teaching   Group work   Whole-class instruction   Independent work   **A** Assessment

For a complete guide to selection support, including support for Advanced students, see the Overview of Resources in the frontmatter.

• To My Dear and Loving Husband

RESOURCES FOR:
- **L1** Special-Needs Students
- **L2** Below-Level Students (Tier 2)
- **L3** On-Level Students (Tier 1)
- **L4** Advanced Students (Tier 1)
- **EL** English Learners
- **All** All Students

Vocabulary/Fluency/Prior Knowledge

EL L1 L2 Reading Warm-ups A and B,
pp. 90–91

Also available for these selections:

EL L1 L2 Vocabulary Warm-ups A and B,
pp. 88–89

All Vocabulary Builder, p. 94

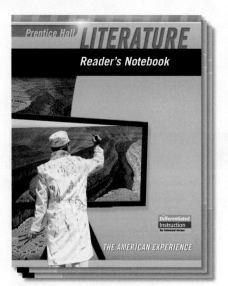

Reader's Notebooks

Pre- and postreading pages for this selection appear in an interactive format in the *Reader's Notebooks*. Each *Notebook* is differentiated for a different group of learners.

The selections in the Adapted and English Learner's versions are abridged.

- **L2 L3** *Reader's Notebook*
- **L1** *Reader's Notebook: Adapted Version*
- **EL** *Reader's Notebook: English Learner's Version*
- **EL** *Reader's Notebook: Spanish Version*

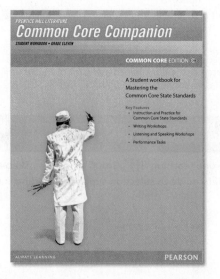

© *Common Core Companion*

Additional instruction and practice for each Common Core State Standard

Selection Support

"To My Dear and Loving Husband" by Anne Bradstreet

Before You Read A: Paraphrasing

Poet's Version	Paraphrase
Then while we live, in love let's so persevere, / That when we live no more, we may live ever.	If we love each other as much as we can while we're alive, then when we die we might love each other forever.

Poet's Version	Paraphrase

Poet's Version	Paraphrase

Graphic Organizer Transparencies
© Pearson Education, Inc. All rights reserved.
17

Graphic Organizer Transparencies

EL L1 L2 Reading: Graphic Organizer A, (partially filled in), p. 17

Also available for these selections:

EL L3 Reading: Graphic Organizer B, p. 18

EL L1 L2 Literary Analysis: Graphic Organizer A (partially filled in), p. 19

EL L3 Literary Analysis: Graphic Organizer B, p. 20

Skills Development/Extension

Unit 1 Resources

Name _____ Date _____

"To My Dear and Loving Husband" by Anne Bradstreet
Reading Strategy: Paraphrasing

The old-fashioned language and sophisticated imagery of Bradstreet's poem can make it difficult to understand. When confronted with a challenging poem or piece of prose, you will often understand it better if you **paraphrase**, or restate ideas in your own words.

Bradstreet's version:
If ever wife was happy in a man,
Compare with me ye women if you can.

Paraphrase:
No woman could be happier with her husband than I am.

DIRECTIONS: *On the lines provided, paraphrase the following excerpts from Bradstreet's poem.*

1. If ever two were one, then surely we.
   _____
   _____

2. I prize thy love more than whole mines of gold,
   Or all the riches that the East doth hold.
   _____
   _____

3. Then while we live, in love let's so persevere.
   That when we live no more, we may life ever.
   _____
   _____
   _____

Unit 1 Resources: A Gathering of Voices
© Pearson Education, Inc. All rights reserved.
93

All Reading: Paraphrasing, p. 93

Also available for these selections:

All Literary Analysis: Puritan Plain Style— Syntax and Inversion, p. 92

EL L3 L4 Support for Writing, p. 95

L4 Enrichment, p. 96

Assessment

Name _____ Date _____

"To My Dear and Loving Husband" by Anne Bradstreet
Selection Test B

Critical Reading *Identify the letter of the choice that best completes the statement or answers the question.*

___ 1. The speaker of "To My Dear and Loving Husband" addresses
   A. her husband.
   B. herself.
   C. the Puritan leadership council.
   D. the Lord.

___ 2. The central idea of Anne Bradstreet's poem is that
   A. other women cannot possibly be as happy as the speaker.
   B. the speaker loves her husband more than she loves God.
   C. heaven will repay the speaker's loving husband with eternal life.
   D. the love the speaker shares with her husband is deep and lasting.

___ 3. Is this first stanza of "To My Dear and Loving Husband" an example of Puritan Plain Style? Why or why not?
   If ever two were one, then surely we./If ever man were lov'd by wife, then thee;/If ever wife was happy in a man,/Compare with me ye women if you can.
   A. No; its lines rhyme.
   B. No; it is about human love, not God's love.
   C. Yes; it usses simple, common words.
   D. Yes; it refers to everyday objects and experiences.

___ 4. What chief emotions does the speaker in Bradstreet's poem express?
   A. respect and admiration for her husband
   B. concern and anxiety about the permanence of her marriage
   C. love for and happiness with her husband
   D. fear of death

___ 5. To paraphrase either poem, which would you do first?
   A. Rewrite the poem in your own words.
   B. Read the information in the footnotes.
   C. Find the subject of each sentence.
   D. Analyze the metaphors in the poem.

___ 6. Which statement below most accurately paraphrases this line from "To My Dear and Loving Husband"?
   If ever man were lov'd by wife, then thee.
   A. I never knew what love meant until I became your wife.
   B. No husband has ever loved his wife more than you love me.
   C. I never have loved you more than I do at this moment.
   D. No wife has ever loved her husband more than I love you.

Unit 1 Resources: A Gathering of Voices
© Pearson Education, Inc. All rights reserved.
103

EL L1 L2 Selection Test B, pp. 103–105

Also available for these selections:

EL L3 L4 Selection Test A, pp. 100–102

L3 L4 Open-Book Test, pp. 97–99

PHLit Online! www.PHLitOnline.com

Online Resources: All print materials are also available online.

- complete narrated selection text
- a thematically related video with writing prompt
- an interactive graphic organizer
- highlighting feature
- access to all student print resources, adapted to individual student needs
- Spanish and English summaries
- adapted selection translations in Spanish

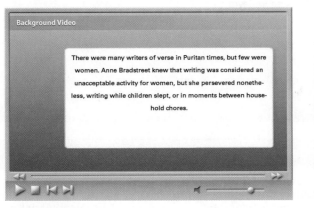

Background Video

There were many writers of verse in Puritan times, but few were women. Anne Bradstreet knew that writing was considered an unacceptable activity for women, but she persevered nonetheless, writing while children slept, or in moments between household chores.

Background Video

Also available:

Get Connected! (thematic video with writing prompt)
All videos are available in Spanish.

Vocabulary Central

Vocabulary Central (tools, activities for studying vocabulary)

Also available:

Writer's Journal (with graphics feature)

❶ Connecting to the Essential Question

1. Review the assignment.

2. Ask students whether they prefer assignments that direct them to focus on community (school, for example) or on their individuality. Then have them write.

3. As students read, have them notice details that refer to private feelings and to community.

❷ Literary Analysis

Introduce the skill.

Think Aloud: Model the Skill

Say to students:

> The book says that a mark of Puritan poetry is inversion. I know inversion from children's rhymes: "A jolly old soul was he" and "He called for his fiddlers three." On page 76, line 9, I see that Anne Bradstreet uses inversion in "Thy love is such I can no way repay."

❸ Reading Strategy

1. Introduce the strategy.

2. Give students **Reading Strategy Graphic Organizer B**, page 18 in *Graphic Organizer Transparencies*, to fill out as they read.

❹ Vocabulary

1. Pronounce each word, giving its definition, and have students say it aloud.

2. For more guidance, see the *Classroom Strategies and Teaching Routines* card for introducing vocabulary.

Before You Read | *To My Dear and Loving Husband*

❶ **Connecting to the Essential Question** The Puritans valued religious devotion, work, and duty over private emotions. Yet, Bradstreet's poems are filled with her feelings. As you read, notice details in this poem that refer to private feelings and those that refer to community or shared belief. Doing so will help as you consider the Essential Question: **What makes American literature American?**

❷ Literary Analysis

The Puritans' beliefs in modesty, hard work, and religious devotion were reflected in all aspects of their lives, from the simple, dark clothes they wore, to the spare furnishings they used, to the literature they wrote. The **Puritan Plain Style** is characterized by short words, direct statements, and references to everyday objects and experiences. Consider the simple, direct statements in these lines from Bradstreet's poem:

> *If ever two were one, then surely we,*
> *If ever man were lov'd by wife, then thee.*

Bradstreet's style may seem less plain to modern readers because of the outdated language, like the use of *thee* for *you*, and the **syntax,** or structure, of her sentences. She sometimes omits words, such as the verb *are* after *we* in the first line above, that we would include today. Her syntax also uses **inversion,** or the placing of sentence elements out of normal position. For example, instead of "let's so persevere in love," she says, "in love let's so persevere."

❸ Reading Strategy

❂ **Preparing to Read Complex Texts** To better understand a poem's *essential meaning*, **paraphrase** it, or restate it in your own words. Rewrite each sentence or clause in language and word order you understand. If necessary, consult the footnotes or a dictionary to clarify unfamiliar terms. Use a graphic organizer like the one shown to help clarify the lines of your paraphrase.

❹ Vocabulary

quench (kwench) *v.* satisfy a thirst (p. 76)

recompense (rek´ əm pens´) *n.* something given or done in return for something else; repayment (p. 76)

manifold (man´ ə fōld´) *adv.* in many ways (p. 76)

persevere (pur´ sə vir´) *v.* continue despite hardship; persist (p. 76)

Poet's Version

My love is such that rivers cannot quench, Nor ought but love from thee, give recompense.

↓

Paraphrase

My love is so strong that rivers cannot relieve its thirst; only your love will satisfy me.

Vocabulary Development

Vocabulary Knowledge Rating
Create a **Vocabulary Knowledge Rating Chart** (in *Professional Development Guidebook*, p. 33) for the vocabulary words on the student page. Give each student a copy of the chart with the words on it. Read the words aloud and have students mark their rating of each in the Before Reading column. When students have completed reading and

discussing the selection, have them take out their **Vocabulary Knowledge Rating Chart** for the selection. Read the words aloud and have students rate their knowledge again in the After Reading column. Clarify any words that are still problematic. Then have students complete the Vocabulary practice at the end of the selection.

 **Vocabulary Central**, featuring tools and activities for studying vocabulary, is available online at **www.PHLitOnline.com.**

❺ Anne Bradstreet (1612–1672)

Author of "To My Dear and Loving Husband"

Anne Bradstreet and her husband, Simon, arrived in the Massachusetts Bay Colony in 1630, when she was only eighteen. Armed with the convictions of her Puritan upbringing, she left behind her hometown of Northampton, England, to start afresh in America. It was not an easy life for Bradstreet, who raised eight children, suffered through multiple illnesses, and faced many hardships.

A Private Writer Made Public Despite the difficulties she endured, Bradstreet was able to devote her spare moments to the very "unladylike" occupation of writing. She wrote for herself, not for publication. Nevertheless, in 1650, John Woodbridge, her brother-in-law, arranged for the publication in England of a collection of her scholarly poems, *The Tenth Muse Lately Sprung Up in America, By a Gentlewoman of Those Parts.* Generally considered to be the first collection of original poetry written in colonial America, the book examined the rights of women to learn and express themselves. Bradstreet's later poems, such as "To My Dear and Loving Husband," are more personal, expressing her feelings about the joys and difficulties of everyday Puritan life. In one, she wrote about her thoughts before giving birth. In another, she wrote about the death of a grandchild.

Bradstreet's poetry reflects the Puritans' knowledge of the stories and language of the Bible, as well as their concern for the relationship between earthly and heavenly life. Her work also exhibits some of the characteristics of the French and English poetry of her day.

In 1956, the poet John Berryman wrote "Homage to Mistress Bradstreet," a long poem that pays tribute to this first American poet.

❻

There is no object that we see; no action that we do; no good that we enjoy; no evil that we feel, or fear, but we may make some spiritual advantage of all: and he that makes such improvement is wise, as well as pious.

To My Dear and Loving Husband **75**

PHLit Online!
www.PHLitOnline.com

Teaching From Technology

Preparing to Read
Go to **www.PHLitOnline.com** in class or in a lab and display the **Get Connected!** slide show for this selection. Have the class brainstorm for responses to the slide show writing prompt, entering ideas in the interactive journal. Then, have students complete their written responses individually in a lab or as homework.

To build background, display the Background and More About the Author features.

Using the Interactive Text
Go to **www.PHLitOnline.com** and display the **Enriched Online Student Edition.** As the class reads the selection or listens to the narration, record answers to side-column prompts using the graphic organizers accessible on the interactive page. Alternatively, have students use the online edition individually, answering the prompts as they read.

🔔 Daily Bellringer

For each class during which you will teach this selection, have students complete one of the five activities for the appropriate week in the *Daily Bellringer Activities* booklet.

Multidraft Reading

To assist struggling readers and to enhance reading for all, apply multidraft reading protocols. For each reading, have students set the purpose indicated:

- **First reading**—identifying key ideas and details and answering any Reading Checks.
- **Second reading**—analyzing craft and structure and responding to the side-column prompts.
- **Third reading**—integrating knowledge and ideas, connecting to other texts and the world, and answering the end-of-selection questions.

For more guidance, refer to the *Classroom Strategies and Teaching Routines* card on multidraft reading.

❺ Background
More About the Author

Anne Dudley was sixteen when she married Simon Bradstreet. The couple immigrated to America and lived in North Andover, Massachusetts. Bradstreet's best poems are those inspired by the rhythms of daily New England life. Her later poems reveal her spiritual growth as she came to embrace Puritan beliefs.

❻ Humanities

Anne Dudley Bradstreet: Colonial American Poet, American etching The single tone of this piece of art seems to reflect the plain style of Puritan life, but it is also the nature of the medium. Etching is a method of engraving in which lines are bitten, or etched, into a surface such as copper by acid. The metal is then covered with one color of ink and pressed against paper to deliver the image.

❶ About the Selection

Simon Bradstreet was often away from home on business for months at a time, and Anne Bradstreet wrote this poem during one of his absences.

❷ Activating Prior Knowledge

Review the first line of Bradstreet's poem, introduced during preteaching. Ask students to respond to it and to discuss whether or not it is a line that would be found *only* in colonial poetry.

Concept Connector ➡

Tell students they will return to their responses after reading the selection.

❸ Reading Strategy

Paraphrasing

1. **Ask** a volunteer to define the term *paraphrase*.
   Answer: To paraphrase is to restate in one's own words.

2. **Ask** students the Reading Strategy question: How would you paraphrase these first two lines?
   Possible response: We form the ideal couple, acting as if we were one person; you are the most beloved of husbands.

❹ Vocabulary

1. Pronounce each word, giving its definition, and have students say it aloud.

2. For more guidance, see the *Classroom Strategies and Teaching Routines* card for introducing vocabulary.

---

❶
❷ # To My Dear an t Loving Husband

Anne Bradstreet

Reading Strategy
Paraphrasing
How would you paraphrase these first two lines?

Vocabulary
quench (kwench) *v.* satisfy a thirst

recompense (rek′ əm pens′) *n.* repayment; something given or done in return for something else

manifold (man′ ə fōld′) *adv.* in many ways

persevere (pʉr′ sə vir′) *v.* persist; be steadfast in purpose

❸ *I*f ever two were one, then surely we.
If ever man were lov'd by wife, then thee;
If ever wife was happy in a man,
Compare with me ye women if you can.

5 I prize thy love more than whole mines of gold,
Or all the riches that the East doth hold.
My love is such that rivers cannot quench,
Nor ought[1] but love from thee, give recompense.
Thy love is such I can no way repay,

10 ❹ The heavens reward thee manifold, I pray.
Then while we live, in love let's so persevere,[2]
That when we live no more, we may live ever.

---

1. **ought** (ôt) *n.* anything whatever.
2. **persevere** pronounced (pʉr′ sə vir′) in the seventeenth century, and thus rhymed with the word *ever*.

76 Beginnings–1800

Ⓒ Text Complexity Rubric

To My Dear and Loving Husband	
Qualitative Measures	
Context/Knowledge Demands	Cultural knowledge demands (faith, love) 1 ② 3 4 5
Structure/Language Conventionality and Clarity	Stanzaic structure; some difficult vocabulary 1 2 3 ④ 5
Levels of Meaning/ Purpose/Concept Level	Accessible (wife's love for husband) 1 2 ③ 4 5
Quantitative Measures	

Lexile	NP	**Text Length**	Word Count: 103
Overall Complexity	**More accessible**		

Reader and Task Suggestions

Preparing to Read the Text
- Using the Background information on TE p. 75, discuss poetry as a vehicle for sharing personal thoughts and emotions.
- Ask students why they might choose poetry as the genre to express their feelings about someone.
- Guide students to use Multidraft Reading strategies to deepen their comprehension (TE p. 75).

Leveled Tasks
Structure/Language If students will have difficulty with the poem's structure, have them read to find the main idea in each stanza. As they reread, ask them to find details that support main ideas.

Evaluating If students will not have difficulty with the poem's structure, have them judge the effect of the poem's exaggeration.

Anne Bradstreet: The Tenth Muse Lately Sprung Up in America, 20th century, LaDonna Gulley Warwick

The artist titled this oil painting after Bradstreet's first published book of poetry, mentioned on page 75 and discussed in more detail on page 78.

1. Tell students that in another poem, Bradstreet writes, "I am obnoxious to each carping tongue, / That says my hand a needle better fits!" Have students paraphrase these lines.

2. **Ask** students how this portrait refutes Bradstreet's critics. **Possible response:** The portrait highlights Bradstreet's role as writer rather than showing her as a stereotype of a woman colonist.

⑥ Critical Viewing

Answer: The painting shows Bradstreet with things that a typical poet of the period would have: a desk, a quill, shelves of books. At the lower right, the painting shows a young child to remind us that Bradstreet was also a mother.

Critical Reading

ⓒ

⑥ ▲ Critical Viewing
How does this painting present Bradstreet as both poet and Puritan housewife? **[Analyze]**

Cite textual evidence to support your responses.

ⓒ 1. **Key Ideas and Details (a)** What does the speaker value more than "whole mines of gold"? **(b) Distinguish:** What other images suggest the richness and abundance of the love the speaker and her husband share?

ⓒ 2. **Key Ideas and Details (a) Analyze:** What is the apparent contradiction in the last two lines? **(b) Draw Conclusions:** What does the last stanza reveal about Puritan beliefs in the afterlife?

ⓒ 3. **Craft and Structure (a)** Note where Bradstreet uses repetition in the first stanza. **(b) Analyze:** How does her use of repetition suggest a growing emotional intensity?

ⓒ 4. **Integration of Knowledge and Ideas** Which aspect of the speaker is more important in this poem—the private or the public self? Use at least two of these Essential Question words in your response: *community, personal, unique, social. [Connecting to the Essential Question: What makes American literature American?]*

To My Dear and Loving Husband **77**

Before students respond, you may wish to have them write a brief objective summary of the selection. As they answer the questions below, remind them to support their answers with evidence from the text.

1. (a) She prizes her husband's love more. (b) Other images include "riches that the East doth hold," "rivers cannot quench," "I can no way repay."

2. (a) The apparent contradiction is their "living" after their lives are over. (b) It indicates that Puritans did believe in an afterlife.

3. (a) Bradstreet repeats the phrase *If ever* and the words *were* and *then.* (b) Repetition suggests the increased weight of an idea.

4. ❓ **Possible response:** Most of the poem shows the speaker's concern with her <u>personal</u> self rather than with the <u>community</u>. The speaker does, however, also show that she accepts the religious community's doctrine of an afterlife.

Concept Connector

Reading Strategy Graphic Organizer
Ask students to review the graphic organizers in which they have paraphrased lines from the poem. Then have them share their organizers and compare the paraphrases they wrote.

Activating Prior Knowledge
Remind students of their responses to the Activating Prior Knowledge activity. Ask them to explain whether their thoughts have changed and if so, how.

❓ Connecting to the Essential Question
Have students compare their responses to the prompt before reading the poem with their thoughts after reading it. Have them work individually or in groups to formulate their new responses. Then lead a class discussion, probing for what students have learned that confirms or invalidates their initial thoughts. Encourage students to cite specific textual details to support their responses.

❼ World Literature in Context

Help students realize that the Muses are still acknowledged from time to time in Western culture. Draw their attention, for example, to the annual Clio awards honoring creative advertising in package design, print, radio, and television

Connect to the Literature Have students read the World Literature in Context feature. Next, present the additional background information above. Then **ask** the Connect to the Literature question: Do you think that Tenth Muse is a fitting title for Anne Bradstreet? Why or why not? **Possible response:** Students will likely acknowledge that, like Sappho and Sor Juana Inés de la Cruz, Anne Bradstreet merits the title Tenth Muse for the creativity that she demonstrated in her own work and for inspiring other women and other poets from her day to this.

The Tenth *Muse*

Title page of *The Tenth Muse* by Anne Bradstreet, London, 1650 ▶

Anne Bradstreet's first book of poetry was published in England under the title *The Tenth Muse Lately Sprung Up in America.* In Greek Mythology, the original nine Muses were goddesses, daughters of Zeus, the ruler of the gods. The Muses were thought to be the source of inspiration for all artists, poets, musicians, dancers — and even philosophers. The Muses each had a specialty, as shown in the chart.

In Greek antiquity, the philosopher Plato referred to Sappho, the noted lyric poet, as The Tenth Muse because her poetry was so beautiful. The label lived through the centuries. Gifted, forward-thinking women writers are sometimes called "Tenth Muse." Anne Bradstreet was hailed as a Tenth Muse, as was her Mexican contemporary, Sor Juana Inés de La Cruz. Sor Juana was a noted poet and playwright, a fierce intellectual, and a woman of faith. She spent most of her adult life as a nun in the Convent of the Order of Saint Jerome. In 1689, an anthology of her poetry was published in Spain titled *The Overflowing of the Castalian Spring, by the Tenth Muse of Mexico.*

CONNECT TO THE LITERATURE

Do you think that Tenth Muse is a fitting title for Anne Bradstreet? Why or why not?

MUSE	SHE INSPIRED
CALLIOPE "… beautiful of voice"	Eloquence and Epic Poetry
ERATO "… amorous"	Love Poetry, Lyrics, and Wedding Songs
CLIO "… glorious"	History
EUTERPE "… charming"	Music and Lyric Poetry
MELPOMENE "… the chanting one"	Tragedy
POLYHYMNIA "… the singer of many hymns"	Sacred Music
TERPSICHORE "… delighted with dance"	Choral Song and Dance
THALIA "… the blossoming one"	Comedy and Pastoral Poetry
URANIA "… the celestial one"	Astronomy

◀ Sappho (c. 630 – c. 570 B.C.) Fresco painting Pompeii, Italy, 1st century A.D.

▼ Dance of Apollo with the Nine Muses (tempera on panel)

Sor Juana Inés de la Cruz, 18th century painting by Miguel Cabrera ▶

Assessment Practice

Summarizing Written Texts (For more practice, see *All-in-One Workbook.*)

Some texts measure students' ability to identify the best summary of a passage. Explain that summarizing is especially useful when reading poetry. After students reread the poem on page 76, have them pick the best summary:

A The speaker wants to live forever with her husband.

B The speaker's love for her husband, which she values more than gold and riches, will never die.

C The speaker owes her husband money.

D The speaker wants heaven to reward her husband.

Choices **A** and **D** make only partially complete claims; **C** presents incorrect information. **B** is the best summary.

Literary Analysis

1. Craft and Structure Use a chart like the one shown to explore aspects of the poem that are typical of the **Puritan Plain Style.**

Style Element	Example
Short Words	
Direct Statements	
Familiar Objects/Experiences	

2. Craft and Structure Which aspects of the poem do not reflect the plainness of the Puritan ethic? Explain.

3. Craft and Structure **(a)** Which lines of the poem have customary **syntax? (b)** Which lines present examples of **inversion?** Explain your answers.

Reading Strategy

4. Paraphrase the last stanza as though you were explaining it to a friend.

PERFORMANCE TASKS
Integrated Language Skills

Vocabulary Acquisition and Use

Word/Phrase Relationships Choose the letter of the situation that best reflects the meaning of the italicized word or phrase. Then, explain your answers.

1. *quench:* **(a)** filling up on snacks before dinner, **(b)** enjoying a glass of cool water after a long walk, **(c)** calming an unruly group of kids

2. *hard-earned recompense*: **(a)** getting a flat tire on the way to the dentist, **(b)** getting a day off after working late, **(c)** cleaning a messy room after a hard day

3. *increase manifold:* **(a)** receiving a small raise, **(b)** adding a drop to a full bucket, **(c)** getting a 300-percent return on an investment

4. *persevere:* **(a)** quitting when you get tired, **(b)** practicing until you improve, **(c)** arguing with a referee

Writing

Explanatory Text Write a brief **essay** in which you interpret the speaker's view of love and reward in this poem. First, review the poem for details relating to luxury and abundance. Then, explain how these images of wealth help the speaker express the depth of her love for her husband. Cite details from the text to support your ideas.

To My Dear and Loving Husband **79**

Common Core State Standards

Writing
2. Write informative/explanatory texts to examine and convey complex ideas, concepts, and information clearly and accurately through the effective selection, organization, and analysis of content.

Language
5. Demonstrate understanding of figurative language, word relationships, and nuances in word meanings.

Answers

1. Examples of short words: "surely," "man," "lov'd," "wife," "happy," "women," "prize," "whole," "live"; examples of direct statements: "I prize thy love more than," "The heavens reward thee manifold, I pray"; examples of familiar objects/ experiences: mines, rivers, "live no more."

2. The personal and emotion-laden subject of a wife's love for a husband and, in the second stanza, the appeal to the senses do not reflect the plainness of the Puritan ethic.

3. (a) and (b) Lines 1–8, 10, and 12 have customary syntax. Line 9 puts the object before the subject and verb, rather than in the more usual position after them. Line 11, as pointed out on page 74, puts the prepositional phrase earlier than usual.

4. **Possible response:** I pray that the heavens will reward you many times over. Let us keep our love strong enough now so that we will merit an afterlife.

Vocabulary Acquisition and Use

1. b: Cool water can quench, or satisfy, the thirst created by a long walk.

2. b: Getting a day off after working late is an example of being repaid for diligence.

3. c: Getting a 300 percent return on an investment represents growth several times over.

4. b: Practicing until you improve is a sign of stick-to-itiveness.

Writing

Evaluate students' interpretive essays using the **Rubrics for Response to Literature,** in *Professional Development Guidebook,* pages 250–251.

79

• Huswifery
Lesson Pacing Guide

ⓒ Administer the Reading and Vocabulary Warm-ups (*Unit 1 Resources*, pp. 106–109) as necessary.

ⓒ Introduce the Literary Analysis concept: Conceit.

• Introduce the Reading Strategy: Adjust Reading Rate.

• Build background with the author and Background features.

• Develop thematic thinking with Connecting to the Essential Question.

ⓒ Teach the selection vocabulary.

DAY 2 **Preteach/Teach/Extend**

• Distribute copies of the appropriate graphic organizer for Literary Analysis (*Graphic Organizer Transparencies*, pp. 21–22).

• Distribute copies of the appropriate graphic organizer for the Reading Strategy (*Graphic Organizer Transparencies*, pp. 23–24).

• Prepare students to read with the Activating Prior Knowledge activities (TE).

• Informally monitor comprehension while students read.

ⓒ Reinforce vocabulary with the Vocabulary notes.

• Assess students' comprehension and mastery of the skills by having them answer the Critical Reading, Literary Analysis, and Reading Strategy questions.

DAY 3 **Assess**

ⓒ Have students complete the Vocabulary practice.

ⓒ Have students complete the Writing activity and write a reflective essay. (You may assign as homework.)

• Administer Selection Test A or B (*Unit 1 Resources*, pp. 118–120 or 121–123).

ⓒ **Common Core State Standards**

Reading Literature 5. Analyze how an author's choices concerning how to structure specific parts of a text contribute to its overall structure and meaning as well as its aesthetic impact.

Writing 2. Write informative/explanatory texts to examine and convey complex ideas, concepts, and information clearly and accurately through the effective selection, organization, and analysis of content.

2.d. Use precise language, domain-specific vocabulary, and techniques such as metaphor, simile, and analogy to manage the complexity of the topic.

Additional Standards Practice
***Common Core Companion**, pp. 54–55; 196–207*

Daily Block Scheduling
Each day in this Lesson Pacing Guide represents a 40–50 minute period. Teachers using block scheduling may combine days to revise pacing. In addition, teachers may differentiate and support core instruction by integrating components for extended and intensive support as students require. See the Guide to Selected Leveled Resources (facing page).

Guide to Selected Leveled Resources

R T I Tier 1 (students performing on level)

		Huswifery
Warm Up	Practice, model, and monitor fluency, working with the whole class or in groups.	Vocabulary and Reading Warm-ups B, *Unit 1 Resources,* pp. 106–107, 109
Comprehension/Skills	Support and monitor comprehension and skills development, having students complete the activities, graphic organizers, and interactive prompts independently or as a class.	• *Reader's Notebook,* adapted instruction and summary EL *Reader's Notebook: English Learner's Version,* adapted instruction and summary • Reading Strategy Graphic Organizer B, *Graphic Organizer Transparencies,* p. 24 • Literary Analysis Graphic Organizer B, *Graphic Organizer Transparencies,* p. 22
Monitor Progress A	Monitor student progress with the differentiated curriculum-based assessment in the *Unit Resources.*	• Selection Test B, *Unit 1 Resources,* pp. 121–123 • Open-Book Test, *Unit 1 Resources,* pp. 115–117
Assess/ Screen A	Assess student progress using Benchmark Test 1.	• Benchmark Test 1, *Unit 1 Resources,* pp. 124–129

R T I Tier 2 (students requiring intervention)

		Huswifery
Warm Up	Practice, model, and monitor fluency in groups or with individuals.	• Vocabulary and Reading Warm-ups A, *Unit 1 Resources,* pp. 106–108 • *Hear It!* Audio CD
Comprehension/Skills	• Support and monitor comprehension and skills development, working in small groups or with individuals. • As students complete the selection in the appropriate version of the *Reader's Notebook,* monitor comprehension frequently with group questions and individual instruction. • Model strategies while guiding students in completing the activities and prompts in the *Reader's Notebook,* as well as the graphic organizers. • Practice skills and monitor mastery with the *Reading Kit* worksheets.	• *Reader's Notebook: Adapted Version,* adapted instruction and summary EL *Reader's Notebook: English Learner's Version,* adapted instruction and summary • Reading Strategy Graphic Organizer A, *Graphic Organizer Transparencies,* p. 23 • Literary Analysis Graphic Organizer A, *Graphic Organizer Transparencies,* p. 21 • *Reading Kit,* Practice worksheets
Monitor Progress A	Monitor student progress with the differentiated curriculum-based assessment in the *Unit Resources* and in the *Reading Kit.*	• Selection Test A, *Unit 1 Resources,* pp. 118–120 • *Reading Kit,* Assess worksheets
Assess/ Screen A	Assess student progress using the Benchmark Test 1.	Benchmark Test 1, *Unit 1 Resources,* pp. 124–129

TIER 3 Tier 3 intervention may require consultation with the student's special-education or dyslexia specialist. For additional support, see the Tier 2 activities and resources listed above.

One-on-one teaching   Group work   Whole-class instruction   Independent work   A Assessment

For a complete guide to selection support, including support for Advanced students, see the Overview of Resources in the frontmatter.

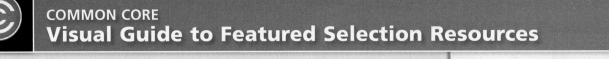

• Huswifery

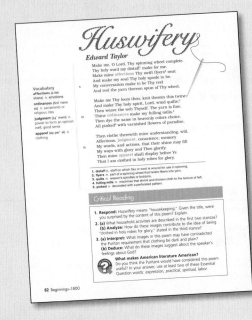

RESOURCES FOR:

- **L1** Special-Needs Students
- **L2** Below-Level Students (Tier 2)
- **L3** On-Level Students (Tier 1)
- **L4** Advanced Students (Tier 1)
- **EL** English Learners
- **All** All Students

Vocabulary/Fluency/Prior Knowledge

All **Vocabulary Builder,** p. 112

Also available for these selections:

EL **L1** **L2** **Vocabulary Warm-ups A and B,** pp. 106–107

EL **L1** **L2** **Reading Warm-ups A and B,** pp. 108–109

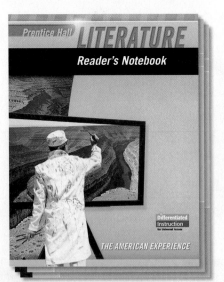

Reader's Notebooks

Pre- and postreading pages for this selection appear in an interactive format in the *Reader's Notebooks.* Each *Notebook* is differentiated for a different group of learners. The selections in the Adapted and English Learner's versions are abridged.

- **L2** **L3** *Reader's Notebook*
- **L1** *Reader's Notebook: Adapted Version*
- **EL** *Reader's Notebook: English Learner's Version*
- **EL** *Reader's Notebook: Spanish Version*

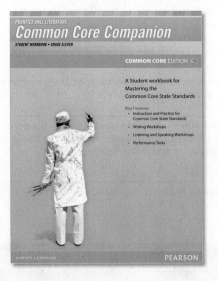

© Common Core Companion

Additional instruction and practice for each Common Core State Standard

Selection Support

Graphic Organizer Transparencies

EL L3 Literary Analysis: Graphic Organizer B, p. 22

Also available for these selections:

EL L1 L2 Literary Analysis: Organizer A, (partially filled in), p. 21

EL L1 L2 Reading: Graphic Organizer A, (partially filled in), p. 23

EL L3 Reading: Graphic Organizer B, p. 24

Skills Development/Extension

Unit 1 Resources

All Literary Analysis: Conceit (Extended Metaphor), p. 110

Also available for these selections:

All Reading: Adjust Reading Rate, p. 111

EL L3 L4 Support for Writing, p. 113

L4 Enrichment, p.114

Assessment

L3 L4 Open-Book Test, pp. 115–117

Also available for these selections:

EL L1 L2 Selection Test A, pp. 118–120

EL L3 L4 Selection Test B, pp. 121–123

PHLit Online!
www.PHLitOnline.com

Online Resources: All print materials are also available online.

- complete narrated selection text
- a thematically related video with writing prompt
- an interactive graphic organizer
- highlighting feature
- access to all student print resources, adapted to individual student needs
- Spanish and English summaries
- adapted selection translations in Spanish

Get Connected!

Also available:

Background Video (thematic video with writing prompt)
All videos are available in Spanish.

Vocabulary Central (tools and activities for studying vocabulary)

Also available:

Writer's Journal (with graphics feature)

❶ 🤔 Connecting to the Essential Question

1. Review the assignment with the class.

2. Ask students for examples of useful poems or songs that teach, or call to action. Then, have students complete the assignment.

3. As students read, have them find details in the poem that stress the usefulness of activity.

❷ Literary Analysis

1. Introduce the skill.

2. Give students **Literary Analysis Graphic Organizer B** *(Graphic Organizer Transparencies,* p. 22) to fill out as they read.

Think Aloud: Model the Skill

Say to students:

To recognize a conceit, or extended metaphor, in a poem, I look for connections among images. A conceit shows how two seemingly different subjects are alike not just in one way but in many ways. When I find an image that conveys a metaphor, I think about how that image and metaphor relate to others in the poem. Doing so helps me to identify an extended metaphor and to better understand the poem's meaning.

❸ Reading Strategy

Introduce the Skill.

❹ Vocabulary

1. Pronounce each word, giving its definition, and have students say it aloud.

2. For more guidance, see the *Classroom Strategies and Teaching Routines* card for introducing vocabulary.

Before You Read | *Huswifery*

❶ Connecting to the Essential Question For most Americans, the values of working hard and being useful are important. Both can be traced back to the Puritans, who believed that all activity should have a practical purpose. As you read this poem, notice details that stress the usefulness of activity. This will help as you consider the Essential Question: **What makes American literature American?**

Common Core State Standards

Reading Literature
5. Analyze how an author's choices concerning how to structure specific parts of a text contribute to its overall structure and meaning as well as its aesthetic impact.

❷ Literary Analysis

A **metaphor** is a figure of speech in which two very different subjects are shown to have a point of similarity. A metaphor may liken an abstract idea, such as love or friendship, to a concrete image:

> Langston Hughes: *"Life is a broken-winged bird."*
> Emily Dickinson: *"Hope is the thing with feathers."*

A **conceit,** also called an **extended metaphor,** is a metaphor taken to its logical limit. With a conceit, the metaphor does not end in a single line or image, but builds throughout the work. In this poem, Taylor uses the poetic structure itself to extend the metaphor of the spinning wheel into a conceit. Most poems are structured in individual **lines** organized into stanzas. A **stanza** is a group of consecutive lines that form a unit. Like a paragraph in prose, a stanza usually introduces and develops a new idea. Use a chart like the one shown to analyze how Taylor builds his conceit line by line and stanza by stanza.

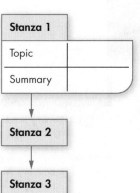

❸ Reading Strategy

Ⓒ Preparing to Read Complex Texts The language of poetry is rich and dense, so you may find poetry more challenging than prose. As you read, monitor your comprehension to make sure you understand how Taylor builds his meaning. If you find the poem difficult, **adjust your reading rate** by slowing down. When you get to a complex image, you may slow down even more and take the time to form a clear, specific picture before you continue reading.

❹ Vocabulary

affections (ə fek´ shənz) *n.* emotions (p. 82)

ordinances (ôrd´′n əns əz) *n.* sacraments or religious rites (p. 82)

judgment (juj´ mənt) *n.* power to form an opinion well; good sense (p. 82)

apparel (əp per´ əl) *n.* clothing (p. 82)

www.PHLitOnline.com

Vocabulary Development

Vocabulary Knowledge Rating

Create a **Vocabulary Knowledge Rating chart** (in *Professional Development Guidebook,* p. 33) for the vocabulary words on the student page. Give each student a copy of the chart with the words on it. Read the words aloud, and have students mark their rating of each in the Before Reading column. When students have completed reading and discussing the selection, have them take out their **Vocabulary Knowledge Rating** charts for the selection. Read the words aloud and have students rate their knowledge again in the After Reading column. Clarify any words that are still problematic. Then have students complete the Vocabulary practice at the end of the selection.

PHLit Online! **Vocabulary Central,** featuring tools and activities for studying vocabulary, is available online at **www.PHLitOnline.com.**

⑤ Edward Taylor (1642–1729)

Author of "Huswifery"

Puritanism was a religious reform movement that began in England in the sixteenth century. The Puritans sought to reform the Church of England and to reshape English society according to their beliefs. These efforts led to both civil strife and government persecution of the Puritans. In response, many Puritans, including Edward Taylor, fled to the American colonies.

Before his emigration to America, Edward Taylor worked as a teacher in England. Upon arriving in Boston in 1668, Taylor entered Harvard College as a sophomore, graduating in 1671. After graduation, he accepted the position of minister and physician in the small frontier farming community of Westfield, Massachusetts, and then walked more than one hundred miles, much of it through snow, to his new home.

Harsh Life in a New World Life in the village of Westfield was filled with hardships. Fierce battles between the Native Americans and the colonists left the community in constant fear. In addition, Taylor experienced many personal tragedies. Five of his eight children died in infancy; then, his wife died while she was still a young woman. He remarried and had five or six more children. (Biographers differ on the exact number.)

Edward Taylor is now generally regarded as the best of the North American colonial poets. Yet, because Taylor thought of his poetry as a form of personal worship, he allowed only two stanzas to be published during his lifetime. Some believe that he chose not to publish his poems because their joyousness and delight in sensory experience ran counter to Puritan attitudes that poetry be for moral instruction only. One of his nineteenth-century descendants donated Taylor's writings to Yale University. The stash of poems was discovered in the 1930s and, in 1939, *The Poetical Works of Edward Taylor* was published. Most of Taylor's poetry, including "Huswifery," uses extravagant comparisons, intellectual wit, and subtle argument to explore religious faith and affection.

> *Oh! that I ever felt what I profess.*
> *'Twould make me then the*
> *happi'st man alive.*

🔔 Daily Bellringer

For each class during which you will teach this selection, have students complete one of the five activities for the appropriate week in the *Daily Bellringer Activities* booklet.

Multidraft Reading

To assist struggling readers and to enhance reading for all, apply multidraft reading protocols. For each reading, have students set the purpose indicated:

- **First reading**—identifying key ideas and details and answering any Reading Checks.
- **Second reading**—analyzing craft and structure and responding to the side-column prompts.
- **Third reading**—integrating knowledge and ideas, connecting to other texts and the world, and answering the end-of-selection questions.

For more guidance, refer to the *Classroom Strategies and Teaching Routines* card on *multidraft reading*.

⑤ Background
More About the Author

Literary critics and students of religion consider Taylor's most important work to be the series of more than two hundred poems called *Preparatory Meditations*. Those poems—as well as "Huswifery"— remind some readers of metaphysical poems by John Donne and George Herbert, which Taylor probably heard during his childhood in England.

PHLit Online! www.PHLitOnline.com

Teaching From Technology

Preparing to Read
Go to **www.PHLitOnline.com** in class or in a lab and display the Get Connected! slide show for this selection. Have the class brainstorm for responses to the slide show writing prompt, entering ideas in the interactive journal. Then, have students complete their written responses individually in a lab or as homework.
To build background, display the Background and More About the Author features.

Using the Interactive Text
Go to **www.PHLitOnline.com** and display the **Enriched Online Student Edition.** As the class reads the selection or listens to the narration, record answers to side-column prompts using the graphic organizers accessible on the interactive page. Alternatively, have students use the online edition individually, answering the prompts as they read.

❶ About the Selection

"Huswifery" combines spinning, weaving, and tailoring into an extended metaphor that expresses Edward Taylor's deep belief in God.

❷ Activating Prior Knowledge

Remind students about the religious concept of salvation, the deliverance from sin. Elicit from students the pathway to salvation in different religions: in Christianity, faith in Jesus; in Judaism, preparation for the arrival of the Messiah in Islam, submission to God.

ASSESS

Answers

1. **(a)** The first two stanzas describe making yarn and weaving it into cloth. **(b)** The images of spinning wheel, distaff, flyers, spool, reel, yarn, loom, twine, quills, fulling mills, and dyeing relate the speaker to the objects and process of cloth making. By thinking and behaving in ways that serve and glorify God, the speaker figuratively wears "holy robes."

2. **(a)** Images include: "dye the same in heavenly colors choice"; "pinked with varnished flowers of paradise"; "their shine." **(b)** They suggest his feelings are intense.

3. **Possible response:** Some Puritans might have considered the poem useful as an <u>expression</u> of <u>spiritual</u> faith. Others might have thought the poem too fanciful or clever.

---

❶❷ Huswifery

Edward Taylor

Make me, O Lord, Thy spinning wheel complete.
Thy holy word my distaff[1] make for me.
Make mine affections Thy swift flyers[2] neat
And make my soul Thy holy spoole to be.
My conversation make to be Thy reel   5
And reel the yarn thereon spun of Thy wheel.

Make me Thy loom then, knit therein this twine:
And make Thy holy spirit, Lord, wind quills:[3]
Then weave the web Thyself. The yarn is fine.
Thine ordinances make my fulling mills.[4]   10
Then dye the same in heavenly colors choice.
All pinked[5] with varnished flowers of paradise.

Then clothe therewith mine understanding, will,
Affections, judgment, conscience, memory
My words, and actions, that their shine may fill   15
My ways with glory and Thee glorify.
Then mine apparel shall display before Ye
That I am clothed in holy robes for glory.

Vocabulary

affections (ə fek´ shənz) *n.* emotions

ordinances (ôrd´'n əns əz) *n.* sacraments or religious rites

judgment (juj´ mənt) *n.* power to form an opinion well; good sense

apparel (əp per´ əl) *n.* clothing

---

1. **distaff** *n.* staff on which flax or wool is wound for use in spinning.
2. **flyers** *n.* part of a spinning wheel that twists fibers into yarn.
3. **quills** *n.* weaver's spindles or bobbins.
4. **fulling mills** *n.* machines that shrink and thicken cloth to the texture of felt.
5. **pinked** *v.* decorated with a perforated pattern.

Critical Reading

Cite textual evidence to support your responses.

1. **Key Ideas and Details (a)** What household activities are described in the first two stanzas? **(b) Analyze:** How do these images contribute to the idea of being "clothed in holy robes for glory," stated in the third stanza?

2. **Key Ideas and Details (a) Interpret:** What images in this poem may have contradicted the Puritan requirement that clothing be dark and plain? **(b) Deduce:** What do these images suggest about the speaker's feelings about God?

3. **Integration of Knowledge and Ideas** Do you think the Puritans would have considered this poem useful? In your answer, use at least two of these Essential Question words: *expression, practical, spiritual, labor.* [Connecting to the Essential Question: What makes American literature American?]

Ⓒ Text Complexity Rubric

Huswifery	
Qualitative Measures	
Context/Knowledge Demands	Puritan poem (Christianity; jargon) 1 2 3 ④ 5
Structure/Language Conventionality and Clarity	Poetic structure; archaic language; extended metaphor 1 2 3 4 ⑤
Levels of Meaning/ Purpose/Concept Level	Challenging (religious devotion) 1 2 3 4 ⑤
Quantitative Measures	
Lexile NP	**Text Length** Word Count: 137
Overall Complexity	**More complex**

Reader and Task Suggestions

Preparing to Read the Text
- Using the Background information on TE p. 81, discuss what is meant by *meditation* and *metaphysical* in regard to poetry.
- Ask students why they might compare their lives to a machine or a technical process. What comparisons would they make, and why?
- Guide students to use Multidraft Reading strategies to deepen their comprehension (TE p. 81).

Leveled Tasks

Structure/Language If students will have difficulty with the metaphor, have them list the steps of clothmaking. As they reread, have students stop after each step and complete this sentence: "When he talks about _____, Taylor means that _____."

Analyzing If students will not have difficulty with the metaphor, discuss Taylor's comparison of God to a master weaver.

Literary Analysis

1. **Craft and Structure (a)** In the first line, what request does the poet make? **(b)** Explain how this is a **metaphor**—what two dissimilar things are being compared? **(c)** What is the point of similarity between the two dissimilar things?

2. **Craft and Structure** Explain how the metaphors developed in each **stanza** build to a **conceit** for the poem as a whole.

Reading Strategy

3. Look back at how you **adjusted your reading rate** as you read the poem. Use a chart like the one shown to classify which lines you read at your usual speed and which you read more slowly. Use your chart to guide a second reading of the poem.

Average speed	More slowly

4. Explain how you integrated footnotes into your readings of the poem.

PERFORMANCE TASKS
Integrated Language Skills

Vocabulary Acquisition and Use

True or False Decide whether each statement below is true or false. Explain each answer.

1. It is always possible to control your **affections,** regardless of the situation.

2. **Ordinances** should be fulfilled with respect and care.

3. Sleep deprivation can impair your **judgment.**

4. Wool, cotton, and polyester are examples of fine **apparel.**

Writing

Explanatory Text Taylor's poem describes the processes of turning raw materials into clothing. It works on two levels—as a description of an ordinary activity and as a metaphor for religious devotion. In a **reflective essay,** describe the procedure of a common household chore and explore how that task suggests a larger, or metaphoric, meaning. Include these elements:

- a complete, step-by-step description of the task from beginning to end
- vivid sensory details that appeal to the five senses
- a thoughtful insight about the meaning the task holds for you

Huswifery **83**

Common Core State Standards

Writing

2. Write informative/explanatory texts to examine and convey complex ideas, concepts, and information clearly and accurately through the effective selection, organization, and analysis of content.

2.d. Use precise language, domain-specific vocabulary, and techniques such as metaphor, simile, and analogy to manage the complexity of the topic.

Answers

1. **(a)** The poet requests that God make him a perfect tool (spinning wheel). **(b)** This metaphor compares a spinning wheel that works for the person who uses it with the poet who desires to devote himself to God. **(c)** Just as the spinning wheel produces what its user intends, the speaker will do God's will.

2. Second stanza: The metaphor compares the poet to a loom. Third stanza: In the metaphor, his words and deeds will be clothed in holiness as a person may be clothed in glowing apparel.

3. Students may be able to move more quickly through the first two stanzas of imperative sentences than through the third stanza, which breaks away from the imperatives.

4. Some students may be able to take in the footnotes in the course of reading the poem; others may have to gain a familiarity with the footnotes before they start line-by-line reading.

Vocabulary Acquisition and Use

1. False. It is not always possible to control your emotions.

2. True. If one is going to participate in sacraments or religious rites, one should do so with respect and care.

3. True. A lack of sleep can reduce one's power to form an opinion well or to display good sense.

4. False. Wool, cotton, and polyester are the materials from which apparel can be made, not kinds of apparel.

Writing

Evaluate students' writing using the **Rubrics for Reflective Essays,** in *Professional Development Guidebook,* pages 293–294.

Assessment Resources

Unit 1 Resources

L1 L2 EL **Selection Test A,** pp. 118–120. Administer Test A to less advanced students.

L3 L4 EL **Selection Test B,** pp. 121–123. Administer Test B to on-level and more advanced students.

L3 L4 **Open-Book Test,** pp. 115–117. As an alternative, give the Open-Book Test.

All **Customizable Test Bank**

All **Self-tests**
Students may prepare for the **Selection Test** by taking the **Self-test** online.

 All assessment resources are available at **www.PHLitOnline.com.**

• *from* Sinners in the Hands of an Angry God
Lesson Pacing Guide

DAY 1 Preteach

ⓒ Administer the Reading and Vocabulary Warm-ups (*Unit 1 Resources*, pp. 130–133) as necessary.

ⓒ Introduce the Literary Analysis concept: Sermons.

• Introduce the Reading Strategy: Using Context Clues.

• Build background with the author and Background features.

• Develop thematic thinking with Connecting to the Essential Question.

ⓒ Teach the selection vocabulary.

DAYS 2–3 Preteach/Teach/Assess

• Distribute copies of the appropriate graphic organizer for the Reading Strategy (*Graphic Organizer Transparencies*, pp. 25–26).

• Distribute copies of the appropriate graphic organizer for Literary Analysis (*Graphic Organizer Transparencies*, pp. 27–28).

• Prepare students to read with the Activating Prior Knowledge activities (TE).

• Informally monitor comprehension while students read.

• Use the Reading Check questions to confirm comprehension.

• Develop students' ability to use context clues using the Reading Strategy prompt.

ⓒ Reinforce vocabulary with the Vocabulary notes.

• Assess students' comprehension and mastery of the skills by having them answer the Critical Reading, Literary Analysis, and Reading Strategy questions.

• Have students complete the Vocabulary Lesson.

DAY 4 Extend/Assess

ⓒ Have students complete the Conventions and Style Lesson.

ⓒ Have students complete the Writing Lesson and write an evaluation of persuasive techniques. (You may assign as homework.)

• Administer Selection Test A or B (*Unit 1 Resources*, pp. 143–145 or 146–148).

ⓒ Common Core State Standards

Reading Informational Text
6. Determine an author's point of view or purpose in a text in which the rhetoric is particularly effective, analyzing how style and content contribute to the power, persuasiveness, or beauty of the text.

Language 3.a. Vary syntax for effect.
4. Determine or clarify the meaning of unknown and multiple-meaning words and phrases based on *grades 11–12 reading content*.
4.a. Use context as a clue to the meaning of a word or phrase.
5. Demonstrate understanding of figurative language, word relationships, and nuances in word meanings.

Writing 1. Write arguments to support claims in an analysis of substantive topics or texts, using valid reasoning and relevant and sufficient evidence.

Additional Standards Practice
***Common Core Companion,* pp. 143–150; 185–195; 322–323; 324–331; 332–335**

Daily Block Scheduling
Each day in this Lesson Pacing Guide represents a 40–50 minute period. Teachers using block scheduling may combine days to revise pacing. In addition, teachers may differentiate and support core instruction by integrating components for extended and intensive support as students require. See the Guide to Selected Leveled Resources (facing page).

Guide to Selected Leveled Resources

			from Sinners in the Hands of an Angry God

Tier 1

Warm Up

Practice, model, and **monitor** fluency, working **with the whole class** or **in groups**.

Vocabulary and Reading Warm-ups B, *Unit 1 Resources,* pp. 130–131, 133

Comprehension/Skills

Support and **monitor** comprehension and skills development, having students complete the activities, graphic organizers, and interactive prompts **independently** or **as a class**.

- *Reader's Notebook,* adapted instruction and summary
- **EL** *Reader's Notebook: English Learner's Version,* adapted instruction and summary
- **Reading Strategy Graphic Organizer B,** *Graphic Organizer Transparencies,* p. 26
- **Literary Analysis Graphic Organizer B,** *Graphic Organizer Transparencies,* p. 28

Monitor Progress

A **Monitor** student progress with the differentiated curriculum-based assessment in the *Unit Resources.*

- **Selection Test B,** *Unit 1 Resources,* pp. 146–148
- **Open-Book Test,** *Unit 1 Resources,* pp. 140–142

Tier 2

			from Sinners in the Hands of an Angry God

Warm Up

Practice, model, and **monitor** fluency **in groups** or **with individuals**.

- **Vocabulary and Reading Warm-ups A,** *Unit 1 Resources,* pp. 130–132
- *Hear It!* **Audio CD**

Comprehension/Skills

- **Support** and **monitor** comprehension and skills development, working **in small groups** or **with individuals**.
- As students complete the selection in the appropriate version of the *Reader's Notebook,* **monitor** comprehension frequently with group questions and individual instruction.
- **Model** strategies while guiding students in completing the activities and prompts in the *Reader's Notebook,* as well as the graphic organizers.
- **Practice** skills and **monitor** mastery with the *Reading Kit* worksheets.

- *Reader's Notebook: Adapted Version,* adapted instruction and summary
- **EL** *Reader's Notebook: English Learner's Version,* adapted instruction and summary
- **Reading Strategy Graphic Organizer A,** *Graphic Organizer Transparencies,* p. 25
- **Literary Analysis Graphic Organizer A,** *Graphic Organizer Transparencies,* p. 27
- *Reading Kit,* Practice worksheets

Monitor Progress

A **Monitor** student progress with the differentiated curriculum-based assessment in the *Unit Resources* and in the *Reading Kit.*

- **Selection Test A,** *Unit 1 Resources,* pp. 143–145
- *Reading Kit,* Assess worksheets

TIER 3 Tier 3 intervention may require consultation with the student's special-education or dyslexia specialist. For additional support, see the Tier 2 activities and resources listed above.

One-on-one teaching Group work Whole-class instruction Independent work **A** Assessment

For a complete guide to selection support, including support for Advanced students, see the Overview of Resources in the frontmatter.

• *from* Sinners in the Hands of an Angry God

from
Sinners in the hands
of an Angry GOD
Jonathan Edwards

BACKGROUND Jonathan Edwards delivered this famous sermon to a congregation in Enfield, Connecticut, in 1741. Surprisingly, he spoke quietly and without emotion. According to one account, he read the six-hour work in a level voice, staring over the heads of his audience at the bell rope that hung against the back wall "as if he would stare it in two." Despite his calm manner, his listeners are said to have screamed in terror, and Edwards had to stop several times to ask for silence.

This is the case of every one of you that are out of Christ: That world of misery, that lake of burning brimstone, is extended abroad under you. There is the dreadful pit of the glowing flames of the wrath of God; there is Hell's wide gaping mouth open; and you have nothing to stand upon, nor anything to take hold of; there is nothing between you and Hell but the air; it is only the power and mere pleasure of God that holds you up.

You probably are not sensible of this; you find you are kept out of Hell, but do not see the hand of God in it: but look at other things, as the good state of your bodily constitution, your care of your own life, and the means you use for your own preservation. But indeed these things are nothing; if God should withdraw his hand, they would avail no more to keep you from falling than the thin air to hold up a person that is suspended in it.

1. **out of Christ** not in God's grace.

Vocabulary
constitution [kän' stə tōō' shən] n. physical makeup of a person

Reading Check
Of what does Edwards believe his congregation is not "sensible"?

from Sinners in the Hands of an Angry God **87**

RESOURCES FOR:
- **L1** Special-Needs Students
- **L2** Below-Level Students (Tier 2)
- **L3** On-Level Students (Tier 1)
- **L4** Advanced Students (Tier 1)
- **EL** English Learners
- **All** All Students

Vocabulary/Fluency/Prior Knowledge

Unit 1 Resources

from "Sinners in the Hands of an Angry God" by Jonathan Edwards
Vocabulary Warm-up Word Lists

Study these words from the selection. Then, complete the activities.

Word List A

doubtless [DOWT lis] *adv.* without any doubt; certainly
The captain will <u>doubtless</u> be at the game.

everlasting [ch ver LAS ting] *adj.* lasting forever; eternal
Empires may go on for centuries, but none is <u>everlasting</u>.

extraordinary [eks TROHR duh ner ee] *adj.* unusual; special
<u>Extraordinary</u> students do more than what is expected.

inconceivable [in kuhn SEE vuh buhl] *adj.* unthinkable
The damage from the huge earthquake was <u>inconceivable</u>.

provoked [pruh VOHKT] *v.* stirred up; made angry
Her speech <u>provoked</u> a strong reaction from her opponent.

uphold [up HOHLD] *v.* support; keep up
This document states the political beliefs that we <u>uphold</u>.

wholly [HOH lee] *adv.* completely; absolutely
I <u>wholly</u> agree with every one of your recommendations.

withheld [with HELD] *v.* held back; kept back; refused
Under questioning, the spy <u>withheld</u> the vital information.

Word List B

abhors [uhb HOHRZ] *v.* hates; detests
My sister <u>abhors</u> that kind of violent television show.

abominable [uh BAHM uhn uh buhl] *adj.* horrible; hateful
The audience gasped at the villain's <u>abominable</u> act.

circumstances [SER kuhm stan suhz] *n.* facts; conditions
The <u>circumstances</u> of this mystery make it hard to solve.

congregation [kahn gre GAY shuhn] *n.* gathering; assembly
The singing of the <u>congregation</u> filled the church.

duration [dyoo RAY shuhn] *n.* length of time; continuation
He was suspended for the <u>duration</u> of the season.

infinite [IN fuh nit] *adj.* endless; without boundaries
As we stared at the stars, the universe seemed <u>infinite</u>.

moderation [mah duh RAY shuhn] *n.* restraint; easing of intensity
The waves kept pounding the shore without <u>moderation</u>.

righteousness [RYT shus nis] *n.* justice; virtue
They chose a judge known for his <u>righteousness</u>.

Unit 1 Resources: A Gathering of Voices
© Pearson Education, Inc. All rights reserved.
130

EL **L1** **L2** **Vocabulary Warm-ups A and B,**
pp. 130–131

Also available for these selections:
EL **L1** **L2** **Reading Warm-ups A and B,**
pp. 132–133
All **Vocabulary Builder,** p. 136

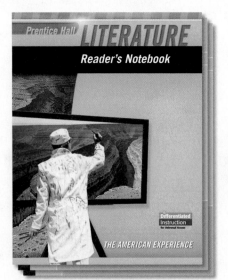

Reader's Notebooks

Pre- and postreading pages for this selection, as well as an excerpt from "Sinners in the Hands of an Angry God," appear in an interactive format in the *Reader's Notebooks*. Each *Notebook* is differentiated for a different group of learners.

The selections in the Adapted and English Learner's versions are abridged.

- **L2** **L3** *Reader's Notebook*
- **L1** *Reader's Notebook: Adapted Version*
- **EL** *Reader's Notebook: English Learner's Version*
- **EL** *Reader's Notebook: Spanish Version*

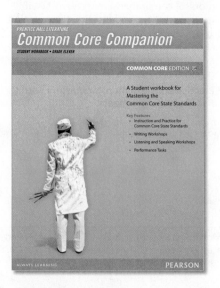

© *Common Core Companion*

Additional instruction and practice for each Common Core State Standard

Selection Support

from *Sinners in the Hands of an Angry God* by Jonathan Edwards

After You Read A: Sermon

"Great waters"

Wrath

"rough winds"

Impact of Edwards's Message

EL L1 L2 Literary Analysis: Graphic Organizer A (partially filled in), p. 27

Also available for these selections:

EL L1 L2 Reading: Graphic Organizer A, (partially filled in), p. 25

EL L3 Reading: Graphic Organizer B, p. 26

EL L3 Literary Analysis: Graphic Organizer B, p. 28

Skills Development/Extension

Name _____ Date _____

from Sinners in the Hands of an Angry God by Jonathan Edwards

Integrated Language Skills: Support for Writing: Evaluation

First, review the persuasive techniques of imagery and theme that Jonathan Edwards uses in his sermon. Then, prepare for writing an **evaluation** by entering important information about each in the graphic organizer below.

Evaluation of Jonathan Edwards's sermon

Examples of Imagery from Edwards's Sermon

Effective or Ineffective? Why?

Examples of Main Themes from Edwards's Sermon

Effective or Ineffective? Why?

On a separate page, use the information from the graphic organizer to write a first draft of your evaluation. Then, revise it to be sure you have included only information related to why Edwards's techniques were either effective or ineffective for his audience.

EL L1 L2 Support for Writing, p. 138

Also available for these selections:

All Literary Analysis: Sermon (Persuasive Oratory), p. 134

All Reading: Use Context Clues, p. 135

EL L3 L4 Grammar and Style, p. 137

L4 Enrichment, p. 139

Assessment

Name _____ Date _____

from Sinners in the Hands of an Angry God by Jonathan Edwards

Selection Test A

Critical Reading *Identify the letter of the choice that best answers the question.*

____ 1. In the selection from *Sinners in the Hands of an Angry God*, what is the author's main intention?
A. to tell his listeners of God's love and mercy
B. to frighten his listeners into seeking salvation
C. to inform his listeners of the life of Jesus Christ
D. to persuade his listeners to form a new church

____ 2. What is the main message of *Sinners in the Hands of an Angry God*?
A. No one has any hope of salvation.
B. Salvation is gained through good deeds.
C. Salvation is gained through Christ.
D. Salvation is gained through prayer.

____ 3. What does Edwards think is true of the members of his congregation in *Sinners in the Hands of an Angry God*?
A. They are all church supporters.
B. They are all sinners.
C. They are all worthy of salvation.
D. They are all saved.

____ 4. Based on context, what does the word *gulf* mean in this passage from *Sinners in the Hands of an Angry God*?
Your wickedness makes you as it were heavy as lead, and to tend downwards with great weight and pressure towards Hell; and if God should let you go, you would immediately sink and swiftly descend and plunge into the bottomless gulf. . . .
A. body of water
B. mountain cave
C. deep pit
D. ocean shore

____ 5. Based on context, what does the word *duration* mean in this passage from *Sinners in the Hands of an Angry God*?
When you look forward, you shall see a long forever, a boundless duration before you, which will swallow up your thoughts and amaze your soul. . . .
A. landscape
B. time period
C. strange sight
D. memory

EL L1 L2 Selection Test A, pp. 143–145

Also available for these selections:

L3 L4 Open-Book Test, pp. 140–142

EL L3 L4 Selection Test B, pp. 146–148

PHLit Online!
www.PHLitOnline.com

Online Resources: All print materials are also available online.

- complete narrated selection text
- a thematically related video with writing prompt
- an interactive graphic organizer
- highlighting feature
- access to all student print resources, adapted to individual student needs
- Spanish and English summaries
- adapted selection translations in Spanish

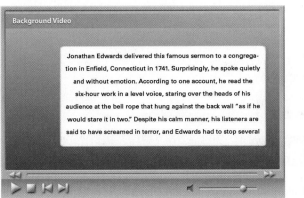

Background Video

Jonathan Edwards delivered this famous sermon to a congregation in Enfield, Connecticut in 1741. Surprisingly, he spoke quietly and without emotion. According to one account, he read the six-hour work in a level voice, staring over the heads of his audience at the bell rope that hung against the back wall "as if he would stare it in two." Despite his calm manner, his listeners are said to have screamed in terror, and Edwards had to stop several

Background Video

Also available:

Get Connected! (thematic video with writing prompt)
All videos available in Spanish.

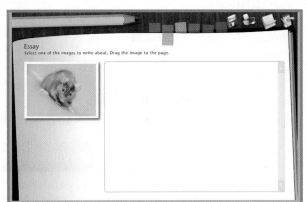

Essay
Select one of the images to write about, Drag the image to the page.

Writer's Journal (with graphics feature)

Also available:

Vocabulary Central (tools and activities for studying vocabulary)

❶ Connecting to the Essential Question

1. Review the assignment.

2. Encourage students to think about speeches they have heard in both important and casual situations. Then, have them complete the assignment.

3. As students read, have them take note of the sermon's most effective passages.

❷ Literary Analysis

Introduce the strategy, using the instruction on the student page.

Think Aloud: Model the Skill

Say to students:

Reading a piece like this out loud, or listening to it read aloud, can help me better appreciate its impact. Reading aloud also allows me to "hear" the speaker's emotions. The impact of Edwards's cry "O sinner! Consider the fearful danger you are in" is greater if it is heard than if it is read silently.

❸ Reading Strategy

1. Introduce the skill, using the instruction on the student page.

2. Give students a copy of **Reading Strategy Graphic Organizer B,** page 26 in *Graphic Organizer Transparencies,* to fill out as they read.

❹ Vocabulary

1. Pronounce each word, giving its definition, and have students say it aloud.

2. For more guidance, see the **Classroom Strategies and Teaching Routines** card for introducing vocabulary.

Before You Read

from *Sinners in the Hands of an Angry God*

❶ Connecting to the Essential Question This sermon had a powerful effect on its original audiences. As you read, note passages that you think most affected listeners. This will help as you consider the Essential Question: **How does literature shape or reflect society?**

❷ Literary Analysis

A **sermon** is broadly defined as a speech given from a pulpit in a house of worship. Like its written counterpart, the essay, a sermon conveys the speaker's message or point of view. As a form of **oratory,** or formal public speaking, sermons almost always display the following elements:

- They are *persuasive*, inspiring listeners to take action.
- They address the needs and concerns of the *audience,* or listeners.
- They *appeal to the emotions*.
- They include *expressive and rhythmic language*.

Often, orators also include images, patterns, characters, or stories from the Bible, myth, or classical literature. These **archetypes** add a deeper dimension for listeners who apply the ancient meanings to the new message. As you read, look for these elements of oratory in the sermon.

❸ Reading Strategy

Ⓒ Preparing to Read Complex Texts As you read, monitor your comprehension of unfamiliar words and look for **context clues**—other words, phrases, and sentences—that can help you understand. For example, take the word *abominable* in this passage: "You are ten thousand times more abominable in his [God's] eyes, than the most hateful venomous serpent is in ours…." Edwards likens the way God views the sinner with the way we view a snake. From this clue, you can figure out that *abominable* must be close in meaning to *disgusting* or *horrible*. As you read, use a chart like the one shown to define other unfamiliar words by using context clues.

❹ Vocabulary

constitution (kän′ stə tōō′ shən) *n.* physical makeup of a person (p. 87)

prudence (prōō′ dəns) *n.* carefulness; caution (p. 88)

omnipotent (äm nip′ ə tənt) *adj.* all-powerful (p. 88)

mediator (mē′ dē ā tər) *n.* one who reconciles opposing groups (p. 89)

induce (in dōōs′) *v.* cause; bring about (p. 89)

Ⓒ Common Core State Standards

Reading Informational Text

6. Determine an author's point of view or purpose in a text in which the rhetoric is particularly effective, analyzing how style and content contribute to the power, persuasiveness, or beauty of the text.

Language

4. Determine or clarify the meaning of unknown and multiple-meaning words and phrases based on *grades 11–12 reading content*.

4.a. Use context as a clue to the meaning of a word or phrase

Difficult Words

↓

Context Clues

↓

Meaning

www.PHLitOnline.com

Vocabulary Development

Vocabulary Knowledge Rating

Create a **Vocabulary Knowledge Rating Chart** (in *Professional Development Guidebook,* p. 33) for the vocabulary words on the student page. Give each student a copy of the chart with the words on it. Read the words aloud and have students mark their rating in the Before Reading column. Urge students to attend to these words as they read and discuss the selection.

In order to gauge how much instruction you need to provide, tally how many students are confident in their knowledge of each word. As students read, point out the words and their context.

 **Vocabulary Central,** featuring tools and activities for studying vocabulary, is available online at **www.PHLitOnline.com.**

❺ Jonathan Edwards (1703–1758)

Author of "Sinners in the Hands of an Angry God"

The sermons of Jonathan Edwards were so filled with "fire and brimstone"—a phrase symbolizing the torments of hell endured by sinners—that his name alone was enough to make many eighteenth-century Puritans shake in their shoes. Yet, Edwards was not just a stone-faced religious zealot. He was also a man who believed in science and reason and who saw in the physical world the proof of God's presence and will.

A Born Preacher This great American theologian was born in East Windsor, Connecticut, where he grew up in an atmosphere of devout discipline. As a young boy, he is said to have demonstrated his religious devotion by preaching sermons to his playmates. He also displayed academic brilliance, learning to speak Latin, Greek, and Hebrew before he was twelve. Edwards entered the Collegiate School of Connecticut (now Yale University) at the age of thirteen and graduated four years later as valedictorian. He went on to earn his master's degree in theology.

The Great Awakening Edwards began his preaching career in 1727 as assistant to his grandfather, Solomon Stoddard. Stoddard was pastor of the church at Northampton, Massachusetts, one of the largest and wealthiest Puritan congregations. Edwards became the church pastor two years later when his grandfather died. Committed to a return to the orthodoxy and fervent faith of the Puritan past, Edwards became one of the leaders of the Great Awakening, a religious revival that swept the colonies in the 1730s and 1740s.

Fall from Favor As pastor of the church at Northampton, Edwards had instituted disciplinary proceedings against members of his congregation for reading what he considered improper books. In his sermons he denounced by name those he considered sinners. Such actions drew criticism and, in 1750, a council representing ten congregations dismissed Edwards as pastor.

After his dismissal, Edwards moved to Stockbridge, Massachusetts, where he preached to the Native Americans and wrote his most important theological works. He continued to preach and write until his death in 1758, shortly after becoming president of the College of New Jersey (now Princeton University). Although in most of his writings Edwards appeals to reason, his emotional sermon "Sinners in the Hands of an Angry God" is by far his most famous work. It demonstrates Edwards's tremendous powers of persuasion and captures the religious fervor of the Great Awakening.

from Sinners in the Hands of an Angry God **85**

Background
❺ More About the Author

As he toiled to strengthen Puritanism against what he saw as new waves of liberalism and rationalism, Jonathan Edwards deeply influenced American religious history. He wrestled continually with the theological issue of free will: If God determines all, how is human free will possible? Edwards concluded that since God gives people the power to choose, they hold responsibility for their acts and will earn God's praise or wrath accordingly. After Edwards left his preaching duties at Northampton, he ministered to the Housatonic Indians and to scattered frontier settlers in New England.

❶ About the Selection

The foundation of Edwards's sermon is the Puritan belief in a life of hard work, self-discipline, and religious devotion. The preacher intended to frighten his listeners into pursuing lives of humility and righteousness in the hope of achieving salvation. What Edwards's listeners probably found most dreadful was the idea of an omniscient God being indifferent to human misery. Moreover, the congregation was surely chilled by the realization that—though their only hope of salvation lay in observing divine laws to the letter—God might dole out mercy according to His whims.

❷ Critical Viewing

Answer: The building reflects values of simplicity and foundational strength.

❷ ▶ **Critical Viewing**
Edwards preached in churches similar to this. What values do you think are reflected in the style of this building? **[Analyze]**

86 Beginnings–1800

ⓒ Text Complexity Rubric

from Sinners in the Hands of an Angry God

Qualitative Measures	
Context/Knowledge Demands	Cultural knowledge demands (Puritanism) 1 2 3 ④ 5
Structure/Language Conventionality and Clarity	Challenging vocabulary; complicated sentences; figurative language 1 2 3 ④ 5
Levels of Meaning/ Purpose/Concept Level	Challenging (Puritan view of God) 1 2 3 4 ⑤

Quantitative Measures			
Lexile	1210L	**Text Length**	Word Count: 1,895
Overall Complexity	**More complex**		

Reader and Task Suggestions

Preparing to Read the Text

- Using the Background information on TE p. 85, discuss the question that concerned Edwards. Encourage students to look for his answer in the sermon.
- Ask students to define *forgiveness*. Discuss why people might need or want forgiveness.
- Guide students to use Multidraft Reading strategies (TE p. 85).

Leveled Tasks

Levels of Meaning If students will have difficulty with the meaning, have them use a chart during a first reading to note details about (1) God's anger toward sin and (2) what sinners can do to receive forgiveness.

Analyzing If students will not have difficulty with the meaning, ask them which aspect of this sermon seemed most persuasive.

① *from*

③ Sinners in the Hands of an Angry GOD

Jonathan Edwards

BACKGROUND Jonathan Edwards delivered this famous sermon to a congregation in Enfield, Connecticut, in 1741. Surprisingly, he spoke quietly and without emotion. According to one account, he read the six-hour work in a level voice, staring over the heads of his audience at the bell rope that hung against the back wall "as if he would stare it in two." Despite his calm manner, his listeners are said to have screamed in terror, and Edwards had to stop several times to ask for silence.

This is the case of every one of you that are out of Christ:[1] That world of misery, that lake of burning brimstone, is extended abroad under you. There is the dreadful pit of the glowing flames of the wrath of God; there is Hell's wide gaping mouth open; and you have nothing to stand upon, nor anything to take hold of; there is nothing between you and Hell but the air; it is only the power and mere pleasure of God that holds you up.

You probably are not sensible of this; you find you are kept out of Hell, but do not see the hand of God in it; but look at other things, as the good state of your bodily constitution, your care of your own life, and the means you use for your own preservation. But indeed these things are nothing; if God should withdraw his hand, they would avail no more to keep you from falling than the thin air to hold up a person that is suspended in it.

---

1. **out of Christ** not in God's grace.

Vocabulary
constitution
(kän′ stə tōō′ shən) *n.*
physical makeup of
a person

④ **Reading Check**

Of what does Edwards believe his congregation is not "sensible"?

from Sinners in the Hands of an Angry God **87**

---

❺ The American Experience

Biblical Imagery

The King James Version of the Bible was preceded in English by Wyclif's Bible (1380), Tyndale's Bible (1525), Coverdale's Bible (1535), Matthew's Bible (1537), Taverner's Bible (1539), the Geneva Bible (1560), and the Bishops' Bible (1568). Also known as the "Authorized Version," the King James Version was composed from 1604 to 1611 by a group of scholars working for King James I. It is widely considered to be the most beautifully written translation of the Judeo-Christian scriptures, and it has had an incalculable effect on English and American literary history.

Connect to the Literature

Encourage students to reflect on contemporary views of God before responding to the question: How do you think a contemporary audience would react to this type of "fire and brimstone" biblical imagery?

Possible responses: A contemporary audience would probably be turned off by Edwards's use of biblical imagery. Today, it is more common for worshippers to view God as loving and benevolent rather than angry and capricious.

❻ Literary Analysis

Sermon and Oratory

1. Ask a volunteer to read the bracketed passage. Have students raise their hands when they hear references to water. List these images on the chalkboard.

2. **Ask** students what mood or feeling is created by these images of water.
   Answer: Students may say that these images suggest threat, violence, or anger.

3. **Ask** students the following question: In what ways do these images of the fury of water help convey Edwards's message?
   Answer: The image of dammed water, rising in volume and power, serves as an effective metaphor for God's potential wrath. It is an image of the possibility of destruction. This is perfect for Edwards's purpose, because it checks his congregation's impulse to rationalize away the possibility of God's judgment.

❺ The American EXPERIENCE

Biblical Imagery

Jonathan Edwards's frightening imagery of God's potential for wrath and destruction recalls stories of fires, floods, and divine retribution in the Old Testament of the King James Bible. While this imagery terrified Edwards's audience, they would have found it quite familiar. In fact, in 1741, when Edwards delivered this sermon, the King James Bible had been in wide circulation for 130 years. The first English version of the Bible to include both the Old and New Testaments, the King James Bible had been produced at the express request of the Puritans in England in 1611. This Bible, with its haunting language and powerful imagery, would have been common daily reading for most of Edwards's listeners.

Connect to the Literature

How do you think a contemporary audience of worshippers would react to this type of "fire and brimstone" biblical imagery?

Vocabulary

prudence (prōō´ dəns)
n. carefulness; caution

omnipotent (äm nip´ ə tənt)
adj. all-powerful

Your wickedness makes you as it were heavy as lead, and to tend downwards with great weight and pressure towards Hell; and if God should let you go, you would immediately sink and swiftly descend and plunge into the bottomless gulf, and your healthy constitution, and your own care and prudence, and best contrivance, and all your righteousness, would have no more influence to uphold you and keep you out of Hell, than a spider's web would have to stop a fallen rock. Were it not for the sovereign pleasure of God, the earth would not bear you one moment . . . The world would spew you out, were it not for the sovereign hand of Him who hath subjected it in hope. There are black clouds of God's wrath now hanging directly over your heads, full of the dreadful storm, and big with thunder; and were it not for the restraining hand of God, it would immediately burst forth upon you. The sovereign pleasure of God, for the present, stays[2] his rough wind; otherwise it would come with fury, and your destruction would come like a whirlwind, and you would be like the chaff of the summer threshing floor.

The wrath of God is like great waters that are dammed for the present; they increase more and more, and rise higher and higher, till an outlet is given; and the longer the stream is stopped, the more rapid and mighty is its course, when once it is let loose. It is true, that judgment against your evil works has not been executed hitherto; the floods of God's vengeance have been withheld; but your guilt in the meantime is constantly increasing, and you are every day treasuring up more wrath; the waters are constantly rising, and waxing more and more mighty; and there is nothing but the mere pleasure of God, that holds the waters back, that are unwilling to be stopped, and press hard to go forward. If God should only withdraw his hand from the floodgate, it would immediately fly open, and the fiery floods of the fierceness and wrath of God, would rush forth with inconceivable fury, and would come upon you with omnipotent power; and if your strength were ten thousand times greater than it is, yea, ten thousand times greater than the strength of the stoutest, sturdiest devil in Hell, it would be nothing to withstand or endure it.

The bow of God's wrath is bent, and the arrow made ready on the string, and justice bends the arrow at your heart, and strains the bow, and it is nothing but the mere pleasure of God, and that of an angry God, without any promise or obligation at all, that keeps the arrow one moment from being made drunk with your blood. Thus all you that never passed under a great change of heart, by the mighty power of the spirit of God upon your souls; all you that were never born again, and made new creatures, and raised from being dead in sin, to

---

2. **stays** (stāz) *v.* restrains.

Enrichment: Investigating Religion and Myth

The Afterlife

Edwards's belief in an afterlife is typical of the followers of most major religions. According to the ancient Greeks, people who led a good life were sent to Elysium, a paradise filled with sunny fields. Ancient Egyptians, too, believed in the afterlife as an agricultural land of plenty. In Norse mythology, heroes slain in battle went to Valhalla. In Buddhism and in Hinduism, the soul is reincarnated (reborn in another body or form) until it achieves a state of spiritual perfection.

Activity: Presentation Encourage students to choose a religion or culture and investigate its beliefs about life after death. Have students examine how these beliefs express human values and emotions. Suggest that they record information in the **Enrichment: Investigating Religion and Myth** worksheet, *Professional Development Guidebook,* page 240. Students can then report their findings in a presentation to the class.

a state of new, and before altogether unexperienced light and life, are in the hands of an angry God. However you may have reformed your life in many things, and may have had religious affections, and may keep up a form of religion in your families and closets,[3] and in the house of God, it is nothing but His mere pleasure that keeps you from being this moment swallowed up in everlasting destruction. However unconvinced you may now be of the truth of what you hear, by and by you will be fully convinced of it.

Those that are gone from being in the like circumstances with you, see that it was so with them; for destruction came suddenly upon most of them; when they expected nothing of it, and while they were saying, peace and safety: now they see, that those things on which they depended for peace and safety, were nothing but thin air and empty shadows.

The God that holds you over the pit of Hell, much as one holds a spider, or some loathsome insect over the fire, abhors you, and is dreadfully provoked: his wrath towards you burns like fire; he looks upon you as worthy of nothing else, but to be cast into the fire; he is of purer eyes than to bear to have you in his sight; you are ten thousand times more abominable in his eyes, than the most hateful venomous serpent is in ours. . . .

O sinner! Consider the fearful danger you are in: it is a great furnace of wrath, a wide and bottomless pit, full of the fire of wrath, that you are held over in the hand of that God, whose wrath is provoked and incensed as much against you, as against many of the damned in Hell. You hang by a slender thread, with the flames of divine wrath flashing about it, and ready every moment to singe it, and burn it asunder; and you have no interest in any mediator, and nothing to lay hold of to save yourself, nothing to keep off the flames of wrath, nothing of your own, nothing that you ever have done, nothing that you can do, to induce God to spare you one moment. . . .

When God beholds the ineffable[4] extremity of your case, and sees your torment to be so vastly disproportioned to your strength, and sees how your poor soul is crushed, and sinks down, as it were, into an infinite gloom; he will have no compassion upon you, he will not forbear the executions of his wrath, or in the least lighten his hand; there shall be no moderation or mercy, nor will God then at all stay his rough wind; he will have no regard to your welfare, nor be at all careful lest you should suffer too much in any other sense, than only that you shall *not suffer beyond what strict justice requires.* . . .

God stands ready to pity you; this is a day of mercy; you may cry now with some encouragement of obtaining mercy. But once the day of mercy is past, your most lamentable and dolorous[5] cries and shrieks

---

3. **closets** *n.* small, private rooms for meditation.
4. **ineffable** (in ef´ ə bəl) *n.* inexpressible.
5. **dolorous** (dō´ lər əs) *adj.* sad; mournful.

Vocabulary
mediator (mē´ dé ā tər) *n.* one who reconciles opposing groups

induce (in dōōs´) *v.* cause; bring about

❽ ☑ Reading Check

According to Edwards, what is "but thin air and empty shadows"?

from Sinners in the Hands of an Angry God **89**

---

❼ Literary Analysis
Sermon and Oratory

1. Have a volunteer read the bracketed passage. Have students count the number of times they hear the word *nothing*.

2. **Ask** students to summarize the message Edwards is trying to convey by using the word *nothing* five times.
   Answer: He is saying that his listeners are powerless and cannot save themselves from God's wrath.

3. Then, **ask** students the following question: What emotional response is Edwards tying to elicit by his use of rhythmic and repetitious language in the passage?
   Answer: Edwards is trying to make his listeners feel a sense of dread.

❽ Reading Check

Answer: Edwards believed that the things that people depended on for peace and safety had no substance, and he compared them to air and shadows.

Differentiated Instruction   for Universal Access

Strategy for Special-Needs Students
Students may benefit from a demonstration of how to use context clues. Invite them to identify a paragraph that includes one or more unfamiliar words or phrases. Write the passage on the board, underlining the difficult words. Then, circle the surrounding context clues that can help students determine the meanings of the unknown words. By reading the challenging words in relationship to the context clues, students may be able to interpret the meaning of the unfamiliar terms.

Enrichment for Gifted/Talented Students
Ask students to find details that distinguish this piece as a sermon. They may cite Edwards's use of religious references or his use of repetition to heighten the sense of the congregants' peril. Also, have students look for examples of figurative language (such as the personification of hell's "wide gaping mouth"), which adds poetic and dramatic impact to the sermon.

Using Context Clues

1. **Ask** a volunteer to read the bracketed passage while the class reads along silently.

2. **Ask** students to identify all words and phrases in the passage that refer to time.
   Answer: Words and phrases should include "moment," "eternity," "look forward," "forever," "duration," and "ever."

3. **Ask** students the Reading Strategy question: What clue does the reference to "forever" provide to the meaning of *boundless*?
   Answer: The word *forever* appears to be synonymous with *boundless,* so *boundless* probably means "without limits."

❿ Literary Analysis

Sermon and Oratory

1. **Invite** students to explain the basic purpose of oratory.
   Answer: Oratory is intended to persuade listeners and to inspire them to take action.

2. **Ask** a student volunteer to read the bracketed passage.

3. **Ask** students: What action is the passage beginning "But this is the dismal case" designed to inspire?
   Answer: This passage is designed to inspire parishioners to repent for their sins and convert their hearts by becoming "born again."

---

will be in vain; you will be wholly lost and thrown away of God, as to any regard to your welfare. God will have no other use to put you to, but to suffer misery; you shall be continued in being to no other end; for you will be a vessel of wrath fitted to destruction; and there will be no other use of this vessel, but to be filled full of wrath. . . .

Thus it will be with you that are in an unconverted state, if you continue in it; the infinite might, and majesty, and terribleness of the omnipotent God shall be magnified upon you, in the ineffable strength of your torments. You shall be tormented in the presence of the holy angels, and in the presence of the Lamb,[6] and when you shall be in this state of suffering, the glorious inhabitants of Heaven shall go forth and look on the awful spectacle, that they may see what the wrath and fierceness of the Almighty is; and when they have seen it, they will fall down and adore that great power and majesty. . . .

Reading Strategy ❾
Using Context Clues
What clue does the reference to "forever" provide to the meaning of *boundless*?

It would be dreadful to suffer this fierceness and wrath of Almighty God one moment; but you must suffer it to all eternity. There will be no end to this exquisite horrible misery. When you look forward, you shall see a long forever, a boundless duration before you, which will swallow up your thoughts and amaze your soul; and you will absolutely despair of ever having any deliverance, any end, any mitigation, any rest at all. . . .

❿ How dreadful is the state of those that are daily and hourly in the danger of this great wrath and infinite misery! But this is the dismal case of every soul in this congregation that has not been born again, however moral and strict, sober and religious, they may otherwise be. Oh that you would consider it, whether you be young or old! . . . Those of you that finally continue in a natural condition, that shall keep you out of Hell longest will be there in a little time! Your damnation does not slumber; it will come swiftly, and, in all probability, very suddenly upon many of you. You have reason to wonder that you are not already in Hell. It is doubtless the case of some whom you have seen and known, that never deserved Hell more than you, and that heretofore appeared as likely to have been now alive as you. Their case is past all hope; they are crying in extreme misery and perfect despair; but here you are in the land of the living and in the house of God, and have an opportunity to obtain salvation. What would not those poor damned hopeless souls give for one day's opportunity such as you now enjoy!

And now you have an extraordinary opportunity, a day wherein Christ has thrown the door of mercy wide open, and stands in calling and crying with a loud voice to poor sinners; a day wherein many are flocking to him, and pressing into the kingdom of God. Many are daily coming from the east, west, north and south; many that were very lately in the same miserable condition that you are in,

---

6. **the Lamb** Jesus.

Think Aloud

Vocabulary: Using Context

Direct students' attention to the word *exquisite* on this page. Use the following "think aloud" to model the skill of using context to infer the meaning of the word. Say to students:

Perhaps I am not sure of the meaning of the word *exquisite*. I have heard the word used before to describe something that is beautiful or perfect: an exquisite sunset, an exquisite painting. But Edwards is talking about an "exquisite horrible misery," which surprises me. When I think about it a little more, I realize that something that is exquisite is also *intense,* and that gives me a clue as to what Edwards is describing: a state of misery that is intense and indescribable and that lasts forever.

are now in a happy state, with their hearts filled with love to him who has loved them, and washed them from their sins in his own blood, and rejoicing in hope of the glory of God. How awful is it to be left behind at such a day! To see so many others feasting, while you are pining and perishing! To see so many rejoicing and singing for joy of heart, while you have cause to mourn for sorrow of heart, and howl for vexation of spirit! . . .

Therefore, let everyone that is out of Christ now awake and fly from the wrath to come. The wrath of Almighty God is now undoubtedly hanging over a great part of this congregation: let everyone fly out of Sodom.[7] "Haste and escape for your lives, look not behind you, escape to the mountain, lest you be consumed."[8]

---

7. **Sodom** (säd´ əm) In the Bible, a city destroyed by fire because of the sinfulness of its people.
8. **"Haste . . . consumed"** from Genesis 19:17, the angels' warning to Lot, the only virtuous man in Sodom, to flee the city before they destroy it.

Critical Reading

1. Key Ideas and Details (a) According to the opening paragraph, what keeps sinners from falling into hell? **(b) Interpret:** According to Edwards, what do his listeners mistakenly feel keeps them from falling into hell?

2. Key Ideas and Details (a) What words in the sermon's title suggest the emotional focus of Edwards's message? **(b) Analyze:** What additional traits does Edwards attribute to God as the sermon progresses?

3. Key Ideas and Details (a) Toward the end of the sermon, what does Edwards say sinners can obtain? **(b) Analyze Cause and Effect:** What must sinners do to obtain these things?

4. Integration of Knowledge and Ideas Given his purpose and the audience of worshipers to whom he spoke, do you think Edwards's sermon was effective? Why or why not?

5. Integration of Knowledge and Ideas This sermon played a significant role in reinvigorating Puritan faith during the 1740s. Why? State your opinion, using at least two of these Essential Question words: *powerful, beliefs, doctrine, faithful.* *[Connecting to the Essential Question: How does literature shape or reflect society?]*

> Cite textual evidence to support your responses.

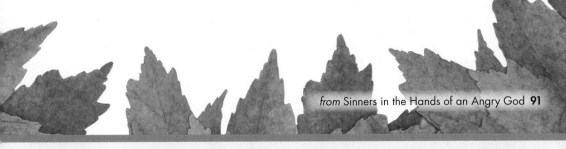

from Sinners in the Hands of an Angry God **91**

Concept Connector

Reading Strategy Graphic Organizer
Ask students to review the graphic organizers with which they have monitored their use of context clues to define difficult words. Then have them share their organizers and compare their conclusions about the meanings of words.

Activating Prior Knowledge
Have students return to their responses in the Activating Prior Knowledge activity. Ask them to explain whether their thoughts have changed and if so, how.

Connecting to the Essential Question
Have students compare the responses they gave to the prompt before reading *Sinners in the Hands of an Angry God* with their thoughts after reading it. Have them work individually or in groups, writing or discussing their thoughts, to define their new responses. Then, lead a class discussion, probing for what students have learned that confirms or invalidates their initial thoughts. Encourage students to cite specific textual details to support their responses.

⑪ Reading Strategy
Using Context Clues
1. Read aloud with students the bracketed passage. Have them listen for images suggesting abundance.
2. Invite a student volunteer to explain what it means to feast.
3. **Ask** students the following question: What clue does the reference to "feasting" provide to the meaning of *perishing*?
Answer: Edwards sets up a series of opposites in this passage. Thus, knowing that *feasting* means "eating a rich and elaborate meal" suggests that *perishing* means "dying," as from lack of nourishment.

ASSESS
Answers

Before students respond, you may wish to have them write a brief objective summary of the selection. As they answer the questions below, remind them to support their answers with evidence from the text.

1. (a) The hand of God prevents the sinner's fall. (b) His listeners mistakenly believe that their behavior keeps them from falling into Hell.

2. (a) The words *angry* and *sinners* suggest the emotional focus of Edwards's message. (b) He presents God as indifferent, contemptuous, and merciless, although capable of pity as well.

3. (a) They can obtain mercy and salvation. (b) To obtain these things, sinners must repent.

4. **Possible response:** Edwards's sermon was highly effective. Even contemporary readers can feel the sting of Edwards's threats

5. **Possible response:** The sermon was important because of the <u>powerful</u> way in which Edwards invoked images of eternal punishment and because of the clear way he stated the <u>doctrine</u> of the faith.

Answers

1. (a) Edwards is trying to convince his audience to repent and save themselves from damnation. (b) "O sinner! Consider the fearful danger you are in . . . ."; "And now you have an extraordinary opportunity. . . ."

2. **Possible answer:** Edwards uses graphic language to convince his listeners to be born again.

3. (a) He appeals to his listeners' fear. (b) His listeners fear damnation and doubt the strength of their faith and virtue.

4. (a) Edwards feels that God will view them as contemptible. (b) He is aware that his audience has been influenced by less strict ways of making moral judgments.

5. **Sample response:** (a) "Therefore, let everyone . . . fly from the wrath to come." (b) In this passage I respond to the direct but dramatic way the author evokes a response.

6. Such images of nature are appropriate because they call to mind similar images from the Bible, and because they are familiar and give listeners a clear idea of the consequences of failing to follow Edwards's message.

7. Edwards's reputation caused people to give greater credence to his message.

8. (a) Possible responses include bow and arrow, fire, and rough wind. (b) These reinforce the idea of God as a hostile force with a means to cause human suffering.

9. (a) *Waxing* means "growing or building." References to water that is "constantly rising" and the words "more and more" indicate something that is getting larger. (b) *Loathsome* means "hateful or repulsive." Holding an insect over a fire indicates that it is not seen in a positive light. *Abhors* means "detests or is disgusted by." If God puts the listener in the category of "some loathsome insect," then *abhor* must be associated with feelings of hatred or disgust. (c) *Mitigation* means "easing" and is synonymous with the other nouns Edwards uses: *rest, deliverance, end* (of suffering).

After You Read

from *Sinners in the Hands of an Angry God*

Literary Analysis

1. **Key Ideas and Details** (a) What message is Edwards conveying in this **sermon? (b)** Note two places where he directly states his purpose and message.

2. **Key Ideas and Details** Explain how Edwards's purpose and message are *persuasive*. What does he want his listeners to do or think?

3. **Craft and Structure** (a) What is the main *emotional appeal* Edwards uses in his effort to move his congregation? (b) Considering Edwards's purpose, why is this an appropriate choice? Explain your answer.

4. **Craft and Structure** (a) What does Edwards seem to feel about those who maintain a "form of religion" or who seem "moral and strict"? (b) How does this part of his message show that Edwards understands his *audience* well?

5. **Craft and Structure** (a) Choose two passages that you find very powerful. (b) Analyze the reasons for your choice: are you responding to the message itself, to the *rhythmic and expressive language* in which it is framed, or to both?

6. **Craft and Structure** Why are images of the destructive power of nature appropriate to Edwards's message?

7. **Integration of Knowledge and Ideas** Do you think Edwards's **oratory** would have been equally effective if he had not had a reputation as a brilliant spiritual leader?

8. **Integration of Knowledge and Ideas** (a) Use a chart like the one shown to identify Biblical **archetypes**—images, patterns, characters, or stories—Edwards uses to describe God's wrath. (b) How does each archetype add to the power of Edwards's message?

Wrath

"Great waters"

Reading Strategy

9. For each item below, **use context clues** to define the italicized words. Then, explain in your own words what each passage means.

   a. "you are every day treasuring up more wrath; the waters are constantly rising, and *waxing* more and more mighty…"

   b. "The God that holds you over the pit of Hell, much as one holds a spider, or some *loathsome* insect over the fire, *abhors* you, and is dreadfully provoked…"

   c. "…and you will absolutely despair of ever having any deliverance, any end, any *mitigation*, any rest at all…"

Common Core State Standards

Writing
1. Write arguments to support claims in an analysis of substantive topics or texts, using valid reasoning and relevant and sufficient evidence. (p. 93)

Language
3.a. Vary syntax for effect. (p. 94)
5. Demonstrate understanding of figurative language, word relationships, and nuances in word meanings. (p. 93)

Assessment Practice

Summarizing Written Texts (For more practice, see *All-in-One Workbook*.)

Many tests require students to identify the best summary of a passage. Present the following and ask students to choose the best summary.

However you may have reformed your life in many things, and may have had religious affections, and may keep up a form of religion in your families and closets, and in the house of God, it is nothing but his mere pleasure that keeps you from being this moment swallowed up in everlasting destruction.

A God can still condemn you even if you live virtuously, pray privately, and go to church.

B God will pardon you if you go to church.

C People should pray and lead virtuous lives.

D People should be religious in order to win God's approval.

B is accurate but incomplete. *C* and *D* are misleading: praying and being religious do not necessarily secure God's grace. *A* is best.

Integrated Language Skills

Vocabulary Acquisition and Use

Word Analysis: Latin Prefix *omni-*

The Latin prefix *omni-* means "all" or "every." *Omnipotent,* then, means "all-powerful." Each of the adjectives below contains the prefix *omni-*. Use the information in parentheses to match each adjective with the situation to which it best applies.

1. omniscient (*sciens* = knowing)
2. omnivorous (*vor* = to eat)
3. omnipresent (*praesens* = present)

a. how a zoologist might describe an animal that eats both meat and plants

b. how a student might describe a brilliant teacher

c. how someone lost in the desert might describe the sun

Vocabulary: Analogies

Analogies show the relationship between pairs of words. Complete each analogy using a word from the vocabulary list on page 84. In each, your choice should create a word pair that matches the relationship between the first two words given. Then, explain your answers.

1. *Brilliant* is to *smart* as _____ is to *powerful.*
2. *Soul* is to *spiritual* as _____ is to *physical.*
3. *Translator* is to *languages* as _____ is to *enemies.*
4. *Argue* is to *reconcile* as _____ is to *prevent.*
5. *Loyalty* is to *faithless* as _____ is to *reckless.*

Writing

Argument A speaker's choice of persuasive techniques should depend on the audience and the occasion. Write an **evaluation** of the persuasive techniques that Edwards uses. Discuss the response he evokes in an audience and the ways he achieves it.

Prewriting To focus your writing, jot down examples of Edwards's uses of imagery, logical reasoning, and emotional appeals. Make sure all of your choices are relevant and provide sufficient support for your claims. Then, write one statement in which you evaluate their effectiveness in reaching an audience.

Drafting Use the statement you wrote as the basis for a strong, focused opening paragraph. Support your main point in the paragraphs that follow.

> **Model: Building Unity**
> Jonathan Edwards appealed to his audience's vulnerability by using powerful, elemental images of nature run amok. His images of air, water, and fire terrified his audience by summoning up mental pictures of unlimited natural destruction.

The paragraph contains a general statement followed by details of specific images used by Edwards.

Revising Read your evaluation as though you are seeing it for the first time. Eliminate any information that is unrelated to the main idea.

Vocabulary Acquisition and Use

1. Introduce the skill, using the instruction on the student page.
2. Have students complete the Word Analysis activity and the Vocabulary practice.

Word Analysis

1. b
2. a
3. c

Vocabulary

1. omnipotent; *omnipotent* and *powerful* are synonymous, as are *brilliant* and *smart.*

2. constitution; just as *soul* refers to a nonmaterial entity, *constitution* has to do with physical existence.

3. mediator; a mediator serves as a "bridge" between enemies, just as a translator connects people who do not share a language.

4. induce; each pair contains words with opposite meanings.

5. prudence; each pair contains words with opposite meanings.

Writing

1. To guide students in writing this evaluation of persuasion, give them the **Support for Writing Lesson** page (*Unit 1 Resources,* p. 156).

2. Students' evaluations should express a clear and definite view of Edwards's achievement in this excerpt from *Sinners in the Hands of an Angry God.* Remind students that the effectiveness of the sermon is related directly to Edwards's Puritan audience, not to a contemporary American one.

3. Students should not only identify Edwards's principal themes, but should also explain how these themes interrelate. Similarly, students should cite the sermon's key images and explain how they reinforce each other.

4. Assess students' evaluations using the **Rubrics for Self Assessment: Persuasive Essay,** *Professional Development Guidebook,* pages 256–257.

Assessment Resources

Unit 1 Resources

L1 L2 EL **Selection Test A,** pp. 143–145. Administer Test A to less advanced students and English learners.

L3 L4 EL **Selection Test B,** pp. 146–148. Administer Test B to on-level and more advanced students.

L3 L4 **Open-Book Test,** pp. 140–142. As an alternative, administer the Open-Book Test.

All **Customizable Test Bank**

All **Self-tests** Students may prepare for the **Selection Test** by taking the **Self-test** online.

 All assessment resources are available at **www.PHLitOnline.com.**

Conventions and Style

Introduce and discuss the skill.

Think Aloud: Model the Skill

Say to students:

Suppose I wanted to go to a certain college. I could say: "College A has a top-rated business program. College A has a great reputation for placing graduates." However, a sentence with correlative conjunctions will make my argument stronger: "College A not only has a top-rated business program, but also a great reputation for placing graduates."

Practice

1. either; or
2. not only; but also
3. whether; or
4. neither; nor
5. both; and
6. Neither the sinner nor the serpent will be spared.
7. He preached to both Puritans and Native Americans.
8. The storm imagery is not only eloquent but also powerful.
9. People could choose either to be saved or to endure eternal suffering.
10. Either He can hold you out of the fire or He can withdraw His hand and let you fall.

Writing and Speaking Conventions

A. **Sample responses:**
1. He expresses both anger and mercy in his speech.
2. Whether we will be miserable or enjoy eternal life will be decided by God.
3. We are called not only to endure suffering but also to rejoice in hope that God will save us.

B. **Sample response:** You say that neither a moral life nor faithful church attendance saves us from God's wrath. Yet Jesus taught forgiveness. I would like to know whether I have misunderstood your words or the words of Jesus.

PH **WRITING COACH**   Grade 11

Students will find additional information on correlative conjunctions in Chapter 13.

Conventions and Style: Correlative Conjunctions

The use of *varied sentence structures* makes your writing more sophisticated and gives it a better flow. If you tend to use many short sentences, combine the ones that express related ideas into longer units. Correlative conjunctions can help you do this. A **correlative conjunction** is a word pair that is used to connect similar words or groups of words. Different correlative conjunctions show different relationships between ideas.

Using Correlative Conjunctions

Choppy Sentences: The sermon was frightening. The sermon was inspiring.
Combined: The sermon was *not only* frightening *but also* inspiring.

Choppy Sentences: The waters will be held back. If not, the flood gates will open.
Combined: *Either* the waters will be held back *or* the floodgates will open.

Common Correlative Conjunctions	
Both/and	Not only/but also
Either/or	Whether/or
Neither/nor	As/as

Tip: Use parallel grammatical structures after both parts of the correlative conjunction.

Ⓒ Writing and Speaking Conventions

A. **Writing** For each word pair, write a sentence in which you link the two words or word groups using a correlative conjunction. Make sure to use the same grammatical structures after both parts of the correlative conjunction.
1. anger—mercy
2. miserable—eternal
3. to endure suffering—to rejoice in hope
   Example: anger—mercy
   Sentence: He can show either anger or mercy.

B. **Speaking** As a member of Edwards's congregation, write and present to the class a response to the sermon. Include two correlative conjunctions.

Practice In items 1–5, fill in the blanks with appropriate correlative conjunctions. In items 6–10, combine the two sentences using a correlative conjunction.

1. _____ the arrow will be released _____ it will not.
2. The sermon appeals _____ to people's fears _____ to their hopes.
3. Who decides _____ a person will go to heaven _____ burn in hell?
4. According to Edwards, _____ moral strictness _____ church attendance will reduce God's wrath.
5. The storm, _____ furious _____ dreadful, can be released at any time.
6. The sinner will not be spared. The serpent will not be spared.
7. He preached to Puritans. He also preached to Native Americans.
8. The storm imagery is eloquent. The storm imagery is powerful.
9. People could choose to be saved. They could choose to endure eternal suffering.
10. He can hold you out of the fire. He can withdraw His hand and let you fall.

PH **WRITING COACH**

Further instruction and practice are available in *Prentice Hall Writing Coach*.

Extend the Lesson

Sentence Modeling

Read this sentence from *Sinners in the Hands of an Angry God*:

Oh that you would consider it, whether you be young or old!

Ask students what they notice about the sentence. Elicit from them that the sentence uses a correlative conjunction. Then, ask what else they notice. They might say it is an oratorical sentence that attempts to persuade listeners, address their concerns, and appeal to their emotions, and that it uses expressive language.

Have students imitate the sentence in a sentence on a topic of their own choosing, matching each grammatical and stylistic feature discussed. Collect the sentences and share them with the class.

A Nation is Born

PART 3

Selection Planning Guide

This section features two contrasting examples of American oratory: Patrick Henry's soaring "Speech in the Virginia Convention" and Benjamin Franklin's wise and adroit "Speech in the Convention." Also included are excerpts from some of the foundational documents of American government and culture: Thomas Jefferson's Declaration of Independence, Thomas Paine's *The American Crisis,* and Benjamin Franklin's *Autobiography.*

Humanities

Portrait of Washington, about 1780, unknown artist

This portrait is distinctive in its relaxed, almost casual presentation of its famously formal subject. Washington rests his arm on the saddle; his knee is bent, and his hand loosely holds the reins. The composition of the painting counterpoises the tall, vertical figure of Washington against the falling curves of the horse to emphasize the stature and strength of the subject.

Use these questions for discussion:

1. What overall impression or mood is created in this portrait of George Washington?
   Possible response: Students may say that Washington's casual pose and the bowed posture of the horse suggest a feeling of calmness and relaxation.

2. What statement about Washington as a leader do you think the artist is making? Use details from the painting to explain your answer.
   Possible response: Washington's expression and relaxed pose suggest that he is a calm and thoughtful leader; his vertical stature suggests confidence and strength.

Monitoring Progress

Before students read the selections in Part 3, administer the **Diagnostic Test 1** (*Unit 1 Resources,* pp. 1–6). This test will determine students' level of readiness for the reading and vocabulary skills.

© Text Complexity: At a Glance

This chart gives a general text complexity rating for the selections in this part of the unit to help guide instruction. For additional text complexity support, see the Text Complexity Rubric at point of use.			
Speech in the Virginia Convention	**More Complex**	To His Excellency, General Washington	**More Complex**
Speech in the Convention	**More Complex**	*from* The Autobiography	**More Complex**
The Declaration of Independence	**More Complex**	Poor Richard's Almanac	**More Accessible**
from The American Crisis	**More Accessible**		

❶ Defining Speeches

1. Remind students that speeches are delivered orally, even though they will read printed versions of speeches.

2. **Ask:** How is a speech different from other nonfiction works, such as an essay?

   Sample responses: Speeches often have greater emotional impact than other nonfiction works. Speeches also draw as much attention to the language they use as to the ideas they express. Because they are spoken aloud, speeches usually give special emphasis to rhythm and other sound devices, unlike essays and other forms of nonfiction.

❷ Types of Speeches

1. Review types of speeches: the political speech, the address, and the sermon. Explain that some of these categories overlap. For example, a president's inaugural address has elements of a political speech and an address.

2. Ask students if they have had any recent experiences with speeches via television or personal attendance. Have volunteers describe the occasion and type of speech encountered.

❸ Rhetorical Devices

Review the types of rhetorical devices described on the student page. Invite volunteers to read aloud the examples. Discuss with students which ones they found particularly effective. Point out that rhetorical devices are not restricted to formal occasions.

❹ Close Read: Rhetorical Devices

Point out examples of highlighted text in the model on page 97. Explain that in each case, the color of the highlighting matches the color of the category in the chart. Details that illustrate a given category are highlighted in the color of that category.

SPEECH IS POWER: SPEECH IS TO PERSUADE, TO CONVERT, TO COMPEL.

— RALPH WALDO EMERSON

❶ Defining Speeches

A **speech** is a nonfiction work that is delivered orally to an audience. Some speeches are fully composed before the speaker reads them aloud. Others are planned in notes or an outline to which the speaker refers as he or she talks.

❷ Types of Speeches
There are countless appropriate settings and purposes for speeches. Common types of speeches include the following:

- **Political Speech:** a speech focusing on an issue relating to government
- **Address:** a formal speech prepared for a special occasion, such as the dedication of a memorial or the inauguration of a new leader
- **Sermon:** a speech intended to provide religious instruction

❸ Rhetorical Devices
Regardless of the occasion, speeches typically include rhetorical devices—patterns of words and ideas that create emphasis, clarify meaning, and stir listeners' emotions. There are numerous rhetorical figures, including the following types.

- **Restatement:** expressing the same ideas using different words
  Abraham Lincoln: "…we can not dedicate—we can not consecrate—we can not hallow—this ground."
- **Anaphora:** repetition of the same word or group of words at the beginning of successive sentences, clauses, or phrases
  Winston Churchill: "We shall go on to the end, we shall fight in France, we shall fight on the seas and oceans…"
- **Rhetorical Questions:** questions asked for effect rather than answers
  Benjamin Franklin: "From such an assembly can a perfect production be expected?"

❹ Close Read: Rhetorical Devices
These rhetorical devices appear in the Model text at right.

Repetition: restating an idea using the same words *Example: "The war is inevitable—and let it come! I repeat it, sir, let it come!" (Patrick Henry)*	**Antithesis:** juxtaposition of strongly contrasting words, images, or ideas *Example: "…ask not what your country can do for you—ask what you can do for your country." (John F. Kennedy)*
Parallelism: repeating a grammatical structure *Example: "With malice toward none; with charity for all…" (Abraham Lincoln)*	**Exclamation:** an emotional statement, often indicated in texts by an exclamation mark *Example: "…as for me, give me liberty or give me death!" (Patrick Henry)*

Extend the Lesson

Evaluating Speeches
Ask students to watch, read, or listen to a contemporary speech—perhaps a political speech, an address at a school function, or a sermon.

Then, have them develop their own set of standards as to what makes that speech—or any speech—effective. Tell them to focus particularly on rhetorical devices and to ask themselves the following questions:

- Am I more drawn to certain rhetorical devices than to others? Why?

  After each student lists his or her standards for an effective speech, have students work in groups to compile their ideas. Work with the class to come up with a comprehensive set of standards.

⑤ Model

About the Text Frederick Douglass (ca. 1818–1895) escaped from slavery and became a writer, orator, and abolitionist. On July 5, 1852, he delivered a speech at a celebration of the signing of the Declaration of Independence. In the speech he states, "This Fourth of July is *yours*, not *mine*. You may rejoice, I must mourn."

---

from "What to the Slave Is the Fourth of July?"
Frederick Douglass

⑥ Fellow Citizens, I am not wanting in respect for the fathers of this republic. The signers of the Declaration of Independence were brave men. They were great men too—great enough to give fame to a great age. It does not often happen to a nation to raise, at one time, such a number of truly great men. The point from which I am compelled to view them is not, certainly, the most favorable; and yet I cannot contemplate their great deeds with less than admiration. They were statesmen, patriots and heroes, and for the good they did, and the principles they contended for, I will unite with you to honor their memory.

They loved their country better than their own private interests; and, though this is not the highest form of human excellence, all will concede that it is a rare virtue, and that when it is exhibited, it ought to command respect. He who will, intelligently, lay down his life for his country, is a man whom it is not in human nature to despise. Your fathers staked their lives, their fortunes, and their sacred honor, on the cause of their country. In their admiration of liberty, they lost sight of all other interests.

⑦ They were peace men; but they preferred revolution to peaceful submission to bondage. They were quiet men; but they did not shrink from agitating against oppression. They showed forbearance; but that they knew its limits. They believed in order; but not in the order of tyranny. With them, nothing was "settled" that was not right. With them, justice, liberty and humanity were "final;" not slavery and oppression. You may well cherish the memory of such men. They were great in their day and generation. Their solid manhood stands out the more as we contrast it with these degenerate times.

⑧ How circumspect, exact and proportionate were all their movements! How unlike the politicians of an hour! Their statesmanship looked beyond the passing moment, and stretched away in strength into the distant future. They seized upon eternal principles, and set a glorious example in their defense. Mark them!

⑨ Fully appreciating the hardship to be encountered, firmly believing in the right of their cause, honorably inviting the scrutiny of an on-looking world, reverently appealing to heaven to attest their sincerity, soundly comprehending the solemn responsibility they were about to assume, wisely measuring the terrible odds against them, your fathers, the fathers of this republic, did, most deliberately, under the inspiration of a glorious patriotism, and with a sublime faith in the great principles of justice and freedom, lay deep the corner-stone of the national superstructure, which has risen and still rises in grandeur around you.

---

⑥ Repetition Repeated use of the word "great" supports the idea that Douglass honors the nation's founders. This allows listeners to more readily accept the argument he will later present that the founders' greatness does not excuse their support of slavery.

⑦ Antithesis Douglass's use of opposing ideas emphasizes the complexity of the founding fathers' beliefs and actions.

⑧ Exclamation Douglass uses exclamation to show the urgency of his feelings and to stir emotion in his audience.

⑨ Parallelism Douglass uses parallelism to add urgency to his accounting of the founding fathers' wisdom and courage.

Extended Study: Speeches **97**

---

⑤ Model
Point out that slavery was still legal in the United States when Douglass delivered this address. Lead students to understand the irony of an escaped slave delivering a speech on Independence Day.

⑥ Repetition
1. Invite a volunteer to read the bracketed passage of text. Point out that Douglass uses the word "great" five times. **Ask:** What other words might Douglass have used in place of "great"?

   Sample responses: *remarkable; accomplished; significant; powerful; famous*

2. Have students experiment reading aloud the passage, using synonyms of their choice in place of "great." Discuss how these changes affect the impact of speech.

⑦ Antithesis
1. Read aloud the bracketed passage. **Ask:** What word indicates antithesis?

   Answer: *but*

2. Encourage students to compose a series of three or four sentences, using opposing ideas about a current political figure or celebrity.

⑧ Exclamation
Remind students that exclamatory sentences often begin with the words *how* or *what*. **Ask:** How would you reword the first sentence of this passage so that it is not an exclamation?

Possible response: All their movements were circumspect, exact, and proportionate.

⑨ Parallelism
Have a volunteer read aloud the bracketed text. **Ask:** What are the parallel elements that Douglass uses in this passage?

Answer: the adverb and verb pairings "Fully appreciating," "firmly believing," "honorably inviting," "reverently appealing," "soundly comprehending," "wisely measuring"

Differentiated
Instruction   for Universal Access

EL Strategies for English Learners
The speeches in this unit may present challenges to students who are learning English. Have students listen to an oral reading of one of the cited speeches on the *Hear It!* **Audio CD** before they read it for themselves. Have them work with partners to break down long sentences into smaller segments. Encourage partners to paraphrase these segments and to have their paraphrases at hand when they listen once again to the oral reading.

Strategies for Gifted/Talented Students
Have students with performing-arts skills read aloud passages from the speeches in this unit. Ask them to tell the class how it felt to deliver the speech—where they had to pay particular attention to the rhythm, when the language was more difficult to enunciate, and where and why they chose to change their pace and volume.

• Speech in the Virginia Convention
• Speech in the Convention
Lesson Pacing Guide

DAY 1 Preteach

- © Administer the Reading and Vocabulary Warm-ups (*Unit 1 Resources,* pp. 149–152) as necessary.
- Introduce the Literary Analysis concept: Persuasive Speeches.
- © Introduce the Reading Strategy: Critiquing Appeal to Audiences.
- Build background with the author and Background features.
- Develop thematic thinking with Connecting to the Essential Question.
- © Teach the selection vocabulary.

DAYS 2–3 Preteach/Teach/Assess

- Distribute copies of the appropriate graphic organizer for the Reading Strategy (*Graphic Organizer Transparencies,* pp. 29–30).
- Distribute copies of the appropriate graphic organizer for Literary Analysis (*Graphic Organizer Transparencies,* pp. 31–32).
- Prepare students to read with the Activating Prior Knowledge activities (TE).
- Informally monitor comprehension while students read.
- Use the Reading Check questions to confirm comprehension.
- © Develop students' understanding of persuasive speeches using the Literary Analysis prompts.
- Develop students' ability to critique persuasive appeals using the Reading Strategy prompt.
- © Reinforce vocabulary with the Vocabulary notes.
- Assess students' comprehension and mastery of the skills by having them answer the Critical Reading, Literary Analysis, and Reading Strategy questions.
- Have students complete the Vocabulary Lesson.

DAY 4 Extend/Assess

- © Have students complete the Writing Lesson and write a compare-and-contrast essay. (You may assign as homework.)
- Administer Selection Test A or B (*Unit 1 Resources,* pp. 161–163 or 164–166).

© Common Core State Standards

Reading Informational Text
6. Determine an author's point of view or purpose in a text in which the rhetoric is particularly effective, analyzing how style and content contribute to the power, persuasiveness, or beauty of the text.
9. Analyze seventeenth-, eighteenth-, and nineteenth-century foundational U.S. documents of historical and literary significance for their themes, purposes, and rhetorical features.

Writing 2. Write informative/explanatory texts to examine and convey complex ideas, concepts, and information clearly and accurately through the effective selection, organization, and analysis of content.
2.a. Introduce a topic; organize complex ideas, concepts, and information so that each new element builds on that which precedes it to create a unified whole.

Language 5. Demonstrate understanding of figurative language, word relationships, and nuances in word meanings.

Additional Standards Practice
Common Core Companion, *pp. 143-150; 170-171; 196-207; 332–335*

Daily Block Scheduling
Each day in this Lesson Pacing Guide represents a 40–50 minute period. Teachers using block scheduling may combine days to revise pacing. In addition, teachers may differentiate and support core instruction by integrating components for extended and intensive support as students require. See the Guide to Selected Leveled Resources (facing page).

Guide to Selected Leveled Resources

Tier 1 (students performing on level)

R T I Tier 1 (students performing on level) | Speech in the Virginia Convention • Speech in the Convention

Warm Up	**Practice, model,** and **monitor** fluency, working **with the whole class** or **in groups**.	Vocabulary and Reading Warm-ups B, *Unit 1 Resources,* pp. 149–150, 152
Comprehension/Skills	**Support** and **monitor** comprehension and skills development, having students complete the activities, graphic organizers, and interactive prompts **independently** or **as a class**.	• *Reader's Notebook,* adapted instruction and summary **EL** *Reader's Notebook: English Learner's Version,* adapted instruction and summary • **Reading Strategy Graphic Organizer B,** *Graphic Organizer Transparencies,* p. 30 • **Literary Analysis Graphic Organizer B,** *Graphic Organizer Transparencies,* p. 32
Monitor Progress	**Monitor** student progress with the differentiated curriculum-based assessment in the *Unit Resources.*	• **Selection Test B,** *Unit 1 Resources,* pp. 164–166 • **Open-Book Test,** *Unit 1 Resources,* pp. 158–160

Tier 2 (students requiring intervention)

R T I Tier 2 (students requiring intervention) | Speech in the Virginia Convention • Speech in the Convention

Warm Up	**Practice, model,** and **monitor** fluency **in groups** or **with individuals**.	• **Vocabulary and Reading Warm-ups A,** *Unit 1 Resources,* pp. 149–151 • *Hear It!* **Audio CD**
Comprehension/Skills	• **Support** and **monitor** comprehension and skills development, working **in small groups** or **with individuals**. • As students complete the selection in the appropriate version of the *Reader's Notebook,* **monitor** comprehension frequently with group questions and individual instruction. • **Model** strategies while guiding students in completing the activities and prompts in the *Reader's Notebook,* as well as the graphic organizers. • **Practice** skills and **monitor** mastery with the *Reading Kit* worksheets.	• *Reader's Notebook: Adapted Version,* adapted instruction and summary **EL** *Reader's Notebook: English Learner's Version,* adapted instruction and summary • **Reading Strategy Graphic Organizer A,** *Graphic Organizer Transparencies,* p. 29 • **Literary Analysis Graphic Organizer A,** *Graphic Organizer Transparencies,* p. 31 • *Reading Kit,* Practice worksheets
Monitor Progress	**Monitor** student progress with the differentiated curriculum-based assessment in the *Unit Resources* and in the *Reading Kit.*	• **Selection Test A,** *Unit 1 Resources,* pp. 161–163 • *Reading Kit,* Assess worksheets

TIER 3 Tier 3 intervention may require consultation with the student's special-education or dyslexia specialist. For additional support, see the Tier 2 activities and resources listed above.

One-on-one teaching **Group work** **Whole class instruction** **Independent work** **A** Assessment

For a complete guide to selection support, including support for Advanced students, see the Overview of Resources in the frontmatter.

• Speech in the Virginia Convention
• Speech in the Convention

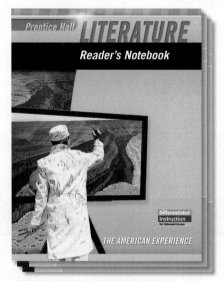

RESOURCES FOR:
- **L1** Special-Needs Students
- **L2** Below-Level Students (Tier 2)
- **L3** On-Level Students (Tier 1)
- **L4** Advanced Students (Tier 1)
- **EL** English Learners
- **All** All Students

Vocabulary/Fluency/Prior Knowledge

EL **L1** **L2** **Reading Warm-ups A and B,** pp. 151–152

Also available for these selections:

EL **L1** **L2** **Vocabulary Warm-ups A and B,** pp. 149–150

All **Vocabulary Builder,** p. 155

Reader's Notebooks

Pre- and postreading pages for these selections appear in an interactive format in the *Reader's Notebooks*. Each *Notebook* is differentiated for a different group of learners. The selections in the Adapted and English Learner's versions are abridged.

- **L2** **L3** *Reader's Notebook*
- **L1** *Reader's Notebook: Adapted Version*
- **EL** *Reader's Notebook: English Learner's Version*
- **EL** *Reader's Notebook: Spanish Version*

© *Common Core Companion*

Additional instruction and practice for each Common Core State Standard

Selection Support

Skills Development/Extension

Assessment

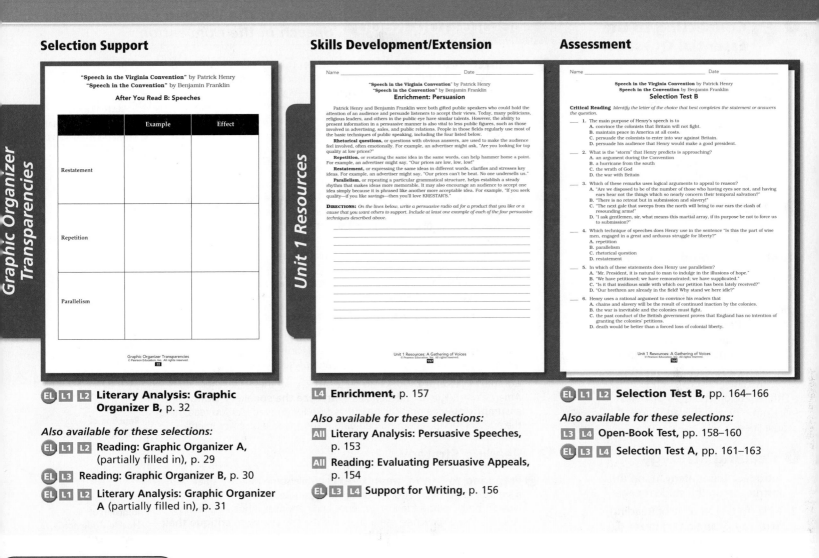

"Speech in the Virginia Convention" by Patrick Henry
"Speech in the Convention" by Benjamin Franklin

After You Read B: Speeches

	Example	Effect
Restatement		
Repetition		
Parallelism		

"Speech in the Virginia Convention" by Patrick Henry
"Speech in the Convention" by Benjamin Franklin
Enrichment: Persuasion

Patrick Henry and Benjamin Franklin were both gifted public speakers who could hold the attention of an audience and persuade listeners to accept their views. Today, many politicians, religious leaders, and others in the public eye have similar talents. However, the ability to present information in a persuasive manner is also vital to less public figures, such as those involved in advertising, sales, and public relations. People in those fields regularly use most of the basic techniques of public speaking, including the four listed below.

Rhetorical questions, or questions with obvious answers, are used to make the audience feel involved, often emotionally. For example, an advertiser might ask, "Are you looking for top quality at low prices?"

Repetition, or restating the same idea in the same words, can help hammer home a point. For example, an advertiser might say, "Our prices are low, low, low!"

Restatement, or expressing the same ideas in different words, clarifies and stresses key ideas. For example, an advertiser might say, "Our prices can't be beat. No one undersells us."

Parallelism, or repeating a particular grammatical structure, helps establish a steady rhythm that makes ideas more memorable. It may also encourage an audience to accept one idea simply because it is phrased like another more acceptable idea. For example, "If you seek quality—if you like savings—then you'll love KRESTAR'S."

DIRECTIONS: On the lines below, write a persuasive radio ad for a product that you like or a cause that you want others to support. Include at least one example of each of the four persuasive techniques described above.

Speech in the Virginia Convention by Patrick Henry
Speech in the Convention by Benjamin Franklin
Selection Test B

Critical Reading Identify the letter of the choice that best completes the statement or answers the question.

___ 1. The main purpose of Henry's speech is to
A. convince the colonists that Britain will not fight.
B. maintain peace in America at all costs.
C. persuade the colonists to enter into war against Britain.
D. persuade his audience that Henry would make a good president.

___ 2. What is the "storm" that Henry predicts is approaching?
A. an argument during the Convention
B. a hurricane from the south
C. the wrath of God
D. the war with Britain

___ 3. Which of these remarks uses logical arguments to appeal to reason?
A. "Are we disposed to be of the number of those who having eyes see not, and having ears hear not the things which so nearly concern their temporal salvation?"
B. "There is no retreat but in submission and slavery!"
C. "The next gale that sweeps from the north will bring to our ears the clash of resounding arms!"
D. "I ask gentlemen, sir, what means this martial array, if its purpose be not to force us to submission?"

___ 4. Which technique of speeches does Henry use in the sentence "Is this the part of wise men, engaged in a great and arduous struggle for liberty?"
A. repetition
B. parallelism
C. rhetorical question
D. restatement

___ 5. In which of these statements does Henry use parallelism?
A. "Mr. President, it is natural to man to indulge in the illusions of hope."
B. "We have petitioned; we have remonstrated; we have supplicated."
C. "Is it that insidious smile with which our petition has been lately received?"
D. "Our brethren are already in the field! Why stand we here idle?"

___ 6. Henry uses a rational argument to convince his readers that
A. chains and slavery will be the result of continued inaction by the colonies.
B. the war is inevitable and the colonies must fight.
C. the past conduct of the British government proves that England has no intention of granting the colonies' petitions.
D. death would be better than a forced loss of colonial liberty.

EL **L1** **L2** **Literary Analysis: Graphic Organizer B,** p. 32

Also available for these selections:

EL **L1** **L2** **Reading: Graphic Organizer A,** (partially filled in), p. 29

EL **L3** **Reading: Graphic Organizer B,** p. 30

EL **L1** **L2** **Literary Analysis: Graphic Organizer A** (partially filled in), p. 31

L4 **Enrichment,** p. 157

Also available for these selections:

All **Literary Analysis: Persuasive Speeches,** p. 153

All **Reading: Evaluating Persuasive Appeals,** p. 154

EL **L3** **L4** **Support for Writing,** p. 156

EL **L1** **L2** **Selection Test B,** pp. 164–166

Also available for these selections:

L3 **L4** **Open-Book Test,** pp. 158–160

EL **L3** **L4** **Selection Test A,** pp. 161–163

PHLit Online!
www.PHLitOnline.com

Online Resources: All print materials are also available online.

- complete narrated selection text
- a thematically related video with writing prompt
- an interactive graphic organizer
- highlighting feature
- access to all student print resources, adapted to individual student needs
- Spanish and English summaries
- adapted selection translations in Spanish

Get Connected!

Also available:

Background Video (thematic video with writing prompt)
All videos available in Spanish.

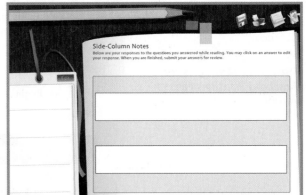

Writer's Journal (with graphics feature)

Also available:

Vocabulary Central (tools and activities for studying vocabulary)

❶ ❓ Connecting to the Essential Question

1. Review the assignment.

2. Ask students if they have ever been inspired by a speech. After discussing their reactions, have them complete the assignment.

3. As students read, have them notice how each speaker stresses the need to deal with realities.

❷ Literary Analysis

Introduce the skills.

Think Aloud: Model the Skill

Say to students:

Repetition can be a powerful device. When his country feared invasion, British prime minister Winston Churchill asserted that "we shall fight in the fields and in the streets, we shall fight in the hills; we shall never surrender." The repetition creates a powerful rhythm. The result is an unforgettable speech.

❸ Reading Strategy

1. Introduce the strategy, using the instruction on the student page.

2. Give students a copy of **Reading Strategy Graphic Organizer B**, page 30 in *Graphic Organizer Transparencies*, to fill out as they read.

❹ Vocabulary

1. Pronounce each word, giving its definition, and have students say it aloud.

2. For more guidance, see the **Classroom Strategies and Teaching Routines** card for introducing vocabulary.

Before You Read | *Speech in the Virginia Convention • Speech in the Convention*

❶ **Connecting to the Essential Question** These speeches prompted great change. Henry's words spurred the American Revolution, and Franklin's helped to shaped our government. As you read, notice how each speaker stresses the need to deal in realities rather than illusions. Doing so will help as you think about the Essential Question: **How does literature shape or reflect society?**

❷ ## Literary Analysis

In these persuasive **speeches,** Henry and Franklin employ many of the **rhetorical devices** defined on page 96, including **restatement, repetition, parallelism,** and **rhetorical questions.** These devices serve to emphasize key points, make speeches memorable, and move listeners' emotions.

Persuasive orators like Henry and Franklin also use **allusions,** references to well-known people or events from history, literature, the Bible, and other sources. For example, in this passage, Patrick Henry alludes to the biblical figure of Judas, who betrayed Jesus "with a kiss":

> *Trust it not, sir; it will prove a snare to your feet. Suffer not yourselves to be betrayed with a kiss.*

As you read, notice examples of rhetorical devices and allusions and analyze how they contribute to the power and persuasiveness of each speech.

Comparing Literary Works To better appreciate these speeches about America's struggle for independence, **analyze the speakers' political assumptions**—the political ideas they take for granted. As you read, note the authors' beliefs about human nature and the role of government.

❸ ## Reading Strategy

ⓒ **Preparing to Read Complex Texts** While some listeners agree with a speaker, others may strongly disagree. A persuasive speech is effective when it both holds a friendly audience and convinces a hostile one. As you read these speeches, use a chart like the one shown to **critique their appeal to friendly and hostile audiences.**

❹ ## Vocabulary

insidious (in´ sid´ ē əs) *adj.* deceitful; treacherous (p. 101)

privileges (priv´ lij əz) *n.* special rights; advantages (p. 102)

vigilant (vij´ ə lənt) *adj.* alert to danger (p. 103)

despotism (des´ pət iz´ əm) *n.* absolute rule; tyranny (p. 105)

salutary (sal´ yoo ter´ ē) *adj.* beneficial; promoting a good purpose (p. 107)

unanimity (yoo´ nə nim´ ə tē) *n.* complete agreement (p. 107)

Common Core State Standards

Reading Informational Text

6. Determine an author's point of view or purpose in a text in which the rhetoric is particularly effective, analyzing how style and content contribute to the power, persuasiveness, or beauty of the text.

9. Analyze seventeenth-, eighteenth-, and nineteenth-century foundational U.S. documents of historical and literary significance for their themes, purposes, and rhetorical features.

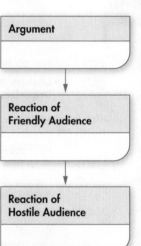

Argument

↓

Reaction of Friendly Audience

↓

Reaction of Hostile Audience

www.PHLitOnline.com

Vocabulary Development

Vocabulary Knowledge Rating

Create a **Vocabulary Knowledge Rating Chart** (*Professional Development Guidebook,* p. 33) for the vocabulary words on the student page. Give each student a copy of the chart with the words on it. Read the words aloud and have students mark their rating in the Before Reading column. Urge students to attend to these words as they read and discuss the selections, because they will rate their knowledge again after they finish reading.

In order to gauge how much instruction you need to provide, tally how many students know (or think they know) a word before reading. As students read, point out the words and their contexts.

PHLit Online! **Vocabulary Central,** featuring tools and activities for studying vocabulary, is available online at **www.PHLitOnline.com.**

Patrick Henry *(1736–1799)*

Author of "Speech in the Virginia Convention"

It was said that Patrick Henry could move his listeners to anger, fear, or laughter more easily than the most talented actor. Remembered most for his fiery battle cry—"Give me liberty or give me death"—Henry is considered to be the most powerful orator of the American Revolution. He helped to inspire colonists to unite in an effort to win their independence from Great Britain.

Voice of Protest In 1765, Henry was elected to the Virginia House of Burgesses. Shortly after his election, he delivered one of his most powerful speeches, declaring his opposition to the Stamp Act. The Stamp Act, which was passed by the British Parliament, required American colonists to pay a tax on every piece of printed paper they used. Legal documents, newspapers, and even playing cards were all subject to the tax. Over the protests of some of its most influential members, the Virginia House adopted Henry's resolutions.

A Call to Arms In 1775, Henry delivered his most famous speech at the Virginia Provincial Convention. While most of the speakers that day argued that the colony should seek a compromise with the British, Henry boldly urged armed resistance to England. His speech had a powerful impact on the audience, feeding the revolutionary spirit that led to the signing of the Declaration of Independence.

In the years that followed, Henry continued to be an important political leader, serving as governor of Virginia and member of the Virginia General Assembly.

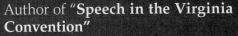

Give me liberty or give me Death!

Speech in the Virginia Convention **99**

🔔 Daily Bellringer

For each class during which you will teach the selections, including the Comparing Literary Works selection, have students complete one of the five activities for the relevant week in the *Daily Bellringer Activities* booklet.

Multidraft Reading

To assist struggling readers and to enhance reading for all, assign the text in chunks as warranted by length and apply multidraft reading protocols. For each reading, have students set the purpose indicated:

- **First reading**—identifying key ideas and details and answering any Reading Checks.
- **Second reading**—analyzing craft and structure and responding to the side-column prompts.
- **Third reading**—integrating knowledge and ideas, connecting to other texts and the world, and answering the end-of-selection questions.

For more guidance, refer to the *Classroom Strategies and Teaching Routines* card on multidraft reading.

⑤ Background
More About the Author

Patrick Henry was no stranger to conflict with the British Crown. In 1765 he had been accused of treason when he delivered his fiery denunciation of the Stamp Act. On that occasion, Henry had referred to two leaders who had been killed for political reasons and declared that King George III might "profit by their example." This shocked the members of the audience so much that they screamed out, accusing Henry of treason. Henry is reported to have made the memorable reply, "If this be treason, make the most of it!"

PHLit Online!
www.PHLitOnline.com

Teaching From Technology

Preparing to Read
Go to www.PHLitOnline.com in class or in a lab and display the **Get Connected!** slide show for these selections. Have the class brainstorm for responses to the slide show writing prompt, entering ideas in the interactive journal. Then, have students complete their written responses individually in a lab or as homework.

To build background, display the Background and More About the Author features.

Using the Interactive Student Edition
Go to www.PHLitOnline.com and display the **Enriched Online Student Edition.** As the class reads the selections or listens to the narration, record answers to side column prompts using the graphic organizers accessible on the interactive page. Alternatively, have students use the online edition individually, answering the prompts as they read.

Speech in the Virginia Convention

① About the Selection

Patrick Henry's speech in the convention played a key role in turning colonial sentiment toward armed rebellion. Henry argues that although colonists have tried every argument in dealing with England, discussion has proved useless.

② Activating Prior Knowledge

Patrick Henry concludes his speech with the famous words "Give me liberty or give me death." Have students spend six or seven minutes freewriting in their journals in response to this question: What is worth dying for?

Concept Connector ➡

Tell students they will return to their responses after reading the selection.

③ Humanities

Patrick Henry Before the Virginia House of Burgesses,
Peter F. Rothermel

In this painting, Peter Rothermel depicts Henry delivering his famous address.

Use this question for discussion:

How has the painter created a dramatic atmosphere?
Answer: Henry is on a platform; his lighted face is set against a dark background; his listeners show animation.

③ *Patrick Henry*

100 Beginnings–1800

Text Complexity Rubric

	Speech in the Virginia Convention	Speech in the Convention
Qualitative Measures		
Context/ Knowledge Demands	Historical knowledge demands (speech) 1 2 ③ 4 5	Historical knowledge demands (speech) 1 2 ③ 4 5
Structure/Language Conventionality and Clarity	Eighteenth-century vocabulary; complicated sentence structure 1 2 3 ④ 5	Eighteenth-century vocabulary; complicated sentence structure 1 2 3 ④ 5
Levels of Meaning/ Purpose/Concept Level	Challenging concept (argues against negotiation in favor of armed rebellion) 1 2 3 ④ 5	Challenging concept (complex reasoning; urges acceptance of Constitution) 1 2 3 ④ 5
Quantitative Measures		
Lexile/Text Length	980L / 1,212 words	1490L / 656 words
Overall Complexity	**More complex**	**More complex**

④ Critical Viewing

Answer: Some students may say that the painting shows dramatic impact, with the speech causing seemingly incredulous individuals to talk among themselves or to rise in reaction. Other students may classify those same depictions as examples of inattention.

BACKGROUND In this famous speech, Patrick Henry denounces the British king and urges the colonists to fight for independence. Making such a declaration took tremendous bravery. England was the world's most powerful country at the time, and the odds against the colonists were overwhelming. If the colonies had failed to win independence, Henry could have been executed for treason.

Mr. President: No man thinks more highly than I do of the patriotism, as well as abilities, of the very worthy gentlemen who have just addressed the house. But different men often see the same subject in different lights; and, therefore, I hope it will not be thought disrespectful to those gentlemen, if, entertaining, as I do, opinions of a character very opposite to theirs, I shall speak forth my sentiments freely and without reserve. This is no time for ceremony. The question before the house is one of awful moment[1] to this country. For my own part, I consider it as nothing less than a question of freedom or slavery. And in proportion to the magnitude of the subject ought to be the freedom of the debate. It is only in this way that we can hope to arrive at truth, and fulfill the great responsibility which we hold to God and our country. Should I keep back my opinions at such a time, through fear of giving offense, I should consider myself as guilty of treason toward my country, and of an act of disloyalty toward the Majesty of Heaven, which I revere above all earthly kings.

Mr. President, it is natural to man to indulge in the illusions of hope. We are apt to shut our eyes against a painful truth, and listen to the song of that siren till she transforms us into beasts.[2] Is this the part of wise men, engaged in a great and arduous struggle for liberty? Are we disposed to be of the number of those who having eyes see not, and having ears hear not,[3] the things which so nearly concern their temporal salvation? For my part, whatever anguish of spirit it may cost, I am willing to know the whole truth; to know the worst and to provide for it.

I have but one lamp by which my feet are guided, and that is the lamp of experience. I know of no way of judging of the future but by the past. And judging by the past, I wish to know what there has been in the conduct of the British ministry for the last ten years to justify those hopes with which gentlemen have been pleased to solace themselves and the house? Is it that insidious smile with which our petition has been lately received? Trust it not, sir; it will prove a snare to your feet. Suffer not yourselves to be betrayed with a kiss.[4]

1. **moment** importance.
2. **listen . . . beasts** In Homer's *Odyssey*, the enchantress Circe transforms men into swine after charming them with her singing.
3. **having eyes . . . hear not** In Ezekiel 12:2, those "who have eyes to see, but see not, who have ears to hear, but hear not" are addressed.
4. **betrayed with a kiss** In Luke 22:47–48, Jesus is betrayed with a kiss.

④ ◄ Critical Viewing
Which details in this painting suggest the power of Patrick Henry's oratory? **[Analyze]**

Literary Analysis
Speeches and Allusions
Why do you think Henry makes allusions to Homer's *Odyssey* and the Bible?

Vocabulary
insidious (in sidʹ ē əs) *adj.* deceitful; treacherous

⑥ Reading Check
Does Henry agree or disagree with those who spoke before him?

Speech in the Virginia Convention **101**

⑤ Literary Analysis
Speeches and Allusions

1. Read the bracketed passage with students. Refer to footnotes to be sure students notice and understand Henry's allusions to the *Odyssey* and the Bible.

2. **Ask** the Literary Analysis question: Why do you think Henry makes allusions to Homer's *Odyssey* and the Bible? **Possible response:** First, students may say that these references are apt examples of Henry's point about ignoring dangerous reality. Second, these allusions have the effect of elevating his argument to epic and theological levels, matching his lofty, serious diction. Third, the references to classic literature and the Bible may be more persuasive to his educated audience than more ordinary examples.

⑥ Reading Check

Answer: Henry disagrees with those who spoke before him.

PHLit Online!

This selection is available in interactive format in the **Enriched Online Student Edition**, at **www.PHLitOnline.com**, which includes a thematically related video with writing prompt and an interactive graphic organizer.

ⓒ Text Complexity: Reader and Task Suggestions

Speech in the Virginia Convention		Speech in the Convention	
Preparing to Read the Text	**Leveled Tasks**	**Preparing to Read the Text**	**Leveled Tasks**
• Using the Background information on TE p. 99, discuss Henry as a firebrand in the years before the American Revolution. • Ask students what kind of language they might use to persuade an uncertain audience. • Guide students to use Multidraft Reading strategies (TE p. 99).	*Structure/Language* If students will have difficulty with structure, have them skim the selection, looking for the persuasive questions that Henry asks. As students reread, have them find an answer for each question. *Analyzing* If students will not have difficulty with structure, have them give an example of parallel language. Discuss how the parallelism reinforces Henry's persuasive appeal.	• Using the information on TE pp. 104–105, discuss Franklin's role after the American Revolution. • Ask students how they would prepare if they knew their speech might be historic. • Guide students to use Multidraft Reading strategies to deepen their comprehension (TE p. 99).	*Structure/Language* If students will have difficulty with syntax, guide them in paraphrasing a few sentences. Encourage students to continue paraphrasing as they reread, focusing on what Franklin suggests about the serious nature of this moment in history. *Evaluating* If students will not have difficulty with syntax, ask them if they think that the speech would have been more persuasive (or more historic) had Franklin not voiced his initial doubts.

Metaphor

1. Remind students that they have studied the concept of metaphor.

2. **Ask** students the Spiral Review question.

   Possible response: Henry speaks directly of a coming "storm" and later mentions the "next gale," which will bring the sound of battles in the north. The "accumulation of navies and armies" resonates like the gathering of clouds. The metaphor reinforces Henry's point that inevitable conflict cannot be escaped but must be prepared for.

❼ Literary Analysis

Speeches and Rhetorical Questions

1. Remind students that asking a rhetorical question is one technique a speaker can use in a speech. Rhetorical questions are questions to which the answer is evident. Because the answer is evident, these questions are often used to make listeners feel as if the speaker's opinions are an inevitable conclusion and to stir their emotions.

2. Have a volunteer read aloud the bracketed passage. Encourage students to think about how these questions make them feel as they listen to them.

3. Then, **ask** students the Literary Analysis question: What is the effect of the five rhetorical questions in this paragraph?

   Answer: These questions counter any possible argument from those who still hesitate about going to war. They also help to stir up the indignation and frustration of the listeners.

Spiral Review
Metaphor Cite details from throughout the speech that liken the growing tensions to an oncoming storm. How does this metaphor add to Henry's message?

Literary Analysis
Speeches and Rhetorical Questions What is the effect of the five rhetorical questions in this paragraph? ❼

Vocabulary
privileges (priv′ lij əz) *n.* special rights; advantages

> The battle, sir, is not to the STRONG alone; it is to the vigilant, the active, the brave.

Ask yourselves how this gracious reception of our petition comports with those warlike preparations which cover our waters and darken our land. Are fleets and armies necessary to a work of love and reconciliation? Have we shown ourselves so unwilling to be reconciled that force must be called in to win back our love? Let us not deceive ourselves, sir. These are the implements of war and subjugation—the last arguments to which kings resort.

I ask gentlemen, sir, what means this martial array, if its purpose be not to force us to submission? Can gentlemen assign any other possible motive for it? Has Great Britain any enemy in this quarter of the world, to call for all this accumulation of navies and armies? No, sir, she has none. They are meant for us: they can be meant for no other. They are sent over to bind and rivet upon us those chains which the British ministry have been so long forging.

And what have we to oppose to them? Shall we try argument? Sir, we have been trying that for the last ten years. Have we anything new to offer upon the subject? Nothing. We have held the subject up in every light of which it is capable; but it has been all in vain. Shall we resort to entreaty and humble supplication? What terms shall we find which have not been already exhausted? Let us not, I beseech you, sir, deceive ourselves longer. Sir, we have done everything that could be done to avert the storm which is now coming on. We have petitioned; we have remonstrated; we have supplicated; we have prostrated ourselves before the throne, and have implored its interposition[5] to arrest the tyrannical hands of the ministry and Parliament. Our petitions have been slighted; our remonstrances have produced additional violence and insult; our supplications have been disregarded; and we have been spurned with contempt from the foot of the throne! In vain, after these things, may we indulge the fond[6] hope of peace and reconciliation. There is no longer any room for hope. If we wish to be free, if we mean to preserve inviolate those inestimable privileges for which we have been so long contending, if we mean not basely to abandon the noble struggle in which we have been so long engaged, and which we have pledged ourselves never to abandon until the glorious object of our contest shall be obtained—we must fight! I repeat it, sir, we must fight! An appeal to arms and to the God of Hosts is all that is left us!

They tell us, sir, that we are weak—unable to cope with so formidable an adversary. But when shall we be stronger? Will it be the next week, or the next year? Will it be when we are totally disarmed, and when a British guard shall be stationed in every house? Shall we gather strength by irresolution and inaction? Shall we acquire the means of effectual resistance by lying supinely on our backs and hugging the delusive phantom of hope until our enemies shall have

---

5. **interposition** intervention.
6. **fond** foolish.

Think Aloud

Critiquing: Appeals
Model the skill of critiquing appeals to hostile audiences. Say to students:

I know that Henry addresses his speech to the president of the Virginia convention, but he seems very aware that his opponents are in the room. Henry responds to them indirectly. First, he only speaks *of* them, not *to* them: I see only references to nameless "gentlemen" and "they." Second, I notice that Henry does not directly attack their ideas as foolish, ignorant, or dangerous. Instead, Henry asks questions.

When I pull out these questions and put them into my own words, I can feel the persuasive power of Henry's rhetoric: Are we closing our eyes to reality? Is military force a sign of good intentions? Has talking worked? Has begging been effective? If we are weak now, will we be stronger tomorrow? Will doing nothing make us stronger? Will lying down discourage our enemies? By analyzing his appeals, I better appreciate the drama of his speech.

bound us hand and foot? Sir, we are not weak, if we make a proper use of those means which the God of nature hath placed in our power. Three millions of people, armed in the holy cause of liberty, and in such a country as that which we possess, are invincible by any force which our enemy can send against us. Besides, sir, we shall not fight our battles alone. There is a just God who presides over the destinies of nations and who will raise up friends to fight our battles for us. The battle, sir, is not to the strong alone;[7] it is to the **vigilant**, the active, the brave. Besides, sir, we have no election;[8] if we were base enough to desire it, it is now too late to retire from the contest. There is no retreat but in submission and slavery! Our chains are forged! Their clanging may be heard on the plains of Boston! The war is inevitable—and let it come! I repeat it, sir, let it come!

It is in vain, sir, to extenuate the matter. Gentlemen may cry, "Peace, peace"—but there is no peace. The war is actually begun! The next gale that sweeps from the north[9] will bring to our ears the clash of resounding arms! Our brethren are already in the field! Why stand we here idle? What is it that gentlemen wish? What would they have? Is life so dear, or peace so sweet, as to be purchased at the price of chains and slavery? Forbid it, Almighty God! I know not what course others may take; but as for me, give me liberty or give me death!

Vocabulary
vigilant (vij′ ə lənt) *adj.*
alert to danger

----

7. **The battle . . . alone** "The race is not to the swift, nor the battle to the strong." (Ecclesiastes 9:11)
8. **election** choice.
9. **The next gale . . . north** In Massachusetts, some colonists had already shown open resistance to the British.

Critical Reading

1. Key Ideas and Details (a) What measures does Henry say the colonists have already tried in their dealings with England? **(b) Analyze:** What examples does he provide to support his position that compromise with the British is not a workable solution?

2. Key Ideas and Details (a) What course of action does Henry want the colonists to take? **(b) Draw Conclusions:** What is Henry's answer to the objection that the colonists are not ready to fight the British?

3. Integration of Knowledge and Ideas (a) Do you think Henry was prepared to stand behind his words when he exclaimed, "Give me liberty or give me death"? Why, or why not? **(b) Deduce:** What does his willingness to make such an assertion reveal about his character? **(c) Extend:** If you had been in his place, would you have made such a statement? Why, or why not?

4. Integration of Knowledge and Ideas Speculate: What types of people living in the colonies at the time of Henry's speech might have reacted negatively to his words? Why?

Cite textual evidence to support your responses.

Speech in the Virginia Convention **103**

❽ Background

More About the Author

From the publication of his 1754 Albany Plan onward, Benjamin Franklin was a tireless advocate for American unity and cooperation. By 1787, however, Franklin was tired. The oldest delegate to the Constitutional Convention, Franklin sometimes drowsed during tedious sessions in the summer heat; too weak to deliver his own speeches, he had them read by others. Despite these difficulties, Franklin played a decisive role in achieving the "Great Compromise" that produced a Congress composed of a Senate and a House of Representatives. His final speech, printed here, remains a masterpiece of persuasion.

❾ About the Selection

Benjamin Franklin uses his years of experience to urge his colleagues to accept the Constitution. Franklin admits that any legal document created by committee will have some inherent weaknesses, although the government will more likely fail because of the people who administer it than because of the document that established it.

❽ BENJAMIN FRANKLIN

(1706–1790)

Author of "Speech in the Convention"

No other colonial American better embodied the promise of America than Benjamin Franklin. Through hard work, dedication, and ingenuity, Franklin was able to rise out of poverty to become a wealthy, famous, and influential person. Although he never received a formal education, Franklin made important contributions in the fields of literature, journalism, science, diplomacy, education, and philosophy.

A Persuasive Diplomat Franklin was a leader in the colonial movement for independence. In 1776, Congress sent him to France to enlist aid for the American Revolution. Franklin's persuasive powers proved effective, as he was able to achieve his goal. This turned out to be a pivotal breakthrough that may have been the deciding factor in the war.

Helping Forge a Nation In 1783, Franklin signed the peace treaty that ended the war and established the new nation. He returned home to serve as a delegate to the Constitutional Convention in Philadelphia. There, as politicians clashed over plans for the new government, Franklin worked to resolve conflicts and ensure ratification of the Constitution.

In spite of his contributions in so many other fields, Franklin is best remembered as a statesman and diplomat. He was the only American to sign all four documents that established the new nation: the Declaration of Independence, the treaty of alliance with France, the peace treaty with England, and the Constitution. (For more on Franklin, see pp. 136–137.)

"I confess, that I do not entirely approve of this Constitution at present..."

Enrichment

The Constitution

Sent to fix the Articles of Confederation, delegates in 1787 instead produced a wholly new document: the Constitution of the United States. The new document, however, did not end the tension between federal authority and states' powers. During the ratification process, *Anti-Federalists* continued to worry about a too-powerful central government. *Federalists* sought to allay concerns by proposing a Bill of Rights.

Activity: Debate Have students conduct research on the Federalists and Anti-Federalists. Suggest that they record information in the **Enrichment: Understanding Political Science** worksheet, *Professional Development Guidebook*, page 237. Have students use this information to stage a mini-debate on the controversy between the groups.

SPEECH *in the* CONVENTION

BENJAMIN FRANKLIN

⑨

⑩ **BACKGROUND** Following the American Revolution, each of the newly independent states created its own constitution. While Congress was able to pass limited laws, it had no power to tax the states or regulate issues, such as trade, that were affected by state boundaries. These problems led to the Constitutional Convention in 1787. Representatives from twelve states met to approve a national constitution. At the age of eighty-one, Benjamin Franklin represented Pennsylvania.

MR. PRESIDENT,

I confess, that I do not entirely approve of this Constitution at present; but, Sir, I am not sure I shall never approve it; for, having lived long, I have experienced many instances of being obliged, by better information or fuller consideration, to change my opinions even on important subjects, which I once thought right, but found to be otherwise. It is therefore that, the older I grow, the more apt I am to doubt my own judgment of others. Most men, indeed, as well as most sects in religion, think themselves in possession of all truth, and that wherever others differ from them, it is so far error. . . . Though many private Persons think almost as highly of their own infallibility as of that of their Sect, few express it so naturally as a certain French Lady, who, in a little dispute with her sister, said, "But I meet with nobody but myself that is *always* in the right." "*Je ne trouve que moi qui aie toujours raison.*"

In these sentiments, Sir, I agree to this Constitution, with all its faults,—if they are such; because I think a general Government necessary for us, and there is no form of government but what may be a blessing to the people, if well administered; and I believe, farther, that this is likely to be well administered for a course of years, and can only end in despotism, as other forms have done before it, when the people shall become so corrupted as to need despotic government, being incapable of any other. I doubt, too, whether any other Convention we can obtain, may be able to make a better constitution; for, when you assemble a number of men, to have the advantage of their joint wisdom, you inevitably assemble with those men all their prejudices, their passions, their errors of opinion, their local interests, and their selfish views. From such an assembly can a *perfect* production be expected? It therefore astonishes me, Sir, to find this

Reading Strategy
Critiquing Appeal to Audiences In his reference to "faults," is Franklin appealing to those who are happy with the Constitution or those who are not? Explain.

Vocabulary
despotism (des´ pət iz´ əm) *n.* absolute rule; tyranny

⑫
Reading Check
What does Franklin confess as he begins his speech?

Speech in the Convention **105**

PROFESSIONAL DEVELOPMENT **Doug Buehl**

▼ **APPLY THE STRATEGY**

"Who Would Say It?" Model "Who would say it?" application with *infallibility* on p.105. When Franklin says "many private Persons think almost as highly of their own *infallibility*," he refers to people who strongly feel that their beliefs are the truth. Who else would say "*infallibility*"? A scientist might say: "The *infallibility* of this process is clear; if followed exactly, the desired results will always be obtained."

Partners should select two of the vocabulary words and brainstorm "who would say" them. Then they create statements using each of the words as they might be put "in play" by individuals they predict would say it. Then, partners share with the class.

For more of Doug Buehl's strategies, see his Professional Development essay, pp. 2a–2b.

TEACH

⑩ **Background**
Delegates at the Convention
Those who represented their states at the Constitutional Convention were some of the most important people in the country. Those who did *not* travel to Philadelphia were also distinguished. Among those invited to serve but who could not or would not attend were Thomas Jefferson, John Adams, Samuel Adams, and Patrick Henry. Henry refused his appointment because of his aversion to strong central government. He would later vigorously oppose ratification of the new Constitution.

⑪ **Reading Strategy**
Critiquing Appeal to Audiences
1. Read the bracketed passage with students.
2. Point out the paradoxical nature of Franklin's expressions of doubt. Most people would say that experience makes them more certain in their judgments. Franklin states the opposite: the more experience he has, the more likely he is to doubt his judgments.
3. **Ask** the Reading Strategy question: In his reference to "faults," is Franklin appealing to those who are happy with the Constitution or those who are not? Explain.
   Answer: Franklin is appealing to those who are dissatisfied with the Constitution. He acknowledges that imperfect delegates have produced an imperfect document.

⑫ **Reading Check**
Answer: Franklin confesses that he does not completely approve of the Constitution as written.

This selection is available in interactive format in the **Enriched Online Student Edition**, at www. PHLitOnline.com, which includes a thematically related video with a writing prompt and an interactive graphic organizer.

105

Whole Class Activity

1. Draw students' attention to the painting on this page. **Ask** students if they recognize any of the individuals portrayed.
Possible response: Students may recognize George Washington, shown in profile on the left; James Madison in the right foreground; and Benjamin Franklin, immediately behind Madison.

2. Point out that all the men pictured are framers of the Constitution. Washington was the presiding officer of the convention; Madison played such a prominent role that he is often described as the Father of the Constitution.

3. **Ask:** What are the dominant elements in the painting?
Answer: The painting is dominated by the figure of a woman, possibly a goddess or spirit representing freedom or America. A large banner bears the opening words of the Constitution, "We the People."

4. **Ask:** How do you interpret the artist's purpose in this painting?
Possible response: The artist intends to identify and honor the people who framed the Constitution and to celebrate the nation that resulted from their work.

⓭

106 Beginnings–1800

Vocabulary Development

Vocabulary Knowledge Rating

When students have completed reading and discussing both selections, have them take out the **Vocabulary Knowledge Rating** charts they worked on earlier. Read the words aloud and have students rate their knowledge of the words again in the After Reading column. Clarify any words that are still problematic. Have students write their own definitions and example or sentence in the appropriate column. Then, have students complete the Vocabulary Lesson at the end of this selection. Encourage students to use the words in further discussion and written work about the selection. Remind them that they will be accountable for these words on the **Selection Test,** *Unit 1 Resources,* pages 161–163 or 164–166.

system approaching so near to perfection as it does; and I think it will astonish our enemies, who are waiting with confidence to hear, that our councils are confounded like those of the builders of Babel, and that our States are on the point of separation, only to meet hereafter for the purpose of cutting one another's throats. Thus I consent, Sir, to this Constitution, because I expect no better, and because I am not sure that it is not the best. The opinions I have had of its *errors* I sacrifice to the public good. I have never whispered a syllable of them abroad. Within these walls they were born, and here they shall die. If every one of us, in returning to our Constituents, were to report the objections he has had to it, and endeavour to gain Partisans in support of them, we might prevent its being generally received, and thereby lose all the salutary effects and great advantages resulting naturally in our favour among foreign nations, as well as among ourselves, from our real or apparent unanimity. Much of the strength and efficiency of any government, in procuring and securing happiness to the people, depends on *opinion,* on the general opinion of the goodness of that government, as well as of the wisdom and integrity of its governors. I hope, therefore, for our own sakes, as a part of the people, and for the sake of our posterity, that we shall act heartily and unanimously in recommending this Constitution, wherever our Influence may extend, and turn our future thoughts and endeavors to the means of having it *well administered.*

On the whole, Sir, I cannot help expressing a wish, that every member of the Convention who may still have objections to it, would with me on this occasion doubt a little of his own infallibility, and, to make manifest our *unanimity,* put his name to this Instrument.

◀ **Critical Viewing** ⑭
How is this painting of the ratifying of the Constitution similar to a literary allusion to classical mythology?
[Analyze]

Vocabulary
salutary (sal´ yōō ter´ ē) *adj.* beneficial; promoting a good purpose

unanimity (yōō´ nə nim´ ə tē) *n.* complete agreement

Critical Reading ©

1. **Key Ideas and Details (a)** Why does Franklin feel that unanimity among the delegates is essential to the success of the United States? **(b) Analyze:** What is his purpose in suppressing his "opinions" for the "public good"?

2. **Key Ideas and Details (a)** According to Franklin, why would any document created by committee be faulty? **(b) Generalize:** What is Franklin saying about human nature?

3. **Craft and Structure (a)** What three reasons does Franklin give for finally agreeing to accept the Constitution? **(b) Evaluate:** How effectively does he convey the thought process that brought him from doubt about the Constitution to a decision to accept it? Explain.

4. **Integration of Knowledge and Ideas** What connections do both Henry and Franklin make between the ability to face hard realities and ideas of loyalty to one's nation? In your response, use at least two of these Essential Question vocabulary words: *patriotism, responsibility, dispute, wisdom.* **[Connecting to the Essential Question: How does literature shape or reflect society?]**

Cite textual evidence to support your responses.

Speech in the Convention **107**

Concept Connector

Reading Strategy Graphic Organizer
Ask students to review the graphic organizers in which they have recorded the reaction of friendly and hostile audiences. Then, have students share their organizers and compare their findings.

Activating Prior Knowledge
Have students return to their responses to the Activating Prior Knowledge activity. Ask them to explain whether their thoughts have changed and if so, how.

Connecting the the Essential Question
Have students compare the responses they gave to the prompt before they completed reading the speeches with their thoughts after reading. Have them work individually or in groups, writing or discussing their thoughts, to formulate their new responses. Then lead a class discussion, probing for what students have learned that confirms or invalidates their initial thoughts. Encourage students to cite specific details to support their responses.

⑭ **Critical Viewing**
Answer: The goddess wears a laurel wreath, a symbol of victory. She carries a Roman *fasces,* birch rods bundled around an axe and wrapped in a ribbon, as a symbol of authority and unity. She is accompanied by an eagle, a symbol of national power.

ASSESS
Answers

Before students respond, you may wish to have them write a brief objective summary of the selection. As they answer the questions below, remind them to support their answers with evidence from the text.

1. (a) Unanimity will show citizens and the world that conflicting political interests do not prevent the nation's officials from working together. (b) Franklin does not want factions to arise as a result of his lingering objections.

2. (a) A committee brings together not just its strengths but also its weaknesses. (b) Franklin implies that people have shortcomings as well as strengths.

3. (a) Franklin asserts that a general government is necessary, that no other convention could make a better constitution, and that enemies of the nation hope for a disagreement among the separate states. (b) Franklin effectively establishes positive reasons for approving the Constitution and diminishes reasons for withholding approval. He does so by pointing out the impossibility of creating a perfect document by a committee and by stressing the importance of showing unanimity.

4. **Possible response:** Both speakers urge their audiences to be realistic as a matter of both patriotism and wisdom. Further, Franklin argues that delegates have a responsibility not to make their doubts and disputes public. For Henry, not to speak his mind is a betrayal of his country. For Franklin, to speak publicly of his misgivings is to betray the common good.

107

Answers

1. Henry: recognize that war is inevitable. Franklin: support the new Constitution.

2. **Sample answers:** Restatement: Example: "We must fight! I repeat it, sir, we must fight! An appeal to arms is all that is left us!" Effect: This emphasizes Henry's argument that there is no alternative to war. Parallelism: "Within these walls they were born, and here they shall die." Effect: The parallel makes discretion seem logical and necessary.

3. (a) Henry: "Shall we try argument?" Franklin: "From such an assembly can a *perfect* production be expected?" (b) Henry clarifies the futility of reasoning with England. Franklin emphasizes realistic expectations.

4. The allusion to sirens suggests that ignoring reality leads to disaster. The reference to Judas's kiss warns against a trap. Franklin's allusion to Babel is a warning that disputes will please America's enemies.

5. (a) Franklin's speech is respectful of others. (b) Henry's rhetoric and emotion might sway a jury.

6. (a) Henry mistrusts governmental power, which can oppress. (b) Franklin believes government is good or bad depending on its people.

7. Henry offers two extremes: liberty or death. The cartoon man calls for one extreme—death—or moderation, which is, by definition, not extreme.

8. **Possible responses:** Students may say that Franklin's calm speech is better at connecting with both types of audiences. Henry's passionate arguments might offend hostile listeners.

9. Henry: His argument that a just God will be on the country's side is aimed at a friendly audience. His "when shall we be stronger?" argument is aimed at his opponents. Franklin: His argument that the Constitution is "so near perfection" appeals to a friendly audience. His acknowledgment of his own doubts is intended for a hostile audience.

10. Henry acknowledges the others' patriotism. Franklin agrees with critics that the new Constitution is not perfect.

108

After You Read

Speech in the Virginia Convention • Speech in the Convention

Literary Analysis

1. **Key Ideas and Details** Explain the persuasive message in each **speech:** What do Henry and Franklin want audiences to think and do?

2. **Craft and Structure** Use a chart like the one shown to note examples and describe the effects of each speaker's use of these **rhetorical devices: restatement, repetition, parallelism.**

	Example	Effect
Restatement		
Repetition		
Parallelism		

3. **Craft and Structure** (a) Identify at least two **rhetorical questions** from these speeches. (b) Explain how each question intensifies the emotion of the speech, clarifies an idea, or emphasizes a point.

4. **Craft and Structure** Explain the meanings each of the following classical and biblical **allusions** add to the speech:
   - Henry's allusion to sirens from Greek mythology
   - Henry's allusion to Judas's betrayal of Jesus in the Bible
   - Franklin's allusion to the builders of the Tower of Babel

5. **Integration of Knowledge and Ideas** (a) How is Franklin's experience as a diplomat reflected in his argument and the types of language he uses? (b) How is Henry's experience as a lawyer reflected in his?

6. **Comparing Literary Works** (a) What **political assumptions** does Henry make about the nature of government? (b) Does Franklin make similar assumptions? Defend and clarify your interpretation with elements from the texts.

7. **Analyzing Visual Information** Explain the humor in the cartoon shown on this page.

Reading Strategy

8. **Critique each speaker's appeal to friendly and hostile audiences.** Which speech do you think was more effective in holding a friendly audience and in reaching a hostile one? Explain your choice.

9. For each speech, note one argument that the speaker designed to appeal to a friendly audience and one intended to reach a hostile audience. Explain your choices.

10. In what ways does each speaker use "concession," or the acknowledgment of opposition arguments?

▼ *"Give me moderation or give me death!"*

"Give me moderation or give me death!"

Common Core State Standards

Writing

2. Write informative/ explanatory texts to examine and convey complex ideas, concepts, and information clearly and accurately through the effective selection, organization, and analysis of content. (p. 109)

2.a. Introduce a topic; organize complex ideas, concepts, and information so that each new element builds on that which precedes it to create a unified whole. (p. 109)

Language

5. Demonstrate understanding of figurative language, word relationships, and nuances in word meanings. (p. 109)

Assessment Practice

Predict Outcomes (For more practice, see *All-in-One Workbook*.)

Practice prediction with this sample test item:

Have we shown ourselves so unwilling to be reconciled that force must be called in to win back our love? These are implements of war and subjugation—the last arguments to which kings resort.

Based on this passage, what will happen if the English assemble their armies and navies?

A The English will remain peaceful.

B The colonists will monitor the English military to avoid armed conflict.

C The English will decrease their show of strength after they threaten the colonists.

D The English will use force against the colonists, and the two sides will go to war.

Based on the text, *D* is the most likely choice.

PERFORMANCE TASKS
Integrated Language Skills

© Vocabulary Acquisition and Use

Relate New Vocabulary to Familiar Words

The word *unanimity* comes from the Latin word *unanimus*, meaning "of one mind." Franklin did not feel the delegates to the Convention would ever be fully "of one mind." The word combines the prefix *uni-*, meaning "one," with the root *-anima-*, which means "being; soul; mind." Both word parts contribute to other words with which you are probably familiar. Write a definition for each word below. Then, explain how the meaning of the prefix or the root contributes to the meaning of each word.

1. animate
2. animation
3. universe
4. unify
5. unique

Vocabulary: Antonyms

For each vocabulary word, choose the letter of the antonym, or word that most closely expresses an opposite meaning. Then, explain your reasoning.

1. despotism **a.** tyranny; **b.** democracy; **c.** cruelty
2. privileges **a.** freedoms; **b.** fees; **c.** penalties
3. salutary **a.** damaging; **b.** beneficial; **c.** insensitive
4. insidious **a.** innocent; **b.** weary; **c.** sinister
5. unanimity **a.** harmony; **b.** discussion; **c.** discord
6. vigilant **a.** careless; **b.** watchful; **c.** forgetful

Writing

© **Explanatory Text** Patrick Henry and Benjamin Franklin were master politicians who knew that success sometimes requires persistence and sometimes requires compromise. Write an **essay** in which you compare and contrast their views about when to compromise and when to stand firm.

Prewriting Review each speech, looking for details related to compromise and persistence. Use a chart like the one shown, or make one of your own design to organize your notes. Then, review your notes for patterns of similarity and difference. Write one sentence that states your *thesis*.

Model: Organizing Notes

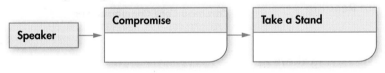

Drafting In your introduction, state the topic and summarize your main points. Then, draft one paragraph about Henry's political approach followed by one paragraph about Franklin's. Support your ideas with quotations.

Revising Reread your essay, making sure you have used sufficient evidence and that your ideas build to a logical conclusion. Check that you have separated longer direct quotations from paragraphs and set off shorter direct quotations with quotation marks.

Extended Study: Integrated Language Skills **109**

Assessment Resources

Unit 1 Resources
- **L1 L2 EL Selection Test A,** pp. 161–163. Administer Test A to less advanced students and English learners.
- **L3 L4 EL Selection Test B,** pp. 164–166. Administer Test B to on-level or more advanced students.
- **L3 L4 Open-Book Test,** pp. 158–160. As an alternative, give the Open-Book Test

- **All Customizable Test Bank**
- **All Self-tests**
  Students may prepare for the **Selection Test** by taking the **Self-test** online.

PHLit Online! All assessment resources are available at **www.PHLitOnline.com**.

Vocabulary Acquisition and Use

1. Introduce the skill, using the instruction on the student page.
2. Have students complete the activity and the practice.

Relate New Vocabulary to Familiar Words

1. "to make lively or alive"; *anima* conveys the sense of being alive.
2. "liveliness"; the root *anim* suggests being alive.
3. "the whole of existing things"; the prefix *uni-* contributes the meaning of oneness or entirety.
4. "make into one"; the prefix *uni-* adds the meaning of oneness.
5. "being one of a kind"; the prefix *uni-* suggests singleness or being one of a kind.

Vocabulary: Antonyms

1. b; *democracy,* government of the people, is the opposite of despotism.
2. c; *penalties,* or punishments, are most unlike privileges.
3. a; *damaging,* or causing harm, is the opposite of salutary.
4. a; something that is *innocent* is most unlike something insidious.
5. c; *discord,* or disagreement, is the opposite of unanimity.
6. a; being *careless* is the opposite of being vigilant.

Writing

1. To guide students, give them the Support for Writing page (*Unit 1 Resources,* p. 156).
2. Review the speeches as a class to identify one relevant quotation for each speaker. Then, have students find additional evidence on their own.
3. Remind students that they should discuss Henry's and Franklin's ideas in separate paragraphs. Those paragraphs should be equal in length and in support.
4. Evaluate students' essays using the **Rubrics for Comparison-and-Contrast Essay,** *Professional Development Guidebook,* pages 260–261.

109

- ## The Declaration of Independence
- ## *from* The American Crisis, Number 1
Lesson Pacing Guide

DAY 1 Preteach

- © Administer the Reading and Vocabulary Warm-ups (*Unit 1 Resources*, pp. 167–170) as necessary.
- © Introduce the Literary Analysis concept: Persuasion.
- • Introduce the Reading Strategy: Analyze Word Choice.
- • Build background with the author and Background features.
- • Develop thematic thinking with Connecting to the Essential Question.
- © Teach the selection vocabulary.

DAYS 2–3 Preteach/Teach/Assess

- • Distribute copies of the appropriate graphic organizer for the Reading Strategy (*Graphic Organizer Transparencies*, pp. 33–34).
- • Distribute copies of the appropriate graphic organizer for Literary Analysis (*Graphic Organizer Transparencies*, pp. 35–36).
- • Prepare students to read with the Activating Prior Knowledge activities (TE).
- • Informally monitor comprehension while students read.
- • Use the Reading Check questions to confirm comprehension.
- © Develop students' understanding of persuasion using the Literary Analysis prompt.
- • Develop students' ability to analyze word choice using the Reading Strategy prompt.
- © Reinforce vocabulary with the Vocabulary notes.
- • Assess students' comprehension and mastery of the skills by having them answer the Critical Reading, Literary Analysis, and Reading Strategy questions.
- © Have students complete the Vocabulary Lesson.

DAY 4 Extend/Assess

- © Have students complete the Writing Lesson and write a persuasive editorial. (You may assign as homework.)
- • Administer Selection Test A or B (*Unit 1 Resources*, pp. 179–181 or 182–184).

© Common Core State Standards

Reading Informational Text
4. Determine the meaning of words and phrases as they are used in a text, including figurative, connotative, and technical meanings; analyze how an author uses and refines the meaning of a key term or terms over the course of a text.
8. Delineate and evaluate the reasoning of seminal U.S. texts and the premises, purposes, and arguments in works of public advocacy.
9. Analyze seventeenth-, eighteenth-, and nineteenth century foundational U.S. documents of historical and literary significance for their themes, purposes, and rhetorical features.

Writing 1. Write arguments to support claims in an analysis of substantive topics or texts, using valid reasoning and relevant and sufficient evidence.

Language 4.b. Identify and correctly use patterns of word changes that indicate different meanings or parts of speech.

Additional Standards Practice
Common Core Companion, pp. 123–130; 170–171; 185–195; 324–331

Daily Block Scheduling
Each day in this Lesson Pacing Guide represents a 40–50 minute period. Teachers using block scheduling may combine days to revise pacing. In addition, teachers may differentiate and support core instruction by integrating components for extended and intensive support as students require. See the Guide to Selected Leveled Resources (facing page).

Guide to Selected Leveled Resources

Tier 1 (students performing on level) | **The Declaration of Independence** • *from* **The American Crisis, Number 1**

Warm Up	**Practice, model,** and **monitor** fluency, working **with the whole class** or **in groups**.	Vocabulary and Reading Warm-ups B, *Unit 1 Resources*, pp. 167–168, 170
Comprehension/Skills	**Support** and **monitor** comprehension and skills development, having students complete the activities, graphic organizers, and interactive prompts **independently** or **as a class**.	• *Reader's Notebook*, adapted instruction and summary **EL** *Reader's Notebook: English Learner's Version*, adapted instruction and summary • **Reading Strategy Graphic Organizer B,** *Graphic Organizer Transparencies*, p. 34 • **Literary Analysis Graphic Organizer B,** *Graphic Organizer Transparencies*, p. 36
Monitor Progress	**A** **Monitor** student progress with the differentiated curriculum-based assessment in the *Unit Resources*.	• **Selection Test B,** *Unit 1 Resources*, pp. 182–184 • **Open-Book Test,** *Unit 1 Resources*, pp. 176–178

Tier 2 (students requiring intervention) | **The Declaration of Independence** • *from* **The American Crisis, Number 1**

Warm Up	**Practice, model,** and **monitor** fluency **in groups** or **with individuals**.	• **Vocabulary and Reading Warm-ups A,** *Unit 1 Resources*, pp. 167–169 • *Hear It!* **Audio CD**
Comprehension/Skills	• **Support** and **monitor** comprehension and skills development, working **in small groups** or **with individuals**. • As students complete the selection in the appropriate version of the *Reader's Notebook*, **monitor** comprehension frequently with group questions and individual instruction. • **Model** strategies while guiding students in completing the activities and prompts in the *Reader's Notebook*, as well as the graphic organizers. • **Practice** skills and **monitor** mastery with the *Reading Kit* worksheets.	• *Reader's Notebook: Adapted Version*, adapted instruction and summary **EL** *Reader's Notebook: English Learner's Version*, adapted instruction and summary • **Reading Strategy Graphic Organizer A,** *Graphic Organizer Transparencies*, p. 33 • **Literary Analysis Graphic Organizer A,** *Graphic Organizer Transparencies*, p. 35 • *Reading Kit*, Practice worksheets
Monitor Progress	**A** **Monitor** student progress with the differentiated curriculum-based assessment in the *Unit Resources* and in the *Reading Kit*.	• **Selection Test A,** *Unit 1 Resources*, pp. 179–181 • *Reading Kit*, Assess worksheets

TIER 3 Tier 3 intervention may require consultation with the student's special-education or dyslexia specialist. For additional support, see the Tier 2 activities and resources listed above.

One-on-one teaching   Group work   Whole class instruction   Independent work   **A** Assessment

For a complete guide to selection support, including support for Advanced students, see the Overview of Resources in the frontmatter.

• The Declaration of Independence
• *from* The American Crisis, Number 1

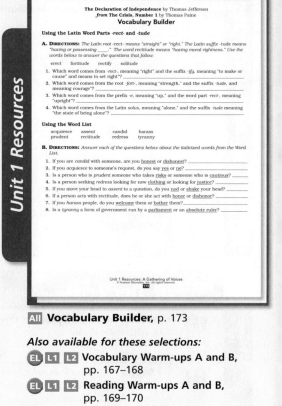

All Vocabulary Builder, p. 173

Also available for these selections:

EL L1 L2 Vocabulary Warm-ups A and B, pp. 167–168

EL L1 L2 Reading Warm-ups A and B, pp. 169–170

RESOURCES FOR:

L1 Special-Needs Students

L2 Below-Level Students (Tier 2)

L3 On-Level Students (Tier 1)

L4 Advanced Students (Tier 1)

EL English Learners

All All Students

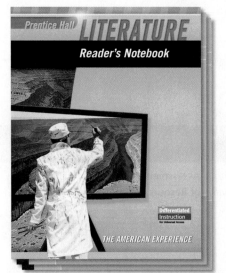

Reader's Notebooks

Pre- and postreading pages for these selections, as well as an excerpt from *The American Crisis,* Number 1, appear in an interactive format in the *Reader's Notebooks*. Each *Notebook* is differentiated for a different group of learners.

The selections in the Adapted and English Learner's versions are abridged.

L2 L3 *Reader's Notebook*

L1 *Reader's Notebook: Adapted Version*

EL *Reader's Notebook: English Learner's Version*

EL *Reader's Notebook: Spanish Version*

© *Common Core Companion*

Additional instruction and practice for each Common Core State Standard

Selection Support

Graphic Organizer Transparencies

EL L1 L2 Reading: Graphic Organizer A, (partially filled in), p. 33

Also available for these selections:

EL L3 Reading: Graphic Organizer B, p. 34

EL L1 L2 Literary Analysis: Graphic Organizer A (partially filled in), p. 35

EL L3 Literary Analysis: Graphic Organizer B, p. 36

Skills Development/Extension

Unit 1 Resources

All Reading: Recognizing Charged Words, p. 172

Also available for these selections:

All Literary Analysis: Persuasion, p. 171

EL L3 L4 Support for Writing, p. 174

L4 Enrichment, p. 175

Assessment

EL L1 L2 Open-Book Test, pp. 176–178

Also available for these selections:

EL L1 L2 Selection Test A, pp. 179–181

EL L3 L4 Selection Test B, pp. 182–184

PHLit Online!
www.PHLitOnline.com

Online Resources: All print materials are also available online.

- complete narrated selection text
- a thematically related video with writing prompt
- an interactive graphic organizer
- highlighting feature
- access to all student print resources, adapted to individual student needs
- Spanish and English summaries
- adapted selection translations in Spanish

Background Video

Also available:

Get Connected! (thematic video with writing prompt)
All videos available in Spanish.

Vocabulary Central (tools and activities for studying vocabulary)

Also available:

Writer's Journal (with graphics feature)

❶ Connecting to the Essential Question

1. Review the assignment with the class.

2. Suggest that students identify real-life examples of their ideals in their discussions. Then, have them complete the assignment.

3. Have students take note of Jefferson's and Paine's ideals as they read.

❷ Literary Analysis

Introduce the skill, using the instruction on the student page.

Think Aloud: Model the Skill

Say to students:

To help me recognize different type of persuasive appeals in literature, I think of some common lines from commercials and their intended effect. "Most doctors recommend" is an appeal to authority. "Starving children need" is an appeal to emotion. "Laboratory tests prove" is an appeal to logic. "Thousands of citizens deserve" is an appeal to ethics.

❸ Reading Strategy

1. Introduce the skill.

2. Give students a copy of **Reading Strategy Graphic Organizer B,** page 34 in *Graphic Organizer Transparencies,* to fill out as they read.

❹ Vocabulary

1. Pronounce each word, giving its definition, and have students say it aloud.

2. For more guidance, see the *Classroom Strategies and Teaching Routines* card for introducing vocabulary.

Before You Read

The Declaration of Independence • from *The American Crisis, Number 1*

❶ **Connecting to the Essential Question** Jefferson and Paine describe ideals that they were willing to fight to protect. As you read, notice the values that both Jefferson and Paine defend. Your observations will help as you reflect on the Essential Question: **What makes American literature American?**

❷ Literary Analysis

Persuasion is writing that presents an *argument*, or message meant to get readers to think or act in a certain way. Effective persuasion uses the following techniques to build arguments:

- *Appeals to emotion* to influence readers' feelings
- *Appeals to logic* to show that an argument is well reasoned
- *Appeals to ethics* to show that an argument is just or fair
- *Appeals to authority* to show that a higher power supports the ideas

As you read, evaluate the reasoning and appeals each writer uses to construct his or her argument.

Comparing Literary Works Jefferson and Paine wrote for different **audiences,** or readers. Some of their readers were friendly and agreed with their ideas, whereas others were hostile and did not. Strong persuasive writers such as Jefferson and Paine attempt to address both types of audience. They anticipate reader concerns and build in counterclaims to address them. As you read, notice how these writers shape their messages to reach different audiences.

❸ Reading Strategy

© **Preparing to Read Complex Texts** When you **analyze word choice,** you study an author's words and observe how he or she uses and refines key terms over the course of a work. Persuasive writers may use words with strong *connotations* or associations to produce an intense emotional response. For example, the *denotation*, or basic meaning, of "evils" and "wrongs" is similar. However, the connotation of "evils" is stronger, making it a *charged or loaded word.* Use a chart like the one shown to note charged words, connotations, and the emotions they evoke.

❹ Vocabulary

candid (kan´ did) *adj.* honest; straightforward (p. 113)

assent (ə sent´) *n.* agreement (p. 113)

harass (hər´ əs) *v.* attack; bother (p. 114)

tyranny (tir´ ə nē) *n.* oppressive power (p. 114)

redress (ri dres´) *n.* compensation for a wrong done (p. 114)

acquiesce (ak´ wē es´) *v.* agree without protest (p. 115)

rectitude (rek´ ti tōōd) *n.* correctness; righteousness (p. 115)

prudent (prōō´ dənt) *adj.* sensible; careful (p. 118)

© **Common Core State Standards**

Reading Informational Text

4. Determine the meaning of words and phrases as they are used in a text, including figurative, connotative, and technical meanings; analyze how an author uses and refines the meaning of a key term or terms over the course of a text.

8. Delineate and evaluate the reasoning in seminal U.S. texts and the premises, purposes, and arguments in works of public advocacy.

9. Analyze seventeenth-, eighteenth-, and nineteenth-century foundational U.S. documents of historical and literary significance for their themes, purposes, and rhetorical features.

Word

↓

Connotation

↓

Emotion

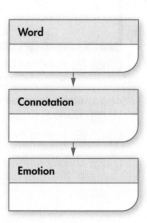

Vocabulary Development

Vocabulary Knowledge Rating

Create a **Vocabulary Knowledge Rating Chart** (in *Professional Development Guidebook,* p. 33) for the vocabulary words on the student page. Give each student a copy of the chart with the words on it. Read the words aloud and have students mark their rating in the Before Reading column. When students have completed reading and discussing the selec-tions, have them take out their **Vocabulary Knowledge Rating** charts for the selections. Read the words aloud and have students rate their knowledge again in the After Reading column. Clarify any words that are still problematic. Then have students complete the Vocabulary Lesson at the end of the selections.

Vocabulary Central, featuring tools and activities for studying vocabulary, is available online at **www.PHLitOnline.com.**

⑤ Thomas Jefferson (1743–1826)

Author of The Declaration of Independence

When you look at all of Thomas Jefferson's achievements, it seems almost nothing was beyond his reach. Not only did he help our nation win its independence and serve as its third president, but he also founded the University of Virginia, helped establish the public school system, designed his own home, invented a type of elevator for sending food from floor to floor, and created the decimal system for American money. He was a skilled violinist, an art enthusiast, and a brilliant writer.

Revolutionary Leader Born into a wealthy Virginia family, Jefferson attended the College of William and Mary and went on to earn a law degree. While serving in the Virginia House of Burgesses, he became an outspoken defender of American rights. When conflict between the colonists and the British erupted into revolution, Jefferson emerged as a leader in the effort to win independence.

Valued Statesman When the war ended, Jefferson served as the American minister to France for several years. He then served as the nation's first secretary of state and second vice president before becoming president in 1801. While in office, Jefferson nearly doubled the size of the nation by authorizing the purchase of the Louisiana Territory from France.

On the morning of July 4, 1826, the fiftieth anniversary of the Declaration of Independence, Jefferson died at the age of 83. John Adams, Jefferson's fellow contributor to the Declaration of Independence, died only several hours after his longtime friend. Adams's last words were "Thomas Jefferson still survives."

The Declaration of Independence **111**

🔔 Daily Bellringer

For each class during which you will teach these selections, have students complete one of the five activities for the appropriate week in the *Daily Bellringer Activities* booklet.

Multidraft Reading

To assist struggling readers and to enhance reading for all, assign the text in chunks as warranted by length and apply multidraft reading protocols. For each reading, have students set the purpose indicated:

- **First reading**—identifying key ideas and details and answering any Reading Checks.
- **Second reading**—analyzing craft and structure and responding to the side-column prompts.
- **Third reading**—integrating knowledge and ideas, connecting to other texts and the world, and answering the end-of-selection questions.

For more guidance, refer to the *Classroom Strategies and Teaching Routines* card on multidraft reading.

Background
⑤ More About the Author

Thomas Jefferson ran for president in the 1796 election but finished second to John Adams. Following the election method in use at the time, Jefferson became vice president. Though he spent nearly all his life in public service, Jefferson actually preferred life on his farm, and in 1809 he retired there permanently. He loved to read and owned a library of 6,400 books. He was also a great writer of letters, and his postretirement correspondence with his former rival and colleague John Adams is a fascinating body of work.

PHLit Online!
www.PHLitOnline.com

Teaching From Technology

Preparing to Read
Go to **www.PHLitOnline.com** in class or in a lab and display the **Get Connected!** slide show for this grouping. Have the class brainstorm for responses to the slide show writing prompt, entering ideas in the interactive journal. Then, have students complete their written responses individually in a lab or as homework.

To build background, display the Background and More About the Authors features.

Using the Interactive Text
Go to **www.PHLitOnline.com** and display the **Enriched Online Student Edition.** As the class reads the selections or listens to the narration, record answers to side-column prompts using the graphic organizers accessible on the interactive page. Alternatively, have students use the online edition individually, answering the prompts as they read.

111

① About the Selection

In this famous battle cry of freedom, Jefferson identifies what he calls "self-evident" truths, pointing out the equality of men and the tenuous contract of government. Then, in a list of the objectionable acts of King George III, arranged from least offensive to most, Jefferson outlines the reasons that the colonials are dissatisfied with their government. Jefferson reaches the reasoned conclusion that every rational means of achieving détente with Britain has failed, and therefore the United States of America must become independent of Britain.

② Activating Prior Knowledge

Set the following scene for students: "Imagine that you are soldiers dressed in ragged clothes. It's winter. Snow and ice surround you. A few of you have light jackets; some are barefoot. All are hungry, huddled in tents without floors. Badly defeated in the last battle, all you can think of is home. What spoken words could keep desperate soldiers such as yourselves fighting for independence?"

Have students write answers to that question in the first person, as a soldier in the Revolutionary War. Discuss their responses. Then, explain that they are about to read two documents that inspired those soldiers.

Concept Connector ➡

Tell students they will return to their responses after reading the selections.

The Declaration of Independence, John Trumbull, Yale University Art Gallery

IN ———S, JULY 4, 1776.

The unanimo——— ———rteen ——ited States of America

①② The Declaration of Independence

Thomas Jefferson

BACKGROUND In 1776, Thomas Jefferson was chosen (with Franklin, Adams, and others) to write a declaration of the colonies' independence from England. The draft presented to the Second Continental Congress was largely Jefferson's work. To his disappointment, however, Congress made changes before approving the document. They dropped Jefferson's condemnation of the British for tolerating a corrupt Parliament, and they struck out a strong statement against slavery.

When in the course of human events, it becomes necessary for one people to dissolve the political bands which have connected them with another, and to assume among the powers of the earth, the separate and equal station to which the laws of nature and of nature's God entitle them, a decent respect to the opinions of mankind requires that they should declare the causes which impel them to the separation.

We hold these truths to be self-evident: that all men are created equal; that they are endowed by their Creator with certain unalienable rights; that among these are life, liberty and the pursuit of happiness; that to secure these rights, governments are instituted among men, deriving their just powers from the consent of the governed; that whenever any form of government

© Text Complexity Rubric

	The Declaration of Independence	*from* The American Crisis, Number 1
Qualitative Measures		
Context/ Knowledge Demands	Historical knowledge demands (document) 1 2 ③ 4 5	Call to arms 1 2 ③ 4 5
Structure/Language Conventionality and Clarity	Eighteenth-century vocabulary and sentence structure 1 2 3 ④ 5	Eighteenth-century vocabulary; complicated sentence structure 1 2 3 ④ 5
Levels of Meaning/ Purpose/Concept Level	Abstract (philosophical ideas) 1 2 3 ④ 5	Accessible (figurative language) 1 2 ③ 4 5
Quantitative Measures		
Lexile/Text Length	1390L / 1,322 words	1200L / 1,000 words
Overall Complexity	**More complex**	**More accessible**

becomes destructive of these ends, it is the right of the people to alter or to abolish it, and to institute new government, laying its foundation on such principles and organizing its powers in such form, as to them shall seem most likely to effect their safety and happiness. Prudence, indeed, will dictate that governments long established should not be changed for light and transient causes; and accordingly all experience hath shown, that mankind are more disposed to suffer while evils are sufferable than to right themselves by abolishing the forms to which they are accustomed. But when a long train of abuses and usurpations, pursuing invariably the same object, evinces a design to reduce them under absolute despotism,[1] it is their right, it is their duty, to throw off such government, and to provide new guards for their future security. Such has been the patient sufferance of these colonies; and such is now the necessity which constrains them to alter their former systems of government. The history of the present king of Great Britain is a history of repeated injuries and usurpations, all having in direct object the establishment of an absolute tyranny over these states. To prove this, let facts be submitted to a candid world.

He has refused his assent to laws the most wholesome and necessary for the public good.

He has forbidden his governors to pass laws of immediate and pressing importance, unless suspended in their operation till his assent should be obtained; and when so suspended, he has utterly neglected to attend to them.

He has refused to pass other laws for the accommodation of large districts of people, unless those people would relinquish the right of representation in the legislature, a right inestimable to them and formidable to tyrants only.

He has called together legislative bodies at places unusual, uncomfortable, and distant from the depository of their public records, for the sole purpose of fatiguing them into compliance with his measures.

He has dissolved representative houses repeatedly, for opposing with manly firmness his invasions on the rights of the people.

He has refused for a long time after such dissolutions to cause others to be elected, whereby the legislative powers, incapable of annihilation, have returned to the people at large for their exercise, the state remaining in the mean time exposed to all the dangers of invasion from without, and convulsions within.

He has endeavored to prevent the population of these states; for that purpose obstructing the laws for naturalization of foreigners, refusing to pass others to encourage their migration hither, and raising the conditions of new appropriations of lands.

He has obstructed the administration of justice, by refusing his assent to laws for establishing judiciary powers.

---

1. **despotism** (des´ pət iz´ əm) *n.* tyranny.

Literary Analysis
Persuasion
Why does Jefferson introduce the idea that one does not change a government for "light" causes?

Vocabulary
candid (kan´ did) *adj.* honest

assent (ə sent´) *n.* agreement

5  **Reading Check**

Why did Jefferson write this long list of facts?

❸ Literary Analysis
Persuasion

1. Draw students' attention to the first bracketed passage. Have students paraphrase the sentence beginning "Prudence, indeed." **Possible response:** Because it is not wise to change governments without serious reasons, people are likely to just go along with things even if they are not entirely fair.

2. Then **ask** students the Literary Analysis question: Why does Jefferson introduce the idea that one does not change a government for "light" causes? **Answer:** Jefferson is arguing that the colonists' reasons for declaring independence are very serious.

❹ Literary Analysis

Persuasion

1. Write the second bracketed passage on the board. Review with students the meaning of the word *candid* and emphasize that Jefferson uses the word in the sense of "unbiased."

2. **Ask** students the following question: What does the statement about submitting facts to a "candid world" suggest about the intended audience? **Possible response:** It suggests that Jefferson believed he was speaking to the world and that he believed the world would judge his words fairly and honestly.

❺ Reading Check

Answer: He wanted to build a strong case against King George III in order to show that the colonists had no choice but to seek independence.

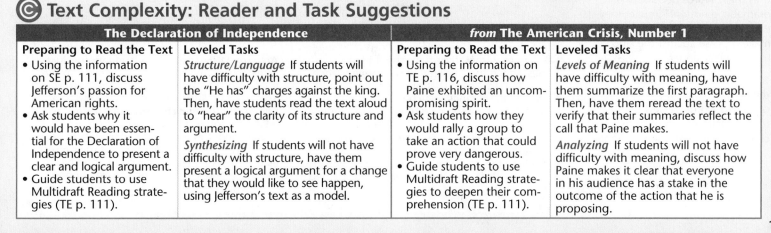

© Text Complexity: Reader and Task Suggestions

The Declaration of Independence		*from* The American Crisis, Number 1	
Preparing to Read the Text	**Leveled Tasks**	**Preparing to Read the Text**	**Leveled Tasks**
• Using the information on SE p. 111, discuss Jefferson's passion for American rights. • Ask students why it would have been essential for the Declaration of Independence to present a clear and logical argument. • Guide students to use Multidraft Reading strategies (TE p. 111).	*Structure/Language* If students will have difficulty with structure, point out the "He has" charges against the king. Then, have students read the text aloud to "hear" the clarity of its structure and argument. *Synthesizing* If students will not have difficulty with structure, have them present a logical argument for a change that they would like to see happen, using Jefferson's text as a model.	• Using the information on TE p. 116, discuss how Paine exhibited an uncompromising spirit. • Ask students how they would rally a group to take an action that could prove very dangerous. • Guide students to use Multidraft Reading strategies to deepen their comprehension (TE p. 111).	*Levels of Meaning* If students will have difficulty with meaning, have them summarize the first paragraph. Then, have them reread the text to verify that their summaries reflect the call that Paine makes. *Analyzing* If students will not have difficulty with meaning, discuss how Paine makes it clear that everyone in his audience has a stake in the outcome of the action that he is proposing.

113

114

6 *The* **American EXPERIENCE**

Philosophical Influence: John Locke and the Social Contract
In writing the Declaration of Independence, Jefferson drew on a theory of government devised by earlier European political thinkers, especially the Englishman John Locke (1632–1704). Locke argued that all people are born with certain *natural rights* that are not the property of governments. Locke's concept of the *social contract* also contributed to Jefferson's notion that governments derive their power from "the consent of the governed." According to Locke, when a ruler breaks the social contract by acting abusively, the people have the right to revolt against his rule. In 1776, that is what the American colonists did.

Connect to the Literature

Where in the Declaration does Jefferson echo Locke's idea that the people have the right to overthrow a government that breaks the social contract?

Vocabulary

harass (hər′ əs) *v.* attack; bother

tyranny (tir′ə nē) *n.* oppressive power

redress (ri dres′) *n.* compensation for a wrong done

Reading Strategy
Analyzing Word Choice
Why do you think Jefferson uses the words "ravaged" and "executioners"?

He has made judges dependent on his will alone, for the tenure of their offices, and the amount and payment of their salaries.

He has erected a multitude of new offices, and sent hither swarms of officers to harass our people and eat out their substance.

He has kept among us in times of peace standing armies without the consent of our legislatures.

He has affected to render the military independent of, and superior to, the civil power.

He has combined with others to subject us to a jurisdiction foreign to our constitution and unacknowledged by our laws, giving his assent to their acts of pretended legislation: for quartering large bodies of armed troops among us; for protecting them by a mock trial from punishment for any murders which they should commit on the inhabitants of these states; for cutting off our trade with all parts of the world; for imposing taxes on us without our consent; for depriving us, in many cases, of the benefits of trial by jury; for transporting us beyond seas to be tried for pretended offenses; for abolishing the free system of English laws in a neighboring province,[2] establishing therein an arbitrary government, and enlarging its boundaries, so as to render it at once an example and fit instrument for introducing the same absolute rule into these colonies; for taking away our charters, abolishing our most valuable laws, and altering fundamentally the forms of our governments; for suspending our own legislatures, and declaring themselves invested with power to legislate for us in all cases whatsoever.

He has abdicated government here, by declaring us out of his protection and waging war against us.

He has plundered our seas, ravaged our coasts, burned our towns, and destroyed the lives of our people.

He is at this time transporting large armies of foreign mercenaries to complete the works of death, desolation, and tyranny, already begun with circumstances of cruelty and perfidy scarcely paralleled in the most barbarous ages, and totally unworthy the head of a civilized nation.

He has constrained our fellow citizens taken captive on the high seas to bear arms against their country, to become the executioners of their friends and brethren, or to fall themselves by their hands.

He has excited domestic insurrections amongst us, and has endeavored to bring on the inhabitants of our frontiers, the merciless Indian savages, whose known rule of warfare is an undistinguished destruction of all ages, sexes, and conditions.

In every stage of these oppressions we have petitioned for redress in the most humble terms. Our repeated petitions have been answered only by repeated injury.

---

2. neighboring province Quebec.

Enrichment: Investigating a Key Person in History

A Spreading Flame of Freedom

When representatives from the thirteen colonies signed the Declaration of Independence, they forged a path that other nations would soon follow. France, which helped the colonists defeat Britain, soon convulsed in revolution.

In Latin America, Simón Bolívar campaigned for independence from Spain in the nineteenth century. He raised an army to liberate what are now the countries of Venezuela, Colombia, Ecuador, Peru, and Bolivia (which was named in his honor).

Activity: Discussion Have students conduct research into the role of Simón Bolívar in the liberation of Latin American countries from Spanish rule. Suggest that they record their findings in the **Enrichment: Investigating a Key Person in History** work sheet, in *Professional Development Guidebook,* page 233. Have them use the results of their research as the basis of a discussion comparing North American and Latin American revolutionary experiences.

A prince whose character is thus marked by every act which may define a tyrant is unfit to be the ruler of a free people.

Nor have we been wanting in attentions to our British brethren. We have warned them from time to time of attempts by their legislature to extend an unwarrantable jurisdiction over us. We have reminded them of the circumstances of our emigration and settlement here. We have appealed to their native justice and magnanimity and we have conjured[3] them by the ties of our common kindred to disavow these usurpations which would inevitably interrupt our connections and correspondence. They too have been deaf to the voice of justice and of consanguinity. We must therefore acquiesce in the necessity which denounces our separation and hold them, as we hold the rest of mankind, enemies in war, in peace friends.

We, therefore, the representatives of the United States of America in general congress assembled, appealing to the Supreme Judge of the world for the rectitude of our intentions, do in the name and by authority of the good people of these colonies, solemnly publish and declare that these united colonies are and of right ought to be free and independent states; that they are absolved from all allegiance to the British Crown, and that all political connection between them and the state of Great Britain is and ought to be totally dissolved; and that as free and independent states, they have full power to levy war, conclude peace, contract alliances, establish commerce, and to do all other acts and things which independent states may of right do.

And for the support of this declaration, with a firm reliance on the protection of divine providence, we mutually pledge to each other our lives, our fortunes and our sacred honor.

---

3. **conjured** v. solemnly appealed to.

Vocabulary
acquiesce (ak′ wē es′) v. agree without protest

rectitude (rek ti t o̅o̅d) n. correctness; righteousness

Critical Reading

©

© 1. **Key Ideas and Details (a)** What points about human rights does Jefferson make at the beginning of the Declaration? **(b) Analyze:** Why does he begin with these observations before addressing the colonists' situation?

© 2. **Craft and Structure (a) Evaluate:** What is the most convincing evidence that Jefferson cites to support his points? Explain. **(b) Evaluate:** How would you rate the overall effectiveness of his argument? Why?

© 3. **Integration of Knowledge and Ideas Synthesize:** The period in which this document was written is often referred to as the Age of Reason because of the emphasis on logic and discipline at the time. What elements of Jefferson's Declaration reflect a faith in reason?

Cite textual evidence to support your responses.

The Declaration of Independence **115**

Differentiated Instruction   for Universal Access

Strategy for Special-Needs Students
Have students work through the selection paragraph by paragraph to find the key ideas in each. Help students identify unfamiliar words or usage *before* they address the content of each paragraph.

Strategy for Less Proficient Readers
Encourage students to break down Jefferson's long sentences. One way to do this is by separating clauses. Using a random complex sentence, demonstrate how to identify and separate clauses. Ask students to paraphrase each clause. Then, help them compose their own sentences using the paraphrasing.

115

⑨ Background
More About the Author

Thomas Paine's words aroused much passion in the hearts of his listeners. Not all of it was positive, however. Many hated Paine. Some found his personality offensive. Others disagreed with his views on religion. Perhaps it was Paine's dislike for compromise that earned him the most enemies.

"I love the man that can **smile in trouble,** that can **gather strength** from distress, and **grow brave** by reflection."

⑨ Thomas Paine (1737–1809)

Author of **The American Crisis, Number 1**

Thomas Paine met Benjamin Franklin in London, and the introduction changed both his life and American history. Paine emigrated to the colonies from England in 1774. With a letter of introduction from Franklin, Paine began a career as a journalist. In January 1776, he published *Common Sense*, in which he argued that Americans must fight for independence. The pamphlet created a national mood for revolution.

Inspiring Essayist Paine enlisted in the American army toward the end of 1776. At that time, the army had just suffered a crushing defeat by the British in New Jersey and had re- treated into Pennsylvania. The soldiers were suf- fering from freezing weather, a shortage of provi- sions, and low morale. Paine was writing the first of a series of essays entitled *The American Crisis*. Washington ordered Paine's essay read to his troops before they crossed the Delaware River to defeat the Hessians at the Battle of Trenton.

In 1787, several years after the end of the American Revolution, Paine traveled to Europe and became involved with the French Revolution. Though he wrote in support of the revolution- ary cause in *The Rights of Man* (1791–1792), he was imprisoned for pleading against the execution of the overthrown French king. While in prison, he began writing *The Age of Reason* (1794), an attack on orga- nized religion. The book turned American public opinion against him, and when he died in 1809, he was a broken man. Years later, however, Paine was once again recognized as a hero of the Revolution.

Enrichment: Building Context

Revolutionary Blockbuster

Colonists began noticing Thomas Paine nearly a year before the dark winter of his *"Crisis"* essay. In early 1776 Paine's pamphlet *Common Sense* made a dramatic impact on colonists and helped set the revolutionary mood. The pamphlet spoke out fervently for complete independence, brooking no compromises or halfway measures. Furthermore, Paine criticized the concept of monarchy and called for the abolition of inherited class status. He said, "the birthday of a new world is at hand," and it was.

Activity: Presentation Have students conduct research into the social context in which Paine wrote. Suggest that they record their findings in the **Enrichment: Building Context** work sheet, in *Professional Development Guidebook*, page 222. Have them use the results of their research as the basis of a presentation that gives listeners further appreciation of the significance of Paine's writing to the revolutionary cause.

PHLit Online!

For more about the author, go online at **www.PHLitOnline.com**.

from THE AMERICAN CRISIS
NUMBER 1
Thomas Paine

These are the times that try men's souls. The summer soldier and the sunshine patriot will, in this crisis, shrink from the service of his country; but he that stands it now, deserves the love and thanks of man and woman. Tyranny, like hell, is not easily conquered; yet we have this consolation with us, that the harder the conflict, the more glorious the triumph. What we obtain too cheap, we esteem too lightly:—'Tis dearness only that gives every thing its value. Heaven knows how to set a proper price upon its goods; and it would be strange indeed, if so celestial an article as Freedom should not be highly rated. Britain, with an army to enforce her tyranny, has declared, that she has a right (*not only to* TAX) but "*to* BIND *us in* ALL CASES WHATSOEVER," and if being *bound in that manner* is not slavery, then is there not such a thing as slavery

10 ▲ Critical Viewing
In what ways does this cartoon mock Great Britain while celebrating the revolutionaries? **[Analyze]**

12 ✓ Reading Check

What does Paine say is not easily conquered?

from The American Crisis, Number 1 **117**

Differentiated Instruction   for Universal Access

Support for Less Proficient Readers
In many places, Paine uses either all capital letters or italicized letters. Explain that Paine uses these techniques to emphasize certain ideas. Thus, when students encounter a phrase such as *"not only to* TAX," they can use the special treatment of the letters to help them construct meaning.

EL Vocabulary for English Learners
Tell students that Paine uses figurative speech—words that have meaning beyond their literal definition—throughout his essay. Model how to decode this figurative language, using the example of the "summer soldier" and the "sunshine patriot." Then, invite volunteers to take turns restating figurative language.

Enrichment for Advanced Readers
In an address to the Continental Congress, George Washington said, "I am wearied to death. I think the game is pretty near up." Have students write a speech as if they were Washington, conveying thoughts *after* reading Paine's essay. Challenge them to quote from the essay and to express renewed dedication.

TEACH

10 Critical Viewing
Answer: The cartoon celebrates the colonial revolutionaries by depicting them as united and strong, while Britain is represented by a single figure of an elderly man who needs a crutch to help him stand.

11 Engaging the Essential Question

1. Point out that a popular form of American political expression is the bumper sticker, a label attached to one's vehicle that offers a pithy statement of values or ideals.

2. Have students review Paine's opening paragraph to identify statements that could serve as bumper sticker ideals.
Possible response: Students may cite "Tyranny, like Hell, is not easily conquered"; "the harder the conflict, the more glorious the triumph"; "What we obtain too cheap, we esteem too lightly"; "'Tis dearness only that gives every thing its value."

3. **Ask** students: How do these statements express values that Paine wants Americans to share? Are these values still important to Americans today?
Possible response: Paine's opening statement emphasizes the cost of freedom. Students may say most Americans still recognize the accuracy of Paine's idea that "freedom is not free."

12 Reading Check
Answer: Paine says that tyranny is not easily conquered.

This selection is available in interactive format in the **Enriched Online Student Edition**, at www.PHLitOnline.com, which includes a thematically related video with a writing prompt and an interactive graphic organizer.

1. Invite a volunteer to stand and speak the words of the bracketed passage.

2. **Ask** students what associations they have with the word *foreign*.
   Possible response: Students may acknowledge associating the word *foreign* with things that are strange or alien to them but also with things that are exciting and interesting.

3. **Ask** students the following question: In what ways might the word *foreign* help Paine inspire the colonists to fight against Britain?
   Possible response: By using it, Paine casts the British as outsiders, when in fact most colonists were of British stock. By distancing the colonists from their adversary, Paine appeals to the colonists' sense of themselves as an emerging nation. Casting Britain as a foreign power rather than as the colonists' legal government helps colonists avoid any sense of disloyalty.

Vocabulary
prudent (proo'dent) *adj.* sensible; careful

11 upon earth. Even the expression is impious, for so unlimited a power can belong only to GOD.

Whether the Independence of the Continent was declared too soon, or delayed too long, I will not now enter into as an argument; my own simple opinion is, that had it been eight months earlier, it would have been much better. . . .

I once felt all that kind of anger, which a man ought to feel, against the mean[1] principles that are held by the Tories:[2] A noted one, who kept a tavern at Amboy, was standing at his door, with as pretty a child in his hand, about eight or nine years old, as most I ever saw, and after speaking his mind as freely as he thought was prudent, finished with this unfatherly expression, "*Well! give me peace in my day.*" Not a man lives on the Continent but fully believes that a separation must some time or other finally take place, and a generous parent would have said, "*If there must be trouble, let it be in my day, that my child may have peace;*" and this single reflection, well applied, is sufficient to awaken every man to duty. Not a place upon earth might be so happy as America. Her situation is remote from all the wrangling world, and she has nothing to do but to trade with them. A man may easily distinguish in himself between temper and principle, and I am as confident, as I am that GOD governs the world, that America will never be happy till she gets clear of foreign dominion. Wars, without ceasing, will break out till that period arrives, and the Continent must in the end be conqueror; for, though the flame of liberty may sometimes cease to shine, the coal never can expire.

13

America did not, nor does not, want force; but she wanted a proper application of that force. Wisdom is not the purchase of a day, and it is no wonder that we should err at first sitting off. From an excess of tenderness, we were unwilling to raise an army, and trusted our cause to the temporary defence of a well meaning militia. A summer's experience has now taught us better; yet with those troops, while they were collected, we were able to set bounds to the progress of the enemy, and, thank GOD! they are again assembling. . . .

. . . I turn with the warm ardour of a friend to those who have nobly stood, and are yet determined to stand the matter out: I call not upon a few, but upon all; not on THIS State or THAT State, but on every State; up and help us; lay your shoulders to the wheel; better have too much force than too little, when so great an object is at stake. Let it be told to the future world, that in the depth of winter, when nothing but hope and virtue could survive, that the city and the country, alarmed at one common danger, came forth to meet and to repulse it. Say not, that thousands are gone, turn out your tens of thousands; throw not the burden of the day upon Providence, but "*show your faith by your works,*" that God may bless you. It matters not where you live, or what rank of life you hold, the evil or the blessing will reach you all. The far and the near, the home counties and the back, the rich and the poor,

---

1. **mean** *adj.* small-minded.
2. **Tories** colonists who remained loyal to Great Britain.

Think Aloud

Literary Analysis: Persuasion
To model recognition and appreciation of the use of persuasion, use the following "think aloud." Say to students:

A common form of persuasion is the rallying cry. The rallying cry is a high-energy message that boils down to "We are all in this together!" Thomas Paine was a master of the rallying cry. As I read his words on the page, I can almost hear him crying out so that all can hear: "I call not upon a few, but upon all; . . . up and help us; lay your shoul- ders to the wheel; better have too much force than too little. . . . Let it be told to the future world, . . . when nothing but hope and virtue could survive, that the city and the country, alarmed at one common danger, came forth to meet and to repulse it." It is no wonder that with such strong calls for unity in the struggle the American colonists eventually prevailed.

shall suffer or rejoice alike. The heart that feels not now, is dead: The blood of his children shall curse his cowardice, who shrinks back at a time when a little might have saved the whole, and made *them* happy. I love the man that can smile in trouble, that can gather strength from distress, and grow brave by reflection. 'Tis the business of little minds to shrink; but he whose heart is firm, and whose conscience approves his conduct, will pursue his principles unto death. My own line of reasoning is to myself as straight and clear as a ray of light. Not all the treasures of the world, so far as I believe, could have induced me to support an offensive war, for I think it murder; but if a thief break into my house, burn and destroy my property, and kill or threaten to kill me, or those that are in it, and to "*bind me in all cases whatsoever*," to his absolute will, am I to suffer it? What signifies it to me, whether he who does it, is a king or a common man; my countryman or not my countryman? whether it is done by an individual villain, or an army of them? If we reason to the root of things we shall find no difference; neither can any just cause be assigned why we should punish in the one case, and pardon in the other. . . .

There are cases which cannot be overdone by language, and this is one. There are persons too who see not the full extent of the evil that threatens them; they solace themselves with hopes that the enemy, if they succeed, will be merciful. It is the madness of folly to expect mercy from those who have refused to do justice; and even mercy, where conquest is the object, is only a trick of war: The cunning of the fox is as murderous as the violence of the wolf; and we ought to guard equally against both.

> These are the times that try men's souls.

Critical Reading

1. Key Ideas and Details (a) In the first paragraph, how does Paine say the "summer soldier" and the "sunshine patriot" will react to the American crisis? Why? **(b) Interpret:** In that same paragraph, with what ideas does Paine justify the struggle of revolution?

2. Key Ideas and Details (a) In the third paragraph, what anecdote, or story, does Paine tell? **(b) Draw Conclusions:** What point is Paine making by relating this anecdote?

3. Integration of Knowledge and Ideas Are the ideals Jefferson and Paine defend in these writings still important to Americans? Explain. In your response, use at least two of these Essential Question words: *patriotism, service, authority, equality. [Connecting to the Essential Question: What makes American literature American?]*

Cite textual evidence to support your responses.

Concept Connector

Reading Strategy Graphic Organizer
Ask students to review the graphic organizers with which they have monitored their comprehension of word choice in the two selections. Then, have students share their organizers and compare their conclusions about the authors' use of connotations.

Activating Prior Knowledge
Have students return to their responses to the Activating Prior Knowledge activity. Ask them to explain whether their thoughts have changed and if so, how.

Connecting to the Essential Question
Have students compare the responses they gave to the prompt before reading the selections with their thoughts afterwards. Have them work individually or in groups, writing or discussing their thoughts, to define their new responses. Then lead a class discussion, probing for what students have learned that confirms or invalidates their initial thoughts. Encourage students to cite specific textual details to support their responses.

Answers

1. **Sample answer:** Jefferson: Emotion: "destroyed the lives of our people." Logic: "Whenever any form of government becomes destructive . . . it is the right of the people to alter or to abolish it." Ethics: "We hold these truths to be self-evident." Authority: "appealing to the Supreme Judge of the world."

2. **Possible response:** (a) Jefferson wants his readers to favor independence; Paine also promotes that cause. (b) Jefferson wants his readers to pledge support for the Declaration. Paine wants readers to support military action.

3. (a) He appeals to anger and distress. (b) Paine appeals more to emotion than to reason. He says, for example, "I once felt all that kind of anger, which a man ought to feel."

4. The anecdote suggests that the parents should act now to leave their children a free country.

5. (a) Jefferson speaks to the world, while Paine speaks to those already fighting. (b) **Possible response:** Students may expect rational arguments in writing for a world audience and more inspirational words for soldiers. (c) Yes. Both documents inspire. Jefferson's is more closely argued; Paine's is more rousing.

6. Jefferson's list refutes the claim that the British are just.

7. **Possible responses:** (a) 1. freedom 2. fairness 3. esteem 4. uncivilized (b) 1. freedom from unjust restraint 2. desrved punishment or reward 3. deserved esteem 4. intolerably cruel (c) 1. *Liberty* evokes a feeling of security and peace. 2. *Justice* evokes a feeling of fairness. 3. *Honor* evokes a feeling of dignity. 4. *Barbarous* evokes feelings of disgust. (d) These words can be loaded depending on context.

8. Both use the terms to mean a despotic ruler and an all-powerful, controlling system.

9. *Supporters* is a kinder word that suggests caretaking, while *thief* suggests a negative image.

10. **Possible response:** Students may agree that some situations are so extreme that even the strongest or most exaggerated words are warranted.

120

The Declaration of Independence • from *The American Crisis, Number 1*

Literary Analysis

1. **Key Ideas and Details** Use a chart like the one shown to identify elements of **persuasion** in these selections. Classify the types of appeals Jefferson and Paine use to advance their arguments.

	Emotion	Logic	Ethics	Authority
Jefferson				
Paine				

2. **Key Ideas and Details** (a) What specific beliefs does each writer want his readers to hold? (b) What actions does each writer want his readers to take? Note details that support your answers.

3. **Craft and Structure** (a) Name two emotions to which Paine appeals in this excerpt. (b) Does he appeal more to emotion or to reason? Support your answer with examples from the text.

4. **Craft and Structure** What persuasive purpose does Paine's anecdote about the Tory serve?

5. **Comparing Literary Works** (a) Who are the intended **audiences** for each of these works? (b) What kinds of supporting evidence would you expect to see in writing meant for each audience? (c) Are your expectations borne out in these selections? Explain your reasoning.

6. **Craft and Structure** Jefferson presents a long list of grievances against King George. What counterclaim do you think the list attempts to answer? Explain.

Reading Strategy

7. **Analyze word choice** by examining *denotation* and *connotation:* (a) Write the denotative meaning of each numbered word below. (b) Write a suggested, or connotative, meaning for each word. (c) Explain the emotions each word evokes in you. (d) Which of these words is charged or loaded? Explain.
   1. liberty   2. justice   3. honor   4. barbarous

8. Both Jefferson and Paine use the charged words "tyrant" and "tyranny" frequently. Do these words carry the same meanings for both writers? Explain.

9. In describing the colonists' British rulers, how does Paine's use of the word "thief" evoke a different response than would the word "supporters"?

10. Paine says, "There are cases which cannot be overdone with language." Do you think this statement is true? Explain your answer.

Common Core State Standards

Writing
1. Write arguments to support claims in an analysis of substantive topics or texts, using valid reasoning and relevant and sufficient evidence. *(p. 121)*

Language
4.b. Identify and correctly use patterns of word changes that indicate different meanings or parts of speech. *(p. 121)*

Assessment Practice

Recognize Cause and Effect (For more practice, see *All-in-One Workbook*.)

To help students understand cause-and-effect relationships, have them reread pages 112–113. Then, ask:

Which of the following actions of the British king was NOT a cause that led to the colonists' creation of the Declaration of Independence?

A his refusal to pass laws created by the colonists

B his dissolution of colonial houses of representatives

C his interference with the administration of justice

D his personal visit to the thirteen colonies

Choices **A**, **B**, and **C** contributed to the Americans' decision to declare independence from Britain. Choice **D** is the correct choice, because it was *not* an action that led to creation of the Declaration.

 All resources are available at **www.PHLitOnline.com**

Integrated Language Skills

© Vocabulary Acquisition and Use

Word Analysis: Latin Word Parts -rect- and -tude

The word "rectitude" combines the Latin root -rect-, meaning "straight," with the suffix -tude, meaning "having or possessing." Thus, a person who displays rectitude possesses ethical or moral straightness. For each item below, notice the meanings of the word parts in parentheses. Combine these meanings with those of the root -rect- or the suffix -tude to write definitions for each numbered word.

1. rectify   (suffix -ify = make, cause)
2. correct   (prefix co- = with)
3. indirect   (prefix in- = without)
4. aptitude   (root -apt- = fit, suited)
5. fortitude   (root -fort- = strength)
6. solitude   (root -sol- = alone)

Vocabulary: True or False

Indicate which of the statements below are true and which are false. Explain your answers.

1. If a child *acquiesces* about being put to bed, she accepts her bedtime.
2. Public support for a radical cause is one form of *tyranny*.
3. There is no need for *redress* if no wrong has been committed.
4. A *candid* opinion is the same as a fact.
5. To judge the *rectitude* of an action, you must consider whether or not it is justified.
6. It is likely that any nation will automatically *assent* to a colony's request for independence.
7. Governments should *harass* citizens who do not agree with specific laws.
8. A *prudent* leader will consider the needs of the public before making a decision.

Writing

© **Argumentative Text** Like Jefferson and Paine, you can change your world with the persuasive use of words. Consider a problem facing your school or community. Write an **editorial** to appear in a local newspaper in which you explain why the situation needs attention and how it should be corrected.

Prewriting List the elements of the problem. Write facts, examples, and explanations that present a solution. Categorize your ideas to identify those that provide strong emotional, logical, and ethical appeals. Consider sources, such as local leaders, whom you might cite in an appeal to authority.

Drafting As you write, structure your ideas so that they flow logically and support them with precise and relevant examples. Demonstrate respect by avoiding name-calling and inappropriate language.

Revising Review your editorial and check that your language is forceful and direct. Replace imprecise or weak language with more persuasive choices.

Model: Revising Language

Separate lounges for upper- and
                      superior
lowerclassmen reflect ~~good~~ planning.
Wise thinkers   ∧
~~Everyone~~ recognizes that each group
         ∧
              age-appropriate
needs a place to pursue ~~their own~~ activities.
                        ∧

Terms such as *superior* and *wise thinkers* add force to the argument. *Age-appropriate* adds more information.

Integrated Language Skills **121**

Assessment Resources

Unit 1 Resources

L1 L2 EL Selection Test A, pp. 179–181. Administer Test A to less advanced students and English learners.

L3 L4 EL Selection Test B, pp. 182–184. Administer Test B to on-level or more advanced students.

L3 L4 Open-Book Test, pp. 176–178. As an alternative, give the Open-Book Test.

All Customizable Test Bank

All Self-tests
Students may prepare for the **Selection Test** by taking the **Self-test** online.

PHLit Online! All assessment resources are available at **www.PHLitOnline.com**.

Answers

Vocabulary Acquisition and Use

1. Introduce the skill, using the instruction on the student page.
2. Have students complete the Word Analysis activity and the Vocabulary practice.

Word Analysis

1. to set straight, to make right
2. to make straight with, or in agreement with, the truth
3. not straight
4. suitability
5. strength
6. condition of being alone

Vocabulary

1. True. The child has agreed.
2. False. Public support shows wide acceptance, which is the opposite of tyranny.
3. True. No compensation is needed in the absence of a wrong.
4. False. An opinion is open to dispute.
5. True. The correctness of an action is determined by whether or not it is justified.
6. False. Nations do not readily give up control of other lands.
7. False. Citizens should be able to voice their disagreement without threats or other trouble.
8. True. A wise leader will consider the full consequences of a decision.

Writing

1. Use the Writing instruction to guide students in developing their proposals. In addition, you may wish to give them the Support for Writing page (*Unit 1 Resources,* p. 174).
2. Remind students to organize their evidence to achieve the greatest impact.
3. Use the **Rubrics for Persuasion,** in *Professional Development Guidebook,* pages 256–257, to evaluate students' work.

• To His Excellency, General Washington
Lesson Pacing Guide

DAY 1 Preteach

ⓒ Administer the Reading and Vocabulary Warm-ups (*Unit 1 Resources*, pp. 185–188) as necessary.

ⓒ Introduce the Literary Analysis concepts: Heroic Couplets.

• Introduce the Reading Strategy: Rereading.

ⓒ Build background with the author and Background features.

• Develop thematic thinking with Connecting to the Essential Question.

ⓒ Teach the selection vocabulary.

DAY 2 Preteach/Teach/Extend

• Distribute copies of the appropriate graphic organizer for the Reading Strategy (*Graphic Organizer Transparencies*, pp. 37–38).

• Distribute copies of the appropriate graphic organizer for Literary Analysis (*Graphic Organizer Transparencies*, pp. 39–40).

• Prepare students to read with the Activating Prior Knowledge activities (TE).

• Informally monitor comprehension while students read.

• Use the Reading Check question to confirm comprehension.

ⓒ Reinforce vocabulary with the Vocabulary notes.

• Assess students' comprehension and mastery of the skills by having them answer the Critical Reading, Literary Analysis, and Reading Strategy questions.

DAY 3 Assess

ⓒ Have students complete the Vocabulary practice.

ⓒ Have students complete the Writing activity and write a persuasive memorandum. (You may assign as homework.)

• Administer Selection Test A or B (*Unit 1 Resources*, pp. 197–199 or 200–202).

ⓒ **Common Core State Standards**

Reading Literature 5. Analyze how an author's choices concerning how to structure specific parts of a text contribute to its overall structure and meaning as well as its aesthetic impact.
9. Demonstrate knowledge of eighteenth-century foundational works of American literature.

Writing 1. Write arguments to support claims in an analysis of substantive topics or texts, using valid reasoning and relevant and sufficient evidence.

Additional Standards Practice
Common Core Companion, *pp. 54–55; 185–195*

Daily Block Scheduling
Each day in this Lesson Pacing Guide represents a 40–50 minute period. Teachers using block scheduling may combine days to revise pacing. In addition, teachers may differentiate and support core instruction by integrating components for extended and intensive support as students require. See the Guide to Selected Leveled Resources (facing page).

Guide to Selected Leveled Resources

R T I Tier 1 (students performing on level)

To His Excellency, General Washington

Warm Up	Practice, **model,** and **monitor** fluency, working **with the whole class** or **in groups.**	**Vocabulary and Reading Warm-ups B,** *Unit 1 Resources,* pp. 185–186, 188
Comprehension/Skills	**Support** and **monitor** comprehension and skills development, having students complete the activities, graphic organizers, and interactive prompts **independently** or **as a class.**	• *Reader's Notebook,* adapted instruction and summary **EL** *Reader's Notebook: English Learner's Version,* adapted instruction and summary • **Reading Skill Graphic Organizer B,** *Graphic Organizer Transparencies,* p. 38 • **Literary Analysis Graphic Organizer B,** *Graphic Organizer Transparencies,* p. 40
Monitor Progress	**Monitor** student progress with the differentiated curriculum-based assessment in the *Unit Resources.*	• **Selection Test B,** *Unit 1 Resources,* pp. 200–202 • **Open-Book Test,** *Unit 1 Resources,* pp. 194–196

R T I Tier 2 (students requiring intervention)

To His Excellency, General Washington

Warm Up	Practice, **model,** and **monitor** fluency **in groups** or **with individuals.**	• **Vocabulary and Reading Warm-ups A,** *Unit 1 Resources,* pp. 185–187 • *Hear It!* **Audio CD**
Comprehension/Skills	• **Support** and **monitor** comprehension and skills development, working **in small groups** or **with individuals.** • As students complete the selection in the appropriate version of the *Reader's Notebook,* **monitor** comprehension frequently with group questions and individual instruction. • **Model** strategies while guiding students in completing the activities and prompts in the *Reader's Notebook,* as well as the graphic organizers. • **Practice** skills and **monitor** mastery with the *Reading Kit* worksheets.	• *Reader's Notebook: Adapted Version,* adapted instruction and summary **EL** *Reader's Notebook: English Learner's Version,* adapted instruction and summary • **Reading Strategy Graphic Organizer A,** *Graphic Organizer Transparencies,* p. 37 • **Literary Analysis Graphic Organizer A,** *Graphic Organizer Transparencies,* p. 39 • *Reading Kit,* Practice worksheets
Monitor Progress	**Monitor** student progress with the differentiated curriculum-based assessment in the *Unit Resources* and in the *Reading Kit.*	• **Selection Test A,** *Unit 1 Resources,* pp. 197–199 • *Reading Kit,* Assess worksheets

TIER 3 Tier 3 intervention may require consultation with the student's special-education or dyslexia specialist. For additional support, see the Tier 2 activities and resources listed above.

One-on-one teaching **Group work** **Whole class instruction** **Independent work** **A Assessment**

For a complete guide to selection support, including support for Advanced students, see the Overview of Resources in the frontmatter.

• To His Excellency, General Washington

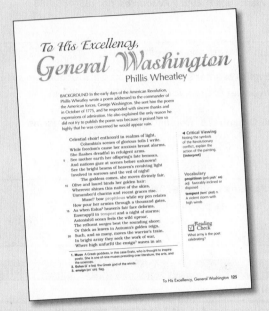

RESOURCES FOR:

- **L1** Special-Needs Students
- **L2** Below-Level Students (Tier 2)
- **L3** On-Level Students (Tier 1)
- **L4** Advanced Students (Tier 1)
- **EL** English Learners
- **All** All Students

Vocabulary/Fluency/Prior Knowledge

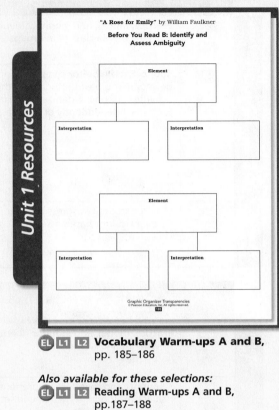

EL L1 L2 Vocabulary Warm-ups A and B, pp. 185–186

Also available for these selections:

EL L1 L2 Reading Warm-ups A and B, pp.187–188

All Vocabulary Builder, p. 191

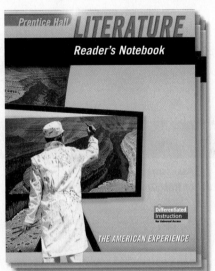

- **L2 L3** *Reader's Notebook*
- **L1** *Reader's Notebook: Adapted Version*
- **EL** *Reader's Notebook: English Learner's Version*
- **EL** *Reader's Notebook: Spanish Version*

Reader's Notebooks

Pre- and postreading pages for this selection appear in an interactive format in the *Reader's Notebooks*. Each *Notebook* is differentiated for a different group of learners.

The selections in the Adapted and English Learner's versions are abridged.

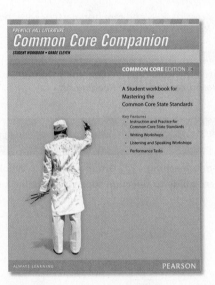

© *Common Core Companion*

Additional instruction and practice for each Common Core State Standard

Selection Support

Graphic Organizer Transparencies

EL **L3** **Reading: Graphic Organizer B**, p. 38

Also available for these selections:

EL **L1** **L2** **Reading: Graphic Organizer A**, (partially filled in), p. 37

EL **L1** **L2** **Literary Analysis: Graphic Organizer A**, (partially filled in), p. 39

EL **L3** **Literary Analysis: Graphic Organizer B**, p. 40

Skills Development/Extension

Unit 1 Resources

EL **L3** **L4** **Reading: Reread to Clarify Meaning**, p. 190

Also available for these selections:

All **Literary Analysis: Heroic Couplets and Archetypal References**, p. 189

EL **L3** **L4** **Support for Writing**, p. 192

L4 **Enrichment**, p. 193

Assessment

EL **L1** **L2** **Selection Test A**, pp. 197–199

Also available for these selections:

L3 **L4** **Open-Book Test**, pp. 194–196

EL **L3** **L4** **Selection Test B**, pp. 200–202

PHLit Online!
www.PHLitOnline.com

Online Resources: All print materials are also available online.

- complete narrated selection text
- a thematically related video with writing prompt
- an interactive graphic organizer
- highlighting feature
- access to all student print resources, adapted to individual student needs
- Spanish and English summaries
- adapted selection translations in Spanish

Get Connected!

Also available:

Background Video (thematic video with writing prompt)
All videos available in Spanish.

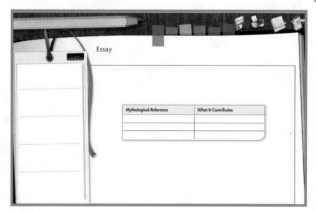

Writer's Journal (with graphics feature)

Also available:

Vocabulary Central (tools and activities for studying vocabulary)

❶ 🅿 **Connecting to the Essential Question**

1. Review the assignment.

2. Invite students to share examples of songs, poems, and films that pay tribute to America and its leaders. Discuss the examples and what they indicate about the qualities desired in a leader. Then, have them complete the assignment.

3. As students read, have them look for details about leadership that have an American "flavor."

❷ **Literary Analysis**

Introduce the skill, using the instruction on the student page.

Think Aloud: Model the Skill

Say to students:

When I read poetry written in pairs of rhyming lines that each contain five unstressed and five stressed syllables, I know that I am reading heroic couplets. Because I know that a heroic couplet expresses a complete thought, I consider the meaning of each individual pair of lines. Then, I apply those ideas as I develop my understanding of the poem as a whole.

❸ **Reading Strategy**

1. Introduce the strategy.

2. Give students **Reading Strategy Graphic Organizer B**, page 38 in *Graphic Organizer Transparencies,* to fill out as they read.

❹ **Vocabulary**

1. Pronounce each word, giving its definition, and have students say it aloud.

2. For more guidance, see the *Classroom Strategies and Teaching Routines* card for introducing vocabulary.

Before You Read | *To His Excellency, General Washington*

❶ **Connecting to the Essential Question** In her poems, Phillis Wheatley often paid tribute to America, its leaders, and the ideals the new country represented to her. As you read, find details that show the qualities Wheatley most admires in George Washington. This will help as you consider the Essential Question: **What makes American literature American?**

❷ **Literary Analysis**

Phillis Wheatley wrote in **heroic couplets,** a traditional *poetic form*, or structure. Heroic couplets were introduced into English literature by the poet Chaucer in the fourteenth century, but they earned their name from their use by sixteenth-century poets in dramatic works about heroes. Heroic couplets have the following elements:

- They are written in a sequence of rhyming *couplets*, or pairs of lines.
- Each couplet expresses a complete thought.
- They have *end rhyme*, or full rhyme at the end of each line.
- They are written in *iambic pentameter*, a meter in which five unstressed syllables are each followed by a stressed syllable.

The influence of traditional literature is also evident in Wheatley's many references to *archetypal figures* from **classical mythology.** In this poem, she even creates a new goddess, Columbia, to symbolize America. As you read, think about how these references add to Wheatley's presentation of Washington as a hero of mythic grandeur.

❸ **Reading Strategy**

© **Preparing to Read Complex Texts** As you read, monitor your comprehension. If you find you are unsure of the meaning of lines or sections, **reread** to clarify your understanding. You may need to reorder words or determine the nouns that confusing pronouns replace. As you reread, use a chart like the one shown to clarify the poem's meaning.

❹ **Vocabulary**

propitious (prō pish′ əs) *adj.* favorably inclined or disposed (p. 125)

tempest (tem′ pist) *n.* a violent storm with high winds (p. 125)

martial (mär′ shəl) *adj.* relating to war (p. 126)

implore (im plôr′) *v.* ask or beg earnestly; plead (p. 126)

pensive (pen′ siv) *adj.* thinking deeply or seriously (p. 126)

lament (lə ment′) *v.* feel sorrow for; mourn (p. 126)

Common Core State Standards

Reading Literature

5. Analyze how an author's choices concerning how to structure specific parts of a text contribute to its overall structure and meaning as well as its aesthetic impact.

9. Demonstrate knowledge of eighteenth-century foundational works of American literature.

Original Sentence

How pour her armies through a thousand gates

Her refers to Columbia. Her armies is the subject of pour.

Clarified Meaning

How Columbia's armies pour through a thousand gates

Vocabulary Development

Vocabulary Knowledge Rating

Create a **Vocabulary Knowledge Rating Chart** (in *Professional Development Guidebook*, p. 33) for the vocabulary words on the student page. Give each student a copy of the chart with the words on it. Read the words aloud, and have students mark their rating of each in the Before Reading column. When students have completed reading and discussing the selec-tion, have them take out their charts for the selection. Read the words aloud and have students rate their knowledge again in the After Reading column. Clarify any words that are still problematic. Then, have students complete the Vocabulary practice at the end of the selection.

 **Vocabulary Central,** featuring tools and activities for studying vocabulary, is available online at **www.PHLitOnline.com.**

Phillis Wheatley (1753?–1784)

Author of "To His Excellency, General Washington"

In an era when few women and even fewer slaves could read and write, Phillis Wheatley, a female slave, became one of the finest American poets of her day. A West African native, Wheatley was brought to America on a slave ship when she was about eight. She was lucky enough to be purchased by a Boston family who valued her intelligence and taught her to read and write. The Wheatleys converted their young slave to Christianity and gave her the Bible, Latin and Greek classics, and contemporary English poetry to read. Soon Wheatley was writing her own verse, publishing her first poem when she was just thirteen.

Fame Abroad at an Early Age In 1770, Wheatley won fame through a poem about the death of a celebrated English clergyman, George Whitehead. Three years later, two British aristocrats helped her publish a volume of poetry in London. Called *Poems on Various Subjects: Religious and Moral,* the book was probably the first published work by an African in the colonies. However, it was not published in America until 1786, two years after Wheatley's death.

A Falling and Rising Star Freed from slavery in 1773, Wheatley's final years were filled with hardship and sorrow. Three of her children died in infancy, and her husband was imprisoned for debt. Though she assembled a second collection of poetry, the manuscript was lost before publication, and Wheatley fell into obscurity as a poet. In the centuries since her death, however, her star has again risen. She is now seen as a noteworthy poet of early America and the first writer of African origin to gain a voice in American literature.

The world is a severe schoolmaster, for its frowns are less dangerous than its smiles and flatteries, and it is a difficult task to keep in the path of wisdom.

To His Excellency, General Washington **123**

Daily Bellringer

For each class during which you will teach this selection, have students complete one of the five activities for the appropriate week in the *Daily Bellringer Activities* booklet.

Multidraft Reading

To assist struggling readers and to enhance reading for all, apply multidraft reading protocols. For each reading, have students set the purpose indicated:

- **First reading**—identifying key ideas and details and answering any Reading Checks.
- **Second reading**—analyzing craft and structure and responding to the side-column prompts.
- **Third reading**—integrating knowledge and ideas, connecting to other texts and the world, and answering the end-of-selection questions.

For more guidance, refer to the *Classroom Strategies and Teaching Routines* card on multidraft reading.

❺ Background
More About the Author

Phillis Wheatley's prominent Massachusetts supporters—led by Governor Thomas Hutchinson—had administered an oral examination to her to persuade themselves of her intellectual and creative capacity. Impressed by her answers, they drafted a two-paragraph letter to the public stating, in part:

> We . . . assure the World, that the POEMS specified in the following Page, were (as we verily believe) written by PHILLIS, a young Negro Girl, who was but a few Years since, brought . . . from Africa.

PHLit Online!
www.PHLitOnline.com

Teaching From Technology

Preparing to Read
Go to **www.PHLitOnline.com** in class or in a lab and display the **Get Connected!** slide show for this selection. Have the class brainstorm for responses to the slide show writing prompt, entering ideas in the interactive journal. Then, have students complete their written responses individually in a lab or as homework.

To build background, display the Background video and the More About the Author feature.

Using the Interactive Text
Go to **www.PHLitOnline.com** and display the **Enriched Online Student Edition.** As the class reads the selection or listens to the narration, record answers to side-column prompts using the graphic organizers accessible on the interactive page. Alternatively, have students use the online edition individually, answering the prompts as they read.

❶ About the Selection

This poem glorifies the Revolutionary cause by personifying America as the goddess Columbia. The poet pictures Columbia as a daughter of Mother Earth, who sympathizes with her daughter as she faces her enemies. The poem then praises George Washington for bravery and goodness; he is the perfect leader for a nation defended by heaven, and he has the moral support of other nations in the war against Britain. The poem asks Washington to proceed, guided by the goddess; and Wheatley suggests that he will be rewarded with a crown, a mansion, and a golden throne.

❷ Humanities

Liberty and Washington, date unknown, Anonymous

This painting, like Wheatley's poem, glorifies Washington. Light bathes the statue and the woman beside it, suggesting purity and inner light. The words on the pedestal echo Wheatley's attitude toward Washington as a leader, diplomat, and hero. Images from the poem—a crown, a wreath of laurels, a flag, and a female figure suggesting the goddess Columbia—also appear in the painting. The goddess tramples the British crown while she places a victory wreath on Washington's head. Use this question for discussion:

> Based on the content of this painting, what would you infer about the painter's attitude about America?
> **Possible response:** The image demonstrates great pride in America and its early leaders.

❸ Activating Prior Knowledge

Tell students that Phillis Wheatley achieved several "firsts." She was a successful female writer when few women authors were recognized. She was African American; that group, too, had been denied literary recognition. She was a slave, and slaves generally could neither read nor write. Ask students how Wheatley's accomplishments influence their expectations about her work.

Concept Connector ➡

Tell students they will return to their responses after reading the selection.

FIRST in WAR,
FIRST in PEACE,
&
FIRST in the HEARTS
OF HIS
COUNTRYMEN.

Liberty and Washington, New York State Historical Association, Cooperstown

Ⓒ Text Complexity Rubric

To His Excellency, General Washington		
Qualitative Measures		
Context/ Knowledge Demands	Poem glorifying the Revolutionary cause 1 2 3 ④ 5	
Structure/Language Conventionality and Clarity	Eighteenth-century diction and syntax; difficult vocabulary 1 2 3 4 ⑤	
Levels of Meaning/ Purpose/Concept Level	Abstract (personification of America) 1 2 3 4 ⑤	
Quantitative Measures		
Lexile/Text Length	NP / 308 words	
Overall Complexity	**More complex**	

To His Excellency, General Washington

Phillis Wheatley

BACKGROUND In the early days of the American Revolution, Phillis Wheatley wrote a poem addressed to the commander of the American forces, George Washington. She sent him the poem in October of 1775, and he responded with sincere thanks and expressions of admiration. He also explained the reason he did not try to publish the poem was because it praised him so highly he was concerned he would appear vain.

> Celestial choir! enthron'd in realms of light,
>   Columbia's scenes of glorious toils I write.
> While freedom's cause her anxious breast alarms,
> She flashes dreadful in refulgent arms.
> 5   See mother earth her offspring's fate bemoan,
> And nations gaze at scenes before unknown!
> See the bright beams of heaven's revolving light
> Involved in sorrows and the veil of night!
>   The goddess comes, she moves divinely fair,
> 10 Olive and laurel binds her golden hair:
> Wherever shines this native of the skies,
> Unnumber'd charms and recent graces rise.
>   Muse![1] bow propitious while my pen relates
> How pour her armies through a thousand gates,
> 15 As when Eolus[2] heaven's fair face deforms,
> Enwrapp'd in tempest and a night of storms;
> Astonish'd ocean feels the wild uproar,
> The refluent surges beat the sounding shore;
> Or thick as leaves in Autumn's golden reign,
> 20 Such, and so many, moves the warrior's train.
> In bright array they seek the work of war,
> Where high unfurl'd the ensign[3] waves in air.

---

1. **Muse** A Greek goddess, in this case Erato, who is thought to inspire poets. She is one of nine muses presiding over literature, the arts, and the sciences.
2. **Eolus** (ē′ ə ləs) the Greek god of the winds.
3. **ensign** (en′ sin) flag.

◀ Critical Viewing

Noting the symbols of the Revolutionary conflict, explain the action of the painting. **[Interpret]**

Vocabulary

propitious (prō pish′ əs) *adj.* favorably inclined or disposed

tempest (tem′ pist) *n.* A violent storm with high winds

Reading Check

What army is the poet celebrating?

❹ Critical Viewing

Answer: Students may note that the goddess tramples the British crown underfoot while she places the laurel wreath, a symbol of victory, on Washington's head. She displays the American flag, while an eagle, another symbol of victory, soars overhead. The painting recognizes Washington's leadership in the victory over Britain.

❺ Reading Strategy

Rereading to Clarify

1. Read aloud the first six lines of the poem to the class.
2. **Ask:** students: Without rereading, can you explain what *arms* means in line 4?
   Possible response: Students may say that they needed to reread the sentence to recognize that *arms* refers to military force rather than Columbia's physical arms.
3. **Ask:** What other elements in these lines might cause you to reread?
   Possible response: Students may want to clarify unusual word order in lines 2, 3, and 5. They may not know the meaning of *refulgent* in line 4 or not understand the reference to *offspring* in line 5.

❻ Reading Check

Answer: She is celebrating the American Revolutionary army.

ⓒ Text Complexity: Reader and Task Suggestions

To His Excellency, General Washington

Preparing to Read the Text	Leveled Tasks
• Using the Background information on TE p. 123, discuss the fact that many Americans found Wheatley's poetic skills both surprising and remarkable. • Ask students to give examples of ways in which people express patriotic feeling. Discuss how some forms of patriotic expression fit certain occasions better than others. • Guide students to use Multidraft Reading strategies to deepen their comprehension (TE p. 123).	*Structure/Language* If students will have difficulty with diction and classical references, guide them in paraphrasing the first few patriotic statements in the poem. After each paraphrase, have them read the lines aloud—first as written, then as paraphrased. As students reread, urge them to apply the same technique to other difficult statements. *Evaluating* If students will not have difficulty with diction and classical references, discuss how well students think that the patriotic sentiment, as expressed by Wheatley, would have been understood and appreciated by readers of the Revolutionary era.

This selection is available in interactive format in the **Enriched Online Student Edition**, at **www.PHLitOnline.com**, which includes a thematically related video with a writing prompt and an interactive graphic organizer.

❼ Literary Analysis

Heroic Couplets

1. Have students read the bracketed couplet aloud. **Ask** them to paraphrase the lines and to identify the person referred to as "thy." **Possible response:** You are famous for your bravery and goodness, and everyone begs for your assistance. Washington is referred to as "thy."

2. Remind the students that a heroic couplet always expresses a complete thought. Review the rhyme and iambic pentameter structure.

ASSESS
Answers

Before students respond, you may wish to have them write a brief objective summary of the selection. As they answer the questions below, remind them to support their answers with evidence from the text.

1. (a) She is described as beautiful (fair), charming, and graceful, with golden hair bound by an olive branch and a laurel wreath. (b) America is beautiful and gracious.

2. (a) The army is compared to the constant beating of waves on the shore during a storm and to the continuous shower of leaves during autumn. (b) **Possible response:** It suggests that the American military forces are powerful and numerous.

3. (a) **Possible response:** The mention of a crown and a throne suggests that the new nation will create a government on the model of Britain's monarchy. (b) He will be its king. (c) It hints at a conflict between those seeking a monarchy and those desiring democracy.

4. ❓ **Possible response:** Wheatley praises Washington's <u>valor</u> and virtue. Today we value the bravery associated with valor, though we do not necessarily see it as a vital aspect of the <u>character</u> of our leaders. We continue to respect virtue but disagree on how to define it.

Shall I to Washington their praise recite?
Enough thou know'st them in the fields of fight.
25 Thee, first in peace and honors,—we demand
The grace and glory of thy martial band.
❼ Fam'd for thy valor, for thy virtues more,
Hear every tongue thy guardian aid implore!
  One century scarce perform'd its destined round,
30 When Gallic⁴ powers Columbia's fury found;
And so may you, whoever dares disgrace
The land of freedom's heaven-defended race!
Fix'd are the eyes of nations on the scales,
For in their hopes Columbia's arm prevails.
35 Anon Britannia⁵ droops the pensive head,
While round increase the rising hills of dead.
Ah! cruel blindness to Columbia's state!
Lament thy thirst of boundless power too late.
  Proceed, great Chief, with virtue on thy side,
40 Thy ev'ry action let the goddess guide.
A crown, a mansion, and a throne that shine,
With gold unfading, WASHINGTON! be thine.

Vocabulary

martial (mär´ shəl) *adj.* relating to war

implore (im plôr´) *v.* ask or beg earnestly; plead

pensive (pen´ siv) *adj.* thinking deeply or seriously

lament (lə ment') *v.* feel sorrow for; mourn

---

4. **Gallic** (gal´ ik) French. The colonists, led by Washington, defeated the French in the French and Indian War (1754–1763).
5. **Britannia** England.

Critical Reading

Cite textual evidence to support your responses.

© 1. **Key Ideas and Details (a)** In lines 9–12, how is Columbia described? **(b) Deduce:** What does this image of Columbia suggest about the speaker's view of America?

© 2. **Key Ideas and Details (a)** In lines 13–20, to what natural phenomenon is the American army compared? **(b) Interpret:** What does this comparison suggest about the power of American military forces in battle?

© 3. **Key Ideas and Details (a)** Which details in the last two lines reflect the influence of the British political system? **(b) Deduce:** What position in a new government does the speaker assume Washington will occupy? **(c) Synthesize:** How do these details hint at the debate about the kind of government to be established after the war?

© 4. **Integration of Knowledge and Ideas** Do the qualities Wheatley attributes to Washington represent typically American values? In your response, use at least two of these Essential Question vocabulary words: *valor, boldness, principles, character.* **[Connecting to the Essential Question: What makes American literature American?]**

Concept Connector

Reading Strategy Graphic Organizer

Ask students to review the graphic organizers with which they have monitored their comprehension of lines and sections of Wheatley's poem. Then have students share their organizers and compare their conclusions about the poet's meaning.

Activating Prior Knowledge

Have students return to their responses to the Activating Prior Knowledge activity. Ask them to explain whether their thoughts have changed and if so, how.

❓ Connecting to the Essential Question

Have students compare their responses to the prompt before reading "To His Excellency, General Washington" with their thoughts after reading the poem. Have them work individually or in groups, writing or discussing their thoughts, to define their new responses. Then lead a class discussion, probing for what students have learned that confirms or invalidates their initial thoughts. Encourage students to cite specific textual details to support their responses.

Literary Analysis

© 1. Craft and Structure To illustrate Wheatley's use of **heroic couplets,** select two lines from the poem. **(a)** Explain what the couplet means. **(b)** Identify the *rhyme.* **(c)** Indicate the patterns of stressed and unstressed syllables.

© 2. Integration of Knowledge and Ideas Use a chart like the one shown to list three **mythological references** in the poem. **(a)** Define each reference. **(b)** Explain what each reference adds to Wheatley's portrayal.

Mythological Reference	What It Contributes

© Common Core State Standards

Writing
1. Write arguments to support claims in an analysis of substantive topics or texts, using valid reasoning and relevant and sufficient evidence.

Reading Strategy

3. Reread lines 35–38 to clarify their meaning. **(a)** To whom or what does the pronoun *thy* in line 38 refer? **(b)** Whose cruel blindness is the speaker talking about?

4. Reread the last four lines. **(a)** To whom does the pronoun *thy* refer? **(b)** Rewrite line 40 in a word order that is easier to understand.

PERFORMANCE TASKS
Integrated Language Skills

© Vocabulary Acquisition and Use

Sentence Completions Complete each sentence with a word from the vocabulary list. Then, explain your choice.
1. We _____ the loss of these brave soldiers.
2. The good weather made it _____ to start the voyage.
3. The soldier knew a lot about _____ matters but little about daily life.
4. Her thoughtful expression reflected her _____ mood.
5. If captured, we must _____ our enemies to treat us with mercy.
6. The ship was tossed back and forth during the _____.

Writing

© Argument A **memo** is a piece of *business writing* that usually begins with these headings: FROM: your name; TO: recipients' names; DATE: date of writing; SUBJECT: your topic. These headings are followed by text organized in paragraphs. Imagine that you are part of the team working on Washington's presidential campaign. Someone has proposed using Wheatley's poem in the campaign. Write a memo supporting or rejecting the idea. Defend your position using details from the poem.

To His Excellency, General Washington **127**

Assessment Resources

Unit 1 Resources
L1 L2 EL Selection Test A, pp. 197–199. Administer Test A to less advanced students.
L3 L4 EL Selection Test B, pp. 200–202. Administer Test B to on-level and more advanced students.
L3 L4 Open-Book Test, pp. 194–196. As an alternative, give the Open-Book Test.

All Customizable Test Bank
All Self-tests
Students may prepare for the **Selection Test** by taking the **Self-test** online.

PHLit Online! All assessment resources are available at **www.PHLitOnline.com.**

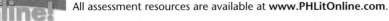

Answers

1. **Possible answer:** (a) The couplet in lines 17–18 describes a stormy ocean that beats upon the shore. (b) *Uproar* and *shore* are the words that rhyme in this couplet. (c) The pattern of stressed and unstressed syllables is the standard iambic pentameter: unstressed syllable, stressed syllable, repeated five times.

2. **Possible answer:** (a) The muse is a goddess figure who inspires artists and poets. Eolus is the Greek god of the winds. (b) The invocation of the muse indicates that the poet is drawing on powers greater than herself to write the poem. The poet's use of Eolus makes the image of the wind and storm much more vivid and exciting.

3. (a) *Thy* refers to Britain and its thirst for power. (b) The speaker is talking about Britain's cruel blindness.

4. (a) *Thy* refers to Washington. (b) **Possible response:** Let the goddess guide every action you take.

Vocabulary Acquisition and Use

1. lament. The speaker is sorrowful about the deaths of soldiers.
2. propitious. It is favorable to begin a journey when the weather is good.
3. martial. A military person would likely know about military subjects.
4. pensive. A person described this way is probably in a serious mood.
5. implore. It would make sense to plead with one's captors about being treated fairly.
6. tempest. Only a large storm can toss a ship at sea.

Writing

Evaluate the students' persuasive memoranda by adapting the **Rubrics for Persuasive Essays** (in *Professional Development Guidebook,* pp. 256–257).

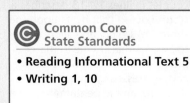

**Common Core
State Standards**

• Reading Informational Text 5
• Writing 1, 10

About the Texts

1. Introduce the texts, using the instruction on the student page.

2. Tell students that they will apply their knowledge of manuals and public service announcements as they read the two documents.

Reading Strategy

1. Introduce the strategy, using the instruction on the student page.

2. Tell students that they will analyze and evaluate information from text features as they read the documents.

Think Aloud: Model the Strategy

Say to students:

Both numbers and bullets help me identify important items of information. When I see a bulleted list, I usually assume that all of the items are equal in importance and that there is no special reason for the order the items are in. When I see a numbered list, I usually assume that the first item is more important than, say, the fifth item, or that the first item is a step that must be done before I proceed to the next.

Content-Area Vocabulary

1. Have students say each word aloud.

2. Use each word in a sentence that makes its meaning clear. Then repeat your sentence with the vocabulary word missing, and have students "fill in the blank."

3. Also see the *Classroom Strategies and Teaching Routines* card for vocabulary.

Reading for Information

Analyzing Functional and Expository Texts

Manual • Public Service Advertisement

About the Texts

A **manual** is an informational document that organizations publish to instruct readers in how to use a product or perform a task. Most manuals contain a statement of purpose; step-by-step instructions; and a list of requirements, tools, regulations, or suggestions.

A **public service advertisement** (PSA) presents information to the general public about issues that affect the common good. Unlike commercial advertisements, PSAs are broadcast or distributed for free. They may appear on posters, in newspapers, or on signs; be broadcast on TV, radio, or podcast; or appear on Web sites.

Reading Strategy

To be effective, functional and expository texts present information clearly so readers can understand and apply the information. To ensure a logical flow of ideas, writers may use specific patterns of organization, including the following structures:

• *Cause and effect* describes the results of an action.

• *Chronological order* identifies the sequence in which steps in a task should be performed.

• *Problem and solution* outlines a problem the text will help readers solve.

Text features—such as headings and subheads, boldface and italic type, bulleted lists, and images—help readers navigate the text. As you read these documents, **evaluate text features,** noting how they emphasize specific sections and help readers grasp the organizational structures. Use a chart like the one shown to identify text features and evaluate their purposes.

Basic Elements			Purpose
Headings and subheads	Yes ☐	No ☐	
Boldfaced or italicized text	Yes ☐	No ☐	
Numbered or bulleted lists	Yes ☐	No ☐	
Photos or illustrations	Yes ☐	No ☐	

**Common Core
State Standards**

**Reading Informational Text
5.** Analyze and evaluate the effectiveness of the structure an author uses in his or her exposition or argument, including whether the structure makes points clear, convincing, and engaging.

Content-Area Vocabulary

These words appear in the selections that follow. They may also appear in other content-area texts.

candidate (kan´ də dāt) *n.* person who seeks election to a political position

legislature (leg´ is lā´ chər) *n.* group of lawmakers who represent a state or nation

candid (kan´ did) *adj.* outspoken; open and sincere

officials (ə fish´ əlz) *n.* people who hold government offices or positions

---

Teaching Resources

Reading Support

L2 L3 *Reader's Notebook*
L1 *Reader's Notebook: Adapted Version*
EL *Reader's Notebook: English Learner's Version*

PHLit Online! All print resources are available at www.PHLitOnline.com.

LEAGUE OF WOMEN VOTERS
Making Democracy Work

HOW TO WATCH A DEBATE

Stay Informed

Sign up for the League's e-newsletter and get all the latest information delivered to your inbox.

> The title indicates the task being addressed.

How to Watch a Debate

> Headings guide readers through a step-by-step process.

Candidate debates have a long history in American politics. At every level of government—from city council to state **legislature**, from Congress to president of the United States—candidates participate in debates to help voters understand who they are and what they stand for.

Watching debates is an important way for voters to learn more about the candidates and the issues before the election, so that they can cast an informed vote. At the same time, voters need to view debates with a careful eye to get the most information. Candidates rehearse thoroughly for debates, making it hard to get **candid**, spontaneous answers. Debates can emphasize form over substance, such as the candidates' appearance instead of their stands on the issues. You may watch a debate and still not get answers to the questions you have about the candidates and issues.

Before the Debate

It will help if you take some time before the debate to

- follow the campaign to learn about the candidates and their backgrounds;
- find out what the important campaign issues are;
- decide what issues are most important to you;
- think about the questions you may have and the information you want to get from the debate to help you in your decision making;
- open your mind to new opinions/impressions of the candidate regardless of party affiliation.

You may want to make plans to get together with friends or family to watch the debate. Watching the debate in a group and discussing it afterward helps to clarify your thoughts about what was said in the debate and how the candidates performed.

Reading for Information: Manual **129**

129

Analyze Text Features

1. Have students review the two bulleted lists of questions under During the Debate.

2. **Ask:** Do these items appear in a significant order, or could they be rearranged without changing meaning? Are some questions more important than others, or are they all of approximately equal importance?
Possible response: Students should recognize that the order of items is not significant and that the questions are roughly equal in importance.

3. Have students review the bulleted list on page 129 and with the same questions in mind. **Ask:** Would bullets or numbers be the better strategy for identifying these items? Explain.
Possible response: Some students may note that the list presents a meaningful sequence of events (follow the campaign, then find out the issues, then decide which are important to you). These students may suggest that numbers would be more appropriate than bullets to emphasize the sequence.

A debate might not include all of the candidates for the office. Before the debate, note which candidates are included and which are not. If all candidates are not participating, try to find out why. Some debates include only candidates who have significant support, on the theory that the voters should be able to compare the candidates with a realistic chance of winning. Others invite all candidates who have qualified for the ballot. Sometimes candidates who are invited choose not to participate. Candidates with a strong lead might refuse to participate because they think there is no advantage to be gained by debating a lesser-known opponent.

During the Debate

When watching the debate, ask yourself questions like these to help you judge the fairness of the debate and the performance of the candidates:

The debate format and questions:

- Does the format give each candidate an equal opportunity to speak and respond to questions?
- Are the questions clear, fair, and equally tough on all candidates?
- Do the questions cover the issues that are important to you?
- Is the moderator in control of the debate? Does the moderator need to say less and let the candidates say more?

Italicized text emphasizes the importance of subheads.

The candidates:

- Do they answer questions directly, or do they evade them or fail to answer the specific question?
- Do they give specifics about their stands on the issues, or do they speak in generalities? Do they support their positions and arguments with facts and figures?
- Do they talk about their own policies and positions, or do they mostly attack their opponents?
- Are their proposals realistic? Can they actually carry out the promises they are making?
- Do they appear sincere, confident, and relaxed?
- Do they show how their backgrounds and experience qualify them to hold the office?
- Are their answers consistent with their previous positions, and if not, do they explain why?
- What image are they trying to create?
- Do their responses appear overly rehearsed or "canned"?

Bulleted lists provide a breakdown of important questions and steps.

Media coverage:

- If you are watching the debate on television, are reaction shots or other techniques used to create a sense of drama or conflict?
- Are you being influenced by comments made by reporters and commentators immediately before and after the debate?

Vocabulary Development

Content-Area Vocabulary: Social Studies

Review the definitions of the content-area vocabulary with students: *candidate, legislature, issues, registration, precinct,* and *provisional.* Then examine each word in its context in one of the documents. For example, point out that *provisional* describes a particular type of ballot that is mentioned in four of the first five paragraphs of "10 Things Every Florida Poll Worker Should Know." This emphasis tells the reader that a provisional ballot is both an important and a sensitive issue. From context in item 5, we learn that provisional ballots will be counted only if certain conditions are met within a short time after the election. This suggests that *provisional* means "temporary" or "for the time being," being made official (or not) at a later time.

Photographs add visual interest.

After the Debate

It will help clarify your thoughts about the candidates and the issues if you take some time after the debate to reflect on what you have just seen and heard. You can do this by

- comparing your impressions with those of others who watched the debate;
- asking yourself, based on the information you got from watching the debate, which candidate appears most qualified for the office;
- identifying the issues on which you agree with a candidate and those on which you disagree, and deciding whether that makes you more or less likely to vote for a particular candidate;
- asking yourself if you learned something new about the issues or the candidate;
- thinking about whether you have more questions about the issues or the candidates that you want to follow up;
- getting more information about the candidates' positions from news reports, candidate Web sites and nonpartisan voter information Web sites; and
- watching later debates for more information or to confirm your current impressions of the candidates.

Conclusion

Candidate debates give voters a chance to hear the candidates speak and respond to their opponents. They give candidates a chance to present their message directly to a wide audience. As a voter, asking yourself the right questions before, during, and after the debate can help you make the most of this opportunity to learn about the candidates and the issues.

A conclusion summarizes the information covered in the manual.

Analyze Text Features

1. After the class has finished reading the entire manual, point out that the document presents twenty-seven bulleted items within three pages. **Ask:** Does the manual present a manageable amount of information to voters, or does it present too much information?
   Possible response: Some students may say that the presentation is thorough and complete, as a manual should be. Others may say that the document overloads voters with more information than they can absorb.

2. **Ask:** If you think that the document presents too much information, in what ways would you suggest it be altered?
   Possible response: Students may suggest reducing the number of bulleted points. Others may suggest a summary at the end of the document that presents only the most essential information for voters.

3. Point out that the manual presents the information in a time-order sequence: before, during, and after. **Ask:** In what other order might this information be presented?
   Possible response: Students may say that the information might be ranked in order of importance, with the most essential factors listed first. The information might also be presented topically, with separate sections for issues, candidate ideas, media coverage, debate performance, and so on.

Enrichment: Analyzing a Historical Event

The Lincoln-Douglas Debates

Seven debates in Illinois in 1858 pitted Abraham Lincoln against Stephen A. Douglas during their campaigns for the Senate. The candidates took turns leading off. The first candidate spoke for an hour; the second spoke for an hour and a half; then the first candidate had a half hour to respond. Those historic debates bear little resemblance to modern presidential debates, which are typically controlled by moderators who pose questions to candidates.

Candidates have only minutes to respond and rarely have a chance to confront opponents with questions of their own.

Activity: Oral Report Have students research impact of the Lincoln-Douglas debates, recording their findings in the **Enrichment: Analyzing a Historical Event** worksheet, *Professional Development Guidebook,* p. 230. Have students report their findings in an oral report to the class.

About Public Service Announcements

1. Before students read "Help North Texas Vote College Program," discuss voting procedures in the local community as students understand them.

2. If necessary, point out that poll workers are citizens trained in voting procedures and rules. On election day, workers oversee voting in polling places, checking the identity and residence of citizens preparing to vote and making sure that every vote is properly cast and accurately counted.

3. Have students read the "Poll Worker Requirements" that appear on the student page, using the side annotation to emphasize details. **Ask:** Why do you think it is so important that poll workers not be elected officials or employees of elected officials?
   Possible response: Students may recognize that this is a key method for preventing anyone from tampering with the votes.

4. **Ask:** What is it important for people to volunteer to be poll workers?
   Answer: Poll workers are needed to make sure that elections run smoothly. If enough people volunteer to be poll workers, there may be delays at voting booths and some polling sites may have to close.

HELP NORTH TEXAS VOTE
COLLEGE PROGRAM

> Headings help readers follow the problem-and-solution organizational structure.

> The problem-and-solution organizational structure is established immediately.

Did You Know?

Not having enough poll workers can force a polling site to close or lead to delays at the voting booth. According to election **officials**, the result could prevent people from exercising their right to vote.

Election Day Is Coming Soon

Sign up to become part of the *Help North Texas Vote College Program* and take on a larger role in the United States election process. The right to vote is the foundation of our democracy, and assuring access in all our communities is critical. Because of this, it is imperative that the election process run smoothly for everyone. A large part of this includes the people that actually work the polls on Election Day. By signing up on the HNTV Web site, you will provide your name to the county in which you are registered to vote, and if there is a need for poll workers in that county, it is very possible that you will be called upon to serve on Election Day.

The Need for Poll Workers

The number of poll workers serving on Election Day is consistently not adequate, according to the election officials in Dallas, Denton, and Tarrant counties. While an inadequate number of poll workers is a significant problem of its own, an added burden results from the lack of bilingual poll workers, including both Spanish and Vietnamese-speaking workers.

How to Become a Poll Worker

It's easy! Sign up on the *Help North Texas Vote* Web site and your information will be transferred to the county in which you are registered. Once the county officials receive your information, they will determine that county's need. Those needed will be called upon to attend poll-worker training. Training is typically held for a few hours over the course of one day. After you are trained, you are qualified to serve as a poll worker on Election Day.

Poll-Worker Requirements

Requirements for election poll workers are similar for Dallas, Denton, and Tarrant counties:

- Workers must be registered to vote in the county where they wish to work.

- Workers must not be an elected official or be an employee of an elected official.

- Workers must be able to arrive at their assigned polling site before the polls open and must remain until the polls are closed and results are either called in or transported.

- Workers should enjoy interaction with the public, be detail-oriented, be able to take direction well, and not be easily distracted.

What's in It for You?

Beyond the opportunity to fulfill a civic duty that aids fellow Texans, there are other advantages to working the polls on Election Day. If you are called and asked to become a poll worker, you will be compensated for your training and the days that you work. Additionally, we encourage students to work with faculty members to arrange criteria for extra credit where applicable.

The average age of a U.S. poll worker is 72, according to the U.S. Election Assistance Commission, and the numbers of active poll workers are dwindling. It has been reported that the current number of poll workers is well short of the 2 million needed for a national election.

Differentiated Instruction   for Universal Access

Support for Less Proficient Readers

The vocabulary of the public service announcement contains a number of words and concepts that may cause difficulty for some students. Read the first paragraph and the "Poll Worker Requirements" aloud to the class, asking students to raise their hands when they need clarification. Students may need explanation of *imperative, elected official, transported,* or *detail-oriented.* Then have students complete the remaining text on their own.

EL Support for English Learners

Some students may be unfamiliar with American voting procedures and political vocabulary. They may need help understanding terms like *polls, county,* and *registered to vote.* Explain that *polls* are places where people can go to vote, and that states are broken into *counties* that include many cities or towns. To be *registered to vote* means that you have completed paperwork demonstrating you are eligible to vote.

Critical Reading

© **1. Key Ideas and Details (a)** Which organizational structure is used in the manual—chronological order, cause-and-effect, or problem-and-solution? Explain. **(b)** Why is this structure appropriate—and common—in a "how-to" text such as this manual?

© **2. Key Ideas and Details** Evaluate the text features used in the manual by considering whether they clarify or obscure the information. Explain your observations.

© **3. Key Ideas and Details (a)** What organizational structure is used in the PSA? **(b)** In what ways do specific text features clarify that structure and emphasize distinct pieces of information?

4. Content-Area Vocabulary (a) Explain how the meaning of the Middle Dutch word *pol* ("head, top") contributes to the meaning of our English word *pollster*. **(b)** Determine the meaning of the following words derived from the same linguistic root: *outpoll, pollee*.

© **Common Core
State Standards**

Writing

1. Write arguments to support claims in an analysis of substantive topics or texts, using valid reasoning and relevant and sufficient evidence.

10. Write routinely over extended time frames and shorter time frames for a range of tasks, purposes, and audiences.

Critical Reading

1. (a) **Answer:** The manual uses the chronological order pattern.
(b) **Answer:** The chronological order pattern guides readers through step-by-step instructions.

2. **Possible response:** The headings guide readers through steps to take before, during, and after the debate. Italicized subheads and bulleted lists help organize long lists of questions.

3. (a) **Answer:** The PSA uses problem-and-solution organization. (b) **Possible response:** The title points to the problem; the subtitle hints at the solution; and the subheadings move readers through the problem and its solution.

4. (a) **Answer:** A pollster is a person who conducts surveys of public opinions; in essence, a pollster counts the number of people, or "heads," who feel a certain way.
(b) **Answer:** To outpoll is to win more votes. A pollee is a person who is asked questions during a vote.

⏱ Timed Writing

Argument [40 minutes]

Format

An **argumentative essay** is not a piece of writing in which you start a fight. An argument is a well-reasoned position or opinion. In an essay, you must explain and support your argument.

These texts provide information intended to get readers more involved in the election process—a key requirement of good **citizenship**. Write an **argumentative essay** in which you take a position about the importance of **civic** involvement. Use evidence from these texts, as well as your own experience and knowledge, to defend your position.

Academic Vocabulary

The prompt asks you to address **citizenship** and **civic** involvement. Focus your response on ideas of community responsibility, rather than on personal benefits.

⏱ Timed Writing

1. Before students begin the assignment, guide them in analyzing key words and phrases in the prompt, using the highlighted notes.

2. Work with students to draw up guidelines for their argumentative essays based on the key words they identified.

3. Have students use the 5-Minute Planner to structure their time.

4. Allow students 40 minutes to complete the assignment. Evaluate their work using the guidelines they have developed.

5-Minute Planner

Complete these steps before you begin to write.

1. Read the prompt carefully. List key words.

2. Draft a thesis that clearly responds to the prompt.

3. Skim the text for details you can use as evidence. **TIP** Organizational structures and text features can be used as evidence if they help support your thesis.

4. Reread the prompt, and draft your essay.

Extend the Lesson

Connecting to the Students' World

To give students more practice with manuals, divide the class into small groups. Ask students to develop a manual for some role, task, or service at school, for example, working the desk in the school office, being a hall monitor, leading a school club, or managing equipment for a sports team. Have students brainstorm for ideas about the tasks and procedures involved. Once the necessary details have been established, students should then decide the order in which the details should be arranged. When the manuals are completed, invite groups to share their manuals with the entire class.

Literary History: Franklin's World

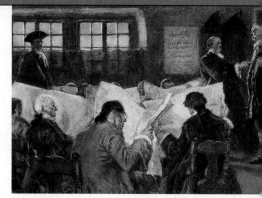

The American Revolution would not have happened when it did without the efforts of colonial newspapers, including those published by the Franklin brothers.

All the News That's Fit to Print

"EXTRA! EXTRA! Read all about it! Newspapers banned! Journalists Jailed! Americans Fight for a Free Press!" Those might have been the headlines blaring from your local newspaper if you had lived in eighteenth-century America. Might have been, that is, if colonial newspapers had used headlines. America's earliest newspapers bore little resemblance to those we know today. They were crudely printed on wooden presses and contained only a clumsy illustration or two. Most were one or two pages, and their stories were often just a list of ship arrivals. Despite their primitive character, these early newspapers laid the groundwork for a uniquely American phenomenon: a free press that could criticize the government.

Trailblazers The first American newspaper, printed in Boston on September 25, 1690, was titled *Publick Occurrences, Both Foreign and Domestick*. The remarkable thing about *Publick Occurrences* was that it existed at all. England had no history of a free and independent press. If a newspaper criticized the crown, it could be shut down. Yet *Publick Occurrences* was published without British approval, and printed stories that the Massachusetts royal governor found offensive. As a result, it lasted exactly one issue.

Americans waited 14 years for another newspaper. In 1704, the Boston *News-Letter* appeared. Approved by the governor of Massachusetts, the *News-Letter* was little more than a British mouthpiece, careful not to offend colonial authorities.

The Franklin Brothers In contrast, other papers sought controversy. For example, the New England *Courant*, founded in 1721 by James Franklin, appeared without British approval. The paper jabbed mercilessly at the royal governor, and eventually landed Franklin in jail. He handed control of the paper to his 16-year-old brother, Benjamin—someone who would play his own significant role in our nation's history.

In 1729, Benjamin Franklin, now living in Philadelphia, founded the Pennsylvania *Gazette*. It was the first newspaper to carry weather reports, interviews, and cartoons, and it became the most successful paper in the colonies.

▲ **Critical Viewing** What does this scene of a coffee house and the facing samples of early newspapers indicate about the role of newspapers in colonial life? **[Analyze]**

Freedom of the Press Is Born A landmark legal case helped establish freedom of the press in America. In 1733, John Peter Zenger, a German immigrant, began publishing the *New York Weekly Journal*. The paper immediately ran afoul of the royal governor by publishing articles critical of his policies. One year later, Zenger was thrown in jail for libel.

In his 1735 trial, Zenger's lawyer, Andrew Hamilton, argued that while Zenger had indeed printed material offensive to the governor, the material was true and, therefore, not libelous. Under British law, even true statements against the government could be legally silenced. Hamilton made an impassioned plea to the jury to defend the "cause of liberty . . . both of exposing and opposing arbitrary power . . . by speaking and writing truth."

The jury found Zenger innocent. As a result of the case, the British stopped prosecuting American journalists, even when their criticisms of the government grew intense in the years leading up to the American Revolution.

Revolutionary Journalists Most historians agree that the American Revolution would not have happened when it did without the efforts of colonial newspapers. Newspapers stoked the flames of revolution, coining phrases like "taxation without representation" and influencing public perception of England as an enemy. When the British Stamp Act of 1765 imposed a heavy tax on all printed materials, the press denounced the legislation and refused to pay the tax. Even though the Stamp Act was repealed in 1766, it united editors and publishers in support of independence. Indeed, in 1776, most newspapers printed the Declaration of Independence on their front page.

During the Revolution, newspapers brought accounts of military developments to an eager readership. By the end of the war, newspapers had gained enormous strength. American newspapers represented something the world had never before seen: a press committed to telling the truth, not pleasing the government.

Speaking and Listening: Media Review

© **Comprehension and Collaboration** Today, electronic media, including TV, the Internet, and even cell phones, provide constant access to news. With a small group, read, watch, and listen to news presented in electronic formats. Divide the labor so that each person is responsible for a different media form. Prepare a set of guiding questions, such as those listed here, to focus your review:

- What is the quality of information provided by each media form?
- Are the same stories presented very differently in different formats?
- Is the coverage across media platforms equally objective and fair?

Organize your observations into a **report** to share with the class.

Extended Study: Benjamin Franklin **135**

Background

John Peter Zenger While he was in prison, Zenger dictated copy and instructions to his workers through a hole in the door. As a result, his newspaper continued to publish throughout his imprisonment, missing only a single issue.

The Zenger verdict was not simply a milestone for American journalism, it was a classic case of jury nullification. The jurors reached their verdict by ignoring existing law and the facts of the case. Their dramatic "not guilty" could not change the legal meaning of libel, but it did discourage colonial governments from taking feisty newspapers to court, allowing "freedom of the press" to continue to grow into an American principle.

Speaking and Listening

Media Review

1. Read the Media Review instructions with the class. You may prefer to create a set of guiding questions as a class before you divide the class into groups, so that everyone is working from a common basis. Here are some additional starter questions: Which electronic medium can present news with the greatest urgency and immediacy? Which medium presents news with the greatest thoroughness? Which medium attracts the widest audience?

2. When the guiding questions are established, divide the class into groups and have the groups assign a different form of news medium to each member.

3. Allow class time for groups to discuss individual findings; then have groups present their conclusions to the class at large.

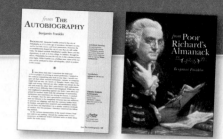

- *from* **The Autobiography**
- *from* **Poor Richard's Almanack**

Lesson Pacing Guide

DAY 1 Preteach

- Ⓒ Administer the Reading and Vocabulary Warm-ups (*Unit 1 Resources*, pp. 203–206) as necessary.
- Ⓒ Introduce the Literary Analysis concepts: Autobiography and Aphorism.
- • Introduce the Reading Strategy: Analyze Cause and Effect.
- • Build background with the Author in Depth and Background features.
- • Develop thematic thinking with Connecting to the Essential Question.
- Ⓒ Teach the selection vocabulary.

DAYS 2–3 Preteach/Teach

- Ⓒ Distribute copies of the appropriate graphic organizer for the Reading Strategy (*Graphic Organizer Transparencies*, pp. 43–44).
- • Distribute copies of the appropriate graphic organizer for Literary Analysis (*Graphic Organizer Transparencies*, pp. 41–42).
- • Prepare students to read with the Activating Prior Knowledge activities (TE).
- • Informally monitor comprehension while students read.
- • Use the Reading Check questions to confirm comprehension.
- Ⓒ Develop students' understanding of autobiography and aphorisms using the Literary Analysis Prompts.
- • Develop students' ability to analyze cause and effect using the Reading Strategy Prompts.
- Ⓒ Reinforce vocabulary with the Vocabulary notes.

DAY 4 Assess

- • Assess students' comprehension and mastery of the skills by having them answer the Critical Reading, Literary Analysis, and Reading Strategy questions.
- Ⓒ Have students complete the Vocabulary Lesson.

DAY 5 Extend/Assess

- • Have students complete the Conventions and Style Lesson.
- Ⓒ Have students complete the Writing Lesson and write an essay analyzing cause and effect. (You may assign as homework.)
- • Have students read and respond to the Critical Commentary.
- • Administer Selection Test A or B (*Unit 1 Resources,* pp. 218–220 or 221–223).

Ⓒ Common Core State Standards

Reading Informational Text 3. Analyze a complex set of ideas or sequence of events and explain how specific individuals, ideas, or events interact and develop over the course of the text.
9. Analyze eighteenth-century foundational U.S. documents of historical and literary significance for their themes, purposes, and rhetorical features.

Writing 2.a. Introduce a topic; organize complex ideas, concepts, and information so that each new element builds on that which precedes it to create a unified whole.
2.c. Use appropriate and varied transitions and syntax to link the major sections of the text, create cohesion, and clarify the relationships among complex ideas and concepts.
2.f. Provide a concluding statement or section that follows from and supports the information or explanation presented.

Language 3.a. Vary syntax for effect.
4.b. Identify and correctly use patterns of word changes that indicate different meanings or parts of speech.
5. Demonstrate understanding of word relationships and nuances in word meanings.

Additional Standards Practice
Common Core Companion, pp. 116–117; 196–207; 322–323; 324–331; 332–335

Daily Block Scheduling
Each day in this Lesson Pacing Guide represents a 40–50 minute period. Teachers using block scheduling may combine days to revise pacing. In addition, teachers may differentiate and support core instruction by integrating components for extended and intensive support as students require. See the Guide to Selected Leveled Resources (facing page).

Guide to Selected Leveled Resources

R T I Tier 1 (students performing on level)
from The Autobiography • from Poor Richard's Almanack

Warm Up	Practice, **model,** and **monitor** fluency, working **with the whole class** or **in groups.**	**Vocabulary and Reading Warm-ups B,** *Unit 1 Resources,* pp. 203–204, 205
Comprehension/Skills	**Support** and **monitor** comprehension and skills development, having students complete the activities, graphic organizers, and interactive prompts **independently** or **as a class.**	• *Reader's Notebook,* adapted instruction and summary **EL** *Reader's Notebook: English Learner's Version,* adapted instruction and summary • **Reading Strategy Graphic Organizer B,** *Graphic Organizer Transparencies,* p. 44 • **Literary Analysis Graphic Organizer B,** *Graphic Organizer Transparencies,* p. 42
Monitor Progress	**A** **Monitor** student progress with the differentiated curriculum-based assessment in the *Unit Resources.*	• **Selection Test B,** *Unit 1 Resources,* pp. 221–223 • **Open-Book Test,** *Unit 1 Resources,* pp. 215–217

R T I Tier 2 (students requiring intervention)
from The Autobiography • from Poor Richard's Almanack

Warm Up	Practice, **model,** and **monitor** fluency **in groups** or **with individuals.**	• **Vocabulary and Reading Warm-ups A,** *Unit 1 Resources,* pp. 203–205 • *Hear It!* Audio CD
Comprehension/Skills	• **Support** and **monitor** comprehension and skills development, working **in small groups** or **with individuals.** • As students complete the selection in the appropriate version of the *Reader's Notebook,* **monitor** comprehension frequently with group questions and individual instruction. • **Model** strategies while guiding students in completing the activities and prompts in the *Reader's Notebook,* as well as the graphic organizers. • **Practice** skills and **monitor** mastery with the *Reading Kit* worksheets.	• *Reader's Notebook: Adapted Version,* adapted instruction and summary **EL** *Reader's Notebook: English Learner's Version,* adapted instruction and summary • **Reading Strategy Graphic Organizer A,** *Graphic Organizer Transparencies,* p. 43 • **Literary Analysis Graphic Organizer A,** *Graphic Organizer Transparencies,* p. 41 • *Reading Kit,* Practice worksheets
Monitor Progress	**A** **Monitor** student progress with the differentiated curriculum-based assessment in the *Unit Resources* and in the *Reading Kit.*	• **Selection Test A,** *Unit 1 Resources,* pp. 218–220 • *Reading Kit,* Assess worksheets

TIER 3 Tier 3 intervention may require consultation with the student's special-education or dyslexia specialist. For additional support, see the Tier 2 activities and resources listed above.

One-on-one teaching   Group work   Whole-class instruction   Independent work   **A** Assessment

For a complete guide to selection support, including support for Advanced students, see the Overview of Resources in the frontmatter.

• *from* The Autobiography
• *from* Poor Richard's Almanack

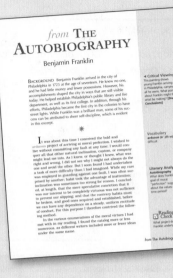

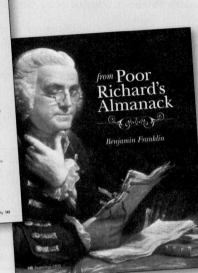

RESOURCES FOR:

L1 Special-Needs Students

L2 Below-Level Students (Tier 2)

L3 On-Level Students (Tier 1)

L4 Advanced Students (Tier 1)

EL English Learners

All All Students

Vocabulary/Fluency/Prior Knowledge

EL **L1** **L2** **Reading Warm-ups A and B,** pp. 205–206

Also available for these selections:

All Vocabulary Builder, p. 211

EL **L1** **L2** **Vocabulary Warm-ups A and B,** pp. 203–204

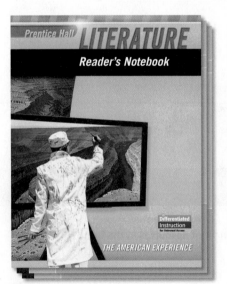

Reader's Notebooks

Pre- and postreading pages for these selections, as well as an excerpt from *The Autobiography,* appear in an interactive format in the *Reader's Notebooks*. Each *Notebook* is differentiated for a different group of learners.

The selections in the Adapted and English Learner's versions are abridged.

L2 **L3** *Reader's Notebook*

L1 *Reader's Notebook: Adapted Version*

EL *Reader's Notebook: English Learner's Version*

EL *Reader's Notebook: Spanish Version*

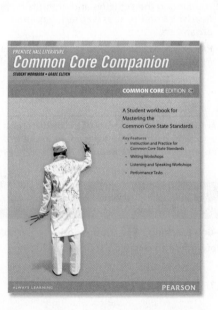

© *Common Core Companion*

Additional instruction and practice for each Common Core State Standard

Selection Support

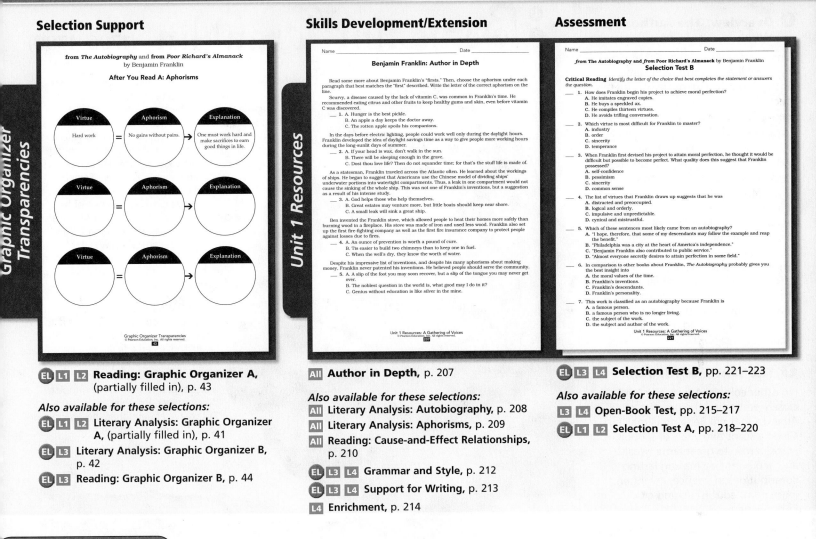

from *The Autobiography* **and** *from* *Poor Richard's Almanack*
by Benjamin Franklin

After You Read A: Aphorisms

Virtue	Aphorism	Explanation
Hard work	No gains without pains.	One must work hard and make sacrifices to earn good things in life.
Virtue	Aphorism	Explanation
Virtue	Aphorism	Explanation

EL L1 L2 Reading: Graphic Organizer A, (partially filled in), p. 43

Also available for these selections:

EL L1 L2 Literary Analysis: Graphic Organizer A, (partially filled in), p. 41

EL L3 Literary Analysis: Graphic Organizer B, p. 42

EL L3 Reading: Graphic Organizer B, p. 44

Skills Development/Extension

Name _____ Date _____

Benjamin Franklin: Author in Depth

Read some more about Benjamin Franklin's "firsts." Then, choose the aphorism under each paragraph that best matches the "first" described. Write the letter of the correct aphorism on the line.

Scurvy, a disease caused by the lack of vitamin C, was common in Franklin's time. He recommended eating citrus and other fruits to keep healthy gums and skin, even before vitamin C was discovered.

___ 1. A. Hunger is the best pickle.
B. An apple a day keeps the doctor away.
C. The rotten apple spoils his companions.

In the days before electric lighting, people could work well only during the daylight hours. Franklin developed the idea of daylight savings time as a way to give people more working hours during the long-sunlit days of summer.

___ 2. A. If your head is wax, don't walk in the sun.
B. There will be sleeping enough in the grave.
C. Dost thou love life? Then do not squander time; for that's the stuff life is made of.

As a statesman, Franklin traveled across the Atlantic often. He learned about the workings of ships. He began to suggest that Americans use the Chinese model of dividing ships' underwater portions into watertight compartments. Thus, a leak in one compartment would not cause the sinking of the whole ship. This was not one of Franklin's inventions, but a suggestion as a result of his intense study.

___ 3. A. God helps those who help themselves.
B. Great estates may venture more, but little boats should keep near shore.
C. A small leak will sink a great ship.

Ben invented the Franklin stove, which allowed people to heat their homes more safely than burning wood in a fireplace. His stove was made of iron and used less wood. Franklin also set up the first fire-fighting company as well as the first fire insurance company to protect people against losses due to fires.

___ 4. A. An ounce of prevention is worth a pound of cure.
B. Tis easier to build two chimneys than to keep one in fuel.
C. When the well's dry, they know the worth of water.

Despite his impressive list of inventions, and despite his many aphorisms about making money, Franklin never patented his inventions. He believed people should serve the community.

___ 5. A. A slip of the foot you may soon recover, but a slip of the tongue you may never get over.
B. The noblest question in the world is, what good may I do in it?
C. Genius without education is like silver in the mine.

Unit 1 Resources

All Author in Depth, p. 207

Also available for these selections:

All Literary Analysis: Autobiography, p. 208

All Literary Analysis: Aphorisms, p. 209

All Reading: Cause-and-Effect Relationships, p. 210

EL L3 L4 Grammar and Style, p. 212

EL L3 L4 Support for Writing, p. 213

L4 Enrichment, p. 214

Assessment

Name _____ Date _____

from The Autobiography **and** *from* Poor Richard's Almanack by Benjamin Franklin
Selection Test B

Critical Reading *Identify the letter of the choice that best completes the statement or answers the question.*

___ 1. How does Franklin begin his project to achieve moral perfection?
A. He imitates engraved copies.
B. He buys a speckled ax.
C. He compiles thirteen virtues.
D. He avoids trifling conversation.

___ 2. Which virtue is most difficult for Franklin to master?
A. industry
B. order
C. sincerity
D. temperance

___ 3. When Franklin first devised his project to attain moral perfection, he thought it would be difficult but possible to become perfect. What quality does this suggest that Franklin possessed?
A. self-confidence
B. pessimism
C. sincerity
D. common sense

___ 4. The list of virtues that Franklin draws up suggests that he was
A. distracted and preoccupied.
B. logical and orderly.
C. impulsive and unpredictable.
D. cynical and mistrustful.

___ 5. Which of these sentences most likely came from an autobiography?
A. "I hope, therefore, that some of my descendants may follow the example and reap the benefit."
B. "Philadelphia was a city at the heart of America's independence."
C. "Benjamin Franklin also contributed to public service."
D. "Almost everyone secretly desires to attain perfection in some field."

___ 6. In comparison to other books about Franklin, *The Autobiography* probably gives you the best insight into
A. the moral values of the time.
B. Franklin's inventions.
C. Franklin's descendants.
D. Franklin's personality.

___ 7. This work is classified as an autobiography because Franklin is
A. a famous person.
B. a famous person who is no longer living.
C. the subject of the work.
D. the subject and author of the work.

EL L3 L4 Selection Test B, pp. 221–223

Also available for these selections:

L3 L4 Open-Book Test, pp. 215–217

EL L1 L2 Selection Test A, pp. 218–220

PHLit Online!
www.PHLitOnline.com

Online Resources: All print materials are also available online.

- complete narrated selection text
- a thematically related video with writing prompt
- an interactive graphic organizer
- highlighting feature
- access to all student print resources, adapted to individual student needs
- Spanish and English summaries
- adapted selection translations in Spanish

Background Video

Also available:

Get Connected! (thematic video with writing prompt)
All videos are available in Spanish.

Writer's Journal (with graphics feature)

Also available:

Vocabulary Central (tools and activities for studying vocabulary)

136d

Background

❶ Overview: The Author's Work

Benjamin Franklin was adept at virtually every literary form of his time. Practical, purposeful prose was his specialty, leavened with humor and a keen sense of audience.

Franklin developed enduring literary characters in "Silence Dogood" and "Poor Richard," but his greatest character, the one that to this day contributes to America's sense of itself, is the Ben Franklin of *The Autobiography.* If he did not invent the rags-to-riches story, Franklin told it best, creating an identity that Americans readily claim as their own: self-made, self-taught, generous, ingenious, thrifty, self-deprecating, good-humored, hard-working, helpful, confident . . . and, of course, humble.

❷ The Writer in His Time

No other colonial American more closely embodied the promise of America that did Benjamin Franklin. Given a scant two years of schooling, Franklin rose to great fame, wealth, and achievement, making lasting contributions in science, invention, journalism, education, and civic improvement.

The dazzle of those accomplishments often obscures the fact that Franklin was also, in the words of the Scottish philosopher David Hume, America's "first great man of letters." Franklin's literary gifts of clarity, brevity, and ironic self-awareness give modern currency both to his aphorisms and to his landmark *Autobiography.*

❶❷ Benjamin Franklin (1706–1790)

From his teen years until his retirement at age forty-two, Benjamin Franklin worked as a printer. He got his start as an apprentice to his brother James Franklin, a Boston printer. By the time he was sixteen, Ben was not only printing, but writing parts of his brother's newspaper. Using the name "Silence Dogood," he wrote letters satirizing daily life and politics in Boston. When he was seventeen, Franklin moved to Philadelphia to open his own print shop. This move gave birth to one of his most enduring contributions to American culture, *Poor Richard's Almanack.* This annual publication, which was published from 1732 to 1757, contained information, observations, and advice and was a colonial bestseller.

The "Write Reputation" Just as he had signed "Silence Dogood" to the letters he wrote for his brother's paper, Franklin created a fictitious author/editor for the *Almanack.* The chatty Richard Saunders, or Poor Richard, first appeared as a dull and foolish astronomer. However, over the years his character developed, becoming more thoughtful, pious, and funny.

Text Complexity Rubric

	from The Autobiography	*from* Poor Richard's Almanack
Qualitative Measures		
Context/ Knowledge Demands	Historical knowledge demands (autobiography) 1 2 ③ 4 5	Aphorisms 1 ② 3 4 5
Structure/Language Conventionality and Clarity	Eighteenth-century vocabulary; complicated sentence structure 1 2 3 ④ 5	Simple vocabulary; familiar sayings 1 ② 3 4 5
Levels of Meaning/ Purpose/Concept Level	Challenging (ideas about achieving virtue) 1 2 3 ④ 5	Accessible (generalizations about life and human nature) 1 2 ③ 4 5
Quantitative Measures		
Lexile/Text Length	1400L / 2,148 words	500L / 242 words
Overall Complexity	**More complex**	**More accessible**

Secret to Success Like most almanacs, *Poor Richard's Almanack* contained practical information about the calendar, the sun and moon, and the weather. It also featured a wealth of homespun sayings and observations, or aphorisms, many of which are still quoted today. It was these aphorisms that made the *Almanack* a bestseller. Franklin included an aphorism at the top or bottom of most of the *Almanack's* pages. The wit and brevity of these sayings allowed him to weave in many moral messages, while also entertaining his readers.

Man of Science When Franklin was forty-two, he retired from the printing business to devote himself to science. He proved to be as successful a scientist as he had been a printer. Over the course of his life, Franklin was responsible for inventing the lightning rod, bifocals, and a new type of stove. He confirmed the laws of electricity, charted the Gulf Stream, and contributed to the scientific understanding of earthquakes and ocean currents. In spite of all these achievements, Franklin is best remembered for his career in politics.

Statesman and Diplomat Franklin played an important role in drafting the Declaration of Independence, enlisting French support during the Revolutionary War, negotiating a peace treaty with Britain, and drafting the United States Constitution. In his later years, he was the United States ambassador to England and then to France. Even before George Washington earned the title, Franklin was considered to be "the father of his country."

The Autobiography Franklin wrote the first section of *The Autobiography* in 1771 when he was sixty-five years old. At the urging of friends, he wrote three more sections—the last shortly before his death—but succeeded in bringing the account of his life only to the year 1759. Though never completed, his *Autobiography*, filled with his opinions and advice, provides not only a record of his achievements but also an understanding of his extraordinary character.

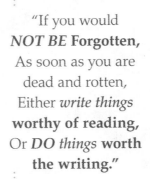

"If you would *NOT BE* **Forgotten,** As soon as you are dead and rotten, Either *write things* **worthy of reading,** Or *DO things* **worth the writing.**"

137

Text Complexity: Reader and Task Suggestions

from The Autobiography		from Poor Richard's Almanack	
Preparing to Read the Text	**Leveled Tasks**	**Preparing to Read the Text**	**Leveled Tasks**
• Using the Background information on TE p. 137, discuss the writing skill that Franklin exhibited when still a teenager. • Ask students why a young person might want to make a list of goals. • Guide students to use Multidraft Reading strategies to deepen their comprehension (TE p. 137).	*Levels of Meaning* If students will have difficulty with meaning, have them paraphrase the list of goals on SE p. 142. Then, have them reread to determine how the list fits into Franklin's account as a whole. *Evaluating* If students will not have difficulty with purpose, have them name one of Franklin's goals. Then, have them explain how they feel about the achievability of that goal.	• Using the information on TE pp. 136–137, discuss how Franklin's sense of humor made him a popular writer. • Ask students if they ever received advice about behavior. Was it helpful? • Guide students to use Multidraft Reading strategies to deepen their comprehension (TE p. 137).	*Levels of Meaning* If students will have difficulty with meaning, have them skim the list, choose one piece of advice, and paraphrase it. As students reread, encourage them to apply the same strategy to each aphorism. *Synthesizing* If students will not have difficulty with concept level, have them suggest a scenario and explain how following Franklin's advice would affect the outcome.

❶ Franklin's Firsts

1. Have students read the text on Franklin's inventions and ideas.

2. Discuss the images shown on the page with students, sharing the following information.

   - The watch is a reference to Daylight Savings Time. Though Franklin is usually credited as the first to propose the idea, DST was not implemented anywhere in the world until the twentieth century.

   - The severed snake is a political cartoon first published by Franklin in 1754. With the caption "Join or Die," this cartoon supported Franklin's view that the colonies needed to work together.

   - The building demonstrates an application of Franklin's lightning rod.

   - The drawing of spectacles is by Franklin to illustrate his idea for bifocal lenses.

   - The musical instrument is Franklin's glass armonica. Mozart and Beethoven are among composers who wrote music for the armonica.

3. After considering all of "Franklin's Firsts," **ask** students: Which of these ideas and inventions do you think is most valuable to society? **Possible response:** Students may note that the lightning rod has produced significant savings of lives and property ever since its invention. Others may attribute a similar benefit to Franklin's ideas for fire departments.

4. You may wish to have interested students find and present additional information about these "firsts" and other Franklin inventions. Students may find Web sites, for example, that reproduce the sounds of the glass armonica and allow users to simulate playing the instrument.

FRANKLIN'S FIRSTS

❶

Benjamin Franklin was an inventions superstar. Practical yet inspired, Franklin never patented his inventions, writing that he was "glad of an opportunity to serve others by any invention of ours; and this we should do freely and generously."

Swim fin/fan: (Ben's childhood) Young Franklin thought he needed a bit more oomph during his swims. To increase his speed in the water, he concocted a fin, shaped like a lily pad, that he wore over his hands.

Fire Department: 1736 Franklin created the first fire department in Philadelphia. Sixteen years later, he set up the first fire insurance company.

Lightning Rod: 1752 Franklin's insight that lightning is a form of electricity led to his design of a pointed metal rod that attached to the top of a building with a wire running into the ground. Elegant and simple, this device reduced property damage and the numbers of lives lost to the fires caused by lightning strikes.

Glass Armonica: 1761 A more sophisticated version of filling up glasses with water and "playing" them by running your fingers around the edge of each, the armonica could produce chords and melodies. These instruments are still in use.

Glass Armonica ▼

Odometer: 1775 As postmaster of Philadelphia, Franklin wanted to boost efficiency by learning which routes were fastest. To measure distances, he attached an instrument to his carriage that counted the rotations of the axles, giving him the information he needed.

Bifocals: 1784 After getting frustrated with the need to keep switching between eyeglasses (one for seeing close up and one for seeing distances), Franklin had each pair cut in half horizontally and put one half of each lens into one frame. Many people use bifocals to this day.

Daylight Savings Time: 1784 Whether in jest or thrift, Franklin invented Daylight Savings Time, an idea that helps us spring forward and fall back each year as we make the most of natural light.

138 Beginnings–1800

Vocabulary Development

Vocabulary Knowledge Rating

Create a **Vocabulary Knowledge Rating Chart** (*Professional Development Guidebook*, p. 33) for the vocabulary words on the next student page. Give each student a copy of the chart with the words on it. Read the words aloud, and have students mark their rating in the Before Reading column. Urge students to attend to these words as they read and discuss the selections.

In order to gauge how much instruction you need to provide, tally how many students know (or think they know) a word before reading. As students read, point out the words and their contexts.

PHLit **Online!** **Vocabulary Central**, featuring tools and activities for studying vocabulary, is available online at **www.PHLitOnline.com**.

Before You Read

from *The Autobiography* •
from *Poor Richard's Almanack*

❷ Connecting to the Essential Question Scholar William L. Andrews has called Franklin's *Autobiography* "the first great American success story." As you read, notice the goals that Franklin set for himself, and think about how they reflect his values. This will help as you reflect on the Essential Question: **What makes American literature American?**

❸ Literary Analysis

The word **autobiography** is composed of three Greek roots: *-auto-*, which means "self," *-bio-*, which means "life," and *-graph-*, which means "write." Hence, an autobiography is a life history written by its subject. To later readers, an autobiography may provide a more intimate view of history than one might find in an official report or political document.

As an elder statesman, Franklin wrote his life story to serve as an example for young people and to offer advice. A similar motivation is at work in his writing of the **aphorisms**—short sayings with a message—for *Poor Richard's Almanack*. Like his life story, the aphorisms help to paint a portrait of Franklin's attitudes and the world he inhabited. As you read, use a chart like the one shown to record details that help you understand Franklin's values and the times in which he lived.

❹ Reading Strategy

Ⓒ Preparing to Read Complex Texts In *The Autobiography*, you will read about Franklin's plan for self-improvement and the changes it made in his life. His plan can be seen as a *cause*, or the reason something happens, while each change may be seen as an *effect*, or the result. Some cause-and-effect relationships are simple.

> **Cause:** Franklin wanted to organize his time
> **Effect:** He prepared a notebook with a 24-hour schedule.

However, other cause-and-effect relationships are more complex. Many events have more than one cause or more than one effect. As you read, **analyze cause and effect** by pausing at important events and deciding, Why did this happen? What occurred as a result?

❺ Vocabulary

arduous (är′ jōō əs) *adj.* difficult (p. 141)

avarice (av′ ə ris) *n.* greed (p. 142)

vigilance (vij′ ə ləns) *n.* watchfulness (p. 143)

incorrigible (in kôr′ ə jə bəl) *adj.* impossible to correct (p. 145)

posterity (päs ter′ ə tē) *n.* all future generations (p. 146)

squander (skwän′ dər) *v.* spend or use wastefully (p. 149)

from The Autobiography • *from Poor Richard's Almanack* **139**

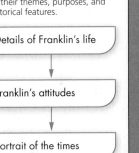

Ⓒ Common Core State Standards

Reading Informational Text

3. Analyze a complex set of ideas or sequence of events and explain how specific individuals, ideas, or events interact and develop over the course of the text.

9. Analyze eighteenth-century foundational U.S. documents of historical and literary significance for their themes, purposes, and rhetorical features.

Details of Franklin's life

↓

Franklin's attitudes

↓

Portrait of the times

Ⓒ Common Core State Standards

• Reading Informational Text 3, 9

• Writing 9, 10

❷ ⓔ Connecting to the Essential Question

1. Review the assignment with the class.

2. Discuss with students specific "American success" stories they have read about or seen in films.

3. As students read, have them note Franklin's goals and think about how they reflect his values.

❸ Literary Analysis

1. Introduce the skill, using the instruction on the student page.

2. Give students a copy of **Literary Analysis Graphic Organizer B,** page 42 in *Graphic Organizer Transparencies,* to fill out as they read.

Think Aloud: Model the Skill

To model drawing conclusions from an autobiography, say to students:

> As I read Franklin's description of his daily routine, I notice that he rises very early and that he schedules virtually every waking hour of his day. This tells me that Franklin is a highly organized person and that he places great importance on the proper use of his time.

❹ Reading Strategy

Introduce the skill, using the instruction on the student page.

❺ Vocabulary

1. Pronounce each word, giving its definition, and have students say it aloud.

2. For more guidance, see the *Classroom Strategies and Teaching Routines* card for vocabulary instruction.

Teaching From Technology

Preparing to Read
Go to **www.PHLitOnline.com** in class or in a lab and display the **Get Connected!** slideshow for these selections. Have the class brainstorm for responses to the slideshow writing prompt, entering ideas in the interactive journal. Then, have students complete their written responses individually, in a lab or as homework.

To build background, display the Background video and More About the Author features.

Using the Interactive Student Edition
Go to **www.PHLitOnline.com** and display the **Enriched Online Student Edition.** As the class reads the selections or listens to the narration, record answers to side column prompts using the graphic organizers accessible on the interactive page. Alternatively, have students use the online edition individually, answering the prompts as they read.

❶ About the Selection

This excerpt shows Franklin's struggle to reach moral perfection, a subject he writes about with the intention that others will imitate the effort. Naming thirteen virtues, Franklin focuses on one at a time, the perfection of one leading to ease of perfecting the next. As years pass, he devotes more time to attaining each virtue before advancing to the next. In telling his story, Franklin displays his fastidious nature, logical thinking, daily organization, and stern self-evaluations.

❷ Activating Prior Knowledge

Ask students to consider what *self-improvement* means. Are people today most interested in improving their health, personal attractiveness, popularity, income, knowledge, skills, or something else? Ask students to predict how Franklin's ideas about self-improvement might be different from today's notions.

Concept Connector ➡

Tell students they will return to their responses after reading the selection.

❸ Visual Connection

1. Tell students that in his *Autobiography,* Franklin paints a slightly ridiculous picture of his arrival in Philadelphia after a long journey by boat. He describes himself as unwashed, shabbily dressed, coat pockets stuffed with extra clothing, carrying a loaf of bread under each arm as he hungrily devours a third.

2. Direct students' attention to the painting on this page. **Ask:** How does this painting compare with Franklin's self-description?
   Possible response: The painting accurately reflects details from Franklin's description, including the loaves of bread. In the painting, Franklin seems serious and dignified, not at all comical.

140 Beginnings–1800

❶ ❷ *from* THE AUTOBIOGRAPHY

Benjamin Franklin

❸ BACKGROUND Benjamin Franklin arrived in the city of Philadelphia in 1723 at the age of seventeen. He knew no one, and he had little money and fewer possessions. However, his accomplishments shaped the city in ways that are still visible today. He helped establish Philadelphia's public library and fire department, as well as its first college. In addition, through his efforts, Philadelphia became the first city in the colonies to have street lights. While Franklin was a brilliant man, some of his success can be attributed to sheer self-discipline, which is evident in this excerpt.

✳

❺ It was about this time I conceived the bold and arduous project of arriving at moral perfection. I wished to live without committing any fault at any time; I would conquer all that either natural inclination, custom, or company might lead me into. As I knew, or thought I knew, what was right and wrong, I did not see why I might not always do the one and avoid the other. But I soon found I had undertaken a task of more difficulty than I had imagined. While my care was employed in guarding against one fault, I was often surprised by another; habit took the advantage of inattention; inclination was sometimes too strong for reason. I concluded, at length, that the mere speculative conviction that it was our interest to be completely virtuous was not sufficient to prevent our slipping; and that the contrary habits must be broken, and good ones acquired and established, before we can have any dependence on a steady, uniform rectitude of conduct. For this purpose I therefore contrived the following method.

In the various enumerations of the moral virtues I had met with in my reading, I found the catalog more or less numerous, as different writers included more or fewer ideas under the same name.

❹ ◀ **Critical Viewing**
This painting shows young Franklin arriving in Philadelphia, carrying all he owns. What point about Franklin might the artist be making? **[Draw Conclusions]**

Vocabulary
arduous (är′ jo͞o əs) *adj.* difficult

Literary Analysis
Autobiography
What does Franklin's goal of moral "perfection" suggest about the values of the time period?

❻ ☑ Reading Check
What project does Franklin undertake?

from The Autobiography **141**

---

❹ **Critical Viewing**
Possible response: Students may say that the artist is portraying a serious, purposeful young Franklin. The straightness of the figure's back suggests discipline and confidence, while the slight downward tilt of the head suggests thoughtfulness.

❺ **Literary Analysis**
Autobiography
1. Have students paraphrase Franklin's attitude toward moral perfection, and write it on the board.
   Possible response: Franklin believes that moral perfection is desirable and can be achieved through hard work.
2. Then, **ask** students the Literary Analysis question: What does Franklin's goal of moral "perfection" suggest about the values of the time period?
   Possible response: It suggests that people of the time period valued hard work and moral behavior very highly. Franklin's belief in these two values encouraged him to try to be "completely virtuous."

❻ **Reading Check**
Answer: He intends to achieve moral perfection through systematic effort.

World Literature

No written work by Socrates exists, so we are dependent on his contemporaries for information about his life. Some of the best sources of information are the early dialogues of his student Plato, who attempted to provide a full picture of Socrates' teaching methods. Socrates became well known for using a method of critical inquiry that explored and often undermined widely held beliefs.

Connect to the Literature
Encourage students to reflect on what they know about Jesus and Socrates before responding to the question.

Ask: Do you see any humor or irony in Franklin's plan for achieving humility—namely, by imitating Jesus and Socrates? Explain.

Possible response: There is some humor in Franklin's plan to achieve humility by imitating Jesus and Socrates in that Jesus and Socrates represent models of perfection. Franklin's confidence that he can attain such lofty levels of humbleness suggests the opposite of humility.

---

❼ LITERATURE IN CONTEXT

World Literature

Socrates
A Greek philosopher and teacher who lived in the fifth century B.C., Socrates pioneered the kind of self-reflection that Benjamin Franklin undertakes with his moral improvement plan. Socrates believed that only through self-knowledge can people achieve virtue. Though he led many Athenians in searching for truth and defining rules for moral conduct, Socrates' criticism of the government resulted in his execution.

Connect to the Literature

Do you see any humor or irony in Franklin's plan for achieving humility—namely, by imitating Jesus and Socrates? Explain.

Vocabulary
avarice (av′ ə ris) *n.* greed

Temperance, for example, was by some confined to eating and drinking, while by others it was extended to mean the moderating every other pleasure, appetite, inclination, or passion, bodily or mental, even to our avarice and ambition. I proposed to myself, for the sake of clearness, to use rather more names, with fewer ideas annexed to each, than a few names with more ideas; and I included under thirteen names of virtues all that at that time occurred to me as necessary or desirable, and annexed to each a short precept, which fully expressed the extent I gave to its meaning.

These names of virtues, with their precepts, were:

1. TEMPERANCE Eat not to dullness; drink not to elevation.
2. SILENCE Speak not but what may benefit others or yourself; avoid trifling conversation.
3. ORDER Let all your things have their places; let each part of your business have its time.
4. RESOLUTION Resolve to perform what you ought; perform without fail what you resolve.
5. FRUGALITY Make no expense but to do good to others or yourself; i.e., waste nothing.
6. INDUSTRY Lose no time; be always employed in something useful; cut off all unnecessary actions.
7. SINCERITY Use no hurtful deceit; think innocently and justly, and, if you speak, speak accordingly.
8. JUSTICE Wrong none by doing injuries, or omitting the benefits that are your duty.
9. MODERATION Avoid extremes; forebear resenting injuries so much as you think they deserve.
10. CLEANLINESS Tolerate no uncleanliness in body, clothes, or habitation.
11. TRANQUILLITY Be not disturbed at trifles, or at accidents common or unavoidable.
12. CHASTITY Rarely use venery but for health or offspring, never to dullness, weakness, or the injury of your own or another's peace or reputation.
13. HUMILITY Imitate Jesus and Socrates.

My intention being to acquire the *habitude* of all these virtues, I judged it would be well not to distract my attention by attempting the whole at once but to fix it on one of them at a time; and, when I should be master of that, then to proceed to another, and so on, till I should have gone through the thirteen; and, as the previous acquisition of some might facilitate the acquisition of certain others, I arranged them with that

❽

Enrichment: Investigating a Key Person in History

Franklin in Philadelphia
Philadelphia was an important center of activity during the period leading up to the American Revolution. It was there that the Declaration of Independence, which established the United States as an independent nation, was written and signed.

Benjamin Franklin became one of Philadelphia's most influential citizens, an instigator of civic improvement. He helped establish the city's public library and volunteer fire department, as well as its first college. Through his efforts, Philadelphia became the first city in the colonies to have street lights.

Activity: Research Have students find further examples of Franklin's efforts to improve life in Philadelphia, recording their findings in the **Enrichment: Investigating a Key Person in History** worksheet, *Professional Development Guidebook,* page 233.

view, as they stand above. *Temperance* first, as it tends to procure that coolness and clearness of head, which is so necessary where constant vigilance was to be kept up, and guard maintained against the unremitting attraction of ancient habits and the force of perpetual temptations. This being acquired and established, *Silence* would be more easy; and my desire being to gain knowledge at the same time that I improved in virtue, and considering that in conversation it was obtained rather by the use of the ears than of the tongue, and therefore wishing to break a habit I was getting into of prattling, punning, and joking, which only made me acceptable to trifling company, I gave *Silence* the second place. This and the next, *Order*, I expected would allow me more time for attending to my project and my studies. *Resolution*, once become habitual, would keep me firm in my endeavors to obtain all the subsequent virtues; *Frugality* and *Industry* freeing me from my remaining debt and producing affluence and independence, would make more easy the practice of *Sincerity* and *Justice*, etc., etc. Conceiving then, that, agreeably to the advice of Pythagoras[1] in his *Golden Verses*, daily examination would be necessary, I contrived the following method for conducting that examination.

I made a little book, in which I allotted a page for each of the virtues. I ruled each page with red ink, so as to have seven columns, one for each day of the week, marking each column with a letter for the day. I crossed these columns with thirteen red lines, marking the beginning of each line with the first letter of one of the virtues, on which line and in its proper column I might mark, by a little black spot, every fault I found upon examination to have been committed respecting that virtue upon that day.

I determined to give a week's strict attention to each of the virtues successively. Thus, in the first week, my great guard was to avoid every[2] the least offense against *Temperance*, leaving the other virtues to their ordinary chance, only marking every evening the faults of the day. Thus, if in the first week I could keep my first line, marked *T*. clear of spots, I supposed the habit of that virtue so much strengthened, and its opposite weakened, that I might venture extending my attention to include the next, and for the following week keep both lines clear of spots. Proceeding thus to the last, I could go through a course complete in thirteen weeks, and four courses in a year. And like him who, having a garden to weed, does not attempt to eradicate all the bad herbs at once, which would exceed his reach and his strength, but works on one of the beds at a time, and, having accomplished the first, proceeds to a second, so I should have, I hoped, the encouraging pleasure of seeing on my pages the progress I made in virtue, by clearing successively my lines of their spots, till in the end, by a number of courses, I should be happy in viewing a clean book, after a thirteen weeks' daily examination. . . .

---

1. **Pythagoras** (pi thag′ ə rəs) Greek philosopher and mathematician who lived in the sixth century B.C.
2. **every** even.

Vocabulary
vigilance (vij′ ə ləns) *n.* watchfulness

Literary Analysis
Autobiography
What does the care with which Franklin makes his book tell you about his character?

Reading Check

10 What does Franklin hope to achieve in 13 weeks?

---

8 Reading Strategy
Analyze Cause and Effect

1. Read the bracketed passage with students.
2. **Ask:** What effect did Franklin expect by placing Temperance at the top of his list and working on this virtue first?
   Answer: Working on Temperance first would give Franklin a cool and clear head, facilitating his concentration on other virtues.

▶ **Monitor Progress Ask:** What might have been the effect if Franklin had ranked the virtues in order of importance, rather than in order of efficiency?
   Possible response: Franklin might have overemphasized the top items on the list and ignored items listed at the bottom.

▶ **Reteach:** If students have difficulty analyzing cause and effect, go over Franklin's explanations in greater detail. He expects Silence will have the effect of improving his knowledge, and that Frugality will have the effect of freeing him from debt.

9 Literary Analysis
Autobiography

1. Read the bracketed passage with students, noting the care with which Franklin describes his book.
2. **Ask:** Why do you think Franklin provides such a detailed description of his book?
   Possible response: Students may suggest that Franklin is proud of his book and wants readers to appreciate its details. He may also want readers to follow his example, and thus provides them with clear directions.
3. **Ask** students the Literary Analysis question: What does the care with which Franklin makes his book tell you about his character?
   Possible response: Students may say that Franklin's care reveals that he is detail-oriented, painstaking, systematic, and methodical.

10 Reading Check

Answer: He hopes to give systematic attention to all thirteen of his listed virtues.

Differentiated
Instruction for Universal Access

Strategy for Less Proficient Readers
Point out to students that in this passage Franklin uses two graphic organizers: a seven-column "scorecard" for each virtue and a two-column daily calendar. Help students understand these two organizers by clarifying their structure and defining any unfamiliar terms. You may wish to work as a class to recreate Franklin's scorecard on the board exactly as he describes it and demonstrate its use, pointing out his deliberate use of red ink for permanent lines and pencil for marks that he could erase from the ivory sheet.

EL Strategy for English Learners
Work with students as a class to define each of Franklin's listed virtues, using dictionaries as necessary. For example, *temperance* may be defined as "moderation"; *silence* may be defined as "reserve or self-restraint." Then, demonstrate the use of a word web to help students understand these concepts. Place the virtue in the center cell, and use outer cells for Franklin's examples and definitions. Help students complete the outer cells with information from the text.

1. Have students read the bracketed passage. Confirm that students understand what it shows.
   Answer: The passage is Franklin's daily schedule, which he uses to organize his day.

2. Focus students' attention on Franklin's guiding questions, which he uses to set the day's agenda and to evaluate his efforts.

3. **Ask:** What insights into Franklin's character does this schedule provide?
   Possible response: The schedule suggests that Franklin is self-motivated, disciplined, and purposeful.

The precept of *Order* requiring that *every part of my business should have its allotted time*, one page in my little book contained the following scheme of employment for the twenty-four hours of a natural day.

The Morning	5	Rise, wash and address Powerful Goodness! Contrive day's business and take the resolution of the day; prosecute the present study, and breakfast.
Question. What good shall I do this day?	6	
	7	
	8	
	9	
	10	Work.
	11	
Noon	12	Read, or overlook my accounts, and dine.
	1	
	2	Work.
	3	
	4	Put things in their places. Supper. Music or diversion, or conversation. Conversation. Examination of the day.
	5	
	6	
Evening	7	
Question. What good have I done today?	8	
	9	
	10	Sleep.
	11	
	12	
Night	1	

⓫

I entered upon the execution of this plan for self-examination, and continued it with occasional intermissions for some time. I was surprised to find myself so much fuller of faults than I had imagined; but I had the satisfaction of seeing them diminish. To avoid the trouble of renewing now and then my little book, which, by scraping out the marks on the paper of old faults to make room for new ones in a new course, became full of holes, I transferred my tables and precepts to the ivory leaves of a memorandum book, on which the lines were drawn with red ink that made a durable stain, and on those lines I marked my faults with a black-lead pencil, which marks I could easily wipe out with a wet sponge. After a while I went through one course only in a year, and afterward only one in several years, till at length I omitted them entirely, being employed in voyages and business abroad, with a multiplicity of affairs that interfered; but I always carried my little book with me.

My scheme of *Order* gave me the most trouble; and I found that, though it might be practicable where a man's business was such as to leave him the disposition of his time, that of a journeyman printer, for instance, it was not possible to be exactly observed by a master, who must mix with the world and often receive people of business at their own hours. *Order,* too, with regard to places for things, papers, etc., I found extremely difficult to acquire. I had not been early accustomed to it, and, having an exceeding good memory, I was not so sensible of the inconvenience attending want of method. This article, therefore, cost me so much painful attention, and my faults in it vexed me so much, and I made so little progress in amendment, and had such frequent relapses, that I was almost ready to give up the attempt, and content myself with a faulty character in that respect, like the man who, in buying an ax of a smith, my neighbor, desired to have the whole of its surface as bright as the edge. The smith consented to grind it bright for him if he would turn the wheel; he turned, while the smith pressed the broad face of the ax hard and heavily on the stone, which made the turning of it very fatiguing. The man came every now and then from the wheel to see how the work went on, and at length would take his ax as it was, without farther grinding. "No," said the smith, "turn on, turn on; we shall have it bright by and by; as yet, it is only speckled." "Yes," says the man, "*but I think I like a speckled ax best.*" And I believe this may have been the case with many, who, having, for want of some such means as I employed, found the difficulty of obtaining good and breaking bad habits in other points of vice and virtue, have given up the struggle, and concluded that "*a speckled ax was best*"; for something, that pretended to be reason, was every now and then suggesting to me that such extreme nicety as I exacted of myself might be a kind of foppery in morals, which, if it were known, would make me ridiculous; that a perfect character might be attended with the inconvenience of being envied and hated; and that a benevolent man should allow a few faults in himself, to keep his friends in countenance.

In truth, I found myself incorrigible with respect to *Order*; and now I am grown old, and my memory bad, I feel very sensibly the want of it. But, on the whole, though I never arrived at the perfection I had been so ambitious of obtaining, but fell far short of it, yet I was, by the endeavor, a better and a happier man than I otherwise should have been if I had not attempted it; as those who aim at perfect writing by imitating the engraved copies, though they never reached the wished-for excellence of those copies, their hand is mended by the endeavor, and is tolerable while it continues fair and legible.

Literary Analysis
Autobiography
What does this anecdote about the man with the ax reveal about Franklin's sense of humor?

Vocabulary
incorrigible (in kôr′ ə jə bəl) *adj.* impossible to correct

13

Which virtue did Franklin hope to achieve by planning each day's activity?

145

Spiral Review

Audience

1. Remind students that they studied the concept of audience.

2. **Ask** students the Spiral Review question.

   Possible response: Franklin intends his essay to be read by future generations. He says he focuses on lessons he has learned so that they may benefit those who come after him.

⑭ Reading Strategy

Analyze Cause and Effect

1. Have students read the bracketed passage. Point out that Franklin, at the age of seventy-nine, is summarizing the results of his lifetime's effort at self-improvement.

2. **Ask:** According to Franklin, what specific effects were caused by his efforts on the virtue of Temperance? Industry and Frugality?

   Answer: Franklin believes striving for Temperance had the effect of giving him health and a good constitution. Working on Industry and Frugality produced the effects of wealth, ease of life, civic usefulness, and a good reputation among educated people.

⑮ The American Experience

Benjamin Franklin in Our World

The practical and inspirational effects of Benjamin Franklin's life continue. Wood-burning stoves based on his design are still in use, as are bifocals, lightning rods, street lights, libraries, and fire departments.

Connect to the Literature Ask students to review what they know about Franklin's character and accomplishments before responding to the question. **Ask:** What would you choose as Benjamin Franklin's most inspiring quality? Explain.

Possible response: Students may cite Franklin's self-discipline, his hard-working nature, his inventiveness, or some other trait.

Spiral Review

Audience For whom is Franklin writing? How do you think his sense of audience helped to shape this account of his life?

Vocabulary
posterity (päs ter ə tē) ⑭
n. all future generations

It may be well my posterity should be informed that to this little artifice, with the blessing of God, their ancestor owed the constant felicity of his life, down to his seventy-ninth year in which this is written. What reverses may attend the remainder is in the hand of Providence; but, if they arrive, the reflection on past happiness enjoyed ought to help his bearing them with more resignation. To *Temperance* he ascribes his long-continued health, and what is still left to him of a good constitution; to *Industry* and *Frugality,* the early easiness of his circumstances and acquisition of his fortune, with all that knowledge that enabled him to be a useful citizen, and obtained for him some degree of reputation among the learned; to *Sincerity* and *Justice,* the confidence of his country, and the honorable employs it conferred upon him; and to the joint influence of the whole mass of the virtues, even in the imperfect state he was able to acquire them, all that evenness of temper, and that cheerfulness in conversation, which makes his company still sought for, and agreeable even to his younger acquaintance. I hope, therefore, that some of my descendants may follow the example and reap the benefit.

Benjamin Franklin National Memorial, The Franklin Institute, Philadelphia, PA ▶

⑮ THE AMERICAN EXPERIENCE

BENJAMIN FRANKLIN
in Our World

In *The Autobiography*, Benjamin Franklin describes his attempts to become a completely virtuous person. Though he thought he failed, Americans *do* view Franklin as a man of many virtues. He was civic-minded, intelligent, inquisitive, practical, and industrious. He embodies much that Americans value, which may be why his image is so visible in our world today. He is, in fact, an American icon.

CONNECT TO THE LITERATURE

What would you choose as Benjamin Franklin's most inspiring quality? Explain.

Cartoon illustration of Ben Franklin from *Liberty's Kids* ▶

Ben Franklin Action Figure ▶   U.S. currency: $100 bill ▲

Enrichment: Investigating Science

The Franklin Institute
The Franklin Institute is living tribute to Franklin's work as scientist. Founded in Philadelphia in 1824, the Institute actively promotes science and scientific education; it also houses the Benjamin Franklin National Memorial.
Activity: Oral Report Have students research the legacy of Franklin's scientific observations involving electricity, weather, and ocean currents. Students may find the online Web site of the Franklin Institute a source of helpful information. Suggest that they record information in the **Enrichment: Investigating Science** worksheet, *Professional Development Guidebook,* page 241. Ask students to prepare oral reports of their findings for the class.

Critical Commentary

Ben Franklin, America's Everyman
William L. Andrews

William L. Andrews, an award-winning scholar and teacher, is the E. Maynard Adams Professor of English at the University of North Carolina, Chapel Hill.

It's not just a coincidence that America's earliest literature is highly auto-biographical. Nor is it by accident that autobiography emerged as a literary form about the same time that the United States became a new nation. Autobiography and America were made for each other.

The revolution in the United States created a new person, as well as a new country. At least that's what the great spokesmen and propagan-dists of the Revolution, especially Thomas Jefferson, Patrick Henry, and Benjamin Franklin, claimed. Franklin, who wore a coonskin cap to the royal courts of Europe, became famous for inventing everything from street lights to eyeglasses. But we read him today because his greatest invention was himself. *The Autobiography* of Benjamin Franklin is the first great American success story: a tale of a poor boy who made good.

A New American Franklin's *Autobiography* has served for many generations as a blueprint for a new American man. This man was ener-getic, adaptable, shrewd, and, as the *Autobiography* makes very clear, success oriented. Industrious, frugal, temperate, orderly, and resolute, Franklin modeled for Americans a hero fulfilled by the work of this world, not longing for deliverance to the next. Yet in Franklin's autobio-graphical mirror his readers could see that success was not to be mea-sured simply by acquiring the goods of this world but by "doing good" for the practical benefit of one's fellow Americans too.

An Achievable Good Franklin's "project of arriving at moral perfec-tion," which he undertook when he was in his mid-twenties, epitomizes his audaciously American can-do spirit in at least two ways. First, it appears that the young Franklin really thought he could divest himself of all his faults simply by putting his mind and will to the task. Second, he seems to have been confident of success by approaching the task as a "project," not unlike some he'd already wrapped up, including the founding of the first lending library and the publication of *Poor Richard's Almanack*. Franklin doesn't hesitate to admit that he failed, but he insists that the effort he exerted was just as valuable to his character develop-ment as his unattained goal. Thus, as if following Poor Richard's counsel to "write injuries in dust, benefits in marble," Franklin's autobiographical account of his perfection project points finally to an achievable good, not an unreachable ideal.

(C) **Key Ideas and Details** According to Andrews, why have generations of Franklin's readers treasured this episode of failure in a life of so many successes?

...his greatest
INVENTION
was himself.

Critical Commentary

1. Have students read Andrews's commentary.

2. Andrews asserts that Franklin's "greatest inventions was himself." **Ask:** Do you agree that there is a sense in which Franklin is a self-invented, or self-made, man? Explain.
   Possible response: Students may note that Franklin began with no money, hardly any edu-cation, little family support, and no influence—yet he rose to great wealth, great accomplish-ment, and great reputation. Since he accomplished all this almost entirely through his own talent and effort, students may agree that Franklin in that sense could be described as self-invented.

3. Williams describes Franklin as "energetic, adaptable, and shrewd."
   Ask students to find examples of each of these qualities in the pas-sage of the *Autobiography* they have just read.
   Possible response: Energetic: Franklin rises at five in the morn-ing and reads and studies when he is not working. Adaptable: When he had trouble erasing marks in his first book, Franklin developed a new book using erasable ivory sheets. Shrewd: Franklin arranged his virtues in an efficient sequence, starting with ones that would have a beneficial effect on his later efforts.

Key Ideas and Details

Answer: Readers treasure the *Autobiography* for providing a new idea of what an American could be. In his moral perfection project, Franklin shows an American "can-do spirit" in his belief that perfection could be achieved by using his mind and his will. Though it did not suc-ceed, this Franklin project (like so many others) produced an achiev-able good.

16 About the Selection

By providing practical wisdom through aphorisms, Benjamin Franklin teaches valuable lessons in brief and easy-to-remember sayings. Though Franklin did not originate most of these aphorisms, his gift for turning a phrase almost always improved them.

17 Humanities

Benjamin Franklin, 1766, by David Martin

Scottish painter David Martin (1737–1797) portrayed many of the most distinguished figures of his time, including the eminent American Benjamin Franklin. Martin completed this famous "thumb portrait" while Franklin was residing in London on a diplomatic mission. Reportedly Franklin himself suggested the pose; he also allowed the artist to show his warts. Franklin liked the result well enough to have a copy of the painting sent to his family in America.

After students have studied the painting, ask this question:

What impression of Franklin do you form by examining this portrait?
Possible response: Students may describe Franklin in this portrait as studious, thoughtful, and dignified. Such details as his pose, facial expression, and the books and papers contribute to this impression.

16
17 *from* Poor
Richard's
Almanack

Benjamin Franklin

148 Beginnings–1800

- Fools make feasts, and wise men eat them.

- Be slow in choosing a friend, slower in changing.

- Keep thy shop, and thy shop will keep thee.

- Early to bed, early to rise, makes a man healthy, wealthy, and wise.

- Three may keep a secret if two of them are dead.

- God helps them that help themselves.

- The rotten apple spoils his companions.

- An open foe may prove a curse; but a pretended friend is worse.

- Have you somewhat to do tomorrow, do it today.

- A true friend is the best possession.

- A small leak will sink a great ship.

- No gains without pains.

- Tis easier to prevent bad habits than to break them.

- Well done is better than well said.

19 | Dost thou love life? Then do not squander time; for that's the stuff life is made of.

- Write injuries in dust, benefits in marble.

- A slip of the foot you may soon recover, but a slip of the tongue you may never get over.

- If your head is wax, don't walk in the sun.

- A good example is the best sermon.

Poor Richard, 1733.
AN
Almanack
For the Year of Chrift
1733,
Being the Firft after LEAP YEAR:

And makes fince the Creation   Years
By the Account of the Eaftern Greeks,   7241
By the Latin Church, when ☉ ent. ♈   6932
By the Con. putation of *W. W.*   5742
By the Roman Chronology   5682
By the Jewifh Rabbies   5494

Wherein is contained
The Lunations, Eclipfes, Judgment of the Weather, Spring Tides, Planets Motions & mutual Afpects, Sun and Moon's Rifing and Setting, Length of Days, Time of High Water, Fairs, Courts, and obfervable Days.
Fitted to the Latitude of Forty Degrees, and a Meridian of Five Hours Weft from *London,* but may without fenfible Error, ferve all the adjacent Places, even from *Newfoundland* to *South-Carolina.*

By *RICHARD SAUNDERS,* Philom.

PHILADELPHIA:
Printed and fold by *B. FRANKLIN,* at the New Printing-Office near the Market.

18 ▲ Critical Viewing
The abbreviation "Philom." is short for *philomath.* The root *-philo-* means "love" and the suffix *-math-* means "learn." Can you infer what the word means? **[Infer Meaning]**

Vocabulary
squander (skwän′ dər) *v.* spend or use wastefully

20 ☑ Reading Check
Which aphorisms offer advice about using time wisely?

from Poor Richard's Almanack **149**

1. (a) He makes a daily calendar with tasks and times outlined. (b) He does not succeed, finding that sometimes he must order tasks around others and that he cannot change his own habit of relying on memory. (c) The anecdote illustrates the exhausting effort involved in the struggle for order, as well as the human tendency to settle for less.

2. (a) He probably felt very determined and optimistic. (b) **Sample answer:** The older Franklin realizes that perfection is unattainable but that the attempt to improve oneself produces real benefits.

3. (a) The following aphorisms concern friendship: "An open foe may prove a curse; but a pretended friend is worse"; "Be slow in choosing a friend, slower in changing"; and "A true friend is the best possession." (b) Yes, he says that real friendship is precious and needs to be guarded with care.

4. (a) He will die of fasting, or lack of nourishment. (b) Franklin might suggest effort or careful planning.

5. **Possible response:** Self-examination can highlight counterproductive behavior, helping one to recognize the need for change.

6. Be sure students make both choices and give clear reasons for their decisions.

7. **Sample answer:** Franklin's quest for self-improvement and his emphasis on <u>practical</u> matters in his aphorisms reflect values that still exist in America. Today's Americans prize <u>individualism</u> and hard work, and they admire people who are <u>thrifty</u>, <u>practical</u>, and <u>humorous</u>.

ρ A good
EXAMPLE
is the best
SERMON.

ρ Hunger is the best pickle.

ρ Genius without education is like silver in the mine.

ρ For want of a nail the shoe is lost; for want of a shoe the horse is lost; for want of a horse the rider is lost.

ρ Haste makes waste.

ρ The doors of wisdom are never shut.

ρ Love your neighbor; yet don't pull down your hedge.

ρ He that lives upon hope will die fasting.

Critical Reading

Cite textual evidence to support your responses.

1. **Key Ideas and Details (a)** What efforts does Franklin make to become more orderly? **(b) Infer:** Is he successful? Explain. **(c) Analyze:** What aspect of his attempt to become more orderly is illustrated by the anecdote of the man with the speckled ax?

2. **Key Ideas and Details (a)** When Franklin began his project, he was a young man. How do you think he felt at the time about his chances of attaining moral "perfection"? **(b) Compare and Contrast:** What insights does Franklin gain about the goal of achieving perfection as he gets older?

3. **Key Ideas and Details (a)** Note three aphorisms that deal directly with friendship. **(b) Analyze:** Is Franklin's message about friendship consistent? Explain.

4. **Key Ideas and Details (a)** According to the aphorism, what happens to a person who "lives upon hope"? **(b) Speculate:** What more reliable value would Franklin say a person can successfully "live upon"?

5. **Integration of Knowledge and Ideas** In what ways can analyzing one's own behavior contribute to personal growth?

6. **Integration of Knowledge and Ideas** With which of Franklin's aphorisms do you most strongly agree and disagree? Why?

7. **Integration of Knowledge and Ideas** In what ways do the goals Franklin sets for himself and the aphorisms he wrote express values that are still widely held in America? Explain. Use at least two of these Essential Question words: *individualism, thrifty, practical, humorous*. *[Connecting to the Essential Question: What makes American literature American?]*

Concept Connector

Literary Analysis Graphic Organizer
Ask students to review the graphic organizers in which they have listed details that reflect Franklin's attitudes and the time in which he lived. Then, have students share their organizers and compare the details they identified.

Activating Prior Knowledge
Have students return to their responses to the Activating Prior Knowledge activity. Ask them to explain whether their thoughts have changed, and if so, how.

Connecting to the Essential Question
Have students compare the responses they gave to the prompt before reading the selections with their thoughts afterward. Have them work individually or in groups, writing or discussing their thoughts, to formulate their new responses. Then, lead a class discussion, probing for what students have learned that confirms or invalidates their initial thoughts. Encourage students to cite specific textual details to support their responses.

㉑ PROVERBS
THE WISDOM OF MANY

◀ Wooden helmet mask with beard (Congo)

The memorable aphorisms that Benjamin Franklin presents in *Poor Richard's Almanack* are grounded in the rich oral tradition of proverbs. A proverb is a traditional saying that offers a practical truth about life, work, love, death, and other universal experiences. Each proverb is a bit of cultural wisdom. A society's proverbs reflect the attitudes and worldviews of its people. Proverbs are handed down through generations and can be used to teach children, offer advice, settle arguments, or even help resolve legal disputes. The proverbs presented here are from various cultures on the African continent.

CONNECT TO THE LITERATURE

What similarities and differences do you notice between the African proverbs and Franklin's aphorisms?

AFRICAN PROVERBS

UGANDA: THE BAGANDA PEOPLE
Where there are no dogs, the wild cats move about freely.

LIBERIA: THE JABO PEOPLE
The butterfly that flies among the thorns will tear its wings.
~
Children are the wisdom of the nation.

SOUTH AFRICA: THE ZULU PEOPLE
There is no foot, which does not stumble.

GHANA: THE ASHANTI PEOPLE
Rain beats on a leopard's skin,
but it does not beat out the spots.
~
One falsehood spoils a thousand truths.

NIGERIA: THE YORUBA PEOPLE
He who is being carried does not
realize how far the town is.

**TANZANIA AND KENYA:
THE MASAI PEOPLE**
The zebra cannot do away with his stripes.
~
Do not repair another man's fence
until you have seen to your own.

Mask with horns (Nigeria) ▶

151

㉑ World Literature Connection

Proverbs: The Wisdom of Many
The universality of proverbs is apparent in similarities of style and meaning across time and culture. The Masai proverb "Do not repair another man's fence until you have seen to your own" has a twin in the biblical saying "Why do you notice the speck in another's eye, but do not notice the log in your own?" and a close relative in the modern saying "People who live in glass houses should not throw stones." Another biblical proverb, "A leopard cannot change its spots" finds two matches: the Ashanti proverb "Rain beats on a leopard's skin, but it does not beat out the spots" and the Masai equivalent, "The zebra cannot do away with his stripes." The Ugandan proverb "Where there are no dogs, the wild cats move about freely" has a familiar ring to Americans, who say "When the cat is away, the mice will play."

Connect to the Literature

After students have reviewed and discussed the proverbs, **ask** the Connect to the Literature question: What similarities and differences do you notice between the African proverbs and Franklin's aphorisms?
Possible response: Students may note that, like Franklin's aphorisms, the African proverbs are simple, brief, and express a practical attitude toward life. Students may note that the Ashanti proverb "One falsehood spoils a thousand truths" is similar to Franklin's "The rotten apple spoils his companions" and "A small leak will sink a great ship."

Students may note, among differences, that the African proverbs put more emphasis on animals and natural events; Franklin's aphorisms focus more on interactions among people.

Vocabulary Development

Vocabulary Knowledge Rating
When students have completed reading and discussing both selections, have them take out the **Vocabulary Knowledge Rating** charts they worked on earlier. Read the words aloud and have students rate their knowledge of the words again in the After Reading column. Clarify any words that are still problematic. Have students write their own definitions and example or sentence in the appropriate column. Then, have students complete the Vocabulary Lesson at the end of these selections. Encourage students to use the words in further discussion and written work about the selections. Remind them that they will be accountable for these words on the **Selection Test,** *Unit 1 Resources,* pages 218–220 or 221–223.

Answers

1. **Possible responses:** (a) Franklin may have hoped that his readers would learn from his failures. (b) Both his efforts and his failures show that self-improvement is beneficial.

2. **Possible responses:** (a) He did not achieve this goal, because at the end he still hopes to impress his descendants. (b) Yes, he seems proud of his book and lists.

3. **Possible response:** Another writer might have pointed out contradictions between his ideals and actions.

4. (a) Franklin's schedule suggests that life included three meals a day, work during morning and afternoon hours, with diversion in the evening. His anecdote of the ax describes a simple business transaction of the day. (b) His account suggests that people of the time valued good character but were ready to ridicule any "foppery of morals."

5. (a) Yes, both reflect concerns for moral behavior. (b) Students may agree that both works reflect the concerns and the wit of the same individual.

6. **Sample answer:** *Virtue:* Industry; *Aphorism:* "Dost thou love life? Then do not squander time; for that's the stuff life is made of." *Explanation:* Both virtue and aphorism stress the value of using time productively.

7. **Possible responses:** An autobiography is written by its subject and tells facts. When the powerful person in the cartoon gathers "creative people" to help him write his autobiography, he misses the point.

8. (a) The man wanted his entire ax to be bright. (b) After exhausting effort, the ax had only a speckled appearance. (c) The cost of change causes the man to settle for less than perfection.

9. **Sample answer:** "A small leak will sink a great ship" suggests that a minor problem can produce a disastrous outcome.

152

After You Read

from *The Autobiography* •
from *Poor Richard's Almanack*

Literary Analysis

1. Key Ideas and Details (a) Why do you think Franklin devoted such a large chunk of his **autobiography** to a discussion of his failures to achieve perfect virtue? **(b)** What message do both his efforts and his failures convey?

2. Key Ideas and Details (a) Do you think Franklin achieved the virtue of humility? Why or why not? **(b)** Do you find any evidence of pride—humility's opposite—in this account of his life?

3. Craft and Structure How do you think *The Autobiography* would be different if it were written about Franklin rather than by him?

4. Integration of Knowledge and Ideas (a) Note two details from this section of *The Autobiography* that reveal an aspect of ordinary, daily life in colonial America. **(b)** In what ways does this excerpt shed light on Franklin's era?

5. Comparing Literary Works (a) Are Franklin's struggles to improve himself related to the advice he offers in the **aphorisms**? **(b)** Do these aphorisms seem to be written by the same person who wrote *The Autobiography*? Why or why not?

6. Integration of Knowledge and Ideas Use a chart like this one to match three aphorisms with virtues from *The Autobiography*. Explain each choice.

Virtue		Aphorism		Explanation
	=		→	

7. Analyzing Visual Information Based on what you know of the genre of autobiography, explain the humor in the cartoon shown on this page.

Reading Strategy

8. Analyze cause and effect in the anecdote about the man with the ax. **(a)** What goal propels the man to take an action? **(b)** What is the result of that action? **(c)** How does that result become the cause of another action or decision?

9. Choose one of Franklin's aphorisms and explain how it suggests a cause-and-effect relationship. For example, "No gains without pains" suggests that only through hard work (cause) can you achieve your goals (effect).

Common Core State Standards

Language
4.b. Identify and correctly use patterns of word changes that indicate different meanings or parts of speech. *(p. 153)*
5. Demonstrate understanding of word relationships and nuances in word meanings. *(p. 153)*

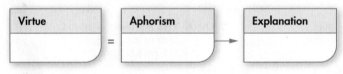

▼ *"I called for you creative people because I feel it's time to begin my autobiography."*

"I called for you creative people because I feel it's time to begin my autobiography."

Assessment Practice

Summarizing Written Texts (For more practice, see the *All-in-One Workbook*.)

In many tests, students will have to identify causes and effects. Use the following sample test item to demonstrate.

> I proposed to myself, for the sake of clearness, to use rather more names [for virtues], with fewer ideas annexed to each, than a few names with more ideas, and I included under thirteen names of virtues all that at that time occurred to me as necessary or desirable . . .

Why did Franklin name more virtues instead of fewer?

A He wanted to be clear.

B He wanted to measure the virtue of his friends.

C He thought thirteen was a lucky number.

D He decided there were only thirteen virtues.

Choices **B** and **C** do not contain any information from the passage. Students may be tempted by choice **D**, but should recognize that **A** is the best answer.

Integrated Language Skills

© **Vocabulary Acquisition and Use**

Word Analysis: Patterns of Word Changes

The noun *vigilance*, meaning "watchfulness," contains the suffix *-ance*. Whenever you see a word with the *-ance* or *-ence* ending, you can be sure it is a noun. That suffix is a *pattern that indicates the word's function*. Words exhibit other patterns that indicate different meanings or functions. Write a definition for each italicized word below. Then, explain the word's function—noun, adjective, or adverb. Based on your answer, identify the letter pattern that indicates the word's function.

1. He was *vigilant* in his efforts to reform.
2. Through the night, the soldier stood watch *vigilantly*.
3. He showed great *avarice* in his drive for wealth.
4. Many great stories exist about *avaricious* characters.

Using Resources to Build Vocabulary

The Language of Failed Attempts
Although Franklin strives for moral perfection, he openly acknowledges his failure to meet his goals. Consider how these words help Franklin describe his failed attempt to be perfect:

debt	reverses
prattle	slipping
punning	temptations
relapses	vexed

Use a print or electronic dictionary to find a meaning for each word as it is used by Franklin. Then, write a short advice column in which you give readers suggestions that will help them avoid failure. Include each word at least once. You might use a question-and-answer format. Vocabulary words may appear in both the questions and answers.

Vocabulary: Analogies

Analogies show the relationships between pairs of words. Complete each analogy using a word from the vocabulary list on page 139. In each, your choice should create a word pair that matches the relationship between the first two words given. Then, explain your answers.

1. *Permission* is to *authorization* as _____ is to *greed*.
2. *Tragedy* is to *comedy* as _____ is to *negligence*.
3. *Contemporary* is to *now* as _____ is to *future*.
4. *Rare* is to *common* as _____ is to *easy*.
5. *Criticize* is to *praise* as _____ is to *save*.
6. *Fresh* is to *trite* as _____ is to *curable*.

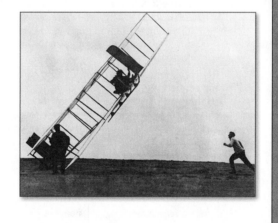

Extended Study: Integrated Language Skills **153**

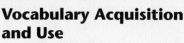
Vocabulary Acquisition and Use

1. Introduce the skill, using the instruction on the student page.
2. Have students complete the Word Analysis activity and the Vocabulary practice.

Word Analysis

1. watchful; adjective; the *-ant* pattern indicates an adjective.
2. in a watchful manner; adverb; the *-ly* pattern indicates an adverb.
3. greed; noun; the *-ice* pattern indicates a noun.
4. greedy; adjective; the *-ious* pattern indicates an adjective.

Vocabulary

1. avarice; *avarice* is a synonym of *greed*, as *permission* is a synonym of *authorization*.
2. vigilance; *vigilance* is an antonym of *negligence*, as *tragedy* is an antonym of *comedy*.
3. posterity; *posterity* is equivalent to *future*, as *contemporary* is equivalent to *now*.
4. arduous; *arduous* is an antonym of *easy*, as *rare* is an antonym of *common*.
5. squander; *squander* is an antonym of *save*, as *criticize* is an antonym of *praise*.
6. incorrigible; *incorrigible* is an antonym of *curable*, as *fresh* is an antonym of *trite*.

Using Resources to Build Vocabulary

Sample Answer:

Dear Mr. Fixit:

My problem is that my business is failing. I am <u>vexed</u> by <u>debt</u>, <u>slipping</u> sales, and the <u>prattle</u> of my competitors. Should I borrow more money or just quit? Signed, In Trouble

Dear Mr. Trouble:

Forgive my <u>punning</u>, but don't borrow, Trouble! Avoid the <u>temptations</u> of quitting or worsening your debt. <u>Reverses</u> and <u>relapses</u> are a part of business life. Remember your goals when you started out. Think of a new way to achieve them.

Writing

You may use this Writing lesson as timed-writing practice, or you may allow students to develop the essay as a writing assignment over several days.

1. Before students begin to work on this assignment, demonstrate the use of the chart by working as a class to identify one effect of Franklin's plan for self-improvement. For example, his focus on the virtue of Temperance (cause) gave Franklin a lifetime of good health (effect).

2. Remind students to establish the relative importance of each of the effects they have identified. Because they will be using an order-of-importance pattern, they should not present effects in the order they appear in *The Autobiography*. They will want to reserve their strongest example for last.

3. Before students begin to revise their drafts, review the chart of transitional words and phrases. Ask volunteers to use each word or phrase in a sentence.

4. Use the **Rubrics for Cause-and-Effect Essays**, *Professional Development Guidebook*, pages 264–265, to evaluate students' work.

154

PERFORMANCE TASKS
Integrated Language Skills

Writing

Informative Text In both life and literature, cause-and-effect relationships are far more complex than "A caused B." Often, one cause has multiple effects. Likewise, an effect can prompt other results, or new effects. In addition, while some effects can be anticipated, many are unforeseen and even surprising. Write an **analytical essay** in which you identify and explain the multiple effects of Benjamin Franklin's plan for self-improvement.

Prewriting Review *The Autobiography*, looking for events, changes, and insights that happened as a result of Franklin's plan. Use a chart like the one shown to identify multiple effects. After completing the chart, rank the effects from most important to least important.

Model: Identifying Multiple Effects

Cause	Effects

Drafting Start with a strong first sentence. You might use one of Franklin's aphorisms as a launching point. In the opening paragraph, state the topic of your essay and your *thesis*, or main idea. Then, follow these steps to structure the body of your essay:

- Describe the effects of Franklin's plan, devoting one paragraph to each effect. Make sure that each paragraph has a clear main idea.
- Follow *order-of-importance organization*, beginning with the least important effect and building toward the most important effect.
- In your conclusion, *summarize* the cause-and-effect relationships you have discussed.

Revising Reread your essay, making sure you have carefully explained the connections among your ideas. Consider reading your essay aloud so that you can hear sections that sound awkward or do not flow logically. Locate points in the text where the addition of *transitional words and phrases* will help clarify the flow of your ideas.

Transitional Words and Phrases	
as a result	outcome
because	since
for the reason that	therefore
in consequence	with the result that

154 Beginnings–1800

Common Core State Standards

Writing
2.a. Introduce a topic; organize complex ideas, concepts, and information so that each new element builds on that which precedes it to create a unified whole.
2.c. Use appropriate and varied transitions and syntax to link the major sections of the text, create cohesion, and clarify the relationships among complex ideas and concepts.
2.f. Provide a concluding statement or section that follows from and supports the information or explanation presented.

Language
3.a. Vary syntax for effect.

Teaching Resources

Unit 1 Resources
L3 L4 **Vocabulary Builder**, p. 211.
L3 L4 **Support for Writing**, p. 213.
L3 L4 **Grammar and Style**, p. 212.
L4 **Enrichment**, p. 214.

All *Professional Development Guidebook*
Rubrics for Self-Assessment: *Cause-and-Effect Essay*, pp. 264–265

All *Common Core Companion,*
pp. 196–207; 322–323

All **Enriched Online Student Edition**
Interactive Grammar Lesson: available under After You Read for this selection
Internet Research Activity: available under After You Read for this selection

PHLit Online! All resources are available at **www.PHLitOnline.com.**

Conventions and Style: Subordinating Conjunctions

To increase the sentence variety in your writing, use subordinating conjunctions to combine short sentences. **Subordinating conjunctions** are words or phrases that join two complete ideas by making one idea subordinate to, or dependent on, the other. When you use **subordination,** you show which idea is more important.

Common Subordinating Conjunctions

after	as though	if	unless
although	because	since	until
as if	before	so that	when
as long as	even though	than	where

Using Subordinating Conjunctions

Short Sentences: Ben Franklin moved to Philadelphia. He had very little money.
Combined: Benjamin Franklin had very little money *when* he moved to Philadelphia.

Short Sentences: Franklin used a pseudonym. Franklin became known as a good writer.
Combined: *Even though* he used a pseudonym, Franklin became known as a good writer.

Short Sentences: He would have to be more careful. He wanted to attain moral perfection.
Combined: He would have to be more careful *if* he wanted to attain moral perfection.

Punctuation Tip: When the dependent clause comes first in a sentence, use a comma between the clauses. When the independent clause comes first, do not separate the clauses with a comma.

© Writing and Speaking Conventions

A. Writing For each item, write a sentence that joins the two ideas using an appropriate subordinating conjunction.

1. he wrote the book—his friends encouraged him
2. Franklin made a chart—he could track his progress
3. you follow these rules—you will be a better person

   Example: He wrote the book *after* his friends encouraged him.

B. Speaking Make up two aphorisms that could each be a refrain for a song. Correctly use subordinating conjunctions in your refrains.

Practice In items 1–5, add a subordinating conjunction to complete each sentence. In items 6–10, combine the two sentences using a subordinating conjunction.

1. Do not speak _____ you have something beneficial to say.
2. Practice temperance _____ you eat and drink.
3. Franklin worked on improving himself _____ it were his life's project.
4. _____ you speak, make sure your words are sincere.
5. _____ a line has no marks, he is improving in that particular category.
6. All things should have a place and time. Order is important.
7. Franklin listed the virtues in a certain order. This way, he could work through them methodically.
8. He tried. He did not achieve moral perfection.
9. People enjoyed the *Almanack*. The proverbs were entertaining.
10. You should use your time wisely. There is never enough of it.

PH WRITING COACH

Further instruction and practice are available in *Prentice Hall Writing Coach*.

Extended Study: Integrated Language Skills **155**

Conventions and Style

1. Introduce and discuss the skill, using the instruction on the student page.
2. Have students complete the Practice and Writing and Speaking Conventions activities.

Practice

1. unless
2. when
3. as if *or* as though
4. When *or* If
5. If *or* Where

Sample answers:

6. All things should have a time and place <u>because</u> order is important.
7. Franklin listed the virtues in a certain order <u>so that</u> he could work through them methodically.
8. <u>Although</u> he tried, he did not achieve moral perfection.
9. People enjoyed the *Almanack* <u>because</u> the proverbs were entertaining.
10. <u>Because</u> there is never enough of it, you should use your time wisely.

Writing and Speaking Conventions

A. Sample answers:

1. He wrote the book <u>because</u> his friends encouraged him.
2. Franklin made a chart <u>so that</u> he could track his progress.
3. <u>If</u> you follow these rules, you will be a better person.

B. Sample answers:

You can't fall in love <u>if</u> you wear a parachute.

You'll know love's work is done <u>when</u> two hearts beat as one.

PH WRITING COACH Grade 11

Students will find additional information on subordinating conjunctions in Chapter 13.

Extend the Lesson

Sentence Modeling

Write the following sentence from the selection on the board

> *Three may keep a secret if two of them are dead.*

Ask students what they notice about this sentence. Elicit from them that the main clause and the subordinate clause are joined by *if*. Now rewrite the sentence, placing the subordinate clause first, followed by a comma. Ask students what they notice about the revised sentence. Lead students to recognize that the revised sentence has lost the jolt of surprise that it had when *dead* was the last word. Have students rewrite Practice items 8, 9, and 10, placing the subordinate clauses both first and last in the sentences. Discuss which is most effective. Finally, have students imitate Franklin's sentence in a sentence on a topic of their own choosing, incorporating each grammatical and stylistic feature discussed. Ask volunteers to share their results with the class.

155

**Ⓒ Common Core
State Standards**

- Reading Informational Text 3
- Writing 9, 10
- Language 6

**❶ Self-Portraits in
American Literature**

1. Have students study the writers listed and their portraits. Invite students to share what they may know about these writers and any of the works that they have read.

2. Point out to students that most of the writers and works listed are represented in this anthology and may be encountered in later reading assignments. Sandra Cisneros, the last writer listed, is the author of the next selection they will read, "Straw Into Gold."

3. Point out that many readers prefer to read "true life" accounts by real people, rather than fiction.
Ask: Why are people attracted to autobiographical accounts?
Possible response: Students may say that some people prefer the authenticity of reading about events that really happened and gaining the personal insights earned by a writer's actual experiences.

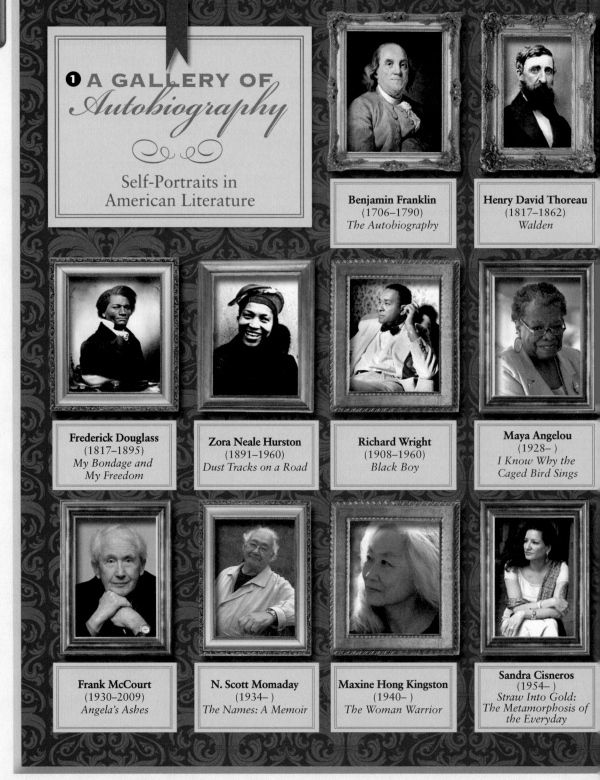

❶ A GALLERY OF
Autobiography

Self-Portraits in
American Literature

Benjamin Franklin
(1706–1790)
The Autobiography

Henry David Thoreau
(1817–1862)
Walden

Frederick Douglass
(1817–1895)
*My Bondage and
My Freedom*

Zora Neale Hurston
(1891–1960)
Dust Tracks on a Road

Richard Wright
(1908–1960)
Black Boy

Maya Angelou
(1928–)
*I Know Why the
Caged Bird Sings*

Frank McCourt
(1930–2009)
Angela's Ashes

N. Scott Momaday
(1934–)
The Names: A Memoir

Maxine Hong Kingston
(1940–)
The Woman Warrior

Sandra Cisneros
(1954–)
*Straw Into Gold:
The Metamorphosis of
the Everyday*

Comparing Literary Works

from *The Autobiography* by Benjamin Franklin • *"Straw Into Gold: The Metamorphosis of the Everyday"* by Sandra Cisneros

❷ Comparing Autobiographies Past and Present

Autobiographical Writing The first autobiography was the *Confessions* of St. Augustine, which was written in Latin sometime around A.D. 400. The form did not appear in English, though, until the late 1700s. It was during this "Golden Age" of nonfiction that Benjamin Franklin wrote his *Autobiography*. In doing so, he created a model for the American success story.

Over the next two centuries, major American autobiographies such as the *Narrative of the Life of Frederick Douglass* (1845) and Zora Neale Hurston's *Dust Tracks on a Road* (1942) paved the way for other related forms of nonfiction. These include *memoirs*, which are smaller in scope and less formal in tone, and *autobiographical essays,* which focus on a small slice of the writer's life in order to explore larger ideas. "Straw Into Gold," by Sandra Cisneros, is an example of an autobiographical essay.

These selections highlight some of the ways that American autobiography has evolved. They reflect vastly different historical periods and cultures as well as changing attitudes toward social status and gender. Despite these differences, both address a powerful American *theme*—success. As you read "Straw Into Gold," use a chart like the one shown to compare and contrast Franklin's and Cisneros's ideas about success.

	Franklin	Cisneros
What is success?		
What are its costs?		
What are its rewards?		

ⓒ Gather Vocabulary Knowledge

Sandra Cisneros uses related forms of the words *venture, nomad,* and *vagabond.* Use a **dictionary** to find each word's part of speech and definition. Then, employ other references to further explore these words:

- **History of Language:** Use a history of English to research each word's origins. Write a paragraph about the word's emergence in English.
- **Book of Quotations:** Use an online or print collection of quotations to find a statement or passage containing one of the words. In a paragraph, explain nuances in meaning that are evident from the context of the quotation.

Comparing References Compare and contrast what you learn about the words from each specialized reference.

ⓒ **Common Core State Standards**

Reading Informational Text
3. Analyze a complex set of ideas or sequence of events and explain how specific individuals, ideas, or events interact and develop over the course of the text.

Language
6. Demonstrate independence in gathering vocabulary knowledge when considering a word or phrase important to comprehension or expression.

PHLit Online!
www.PHLitOnline.com

from The Autobiography • Straw Into Gold: The Metamorphosis of the Everyday **157**

❷ Comparing Autobiographies Past and Present

1. Introduce autobiographical writing, using the instruction on the student page.

2. Encourage students to use a chart similar to the one shown to record similarities and differences they find in Franklin's and Cisneros's ideas about success.

Think Aloud: Model the Skill

Say to students:

When I am reading and comparing autobiographical narratives, I focus on how the writers' thinking changes from the time they experience an event to the time, perhaps years later, when they write about it. For example, as a young man Franklin was confident that moral perfection was possible. By the time he wrote about his attempts at moral improvement in the *Autobiography,* an older Franklin realized that perfection was impossible, though trying to be a better person produced many benefits.

❸ Gather Vocabulary Knowledge

Have online and print resources available for students to use as they research word origins and quotations. Display the proverb "Nothing ventured, nothing gained" and discuss with students how the contrast in the quotation helps them understand the meaning of *ventured* in this context.

Teaching Resources

The following resources can be used to enrich, extend, or differentiate the instruction.

All *Unit 1 Resources,* pp. 224–226

All Enriched Online Student Edition

All *Common Core Companion,* pp. 61–67, 116–122, 261–276

PHLit Online! All resources are available online at **www.PHLitOnline.com.**

Daily Bellringer

For each class during which you will teach this selection, have students complete one day of the five activities remaining for the appropriate week in the *Daily Bellringer Activities* booklet.

Multidraft Reading

To assist struggling readers and to enhance reading for all, assign the text in chunks as warranted by length and apply multidraft reading protocols. For each reading, have students set the purpose indicated:

- **First reading**—identifying key ideas and details and answering any Reading Checks.

- **Second reading**—analyzing craft and structure and responding to the side-column prompts.

- **Third reading**—integrating knowledge and ideas, connecting to other texts and the world, and answering the end-of-selection questions.

For more guidance, refer to the *Classroom Strategies and Teaching Routines* card on multidraft reading.

---

❹ Background

More About the Author

As a young girl, Sandra Cisneros felt the lack of a "normal" childhood like the ones she saw on television shows such as *Leave It to Beaver* and *Father Knows Best.* She had, she says, "seven fathers," or six brothers and a father, and was lonely for a sister and female friends.

Cisneros did not take writing seriously until her first creative writing class in college. She deliberately developed a writing style different from that of her classmates.

In "Ghosts and Voices: Writing From Obsession," Cisneros writes, "If I were asked what it is I write about, I would have to say I write about those ghosts that haunt me, that will not let me sleep, of that which even memory does not like to mention."

❹ Sandra Cisneros (b. 1954)

Author of "Straw Into Gold: The Metamorphosis of the Everyday"

Sandra Cisneros was born in Chicago into a large Mexican American family. Because her family was poor, Cisneros moved frequently and lived for the most part in small, cramped apartments. To cope with these conditions, she retreated into herself and spent much of her time reading fairy tales and classic literature.

Embracing Her Heritage Cisneros attended Loyola University in Chicago and, later, the prestigious Writer's Workshop at the University of Iowa. During her college years, Cisneros met writers from many other backgrounds. At first uncomfortable about her family's struggles, she soon realized that her heritage provided her with something unique. She began writing about her childhood in a book of connected short stories. *The House on Mango Street,* published in 1984, ushered Cisneros into the literary limelight.

Charting Her Success Cisneros's second book, *Woman Hollering Creek* (1991), confirmed her status as an important American writer. Since then, Cisneros has penned dozens of books, essays, poems, articles, and collections. Her most recent novel, *Caramelo* (2002), was selected for the Today Show Book Club and as notable book of the year by *The New York Times Book Review,* among others. Of her desire to write about her family and community, Cisneros has said, "I feel like a cartographer; I'm determined to fill a literary void."

All Autobiography? Translated into more than a dozen languages and taught in schools and universities around the world, Cisneros's works have not only filled a literary void, but charted new territory for writers who work in a semi-autobiographical vein. Frequently asked whether her fictional stories are "true" and whether she is their "main character," Cisneros responds: *"Yes, but no. . . . . I write what I see . . . or what happened to me that I can't forget, but also what happened to others I love, or what strangers have told me happened to them. . . . I take all of this and cut and paste it together to make a story, because in real life a story doesn't have shape, and it's the writer that gives it a beginning, a middle, and an end."*

①② STRAW INTO GOLD:
The Metamorphosis Of The Everyday

SANDRA CISNEROS

BACKGROUND The term "essay" from ❸ the French *essai,* meaning "try," historically described an exploratory piece of writing that lacked finish. Eventually, the essay lost its original "unfinished" sense and became a polished form of writing. Here, Sandra Cisneros recounts part of her own growth from "unfinished" to accomplished writer.

When I was living in an artists' colony in the south of France, some fellow Latin-Americans who taught at the university in Aix-en-Provence[1] invited me to share a home-cooked meal with them. I had been living abroad almost a year then on an NEA[2] grant, subsisting mainly on French bread and lentils while in France so that my money could last longer. So when the invitation to dinner arrived, I accepted without hesitation. Especially since they had promised Mexican food.

---

1. **Aix-en-Provence** (eks än prō väns´) city in southeastern France.
2. **NEA** National Endowment for the Arts.

Straw Into Gold: The Metamorphosis of the Everyday **159**

4 Comparing Autobiographies

1. Have students review the bracketed passage. **Ask:** What two challenges does Cisneros link together in this passage? **Answer:** Cisneros must make corn tortillas for the first time in her life, and she must write a critical essay for her MFA exam.

2. Then, **ask** the Comparing Autobiographies question: Are the challenges Cisneros describes similar in any way to those Franklin set for himself? Explain. **Possible responses:** Some students may note that both Cisneros and Franklin face experiences that are new to them. Cisneros has never written a critical essay or made corn tortillas; Franklin has never tried a program of moral improvement. The challenges of each require a step-by-step process. Other students may stress differences: Cisneros's challenges are imposed by others; Franklin's are imposed by himself. Cisneros's challenges involve skill and knowledge; Franklin's challenges involve self-control and behavior.

Comparing Autobiographies

Are the challenges Cisneros describes similar in any way to those Franklin set for himself? Explain.

Vocabulary

intuitively (in tōō′ i tiv lē) *adv.* without having to be taught; instinctively

capable (kā′ pə bəl) *adj.* having the skills needed to do something

---

What I didn't realize when they made this invitation was that I was supposed to be involved in preparing this meal. I guess they assumed I knew how to cook Mexican food because I was Mexican. They wanted specifically tortillas, though I'd never made a tortilla in my life.

It's true I had witnessed my mother rolling the little armies of dough into perfect circles, but my mother's family is from Guanajuato,[3] *provinciales*,[4] country folk. They only know how to make flour tortillas. My father's family, on the other hand, is chilango,[5] from Mexico City. We ate corn tortillas but we didn't make them. Someone was sent to the corner tortilleria to buy some. I'd never seen anybody make corn tortillas. Ever.

4 Well, somehow my Latino hosts had gotten a hold of a packet of corn flour, and this is what they tossed my way with orders to produce tortillas. *Asi como sea.* Any ol' way, they said and went back to their cooking.

Why did I feel like the woman in the fairy tale who was locked in a room and ordered to spin straw into gold? I had the same sick feeling when I was required to write my critical essay for my MFA[6] exam—the only piece of noncreative writing necessary in order to get my graduate degree. How was I to start? There were rules involved here, unlike writing a poem or story, which I did intuitively. There was a step-by-step process needed and I had better know it. I felt as if making tortillas, or writing a critical paper for that matter, were tasks so impossible I wanted to break down into tears.

Somehow though, I managed to make those tortillas—crooked and burnt, but edible nonetheless. My hosts were absolutely ignorant when it came to Mexican food; they thought my tortillas were delicious. (I'm glad my mama wasn't there.) Thinking back and looking at that photograph documenting the three of us consuming those lopsided circles I am amazed. Just as I am amazed I could finish my MFA exam (lopsided and crooked, but finished all the same). Didn't think I could do it. But I did.

I've managed to do a lot of things in my life I didn't think I was capable of and which many others didn't think me capable of either.

Especially because I am a woman, a Latina, an only daughter in a family of six men. My father would've liked to

---

3. **Guanajuato** (gwä′ nä hwä′ tō) state in central Mexico.
4. **provinciales** (prō bēn sē ä′ lās) "country folk" (Spanish).
5. **chilango** (chē län′ gō) "city folk" (Spanish).
6. **MFA** Master of Fine Arts.

Think Aloud

Vocabulary: Using Context
Point out to students that the subtitle of this essay, "The Metamorphosis of the Everyday" includes a word they may not know. Say to students:

I may not know the meaning of *metamorphosis,* but I notice that it contains *morph.* I know that in movies, *morphing* describes a special effect in which something completely changes shape. I notice that the title, "Straw Into ...Gold," refers to a complete change. I also see that the title page includes the image of a butterfly emerging from a cocoon, another example of something (a caterpillar) transforming into something else (a butterfly). I think *metamorphosis* refers to a complete change or transformation.

5

La molendera (The grinder), Diego Rivera (1886–1957), 1926, oil on canvas, Museo Nacional de Arte Moderno, Instituto Nacional de Bellas Artes, Mexico City, D.F., Mexico, ©Banco de Mexico Diego Rivera & Frida Kahlo Museums Trust, Av. Cinco de Mayo No. 2, Col. Centro, Del. Cuauhtemoc 06059, Mexico, D.F., reproduction authorized by the Instituto Nacional de Bellas Artes y Literatura.

6 ◀ **Critical Viewing**
Judging from this painting by Mexican artist Diego Rivera, explain the challenge tortilla making would present to someone who had never done it before. **[Connect]**

Vocabulary
taboo (ta boo´) *n.* something forbidden within a particular society or culture

have seen me married long ago. In our culture, men and women don't leave their father's house except by way of marriage. I crossed my father's threshold with nothing carrying me but my own two feet. A woman whom no one came for and no one chased away.

To make matters worse, I had left before any of my six brothers had ventured away from home. I had broken a terrible taboo. Somehow, looking back at photos of myself as a child, I wonder if I was aware of having begun already my own quiet war.

I like to think that somehow my family, my Mexicanness, my poverty all had something to do with shaping me into a writer. I like to think my parents were preparing me all along for my life as an artist even though they didn't know it. From my father I inherited a love of wandering. He was born in Mexico City but as a young man he traveled into the U.S. vagabonding. He eventually was drafted and thus became a citizen. Some of the stories he has told about his first months in the U.S. with little or no English surface in my stories in *The House on Mango Street* as well as others I have in mind to write in the future. From him I inherited a sappy heart. (He still cries when he watches the Mexican soaps—especially if they deal with children who have forsaken their parents.)

7 **Reading Check**
What Mexican dish was Cisneros asked to prepare?

Straw Into Gold: The Metamorphosis of the Everyday **161**

5 **Humanities**

The Grinder, 1924, Diego Rivera

Diego Rivera (1886–1957) was a Mexican artist best known for densely populated, detail-filled public murals that display the culture, life, and history of Mexico. Rivera studied modern art in Europe and became influential in the Cubism movement. On return to Mexico, he took a new direction as a muralist, blending modern art with ancient Mexican traditions. His distinctive style presents figures that are at once simple and epic, characteristics that are evident in his subject in *The Grinder.* Use these questions for discussion:

1. The figure of the woman dominates this painting. What do you think Rivera is suggesting by focusing so completely on the woman?
   Possible response: Students may suggest that the strong visual emphasis on the woman makes her seem important, even heroic. Rivera may intend to honor the woman's simple but vital work in preparing food.

2. Based on details in the painting, what impression do you have of the woman?
   Possible response: Some students may say that the woman's figure, posture, and facial expression show physical strength, dignity, and purpose. Other students may find in her bowed head and seemingly closed eyes a passive acceptance of drudgery.

6 **Critical Viewing**

Possible response: Students may suggest that someone unfamiliar with the process would lack the skill to grind the corn to the necessary fineness or to effectively operate the stove shown in the painting.

7 **Reading Check**

Answer: Cisneros was asked to prepare corn tortillas.

161

1. Read aloud the bracketed passage. **Ask:** What does Cisneros mean by "hunger" in this passage?

Answer: Students should recognize that Cisneros is referring to a yearning, desire, or longing that has nothing to do with physical appetite.

2. **Ask** the Comparing Autobiographies question: Why do you think Cisneros does not go into greater detail about the nature of her "hunger"?

Answer: Cisneros probably cannot go into greater detail because she is too young and inexperienced to recognize this feeling as a need for personal expression, or as ambition, dissatisfaction, or a longing for change or adventure.

▶ **Monitor Progress** Have students consider the Franklin excerpt in terms of "hunger." **Ask:** Does Franklin's quest for moral perfection suggest that he, too, is experiencing a hunger? **Possible response:** Students may say that Franklin's deep study of virtue and his highly organized and continuous program of moral perfection reflect a "hunger" for self-improvement. Though Franklin's tone throughout is matter-of-fact, his extraordinary efforts to be good—in no less than thirteen categories—may be evidence of a yearning or longing.

Vocabulary
nostalgia (nä stal´jə) *n.*
a longing for something

Comparing Autobiographies
Why do you think Cisneros does not go into greater detail about the nature of her "hunger"?

162 Beginnings–1800

My mother was born like me—in Chicago but of Mexican descent. It would be her tough, streetwise voice that would haunt all my stories and poems. An amazing woman who loves to draw and read books and can sing an opera. A smart cookie.

When I was a little girl we traveled to Mexico City so much I thought my grandparents' house on La Fortuna, Number 12, was home. It was the only constant in our nomadic ramblings from one Chicago flat to another. The house on Destiny Street, Number 12, in the colonia Tepeyac,[7] would be perhaps the only home I knew, and that nostalgia for a home would be a theme that would obsess me.

My brothers also figured greatly in my art. Especially the oldest two; I grew up in their shadows. Henry, the second oldest and my favorite, appears often in poems I have written and in stories which at times only borrow his nickname, Kiki. He played a major role in my childhood. We were bunkbed mates. We were co-conspirators. We were pals. Until my oldest brother came back from studying in Mexico and left me odd-woman-out for always.

What would my teachers say if they knew I was a writer? Who would've guessed it? I wasn't a very bright student. I didn't much like school because we moved so much and I was always new and funny-looking. In my fifth-grade report card, I have nothing but an avalanche of C's and D's, but I don't remember being that stupid. I was good at art and I read plenty of library books and Kiki laughed at all my jokes. At home I was fine, but at school I never opened my mouth except when the teacher called on me, the first time I'd speak all day.

When I think how I see myself, it would have to be at age eleven. I know I'm thirty-two on the outside, but inside I'm eleven. I'm the girl in the picture with skinny arms and a crumpled shirt and crooked hair. I didn't like school because all they saw was the outside me. School was lots of rules and sitting with your hands folded and being very afraid all the time. I liked looking out the window and thinking. I liked staring at the girl across the way writing her name over and over again in red ink. I wondered why the boy with the dirty collar in front of me didn't have a mama who took better care of him.

I think my mama and papa did the best they could to keep us warm and clean and never hungry. We had birthday and graduation parties and things like that, but there was another hunger that had to be fed. There was a hunger I didn't even have a name for. Was this when I began writing?

---

7. **colonia Tepeyac** (cô lō´ nēä tä pä´ yäc) district of Mexico City.

162

In 1966 we moved into a house, a real one, our first real home. This meant we didn't have to change schools and be the new kids on the block every couple of years. We could make friends and not be afraid we'd have to say goodbye to them and start all over. My brothers and the flock of boys they brought home would become important characters eventually for my stories—Louie and his cousins, Meme Ortiz and his dog with two names, one in English and one in Spanish.

My mother flourished in her own home. She took books out of the library and taught herself to garden, producing flowers so envied we had to put a lock on the gate to keep out the midnight flower thieves. My mother is still gardening to this day.

This was the period in my life, that slippery age when you are both child and woman and neither, I was to record in *The House on Mango Street*. I was still shy. I was a girl who couldn't come out of her shell.

How was I to know I would be recording and documenting the women who sat their sadness on an elbow and stared out a window? It would be the city streets of Chicago I would later record, but from a child's eyes.

I've done all kinds of things I didn't think I could do since then. I've gone to a prestigious university, studied with famous writers, and taken away an MFA degree. I've taught poetry in the schools in Illinois and Texas. I've gotten an NEA grant and run away with it as far as my courage would take me. I've seen the bleached and bitter mountains of the Peloponnesus.[8] I've lived on a Greek island. I've been to Venice[9] twice. In Rapallo, I met Ilona once and forever and took her sad heart with me across the south of France and into Spain.

I've lived in Yugoslavia. I've been to the famous Nice[10] flower market behind the opera house. I've lived in a village in the pre-Alps[11] and witnessed the daily parade of promenaders.

I've moved since Europe to the strange and wonderful country of Texas, land of polaroid-blue skies and big bugs. I met a mayor with my last name. I met famous Chicana/o artists and writers and *politicos*.[12]

Texas is another chapter in my life. It brought with it the Dobie-Paisano Fellowship, a six-month residency on a 265-acre ranch. But most important Texas brought Mexico back to me.

---

8. **Peloponnesus** (pel´ ə pə nē´ səs) peninsula forming the southeastern part of the Greek mainland.
9. **Venice** (ven´ is) seaport in northern Italy.
10. **Nice** (nēs) seaport and resort in southeastern France.
11. **pre-Alps** foothills of the Alps, a mountain range in south-central Europe.
12. **politicos** (pō lē´ tē cōs) "politicians" (Spanish).

Vocabulary

flourished (flʉr´ isht) *v.* grew strong, healthy, and happy; prospered

10  Reading Check

What happened to change Cisneros's life in 1966?

---

9 **Comparing Autobiographies**

1. Remind students that Franklin's *Autobiography* presents the viewpoint of an older man describing the activities of his younger self. This perspective allows Franklin to show both the ambitious idealism of his youth and his "older but wiser" thoughts about attaining perfect virtue.

2. Have students read the bracketed passage. Then, **ask:** At what age is Cisneros "on the outside" as she writes this essay? How old does she feel inside?
   Answer: Cisneros is thirty-two on the outside, but she feels like eleven on the inside.

3. **Ask:** What differences exist between Cisneros's outside and inside selves?
   Possible response: As a child, Cisneros feels that she is seen as a quiet student with below-average grades. Because her family moves so much, she always feels "new and funny-looking." On the inside (or at home), Cisneros is confident in her artistic talent and her sense of humor; she is a reader of library books and asks herself imaginative questions.

4. **Ask** students whether they feel Cisneros's sense of having an "inside" and an "outside" self, or of feeling a different age than one's actual years, is unique or unusual.
   Possible responses: Students' answers will vary based on their own life experiences. Some students may report having similar feelings to those described by Cisneros.

10 **Reading Check**
Answer: In 1966 Cisneros's family moved into a house, their first real home.

Differentiated Instruction for Universal Access

Support for Special-Needs Students
Bring a globe or world map to class and work with students to identify the places in Europe that Cisneros lived in or visited. Locate the places in North America where she was born (Chicago), went to school (Iowa), taught (Illinois and Texas), and visited relatives (Mexico City).

Enrichment for Gifted/Talented Students
In a sense, Cisneros presents her life story as a kind of roadmap of places she has lived in and visited. Ask students to create a poster-sized world map that shows all the places she mentions in her essay. Using details from the essay and further research, have students annotate the map with information about what Cisneros did (studied, taught, wrote, lectured) at each place.

Before students respond, you may wish to have them write a brief objective summary of the selection. As they answer the questions below, remind them to support their answers with evidence from the text.

1. (a) Being asked to make corn tortillas brings to Cisneros's mind the woman who had to spin straw into gold. (b) She is trying to point out that difficult experiences can be valuable. (c) Cisneros drew from her good and bad experiences to become a writer, thus turning straw into gold.

2. (a) Cisneros left home without being married. Girls were expected to remain with their parents until they wed. (b) The enemy in Cisneros's quiet war is traditional definitions of what women are supposed to do and be.

3. (a) Cisneros feels that she is eleven "on the inside." (b) At eleven, she appeared to be quiet and timid, with limited intelligence and imagination. Inside she is thoughtful, bright, observant, and rebellious.

4. (a) Traditional expectations for a Latina from a poor family were obstacles for Cisneros. (b) Cisneros's family acquired a home and stopped traveling so much. She went to college and discovered her gift for writing. She developed her own voice as a writer and drew on her experiences for subject matter.

5. (a) The main point of the essay is that writers draw on their life experiences ("straw") to make literature ("gold"). Cisneros demonstrates this with examples from her own life. (b) Students may comment on learning from one's life experiences.

Sitting at my favorite people-watching spot, the snaky Woolworth's counter across the street from the Alamo,[13] I can't think of anything else I'd rather be than a writer. I've traveled and lectured from Cape Cod to San Francisco, to Spain, Yugoslavia, Greece, Mexico, France, Italy, and finally today to Seguin, Texas. Along the way there is straw for the taking. With a little imagination, it can be spun into gold.

---

13. **the Alamo** (al′ ə mō′) mission in San Antonio, Texas, that was the scene of a famous battle between Texans and Mexican troops in 1836.

Critical Reading

Cite textual evidence to support your responses.

1. **Key Ideas and Details (a)** Which experience reminds Cisneros of the story of the woman who had to spin straw into gold? **(b) Interpret:** What point is she trying to make through this anecdote? **(c) Connect:** What connections does Cisneros draw between this story and her life?

2. **Key Ideas and Details (a)** What was the taboo Cisneros broke when she left her family home? **(b) Analyze:** Who was the enemy in the "quiet war" Cisneros had begun?

3. **Key Ideas and Details (a)** How old is Cisneros "on the inside"? **(b) Analyze:** In what ways does her description of herself at that age represent a divide between her inner sense of self and her external realities?

4. **Key Ideas and Details (a)** Which obstacles stood in the way of Cisneros's becoming a writer? **(b) Analyze:** What circumstances contributed to her success?

5. **Key Ideas and Details (a)** What is the main point of the essay? Support your answer. **(b) Apply:** In what ways could you apply Cisneros's message to your own life?

After You Read | from *The Autobiography* • *Straw Into Gold*

Comparing Autobiography Past and Present

1. **Key Ideas and Details** **(a)** What facts about Franklin do you learn from reading his **autobiography** on pages 141–146? **(b)** What facts about Cisneros do you learn from reading her **autobiographical essay**?

2. **Key Ideas and Details** What information other than basic facts do you learn about each writer from these works? Cite details to support your answers.

3. **Key Ideas and Details** **(a)** What details does Cisneros include that you would find surprising in Franklin's writing? **(b)** Is this due to the time period, the writer's gender, the writer's cultural background, or another element? Explain.

4. **Integration of Knowledge and Ideas** **(a)** Judging from these two texts, how has American autobiography changed from the eighteenth to the twenty-first centuries? **(b)** In what ways is the genre the same? Support your answers with details from the texts.

Timed Writing

Explanatory Text: Essay

Even though Franklin and Cisneros faced different obstacles, the *theme* of success—how to achieve it, what it is, and what it means—is a key element in both of their autobiographical works.

Assignment: Write an **essay** in which you *compare and contrast* each writer's ideas about success. Cite evidence from the texts to support your ideas. Use these questions to focus your analysis. **[40 minutes]**

- What challenges does each writer face? Are the challenges self-imposed, or do they come from without?
- What conclusions about success does each writer draw?
- Do these autobiographical works reveal connections between American identity and ideas of achievement or success?

Organize your ideas logically. You might focus on the features of one selection and then the features of the other. Alternatively, you might focus on points of similarity and difference, moving back and forth between the two selections.

5-Minute Planner

Complete these steps before you begin to write:

1. Read the assignment carefully. List key words and phrases.
2. Scan the autobiographies for evidence that relates to the ideas in your list. **TIP** As you scan the texts, jot down quotations or details that you might use in your essay.
3. Create a rough outline for your essay.
4. Reread the prompt, and draft your essay.

from The Autobiography • Straw Into Gold: The Metamorphosis of the Everyday **165**

Common Core State Standards

Writing

9. Draw evidence from literary or informational texts to support analysis, reflection, and research.

10. Write routinely over extended time frames and shorter time frames for a range of tasks, purposes, and audiences.

USE ACADEMIC VOCABULARY

As you write, use academic language, including the following words or their related forms:

    categorize
    examine
    insight
    perception

For more on academic language, see the vocabulary charts in the introductory unit in this book.

Answers

Comparing Autobiographies Past and Present

1. **(a) Sample response:** Franklin was a journeyman printer when he identified thirteen virtues and kept records of his efforts to achieve them. **(b)** Cisneros was the only daughter in a large Mexican American family. Born in Chicago, she has lived in many different places; she earned an MFA degree and has published several books.

2. **Sample response:** Franklin's habits show that he is both logical and methodical. By leaving home, Cisneros shows that she is independent.

3. **(a)** Cisneros includes more discussion of her feelings and relationships; Franklin's focus on his own self-improvement seems to preclude references to others. **(b) Possible response:** Some students may note that writers in Franklin's time were more formal than modern writers.

4. **Possible responses: (a)** Students may note than modern autobiography is both more informal in style and more personal in scope than autobiography in the eighteenth century. **(b)** Frankness is valued in both. Both Franklin and Cisneros give facts about their lives and share even details that show them at a disadvantage, such as Franklin's failures and Cisneros's shyness.

Timed Writing

1. Teach the Academic Vocabulary. Discuss the words, as well as their related forms, including *category, examination,* and *interpretation.* Review with students the vocabulary they learned before reading the selection, and encourage them to use *venture, vagabond,* and *nomad* when discussing the challenges Cisneros faced.

2. Use the prompt to help students identify elements and qualities their comparison and contrast essay should have:

   - A thesis statement about the relationship between the ideas of success in the two works
   - Specific examples of the challenges each writer faced and how they shaped his or her ideas about success

- Evidence, including text details, to support the thesis statement
- A logical organization that makes the similarities and differences clear

Encourage students to focus on these points when they are planning and revising their essays.

Tell students they will have 40 minutes to plan and write the essay. Call students' attention to the 5-Minute Planner. Encourage students to budget their time to allow 5 minutes for outlining, 5 minutes for identifying some initial supporting text references in the works, and 10 minutes for revision and proofreading.

• *from* The Interesting Narrative of the Life of Olaudah Equiano
Lesson Pacing Guide

DAY 1 Preteach

- © Administer the Reading and Vocabulary Warm-ups (*Unit 1 Resources,* pp. 231–234) as necessary.
- © Introduce the Literary Analysis concept: Slave Narrative.
- • Introduce the Reading Strategy: Summarize.
- © Build background with the author and Background features.
- • Develop thematic thinking with Connecting to the Essential Question.
- © Teach the selection vocabulary.

DAYS 2–3 Preteach/Teach/Assess

- • Distribute copies of the appropriate graphic organizer for the Reading Strategy (*Graphic Organizer Transparencies,* pp. 47–48).
- • Distribute copies of the appropriate graphic organizer for Literary Analysis (*Graphic Organizer Transparencies,* pp. 49–50).
- • Prepare students to read with the Activating Prior Knowledge activities (TE).
- • Informally monitor comprehension while students read.
- • Use the Reading Check questions to confirm comprehension.
- • Reinforce vocabulary with the Vocabulary notes.
- • Assess students' comprehension and mastery of the skills by having them answer the Critical Reading, Literary Analysis, and Reading Strategy questions.
- © Have students complete the Vocabulary Lesson.

DAY 4 Extend/Assess

- © Have students complete the Writing Lesson and write a museum placard. (You may assign as homework.)
- • Have students read and respond to the Contemporary Commentary.
- • Administer Selection Test A or B (*Unit 1 Resources,* pp. 243–245 or 246–248).

© Common Core State Standards

Reading Informational Text
2. Determine two or more central ideas of a text and analyze their development over the course of the text, including how they interact and build on one another to provide a complex analysis; provide an objective summary of the text.
9. Analyze eighteenth-century foundational U.S. documents of historical and literary significance for their themes, purposes, and rhetorical features.

Writing 7. Conduct short as well as more sustained research projects to answer a question or solve a problem; narrow or broaden the inquiry when appropriate; synthesize multiple sources on the subject, demonstrating understanding of the subject under investigation.

Language 4.d. Verify the preliminary definition of the meaning of a word or phrase.

Additional Standards Practice
Common Core Companion, *pp. 103–110; 240–244; 324–331*

Daily Block Scheduling
Each day in this Lesson Pacing Guide represents a 40–50 minute period. Teachers using block scheduling may combine days to revise pacing. In addition, teachers may differentiate and support core instruction by integrating components for extended and intensive support as students require. See the Guide to Selected Leveled Resources (facing page).

Guide to Selected Leveled Resources

R T I **Tier 1** (students performing on level)

from The Interesting Narrative of the Life of Olaudah Equiano

Warm Up	Practice, model, and monitor fluency, working with the whole class or in groups.	Vocabulary and Reading Warm-ups B, *Unit 1 Resources,* pp. 231–232, 234
Comprehension/Skills	Support and monitor comprehension and skills development, having students complete the activities, graphic organizers, and interactive prompts independently or as a class.	• *Reader's Notebook,* adapted instruction and summary EL *Reader's Notebook: English Learner's Version,* adapted instruction and summary • Reading Strategy Graphic Organizer B, *Graphic Organizer Transparencies,* p. 48 • Literary Analysis Graphic Organizer B, *Graphic Organizer Transparencies,* p. 50
Monitor Progress A	Monitor student progress with the differentiated curriculum-based assessment in the *Unit Resources.*	• Selection Test B, *Unit 1 Resources,* pp. 246–248 • Open-Book Test, *Unit 1 Resources,* pp. 240–242
Assess/ Screen A	Assess student progress using Benchmark Test 1.	• Benchmark Test 2, *Unit 1 Resources,* pp. 258–267

R T I **Tier 2** (students requiring intervention)

from The Interesting Narrative of the Life of Olaudah Equiano

Warm Up	Practice, model, and monitor fluency in groups or with individuals.	• Vocabulary and Reading Warm-ups A, *Unit 1 Resources,* pp. 231–233 • *Hear It!* Audio CD
Comprehension/Skills	• Support and monitor comprehension and skills development, working in small groups or with individuals. • As students complete the selection in the appropriate version of the *Reader's Notebook,* monitor comprehension frequently with group questions and individual instruction. • Model strategies while guiding students in completing the activities and prompts in the Reader's Notebook, as well as the graphic organizers. • Practice skills and monitor mastery with the *Reading Kit* worksheets.	• *Reader's Notebook: Adapted Version,* adapted instruction and summary EL *Reader's Notebook: English Learner's Version,* adapted instruction and summary • Reading Strategy Graphic Organizer A, *Graphic Organizer Transparencies,* p. 47 • Literary Analysis Graphic Organizer A, *Graphic Organizer Transparencies,* p. 49 • *Reading Kit,* Practice worksheets
Monitor Progress A	Monitor student progress with the differentiated curriculum-based assessment in the *Unit Resources* and in the *Reading Kit.*	• Selection Test A, *Unit 1 Resources,* pp. 243–245 • *Reading Kit,* Assess worksheets
Assess/ Screen A	Assess student progress using the Benchmark Test 1.	Benchmark Test 1, *Unit 1 Resources,* pp. 124–129

TIER 3 Tier 3 intervention may require consultation with the student's special-education or dyslexia specialist. For additional support, see the Tier 2 activities and resources listed above.

One-on-one teaching Group work Whole-class instruction Independent work A Assessment

For a complete guide to selection support, including support for Advanced students, see the Overview of Resources in the frontmatter.

• *from* The Interesting Narrative of the Life of Olaudah Equiano

RESOURCES FOR:

L1 Special-Needs Students

L2 Below-Level Students (Tier 2)

L3 On-Level Students (Tier 1)

L4 Advanced Students (Tier 1)

EL English Learners

All All Students

Vocabulary/Fluency/Prior Knowledge

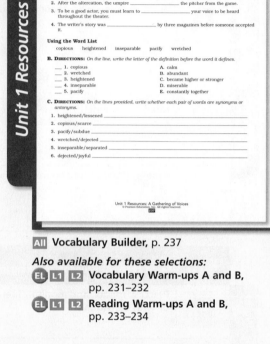

All Vocabulary Builder, p. 237

Also available for these selections:

EL **L1** **L2** Vocabulary Warm-ups A and B, pp. 231–232

EL **L1** **L2** Reading Warm-ups A and B, pp. 233–234

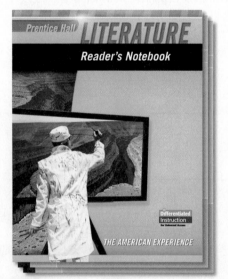

Reader's Notebooks

Pre- and postreading pages for this selection, as well as an excerpt from *The Interesting Narrative of the Life of Olaudah Equiano*, appear in an interactive format in the *Reader's Notebooks*. Each *Notebook* is differentiated for a different group of learners.

The selections in the Adapted and English Learner's versions are abridged.

L2 **L3** *Reader's Notebook*

L1 *Reader's Notebook: Adapted Version*

EL *Reader's Notebook: English Learner's Version*

EL *Reader's Notebook: Spanish Version*

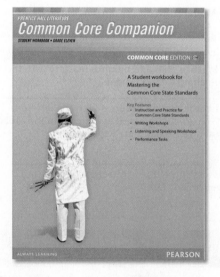

© *Common Core Companion*

Additional instruction and practice for each Common Core State Standard

Selection Support

EL L3 **Literary Analysis: Graphic Organizer B**, p. 50

Also available for these selections:

EL L1 L2 **Reading: Graphic Organizer A,** (partially filled in), p. 47

EL L3 **Reading: Graphic Organizer B,** p. 48

EL L1 L2 **Literary Analysis: Graphic Organizer A,** (partially filled in) p. 49

Skills Development/Extension

L4 **Enrichment,** p. 239

Also available for these selections:

All **Literary Analysis: Slave Narratives,** p. 235

All **Reading: Summarizing,** p. 236

EL L3 L4 **Support for Writing,** p. 238

Assessment

L3 L4 **Open-Book Test,** pp. 240–242

Also available for these selections:

EL L1 L2 **Selection Test B,** pp. 243–245

EL L3 L4 **Selection Test B,** pp. 246–248

PHLit Online!
www.PHLitOnline.com

Online Resources: All print materials are also available online.

- complete narrated selection text
- a thematically related video with writing prompt
- an interactive graphic organizer
- highlighting feature
- access to all student print resources, adapted to individual student needs
- Spanish and English summaries
- adapted selection translations in Spanish

Get Connected!

Also available:

Background Video (thematic video with writing prompt)
All videos available in Spanish.

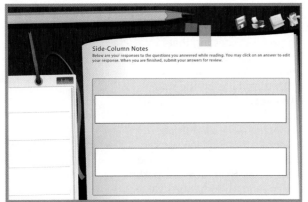

Writer's Journal (with graphics feature)

Also available:

Vocabulary Central (tools and activities for studying vocabulary)

Themes Across Centuries
William L. Andrews

1. Tell students that William L. Andrews, a well-known historian, writes about Olaudah Equiano's harrowing description of the "Middle Passage"—the experience of Africans being transported from their native lands to the New World on slave ships.

2. Use the *See It!* DVD to introduce William L. Andrews. Show Segment 2 to provide insights into his study of Olaudah Equiano. After the students have watched the segment, **ask:** How does this video segment with Andrews show the importance of diligence in historical scholarship?
Answer: Andrews mentions that recently doubt has arisen about Equiano's claim that he was born in Africa. New versions of the account of Equiano's life must indicate this new doubt.

The Middle Passage

1. Have students read Andrews's comments about how Equiano re-creates the horrors of a slave ship for white readers.

2. Andrews explains that the Africans' passage across the Atlantic Ocean was a horrific experience in which hundreds of thousands perished. Andrews notes that hardly anyone who survived the trip wrote about it, so that Equiano's account is particularly valuable.

3. **Ask:** What point does Andrews make by suggesting that Equiano's readers identified more with the African narrator than with the whites on the ship?
Answer: Andrews's comment about Equiano's reversal of expected racial identification suggests that Equiano wanted his readers to see that humaneness rather than race is important when judging someone's value.

Themes Across Centuries: Scholar's Insights

William L. Andrews Introduces
The Interesting Narrative of
THE LIFE OF OLAUDAH EQUIANO

A Rare Firsthand Account of the Middle Passage One of the most astonishing facts about the Middle Passage—the Atlantic crossing of enslaved Africans to the Americas—is that, although millions of Africans endured it, and as many as one in eight died from it, history has preserved almost no firsthand accounts of it. *The Interesting Narrative of the Life of Olaudah Equiano* contains one of the rare detailed reports of the catastrophic journey that survives in English. Imagine how hard it would be for someone who had been through such a horrifying experience to write about it. Writing about past trauma almost certainly requires a person to relive it.

A Virtual Tour of the Slave Ship Equiano's account of the Middle Passage directly thrusts his reader, who Equiano expected would be either English or American, into a terrifying situation. Whatever Equiano's white readers thought about slavery, we can be pretty sure that they didn't want to think about how the Africans got to the Americas. By taking his reader on a virtual tour of the slave ship above and below decks, Equiano seems determined to confront his reader with the hideous—and generally hidden—truth about life aboard a slave ship.

The first stop is the ship's suffocating hold, where its human cargo was stored for most of the transatlantic voyage. Here we can see, hear, feel, and, especially, smell how "loathsome" a place it really was. Hell on earth would not be too strong a term to describe the hold of a slave ship.

Equiano doesn't confine us long in the miserable hold before taking us up into the fresh air, where we might hope for some relief from the horrors we've experienced. However, we soon find ourselves accompanied by dying Africans who've been brought up to the deck to perish of the illnesses they've contracted in the hold. Meanwhile, the European ship hands merely watch and wait, supremely indifferent to the suffering they witness.

About the Author

William L. Andrews is the series editor of North American Slave Narratives, Beginnings to 1920. His book *To Tell a Free Story* is a history of African American autobiography up to 1865.

Teaching Resources

The following resources can be used to enrich or extend the instruction for Themes Across Centuries.

Unit 1 Resources
  Themes Across Centuries, p. 229
  Listening and Viewing, p. 230
See It! DVD
  William L. Andrews, Segment 2

PHLit Online! All resources are available at www.PHLitOnline.com.

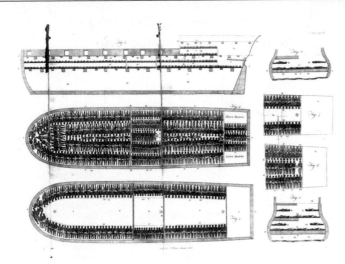

◀ **Critical Viewing**
What do these design drawings of a slave ship tell you about slave traders' attitudes toward their captives? **[Analyze]**

Identifying With the Abused Africans The cruelty of the whites aboard the slave ship must have shocked Equiano's readers, particularly since, as whites themselves, they would likely have felt more in common with the Europeans on the ship than the Africans. But Equiano's storytelling gradually alienates his reader from the brutal whites while helping the reader to identify with the abused Africans.

Through the point of view of the ten-year-old African narrator, we inevitably feel the same shock and dread that the innocent African boy felt. Our sympathy with the narrator goes beyond pitying him as a victim, however. We follow as the curious African boy steps forward to take a peek through the ship's quadrant. As an unimagined world opens up to him, we realize that no matter how unjustly that new world may treat him in the future, Equiano the inquisitive, resilient traveler, will survive.

Thinking About the Commentary ©

1. **Key Ideas and Details (a)** What was the Middle Passage? **(b) Speculate:** Why do you think firsthand accounts of it are so rare?

2. **Key Ideas and Details (a)** What does Equiano show readers? **(b) Infer:** What do you think was his purpose in conducting this "virtual tour"?

As You Read *The Interesting Narrative of the Life of Olaudah Equiano . . .*

3. **Key Ideas and Details** Identify details that justify Andrews's description of Equiano as "inquisitive" and "resilient."

167

❶ Connecting to the Essential Question

1. Review the assignment.
2. Ask students to think of cases in which someone's personal experience influenced public opinion. Then, have them complete the assignment.
3. As students read, have them note details that make strong emotional impressions. Such details are likely to affect public opinion.

❷ Literary Analysis

Introduce the skill, using the instruction on the student page.

Think Aloud: Model the Skill

Say to students:

When I read about extreme situations, I pay attention to sensory words—details that tell me about sights, sounds, touch, tastes, and smells. In Equiano's first paragraph, I notice "noises," "stench," "heat," and "suffocated." These details make his experience more real and more affecting to me.

❸ Reading Strategy

1. Introduce the strategy, using the instruction on the student page.
2. Give students a copy of **Reading Strategy Graphic Organizer B,** page 48 in *Graphic Organizer Transparencies,* to fill out as they read.

❹ Vocabulary

1. Pronounce each word, giving its definition, and have students say it aloud.
2. For more guidance, see the *Classroom Strategies and Teaching Routines* card for introducing vocabulary.

168

Before You Read

from *The Interesting Narrative of the Life of Olaudah Equiano*

❶ Connecting to the Essential Question Olaudah Equiano wrote about a personal ordeal. In doing so, he helped to shift public opinion on the issue of slavery. As you read, focus on details in Equiano's writing that you think would have been especially effective in changing public opinion. This will help as you consider the Essential Question: **How does literature shape or reflect society?**

❷ Literary Analysis

A **slave narrative** is an autobiographical account of a person's life as a slave. Written when slavery was a legal practice, most slave narratives have an implicit persuasive purpose: to expose the evils of slavery and, in so doing, turn the public against it. Equiano's account speaks powerfully against the slave trade. His style includes descriptive language that appeals to readers' emotions. Notice, for example, how descriptive words such as "shrieks" and "groans" evoke readers' sympathy and outrage in this description of the slave ship that brought Equiano from Africa:

> *The shrieks of the women, and the groans of the dying, rendered the whole a scene of horror almost inconceivable.*

As you read, recognize details that both convey Equiano's perceptions and experiences and register as strong emotional appeals against the institution of slavery. Consider how each detail contributes to the implicit case Equiano is building against the entire institution of slavery.

❸ Reading Strategy

Preparing to Read Complex Texts Some literature written long ago may be challenging to read. You can improve your comprehension by **summarizing to identify the main, or central, idea.** To do so, identify only the most important ideas and details in a passage. Include key information from the beginning, middle, and end. Then, gather that information into a brief statement. As you read, use a chart like the one shown to summarize.

❹ Vocabulary

copious (kō′ pē əs) *adj.* plentiful; abundant (p. 172)

wretched (rech′ id) *adj.* deeply distressed; miserable (p. 172)

dejected (dē jek′ tid) *adj.* in low spirits; downcast; depressed (p. 173)

inseparable (in sep′ ə rə bəl) *adj.* not able to be divided; linked (p. 173)

heightened (hīt′ ənd) *v.* raised the level of (p. 174)

pacify (pas′ ə fī′) *v.* calm or soothe (p. 175)

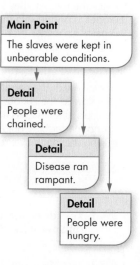

Main Point
The slaves were kept in unbearable conditions.

Detail
People were chained.

Detail
Disease ran rampant.

Detail
People were hungry.

PHLit Online!
www.PHLitOnline.com

Common Core State Standards

Reading Informational Text
2. Determine two or more central ideas of a text and analyze their development over the course of the text, including how they interact and build on one another to provide a complex analysis; provide an objective summary of the text.
9. Analyze eighteenth-century foundational U.S. documents of historical and literary significance for their themes, purposes, and rhetorical features.

168 Beginnings–1800

Vocabulary Development

Vocabulary Knowledge Rating
Create a **Vocabulary Knowledge Rating Chart** (*Professional Development Guidebook,* p. 33) for the vocabulary words on the student page. Give each student a copy of the chart with the words on it. Read the words aloud and have students mark their rating in the Before Reading column. Urge students to attend to these words as they read and discuss the selection.

In order to gauge how much instruction you need to provide, tally how many students are confident in their knowledge of each word. As students read, point out the words and their context.

PHLit Online! **Vocabulary Central,** featuring tools and activities for studying vocabulary, is available online at **www.PHLitOnline.com**.

⑤ Olaudah Equiano
(1745–1797)

Author of *The Interesting Narrative of the Life of Olaudah Equiano*

When it was first published in 1789, the autobiography of Olaudah Equiano (ō lä ōō′dā ek′wē ä′ nō) created a sensation. A best seller on both sides of the Atlantic, it made society face the cruelties of slavery and contributed to the banning of the slave trade in both the United States and England.

Childhood Interrupted The son of a West African tribal elder, Olaudah Equiano might have followed in his father's footsteps had he not been sold into slavery. Instead, when he was eleven years old, he and his sister were kidnapped from their home and sold to British slave traders. Separated from his sister, Equiano—like millions of other Africans—was shipped across the Atlantic Ocean under horrendous conditions. He was taken first to the West Indies and later brought to Virginia, where he was purchased by a British captain and employed at sea.

The Struggle for Liberty Renamed Gustavus Vassa, Equiano was enslaved for nearly ten years. After managing his master's finances and making his own money in the process, he amassed enough to buy his own freedom. In later years, he settled in England and devoted himself to the abolition of slavery. In addition to writing his two-volume autobiography to publicize the plight of slaves, he lectured and rallied public sympathies against the cruelties of slavery. He was also involved in the founding of Sierra Leone, the famous British colony established on the west coast of Africa for freed British slaves.

> *I believe there are few events in my life, which have not happened to many: it is true the incidents of it are numerous; and, did I consider myself an European, I might say my sufferings were great: but when I compare my lot with that of most of my countrymen, I regard myself as a particular favorite of Heaven, and acknowledge the mercies of Providence in every occurrence of my life.*

from The Interesting Narrative of the Life of Olaudah Equiano **169**

🔔 Daily Bellringer

For each class during which you will teach this selection, have students complete one of the five activities for the appropriate week in the *Daily Bellringer Activities* booklet.

Multidraft Reading

To assist struggling readers and to enhance reading for all, assign the text in chunks as warranted by length and apply multidraft reading protocols. For each reading, have students set the purpose indicated:

- **First reading**—identifying key ideas and details and answering any Reading Checks.
- **Second reading**—analyzing craft and structure and responding to the side-column prompts.
- **Third reading**—integrating knowledge and ideas, connecting to other texts and the world, and answering the end-of-selection questions.

For more guidance, refer to the *Classroom Strategies and Teaching Routines* card on multidraft reading.

⑤ Background
More About the Author

In the Ibo language, the author's name means "well-spoken leader," and after his years of slavery, Olaudah Equiano lived up to his name—not only publishing his acclaimed *Interesting Narrative*, but also playing a prominent role in the British abolitionist movement. Equiano lectured, protested, and personally petitioned the British Parliament to outlaw slavery.

PHLit Online! www.PHLitOnline.com
Teaching From Technology

Preparing to Read
Go to **www.PHLitOnline.com** in class or in a lab and display the **Get Connected!** slide show for this selection. Have the class brainstorm for responses to the slide show writing prompt, entering ideas in the interactive journal. Then, have students complete their written responses individually, in a lab or as homework.

To build background, display the Background and More About the Authors features.

Using the Interactive Text
Go to **www.PHLitOnline.com** and display the **Enriched Online Student Edition**. As the class reads the selection or listens to the narration, record answers to side-column prompts using the graphic organizers accessible on the interactive page. Alternatively, have students use the online edition individually, answering the prompts as they read.

❶❷from
The Interesting Narrative of
——THE LIFE OF——
OLAUDAH EQUIANO

170 Beginnings–1800

❶ About the Selection

Like Harriet Beecher Stowe's explosive, best-selling novel *Uncle Tom's Cabin* (1853), Equiano's work had a significant effect on the institution of slavery. By exposing the cruelty of slavery, both works contributed to its eventual demise in the United States. Unlike Stowe's work, *The Interesting Narrative* is a firsthand account of an actual event. Equiano communicates heinous details of the slave trade vividly but simply.

❷ Activating Prior Knowledge

Students are probably familiar with common expressions that use the term *slave* and inadvertently trivialize the horrors of slavery. You might ask students if they have ever heard—or used—expressions such as *to slave over homework* or *a slave to fashion*.

Invite students to empathize with victims of slavery by imagining being forcibly captured and then hauled like cargo for many weeks in the dark and airless hold of a ship. Ask them to write an imaginary journal entry that expresses their thoughts upon being freed from that experience.

Concept Connector ▸

Tell students they will return to their responses after reading the selection.

Ⓒ Text Complexity Rubric

from The Interesting Narrative of the Life of Olaudah Equiano	
Qualitative Measures	
Context/Knowledge Demands	Slavery; historical knowledge demands 1 2 ③ 4 5
Structure/Language Conventionality and Clarity	Challenging vocabulary; long sentences 1 2 3 ④ 5
Levels of Meaning/Purpose/Concept Level	Accessible (description of a slave ship) 1 2 ③ 4 5
Quantitative Measures	

Lexile	1240L	**Text Length**	Word Count: 1,129
Overall Complexity	**More accessible**		

Reader and Task Suggestions

Preparing to Read the Text

- Using the Background information on TE p. 169, discuss the meaning of Equiano's name.
- Ask students why it would be important for the survivor of a terrible crime to tell his or her story clearly and vividly.
- Guide students to use Multidraft Reading strategies to deepen their comprehension (TE p. 169).

Leveled Tasks

Structure/Language If students will have difficulty with the vocabulary or syntax, have them first read to identify and find definitions for unfamiliar words.

Synthesizing If students will not have difficulty with the vocabulary or syntax, have students imagine whether a movie of Equiano's ordeal would have the same intensity as his writing.

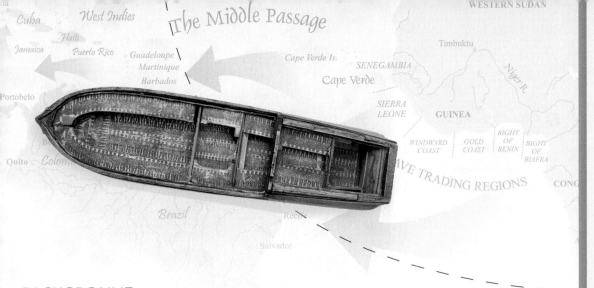

The Middle Passage

BACKGROUND In the first several chapters of his narrative, Olaudah Equiano describes how slave traders kidnapped him and his sister from their home in West Africa and transported them to the African coast. During this six- or seven-month journey, Equiano was separated from his sister and held at a series of way stations. After reaching the coast, Equiano was shipped with other slaves to North America. The following account describes this horrifying journey.

4 ◀ ▲ **Critical Viewing**
In what ways do these images of slave ships help prove Equiano's point that the slavers were motivated by extreme greed? **[Verify]**

A̲t last when the ship we were in, had got in all her cargo, they made ready with many fearful noises, and we were all put under deck, so that we could not see how they managed the vessel. But this disappointment was the least of my sorrow. The stench of the hold while we were on the coast was so intolerably loathsome, that it was dangerous to remain there for any time, and some of us had been permitted to stay on the deck for the fresh air; but now that the whole ship's cargo were confined together, it became absolutely pestilential. The closeness of the place, and the heat of the climate, added to the number in the ship, which was so crowded that each had scarcely room to turn himself, almost suffocated us.

5  Reading Check

According to Equiano, why does the hold become "pestilential"?

from The Interesting Narrative of the Life of Olaudah Equiano **171**

❻ Humanities

Slaves Below Deck (detail), Lt. Francis Meynell

This picture depicts a scene aboard a Spanish slave ship on its way to the West Indies. Use this question for discussion:

> Do you think Meynell or Equiano more vividly captures the horror of the voyage? Explain.
>
> **Possible response:** Students may say Equiano's description seems more horrible than the scene portrayed in the painting because it tells of the stench, the pain of the shackles, and the mistreatment that captives endured—none of which is immediately evident in the painting.

❼ Critical Viewing

Answer: Students may say that the painting is less dire than the scenes Equiano describes. Students may point to details such as the apparent lack of shackles and air and light reaching into the hold from the deck above.

❽ Scholar's Insight

1. Direct students' attention to Andrews's remark about Equiano's word choice. Tell students that writers select words or phrases to produce a desired effect.

2. Read the bracketed passage. **Ask** students how Equiano's word choice would affect his audience.
   Possible response: Equiano's word choice would appeal to the readers' emotions, and it also helps point out the faults of the slave traders.

❻

❼ **Critical Viewing ▶**
The artist portrays conditions on a slave ship. Compare and contrast this image with the scene that Equiano describes. **[Compare and Contrast]**

Slaves Below Deck (detail), Lt. Francis Meynell, National Maritime Museum, Greenwich

Vocabulary

copious (kō′ pē əs) *adj.* plentiful; abundant

wretched (rech′ id) *adj.* deeply distressed; miserable

William L. Andrews
Scholar's Insight
The wasteful greed of European slave traders makes them so callous that they don't even care about the profits they lose when slaves die in transit aboard their ships. The words *improvident avarice* help Equiano portray slavery as both inhuman and unprofitable.

❽

This produced copious perspirations, so that the air soon became unfit for respiration, from a variety of loathsome smells, and brought on a sickness among the slaves, of which many died—thus falling victims to the improvident avarice, as I may call it, of their purchasers. This wretched situation was again aggravated by the galling of the chains, now become insupportable, and the filth of the necessary tubs, into which the children often fell, and were almost suffocated. The shrieks of the women, and the groans of the dying, rendered the whole a scene of horror almost inconceivable. Happily perhaps, for myself, I was soon reduced so low here that it was thought necessary to keep me almost always on deck; and from my extreme youth I was not put in fetters.[1] In this situation I expected every hour to share the fate of my companions, some of whom were almost daily brought upon deck at the point of death, which I began to hope would soon put an end to my miseries. Often did I think many of the inhabitants of the deep much more happy than myself.

---

1. fetters (fet′ ərz) *n.* chains.

Enrichment: Analyzing Film

History at the Movies

The 2007 film *Amazing Grace* tells the story of the abolition of the British slave trade. William Wilberforce (1759–1833), a member of Parliament, fought to outlaw the trade for twenty years. His allies included Olaudah Equiano, who is a minor but important character in the film, and John Newton (1725–1807). Newton, a former slave trader, renounced his deeds and wrote the hymn "Amazing Grace." Like many films based on history, *Amazing Grace* takes some liberties to facilitate the narrative, but it is above all an inspiring film about the capacity of people to change the world.

Activity: Film Analysis Have students watch *Amazing Grace* and study the techniques used to tell the story effectively. Suggest that they record their findings in the **Enrichment: Analyzing Film** worksheet, *Professional Development Guidebook,* page 226. Have them use their analysis as the basis of a presentation about how contemporary film treats history.

I envied them the freedom they enjoyed, and as often wished I could change my condition for theirs. Every circumstance I met with, served only to render my state more painful, and heightened my apprehensions, and my opinion of the cruelty of the whites.

One day they had taken a number of fishes; and when they had killed and satisfied themselves with as many as they thought fit, to our astonishment who were on deck, rather than give any of them to us to eat, as we expected, they tossed the remaining fish into the sea again, although we begged and prayed for some as well as we could, but in vain; and some of my countrymen, being pressed by hunger, took an opportunity, when they thought no one saw them, of trying to get a little privately; but they were discovered, and the attempt procured them some very severe floggings. One day, when we had a smooth sea and moderate wind, two of my wearied countrymen who were chained together (I was near them at the time), preferring death to such a life of misery, somehow made through the nettings and jumped into the sea; immediately, another quite dejected fellow, who, on account of his illness, was suffered to be out of irons, also followed their example; and I believe many more would very soon have done the same, if they had not been prevented by the ship's crew, who were instantly alarmed. Those of us that were the most active, were in a moment put down under the deck; and there was such a noise and confusion amongst the people of the ship as I never heard before, to stop her, and get the boat out to go after the slaves. However, two of the wretches were drowned, but they got the other, and afterwards flogged him unmercifully, for thus attempting to prefer death to slavery. In this manner we continued to undergo more hardships than I can now relate, hardships which are inseparable from this accursed trade. Many a time we were near suffocation from the want of fresh air, which we were often without for whole days together. This, and the stench of the necessary tubs, carried off many.

William L. Andrews
❾ Scholar's Insight
The inexplicable cruelty of the Europeans, contrasted with the pleading and praying of the Africans, is designed to challenge the prejudices of Equiano's readers. These readers would have expected the supposedly heathen Africans, not the Christian Europeans, to be indifferent to human need. ❿

Vocabulary
dejected (dē jek´ tid) *adj.* in low spirits; downcast; depressed

inseparable (in sep´ ə rə bəl) *adj.* not able to be divided; linked

⓫ Reading Check
What do some slaves do to escape the misery of the Middle Passage?

from The Interesting Narrative of the Life of Olaudah Equiano **173**

---

❾ Scholar's Insight
1. Read the insight note to students. Have students share their ideas about how Christian readers would react to the bracketed passage.
2. **Ask** if they feel this passage would change European stereotypes of the Africans.
   Possible response: Some students may feel the description of the Africans praying would erase prejudices. Others may feel that readers would only be momentarily swayed from their beliefs.

❿ Literary Analysis
Slave Narrative
1. Read aloud with students the long sentence on this page that starts with "One day they had taken." Encourage students to identify two distinct injustices that are presented in this passage.
   Answer: Injustices include the crew's throwing food overboard rather than allowing the captives to eat it and the crew's flogging captives for trying to get something to eat.
2. **Ask:** What is the effect of these floggings on the readers' emotions?
   Answer: Most readers will feel disgust, anger, or sadness while reading descriptions of flogging.

⓫ Reading Check
Answer: Some choose to jump into the ocean and drown rather than continue to endure the torture of the Middle Passage.

Economics

Between 1500 and 1800, about 15 million Africans were captured and shipped as captives to the Western Hemisphere. Historians estimate that nearly 2 million people died during the Middle Passage before reaching the slave traders' destinations. You may wish to point out that Equiano and others spent months in transit prior to boarding the ship itself—and that they then spent several weeks on board before setting sail. Often pairs of adult captives were chained together at the ankles and wrists, and the shackles were removed only when one of the pair became very sick or died.

Connect to the Literature

Encourage students to examine Equiano's word choice. Then, **ask** the Connect to the Literature question: What seems to be Equiano's attitude toward the captives who preferred death to slavery?

Possible response: Equiano calls the captives who chose to jump into the sea "*wretches,*" which indicates that he understood that they were distressed. He also says many others may have done the same thing, but he does not say that he wished to follow the escaped captives to death. Equiano's attitude appears to be one of separateness. He does not see himself as being part of the group he describes. This attitude may be a means of protecting himself.

---

⑫ The
American
EXPERIENCE

ECONOMICS

The Slave Trade

While some people came to the Western Hemisphere in search of a better life, others were brought against their will to be sold as slaves. The map shown here indicates the major slave trade routes.

The Atlantic crossing, known as the Middle Passage, was brutal. Africans were chained below decks in cramped, filthy spaces. Overcrowding, disease, and despair claimed many lives. Some Africans mutinied; others tried to starve themselves or jump overboard.

Connect to the Literature

What seems to be Equiano's attitude toward the captives who preferred death to slavery?

Atlantic Slave Trade Routes
❖ 1502–1870 ❖

Vocabulary
heightened (hīt´ ənd) *v.* raised the level of

During our passage, I first saw flying fishes, which surprised me very much; they used frequently to fly across the ship, and many of them fell on the deck. I also now first saw the use of the quadrant;[2] I had often with astonishment seen the mariners make observations with it, and I could not think what it meant. They at last took notice of my surprise; and one of them, willing to increase it, as well as to gratify my curiosity, made me one day look through it. The clouds appeared to me to be land, which disappeared as they passed along. This heightened my wonder; and I was now more persuaded than ever, that I was in another world, and that every thing about me was magic. At last, we came in sight of the island of Barbados, at which the whites on board gave a great shout, and made many signs of joy to us. We did not know what to think of this; but as the vessel drew nearer, we plainly saw the harbor, and other ships of different kinds and sizes, and we soon anchored amongst them, off Bridgetown.[3] Many merchants and planters now came on board, though it was in the evening. They put us in separate parcels,[4] and examined us attentively. They also made us jump, and pointed to the land, signifying we were to go there.

> 2. **quadrant** (kwä´ drənt) *n.* an instrument used by navigators to determine the position of a ship.
> 3. **Bridgetown** *n.* the capital of Barbados.
> 4. **parcels** (pär´ səlz) *n.* groups.

Differentiated
Instruction for Universal Access

Culturally Responsive Instruction

Culture Connection Some students may feel that Equiano portrays European slave traders as outright evil men who are representative of their race, religion, and nations. Remind them that Equiano himself, after purchasing his freedom, joined the British abolitionist movement and worked with English men and women such as William Wilberforce, John Wesley, Hannah More, and Josiah Wedgwood to bring an end to the British slave trade. Despite his pride in his homeland, Equiano also had harsh words for Africans who participated in the slave trade. In his quest to bring an end to slavery, Equiano saw beyond the bounds of race, religion, and nationality. Discuss with students the possible consequences of stereotyping or making overly broad generalizations about groups of people.

We thought by this, we should be eaten by these ugly men, as they appeared to us; and, when soon after we were all put down under the deck again, there was much dread and trembling among us, and nothing but bitter cries to be heard all the night from these apprehensions, insomuch, that at last the white people got some old slaves from the land to pacify us. They told us we were not to be eaten, but to work, and were soon to go on land, where we should see many of our country people. This report eased us much. And sure enough, soon after we were landed, there came to us Africans of all languages.

We were conducted immediately to the merchant's yard, where we were all pent up together, like so many sheep in a fold, without regard to sex or age. . . . We were not many days in the merchant's custody, before we were sold after their usual manner, which is this: On a signal given (as the beat of a drum), the buyers rush at once into the yard where the slaves are confined, and make choice of that parcel they like best. . . .

Vocabulary
pacify (pas′ ə fi′) v. to calm or soothe

William L. Andrews
Scholar's Insight
This reversal of the well-established European stereotype of the African as cannibal is one of Equiano's most effective ironies.

Critical Reading ©

© 1. **Key Ideas and Details (a)** Why does Equiano blame the illness aboard the ship on the "improvident avarice" of the traders? **(b) Infer:** How do the white crewmen view their captives? **(c) Draw Conclusions:** What does the treatment of the slaves reveal about the captors' attitudes toward human life?

© 2. **Key Ideas and Details (a)** How does Equiano's age affect his experiences during the voyage? **(b) Infer:** How do you think he felt about his experience compared to the fate of other captives on the ship?

© 3. **Craft and Structure** How does Equiano show his great zest for life despite his assertion that he wants to die? Provide examples from the selection.

© 4. **Integration of Knowledge and Ideas** What do you think the public of Equiano's day learned about the "accursed trade" of slavery that it may not have known before reading this narrative? In your response, use at least two of these Essential Question vocabulary words: *awareness, compassion, inhumane, avarice.* *[Connecting to the Essential Question: How does literature shape or reflect society?]*

Cite textual evidence to support your responses.

from The Interesting Narrative of the Life of Olaudah Equiano **175**

Concept Connector

Reading Strategy Graphic Organizer
Ask students to review the graphic organizers in which they have summarized the main idea or essential message. Then, have students share their organizers and compare summaries.

Activating Prior Knowledge
Have students return to their responses to the Activating Prior Knowledge activity. Ask them to explain whether their thoughts have changed and if so, how.

Connecting to the Essential Question
Have students compare the responses they gave to the prompt before they completed reading the selection with their thoughts after reading it. Have them work individually or in groups, writing or discussing their thoughts, to formulate their new responses. Then, lead a class discussion, probing for what students have learned that confirms or invalidates their initial thoughts. Encourage students to cite specific textual details to support their responses.

⑬

⑬ **Scholar's Insight**

1. Review the meaning of *irony*. Tell students that irony is a technique that involves surprising and sometimes amusing contradictions.

2. Read the Scholar's Insight note to students. **Ask** them what is ironic about the bracketed passage. **Possible response:** Most Europeans felt that Africans were cannibals. It is ironic that the Africans think the men on the ship are going to eat them.

ASSESS
Answers

Before students respond, you may wish to have them write a brief objective summary of the selection. As they answer the questions below, remind them to support their answers with evidence from the text.

1. (a) Equiano believes that the traders' greed has led them to load the ships with too many captives, causing unsanitary conditions and deadly illness. (b) The white crewmen view their captives as little more than cargo. (c) The captors do not seem to believe their prisoners are human, seeing them only as property to be transported and sold.

2. (a) Equiano was granted certain privileges because of his age. For example, he was often kept on deck rather than in the cramped quarters below. (b) He probably felt fortunate to be spared some of the degradation suffered by the other captives.

3. **Possible response:** His zest for life is apparent in his alert descriptions of events and in his curiosity about the quadrant. His mind and spirit have not been dulled by his oppression.

4. **Possible response:** Equiano's book increased public <u>awareness</u> of the cruelty of the slave trade, which caused some people to respond with <u>compassion</u> and join the abolitionist movement. Students may note that the response to Equiano's book demonstrates the power of literature to shape society.

Answers

1. (a) Captives were half-starved and chained in the crowded, hot, suffocating hold of a ship. (b) The captives felt complete despair. Many expressed a desire to die. (c) The author is giving readers a sense of the injustice and cruelty of the slave trade.

2. (a) **Possible response:** The traders give captives very little living space on board ship. They routinely beat them. (b) Many would be repulsed, but others might feel that this treatment is necessary.

3. (a) The traders allow Equiano to use the quadrant. They allow younger captives to be kept out of chains and above deck. (b) The traders' main motivation is to deliver as many healthy captives as possible. (c) **Possible response:** The traders' concern for making money is genuine, but their concern for their prisoners is not.

4. (a) **Possible response:** Students may cite "so intolerably loathsome," "absolutely pestilential," and "wretched situation." (b) These emotional appeals encourage the reader to empathize with the captives.

5. **Possible response:** Students may say that if victims share their experiences, these accounts are more likely to prevent further injustices.

6. (a) Summaries should include the following main points: Olaudah Equiano traveled across the Atlantic Ocean in a slave ship. The conditions on board were detestable. The crew treated the captives as less than human, often flogging them for minor trespasses. (b) **Possible response:** The slave trade is cruel and unjust and should be abolished.

7. **Possible response:** Delete the last sentence of the summary. Add: Almost every day, more captives died.

8. (a) When the ship arrived on shore, the frightened captives were brought to auction and sold. (b) **Possible response:** The captives are considered nothing more than property to be owned by others.

176

Literary Analysis

© 1. **Key Ideas and Details** (a) In his **slave narrative,** which physical hardships does Equiano say the captives suffered during the Middle Passage? (b) What emotional torments does he describe? (c) In what ways do these descriptions serve as appeals to readers' emotions? Explain.

© 2. **Key Ideas and Details** (a) Cite two examples of the slave traders' cruelty to the slaves. (b) What effect do you think this information would have had on readers in Equiano's day?

© 3. **Key Ideas and Details** (a) Cite two examples that show the slave traders' concern for the slaves. (b) What seems to motivate this concern? (c) Would you say this is genuine concern or something else? Explain.

© 4. **Craft and Structure** (a) Using a chart like the one shown, identify three examples of *descriptive language* in the narrative. (b) Explain how each example serves as a strong emotional appeal to the reader.

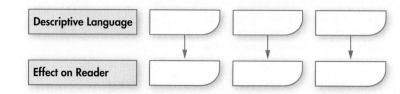

© 5. **Integration of Knowledge and ideas** Do you think it is better for people who are victims of injustice to record and even publicize their experiences or to maintain their privacy? Explain your answer.

Reading Strategy

6. (a) In **summarizing** the excerpt as a whole, what three central ideas would you include? (b) What is the single most essential message of Equiano's autobiographical account?

7. A summary of the first paragraph of the excerpt appears below. Revise this summary by deleting one piece of information that is not important enough to include, and adding one detail that is too important to omit.

> *On the ship that took Equiano from Africa to the Americas, the slaves were kept in miserable conditions. It was hot and crowded. People were chained. Equiano wished he were a fish or another inhabitant of the deep.*

8. (a) Summarize the events that occur after the ship reaches Bridgetown. (b) What is the central idea or essential message in that section of the narrative?

© **Common Core State Standards**

Writing
7. Conduct short as well as more sustained research projects to answer a question or solve a problem; narrow or broaden the inquiry when appropriate; synthesize multiple sources on the subject, demonstrating understanding of the subject under investigation. (p. 177)

Language
4.d. Verify the preliminary definition of the meaning of a word or phrase. (p. 177)

Assessment Practice

Summarizing Written Texts: Implied Main Idea (For more practice, see the *All-in-One Workbook*.)
When the main idea is not directly stated, students must infer the main focus of the passage. Some tests require students to identify the implied main idea of a reading passage. Have the students reread the opening paragraph of the selection, which begins on page 171. Then have them choose the implied main idea of the paragraph from the following responses:

A Most slaves were kept in the hold below the deck.

B Death seemed better than life to slaves on the African slave ships.

C Slave ships from Africa were filthy, overcrowded, and cruelly managed, which caused many slaves to sicken and die.

D Equiano wrote a journal about life on an African slave ship.

Choice **A** is a supporting detail, and choices **B** and **D** present background information. Choice **C** contains the implied main idea.

Integrated Language Skills

Vocabulary Acquisition and Use

Word Analysis: Latin Root *-ject-*

The word *dejected* contains the Latin root *-ject-*, which means "throw." Someone who is *dejected* is thrown down, or downcast, by disappointment or sorrow. Use context clues and knowledge of the root *-ject-* to explain the meaning of each italicized word below. Also make clear how the word's meaning reflects the meaning of the root.

1. I was disappointed when the publisher *rejected* my manuscript.
2. The nurse gave me an *injection* in my arm.
3. Tanya *projected* her voice across the room.
4. We did not know the answer, but we offered our *conjectures* in a brainstorming session.
5. Pablo and Luisa were conversing when Celia *interjected* some remarks.
6. The guard *ejected* the misbehaving children.

Vocabulary: Categorize Key Vocabulary

Review the list of vocabulary words on page 168. Then, analyze the relationship between the italicized word and the words that follow it in each item below. For each grouping, determine a logical category, such as *synonyms*, *antonyms and synonyms*, or another category that you can defend. Explain your reasoning. Consult a dictionary if necessary.

1. *copious,* sparse, meager
2. *wretched,* desolate, pitiful
3. *dejected,* cheerful, lively
4. *inseparable,* divisible, isolated
5. *heightened,* sensitive, keen
6. *pacify,* agitate, incite

Writing

Ⓒ **Informative Text** Write the information for a large **museum placard** that visitors might read at the beginning of a museum exhibit about Olaudah Equiano and the slave trade during the eighteenth century. Use details from Equiano's narrative, as well as facts and data about the North American slave trade that you gather through research in other sources.

Prewriting Conduct research at the library or online to find public documents that *verify and clarify facts* and observations Equiano presents in his narrative. Organize your findings, perhaps drawing a map to trace the slave trade routes or marking dates and other key details on a timeline. Identify any *specialized vocabulary* you may need to define in order to make the material clear to a general reader.

Drafting As you draft, *consider your audience and purpose.* Begin with strong information, such as a startling anecdote or fact, that will draw the public into the exhibit. Remember that your audience probably has little prior knowledge about your topic. Use a chart like the one shown to anticipate readers' questions.

Revising Review your work, making sure you have clarified all unfamiliar facts or data. Add explanations as needed.

Model: Assessing Audience Knowledge

Detail	Prior Knowledge?	Action
Location of West Africa	Probably not	Explain
Average duration of Middle Passage	No	Provide data

Integrated Language Skills **177**

1. turned down; it was "thrown back."
2. shot or needle; the medicine is "thrown" into the body.
3. spoke loudly; she "threw" her voice out.
4. speculated; we looked for an explanation by "throwing" various ideas around.
5. inserted; she "threw" her comments in suddenly.
6. forced to leave; he "threw" them out.

Vocabulary

1. antonyms; *copious* means "plentiful"; *sparse* and *meager* mean the opposite.
2. synonyms; all have meanings related to being miserable.
3. antonyms; *dejected* means "downcast"; *cheerful* and *lively* mean the opposite.
4. antonyms; things that are inseparable cannot be divided, which is the opposite of *divisible.* Something that is isolated is by itself.
5. synonyms; all refer to sharp levels of intensity.
6. antonyms; *pacify* means "to bring peace or calm"; *agitate* and *incite* mean the opposite.

Writing

1. To guide students in writing this museum placard, give them the Support for Writing page (*Unit 1 Resources,* p. 238).
2. Use the Writing instruction to guide students in developing their placards.
3. Remind the students to organize their information in a way that is clear and accessible. It should be readily grasped in a single reading.
4. Use the **General Writing Rubrics,** *Professional Development Guidebook,* pages 282–283, to evaluate students' work.

Assessment Resources

Unit 1 Resources

L1 L2 EL **Selection Test A, pp. 243–245.** Administer Test A to less advanced students and English learners.

L3 L4 EL **Selection Test B, pp. 246–248.** Administer Test B to on-level or more advanced students.

L3 L4 **Open-Book Test, pp. 240–242.** As an alternative, give the Open-Book Test.

All **Customizable Test Bank**

All **Self-tests**
Students may prepare for the **Selection Test** by taking the **Self-test** online.

All assessment resources are available at **www.PHLitOnline.com.**

COMMON CORE ▪ RESEARCH PROJECT

Primary Sources

Letter	Letter	Floor Plan
Letter from the President's House	Letter from the New White House	President's House

© **Common Core State Standards**

Reading Informational Text 9. Analyze seventeenth-, eighteenth-, and nineteenth-century foundational U.S. documents of historical and literary significance for their themes, purposes, and rhetorical features.

© **Common Core State Standards**

• Reading Informational Text 9
• Writing 7, 8
• Language 6

❶ About the Text Forms

1. Introduce the forms, using the instruction on the student page.

2. Explain that the value of letters as a source of information—the fact that the writer is a witness of events—is also a potential draw-back. Participants in events may have incomplete knowledge or suffer from biases.

3. Point out that, as counterweight to this concern, primary sources can be checked against one another. For example, Abigail Adams's claims about the White House can be double-checked against Latrobe's floor plan.

❷ Reading Strategy

Introduce the strategy.

Think Aloud: Model the Skill

Say to students:

If a writer records the parties and fashions of his day, I realize he has a perspective on his world—he approves of its pursuit of fun. When I read another writer of the time complaining about the indulgences of the wealthy, I realize that this writer has a different perspec-tive—he views the same events negatively. Finally, if I learn that the second writer was influenced by religious views of the day, I understand the sources of his per-spective.

❸ What is the relationship between literature and place?

Tell students to look for details that show the feelings in their new home as well as their hopes for the future.

PH WRITING COACH | Grade 11

Students will find additional instruction on research writing in Chapter 11.

❶ About the Text Forms

Today, you might send an IM or an e-mail to a distant friend, or simply make a phone call. In the past, though, people relied on **letters** to keep in touch. Private letters tend to be informal, spontaneous, and intended only for the reader to whom they are addressed. Most letters are not meant for publication. However, some letters, such as these by John and Abigail Adams, contain firsthand accounts of historical events and so are regarded as important primary source documents.

A **floor plan** is a diagram of one level of a building shown from an aer-ial point of view. It is usually drawn to scale and shows the relationships between rooms and other features. While this floor plan is an interesting primary source document in its own right, you may also use it to *verify and clarify* information the Adamses include in their letters.

❷ Reading Strategy

A writer's circumstances and point of view are often referred to as his or her "perspective." **Analyzing a writer's perspective** in a primary source document can help you step more fully into the time period in which he or she lived. For example, these letters describe the White House as it is being built. As you read, picture the structure exactly as the writers describe it. Analyze the perspectives using questions such as these:

- Does the writer have positive or negative feelings about the subject?
- Are broader *philosophical, religious, ethical, social, or historical events* influencing his or her perspective?
- Does the perspective seem appropriate, given the circumstances?

❸ What is the **relationship** between literature and *place?*

Today, the White House is recognized as a symbol of power and democ-racy, but in 1800 it was just an unfinished structure. As you inspect these texts, notice details that express how the President and First Lady felt in such an environment as well as their hopes for the future.

Teaching Resources

Unit 1 Resources
Primary Source worksheet, p. 249
Vocabulary Builder, p. 250

Professional Development Guidebook
Enrichment, pp. 33, 223, 237

Common Core Companion,
pp. 170–171

PHLit Online! www.PHLitOnline.com.

❹ Note-Taking Guide

Primary source documents are a rich source of information for researchers. As you read these documents, use a note-taking guide like the one shown to organize relevant and accurate information.

1 Type of Document (check one)
☐ Newspaper   ☐ Advertisement   ☐ Telegram   ☐ Letter
☐ Floor Plan   ☐ Diary or Journal   ☐ E-mail   ☐ Report

2 Date(s) of Document _____

3 Author of Document _____

4 Who is the intended audience for the work? _____
_____

5 What is the main subject of this work? _____
_____

6 List three observations or details in this document that you think are important:
  a _____
  b _____
  c _____

7 Based on your answers to items 4–6, how would you describe the writer's perspective on the subject?
_____
_____

Reading Strategy
Analyzing a Writer's Perspective
A writer's perspective is often affected by his or her audience. As you study each document, ask yourself whether the relationship between writer and audience is intimate or formal, and how this relationship influences the work's content.

This guide was adapted from the **U.S. National Archives** document analysis worksheet.

❺ Vocabulary

account (ə count´) *n.* a report or description (p. 181)

commissioners (kə mish´ ə nərz) *n.* government officials (p. 181)

inspection (in spek´ shən) *n.* examination (p. 181)

unabated (un ə bāt´ əd) *adj.* not lessened or reduced (p. 181)

interspersed (in´ tər spʉrst´) *v.* placed here and there (p. 182)

scale (skāl) *n.* the extent or size of something (p. 182)

establishment (ə stab´ lish mənt) *n.* a household or business (p. 182)

contract (kän´ trakt´) *n.* a written agreement (p. 183)

procure (prō kyoor´) *v.* bring about through some effort (p. 183)

recourse (rē´ kôrs´) *n.* access to a form of help or aid (p. 183)

❹ Note-Taking Guide

1. As a class, review the instructions on the student page about the note-taking guide.

2. Emphasize question 4 in the guide by having a student read the Reading Strategy note in the margin of the student page.

3. Encourage students to use a similar guide as they read the primary sources in this set. Point out that they may customize their note-taking guide to fit the particular needs of the reading assignment.

❺ Vocabulary

1. Pronounce each word, giving its definition; have students say it aloud.

2. Also see the *Classroom Strategies and Teaching Routines* card for introducing vocabulary.

Vocabulary Development

Vocabulary Knowledge Rating
Create a **Vocabulary Knowledge Rating Chart** (in *Professional Development Guidebook,* p. 33) for the vocabulary words on the student page. Give each student a copy of the chart with the words on it. Read the words aloud and have students mark their rating of each in the Before Reading column. When students have completed reading and discussing the group of selections, have them take out their **Vocabulary Knowledge Rating** charts. Read the words aloud and have students rate their knowledge again in the After Reading column. Clarify any words that are still problematic. Then, have students complete the Vocabulary practice at the end of the selections.

❻ THE STORY BEHIND THE DOCUMENTS

John Adams was nearing the end of his first and only term as president of the United States when he wrote this particular letter to his wife, Abigail. It has been noted that theirs was one of the great love stories of American history. Not only in the first letter here but in hundreds of other letters, he addressed her as "My Dearest Friend"; she described him as "the tenderest of husbands." Interestingly, Abigail's mother, it is said, thought her daughter was marrying beneath her.

Of all the letters Abigail wrote to her husband, perhaps the one most quoted contains her admonition of March 31, 1776, that John "remember the ladies" while working out the government of the former colonies at the Continental Congress in Philadelphia. (See more of the quotation in the Enrichment note on p. 182.)

The British architect and civil engineer Latrobe is actually more famous for his work on the U.S. Capitol; although he succeeded James Hoban as architect for the White House, his work halted abruptly, first for financial reasons and then because the British burned the White House in 1814. Hoban returned to work there in 1815; in 1826, he added the semicircular south portico that Latrobe had planned and in 1829 completed the rectangular north portico that Latrobe had envisioned.

President John Adams

Abigail Adams

Benjamin Henry Latrobe

In 1790—two years after the ratification of the Constitution and one year after George Washington was elected the nation's first president—the U.S. Congress passed the Residence Act. This act established a permanent national capital in a 10-square-mile tract of land along the Potomac River. Washington himself selected the site for the President's House, later known as the White House, in a wooded area on the banks of the river. In 1792, a competition was held to choose an architect for the presidential residence. It was hoped that the design would reflect the nation's noble ideals. Irishman James Hoban (1762–1831) won the competition.

Hoban's design for the President's House was a basic rectangular structure. The classic simplicity of this design would allow later presidents to make alterations according to the needs of the day. Thomas Jefferson, for one, would ask architect **Benjamin Henry Latrobe (1764–1820)** to complete and extend Hoban's design. Latrobe transformed Hoban's boxy original into the grand house with columns and covered entrances that today is widely recognized as the home of the President of the United States.

Construction of the original President's House began on October 13, 1792. The house would not near completion until some eight years later, when the second President of the United States, **President John Adams (1735–1826)** and his wife **Abigail Smith Adams (1744–1818)** took up residence there in November, 1800. Although their stay in the house would be brief, the Adamses graciously made do with less-than-perfect living conditions. Many of the walls were still unplastered. A giant hole marked the place where the grand staircase would someday be, and the six out of thirty-six rooms that were habitable were poorly lit and drafty. To keep the house even mildly warm, President Adams paid for firewood out of his own pocket. Unwilling to have the president's laundry hung about the yard, Abigail had lines strung in the large, unfinished East Room.

These were trying times for the Adamses. John was on the brink of losing his reelection to Thomas Jefferson, and Abigail had been ill. The couple was no doubt bolstered by their close companionship, a relationship documented in their letters. Throughout their courtship and marriage, John and Abigail wrote more than one thousand letters to one another. Although their letters are often affectionate and even playful, they also reflect the couple's underlying awareness that they were key players in the unfolding of history.

© Text Complexity Rubric

	Letter from the President's House	Letter to Her Daughter from the New White House	Floor Plan of the President's House
Qualitative Measures			
Context/ Knowledge Demands	Thoughts of the second president 1 2 ③ 4 5	Thoughts and feelings of the first lady 1 2 ③ 4 5	White House architectural plan 1 ② 3 4 5
Structure/Language Conventionality and Clarity	Mostly straightforward, short sentences 1 ② 3 4 5	Long sentences with embedded clauses 1 2 ③ 4 5	Annotations to a floor plan; some technical terms 1 2 ③ 4 5
Levels of Meaning/ Purpose/Concepts	Accessible (report on White House stay) 1 2 ③ 4 5	Accessible (description of daily events) 1 2 ③ 4 5	Abstract (labeled diagram) 1 ② 3 4 5
Quantitative Measures			
Lexile/Text Length	980L / 246 words	1120L / 759 words	NP / 88 words
Overall Complexity	**More accessible**	**More accessible**	**More accessible**

Letter from the
PRESIDENT'S HOUSE

John Adams

BACKGROUND As John Adams wrote this letter, the outcome of the election of 1801, in which Thomas Jefferson was his opponent, was still uncertain. Anxious for the company and consolation of his wife, Adams seems to sense that defeat is likely.

President's house,
Washington City,
Nov. 2. 1800

My Dearest Friend,

We arrived here last night, or rather yesterday, at one o Clock and here we dined and Slept. The Building is in a State to be habitable. And now we wish for your Company. The Account you give of the melancholly State of our dear Brother Mr. Cranch [1] and his family is really distressing and must severely afflict you. I most cordially Sympathize with you and them. I have seen only Mr. Marshall and Mr. Stoddert, General Wilkinson and the two Commissioners Mr. Scott and Mr. Thornton. [2] I shall say nothing of public affairs. I am very glad you consented to come on, for you would have been more anxious at Quincy [3] than here, and I, to all my other Solicitudines Mordaces as Horace [4] calls them i.e. "biting Cares" should have added a great deal on your Account. Besides it is fit and proper that you and I should retire together and not one before the other. Before I end my Letter I pray Heaven to bestow the best of Blessings on this House and all that shall hereafter inhabit it. May none but honest and wise Men ever rule under this roof. I shall not attempt a description of it. You will form the best Idea of it from Inspection. Mr. Brisler [5] is very anxious for the arrival of the Man and Women and I am much more so for that of the Ladies. I am with unabated Confidence and affection your

John Adams

Vocabulary
account (ə count´) *n.* a report or description

commissioners (kə mish´ ə nərz) *n.* government officials

inspection (in spek´ shən) *n.* examination

unabated (un ə bā´ təd) *adj.* not lessened or reduced

▲ sample of John Adams's handwriting

1. **Richard Cranch** President Adams's brother-in-law.
2. **Mr. Marshall. . . Mr. Thornton** Various officials and cabinet members.
3. **Quincy** the Adamses' hometown in Massachusetts.
4. **Horace** classical Roman poet.
5. **John Brisler** President Adams's servant.

Letter from the President's House **181**

---

❸ Background

Washington, D.C.

In his last months as president, John Adams and his wife, Abigail, became the first couple to live in the White House (not yet known by that title). At the time, the city of Washington consisted of a few public buildings and a scattered collection of crude residences. This letter to Adams's daughter describes the unfinished White House and captures the essence of life in the new nation.

❹ Primary Sources

Letters

1. Draw students' attention to the bracketed passage.

2. **Ask** students the following question: Why would this comment about "ladies" be found only in a private letter, never in one intended as public?

   Answer: Adams's personal opinions of the ladies' hometown of Georgetown, in comparison with Milton, Massachusetts, are uncomplimentary and would not belong in a public document.

---

❸ Letter to Her Daughter from the
NEW WHITE HOUSE

Abigail Adams

Washington,
21 November, 1800

My Dear Child:

I arrived here on Sunday last, and without meeting with any accident worth noticing, except losing ourselves when we left Baltimore and going eight or nine miles on the Frederick road, by which means we were obliged to go the other eight through woods, where we wandered two hours without finding a guide or the path. Fortunately, a straggling black came up with us, and we engaged him as a guide to extricate us out of our difficulty; but woods are all you see from Baltimore until you reach the *city*, which is only so in name. Here and there is a small cot, without a glass window, interspersed amongst the forests, through which you travel miles without seeing any human being. In the city there are buildings enough, if they were compact and finished, to accommodate Congress and those attached to it; but as they are, and scattered as they are, I see no great comfort for them. The river, which runs up to Alexandria,[1] is in full view of my window, and I see the vessels as they pass and repass. The house is upon a grand and superb **scale**, requiring about thirty servants to attend and keep the apartments in proper order, and perform the ordinary business of the house and stables; an **establishment** very well proportioned to the President's salary. The lighting of the apartments, from the kitchen to parlors and chambers, is a tax indeed; and the fires we are obliged to keep to secure us from daily agues is another very cheering comfort. To assist us in this great castle, and render less attendance necessary, bells are wholly wanting, not one single one being hung through the whole house, and promises are all you can obtain. This is so great an inconvenience, that I know not what to do, or how to do. The ladies from Georgetown[2] and in the city have many of them visited me. Yesterday I returned fifteen visits—but such a place as Georgetown appears—why, our Milton[3] is beautiful. But no comparisons—if they will put me up some bells and let me have wood enough to keep fires, I design to be pleased. I could content myself almost anywhere three

Vocabulary

interspersed (in´ tər spʉrst´) *v.* placed here and there

scale (skāl) *n.* the extent or size of something

establishment (ə stab´ lish mənt) *n.* a household or business

---

1. **Alexandria** city in northeastern Virginia.
2. **Georgetown** section of Washington, D.C.
3. **Milton** town in Massachusetts.

Enrichment: Investigating a Key Person in History

Adams and Women's Rights

John Adams was impressed with young Abigail's independent mind. In 1776 Abigail wrote to her husband of her vision of a new independence for women. "And by the way, in the new code of laws, which I suppose it will be necessary for you to make, I desire you would remember the ladies. . . . Do not put such unlimited power in the hands of the husbands. Remember, all men would be tyrants if they could."

Activity: Biographical Sketch Have students conduct research on the concerns Abigail Adams had about women's rights. Suggest that they record the limitations on nineteenth-century women's voting, property, and other rights in the **Enrichment: Investigating a Key Person in History** worksheet, *Professional Development Guidebook,* page 233. Have students use the results of their research to write a sketch about Abigail Adams.

months; but, surrounded with forests, can you believe that wood is not to be had because people cannot be found to cut and cart it? Briesler entered into a **contract** with a man to supply him with wood. A small part, a few cords only, has he been able to get. Most of that was expended to dry the walls of the house before we came in, and yesterday the man told him it was impossible for him to **procure** it to be cut and carted. He has had **recourse** to coals; but we cannot get grates made and set. We have, indeed, come into a new country. You must keep all this to yourself, and, when asked how I like it, say that I write you the situation is beautiful, which is true. The house is made habitable, but there is not a single apartment finished, and all withinside, except the plastering, has been done since Briesler came. We have not the least fence, yard, or other convenience without and the great unfinished audience room I make a drying-room of, to hang up the clothes in. The principal stairs are not up, and will not be this winter. Six chambers are made comfortable; two are occupied by the President and Mr. Shaw; two lower rooms, one for a common parlor, and one for a levee room. Upstairs there is the oval room, which is designed for the drawing room, and has the crimson furniture in it. It is a very handsome room now; but, when completed, it will be beautiful. If the twelve years, in which this place has been considered as the future seat of government had been improved, as they would have been if in New England, very many of the present inconveniences would have been removed. It is a beautiful spot, capable of every improvement, and, the more I view it, the more I am delighted with it. Since I sat down to write, I have been called down to a servant from Mount Vernon,[4] with a billet[5] from Major Custis, and a haunch of venison, and a kind, congratulatory letter from Mrs. Lewis, upon my arrival in the city, with Mrs. Washington's love, inviting me to Mount Vernon, where, health permitting, I will go before I leave this place. Affectionally, your mother,

Abigail Adams

---

4. **Mount Vernon** home of George Washington, located in northern Virginia.
5. **billet** (bil´ it) *n.* brief letter.

Vocabulary

contract (kän´ trakt´) *n.* a written agreement

procure (prō kyoor´) *v.* to bring about through some effort

recourse (rē´ kôrs´) *n.* access to a form of help or aid

Primary Sources
Letters
In what ways does Mrs. Adams's statement about coming into a "new country" suggest a moment in time that is both historically and personally significant?

American stagecoach, mid-nineteenth century ▼

WILLIAMSVILLE & EAST DOVER.

U.S. MAIL

Letter to Her Daughter from the New White House **183**

⑤ Primary Sources
Letters

1. Draw students' attention to the bracketed passage.

2. **Ask** students the Primary Sources question: In what ways does Mrs. Adam's statement about coming into a "new country" suggest a moment in time that is both historically and personally significant?
   Answer: Historically, the United States, a very young country, was claiming a previously unused area as its brand-new capital. Personally, the move to Washington was an adventure for Abigail Adams; it represented a very different kind of life from the one she had led in refined, cultivated Boston.

Differentiated Instruction for Universal Access

Enrichment for Advanced Readers
John Adams's term as president was filled with controversy, as was the election of 1800, which was finally decided by the House of Representatives. Have students choose among the following issues to research and then to write about in a brief report: the XYZ affair, the Alien and Sedition Acts, or the development of political parties.

Enrichment for Gifted/Talented Students
Have students script the scene in which Abigail Adams arrives at the White House for the first time and is greeted by her husband. Students should create the dialogue between the wife and husband as he welcomes her and shows her around the new house.

Analyzing a Writer's Perspective

1. Remind students that analyzing a writer's perspective will help them understand the writer's time period.

2. **Ask** the following question: Do Latrobe's notes on this page and the next focus on the weaknesses of the house or its strengths? How so?
   Answer: Students should see that the notes call out omissions and problems: "This staircase is not yet put up"; "entirely unfinished"; "the ceiling has given way"; "Wooden platform"; "rough post and rail fence"; "mere vestibule."

3. **Ask** students to speculate about how Americans of the time might have felt about an "entirely unfinished" public audience chamber in their leader's residence.
   Possible responses: Some Americans might have felt that their nation should be represented with dignity and that it was unbecoming for the president to lack a stately reception area for guests. At the same time, the fact that the house remained unfinished for so long indicates that there was little public concern about its condition.

© **COMMON CORE ▪ RESEARCH PROJECT**

Floor Plan of the
PRESIDENT'S HOUSE
Benjamin Henry Latrobe

Shown here is a floor plan of the President's House as it existed in 1803. Latrobe created this floor plan as a proposal for work that remained to be done on the house. Below is a detail showing all the rooms on the first floor; at right is the entire original drawing, including Latrobe's comments. Latrobe's original notations are blurred with age.

❻

▼ Detail of Latrobe drawing

Latrobe's Notations

❶ Public dining room
❷ Porters Lodge
❸ Private stairs
❹ Hall
❺ Staircase
❻ This staircase is not yet put up
❼ Library & Cabinet
❽ President's antechamber
❾ Drawing room
❿ Common dining Room
⓫ Public audience chamber; entirely unfinished;
⓬ the ceiling has given way
⓭ Wooden platform

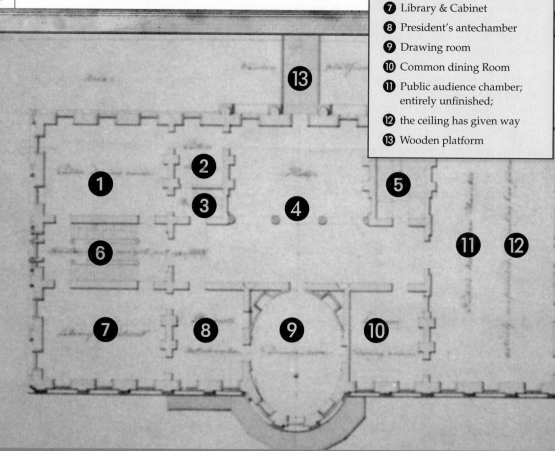

Enrichment: Investigating Artistic Schools and Movements

Neoclassicism

The original Hoban plan for the White House was categorized as neoclassical. As pointed out in student and teacher edition notes, the building was added to and reconsidered in the thirty years after the Adamses' residence there. Then, both in 1902 and after World War II, the building saw further major work.

Activity: Architectural Illustration Have students teach themselves about neoclassicism in architecture. Suggest that they record their

findings in the **Enrichment: Investigating Artistic Schools and Movements** work sheet, *Professional Development Guidebook,* page 220. Students should pass on their findings about neoclassicism to classmates by sharing previously published drawings and photographs or illustrations they make themselves.

Latrobe's notes above and below the drawing contain observations about the President's House and its grounds. The drawing is signed and dated.

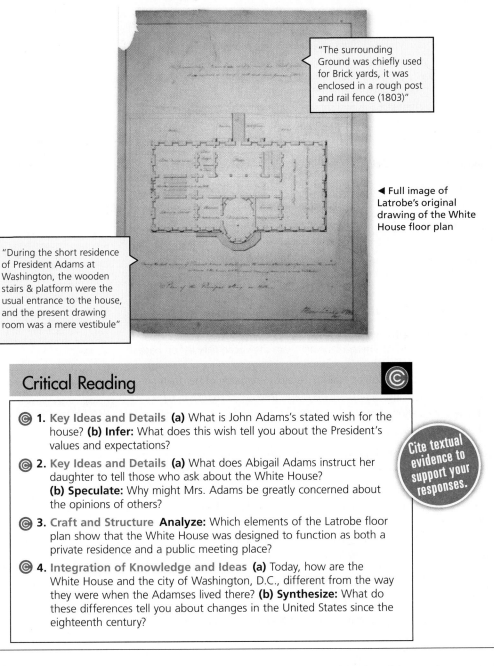

"The surrounding Ground was chiefly used for Brick yards, it was enclosed in a rough post and rail fence (1803)"

◄ Full image of Latrobe's original drawing of the White House floor plan

"During the short residence of President Adams at Washington, the wooden stairs & platform were the usual entrance to the house, and the present drawing room was a mere vestibule"

Critical Reading

1. Key Ideas and Details (a) What is John Adams's stated wish for the house? **(b) Infer:** What does this wish tell you about the President's values and expectations?

2. Key Ideas and Details (a) What does Abigail Adams instruct her daughter to tell those who ask about the White House?
(b) Speculate: Why might Mrs. Adams be greatly concerned about the opinions of others?

3. Craft and Structure Analyze: Which elements of the Latrobe floor plan show that the White House was designed to function as both a private residence and a public meeting place?

4. Integration of Knowledge and Ideas (a) Today, how are the White House and the city of Washington, D.C., different from the way they were when the Adamses lived there? **(b) Synthesize:** What do these differences tell you about changes in the United States since the eighteenth century?

Cite textual evidence to support your responses.

Answers

1. **(a)** John Adams prays that the house and its future inhabitants will be blessed. **(b)** This prayer tells us that the president thought not only about himself but also about the future, when he expected others to take his place.

2. **(a)** She tells her daughter to say that the White House is located in a beautiful area. **(b)** Students should infer that as First Lady, Adams occupied a political position in which the opinions of others carried great weight.

3. Possible response: The notation "Private dining room" acknowledges that part of the residence was not open to the public. The labels "Public dining room" and "Public audience chamber" indicate the house belonged to all Americans.

4. Possible responses: **(a)** The White House today is somewhat larger than in the Adamses' day, while the city of Washington, D.C., is now dense with buildings, both governmental and private. **(b)** The number of people who work in and need access to the White House, as well as the number of people working in government in general, has grown enormously.

Answers

Comparing Primary Sources

1. (a) The intended audience for John Adams's letter was his wife; for Abigail Adams's letter, her daughter; for Latrobe's floor plan/ notes, whomever he reported to. (b) Addressing Mrs. Adams, President Adams expresses personal feelings; addressing her daughter, Mrs. Adams is frank; addressing higher-ups, Latrobe shows how much work remains.

2. **Sample answers:** (a) John Adams: "I shall not attempt a description of it"; Abigail Adams: "the . . . audience room I make a drying-room of"; Latrobe: "the ceiling has given way." (b) John: respect, concern; Abigail: patience; Latrobe: objectivity.

3. **Possible response:** Latrobe's notes clarify what John means when he says the building is in a "State to be habitable"—portions are unfinished.

Vocabulary Acquisition and Use

1. an account
2. interspersed
3. establishment
4. unabated
5. <u>Commissioners</u> work in a state capitol, near the government.
6. Restaurant owners might prepare for an <u>inspection</u> by thoroughly cleaning the premises.
7. City planners are more concerned with <u>scale</u> as they consider how buildings fit their locations.
8. A <u>contract</u>, or written agreement, is necessary in business situations but usually not between friends.
9. A political campaign should <u>procure</u>, or bring about, votes.
10. In America, even if you break a law, you have <u>recourse</u> to other laws to protect yourself.

Etymology Study: The noun *contract* refers to a document that draws people together to do something; the verb *contract* refers to the action of drawing parties together for an agreed-on end. The prefixes *com-* and *con-* show up in *commission, committee, compile, connotation*; *trahare* is part of *traction, distraction, subtract,* and *extract.*

Letters • Floor Plan

Comparing Primary Sources

Refer to your Note-Taking Guide to answer these questions.

1. **(a)** Who is the intended audience for each document? **(b)** How did the audience probably influence the type and style of information presented in the **letters** and the **floor plan**?

2. **(a)** Use a chart like the one shown to identify one important detail or observation from each document. **(b)** What **perspective** toward the President's House does each detail or observation reflect?

Source	Detail or Observation	Attitude It Reveals
John Adams		
Abigail Adams		
Benjamin Latrobe		

3. Which details do the Adamses present in their letters that you can verify or clarify by reviewing the floor plan and its notes? Explain.

© Vocabulary Acquisition and Use

Synonyms For each item, replace the italicized word with a synonym, or word of similar meaning, from the vocabulary list on page 179. Use each word once.

1. In a letter to her mother, Holly gave a(n) *description* of her train ride.
2. The scenery consisted of farmhouses with cows *scattered* in between.
3. The train station was a primitive *structure* with no indoor plumbing.
4. Holly felt *strong* pleasure at the idea of a week in the country.

Content-Area Vocabulary Answer each question. Explain your answers.

5. Do *commissioners* most likely work at a school or a state capitol?
6. How might restaurant owners prepare for an *inspection*?
7. Which group is more concerned with *scale*, city planners or dancers?
8. Would you use a *contract* to get a ride from a friend?
9. Should a successful campaign *procure* votes or voters?
10. Would you have *recourse* to the law if you had broken it?

Etymology Study The word *contract* comes from the Latin words *com*, which means "together," and *trahare*, which means "to draw." Explain how these meanings relate to both the noun and the verb form of *contract*. Then, use a dictionary to locate other words with the same Latin word parts.

Writing

7. Conduct short as well as more sustained research projects to answer a question or solve a problem; narrow or broaden the inquiry when appropriate; synthesize multiple sources on the subject, demonstrating understanding of the subject under investigation.

8. Gather relevant information from multiple authoritative print and digital sources, using advanced searches effectively; assess the strengths and limitations of each source in terms of the task, purpose, and audience; integrate information into the text selectively to maintain the flow of ideas, avoiding plagiarism and overreliance on any one source and following a standard format for citation.

Language

6. Acquire and use accurately general academic and domain-specific words and phrases, sufficient for reading, writing, speaking, and listening at the college and career readiness level; demonstrate independence in gathering vocabulary knowledge when considering a word or phrase important to comprehension or expression.

Assessment Practice

Recognize Cause and Effect (For more practice, see *All-in-One Workbook*.)

Successful readers understand that causal relationships are sometimes signaled by transitions such as *since* or *because*. Use the following example to help students identify signal words as they look for causal relationships.

> . . . if they will . . . let me have wood enough to keep fires, I design to be pleased. I could content myself almost anywhere three months; but surrounded with forests, can you believe that wood is not to be had

because people cannot be found to cut and cart it?

Why does Abigail Adams lack firewood?

A There were no forests nearby.
B There was no one to cut the wood.
C Washingtonians did not use firewood.
D Abigail Adams preferred coal.

Choices **A**, **C**, and **D** contain inaccurate information. **B** states the cause given in the text.

Research Task

Topic: The Changing White House

Like America itself, the White House has come a long way since Abigail Adams hung her family's clothes to dry in "the great unfinished audience room." Starting with what you have learned from the Adams letters and the Latrobe floor plan, research the history of the building.

Assignment: Construct an annotated and illustrated timeline of the White House. Include each of these types of items:

- Architectural changes and additions
- Technological changes and additions
- Historical events that altered the building
- Influential presidents and first ladies
- Visual images—photos, drawings, diagrams

Formulate a research plan. Locate authoritative print and electronic resources on the history of the White House. Identify key points to feature on your timeline and choose the most useful sources to cite.

Narrow the inquiry. Focus your research by listing questions, such as the following: When was electrical wiring installed? Who changed the house the most? What do specific changes to the White House say about our changing culture? Work to answer your specific questions.

Gather sources. Assemble the information in a systematic way, taking accurate notes, and separating factual data from opinions. Make sure to follow appropriate principles of citation (see pp. R21–R23 for details on how to cite varied sources.)

Synthesize multiple sources. When you synthesize information, you assemble data from varied sources and organize it into a unified presentation. As you work, critique your process. You may need to discard some details or continue researching to find additional information.

Model: Synthesizing Information with a Flexible Timeline

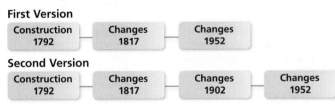

First Version

| Construction 1792 | Changes 1817 | Changes 1952 |

Second Version

| Construction 1792 | Changes 1817 | Changes 1902 | Changes 1952 |

Present your ideas. Make sure your timeline contains all of the essential information. Then, add annotations, quotations, and visuals.

RESEARCH TIP

As you research, you may find it helpful to distinguish between interior and exterior changes to the White House.

Use a checklist like the one shown to evaluate your work.

Research Checklist

☐ Have I addressed all of my research questions?

☐ Have I clearly shown changes over time?

☐ Do my annotations support the basic facts?

☐ Do my visuals clearly illustrate historical changes?

The Changing White House

Introduce the Assignment

1. Review the assignment. Explain that an annotated timeline should include dates of significant events, as well as quotes, images, and short summaries of events.

2. Refer students to the timeline on pp. 4–13 as a model. Point out that the assignment requires longer annotations, or explanations, than are given on this timeline.

3. Using the list of items on the student page, students should formulate a research plan. To aid students, help them to ask open-ended research questions, such as "Have any changes been made based on similar buildings in other countries?"

Guide Student Research

1. Using the library and the Internet, students should locate a range of relevant sources. Point out that it is often helpful to find different accounts of the same event, both to ensure the accuracy of the information and to gain a full perspective.

2. Suggest that students begin their research with secondary sources such as history books and encyclopedias in order to get "the big picture" from scholars who have studied the primary sources. Then, they can move on to research relevant and recommended primary sources for support.

Think Aloud: Model Separating Fact From Opinion

Say to students:

When I am unsure if a piece of information is the author's opinion, I ask myself, "Could someone else have another opinion about it?" For example, in the statement "In 1814 the British Army set the White House on fire, forever changing the country's perception of its premier building," I know the date and the participants are facts. But another researcher might disagree that the fire affected public opinion, which tells me that part of the statement is an author's opinion.

Guide Student Writing

1. Students should put their data in chronological order and synthesize, or combine information relating to the same topic.

2. Encourage students to evaluate the relevance of their information and discard information as needed.

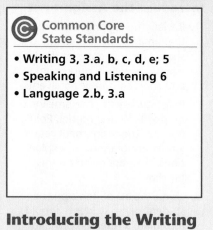

Common Core State Standards

- **Writing 3, 3.a, b, c, d, e; 5**
- **Speaking and Listening 6**
- **Language 2.b, 3.a**

Introducing the Writing Assignment

Review the assignment and the criteria, using the instruction on the student page.

What Do You Notice?

1. Read the excerpt from *The Interesting Narrative of the Life of Olaudah Equiano*. Discuss the passage with students.

2. Have a student read the highlighted sentences aloud. **Ask** what makes the writing special. (**Possible responses:** its vivid verbs; its concrete details; its careful punctuation)

3. Direct students' attention to the punctuation in the first highlighted sentence. Then, **ask** why the writer uses a semicolon to join the two main clauses. (**Answer:** Since the ideas expressed in the clauses are closely related, the writer uses a semicolon to join the main clauses. If the two ideas were not closely related, the writer should have put them in separate sentences.)

4. Have students consider why the writer did not use a comma instead of a semicolon to join the two main clauses. (**Answer:** By using a comma to join the two main clauses, the writer would have created a run-on sentence.)

5. Suggest that students use semicolons in their narratives to join main clauses with closely related ideas.

Susan Power on Autobiographical Writing

Show students Segment 3 on Susan Power on the *See It!* DVD or via the link in the **Enriched Online Student Edition** at www.PHLitOnline.com. Discuss Power's comments about how she grounds her fictional writing in real-life events.

188

Write a Narrative

Autobiographical Narrative Writers are often told to write about what they know. This advice has produced some of the best stories in literature. While some are pure works of imagination, others are true tales about the writer's own life. Such nonfiction stories are called autobiographical narratives. Autobiographical narratives often use the same types of narrative techniques you are used to seeing in works of fiction. Follow the steps outlined in this workshop to write your own autobiographical narrative.

Assignment Write an autobiographical narrative about a special or memorable experience.

What to Include Your autobiographical narrative should include the following elements:

- You, the writer, as the main character and other developed characters
- A clear depiction of a problem or situation
- An insight about the experience, an expression of its significance
- A logical organization that builds a smooth progression of events
- Narrative techniques that bring events, settings, and people to life
- Error-free conventions, including correct use of capitalization

To preview the criteria on which your autobiographical narrative may be assessed, see the rubric on page 195.

> To get a feel for autobiographical narratives, read this mentor text. Notice how Olaudah Equiano explains what happened to him and how he felt about it. For the complete text, see pages 171–175.
>
> ### *from:* The Interesting Narrative of the Life of Olaudah Equiano
>
> *During our passage, I first saw flying fishes, which surprised me very much; they used frequently to fly across the ship, and many of them fell on the deck. I also now first saw the use of the quadrant; I had often with astonishment seen the mariners make observations with it, and I could not think what it meant. They at last took notice of my surprise; and one of them, willing to increase it, as well as to gratify my curiosity, made me one day look through it. The clouds appeared to me to be land, which disappeared as they passed along. This heightened my wonder…*

Common Core State Standards

Writing

3. Write narratives to develop real or imagined experiences or events using effective techniques, well-chosen details, and well-structured event sequences.

3.a. Engage and orient the reader by setting out a problem, situation, or observation and its significance, establishing one or multiple point(s) of view, and introducing a narrator and/or characters; create a smooth progression of experiences or events.

5. Develop and strengthen writing as needed by planning, revising, editing, rewriting, or trying a new approach, focusing on addressing what is most significant for a specific purpose and audience.

www.PHLitOnline.com

WRITE GUY
Jeff Anderson, M.Ed.

What Do You Notice?

Read the highlighted sentences several times. Then, with a partner, discuss the qualities that make them special. You might consider the following elements:

- Word choice
- Emotional appeal
- Structure
- Use of punctuation

Share your group's observations with the class.

Teaching Resources

The following resources can be used to enrich or extend the instruction.

All *Unit 1 Resources*
Writing Workshop, pp. 253–254

All *Common Core Companion,* pp. 208–218; 226–227

All *Professional Development Guidebook*
Rubric for Self-Assessment:
Autobiographical Narrative, pp. 248–249

All *Graphic Organizer Transparencies*
Rubric for Self Assessment:
Autobiographical Narrative, p. 53

All *See It!* DVD
Susan Power, Segments 3 and 4

PHLit Online! All resources, including print and video, are available online at www.PHLitOnline.com

Prewriting and Planning

Choosing Your Topic

Choose an event from your life that is meaningful to you, interesting to readers, and not awkward or painful to share. It may be an experience that showed you a different aspect of yourself, solved a problem, or gave you a new perspective. To find a topic, use one of these strategies:

- **Interview yourself.** List ten questions you might ask a stranger about his or her life. Add follow-up questions that would help you get deeper answers. Then, use your list to interview yourself.

> **Model: Interviewing Yourself**
>
> **Main Question:** What was the most surprising thing that ever happened to you?
> **Follow-Ups:** How did you react? Would you react the same way today? Why or why not?

- **Make memory notes.** Go through a photo album or scrapbook and jot down notes about the events recorded there. Add details about what you did and how you felt at those times. Talk to a relative who might remember those moments from a different perspective.

Narrowing Your Topic

Find the turning point. Once you have chosen a basic topic, sharpen your focus. Narrow in on a moment—something that became a turning point in your life. Use an event chart like the one shown to locate such a key event. In the chart shown, the writer has highlighted the turning point in yellow.

| We moved to CA when Dad got a promotion. | → | Lost my friends; felt afraid of new situations | → | Mom gave us surfboards and lessons. | → | I began to love the ocean. | → | I decided to study oceanography in college. |

Gathering Details

Engage and orient the reader. Your purpose in writing is to explore your thoughts and feelings about an experience and to share your insights with readers. Once you have chosen a topic, gather details that will help your readers understand your meaning. To do so, answer questions like the following:

- What *background information* do my readers need to have in order to understand my experience?
- What *descriptive details* will bring my experience to life for my readers?
- What do readers need to know about what this experience means to me?

Writing Workshop **189**

Prewriting and Planning

1. Introduce the prewriting strategies, using the instruction on the student page.
2. Have students apply the strategies to choose and narrow a topic.

Teaching the Strategies

1. Explain to students that the events of their narratives do not necessarily have to be told in chronological order, but putting these events on a timeline will help them organize their thoughts.
2. Explain that research may be needed if students refer to factual events with details they do not recall or if they need to clarify for their readers the context in which they are writing.

Think Aloud: Model Narrowing Your Topic

Model narrowing the topic, using the following "think aloud." Say to students:

> Now that I have several possible events and ideas to write about, I need to choose what I want to concentrate on. Which item on my list represents a turning point for me? I look for the event or issue that changed me or made me think about things differently.

Six Traits Focus

✔	Ideas		Word Choice
✔	Organization		Sentence Fluency
	Voice		Conventions

PH **WRITING COACH** Grade 11

Students will find additional information on writing an autobiographical narrative in Chapter 5.

1. Introduce the drafting strategies, using the instruction on the student page.
2. Have students apply the strategies as they draft.

Teaching the Strategies

1. Instruct students to hint at the conflict in the opening of their drafts before telling how it began, developed, and was resolved.

2. Explain that because the climax is a story's most interesting and suspenseful moment, it is the most important point in a story. Therefore, all the details that come before the climax should help build up to the climax.

3. Before students think about their lead, suggest that they identify the focal point of the narrative. For example, is it the setting, a person, or an event? Tell students to write their compelling lead around this central point.

4. Discuss how dialogue can help the reader understand characters and how it can increase suspense and develop the conflict. Emphasize, however, that dialogue should not be included unless it contributes directly to the main idea and plot of the narrative.

5. Remind students that each time a new character begins speaking, they should start a new paragraph. The paragraph might include just the words of the character, or it might also include a description of the character or a commentary on the words spoken.

Six Traits Focus

✔	Ideas		Word Choice
✔	Organization		Sentence Fluency
	Voice		Conventions

190

Drafting

Shaping Your Writing

Order events. Most autobiographical narratives relate events in *chronological order*, or the sequence in which they happened. They also center on a *conflict*, or problem, that is somehow resolved. As the conflict develops, the tension should increase until it reaches the *climax,* or point of greatest intensity. After that, the tension should decrease as you move toward the ending, or *resolution*. Within this overall structure, consider using narrative techniques. For example, you may jump back in time with a *flashback* or forward in time with a *flash-forward*. Use a plot diagram like the one shown here to order your events.

Begin with a strong lead. Write a simple but intriguing sentence that catches the reader's curiosity. Notice how these lead sentences *foreshadow*, or drop hints about the story to follow:

- *My grandfather walked in and suddenly the room was silent.*
- *My dog probably wouldn't want me to tell you this story.*

Provide a meaningful conclusion. End your narrative with a reflection, observation, or insight that confirms the importance of the experience.

Providing Elaboration

Use thought shots. As you write, follow these steps to expand your ideas:

- Scan your draft for uses of the word *I*. For each one, ask yourself how you reacted to what you described.
- For each reaction, draw a circle, or *thought shot*, in the margin. Inside the circle, jot details about what you saw, heard, felt, or thought.

Climax
Show the conflict at its height.

Build the intensity of the conflict. — Rising Action / Falling Action — Start to end the conflict.

Exposition
Introduce the situation and conflict.

Resolution
Settle the conflict.

Model: Using "Thought Shots"

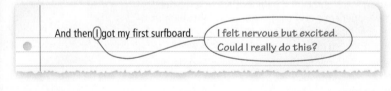

And then ⓘ got my first surfboard. | I felt nervous but excited. Could I really do this?

Include dialogue. One of the best ways to make your writing more vivid is to include dialogue. People's words bring them alive as characters and help advance the story's conflict and climax.

Common Core State Standards

Writing

3.b. Use narrative techniques such as dialogue, pacing, description, reflection, and multiple plot lines, to develop experiences, events, and/or characters.

3.c. Use a variety of techniques to sequence events so that they build on one another to create a coherent whole and build toward a particular tone and outcome.

3.e. Provide a conclusion that follows from and reflects on what is experienced, observed, or resolved over the course of the narrative.

Strategies for
Using Technology in Writing

Encourage students to write their narratives on computers. Composing on a computer facilitates writing by allowing students to put down their thoughts quickly as they develop. Students can easily go forward and backward in the text to add, delete, or move around ideas.

Students can also take advantage of the reviewing feature on many word-processing programs; this will enable them to enter comments that are not part of the text. (The reviewing feature is accessible as a tool bar option.) Students can use this feature to enter "thought shots" or other ideas that they want to think more about before incorporating them into the text.

Writers on Writing

Susan Power On Choosing the Right Words

Susan Power is the author of "Museum Indians" (p. 34).

Beginnings are always difficult for me. I'll have an idea for a story, or, as in this excerpt from a nonfiction essay, a memory from childhood, but I won't know where to start. Here I wanted to write about the body of water where I'd spent many happy hours—Lake Michigan. Should I begin with hard facts, its depth and circumference? No. After many drafts, I began with my mother's stories.

"Finding the precise word can be tricky."

—Susan Power

from "Chicago Waters," from *Roofwalker*

My mother used to say that by the time I was an old woman, Lake Michigan would be the size of a silver dollar. She pinched her index finger with her thumb to show me the pitiful dimensions.

"People will gather around the tiny lake, what's left of it, and cluck over a spoonful of water," she told me.

I learned to squint at the 1967 shoreline until I had carved away the structures and roads built on landfill and could imagine the lake and its city as my mother found them in 1942 when she arrived in Chicago. I say *the lake and its city* rather than *the city and its lake*, because my mother taught me another secret: the city of Chicago belongs to Lake Michigan.

But which of my mother's pronouncements to believe? That Chicago would swallow the Midwestern sea, smother it in concrete, or that the lake wielded enough strength to outpolitick even Mayor Richard Daley?

Mayor Daley, Sr. is gone now, but the lake remains, alternately tranquil and riled, changing colors like a mood ring. I guess we know who won.

When my mother watches the water from her lakeside apartment building, she still sucks in her breath. "You have to respect the power of that lake," she tells me. And I do now. I do.

> I mention that I'm looking at "the 1967 shoreline" so the reader will know the time frame, when I was a child.

> I rely on the dictionary and thesaurus to help me find the precise, specific word. First I tried *sayings*, but that didn't exhibit my mother's strength as much as *pronouncements*.

> Wrestling with word choice again, I used *beat* initially but later selected *outpolitick*— more appropriate when describing a politician.

Writing Workshop **191**

Susan Power on Choosing the Right Words

Review the passage on the student page with the class using Susan Power's comments to deepen students' understanding of the process of writing an autobiographical narrative.

Teaching From the Professional Model

1. Show students Segment 4 of Susan Power on the *See It!* **DVD** or from this page in the **Enriched Online Student Edition**. Discuss how incorporating autobiographical events into her writing has acted as a tool of self-discovery for Power.

2. **Ask** students why *pronouncements* is a better word choice in Power's narrative than *sayings*. **Possible response:** *Pronouncements* is a more specific word, and it better conveys the mother's strength and authority. *Sayings* is bland and imprecise.

3. **Ask** students to explain why autobiographical writing could benefit from the kinds of adjustments Power made in the excerpt from *Roofwalker*. **Possible response:** An autobiographical narrative vividly describes a real-life event to readers. Specific, precise words that fit the context of the narrative help bring the event to life.

4. Have students identify how Power makes a connection between the past and the present. **Answer:** At the end of the excerpt, she says that she now "respects the power of the lake," as her mother once told her to do.

191

Revising

1. Introduce the revising strategies, using the instruction on the student page.

2. Have students apply the strategies as they revise.

Teaching the Strategies

1. If time permits, allow students to wait twenty-four hours before they begin to revise their drafts. Explain that time away from a piece of writing helps the writer see his or her work with fresh eyes and renewed attention.

2. Point out that the connection to the present does not have to appear at any particular point in the narrative. It can occur at the beginning, at the end, or in comments throughout the narrative.

3. Point out that transitional words that show a shift in time and a connection of ideas help make connections between the past and the present. In the Model, explain that the word *Eventually* introduces a phrase explaining how the writer changed.

4. Write these sentences on the board, and **ask** students to expand the sentences to provide more information about the characters.

   My grandmother was a cheerful and happy woman.

   The guest arrived late and seemed upset.

   Sample answer:

   My grandmother was a merry woman who loved to prepare delicious feasts for her husband and appreciative friends, children, and grandchildren.

   The guest arrived late, pale and out of breath, and told us she had just seen something very strange.

Six Traits Focus

✔	Ideas	✔	Word Choice
✔	Organization		Sentence Fluency
	Voice		Conventions

Revising

Revising Your Overall Structure

Connect the past to the present. Your autobiographical narrative should show how the experience you are describing helped you become the person you are today. Make sure you have included details that help the reader understand what you learned or how you changed as a direct result of the experience you narrate. To strengthen those connections even more, follow these steps:

- Highlight passages in your draft that state or hint at how the experience affected you in a long-term way.
- ✔ Put a check mark beside those passages that could be clearer or explained better.
- Strengthen the checked passages by adding transitions to clarify connections, sensory details to make them more vivid, or a better explanation.

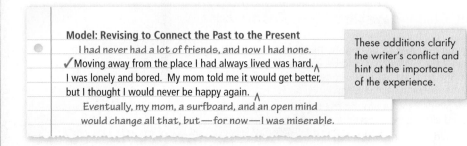

Model: Revising to Connect the Past to the Present

I had never had a lot of friends, and now I had none.

✓ Moving away from the place I had always lived was hard. ∧ I was lonely and bored. My mom told me it would get better, but I thought I would never be happy again. ∧

Eventually, my mom, a surfboard, and an open mind would change all that, but—for now—I was miserable.

These additions clarify the writer's conflict and hint at the importance of the experience.

Revising Your Sentences

Use subordination to give characters depth. Carefully reread the sentences that introduce the people in your story. If they seem bland and uninformative, use subordinate clauses to expand simple sentences and provide more information about who your characters are, what they are like, and how they affect the events of your narrative.

Simple Sentence: Alison taught me how to surf.

Complex Sentence: Alison, my mother's best friend, saw me fumbling in the waves, so she took pity on me and taught me how to surf.

Simple Sentence: She helped me a lot.

Complex Sentence: By showing that someone cared, she helped me a lot.

Peer Review: Have a partner review your draft, identifying sentences that introduce or describe characters. Answer questions your partner poses about the characters' personalities, their behavior or statements, and their roles in your narrative. Use your answers to expand the sentences your partner identified.

 **Common Core State Standards**

Writing
3.d. Use precise words and phrases, telling details, and sensory language to convey a vivid picture of the experiences, events, setting, and/or characters.

Language
3.a. Vary syntax for effect.

Strategies for *Using Technology in Writing*

When they reach the revision stage, students using word-processing software may want to set their line spacing at double or even triple spacing before printing copies of their drafts. The extra spacing allows plenty of space to make changes between the lines, and the hard copy allows students to spread the pages out and look at the essay as a whole, rather than seeing only a few lines of it at once on a screen.

Students should then transfer the changes to the electronic file.

Encourage students to save a version of their draft so that they can compare it to the revised version. Having a copy of previous versions will also allow them to go back to an earlier version if they decide some of the original passages were better before changes were made.

| Word Choice | Ideas | Conventions | Sentence Fluency | Voice | Organization |

Developing Your Style

Improving Word Choice

If your writing is not as clear, sharp, or fresh as it should be, a careful look at your **word choice** might help. The use of strong verbs, precise nouns, and specific adjectives will make your writing come alive. It will also help you avoid clichés and say exactly what you mean.

Dull, Vague Words	Lively, Precise Words
The dog ran through the woods.	The terrier bounded through the underbrush.
I fell into the rough water.	I tumbled into the churning foam.
People yelled at the mayor.	Irate citizens harangued the mayor.

Find It in Your Reading

Read the excerpt from *The Interesting Narrative of the Life of Olaudah Equiano* on page 171.

1. Identify at least one specific noun, active verb, vivid adjective, and effective adverb.
2. Make a list of the words and identify their parts of speech.
3. Choose one word you think is a particularly good choice. Write a sentence or two in which you explain your reasons.

PH WRITING COACH

Further instruction and practice are available in *Prentice Hall Writing Coach*.

Apply It to Your Writing

Review the draft of your autobiographical narrative. Follow these steps for each paragraph:

1. Underline any nouns or verbs that seem vague or weak. Note each use of the verb *to be* (*am, is, are, was,* and *were*). In the margin, jot down a few interesting alternates for each bland word, and then choose the best replacement.
2. Highlight phrases that are wordy, and think about what you are really trying to say. Then, find one or two punchy words that mean the same thing but express your idea more forcefully.
3. Check to see if there are any sentences with no underlining or highlighting. Take a look at these sentences again. Challenge yourself to find places where you could add vivid words to create a clearer picture or convey a stronger attitude.

Developing Your Style

1. Introduce the style points to students, using the instruction on the student page.
2. Have students complete the Find It in Your Reading and Apply It to Your Writing activities.

Teaching the Strategies

1. Ask volunteers to provide example sentences from their drafts. Have the class identify the nouns, verbs, adjectives, and adverbs.
2. Guide the class in finding alternative word choices for the example sentences. Ask students to explain why one word fits the context of the sentence better than another.
3. As students apply the skill to their own writing, have them work in pairs to help each other in replacing dull, vague words with more dynamic and precise ones.

Think Aloud: Model Word Choice

Model the strategy of choosing better words, using the following "think aloud." Say to students:

I want to use words in my narrative that will help the reader see and feel what I experienced. First I look over the narrative to make sure that it employs active verbs whenever possible. In a sentence such as "We were in the woods that day looking for mushrooms," I might replace the limp "were in" with the more active "were tramping through." Then I make a list of words or phrases that fail to clearly express what I saw and felt. I try to come up with some more lively alternatives.

Six Traits Focus

Ideas		✔ Word Choice	
Organization		Sentence Fluency	
Voice		Conventions	

PH WRITING COACH | Grade 11

Students will find additional instruction on parts of speech in Chapter 13.

Differentiated Instruction for Universal Access

EL Strategy for English Learners

Students with more limited vocabularies should be advised to use a thesaurus for help in finding alternative word choices. Caution students against taking words from a thesaurus without also evaluating their meaning in a dictionary; explain that the words listed may not be exact synonyms.

Strategy for Advanced Writers

Review with students how words with similar meanings can have different connotations; use the words *cheap, inexpensive, thrifty,* and *penny-pinching* to illustrate how different words appeal to a reader's emotions. Have students work in pairs to identify the connotations of key descriptive words and, if necessary, replace the words with those that better fit the tone and context of the narrative.

Student Model

Review the Student Model with the class, using the annotations to analyze the writer's incorporation of the elements of a good autobiographical narrative.

Teaching the Strategies

1. Explain that the Student Model is a sample and that their autobiographical narratives may be longer.

2. Point out that Branden has centered her narrative around a crucial event in her childhood. This may give students ideas for topics of their own.

3. Have students discuss the details with which Branden sets the scene. Have them list specific details that they will use in their own essays.

4. **Ask** students how the essay would have been affected if Branden had not quoted from the poem.
   Possible response: Being able to read the poem themselves makes readers much more likely to identify with Branden's reaction to it.

5. Emphasize that the dialogue is a much more powerful way of showing the scene than merely telling the reader what happened. Point out that the dialogue gives insight into the feelings of the characters and makes the scene immediate—almost as though it is happening right now.

6. Have a student read aloud the final paragraph of the narrative. Help students see that Branden states the reason she chose her topic and that she connects her experience to a broader statement about human life with a reference to "the poignancy of art."

Connecting to Real-life Writing

Explain to students that they will use autobiographical writing in many ways throughout their lives. They will find, for example, that many college applications require students to write essays on a given topic. Frequently, these essay topics are autobiographical. Likewise, cover letters for job applications are concise autobiographical essays that include only certain relevant details.

Student Model: Branden Boyer-White, Palm Springs, CA

Discovering Poetry

My mother was a night owl. She worked nights as a nurse at the hospital. She liked it; the schedule suited her. The nights she was off, she maintained her nocturnal routine—active at night and asleep in the early part of the day.

One early morning, I went into the living room to find my mother reading a thick book called *Best Loved Poems to Read Again and Again*. My interest was piqued solely by the fact that the word *Poems* appeared in big, hot pink letters.

"Is it good?" I asked her.

"Yeah," she answered. "There's one you'll really like." She began to thumb through the grainy white pages. She finally stopped and asked, "Ready?" I certainly was! I leaned forward.

"'Patty Poem,'" she read the title. *Who is Patty?* my mind buzzed. The poem began:

> She never puts her toys away,
> Just leaves them scattered where they lay, . . .

The poem was just three short stanzas. The final one came quickly:

> When she grows and gathers poise,
> I'll miss her harum-scarum noise,
> And look in vain for scattered toys,
>   And I'll be sad.

A terrible sorrow washed over me. Whoever Patty was, she was a dreadful, mean girl. Then, the bombshell.

"It's you, honey," my mother sentimentalized.

To my mother, the poem captured a parent's nostalgic love when her child grows up and leaves. To me, the "she" in the poem was a horror. It was my mama who would be sad. It was so terrible I burst into tears.

"What's wrong?" my mother asked.

"Oh Mama," I babbled. "I don't want to grow up ever!"

She smiled. "Honey, it's okay. You're not growing up anytime soon. And when you do, I'll still love you, okay?"

"Okay," I hiccuped. My panic had subsided. But I could not stop thinking about that silly poem. After what seemed like a safe amount of time, I read the poem again and was mystified. It all fit so well together, like a puzzle. The language was simple, so simple I could plainly understand its meaning, yet it was still beautiful. I was now transfixed by the idea of poetry, words that had the power to make or break a person's world. . . .

I have since fallen in love with other poems, but "Patty Poem" remains my poem. It was my first, and it will be mine to the end, because it brought me my love for poetry. This is a great testimony to the poignancy of the art. After all, "Patty Poem" gave me my love for poetry not because it was the verse that lifted my spirits, but because it was the one that hurt me the most.

> Branden uses concrete details to set the scene.

> Excerpts from the poem help readers understand the writer's emotional reaction to what she heard.

> Dialogue makes the narrative more realistic and poignant.

> Branden clearly demonstrates the significance of this experience.

194 Beginnings–1800

Strategies for Writing Dialogue

Have students work with partners when revising dialogue. Tell them to read the dialogue aloud and then discuss the following questions:

- Is the dialogue realistic?

- Do the quotes stand alone, or do you need to add an explanation to make the thought complete?

- Does the dialogue capture any dialect or speech mannerisms of the character?

- Have you described the speaker's hand gestures or facial expressions?

- Have you described the speaker's tone of voice or attitude?

Tell students to reproduce the quotations as accurately as they can recall. Caution them against making up dialogue. If they cannot remember the exact words, suggest that they paraphrase them.

Editing and Proofreading

Check your narrative for errors in grammar, usage, punctuation, and spelling.

Focus on capitalization. Double-check the capitalization of names and places. Common nouns name general categories and are lowercase. Proper nouns name specific people, places, or things and are capitalized.

Focus on spelling. The one-syllable word *full* has two *l*'s. However, the suffix *-ful* has only one *l*. The orthographic, or spelling, rule is as follows: Words with two or more syllables, like *cheerful* and *successful*, end with the one-*l* suffix. Check your spelling of any words that end with this suffix.

Spiral Review: Conventions Earlier in this unit, you learned about coordinating conjunctions (p. 31), correlative conjunctions (p. 94), and subordinating conjunctions (p. 155). Check your narrative to be sure you have used those conventions correctly.

Publishing, Presenting, and Reflecting

Consider one of the following ways to share your writing.

Deliver an oral presentation. Turn your narrative into an oral presentation and deliver it to the class. To do so, mark up a copy of your finished work, underlining words and phrases to emphasize. Also, identify places where you can add drama by changing your tone of voice or pausing. If you wish, choose photographs to display as a backdrop.

Create an illustrated class anthology. With classmates, combine several narratives in a binder. Include photographs or artwork that capture the mood or setting of each narrative.

Reflect on your writing. In a writer's journal, jot down your thoughts about the experience of writing an autobiographical narrative. Begin by answering these questions: *Which part of the process did you enjoy most and least? Did the work make you look at your life differently? If so, how?*

Rubric for Self-Assessment

Evaluate your reflective essay using the following criteria and rating scale.

Criteria	Rating Scale
	not very *very*
Focus: How clearly do you depict the conflict, its resolution, and your insight?	1 2 3 4 5
Organization: How clear and logical is the progression of events?	1 2 3 4 5
Support/Elaboration: How well do you build on your ideas with details and reactions?	1 2 3 4 5
Style: How effectively do you vary sentences and add details to bring characters alive?	1 2 3 4 5
Conventions: How correct are your grammar and mechanics, especially your use of capitalization?	1 2 3 4 5

Common Core State Standards

Language
2.b. Spell correctly.
Speaking and Listening
6. Adapt speech to a variety of contexts and tasks.

PH WRITING COACH

Further instruction and practice are available in *Prentice Hall Writing Coach*.

Editing and Proofreading

1. Introduce the editing and proofreading focuses, using the instruction on the student page.

2. Have students read their autobiographical narratives carefully, marking them for line edits, including changes in word choice and corrections in grammar, spelling, and punctuation. Make sure they check for errors of the type noted in the lesson focus and the Spiral Review.

Teaching the Strategies

1. If students have composed their narratives on a computer, tell them to print a hard copy to edit and proofread.

2. Have students exchange papers and read for errors in spelling and grammar.

Six Traits Focus

Ideas		Word Choice	
Organization		Sentence Fluency	✔
Voice		Conventions	✔

ASSESS

Publishing, Presenting, and Reflecting

1. Suggest that students planning an oral presentation practice reading their narratives in front of a mirror.

2. Encourage students to place their anthologies in a display in the classroom or in the library.

3. To help students reflect on their writing, ask them to brainstorm for additional questions that will explore their experience with writing an autobiographical narrative.

4. After they complete their journal entries, have students meet in small groups to discuss and compare their answers.

Strategies for Test Taking

When students encounter test prompts that ask them to write autobiographical essays, remind them not to waste too much time agonizing over a topic. Students should read the test prompt carefully to determine whether it sets any limits on the topic. Then they should choose a topic that they know well and move ahead to the prewriting phase. Remind students to leave enough time to reread their essays and to revise them with requirements given in the prompt.

**Common Core
State Standards**

• Speaking and Listening 3

Types of Content and Positions

1. Present the four types of speech, using the instruction and chart on the student page.

2. As students examine the example column, point out that each is an assertion that must be supported. **Ask** students how each example might be supported.
Possible response: Fact: Eyewitnesses or photographs might show that the defendant fled. Value: One or several music experts might be cited to establish the eminence of jazz. Problem: Statistics, examples, and testimony might demonstrate the parking problem. Policy: A list of potential benefits to students, backed by opinions of language experts, might support the Latin requirement.

Types of Appeals and Evidence

1. Present the three types of appeals. Tell students that although they may not know the Greek terminology, they routinely use the three types of appeals in daily efforts to persuade: ethos: "Hey! I'm being serious!"; pathos: "Are you going to make me do it all by myself?"; logos: "The job will go faster if you help me."

2. After you have discussed appeals and evidence, ask students to review the sermon of Jonathan Edwards (p. 87) and the speeches of Patrick Henry (p. 100) and Benjamin Franklin (p. 105) to find examples of each type.

Evaluate Persuasive Speech

Persuasive speech, also called *argument*, is the language people use when they want to convince us to think or act in a certain way. Advertisers use it to spread interest in their products; lawyers use it to establish the innocence of clients; and politicians use it to attract our support.

Types of Content and Positions

There are four main types of argumentation, or persuasive speech: propositions of fact, value, problem, and policy. All use language, reasoning, and proof differently in order to achieve specific ends.

Propositions	What They Establish	Examples
Fact	That something is so, or has happened	In fact, the defendant fled the scene.
Value	That something is good or bad, better or worse	Jazz is America's best music.
Problem	That something is a problem	The parking situation is a problem because…
Policy	That something should be done	Latin should be a required subject.

Types of Appeals and Evidence

Persuasive Appeals More than 2,000 years ago, Aristotle identified three types of appeals, or techniques, that can occur in any argument:

- **Ethos, or appeal to authority,** cites the speaker's credibility, or authority; for example, a noted scientist discussing issues in medical ethics.

- **Pathos, or appeal to sympathy,** engages the audience's emotions.

- **Logos, or appeal to logic,** applies reasoning and facts to build convincing arguments.

Some strategies may be more useful than others in certain situations. For example, a speaker asking for donations may use pathos more than logos.

Evidence Effective arguments employ strong evidence.

- **Facts:** data, statistical information, scientific observations
- **Anecdotes:** stories that illustrate a point
- **Expert Testimony:** statements by people who are widely viewed as authorities on a subject

When listening to persuasive speech, identify the speaker's position and evaluate the quality of the evidence he or she uses to support ideas.

**Common Core
State Standards**

**Speaking and Listening
3.** Evaluate a speaker's point of view, reasoning, and use of evidence and rhetoric, assessing the stance, premises, links among ideas, word choice, points of emphasis, and tone used.

Negative Persuasive Techniques

Logical fallacies are types of reasoning that may seem convincing but contain inherent flaws. Be alert to arguments built on such faulty reasoning.

- **Ad Hominem:** an attack on a person's character, not his or her ideas
- **False Causality:** an assumption that because A happened before B, A caused B
- **Red Herring:** something a speaker tosses into an argument to distract listeners from a more important issue or question
- **Overgeneralization:** a conclusion based on too little evidence
- **Bandwagon:** the assumption that something is right because it is popular

Propaganda, another negative technique, presents one-sided information and does not fairly represent an opposing view. It aims to win, but not to educate or invite discussion.

Activities: Evaluate Persuasive Speech

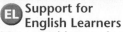 **Comprehension and Collaboration** For both activities, use an evaluation form like the one shown below.

A. Watch or listen to a persuasive speech. You may listen to a speech given by a classmate, find one in a movie, or locate one on the Internet.

B. With a partner, select two speeches that argue similar propositions but to different audiences. Critique their uses of appeals and evidence. Notice whether they use any negative persuasive techniques, and to what effect.

Evaluation Form for Persuasive Speech

Name of Speech _____

Media Type _____

Intended Audience _____

Purpose _____

Type of Proposition _____

Types of Appeals:

      Ethos: ☐ Example: _____

      Pathos: ☐ Example: _____

      Logos: ☐ Example: _____

Specific Forms of Evidence: _____

Special Uses of Language: _____

Negative Persuasive Techniques: no ☐   yes ☐

      Which Ones? _____

Negative Persuasive Techniques

1. **Present** logical fallacies, using the instruction on the student page.
2. **Ask** students which of these fallacies, in their own experience, are more common in discussions, arguments, and speeches. **Possible response:** Students may say that ad hominem attacks, overgeneralizations, and bandwagon arguments are common in everyday persuasive experiences.

Activities: Evaluate Persuasive Speech

1. Allow students to choose the evaluation activity, or assign your preference to the class. The sample evaluation form on the student page is relevant to either activity.
2. To provide a more structured menu of speeches for students to select, you may wish to give them a list of speeches from which to choose, including Internet addresses for those available online.
3. Allow class time for volunteers to present their evaluations to the class.

Differentiated Instruction — for Universal Access

Support for Special-Needs Students

Activity A will be the better option for some students. To provide more structure for these students, select a short accessible speech and show it to the class. Pause the speech at intervals to ask students to summarize what the speaker has said and to identify persuasive techniques and logical fallacies. Work through the evaluation as a class.

EL Support for English Learners

Many notable speeches are available in print as well as in audio or video recordings. You may wish to direct English learners to speeches for which a printed text is available. Encourage them to listen to the speech twice. The first time they should read along in the text; the second time they should set aside the text and focus on the speaker's persuasive techniques.

197

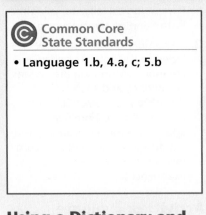
Using a Dictionary and Thesaurus

1. Teach the skills, using the instruction and samples on the student page.

2. If possible, demonstrate the use of an electronic dictionary via computers in a lab or the classroom.

Think Aloud: Model the Skills

Say to students:

When I look up a word, I always check the etymology, where the word comes from. Often a word's origin grabs my interest and helps me remember the meaning. For example, I learn that *portend* comes from the Latin for "extend; stretch." When I think of the fact that *portend* means "indicating beforehand," I imagine an arm *stretching* ahead, pointing to the future. I can also imagine the "stretch" in other "tend" words, such as *tendency* ("pattern, habit, or the direction in which something always *stretches*"), *pretend* ("*stretch* the truth"), and *intend* ("plan, mean, or *stretch* from where you are now into the future").

Vocabulary Workshop

Using a Dictionary and Thesaurus

A **dictionary** is a reference work containing words and information about them. Dictionaries can help you find the exact meaning of a word or understand the different ways in which a word might be used. A print dictionary is arranged alphabetically. To use an **electronic dictionary,** you enter the word for which you are searching. **Specialized dictionaries** are those that define terms used in a particular field, such as law or business.

Sample Dictionary Entry

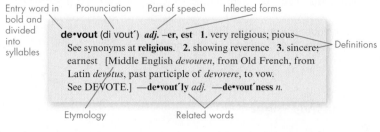

Sample Thesaurus Entry

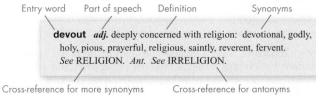

A **thesaurus** is a book of synonyms, or words with similar meanings. All of the synonyms listed for a word share denotation, or surface meaning, but their connotations, or shades of meaning, will probably vary. When writing, use a thesaurus to help vary your word choice. However, check your choices in a dictionary to make sure both their denotative and connotative meanings accurately represent your ideas.

Practice

Directions: Refer to the sample entries to answer questions 1 and 2. Use a print or electronic dictionary and thesaurus to answer question 3.

1. Trace the path by which the word *devout* entered the English language. Explain whether its meaning has changed or stayed the same.

2. **(a)** Analyze the context to determine which synonym for *devout* best completes this sentence: *Their hushed voices showed the pilgrims'___ attitude.* **(b)** Explain the nuances in word meanings that allowed you to make your choice.

3. Find two synonyms for *earnest* that have positive connotations and two that have negative connotations. For each synonym, write a sentence that reflects its connotative meaning.

Practice

Answers

1. *Devout* is derived from the Middle English *devouren,* which in turn came from Old French, which took it from the Latin word *devotus,* a form of the verb *devovere,* "to vow."

2. **Sample responses:** (a) reverent; (b) The word *reverent* best fits with "hushed voices"; the other synonyms have more intensity than context requires.

3. **Sample response:** Synonyms of *earnest* that have positive connotations include *serious* and *determined.* Synonyms that have negative connotations include *staid* and *rigid.* Sample sentences: His <u>serious</u> expression told us that he really meant his criticism.
The explorers made a <u>determined</u> effort to climb the ridge.
The host's <u>staid</u> behavior disappointed fun-seekers at the party.
Given her <u>rigid</u> beliefs, it is unlikely that she will compromise.

Vocabulary Acquisition and Use: Context Clues

Context clues are words or phrases that help readers clarify the meanings of unfamiliar words in a text. Even fluent readers may not always know the dictionary definition of every word they read. By using context clues, readers make educated guesses, or inferences, about unfamiliar word meanings. This skill is often assessed on standardized tests.

Practice

This exercise is modeled after the Sentence Completion questions that appear in the Reading Comprehension section of the SAT.

Directions: Each of the following sentences is missing one or two words. Choose the word or set of words that best completes each sentence.

> **Test-Taking Tip**
> Immediately rule out any answer choices you *know* are wrong.

1. Many colonists felt that more ___?___ was necessary before war against Britain was declared.
   - **A.** disposition
   - **B.** provision
   - **C.** oblivion
   - **D.** deliberation
   - **E.** recompense

2. Revolutionaries such as Thomas Paine attempted to rouse the colonists' ___?___ desires for freedom and self-determination.
   - **A.** brittle
   - **B.** unconscious
   - **C.** tempered
   - **D.** omnipotent
   - **E.** vigilant

3. Paine and others argued that only a full split with Britain would create a peaceful world for ___?___.
   - **A.** posterity
   - **B.** tyranny
   - **C.** unanimity
   - **D.** diversity
   - **E.** urgency

4. With no sign of ___?___ for their complaints, colonial leaders declared independence from the crown.
   - **A.** privilege
   - **B.** vigilance
   - **C.** redress
   - **D.** peril
   - **E.** allegiance

5. Though the ___?___ of war would last for years, few would ___?___ the freedom it secured.
   - **A.** tempest . . . lament
   - **B.** assent . . . implore
   - **C.** tempest . . . relent
   - **D.** apparel . . . implore
   - **E.** privileges . . . redress

6. Nevertheless, the work of crafting a ___?___ for the new nation proved ___?___.
   - **A.** judgment . . . incorrigible
   - **B.** mediator . . . prudent
   - **C.** provision . . . copious
   - **D.** constitution . . . arduous
   - **E.** judgment. . . pensive

Test-Taking Practice

In this Assessment Workshop (pp. 200–203), students apply the skills in Unit 1. The practice is divided into three sections.

1. Before assigning each section, review the relevant unit skills with students. Discuss the characteristics of each type of test and specific strategies for test questions, using the instruction that precedes each practice.

2. Set a time limit for the multiple-choice items in each practice, allowing a little more than 1 minute per question. Use the designated time allowance set for the Timed Writing section.

3. Administer each section. Have students write the starting time at the top of their papers. When half of the time for the multiple-choice items has run out, ask students to write the time next to the answer on which they are working. Have them make similar notes when three-quarters of the time has expired and again when time is up. Follow a similar procedure for the Timed Writing assignment.

4. Review with students the pacing reflected in their notes.

Reteaching

Have students complete each practice. Then use the Reteach charts to determine which skills require reteaching, based on the items students answer incorrectly. Reteach these skills prior to assigning **Benchmark Test 2** (*Unit 1 Resources*, pp. 258–267).

Reteach

Question	Pages to Reteach
1	148, 158
2	148, 158
3	206, 214
4	78, 83
5	136, 146
6	56, 57
7	78, 83
8	206, 214
9	148, 158
10	94, 104

200

Test-Taking Practice

Reading Test: Social Science Passages

Social science reading passages are one type of reading selection found on standardized tests. The social sciences include disciplines such as anthropology, economics, geography, history, political science, and psychology. These passages tend to be tightly written and logically organized. They are informational, but they also express the author's point of view either directly or indirectly. Questions following these passages usually address elements such as structure, main idea, or author's purpose.

Common Core State Standards

RI.11-12.1, RI.11-12.4, RI.11-12.6; L.11-12.1, L.11-12.2, L.11-12.3, L.11-12.4.a

[For the full wording of the standards, see the standards chart in the front of your textbook.]

Practice

This exercise is modeled after the ACT Reading Test, Social Science section.

Directions: Read the following passage, taken from *The American Crisis* by Thomas Paine. Then, choose the best answer to each question.

I once felt all that kind of anger, which a man ought to feel, against the mean principles that are held by the Tories: a noted one, who kept a tavern at Amboy, was standing at this door, with as pretty a child in his hand, about eight or nine years old, as I ever saw, and after speaking his
5   mind as freely as he thought was prudent, finished with this unfatherly expression, *"Well! give me peace in my day."* Not a man lives on the continent but fully believes that a separation must some time or other finally take place, and a generous parent should have said, *"If there must be trouble let it be in my day, that my child may have peace"*;
10   and this single reflection, well applied, is sufficient to awaken every man to duty. . . .
    I turn with the warm ardor of a friend to those who have nobly stood, and are yet determined to stand the matter out: I call not upon a few, but upon all; not on *this* state or *that* state, but on *every* state;
15   up and help us; lay your shoulders to the wheel; better have too much force than too little, when so great an object is at stake. Let it be told to the future world, that in the depth of winter, when nothing but hope and virtue could survive, that the city and the country, alarmed at one common danger, came forth to meet and to repulse it. Say not
20   that thousands are gone, turn out your tens of thousands; throw not the burden of the day upon Providence, but *"show your faith by your works,"* that God may bless you. It matters not where you live, or what rank of life you hold, the evil or the blessing will reach you all.

Strategy

Scan, then read.

- **First, scan the passage.** Take 20 seconds to skim the text. Look for a main topic and a few key terms.

- **Second, read the passage in full.** Ask yourself: *What is the author's purpose? What information is most important?*

Strategies for Test Taking

Tell students that when reading the choices in a multiple-choice question, they should avoid the distraction of a choice that includes accurate but unimportant information. For example, choice B in the sample question mentions "British law," and the passage mentions that Britain claims the right to "tax" and "bind."

A student working too quickly might decide to select choice B because it seems to cite a detail from the passage. However, choice B is incidental information and does not express Paine's main purpose. Choice D correctly expresses the main purpose.

1. The author includes the story about the father and child in order to:
   A. entertain his readers.
   B. shame his readers into action.
   C. stir up noble feelings in his readers.
   D. persuade his readers to do nothing.

2. The author uses the word *unfatherly* in reference to the tavern owner because he feels the man is:
   F. putting his child in danger.
   G. being selfish.
   H. behaving immaturely.
   J. ignoring his child.

3. What is the best summary of this passage?
   A. Let us band together to defend ourselves.
   B. We must labor to improve the lives of our children.
   C. The separation of one continent from another is inevitable.
   D. If we do good deeds, we will be blessed.

4. In the phrase "lay your shoulders to the wheel," what does the wheel symbolize?
   F. the Tories
   G. one's fellow soldiers
   H. Thomas Paine himself
   J. the task of war

5. When the author writes "I call not upon a few, but upon all; not on *this* state or *that* state, but on *every* state," which rhetorical device is he using?
   A. repetition
   B. restatement
   C. a rhetorical question
   D. an allusion

6. This passage LEAST resembles:
   F. a speech.
   G. an origin myth.
   H. a political document.
   J. a sermon.

7. According to the passage, what kind of anger does Paine believe is justified?
   A. anger at Tories
   B. anger at low-minded principles
   C. anger at bad parents
   D. anger at those who show little faith

8. Based on the passage, Paine's approach to his topic can best be characterized as:
   F. flexible and unbiased.
   G. contemplative and expansive.
   H. skeptical and tentative.
   J. passionate and uncompromising.

9. When the author urges his readers to "'*show your faith by your works,*' that God may bless you," he is using:
   A. a logical appeal.
   B. an emotional appeal.
   C. an ethical appeal.
   D. a political appeal.

10. Paine's overall purpose in this passage is to:
    F. urge Tories to defend themselves against abuse and ignorance.
    G. entertain soldiers who have recently returned from war.
    H. persuade colonists to fight in the cause of freedom.
    J. provide religious instruction to those who are troubled by anger.

GO ON

Test-Taking Practice **201**

Differentiated
Instruction   for Universal Access

EL Support for English Learners
Read the entire passage with the class and help students summarize each paragraph. Review the ten questions, making sure that students understand "summary" in question 3, "symbolize" in question 4, and "rhetorical device" in question 5. Allow students to ask clarifying questions about any of the question choices, being careful not to reveal correct answers. Once students understand the questions, have them complete the test on their own. Allow 5 minutes for reading the passage and 12 minutes for the questions.

Reading Test
Social Science Passages

1. Introduce the skill, using the instruction on page 200. Be sure students understand the strategy set off in the boxed section.

2. Read the sample test passage to students, pointing out the side comments on logic words and pronoun clues.

3. Analyze the sample question with the class, discussing each choice.

4. You may wish to go over the first test item with students before they take the test. Have students read the first paragraph silently. Then, as a class, analyze each choice in the first test item.

   A—Paine wants to "awaken," not entertain, his readers. (Eliminate)

   B—Shame is directed at the Tory father, not at the reader. (Eliminate)

   C—Correct answer. Paine wants readers to act now so that their children might live in peace.

   D—Paine wants to awaken every man "to duty," not to "do nothing." (Eliminate)

5. Assign the Practice exercise. Have students read the passage and answer the questions on their own. Allow 15 minutes for this process, and announce to students when they have 5 minutes and 1 minute remaining.

Answers
1. C
2. G
3. A
4. J
5. B
6. G
7. B
8. J
9. C
10. H

Grammar and Writing

Editing in Context:

1. Introduce the skill, using the instruction on the student page. Be sure students understand the strategy set off in the boxed section.

2. Read the first paragraph of the Practice passage; then go over the first test item with students, modeling the "try out each answer" strategy.

3. Point out that the original sentence seems to contrast "statesman" with "scientist," but the emphasis in the paragraph is that Franklin was both. A change is required, so choice A is eliminated. Choice B incorrectly asserts that Franklin was "either" a statesman or a scientist; B is eliminated. Choice C correctly states that Franklin was both a statesman and a scientist. Choice D lacks a verb and uses the incorrect combination of "whether . . . nor"; D is eliminated. Choice C is therefore the best alternative.

4. Have students complete questions 2–7 on their own. Allow students 8 minutes to complete the questions.

Grammar and Writing: Editing in Context

In some tests you will encounter a passage with numbered sentences or parts of sentences, some of which contain errors in grammar, style, and usage. Your task is to choose the best version of the sentence from the choices offered. Some questions may also refer to the passage as a whole.

Practice

This exercise is modeled after the ACT English Test.

Directions: For each underlined sentence or portion of a sentence, choose the best alternative. If an item asks a question about the underlined portion, or about the passage as a whole, choose the best answer to the question.

[1]

Most people know that the mature Franklin <u>was an important statesman but also</u> an innovative scientist. What they may *not* know is that even the young Franklin lived a noteworthy life.

[2]

As one of seventeen children and the son of a poor soap maker, the odds were against young Ben. ☐2 As a small boy, he taught himself to read; and though he had only two years of formal education, he stored the knowledge away for future use. <u>When</u> he was apprenticed at age twelve to his brother, a printer, Franklin took his education into his own hands. He spent his spare moments copying essays out of a discarded literary magazine, translating them into poetry, translating them back into prose, and then memorizing them. He knew that good writing <u>was rare, and could</u> lead him to both fame and fortune.

[3]

Finally, at age sixteen, Franklin saw himself in print. Adopting the persona of a widow named Silence Dogood, he penned a series of essays that poked fun at various aspects of colonial <u>life that included</u> education, etiquette, and fashion. All fourteen essays were printed in his brother's newspaper, the *New-England Courant*. In fact, readers were so charmed by Silence Dogood that the nonexistent widow received several written proposals of marriage. ☐6

Strategy

Try out each answer. Mentally test each answer before you choose one of them. The one that sounds the best is probably correct.

Strategies for
Test Taking

Point out to students that in editing in-context tests such as the one on this page, some test items simply list choices; students, following the general directions, are expected to choose the best alternative. Items 1, 4, and 5 are of this type.

Other test items are preceded by questions. Often these involve descriptions of the writer's thoughts, sometimes describing a deletion or quoting an insertion the writer is planning to make. Items 2 and 6 are of this type. Tell students to read these questions twice, making sure they understand exactly what change the writer is contemplating before testing out the item's choices.

Since these questions may take more time, students might work through the "short" test items first and then go back to the more detailed test items. Also, if students complete the test with time remaining, they should review their answers to the detailed test items.

1. **A.** NO CHANGE
   B. either an important statesman or
   C. both an important statesman and
   D. whether an important statesman nor

2. At this point, the writer is considering inserting the following: Nevertheless, he proved self-reliant from early on. Should the writer make this insertion?
   F. No, because the sentence directly expresses the essay's main idea.
   G. No, because the sentence distracts from the paragraph's main focus.
   H. Yes, because the sentence refers to Franklin's later writings.
   J. Yes, because the sentence provides a transition between two ideas.

3. What is the function of this word?
   A. It has no function and should be deleted.
   B. It is used as a subordinating conjunction.
   C. It is used as a correlative conjunction.
   D. It is used as a coordinating conjunction.

4. **F.** NO CHANGE
   G. is rare, but could
   H. was rare, as if it could
   J. though rare, could

5. **A.** NO CHANGE
   B. life and which included
   C. life, yet including
   D. life, including

6. Upon reviewing paragraph 3, the writer considers deleting the preceding sentence. If the writer were to delete the sentence, the paragraph would primarily lose:
   F. a humorous commentary that helps underscore Franklin's success.
   G. a colorful detail that shows how naive eighteenth-century readers were.
   H. a good-natured hint that Franklin's writing may have lacked clarity.
   J. nothing; it should be deleted.

7. This question asks about the passage as a whole.
   Review paragraphs 1 through 3. The text structure of this passage is:
   A. cause and effect.
   B. chronological order.
   C. problem and solution.
   D. comparison and contrast.

 Timed Writing: Position Statement [25 minutes]

Consider these two commentaries on success:

I wished to live without committing any fault at any time; I would conquer all that either natural inclination, custom, or company might lead me into.

—Benjamin Franklin, *Autobiography*

I've managed to do a lot of things in my life I didn't think I was capable of and which many others didn't think me capable of either.

—Sandra Cisneros, "Straw Into Gold"

In your view, is success doing something perfectly, or doing something new and unexpected? Write an essay in which you develop your point of view on this issue. Support your position with reasoning and examples taken from your reading, studies, or experience.

Academic Vocabulary

An **issue** is a debatable idea. There is no right or wrong opinion. Choose the position for which you can offer the strongest support.

STOP

Test-Taking Practice **203**

Answers

1. C
2. J
3. B
4. F
5. D
6. F
7. B

Timed Writing
Position Statement

1. Go over the two paragraphs of the timed writing assignment on the student page.

2. Tell students that they can quickly formulate a thesis statement for their position by completing one of the following sentence starters: "I agree that . . . ." or "I disagree that . . . ." Students should complete the statement with language from assignment.

3. Encourage students to budget adequate time for prewriting and revising/editing. Students should spend about 8 minutes in the prewriting stage, 12 minutes drafting, and 5 minutes revising and editing. Reinforce this by announcing elapsed time at the 8-, 12-, and 20-minute marks as students respond to the assignment.

4. Use the **Rubrics for Writing for Assessment Essays** in *Professional Development Guidebook,* pages 258–259, to evaluate students' work.

Benchmark

Reteach skills as indicated by students' performance, following the Reteach charts on pages 200 and 203. Then administer the end-of-unit **Benchmark Test** 2 (*Unit 1 Resources,* pp. 258–267). Follow the **Interpretation Guide** for the test (*Unit 1 Resources,* p. 271) to assign reteaching pages as necessary in the *Reading Kit.* Use the built-in tracking software at www. PHLitOnline.com to automatically assign these pages.

Reteach

Question	Pages to Reteach
1	69
2	230
3	193
4	69
5	230
6	190
7	190

The **Benchmark Tests** and **Success Tracker** are available online at www.PHLitOnline.com.

Performance Tasks

Assigning Tasks/Reteaching Skills

Use the chart below to choose appropriate Performance Tasks by identifying which tasks assess lessons in the textbook that you have taught. Use the same lessons for reteaching when students' performance indicates a failure to fully master a standard. For additional instruction and practice, assign the *Common Core Companion* pages indicated for each task.

Task	Where Taught/ Pages to Reteach	Common Core Companion Pages
1	18, 32–33, 166	15–27, 261–268, 322–323
2	168	103–115, 261–268, 322–323
3	56, 110, 168	170–176, 261–268
4	56, 100, 105, 110	75–81, 261–268, 304–305
5	56, 100, 105, 110	163–169, 277–285
6	110	123–135, 297–303

Assessment Pacing

In assigning the Writing Tasks on this student page, allow a class period for the completion of a task. As an alternative, assign tasks as homework. In assigning the Speaking and Listening Tasks on the facing page, consider having students do any required preparation as a homework assignment. Then, allow a class period for the presentations themselves.

Evaluating Performance Tasks

Use the rubric at the bottom of this Teacher Edition page to evaluate students' mastery of the standards as demonstrated in their Performance Task responses. Review the rubric with students before they begin work so they know the criteria by which their work will be evaluated.

Performance Tasks

Follow the instructions to complete the tasks below as required by your teacher. As you work on each task, incorporate both general academic vocabulary and literary terms you learned in this unit.

Common Core State Standards

RL.11-12.2, RL.11-12.9; RI.11-12.2, RI.11-12.4, RI.11-12.8, RI.11-12.9; W.11-12.9.a, W.11-12.9.b, W.11-12.10; SL.11-12.1.a, SL.11-12.1.b, SL.11-12.4, SL.11-12.5; L.11-12.2.b, L.11-12.3.a
[For the full wording of the standards, see the standards chart in the front of your textbook.]

Writing

Task 1: Literature [RL.11-12.2; W.11-12.9.a; L.11-12.3.a]
Analyze the Development of Theme

*Write an **essay** in which you determine two or more themes in a literary work from this unit.*

- Identify at least two themes in the work. Analyze how each theme is introduced and developed.
- Discuss similarities and differences among the insights each theme expresses.
- Note ways in which the themes interact and build on one another, and discuss how this interaction creates a complex account or deeper meaning.
- To ensure that readers understand your analysis, include an objective summary of each literary work.
- Vary your syntax by using coordinating or correlative conjunctions to combine short, choppy sentences.

Task 2: Informational Text [RI.11-12.2; W.11-12.9.b; L.11-12.3.a]
Analyze the Development of Central Ideas

*Write an **essay** in which you analyze the development of two or more central ideas in a work of literary nonfiction from this unit.*

- Clearly identify and explain at least two central ideas expressed in the work.
- Discuss how the author introduces and develops each idea.
- Identify specific details that shape and refine each central idea.

204 Beginnings–1800

- Consider how the central ideas interact and build on one another to create a complex analysis of a topic.
- To ensure that readers understand your analysis, include an objective summary of the work.
- Vary your syntax by using subordinating conjunctions to combine sentences.

Task 3: Informational Text [RI.11-12.9; W.11-12.9.b; L.11-12.2.b]
Analyze Foundational U.S. Documents for Themes, Purposes, and Rhetorical Features

*Write an **essay** in which you analyze one of the foundational U.S. documents that appears in this unit, identifying its theme, purpose, and key rhetorical features.*

- Explain which document you chose and why you chose it.
- Identify the theme, or central idea, expressed in the document. If there are multiple themes or ideas, explain what they are and how they interact.
- Discuss the author's main purpose for writing as well as any secondary purposes.
- Analyze notable rhetorical features, considering how they help communicate the themes and advance the author's purpose for writing.
- Add to the strength of your writing and the clarity of your ideas by using strong verbs, precise nouns, and specific adjectives. Spell correctly.

Performance Task Rubric: Standards Mastery	Rating Scale				
	not very				very
Critical Thinking: How clearly and consistently does the student pursue the specific mode of reasoning or discourse required by the standard, as specified in the prompt (e.g., comparing and contrasting, analyzing, explaining)?	1	2	3	4	5
Focus: How well does the student understand and apply the focus concepts of the standard, as specified in the prompt (e.g., development of theme or of complex characters, effects of structure, and so on)?	1	2	3	4	5
Support/Elaboration: How well does the student support points with textual or other evidence? How relevant, sufficient, and varied is the evidence provided?	1	2	3	4	5
Insight: How original, sophisticated, or compelling are the insights the student achieves by applying the standard to the text(s)?	1	2	3	4	5
Expression of Ideas: How well does the student organize and support ideas? How well does the student use language, including word choice and conventions, in the expression of ideas?	1	2	3	4	5

Speaking and Listening

Task 4: Literature [RL.11-12.9; W.11-12.9.a; SL.11-12.5]

Demonstrate Knowledge of Foundational Works of American Literature

*With a partner, deliver an **oral presentation** in which you analyze how two or more literary works from this unit treat similar themes or topics.*

- Explain which works you will discuss and why you chose them.
- Identify the topics each work addresses and describe how each work presents characters, settings, and ideas.
- Explain the theme each work expresses and analyze the reasons for any similarities or differences.
- Incorporate digital media that enhances your presentation. For example, consider images, audio, graphics, or textual elements that help illustrate and clarify your ideas or those expressed in the works under discussion.

Task 5: Informational Texts [RI.11-12.8; SL.11-12.1.a, SL.11-12.1.b]

Evaluate the Reasoning in Seminal U.S. Texts

*Conduct a **panel discussion** in which you delineate and evaluate the reasoning in a seminal U.S. text from this unit.*

- Assign each member of the panel a specific role in the discussion.
- Each presenter should address at least one of the following elements: the text to be discussed and the reasons for the choice; the author's purpose for writing; the author's premises, reasoning, and arguments; the ways in which the author builds transitions and establishes meaningful connections among ideas; the types of evidence the author uses to support ideas and the quality of that evidence.
- As a group, ensure that the discussion is civil and democratic, or equally shared.
- As a group, ensure that each panel member has read the materials and completed any research needed to participate fully.

Task 6: Informational Text [RI.11-12.4; SL.11-12.4]

Determine the Meaning of Words and Phrases as They Are Used in a Text

*With a partner, conduct a **colloquy**, or formal discussion, about the meaning of a key term as it is used and refined in a text from this unit.*

- Explain which text you chose and why you chose it. Identify the key term you will discuss and explain why it is essential to the author's ideas.
- Discuss how the author introduces and defines the key term. Explain how the author then develops and refines that definition.
- Consider how the author incorporates connotations, or nuances, in the term's meaning as well as any figurative or technical meanings.
- As you speak, present information, findings, and evidence clearly so that listeners can follow your line of reasoning.
- Make sure your use of language, speaking style, and content are appropriate for a formal discussion.

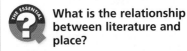

What is the relationship between literature and place?

First Encounters When Europeans first arrived in North America, the native peoples had been living here for thousands of years. The first encounters between various groups not only affected the early settlements but continue to resonate in our society.

Assignment Choose at least two writers from this unit who describe an early encounter between two different groups. Write a **comparison-and-contrast essay** about the perspectives reflected in each text.

Performance Tasks **205**

205

Independent Reading

Titles featured on the Independent Reading pages at the end of each unit represent a range of reading, including stories, dramas, and poetry, as well as literary nonfiction and other types of informational text. Throughout, labels indicate the works that are CCSS Exemplar Texts. Choosing from among these featured titles will help students read works at increasing levels of text complexity in the grades 11–12 text complexity band.

Using Literature Circles

A literature circle is a temporary group in which students independently discuss a book.

Use the guidance in the *Professional Development Guidebook*, pp. 47–49, as well as the teaching notes on the facing page, for additional suggestions for literature circles.

© Meeting Unit 1 CCS Standards

Students can use books listed on this page to apply and reinforce their mastery of the CCS Standards covered in this unit.

Introducing Featured Titles

Have students choose a book or books for independent reading. Assist them by previewing the titles, noting their subject matter and level of difficulty. **Note:** Before recommending a work to students, preview it, taking into account the values of your community as well as the maturity of your students.

Featured Titles

In this unit, you have read a variety of precolonial and early American literature. Continue to read works related to this era on your own. Select books that you enjoy, but challenge yourself to explore new topics, new authors, and works offering varied perspectives or approaches. The titles suggested below will help you get started.

LITERATURE

Native American Literature
Pearson Prentice Hall

Anthology The literature of Native Americans is a rich collection of myths, legends, poems, histories, personal experiences, dreams, and songs. More than fifty such selections are collected in this anthology.

The Complete Writings
Phillis Wheatley   EXEMPLAR TEXT ©

Poetry Wheatley was the first enslaved African and the third woman in the United States to publish a book of poems. Wheatley's verse, including the poem "On Being Brought From Africa to America," explores religion, death, and the struggles of enslaved Africans.

[Wheatley's poem, "To His Excellency, General Washington," appears on p. 124 of this book. Build knowledge by reading Wheatley's complete works.]

INFORMATIONAL TEXTS

Historical Texts

Chronicle of the Narváez Expedition
Alvar Núñez Cabeza de Vaca;
translated by Fanny Bandelier

Narrative Account In the early sixteenth century, Spain sent the Narváez expedition to what is now the southern United States to claim vast territories for the Spanish empire. Cabeza de Vaca, who went on this journey, describes the fate of the nine-year expedition.

[An excerpt from de Vaca's account appears on p. 48 of this book. Build knowledge by reading the full text.]

Letters From an American Farmer
J. Hector St. John de Crevecoeur;
translated by Gerald Bevan

Epistolary Letters Early America's physical and cultural landscape is captured in these impassioned and engaging epistles, or essays fashioned as letters.

The Interesting Narrative of The Life of Olaudah Equiano
Olaudah Equiano

Autobiography Written in 1789, Equiano's autobiography is one of the most widely read "slave narratives." The author describes his childhood in eighteenth-century Guinea, Africa, where he was first enslaved. He also recounts his later experiences as a freedman and abolitionist in the United States.

[An excerpt from Equiano's autobiography appears on p. 170 of this book. Build knowledge by reading the full text.]

Democracy in America
Alexis de Tocqueville;
translated by Gerald Bevan   EXEMPLAR TEXT ©

Political Science In 1831, Alexis de Tocqueville, a twenty-five year old Frenchman, traveled throughout the United States for nine months. He had been sent by his government to observe American prisons, but he wound up taking notes about all aspects of American society. The resulting two-volume work, published in 1835 and 1840, is now a classic of political science.

Contemporary Scholarship

American Colonies: The Settling of North America
Alan Taylor

History The settling of the American colonies was not a simple story but an interweaving of many narratives. Pulitzer Prize–winning author Alan Taylor does justice to this multifaceted history by explaining the roles that different peoples played in this process.

1776
David McCullough   EXEMPLAR TEXT ©

History Esteemed historian McCullough describes the turbulence and promise of this most important year in American history.

© Text Complexity: Aligning Texts With Readers and Tasks

TEXTS	READERS AND TASKS
• *Native American Literature* • *Chronicle of the Narváez Expedition*	**Below-Level Readers** Allow students to focus on reading for content, and challenge them to interpret multiple perspectives.
• *Letters from an American Farmer* • *The Interesting Narrative of the Life of Olaudah Equiano* • *American Colonies: The Settling of North America* • *The Complete Writings of Phyllis Wheatley*	**Below-Level Readers** Challenge students as they read for content. **On-Level Readers** Allow students to focus on reading for content, and challenge them to interpret multiple perspectives. **Advanced Readers** Allow students to focus on interpreting multiple perspectives.
• *1776* (Lexile: 1300L) • *Democracy in America* (Lexile: 1310L)	**On-Level Readers** Challenge students as they read for content. **Advanced Readers** Allow students to focus on reading for content, and challenge them to interpret multiple perspectives.

Preparing to Read Complex Texts

Reading for College and Career In both college and the workplace, readers must analyze texts independently, draw connections among works that offer varied perspectives, and develop their own ideas and informed opinions. The questions shown below, and others that you generate on your own, will help you more effectively read and analyze complex college-level texts.

Common Core State Standards

Reading Literature/Informational Text
10. By the end of grade 11, read and comprehend literature, including stories, dramas, and poems, and literary nonfiction, in the grades 11-CCR text complexity band proficiently, with scaffolding as needed at the high end of the range.

When reading analytically, ask yourself...

- What idea, experience, or story seems to have compelled the author to write? Has the author presented that idea, experience, or story in a way that I, too, find compelling?
- How might the author's era, social status, belief system, or personal experiences have affected the point of view he or she expresses in the text?
- How do my circumstances affect what I understand and feel about this text?
- What key idea does the author state explicitly? What key idea does he or she suggest or imply? Which details in the text help me to perceive implied ideas?
- Do I find multiple layers of meaning in the text? If so, what relationships do I see among these layers of meaning?
- Do I find the text believable and convincing? Why or why not?

Key Ideas and Details

- What patterns of organization or sequences do I find in the text? Do these patterns help me understand the ideas better? If so, how?
- What do I notice about the author's style, including his or her diction, uses of imagery and figurative language, and syntax?
- Do I like the author's style? Is the author's style memorable? Why or why not?
- What emotional attitude does the author express toward the topic, the story, or the characters? Does this attitude seem appropriate? Why or why not?
- What emotional attitude does the author express toward me, the reader? Does this attitude seem appropriate? Why, or why not?
- What do I notice about the author's voice—his or her personality on the page? Do I like this voice? Does it make me want to read on?

Craft and Structure

- Is the work fresh and original? How do I know?
- Do I agree with the author's ideas entirely or are there elements I find unconvincing?
- Do I disagree with the author's ideas entirely, or are there elements I can accept as true?
- How does this text relate to others I have read on the same or a similar topic?
- Based on my knowledge of American literature, history, and culture, does this work seem distinctly American? Why, or why not?

Integration of Ideas

Text Complexity: Reader and Task Support Suggestions

INDEPENDENT READING

Increased Support Suggest that students choose a book that they feel comfortable reading and one that is a bit more challenging.

Pair a more proficient reader with a less proficient reader and have them work together on the more challenging text. Partners can prepare to read the book by reviewing questions on this student page. They can also read difficult passages together, sharing questions and insights. They can use the questions on the student page to guide after-reading discussion.

Increased Challenge Encourage students to integrate knowledge and ideas by combining the Essential Questions and the unit concepts in their approach to two or more featured titles.

For example, students might consider the contrast between Olaudah Equiano's and Alexis de Tocqueville's experience of the United States. Students can focus on how these very different views of America affect each writer's ideas and writing style.

Preparing to Read Complex Texts

1. Tell students they can be attentive readers by bringing their experience and imagination to the texts they read and by actively questioning those texts. Explain that the questions they see on the student page are examples of types of questions to ask about works of fiction and nonfiction.

2. Point out that, like writing, reading is a "multidraft" process, involving several readings of complete works or passages, revising and refining one's understanding each time.

Key Ideas and Details

3. Review and amplify the fifth bulleted point in the Key Ideas and Details box. **Ask:** What details in the text reveal the relationship between these layers of meaning?

   Possible response: Students may point out that certain themes are connected to the storylines of different characters, or that a theme is set up by one character's storyline and resolved by another's.

Craft and Structure

4. **Ask:** Why might an author vary his or her style from story to story or book to book?

   Possible response: The writing style can contribute to the reader's understanding of the ideas and themes of a piece. Different ideas and themes will be most effectively conveyed using different writing styles.

Integration of Ideas

5. Review and amplify the second and third bulleted points in the Integration of Ideas box. **Ask:** Why might it be useful to keep track of the ideas that you agree or disagree with in a text?

   Possible response: This will help you separate your feelings about the author's style and technique from the ideas presented.

6. Finally, explain to students that they should cite key ideas and details, examples of craft and structure, or instances of the integration of ideas as evidence to support their points during a discussion of fiction, nonfiction, or poetry. After hearing the evidence, the group might reach a consensus or might agree to disagree.

© Common Core
State Standards

- Reading Literature 1, 2, 3, 4, 5, 6
- Writing 1, 1.a, 2, 2.b, c; 3, 3.c, d; 4
- Language 1, 2.a, 4, 4.b, c, d; 5

A Growing Nation
Literature of the American Renaissance

". . . America is a land of wonders, in which everything is in constant motion and every change seems an improvement. . ."

- Alexis de Tocqueville

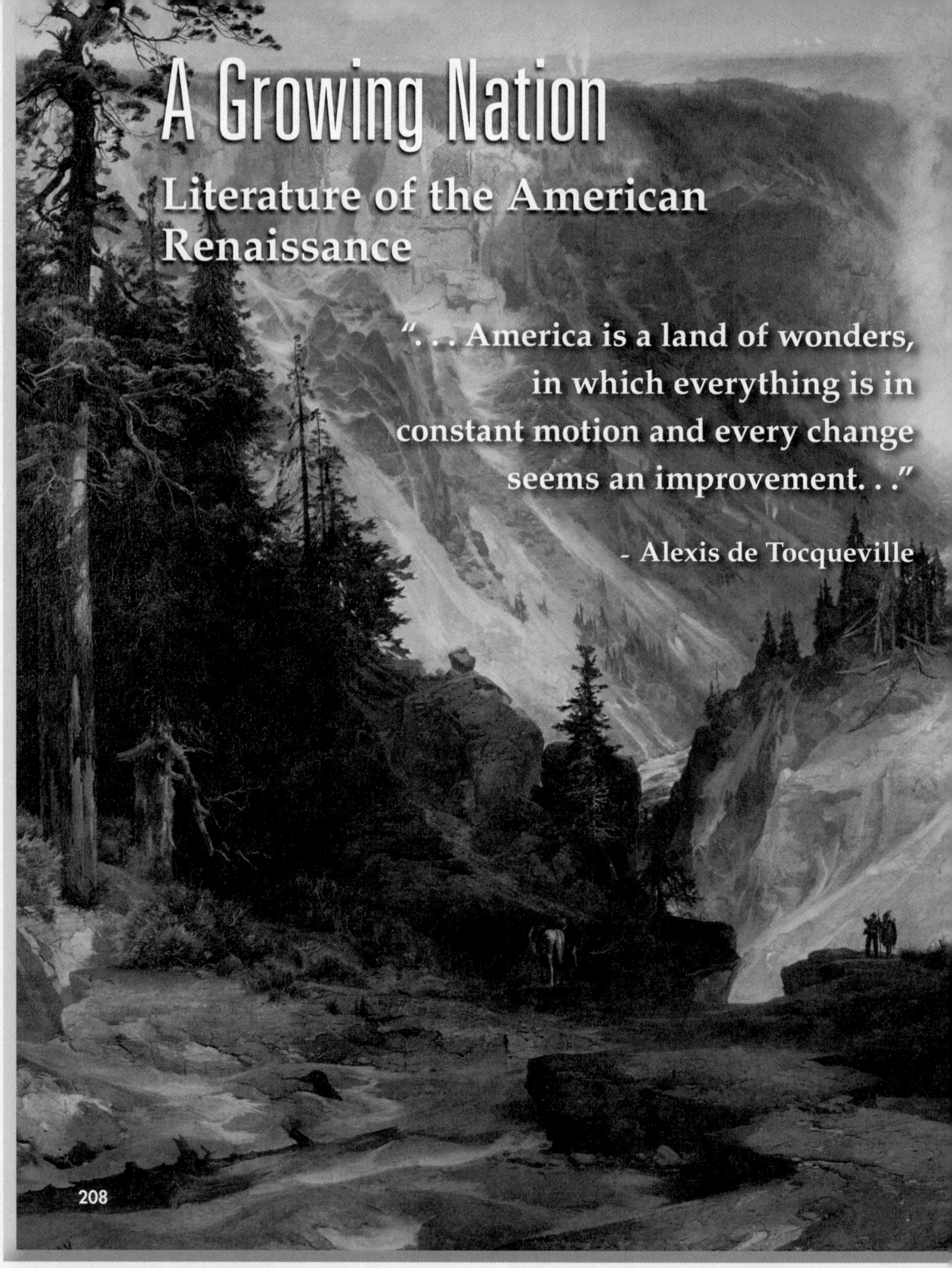

208

PHLit Online!
www.PHLitOnline.com

Teaching From Technology

Enriched Online Student Edition
- full narration of selections
- interactive graphic organizers
- linked **Get Connected** and **Background** videos
- all work sheets and other student resources

Professional Development
- the *Professional Development Guidebook* online
- additional professional-development essays by program authors

Planning, Assigning, and Monitoring
- software for online assignment of work to students, individually or to the whole class
- a system for tracking and grading student work

www.PHLitOnline.com

Hear It!
- Selection summary audio
- Selection audio

See It!
- Author video
- Essential Question video
- Get Connected videos
- Background videos
- More about the authors
- Illustrated vocabulary words
- Vocabulary flashcards

Do It!
- Interactive journals
- Interactive graphic organizers
- Grammar tutorials
- Interactive vocabulary games
- Test practice

209

Introduce Unit 2

1. Direct students' attention to the title of the unit, including the time period covered. Have a volunteer read the quotation. **Ask:** What does the quotation suggest about attitudes of the period? **Possible response:** The quotation suggests that newcomers could be awed by the new nation.

2. Discuss the artwork, *Grand Canyon of the Yellowstone*, 1872, by Thomas Moran. **Ask:** What does this painting suggest about America? **Possible response:** Students may say that the painting evokes the vastness, beauty, and ruggedness of the American landscape.

3. Have students speculate about the literature of the period, given the quotation and the art. **Possible response:** The literature of the period is likely to explore the wonders of America both as a landscape and as a land of change and opportunity.

Unit Resources

Unit 2 Resources includes these pages:

➤ **Benchmark Tests** assess and monitor student progress.

➤ **Vocabulary and Reading Warm-ups** provide additional vocabulary support, based on Lexile rankings, for each selection. "A" **Warm-ups** are for students reading two grades below level. "B" **Warm-ups** are for students reading one grade below level.

➤ **Selection Support**
- **Reading Skill**
- **Literary Analysis**
- **Vocabulary Builder**
- **Support for Writing**
- **Enrichment**

Unit Features

Unit Author
Gretel Ehrlich helps introduce the period in the unit introduction, provides a Contemporary Commentary on literature in the unit, and offers insight in the Writing Workshop.

Extended Studies
Students explore in depth the works of Edgar Allan Poe, accompanied by links to contemporary culture, a Critical Commentary, and a Comparing Literary Works feature.

Comparing Literary Works
Students compare classic and contemporary literary works.

Primary Sources
Students engage the documents that recorded history as it was made.

Informational Texts
Students learn to use and evaluate various types of informational text.

Themes Across Centuries
Students discover links between canonical literature and the contemporary world.

All worksheets and other student resources are also available online at www.PHLitOnline.com.

CLASSROOM STRATEGIES

Engaging Students in English **Jeff Anderson**

> "Inviting students in, as well as modeling and encouraging connections to present day culture can aid in making literature of the past seem more relevant to today.

Let's face it. Classroom management goes more smoothly when students are engaged. Sounds simple, right? But just how does an English teacher engage the typical high school student in the English classroom? Inviting students in, as well as modeling and encouraging connections to present day culture, can aid in making literature of the past seem more relevant to today. Scoffing at today's latest technology doesn't invite kids in, but listening to what they find appealing and what they connect to can help us build a bridge between academics and life outside school.

Practical Ways to Invite Students to Share Thinking

To make literature a bit more inviting, you don't need to do back flips (though that couldn't hurt), nor do you need elaborate grouping strategies. Nope. You just need a few engaging processes and questions up your sleeve, to pull out at a moment's notice. A few things that will work no matter what you're reading. And once you have students responding, you need to make sure what you say will keep them responding.

Turn and Talk

Put the kids in groups. It's the mantra of classroom management gurus, but sometimes it's hard to manage in real classrooms. One safe way to start is to have students turn and talk to one person. It's a simple, elegant process that's easy to manage:

- Pose a question
- Direct students to turn and talk for a designated time
- Share a few responses

Talk aids us in making sense of literature. When one question is asked and only one student answers, not everyone benefits or engages. With turn and talk, the high threat of looking foolish in front of your peers is reduced, and everyone is expected to say something to someone next to them.

What Sticks with You?

Barry Lane introduced me to what is quite possibly my favorite question: What sticks with you? Read a passage, a poem, an entire short story and ask students, "What sticks with you? What word or phrase sticks with you?"

If students aren't saying anything, then model what a response could sound like. We know that kids may become disengaged for many reasons. We can assume that an effective model will bring kids along—if not this time, the next time.

We all want to be in a safe place where our answers and thoughts will be valued. Acceptance has to be shown to get kids to open up. This question allows students to be right. It's what sticks with you—whatever that is. When students answer this question, they tend to point out powerful words (verbs, specific nouns) and phrases (images, dialogue, punctuation). Here we are. In a non-threatening way we're talking about diction and all sorts of literary devices.

Even if we add some depth to the responses, they are springing forth from the students—not the teachers. And that's the secret to engaging high school students: Listening to their responses and building from them, finding what is relevant to students and connecting that to what they need to know.

Encouraging Adolescent Writers and Readers

If students don't believe they have a possibility of success in something, they disengage. Who likes doing something they know they will never be able to master? Part of our job as English teachers is to help students believe they can bring something to the table in our literary discussions and in their writing.

Accept student errors as part of the process. Often students disengage from literature and writing for fear of being wrong. Think about the way you frame responses.

Instead of: a negative response to an answer you perceive as off the wall (*Once again, not paying attention. Did we read the same story?*)

Try: repeating their answers back to be sure you understood (*That's something I hadn't thought of. What made you think that?*)

Instead of: devaluing students' connections with popular culture (*Oh, great, another teenager who thinks texting is important. Writing is becoming a joke because of these things.*)

Try: looking for connections with these "other" forms of literacy such as text messaging and emailing (*You already know complex systems. All of you who text message know what each character you type means. Grammar has meaning just like that. It's so your reader understands you.*)

Instead of: marking all errors in students papers with your red pen. (*You need to edit your paper. You're just not thinking!*)

Try: Honoring the thinking behind the mistake. Scavenge for evidence of what the student knows and what thinking he or she is showing. '*When I was thirteen years old' does have a pause after it. How'd you know?*" After honoring their thought process, tell them that the way we show that pause is with a comma.

The words we choose when giving feedback to students have a great impact on their future attempts. We are teachers of words, and it is important that we make careful choices about what we say to and about our students.

Jeff Anderson

Jeff Anderson has written two books and numerous articles on teaching grammar and editing in context. NCTE honored him with the Paul and Kate Farmer *English Journal* Writing Award in 2006. He continues to work in classrooms and do staff development for teachers.

Supporting Research

Anderson, Jeff. *Mechanically inclined: building grammar, usage, and style into writer's workshop.* Portland: Stenhouse, 2005.

Johnston, Peter. *Choice words.* Portland: Stenhouse, 2004.

Lane, Barry. *After the end.* Portsmouth, Heinemann, 1992.

Tovani, Cris. *I read it, but I don't get it.* Portland: Stenhouse, 2000.

Reading the Unit Introduction

A Growing Nation

Explain to students that this unit covers American literature from 1800 to 1870, a period during which the nation expanded and awoke to its cultural identity. The Unit Introduction includes these components:

- a **Snapshot** offering a quick glimpse at the period;
- a **Historic Background** section discussing major events;
- a **Timeline** that runs decade by decade;
- a **Unit Essay** examining the literature of the period through the lens of three Essential Questions;
- **Following-Through** activities;
- a **Contemporary Commentary**.

Introducing the Essential Questions

1. Introduce each of the Essential Questions on the student page.

2. Show the **Essential Question** video on the *See It!* DVD. Help students relate the Essential Questions to the unit and their own experiences by asking the following:
   Literature and Place What reasons would lead you to move from your home to a distant place? How would you feel about the new place?
   Literature and Society Name a contemporary performer whose lyrics celebrate individuality. How attractive do you find this performer's view of life?
   American Literature Think of a contemporary person or character who is distinctly American. What qualities make up this person's "American-ness"?

3. Explain to students that the ideas they have considered in answering these questions also apply to the history of the American Renaissance. Have them begin reading the Unit Introduction, telling them to look as they read for ideas related to their answers.

Snapshot of the Period

1804 Filter Coffee Pot

In 1831, the French writer Alexis de Tocqueville (shown at right) traveled to America to write about its prisons. He was so enchanted by the bustling spirit of the young nation that he chose to write instead about American culture. While he celebrated the country's energy, Tocqueville also noted that America "has produced very few writers of distinction … [The literature of England] still darts its rays into the forests of the New World." By 1870, industrialism, population growth, economic changes, and the Civil War had all aged the nation's spirit. Along with that maturity came a new generation of writers who were the equal of any Europe had produced. Irving, Poe, Emerson, Thoreau, Dickinson, Whitman, and others shone their distinctly American light into and far beyond the "forests of the New World."

Hawthorne   **Whitman**   **Poe**   **Emerson**   **Dickinson**   **Thoreau**

As you read the selections in this unit, you will be asked to think about them in view of three key questions:

What is the **relationship** between literature and *place?*

How does **literature** shape or reflect *society?*

What makes **American** literature *American?*

Teaching Resources

The following resources can be used to support, enrich, or extend the instruction.

Unit 2 Resources
Names and Terms to Know, p. 2
Essential Question, pp. 3–5
Following Through, p. 6
All *Common Core Companion,*
pp. 10–16; 33–38

All *Professional Development Guidebook*
Cross-Curricular Enrichment, pp. 65, 225, 228, 230

All *See It!* DVD
Essential Question Video: Unit 2, Gretel Ehrlich, Segment 2

PHLit Online!   All resources are available at **www.PHLitOnline**.com

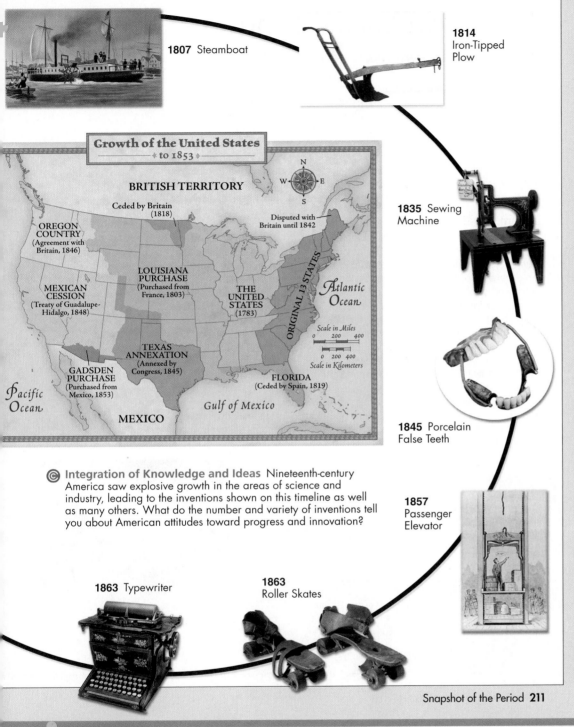

1807 Steamboat

1814 Iron-Tipped Plow

1835 Sewing Machine

1845 Porcelain False Teeth

1857 Passenger Elevator

1863 Typewriter

1863 Roller Skates

Growth of the United States
to 1853

BRITISH TERRITORY

Ceded by Britain (1818)

Disputed with Britain until 1842

OREGON COUNTRY (Agreement with Britain, 1846)

MEXICAN CESSION (Treaty of Guadalupe-Hidalgo, 1848)

LOUISIANA PURCHASE (Purchased from France, 1803)

THE UNITED STATES (1783)

ORIGINAL 13 STATES

Atlantic Ocean

TEXAS ANNEXATION (Annexed by Congress, 1845)

GADSDEN PURCHASE (Purchased from Mexico, 1853)

FLORIDA (Ceded by Spain, 1819)

Pacific Ocean

MEXICO

Gulf of Mexico

Scale in Miles
0   200   400

Scale in Kilometers
0   200   400

© **Integration of Knowledge and Ideas** Nineteenth-century America saw explosive growth in the areas of science and industry, leading to the inventions shown on this timeline as well as many others. What do the number and variety of inventions tell you about American attitudes toward progress and innovation?

Snapshot of the Period **211**

TEACH

Background

History

Tell students that de Tocqueville's (1805–1859) investigations of American prisons took him all over the United States, and his writings offer a detailed portrait of America as it was in the early 1830s. His comments about America were not always flattering, for example, " I know of no other country where love of money has such a grip on men's hearts."

Critical Viewing

Interpret Illustrations

1. Draw students' attention to the inventions shown on this page. **Ask** the question on the student page: What do the number and variety of inventions tell you about American attitudes towards innovation and progress? **Possible response:** The many diverse inventions show that Americans strongly encouraged innovation and progress.

2. Then **ask** students to explain how one of the inventions promoted productivity. **Possible response:** The sewing machine allowed clothes to be manufactured in large quantities.

Critical Viewing

Draw Conclusions

Divide students into small groups to examine the map and draw conclusions from it. Have each group come up with three conclusions about America's growth during this time. **Sample answers:** The progression was generally westward; the Louisiana Purchase was the biggest single addition to the country; America's borders reached from the Atlantic to the Pacific Ocean.

Differentiated Instruction   for Universal Access

Support For Less Proficient Readers

Before students read the Unit Introduction, distribute copies of the **Names and Terms to Know** work sheet (*Unit 2 Resources,* p. 2). Ask students to preview the work sheet. On the board, list the names and terms from the work sheet's Answer Key. Tell students to watch for these names and terms as they read the Unit Introduction. As students read the Unit Introduction, have them look for each name and term you have listed, and ask them to supply a clue to help remember its significance. Write each clue on the board next to the name or term it applies to. Finally, when students have finished reading the Unit Introduction, erase the names on the board and have the class complete the work sheet, referring back to the Unit Introduction.

PHLit Online!

Show or assign the **Essential Question** video for Unit 2 online at www.PHLitOnline.com.

211

The Historical Background section discusses the most significant events of this period: the physical expansion of the nation; the rise of industry and improvements in transportation; the spread of democracy—and its shortfalls (the lack of female suffrage, forced Native American removal, continued enslavement of African Americans); and the new country's international involvements.

1. Point out that the story of this period is the story of westward expansion.

2. Have students read the Background. Then **ask** them to decide whether the following events were the results or the causes of expansion, or whether they were both: the Louisiana Purchase, the forced removal of Native Americans, the Mexican War, the California gold rush, and slavery.
Sample response: The Louisiana Purchase added territory and so was a cause of westward expansion. The conflicts with Native Americans were the results of westward expansion. The Mexican War and California gold rush were both results of the movement west and causes of further expansion. Slavery existed from colonial times, but supporters and opponents of slavery fought over dominating the new territories; so, the escalating conflict over slavery was a result of expansion.

Teaching the Timeline

Tell students that the Timeline for 1800–1870 appears on pages 212–221 of this Unit Introduction. Each portion of the Timeline identifies and illustrates several major events in the United States and the world for that period.

Critical Viewing

1. Call students' attention to the illustration of the Lewis and Clark expedition on the Timeline.

2. **Ask** students what aspect of the expedition is emphasized.
Possible response: It emphasizes the cooperative relations between the explorers and the Native American tribes.

Historical Background

The American Renaissance (1800–1870)

The European Renaissance—the magnificent rebirth of classical art and learning—took place in the fourteenth, fifteenth, and sixteenth centuries. The American version—not a "rebirth" as much as a first flowering—took place in the first half of the nineteenth century. During these years, the nation came of age and entered its literary and cultural maturity.

Two turn-of-the-century events symbolized America's growing up. In 1800 the nation's capital was moved from Philadelphia to Washington, D.C., establishing a unique political center for a unique republic. In the same year, Americans founded the first cultural institution in the capital, the Library of Congress, a storehouse of law, scholarship, and creativity.

Steam, Steel, and Spirit

Underpinning the American cultural renaissance was sheer physical and technological growth. In 1803, Thomas Jefferson doubled the nation's size by signing the Louisiana Purchase. With the expansion of size came an expansion of spirit, an upsurge of national pride and self-awareness. Improved transportation helped bind the old and the new states together. Canals, turnpikes, and especially railroads—"the iron horse"—multiplied. Steamboats and sailing packets sped people and goods to their destinations. Everyone and everything was on the move. After California was added to the nation, the Gold Rush of 1849 drew hundreds of thousands of hopeful people to the western edge of the continent.

Major advances in technology spurred social and cultural change. Factories sprang up all over the Northeast, creating new industries, new kinds of jobs, and plenty of economic profit. The steel plow and the reaper encouraged more aggressive frontier settlement by making farming practical on the vast, sod-covered grasslands. The telegraph made almost instant communication possible across America's great distances.

TIMELINE

1803: Louisiana Purchase extends the nation's territory to the Rocky Mountains.

1800

"The object of our mission is to explore the Missouri River"
—*Thomas Jefferson*

▲ **1804:** Lewis and Clark begin expedition exploring and mapping vast regions of the West.

Enrichment: Investigating Geography

Old New York

In the 1600s, the Dutch settled the southern tip of Manhattan Island, which eventually turned into New York City. In the city's early days, an area in southern Manhattan became known as Greenwich Village because it was actually a suburb—a "village" compared to the more populous area to the south of it. However, by 1820, Greenwich Village was absorbed into the rapidly growing city, which reached from the tip of the island to as far north as 14th Street.

Today's New York extends north for hundreds of blocks beyond 14th Street.

Activity: Geography Report Have students use the **Investigating Geography** work sheet, in *Professional Development Guidebook,* page 228, to help them compare the boundaries of old New York to those of the contemporary city. Then ask them to report their findings to the class.

The Slow March of Democracy

The 1828 election of Andrew Jackson, "the People's President," ushered in the era of the common man, as property requirements for voting began to be eliminated. Only white males, however, benefited from these democratic advances. Little political attention was paid to women, and most African Americans remained enslaved. The tragic policy of "Indian removal" forced the westward migration of Native Americans as their tribal lands were confiscated. On the 1838 "Trail of Tears," for example, thousands of Cherokee perished on the trek from Georgia to Oklahoma.

On the World Stage

The first decades of the 1800s were hopeful ones. The War of 1812 convinced Europeans that the United States was on the world stage to stay. The Monroe Doctrine of 1823 warned Europe not to intervene in the new Latin American nations. In the 1830s, the U.S. became embroiled in a conflict over the secession of Texas from Mexico. When Texas was admitted to the Union in 1845, the resulting war with Mexico ended in a United States victory, adding more territory to the nation, including California.

Winds of Change

At mid-century the United States faced trouble as well as promise. The new prosperity unleashed fierce competition, leading to factories scarred by child labor and unsafe working conditions. Women's rights gained some ground, but the deepest social divide remained slavery. Advocates of states' rights argued that the federal government could not bend states to its will. Abolitionists, on the other hand, insisted that slavery was morally wrong. In 1861, the gathering storm finally burst into civil war.

Key Historical Theme: Coming of Age

- Physical expansion and technological progress lay the foundation for an American cultural flowering.
- Democracy advanced, although women, Native Americans, and African Americans did not fully share in it.
- The conflict over slavery eventually led to civil war.

1807: Robert Fulton's steamboat makes first trip from New York City to Albany. ▶

1810

◀ **1804: France** Napoleon Bonaparte declares himself emperor.

Historical Background **213**

Connecting to the Literature

1. Point out that the seminal essay "On Civil Disobedience" (p. 388), by Henry David Thoreau (1817–1862), grew from his objections to the Mexican War and his refusal to pay taxes to support it.

2. During this time, America's economy expanded overseas. The great novel *Moby-Dick* (p. 336) by Herman Melville (1819–1891) depicts the whaling trade and is set largely on the open sea.

Background

History

James Marshall found gold at Sutter's mill in California in January of 1848. In a few days, word of the gold strike spread to San Francisco. Carpenters threw down their tools, bakers left their loaves to burn, and schools emptied as teachers joined the rush to the gold fields.

The news quickly spread outward from San Francisco. More than 80,000 Americans, Europeans, and South Americans made the long journey to California in 1849. They became known as "forty-niners."

Key Historical Theme

1. Explain to students that this section of the Historical Background points out three major historical developments from the whole period.

2. **Ask** students to come up with a short headline-type phrase for each point to help jog their memories.
   Sample answer: "America Grows Up"; "More Democracy (for Some)"; "A Nation Divided."

Differentiated Instruction for Universal Access

Strategy for Less Proficient Readers
Ask each student to become an expert on a particular section of the Historical Background by reading it several times and devising a comprehension test on it.

EL Support for English Learners
Draw a rough outline of the United States on the chalkboard. As students read about each new surge of expansion, shade in and date newly acquired territory so that students can see the course of growth.

Strategy for Advanced Readers
Challenge students to find links between this historical period and their own times. Students can look for parallels or cause-and-effect relationships. For example, how did the Louisiana Purchase encourage people to settle the West?

213

As students read The American Renaissance, they will examine its information through the lens of three Essential Questions. Each Essential Question is broken down into "steppingstone" questions. Work through each steppingstone question with the class. Then have students pose answers to each Essential Question as it applies to the period.

What is the relationship between literature and place?

1. Before they read this section of the essay, tell students that from 1800 to 1870, more than at any other time, Americans connected their lives with the land they were discovering.

2. Have students read this section of the essay. Then pose the first steppingstone question. **Ask:** What did Americans discover as they explored the continent? **Possible response:** They found a challenging and varied terrain that included mountains, forests, plains; hostile Native American tribes; opportunities such as fertile land and valuable resources.

3. Then **ask** the second steppingstone question: What attitudes developed toward the American land? **Possible response:** People felt the desire to possess the riches of the land. They also felt awe in the expanse and beauty of the landscape.

(continued on p. 215)

Critical Viewing

1. Direct students to the illustration on the Timeline of Francis Scott Key (1779–1843) at Fort McHenry (p. 214). Explain that Key composed "The Star-Spangled Banner" in 1814 after witnessing the British attack on Fort McHenry during the War of 1812.

2. **Ask** students to identify phrases from the national anthem that could be connected with the battle shown in the illustration. **Possible response:** Students may cite "o'er the ramparts we watched"; "perilous fight"; "the rockets' red glare"; "the bombs bursting in air."

Essential Questions Across Time
The American Renaissance (1800–1870)

 What is the relationship between literature and *place?*

ESSENTIAL QUESTION VOCABULARY

These Essential Question words will help you think and write about literature and place:

barrier (bar´ē ər) *n.* something that prevents movement or separates

acquisition (ak´wə zish´ən) *n.* the act of obtaining something

exploration (eks´ plə rā´ shən) *n.* investigation of new lands

What did Americans discover as they explored the continent?
Starting as thirteen eastern seaboard colonies, hemmed in by mountain barriers blocking easy access to the interior, the United States gradually extended itself west. The Louisiana Purchase in 1803, the Mexican Cession of 1848, and the additions of Texas and the Oregon Territory filled out the nation and needed to be explored, surveyed, documented, and celebrated.

Size and Diversity Americans were inspired by the sheer size of the land. Vast open prairies in the Midwest, demanding deserts in the Southwest, unbroken forests in the Northwest, grand mountains and canyons in the West—the land ended only at an ocean. Explorers and settlers found countless natural resources. It seemed enough to last forever.

What attitudes developed toward the American land?
Commerce Americans covered the continent in a spirit of acquisition and pride of ownership. The land seemed to demand optimism and practical invention, calling continuously for one more step west. With exploration came exploitation. Commercial possibilities were as wide as the landscape.

Grandeur At the same time, many Americans developed an attitude that went beyond practical matters. The land struck them with awe. To them its spiritual possibilities, not its commercial ones, were as wide as the landscape. Its physical grandeur inspired them to reach for the sublime.

TIMELINE

1813: England Jane Austen publishes *Pride and Prejudice.* ▶

1810

1812: U.S. declares war on Great Britain; early battles in War of 1812 are at sea.

▲ **1814:** Bombardment of Fort McHenry inspires Francis Scott Key to write "The Star-Spangled Banner."

214 A Growing Nation (1800–1870)

Vocabulary Development

 Essential Question Vocabulary
Students will be expected to use Essential Question Vocabulary (introduced on pp. 214, 216, and 219) when they talk and write about the Essential Questions. Introduce the vocabulary as students complete each section of this Unit Introduction. Then, have students complete sentence starters like the following to help them internalize this vocabulary.

One very large **acquisition** made by the United States was _____.
(**Sample answer:** the Louisiana Purchase)

One kind of **technology** that changed the way people communicated across long distances was _____ . (**Sample answer:** the telegraph)

Colloquial English is different from formal English in that it _____.
(**Sample answer:** includes more contractions.)

How did these attitudes show up in literature?

An American Mythology Explorers such as Meriwether Lewis and Captain William Clark recorded the facts of their expeditions in colorful words and drawings that made the farthest reaches of the continent accessible to every American, at least in imagination. Fiction writers Washington Irving and James Fenimore Cooper helped to create an American mythology by setting tales in the forests, towns, and outposts of the American landscape. In his exciting narrative poems, Henry Wadsworth Longfellow populated the wilderness with colonial Americans, Native Americans, and Revolutionary War heroes.

The American Masters The greatest of American writers—those whose work created the American Renaissance—were all profoundly involved in the American landscape. Edgar Allan Poe, Nathaniel Hawthorne, and Herman Melville saw the dark side of the wilderness, while Ralph Waldo Emerson and Henry David Thoreau emphasized its sublimity. Emily Dickinson explored the universal qualities of her local landscape, while Walt Whitman merged his all-encompassing self with the entire nation.

Nature and Culture The American place affected a wide variety of cultural figures. Thomas Cole and the other Hudson River painters based their work on the romantic and sublime features of the landscape. John James Audubon applied both science and art to American wildlife. Frederick Law Olmsted even found a way to bring nature into the city with his landscape design of New York City's Central Park.

The American EXPERIENCE

CLOSE-UP ON HISTORY

Sacajawea, Guide for Lewis and Clark

In 1804, a Shoshone woman named Sacajawea was staying with the Mandan Indians near present-day Bismarck, North Dakota. Meriwether Lewis and William Clark, who had been asked by President Thomas Jefferson to explore the new lands of the Louisiana Purchase, were spending the winter with the Mandans. Sacajawea offered to guide them in the spring across the Rocky Mountains, where the Shoshones lived. She knew the region well and she could translate for them in their encounters with different Indian tribes.

Sacajawea contributed greatly to the success of the expedition, gathering wild vegetables and advising the men where to fish and hunt. She also knew about the healing qualities of different herbs. When the party reached the mountains, Sacajawea recognized the lands of her people, and she persuaded her relatives to support the expedition with food and horses.

After crossing the Rockies, the explorers reached the west coast and returned to St. Louis in 1806. Thanks largely to Sacajawea, their relations with Indians had been almost entirely peaceful. Sadly, however, the westward movement inspired by the expedition would eventually lead to "Indian removal" and confiscation of Indian lands.

1817: William Cullen Bryant publishes early draft of "Thanatopsis" in a Boston magazine. ▶

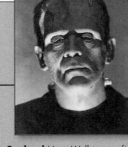

1818: **England** Mary Wollstonecraft Shelley creates a legend with *Frankenstein*. ▲

— **1820** —

The American Experience

Close-Up on History

1. Have students read the sidebar feature about Sacajawea.

2. Share the following information with students: Sacajawea had a difficult life. Warriors from another tribe took her from her family when she was about 12 years old. They sold her to a French-Canadian trader, who married her but treated her as an inferior. It was his idea to join Lewis and Clark. Sacajawea was only about 18 years old when she, her husband, and her infant son left home with the expedition.

3. **Ask** students to share stories they have heard about Sacajawea.
   Possible responses: She joined the expedition on her own; she fell in love with an explorer. Discuss with students why people might have perpetuated these stories.
   Possible answer: People may have preferred to view Sacajawea as a symbol of the grandeur of the west rather than as a person who had faced difficulty in part because of European settlers.

? Teaching the Essential Questions (cont.)

4. **Ask** the final steppingstone question: How did these attitudes show up in literature?
   Sample answer: Some writers (Lewis, Powell) celebrated the land's beauty, while others (Irving, Cooper, Longfellow) spun a new American mythology in fiction and poetry narratives. Some American masters (Poe, Hawthorne, Melville) responded to the dark side of the mysterious land, while others (Emerson, Thoreau) wrote of its sublimity or found a personal spiritual connection with the place they called home (Dickinson, Whitman).

Applying the Essential Questions

1. Summarize the class discussion of the three steppingstone questions on pages 214–215.

2. Then **ask** students how the answer to this Essential Question might differ today, that is, how Americans' attitude toward their land in 1800–1870 might be different from our attitudes today.
   Possible response: Nineteenth-century Americans were making fresh discoveries about a terrain that we now know well, and so they probably were more excited about the land and more intimately involved with the physical land than we are today, in activities such as farming and in traveling without the benefit of trains, planes, or cars. On the other hand, earlier Americans were probably less aware than we are of the harmful effects of their settlement on the environment and other people, such as Native Americans.

Teaching the Essential Question

How does literature shape or reflect society?

1. Before they read this section, explain to students that from 1800 to 1870, this nation changed from a largely agricultural society to a more industrialized one as cities grew and technology brought people closer together.

2. Have students read this section of the essay. Then **ask** the first stepping-stone question: What social forces shaped America during the period?

Possible response: New technology (the steamboat, the telegraph, and other improvements) sped up travel and communications, made daily life easier, and increased productivity. As people clustered in larger towns and cities, they became more aware of how others lived and thought, and this awareness helped fuel social movements, such as abolitionism and women's rights. The spread of democracy—indicated by the rise of the "little man" in the presidency of Andrew Jackson—gave more people access to political power. The antislavery movement affected politics (and vice versa), as territories turned into new states and were entered into either the slavery or the antislavery camp.

(continued on p. 217)

Critical Viewing

Draw Conclusions

1. Draw students' attention to the map on the Timeline illustrating the Missouri Compromise of 1820.

2. **Ask** students: What does the map on the Timeline show about the impact of the Missouri Compromise on the nation as a whole?

Possible response: The map shows a clear division between states and territories where slavery was allowed and where it was banned—in part, the result of the Missouri Compromise. The free area (shown in green and yellow) is much larger than the area where slavery was permitted. Slavery was an issue that divided the nation.

216

© COMMON CORE ▪ MULTIPLE PERSPECTIVES ON THE ERA

How does literature shape or reflect *society?*

What social forces shaped America during this period?

Technology Bigger, better, stronger, faster—everything in America was rolling on the fast track, especially on the iron network of railroad tracks that crisscrossed the country. Railroads allowed farmers to get their crops to larger markets, and they made almost every corner of America a potential market. Factories made cities grow, and cities then built more factories. Shipbuilding, fishing, and whaling flourished. Inventions of all kinds made life easier: the telegraph and Morse code, the steamboat, the reaper, vulcanized rubber, powerful looms and lathes, the sewing machine, the elevator. Even the word *technology* was coined during this period.

Democracy As the nineteenth century moved forward in America, the right to vote was still largely restricted to white males who owned land. The election of Andrew Jackson as president and the rise of Jacksonian Democracy, however, signaled the rise of the common man to positions of unprecedented power. It was no longer necessary to be wealthy and highly educated to wield political authority in America. At the same time, the women's rights movement gained momentum, spurred on by the Seneca Falls Convention in 1848. Native Americans, on the other hand, felt the continuing hardship of forced removal from their traditional homelands.

Slavery The institution of slavery remained the most profound controversy in America. Eventually, slavery would be the social and political issue that would have the greatest effect on the lives—and deaths—of Americans.

What did nineteenth-century Americans read?

Americans had broken away from Britain politically, but they still devoured British literature, including the adventure tales of Walter Scott and the serial novels of Charles Dickens. However, no British author came close in popularity to two Americans. Harriet Beecher Stowe's anti-slavery novel *Uncle Tom's Cabin* became a national—and international—phenomenon, and Longfellow became the best-selling poet in the English language.

> **ESSENTIAL QUESTION VOCABULARY**
>
> These Essential Question words will help you think and write about literature and society:
>
> **market** (mär´ kit) *n.* region in which goods can be bought and sold
>
> **invention** (in ven´ shən) *n.* something originated by experiment; new device
>
> **technology** (tek näl´ ə jē) *n.* scientific or industrial methods or products

TIMELINE

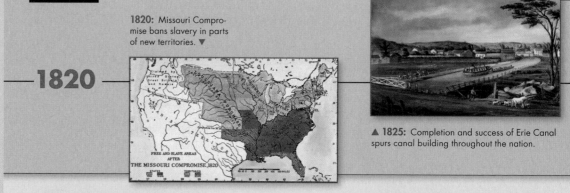

1820

1820: Missouri Compromise bans slavery in parts of new territories. ▼

▲ **1825:** Completion and success of Erie Canal spurs canal building throughout the nation.

FREE AND SLAVE AREAS AFTER THE MISSOURI COMPROMISE, 1820

216 A Growing Nation (1800–1870)

Think Aloud

Vocabulary: Using Context

Direct students' attention to the word *unprecedented* in the sentence on this page: "The election of Andrew Jackson as president and the rise of Jacksonian Democracy, however, signaled the rise of the "common man" to positions of *unprecedented* power." Use the following "think aloud" to model the skill of using context to infer the meaning of the word. Say to students:

When I read the sentence, I realize that the writer is using *unprecedented* to describe some increase in the power of the "common man." The writer says that Jackson's election marked "the rise of the 'common man' to positions of unprecedented power." The next sentence says, "It was no longer necessary to be wealthy and highly educated to wield political authority in America." The words *rise* and *no longer necessary* suggest that this increase in power was happening for the first time. So I think *unprecedented* refers to something important that had not happened before.

What did American writers want to achieve?

The Social Vision Thomas Jefferson's vision of America was grand, and the Louisiana Purchase helped make that vision a reality. The reports sent by Lewis and Clark and other explorers encouraged the country's physical, political, and commercial growth. At the same time, American journalism fed the idea that the New World could rival the Old World in every way. In lectures, essays, speeches, debates, pamphlets, editorials, and songs, Americans presented what they thought and felt about women's rights, slavery, treatment of Native Americans, land use, immigration, trade, and taxes. Public writing enabled America to define a public self.

The Romantic Vision Romanticism made clear that exploration of the private self was as important as exploration of the land. In prose and poetry, American writers described individual quests for self-definition. Romantic writers elevated imagination over reason, feeling over fact, and nature above all. The fantastical tales of Washington Irving and Edgar Allan Poe, and the agonized heroes of Nathaniel Hawthorne and Herman Melville made the Romantic vision an essential part of the American Renaissance.

The Transcendental Vision Literature, philosophy, and religion merged in New England Transcendentalism, producing a native blend that was Romantic, intuitive, and ethically engaged. For Transcendentalists, real truths lay outside sensory experience. Ralph Waldo Emerson explored those truths in brilliant, wide-ranging essays. Henry David Thoreau put his finger on those truths by merging nature writing and spiritual autobiography. Thoreau's *Walden* remains central to American literature.

The American EXPERIENCE

A LIVING TRADITION

Walden Pond and Tinker Creek

About 120 years after Thoreau embarked on the experiment of living "alone, in the woods … on the shore of Walden Pond," Annie Dillard undertook a similar experiment with nature and solitude: "I live by a creek, Tinker Creek, in a valley in Virginia's Blue Ridge." Just as Thoreau wrote *Walden* to describe his experiences, she, too, wrote a book about what she saw and thought, the best-selling *Pilgrim at Tinker Creek*. Near the beginning of the book, she describes the home base for her observations:

"An anchorite's hermitage [hermit's secluded retreat] is called an anchor-hold; some anchor-holds were simple sheds clamped to the side of a church like a barnacle to a rock. I think of this house clamped to the side of Tinker Creek as an anchor-hold. It holds me at anchor to the rock bottom of the creek itself and it keeps me steadied in the current, as a sea anchor does, facing the stream of light pouring down. It's a good place to live; there's a lot to think about. The creeks—Tinker and Carvin's—are an active mystery, fresh every minute."

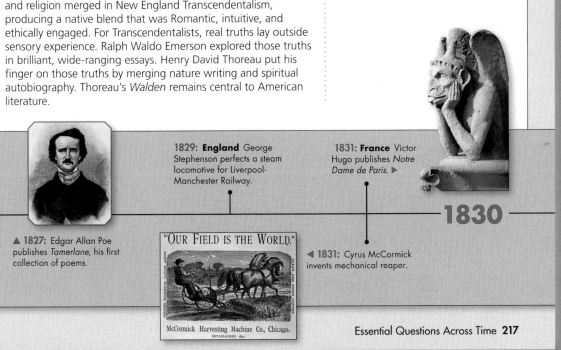

1829: **England** George Stephenson perfects a steam locomotive for Liverpool-Manchester Railway.

1831: **France** Victor Hugo publishes *Notre Dame de Paris.* ▶

1830

▲ 1827: Edgar Allan Poe publishes *Tamerlane*, his first collection of poems.

"OUR FIELD IS THE WORLD."

McCormick Harvesting Machine Co., Chicago.
ESTABLISHED 1831.

◀ 1831: Cyrus McCormick invents mechanical reaper.

3. Have students read this section of the essay. Then **ask** the second steppingstone question: What did nineteenth-century Americans read?

   Possible answer: Americans read contemporary British authors (including Walter Scott and Charles Dickens); Harriet Beecher Stowe's influential bestseller *Uncle Tom's Cabin*.

4. **Ask** the third steppingstone question on this student page: What did American writers want to achieve?

   Answer: American writers wrote to give voice to the American experience and America's "public self": physical and economic growth; an increasingly democratic American society; and the political issues of their day (abolitionism, women's rights). They also expressed the quest of individuals to define themselves. The Romantics celebrated nature and self-definition. Romanticism valued imagination and emotion over reason. The Transcendental movement, led by Ralph Waldo Emerson and Henry David Thoreau, applied Romantic thought to American values such as self-reliance.

The American Experience

A Living Tradition

1. Explain that the writings of Henry David Thoreau affected many influential later writers and leaders. His masterpiece *Walden* inspired contemporary American writers such as Annie Dillard, Gretel Ehrlich, and Diane Ackerman. Thoreau's views on social change had great influence on such modern leaders as Martin Luther King, Jr., (1929–1968) and Mohandas Gandhi (1869–1948).

2. **Ask** students how Thoreau has influenced some aspect of twentieth-century life.

Possible response: Thoreau's social ideas helped fuel the civil rights movement led by King, which produced major social changes in the United States in the late twentieth century.

217

Applying the Essential Questions

1. Summarize discussion of the three steppingstone questions on pages 216–217.

2. Then **ask** students whether they would have found living during such a restless period exciting or unsettling. Have them support their answers with examples.
   Possible answer: Seeing the country grow from an agricultural to an industrial nation, with rapid progress in travel and communication, would be stimulating. It would be inspiring to be part of the reform movements.

Contemporary Connection

1. Have students read the feature about Emily Dickinson. If they are unfamiliar with the term muse, refer them to the feature on Anne Bradstreet on p. 78.

2. Have students discuss which of the three video game designs they would have chosen as the winner, and why. Encourage students to revisit their decision after they read Dickinson's biography and poetry on pages 404–421.

Critical Viewing

Draw Conclusions

1. Call students' attention to this page's Timeline image of the Trail of Tears. Explain that it refers to the 800-mile march of 16,000 Cherokee people from Georgia to the Indian Territory (now Oklahoma); over 5,000 died.

2. **Ask:** What does the image imply about the conditions on the march?
   Answer: Women and children huddle in blankets, suggesting they are suffering severe hardships.

The American EXPERIENCE

CONTEMPORARY CONNECTION

EMILY DICKINSON: POET, RECLUSE . . . GAMER?

In 2005, three prominent video-game designers set themselves a challenge to create games based on something surprising: the poetry of Emily Dickinson.

Clint Hocking, lead designer of *Splinter Cell*, created a game called *Muse*. Players would collect symbols based on Dickinson's Massachusetts. They would then assemble the symbols to make poems within a certain amount of time.

Peter Molyneux, designer of *Black & White*, created a game using a house modeled on Dickinson's. Players would wander around the house, trying to unlock Dickinson's experiences.

Will Wright, creator of *The Sims*, believes that Dickinson and hi-tech are a natural combination. "If she were alive today," he said, "she'd be an Internet addict, and she'd probably have a really amazing blog." The game Wright designed would be stored on a USB flash drive. The player and Emily would write to each other. Emily would appear randomly with IMs, e-mails, or desktop appearances. Ultimately, she could delete herself from the memory stick.

Wright's game won the challenge.

TIMELINE

1835

1837: Samuel F.B. Morse patents electromagnetic telegraph. ▶

1838: U.S. Army marches Cherokees of Georgia on long "Trail of Tears" to Oklahoma. ▶

1841: Antarctica is first explored by Englishman James Ross. ▶

1842: Asia Hong Kong becomes a British colony.

218 A Growing Nation (1800–1870)

Enrichment: Analyzing a Historic Event

Seneca Falls and Women's Rights

The famous 1848 Women's Rights convention in Seneca Falls, New York, had its impetus in an antislavery convention in London eight years before. Lucretia Mott (1793–1880) and Elizabeth Cady Stanton (1815–1902), American abolitionists, had been refused admittance to the London meeting because they were women. In response, they organized the Seneca Falls Convention, where Stanton drafted eleven resolutions arguing that women should be granted the same rights as men, including one declaring that women should have the right to vote. Mott, shocked, said to her friend, "Why, Lizzie, thee will make us ridiculous." It was not until 1920 that American women could vote in a national election.

Activity: Research Have students make a list of research topics relating to the Seneca Falls Convention, using the **Enrichment: Analyzing a Historical Event** work sheet from the *Professional Development Guidebook,* page 230, to guide them.

What makes American literature *American?*

What qualities made American literature sound American?

American English Most Americans, descended from English colonists, spoke English, but gradually the American way of speaking and writing took on many unique features. Dialects, the products of local communities, developed around the country, and local grammar and syntax often drove out standard British English. Spanish, French, Dutch, and Native American languages added to the mix, and Americans coined new words to describe their land, weather, plants, animals, and ways of daily life.

Triumph of the Colloquial American English, both spoken and written, became more colloquial, or informal, than British English. Contractions such as *can't, don't,* and *couldn't* were acceptable. Colorful idioms enlivened everyday speech. Americans might *set a spell, take a fork in a road,* or *bark up the wrong tree.* The British thought that Americans were ruining the language, but, like the nation itself, American English was intensely alive to change, variety, and new additions.

The "Barbaric Yawp" During the American Renaissance, American writers found their own voices. Emerson, Thoreau, Poe, Dickinson—each contributed to a recognizably American style, but no one sounded as utterly American as Walt Whitman. He was unafraid to sound his "barbaric yawp" across the continent. His style incorporated the plain and the elegant, the high and the low, the foreign and the native. It mixed grand opera, political oratory, journalistic punch, everyday conversation, and biblical cadences. Whitman's sound was the American sound.

What literary character types emerged during this period?

The Frontiersman As the frontier continued to open, the men and women who faced it head-on entered into the nation's literary imagination. Real-life backwoodsmen such as Daniel Boone and Davy Crockett were mythologized in almanacs and folktales, and Americans delighted in tall tales about

> **ESSENTIAL QUESTION VOCABULARY**
>
> These Essential Question words will help you think and write about American literature:
>
> **individualist** (in´də vij´ oo əl ist) *n.* one who lives life his or her own way, not influenced by others
>
> **colloquial** (kə lō´kwē əl) *adj.* conversational; informal
>
> **self-reliant** (self-ri li´ənt) *adj.* depending upon one's own judgments and abilities

1845: Ireland Famine results from failure of potato crop.

1848: Gold Rush begins in California. ▶

1848: Mexican War ends; United States expands borders.

1850

1845: Florida becomes the twenty-seventh state in the United States.

◀ **1848: Women's Rights Convention** held in Seneca Falls, New York.

1848: Karl Marx and Friedrich Engels publish *The Communist Manifesto.*

Essential Questions Across Time **219**

Teaching the Essential Question

What makes American literature American?

1. Before students read this section of the essay, point out that although each American writer is a unique individual, the experiences of these writers as Americans give them a common identity. For example, no European author could claim the American frontier, with its perennial promise of something new or the American pattern of moving on and starting over.

2. **Ask** the first steppingstone question on page 219: What qualities made American literature sound American?
   Possible response: American writers used ever-changing colloquial styles, slang, local dialects, and colorful vocabulary. Many broke with standard British grammar.

3. Then **ask** the second steppingstone question: What literary character types emerged during the American Renaissance?
   Possible response: New character types included scouts, frontiersmen, riverboat men, and pioneers. Regional and ethnic character types (and stereotypes) appeared in American literature. Typical American heroes were Romantic rebels and individualists, seekers and dreamers.

(continued on p. 220)

Differentiated Instruction for Universal Access

Culturally Responsive Instruction

Have students choose three of the following common English words and have them come up with alternative words with the same meaning from slang, nonstandard English, or another language. Encourage students who are listing words in the same language to compare their terms and create a minidictionary.

bad	*good*	*beautiful*
home	*enemy*	*love*
friend	*scary*	*fun*

219

Background

Literature

Tell students that Nathaniel Hawthorne (1804–1864) and Herman Melville (1819–1891) were good friends for a brief period. In 1850—the year that Hawthorne's greatest work, *The Scarlet Letter*, was published—the two men attended a picnic. When a thunderstorm interrupted the gathering, they had the chance to spend some time together.

Melville published his great novel *Moby-Dick* soon after, in 1851. In stark contrast to Hawthorne's book, Melville's would not receive its due until many years later. Hurt, Melville sought reassurance from Hawthorne. The friendship continued until around 1852, when it cooled for reasons that are not known.

Teaching the Essential Questions

(cont.)

4. **Ask** students the final stepping-stone question, on this page: What literary themes emerged during this era?
   Possible response: Typical American themes included "westering," or reflecting on the frontier; self-reliance and individualism; Transcendentalism; Romantic fascination with nature and the individual spirit

the superhuman lumberjack Paul Bunyan, the rowdy riverboat man Mike Fink, and the African American steel-driver John Henry. In fiction, the essential frontiersman was Natty Bumppo, the hero of James Fenimore Cooper's *Leatherstocking Tales*. At one with the wilderness, these hardy characters helped define the American identity as bold, self-reliant, and "uncorrupted" by civilization.

The Romantic Individualist Romanticism emphasized the individual over the institution and the person over the community. The American Romantic hero took many forms. In *The Scarlet Letter*, Nathaniel Hawthorne's Hester Prynne dared to put love and honor over the repressive rule of her town. In *Moby-Dick*, Herman Melville's Captain Ahab let nothing stand in the way of his obsession with the white whale. In *Leaves of Grass*, Walt Whitman's ecstatic self celebrated its own joyful existence at the center of the universe.

The Transcendental Seeker One type of Romantic individualist was the person who sought to reach the sublime, a feeling of oneness with all that is beautiful and good. This private soul craved unity with the Oversoul, a universal force that might be identified as the mind of God. As Emerson wrote, "the individual is the world," and an individual could reach the sublime through the world of nature. Emerson and Thoreau defined this character type, but other writers and artists contributed to the quest for the sublime. Margaret Fuller edited the Transcendentalist magazine *The Dial*, and the Hudson River school of visual artists painted landscapes that inspired a sense of the sublime in all who saw them.

What literary themes emerged during this era?

Westering The myth of America began as "a city upon a hill," but by the nineteenth century it had become "the garden of the world." The sheer bulk of the continent, with its treasury of natural resources, made continuous Western expansion a fundamental part of the national identity. Many Americans considered this movement west as a continental destiny. It became the right and duty of Americans to explore, expand, and exploit. However, if America was a garden, it was one being invaded by machines. This is a theme that continues to resonate in American literature.

TIMELINE

1850: Nathaniel Hawthorne publishes *The Scarlet Letter*.

1851: Herman Melville publishes *Moby-Dick*.

1850

1850: England Elizabeth Barrett Browning publishes *Sonnets from the Portuguese.* ▶

1851: Nathaniel Hawthorne publishes *The House of Seven Gables.*

1851: Australia Gold discovered in New South Wales.

Enrichment: Understanding Economics

Francis Lowell and American Industry

In the War of 1812, Britain's blockade of the United States provided a boost to American industry. Cut off from foreign supplies, Americans had to produce more goods themselves.

On a tour of British textile mills, a Boston merchant named Francis Cabot Lowell saw that workers at one factory spun thread while workers at another wove it into cloth. Lowell thought it would be more efficient to combine the spinning and weaving tasks under one roof.

Lowell and several partners built a textile mill in Waltham, Massachusetts. The nearby Charles River powered the machines that turned the raw cotton into finished cloth. **Activity:** Have students use the **Understanding Economics** work sheet, in *Professional Development Guidebook,* page 225, to help them list questions to guide an investigation of the cotton economy as it affected New England, the South, and the nation as a whole.

Bright and Dark Romanticism Romanticism had two faces, one bright and optimistic, the other dark and shadowed by evil. Emerson and Thoreau emphasized "the sun is but a morning star" aspect of Romanticism. They saw human beings as fundamentally good. Poe, Hawthorne, and Melville, on the other hand, were deeply disturbed by what they saw in the human heart. They believed that crime, cruelty, guilt, and self-destruction were the true earmarks of human nature. During the American Renaissance, writers explored both sides of the Romantic impulse.

Self-Reliance "Trust thyself," Emerson advised. Think for yourself, and act on what you think. "Live deliberately," Thoreau advised. Make your own choices, and do not let others choose for you. These principles had been built into American democracy, and they became fundamental themes of American culture. What applied to individuals also applied to the nation as a whole. The eighteenth century had seen the Declaration of Independence. The nineteenth century saw declarations of cultural independence. Self-reliance is key to why the American Renaissance happened at all. Literary culture had begun to grow; journalism and education prepared the ground. But it was extraordinary individuals who made it happen—self-reliant men and women who thought for themselves and refused to let social, political, religious, or cultural institutions overwhelm them.

The American EXPERIENCE

DEVELOPING AMERICAN ENGLISH

The Truth About O.K. by Richard Lederer

Americans seem to have a passion for stringing initial letters together. We use *A.M.* and *P.M.* to separate light from darkness and *B.C.* and *A.D.* to identify vast stretches of time. We may listen to a deejay or veejay on *ABC* or *MTV*, or a crusading *DA* quoting the *FBI* on *CNN*.

Perhaps the most widely understood American word in the world is *O.K.* The explanations for its origin have been imaginative and various. Some claim that *O.K.* is a version of the Choctaw affirmative *okeh*. Others assert that it is short for the Greek *olla kalla* ("all good") or *Orrin Kendall* crackers or chief *Old Keukuk*.

The truth is that in the 1830s there was a craze for initialisms, like our currently popular *T.G.I.F.* and *F.Y.I.* The fad went so far as to generate letter combinations of intentional misspellings: *K.Y.* for "know use," *O.W.* for "oll wright." *O.K.* for "oll korrect" followed.

Ultimately, *O.K.* survived because of a presidential nickname. President Martin Van Buren was born in Kinderhook, New York, and dubbed "Old Kinderhook." "O.K." became the rallying cry of the Old Kinderhook Club that supported him for re-election in 1840. Van Buren was defeated, but the word honoring his name remains what H. L. Mencken identified as "the most shining and successful Americanism ever invented."

1. Summarize the discussion of the Essential Question on pages 219–221.

2. Then **ask:** Compare the American identity portrayed in nineteenth-century American literature with the American identity today. Are we still individualists?
   Possible response: Americans are still individualists, although we are now influenced by trends spread by the mass media. Most contemporary Americans still believe that it is possible for each person to shape his or her own destiny.

Critical Viewing
Applying Math Skills

1. Call students' attention to the advertisement on the Timeline for Harriet Beecher Stowe's novel *Uncle Tom's Cabin*.

2. Clarify that the novel was sold as a two-volume set. **Ask:** How many novel sets were sold, according to the ad?
   Answer: 135,000 novel (sets).

3. **Ask:** Since the United States population was about 23 million at that time, what percentage of Americans had bought the novel, expressed in a decimal?
   Answer: About .59%, or .0059. bought the novel.

4. Then **ask:** What would the equivalent sales figure be for today's population of 300 million?
   Answer: 1.77 million.

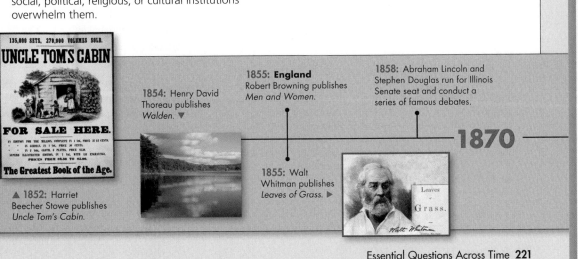

135,000 SETS, 270,000 VOLUMES SOLD.

UNCLE TOM'S CABIN

FOR SALE HERE.

The Greatest Book of the Age.

▲ **1852:** Harriet Beecher Stowe publishes *Uncle Tom's Cabin.*

1854: Henry David Thoreau publishes *Walden.* ▼

1855: England
Robert Browning publishes *Men and Women.*

1855: Walt Whitman publishes *Leaves of Grass.* ▶

1858: Abraham Lincoln and Stephen Douglas run for Illinois Senate seat and conduct a series of famous debates.

1870

Leaves of Grass.

The American Experience
Development of American English

1. Before students read Lederer's feature, tell them that the term *OK* has been around for over 150 years. Then have students read the feature explaining its origin.

2. **Ask** students why the term *OK* became so useful that H. L. Mencken called it "the most shining and successful Americanism."
   Possible response: *OK* means the same as "yes," but it has a punchier, more expressive sound. Because it is abbreviated, it also seems modern.

3. **Ask** students to list several contemporary terms made up entirely of initials.
   Sample answer: *CU* ("see you"), *BRB* ("be right back"), *TGIF* (thank God it's Friday), *FYI* ("for your information"), *BTW* ("by the way").

Recent Scholarship

Gretel Ehrlich

1. Gretel Ehrlich, a nature writer, introduces the unit and provides insights into the philosophy of Henry David Thoreau.

2. Have students read the Meet the Author feature about Gretel Ehrlich. Tell students that Ehrlich spent seven years living on the Arctic island of Greenland, an experience she wrote about in *The Cold Heaven*. Her earlier book, *A Match to the Heart*, was inspired by her experience of being struck by lightning.

3. Use the *See It!* **DVD** to introduce Gretel Ehrlich. Show Segment 1 to provide insights into her career as a nature writer.

4. After students have watched the segment, **ask:** How did Ehrlich's shyness as a child help her later as a writer?
   Possible response: She learned to be a good listener and observer.

Inspired by Nature

Gretel Ehrlich

We are all born on a particular spot on the planet with its unique seasons, weather, and topography. Mountains, rivers, rocks, storms, glaciers, skies, trees, and grasses, as well as all living things, help shape who we are, how we see, how we move through our days, and how we know who we are. Those of us who have been called "nature writers" are simply people who observe and write about the living planet, who witness the birth and death of its residents, who understand that we all share the earth equally, and who tell the stories that come from the earth.

About the Author

Gretel Ehrlich was born in California. She worked as a ranch hand, a sheepherder, a a documentary filmmaker. As a writer, she has been profoundly influenced by living Wyoming, a place of intense extremes an breathtaking beauty. Ehrlich is the author 13 books, including three collections of es a memoir, and three books of poetry. Her many honors include the 2010 PEN Thore. Award. She is best known for her nature ing, which has focused most recently on island of Greenland.

All video resources are available online at www.PHLitOnline.com.

From Natural Fact Comes Human Meaning

The Inuit people of northern Greenland have a word, *sila*, that means "the power of nature, weather, and human and animal consciousness as one and the same": no separation between the "emotional weather" inside ourselves and the natural forces on the outside that affect us. Nature writers are always writing about two things at once: the ecosystem and continent that is our mind and body, and the greater one of the world surrounding us. They show us how human meaning can come from natural fact.

A One-Room Cabin on Walden Pond

Henry David Thoreau was one of the great natural history writers of all time. Broken-hearted over a lost love, he went to live on Walden Pond in Concord, Massachusetts, for two years and two months. His friend and mentor, Ralph Waldo Emerson, a brilliant essayist, bought an eleven-acre field on the north shore of the pond, and in March of 1845, Thoreau, with Emerson's encouragement, built a ten-by-fifteen-foot one-room cabin. Then, he borrowed a horse and plow and planted two acres in white beans, corn, and potatoes.

An Inventory of the Natural World

Thoreau was twenty-eight at the time, and he wanted to be free from the constraints of family and society. Reading widely, walking locally, writing obsessively—those were his priorities. He was not a great adventurer—others at the time were searching for the Northwest Passage in the Arctic, sailing the seas of the world, traveling by covered wagon across the country. Thoreau knew that his inventory of the natural world and his insights into human consciousness could be achieved right where he was: on Walden Pond. He wanted to live simply and quietly, to live deeply, to listen and observe, to become intimate with a place. In so doing, he allowed the outer landscape to shape the prose that came from within.

Where We Live Holds the Secrets of the Universe

"I went to the woods because I wished to live deliberately," he wrote, "to front only the essential facts of life, and see if I could not learn what it had to teach, and not, when I came to die, discover that I had not lived." What we learn from Thoreau's life and writings is that anywhere we happen to live is good enough. We don't have to go to some exotic place to find ourselves or understand the world. It's all right here, for each of us. Each place holds all the secrets of the universe, the history of the world in a raindrop.

ⓒ Collaboration: Speaking and Listening

One lesson of Thoreau's writing, according to Gretel Ehrlich, is that natural wonders exist in every corner of the natural world:

"What we learn from Thoreau's life and writings is that anywhere we happen to live is good enough... Each place holds all the secrets of the universe, the history of the world in a raindrop."

Hold a **small group discussion** about Ehrlich's ideas in the quoted passage. Decide whether you agree or disagree with her statement. Select a point person to share your ideas with the class.

Collaboration: Speaking and Listening

1. Review the assignment with students.
2. Divide the class into small groups, and have students discuss the passages. Have representatives of each group present the group's ideas to the class.
3. Open up the discussion to the whole class. Write on the board the sentence "Everywhere we happen to live is good enough." Then invite students to indicate whether they agree or disagree and to share their reasons.
4. To help conduct the discussion, use the **Discussion Guide** in the *Professional Development Guidebook,* page 65.

COMMON CORE ▪ MULTIPLE PERSPECTIVES ON THE ERA

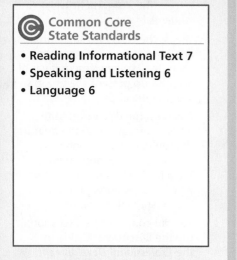

© **Common Core
State Standards**

- Reading Informational Text 7
- Speaking and Listening 6
- Language 6

Integrate and Evaluate Information

1. Review the chart assignment with the class. Then, ask students to use the Activity I chart in the **Following Through** worksheet (p. 6 in *Unit 2 Resources*) to complete this activity.

   Possible response: *American Literature: Key Concept—* individualism; *Key Author—* Whitman. *Literature and Society Key Concept—*social change and reform movements; *Key Author—* Harriet Beecher Stowe.

2. **Possible response:** The illustration of the Erie Canal on p. 216 adds to the understanding of the rapid development of technology. The photograph on p. 221 of Walden Pond adds to the understanding of Thoreau's experience after leaving the constraints of family and society behind.

3. **Possible responses:** One attitude that developed toward the American land and its settlement was the spirit of commerce. New forms of transportation expanded settlement and created new markets. Another attitude was awe at the grandeur and the size and diversity of the land with its abundant natural resources. Most students will say that these attitudes have helped shape contemporary American culture, which values technology and sees the country as a place of opportunity.

4. **Possible responses:** Ehrlich has much in common with transcendental seekers such as Emerson and Thoreau. Her ideas challenge

224

Integrate and Evaluate Information

1. Use a chart like the one shown to determine the key ideas expressed in the Essential Question essays on pages 214–221. Fill in two ideas related to each Essential Question and note the authors most closely associated with each concept. One example has been done for you.

Essential Question	Key Concept	Key Author
Literature and Place	A kinship with nature	Thoreau
American Literature		
Literature and Society		

2. How do the visual sources in this section—artifacts, paintings, photographs, and illustrations—add to your understanding of the ideas expressed in words? Cite specific examples.

3. The vast, unexplored American West sparked the American imagination. Describe some of the different attitudes that developed toward the American land and its settlement, citing evidence from the multiple sources on pages 210–223. In your view, have these attitudes helped shape contemporary American culture? If so, how? If not, why not?

© 4. **Address a Question** In her discussion of Thoreau, Gretel Ehrlich writes: "We don't have to go to some exotic place to find ourselves or understand our world…. Each place holds all the secrets of the universe." How might this idea challenge certain values, such as the importance of progress, innovation, and expansion, that are often seen as essentially American? Integrate information from this textbook and other sources to support your ideas.

Speaking and Listening: Slide Presentation

During the nineteenth century, technology leaped forward. Using a variety of print and electronic resources, research one of the following nineteenth-century inventions. Then, write and deliver a **slide presentation** that explores the impact of the invention on American life:

- the mechanical reaper
- the cotton gin
- the steam locomotive
- the telegraph
- the bicycle

Your slide presentation should answer the following questions: What aspects of American life did the invention affect or change? What ripple effects did the invention cause? Whom did the invention most benefit? Whom, if anyone, did the invention harm?

© **Solve a Research Problem** This assignment requires you to understand and integrate technical terms into your writing. To do so, find reliable print and online sources for definitions and explanations. Also, consult writings by scientists, inventors, and historians. As you present, make sure to explain technical terms that may be unfamiliar to your audience.

224 A Growing Nation (1800–1870)

© **Common Core
State Standards**

Reading Informational Text
7. Integrate and evaluate multiple sources of information presented in different media or formats as well as in words in order to address a question or solve a problem.

Speaking and Listening
6. Adapt speech to a variety of contexts and tasks.

Language
6. Acquire and use accurately general academic and domain-specific words and phrases.

ESSENTIAL QUESTION VOCABULARY

Use these words in your responses:

Literature and Place
barrier
acquisition
exploration

American Literature
individualist
colloquial
self-reliant

Literature and Society
market
invention
technology

the value of the importance of progress, invention, and expansion; nonetheless, these have been essential to the settlement of the United States and the creation of modern U.S. society.

Speaking and Listening

1. Have students analyze the activity and identify its key terms: *invention, research, impact, benefit,* and *harm.*

2. Then, have students complete Activity II in the **Following Through** worksheet (p. 6) in *Unit 2 Resources.*

Fireside and Campfire

PART 1

225

Text Complexity: At a Glance

This chart gives a general text complexity rating for the selections in this part of the unit to help guide instruction. For additional text complexity support, see the Text Complexity Rubric at point of use.

The Devil and Tom Walker	**More Complex**	Thanatopsis	**More Complex**
from The Song of Hiawatha	**More Accessible**	Old Ironsides	**More Accessible**
The Tide Rises, the Tide Falls	**More Accessible**		

Selection Planning Guide

The selections in this section reflect the literary and territorial expansion of the United States in the nineteenth century. Students will enjoy reading "The Devil and Tom Walker" by Washington Irving, one of the first of a new breed of purely American writers. The popular works of the Fireside Poets—Longfellow, Holmes, and Whittier—break new ground in American literature.

Humanities

Winter in Malden, Massachusetts, 1864, Joseph Morviller (1800–1870)

Born in Paris, Joseph Morviller studied art in France and England. He immigrated to Boston, Massachusetts, in 1852 and established himself as a landscape painter specializing in scenes of New England winter.

Use the following questions for discussion:

1. Though its setting is a snow-filled forest in winter, how does the painting create an impression of warmth?
   Possible response: The color scheme of the painting is dominated not by frosty whites, but by the warm brown tones of the trees. Sunlight adds tints of pink, gold, and orange, increasing the "temperature" of the scene.

2. What overall feeling does this painting suggest to you? What details contribute to this feeling?
   Possible response: Students may say that, despite the wintry outdoor setting, the painting conveys a feeling of comfort and coziness. Details such as the warm colors, the smoke rising from the cabin, and the sheltering formation of the trees contribute to this feeling.

Monitoring Progress

Before students read "The Devil and Tom Walker," refer to the results for the **Vocabulary in Context** items on **Benchmark Test 2** (*Unit 1 Resources,* p. 265–267). Use this diagnostic portion of the test to guide your choice of selections to teach, as well as the depth of prereading preparation you will provide, based on students' readiness for the reading and vocabulary skills.

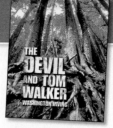

• The Devil and Tom Walker
Lesson Pacing Guide

DAY 1 Preteach

- © Administer the Reading and Vocabulary Warm-ups (*Unit 2 Resources*, pp. 7–10) as necessary.
- © Introduce the Literary Analysis concepts: Characterization.
- • Introduce the Reading Strategy: Evaluate the Influences of the Historical Period.
- © Build background with the author and Background features.
- • Develop thematic thinking with Connecting to the Essential Question.
- © Teach the selection vocabulary.

DAYS 2–3 Preteach/Teach/Assess

- • Distribute copies of the appropriate graphic organizer for the Reading Strategy (*Graphic Organizer Transparencies*, pp. 54–55).
- • Distribute copies of the appropriate graphic organizer for Literary Analysis (*Graphic Organizer Transparencies*, pp. 56–57).
- • Prepare students to read with the Activating Prior Knowledge activities (TE).
- • Informally monitor comprehension while students read.
- • Use the Reading Check question to confirm comprehension.
- © Develop students' understanding of Characterization using the Literary Analysis prompts.
- • Develop students' ability to Evaluate the Influences of the Historical Period using the Reading Strategy prompts.
- © Reinforce vocabulary with the Vocabulary notes.
- • Assess students' comprehension and mastery of the skills by having them answer the Critical Reading, Literary Analysis, and Reading Strategy questions.
- © Have students complete the Vocabulary Lesson.

DAY 4 Extend/Assess

- © Have students complete the Writing Lesson and write a modern retelling of a story. (You may assign as homework.)
- • Administer Selection Test A or B (*Unit 2 Resources*, pp. 19–21 or 22–24).

© Common Core State Standards

Reading Literature 3. Analyze the impact of the author's choices regarding how to develop and relate elements of a story or drama (e.g., where a story is set, how the characters are introduced and developed).
9. Demonstrate knowledge of eighteenth-century foundational works of American literature.

Writing 3. Write narratives to develop real or imagined experiences or events using effective technique, well-chosen details, and well-structured event sequences.
3.d. Use precise words and phrases, telling details, and sensory language to convey a vivid picture of the experiences, events, setting, and/or characters.

Language 2.a. Observe hyphenation conventions.
4.b. Identify and correctly use patterns of word changes that indicate different meanings or parts of speech.

Additional Standards Practice
Common Core Companion, pp. 28–35; 75–86; 208–218; 318–321; 324–331

Daily Block Scheduling
Each day in this Lesson Pacing Guide represents a 40–50 minute period. Teachers using block scheduling may combine days to revise pacing. In addition, teachers may differentiate and support core instruction by integrating components for extended and intensive support as students require. See the Guide to Selected Leveled Resources (facing page).

Guide to Selected Leveled Resources

R T I Tier 1 (students performing on level)

The Devil and Tom Walker

Warm Up	Practice, model, and monitor fluency, working with the whole class or in groups.	Vocabulary and Reading Warm-ups B, *Unit 2 Resources,* pp. 7–8, 10
Comprehension/Skills	Support and monitor comprehension and skills development, having students complete the activities, graphic organizers, and interactive prompts independently or as a class.	• *Reader's Notebook,* adapted instruction and summary **EL** *Reader's Notebook: English Learner's Version,* adapted instruction and summary • **Reading Strategy Graphic Organizer B,** *Graphic Organizer Transparencies,* p. 55 • **Literary Analysis Graphic Organizer B,** *Graphic Organizer Transparencies,* p. 57
Monitor Progress	Monitor student progress with the differentiated curriculum-based assessment in the *Unit Resources.*	• **Selection Test B,** *Unit 2 Resources,* pp. 22–24 • **Open-Book Test,** *Unit 2 Resources,* pp. 16–18

R T I Tier 2 (students requiring intervention)

The Devil and Tom Walker

Warm Up	Practice, model, and monitor fluency in groups or with individuals.	• **Vocabulary and Reading Warm-ups A,** *Unit 2 Resources,* pp. 7–9 • *Hear It!* **Audio CD**
Comprehension/Skills	• **Support** and **monitor** comprehension and skills development, working **in small groups** or **with individuals.** • As students complete the selection in the appropriate version of the *Reader's Notebook,* monitor comprehension frequently with group questions and individual instruction. • Model strategies while guiding students in completing the activities and prompts in the *Reader's Notebook,* as well as the graphic organizers. • Practice skills and monitor mastery with the *Reading Kit* worksheets.	• *Reader's Notebook: Adapted Version,* adapted instruction and summary **EL** *Reader's Notebook: English Learner's Version,* adapted instruction and summary • **Reading Strategy Graphic Organizer A,** *Graphic Organizer Transparencies,* p. 54 • **Literary Analysis Graphic Organizer A,** *Graphic Organizer Transparencies,* p. 56 • *Reading Kit,* Practice worksheets
Monitor Progress	Monitor student progress with the differentiated curriculum-based assessment in the *Unit Resources* and in the *Reading Kit.*	• **Selection Test A,** *Unit 2 Resources,* pp. 19–21 • *Reading Kit,* Assess worksheets

TIER 3 Tier 3 intervention may require consultation with the student's special-education or dyslexia specialist. For additional support, see the Tier 2 activities and resources listed above.

One-on-one teaching ▪ Group work ▪ Whole class instruction ▪ Independent work ▪ Assessment
For a complete guide to selection support, including support for Advanced students, see the Overview of Resources in the frontmatter.

• The Devil and Tom Walker

THE DEVIL AND TOM WALKER
WASHINGTON IRVING

RESOURCES FOR:

- **L1** Special-Needs Students
- **L2** Below-Level Students (Tier 2)
- **L3** On-Level Students (Tier 1)
- **L4** Advanced Students (Tier 1)
- **EL** English Learners
- **All** All Students

Vocabulary/Fluency/Prior Knowledge

Unit 2 Resources

> "The Devil and Tom Walker" by Washington Irving
> **Vocabulary Warm-up Word Lists**
>
> *Study these words from the selection. Then, complete the activities.*
>
> **Word List A**
>
> **consequence** [KAHN suh kwents] *n.* result; effect
> As a consequence of your carelessness, we have no more water.
>
> **elapsed** [ee LAPST] *v.* passed; went by
> Five minutes elapsed before they returned.
>
> **indifference** [In DIF uhr uhnts] *n.* not caring; lack of interest
> They showed indifference and paid no attention to the screaming fans.
>
> **meager** [MEE ger] *adj.* very thin; inadequate
> Such a meager salary for this tough job is unfair.
>
> **notorious** [noh TOR ee us] *adj.* having a bad reputation; infamous
> That government was notorious for corruption and injustice.
>
> **prior** [PRY er] *adj.* previous; coming before
> Her prior service in the military helped her get the job.
>
> **prone** [PROHN] *adj.* inclined (to)
> Because he did everything so fast, he was prone to having accidents.
>
> **zeal** [ZEEL] *n.* great enthusiasm; passion
> The candidate wanted campaign workers with plenty of zeal.
>
> **Word List B**
>
> **contradiction** [kahn truh DIK shun] *n.* something opposite; denial
> This evidence is a contradiction of what we thought was true.
>
> **disclosed** [dis KLOHZD] *v.* showed; revealed
> The witness finally disclosed the fact that he had not been there.
>
> **precaution** [pree KAW shun] *n.* care taken in advance
> We took every precaution to avoid running out of supplies.
>
> **prevalent** [PRE vuh lent] *adj.* widely existing; most common
> The prevalent attitude around here is that the mayor is doing a good job.
>
> **squeamish** [SKWEEM ish] *adj.* easily nauseated or offended
> If you are squeamish, you may want to avoid this graphic documentary.
>
> **steadfastly** [STED fast lee] *adv.* with firmness; without changing
> The soldier remained at his post steadfastly throughout the night.
>
> **strenuous** [STREN yoo us] *adj.* demanding great effort or energy
> Before strenuous exercise, be sure to warm up and stretch.
>
> **uppermost** [UP uhr mohst] *adj.* highest; first
> Protecting ourselves from danger was uppermost in our minds.
>
> Unit 2 Resources: A Growing Nation
> © Pearson Education, Inc. All Rights Reserved.
> 7

EL **L1** **L2** **Vocabulary Warm-ups A and B,** pp. 7–8

Also available for these selections:

EL **L1** **L2** **Reading Warm-ups A and B,** pp. 9–10

All **Vocabulary Builder,** p. 13

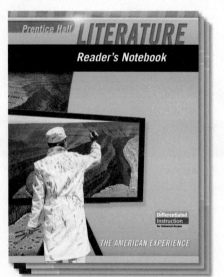

Prentice Hall LITERATURE
Reader's Notebook
Differentiated Instruction for Universal Access
THE AMERICAN EXPERIENCE

Reader's Notebooks

Pre- and postreading pages for this selection, as well as "The Devil and Tom Walker," appear in an interactive format in the *Reader's Notebooks*. Each *Notebook* is differentiated for a different group of learners.

The selections in the Adapted and English Learner's versions are abridged.

- **L2** **L3** *Reader's Notebook*
- **L1** *Reader's Notebook: Adapted Version*
- **EL** *Reader's Notebook: English Learner's Version*
- **EL** *Reader's Notebook: Spanish Version*

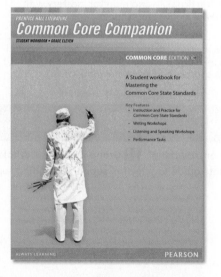

PRENTICE HALL LITERATURE
Common Core Companion
STUDENT WORKBOOK • GRADE ELEVEN
COMMON CORE EDITION ©

A Student workbook for Mastering the Common Core State Standards

Key Features
- Instruction and Practice for Common Core State Standards
- Writing Workshops
- Listening and Speaking Workshops
- Performance Tasks

ALWAYS LEARNING
PEARSON

© *Common Core Companion*

Additional instruction and practice for each Common Core State Standard

Selection Support

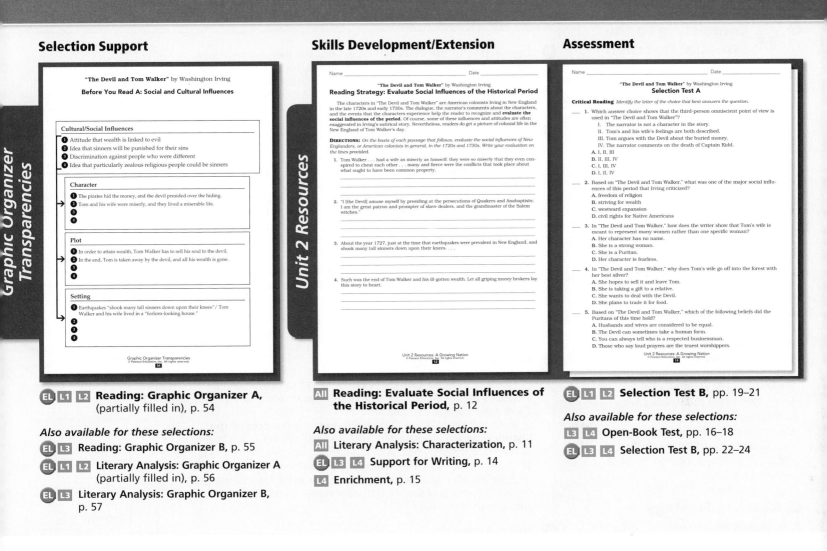

"The Devil and Tom Walker" by Washington Irving

Before You Read A: Social and Cultural Influences

Cultural/Social Influences
❶ Attitude that wealth is linked to evil
❷ Idea that sinners will be punished for their sins
❸ Discrimination against people who were different
❹ Idea that particularly zealous religious people could be sinners

Character
❶ The pirates hid the money, and the devil presided over the hiding.
❷ Tom and his wife were miserly, and they lived a miserable life.
❸
❹

Plot
❶ In order to attain wealth, Tom Walker has to sell his soul to the devil.
❷ In the end, Tom is taken away by the devil, and all his wealth is gone.
❸
❹

Setting
❶ Earthquakes "shook many tall sinners down upon their knees" / Tom Walker and his wife lived in a "forlorn-looking house."
❷
❸
❹

Graphic Organizer Transparencies
© Pearson Education, Inc. All rights reserved.
54

EL L1 L2 Reading: Graphic Organizer A, (partially filled in), p. 54

Also available for these selections:

EL L3 Reading: Graphic Organizer B, p. 55

EL L1 L2 Literary Analysis: Graphic Organizer A (partially filled in), p. 56

EL L3 Literary Analysis: Graphic Organizer B, p. 57

Skills Development/Extension

Name _____ Date _____

"The Devil and Tom Walker" by Washington Irving
Reading Strategy: Evaluate Social Influences of the Historical Period

The characters in "The Devil and Tom Walker" are American colonists living in New England in the late 1720s and early 1730s. The dialogue, the narrator's comments about the characters, and the events that the characters experience help the reader to recognize and **evaluate the social influences of the period.** Of course, some of these influences and attitudes are often exaggerated in Irving's satirical story. Nevertheless, readers do get a picture of colonial life in the New England of Tom Walker's day.

DIRECTIONS: *On the basis of each passage that follows, evaluate the social influences of New Englanders, or American colonists in general, in the 1720s and 1730s. Write your evaluation on the lines provided.*

1. Tom Walker . . . had a wife as miserly as himself; they were so miserly that they even conspired to cheat each other . . . many and fierce were the conflicts that took place about what ought to have been common property.

2. "I [the Devil] amuse myself by presiding at the persecutions of Quakers and Anabaptists; I am the great patron and prompter of slave dealers, and the grandmaster of the Salem witches."

3. About the year 1727, just at the time that earthquakes were prevalent in New England, and shook many tall sinners down upon their knees. . . .

4. Such was the end of Tom Walker and his ill-gotten wealth. Let all griping money brokers lay this story to heart.

Unit 2 Resources: A Growing Nation
© Pearson Education, Inc. All rights reserved.
12

All Reading: Evaluate Social Influences of the Historical Period, p. 12

Also available for these selections:

All Literary Analysis: Characterization, p. 11

EL L3 L4 Support for Writing, p. 14

L4 Enrichment, p. 15

Assessment

Name _____ Date _____

"The Devil and Tom Walker" by Washington Irving
Selection Test A

Critical Reading *Identify the letter of the choice that best answers the question.*

___ 1. Which answer choice shows that the third-person omniscient point of view is used in "The Devil and Tom Walker"?
  I. The narrator is not a character in the story.
  II. Tom's and his wife's feelings are both described.
  III. Tom argues with the Devil about the buried money.
  IV. The narrator comments on the death of Captain Kidd.
  A. I, II, III
  B. II, III, IV
  C. I, III, IV
  D. I, II, IV

___ 2. Based on "The Devil and Tom Walker," what was one of the major social influences of this period that Irving criticized?
  A. freedom of religion
  B. striving for wealth
  C. westward expansion
  D. civil rights for Native Americans

___ 3. In "The Devil and Tom Walker," how does the writer show that Tom's wife is meant to represent many women rather than one specific woman?
  A. Her character has no name.
  B. She is a strong woman.
  C. She is a Puritan.
  D. Her character is fearless.

___ 4. In "The Devil and Tom Walker," why does Tom's wife go off into the forest with her best silver?
  A. She hopes to sell it and leave Tom.
  B. She is taking a gift to a relative.
  C. She wants to deal with the Devil.
  D. She plans to trade it for food.

___ 5. Based on "The Devil and Tom Walker," which of the following beliefs did the Puritans of this time hold?
  A. Husbands and wives are considered to be equal.
  B. The Devil can sometimes take a human form.
  C. You can always tell who is a respected businessman.
  D. Those who say loud prayers are the truest worshippers.

Unit 2 Resources: A Growing Nation
© Pearson Education, Inc. All rights reserved.
19

EL L1 L2 Selection Test B, pp. 19–21

Also available for these selections:

L3 L4 Open-Book Test, pp. 16–18

EL L3 L4 Selection Test B, pp. 22–24

Online Resources: All print materials are also available online.

- complete narrated selection text
- a thematically related video with writing prompt
- an interactive graphic organizer
- highlighting feature
- access to all student print resources, adapted to individual student needs
- Spanish and English summaries
- adapted selection translations in Spanish

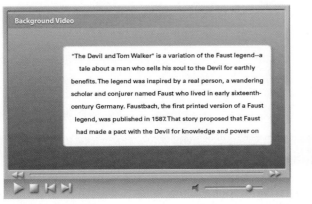

Background Video

"The Devil and Tom Walker" is a variation of the Faust legend--a tale about a man who sells his soul to the Devil for earthly benefits. The legend was inspired by a real person, a wandering scholar and conjurer named Faust who lived in early sixteenth-century Germany. Faustbach, the first printed version of a Faust legend, was published in 1587. That story proposed that Faust had made a pact with the Devil for knowledge and power on

Background Video

Also available:

Get Connected! (thematic video with writing prompt)
All videos available in Spanish.

Vocabulary Central

Vocabulary Central (tools and activities for studying vocabulary)

Also available:

Writer's Journal (with graphics feature)

❶ Connecting to the Essential Question

1. Review the assignment.

2. Prepare students to write by discussing the impact of sudden wealth on real people or fictional characters.

3. As students read, have them look for both direct and implied criticism of selfishness and greed.

❷ Literary Analysis

Introduce the skill, using the instruction on the student page.

Think Aloud: Model the Skill

Say to students:

Indirect characterization makes me a more active and alert reader. Take this example: "'I am not c-c-cold,' Carol shivered." This brief sentence offers me two details and a mystery: I know Carol is cold; I know she denies it; I wonder why. I am a more engaged reader than if the writer had told me directly that "Carol is too proud to admit she is cold." As you read, be alert to what writers *show* you.

❸ Reading Strategy

1. Introduce the strategy.

2. Give students a copy of **Reading Strategy Graphic Organizer B**, page 55 in *Graphic Organizer Transparencies,* to fill out as they read.

Think Aloud: Model the Skill

Say to students:

When I notice a surprising or untypical action by a character, I look for an underlying influence of the historical period. For example, Tom Walker—who would do anything for money—refuses to engage in the slave trade. That detail tells me that attitudes in colonial Massachusetts were so opposed to the slave trade that even heartless Tom Walker balks.

❹ Vocabulary

1. Pronounce each word, giving its definition; have students say it aloud.

2. For more guidance, see the *Classroom Strategies and Teaching Routines* card for vocabulary.

Before You Read   *The Devil and Tom Walker*

❶ **Connecting to the Essential Question** This dark yet comic story centers on greedy Tom Walker, who cares only for himself in his pursuit of riches. As you read, look for details that criticize selfishness and greed. This will help as you consider the Essential Question: **How does literature shape or reflect society?**

❷ **Literary Analysis**

Characterization is the creation and development of a character. In **direct characterization,** a writer tells you what a character is like. In **indirect characterization,** the writer reveals a character's personality through the character's speech, thoughts, actions, appearance, and other characters' reactions. For example, Irving uses direct characterization when he tells the reader that Tom Walker was "not a man to be troubled with any fears." He uses indirect characterization in Tom's reply to the Devil, who has threateningly suggested that Tom is trespassing:

> *"Your grounds!" said Tom with a sneer, "no more your grounds than mine; they belong to Deacon Peabody."*

Indirect characterization provides valuable information and adds to a story's action, drama, or humor. As you read, notice Irving's use of characterization.

❸ **Reading Strategy**

© **Preparing to Read Complex Texts** Works of fiction are often shaped by the concerns of the historical period in which they are set. These may involve philosophical trends, religious beliefs, ethical issues, or social problems. As you read, **evaluate the influences of the historical period** on characters, plot, and settings. For example, the characters in this story hold attitudes common to New Englanders in the 1720s, when the story is set. Through his narrator, Irving criticizes some of those attitudes while accepting others. Use a chart like the one shown to track the effects of specific cultural attitudes on the characters, plot, and settings of this story.

❹ **Vocabulary**

prevalent (prev´ ə lənt) *adj.* widely existing or occurring (p. 229)

discord (dis´ kôrd´) *n.* lack of harmony; conflict (p. 230)

treacherous (trech´ ər əs) *adj.* dangerous (p. 230)

extort (eks tôrt´) *v.* obtain by threat or violence (p. 236)

ostentation (äs´ tən tā´ shən) *n.* boastful display (p. 237)

parsimony (pär´ sə mō´ nē) *n.* stinginess (p. 237)

Common Core
State Standards

Reading Literature
3. Analyze the impact of the author's choices regarding how to develop and relate elements of a story or drama (e.g., where a story is set, how the characters are introduced and developed).
9. Demonstrate knowledge of nineteenth-century foundational works of American literature.

Cultural/Social Influences

Character

Plot

Setting

www.PHLitOnline.com

226 A Growing Nation (1800–1870)

Vocabulary Development

Vocabulary Knowledge Rating
Create a **Vocabulary Knowledge Rating** chart (*Professional Development Guidebook,* p. 33) for the vocabulary words on the student page. Give each student a copy of the chart with the words on it. Read the words aloud, and have students mark their rating in the Before Reading column. Urge students to attend to these words as they read and discuss the selection.

In order to gauge how much instruction is needed, tally how many students are confident in their knowledge of each word. As students read, point out the words and their context.

 **Vocabulary Central,** featuring tools and activities for vocabulary, is available at **www.PHLitOnline.com.**

⑤ Washington Irving (1783–1859)

Author of "The Devil and Tom Walker"

Named after President George Washington, Washington Irving became the first American fiction writer to achieve an international reputation. Irving was born into a wealthy New York family right at the close of the American Revolution. Although he planned to be a lawyer, he grew more interested in travel and writing and devoted his life to both pursuits.

A Career Blooms From 1807 to 1808, Irving wrote satirical essays under the pen name Jonathan Oldstyle. With his brother William, he anonymously published the magazine *Salmagundi*, named after a spicy appetizer. In 1809, he produced his first major work, *A History of New York From the Beginning of the World to the End of the Dutch Dynasty*. This humorous examination of New York in colonial times made Irving so famous that to this day native New Yorkers are known as "Knickerbockers" after Diedrich Knickerbocker, the character Irving created to narrate the work.

Americanizing Europe's Folklore Traveling in Europe from 1815 to 1832, Irving encountered European folklore that helped inspire his own writing. Two of his best-known works, "The Legend of Sleepy Hollow" and "Rip Van Winkle," turn German folk tales into distinctly American narratives set in New York's Hudson Valley. Their main characters—Ichabod Crane, the nervous Sleepy Hollow schoolteacher harassed by a headless horseman, and Rip Van Winkle, the lazy colonist who slept for decades—have become classic figures of American literature.

I am endeavoring to serve my country. Whatever I have written has been written with the feelings and published as the writing of an American. . . . If I can do any good in this world it is with my pen.

The Devil and Tom Walker **227**

🔔 Daily Bellringer

For each class during which you will teach this selection, have students complete one of the five activities for the appropriate week in the *Daily Bellringer Activities* booklet.

Multidraft Reading

To assist struggling readers and to enhance reading for all, assign the text in chunks as warranted by length and apply multidraft reading protocols. For each reading, have students set the purpose indicated:

- **First reading**—identifying key ideas and details and answering any Reading Checks.
- **Second reading**—analyzing craft and structure and responding to the side-column prompts.
- **Third reading**—integrating knowledge and ideas, connecting to other texts and the world, and answering the end-of-selection questions.

For more guidance, refer to the *Classroom Strategies and Teaching Routines* card, **Multidraft Reading**.

⑤ Background
More About the Author

Although Washington Irving's comic look at New York—usually referred to as *Knickerbocker's History of New York*—made him famous, it also offended many leading families by poking fun at their ancestors and heritage. Perhaps hoping to alleviate American criticism about his time spent abroad, Irving went to work for the United States government in Europe. He served as an American diplomat first in Spain and later in London.

PHLit Online!
www.PHLitOnline.com

Teaching From Technology

Preparing to Read
Go to **www.PHLitOnline.com** in class or in a lab and display the Get Connected! slide show for this selection. Have the class brainstorm for responses to the slide show writing prompt, entering ideas in the interactive journal. Then have students complete their written responses individually in a lab or as homework.

To build background, display the Background and More About the Author features.

Using the Interactive Text
Go to **www.PHLitOnline.com** and display the **Enriched Online Student Edition**. As the class reads the selection or listens to the narration, record answers to side-column prompts using the graphic organizers accessible on the interactive page. Alternatively, have students use the online edition individually, answering the prompts as they read.

❶ About the Selection

Set in colonial Massachusetts, this story is a humorous tale of the consequences of a miser's pact with the Devil. Tight-fisted Tom Walker meets the Devil in a swampy forest and, tempted by the prospect of untold wealth, eventually enters into a deal with him. Riches make Walker greedier, as he begins a campaign to fleece his neighbors of their property. Later in life, Tom begins to fear for his mortal soul and reforms. As rigid in his piety as he was in his avarice, he is still unable to stave off the inevitable when the Devil returns to collect.

❷ Activating Prior Knowledge

Have students discuss the following statement: "The desire for wealth can make people hard and unfeeling." Note how many students agree with the statement and how many disagree with it at this point.

Concept Connector ➡

Tell students that they will revisit the statement about the effects of wealth after reading the selection and that you will poll them again.

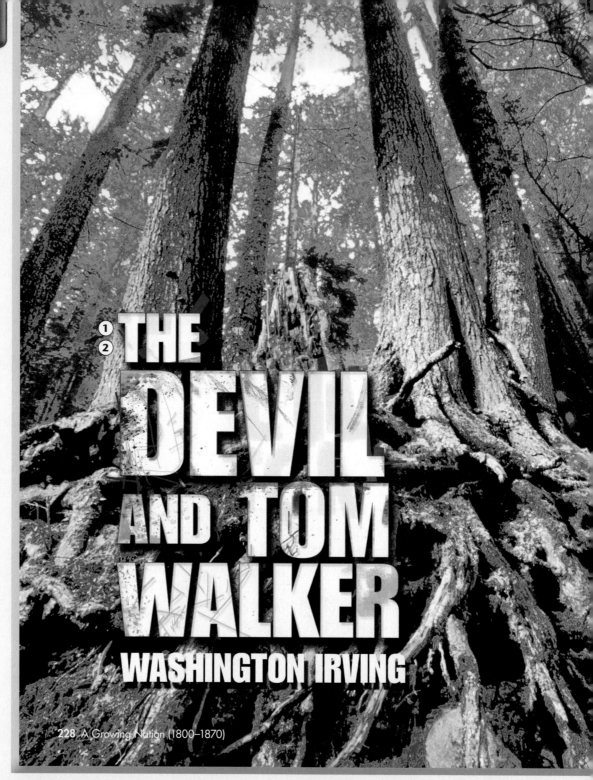

❶ ❷ THE DEVIL AND TOM WALKER

WASHINGTON IRVING

228 A Growing Nation (1800–1870)

Ⓒ Text Complexity Rubric

The Devil and Tom Walker	
Qualitative Measures	
Context/Knowledge Demands	Colonial era; historical knowledge demands 1 2 ③ 4 5
Structure/Language Conventionality and Clarity	Some long sentences in description and narrative; accessible dialogue 1 2 ③ 4 5
Levels of Meaning/ Purpose/Concept Level	Accessible (greed, usury, materialism, evil punished) 1 ② 3 4 5
Quantitative Measures	
Lexile	1130L	**Text Length**	Word Count: 4,765
Overall Complexity	**More complex**

Reader and Task Suggestions

Preparing to Read the Text

- Using the information on SE p. 227, discuss Irving's interest in colonial America.
- Ask students to think of a story set in a faraway time or place. How could that story be retold to represent what "American" means to people today?
- Guide students to use Multidraft Reading strategies to deepen their comprehension (TE p. 227).

Leveled Tasks

Knowledge Demands If students will have difficulty with the context, have them refer to the headnote as they read. Then, have them reread to identify elements that seem clearly "American."

Analyzing If students will not have difficulty with the context, have them focus on how Irving created a distinctly "American" Devil.

This story appeared in 1824, when the American economy was booming. Advances in technology and transportation and the rapid growth of cities created large markets for goods. For the first time, manufactured items were widely available and people had money to buy them. Irving's story retells the European tale of Faust, a scholar who sold his soul for wisdom. Tom Walker, Washington Irving's American Faust, has no interest in wisdom; he is simply after riches. Irving may have set this story in an earlier America, but he revealed the materialism of his own era.

A few miles from Boston in Massachusetts, there is a deep inlet, winding several miles into the interior of the country from Charles Bay, and terminating in a thickly wooded swamp or morass. On one side of this inlet is a beautiful dark grove; on the opposite side the land rises abruptly from the water's edge into a high ridge, on which grow a few scattered oaks of great age and immense size. Under one of these gigantic trees, according to old stories, there was a great amount of treasure buried by Kidd the pirate.[1] The inlet allowed a facility to bring the money in a boat secretly and at night to the very foot of the hill; the elevation of the place permitted a good look-out to be kept that no one was at hand; while the remarkable trees formed good landmarks by which the place might easily be found again. The old stories add, moreover, that the Devil presided at the hiding of the money, and took it under his guardianship; but this it is well known he always does with buried treasure, particularly when it has been ill-gotten.

Be that as it may, Kidd never returned to recover his wealth; being shortly after seized at Boston, sent out to England, and there hanged for a pirate.

About the year 1727, just at the time that earthquakes were prevalent in New England, and shook many tall sinners down upon their knees, there lived near this place a meager, miserly fellow, of the name of Tom Walker. He had a wife as miserly as himself: they were so miserly that they even conspired to cheat each other. Whatever the woman could lay hands on, she hid away; a hen could not cackle but she was on the alert to secure the new-laid egg. Her husband was continually prying about to detect her secret hoards, and many and fierce were the conflicts that took place about what ought to have been common property.

---

1. **Kidd the pirate** Captain William Kidd (1645–1701).

Reading Strategy
Evaluate Influences of the Historical Period
What does this reference to the Devil and treasure suggest about period attitudes toward wealth?

Vocabulary
prevalent (prev′ ə lənt)
adj. widely existing or occuring

❹ Reading Check
What is buried under one of the gigantic trees?

The Devil and Tom Walker **229**

Possible response: Students may cite the few bare trees, the absence of chimney smoke, and an air of emptiness and isolation about the cabin as similar to the characteristics of Tom Walker's house. Students may note that the cabin does not necessarily convey the sense of "starvation" and unwelcome that the Walker house does.

❻ Literary Analysis

Characterization

1. Review the bracketed passage with the class. Ask students to identify examples of direct characterization in the passage.
   Answer: Readers are told that Tom's wife is a "tall termagant" with a loud voice, strong arm, and fierce temper.

2. Then **ask** students to identify examples of indirect characterization.
   Answer: Marks on Tom's face suggest that his wife sometimes attacks him physically. Their strife frightens passers-by.

❺ ▲ Critical Viewing
How does this picture compare to Irving's description of the Walkers' home? **[Compare and Contrast]** ❻

Vocabulary

discord (dis´ kôrd´) *n.* lack of harmony; conflict

treacherous (trech´ ər əs) *adj.* dangerous

They lived in a forlorn-looking house that stood alone, and had an air of starvation. A few straggling savin trees, emblems of sterility, grew near it; no smoke ever curled from its chimney; no traveler stopped at its door. A miserable horse, whose ribs were as articulate as the bars of a gridiron, stalked about a field, where a thin carpet of moss, scarcely covering the ragged beds of puddingstone, tantalized and balked his hunger; and sometimes he would lean his head over the fence, look piteously at the passerby, and seem to petition deliverance from this land of famine.

The house and its inmates had altogether a bad name. Tom's wife was a tall termagant,[2] fierce of temper, loud of tongue, and strong of arm. Her voice was often heard in wordy warfare with her husband; and his face sometimes showed signs that their conflicts were not confined to words. No one ventured, however, to interfere between them. The lonely wayfarer shrunk within himself at the horrid clamor and clapperclawing;[3] eyed the den of discord askance; and hurried on his way, rejoicing, if a bachelor, in his celibacy.

One day that Tom Walker had been to a distant part of the neighborhood, he took what he considered a shortcut homeward, through the swamp. Like most shortcuts, it was an ill-chosen route. The swamp was thickly grown with great gloomy pines and hemlocks, some of them ninety feet high, which made it dark at noonday, and a retreat for all the owls of the neighborhood. It was full of pits and quagmires, partly covered with weeds and mosses, where the green surface often betrayed the traveler into a gulf of black, smothering mud; there were also dark and stagnant pools, the abodes of the tadpole, the bullfrog, and the watersnake; where the trunks of pines and hemlocks lay half-drowned, half-rotting, looking like alligators sleeping in the mire.

Tom had long been picking his way cautiously through this treacherous forest; stepping from tuft to tuft of rushes and roots, which afforded precarious footholds among deep sloughs; or pacing carefully, like a cat, along the prostrate trunks of trees; startled now and then by the sudden screaming of the bittern, or the quacking of a wild duck, rising on the wing from some solitary pool. At length he arrived at a piece of firm ground, which ran out like a peninsula into the deep bosom of the swamp. It had been one of the strongholds of the Indians during their wars with the first colonists. Here they had thrown up a kind of fort, which they had looked upon as almost impregnable, and had used as a place of refuge for their squaws and children. Nothing remained of the old Indian fort but a few embankments, gradually sinking to the level of the surrounding earth, and already overgrown in part by oaks and other forest trees, the foliage of which formed a contrast to the dark pines and hemlocks of the swamp.

2. **termagant** (tur´ mə gənt) *n.* quarrelsome woman.
3. **clapperclawing** (klap´ ər klô´ iŋ) *n.* clawing or scratching.

Think Aloud

Vocabulary: Using Context
Point out the word *impregnable* in the last paragraph. Use the following "think aloud" to model the skill of using context to infer the meaning of the word. Say to students:

I may not immediately know the meaning of *impregnable*, but I know that it is being used to describe a kind of fort. In the preceding sentence the place is called a "stronghold" that was built during a time of war. This gives me a sense that *impregnable* may have something to do with a protected, defendable place. When I read that warriors had sheltered their women and children there, I know that they must have regarded the fort as the safest possible place. Therefore, I think *impregnable* means something like "safe from attack" or "unable to be attacked."

It was late in the dusk of evening when Tom Walker reached the old fort, and he paused there awhile to rest himself. Anyone but he would have felt unwilling to linger in this lonely, melancholy place, for the common people had a bad opinion of it, from the stories handed down from the time of the Indian wars; when it was asserted that the savages held incantations here, and made sacrifices to the evil spirit.

Tom Walker, however, was not a man to be troubled with any fears of the kind. He reposed himself for some time on the trunk of a fallen hemlock, listening to the boding cry of the tree toad, and delving with his walking staff into a mound of black mold at his feet. As he turned up the soil unconsciously, his staff struck against something hard. He raked it out of the vegetable mold, and lo! a cloven skull, with an Indian tomahawk buried deep in it, lay before him. The rust on the weapon showed the time that had elapsed since this deathblow had been given. It was a dreary memento of the fierce struggle that had taken place in this last foothold of the Indian warriors.

"Humph!" said Tom Walker, as he gave it a kick to shake the dirt from it.

"Let that skull alone!" said a gruff voice. Tom lifted up his eyes, and beheld a great black man seated directly opposite him, on the stump of a tree. He was exceedingly surprised, having neither heard nor seen anyone approach; and he was still more perplexed on observing, as well as the gathering gloom would permit, that the stranger was neither Negro nor Indian. It is true he was dressed in a rude half-Indian garb, and had a red belt or sash swathed round his body; but his face was neither black nor copper color, but swarthy and dingy, and begrimed with soot, as if he had been accustomed to toil among fires and forges. He had a shock of coarse black hair, that stood out from his head in all directions, and bore an ax on his shoulder.

He scowled for a moment at Tom with a pair of great red eyes.

"What are you doing on my grounds?" said the black man, with a hoarse growling voice.

"Your grounds!" said Tom with a sneer, "no more your grounds than mine; they belong to Deacon Peabody."

"Deacon Peabody be d—d," said the stranger, "as I flatter myself he will be, if he does not look more to his own sins and less to those of his neighbors. Look yonder, and see how Deacon Peabody is faring."

Tom looked in the direction that the stranger pointed, and beheld one of the great trees, fair and flourishing without, but rotten at the core, and saw that it had been nearly hewn through, so that the first high wind was likely to blow it down. On the bark of the tree was scored the name of Deacon Peabody, an eminent man, who had waxed wealthy by driving shrewd bargains with the Indians. He now looked round, and found most of the tall trees marked with the name of some great man of the colony, and all more or less scored by the ax. The one on which he had been seated, and which had evidently just been hewn down, bore the name of Crowninshield: and he recollected a mighty

Reading Strategy
Evaluate Influences of the Historical Period
What do details in the first two paragraphs on this page reveal about colonial attitudes toward Native Americans?

⑨ ☑ Reading Check

Where does Tom pause to rest?

The Devil and Tom Walker **231**

⑦ **Reading Strategy**
Evaluate Influences of the Historical Period

1. Point out the word *savages* and ask students to share their associations with it. Then **ask** them what they associate with the ritual of making sacrifices.
Answer: Most students will associate the word *savages* with people known for crude ways of living, superstitious beliefs, fierceness, and violence. Most will associate the custom of making sacrifices with cultures that are called primitive.

2. **Ask** students the Reading Strategy question: What do the details in these two paragraphs reveal about colonial attitudes toward Native Americans?
Answer: The colonists stereotyped the Native Americans as violent people who practiced ceremonies involving magical chants and sacrifices to evil spirits.

⑧ **Literary Analysis**
Characterization

Direct students to the bracketed passage. **Ask:** What do you learn about Tom's feelings through direct characterization?
Answer: Tom is both "surprised" and "perplexed" by the sudden appearance of a stranger in the gathering dark.

▶ **Monitor progress:** What do you learn about Tom's feelings through indirect characterization?
Answer: Tom shows that he is unafraid by standing his ground and even sneering in response to the stranger's challenge.

▶ **Reteach:** If students still have difficulty distinguishing between direct and indirect characterization, have them reread the second paragraph on the page. Point out that the first sentence directly *tells* the reader that Tom is not afraid of being in an eerie place. The rest of the paragraph *shows* the reader that Tom is not afraid: He relaxes on a fallen tree, pokes at the dirt, and mutters only "Humph!" when he turns up a human skull.

⑨ **Reading Check**
Answer: Tom pauses to rest at the site of an old fort.

Differentiated Instruction for Universal Access

EL Support for English Learners
Tell students that Irving's very long sentences may be difficult to understand. Point out, however, that it is Irving's style to make frequent use of semicolons to link clauses. Encourage students to break down long sentences into more comprehensible parts by separating them at the semicolons. Have them read each clause for meaning before proceeding to the next clause.

Enrichment for Gifted/Talented Students
Ask students to identify the features that suggest the stranger is ominous, evil, perhaps the Devil. Students may point to the stranger's coarse black hair that stood out "in all directions," his soot-begrimed face, "hoarse growling voice," and red eyes. Ask students to research other physical details attributed to the Devil in literature and in art, for example, red skin, fangs, horns, and tail. Students might make a composite drawing of the Devil that includes and labels all the physical features they have discovered.

1. Direct students' attention to the bracketed passage. Point out that this paragraph includes the Devil's boasts, but it also includes critical commentary about colonial culture.

2. **Ask** students: What statement about Massachusetts's cultural attitudes is Irving making in this passage?
   Possible response: Irving is condemning the colonists' mistreatment of others. By directly linking the Devil to the colonists' extermination of Native Americans, persecution of Quakers and Anabaptists, slave dealing, and execution of the Salem "witches," Irving is emphasizing the evil of these events.

⑪ **Literary Analysis**

Characterization

1. Have a volunteer read the bracketed passage.

2. **Ask** the Literary Analysis question: Identify the direct characterization in the paragraph beginning "Such was the opening of this interview."
   Answer: The reader is told directly that Tom is "hard-minded," not "daunted," and is not afraid of the Devil.

"And pray, who are you, ⑩ if I may be so bold?" said Tom.

⑪

Literary Analysis
Characterization
Identify the direct characterization in the paragraph beginning "Such was the opening of this interview . . ."

---

rich man of that name, who made a vulgar display of wealth, which it was whispered he had acquired by buccaneering.

"He's just ready for burning!" said the black man, with a growl of triumph. "You see I am likely to have a good stock of firewood for winter."

"But what right have you," said Tom, "to cut down Deacon Peabody's timber?"

"The right of a prior claim," said the other. "This woodland belonged to me long before one of your white-faced race put foot upon the soil."

"And pray, who are you, if I may be so bold?" said Tom.

"Oh, I go by various names. I am the wild huntsman in some countries; the black miner in others. In this neighborhood I am known by the name of the black woodsman. I am he to whom the red men consecrated this spot, and in honor of whom they now and then roasted a white man, by way of sweet-smelling sacrifice. Since the red men have been exterminated by you white savages, I amuse myself by presiding at the persecutions of Quakers and Anabaptists;[4] I am the great patron and prompter of slave dealers, and the grandmaster of the Salem witches."

"The upshot of all which is, that, if I mistake not," said Tom, sturdily, "you are he commonly called Old Scratch."

"The same, at your service!" replied the black man, with a half-civil nod.

Such was the opening of this interview, according to the old story; though it has almost too familiar an air to be credited. One would think that to meet with such a singular personage, in this wild, lonely place, would have shaken any man's nerves; but Tom was a hard-minded fellow, not easily daunted, and he had lived so long with a termagant wife, that he did not even fear the Devil.

It is said that after this commencement they had a long and earnest conversation together, as Tom returned homeward. The black man told him of great sums of money buried by Kidd the pirate, under the oak trees on the high ridge, not far from the morass. All these were under his command, and protected by his power, so that none could find them but such as propitiated his favor. These he offered to place within Tom Walker's reach, having conceived an especial kindness for him; but they were to be had only on certain conditions. What these conditions were may easily be surmised, though Tom never disclosed them publicly. They must have been very hard, for he required time to think of them, and he was not a man to stick at trifles where money was in view. When they had reached the edge of the swamp, the stranger paused—"What proof have I that all you have been telling me is true?" said Tom. "There is my signature," said the black man, pressing his finger on Tom's forehead. So saying, he turned off among the thickets of the swamp, and seemed, as Tom

---

4. Quakers and Anabaptists two religious groups that were persecuted for their beliefs.

Enrichment: Analyzing Historical Patterns, Trends, and Periods

Puritans Versus Quakers
The Puritans obtained a royal charter and established the Massachusetts Bay Colony in the Boston area in 1629. Blending piety with practicality, the colony prospered and expanded into what are now Massachusetts and Connecticut. However, their progress brought increased friction with Native Americans and with other religious sects in their midst. Quakers, for example, believed in pacifism, justice, charity, and spiritual equality for all, including Native Americans. For those beliefs and for criticizing Puritan treatment of Native Americans, Quakers were persecuted in Massachusetts; four were executed. Many Quakers emigrated to Pennsylvania, where they thrived.

Activity: Research Ask students to compare Puritan and Quaker attitudes toward Native Americans in colonial times, recording their findings in the **Enrichment: Analyzing Historical Patterns, Trends, and Periods** worksheet, in *Professional Development Guidebook*, page 231.

said, to go down, down, down, into the earth, until nothing but his head and shoulders could be seen, and so on, until he totally disappeared.

When Tom reached home, he found the black print of a finger, burnt, as it were, into his forehead, which nothing could obliterate.

The first news his wife had to tell him was the sudden death of Absalom Crowninshield, the rich buccaneer. It was announced in the papers with the usual flourish, that "A great man had fallen in Israel."[5]

Tom recollected the tree which his black friend had just hewn down, and which was ready for burning, "Let the freebooter roast," said Tom, "who cares!" He now felt convinced that all he had heard and seen was no illusion.

He was not prone to let his wife into his confidence; but as this was an uneasy secret, he willingly shared it with her. All her avarice was awakened at the mention of hidden gold, and she urged her husband to comply with the black man's terms and secure what would make them wealthy for life. However Tom might have felt disposed to sell himself to the Devil, he was determined not to do so to oblige his wife; so he flatly refused, out of the mere spirit of contradiction. Many and bitter were the quarrels they had on the subject, but the more she talked, the more resolute was Tom not to be damned to please her.

At length she determined to drive the bargain on her own account, and if she succeeded, to keep all the gain to herself. Being of the same fearless temper as her husband, she set off for the old Indian fort towards the close of a summer's day. She was many hours absent. When she came back, she was reserved and sullen in her replies. She spoke something of a black man, whom she had met about twilight, hewing at the root of a tall tree. He was sulky, however, and would not come to terms: she was to go again with a propitiatory offering, but what it was she forbore to say.

The next evening she set off again for the swamp, with her apron heavily laden. Tom waited and waited for her, but in vain; midnight came, but she did not make her appearance: morning, noon, night returned, but still she did not come. Tom now grew uneasy for her safety, especially as he found she had carried off in her apron the silver teapot and spoons, and every portable article of value. Another night elapsed, another morning came; but no wife. In a word, she was never heard of more.

What was her real fate nobody knows, in consequence of so many pretending to know. It is one of those facts which have become confounded by a variety of historians. Some asserted that she lost her way among the tangled mazes of the swamp, and sank into some pit or slough; others, more uncharitable, hinted that she had eloped with the household booty, and made off to some other province;

Literary Analysis
Characterization
What does Mrs. Walker's reaction to Tom's news reveal about her character?

13 ☑ Reading Check

What does Tom's wife determine to do?

5. **A . . . Israel** a reference to II Samuel 3:38 in the Bible. The Puritans often called New England "Israel."

The Devil and Tom Walker **233**

12 **Literary Analysis**
Characterization

1. Direct students to the bracketed passage. **Ask:** How does Mrs. Walker react when Tom tells her about his encounter with the Devil?
   Answer: Mrs. Walker's greediness is awakened. She urges her husband to make the bargain with the Devil; when Tom refuses, she sets off to make her own bargain.

2. **Ask** the Literary Analysis question: What does Mrs. Walker's reaction to Tom's news reveal about her character?
   Possible response: Mrs. Walker's reaction suggests that she is both greedier than her husband and less cautious. Her attempt to make her own bargain shows that she is independent and unafraid of the Devil.

13 **Reading Check**

Answer: She determines to make her own bargain with the Devil.

Evaluate Influences of the Historical Period

1. Discuss with students how a present-day community might react when a person suddenly goes missing without explanation. What speculations occur?
Possible response: Students may say that people in the community might worry that the missing person has been killed or kidnapped. Some might believe that the person has run away. It is unlikely people would wonder about possible supernatural explanations.

2. Refer students to the bracketed passage, which begins on page 233. **Ask:** What different cultural attitudes do you see in the many stories about what might have happened to Mrs. Walker?
Answer: The stories about Mrs. Walker's disappearance reveal logical, skeptical, and supernatural attitudes. For some, the most likely explanation is that the woman simply became lost in the swamp and sank. Others suggest that Mrs. Walker ran away with the family wealth. Still others have supernatural speculations: that Mrs. Walker was lured into a fatal quagmire by the Devil or was robbed and murdered by the Devil. Ironically, it is the least rational attitude that points to the true explanation.

⓯ **Critical Viewing**

Possible response: Vultures are literal and symbolic signs of death. The presence of the vulture with Mrs. Walker's apron is a clear signal that she is dead.

⓯ ▼ **Critical Viewing**
The narrator describes "a great vulture" and a checked apron hanging in a tree. What do you think happened to Tom Walker's wife? **[Infer]**

⓮ while others surmised that the tempter had decoyed her into a dismal quagmire, on the top of which her hat was found lying. In confirmation of this, it was said a great black man, with an ax on his shoulder, was seen late that very evening coming out of the swamp, carrying a bundle tied in a checked apron, with an air of surly triumph.

The most current and probable story, however, observes that Tom Walker grew so anxious about the fate of his wife and his property, that he set out at length to seek them both at the Indian fort. During a long summer's afternoon he searched about the gloomy place, but no wife was to be seen. He called her name repeatedly, but she was nowhere to be heard. The bittern alone responded to his voice, as he flew screaming by; or the bullfrog croaked dolefully from a neighboring pool. At length, it is said, just in the brown hour of twilight, when the owls began to hoot, and the bats to flit about, his attention was attracted by the clamor of carrion crows hovering about a cypress tree. He looked up, and beheld a bundle tied in a checked apron, and hanging in the branches of the tree, with a great vulture perched hard by, as if keeping watch upon it. He leaped with joy; for he recognized his wife's apron, and supposed it to contain the household valuables.

"Let us get hold of the property," said he, consolingly to himself, "and we will endeavor to do without the woman."

As he scrambled up the tree, the vulture spread its wide wings, and sailed off screaming into the deep shadows of the forest. Tom seized the checked apron, but woeful sight! found nothing but a heart and liver tied up in it!

Such, according to the most authentic old story, was all that was to be found of Tom's wife. She had probably attempted to deal with the black man as she had been accustomed to deal with her husband; but though a female scold is generally considered a match for the Devil, yet in this instance she appears to have had the worst of it. She must have died game, however; for it is said Tom noticed many prints of cloven feet deeply stamped about the tree, and found handfuls of hair, that looked as if they had been plucked from the coarse black shock of the woodsman.

Enrichment: Understanding Economics

Loan Practices

Interest is the cost of borrowing money, usually charged as an annual percentage of the amount borrowed. For example, a loan of $100 at a 2 percent simple interest rate requires a repayment of $102 after a year. Interest rates can vary widely over time, depending on economic conditions. Irving provides a detailed description of such conditions in the bracketed passage on page 236.

Usury is the charging of extremely high interest rates. In Irving's story, the Devil seeks a rate of 2 percent a month, or 24 percent a year, an exorbitant rate. Tom Walker's rates, which add up to 48 percent a year, are even worse.

Activity: Research Ask students to investigate contemporary interest rates, how they are set and how they are influenced by local and national economic conditions. Suggest that they use the **Enrichment: Understanding Economics** worksheet, in *Professional Development Guidebook,* page 225 to record their findings.

Tom knew his wife's prowess by experience. He shrugged his shoulders, as he looked at the signs of a fierce clapper-clawing. "Egad," said he to himself, "Old Scratch must have had a tough time of it!"

Tom consoled himself for the loss of his property, with the loss of his wife, for he was a man of fortitude. He even felt something like gratitude towards the black woodsman, who, he considered, had done him a kind-ness. He sought, therefore, to cultivate a further acquaintance with him, but for some time without success; the old blacklegs played shy, for whatever people may think, he is not always to be had for calling for: he knows how to play his cards when pretty sure of his game.

At length, it is said, when delay had whetted Tom's eagerness to the quick, and prepared him to agree to any-thing rather than not gain the promised treasure, he met the black man one evening in his usual woodsman's dress, with his ax on his shoulder, sauntering along the swamp, and humming a tune. He affected to receive Tom's advances with great indifference, made brief replies, and went on humming his tune.

By degrees, however, Tom brought him to business, and they began to haggle about the terms on which the former was to have the pirate's treasure. There was one condi-tion which need not be mentioned, being generally under-stood in all cases where the Devil grants favors; but there were others about which, though of less importance, he was inflexibly obstinate. He insisted that the money found through his means should be employed in his service. He proposed, therefore, that Tom should employ it in the black traffic; that is to say, that he should fit out a slave ship. This, however, Tom resolutely refused: he was bad enough in all conscience, but the Devil himself could not tempt him to turn slave-trader.

Finding Tom so squeamish on this point, he did not insist upon it, but proposed, instead, that he should turn usurer; the Devil being extremely anxious for the increase of usurers, looking upon them as his peculiar[6] people.

To this no objections were made, for it was just to Tom's taste.

"You shall open a broker's shop in Boston next month," said the black man.

"I'll do it tomorrow, if you wish," said Tom Walker.

---

6. **peculiar** particular; special.

18 **Reading Check**
What service does Tom refuse to provide for the Devil?

Engaging the Essential Question

19 **?**

How does literature shape or reflect society?

1. Have students reread the Background note that precedes the story on page 229, and then direct them to the bracketed passage.

2. **Ask** students to identify details in the passage that criticize selfishness and greed.
   Answer: During Governor Belcher's term, people heavily invested in land and settlements, hoping for sudden wealth. When these greedy schemes failed, people fell into "hard times" and were exploited by Tom Walker. Irving uses words such as "needy," "gambling," "dreaming," "thriftless," and "desperate" to describe Tom's victims.

3. **Ask:** Why do you think Irving describes these economic conditions in such great detail, when they were ancient history even to his readers in 1820? What influence does he hope these details will have on his readers?
   Possible response: Students may suggest that Irving includes these details as a warning to his prosperous, materialistic readers, hoping to influence them to avoid the dangers of greedily pursuing wealth.

Vocabulary
extort (eks tôrt′)
v. to obtain by threat or violence

"You shall lend money at two per cent a month."

"Egad, I'll charge four!" replied Tom Walker.

"You shall extort bonds, foreclose mortgages, drive the merchant to bankruptcy—"

"I'll drive him to the D——l," cried Tom Walker.

"You are the usurer for my money!" said the blacklegs with delight. "When will you want the rhino?"[7]

"This very night."

"Done!" said the Devil.

"Done!" said Tom Walker. So they shook hands and struck a bargain.

A few days' time saw Tom Walker seated behind his desk in a countinghouse in Boston.

His reputation for a ready-moneyed man, who would lend money out for a good consideration, soon spread abroad. Everybody remembers the time of Governor Belcher,[8] when money was particularly scarce. It was a time of paper credit. The country had been deluged with government bills; the famous Land Bank[9] had been established; there had been a rage for speculating; the people had run mad with schemes for new settlements, for building cities in the wilderness; land jobbers[10] went about with maps of grants, and townships, and El Dorados,[11] lying nobody knew where, but which everybody was ready to purchase. In a word, the great speculating fever which breaks out every now and then in the country, had raged to an alarming degree, and everybody was dreaming of making sudden fortunes from nothing. As usual the fever had subsided; the dream had gone off, and the imaginary fortunes with it; the patients were left in doleful plight, and the whole country resounded with the consequent cry of "hard times."

At this propitious time of public distress did Tom Walker set up as usurer in Boston. His door was soon thronged by customers. The needy and adventurous, the gambling speculator, the dreaming land jobber, the thriftless tradesman, the merchant with cracked credit, in short, everyone driven to raise money by desperate means and desperate sacrifices, hurried to Tom Walker.

Thus Tom was the universal friend of the needy, and acted like a "friend in need"; that is to say, he always exacted good pay and good security. In proportion to the distress of the applicant was the hardness of his terms. He accumulated bonds and mortgages; gradually squeezed his customers closer and closer, and sent them

19

---

7. **rhino** (rī′ nō) slang term for money.
8. **Governor Belcher** Jonathan Belcher, the governor of Massachusetts Bay Colony from 1730 through 1741.
9. **Land Bank** a bank that financed transactions in real estate.
10. **land jobbers** people who bought and sold undeveloped land.
11. **El Dorados** (el′ də rä′ dōz) *n.* places that are rich in gold or opportunity. El Dorado was a legendary country in South America sought by early Spanish explorers for its gold and precious stones.

at length, dry as a sponge, from his door.

In this way he made money hand over hand, became a rich and mighty man, and exalted his cocked hat upon 'Change.[12] He built himself, as usual, a vast house, out of ostentation; but left the greater part of it unfinished and unfurnished, out of parsimony. He even set up a carriage in the fullness of his vainglory, though he nearly starved the horses which drew it; and as the ungreased wheels groaned and screeched on the axletrees, you would have thought you heard the souls of the poor debtors he was squeezing.

As Tom waxed old, however, he grew thoughtful. Having secured the good things of this world, he began to feel anxious about those of the next. He thought with regret on the bargain he had made with his black friend, and set his wits to work to cheat him out of the conditions. He became, therefore, all of a sudden, a violent churchgoer. He prayed loudly and strenuously, as if heaven were to be taken by force of lungs. Indeed, one might always tell when he had sinned most during the week, by the clamor of his Sunday devotion. The quiet Christians who had been modestly and steadfastly traveling Zionward,[13] were struck with self-reproach at seeing themselves so suddenly outstripped in their career by this new-made convert. Tom was as rigid in religious as in money matters; he was a stern supervisor and censurer of his neighbors, and seemed to think every sin entered up to their account became a credit on his own side of the page. He even talked of the expediency of reviving the persecution of Quakers and Anabaptists. In a word, Tom's zeal became as notorious as his riches.

Still, in spite of all this strenuous attention to forms, Tom had a lurking dread that the Devil, after all, would have his due. That he might not be taken unawares, therefore, it is said he always carried a small Bible in his coat pocket. He had also a great folio Bible on his countinghouse desk, and would frequently be found reading it when people called on business; on such occasions he would lay his green spectacles in the book, to mark the place, while he turned round to drive some usurious bargain.

Some say that Tom grew a little crackbrained in his old days, and that fancying his end approaching, he had his horse newly shod, saddled and bridled, and buried with his feet uppermost; because he supposed that at the last day the world would be turned upside down, in which case he should find his horse standing ready for mounting, and he was determined at the worst to give his old friend a run for it. This, however, is probably a mere old wives' fable. If he really did take such a precaution, it was totally superfluous; at least so says the authentic old legend, which closes his story in the following manner.

---

12. **'Change** exchange where bankers and merchants did business.
13. **Zionward** (zī′ ən wərd) toward heaven.

The Devil and Tom Walker **237**

Vocabulary
ostentation (äs′ tən tā′ shən) *n.* boastful display
parsimony (pär′ sə mō′ nē) *n.* stinginess

Reading Strategy
Evaluate Influences of the Historical Period
How do religious attitudes of the day inform Tom's feelings as he gets older?

Literary Analysis
Characterization What do you learn about Tom's character from the narrator's description of his religious zeal?

22 Reading Check
As he gets older, what does Tom always carry in his pocket?

---

20 Reading Strategy
Evaluate Influences of the Historical Period

1. Before students read the bracketed passage, discuss religious beliefs about the afterlife. The common belief of Christians in Tom Walker's time was that all people face a judgment when they die: Righteous believers go to heaven for eternity; unbelievers and the wicked go to hell. Remind students that in his bargain, Tom has already agreed that he is going to the Devil. Then have students read the bracketed passage.

2. **Ask** students the Reading Strategy question: How do religious attitudes of the day inform Tom's feelings as he gets older? **Answer:** As he ages, Tom begins to think of the next world and the fate that awaits him when he dies: Because of his evil bargain he knows that he is literally going to the Devil. Anxious and filled with regret, Tom becomes a "violent churchgoer" in hopes of cheating the Devil.

21 Literary Analysis
Characterization

1. Have students read the bracketed passage carefully. Tell them to watch for an implied comparison as they read.

2. **Ask** students the Literary Analysis question: What do you learn about Tom's character from the narrator's description of his religious zeal? **Possible response:** You learn that Tom is as rigid, narrow minded, and cold hearted in his religiosity as he is in his money-making. Irving illustrates this similarity at the end of the passage by showing Tom turn from reading the Bible to make "some usurious bargain."

22 Reading Check
Answer: Tom always carries a small Bible in his pocket.

Differentiated Instruction for Universal Access

Enrichment for all Students
Tell students that the twentieth-century writer Stephen Vincent Benét wrote a version of the Irving story in which a New England man, facing the same dilemma as Tom Walker, finds a lawyer—the famous Daniel Webster—to defend him against the Devil in a jury trial.

Invite the class to set up a trial situation for Tom Walker. Several students can act as prosecutors enforcing the bargain; others can act as defense attorneys trying to free Tom from his obligation. Other roles might include Tom Walker and witnesses for the prosecution and defense. You or an appointed student might act as judge, making sure that all information presented in the trial is based on details in the story. Allow students time to prepare for trial; then stage the event in class.

1. Direct students' attention to the final three paragraphs of the story.

2. **Ask** students to describe and explain the attitude of "the good people of Boston" to Tom Walker's dramatic disappearance.
Answer: The people "shrugged their shoulders" at Tom's disappearance. Their casual response may be due to the fact that they are familiar with supernatural creatures and devilish tricks.

3. **Ask** students: Do you think Irving is implicitly criticizing people's attitudes in colonial Massachusetts?
Possible response: Some students may say that Irving is criticizing only greedy moneylenders like Tom, not colonial people in general. Others may say that Irving feels that "the good people of Boston" are too familiar with evil and greed and need to learn a lesson from Tom Walker's fate.

One hot summer afternoon in the dog days, just as a terrible black thunder-gust was coming up, Tom sat in his countinghouse in his white linen cap and India silk morning gown. He was on the point of foreclosing a mortgage, by which he would complete the ruin of an unlucky land speculator for whom he had professed the greatest friendship. The poor land jobber begged him to grant a few months' indulgence. Tom had grown testy and irritated, and refused another day.

"My family will be ruined and brought upon the parish," said the land jobber.

"Charity begins at home," replied Tom; "I must take care of myself in these hard times."

"You have made so much money out of me," said the speculator.

Tom lost his patience and his piety—"The Devil take me," said he, "if I have made a farthing!"

Just then there were three loud knocks at the street door. He stepped out to see who was there. A black man was holding a black horse, which neighed and stamped with impatience.

"Tom, you're come for," said the black fellow, gruffly. Tom shrunk back, but too late. He had left his little Bible at the bottom of his coat pocket, and his big Bible on the desk buried under the mortgage he was about to foreclose: never was sinner taken more unawares. The black man whisked him like a child into the saddle, gave the horse the lash, and away he galloped, with Tom on his back, in the midst of the thunderstorm. The clerks stuck their pens behind their ears, and stared after him from the windows. Away went Tom Walker, dashing down the streets, his white cap bobbing up and down, his morning gown fluttering in the wind, and his steed striking fire out of the pavement at every bound. When the clerks turned to look for the black man he had disappeared.

Tom Walker never returned to foreclose the mortgage. A countryman who lived on the border of the swamp, reported that in the height of the thunder-gust he had heard a great clattering of hoofs and a howling along the road, and running to the window caught sight of a figure, such as I have described, on a horse that galloped like mad across the fields, over the hills and down into the black hemlock swamp towards the old Indian fort; and that shortly after a thunderbolt falling in that direction seemed to set the whole forest in a blaze.

The good people of Boston shook their heads and shrugged their shoulders, but had been so much accustomed to witches and goblins and tricks of the Devil, in all kind of shapes from the first settlement of the colony, that they were not so much horror struck as might have been expected. Trustees were appointed to take charge of Tom's effects. There was nothing, however, to administer upon.

23

Vocabulary Development

Vocabulary Knowledge Rating
When students have completed reading and discussing both selections, have them take out the **Vocabulary Knowledge Rating** charts they worked on earlier. Read the words aloud and have students rate their knowledge of the words again in the After Reading column. Clarify any words that are still problematic. Have students write their own definitions and example or sentence in the appropriate column. Then have students complete the Vocabulary Lesson at the end of this selection. Encourage students to use the words in further discussion and written work about the selections. Remind them that they will be accountable for these words on the **Selection Test,** *Unit 2 Resources,* pages 19–21 or 22–24.

On searching his coffers all his bonds and mortgages were found reduced to cinders. In place of gold and silver his iron chest was filled with chips and shavings; two skeletons lay in his stable instead of his half-starved horses, and the very next day his great house took fire and was burned to the ground.

Such was the end of Tom Walker and his ill-gotten wealth. Let all griping money brokers lay this story to heart. The truth of it is not to be doubted. The very hole under the oak trees, whence he dug Kidd's money, is to be seen to this day; and the neighboring swamp and old Indian fort are often haunted in stormy nights by a figure on horseback, in morning gown and white cap, which is doubtless the troubled spirit of the usurer. In fact, the story has resolved itself into a proverb, and is the origin of that popular saying, so prevalent throughout New England, of "The Devil and Tom Walker."

Critical Reading

Cite textual evidence to support your responses.

1. **Key Ideas and Details (a)** What does the Devil offer Tom Walker? **(b) Analyze:** Why does Tom at first refuse?

2. **Key Ideas and Details (a)** What happens to Tom's wife? **(b) Interpret:** What do you learn about Tom, based on his reaction to the loss of his wife?

3. **Key Ideas and Details (a)** What agreement does Tom Walker ultimately make with the Devil? **(b) Draw Conclusions:** As the story progresses, why do you think Tom begins to go to church and carry a Bible with him at all times?

4. **Key Ideas and Details (a)** What does Tom do to cause the narrator to call him a "violent churchgoer"? **(b) Interpret:** In what way is Tom's approach to religion similar to his approach to financial dealings?

5. **Integration of Knowledge and Ideas (a) Take a Position:** Do you feel that Tom Walker deserved his fate? Explain. **(b) Defend:** Would you have felt more sympathy for Tom if he, like the original Faust, had sold his soul for knowledge instead of money? Explain.

6. **Integration of Ideas and Knowledge** Judging from the events of this story, what do you think Washington Irving might say about the effects of greed on society? In your response, use at least two of these Essential Question words: *avarice, failure, divide, charitable*. *[Connecting to the Essential Question: How does literature shape or reflect society?]*

The Devil and Tom Walker **239**

Concept Connector

Reading Strategy Graphic Organizer
Ask students to review the graphic organizers in which they have listed details that reflect specific cultural attitudes. Then have students share their organizers and compare the details and attitudes they identified.

Activating Prior Knowledge
Remind students of their agreement or disagreement with the statement that the desire for wealth can make people hard and unfeeling. Ask them to explain whether their thoughts have changed, and if so, how.

 Writing About the Essential Question
Have students compare their responses to the prompt before reading the selection with their thoughts after reading it. Have them work individually or in groups, writing or discussing their thoughts, to define their new responses. Then lead a class discussion, probing for what students have learned that confirms or invalidates their initial thoughts. Encourage students to cite specific textual details to support their responses.

Answers

1. Tom is crafty, selfish, and greedy.

2. (a) **Sample answer:** Trait: callousness. Details: Tom mistreats horses; he is indifferent to his wife's death; he voluntarily doubles the Devil's interest rate; he is merciless with his customers. (b) **Possible response:** Tom is bold, greedy, selfish, stingy, and callous.

3. (a) Tom's wife is tall, strong, bad tempered, loud, and as greedy as her husband. (b) The couple's disputes are loud; they are heard by outsiders. Their disputes are physical; Tom's face shows marks of fighting.

4. (a) The condition of the home suggests that the Walkers are careless, miserly, and unwelcoming. (b) Tom's second home shows that he is proud enough to build a showy house but is too cheap to furnish it properly.

5. The narrator's sardonic tone signals that he is amused by the Walkers as thoroughly as he is offended by their meanness and greed. He seems to admire their fearlessness—Tom's poise on first meeting the Devil, Mrs. Walker "dying game"—but is critical of all else, including their marriage.

6. (a) Characters driven by desire for wealth include the Walkers and the incidental figures Deacon Peabody and Crowninshield. (b) Tom, once rich, builds a great house to show off his wealth. (c) Since Tom comes to a bad end, the plot is a tutorial on the dangers of greed.

7. Irving's scathing portraits of greedy characters is one form of his criticism, but he also ridicules the foolish speculators of the Belcher era.

8. (a) The narrator's casual use of "savages" suggests that colonists commonly used this term. The reference to Deacon Peabody alludes to the economic exploitation of Native Americans by colonists. (b) Irving strongly criticizes these views as evil, most clearly by linking them to the Devil.

Literary Analysis

1. **Key Ideas and Details** Identify three things you learn about Tom Walker through **direct characterization.**

2. **Key Ideas and Details** **(a)** Use a chart like the one shown to record dialogue, thoughts, actions, and other details that help reveal the key traits of Tom's personality. **(b)** What do these examples of **indirect characterization** show to be his chief personality traits?

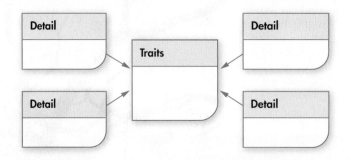

3. **Key Ideas and Details** **(a)** Describe Tom's wife based on the narrator's comments. **(b)** What do you learn about the relationship of Tom and his wife through indirect characterization? Explain.

4. **Key Ideas and Details** **(a)** What does the Walkers' home early in the story show about their personalities and values? **(b)** What does the home Tom builds later show about him?

5. **Craft and Structure** How would you describe the narrator's attitude toward Tom and his wife—for example, does he admire them? Is he amused by them? Cite details to support your answer.

Reading Strategy

6. **Evaluate the influences of the historical period on characters, plot, and settings** by identifying elements of the story that reflect an excessive concern for wealth in 1720s New England. **(a)** Note two characters who are driven by a desire for wealth. **(b)** Note at least one setting that demonstrates characters' concerns for the appearance of wealth. **(c)** Explain how the plot as a whole can be seen as an exploration of the dangers of excessive concern for wealth.

7. Does Irving effectively criticize this attitude? Cite details to support your evaluation.

8. **(a)** What does the story reveal about social attitudes toward Native Americans among New Englanders of European background in the 1720s? **(b)** Does Irving criticize these views? Cite story details to illustrate your thoughts.

Common Core State Standards

Writing

3. Write narratives to develop real or imagined experiences or events using effective technique, well-chosen details, and well-structured event sequences. *(p. 241)*

3.d. Use precise words and phrases, telling details, and sensory language to convey a vivid picture of the experiences, events, setting, and/or characters. *(p. 241)*

Language

2.a. Observe hyphenation conventions. *(p. 241)*

Assessment Practice

Make Inferences and Generalizations (For more practice, see *All-in-One Workbook.*)

An inference is a reasonable guess based on facts. Use this sample test item:

> A miserable horse, whose ribs were as articulated as the bars of a gridiron, stalked about a field . . . and sometimes he would lean his head over the fence . . . and seem to petition deliverance from this land of famine.

According to the passage, why might the horse be so miserable?

A He misses his former owner.

B He is kept in the barn all day.

C He lives in the country.

D He is starving.

The excerpt makes no mention of any information found in choices **A, B,** and **C.** The horse's ribs show, and the author describes a "land of famine." Students should infer that the horse is not well fed and should choose **D.**

240

© Vocabulary Acquisition and Use

Word Analysis: Latin Prefix *ex-*

When used without a hyphen, the Latin prefix *ex-* means "out; out of; away from." In the word *extort*, for example, it combines with the Latin root *-tort-*, meaning "twist," to form a verb meaning "to twist out of" or "to force." For each item below, form a word that combines the prefix *ex-* with the specified Latin root. You may need to make small changes to the spelling of the root. Explain the meaning of each word you form.

1. *-clam-*, "to cry; to shout"
2. *-hal-*, "to breathe"
3. *-tend-*, "to stretch"

When the prefix *ex-* is used with a hyphen, it means "former," as in ex-Governor. Write three words that correctly use the prefix *ex-* with a hyphen.

Vocabulary: Sentence Completions

Use a word from the vocabulary list on page 226 to complete each sentence, and explain your choice. Use each word only once.

1. Walking on that crumbling bridge is _____.
2. During those years of _____, politicians quarreled all the time.
3. Hurricanes in the Gulf of Mexico are _____ in summer but rare in winter.
4. The building's gold trim and ornate stone carvings were marks of _____.
5. The miser's _____ irritated his neighbors.
6. He would _____ money by threatening to harm those who would not pay.

Writing

© **Narrative Text** Write a new version of Irving's **story**, updating it in a way that addresses a modern audience. Keep Irving's theme and the conflict of someone selling his or her soul to the devil for worldly gain.

Prewriting Use a two-column chart to plan your story. Reread Irving's tale, listing plot events, characters, and settings in the left column. Put a check next to details you want to update. Then, decide on the best way to update those details and write your ideas in the right-hand column. Finally, write down ideas for sensory details that will bring the new settings and characters to life for the reader.

Drafting Write your story using the updated details. Pay particular attention to the *concrete sensory details* you listed and take care to describe the specific actions, movements, gestures, and feelings of the characters. Consider using *interior monologue,* in which a character shares his or her thoughts with the reader but keeps them hidden from other characters.

Revising Confirm that your new version balances the original story elements with new details. Check to see that the conflict and message are the same, while the language and setting reflect today's world.

> **Model: Updating a Story**
> Tom was sitting at his computer, downloading promissory notes. Suddenly, he saw a pair of beady eyes glaring at him from the screen. Then, pixel by pixel, a strange-looking face took shape.
>
> While maintaining the intent of the story, modern elements such as "pixel" and "computer" update the setting.

Vocabulary Acquisition and Use

1. Introduce the skill, using the instruction on the student page.
2. Have students complete the Word Analysis activity and the Vocabulary practice.

Word Analysis:
Sample answers:

1. exclaim. To <u>exclaim</u> means "to shout out."
2. exhale. To <u>exhale</u> means "to breathe out."
3. extend. To <u>extend</u> means "to stretch out or lengthen."

   ex-Senator, ex-patriot, ex-cheerleader

Vocabulary:

1. treacherous. It would be dangerous or <u>treacherous</u> to walk on a crumbling bridge.
2. discord. An era when politicians constantly quarreled would be a time of conflict or <u>discord</u>.
3. prevalent. Hurricanes are quite common or <u>prevalent</u> in summer.
4. ostentation. Gold trim and carved stone are showy displays or <u>ostentation</u>.
5. parsimony. A miser's stinginess or <u>parsimony</u> could be irritating.
6. extort. "To threaten harm to get something" is the definition of <u>extort</u>.

Writing

1. To guide students in retelling the Tom Walker story, give them the Support for Writing page (*Unit 2 Resources,* p. 14).
2. Remind students it is not necessary to replicate every event from Irving's story, but their updated stories should retain the theme of greed, include a devilish bargain, and show the bargain's outcome.
3. Use the **Rubrics for Short Story**, in *Professional Development Guidebook,* pages 252–253, to evaluate students' work.

Assessment Resources

Unit 1 Resources,

L1 L2 EL **Selection Test A,** pp. 19–21. Administer Test A to less advanced students and English learners.

L3 L4 EL **Selection Test B,** pp. 22–24. Administer Text B to on-level or more advanced students.

L3 L4 **Open-Book Test,** pp. 16–18. As an alternative, administer the Open-Book Test

All **Customizable Test Bank**

All **Self-tests**
Students may prepare for the **Selection Test** by taking the **Self-test** online.

All assessment resources are available at **www.PHLitOnline.com**.

241

❶ **About the Text Forms**

Introduce the forms, using the instruction on the student page.

Think Aloud: Model the Skill

Say to students:

It helps me to think of a *commission* as a license. Just as my driver's license gives me legal authority to operate a car, Lewis's commission gives him legal authority to enlist men, buy supplies, and represent the United States.

A *field report* is like a log or diary, a current record of what is being accomplished. Lewis uses his field report not only to record data and discoveries but also to show how he is completing his assignments.

❷ **Reading Strategy**

Introduce the strategy, using the instruction on the student page.

Think Aloud: Model the Skill

Say to students:

To determine the writer's purpose in writing a document, I start with the title of the work as well as with the place where it appears and any available introductory material. For example, the title "Commission of Meriwether Lewis" tells me a good deal. I know that *commission* means "authorization," so I know that Jefferson's general purpose is to authorize certain actions. As I read the document, I learn more about his specific purpose from his own statements.

Primary Sources

Government Document
Commission of Meriwether Lewis

Field Report
Crossing the Great Divide

❶ **About the Text Forms**

The word *commission* has different meanings in different contexts. In a financial context, it refers to a payment based on percentages of a sale; in a legal context, it refers to the perpetration of a crime. When referring to a written work, a **commission** is a type of **government document** in which an official person or institution assigns a special task to someone. In this commission, Thomas Jefferson, then president of the United States, describes Meriwether Lewis's main goal and assigns him specific responsibilities. The language Jefferson uses reflects his position as leader of the young country, as well as an almost scientific curiosity about the vast territories acquired in the Louisiana Purchase.

A **field report** is a first hand record of observations and data written by researchers or explorers at the site of their work, or "in the field." Field reports present objective information and may also contain notes on personal thoughts. Depending on their subjects, writers of field reports may use *specialized scientific or technical language*, as well as graphs, charts, maps, or illustrations. Lewis's detailed report reflects his commitment to meeting Jefferson's expectations.

❷ **Reading Strategy**

The *general purpose* of any written work may be *to inform, to entertain, to persuade, to describe*, or *to reflect*. The documents you are about to read were written to inform. However, their *specific purposes* and intended *audiences,* or readers, are different. Jefferson was sending Lewis on a mission. His commission describes the details of the task. Lewis was reporting his progress to his boss. As you read, **identify the writer's purpose** and the ways in which it shapes the text.

❸ 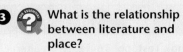 **What is the relationship between** *literature* **and** *place?*

Reading these documents will help you understand how some nineteenth-century Americans felt about the vast continent they were beginning to explore. Notice details that show President Jefferson's interest in the resources provided by the new lands. Also, note details that tell you what Meriwether Lewis felt as he explored the wilderness.

www.PHLitOnline.com

---

❸ **What is the relationship between literature and place?**

Tell students to look for details as they read that will help them answer the Essential Question, including details that show Jefferson's interest in natural resources and details that show Lewis's feelings as he explores.

❹ Note-Taking Guide

Primary source documents are a rich source of information for researchers. As you read these documents, use a note-taking guide like the one shown to systematically organize relevant and accurate information.

1 Type of Document (check one)
☐ Newspaper ☐ Letter ☐ Map ☐ Memorandum ☐ Press release
☐ Report ☐ Government document ☐ E-mail ☐ Advertisement ☐ Other

2 Date(s) of Document _____

3 Author of Document _____
Author's Position or Title _____

4 Audience: For whom was the document written? _____

5 Purpose and Importance: ◀ ┈┈┈┈┈┈┈┈┈┈┈┈┈┈

   a Why was this document written? _____
   Write down two details that support your answer: _____
   _____

   b List two important ideas, statements, or observations from this document: ___
   _____

   c What does this document show about life in the time and place in which it was written? _____
   _____

Reading Strategy
Purpose
A primary-source document may be written for more than one reason, or purpose. As you read, think about the different purposes each document may have served.

This guide was adapted from **U.S. National Archives** document-analysis worksheets.

❺ Vocabulary

celestial (sə les′ tē əl) *adj.* of or in the sky, as planets or stars (p. 245)

practicable (prak′ ti kə bəl) *adj.* practical; possible (p. 245)

latitude (lat′ ə tood′) *n.* distance north or south from the equator (p. 245)

longitude (län′ jə tood) *n.* distance east or west on the earth's surface (p. 245)

membranes (mem′ branz′) *n.* thin, soft layers serving as coverings or linings (p. 247)

conciliatory (kən sil′ ē ə tôr′ ē) *adj.* intended to make peace or to reconcile; friendly (p. 249)

discretion (dis kre′ shən) *n.* judgment (p. 249)

dispatched (di spach'd′) *v.* sent off, usually on official business (p. 251)

prospect (pros′ spekt) *n.* something hoped for or expected (p. 251)

conspicuous (kən spik′ yoo əs) *adj.* obvious; easy to see or perceive (p. 252)

Primary Sources: Government Document/Field Report **243**

PRETEACH

❹ Note-Taking Guide

1. As a class, review the instruction on the student page about the note-taking guide.

2. Emphasize question 5 on the guide by having a student read the Reading Strategy note in the margin of the student page.

3. Encourage students to use a similar guide as they read the primary sources in this set. Point out that they may customize their note-taking guides to fit the particular needs of the reading assignment.

❺ Vocabulary

1. Pronounce each word, giving its definition; have students say it aloud.

2. Also see the *Classroom Strategies and Teaching Routines* card for vocabulary.

Vocabulary Development

Vocabulary Knowledge Rating
Create a **Vocabulary Knowledge Rating chart** (*Professional Development Guidebook,* p. 33) for the vocabulary words on the student page. Give each student a copy of the chart with the words on it. Read the words aloud, and have students mark their rating of each in the Before Reading column. When students have completed reading and discussing the selections, have them take out their **Vocabulary Knowledge Rating** charts for the selections. Read the words aloud and have students rate their knowledge again in the After Reading column. Clarify any words that are still problematic. Then have students complete the Vocabulary practice at the end of the selections.

6 Background

The Story Behind the Documents

Thomas Jefferson had a mentoring friendship with Meriwether Lewis. The two Virginians had much in common. Both had lost their fathers early in life, both had wide-ranging intellects, and both had aspirations beyond the equestrian preoccupations typical of most Virginia gentlemen of their time. Given their friendship, Jefferson's appointment of Lewis to lead the expedition might have seemed pure favoritism. In fact, no presidential appointment in history has been more apt or better fulfilled than Jefferson's choice of Meriwether Lewis.

Jefferson's interest in exploring the West began long before his Louisiana Purchase. In 1792 an American sea captain arrived at the mouth of a river flowing into the Pacific. He named the river for his ship, *Columbia,* and determined its latitude and longitude. That location, the possible end point of America, captured Jefferson's imagination. With others, Jefferson raised a subscription to send one or two explorers overland to reach the mouth of the Columbia River. Meriwether Lewis, then only a teenager, heard of the project and volunteered. Jefferson chose instead a French botanist, who turned out to be a secret agent and had to be recalled.

6 THE STORY BEHIND THE DOCUMENTS

President Thomas Jefferson

Captain Meriwether Lewis

As the 19th century dawned, Ohio was the westward frontier of the United States, but that was not long to be. In 1803, **President Thomas Jefferson (1743–1826),** then the nation's third president, negotiated with France to buy a tract of land extending from the southern coast of Louisiana north into what is now Canada. This vast expanse included all of present-day Arkansas, Missouri, Iowa, Oklahoma, Kansas, and Nebraska. It also included parts of Minnesota, most of North and South Dakota, northeastern New Mexico, northern Texas, and portions of Colorado, Montana, and Wyoming. This enormous real-estate deal became known as **The Louisiana Purchase** and was one of the defining achievements of Thomas Jefferson's presidency. In a single treaty, Jefferson added more than 800,000 uncharted square miles to the holdings of the nation, effectively doubling the size of the country.

Jefferson had long wanted to pursue exploration of the Pacific Northwest. The completion of the Louisiana Purchase strengthened his resolve. He convinced Congress to allocate $2,500 to fund an expedition, writing:

The river Missouri, and Indians inhabiting it, are not as well known as rendered desirable by their connection with the Mississippi, and consequently with us. . . . An intelligent officer, with ten or twelve chosen men. . . might explore the whole line, even to the Western Ocean. . . .

The "intelligent officer" he had in mind was his secretary, **Captain Meriwether Lewis (1774–1809).** On June 20, 1803, Jefferson wrote Lewis's commission to lead an expedition. He assigned Lewis the job of exploring the new territories with the particular objective of finding a water route from the Missouri River to the Pacific Ocean. Jefferson instructed Lewis to collect scientific data along the way, trace the boundaries of the Louisiana Territory, and claim the Oregon Territory for the United States. He also charged Lewis with the responsibility of recording almost every detail of his experiences.

Lewis had honed his leadership skills in the army. In preparation for the journey, he studied botany, biology, and cartography (map making). **Captain William Clark** became co-leader of the group, which numbered thirty-three people and one Newfoundland dog. Between 1804 and 1806, the team—which was known as **The Corps of Discovery**—completed an 8,000-mile trek from St. Louis to the source of the Missouri River, across the Rocky Mountains to the Pacific coast, and back to Missouri. Lewis started writing his report in May of 1804. Clark also maintained a journal in which he drew pictures of the people, plants, and animals the expedition encountered.

244 A Growing Nation (1800–1870)

© Text Complexity Rubric

	Commission of Meriwether Lewis	Crossing the Great Divide
Qualitative Measures		
Context/ Knowledge Demands	Official document; historical knowledge demands 1 2 ③ 4 5	Explorer's field report 1 2 ③ 4 5
Structure/Language Conventionality and Clarity	Lengthy sentences with clear structure; some difficult vocabulary 1 2 3 ④ 5	Simple sentence structure 1 2 ③ 4 5
Levels of Meaning/ Purpose/Concept Level	Accessible (listing of expectations) 1 2 ③ 4 5	Accessible (Lewis's negotiations) 1 2 ③ 4 5
Quantitative Measures		
Lexile/Text Length	1340L / 1,311 words	1450L / 484 words
Overall Complexity	**More complex**	**More accessible**

Commission of
MERIWETHER LEWIS

Thomas Jefferson

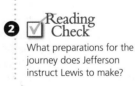

▲ Compass used by Lewis and Clark

To Meriwether Lewis,

Esquire, captain of the first regiment of infantry of the United States of America: Your situation as secretary of the president of the United States, has made you acquainted with the objects of my confidential message of January 18, 1803, to the legislature; you have seen the act they passed, which, though expressed in general terms, was meant to sanction those objects, and you are appointed to carry them into execution.

Instruments for ascertaining by celestial observations the geography of the country, through which you will pass, have been already provided. Light articles for barter, and presents among the Indians, arms for your attendants, say for from ten to twelve men, boats, tents, and other traveling apparatus, with ammunition, medicine, surgical instruments and provisions you will have prepared with such aids as the Secretary at War can yield in his department; and from him also you will receive authority to engage among our troops, by voluntary agreement, the number of attendants above-mentioned, over whom you, as their commanding officer, are invested with all the powers the laws give in such a case...

The object of your mission is to explore the Missouri river, and such principal streams of it, as, by its course and communication with the waters of the Pacific ocean, whether the Columbia, Oregan [*sic*], Colorado, or any other river, may offer the most direct and practicable water-communication across the continent, for the purposes of commerce.

Beginning at the mouth of the Missouri, you will take observations of latitude and longitude, at all remarkable points on the river, and especially at the mouths of rivers, at rapids, at islands, and other places and objects distinguished by such natural marks and characters, of a durable kind, as that they may with certainty be recognized hereafter. The courses of the river between these points of observation may

Vocabulary

celestial (sə lesʹ tē əl)
adj. of or in the sky, as planets or stars

practicable (prakʹ ti kə bəl)
adj. practical; possible

latitude (latʹə to͞odʹ)
n. distance north or south from the equator

longitude (länʹjə to͞od)
n. distance east or west on the earth's surface

② Reading Check ✓

What preparations for the journey does Jefferson instruct Lewis to make?

---

❶ Primary Source

1. Read the first paragraph to students in your "official" voice.

2. **Ask** students: What official language do you find in the first paragraph of this document?
Answer: Lewis is addressed by title (esquire) and rank (captain). Jefferson uses formal phrasing to establish the background of his assignment: "Your situation . . . has made you acquainted with the objects of my confidential message." The paragraph includes many official terms such as "regiment," "legislature," "president of the United States," and "act"; it concludes with official verbs, "to sanction" and "are appointed."

3. **Ask** students what this official language indicates about the nature of the document.
Possible response: It shows that the document represents an official action, one with the authority of the government behind it.

❷ Reading Check

Answer: Jefferson tells Lewis to obtain equipment and provisions, including articles for barter and gifts, boats, tents, ammunition, and medical equipment. Lewis is also to recruit volunteers from the army to accompany him.

ⓒ Text Complexity: Reader and Task Suggestions

Commission of Meriwether Lewis		Crossing the Great Divide	
Preparing to Read the Text	**Leveled Tasks**	**Preparing to Read the Text**	**Leveled Tasks**
• Using the information on TE p. 244, discuss Jefferson's choice of Lewis to lead the expedition. • Ask students why it would be important for Jefferson to spell out his expectations for this expedition.	*Structure/Language* If students will have difficulty with the vocabulary or syntax, have them first read to identify and define unfamiliar words. Then, have them read the text aloud to "hear" Jefferson's voice in the expectations. *Synthesizing* If students will not have difficulty with vocabulary and syntax, ask them to imagine an exploration of Mars. Have students use Jefferson's text as a model for spelling out a few expectations for this future expedition.	• Using the Background information on TE p. 251, discuss the expedition's relationship with Native Americans. • Ask students why a field report would be helpful for people who might plan to travel to an area in the future.	*Levels of Meaning* If students will have difficulty with the meaning, have them summarize the first paragraph. As students reread, have them add details that they consider helpful. *Analyzing* If students will not have difficulty with the meaning, discuss the second paragraph of the field report. Ask, "How is the speech meant to be helpful to Native Americans and the government?"

❸ Background

Louisiana

The map on this page gives more precise boundaries to the Louisiana Territory than it actually had at the time of Jefferson's commission. No American or European had ever set foot in the northwestern areas of the Territory, much less mapped it accurately. "Louisiana" was defined as the western half of the Mississippi River drainage—that is, all western lands that contain rivers flowing into the Mississippi, including the Missouri River and all its tributaries. With that loose understanding of its dimensions, the territory passed among Spain, France, and the United States.

❹ Primary Source: Map

Possible response: Students may note the contrast between the undefined mass of "Louisiana" and the highly defined eastern portion of the continent as an explanation for Jefferson's desire to explore and map the territory. Students may also say that Jefferson might be anxious to establish legal boundaries because of possible competition from the neighboring powers of Britain and Spain. The map also makes clear the necessity for American control of the land between the Louisiana Territory and the mouth of the Columbia River. (On the map, the Columbia passes between the letters *E* and *G* of OREGON.)

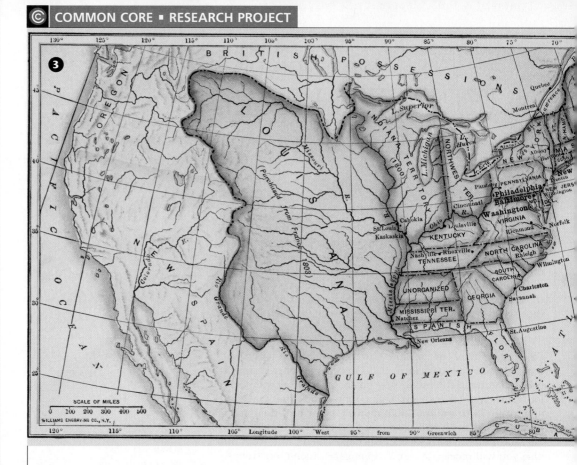

❹ ▲ **Primary Source: Map**
How does this period map clarify your understanding of Jefferson's interest in the newly acquired lands? **[Connect]**

be supplied by the compass, the log-line, and by time, corrected by the observations themselves. The variations of the needle, too, in different places, should be noticed.

The interesting points of the portage between the heads of the Missouri, and of the water offering the best communication with the Pacific Ocean, should also be fixed by observation; and the course of that water to the ocean, in the same manner as that of the Missouri.

❺ Your observations are to be taken with great pains and accuracy; to be entered distinctly and intelligibly for others as well as yourself; to comprehend all the elements necessary, with the aid of the usual tables, to fix the latitude and longitude of the places at which they were taken; and are to be rendered to the war-office, for the purpose of having the calculations made concurrently by proper persons within the United States. Several copies of these, as well as of your other notes, should be made at leisure times, and put into

246 A Growing Nation (1800–1870)

Enrichment: Investigating Science

Lewis's Many Hats

Lewis was appointed to lead an exploration, but Jefferson's commission specified many additional responsibilities: navigator, astronomer, recording secretary, ambassador, commercial agent, meteorologist, ethnologist, botanist, zoologist, geologist, and doctor. With no formal medical training, Lewis treated the injuries and diseases of the dozens of people in his care over the course of two years in dangerous wilderness. Amazingly, he lost only one patient:

Sergeant Charles Floyd died of what is now thought to have been appendicitis.

Activity: Research Ask individual students to research the state of scientific understanding in Lewis's time, focusing on one specific discipline (astronomy, botany, or geology, for example). Suggest that they record their findings in the **Enrichment: Investigating Science** work sheet, in *Professional Development Guidebook,* page 241.

the care of the most trustworthy of your attendants to guard, by multiplying them against the accidental losses to which they will be exposed. A further guard would be, that one of these copies be on the cuticular membranes of the paper-birch, as less liable to injury from damp than common paper.

The commerce which may be carried on with the people inhabiting the line you will pursue, renders a knowledge of those people important. You will therefore endeavor to make your self acquainted, as far as a diligent pursuit of your journey shall admit, with the names of the nations and their numbers;

The extent and limits of their possessions;
Their relations with other tribes or nations;
Their language, traditions, monuments;
Their ordinary occupations in agriculture, fishing, hunting, war, arts, and the implements for these;
Their food, clothing, and domestic accommodations;
The diseases prevalent among them, and the remedies they use;
Moral and physical circumstances which distinguish them from the tribes we know;
Peculiarities in their laws, customs, and dispositions;
And articles of commerce they may need or furnish, and to what extent.

And, considering the interest which every nation has in extending and strengthening the authority of reason and justice among the people around them, it will be useful to acquire what knowledge you can of the state of morality, religion, and information among them; as it may better enable those who may endeavor to civilize and instruct them, to adapt their measures to the existing notions and practices of those on whom they are to operate.

Other objects worthy of notice will be—The soil and face of the country, its growth and vegetable productions, especially those not of the United States;

The animals of the country generally, and especially those not known in the United States;
The remains and accounts of any which may be deemed rare or extinct;
The mineral productions of every kind, but more particularly metals, limestone, pitcoal, and saltpeter; salines and mineral waters, noting the temperature of the last, and such circumstances as may indicate their character;

Vocabulary
membranes (mem′ branz′) *n.* thin, soft layers serving as coverings or linings

Captain Clark's magnet and compass ▼

6 ☑ Reading Check

What does Jefferson tell Lewis to look for between the heads of the Missouri River and the Pacific Ocean?

Primary Sources: Government Document **247**

247

❼ Background

Secrets of the Expedition

The first paragraph of Jefferson's commission has an unexpected air of secrecy and discretion. Jefferson speaks of a "confidential message to the legislature" and notes that the authorizing act was "expressed in general terms." The discretion was necessary: Jefferson was preparing to explore Louisiana long before he learned that France was willing to sell the region. As originally planned, Lewis would be exploring territory that was not only unknown but also literally foreign.

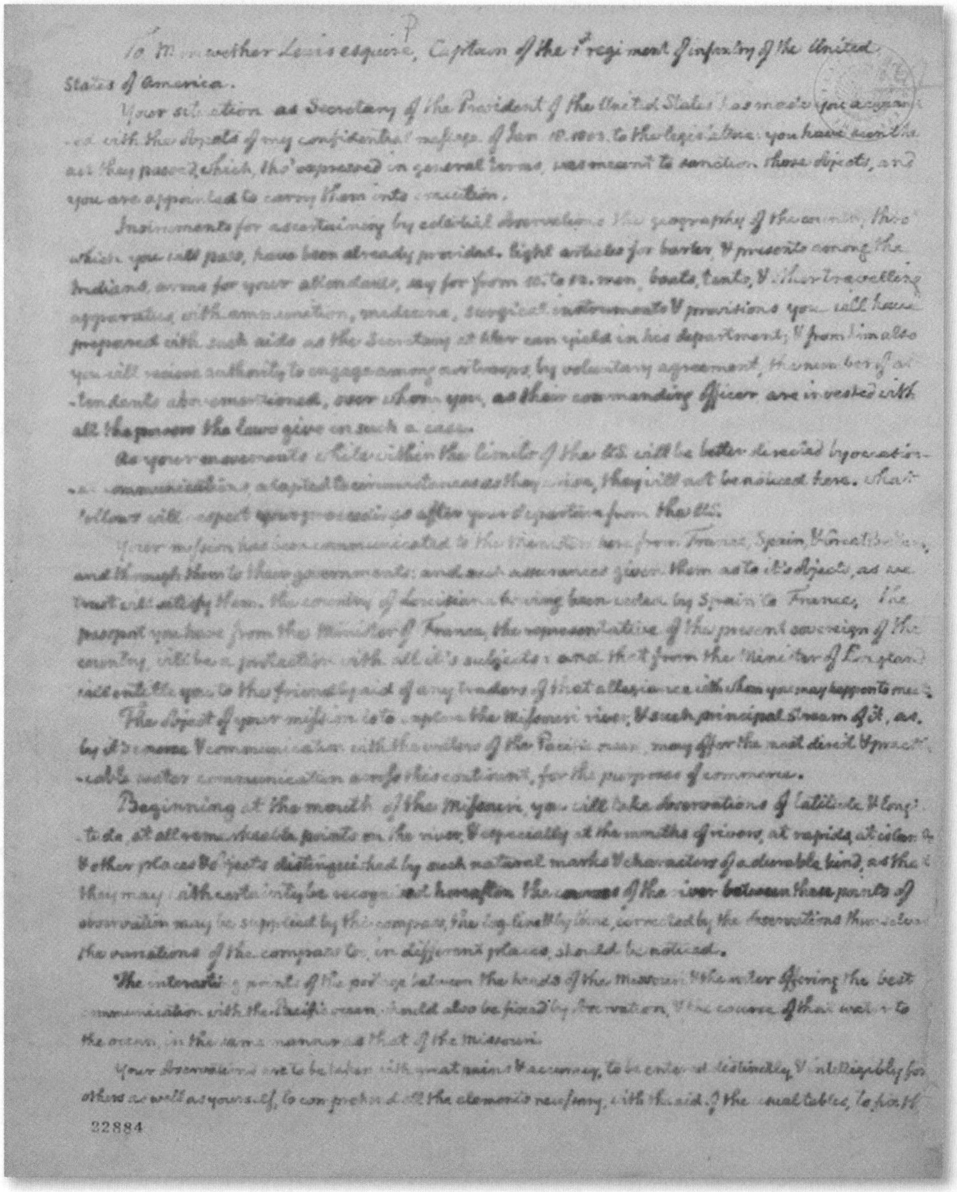

Congress authorized the expedition on February 28, 1803. Lewis began buying supplies in March. France, negotiating with Jefferson's government for the sale of New Orleans, surprised everyone by putting the entire Territory on offer on April 11th. The treaty sealing the deal was signed on May 2, 1803.

On July 4, 1803, the American public—and Meriwether Lewis—learned about the Louisiana Purchase. The next day Lewis left Washington, headed west. By the time the official transfer of power occurred on December 20, 1803, the Corps of Discovery was in winter camp near St. Louis.

❼

To Meriwether Lewis esquire, Captain of the 1st regiment of infantry of the United States of America.

Your situation as Secretary of the President of the United States has made you acquainted with the objects of my confidential message of Jan. 18. 1803. to the legislature; you have seen the act they passed, which, tho' expressed in general terms, was meant to sanction those objects, and you are appointed to carry them into execution.

Instruments for ascertaining by celestial observations the geography of the country thro' which you will pass, have been already provided. light articles for barter, & presents among the Indians, arms for your attendants, say for from 10 to 12 men, boats, tents, & other travelling apparatus, with ammunition, medecine, surgical instruments & provisions you will have prepared with such aids as the Secretary at War can yield in his department; & from him also you will recieve authority to engage among our troops, by voluntary agreement, the number of attendants above mentioned, over whom you, as their commanding officer are invested with all the powers the laws give in such a case.

As your movements while within the limits of the U.S. will be better directed by occasional communications, adapted to circumstances as they arise, they will not be noticed here. what follows will respect your proceedings after your departure from the U.S.

Your mission has been communicated to the Ministers here from France, Spain, & Great Britain, and through them to their governments; and such assurances given them as to it's objects, as we trust will satisfy them. the country of Louisiana having been ceded by Spain to France, the passport you have from the Minister of France, the representative of the present sovereign of the country, will be a protection with all it's subjects: and that from the Minister of England will entitle you to the friendly aid of any traders of that allegiance with whom you may happen to meet.

The object of your mission is to explore the Missouri river, & such principal stream of it, as, by it's course & communication with the waters of the Pacific ocean, may offer the most direct & practicable water communication across this continent, for the purposes of commerce.

Beginning at the mouth of the Missouri, you will take observations of latitude & longitude, at all remarkeable points on the river, & especially at the mouths of rivers, at rapids, at islands, & other places & objects distinguished by such natural marks & characters of a durable kind, as that they may with certainty be recognised hereafter. the courses of the river between these points of observation may be supplied by the compass, the log-line & by time, corrected by the observations themselves. the variations of the compass too, in different places, should be noticed.

The interesting points of the portage between the heads of the Missouri & the water offering the best communication with the Pacific ocean, should also be fixed by observation, & the course of that water to the ocean, in the same manner as that of the Missouri.

Your observations are to be taken with great pains & accuracy, to be entered distinctly, & intelligibly for others as well as yourself, to comprehend all the elements necessary, with the aid of the usual tables, to fix

22884

▲ Shown above is the original letter of commission President Jefferson wrote to Captain Lewis. The clarity of Jefferson's handwriting has been blurred by time.

Volcanic appearances;

Climate, as characterized by the thermo-meter, by the proportion of rainy, cloudy, and clear days; by lightning, hail, snow, ice; by the access and recess of frost; by the winds prevailing at different seasons; the dates at which particular plants put forth, or lose their flower or leaf; times of appearance of particular birds, reptiles or insects....

In all your [dealings] with the natives, treat them in the most friendly and conciliatory manner which their own conduct will admit; allay all jealousies as to the object of your journey; satisfy them of its innocence; make them acquainted with the position, extent, character, peaceable and commercial dispositions of the United States; of our wish to be neighborly, friendly, and useful to them, and of our dispositions to a commercial [relationship] with them; confer with them on the points most convenient as mutual emporiums, and the articles of most desirable interchange for them and us. If a few of their influential chiefs, within practicable distance, wish to visit us, arrange such a visit with them, and furnish them with authority to call on our officers on their entering the United States, to have them conveyed to this place at the public expense. If any of them should wish to have some of their young people brought up with us, and taught such arts as may be useful to them, we will receive, instruct, and take care of them. Such a mission, whether of influential chiefs, or of young people, would give some security to your own party. Carry with you some matter of the kine-pox; inform those of them with whom you may be of its efficacy as a preservative from the small-pox, and instruct and encourage them in the use of it. This may be especially done wherever you winter.

As it is impossible for us to foresee in what manner you will be received by those people, whether with hospitality or hostility, so is it impossible to prescribe the exact degree of perseverance with which you are to pursue your journey. We value too much the lives of citizens to offer them to probable destruction. Your numbers will be sufficient to secure you against the unauthorized opposition of individuals, or of small parties; but if a superior force, authorized, or not authorized, by a nation, should be arrayed against your further passage, and inflexibly determined to arrest it, you must decline its further pursuit and return. In the loss of yourselves we should lose also the information you will have acquired. By returning safely with that, you may enable us to renew the essay with better calculated means. To your own discretion, therefore, must be left the degree of danger you may risk, and the point at which you should decline, only saying, we wish you to err on the side of your safety, and to bring back your party safe, even if it be with less information. . . .

Vocabulary
conciliatory (kən sil′ ē ə tôr′ ē) *adj.* intended to make peace or to reconcile; friendly

Primary Sources
Commission In what ways do Jefferson's instructions to Lewis regarding the native peoples show his official interest in matters of public concern?

Vocabulary
discretion (dis kre′ shən) *n.* judgment

Primary Sources: Government Document **249**

❽ Primary Sources
Commission

1. Before directing students to the bracketed passage, point out that earlier in the commission, Jefferson requires Lewis to gather detailed information about native people he encounters. In this passage, Jefferson gives detailed instructions for relating to native people. **Ask:** Why do you think Jefferson gives such detailed instructions about dealing with native peoples? **Possible response:** Jefferson is aware that in most cases, Lewis will be the first representative of the United States that these people have ever seen, and he wants their initial meetings to be as positive and fruitful as possible.

2. **Ask** the Primary Sources question: In what ways do Jefferson's instructions to Lewis regarding the native peoples show his official interest in matters of public concern? **Possible response:** Students may note that almost all of Jefferson's instructions relate directly to public concern and national interest. He wants to secure peace with the native peoples; he wants them to understand the powers and purposes of the United States; he wants to establish trade relations that will benefit American commerce. To cement strong relationships, Jefferson plans to honor their leaders and to offer education for their children.

❾ Background
Stopping the Expedition

Jefferson's instructions anticipate that "a nation" might attempt to stop the expedition. When a spy informed Spanish officials that Lewis's expedition had set out from St. Louis, they feared that its real objectives were Spanish gold and silver mines in the Southwest. Over a two-year period, New Spain sent out four armed groups to find and capture the Corps of Discovery; none came close.

249

⑩ Background

The Great Divide

The Great Divide, also called the Continental Divide, is the ridge of land separating rivers (such as the Missouri) that flow into the Gulf of Mexico from rivers (such as the Columbia) that flow into the Pacific Ocean. Any hope of a Northwest Passage required that the portage, or land journey, between the Missouri and Columbia rivers be relatively short and easy. At this point in Lewis's journal, he still believes an easy crossing of the Great Divide is possible.

⑪ Humanities

Lewis and Clark With Sacagawea at the Great Falls of the Missouri, Olaf Seltzer

In the spring of 1805, Meriwether Lewis became the first white man to behold the Great Falls. He was suitably impressed—"the grandest sight I ever beheld"—but he also wrote about several difficult events in the vicinity of the falls, including Sacagawea's illness, a dangerous encounter with a grizzly, and a grueling portage around the falls.

Olaf Seltzer portrays Sacagawea with her baby, Captain Clark in uniform, and Captain Lewis in buckskin. The man carrying the rifle is York, the only African American in the Corps of Discovery. Use the following question for discussion:

> If you were Lewis, what sensory details would you include in your description of the Great Falls?

Possible response: Students might include the roaring sound of the falls, the sense of damp mist in the air, and the sight of white water.

⑩ Crossing the GREAT DIVIDE

Meriwether Lewis

⑪

Lewis and Clark With Sacagawea at the Great Falls of the Missouri,
Olaf Seltzer, The Thomas Gilcrease Institute of Art, Tulsa, Oklahoma

250 A Growing Nation (1800–1870)

Enrichment: Investigating a Key Person in History

Sacagawea's Reunion

Lewis's account of August 17, 1805, severely understates one of the most amazing moments of the entire expedition. Lewis is about to negotiate with the Shoshone chief Cameahwait, hoping to obtain enough horses and supplies to complete his journey, when Sacagawea realizes that *Cameahwait is her long-lost brother!* This discovery instantly improves the negotiation's prospects, and Cameahwait provides the expedition with what it needs.

As a girl, Sacagawea had been captured by a Hidatsa war party. At the time she joined the expedition she was about fifteen years old.

Activity: Research Ask students to evaluate the key role Sacagawea played in the success of the expedition. Suggest that students take notes in the **Enrichment: Investigating a Key Person in History** work sheet, in *Professional Development Guidebook,* page 233.

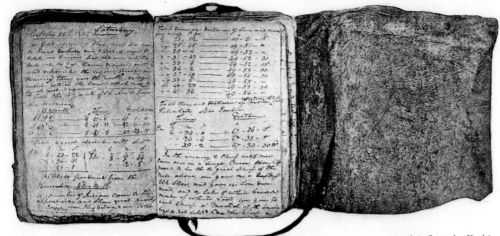

▸▲ Captain Clark's journal is shown here both closed (left) and open (right).

Saturday, August 17th, 1805

This morning I arose very early and dispatched Drewyer and the Indian down the river. Sent Shields to hunt. I made McNeal cook the remainder of our meat which afforded a slight breakfast for ourselves and the Chief. Drewyer had been gone about 2 hours when an Indian who had straggled some little distance down the river returned and reported that the white men were coming, that he had seen them just below. They all appeared transported with joy, and the chief repeated his fraternal hug. I felt quite as much gratified at this information as the Indians appeared to be. Shortly after Capt. Clark arrived with the Interpreter Charbono, and the Indian woman, who proved to be a sister of the Chief Cameahwait. The meeting of those was really affecting, particularly between Sah-ca-ga-we-ah and an Indian woman, who had been taken prisoner at the same time with her, and who had afterwards escaped from the Minnetares and rejoined her nation. At noon the canoes arrived, and we had the satisfaction once more to find ourselves all together, with a flattering prospect of being able to obtain as many horses shortly as would enable us to prosecute our voyage by land should that by water be deemed unadvisable.

Vocabulary
dispatched (di spach'd')
v. sent off, usually on official business

Vocabulary
prospect (pros' spekt)
n. something hoped for or expected

Reading Check
What information does the Indian bring to Lewis and his group?

◀ **Primary Source: Art** What does this painting of Lewis and Clark with Sacagawea suggest about the relationships among the people in it? Does Lewis's journal support the suggestion? **[Infer; Support]**

---

⑫ **Background**

The Negotiation

Chief Cameahwait met Lewis under difficult circumstances. The Shoshone had recently been driven into the mountains by their better-armed enemies, losing tepees and supplies. Lacking food and shelter, they were anxious to get to their buffalo-hunting grounds.

Cameahwait may have hoped to obtain muskets that would improve his people's prospects in hunting and warfare. Lewis, however, had strict instructions from Jefferson against trading firearms.

⑬ **Primary Source: Art**

Possible response: Students may note that the figures in the painting appear to be at ease with one another. The text, which describes the explorers' friendship with and dependence on Native Americans, is reflected in the painting.

⑭ **Reading Check**

Answer: He has seen a small part of their group, including both Captain Clark and his interpreters, on the way back to the main camp.

Differentiated Instruction   for Universal Access

Culturally Responsive Instruction

To engage students' own cultural resources, have small groups of students role-play Lewis and Cameahwait's meeting, employing strategies they would use to strike a bargain with a stranger.

First, review the situation in the text: Lewis needs help if he is to complete his mission; he has much to offer Cameahwait eventually, but little to give immediately. Cameahwait has never met Lewis and has little reason to trust him.

Next have students brainstorm for ways to handle such a meeting, to get along with a stranger, and to get the best deal. Have students meet in small groups to develop their role plays.

After each group role-plays their negotiation, members should briefly discuss the bargaining tactics they used. When all groups have presented, have the class compare the tactics used in role-playing with the actual exchange reported in Lewis's field report.

⓯ Primary Source: Art

Answer: The size of the sketch suggests that Clark wished to make the image large enough to show details. The placement of the image inside the field report's text reveals that he needed to use each piece of paper completely—he could not obtain more until he returned to the East.

⓰ Reading Strategy

Identifying the Writer's Purpose

1. As a class, return to Jefferson's commission to review his instructions about how Lewis was to treat native peoples. As students list specific details, write them on the board.

2. Then have students review the bracketed passage. **Ask** the Reading Strategy question: Which of Lewis's specific purposes for writing are evident in this paragraph?
Possible response: Lewis's specific purpose in this passage is to show that he was faithfully following Jefferson's instructions regarding contact with native peoples.

3. Finally, **ask** students if they believe Jefferson would have been satisfied with Lewis's treatment of Cameahwait and his people.
Possible response: Students may agree that Jefferson would have approved of Lewis's performance. Lewis has treated Cameahwait and his people with care and dignity, giving them food and creating shade for them to sit in. He tells them of the strength and friendliness of his own government, points out to Cameahwait's people the positive benefits of his mission, and echoes Jefferson's emphasis on the mutual value of trade and commerce.

© **COMMON CORE • RESEARCH PROJECT**

⓯ ▲ **Primary Source: Art** What do the placement and size of these sketches in William Clark's journal reveal about his purpose in making them? **[Interpret]**

Reading Strategy
Identifying Writer's Purpose Which of Lewis's specific purposes for writing are evident in this paragraph?

Vocabulary
conspicuous (kən spik′ yōō əs) *adj.* obvious; easy to see or perceive

We now formed our camp just below the junction of the forks on the Lard. side[1] in a level smooth bottom covered with a fine turf of greensward. Here we unloaded our canoes and arranged our baggage on shore; formed a canopy of one of our large sails and planted some willow brush in the ground to form a shade for the Indians to sit under while we spoke to them, which we thought it best to do this evening. Accordingly about 4 P.M. we called them together and through the medium of Labuish, Charbono and Sah-ca-ga-we-ah, we communicated to them fully the objects which had brought us into this distant part of the country, in which we took care to make them a **conspicuous** object of our own good wishes and the care of our government.

---

1. **Lard. side** abbreviation for larboard, the port side of a ship. From their perspective, they camped on the left side of the river.

252 A Growing Nation (1800–1870)

Enrichment: Investigating Geography

A Desperate Crossing

After being supplied by Cameahwait, the expedition set off to cross the Great Divide and connect to the Columbia River system. What they discovered and endured over the next few weeks killed any hope of a Northwest Passage. The distance between the Missouri and the Columbia rivers was no portage, but a gap of three hundred and forty miles, much of it rugged mountain terrain. Half-lost, exhausted, and near starvation, the expedition might have collapsed entirely but for a fortunate encounter with a band of Nez Percé, who supplied the exploring party with sufficient food and guidance to get them over the divide.

Activity: Map-Making Ask students to make a map tracing the expedition's route from the meeting with Cameahwait to the Pacific coast. Tell students to be sure to include details about the terrain the expedition encountered, making notes in the **Enrichment: Investigating Geography** work sheet, in *Professional Development Guidebook,* page 228.

We made them sensible of their dependence on the will of our government for every species of merchandise as well for their defense and comfort; and apprised them of the strength of our government and its friendly dispositions towards them. We also gave them as a reason why we wished to penetrate the country as far as the ocean to the west of them was to examine and find out a more direct way to bring merchandise to them. That as no trade could be carried on with them before our return to our homes that it was mutually advantageous to them as well as to ourselves that they should render us such aids as they had it in their power to furnish in order to hasten our voyage and of course our return home.

Sextant used for celestial navigation by the expedition ▶

⓱ ▲ Primary Source: Art
Why do you think Clark used less detail in these sketches than in his drawings of plants and animals? **[Infer]**

Critical Reading

Cite textual evidence to support your responses.

Ⓒ 1. Key Ideas and Details (a) In the Commission, what information did Jefferson tell Lewis to write out in multiple copies? **(b)** To what office of the government was Lewis instructed to render these copies? **(c) Infer:** What do these instructions suggest about the importance of this information to Jefferson and the United States government? Explain.

Ⓒ 2. Key Ideas and Details (a) In his report, how did Lewis feel about being reunited with his party? **(b) Analyze:** What are his reasons for feeling as he did?

Ⓒ 3. Key Ideas and Details (a) Note two tasks that Jefferson instructed Lewis to perform. **(b) Evaluate:** Judging from this excerpt, how well do you think Lewis fulfilled his assignment?

Ⓒ 4. Integration of Knowledge and Ideas (a) What did Lewis tell the Indians to expect from the United States government? **(b) Speculate:** In what ways does his dialogue with the Indians reflect specific instructions from Jefferson?

⓱ Primary Source: Art

Possible response: In his drawings of plants and animals, Clark was presenting discoveries new to science; each detail of the drawings was scientifically important. The simple sketches in this drawing are sufficient for their purposes: to show a device or the profile of a head.

ASSESS

Answers

1. (a) Jefferson wants multiple copies of Lewis's observations of latitude and longitude. (b) Copies were to be sent to the war office. (c) **Possible response:** The instructions suggest that the information is vital both to the military for defense of the new territory and to the government for establishing legal claims.

2. (a) Lewis is pleased and relieved. (b) He now has hopes of obtaining enough horses to continue.

3. (a) Students may note that Lewis is to form an exploring team to explore the Missouri River, seeking a water route across the continent; to record latitudes and longitudes; to record data about soils, minerals, plants, animals, and weather; and to establish friendly relations with native peoples. (b) Students may agree that the excerpt demonstrates that Lewis is fulfilling his assignment. His negotiation with Cameahwait shows that he is attentive to Jefferson's expectations.

4. (a) He told them to expect merchandise, defense, and "comfort." (b) Lewis's conduct with Cameahwait reflects the commission's requirement that he be friendly; that he explain the purpose of his journey; and that he describe the peaceful intentions of the United States government.

Comparing Primary Sources

1. (a) Jefferson addresses Lewis by formal rank and title. He cites the official act that authorizes Lewis's mission. (b) Lewis is writing as an official.

2. (a) **Sample answer:** Jefferson statement: "Carry with you some matter of the kine-pox"; Life: People knew the dangers of smallpox and had a means of prevention. (b) **Possible response:** Students may learn more from the commission, due to its range of subjects and detailed explanations.

3. (a) **Sample answer:** Jefferson wants to establish trade. (b) Lewis promotes trade in his talks with Cameahwait.

4. (a) **Possible response:** Similarities: focus on diplomatic and commercial issues. Differences: Lewis does not touch on exploration, mapping, or studies of animal life. (b) Differences are explained by the limited scope of the Lewis document.

Vocabulary Acquisition and Use

1. The <u>conspicuous</u> way he shows off his new wealth shows that he lacks <u>discretion</u>.

2. As the village faced the <u>prospect</u> of starvation, the chief <u>dispatched</u> messengers for help.

3. To allow defeated soldiers to keep weapons would be a <u>conciliatory</u> gesture, but not a <u>practicable</u> way of ending the war.

4. As one who studies the stars, an astronomer would be more interested in <u>celestial</u> bodies than would a biologist.

5. No, a city cannot change its <u>latitude</u>, its distance from the equator.

6. Yes, <u>longitude</u>, one's east-west position on the earth or ocean, is important to a sailor.

7. No, bark does not have the thin, soft qualities of a <u>membrane</u>.

8. No, <u>minerals</u> do not grow, breathe, or reproduce.

Etymology Study The root of *terrestrial* is *terra*, the Latin word for "earth." The adjective *terrestrial* means "having to do with the earth; of the earth." Words that share the same root include *terrace, territory,* and *terrain*.

254

Government Document • Field Report

Comparing Primary Sources

Refer to your Note-Taking Guide to complete these questions.

1. **(a)** Find two details from the commission that show Jefferson is writing as a government official, not a private person. **(b)** In this excerpt, is Lewis writing from an official or a personal perspective? Explain.

2. **(a)** Using a chart like the one shown, identify one statement from each document and explain what it shows about life in the early 1800s. **(b)** From which document do you learn more? Explain.

Author	Statement	Life in early 1800s
Jefferson		
Lewis		

3. **(a)** Note one fact you learn from the commission about Jefferson's reasons for exploring the new lands. **(b)** Locate one statement in Lewis's report that *verifies or clarifies* that fact. Explain your choice.

4. **(a)** Identify two similarities and two differences in how these documents describe the Lewis and Clark expedition. **(b)** Explain the reasons for these similarities and differences.

© Vocabulary Acquisition and Use

Use New Words Correctly For each word pair, write a sentence in which you use both words correctly.

1. conspicuous/discretion
2. prospect/dispatched
3. conciliatory/practicable

Content-Area Vocabulary Answer each question. Then, explain your reasoning.

4. Would an astronomer or a biologist be more interested in *celestial* bodies?
5. Can a city change its *latitude*?
6. Would a sailor be concerned about *longitude*?
7. Would the outer bark of a tree be considered a *membrane*?
8. Can a *mineral* be a living organism?

Etymology Study The word *celestial* comes from the Latin word *caelestis,* which means "heaven" or "sky." It often appears in opposition to the word *terrestrial*. Research the history of the word *terrestrial,* locate its root, and write a definition. Then, identify two other words that share the same root.

© Common Core State Standards

Writing

7. Conduct short as well as more sustained research projects to answer a question or solve a problem; narrow or broaden the inquiry when appropriate; synthesize multiple sources on the subject, demonstrating understanding of the subject under investigation. *(p. 255)*

8. Gather relevant information from multiple authoritative print and digital sources, using advanced searches effectively; assess the strengths and limitations of each source in terms of the task, purpose, and audience; integrate information into the text selectively to maintain the flow of ideas, avoiding plagiarism and overreliance on any one source and following a standard format for citation. *(p. 255)*

Assessment Practice

Make Inferences and Generalizations (For more practice, see *All-in-One Workbook*.)

Many tests ask students to make inferences about implied information. Use this sample test item.

Why does Lewis emphasize the U.S. government's "friendly disposition" toward the Native Americans in his meeting with them?

A He wants them to help his expedition.

B He wants to join their community.

C He wants them to join the United States.

D He wants to take their land.

Choices **B, C,** and **D** are not supported by the passage. Lewis explains that if the Native Americans help the explorers reach the Pacific Ocean and then return home, the government will provide them with many benefits. Thus, choice **A** is correct.

Research Task

Topic: The Life of Sacagawea

Sacagawea, the Shoshone woman who traveled with Lewis and Clark, was an invaluable source of help and information to the explorers. While some parts of Sacagawea's life are well documented, there is scarce and sometimes conflicting information about other periods of her life. She is, therefore, an intriguing topic for research.

Assignment: Write a biographical narrative designed as a **book for young readers** on the life of Sacagawea. As you research, differentiate between the theories about Sacagawea and the evidence that supports them. Determine the quality of the evidence you find for each theory in order to decide whether to include that information in your narrative.

Formulate a research plan. Working alone or in a group, formulate questions, such as the following, to answer through research:

- What are the basic facts of Sacagawea's life?
- What did she do on the Lewis and Clark expedition?
- What happened to her after the expedition?
- How does the popular cultural view of Sacagawea differ from the provable facts?

Gather sources. Use online and library sources to follow your research plan and find answers to your questions. Collect the information in a systematic way, grouping items about Sacagawea in categories such as "Family," "Accomplishments," and "Personal Qualities."

Synthesize information. When you synthesize information, you evaluate, assemble, and combine it in order to create a cogent argument—in this case, a reliable biography. Use a graphic organizer like the one shown to differentiate between theories about Sacagawea and the weak or strong evidence that supports them.

Model: Differentiating Between Theories and Evidence

Theory	**Evidence**	**Evaluation of Evidence**
Sacagawea was calm and brave under pressure.	Personal diaries of members of the expedition agree.	Strong, reliable first-hand evidence from multiple sources.

Organize and present ideas. As you write, remember that you are addressing young readers. This means you may use shorter sentences and easier vocabulary and should plan to include useful visuals. However, a narrative for young readers should never be so simplified that it becomes incorrect or misleading. Make sure your facts are accurate according to the best sources. Include a Works Cited list in which you cite your sources, both print and electronic, correctly. (For more information on correct citations, see page R21 in this textbook.)

> **RESEARCH TIP**
> Pay careful attention to sources of online information. A Web site administered by a university or a recognized scholar is likely to be more reliable than one sponsored by a blogger, a club, a commercial company, or a popular media outlet.

Use a checklist like the one shown to be sure your research results in a reliable biographical narrative.

> **Research Checklist**
> ☐ Have I answered all my research questions?
> ☐ Have I differentiated between theories and evidence?
> ☐ Have I included strong evidence throughout?
> ☐ Do my visuals adequately illustrate the narrative?

Research Task **255**

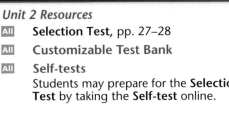

The Song of Hiawatha • The Tide Rises, The Tide Falls • Thanatopsis • Old Ironsides
Lesson Pacing Guide

DAY 1 Preteach

- © Administer the Reading and Vocabulary Warm-ups (*Unit 2 Resources*, pp. 29–32) as necessary.
- © Introduce the Literary Analysis concepts: Meter.
- • Introduce the Reading Strategy: Summarize.
- © Build background with the author and Background features.
- • Develop thematic thinking with Connecting to the Essential Question.
- © Teach the selection vocabulary.

DAY 2 Preteach/Teach/Extend

- • Distribute copies of the appropriate graphic organizer for the Reading Strategy (*Graphic Organizer Transparencies*, pp. 60–61).
- • Distribute copies of the appropriate graphic organizer for Literary Analysis (*Graphic Organizer Transparencies*, pp.62–63).
- • Prepare students to read with the Activating Prior Knowledge activities (TE).
- • Informally monitor comprehension while students read.
- • Use the Reading Check question to confirm comprehension.
- © Develop students' understanding of meter using the Literary Analysis prompts.
- • Develop students' ability to summarize using the Reading Strategy prompts.
- © Reinforce vocabulary with the Vocabulary notes.
- • Assess students' comprehension and mastery of the skills by having them answer the Critical Reading, Literary Analysis, and Reading Strategy questions.

DAY 3 Assess

- © Have students complete the Vocabulary activities.
- © Have students complete the Writing lesson and write o compare literary works. (You may assign as homework.)
- • Administer Selection Test A or B (*Unit 2 Resources,* pp. 41–43 or 44–46).

© Common Core State Standards

Reading Literature 2. Determine two or more themes or central ideas of a text and analyze their development over the course of the text, including how they interact and build on one another to produce a complex account; provide an objective summary of the text.
5. Analyze how an author's choices concerning how to structure specific parts of a text contribute to its overall structure and meaning as well as its aesthetic impact.

Writing 2. Write informative texts to examine and convey complex ideas, concepts, and information clearly and accurately through the effective selection, organization, andanalysis of content.

Language 5. Demonstrate understanding of word relationships.

Additional Standards Practice
Common Core Companion, pp. 15–22; 54–55; 196–207; 332–335

Daily Block Scheduling
Each day in this Lesson Pacing Guide represents a 40–50 minute period. Teachers using block scheduling may combine days to revise pacing. In addition, teachers may differentiate and support core instruction by integrating components for extended and intensive support as students require. See the Guide to Selected Leveled Resources (facing page).

Guide to Selected Leveled Resources

R T I Tier 1 (students performing on level)

from The Song of Hiawatha • The Tide Rises, The Tide Falls • Thanatopsis • Old Ironsides

Warm Up	Practice, **model**, and **monitor** fluency, working **with the whole class** or **in groups**.	Vocabulary and Reading Warm-ups B, *Unit 2 Resources,* pp. 29–30, 32
Comprehension/Skills	**Support** and **monitor** comprehension and skills development, having students complete the activities, graphic organizers, and interactive prompts **independently** or **as a class**.	• *Reader's Notebook,* adapted instruction and summary **EL** *Reader's Notebook: English Learner's Version,* adapted instruction and summary • **Reading Strategy Graphic Organizer B,** *Graphic Organizer Transparencies,* p. 61 • **Literary Analysis Graphic Organizer B,** *Graphic Organizer Transparencies,* p. 63
Monitor Progress	**Monitor** student progress with the differentiated curriculum-based assessment in the *Unit Resources.*	• **Selection Test B,** *Unit 2 Resources,* pp. 44–46 • **Open-Book Test,** *Unit 2 Resources,* pp. 38–40

R T I Tier 2 (students requiring intervention)

from The Song of Hiawatha • The Tide Rises, The Tide Falls • Thanatopsis • Old Ironsides

Warm Up	Practice, **model,** and **monitor** fluency **in groups** or **with individuals**.	• *Vocabulary and Reading Warm-ups A, Unit 1 Resources,* pp. 29–31 • *Hear It!* Audio CD
Comprehension/Skills	• **Support** and **monitor** comprehension and skills development, working **in small groups** or **with individuals**. • As students complete the selection in the appropriate version of the *Reader's Notebook,* **monitor** comprehension frequently with group questions and individual instruction. • **Model** strategies while guiding students in completing the activities and prompts in the *Reader's Notebook,* as well as the graphic organizers. • **Practice** skills and **monitor** mastery with the *Reading Kit* worksheets.	• *Reader's Notebook: Adapted Version,* adapted instruction and summary **EL** *Reader's Notebook: English Learner's Version,* adapted instruction and summary • **Reading Strategy Graphic Organizer A,** *Graphic Organizer Transparencies,* p. 60 • **Literary Analysis Graphic Organizer A,** *Graphic Organizer Transparencies,* p. 62 • *Reading Kit,* Practice worksheets
Monitor Progress	**Monitor** student progress with the differentiated curriculum-based assessment in the *Unit Resources* and in the *Reading Kit.*	• **Selection Test A,** *Unit 2 Resources,* pp. 41–43 • *Reading Kit,* Assess worksheets

TIER 3 Tier 3 intervention may require consultation with the student's special education or dyslexia specialist For additional support, see the Tier 2 activities and resources listed above.

One-on-one teaching   Group work   Whole class instruction   Independent work   Assessment

For a complete guide to selection support, including support for Advanced students, see the Overview of Resources in the frontmatter.

from The Song of Hiawatha
• The Tide Rises, The Tide Falls
• Thanatopsis • Old Ironsides

RESOURCES FOR:

- **L1** Special-Needs Students
- **L2** Below-Level Students (Tier 2)
- **L3** On-Level Students (Tier 1)
- **L4** Advanced Students (Tier 1)
- **EL** English Learners
- **All** All Students

Vocabulary/Fluency/Prior Knowledge

EL L1 L2 Reading Warm-ups A and B, pp. 31–32

Also available for these selections:

EL L1 L2 Vocabulary Warm-ups A and B, pp. 29–30

All Vocabulary Builder, p. 35

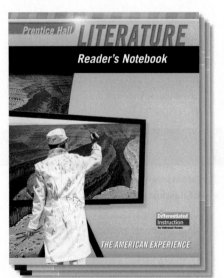

Reader's Notebooks

Pre- and postreading pages for these selections appear in an interactive format in the *Reader's Notebooks.* Each *Notebook* is differentiated for a different group of learners. The selections in the Adapted and English Learner's versions are abridged.

- **L2 L3** *Reader's Notebook*
- **L1** *Reader's Notebook: Adapted Version*
- **EL** *Reader's Notebook: English Learner's Version*
- **EL** *Reader's Notebook: Spanish Version*

© *Common Core Companion*

Additional instruction and practice for each Common Core State Standard

Graphic Organizer Transparencies

from *The Song of Hiawatha* and "The Tide Rises, The Tide Falls"
by Henry Wadsworth Longfellow
"Thanatopsis" by William Cullen Bryant
"Old Ironsides" by Oliver Wendell Holmes

Before You Read B: Summarizing

Key Details of *Hiawatha*	Key Details of "Thanatopsis"
Stanza __:	Stanza __:
Stanza __:	Stanza __:
Stanza __:	Stanza __:
Stanza __:	Stanza __:

Summary	Summary

Key Details of "The Tide"	Key Details of "Old Ironsides"
Stanza __:	Stanza __:
Stanza __:	Stanza __:
Stanza __:	Stanza __:

Summary	Summary

EL L3 Reading: Graphic Organizer B, p. 61

Also available for these selections:

EL L1 L2 Reading: Graphic Organizer A,
(partially filled in), p. 60

EL L1 L2 Literary Analysis: Graphic Organizer A,
(partially filled in), p. 62

EL L3 Literary Analysis: Graphic Organizer B,
p. 63

Unit 2 Resources

Name _____ Date _____

from "The Song of Hiawatha" and "The Tide Rises, The Tide Falls"
by Henry Wadsworth Longfellow
"Thanatopsis" by William Cullen Bryant
"Old Ironsides" by Oliver Wendell Holmes

Literary Analysis: Meter

The **meter** of a poem is the rhythmic pattern created by the arrangement of stressed and unstressed syllables. The basic unit of meter is the **foot**, which usually consists of one stressed syllable and one or more unstressed syllables. The most common foot in English-language poetry is the **iamb**, an unstressed syllable followed by a stressed syllable, as in the word *today*.

The type and number of feet per line determine the poem's meter. For example, a pattern of three iambs per line is called **iambic trimeter**; four iambs per line, **iambic tetrameter**; five iambs per line, **iambic pentameter**. The process of analyzing a poem's meter is called **scansion**, or **scanning** the poem. Here are examples of scanned lines.

| **Iambic tetrameter:** | Beneath it rung the battle shout |
| **Iambic pentameter:** | To him who in the love of Nature holds |

DIRECTIONS: *Scan the following stanza of "Old Ironsides" by marking the stressed and unstressed syllables. Then, describe the metrical pattern of the poem on these lines:*

_____

_____

Oh, better that her shattered hulk

Should sink beneath the wave;

Her thunders shook the mighty deep,

And there should be her grave;

Nail to the mast her holy flag,

Set every threadbare sail,

And give her to the god of storms,

The lightning and the gale!

All Literary Analysis: Meter, p. 33

Also available for these selections:

All Reading Summarizing to Repair Comprehension, p. 34

EL L3 L4 Support for Writing, p. 36

L4 Enrichment, p. 37

Name _____ Date _____

from "The Song of Hiawatha" and "The Tide Rises,
The Tide Falls" by Henry Wadsworth Longfellow
"Thanatopsis" by William Cullen Bryant
"Old Ironsides" by Oliver Wendell Holmes

Selection Test B

Critical Reading *Identify the letter of the choice that best completes the statement or answers the question.*

___ 1. In line 1 of the prologue to "The Song of Hiawatha," what is the meaning of the question "whence these stories"?
A. "When will you tell us these stories?"
B. "Why should I tell you these stories?"
C. "Where did these stories come from?"
D. "Are these stories fact or fiction?"

___ 2. Longfellow believes that Native American tales derive their power from what source?
A. the skill of the storytellers, who are clever at plot and characterization
B. nature itself, whose spirit is expressed in native peoples and their cultures
C. great deeds of warfare, conquest, and nobility
D. Europe, where Longfellow learned about myths and folk tales

___ 3. The title "Thanatopsis" means
A. a vision of death.
B. the process of decaying.
C. a metamorphosis or transformation.
D. a feeling of euphoria or well-being.

___ 4. According to the speaker in "Thanatopsis," what will happen to him after death?
A. His soul will go to heaven.
B. His spirit will cease to exist.
C. His body will be preserved in the earth.
D. His body will become part of nature.

___ 5. Bryant's line "Shall send his roots abroad, and pierce thy mold" is an example of iambic ___.
A. trimeter
B. tetrameter
C. pentameter
D. hexameter

___ 6. "Old Ironsides" was the nickname of
A. the *U.S.S. Constitution*, a War of 1812 battleship.
B. the *Clermont*, an early steamship.
C. the *Titanic*, a famous luxury liner.
D. Oliver Wendell Holmes.

EL L3 L4 Selection Test B, pp. 44–46

Also available for these selections:

L3 L4 Open-Book Test, pp. 38–40

EL L1 L2 Selection Test A, pp. 41–43

PHLit Online!
www.PHLitOnline.com

Online Resources: All print materials are also available online.

- complete narrated selection text
- a thematically related video with writing prompt
- an interactive graphic organizer
- highlighting feature
- access to all student print resources, adapted to individual student needs
- Spanish and English summaries
- adapted selection translations in Spanish

Get Connected! (thematic video with writing prompt)

Also available:

Background Video
All videos are available in Spanish.

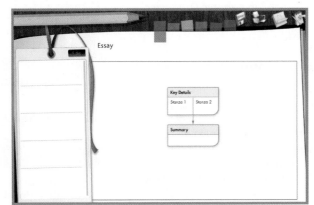

Writer's Journal (with graphics feature)

Also available:

Vocabulary Central (tools and activities for studying vocabulary)

① ❓ Connecting to the Essential Question

1. Review the assignment.

2. Ask students who deserves the label "American hero." Have students complete the assignment.

3. As students read, have them notice the praise of American people and places.

② Literary Analysis

Introduce the skills, using the instruction on the student page.

Think Aloud: Model the Skill

Say to students:

In a poem, meter can vary a bit from line to line. Here are the first lines of "Paul Revere's Ride"; watch my finger point for each stressed syllable:

Listen, my children, and you shall hear

Of the midnight ride of Paul Revere,

On the eighteenth of April in seventy-five;

Some listeners say that the meter reminds them of hoof beats and excitement.

③ Reading Strategy

1. Introduce the strategy.

2. Give students a copy of **Reading Strategy Graphic Organizer B**, page 61 in *Graphic Organizer Transparencies,* to fill out as they read.

Think Aloud: Model the Skill

Say to students:

A summary is a brief version in your own words of what you read. It includes *both* the main ideas *and* details. I can summarize the lines in "Paul Revere's Ride" by saying, "The speaker will report the historical event of April 18, 1775."

④ Vocabulary

1. Pronounce each word, giving its definition, and have students say it aloud.

2. See also the *Classroom Strategies and Teaching Routines* card for introducing vocabulary.

Before You Read

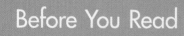

from *The Song of Hiawatha* •
The Tide Rises, The Tide Falls •
Thanatopsis • Old Ironsides

① **Connecting to the Essential Question** The Fireside Poets' work helped to create a mythology of early American heroes. As you read, notice details that praise or celebrate American settings or characters. This will help as you consider the Essential Question: **What makes American literature American?**

② ## Literary Analysis

In poetry, the systematic arrangement of stressed (´) and unstressed (ˇ) syllables is called **meter.** The basic unit of meter is the **foot,** which usually consists of one stressed and one or more unstressed syllables. The most frequently used foot in American verse is the *iamb*—one unstressed syllable followed by a stressed syllable. The type and number of feet in the lines of a poem determine its meter. For example, a pattern of five iambs per line is known as *iambic pentameter,* as in this line from Bryant's "Thanatopsis":

> The youth in life's green spring, and he who goes

In "The Song of Hiawatha," Longfellow uses the *trochee*, a stressed syllable followed by an unstressed syllable. This line has four trochees, a meter called *trochaic tetrameter*:

> Ye who love the haunts of Nature

Comparing Literary Works The meter of a poem can affect the **mood,** or emotional quality, it evokes in a reader. Meter can also contribute to a poem's meaning. For example, the drum-like rhythm of the trochees in "The Song of Hiawatha" reflects the Native American subject and adds to the poem's intensity. To better hear and understand these metered poems, read them aloud, listening for patterns. Identify the meter and compare the moods each helps to evoke. For each poem, consider how the meter contributes to the work's overall meaning.

③ ## Reading Strategy

© **Preparing to Read Complex Texts** To check your understanding of what you have read, **summarize** the work or parts of the work by briefly stating the main ideas and supporting details in your own words. As you read, use a graphic organizer like the one shown to summarize each poem.

④ ## Vocabulary

efface (ə fās´) *v.* erase, wipe out (p. 260)

eloquence (el´ ə kwəns) *n.* expressiveness (p. 262)

pensive (pen´ siv) *adj.* expressing deep thoughtfulness (p. 263)

venerable (ven´ ər ə bəl) *adj.* worthy of respect (p. 263)

© **Common Core State Standards**

Reading Literature
5. Analyze how an author's choices concerning how to structure specific parts of a text contribute to its overall structure and meaning as well as its aesthetic impact.

Key Details	
Stanza 1	Stanza 2

Summary

www.PHLitOnline.com

Vocabulary Development

Vocabulary Knowledge Rating

Create a **Vocabulary Knowledge Rating Chart** (*Professional Development Guidebook*, p. 33) for the vocabulary words on the student page. Give each student a copy of the chart with the words on it. Read the words aloud, and have students mark their rating in the Before Reading column. Urge students to attend to these words as they read and discuss the selections, because they will rate their knowledge of the words again after they finish reading.

In order to gauge how much instruction you need to provide, tally how many students know (or think they know) a word before reading. As students read, point out the words and their context.

Vocabulary Central, featuring tools and activities for studying vocabulary, is available online at **www.PHLitOnline.com.**

5 Henry Wadsworth Longfellow (1807–1882)

Author of "The Song of Hiawatha"; "The Tide Rises, The Tide Falls"

Henry Wadsworth Longfellow enjoyed a long and successful career as a poet, publishing his first collection of poems, *Voices in the Night,* in 1839. By writing poetry that soothed and encouraged readers, Longfellow became the first American poet to reach a wide audience and create a national interest in poetry. His popular anthology *The Poets and Poetry of Europe,* published in 1845, accomplished his goal of bringing non-English poetry to the ordinary American reader.

Born and raised in Portland, Maine, Longfellow graduated from Bowdoin College and went on to teach modern languages at Harvard University for eighteen years, often writing and publishing his own textbooks for his classes. He also translated foreign literature into English, finding in foreign poetry inspirational models for his own work.

Longfellow experimented with adapting traditional European verse forms and themes to uniquely American subjects. Many of his narrative poems, such as "The Song of Hiawatha" (1855), "The Courtship of Miles Standish" (1858), and "Paul Revere's Ride" (1860), gave a romanticized view of America's early history and democratic ideals.

The Poet's Legacy Longfellow's poetry has been criticized for being overly optimistic and sentimental. Yet it was his optimism and sentimentality that made Longfellow the most popular poet of his day. In fact, Longfellow was so popular in his time that his seventy-fifth birthday was celebrated as if it were a national holiday.

"Talk not of wasted affection; affection never was wasted."

Daily Bellringer

For each class during which you will teach these selections, have students complete one of the five activities for the appropriate week in the ***Daily Bellringer Activities*** booklet.

Multidraft Reading

To assist struggling readers and to deepen the reading experience for all, apply multidraft reading protocols. For each reading, have students set the purpose indicated:

- **First reading**—identifying key ideas and details and answering any Reading Checks.
- **Second reading**—analyzing craft and structure and responding to the side-column prompts.
- **Third reading**—integrating knowledge and ideas, connecting to other texts and the world, and answering the end-of-selection questions.

For more guidance, refer to the ***Classroom Strategies and Teaching Routines*** card, **Multidraft Reading.**

5 Background

More About the Author

Longfellow showed his literary promise early. He published his first poem when he was only thirteen and entered Bowdoin College at age fifteen. In a letter written from college to his father, Longfellow declared his wish to spend his life writing.

Longfellow's childhood home in Portland, Maine, was located at the seashore. Perhaps this fact explains the poet's lifelong knowledge of and interest in the sea. "The Tide Rises, The Tide Falls" (p. 260) is only one of several poems Longfellow wrote about the sea.

PHLit Online! www.PHLitOnline.com

Teaching From Technology

Preparing to Read

Go to **www.PHLitOnline.com** in class or in a lab and display the Get Connected! slide show for these selections. Have the class brainstorm for responses to the slide show writing prompt, entering ideas in the interactive journal. Then have students complete their written responses individually in a lab or as homework.

To build background, display the Background and More About the Author features.

Using the Interactive Text

Go to **www.PHLitOnline.com** and display the **Enriched Online Student Edition.** As the class reads the selections or listens to the narration, record answers to side-column prompts using the graphic organizers accessible on the interactive page. Alternatively, have students use the online edition individually, answering the prompts as they read.

❶ About the Selection

The prologue to "The Song of Hiawatha" sets the stage by defending the authority of the poem proper.

❷ Activating Prior Knowledge

Have some students bring in a recording or lyrics of a contemporary song that has special meaning to them. Ask volunteers to share and discuss their songs.

Explain to students that the poets whose work they are about to read popularized poetry as family entertainment. The poems express the values, emotions, and concerns of those who lived in America in the nineteenth century.

❸ Reading Strategy

Summarizing

1. Remind students that a summary must be in a reader's own words.

2. **Ask** students to respond to the Reading Strategy prompt: In two sentences, summarize the question and answer in lines 1–20. **Possible response:** The speaker asks, "What is the source of these sense-tingling legends?" The source is the region itself.

Reading Strategy
Summarizing In two sentences, summarize the question and answer in lines 1–20.

❶ from
❷ *The Song of*
HIAWATHA
Henry Wadsworth Longfellow

BACKGROUND "The Song of Hiawatha" is a long narrative poem based on a legend of the Ojibway, a Native American people of the Great Lakes region. Hiawatha was actually an Iroquois chief who joined with Dekanawidah (page 41) in efforts to unite the Iroquois people. In the Ojibway version, Hiawatha takes on godlike, heroic qualities. Published in 1855, Longfellow's famous poem contains over twenty sections recounting Hiawatha's adventures. The following lines are from the prologue, or introduction, to the poem.

Prologue

Should you ask me, whence these stories?
Whence these legends and traditions,
With the odours of the forest,
With the dew and damp of meadows,
5   With the curling smoke of wigwams,
With the rushing of great rivers,
With their frequent repetitions,
And their wild reverberations,
As of thunder in the mountains?

❸

10   I should answer, I should tell you:
`From the forests and the prairies,
From the great lakes of the Northland,
From the land of the Ojibways,
From the land of the Dacotahs,[1]
15   From the mountains, moors, and fenlands,[2]
Where the heron, the Shuh-shuh-gah,[3]
Feeds among the reeds and rushes,
I repeat them as I heard them
From the lips of Nawadaha,
20   The musician, the sweet singer.'

---

1. **Dacotahs** *n.* a Native American people living near the Ojibway; usually spelled *Dakotas*. Minniehaha, Hiawatha's wife in Longfellow's poem, is Dacotah.
2. **moors . . . fenlands** swampy areas.
3. **Shuh-shuh-gah** Longfellow's attempt to spell the Ojibway word for the great blue heron, a large water bird.

258 A Growing Nation (1800–1870)

© Text Complexity Rubric

	from The Song of Hiawatha	The Tide Rises, the Tide Falls	Thanatopsis	Old Ironsides
Qualitative Measures				
Context/ Knowledge Demands	Retelling of legend 1 2 ③ 4 5	Early-American romantic poem 1 ② 3 4 5	Focus on death and nature 1 2 ③ 4 5	Famous poem about warship 1 2 ③ 4 5
Structure/Language Conventionality and Clarity	Poetic syntax; vocabulary 1 2 ③ 4 5	Accessible 1 ② 3 4 5	Poetic diction and syntax; some challenging vocabulary 1 2 3 ④ 5	Declamatory 1 2 ③ 4 5
Levels of Meaning/ Purpose/Concepts	Accessible (setting of poem) 1 ② 3 4 5	Accessible (metaphors) 1 2 ③ 4 5	Challenging (death) 1 2 3 ④ 5	Accessible (plea for ship) 1 ② 3 4 5
Quantitative Measures				
Lexile/Text Length	NP / 238 words	NP / 101 words	NP / 635 words	NP / 143 words
Overall Complexity	**More accessible**	**More accessible**	**More complex**	**More accessible**

Ye who love the haunts of Nature,
Love the sunshine of the meadow,
Love the shadow of the forest,
Love the wind among the branches,
25 And the rain-shower and the snowstorm,
And the rushing of great rivers
Through their palisades⁴ of pine-trees,
And the thunder in the mountains,
Whose innumerable echoes
30 Flap like eagles in their eyries;⁵
Listen to these wild traditions,
To this Song of Hiawatha!

    Ye who love a nation's legends,
Love the ballads of a people,
35 That like voices from afar off
Call to us to pause and listen,
Speak in tones so plain and childlike,
Scarcely can the ear distinguish
Whether they are sung or spoken;
40 Listen to this Indian Legend,
To this Song of Hiawatha!

---

4. **palisades** (pal´ ə sādz) *n.* stakes of a fence; used figuratively here.
5. **eyries** (ā´ ər ēz *or* ē´ rēz) *n.* high nests; often spelled *aeries*.

Critical Reading

©

© **1. Key Ideas and Details (a)** According to this prologue, what are the sources of the Hiawatha legend? **(b) Analyze:** What details in lines 1–20 stress the authenticity of this retelling?

© **2. Key Ideas and Details (a)** What attitude toward nature does the prologue say a reader who appreciates "The Song of Hiawatha" will have? **(b) Analyze:** What attitude toward nature does the prologue convey?

© **3. Key Ideas and Details (a)** What attitude toward traditional legends and ballads is expressed in this prologue? **(b) Evaluate:** Based on this prologue, what values do you think the poem will express?

Cite textual evidence to support your responses.

from The Song of Hiawatha **259**

---

④ Literature in Context
Literary Connection
In addition to being known as the Fireside Poets, this group was also called the Schoolroom Poets or the Household Poets. While some readers level the charge of sentimentalism and Victorianism against these poets, they have had an impressive longevity; lines by them are still quoted in the twenty-first century. In addition to the American legends and domestic scenes these poets favored, they also addressed contemporary politics at times—for example, in "Old Ironsides" (p. 267).

Connect to the Literature Have students read Literature in Context; next, share the facts given above. Then **assign** the Connect to the Literature prompt: List three qualities that make the Fireside Poets well suited to oral tradition.

Answer: Their poems often have clear rhymes and easily discernible rhythms, and sometimes they contain elements of storytelling, such as characters, settings, and plots.

ASSESS

Answers

Remind students to support their answers with evidence from the text.

1. (a) The lines stress how land and nature are deeply ingrained in the story of Hiawatha. (b) The speaker says that he heard the traditions about Hiawatha from the Native American musician Nawadaha.

2. (a) The prologue says that a reader who appreciates the prologue will love nature. (b) The prologue reflects a respectful, admiring attitude toward nature.

3. (a) The prologue encourages respect for traditional legends and ballads. (b) **Possible response:** Students may say that those who love nature and uplifting legends of heroes will like the poem.

© Text Complexity: Reader and Task Suggestions

Preparing to Read the Texts	*from* **The Song of Hiawatha, Old Ironsides**	**The Tide Rises, the Tide Falls**	**Thanatopsis**
• Using the information on TE pp. 258–259, discuss the influence of the Fireside Poets. • Ask students how traditions help people stay in touch with their history and values. • Guide students to use Multidraft Reading strategies to deepen their comprehension (TE p. 257).	**Leveled Tasks** *Knowledge Demands* If students will have difficulty with context, have them refer to the headnotes as they read. Then, have them reread to determine how each poem calls readers to remember America's history. *Analyzing* If students will not have difficulty with context, have them discuss the tone in each of the poems.	**Leveled Tasks** *Levels of Meaning* If students will have difficulty with the meaning, have them note mentions of time. As they reread, have them relate that information to the traditional symbol of time as an ocean. *Synthesizing* If students will not have difficulty with the meaning, have them suggest other formats in which the message of valuing time could be effectively expressed.	**Leveled Tasks** *Structure/Language* If students will have difficulty with diction, have them paraphrase lines 31–37 as a statement about the value of honoring the dead. Have them apply the same technique to other passages. *Evaluating* If students will not have difficulty with diction, discuss how well the values in this poem fit modern times.

❺ The Tide Rises, The Tide Falls

Henry Wadsworth Longfellow

Literary Analysis
Meter How does the broken meter in lines 1, 5, 10, and 15 reflect the content of those lines?

Vocabulary
efface (ə fās′) v. erase; wipe out

The tide rises, the tide falls.
The twilight darkens, the curlew[1] calls;
Along the sea sands damp and brown
The traveler hastens toward the town,
5   And the tide rises, the tide falls.

Darkness settles on roofs and walls,
But the sea, the sea in the darkness calls:
❻ The little waves, with their soft, white hands,
Efface the footprints in the sands,
10   And the tide rises, the tide falls.

The morning breaks; the steeds in their stalls
Stamp and neigh, as the hostler[2] calls:
The day returns, but nevermore
Returns the traveler to the shore,
15   And the tide rises, the tide falls.

1. **curlew** (kʉr′ lōō) n. large wading bird associated with evening.
2. **hostler** (häs′ lər) n. person tending the horses at an inn or a stable.

260

William Cullen Bryant (1794–1878)

Author of "Thanatopsis"

As a journalist and political activist, William Cullen Bryant fought to ensure that industrialization did not obscure America's democratic values. Bryant began writing poetry at the age of nine and drafted the first version of "Thanatopsis," his most famous poem, when he was only nineteen. To support himself, Bryant practiced law for ten years while continuing to write poetry in his spare time. In 1825, he moved to New York City and became a journalist; by 1829, he had become editor-in-chief and part owner of the New York newspaper the *Evening Post.*

Voice for Justice Bryant used his position as an influential journalist to defend human rights and personal freedoms. He was an outspoken advocate of women's rights and a passionate foe of slavery. Bryant was the first American poet to win worldwide critical acclaim, and his work helped establish the Romantic Movement in America.

Romantic Influence Romanticism was an artistic and philosophical movement that stressed emotion over reason and celebrated individuality and the human imagination. Critical of science and the new industrial age, Romantic writers turned instead to nature as a source of spiritual comfort and guidance. Bryant was influenced by the work of the British Romantics William Wordsworth and Samuel Taylor Coleridge, whose 1798 publication of *Lyrical Ballads* revolutionized British poetry. After reading Wordsworth and Coleridge, Bryant incorporated aspects of romanticism into his poem "Thanatopsis."

> *"To* me it seems that one of the most important requisites for a great poet is a luminous style.*"*

Thanatopsis **261**

❶ Background

More About the Author

William Cullen Bryant helped establish an American literary tradition by producing poems that were a match for the work of the best European poets of his day. Perhaps his early lessons in Greek and Latin, taught by his country-doctor father, gave him added linguistic dexterity. Certainly his father helped launch Bryant's career by submitting "Thanatopsis" and another poem to a Boston magazine. Shocked that an American could draft such compelling verse, the magazine nonetheless published Bryant's poem in its first version—minus some of the introductory lines and the final stanza.

Differentiated Instruction   for Universal Access

Support for Special-Needs Students
To help students appreciate "Thanatopsis" (p. 262), focus on its rhythm before addressing its meaning. Have students listen to Bryant's poem on the *Hear It!* Audio CD. Discuss students' reactions to hearing the poem. Then guide them in reading the poem for meaning.

Vocabulary for Less Proficient Readers
Students may find the poetic language of "Thanatopsis" (p. 262) challenging. Point out some examples in lines 8 and 14 (*ere* and *list,* meaning "before" and "listen"). Explain that poetic language includes words such as these for the sake of rhyme or meter.

Enrichment for Gifted/Talented Students
Encourage students to locate in books of fine art or on the Internet alternatives for the painting on page 262. Guide students either generally to the Hudson River school of painters or specifically to *Kindred Spirits,* a painting by Asher B. Durand that shows the poet Bryant and the landscape painter Thomas Cole.

For more about the author, go online at www.PHLitOnline.com.

❶ About the Selection

"Thanatopsis" presents the poet's thoughts on death and its links to nature. Nature brings joy and comfort to those who love it. When people think of death, nature teaches them that everyone and everything must die and become part of the earth again. As all of nature is intertwined, so are the bodies and spirits of all who die. Death need not be feared or despised.

❷ Critical Viewing

Possible response: The painting captures the overwhelming magnitude of nature but does not intimidate. The stillness of the scene and the muted colors show only the benign side of nature.

❶ *Thanatopsis*
William Cullen Bryant

❷ ▲ Critical Viewing
What moods or emotions does this painting capture for you? Explain. **[Interpret]**

Vocabulary
eloquence (el´ ə kwəns)
n. expressiveness

BACKGROUND The poem's title, which comes from Greek, means "a view or meditation on death." Bryant wrote his first draft of "Thanatopsis" while still a teenager, revised it often, and published his final longer version in 1821.

> To him who in the love of Nature holds
> Communion[1] with her visible forms, she speaks
> A various language; for his gayer hours
> She has a voice of gladness, and a smile
> 5   And eloquence of beauty, and she glides
> Into his darker musings, with a mild
> And healing sympathy, that steals away
> Their sharpness, ere[2] he is aware. When thoughts
> ❸ Of the last bitter hour come like a blight
> 10 Over thy spirit, and sad images
> Of the stern agony, and shroud, and pall,
> And breathless darkness, and the narrow house,[3]
> Make thee to shudder, and grow sick at heart—
> Go forth, under the open sky, and list
> 15 To Nature's teachings, while from all around—
> Earth and her waters, and the depths of air—
> Comes a still voice—Yet a few days, and thee

---

1. **Communion** (kə myo͞on´yən) *n.* the act of sharing one's thoughts; intimate conversation.
2. **ere** (er) *conj.* before.
3. **narrow house** coffin.

Enrichment: Investigating Culture

Cultural Views of Death

In the course of human history, different cultures have held different views of death, the subject of this poem. In many ancient civilizations, death was seen as a passage to another life. The Egyptians built huge pyramids as tombs for their pharaohs and stocked them with all the comforts needed for the afterlife.

In some African cultures, men are buried on their right sides, facing east, so the rising sun will wake them in the afterlife to hunt and farm. Women are buried facing west, so the setting sun will remind them to prepare the evening meal.

Activity: Research Encourage interested students to investigate the beliefs and practices about death that mark a contemporary ethnic, national, or religious community. Suggest that they record their findings in the **Enrichment: Investigating Culture** work sheet, in *Professional Development Guidebook*, page 223.

The all-beholding sun shall see no more
In all his course; nor yet in the cold ground,
20 Where thy pale form was laid, with many tears,
Nor in the embrace of ocean, shall exist
Thy image. Earth, that nourished thee, shall claim
Thy growth, to be resolved to earth again,
And, lost each human trace, surrendering up
25 Thine individual being, shalt thou go

4 To mix forever with the elements,
To be a brother to the insensible rock
And to the sluggish clod, which the rude swain
Turns with his share,[4] and treads upon. The oak
30 Shall send his roots abroad, and pierce thy mold.

5 | Yet not to thine eternal resting place
Shalt thou retire alone, nor couldst thou wish
Couch[5] more magnificent. Thou shalt lie down
With patriarchs of the infant world—with kings,
35 The powerful of the earth—the wise, the good,
Fair forms, and hoary seers of ages past,
All in one mighty sepulcher.[6] The hills
Rock-ribbed and ancient as the sun—the vales
Stretching in pensive quietness between;
40 The venerable woods—rivers that move
In majesty, and the complaining brooks
That make the meadows green; and, poured round all,
Old Ocean's gray and melancholy waste—
Are but the solemn decorations all
45 Of the great tomb of man. The golden sun,
The planets, all the infinite host of heaven,
Are shining on the sad abodes of death,
Through the still lapse of ages. All that tread
The globe are but a handful to the tribes
50 That slumber in its bosom. Take the wings
Of morning,[7] pierce the Barcan[8] wilderness,
Or lose thyself in the continuous woods
Where rolls the Oregon,[9] and hears no sound,
Save his own dashings—yet the dead are there:
55 And millions in those solitudes, since first
The flight of years began, have laid them down
In their last sleep—the dead reign there alone.

---

4. **clod, which . . . share** lump of earth, which the simple country youth turns with his plow-share.
5. **Couch** bed.
6. **sepulcher** (sep´ əl kər) *n.* tomb.
7. **Take . . . morning** a reference to Psalm 139:9.
8. **Barcan** (bär´ kən) *adj.* referring to Barca, a desert region in North Africa.
9. **Oregon** river flowing between Oregon and Washington State, now called the Columbia River.

Thanatopsis **263**

Literary Analysis
Meter Identify two places in the first fifteen lines where the poem does not use perfect iambic pentameter.

Literary Analysis
Mood Describe the shift in mood that occurs in line 31.

Vocabulary
pensive (pen´ siv) *adj.* expressing deep thoughtfulness

venerable (ven´ ər ə bəl) *adj.* worthy of respect

Reading Check

6 Who has "a voice of gladness" and a "healing sympathy"?

---

3 **Literary Analysis**
Meter
1. Before addressing the text, have students review the instruction about meter on page 256.
2. **Ask** students to respond to the first Literary Analysis prompt: Identify two places in the first fifteen lines where the poem does not use perfect iambic pentameter.
Answer: Lines 9 and 14 break from strict iambic pentameter in order to provide a more natural reading. To apply iambic pentameter to line 9 yields, for example, *Of* the *last* bit*ter* hour *come* like *a* **blight** (with italics representing unstressed syllables and bold type representing stressed syllables) instead of the more natural-sounding *Of the* last bit*ter* hour come *like a* **blight**.

4 **Critical Thinking**
Criticize
1. Draw students' attention to the sentence that runs from line 22 through line 29.
2. **Ask** students what they think of Bryant's description of the fate of human bodies.
Possible response: Some students will choose to comment on Bryant's scientific understanding of decomposition; others will choose to comment on his poetic accomplishment.

5 **Literary Analysis**
Mood
1. Read aloud the bracketed line.
2. **Ask** students to respond to the second Literary Analysis prompt: Describe the shift in mood that occurs in line 31.
Possible response: Here the mood becomes hopeful and positive as the poet describes an eternal resting place, in contrast to the previous lines in which the mood was somber and even grim in discussing earthly burial.

6 **Reading Check**
Answer: Nature has a voice of gladness and a healing sympathy.

Differentiated Instruction for Universal Access

Strategy for Less Proficient Readers
Point out Bryant's extensive use of figurative language. Review the definition of *metaphor*: a thing spoken of as though it were something else. For example, the poet describes the earth metaphorically as "the great tomb of man" (line 45). Help students locate and decipher other metaphors in "Thanatopsis."

EL Strategy for English Learners
Tell students that Bryant personifies Earth, nature, and the ocean in this poem. Review with students that in using personification, poets attribute human qualities to nonhuman objects. Help students understand that with personification Bryant can portray Earth having feelings or taking actions.

Strategy for Advanced Readers
Challenge students to develop a character analysis of nature as Bryant portrays it. What feelings does he ascribe to Earth? Is Earth seen as beautiful and inviting or as threatening? Ask volunteers to read their analyses aloud for the class. Poll the class to see how many students agree with each writer's interpretation.

263

1. Read aloud the bracketed text to convey its final uplifting mood.

2. **Ask** students to respond to the Reading Strategy prompt: Briefly state the poet's message in the final nine lines of the poem. **Possible response:** Death comes to all; you can accept it peacefully.

▶ **Monitor Progress:** Before asking students to read their summaries aloud, circulate and read some silently yourself.

▶ **Reteach:** If students have trouble, reread the lines aloud, eliminating the subordinate clauses in lines 74–76 and stressing "go not" and "but . . . approach."

ASSESS

Answers

Before students respond, you may wish to have them write a brief objective summary of the selection. As they answer the questions below, remind them to support their answers with evidence from the text.

1. (a) The second stanza mentions the wiping out of footprints in the sand; the third says, ". . . nevermore / Returns the traveler to the shore." While other interpretations are possible, these details do suggest the death of the traveler. (b) The contrast between the disappearing traveler and the constant waves suggests that individuals may die but nature is never ending.

2. (a) He or she will die, be buried, and become part of nature's elements. (b) They describe a buried body's return to the earth.

3. (a) The poet conveys his own philosophy, or "vision," of death: that mortal humans must die and become part of immortal nature. (b) **Possible response:** Through nature, we come to understand our place in the life cycle and how, with our deaths, our bodies return to it.

So shalt thou rest, and what if thou withdraw
In silence from the living, and no friend
60 Take note of thy departure? All that breathe
Will share thy destiny. The gay will laugh
When thou art gone, the solemn brood of care
Plod on, and each one as before will chase
His favorite phantom; yet all these shall leave
65 Their mirth and their employments, and shall come
And make their bed with thee. As the long train
Of ages glide away, the sons of men,
The youth in life's green spring, and he who goes
In the full strength of years, matron and maid,
70 The speechless babe, and the gray-headed man—
Shall one by one be gathered to thy side,
By those, who in their turn shall follow them.

    So live, that when thy summons comes to join
The innumerable caravan, which moves
75 To that mysterious realm, where each shall take
His chamber in the silent halls of death,
❼ Thou go not, like the quarry-slave at night,
Scourged[10] to his dungeon, but, sustained and soothed
By an unfaltering trust, approach thy grave,
80 Like one who wraps the drapery of his couch
About him, and lies down to pleasant dreams.

Reading Strategy
Summarizing
Briefly state the poet's message in the final nine lines of the poem.

---

10. Scourged (skûrjd) *v.* whipped.

Critical Reading

Cite textual evidence to support your responses.

© 1. **Key Ideas and Details** **(a) Analyze:** Which details in the second and third stanzas of "The Tide Rises…" suggest that the traveler has died? **(b) Interpret:** What does the contrast between the traveler and the waves suggest about human life?

© 2. **Craft and Structure** **(a)** What does the "still voice" in line 17 of "Thanatopsis" say will happen to the individual being? **(b) Analyze:** In what ways do the images in lines 27–30 reinforce this idea?

© 3. **Integrate Ideas and Knowledge** **(a) Connect:** Explain the connection between Bryant's poem and its title, which combines the Greek words *thanatos* ("death") and *opsis* ("view or vision"). **(b) Draw Conclusions:** What is the speaker's overall attitude toward death and the role nature plays in it?

Vocabulary Development

Vocabulary Knowledge Rating
When students have completed reading and discussing the Longfellow and Bryant poems, have them take out their **Vocabulary Knowledge Rating** charts for the poems. Read the words aloud and have students rate their knowledge of the words again in the After Reading column. Clarify any words that are still problematic. Have students write their own definitions and example or sentence in the appropriate column. Then have students complete the Vocabulary practice on page 268. Encourage students to use the words in further discussion and written work about the selections. Remind them that they will be accountable for these words on the **Selection Test**, *Unit 2 Resources*, pages 41–43 or 44–46.

❶ OLIVER WENDELL HOLMES *(1809–1894)*

Author of "Old Ironsides"

Another of the so-called Fireside Poets, Oliver Wendell Holmes penned humorous and celebratory verse with wide audience appeal. Famous for prose as well as poetry, he was also a significant figure in the world of medicine, serving as a professor of anatomy and physiology as well as dean of the Harvard Medical School and producing many important medical tracts.

A Cambridge Man A descendant of the poet Anne Bradstreet (page 75), Holmes grew up near Harvard in Cambridge, Massachusetts, where his father was a Congregationalist minister. After a brief flirtation with the law, he switched to medicine, studying at Harvard and also for two years in Paris. He obtained his medical degree in 1836, the same year he published his first collection of poetry.

A Keen Wit Whether lecturing at Harvard or rubbing elbows with Emerson, Longfellow, and other leading writers of the day, Holmes was known for his brilliant skills as a speaker. He found a way to exhibit those skills in written form in his best-known prose work, *The Autocrat of the Breakfast-Table*, a series of supposed dinner-table conversations at a fictional Boston boarding house that wittily examine a wide range of interesting topics. The popular work was serialized in *The Atlantic Monthly*, the influential magazine of art, literature, and politics that Holmes helped found with his friend and fellow Fireside Poet James Russell Lowell.

> "ONE'S MIND, ONCE STRETCHED BY A NEW IDEA, NEVER REGAINS ITS ORIGINAL DIMENSIONS."

Old Ironsides **265**

❶ Background
More About the Author

Although nationally recognized for his poetry, Oliver Wendell Holmes took greater pride in his medical achievements. In particular, his ideas about improving medical practices in childbirth—doctors washing their hands and wearing sterile clothing to deliver babies—saved many lives. Holmes's medical students loved him as much as did the readers of his poetry. As a result, he always taught his classes at times when students would be most tired—Holmes's witty style kept them interested!

Differentiated Instruction for Universal Access

Culturally Responsive Instruction
Culture Focus The author of "Old Ironsides" (p. 267) had a first name (Oliver), a middle name (Wendell), and a last name (Holmes). In this case, the middle name was his mother's last name before she married Holmes's father.

Non-Hispanics in the United States are learning that many Hispanics use another system of naming; instead of one last name, this system involves two surnames, or *apellidos*. Here is an example:

Father's name: Oscar Vélez Márquez
Mother's name: Rosa Quinones García
Child's name: Jaime Vélez Quinones

The child's first surname is his father's first surname; the child's second surname is his mother's first surname. With students, examine variations on this system that Americans now encounter among friends and relatives from Hispanic and other cultures.

265

Written when the War of 1812 was still a living memory, the poem "Old Ironsides" pays homage to the valiant role the ship U.S.S. *Constitution* played in American history—particularly, during the war. The poet pleads to let the ship sink at sea rather than suffer ignominious demolition.

❷ Background

U.S.S. *Constitution*

This forty-four-gun frigate, ordered built by President George Washington and completed in 1797, first won fame battling Barbary pirates in Tripoli, a victory celebrated in the Marine Corps hymn. The *Constitution,* nicknamed Old Ironsides, is probably best remembered for its role in the War of 1812, when it won decisive victories in single-ship duels against British frigates.

Though Oliver Wendell Holmes helped save the *Constitution* from peril, a century later it was in danger again. The deteriorating ship was in need of major repairs. This time, America's schoolchildren came to the rescue by collecting money to restore the ship to its original condition. The restored *Constitution* is still on display at Charlestown Navy Yard, Charlestown, Massachusetts.

❶ OLD IRONSIDES

Oliver Wendell Holmes

266 A Growing Nation (1800–1870)

Concept Connector

Reading Strategy Graphic Organizer
Ask students to review the graphic organizer in which they summarized a work and listed supporting details. Then have them share their organizers and compare summaries and supporting details.

Activating Prior Knowledge
Have students return to their responses to the Activating Prior Knowledge activity (p. 258). Ask students to reconsider how well the writers of the contemporary lyrics give voice to the concerns and ideals of the students' generation.

Connecting to the Essential Question
Have students compare their responses to the prompt before reading the poems with their thoughts after reading them. Have them work individually or in groups, writing or discussing their thoughts, to decide if they would now cite different fictional characters or real people as American heroes and to explain why.

② BACKGROUND The battleship *Constitution* earned its nickname of "Old Ironsides" for withstanding British attacks during the War of 1812. By 1830, having outworn its usefulness, the ship was slated for demolition. Holmes **③** wrote this poem to protest this decision. The popular verse saved the ship and won Holmes early fame as a poet.

> Ay, tear her tattered ensign[1] down!
>   Long has it waved on high,
> And many an eye has danced to see
>   That banner in the sky;
> 5   Beneath it rung the battle shout,
>   And burst the cannons roar;—
> **⑤** The meteor of the ocean air
>   Shall sweep the clouds no more.
>
> Her deck, once red with heroes' blood,
> 10   Where knelt the vanquished foe,
> When winds were hurrying o'er the flood,
>   And waves were white below,
> No more shall feel the victor's tread,
>   Or know the conquered knee;—
> 15 The harpies[2] of the shore shall pluck
>   The eagle of the sea!
>
> Oh, better that her shattered hulk
>   Should sink beneath the wave;
> Her thunders shook the mighty deep,
> 20   And there should be her grave;
> Nail to the mast her holy flag.
>   Set every threadbare sail,
> And give her to the god of storms,
>   The lightning and the gale!

---

1. **ensign** (en´ sin') *n.* the national flag displayed on a ship.
2. **harpies** (här´ pēz) *n.* a term for greedy, grasping people that comes from the name of the sharp-clawed half-bird, half-woman monsters in Greek mythology.

Critical Reading

Cite textual evidence to support your responses.

© 1. **Key Ideas and Details** (a) **Infer:** Who or what are "the harpies of the shore" in line 15? (b) **Interpret:** What does the word *harpies* suggest about their motives in demolishing the ship?

© 2. **Key Ideas and Details** (a) **Draw Conclusions:** Why does the speaker think it would be better to let the ship sink? (b) **Evaluate:** Do you agree? Explain.

© 3. **Integration of Knowledge and Ideas** How is the subject matter of the poems in this grouping distinctly American? In your response, use at least two of these Essential Question words: *native, heroic, landscape.* [**Connecting to the Essential Question: What makes American literature American?**]

Old Ironsides **267**

Assessment Practice

Make Inferences and Generalizations (For more practice, see *All-in-One Workbook.*)

Many tests require students to make valid generalizations based on specific evidence in a text. Explain that to be valid, a generalization must be supported by information found in the passage. Use this sample test item.

Which of the following most accurately describes Old Ironsides's record of service?

A inactive
B unremarkable
C distinguished
D brief

A, B, and *D* are not supported by the poem. The ship survived difficult battles and won many victories at sea. Therefore, **C** is correct.

---

④ ◄ Critical Viewing
To celebrate the 200th anniversary of her 1797 launch, the U.S.S. *Constitution* took a five-hour sail around Massachusetts Bay in 1997. The ship had not sailed in more than 116 years. Which lines from the poem still apply to "Old Ironsides" today? [**Apply**]

Literary Analysis
Meter Identify the three-syllable foot that breaks the iambic meter in line 7.

---

③ **Engaging the Essential Question**

1. Remind students of the explanation on page 259 that the Fireside Poets did not develop innovative forms of poetry.

2. **Ask** students: What then might justify calling "Old Ironsides" uniquely American?
Possible response: The poem celebrates a symbol of American might and success. The poem calls for the people to take matters into their own hands, rather than to accept the demolition.

④ Critical Viewing

Answer: Only lines 3–4—about viewers admiring the ship's flag—are applicable.

⑤ Literary Analysis
Meter

1. Ask students to listen to the rhythm of lines 7 and 8 as you read them aloud.

2. **Ask** students to respond to the Literary Analysis prompt: Identify the three-syllable foot that breaks the iambic meter in line 7.
Answer: The three-syllable word *meteor* breaks the iambic pattern.

ASSESS/EXTEND

Answers

Before students respond, you may wish to have them write a brief objective summary of the selection. As they answer the questions below, remind them to support their answers with evidence from the text.

1. (a) The "harpies of the shore" are those who would demolish the ship. (b) *Harpies* suggests that the people interested in demolition have a profit motive.

2. (a) He thinks letting the ship sink would be less disrespectful than demolishing it. (b) **Possible response:** Most students, roused by Holmes's rallying cry, would probably agree with him.

3. **Possible response:** The poems celebrate the American landscape, the experiences of native peoples, and a naval vessel of the heroic past.

267

Answers

1. (a) Should you ask me, whence these stories? Whence these legends and traditions,

   (b) **Possible response:** The meter establishes a natural, inviting mood.

2. (a) From lines 3–24, all the odd-numbered lines are in iambic tetrameter. (b) All the even-numbered lines are in iambic trimeter. (c) **Possible response:** Starting with an inexact meter and then breaking into a regular foot keeps listeners attentive.

3. (a) **Sample response:** "Thanatopsis," line 58: iamb; five feet; iambic pentameter; "Old Ironsides," line 9: iamb; four feet; iambic tetrameter
   (b) Iambic meters are closest to natural speech, with its alternating unstressed and stressed syllables.

4. **Possible response:** (a) The speaker announces that he will give a reliable account of the life of Hiawatha. (b) Supporting details tell where the speaker heard the stories, who his source was, and who will appreciate them. (c) The excerpt raises the listeners' question (where do the stories of Hiawatha come from?), answers the question (from the place where Nawadaha lives), and announces who should listen (those who love nature and "a nation's legends").

Vocabulary Acquisition and Use

1. b. *Venerable* means "well regarded"; antonym is *disregarded.*

2. b. *Efface* means "erase"; antonym is *insert.*

3. a. Eloquence means "expressiveness"; antonym is *slurring.*

4. a. *Pensive* means "deeply thoughtful"; antonym is *shallow.*

Writing

Evaluate students' essays using the **Rubrics for Explanatory Text,** in *Professional Development Guidebook,* pages 260–261.

268

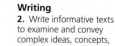

Literary Analysis

Common Core State Standards

Writing
2. Write informative texts to examine and convey complex ideas, concepts, and information clearly and accurately through the effective selection, organization, and analysis of content.

Language
5. Demonstrate understanding of word relationships.

1. **Craft and Structure (a)** Copy the first two lines of "The Song of Hiawatha" and mark the syllables to show the **meter** (trochaic tetrameter). **(b)** What **mood** does line after line of trochaic tetrameter help establish? Explain.

2. **Craft and Structure (a)** In "Old Ironsides," which lines are in iambic tetrameter (four iambs)? **(b)** Which are in iambic trimeter (three iambs)? **(c)** The first two lines do not follow the exact metrical pattern. What effect does breaking the meter create?

3. **Craft and Structure (a)** Using a chart like the one shown, analyze the meter of two lines of poetry. **(b)** Which meter sounds the most like natural speech? Explain.

Line #	Stresses	# of feet		Meter
58 (Thanatopsis)				
9 (Old Ironsides)				

Reading Strategy

4. **(a)** What is the main idea of the excerpt from "The Song of Hiawatha"? **(b)** What are three supporting details? **(c)** **Summarize** the excerpt.

PERFORMANCE TASKS
Integrated Language Skills

Vocabulary Acquisition and Use

Antonyms For each numbered word, choose the letter of its antonym, or word of opposite meaning. Then, explain your choice.

1. venerable   **(a)** greedy **(b)** disregarded **(c)** quick **(d)** current
2. efface   **(a)** clarify **(b)** insert **(c)** retire **(d)** loose
3. eloquence   **(a)** slurring **(b)** persuasive **(c)** powerful **(d)** fearful
4. pensive   **(a)** shallow **(b)** deep **(c)** curious **(d)** creative

Writing

Informative Text Choose two passages from the poems you have just read that evoke distinct moods in the reader. The passages should be between five and ten lines long. Write a **compare-and-contrast essay** in which you describe the mood evoked by each passage and discuss the *stylistic devices* the poet uses to create those moods. For example, in addition to meter, consider each poem's subject, striking images or word choices, and other aspects that you find noteworthy. Support your comparisons and contrasts with details from the passages.

Assessment Resources

Unit 2 Resources

L1 L2 EL Selection Test A, pp. 41–43. Administer Test A to less advanced students.

L3 L4 EL Selection Test B, pp. 44–46. Administer Test B to on-level and more advanced students.

L3 L4 Open-Book Test, pp. 38–40. As an alternative, administer the Open-Book Test.

All Customizable Test Bank

All Self-tests
Students may prepare for the **Selection Test** by taking the **Self-test** online.

PHLit Online! All assessment resources are available at **www.PHLitOnline.com.**

Shadows of the Imagination

PART 2

269

Text Complexity: At a Glance

This chart gives a general text complexity rating for the selections in this part of the unit to help guide instruction. For additional text complexity support, see the Text Complexity Rubric at point of use.			
The Minister's Black Veil	**More Complex**	The Raven	**More Accessible**
The Fall of the House of Usher	**More Complex**	*from* Moby-Dick	**More Complex**

Selection Planning Guide

The selections in this section deal with the ominous side of human emotions. Here we find tortured individuals ruled by the menacing shadows of their imaginations. In Hawthorne's "The Minister's Black Veil," a young clergyman unexpectedly and without explanation screens himself from others for the rest of his life. Poe's "The Fall of the House of Usher" introduces Roderick Usher, a tormented figure who knows he is losing his mind and tries desperately to escape death. In "The Raven," Poe presents a man whose grief for his deceased beloved knows no bounds. The last selection provides a close-up of obsession at its most dangerous. In an excerpt from the novel *Moby-Dick*, Captain Ahab is driven to revenge at any cost, including the lives of his crew and himself.

Visual Connections

1. Open discussion of this oil painting by asking students: What do you see in this painting?
   Possible response: Students may say that they see a woman in a dense thicket being harassed or pursued by several black birds.

2. What do you think is the woman's emotional state? Explain.
   Possible response: Such details as the woman's hands at her face, her expression, and her falling pose indicate a high level of fear, panic, or other stressful emotion.

3. If you were to interpret this painting symbolically, what do you think the thicket represents? The birds?
   Possible response: Students may say that the thicket represents difficult circumstances that seem to trap the woman. The birds may represent fears or bad memories that haunt the woman.

4. What title would you give to this painting?
   Sample answers: *Panic Attack; Lost in the Woods; No Escape*

Monitoring Progress

Before students read the poetry selections, refer to students' results on the **Vocabulary in Context** section of **Benchmark Test 2** (*Unit 4 Resources,* pp. 265–267). Use this diagnostic portion of the test to guide your choice of selections to teach.

• The Minister's Black Veil
Lesson Pacing Guide

DAY 1 Preteach

- ⓒ Administer the Reading and Vocabulary Warm-ups (*Unit 2 Resources*, pp. 47–50) as necessary.
- ⓒ Introduce the Literary Analysis concepts: Parable and Symbol.
- • Introduce the Reading Strategy: Drawing Inferences.
- ⓒ Build background with the author and Background features.
- • Develop thematic thinking with Connecting to the Essential Question.
- ⓒ Teach the selection vocabulary.

DAYS 2–3 Preteach/Teach/Assess

- • Distribute copies of the appropriate graphic organizer for the Reading Strategy (*Graphic Organizer Transparencies*, pp. 64–65).
- • Distribute copies of the appropriate graphic organizer for Literary Analysis (*Graphic Organizer Transparencies*, pp. 66–67).
- • Prepare students to read with the Activating Prior Knowledge activities (TE).
- • Informally monitor comprehension while students read.
- • Use the Reading Check question to confirm comprehension.
- ⓒ Develop students' understanding of parable and symbol using the Literary Analysis prompts.
- • Develop students' ability to draw inferences using the Reading Strategy prompts.
- ⓒ Reinforce vocabulary with the Vocabulary notes.
- • Assess students' comprehension and mastery of the skills by having them answer the Critical Reading, Literary Analysis, and Reading Strategy questions.
- • Have students complete the Vocabulary Lesson.

DAY 4 Extend/Assess

- ⓒ Have students complete the Conventions and Style Lesson.
- ⓒ Have students complete the Writing Lesson and write an interpretive essay about ambiguity. (You may assign as homework.)
- • Administer Selection Test A or B (*Unit 2 Resources,* pp. 60–62 or 63–65).

ⓒ Common Core State Standards

Reading Literature 1. Cite strong and thorough textual evidence to support analysis of what the text says explicitly as well as inferences drawn from the text, including determining where the text leaves matters uncertain.

Writing 2. Write explanatory texts to examine and convey complex ideas, concepts, and information clearly and accurately through the effective selection, organization, and analysis of content.
2.b. Develop the topic thoroughly by selecting the most significant and relevant facts, concrete details, quotations, or other information and examples appropriate to the audience's knowledge of the topic.
2.c. Use appropriate and varied transitions and syntax to link the major sections of the text, create cohesion, and clarify the relationships among complex ideas and concepts.

Language 1. Demonstrate command of the conventions of standard English grammar and usage when writing or speaking.
5. Demonstrate understanding of word relationships.

Additional Standards Practice
Common Core Companion, pp. 2–9; 196–207; 314–317; 332–335

Daily Block Scheduling
Each day in this Lesson Pacing Guide represents a 40–50 minute period. Teachers using block scheduling may combine days to revise pacing. In addition, teachers may differentiate and support core instruction by integrating components for extended and intensive support as students require. See the Guide to Selected Leveled Resources (facing page).

Guide to Selected Leveled Resources

RTI Tier 1 (students performing on level)

"The Minister's Black Veil"

Warm Up	Practice, **model**, and **monitor** fluency, working **with the whole class** or **in groups**.	Vocabulary and Reading Warm-ups B, *Unit 2 Resources*, pp. 47–48, 50
Comprehension/Skills	**Support** and **monitor** comprehension and skills development, having students complete the activities, graphic organizers, and interactive prompts **independently** or **as a class**.	• *Reader's Notebook*, adapted instruction and summary **EL** *Reader's Notebook: English Learner's Version*, adapted instruction and summary • **Reading Strategy Graphic Organizer B**, *Graphic Organizer Transparencies*, p. 65 • **Literary Analysis Graphic Organizer B**, *Graphic Organizer Transparencies*, p. 67
Monitor Progress A	**Monitor** student progress with the differentiated curriculum-based assessment in the *Unit Resources*.	• **Selection Test B**, *Unit 2 Resources*, pp. 63–65 • **Open-Book Test**, *Unit 2 Resources*, pp. 57–59

RTI Tier 2 (students requiring intervention)

"The Minister's Black Veil"

Warm Up	Practice, **model**, and **monitor** fluency **in groups** or **with individuals**.	• *Vocabulary and Reading Warm-ups A*, *Unit 2 Resources*, pp. 47–49 • *Hear It!* Audio CD
Comprehension/Skills	• **Support** and **monitor** comprehension and skills development, working **in small groups** or **with individuals**. • As students complete the selection in the appropriate version of the *Reader's Notebook*, **monitor** comprehension frequently with group questions and individual instruction. • **Model** strategies while guiding students in completing the activities and prompts in the *Reader's Notebook*, as well as the graphic organizers. • **Practice** skills and **monitor** mastery with the *Reading Kit* worksheets.	• *Reader's Notebook: Adapted Version*, adapted instruction and summary **EL** *Reader's Notebook: English Learner's Version*, adapted instruction and summary • **Reading Skill Graphic Organizer A**, Graphic Organizer Transparencies, **p. 64** • **Literary Analysis Graphic Organizer A**, *Graphic Organizer Transparencies*, p. 66 • *Reading Kit*, Practice worksheets
Monitor Progress A	**Monitor** student progress with the differentiated curriculum-based assessment in the *Unit Resources* and in the *Reading Kit*.	• **Selection Test A**, *Unit 2 Resources*, pp. 60–62 • *Reading Kit*, Assess worksheets

TIER 3 Tier 3 intervention may require consultation with the student's special-education or dyslexia specialist. For additional support, see the Tier 2 activities and resources listed above.

One-on-one teaching   Group work   Whole-class instruction   Independent work   A Assessment

For a complete guide to selection support, including support for Advanced students, see the Overview of Resources in the frontmatter.

• The Minister's Black Veil

RESOURCES FOR:
- **L1** Special-Needs Students
- **L2** Below-Level Students (Tier 2)
- **L3** On-Level Students (Tier 1)
- **L4** Advanced Students (Tier 1)
- **EL** English Learners
- **All** All Students

Vocabulary/Fluency/Prior Knowledge

Name _____ Date _____

"The Minister's Black Veil" by Nathaniel Hawthorne
Vocabulary Builder

Using the Root -path-

A. DIRECTIONS: *The word root -path- means "feeling, suffering, or disease." Keep that in mind as you answer the following questions on the lines provided.*

1. *Pathology* is a branch of medicine. With what issues in medicine do you think it is concerned?

2. The prefix *anti-* means "against." If you felt extreme *antipathy* toward another person, would you want that person to be your friend? Explain.

3. The prefix *sym-* means "with." If your friend suffered a terrible disappointment, how would you show that you were *sympathetic*?

Using the Word List

imperceptible   impertinent   inanimate   obstinacy   pathos   venerable

B. DIRECTIONS: *Revise each sentence so that the underlined vocabulary word is used in a logical way. Be sure to keep the vocabulary word in your revision.*

Example: The starving animal just picked at the food that was offered.
Revision: The starving animal gobbled up the food that was offered.

1. Because of Megan's obstinacy, she was always willing to change her mind for good reasons.

2. No one had any respect for the venerable old man.

3. The inanimate object jumped all over the room.

4. The audience laughed uproariously at the pathos in the play.

5. The impertinent child showed great respect to his elders.

6. The sound of the lion's roar was imperceptible from twenty feet away.

Unit 2 Resources: A Growing Nation
© Pearson Education, Inc. All rights reserved.
53

Unit 2 Resources

All Vocabulary Builder, p. 53

Also available for these selections:
- **EL L1 L2** Vocabulary Warm-ups A and B, pp. 47–48
- **EL L1 L2** Reading Warm-ups A and B, pp. 49–50

Reader's Notebooks

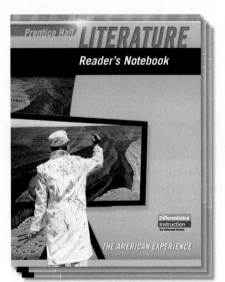

Pre- and postreading pages for this selection appear in an interactive format in the *Reader's Notebooks*. Each *Notebook* is differentiated for a different group of learners.
The selections in the Adapted and English Learner's versions are abridged.

- **L2 L3** *Reader's Notebook*
- **L1** *Reader's Notebook: Adapted Version*
- **EL** *Reader's Notebook: English Learner's Version*
- **EL** *Reader's Notebook: Spanish Version*

© Common Core Companion
Additional instruction and practice for each Common Core State Standard

PRENTICE HALL LITERATURE
Common Core Companion
STUDENT WORKBOOK • GRADE ELEVEN

COMMON CORE EDITION ©

A Student workbook for Mastering the Common Core State Standards

Key Features
- Instruction and Practice for Common Core State Standards
- Writing Workshops
- Listening and Speaking Workshops
- Performance Tasks

ALWAYS LEARNING   PEARSON

Selection Support

EL L1 L2 Literary Analysis: Graphic Organizer A (partially filled in), p. 66

Also available for these selections:

EL L1 L2 Reading: Graphic Organizer A, (partially filled in), p. 64

EL L3 Reading: Graphic Organizer B, p. 65

EL L3 Literary Analysis: Graphic Organizer B, p. 67

Skills Development/Extension

EL L3 L4 Support for Writing, p. 55

Also available for these selections:

All Literary Analysis: Parable and Symbol, p. 51

All Reading: Draw Inferences to Determine Essential Meaning, p. 52

EL L3 L4 Grammar and Style, p. 54

L4 Enrichment, p. 56

Assessment

L3 L4 Open-Book Test, pp. 57–59

Also available for these selections:

EL L1 L2 Selection Test A, pp. 60–62

EL L3 L4 Selection Test B, pp. 63–65

PHLit Online!
www.PHLitOnline.com

Online Resources: All print materials are also available online.

- complete narrated selection text
- a thematically related video with writing prompt
- an interactive graphic organizer
- highlighting feature
- access to all student print resources, adapted to individual student needs
- Spanish and English summaries
- adapted selection translations in Spanish

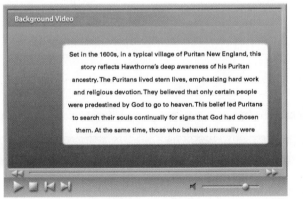

Background Video

Set in the 1600s, in a typical village of Puritan New England, this story reflects Hawthorne's deep awareness of his Puritan ancestry. The Puritans lived stern lives, emphasizing hard work and religious devotion. They believed that only certain people were predestined by God to go to heaven. This belief led Puritans to search their souls continually for signs that God had chosen them. At the same time, those who behaved unusually were

Background Video

Also available:

Get Connected! (thematic video with writing prompt)
All videos are available in Spanish.

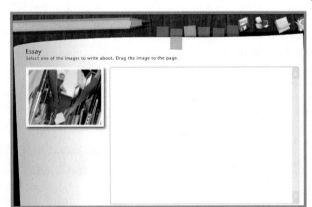

Essay
Select one of the images to write about. Drag the image to the page.

Writer's Journal (with graphics feature)

Also available:

Vocabulary Central (tools and activities for studying vocabulary)

❶ Connecting to the Essential Question

1. Review the assignment with the class.

2. Tell students about a curious aspect of the community in which you grew up. Then have them complete the assignment.

3. Point out to students that attitudes in the story can be inferred from characters' thoughts and actions.

❷ Literary Analysis

Introduce the strategy, using the instruction on the student page.

Think Aloud: Model the Skill

Say to students:

I've learned from the "school of hard knocks," but some of my best lessons emerge from stories. A lesson in story form can be indelible because I relate to characters and see a picture of cause and effect. I know others may draw very different lessons from the same story.

❸ Reading Strategy

1. Introduce the skill, using the instruction on the student page.

2. Give students a copy of **Literary Analysis Graphic Organizer B,** page 65 in *Graphic Organizer Transparencies,* to fill out as they read.

Think Aloud

Say to students:

If a dove lands in a tree near a battlefield, I should draw an inference about peace. And when more than one inference can be drawn, things get very interesting.

❹ Vocabulary

1. Pronounce each word, giving its definition, and have students say it aloud.

2. For more guidance, see the *Classroom Strategies and Teaching Routines* card for introducing vocabulary.

Before You Read | *The Minister's Black Veil*

❶ Connecting to the Essential Question Nathaniel Hawthorne wrote about America's Puritan past with puzzlement and shame but also with fascination. As you read this story, notice details that express specific attitudes toward Puritan New England. This will help as you consider the Essential Question: **What is the relationship between literature and place?**

❷ Literary Analysis

Hawthorne called "The Minister's Black Veil" a **parable,** or story that teaches a moral lesson. However, unlike religious parables such as those in the Bible, Hawthorne's parable teaches a lesson full of **ambiguity,** or uncertain meaning. Much of the ambiguity stems from the story's use of a symbol that is subject to different interpretations. A **symbol** is an object, setting, or even a character that has meaning as itself but also stands for something greater—often an abstract idea. The central symbol in this story is an article of clothing that the main character vows never to remove:

> Swathed about his forehead, and hanging down over his face … Mr. Hooper had on a black veil.

The veil's meaning is a mystery for both the characters in the story and the reader. As you read, look for details that will help you decide on your own interpretation of this ambiguous symbol.

❸ Reading Strategy

Ⓒ **Preparing to Read Complex Texts** An inference is a logical guess you make about aspects of a text that are not explicitly, or directly, stated. You draw inferences by applying your own life experience to story details. To *interpret the essential meaning* of this story, **draw inferences** by noting descriptions, dialogue, and characters' actions and assessing them in view of your own understanding of human nature. As you read, use a chart like the one shown to draw inferences.

❹ Vocabulary

inanimate (in an′ ə mit) *adj.* not alive; lifeless (p. 274)

venerable (ven′ ər ə bəl) *adj.* commanding respect (p. 274)

pathos (pa′ thäs′ *or* thōs′) *n.* quality that arouses pity, sorrow, or sympathy in others (p. 275)

impertinent (im pʉr′ tə nənt) *adj.* not showing proper respect; saucy (p. 278)

obstinacy (äb′ stə nə sē) *n.* stubbornness (p. 279)

imperceptible (im′ pər sep′ tə bel) *adj.* not easy to perceive; unnoticeable (p. 283)

Ⓒ **Common Core State Standards**

Reading Literature
1. Cite strong and thorough textual evidence to support analysis of what the text says explicitly as well as inferences drawn from the text, including determining where the text leaves matters uncertain.

Description/Dialogue
"A sad smile gleamed faintly from beneath the black veil, . . ."

Inference
The minister has suffered a loss.

Vocabulary Development

Vocabulary Knowledge Rating

Create a **Vocabulary Knowledge Rating chart** (*Professional Development Guidebook,* p. 33) for the vocabulary words on the student page. Give each student a copy of the chart with the words on it. Read the words aloud, and have students mark their rating in the Before Reading column. Urge students to attend to these words as they read and discuss the selection.

In order to gauge how much instruction you need to provide, tally how many students are confident in their knowledge of each word. As students read, point out the words and their context.

 **Vocabulary Central,** featuring tools and activities for studying vocabulary, is available online at **www.PHLitOnline.com.**

⑤ Nathaniel Hawthorne
(1804–1864)

Author of "The Minister's Black Veil"

Sometimes called an "anti-Transcendentalist," Nathaniel Hawthorne admired Transcendentalists like Ralph Waldo Emerson but could not adopt their optimistic world view. Instead, as the descendant of New England Puritans who prosecuted witches and persecuted Quakers, Hawthorne was shaped by a sense of inherited guilt that gave him a darker vision. He believed that evil was a powerful force in the world, a sentiment that infuses most of his fiction.

A Shaky Start Hawthorne was born in Salem, Massachusetts, 112 years after the famous witchcraft trials in which one of his ancestors was a judge. After graduating from Bowdoin (bō´din) College in Maine, he secluded himself in his mother's home, determined to become a writer. In 1828 he published a novel, *Fanshawe*, but was so displeased with the effort that he tried to burn all the copies. Continuing to toil at his craft, he produced a story collection, *Twice-Told Tales* (1837), that won him critical regard but sold poorly.

Struggling to Earn a Living Hawthorne lived briefly at the Transcendentalist commune at Brook Farm and then at the Old Manse in Concord, Massachusetts, where he produced another story collection, *Mosses from an Old Manse* (1846). Still, to support his family, he was forced to accept a political post at the custom house back in Salem. A change of administrations lost him the job, but his stint there helped inspire his masterpiece, *The Scarlet Letter* (1850), a novel of sin and guilt among the early Puritans.

A Final Appointment When his college friend, Franklin Pierce, became president, Hawthorne was named American consul in Liverpool, England. He spent several years abroad, his travels in Italy inspiring his novel *The Marble Faun* (1860). Four years later, on a tour of New Hampshire with Franklin Pierce, Hawthorne died suddenly in his sleep.

> *"Happiness is a butterfly, which when pursued, is always just beyond your grasp, but which, if you will sit down quietly, may alight upon you."*

The Minister's Black Veil **271**

▷ Daily Bellringer

For each class during which you will teach this selection, have students complete one of the five activities for the appropriate week in the *Daily Bellringer Activities* booklet.

▌ Multidraft Reading

To assist struggling readers and to enhance reading for all, assign the text in chunks as warranted by length and apply multidraft reading protocols. For each reading, have students set the purpose indicated:

- **First reading**—identifying key ideas and details and answering any Reading Checks.
- **Second reading**—analyzing craft and structure and responding to the side-column prompts.
- **Third reading**—integrating knowledge and ideas, connecting to other texts and the world, and answering the end-of-selection questions.

For more guidance, refer to the *Classroom Strategies and Teaching Routines* card, **Multidraft Reading.**

⑤ Background
More About the Author

Nathaniel Hawthorne was a keen observer of the human condition and a master of symbolism. As he wrote throughout his life, he met nearly always with the same result—critical acclaim coupled with monetary failure. The literary critic Edward H. Davidson has written: "That a century after he lived he should be included in a collection of major writers of America would have baffled Hawthorne. . . . Hawthorne himself had been so consistently ignored, that to be a subject for literary study . . . and to be termed a 'classic' among American writers, would have seemed nothing short of grotesque. . . . Indeed, his literary reputation has maintained its high place more steadily than that of any other major American writer."

❶ About the Selection

In this parable, Mr. Hooper, a highly respected minister in a small Puritan community, suddenly appears wearing a black veil. He vows never to remove this mask but offers no explanation for this choice. The veil has a powerful, gloomy effect on his parishioners. They are stunned and unable to ask Mr. Hooper directly why he is wearing it; his fiancée turns from him because of the veil. The veil's symbolic meaning—a reminder of the secret sins each soul carries to the grave—is revealed through the speech and actions of Mr. Hooper and his parishioners, as well as in his deathbed explanation.

❷ Activating Prior Knowledge

Write the following quotation on the chalkboard:

"But what has good Parson Hooper got upon his face?" cried the sexton in astonishment.

When Mr. Hooper appears one day wearing a black veil, it causes quite a stir among his congregation. Invite students to imagine that someone they know, suddenly and without explanation, makes a drastic change to her or his appearance. Ask them to predict how they would react. What might they wish to ask or say to this person?

Concept Connector ➔

Tell students they will return to their responses after reading the selection.

❶
❷ The **Minister's**
BLACK VEIL

272

A PARABLE 🙠 NATHANIEL HAWTHORNE

Ⓒ Text Complexity Rubric

The Minister's Black Veil	
Qualitative Measures	
Context/Knowledge Demands	Nineteenth-century tale; historical context demands 1 2 3 ④ 5
Structure/Language Conventionality and Clarity	Challenging dialogue; dense, formal narration 1 2 ③ 4 5
Levels of Meaning/ Purpose/Concept Level	Challenging (abstract concepts of sin and guilt) 1 2 3 4 ⑤
Quantitative Measures	
Lexile	1250L
Text Length	Word Count: 5,160
Overall Complexity	**More complex**

Reader and Task Suggestions

Preparing to Read the Text

- Using the Background information on TE p. 271, discuss what it means to be "a keen observer of the human condition."
- Ask students how guilt can color a person's behavior.
- Guide students to use Multidraft Reading strategies to deepen their comprehension (TE p. 271).

Leveled Tasks

Levels of Meaning If students will have difficulty with the meaning, have them focus on Mr. Hooper's conversation with Elizabeth. Then, have them reread to see how guilt emerges throughout the story.

Analyzing If students will not have difficulty with the meaning, have them discuss whether guilt is the best explanation for the minister's veil.

BACKGROUND Set in the 1600s, in a typical village of Puritan New England, this story reflects Nathaniel Hawthorne's deep awareness of his Puritan ancestry. The Puritans lived stern lives, emphasizing hard work and religious devotion. They believed that only certain people were predestined, or chosen, by God to go to heaven. This belief led them to search their souls continually for signs that God had selected them. At the same time, those who behaved unusually were often thought to be controlled by evil forces. This attitude contributed to the Salem witchcraft trials of 1692, during which at least twenty accused witches were executed. In this story, Hawthorne explores how such attitudes probably led to other, more commonplace acts of cruelty.

The sexton[1] stood in the porch of Milford meeting-house, pulling busily at the bell rope. The old people of the village came stooping along the street. Children, with bright faces, tripped merrily beside their parents, or mimicked a graver gait, in the conscious dignity of their Sunday clothes. Spruce bachelors looked sidelong at the pretty maidens, and fancied that the Sabbath sunshine made them prettier than on weekdays. When the throng had mostly streamed into the porch, the sexton began to toll the bell, keeping his eye on the Reverend Mr. Hooper's door. The first glimpse of the clergyman's figure was the signal for the bell to cease its summons.

"But what has good Parson Hooper got upon his face?" cried the sexton in astonishment.

All within hearing immediately turned about, and beheld the semblance of Mr. Hooper, pacing slowly his meditative way towards the meetinghouse. With one accord they started, expressing more wonder than if some strange minister were coming to dust the cushions of Mr. Hooper's pulpit.

"Are you sure it is our parson?" inquired Goodman[2] Gray of the sexton.

"Of a certainty it is good Mr. Hooper," replied the sexton. "He was to have exchanged pulpits with Parson Shute, of Westbury; but Parson Shute sent to excuse himself yesterday, being to preach a funeral sermon."

---

1. **sexton** (seks´ tən) *n.* person in charge of the maintenance of a church.
2. **Goodman** title of respect similar to "Mister."

3 ◀ **Critical Viewing**
How might a community react if a respected person were to wear a veil like the one shown in this illustration? **[Speculate]**

4 ☑ Reading Check
As the story begins, what weekly event is about to take place?

The Minister's Black Veil **273**

3 **Critical Viewing**

Possible response: Students may respond that the community would react by feeling threatened, antagonized, or amused. They might take action for or against the person in question.

4 **Reading Check**

Answer: Mr. Hooper's regular Sunday church service is about to begin at Milford meetinghouse.

Parable

1. Slowly read aloud the first paragraph on this page. Encourage students to listen for descriptive details about Mr. Hooper, the veil, and the reactions of the townspeople.

2. **Ask** students the following question: What does this first detailed description of the veil indicate about its effect on the community?
Answer: The description makes the veil seem strange and significant.

❻ Literary Analysis

Parable and Symbol

1. Remind students that when an object takes on significance outside itself and stands for something greater, it is being used as a symbol.

2. Ask one or more student volunteers to read aloud carefully the bracketed passage. Urge students to take note of how Hawthorne has chosen to describe the effect of the veil.

3. **Ask** students the Literary Analysis question: The passage beginning "That mysterious emblem" is the first suggestion that the veil is a symbol. What might the veil symbolize?
Answer: Hawthorne's descriptions delineate how the veil creates an "unnatural" separation between Mr. Hooper and the subject of his current attention (speaking the psalm, reading the page of the Bible, looking up to God). Thus the veil may symbolize something that has come between the minister and ordinary life.

Vocabulary
inanimate (in anʹ ə mit) *adj.*
not alive; lifeless

❺

"He has changed himself into something awful, only by hiding his face."

☙

Vocabulary
venerable (venʹ ər ə bəl)
adj. commanding respect

Literary Analysis
Parable and Symbol
The passage beginning "That mysterious emblem" is the first suggestion that the veil is a symbol. What might the veil symbolize?

❻

The cause of so much amazement may appear sufficiently slight. Mr. Hooper, a gentlemanly person, of about thirty, though still a bachelor, was dressed with due clerical neatness, as if a careful wife had starched his band, and brushed the weekly dust from his Sunday's garb. There was but one thing remarkable in his appearance. Swathed about his forehead, and hanging down over his face, so low as to be shaken by his breath, Mr. Hooper had on a black veil. On a nearer view it seemed to consist of two folds of crape,[3] which entirely concealed his features, except the mouth and chin, but probably did not intercept his sight, further than to give a darkened aspect to all living and inanimate things. With this gloomy shade before him, good Mr. Hooper walked onward, at a slow and quiet pace, stooping somewhat, and looking on the ground, as is customary with abstracted men, yet nodding kindly to those of his parishioners who still waited on the meetinghouse steps. But so wonderstruck were they that his greeting hardly met with a return.

"I can't really feel as if good Mr. Hooper's face was behind that piece of crape," said the sexton.

"I don't like it," muttered an old woman, as she hobbled into the meetinghouse. "He has changed himself into something awful, only by hiding his face."

"Our parson has gone mad!" cried Goodman Gray, following him across the threshold.

A rumor of some unaccountable phenomenon had preceded Mr. Hooper into the meetinghouse, and set all the congregation astir. Few could refrain from twisting their heads towards the door; many stood upright, and turned directly about; while several little boys clambered upon the seats, and came down again with a terrible racket. There was a general bustle, a rustling of the women's gowns and shuffling of the men's feet, greatly at variance with that hushed repose which should attend the entrance of the minister. But Mr. Hooper appeared not to notice the perturbation of his people. He entered with an almost noiseless step, bent his head mildly to the pews on each side, and bowed as he passed his oldest parishioner, a white-haired great-grandsire, who occupied an armchair in the center of the aisle. It was strange to observe how slowly this venerable man became conscious of something singular in the appearance of his pastor. He seemed not fully to partake of the prevailing wonder, till Mr. Hooper had ascended the stairs, and showed himself in the pulpit, face to face with his congregation, except for the black veil. That mysterious emblem was never once withdrawn. It shook with his measured breath, as he gave out the psalm; it threw its obscurity between him and the holy page, as he read the Scriptures; and while he prayed, the veil lay heavily on his uplifted countenance. Did he seek to hide it from the dread Being whom he was addressing?

---

3. **crape** (krāp) *n.* piece of black cloth worn as a sign of mourning.

Enrichment: Analyzing Themes and Symbols

Veils
A veil is "a piece of light fabric, as of net or gauze, worn especially by women over the face or head or draped from a hat to conceal, protect, or enhance the face." Veils are worn for a variety of reasons—for example, to express modesty or mourning—in different cultures. They are worn often at weddings, funerals, and other religious ceremonies.
Activity: Presentation Encourage students to find out more about why, when, how, and by whom veils are worn in different cultures.

Have them choose a particular usage of the veil and speculate about its symbolic meaning. Suggest that they record information in the **Enrichment: Analyzing Themes and Symbols** work sheet, in *Professional Development Guidebook,* page 243. Students can then report their findings to the class and initiate a discussion comparing Hawthorne's symbolic use of the veil with that of the usage they have studied.

Such was the effect of this simple piece of crape, that more than one woman of delicate nerves was forced to leave the meetinghouse. Yet perhaps the palefaced congregation was almost as fearful a sight to the minister, as his black veil to them.

Mr. Hooper had the reputation of a good preacher, but not an energetic one: he strove to win his people heavenward by mild, persuasive influences, rather than to drive them thither by the thunders of the Word. The sermon which he now delivered was marked by the same characteristics of style and manner as the general series of his pulpit oratory. But there was something, either in the sentiment of the discourse itself, or in the imagination of the auditors, which made it greatly the most powerful effort that they had ever heard from their pastor's lips. It was tinged, rather more darkly than usual, with the gentle gloom of Mr. Hooper's temperament. The subject had reference to secret sin, and those sad mysteries which we hide from our nearest and dearest, and would fain conceal from our own consciousness, even forgetting that the Omniscient[4] can detect them. A subtle power was breathed into his words. Each member of the congregation, the most innocent girl, and the man of hardened breast, felt as if the preacher had crept upon them, behind his awful veil, and discovered their hoarded iniquity of deed or thought. Many spread their clasped hands on their bosoms. There was nothing terrible in what Mr. Hooper said, at least, no violence; and yet, with every tremor of his melancholy voice, the hearers quaked. An unsought pathos came hand in hand with awe. So sensible were the audience of some unwonted attribute in their minister, that they longed for a breath of wind to blow aside the veil, almost believing that a stranger's visage would be discovered, though the form, gesture, and voice were those of Mr. Hooper.

At the close of the services, the people hurried out with indecorous confusion, eager to communicate their pent-up amazement, and conscious of lighter spirits the moment they lost sight of the black veil. Some gathered in little circles, huddled closely together, with their mouths all whispering in the center; some went homeward alone, wrapt in silent meditation; some talked loudly, and profaned the Sabbath day with ostentatious laughter. A few shook their sagacious heads, intimating that they could penetrate the mystery; while one or two affirmed that there was no mystery at all, but only that Mr. Hooper's eyes were so weakened by the midnight lamp, as to require a shade. After a brief interval, forth came good Mr. Hooper also, in the rear of his flock. Turning his veiled face from one group to another, he paid due reverence to the hoary heads, saluted the middle-aged with kind dignity as their friend and spiritual guide, greeted the young with mingled authority and love, and laid his hands on the little children's heads to bless them. Such was always

---

4. Omniscient (äm niʹ shənt) all-knowing God.

Reading Strategy
Drawing Inferences
Has Mr. Hooper truly changed? What inferences can you draw based on this description of his sermon?

Vocabulary
pathos (paʹ thäsʹ or thōsʹ) *n.* quality that arouses pity, sorrow, or sympathy in others

8 Reading Check
What change has occurred in Mr. Hooper's appearance?

Differentiated Instruction for Universal Access

⑨ The American Experience

Jonathan Edwards, Puritans, and Sermons of Fear

In *Jonathan Edwards, Pastor,* author Patricia Tracy discusses how Edwards achieved the "terrifying effects" of his sermon: "Although it conveys the reek of brimstone, the sermon does not say that God will hurl man into everlasting fires—on the contrary, doom will come from God's indifference . . . . He holds man above the pit as by a spider's thread, and should He become weary of protecting worthless man, that abominable insect will drop of his own weight. Man's preservation lay in God's whim of mercy, and the terror of this message derived from the insecurity of being temporarily protected by an all-powerful being who had an infinite anger. (Was the control of such strong feelings something that Edwards's audience found difficult to understand or to trust?)" Tracy suggests that because the Puritans held such a dim view of human beings' ability to control their feelings, they were all the more anxious about God's ability to control his anger.

Connect to the Literature Have a volunteer read the note aloud. Then **ask** students the Connect to the Literature question: People in Mr. Hooper's congregation are taught to fear eternal damnation—and to look for signs of evil in themselves and others. Why would they be inclined to fear anything that appears to be a mark of sin?

Possible response: People might fear something that appears to be a mark of sin because it could signify damnation despite an individual's apparent goodness or religious observance.

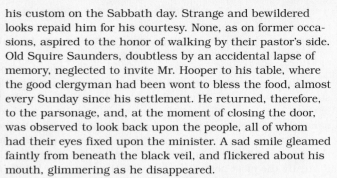

⑨ The American EXPERIENCE

Jonathan Edwards, Puritans, and Sermons of Fear

The congregation's fear of Mr. Hooper's veil recalls Jonathan Edwards, one of the greatest preachers of the colonial period. Edwards used his sermons to inspire fear of eternal damnation in the minds of his listeners. He insisted that the evidence they saw as proof of God's grace in their lives was false. According to Edwards, personal comfort, success, health, and a sense of being a good person were no proof that one was saved. Rather, these satisfactions in the earthly realm were mere distractions, providing comfort, but no substance, to the ignorant.

Though Hawthorne describes Mr. Hooper as a mild and benevolent preacher—certainly no spouter of fire-and-brimstone like Edwards—his veil inspires a similar fear and trembling among the villagers. You can read an excerpt of Jonathan Edwards's "Sinners in the Hands of an Angry God" on page 86.

Connect to the Literature

People in Hooper's congregation are taught to fear eternal damnation and to look for signs of evil in themselves and others. Why would they be inclined to fear anything that appears to be a mark of sin?

276 A Growing Nation (1800–1870)

his custom on the Sabbath day. Strange and bewildered looks repaid him for his courtesy. None, as on former occasions, aspired to the honor of walking by their pastor's side. Old Squire Saunders, doubtless by an accidental lapse of memory, neglected to invite Mr. Hooper to his table, where the good clergyman had been wont to bless the food, almost every Sunday since his settlement. He returned, therefore, to the parsonage, and, at the moment of closing the door, was observed to look back upon the people, all of whom had their eyes fixed upon the minister. A sad smile gleamed faintly from beneath the black veil, and flickered about his mouth, glimmering as he disappeared.

"How strange," said a lady, "that a simple black veil, such as any woman might wear on her bonnet, should become such a terrible thing on Mr. Hooper's face!"

"Something must surely be amiss with Mr. Hooper's intellects," observed her husband, the physician of the village. "But the strangest part of the affair is the effect of this vagary, even on a sober-minded man like myself. The black veil, though it covers only our pastor's face, throws its influence over his whole person, and makes him ghost-like from head to foot. Do you not feel it so?"

"Truly do I," replied the lady; "and I would not be alone with him for the world. I wonder he is not afraid to be alone with himself!"

"Men sometimes are so," said her husband.

The afternoon service was attended with similar circumstances. At its conclusion, the bell tolled for the funeral of a young lady. The relatives and friends were assembled in the house, and the more distant acquaintances stood about the door, speaking of the good qualities of the deceased, when their talk was interrupted by the appearance of Mr. Hooper, still covered with his black veil. It was now an appropriate emblem. The clergyman stepped into the room where the corpse was laid, and bent over the coffin, to take a last farewell of his deceased parishioner. As he stooped, the veil hung straight down from his forehead, so that, if her eyelids had not been closed forever, the dead maiden might have seen his face. Could Mr. Hooper be fearful of her glance, that he so hastily caught back the black veil? A person who watched the interview between the dead and living, scrupled not to affirm, that, at the instant when the clergyman's features were disclosed,

---

Enrichment: Investigating Career Connections

The Clergy

Like most members of the clergy—such as ministers, rabbis, and priests—Mr. Hooper is a central figure in his community. In addition to offering religious instruction and counseling to their congregations, the clergy preside over weddings, funerals, and other rites of passage. Many are involved in education and social service. Today, as in Mr. Hooper's time, a minister's words and actions can be heard and seen by the public at large.

Activity: Interview Have students interview members of the clergy in your area to learn about their responsibilities. Suggest that students record information in the **Enrichment: Investigating Career Connections** work sheet, in *Professional Development Guidebook*, page 221. Students can then compare notes and identify characteristics demonstrated by clergy in their leadership roles.

the corpse had slightly shuddered, rustling the shroud and muslin cap, though the countenance retained the composure of death. A superstitious old woman was the only witness of this prodigy. From the coffin Mr. Hooper passed into the chamber of the mourners, and thence to the head of the staircase; to make the funeral prayer. It was a tender and heart-dissolving prayer, full of sorrow, yet so imbued with celestial hopes, that the music of a heavenly harp, swept by the fingers of the dead, seemed faintly to be heard among the saddest accents of the minister. The people trembled, though they but darkly understood him when he prayed that they, and himself, and all of mortal race, might be ready, as he trusted this young maiden had been, for the dreadful hour that should snatch the veil from their faces. The bearers went heavily forth, and the mourners followed, saddening all the street, with the dead before them, and Mr. Hooper in his black veil behind.

"Why do you look back?" said one in the procession to his partner.

"I had a fancy," replied she, "that the minister and the maiden's spirit were walking hand in hand."

"And so had I, at the same moment," said the other.

That night, the handsomest couple in Milford village were to be joined in wedlock. Though reckoned a melancholy man, Mr. Hooper had a placid cheerfulness for such occasions, which often excited a sympathetic smile where livelier merriment would have been thrown away. There was no quality of his disposition which made him more beloved than this. The company at the wedding awaited his arrival with impatience, trusting that the strange awe, which had gathered over him throughout the day, would now be dispelled. But such was not the result. When Mr. Hooper came, the first thing that their eyes rested on was the same horrible black veil, which had added deeper gloom to the funeral, and could portend nothing but evil to the wedding. Such was its immediate effect on the guests that a cloud seemed to have rolled duskily from beneath the black crape, and dimmed the light of the candles. The bridal pair stood up before the minister. But the bride's cold fingers quivered in the tremulous hand of the bridegroom, and her deathlike paleness caused a whisper that the maiden who had been buried a few hours before was come from her grave to be married. If ever another wedding were so dismal, it was that famous one where they tolled the wedding knell.[5] After performing the ceremony, Mr. Hooper raised a glass of wine to his lips, wishing happiness to the new-married couple in a strain of mild pleasantry that ought to have brightened the features of the guests, like a cheerful gleam from the hearth. At that instant, catching a glimpse of his figure in the looking glass, the black veil involved his own spirit in the horror with which it overwhelmed all others. His frame shuddered, his lips grew white, he spilt the untasted wine upon

---

5. **If . . . knell** reference to Hawthorne's short story "The Wedding Knell." A knell is the slow ringing of a bell, as at a funeral.

Reading Strategy
Drawing Inferences
What inferences can you draw from this dialogue about the veil's intensifying impact on the villagers?

12 **Reading Check**
How does Mr. Hooper's veil affect the wedding party?

The Minister's Black Veil **277**

10 **Reading Strategy**
Drawing Inferences

1. Have two students read this dialogue in quiet, discreet voices.

2. Encourage students to pay attention to the reference to the spirit of the dead maiden. Have them consider why the villager might have made this statement.

3. Then **ask** students the Reading Strategy question: What inferences can you draw from this dialogue about the veil's increasing impact on the villagers?
Answer: A reader might infer that the veil has started to work on the villagers' imaginations. Though the minister has said nothing yet regarding the meaning of the veil, parishioners are creating increasingly detailed scenarios that might explain the veil and Mr. Hooper's behavior.

11 **Critical Thinking**
Compare and Contrast

1. Ask students to brainstorm a list of words, phrases, ideas, and feelings they associate with the word *wedding*.

2. **Ask** students: Why might the fearful effect of the black veil be more intense at the wedding than at the funeral?
Possible response: People expect such dismal attire (as well as sadness) at a funeral. A wedding, however, is ordinarily a time of joy. Therefore, the minister's black veil at the wedding inverts everyone's sense of normalcy and makes the veil's effect even more upsetting than it would be at a funeral.

12 **Reading Check**
Answer: The veil reminds the members of the wedding party of death and gives them a feeling of horror.

277

⑬ Reading Strategy

Drawing Inferences

1. Ask the students to listen for characteristics of Mr. Hooper's congregation *as a group.* Then read the bracketed text out loud.

2. **Ask:** How would you describe the "personality" of the congregation before Mr. Hooper started wearing the veil?
   Possible response: They sound like a lively group of people who enjoy participation and are not afraid to give advice to their minister.

3. Point out that the parishioners seem less inclined to engage with Mr. Hooper after he starts wearing the veil. **Ask:** What inference might a reader make about the congregation based on this change?
   Possible response: A reader might infer that the congregation feels inhibited or antagonized by Mr. Hooper's action and is therefore less likely to participate in the way they used to.

⑭ Literary Analysis

Parable

1. Direct students to the bracketed passage. Encourage them to look carefully for details that reveal the character of Mr. Hooper's fiancée.

2. **Ask** students the following question: What might these details about Mr. Hooper's fiancée add to the parable's moral?
   Answer: The description of how directly and simply Mr. Hooper's fiancée approaches the topic of the veil and the revelation that the minister refuses to explain his reasons even to her reinforce the symbolic power of the veil.

Vocabulary
impertinent (im pur´ tə nənt)
adj. not showing proper respect; saucy

the carpet, and rushed forth into the darkness. For the Earth, too, had on her Black Veil.

The next day, the whole village of Milford talked of little else than Parson Hooper's black veil. That, and the mystery concealed behind it, supplied a topic for discussion between acquaintances meeting in the street, and good women gossiping at their open windows. It was the first item of news that the tavernkeeper told to his guests. The children babbled of it on their way to school. One imitative little imp covered his face with an old black handkerchief, thereby so affrighting his playmates that the panic seized himself, and he well nigh lost his wits by his own waggery.

It was remarkable that of all the busybodies and impertinent people in the parish, not one ventured to put the plain question to Mr. Hooper, wherefore he did this thing. Hitherto, whenever there appeared the slightest call for such interference, he had never lacked advisers, nor shown himself averse to be guided by their judgment. If he erred at all, it was by so painful a degree of self-distrust that even the mildest censure would lead him to consider an indifferent action as a crime. Yet, though so well acquainted with this amiable weakness, no individual among his parishioners chose to make the black veil a subject of friendly remonstrance. There was a feeling of dread, neither plainly confessed nor carefully concealed, which caused each to shift the responsibility upon another, till at length it was found expedient to send a deputation of the church, in order to deal with Mr. Hooper about the mystery, before it should grow into a scandal. Never did an embassy so ill discharge its duties. The minister received them with friendly courtesy, but became silent, after they were seated, leaving to his visitors the whole burden of introducing their important business. The topic, it might be supposed, was obvious enough. There was the black veil swathed round Mr. Hooper's forehead, and concealing every feature above his placid mouth, on which, at times, they could perceive the glimmering of a melancholy smile. But that piece of crape, to their imagination, seemed to hang down before his heart, the symbol of a fearful secret between him and them. Were the veil but cast aside, they might speak freely of it, but not till then. Thus they sat a considerable time, speechless, confused, and shrinking uneasily from Mr. Hooper's eye, which they felt to be fixed upon them with an invisible glance. Finally, the deputies returned abashed to their constituents, pronouncing the matter too weighty to be handled, except by a council of the churches, if, indeed, it might not require a general synod.[6]

But there was one person in the village unappalled by the awe with which the black veil had impressed all beside herself. When the deputies returned without an explanation, or even venturing to demand one, she, with the calm energy of her character, determined to chase away the strange cloud that appeared to be settling round Mr. Hooper,

---

6. **synod** (sin´ əd) *n.* high governing body in certain Christian churches.

Think Aloud

Reading Strategy: Breaking Down Long Sentences

To model the process of breaking down long sentences, use the following "think aloud." Write the sentence beginning "There was a feeling of dread" (p. 278) on the chalkboard. Say to students:

Perhaps this long sentence is Hawthorne's way of showing us the congregation's confusion and fear about Mr. Hooper's black veil. He takes a long path to describe the decision to send a group to confront him. Breaking down this sentence to improve our understanding also reveals traits of the congregation as a group: They don't hide their feelings, but they also don't talk about them. They don't want to take the initiative, but they don't force it on others. They are concerned about appearances. We need to keep track of the subjects and verbs of long sentences like this one, but at the same time we should be looking at what it says about characters. From that perspective, Hawthorne says a lot in this sentence—in very *few* words.

every moment more darkly than before. As his plighted wife,[7] it should be her privilege to know what the black veil concealed. At the minister's first visit, therefore, she entered upon the subject with a direct simplicity, which made the task easier both for him and her. After he had seated himself, she fixed her eyes steadfastly upon the veil, but could discern nothing of the dreadful gloom that had so overawed the multitude: it was but a double fold of crape, hanging down from his forehead to his mouth, and slightly stirring with his breath.

"No," said she aloud, and smiling, "there is nothing terrible in this piece of crape, except that it hides a face which I am always glad to look upon. Come, good sir, let the sun shine from behind the cloud. First lay aside your black veil; then tell me why you put it on."

Mr. Hooper's smile glimmered faintly.

"There is an hour to come," said he, "when all of us shall cast aside our veils. Take it not amiss, beloved friend, if I wear this piece of crape till then."

"Your words are a mystery, too," returned the young lady. "Take away the veil from them, at least."

"Elizabeth, I will," said he, "so far as my vow may suffer me. Know, then, this veil is a type and a symbol, and I am bound to wear it ever, both in light and darkness, in solitude and before the gaze of multitudes, and as with strangers, so with my familiar friends. No mortal eye will see it withdrawn. This dismal shade must separate me from the world: even you, Elizabeth, can never come behind it!"

"What grievous affliction hath befallen you," she earnestly inquired, "that you should thus darken your eyes forever?"

"If it be a sign of mourning," replied Mr. Hooper, "I, perhaps, like most other mortals, have sorrows dark enough to be typified by a black veil."

"But what if the world will not believe that it is the type of an innocent sorrow?" urged Elizabeth. "Beloved and respected as you are, there may be whispers that you hide your face under the consciousness of secret sin. For the sake of your holy office, do away this scandal!"

The color rose into her cheeks as she intimated the nature of the rumors that were already abroad in the village. But Mr. Hooper's mildness did not forsake him. He even smiled again—that same sad smile, which always appeared like a faint glimmering of light, proceeding from the obscurity beneath the veil.

"If I hide my face for sorrow, there is cause enough," he merely replied; "and if I cover it for secret sin, what mortal might not do the same?"

And with this gentle, but unconquerable *obstinacy* did he resist all her entreaties. At length Elizabeth sat silent. For a few moments she appeared lost in thought, considering, probably, what new methods might be tried to withdraw her lover from so dark a fantasy,

7. **plighted wife** fiancée.

> *"There is an hour to come," said he, "when all of us shall cast aside our veils."*
>
> ◯

Reading Strategy
Drawing Inferences
In his reply to Elizabeth, what does Mr. Hooper suggest about the veil's meaning?

Vocabulary
obstinacy (äb′ stə nə sē) *n.* stubbornness

16 ✓ Reading Check
Are the villagers able to confront Mr. Hooper directly about the veil?

The Minister's Black Veil **279**

---

15 **Reading Strategy**
Drawing Inferences

1. Ask two students to read aloud the dialogue between Mr. Hooper and his fiancée.

2. Then **ask** students the Reading Strategy question: In his reply to Elizabeth, what does Mr. Hooper suggest about the veil's meaning? **Possible response:** He suggests that the veil possesses a deep, serious, and universal meaning. Moreover, he implies that its meaning relates to the contrast between his relationship with God and his relationship with human society.

▶ **Monitor Progress Ask** students to explain what Mr. Hooper's responses say about Hawthorne's view of humanity.
Answer: Hawthorne seems to believe that people everywhere know sorrow but, more importantly, that they live burdened with secret sins.

16 **Reading Check**

Answer: The villagers attempt, but are unable, to confront Mr. Hooper about the veil.

Differentiated
Instruction   for Universal Access

Support for Special-Needs Students
Some students may need help focusing on the central ideas underlying this pivotal scene between Elizabeth and Mr. Hooper. Read the scene aloud, stopping to clarify and discuss, first, how Elizabeth tries to elicit an explanation from Mr. Hooper by using a simple, direct approach based on her position as his beloved and fiancée; and second, by suggesting that if the veil leads people to believe that he is hiding a secret sin, a scandal could easily erupt.

Then spend time discussing with students Mr. Hooper's question "what mortal might not do the same?" Help students see that he expresses the belief (no doubt Hawthorne's own) that people everywhere carry the consciousness of their own sins with them.

279

⑰ Humanities

Winter Sunday in Norway, Maine,
artist unknown

This painting is by an anonymous folk artist. Folk artists provide a link between the past and the present by reflecting social history. Folk art paintings offer intimate views of events through the eyes of ordinary people. Thus, images in folk art tend to be simple, homey, deeply felt, and untutored. Folk art incorporates common scenes and materials, native designs, and artisanship. Use these questions for discussion:

1. How would you describe the mood of this scene?
   Possible response: Students may say that it is a dreary, somber winter day in a small town where the church plays a prominent role. Students may notice that the insides of the church and houses are as colorless as the bleak landscape.

2. What seems to be missing from this scene?
   Possible response: Students may notice that no smoke comes from the chimneys and that there appears to be a lack of warmth inside and out.

⑱ Critical Viewing

Answer: Students may point out that the painting's cold, gray, and gloomy setting, as well as the stiff, proper appearance of the people, reflect the story's feeling of formality and the overriding presence of sin as symbolized by the black veil.

⑲ Reading Strategy

Drawing Inferences

1. Have a volunteer read the bracketed text. Then help students summarize the reactions of various townspeople and acquaintances of Mr. Hooper, as described by Hawthorne so far.

2. **Ask** students the following question: What can you infer about the people in the community based on their fear of Mr. Hooper's veil?
   Possible response: One might infer that Milford residents are guilt ridden, superstitious, or reluctant to admit the possibility of shame or sin in themselves or in those around them.

⑰

Winter Sunday in Norway, Maine, Unidentified artist, New York Historical Association, Cooperstown

⑱ ▲ **Critical Viewing**
In what ways does the atmosphere in this painting reflect the mood of the story? **[Connect]**

which, if it had no other meaning, was perhaps a symptom of mental disease. Though of a firmer character than his own, the tears rolled down her cheeks. But in an instant, as it were, a new feeling took the place of sorrow: her eyes were fixed insensibly on the black veil, when, like a sudden twilight in the air, its terrors fell around her. She arose, and stood trembling before him.

"And do you feel it then, at last?" said he mournfully.

She made no reply, but covered her eyes with her hand, and turned to leave the room. He rushed forward and caught her arm.

"Have patience with me, Elizabeth!" cried he, passionately. "Do not desert me, though this veil must be between us here on earth. Be mine, and hereafter there shall be no veil over my face, no darkness between our souls! It is but a mortal veil—it is not for eternity! O! you know not how lonely I am, and how frightened, to be alone behind my black veil. Do not leave me in this miserable obscurity forever!"

"Lift the veil but once, and look me in the face," said she.

"Never! It cannot be!" replied Mr. Hooper.

"Then farewell!" said Elizabeth.

⑲ ↓ She withdrew her arm from his grasp, and slowly departed, paus-

280 A Growing Nation (1800–1870)

---

ing at the door, to give one long shuddering gaze, that seemed almost to penetrate the mystery of the black veil. But, even amid his grief, Mr. Hooper smiled to think that only a material emblem had separated him from happiness, though the horrors, which it shadowed forth, must be drawn darkly between the fondest of lovers. From that time no attempts were made to remove Mr. Hooper's black veil, or, by a direct appeal, to discover the secret which it was supposed to hide. By persons who claimed a superiority to popular prejudice, it was reckoned merely an eccentric whim, such as often mingles with the sober actions of men otherwise rational, and tinges them all with its own semblance of insanity. But with the multitude, good Mr. Hooper was irreparably a bugbear.[8] He could not walk the street with any peace of mind, so conscious was he that the gentle and timid would turn aside to avoid him, and that others would make it a point of hardihood to throw themselves in his way. The impertinence of the latter class compelled him to give up his customary walk at sunset to the burial ground; for when he leaned pensively over the gate, there would always be faces behind the gravestones, peeping at his black veil. A fable went the rounds that the stare of the dead people drove him thence. It grieved him, to the very depth of his kind heart, to observe how the children fled from his approach, breaking up their merriest sports, while his melancholy figure was yet afar off. Their instinctive dread caused him to feel more strongly than aught else, that a preternatural[9] horror was interwoven with the threads of the black crape. In truth, his own antipathy to the veil was known to be so great that he never willingly passed before a mirror, nor stooped to drink at a still fountain, lest, in its peaceful bosom, he should be affrighted by himself. This was what gave plausibility to the whispers, that Mr. Hooper's conscience tortured him for some great crime too horrible to be entirely concealed, or otherwise than so obscurely intimated. Thus, from beneath the black veil, there rolled a cloud into the sunshine, an ambiguity of sin or sorrow, which enveloped the poor minister, so that love or sympathy could never reach him. It was said that ghost and fiend consorted with him there. With self-shudderings and outward terrors, he walked continually in its shadow, groping darkly within his own soul or gazing through a medium that saddened the whole world. Even the lawless wind, it was believed, respected his dreadful secret, and never blew aside the veil. But still good Mr. Hooper sadly smiled at the pale visages of the worldly throng as he passed by.

Among all its bad influences, the black veil had the one desirable effect, of making its wearer a very efficient clergyman. By the aid of his mysterious emblem—for there was no other apparent cause—he became a man of awful power over souls that were in agony for sin. His converts always regarded him with a dread peculiar to them-

---

8. **bugbear** *n.* something causing needless fear.
9. **preternatural** (prēt´ ər nāch´ ər əl) *adj.* supernatural.

Literary Analysis
Parable What message is conveyed by the passage beginning "But, even amid his grief,…"?

Reading Strategy
Drawing Inferences
Based on this description of the townspeople's reactions, what inferences can you draw about Mr. Hooper's happiness in life?

22 **Reading Check**
What one desirable effect does the veil have?

The Minister's Black Veil **281**

20 **Literary Analysis**
Parable

1. **Read aloud** the bracketed sentence.

2. **Ask** students the Literary Analysis question: What message is conveyed by the passage beginning, "But, even amid his grief. . ."?
Answer: Hawthorne's pessimistic view of human nature is revealed. Marital bliss is denied the minister and his fiancée because of his refusal to provide a direct answer about the veil. Thus, a "material emblem" destroys happiness. Hawthorne may be suggesting that true happiness is impossible in this imperfect material world.

21 **Reading Strategy**
Drawing Inferences

1. **Read aloud** with students the bracketed passage.

2. **Ask** students the Reading Strategy question: Based on this description of the townspeople's reactions, what inferences can you draw about Mr. Hooper's happiness in life?
Possible response: Mr. Hooper is miserable, not only for his own friendless isolation, but for the distress he causes in those he meets.

22 **Reading Check**

Answer: The veil has the effect of making Mr. Hooper a more efficient clergyman.

Differentiated
Instruction   for Universal Access

Support for Special-Needs Students
Students may need help to understand why the black veil makes Mr. Hooper "a very efficient clergyman." After reading aloud the paragraph beginning "Among all its bad influences," use discussion to guide students to understand the effect the veiled minister has upon people who suffer from overwhelming guilt. For these people, the minister's veil symbolizes their own sense of sin, suffering, and shame.

Enrichment for Advanced Readers
Point out that Mr. Hooper is a religious leader commanding the utmost respect. Yet his action throws the village into confusion and anxiety. Invite students to stage a debate on whether a leader has the right to take such an action. Should a leader publicly acknowledge his or her own wrongdoing while continuing to serve in an official capacity? Students may wish to conduct research to support their viewpoints. History provides ample evidence for and against the rights and responsibilities of leaders.

281

23 **Humanities**

Humanities

The Puritan, 1898, by Frank E. Schoonover

Frank Schoonover (1877–1972) was an American illustrator for magazines and books, such as *LaFitte, the Pirate of the Gulf,* and the Hopalong Cassidy series of westerns. His paintings show great precision and detail. This portrait accurately illustrates Puritan garb and conveys the subject's austere Puritan attitude. Use these questions for discussion:

1. This is a formal portrait, one in which the subject was posed by the artist. How does this concept echo Mr. Hooper's personality?
   Answer: The rigid pose suggests obedience to the will of the artist. Likewise, Mr. Hooper stands rigidly by his decision to never remove the veil or discuss its meaning.

2. Would the man in this portrait seem at home or out of place in the scene depicted in the painting on page 280? Explain your answer.
   Possible response: He would probably feel at home because the rigidity of the scene in the other painting would match his own bearing.

24 **Critical Viewing**

Answer: The dark, somber colors and the formal pose of the subject reflect the foreboding and mysterious mood of the story.

The Puritan, Frank E. Schoonover

24 ▲ **Critical Viewing**
Does this image of a Puritan reflect Mr. Hooper's character? Explain.
[Connect]

selves, affirming, though but figuratively, that, before he brought them to celestial light, they had been with him behind the black veil. Its gloom, indeed, enabled him to sympathize with all dark affections. Dying sinners cried aloud for Mr. Hooper, and would not yield their breath till he appeared; though ever, as he stooped to whisper consolation, they shuddered at the veiled face so near their own. Such were the terrors of the black veil, even when Death had bared his visage! Strangers came long distances to attend service at his church, with the mere idle purpose of gazing at his figure, because it was forbidden them to behold his face. But many were made to quake ere they departed! Once, during Governor Belcher's[10] administration, Mr. Hooper was appointed to preach the election sermon. Covered with his black veil, he stood before the chief magistrate, the council, and the representatives, and wrought so deep an impression that the legislative measures of that year were characterized by all the gloom and piety of our earliest ancestral sway.

In this manner Mr. Hooper spent a long life, irreproachable in outward act, yet shrouded in dismal suspicions; kind and loving, though unloved, and dimly feared; a man apart from men, shunned in their health and joy, but ever summoned to their aid in mortal anguish. As years wore on, shedding their snows above his sable veil, he acquired a name throughout the New England churches, and they called him Father Hooper. Nearly all his parishioners, who were of mature age when he was settled, had been borne away by many a funeral: he had one congregation in the church, and a more crowded one in the churchyard; and having wrought so late into the evening, and done his work so well, it was now good Father Hooper's turn to rest.

Several persons were visible by the shaded candlelight, in the death chamber of the old clergyman. Natural connections[11] he had none. But there was the decorously grave, though unmoved physician, seeking only to mitigate the last pangs of the patient whom he could not save. There were the deacons, and other eminently pious members of his church. There, also, was the Reverend Mr. Clark, of Westbury, a young and zealous divine, who had ridden in haste to pray by the bedside of the expiring minister. There was the nurse, no hired handmaiden of death, but one whose calm affection had endured thus long in secrecy, in solitude, amid the chill of age, and would not perish, even at the dying hour. Who, but Elizabeth! And there lay the hoary head of good Father Hooper upon the death pillow, with the black veil still swathed

---

10. **Governor Belcher** Jonathan Belcher (1682–1757), the royal governor of the Massachusetts Bay Colony, from 1730 to 1741.
11. **Natural connections** relatives.

Vocabulary Development

Vocabulary Knowledge Rating
When students have completed reading and discussing the selection, have them take out their **Vocabulary Knowledge Rating** charts for the story. Read the words aloud and have students rate their knowledge of words again in the After Reading column. Clarify any words that are still problematic. Have students write their own definitions and example or sentence in the appropriate column. Then have students complete the Vocabulary Lesson at the end of the selection. Encourage students to use the words in further discussion and written work about the selection. Remind them that they will be accountable for these words on the **Selection Test,** *Unit 2 Resources,* pages 60–62 or 63–65.

about his brow, and reaching down over his face, so that each more difficult gasp of his faint breath caused it to stir. All through life that piece of crape had hung between him and the world: it had separated him from cheerful brotherhood and woman's love, and kept him in that saddest of all prisons, his own heart; and still it lay upon his face, as if to deepen the gloom of his darksome chamber, and shade him from the sunshine of eternity.

For some time previous, his mind had been confused, wavering doubtfully between the past and the present, and hovering forward, as it were, at intervals, into the indistinctness of the world to come. There had been feverish turns, which tossed him from side to side, and wore away what little strength he had. But in his most convulsive struggles, and in the wildest vagaries of his intellect, when no other thought retained its sober influence, he still showed an awful solicitude lest the black veil should slip aside. Even if his bewildered soul could have forgotten, there was a faithful woman at his pillow, who, with averted eyes, would have covered that aged face, which she had last beheld in the comeliness of manhood. At length the death-stricken old man lay quietly in the torpor of mental and bodily exhaustion, with an imperceptible pulse, and breath that grew fainter and fainter, except when a long, deep, and irregular inspiration seemed to prelude the flight of his spirit.

The minister of Westbury approached the bedside.

"Venerable Father Hooper," said he, "the moment of your release is at hand. Are you ready for the lifting of the veil that shuts in time from eternity?"

Father Hooper at first replied merely by a feeble motion of his head; then, apprehensive, perhaps, that his meaning might be doubtful, he exerted himself to speak.

"Yea," said he, in faint accents, "my soul hath a patient weariness until that veil be lifted."

"And is it fitting," resumed the Reverend Mr. Clark, "that a man so given to prayer, of such a blameless example, holy in deed and thought, so far as mortal judgment may pronounce; is it fitting that a father in the church should leave a shadow on his memory, that may seem to blacken a life so pure? I pray you, my venerable brother, let not this thing be! Suffer us to be gladdened by your triumphant aspect as you go to your reward. Before the veil of eternity be lifted, let me cast aside this black veil from your face!"

And thus speaking, the Reverend Mr. Clark bent forward to reveal the mystery of so many years. But, exerting a sudden energy, that made all the beholders stand aghast, Father Hooper snatched both his hands from beneath the bedclothes, and pressed them strongly on the black veil, resolute to struggle, if the minister of Westbury would contend with a dying man.

"Never!" cried the veiled clergyman. "On earth, never!"

"Dark old man!" exclaimed the affrighted minister, "with what horrible crime upon your soul are you now passing to the judgment?"

Vocabulary
imperceptible (im′ pər sep′ tə bel) *adj.* not easy to perceive; unnoticeable

Literary Analysis
Parable and Symbol
What does the minister of Westbury's question suggest about the veil's symbolic meaning?

27

On his deathbed, does Mr. Hooper wish the veil to be removed?

The Minister's Black Veil **283**

---

25 **Literary Analysis**
Parable

1. Spend time reading aloud and discussing the bracketed text. Help students recognize that Hawthorne is setting the stage for the story's climactic scene.

2. **Ask** students the following question: What message is Hawthorne conveying in his description of the veil as a partition, setting Mr. Hooper off from "cheerful brotherhood"?
   Possible response: Hawthorne highlights an awful irony: although Mr. Hooper wears a veil symbolizing the guilt and sin that all people share, the veil separates him from humanity.

26 **Literary Analysis**
Parable and Symbol

1. Read aloud the bracketed passage to students. **Ask:** What does the minister of Westbury mean when he says that the moment of Mr. Hooper's "release" is near?
   Answer: Mr. Hooper is about to die.

2. Spend time discussing the question the minister asks Mr. Hooper, "Are you ready for the lifting of the veil that shuts in time from eternity?" Help students realize that in this solemn moment he alludes to the lifting of the veil between life and death—"time and eternity"—more than he does to the physical veil worn by Mr. Hooper.

3. **Ask** students the Literary Analysis question: What does the minister of Westbury's question suggest about the veil's symbolic meaning?
   Possible response: Students may say that it suggests that the veil symbolizes the division or veil between life and death.

27 **Reading Check**

Answer: Mr. Hooper musters all his remaining strength to resist having the veil removed from his face before death.

283

Characterization

1. Remind students that they studied the concept of characterization.

2. Have students reread Mr. Hooper's monologue. Then **ask** students the Spiral Review question.

   Possible response: Mr. Hooper's monologue shows his dedication and motivation to teaching an important lesson by wearing the veil—that all people must face their own secret sins.

ASSESS

Answers

Before students respond, you may wish to have them write a brief objective summary of the selection. As they answer the questions below, remind them to support their answers with evidence from the text.

1. (a) His congregation held him in high esteem. (b) The veil separates him from them; they grow fearful of him and of his apparent secret. Also, the performance of his ordinary duties as a minister begins to have a greater and keener impact on the members of his congregation.

2. (a) The sermon's subject is secret sin. (b) His sermon arouses feelings of guilt, fear, and remorse. (c) The minister's wearing of an unexplained black veil is shocking and provocative, and it causes his listeners to react in unexpected, dramatic ways.

3. (a) The "lawless wind" seems to respect Mr. Hooper's choice to wear the veil by never blowing it aside. (b) Nature's reaction adds credibility and purposefulness to Mr. Hooper's choice to wear the veil.

4. **Possible response:** Hawthorne's portrait seems to be more accurate than <u>severe</u>. He portrays a Puritan <u>community</u> that is influenced by <u>powerful</u> concepts of sin and guilt. In the literature of Hawthorne, New England is a landscape of moral <u>struggle.</u>

Father Hooper's breath heaved; it rattled in his throat; but, with a mighty effort, grasping forward with his hands, he caught hold of life, and held it back till he should speak. He even raised himself in bed; and there he sat, shivering with the arms of death around him, while the black veil hung down, awful, at that last moment, in the gathered terrors of a lifetime. And yet the faint, sad smile, so often there, now seemed to glimmer from its obscurity, and linger on Father Hooper's lips.

"Why do you tremble at me alone?" cried he, turning his veiled face round the circle of pale spectators. "Tremble also at each other! Have men avoided me, and women shown no pity, and children screamed and fled, only for my black veil? What, but the mystery which it obscurely typifies, has made this piece of crape so awful? When the friend shows his inmost heart to his friend; the lover to his best beloved; when man does not vainly shrink from the eye of his Creator, loathsomely treasuring up the secret of his sin; then deem me a monster, for the symbol beneath which I have lived, and die! I look around me, and, lo! on every visage a Black Veil!"

While his auditors shrank from one another, in mutual affright, Father Hooper fell back upon his pillow, a veiled corpse, with a faint smile lingering on the lips. Still veiled, they laid him in his coffin, and a veiled corpse they bore him to the grave. The grass of many years has sprung up and withered on that grave, the burial stone is moss-grown, and good Mr. Hooper's face is dust; but awful is still the thought that it moldered beneath the Black Veil!

Critical Reading

1. **Key Ideas and Details (a)** How did his congregation regard Mr. Hooper before he began wearing the veil? **(b) Analyze:** In what ways does the veil affect Mr. Hooper's relationship with his congregation?

2. **Key Ideas and Details (a)** What is the subject of Mr. Hooper's sermon on the day he first wears the veil? **(b) Compare and Contrast:** What emotions does Mr. Hooper evoke in his congregation that he never did before? **(c) Draw Conclusions:** To what do you attribute Mr. Hooper's newfound ability to affect his listeners?

3. **Craft and Structure (a)** According to the narrator, how does the "lawless wind" respond to the veil? **(b) Draw Conclusions:** Why is it significant that nature, as represented by the wind, has this reaction?

4. **Integration of Knowledge and Ideas** Does the portrait this story paints of Puritan New England seem too sympathetic, too harsh, or simply accurate? Explain. In your response, use at least two of these Essential Question words: *severe, powerful, community, struggle. [Connecting to the Essential Question: What is the relationship between literature and place?]*

Concept Connector

Reading Strategy Graphic Organizer
Ask students to review the graphic organizers with which they listed details to make inferences. Then have students share their organizers and compare their conclusions about the meanings of words.

Activating Prior Knowledge
Have students return to their responses to the Activating Prior Knowledge activity. Ask them to explain whether their thoughts have changed and if so, how.

Writing About the Essential Question
Have students compare their responses to the prompt before they completed reading "The Minister's Black Veil" with their thoughts after reading it. Have them work individually or in groups, writing or discussing their thoughts, to define their new responses. Then lead a class discussion, probing for what students have learned that confirms or invalidates their initial thoughts. Encourage students to cite specific textual details to support their responses.

Literary Analysis

1. **Key Ideas and Details** A **parable** is a story that conveys a message. What message does this story convey? Support your answer with details from the text.

2. **Craft and Structure** **(a)** By calling this story a parable, what expectations does Hawthorne set up for the reader? **(b)** Does the story meet those expectations? Explain your response.

3. **Craft and Structure** What does Hawthorne's parable show about the way communities may treat those who are different or behave oddly? Explain your answer.

4. **Integration of Knowledge and Ideas** Hawthorne never makes clear why Mr. Hooper chooses to wear the veil. **(a)** By leaving the causes of Mr. Hooper's choice uncertain, what might he be saying about relationships among people? **(b)** Do you agree with this implicit message? Explain.

5. **Craft and Structure** Explain how the veil might be a **symbol** of each of these abstract ideas: **(a)** sin or guilt, **(b)** sorrow or mourning, **(c)** isolation, **(d)** the mystery of the self. Use a chart like the one shown to gather details from the story that support each interpretation.

Sin/Guilt	Sorrow/Mourning	Isolation	Mystery

6. **Craft and Structure** **(a)** In addition to the veil, identify at least one other possible symbol in the story. **(b)** Explain what this additional symbol might represent.

7. **Craft and Structure** Do you think Hawthorne's intentional use of **ambiguity,** or uncertain meaning, makes the story more or less effective? Explain your reasoning.

Reading Strategy

8. **(a)** From the description in the opening paragraph, **draw inferences** about the town of Milford's physical setting and its inhabitants. **(b)** How critical is the setting to the essential meaning of this story?

9. **(a)** Based on her actions in the story, what inferences can you draw about Elizabeth's personality and overall character? **(b)** Explain which of her actions lead you to draw your inferences.

10. On his deathbed, when Mr. Clark asks him to remove the black veil, Mr. Hooper replies, "On earth, never!" **(a)** What inference can you draw about when he *will* remove the veil? **(b)** What does this inference suggest about the essential meaning or significance of the veil?

Common Core State Standards

Writing
2.b. Develop the topic thoroughly by selecting the most significant and relevant facts, concrete details, quotations, or other information and examples appropriate to the audience's knowledge of the topic. *(p. 286)*

2.c. Use appropriate and varied transitions and syntax to link the major sections of the text, create cohesion, and clarify the relationships among complex ideas and concepts. *(p. 286)*

Language
1. Demonstrate command of the conventions of standard English grammar and usage when writing or speaking. *(p. 287)*

3.a. Vary syntax for effect. *(p. 287)*

5. Demonstrate understanding of word relationships. *(p. 286)*

The Minister's Black Veil 285

Assessment Practice

Make Inferences and Generalizations (For more practice, see *All-in-One Workbook.*)

Many tests require students to make generalizations—that is, general statements based on specific information from the written passage. A generalization is a general idea that is supported by textual evidence. Use the following sample question about Hawthorne's story to show students how to make generalizations about a written text.

What effect does the appearance of Mr. Hooper's black veil have on his congregation?

A They are afraid and confused.
B They are indifferent.
C They are quietly supportive.
D They are angry and violent.

Choices **B**, **C**, and **D** contain information not found in the text. **A** is correct. The veil is mysterious and makes Mr. Hooper appear more threatening and powerful.

Answers

1. **Possible response:** This story conveys the message that all people are marked by sin, as Mr. Hooper indicates when he says, "I look around me and lo! on every visage a Black Veil!"

2. (a) He sets up the expectation that the story will have a lesson. (b) It meets that expectation by providing a lesson that can be interpreted in different ways.

3. Communities sometimes keep a distance from people who are different, as Mr. Hooper is.

4. **Sample answer:** (a) He might be saying that no one can ever fully know another person. (b) I agree, because most people never reveal themselves completely to others.

5. **Possible response:** (a) Mr. Clark highlights the guilt symbolism by asking what "horrible crime" Mr. Hooper is carrying. (b) Mr. Hooper tells Elizabeth that there is great cause for sorrow. (c) Mr. Hooper is isolated when Elizabeth ends their engagement. (d) Elizabeth finds Mr. Hooper's explanation a mystery.

6. **Possible response:** (a) The wind is a possible symbol. (b) It symbolizes nature and, by failing to lift the veil, it makes the veil seem supernatural.

7. **Possible response:** Ambiguity makes the story more thought provoking. Readers must search for Mr. Hooper's motives.

8. (a) Readers might infer that the town is small and most or all of its residents attend church. (b) The setting is very critical because in a small town that is set in its ways, Mr. Hooper's action is even more striking and curious.

9. (a) Elizabeth thinks for herself. (b) Her choice to end her engagement to Mr. Hooper led to this inference.

10. (a) Mr. Hooper believes he will remove the veil after his death, when he stands in judgment before God. (b) This belief suggests that nothing was more important to Mr. Hooper than his commitment to wear the veil.

Vocabulary Acquisition and Use

1. Introduce the skill, using the instruction on the student page.

2. Have students complete the Word Analysis activity and the Vocabulary practice.

Word Analysis

1. d. I have <u>empathy</u> for my friend who failed a test, because I have had similar experiences.

2. e. The injured dog was a <u>pathetic</u> sight, so I tried to help.

3. b. The doctor tested for a certain <u>pathogen</u> and cured the disease.

4. c. Without the science of <u>pathology</u> we would be unable to treat some sicknesses.

5. a. The taxi driver was not <u>sympathetic</u> when our flight was late.

Vocabulary

1. c. An inanimate object is not a living thing.

2. a. This type of person is respected and considered to be wise.

3. c. A movement as small as a blink might not be visible to the eye.

4. b. A tragic play is most likely to bring out sorrow or pity.

5. d. Teasing is not respectful behavior.

6. d. Stubbornness and obstinacy are similar qualities.

Writing

1. To guide students in writing this explanatory text, give them the **Support for Writing Lesson** page (*Unit 2 Resources*, p. 55).

2. Students' essays should demonstrate a clear understanding of the concept of ambiguity. Their use of direct quotations from "The Minister's Black Veil" should support their interpretation and move it forward. Remind them to use quotations accurately.

3. Assess students' evaluations using the **Rubrics for Response to Literature**, in *Professional Development Guidebook*, pages 250–251.

Ⓒ Vocabulary Acquisition and Use

Word Analysis: Greek Root -path-

The word *pathos* contains the Greek root *-path-*, which means "suffering," "feeling," or "disease." Although the root appears in words related to the emotions, it is often found in *scientific and medical terminology*. Match each *-path-* word on the left with its definition on the right. Then, use each word in a sentence.

1. empathy   **(a)** caring about the feelings and suffering of others

2. pathetic   **(b)** a microorganism that causes disease

3. pathogen   **(c)** the branch of medicine that studies the nature of disease

4. pathology   **(d)** ability to experience the emotions of another person

5. sympathetic   **(e)** arousing feelings of pity in others; pitiful

Vocabulary: Word/Phrase Relationships

For each item, indicate the letter of the choice that best illustrates the phrase containing the italicized word. Explain your thinking.

1. an *inanimate* object: **(a)** a flower **(b)** a puppy **(c)** a rock **(d)** a dancer

2. a *venerable* figure: **(a)** a village elder **(b)** a criminal **(c)** an insect **(d)** a spoiled brat

3. a nearly *imperceptible* movement: **(a)** a twirl **(b)** a lurch **(c)** a blink **(d)** a stride

4. a play full of *pathos:* **(a)** a comedy **(b)** a tragedy **(c)** a fantasy **(d)** a farce

5. an *impertinent* act: **(a)** bowing **(b)** smiling **(c)** shaking hands **(d)** teasing

6. a creature of *obstinacy:* **(a)** a fickle friend **(b)** a puzzled student **(c)** a timid mouse **(d)** a stubborn mule

Writing

Ⓒ **Explanatory Text** Like Mr. Hooper's congregation, critics and general readers alike have puzzled over the uncertainties of the black veil in Hawthorne's story. Write an **interpretive essay** in which you explore the veil's significance. Explain the ambiguity that surrounds the veil, and give your own interpretation of its meaning.

Prewriting Reread the story, listing descriptions, dialogue, and character's actions relating to the veil. Review the details you listed, and look for relationships among them. Then, write a sentence in which you state your interpretation of the veil's meaning. Underline the details on your list that point to your interpretation.

Drafting Begin with a statement about the veil's ambiguity and the meaning that you give it. Then, defend your interpretation using the details you underlined as supporting evidence. *Use transitions* such as *first*, *next*, *in addition*, and *finally* to make the sequence of your examples clear.

Revising Reread your essay and make sure you have included enough passages or details from the story to support your ideas. Add additional direct quotations as needed to strengthen your work.

> **Model: Using Exact Quotations**
> Hawthorne never tells us why Parson Hooper decides to
> , which Hawthorne *describes as a "gloomy shade,"*
> wear the veil. We know only that the veil conceals his entire
> face except for his chin and mouth.
>
> The most effective way to cite details from a literary work is to use word-for-word quotations.

Assessment Resources

Unit 2 Resources

[L1] [L2] [EL] **Selection Test A**, pp. 60–62. Administer Test A to less advanced students.

[L3] [L4] [EL] **Selection Test B**, pp. 63–65. Administer Test B to on-level and more advanced students.

[L3] [L4] **Open-Book Test**, pp. 57–59. As an alternative, give the Open-Book Test.

[All] **Customizable Test Bank**

[All] **Self-tests**
Students may prepare for the **Selection Test** by taking the **Self-test** online.

PHLit Online!   All assessment resources are available at www.PHLitOnline.com.

Conventions and Style: Adjective and Adverb Clauses

Sentence variety and flow are important elements of all good writing. Add to the fluidity of your writing by combining sentences with adjective or adverb clauses. An **adjective clause** is a subordinate clause that modifies a noun or pronoun by telling *what kind* or *which one*. An **adverb clause** is a subordinate clause that modifies a verb, adjective, adverb, or verbal by telling *where, when, in what way, to what extent, under what condition,* or *why.*

Starter Words for Types of Clauses

Adjective Clause: the relative pronouns *that, which, who, whom,* and *whose;* the relative adverbs *where, when*

Adverb Clause: the subordinating conjunctions *after, although, because, even though, so that, though, when*

Using Clauses to Combine Sentences

Choppy: The Puritans valued self-discipline. The Puritans devoted their lives to hard work.
Combined with adjective clause: The Puritans, *who valued self-discipline,* devoted their lives to hard work.

Choppy: People saw Mr. Hooper in his veil. People felt shocked.
Combined with adverb clause: People felt shocked *when they saw Mr. Hooper in his veil.*

Practice In items 1–5, identify each adjective clause or adverb clause. State what type of clause it is and tell what word or words it modifies. In items 6–10, use an adjective or adverb clause to combine the two sentences.

1. The sexton, who was the first to see Mr. Hooper, cried out in astonishment.
2. The sight that drew everyone's attention was a black veil.
3. The congregation stirred as the minister entered the church.
4. Although the villagers were curious, no one asked him about the veil.
5. As long as Mr. Hooper lived, he kept the veil on his face.
6. He would not remove the veil. His fiancée pleaded with him.
7. He would not answer Elizabeth's questions. Elizabeth left.
8. Through the veil, they could sometimes see a smile. The smile was melancholy.
9. The children were also there. The children seemed more frightened than the adults.
10. The mysterious preacher's sermon was powerful. The preacher's sermon upset his parishioners.

© Writing and Speaking Conventions

A. Writing Use each subordinate clause in a sentence. Tell what word the clause modifies and what type of clause it is.

1. who had died young
2. which hid most of his face
3. after he delivered the sermon

   Example: who loved him
   Sentence: Elizabeth, who loved him, never understood Mr. Hooper's choice.
   Word Modified: Elizabeth; **Type of Clause:** adjective

B. Speaking Write and present to the class a eulogy to be read at Father Hooper's funeral. Include at least one adjective clause and one adverb clause.

PH WRITING COACH

Further instruction and practice are available in *Prentice Hall Writing Coach.*

Extend the Lesson

Adjective and Adverb Clauses

In turn, read each of these sentences from "The Minister's Black Veil."

> When Mr. Hooper came, the first thing that their eyes rested on was the same horrible black veil, which had added deeper gloom to the funeral, and could portend nothing but evil to the wedding.

> The black veil, though it covers only our pastor's face, throws its influence over his whole person and makes him ghostlike from head to foot.

For each sentence, ask students what they notice about it. Elicit from them that the first sentence uses an adjective clause and the second uses an adverb clause.

Have students imitate one of Hawthorne's sentences in a sentence on a topic of their own choosing, using either an adjective or adverb clause. Collect the sentences and share them with the class.

Conventions and Style

Introduce and discuss the skill, using the instruction on the student page.

Practice

1. *who was the first to see Mr. Hooper;* adjective clause; *sexton*
2. *that drew everyone's attention;* adjective clause; *sight*
3. *as the minister entered the church;* adverb clause; *stirred*
4. *Although the villagers were curious;* adverb clause; *asked*
5. *As long as Mr. Hooper lived;* adverb clause; *kept*
6. Although his fiancée pleaded with him, he would not remove the veil. (adverb clause)
7. Because he would not answer Elizabeth's questions, she left. (adverb clause)
8. Through the veil, they could sometimes see a smile that was melancholy. (adjective clause)
9. The children, who were also there, seemed more frightened than the adults. (adjective clause)
10. The mysterious preacher's sermon, which upset his parishioners, was powerful. (adjective clause)

Writing and Speaking Conventions

A. Sample responses:

1. His mother, who had died young, taught him a memorable lesson. Adjective clause; modifies *mother.*
2. The veil, which hid most of his face, gave him a disturbing and mysterious appearance. Adjective clause; modifies *veil.*
3. After he delivered the sermon, the minister went home alone. Adverb clause; modifies *went.*

B. Sample response:

Today we honor a man who, <u>although he hid his face from us,</u> cared for us like a parent. Reverend Hooper, <u>who kept his secret and his promise all his life,</u> has gone on to his just reward.

PH WRITING COACH   Grade 11

Students will find further information on adjective and adverb clauses in Chapter 15.

The Fall of the House of Usher •
The Raven
Lesson Pacing Guide

DAY 1 Preteach

- Ⓒ Administer the Reading and Vocabulary Warm-ups (*Unit 2 Resources*, pp. 66–69) as necessary.
- Ⓒ Introduce the Literary Analysis concepts: Gothic Literature and Single Effect.
- Introduce the Reading Strategy: Break down long sentences.
- Ⓒ Build background with the Author in Depth and Background features.
- Develop thematic thinking with Connecting to the Essential Question.
- Ⓒ Teach the selection vocabulary.

DAYS 2–3 Preteach/Teach/Extend

- Distribute copies of the appropriate graphic organizer for the Reading Strategy (*Graphic Organizer Transparencies*, pp. 68–69).
- Distribute copies of the appropriate graphic organizer for Literary Analysis (*Graphic Organizer Transparencies*, pp. 70–71).
- Prepare students to read with the Activating Prior Knowledge activities (TE).
- Informally monitor comprehension while students read.
- Use the Reading Check question to confirm comprehension.
- Ⓒ Develop students' understanding of Gothic Literature and Single Effect using the Literary Analysis prompts.
- Develop students' ability to break down long senteces using the Reading Strategy prompts.
- Ⓒ Reinforce vocabulary with the Vocabulary notes.
- Ⓒ Reinforce unit vocabulary with the Vocabulary notes.

DAY 4 Assess

- Assess students' comprehension and mastery of the skills by having them answer the Critical Reading, Literary Analysis, and Reading Strategy questions.
- Ⓒ Have students complete the Vocabulary Lesson

DAY 5 Extend/Assess

- Ⓒ Have students complete the Conventions and Style Lesson.
- Ⓒ Have students complete the Writing Lesson and write an essay evaluating different critical views. (You may assign as homework.)
- Have students read and respond to the Contemporary Commentary.
- Administer Selection Test A or B (*Unit 2 Resources*, pp. 81–83 or 84–86).

Ⓒ Common Core State Standards

Reading Literature 1. Cite strong and thorough textual evidence to support analysis of what the text says explicitly as well as inferences drawn from the text, including determining where the text leaves matters uncertain.

3. Analyze the impact of the author's choices regarding how to develop and relate elements of a story.

9. Demonstrate knowledge of nineteenth-century foundational works of American literature, including how two or more texts from the same period treat similar themes or topics.

Writing 2.c. Use appropriate and varied transitions and syntax to link the major sections of the text, create cohesion, and clarify the relationships among complex ideas and concepts.

9.a. Apply *grades 11–12 Reading standards* to literature.

Language 1. Demonstrate command of the conventions of standard English grammar and usage when writing or speaking.

4.b. Identify and correctly use patterns of word changes that indicate different meanings or parts of speech.

4.c. Consult general and specialized reference materials, both print and digital, to find the pronunciation of a word or determine or clarify its precise meaning or its standard usage.

Additional Standards Practice
***Common Core Companion**, pp. 2–9; 28–35; 75–76; 196–207; 261–266; 314–317; 324–331*

Daily Block Scheduling
Each day in this Lesson Pacing Guide represents a 40–50 minute period. Teachers using block scheduling may combine days to revise pacing. In addition, teachers may differentiate and support core instruction by integrating components for extended and intensive support as students require. See the Guide to Selected Leveled Resources (facing page).

Guide to Selected Leveled Resources

R T I Tier 1 (students performing on level)

The Fall of the House of Usher • The Raven

Warm Up	**Practice, model,** and **monitor** fluency, working **with the whole class** or **in groups**.	Vocabulary and Reading Warm-ups B, *Unit 2 Resources,* pp. 66–67, 69
Comprehension/Skills	**Support** and **monitor** comprehension and skills development, having students complete the activities, graphic organizers, and interactive prompts **independently** or **as a class**.	• *Reader's Notebook,* adapted instruction and summary **EL** *Reader's Notebook: English Learner's Version,* adapted instruction and summary • **Reading Strategy Graphic Organizer B,** *Graphic Organizer Transparencies,* p. 69 • **Literary Analysis Graphic Organizer B,** *Graphic Organizer Transparencies,* p. 71
Monitor Progress [A]	**Monitor** student progress with the differentiated curriculum-based assessment in the *Unit Resources.*	• **Selection Test B,** *Unit 2 Resources,* pp. 84–86 • **Open-Book Test,** *Unit 2 Resources,* pp. 78–80

R T I Tier 2 (students requiring intervention)

The Fall of the House of Usher • The Raven

Warm Up	**Practice, model,** and **monitor** fluency **in groups** or **with individuals**.	• **Vocabulary and Reading Warm-ups A,** *Unit 2 Resources,* pp. 66–68 • *Hear It!* Audio CD
Comprehension/Skills	• **Support** and **monitor** comprehension and skills development, working **in small groups** or **with individuals**. • As students complete the selection in the appropriate version of the *Reader's Notebook,* **monitor** comprehension frequently with group questions and individual instruction. • **Model** strategies while guiding students in completing the activities and prompts in the *Reader's Notebook,* as well as the graphic organizers. • **Practice** skills and **monitor** mastery with the *Reading Kit* worksheets.	• *Reader's Notebook: Adapted Version,* adapted instruction and summary **EL** *Reader's Notebook: English Learner's Version,* adapted instruction and summary • **Reading Strategy Graphic Organizer A,** *Graphic Organizer Transparencies,* p. 68 • **Literary Analysis Graphic Organizer A,** *Graphic Organizer Transparencies,* p. 70 • *Reading Kit,* Practice worksheets
Monitor Progress [A]	**Monitor** student progress with the differentiated curriculum-based assessment in the *Unit Resources* and in the *Reading Kit.*	• **Selection Test A,** *Unit 2 Resources,* pp. 81–83 • *Reading Kit,* Assess worksheets

TIER 3 Tier 3 intervention may require consultation with the student's special-education or dyslexia specialist. For additional support, see the Tier 2 activities and resources listed above.

 One-on-one teaching   Group work   Whole class-instruction   Independent work   [A] Assessment

For a complete guide to selection support, including support for Advanced students, see the Overview of Resources in the frontmatter.

The Fall of the House of Usher
• The Raven

RESOURCES FOR:

- **L1** Special-Needs Students
- **L2** Below-Level Students (Tier 2)
- **L3** On-Level Students (Tier 1)
- **L4** Advanced Students (Tier 1)
- **EL** English Learners
- **All** All Students

Vocabulary/Fluency/Prior Knowledge

"The Fall of the House of Usher" and "The Raven" by Edgar Allan Poe
Vocabulary Warm-up Word Lists

Study these words from the selections. Then, complete the activities.

Word List A

alternately [AWL tuhr nuht lee] *adv.* in succession; taking turns
Tom was alternately hopeful and pessimistic, and could not make up his mind.

boon [BOON] *n.* welcome benefit; favor
The high grade on his math exam was a boon to James, giving him encouragement.

enchantment [en CHANT muhnt] *n.* state of being charmed; magical spell
During the concert, the flute solo was a delightful source of enchantment.

ghastly [GAST lee] *adj.* horrible; frightful
The television pictures of the war casualties were ghastly.

maturity [muh CHOOR uh tee] *n.* state or quality of being full-grown
In maturity, a full-grown male Bengal tiger weighs about 450 pounds.

similarly [SIM uh luhr lee] *adv.* likewise
Homer's *Iliad* is an epic poem; similarly, *Beowulf* is also an epic focusing on a hero.

sinister [SIN is tuhr] *adj.* threatening harm or evil
We could tell that the villain in that TV show had sinister intentions.

somber [SOM buhr] *adj.* dark and gloomy; depressed
The solemn music at the funeral put everyone in a somber mood.

Word List B

acuteness [uh KYOOT nis] *n.* sharpness; keenness
The acuteness of most dogs' hearing surpasses human abilities.

apathy [AP uh thee] *n.* lack of interest or feeling; indifference
The class listened with apathy to the speaker.

demeanor [duh MEEN uhr] *n.* outward behavior or conduct
Sarah was known for her shy demeanor.

gradual [GRAD yoo uhl] *adj.* taking place by slow steps or degrees
Progress on that issue will have to be gradual and can't be achieved overnight.

inaccessible [in ak SES uh buhl] *adj.* impossible to reach or enter
Their house is inaccessible except by helicopter.

sensibility [sen si BIL uh tee] *n.* capacity for being affected emotionally
Pete was respected for his sensibility to other people's problems.

solace [SAHL uhs] *n.* comfort; consolation
The old man found solace in the visit of his grandchildren.

succumbed [suh KUMD] *v.* yielded to; gave way; submitted to
Debbie succumbed to temptation and ordered a chocolate ice cream soda.

Unit 2 Resources: A Growing Nation
© Pearson Education, Inc. All rights Reserved.

(Unit 2 Resources — side tab)

EL **L1** **L2** **Vocabulary Warm-ups A and B,**
pp. 66–67

Also available for these selections:

EL **L1** **L2** **Reading Warm-ups A and B,**
pp. 68–69

All **Vocabulary Builder,** p. 74

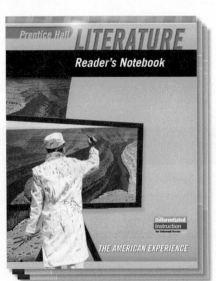

Reader's Notebooks

Pre- and postreading pages for these selections, as well as "The Raven," appear in an interactive format in the *Reader's Notebooks.* Each *Notebook* is differentiated for a different group of learners.

The selections in the Adapted and English Learner's versions are abridged.

- **L2** **L3** *Reader's Notebook*
- **L1** *Reader's Notebook: Adapted Version*
- **EL** *Reader's Notebook: English Learner's Version*
- **EL** *Reader's Notebook: Spanish Version*

© *Common Core Companion*

Additional instruction and practice for each Common Core State Standard

Selection Support

Gothic Element	"The Fall of the House of Usher"	"The Raven"
Setting		
Characterization		
Violence		
The Supernatural		

Graphic Organizer Transparencies
© Pearson Education, Inc. All rights reserved. **71**

EL **L3** **Literary Analysis: Graphic Organizer B**, p. 71

Also available for these selections:

EL **L1** **L2** Reading: Graphic Organizer A, (partially filled in), p. 68

EL **L3** Reading: Graphic Organizer B, p. 69

EL **L1** **L2** Literary Analysis: Graphic Organizer A (partially filled in), p. 70

Skills Development/Extension

Unit 2 Resources

Name _____ Date _____

"The Fall of the House of Usher" and "The Raven" by Edgar Allan Poe
Edgar Allan Poe: Biography

The sad, colorful life of Edgar Allan Poe made him America's first tormented genius. A writer of haunting poetry, brilliant detective fiction and thrilling horror stories, and insightful literary criticism, Poe unfortunately knew only limited success in his lifetime. Yet he eventually became one of the most popular American writers, largely due to his ability to call up the dark, unknown side of human experience.

A. Directions: *Edgar Allan Poe has been the subject of many plays, films, and other works. Imagine that you are helping to create a documentary about Poe's life and career. Write a brief summary of each part of Poe's life. Then, suggest a visual or two to use to illustrate each part.*

Part I (childhood): "Orphan Raised Overseas"—**Summary:** _____

Suggested visual(s): _____

Part II (military): "The Poet in the Army"—**Summary:** _____

Suggested visual(s): _____

Part III (literary career): "Turning to Fiction and Criticism"—**Summary:** _____

Suggested visual(s): _____

Part IV (last years): "A Sad End"—**Summary:** _____

Suggested visual(s): _____

B. Directions: *Imagine that you are Edgar Allan Poe being interviewed. Give his responses to the following questions.*

Interviewer: You were raised in England and spent time in the army when you started your writing career. What experiences in your life influenced your work?

Poe: _____

Interviewer: Mr. Poe, what sort of reader do you think will be drawn to your stories and poems?

Poe: _____

Interviewer: Finally, Mr. Poe, what qualities do you think are distinctly American? How do you show these qualities in your writings?

Poe: _____

Unit 2 Resources: A Growing Nation
© Pearson Education, Inc. All rights reserved. **70**

All **Author in Depth**, p. 70

Also available for these selections:

All Reading: Break Down Long Sentences, p. 73

All Literary Analysis: Single Effect, p. 71

All Literary Analysis: Gothic Style, p. 72

EL **L3** **L4** Support for Writing, p. 76

EL **L3** **L4** Grammar and Style, p. 75

L4 Enrichment, p. 77

Assessment

Name _____ Date _____

"The Fall of the House of Usher" and "The Raven" by Edgar Allan Poe
Selection Test A

Critical Reading *Identify the letter of the choice that best answers the question.*

_____ 1. In "The Fall of the House of Usher," which word best describes the single effect created by the opening description of the house?
A. interest
B. gloom
C. enthusiasm
D. sorrow

_____ 2. Which choice below best restates this long sentence from "The Fall of the House of Usher"?
Feeble beams of encrimsoned light made their way through the trellised panes, and served to render sufficiently distinct the more prominent objects around; the eye, however, struggled in vain to reach the remoter angles of the chamber or the recesses of the vaulted and fretted ceiling.
A. Not enough light came through the windowpanes, and I had trouble seeing even the larger objects in the room.
B. The light that came through the windows was so dim that it made everything in the room seem shadowy.
C. The dim light coming through the windows lit up the larger objects, but my eye could not see anything in the corners of the room.
D. The reddish light coming through the windows helped my eyes focus on everything in the room.

_____ 3. In "The Fall of the House of Usher," what does the narrator find to be the explanation for his host's sad situation?
A. the condition of the old house
B. the unending gloomy weather
C. his sister's mortal illness
D. his own failing health

_____ 4. What gothic element may be seen in details such as the black tarn, decayed trees, and vacant, eyelike windows of Usher's house?
A. macabre or violent incidents
B. bleak or remote settings
C. characters in psychological and/or physical torment
D. strong language full of dangerous meanings

Unit 2 Resources: A Growing Nation
© Pearson Education, Inc. All rights reserved. **81**

EL **L1** **L2** **Selection Test A**, pp. 81–83

Also available for these selections:

L3 **L4** Open-Book Test, pp. 78–80

EL **L3** **L4** Selection Test B, pp. 84–86

PHLit Online!
www.PHLitOnline.com

Online Resources: All print materials are also available online.

- complete narrated selection text
- a thematically related video with writing prompt
- an interactive graphic organizer
- highlighting feature
- access to all student print resources, adapted to individual student needs
- Spanish and English summaries
- adapted selection translations in Spanish

Get Connected! (thematic video with writing prompt)

Also available:

Background Video
All videos are available in Spanish.

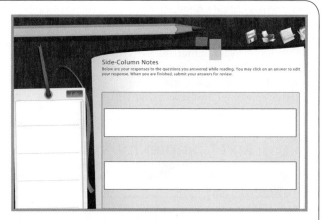

Writer's Journal (with graphics feature)

Also available:

Vocabulary Central (tools and activities for studying vocabulary)

❶ Background

Overview: The Author's Work

Edgar Allan Poe's writing contains a fascinating duality. On one hand, Poe was an idealist whose sensitivity led him to write touching lyrics, most notably "Annabel Lee." Yet he was intrigued by dark escapes from reality as well. He was irresistibly drawn to eerie thoughts, impulses, and fears in writing his daring tales of wickedness, crime, and death.

Gifted and tortured, Poe made a lasting contribution to American letters in his short stories, poems, and critical essays. He is often credited as the inventor of the detective story and a leading pioneer of the modern thriller.

The Writer in His Time

Poe lived during a period of great American expansion. A year after his birth, the United States Census recorded over 7 million people living in the country. By 1850, a year after Poe's death, the population had more than tripled. During his lifetime, cities mushroomed and a system of canals and railroads was built to link distant parts of the growing country.

The nation was also growing culturally. In 1820 the Englishman Sydney Smyth could ask, "In the four quarters of the globe, who reads an American book? Or goes to an American play?" Poe's generation, from Herman Melville (1819–1891) to Nathaniel Hawthorne (1804–1864) to Ralph Waldo Emerson (1803–1882), had begun to answer that question, laying a foundation of internationally recognized classic American literature.

❶❷ EDGAR ALLAN POE (1809–1849)

When Edgar Allan Poe died, Rufus Griswold, an editor and fellow writer who had an uneasy relationship with Poe, wrote a slanderous obituary that began, "Edgar Allan Poe is dead . . . . This announcement will startle many, but few will be grieved by it" (*New York Tribune*, October 9, 1849, p. 2). He went on to claim that Poe had been expelled from college, that he had neither good friends nor good qualities, and that he committed flagrant acts of plagiarism. Suspicious of this unconventional obituary, some speculated that Poe orchestrated the death notice himself to keep his name in the public eye. Yet, Poe's real life was almost as dark and dismal as the false obituary described it.

A TROUBLED CHILDHOOD Poe was born in Boston in 1809, the son of impoverished traveling actors. Shortly after Poe's birth, his father deserted the family; a year later, his mother died. Young Edgar was taken in—though never formally adopted—by the family of John Allan, a wealthy Virginia merchant. Poe lived with the Allans in England from 1815 to 1820, when they returned to the United States. It was from John Allan that Poe received his middle name. The Allans also provided for Poe's education; however, when his stepfather refused to pay Poe's large gambling debts at the University of Virginia, the young man was forced to leave the school.

BUILDING A LITERARY CAREER
In 1827, after joining the army under an assumed name, Poe published his first volume of poetry, *Tamerlane and Other Poems*. Two years later, he published a second volume, *Al Aaraaf*. In 1830, John Allan helped Poe win an appointment to the United States Military Academy at West Point. Within a year, however, Poe was expelled for academic violations, and his dismissal resulted in an irreparable break with his stepfather.

288 A Growing Nation (1800–1870)

❼ Text Complexity Rubric

	The Fall of the House of Usher	The Raven
Qualitative Measures		
Context/ Knowledge Demands	Early tale of horror; historical knowledge demands 1 2 ③ 4 5	Famous nineteenth-century narrative poem 1 2 ③ 4 5
Structure/Language Conventionality and Clarity	Long, intricate sentence structures; challenging vocabulary 1 2 3 ④ 5	Accessible (narrative poem); average vocabulary 1 2 ③ 4 5
Levels of Meaning/ Purpose/Concept Level	Challenging (descent into madness caused by guilt and grief) 1 2 3 ④ 5	Challenging (speaker's monologue about loss, grief, and madness) 1 2 3 ④ 5
Quantitative Measures		
Lexile/Text Length	1410L / 7,162 words	NP / 1,125 words
Overall Complexity	**More complex**	**More accessible**

STRUGGLING, WITH LITTLE REWARD During the second half of his short life, Poe pursued a literary career in New York, Richmond, Philadelphia, and Baltimore, barely supporting himself by writing and working as an editor for several magazines. After his third volume of poetry, *Poems* (1831), failed to bring him either money or acclaim, he turned from poetry to fiction and literary criticism. Five of his short stories were published in newspapers in 1832, and in 1838 he published his only novel, *The Narrative of Arthur Gordon Pym*.

AN UNHAPPY ENDING Although his short stories gained him some recognition, and his poem "The Raven" (1845) was greeted with enthusiasm, Poe could never escape from poverty. He suffered from bouts of depression and madness. His beloved wife, Virginia, seemed to be his one source of happiness. In 1846, he wrote these words to her: "[M]y little darling wife you are my greatest and only stimulus now, to battle with this uncongenial, unsatisfactory and ungrateful life…." Virginia died in 1847, at the age of 24. Some critics believe that Poe's despair over Virginia's lingering illness and death explains his fascination with doomed female characters, such as the lost Lenore of "The Raven" and the tormented Madeline Usher of "The Fall of the House of Usher." Two years after Virginia's death, Poe died in Baltimore, alone and unhappy.

A BOUNTIFUL LEGACY Since his death, Poe's work has been a magnet for attention and has influenced writers and artists of all types. His story "The Murders in the Rue Morgue" is widely accepted as the first detective story, making Poe the founder of an entire literary and theatrical genre. His psychological thrillers have been imitated by scores of modern writers, translated into nearly every language, and adapted for dozens of films. Since 1946, the Mystery Writers of America have honored their best and brightest by conferring upon them the Edgar Award for achievement in mystery writing. Today, Poe is regarded as a brilliant original whose tireless exploration of altered mental states and the dark side of human nature changed the landscape of literature, both in America and around the world.

> ALL THAT WE SEE OR SEEM, IS BUT A DREAM WITHIN A DREAM.
>
> *Edgar A. Poe.*

Extended Study: Edgar Allan Poe **289**

Daily Bellringer

For each class during which you will teach the selections, including the Comparing Literary Works selection, have students complete one of the five activities for the appropriate week in the *Daily Bellringer Activities* booklet.

Multidraft Reading

To assist struggling readers and to enhance reading for all, assign the text in chunks as warranted by length and apply multidraft reading protocols. For each reading, have students set the purpose indicated:

- **First reading**—identifying key ideas and details and answering any Reading Checks.
- **Second reading**—analyzing craft and structure and responding to the side-column prompts.
- **Third reading**—integrating knowledge and ideas, connecting to other texts and the world, and answering the end-of-selection questions.

For more guidance, refer to the *Classroom Strategies and Teaching Routines* card, **Multidraft Reading**.

❷ **Background**

More About the Author

There is a Gothic symmetry to the fact that a writer who dwelled obsessively on mystery and death would himself die a mysterious death. On September 28, 1849, Poe was found unconscious outside a Baltimore inn, dressed in tattered, ill-fitting clothes and shoes. He died in a hospital on October 7. Some have attributed Poe's death to a drinking binge, to a mugging or kidnapping, or to disease, perhaps cholera. None of these theories has resolved the mystery of Poe's death.

ⓒ Text Complexity: Reader and Task Suggestions

The Fall of the House of Usher		The Raven	
Preparing to Read the Text	**Leveled Tasks**	**Preparing to Read the Text**	**Leveled Tasks**
• Using the information on TE pp. 288–289, discuss how Poe's writings differed from those of many of his contemporaries. • Ask students how they might tell a story that shows a leading character losing his or her sanity. • Guide students to use Multidraft Reading strategies (TE p. 289).	*Structure/Language* If students will have difficulty with vocabulary and syntax, guide them through the narrator's account on SE p. 299. Then, have them reread to determine how that account fits into Usher's descent into insanity. *Evaluating* If students will not have difficulty with vocabulary and syntax, ask, "Would Usher's insanity have been easier to understand if Poe had written the story differently? If so, how do you think Poe should have written it?"	• Using the information on SE p. 311, discuss the mood Poe wanted to convey in "The Raven." • Ask students why they think that the idea of being "haunted" intrigues many readers. • Guide students to use Multidraft Reading strategies to deepen their comprehension (TE p. 289).	*Levels of Meaning* If students will have difficulty with the poem's meaning, have them look for details in the first three stanzas that suggest that the speaker feels haunted. Then, have them reread to see how Poe develops that idea. *Synthesizing* If students will not have difficulty with the poem's meaning, ask them how they would retain the feeling of being haunted if they were presenting the narrative as a film.

289

❶ Poe and Pop Culture

1. Have students read the text on Poe's cultural impact.

2. Ask them to identify the artifacts on the page. You may wish to point out that the Baltimore Ravens, represented by the football helmet, are the only National Football League team named for a literary creation. (In the National Basketball Association, the New York Knicks share a similar distinction; their name is derived from Diedrich Knickerbocker, a literary character created by Washington Irving.)

3. Ask students to discuss their own interactions with movies, television programs, songs, or cartoons that are based on or allude to the work of Edgar Allan Poe.

4. You may wish to have interested students present Poe artifacts to the class. For example, students may wish to find and play examples of the Poe-related songs by the musicians listed in the text.

❶ POE & POP CULTURE

Ever since his death in 1849, Poe's legend has grown. He has become a pop icon—a status usually reserved for movie stars or musicians. Consider this sampling of Poe's modern-day appearances:

- Poe is pictured on the Beatles' famous Sergeant Pepper album cover, and is referred to in the lyrics of "I Am the Walrus."

- Other musicians who have recorded Poe-related songs include Lou Reed, Joan Baez, Judy Collins, Iron Maiden, Good Charlotte, Public Enemy, Green Day, the Alan Parsons Project, and Japanese pop star Utada Hikaru.

- The 1990 Halloween edition of the TV show The Simpsons featured "The Raven." Poe is credited as a writer on the episode.

- Dozens of movies have been based on Poe's stories, including the famous films directed by Roger Corman.

- The Baltimore Ravens football team takes its name from Poe's famous poem.

- In the 1960s sitcom The Munsters, a raven often emerged from a cuckoo clock to squawk, "Nevermore, Nevermore."

Nevermore Nevermore

VINCENT PRICE
THE MASQUE OF THE RED DEATH
HAZEL COURT
JANE ASHER

EDGAR ALLAN POE

290 A Growing Nation (1800–1870)

Vocabulary Development

Vocabulary Knowledge Rating
Create a **Vocabulary Knowledge Rating chart** (*Professional Development Guidebook,* p. 33) for the vocabulary words on the student page. Give each student a copy of the chart with the words on it. Read the words aloud, and have students mark their rating in the Before Reading column. Urge students to attend to these words as they read and discuss the selections, because they will rate their knowledge again after they finish reading.

In order to gauge how much instruction you need to provide, tally how many students know (or think they know) a word before reading. As students read, point out the words and their contexts.

PHLit Online! Vocabulary Central, featuring tools, activities, and songs for studying vocabulary, is available online at **www.PHLitOnline.com**.

Before You Read

The Fall of the House of Usher • The Raven

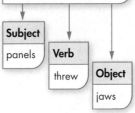

② Connecting to the Essential Question Poe explored boundaries between reality and dreamlike states. The settings in his stories and poems are fantastic mental landscapes. As you read, find details that portray the setting as unreal or dreamlike. This will help as you think about the Essential Question: **What is the relationship between literature and place?**

❸ Literary Analysis

This story and poem are examples of **Gothic literature,** a literary genre that began in England in the late 1700s. The word "Gothic" came from architecture, where it describes castles and cathedrals that served as the mysterious settings for early Gothic fiction. The Gothic style, which has the following elements, appealed to Edgar Allan Poe's dark view of the world:

- Bleak or remote settings
- Macabre or violent incidents
- Characters in psychological and/or physical torment
- Supernatural or otherworldly elements
- Strong language full of dangerous meanings

Poe's literary contributions extend beyond his stories. He was an important critic, who argued that a narrative should achieve a "certain unique or **single effect.**" He felt that every detail in a short story, play, or poem, should contribute to one impression. In Poe's work, the single effect is usually one of fear and a disturbing ambiguity about what is real. As you read, notice Gothic elements in both works that contribute to a single, unified effect.

❹ Reading Strategy

Ⓒ Preparing to Read Complex Texts As you read, *monitor your comprehension* of Poe's complex sentences. If you are unsure of the meaning, **break down long sentences** into logical parts. First, look for a sentence's subject and verb. Then, look for clues in punctuation, conjunctions, and modifiers. Use a chart like the one shown to break Poe's intricate sentences into smaller parts.

❺ Vocabulary

importunate (im pör´ che nit) *adj.* insistent (p. 294)

munificent (myoo nif´ ə sənt) *adj.* generous (p. 296)

equivocal (i kwiv´ ə kəl) *adj.* having more than one possible interpretation (p. 296)

specious (spē´ shəs) *adj.* seeming to be but not actually sound (p. 297)

anomalous (ə näm´ ə ləs) *adj.* odd; out of the ordinary (p. 299)

sentience (sen´ shəns) *n.* capacity for feeling (p. 303)

Ⓒ Common Core State Standards

Reading Literature

1. Cite strong and thorough textual evidence to support analysis of what the text says explicitly as well as inferences drawn from the text, including determining where the text leaves matters uncertain.

3. Analyze the impact of the author's choices regarding how to develop and relate elements of a story.

9. Demonstrate knowledge of nineteenth-century foundational works of American literature, including how two or more texts from the same period treat similar themes or topics.

Sentence

As if … there had been found the potency of a spell, the huge antique panels to which the speaker pointed threw slowly back, upon the instant, their ponderous and ebony jaws.

Subject → panels

Verb → threw

Object → jaws

PHLit Online!
www.PHLitOnline.com

The Fall of the House of Usher • The Raven **291**

PHLit Online!
www.PHLitOnline.com

Teaching From Technology

Preparing to Read
Go to **www.PHLitOnline.com** in class or in a lab and display the Get Connected! slide show for these selections. Have the class brainstorm for responses to the slide show writing prompt, entering ideas in the interactive journal. Then have students complete their written responses individually in a lab or as homework.

To build background, display the Background video and More About the Author features.

Using the Interactive Student Edition
Go to **www.PHLitOnline.com** and display the **Enriched Online Student Edition.** As the class reads the selections or listens to the narration, record answers to side-column prompts using the graphic organizers accessible on the interactive page. Alternatively, have students use the online edition individually, answering the prompts as they read.

---

② Connecting to the Essential Question

1. Review the assignment with the class.

2. Ask students to describe stories and films that they have read or seen that have unreal settings. What characteristics do these works have in common?

3. As students read, have them note details that contribute to an unreal or dreamlike setting.

❸ Literary Analysis

1. Introduce the skill, using the instruction on the student page.

2. Challenge students to consider as they read whether Poe achieves a single unifying effect in "The Fall of the House of Usher."

❹ Reading Strategy

1. Introduce the skill, using the instruction on the student page.

2. Give students a copy of **Reading Strategy Graphic Organizer B**, page 69 in *Graphic Organizer Transparencies*, to fill out as they read.

Think Aloud: Model the Strategy

Model the strategy of breaking down sentences. Write the first sentence from "The Fall of the House of Usher" on the chalkboard. Say to students:

> When I read a long sentence like this one, I first look for the main action, expressed in the main subject and verb. I know that the first two phrases, beginning with "during" and "when," do not express the main action. Instead, they tell *when* the main action occurs. Reading on, I realize that the two main actions are expressed in the words "had been passing" and "found myself," which share the main subject, "I."

❺ Vocabulary

1. Pronounce each word, giving its definition, and have students say it aloud.

2. For more guidance, see the *Classroom Strategies and Teaching Routines* card for vocabulary instruction.

❶ About the Selection

In Poe's classic journey into the inner reaches of a decaying mind, the narrator honors a request from a boyhood friend to visit him during an oppressive illness. The narrator arrives at a remote, gloomy mansion next to a dark lake and finds Roderick Usher in poor physical and mental health. The apparent death of Usher's twin sister leads to days of tormented suspense and a shocking final outcome.

❷ Activating Prior Knowledge

Have students think about eerie or mysterious stories they have read or films they have seen. Ask them to give quick, one-word descriptions of what they expect to experience in such works; write their responses on the chalkboard. When the list is complete, ask students to read "The Fall of the House of Usher" to see how many of their eerie expectations are met by Poe's story.

Concept Connector ➡

Tell students that they will return to their list of expectations after they have read the story.

❸ Background

Working Life

Poe would have starved on his earnings from the poetry and fiction he wrote. Like hundreds of writers before and after him, Poe supported his art by working as an editor, journalist, and reviewer. Among many other American writers who earned their living—and honed their talent—as editors and journalists are Stephen Crane, Langston Hughes, Mark Twain, and Ernest Hemingway.

❹ Critical Viewing

Possible response: Students may say that events in the story may take place in a castlelike or dungeonlike setting and that a woman will be involved. Her dress suggests that the story is set in the distant past.

❹ ▲ **Critical Viewing**
What does this opening illustration suggest about the events that will take place in this story? **[Predict]**

292 A Growing Nation (1800–1870)

THE FALL OF THE
HOUSE
OF
USHER

EDGAR ALLAN POE

1
2

3 BACKGROUND In 1839, Edgar Allan Poe lived in Philadelphia and became coeditor of *Burton's Gentleman's Magazine*, a journal that published essays, fiction, reviews, and poems, as well as articles on sailing, hunting, and cricket. Poe's articles ran the gamut of topics. He explained the parallel bars, mused about the mysteries of Stonehenge, and reviewed more than eighty books on varied topics. It was in this magazine that he first published "The Fall of the House of Usher."

Son Coeur est un luth suspendu:
Sitôt qu'on le touche il résonne.[1]

5 During the whole of a dull, dark, and soundless day in the autumn of the year, when the clouds hung oppressively low in the heavens, I had been passing alone, on horseback, through a singularly dreary tract of country, and at length found myself, as the shades of evening drew on, within view of the melancholy House of Usher. I know not how it was—but, with the first glimpse of the building, a sense of insufferable gloom pervaded my spirit. I say insufferable; for the feeling was unrelieved by any of that half-pleasurable, because poetic, sentiment, with which the mind usually receives even the

6 **Reading Check**
What does the narrator feel at his first glimpse of the House of Usher?

1. ***Son . . . résonne*** "His heart is a lute strung tight: As soon as one touches it, it resounds." From "Le Refus" by Pierre Jean de Béranger (1780–1857).

The Fall of the House of Usher **293**

---

5 **Literary Analysis**
Gothic Literature
1. Read aloud the first three sentences of the story to the class, stressing as you read the words that convey a gloomy feeling.
2. Have the class review the three sentences, looking for details that correspond to Gothic style. Write student ideas on the board.
   Possible response: Students may cite such details as "dull, dark, and soundless day"; "clouds hung oppressively low"; "alone"; "the melancholy House"; "insufferable gloom"; "desolate or terrible."
3. **Ask** students: What mood or feeling has Poe established in the opening three sentences of his story?
   Possible response: Poe's first three sentences create a sense of oppressive gloom.

6 **Reading Check:**
Answer: The narrator has an unbearable feeling of gloom.

293

Breaking Down Long Sentences

1. Have two student volunteers read aloud the sentence beginning "It was possible, I reflected."

2. **Ask** students: What are the subjects and verbs in that sentence?
Answer: The sentence's subjects and verbs are: *It/was; I/reflected; arrangement/would be; I/reined . . . and gazed; that/lay.*

3. **Ask** students to paraphrase this sentence.
Sample Answer: I thought that if the house and its surroundings were seen from another point of view, they might appear less grim, but when I looked at them reflected in the lake, they looked even worse.

❽ Critical Viewing:

Answer: Details in the painting that reflect the narrator's impressions include a dark, oppressive sky, the bleak walls and vacant windows of the house, and the decayed trees.

> THERE WAS AN ICINESS, A SINKING, A SICKENING OF THE HEART.

❼

Vocabulary
importunate (im pôr´ che nit) *adj.* insistent

❽ ▶ Critical Viewing
Which details in this illustration reflect the description of the narrator's first impression of the house?
[Connect]

sternest natural images of the desolate or terrible. I looked upon the scene before me—upon the mere house, and the simple landscape features of the domain—upon the bleak walls—upon the vacant eyelike windows—upon a few rank sedges[2]—and upon a few white trunks of decayed trees—with an utter depression of soul, which I can compare to no earthly sensation more properly than to the after-dream of the reveler upon opium—the bitter lapse into everyday life—the hideous dropping off of the veil. There was an iciness, a sinking, a sickening of the heart—an unredeemed dreariness of thought which no goading of the imagination could torture into aught[3] of the sublime. What was it—I paused to think—what was it that so unnerved me in the contemplation of the House of Usher? It was a mystery all insoluble; nor could I grapple with the shadowy fancies that crowded upon me as I pondered. I was forced to fall back upon the unsatisfactory conclusion, that while, beyond doubt, there are combinations of very simple natural objects which have the power of thus affecting us, still the analysis of this power lies among considerations beyond our depth. It was possible, I reflected, that a mere different arrangement of the particulars of the scene, of the details of the picture, would be sufficient to modify, or perhaps to annihilate its capacity for sorrowful impression; and, acting upon this idea, I reined my horse to the precipitous brink of a black and lurid tarn[4] that lay in unruffled luster by the dwelling, and gazed down—but with a shudder even more thrilling than before—upon the remodeled and inverted images of the gray sedge, and the ghastly tree stems, and the vacant and eyelike windows.

Nevertheless, in this mansion of gloom I now proposed to myself a sojourn of some weeks. Its proprietor, Roderick Usher, had been one of my boon companions in boyhood; but many years had elapsed since our last meeting. A letter, however, had lately reached me in a distant part of the country—a letter from him—which, in its wildly **importunate** nature, had admitted of no other than a personal reply. The MS[5] gave evidence of nervous agitation. The writer spoke of acute bodily illness—of a mental disorder which oppressed him—and of an earnest desire to see me, as his best and indeed his only personal friend, with a view of attempting, by the cheerfulness of my society, some alleviation of his malady. It was the manner in which all this, and much more, was said—it was the apparent *heart* that went with his request—which allowed me no room for hesitation; and I accordingly obeyed forthwith what I still considered a very singular summons.

Although, as boys, we had been even intimate associates, yet I really knew little of my friend. His reserve had been always excessive and habitual. I was aware, however, that his very ancient family had

2. **sedges** (sej´ iz) *n.* grasslike plants.
3. **aught** (ôt) anything.
4. **tarn** (tärn) *n.* small lake.
5. **MS.** *abbr.* manuscript.

Think Aloud

Vocabulary: Using Context
Direct students' attention to the word *insufferable* on page 293. Using a "think-aloud" process, model how to use context to infer the meaning of an unknown word. Say to students:

I'm going to think aloud to show you how I would figure out the meaning of *insufferable* from its context.

In this sentence, *insufferable* is being used to describe the gloomy feeling the narrator experiences when he first sees the House of Usher.

In the next sentence, the narrator deliberately repeats the word ("I say insufferable"); his use of the word *for* indicates that an explanation will follow. The narrator then implies that the feeling is a completely negative one because it is "unrelieved" by any "half-pleasurable" feeling that one would normally expect. Since the context suggests such a strongly negative meaning, I think *insufferable* must mean "deeply unpleasant" or "unbearable."

❾ Humanities

"I at length . . ." Edgar Allan Poe's Tales of Mystery and Imagination, 1935, by Arthur Rackham

London-born Arthur Rackham (1867–1939) was one of the best-known illustrators of his day, and his work is still familiar to millions of readers. Some of his most famous works are the illustrations for *Grimms' Fairy Tales* (1900) and for limited editions of German legends and Christmas stories. Rackham's imaginative, fanciful style was well suited to whimsical, grotesque, and gruesome subjects. For example, his use of form and color in this illustration for "The Fall of the House of Usher" dramatically captures the tortured mood of the story. Use the following questions for discussion:

1. How does the mood of Rackham's painting compare with the mood of Poe's opening paragraphs?
   Possible response: Students may say that both painting and story share a gloomy, sad, and lonely mood.

2. Rackham's trees have twisted and misshapen trunks. How do the trees contribute to the overall effect of the scene?
   Possible response: Students may say that the leafless, branchless trunks suggest death. The hollows of the trees may suggest contorted faces or monstrous jaws to some students.

The Fall of the House of Usher **295**

Differentiated Instruction for Universal Access

Support for Special-Needs Students
Have students in small groups listen as you read the story's opening paragraphs. Point out that, despite all the gloom described in the opening passages, the narrator plans to stick to his decision to stay for some weeks. Have students discuss why he makes this choice. Encourage them to see that he may feel loyalty to his old friend, that he may not want to let the gloom frighten him away, or that his curiosity may compel him to stay on.

Enrichment for Advanced Readers
Challenge students to trace and analyze a common theme in Poe's work: a narrator preyed upon by malevolent outside forces as well as by his own disordered or obsessive thoughts or those of another character. Have students look for examples of such outside forces in this story and in the poem that follows.

Vocabulary
munificent
(myo͞o nif´ ə sənt)
adj. generous

Vocabulary
equivocal (i kwiv´ ə kəl) ❿
adj. having more than one possible interpretation

Literary Analysis ⓫
Gothic Literature
How do the setting and mood of the story so far reflect Gothic literary style?

been noted, time out of mind, for a peculiar sensibility of temperament, displaying itself, through long ages, in many works of exalted art, and manifested, of late, in repeated deeds of **munificent** yet unobtrusive charity, as well as in a passionate devotion to the intricacies, perhaps even more than to the orthodox and easily recognizable beauties, of musical science. I had learned, too, the very remarkable fact, that the stem of the Usher race, all time-honored as it was, had put forth, at no period, any enduring branch: in other words, that the entire family lay in the direct line of descent, and had always, with very trifling and very temporary variations, so lain. It was this deficiency, I considered, while running over in thought the perfect keeping of the character of the premises with the accredited character of the people, and while speculating upon the possible influence which the one, in the long lapse of centuries, might have exercised upon the other—it was this deficiency, perhaps of collateral issue,[6] and the consequent undeviating transmission, from sire to son, of the patrimony[7] with the name, which had, at length, so identified the two as to merge the original title of the estate in the quaint and **equivocal** appellation of the "House of Usher"—an appellation which seemed to include, in the minds of the peasantry who used it, both the family and the family mansion.

I have said that the sole effect of my somewhat childish experiment—that of looking down within the tarn—had been to deepen the first singular impression. There can be no doubt that the consciousness of the rapid increase of my superstition—for why should I not so term it?—served mainly to accelerate the increase itself. Such, I have long known, is the paradoxical law of all sentiments having terror as a basis. And it might have been for this reason only, that, when I again uplifted my eyes to the house itself, from its image in the pool, there grew in my mind a strange fancy—a fancy so ridiculous, indeed, that I but mention it to show the vivid force of the sensations which oppressed me. I had so worked upon my imagination as really to believe that about the whole mansion and domain there hung an atmosphere peculiar to themselves and their immediate vicinity—an atmosphere which had no affinity with the air of heaven, but which had reeked up from the decayed trees, and the gray wall, and the silent tarn—a pestilent and mystic vapor, dull, sluggish, faintly discernible and leaden-hued.

Shaking off from my spirit what *must* have been a dream, I scanned more narrowly the real aspect of the building. Its principal feature seemed to be that of an excessive antiquity. The discoloration of ages had been great. Minute fungi overspread the whole exterior, hanging in a fine tangled web-work from the eaves. Yet all this was apart from any extraordinary dilapidation. No portion of the masonry had fallen; and there appeared to be a wild inconsistency between

---

6. **collateral** (kə lat´ ər əl) **issue** descended from the same ancestors but in a different line.
7. **patrimony** (pat´ rə mō´ nē) *n.* property inherited from one's father.

its still perfect adaptation of parts, and the crumbling condition of the individual stones. In this there was much that reminded me of the specious totality of old woodwork which has rotted for long years in some neglected vault, with no disturbance from the breath of the external air. Beyond this indication of extensive decay, however, the fabric gave little token of instability. Perhaps the eye of a scrutinizing observer might have discovered a barely perceptible fissure, which, extending from the roof of the building in front, made its way down the wall in a zigzag direction, until it became lost in the sullen waters of the tarn.

Noticing these things, I rode over a short causeway to the house. A servant in waiting took my horse, and I entered the Gothic[8] arch-way of the hall. A valet, of stealthy step, then conducted me, in silence, through many dark and intricate passages in my progress to the studio of his master. Much that I encountered on the way contributed, I know not how, to heighten the vague sentiments of which I have already spoken. While the objects around me—while the carvings of the ceilings, the somber tapestries of the walls, the ebon blackness of the floors, and the phantasmagoric[9] armorial trophies which rattled as I strode, were but matters to which, or to such as which, I had been accustomed from my infancy—while I hesitated not to acknowledge how familiar was all this—I still wondered to find how unfamiliar were the fancies which ordinary images were stirring up. On one of the staircases, I met the physician of the family. His countenance, I thought, wore a mingled expression of low cunning and perplexity. He accosted me with trepidation and passed on. The valet now threw open a door and ushered me into the presence of his master.

The room in which I found myself was very large and lofty. The windows were long, narrow, and pointed, and at so vast a distance from the black oaken floor as to be altogether inaccessible from within. Feeble gleams of encrimsoned light made their way through the trellised panes, and served to render sufficiently distinct the more prominent objects around; the eye, however, struggled in vain to reach the remoter angles of the chamber, or the recesses of the vaulted and fretted[10] ceiling. Dark draperies hung upon the walls. The general furniture was profuse, comfortless, antique, and tattered. Many books and musical instruments lay scattered about, but failed to give any vitality to the scene. I felt that I breathed an atmosphere of sorrow. An air of stern, deep, and irredeemable gloom hung over and pervaded all.

Upon my entrance, Usher arose from a sofa on which he had been lying at full length, and greeted me with a vivacious warmth which

Vocabulary
specious (spē´ shəs) *adj.* seeming to be but not actually sound

❸ ✓ Reading Check

What flaw in the house might a careful observer find?

---

8. **Gothic** *adj.* high and ornate.
9. **phantasmagoric** (fan taz´ mə gôr´ ik) *adj.* fantastic or dreamlike.
10. **fretted** (fret´ id) *adj.* ornamented with a pattern of small, straight, intersecting bars.

The Fall of the House of Usher **297**

❶❷ ? **Engaging the Essential Question**

What is the relationship between literature and place?

1. Have students read the bracketed passage, the description of a room in Usher's mansion.

2. Point out to students that Poe has now described three places in order of diminishing size: a natural landscape; a mansion within that landscape; and, finally, a room within that mansion.

3. **Ask** students: What similarities do you find in the descriptions of the three places? What similar effect do these places have on the narrator?
Possible response: Students may note that, in keeping with Poe's intent to achieve a single effect, all three settings share a sense of gloom, melancholy, bleakness, and decay. All three setting cast a pall over the narrator's spirit; in the room, the narrator feels that he is breathing sorrow.

4. Finally, **ask** students: What do these descriptions of setting suggest to you about the "power of place" in a work of literature?
Possible response: Students may say that descriptions of place can play a powerful role in establishing mood and atmosphere in a work of literature. Poe certainly uses "power of place" to the fullest extent to infuse his story with feelings of eeriness and melancholy.

❸ **Reading Check**

Answer: A barely visible crack runs down the front of the building from the roof to the waterline.

⓮ Literary Analysis

Gothic Literature and Single Effect

1. Slowly read aloud this detailed description of Roderick Usher's appearance.

2. Help students with the complexity of Poe's descriptive prose by encouraging them to keep close track of the focus on Usher's features and on the effect created by these details.

3. Invite students to find parallels between the descriptions of Roderick Usher and those of the house. Explain to students that this likeness is another example of Poe's use of single effect.
Possible responses: Usher's weblike hair is like the tangled web of fungi on the house; the ghastly pallor of his skin is like the house's bleak walls.

⓯ Reading Strategy

Breaking Down Long Sentences

1. Direct students to the bracketed sentence describing Usher's hair. **Ask** students to find the subjects and verbs in this compound sentence.
Answer: The subject of the first main clause is "hair"; the verb is "had been suffered to grow." The subject of the second clause is "I"; the verb is "could not connect."

2. **Ask** students to respond to the Reading Strategy prompt: In your own words, restate the meaning of the sentence beginning with "The silken hair. . ."
Sample answer: His silky hair had grown out carelessly and floated lightly around his face; though I tried, I could not imagine that amazing hair to be ordinary or normal.

Reading Strategy
Breaking Down Long Sentences In your own words, restate the meaning of the sentence beginning "The silken hair. . ."

had much in it, I at first thought, of an overdone cordiality—of the constrained effort of the *ennuyé*[11] man of the world. A glance, however, at his countenance convinced me of his perfect sincerity. We sat down; and for some moments, while he spoke not, I gazed upon him with a feeling half of pity, half of awe. Surely, man had never before so terribly altered, in so brief a period, as had Roderick Usher! It was with difficulty that I could bring myself to admit the identity of the wan being before me with the companion of my early boyhood. Yet the character of his face had been at all times remarkable. A cadaverousness of complexion; an eye large, liquid, and luminous beyond comparison; lips somewhat thin and very pallid, but of a surpassingly beautiful curve; a nose of a delicate Hebrew model, but with a breadth of nostril unusual in similar formations; a finely molded chin, speaking, in its want of prominence, of a want of moral energy; hair of a more than weblike softness and tenuity—these features, with an inordinate expansion above the regions of the temple, made up altogether a countenance not easily to be forgotten. And now in the mere exaggeration of the prevailing character of these features, and of the expression they were wont to convey, lay so much of change that I doubted to whom I spoke. The now ghastly pallor of the skin, and the now miraculous luster of the eye, above all things startled and even awed me. The silken hair, too, had been suffered to grow all unheeded, and as, in its wild gossamer texture, it floated rather than fell about the face, I could not, even with effort, connect its Arabesque[12] expression with any idea of simple humanity.

In the manner of my friend I was at once struck with an incoherence—an inconsistency; and I soon found this to arise from a series of feeble and futile struggles to overcome an habitual trepidancy—an excessive nervous agitation. For something of this nature I had indeed been prepared, no less by his letter than by reminiscences of certain boyish traits, and by conclusions deduced from his peculiar physical conformation and temperament. His action was alternately vivacious and sullen. His voice varied rapidly from a tremulous indecision (when the animal spirits seemed utterly in abeyance) to that species of energetic concision—that abrupt, weighty, unhurried, and hollow-sounding enunciation—that leaden, self-balanced, and perfectly modulated guttural utterance, which may be observed ▼

11. *ennuyé* (än´ wē ā´) *adj.* bored (French).
12. **Arabesque** (ar´ ə besk´) *adj.* of complex and elaborate design.

298 A Growing Nation (1800–1870)

in the lost drunkard, or the irreclaimable eater of opium, during the periods of his most intense excitement.

It was thus that he spoke of the object of my visit, of his earnest desire to see me, and of the solace he expected me to afford him. He entered, at some length, into what he conceived to be the nature of his malady. It was, he said, a constitutional and a family evil and one for which he despaired to find a remedy—a mere nervous affection,[13] he immediately added, which would undoubtedly soon pass off. It displayed itself in a host of unnatural sensations. Some of these, as he detailed them, interested and bewildered me; although, perhaps, the terms and the general manner of their narration had their weight. He suffered much from a morbid acuteness of the senses; the most insipid food was alone endurable; he could wear only garments of certain texture; the odors of all flowers were oppressive; his eyes were tortured by even a faint light; and there were but peculiar sounds, and these from stringed instruments, which did not inspire him with horror.

To an anomalous species of terror I found him a bounden slave. "I shall perish," said he, "I *must* perish in this deplorable folly. Thus, thus, and not otherwise, shall I be lost. I dread the events of the future, not in themselves, but in their results. I shudder at the thought of any, even the most trivial, incident, which may operate upon this intolerable agitation of soul. I have, indeed, no abhorrence of danger, except in its absolute effect—in terror. In this unnerved, in this pitiable, condition I feel that the period will sooner or later arrive when I must abandon life and reason together, in some struggle with the grim phantasm, FEAR."

I learned, moreover, at intervals, and through broken and equivocal hints, another singular feature of his mental condition. He was enchained by certain superstitious impressions in regard to the dwelling which he tenanted, and whence, for many years, he had never ventured forth—in regard to an influence whose supposititious[14] force was conveyed in terms too shadowy here to be restated—an influence which some peculiarities in the mere form and substance of his family mansion had, by dint of long sufferance, he said, obtained over his spirit—an effect which the physique of the gray walls and turrets, and of the dim tarn into which they all looked down, had at length, brought about upon the morale of his existence.

He admitted, however, although with hesitation, that much of the peculiar gloom which thus afflicted him could be traced to a more natural and far more palpable origin—to the severe and long-continued illness—indeed to the evidently approaching dissolution—of a tenderly beloved sister, his sole companion for long years, his last and only relative on earth. "Her decease," he said, with a bitterness

---

13. **affection** affliction.
14. **supposititious** (sə päz′ ə tish′ əs) *adj.* supposed.

Literary Analysis
Gothic Literature
In what ways do Usher's mental state and the house itself typify a work of Gothic literature?

Vocabulary
anomalous (ə näm′ ə ləs) *adj.* odd; out of the ordinary

17 **Reading Check**
In what ways has Roderick Usher changed since the narrator last saw him?

The Fall of the House of Usher **299**

---

16 Literary Analysis

Gothic Literature

1. Ask students to summarize Roderick Usher's mental state. Students' responses should focus on his nervousness, distraction, hypersensitivity, and apparent weakness of spirit.

2. Then have students characterize the condition and appearance of the Usher house in a single sentence. Students' responses might focus on the grimness of the building and its situation, the layer of moss covering the entire house, and so forth.

3. Ask students the Literary Analysis question: In what ways do Usher's mental state and the house itself typify a work of Gothic literature? **Answer:** Both are characterized by gloom, distress, and decay, which are basic elements of Gothic literature.

17 Reading Check

Answer: Usher has grown pale, and each of his facial features has been exaggerated by time. Especially notable are his "ghastly pallor," the "miraculous luster of the eye," and disheveled "silken hair."

Differentiated Instruction for Universal Access

Culturally Responsive Instruction
Culture Connection After students have reviewed the characteristics of traditional Gothic fiction, point out that many cultures offer stories and tales that present terrifying situations, supernatural elements, and fearsome creatures equivalent to the ghosts, vampires, and Frankenstein monsters of Gothic lore.

Invite students to share information about the "Gothic" tradition in their home cultures.

For example, they might briefly describe a horror story or describe images of monsters or other supernatural creatures. After everyone has shared these details, encourage the class to identify similarities and differences among these traditions. Then have the class address the issue of why "scary stories" have such a broad appeal in all cultures.

Gothic Literature and Single Effect

1. Direct students to the bracketed passage, pointing out that this is the first and only time the narrator sees Madeline before she succumbs to her illness.

2. **Ask:** How does the narrator react to this glimpse of Usher's sister?
Answer: The narrator feels astonishment, dread, and a "sensation of stupor." He is essentially shocked, frightened, and dazed by his brief look at Madeline.

3. Note to students that the narrator himself cannot explain his feelings on seeing Madeline.
Ask: How would you explain the narrator's reaction?
Possible response: Students may note that Usher is in the act of describing his sister's imminent death when she herself passes through the room—this sudden coincidence may have unnerved the narrator. The narrator's unusually intense reaction may also be a symptom of his own delicate mental state.

which I can never forget, "would leave him (him, the hopeless and the frail) the last of the ancient race of the Ushers." While he spoke, the lady Madeline (for so was she called) passed through a remote portion of the apartment, and, without having noticed my presence, disappeared. I regarded her with an utter astonishment not unmingled with dread; and yet I found it impossible to account for such feelings. A sensation of stupor oppressed me as my eyes followed her retreating steps. When a door, at length, closed upon her, my glance sought instinctively and eagerly the countenance of the brother; but he had buried his face in his hands, and I could only perceive that a far more than ordinary wanness had overspread the emaciated fingers through which trickled many passionate tears.

The disease of the lady Madeline had long baffled the skill of her physicians. A settled apathy, a gradual wasting away of the person, and frequent although transient affections of a partially cataleptical[15] character were the unusual diagnosis. Hitherto she had steadily borne up against the pressure of her malady, and had not betaken herself finally to bed; but on the closing in of the evening of my arrival at the house, she succumbed (as her brother told me at night with inexpressible agitation) to the prostrating power of the destroyer; and I learned that the glimpse I had obtained of her person would thus probably be the last I should obtain—that the lady, at least while living, would be seen by me no more.

For several days ensuing, her name was unmentioned by either Usher or myself; and during this period I was busied in earnest endeavors to alleviate the melancholy of my friend. We painted and read together, or I listened, as if in a dream, to the wild improvisations of his speaking guitar. And thus, as a closer and still closer intimacy admitted me more unreservedly into the recesses of his spirit, the more bitterly did I perceive the futility of all attempt at cheering a mind from which darkness, as if an inherent positive quality, poured forth upon all objects of the moral and physical universe in one unceasing radiation of gloom.

I shall ever bear about me a memory of the many solemn hours I thus spent alone with the master of the House of Usher. Yet I should fail in any attempt to convey an idea of the exact character of the studies, or of the occupations, in which he involved me, or led me the way. An excited and highly distempered ideality[16] threw a sulfureous[17] luster over all. His long improvised dirges will ring forever in my ears. Among other things, I hold painfully in mind a certain singular perversion and amplification

---

15. **cataleptical** (kat´ əl ep´ tik əl) *adj.* in a state in which consciousness and feeling are suddenly and temporarily lost and the muscles become rigid.
16. **ideality** (ī dē al´ i tē) *n.* something that is ideal and has no reality.
17. **sulfureous** (sul fyoor´ ē əs) *adj.* greenish-yellow.

300 A Growing Nation (1800–1870)

of the wild air of the last waltz of von Weber.[18] From the paintings over which his elaborate fancy brooded, and which grew, touch by touch, into vaguenesses at which I shuddered the more thrillingly, because I shuddered knowing not why—from these paintings (vivid as their images now are before me) I would in vain endeavor to educe more than a small portion which should lie within the compass of merely written words. By the utter simplicity, by the nakedness of his designs, he arrested and overawed attention. If ever mortal painted an idea, that mortal was Roderick Usher. For me at least, in the circumstances then surrounding me, there arose out of the pure abstractions which the hypochondriac contrived to throw upon his canvas, an intensity of intolerable awe, no shadow of which felt I ever yet in the contemplation of the certainly glowing yet too concrete reveries of Fuseli.[19]

One of the phantasmagoric conceptions of my friend, partaking not so rigidly of the spirit of abstraction, may be shadowed forth, although feebly, in words. A small picture presented the interior of an immensely long and rectangular vault or tunnel, with low walls, smooth, white and without interruption or device. Certain accessory points of the design served well to convey the idea that this excavation lay at an exceeding depth below the surface of the earth. No outlet was observed in any portion of its vast extent, and no torch or other artificial source of light was discernible; yet a flood of intense rays rolled throughout, and bathed the whole in a ghastly and inappropriate splendor.

I have just spoken of that morbid condition of the auditory nerve which rendered all music intolerable to the sufferer, with the exception of certain effects of stringed instruments. It was, perhaps, the narrow limits to which he thus confined himself upon the guitar which gave birth, in great measure, to the fantastic character of his performances. But the fervid facility of his impromptus could not be so accounted for. They must have been, and were, in the notes, as well as in the words of his wild fantasias (for he not unfrequently accompanied himself with rhymed verbal improvisations), the result of that intense mental collectedness and concentration to which I have previously alluded as observable only in particular moments of the highest artificial excitement. The words of one of these rhapsodies I have easily remembered. I was, perhaps, the more forcibly impressed with it as he gave it because, in the under or mystic current of its meaning, I fancied that I perceived, and for the first time, a full consciousness on the part of Usher of the tottering of his lofty reason upon her throne. The verses, which were entitled "The Haunted Palace," ran very nearly, if not accurately, thus:

---

18. **von Weber** (fôn vā´ bər) Karl Maria von Weber (1786–1826), a German Romantic composer whose music was highly emotional and dramatic.
19. **Fuseli** (foō ze´ lē) Johann Heinrich Fuseli (1741–1825), also known as Henry Fuseli, Swiss-born painter who lived in England and was noted for his depictions of dreamlike and sometimes nightmarish images.

19 ◄ Critical Viewing
Which of the qualities described by the narrator are captured in this illustration of Madeline Usher? **[Interpret]**

Literary Analysis
Gothic Literature and Single Effect What effect does this description of Usher's artwork help to create? Explain.

21 Reading Check
What conclusion does the narrator draw about Usher's mental state?

㉒ Literary Analysis
Gothic Literature and Single Effect

1. As students review the poem, remind them that the narrator identifies these stanzas as the lyrics to a ballad sung by Roderick Usher.

2. Guide students to notice the ways the poem reflects the same atmosphere and emotions as those in the story. In this way the verse reinforces Poe's intended single effect.

3. **Ask** students the Literary Analysis question: Which details of this poem mirror the narrator's sense of Usher's mental instability? **Possible response:** Students may say that "evil things, in robes of sorrow" reflects Usher's uncontrollable grief. "Vast forms" and "hideous throng" may refer to the wild, disordered thoughts of a deranged mind.

Literary Analysis
Gothic Literature and Single Effect Which details of this poem mirror the narrator's sense of Usher's mental instability?

I

In the greenest of our valleys,
      By good angels tenanted,
Once a fair and stately palace—
      Radiant palace—reared its head.
In the monarch Thought's dominion—
      It stood there!
Never seraph[20] spread a pinion
      Over fabric half so fair.

II

Banners yellow, glorious, golden,
      On its roof did float and flow
(This—all this—was in the olden
      Time long ago)
And every gentle air that dallied,
      In that sweet day,
Along the ramparts plumed and pallid,
      A winged odor went away.

㉒

III

Wanderers in that happy valley
      Through two luminous windows saw
Spirits moving musically
      To a lute's well-tunéd law;
Round about a throne, where sitting
      (Porphyrogene!)[21]
In state his glory well befitting,
      The ruler of the realm was seen.

IV

And all with pearl and ruby glowing
      Was the fair palace door,
Through which came flowing, flowing, flowing
      And sparkling evermore,
A troop of Echoes whose sweet duty
      Was but to sing,
In voices of surpassing beauty,
      The wit and wisdom of their king.

---

20. **seraph** (ser´ əf) angel.
21. **Porphyrogene** (pôr fər ō jēn´) born to royalty or "the purple."

302 A Growing Nation (1800–1870)

V

> But evil things, in robes of sorrow,
>   Assailed the monarch's high estate;
> (Ah, let us mourn, for never morrow
>   Shall dawn upon him, desolate!)
> And, round about his home, the glory
>   That blushed and bloomed
> Is but a dim-remembered story
>   Of the old time entombed.

㉓

VI

> And travelers now within that valley,
>   Through the red-litten[22] windows see
> Vast forms that move fantastically
>   To a discordant melody;
> While, like a rapid ghastly river,
>   Through the pale door,
> A hideous throng rush out forever,
>   And laugh—but smile no more.

I well remember that suggestions arising from this ballad led us into a train of thought wherein there became manifest an opinion of Usher's which I mention not so much on account of its novelty (for other men have thought thus), as on account of the pertinacity with which he maintained it. This opinion, in its general form, was that of the **sentience** of all vegetable things. But, in his disordered fancy the idea had assumed a more daring character, and trespassed, under certain conditions, upon the kingdom of inorganization.[23] I lack words to express the full extent, or the earnest abandon of his persuasion. The belief, however, was connected (as I have previously hinted) with the gray stones of the home of his forefathers. The conditions of the sentience had been here, he imagined, fulfilled in the method of collocation of these stones—in the order of their arrangement, as well as in that of the many fungi which overspread them, and of the decayed trees which stood around—above all, in the long undisturbed endurance of this arrangement, and in its reduplication in the still waters of the tarn. Its evidence—the evidence of the sentience—was to be seen, he said (and I here started as he spoke), in the gradual yet certain condensation of an atmosphere of their own about the waters and the walls. The result was discoverable, he added, in that silent yet importunate and terrible influence which for centuries had **㉔** molded the destinies of his family, and which made him what I now saw him—what he was. Such opinions need no comment, and I will make none.

---

22. litten lighted.
23. inorganization (in´ ôr gə ni zā´ shən) *n.* inanimate objects.

Vocabulary
sentience (sen´ shəns) *n.*
capacity of feeling

Reading Check ☑
What is "The Haunted Palace"?

The Fall of the House of Usher **303**

㉓ Background
"The Haunted Palace"
Poe wrote "The Haunted Palace" and published it five months before it appeared in this short story. Some scholars believe it is possible that the poem inspired the tale. In one of his letters, Poe says that the palace in the poem's title symbolizes the human mind: "by the Haunted Palace I mean to imply a mind haunted by phantoms—a disordered brain." In the story itself, the narrator states his belief that by singing the song, Usher is acknowledging that he is losing his mind.

㉔ Reading Check
Answer: "The Haunted Palace" is a ballad sung by Roderick Usher. The lyrics of the song describe the mysterious, desolate palace of a doomed king.

Differentiated Instruction   for Universal Access

EL **Support for English Learners**
Help students read the poem stanza by stanza, identifying subjects and verbs and analyzing unusual sentence structures. Encourage students to color-code rhyming words at the ends of lines and to take note of Poe's use of sound devices (such as the many examples of repetition and alliteration). Finally, invite students to work in pairs to read the poem aloud. Partners might proceed by reading alternate stanzas.

Enrichment for Gifted/Talented Students
The narrator reports that guitar playing was the only form of music that Roderick Usher could tolerate, and he sings "The Haunted Palace" to the accompaniment of that instrument. Ask students who play the guitar to adapt or compose a melody for the lyrics of "The Haunted Palace." They may wish to collaborate with students with singing ability to present a performance of the poem to the class.

Breaking Down Long Sentences

1. Begin by reading aloud each of this paragraph's first two sentences, encouraging students to visualize Poe's descriptions of physical actions and other details. Make sure students understand the difference between a coffin and a vault ("a burial chamber or other underground storage compartment").

2. Invite one or more students to read aloud the sentence beginning "The vault in which we placed it. . ."

3. **Ask** students to respond to the Reading Strategy prompt: Clarify the main idea of the sentence beginning "The vault in which we placed it."
   Answer: The vault where Madeline's body will be temporarily entombed is dark, small, damp, and long unused. (Students may also note the location of the vault directly below the room where the narrator sleeps.)

HE STATED HIS INTENTION OF PRESERVING HER CORPSE FOR A FORTNIGHT.

Reading Strategy
Breaking Down Long Sentences
Clarify the main idea of the sentence beginning "The vault in which we placed it. . ."
25

Our books—the books which, for years, had formed no small portion of the mental existence of the invalid—were, as might be supposed, in strict keeping with this character of phantasm. We pored together over such works as the *Ververt et Chartreuse*[24] of Gresset; the *Belphegor* of Machiavelli; the *Heaven and Hell* of Swedenborg; the *Subterranean Voyage of Nicholas Klimm* by Holberg; the *Chiromancy* of Robert Flud, of Jean D'Indaginé and of De la Chambre; the *Journey into the Blue Distance* of Tieck; and the *City of the Sun* of Campanella. One favorite volume was a small octavo edition of the *Directorium Inquisitorium*, by the Dominican Eymeric de Gironne; and there were passages in Pomponius Mela, about the old African Satyrs and Œgipans, over which Usher would sit dreaming for hours. His chief delight, however, was found in the perusal of an exceedingly rare and curious book in quarto Gothic—the manual of a forgotten church—the *Vigilae Mortuorum secundum Chorum Ecclesiae Maguntinae.*

I could not help thinking of the wild ritual of this work, and of its probable influence upon the hypochondriac, when, one evening, having informed me abruptly that the lady Madeline was no more, he stated his intention of preserving her corpse for a fortnight (previously to its final interment), in one of the numerous vaults within the main walls of the building. The worldly reason, however, assigned for this singular proceeding, was one which I did not feel at liberty to dispute. The brother had been led to his resolution (so he told me) by consideration of the unusual character of the malady of the deceased, of certain obtrusive and eager inquiries on the part of her medical men, and of the remote and exposed situation of the burial ground of the family. I will not deny that when I called to mind the sinister countenance of the person whom I met upon the staircase, on the day of my arrival at the house, I had no desire to oppose what I regarded as at best but a harmless, and by no means an unnatural precaution.

At the request of Usher, I personally aided him in the arrangements for the temporary entombment. The body having been encoffined, we two alone bore it to its rest. The vault in which we placed it (and which had been so long unopened that our torches, half smothered in its oppressive atmosphere, gave us little opportunity for investigation) was small, damp, and entirely without means of admission for light; lying, at great depth, immediately beneath that portion of the building in which was my own sleeping apartment. It had been used, apparently, in remote feudal times, for the worst purposes of a donjon-keep, and, in later days, as a place of deposit for powder, or some other highly combustible substance, as a portion of its floor, and the whole interior of a long archway through which we reached it, were carefully sheathed with copper. The door, of massive

---

24. *Ververt et Chartreuse*, etc. All the books listed deal with magic or mysticism.

Enrichment: Investigating Psychology

What Was Usher's Problem?
Roderick Usher acknowledges that he has a "mental disorder"—but he seems to have enough symptoms for three patients: pallor; weight loss; poor grooming; altered speech; nervous agitation; mood swings; obsessive behavior; hypersensitivity to light; changed appetite; aversion to most odors, textures, and sounds; aversion to most music; free-floating anxiety. How would a modern therapist or psychologist view Usher's symptoms?

Activity Discussion: Have students research the field of clinical psychology to find out how therapists treat patients with symptoms similar to those that Usher exhibits in the story. Students may record information in the **Enrichment: Investigating Psychology** work sheet, in *Professional Development Guidebook,* page 239. Then, as a class, discuss how a modern therapist might have treated Roderick Usher.

iron, had been, also, similarly protected. Its immense weight caused an unusually sharp, grating sound, as it moved upon its hinges.

Having deposited our mournful burden upon trestles within this region of horror, we partially turned aside the yet unscrewed lid of the coffin, and looked upon the face of the tenant. A striking similitude between the brother and sister now first arrested my attention; and Usher, divining, perhaps, my thoughts, murmured out some few words from which I learned that the deceased and himself had been twins, and that sympathies of a scarcely intelligible nature had always existed between them. Our glances, however, rested not long upon the dead—for we could not regard her unawed. The disease which had thus entombed the lady in the maturity of youth, had left, as usual in all maladies of a strictly cataleptical character, the mockery of a faint blush upon the bosom and the face, and that suspiciously lingering smile upon the lip which is so terrible in death. We replaced and screwed down the lid, and, having secured the door of iron, made our way, with toil, into the scarcely less gloomy apartments of the upper portion of the house.

And now, some days of bitter grief having elapsed, an observable change came over the features of the mental disorder of my friend. His ordinary manner had vanished. His ordinary occupations were neglected or forgotten. He roamed from chamber to chamber with hurried, unequal, and object-less step. The pallor of his countenance had assumed, if possible, a more ghastly hue—but the luminousness of his eye had utterly gone out. The once occasional huskiness of his tone was heard no more; and a tremulous quaver, as if of extreme terror, habitually characterized his utterance. There were times, indeed, when I thought his unceasingly agitated mind was laboring with some oppressive secret, to divulge which he struggled for the necessary courage. At times, again, I was obliged to resolve all into the mere inexplicable vagaries[25] of madness, for I beheld him gazing upon vacancy for long hours, in an attitude of the profoundest attention, as if listening to some imaginary sound. It was no wonder that his condition terrified—that it infected me. I felt creeping upon me, by slow yet uncertain degrees, the wild influences of his own fantastic yet impressive superstitions.

It was, especially, upon retiring to bed late in the night of the seventh or eighth day after the placing of the lady Madeline within the donjon, that I experienced the full power of such feelings. Sleep came not near my couch—while the hours waned and waned away. I struggled to reason off the nervousness which had dominion over me. I endeavored to believe that much, if not all of what I felt, was due to the bewildering influence of the gloomy furniture of the room—of the dark and tattered draperies, which, tortured

27  **Reading Check**

What does the narrator notice about Madeline's appearance in her coffin?

---

25. vagaries (vā´ ger ēz) *n.* odd, unexpected actions or notions.

26 **Critical Thinking**

Speculate

1. Ask students to recall Roderick Usher's behavior and appearance earlier in the story. Students should remember Usher's nervousness and apparent ill health.

2. Read aloud the bracketed paragraph beginning "And now, some days of bitter grief." **Ask** students to speculate about what may have caused this deterioration in Roderick Usher.
   Answer: Students may say that grief has overwhelmed him, that his twin's death has made him fear for his own life, and that he is harboring a terrible secret that torments him.

27 **Reading Check**

Answer: The narrator notices Madeline's strong resemblance to her brother as well as the way her face retains a slight smile and a faint blush of color.

1. Have a student volunteer read aloud the paragraph beginning "It was, especially," which begins on page 305. Encourage other students to listen carefully for descriptions of the narrator's physical and mental condition.

2. Then, **ask** students the Literary Analysis question: Which elements of Gothic literature are present in this description of the narrator's sleepless night?
Answer: The narrator's room is a gloomy, morbid setting; he hears strange and eerie sounds in the night, which increase his sense of horror. His physical and mental symptoms have begun to feed one another in a destructive, cyclical manner.

Literary Analysis
Gothic Literature
Which elements of Gothic literature are present in this description of the narrator's sleepless night?

❷❽

into motion by the breath of a rising tempest, swayed fitfully to and fro upon the walls, and rustled uneasily about the decorations of the bed. But my efforts were fruitless. An irrepressible tremor gradually pervaded my frame; and, at length, there sat upon my very heart an incubus[26] of utterly causeless alarm. Shaking this off with a gasp and a struggle, I uplifted myself upon the pillows, and, peering earnestly within the intense darkness of the chamber, hearkened—I know not why, except that an instinctive spirit prompted me—to certain low and indefinite sounds which came, through the pauses of the storm, at long intervals, I knew not whence. Overpowered by an intense sentiment of horror, unaccountable yet unendurable, I threw on my clothes with haste (for I felt that I should sleep no more during the night), and endeavored to arouse myself from the pitiable condition into which I had fallen by pacing rapidly to and fro through the apartment.

I had taken but few turns in this manner, when a light step on an adjoining staircase arrested my attention. I presently recognized it as that of Usher. In an instant afterward he rapped, with a gentle touch, at my door, and entered, bearing a lamp. His countenance was, as usual, cadaverously wan—but, moreover, there was a species of mad hilarity in his eyes—an evidently restrained hysteria in his whole demeanor. His air appalled me—but anything was preferable to the solitude which I had so long endured, and I even welcomed his presence as a relief.

"And you have not seen it?" he said abruptly, after having stared about him for some moments in silence—"you have not then seen it?—but, stay! you shall." Thus speaking, and having carefully shaded his lamp, he hurried to one of the casements, and threw it freely open to the storm.

The impetuous fury of the entering gust nearly lifted us from our feet. It was, indeed, a tempestuous yet sternly beautiful night, and one wildly singular in its terror and its beauty. A whirlwind had apparently collected its force in our vicinity; for there were frequent and violent alterations in the direction of the wind; and the exceeding density of the clouds (which hung so low as to press upon the turrets of the house) did not prevent our perceiving the lifelike velocity with which they flew careering from all points against each other, without passing away into the distance. I say that even their exceeding density did not prevent our perceiving this—yet we had no glimpse of the moon or stars, nor was there any flashing forth of the lightning. But the under surfaces of the huge masses of agitated vapor, as well as all terrestrial objects immediately around us, were glowing in the unnatural light of a faintly luminous and distinctly visible gaseous exhalation which hung about and enshrouded the mansion.

"You must not—you shall not behold this!" said I, shuddering,

---

26. incubus (in′ kyə bəs) *n.* something nightmarishly burdensome.

Enrichment: Analyzing Film

Film Adaptations of Poe's Work
The vivid images in Edgar Allan Poe's stories and poems and his exploration of macabre, gruesome, and chilling themes have made his literary works appealing to filmmakers. Several of Poe's works have been adapted more than once. Films based on Poe's works include *The Raven* (1935, 1963), *The Tell-Tale Heart* (1962), *The Fall of the House of Usher* (1982), *Murders in the Rue Morgue* (1932, 1971, 1986), *The Masque of the Red Death* (1964, 1989), and *The Pit and the Pendulum* (1961).

Activity: Analyze a Film Invite students to read a poem or tale by Poe and then to watch a film adaptation of it, recording their responses in the **Enrichment: Analyzing Film** work sheet, in *Professional Development Guidebook,* page 226. Ask students to write a critical essay that analyzes the strengths and weaknesses of the film version.

to Usher, as I led him, with a gentle violence, from the window to a seat. "These appearances, which bewilder you, are merely electrical phenomena not uncommon—or it may be that they have their ghastly origin in the rank miasma²⁷ of the tarn. Let us close this casement:—the air is chilling and dangerous to your frame. Here is one of your favorite romances. I will read, and you shall listen:—and so we will pass away this terrible night together."

The antique volume which I had taken up was the *Mad Trist* of Sir Launcelot Canning;²⁸ but I had called it a favorite of Usher's more in sad jest than in earnest; for, in truth, there is little in its uncouth and unimaginative prolixity which could have had interest for the lofty and spiritual ideality of my friend. It was, however, the only book immediately at hand; and I indulged a vague hope that the excitement which now agitated the hypochondriac, might find relief (for the history of mental disorder is full of similar anomalies) even in the extremeness of the folly which I should read. Could I have judged, indeed, by the wild overstrained air of vivacity with which he hearkened, or apparently hearkened, to the words of the tale, I might well have congratulated myself upon the success of my design.

I had arrived at that well-known portion of the story where Ethelred, the hero of the Trist, having sought in vain for peaceable admission into the dwelling of the hermit, proceeds to make good an entrance by force. Here, it will be remembered, the words of the narrative run thus:

"And Ethelred, who was by nature of a doughty heart, and who was now mighty withal, on account of the powerfulness of the wine which he had drunken, waited no longer to hold parley with the hermit, who, in sooth, was of an obstinate and maliceful turn, but feeling the rain upon his shoulders, and fearing the rising of the tempest, uplifted his mace outright, and, with blows, made quickly room in the plankings of the door for his gauntleted hand; and now pulling therewith sturdily, he so cracked, and ripped, and tore all asunder, that the noise of the dry and hollow-sounding wood alarumed and reverberated throughout the forest."

At the termination of this sentence I started and, for a moment, paused; for it appeared to me (although I at once concluded that my excited fancy had deceived me)—it appeared to me that, from some very remote portion of the mansion, there came, indistinctly to my ears, which might have been, in its exact similarity of character, the echo (but a stifled and dull one certainly) of the very cracking and ripping sound which Sir Launcelot had so particularly described. It was, beyond doubt, the coincidence alone which had arrested my attention; for, amid the rattling of the sashes of the casements, and the ordinary commingled noises of the still increasing storm, the sound, itself, had nothing, surely, which should have interested or

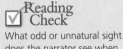

30 ☑ **Reading Check**
What odd or unnatural sight does the narrator see when the curtains are opened?

---

27. **miasma** (mī az′ me) *n.* unwholesome atmosphere.
28. ***Mad Trist* of Sir Launcelot Canning** fictional book and author.

> "YOU MUST NOT—YOU SHALL NOT BEHOLD THIS!"

29 Literary Analysis
Gothic Literature

1. Review the bracketed paragraphs with the class. **Ask:** What startling coincidence does the narrator experience as he is reading? **Answer:** As the narrator is reading about a cracking, tearing sound in the story, he actually hears the same sound within the mansion.

2. Point out that earlier in the story Usher had told the narrator about his belief that the mansion had a mysterious living connection to Usher's family.

3. **Ask** students: At this point in the story, do you think this mysterious noise is a coincidence? Why or why not? **Possible response:** Most students may say that the noise has an eerie, mysterious meaning rather than being a simple coincidence.

4. Tell students to watch for additional Gothic effects as the narrator continues to read the story.

30 Reading Check

Answer: The narrator sees strangely dense clouds, whirlwinds, and other effects of a terrible storm taking place on a "sternly beautiful night."

Differentiated
Instruction for Universal Access

EL Support for English Learners
Students struggling with Poe's nineteenth-century prose may need extra help with the passages from *Mad Trist*, a story-within-the story that presents an even more "antique" style and vocabulary. Read the Ethelred passages aloud to the class, pausing as needed to define such archaisms as *doughty* ("brave"); *hold parley* ("discuss terms"); *mace* ("metal club"); *gauntleted* ("armor-gloved"); *sore enraged* ("extremely angry"); *brazen* ("made of brass"); *in sooth* ("truthfully"); *tarried not* ("did not stay").

Enrichment for Advanced Readers
Tell students that whirlpools and whirlwinds are recurring symbols in Poe stories. Because they draw things toward their center, whirlpools and whirlwinds symbolize destructive collapse. Have students read and report on another piece of Poe's short fiction that uses whirling imagery, such as "A Descent Into the Maelstrom." Students should be able to summarize the story and explain how this particular imagery relates to the story's plot, themes, or characters.

1. Read aloud for students the paragraph beginning "And now, the champion." Remind students that these words are being read aloud to Roderick Usher by the narrator from a book called *Mad Trist*.

2. **Ask** students to respond to the Reading Strategy prompt: Summarize the action of the paragraph-long sentence beginning "And now, the champion." **Sample Answer:** Ethelred thinks of the magical shield, removes the dragon's corpse, and walks toward the shield hanging on the castle wall, during which time the shield crashes to the floor at his feet.

disturbed me. I continued the story:

"But the good champion Ethelred, now entering within the door, was sore enraged and amazed to perceive no signal of the maliceful hermit; but, in the stead thereof, a dragon of a scaly and prodigious demeanor, and of a fiery tongue, which sate in guard before a palace of gold, with a floor of silver; and upon the wall there hung a shield of shining brass with this legend enwritten—

> Who entereth herein, a conqueror
> hath bin;
> Who slayeth the dragon, the shield
> he shall win.

And Ethelred uplifted his mace, and struck upon the head of the dragon, which fell before him, and gave up his pasty breath, with a shriek so horrid and harsh, and withal so piercing, that Ethelred had fain to close his ears with his hands against the dreadful noise of it, the like whereof was never before heard."

Here again I paused abruptly, and now with a feeling of wild amazement—for there could be no doubt whatever that, in this instance, I did actually hear (although from what direction it proceeded I found it impossible to say) a low and apparently distant, but harsh, protracted, and most unusual screaming or grating sound—the exact counterpart of what my fancy had already conjured up for the dragon's unnatural shriek as described by the romancer.

Oppressed, as I certainly was, upon the extraordinary coincidence, by a thousand conflicting sensations, in which wonder and extreme terror were predominant, I still retained sufficient presence of mind to avoid exciting, by an observation, the sensitive nervousness of my companion. I was by no means certain that he had noticed the sounds in question; although, assuredly, a strange alteration had, during the last few minutes, taken place in his demeanor. From a position fronting my own, he had gradually brought round his chair; so as to sit with his face to the door of the chamber; and thus I could but partially perceive his features, although I saw that his lips trembled as if he were murmuring inaudibly. His head had dropped upon his breast—yet I knew that he was not asleep, from the wide and rigid opening of the eye as I caught a glance of it in profile. The motion of his body, too, was at variance with this idea—for he rocked from side to side with a gentle yet constant and uniform sway. Having rapidly taken notice of all this, I resumed the narrative of Sir Launcelot, which thus proceeded:

"And now, the champion, having escaped from the terrible fury of the dragon, bethinking himself of the brazen shield, and of the breaking up of the enchantment which was upon it, removed the carcass from out of the way before him, and approached valorously over the silver pavement of the castle to where the shield was upon the wall; which in sooth tarried not for his full coming, but fell down at his feet

Reading Strategy

Breaking Down Long Sentences

Summarize the action of the paragraph-long sentence beginning "And now, the **31** champion. . ."

Enrichment: Investigating Health and Medicine

A Matter of Life or Death

The fear of being buried alive is not merely a clinical condition—taphephobia—or the stuff of urban legends. In Usher's time medical science had only a few basic techniques for detecting breath and pulse. One method, for example, was to hold a mirror to the patient's nostrils and mouth to check for the telltale fog of breath. Incidents of premature burial, though very rare, have occurred; inventors in the past devised "safety coffins" variously equipped with glass panels, air tubes, and signaling devices.

Activity: Research Ask students what would happen if Madeline "died" in the present day. What methods would doctors use to determine the absence of life? Have students research the equipment and techniques used by modern doctors to establish the presence—and absence—of "vital signs." Have them record their findings in the **Enrichment: Investigating Health and Medicine** work sheet, in *Professional Development Guidebook*, page 229.

upon the silver floor, with a mighty great and terrible ringing sound."

No sooner had these syllables passed my lips, than—as if a shield of brass had indeed, at the moment, fallen heavily upon a floor of silver—I became aware of a distinct, hollow, metallic, and clangorous, yet apparently muffled, reverberation. Completely unnerved, I leaped to my feet; but the measured rocking movement of Usher was undisturbed. I rushed to the chair in which he sat. His eyes were bent fixedly before him, and throughout his whole countenance there reigned a stony rigidity. But, as I placed my hand upon his shoulder, there came a strong shudder over his whole person; a sickly smile quivered about his lips; and I saw that he spoke in a low, hurried, and gibbering murmur, as if unconscious of my presence. Bending closely over him I at length drank in the hideous import of his words.

"Not hear it?—yes, I hear it, and have heard it. Long—long— long—many minutes, many hours, many days, have I heard it—yet I dared not—oh, pity me, miserable wretch that I am!—I *dared* not—I dared not speak! *We have put her living in the tomb!* Said I not that my senses were acute? I *now* tell you that I heard her first feeble movement in the hollow coffin. I heard them—many, many days ago—yet I dared not—*I dared not speak!* and now—tonight—Ethelred—ha! ha!—the breaking of the hermit's door, and the death cry of the dragon, and the clangor of the shield—say, rather, the rending of her coffin, and the grating of the iron hinges of her prison, and her struggles within the coppered archway of the vault! Oh! wither shall I fly? Will she not be here anon? Is she not hurrying to upbraid me for my haste? Have I not heard her footstep on the stair? Do I not distinguish that heavy and horrible beating of her heart? Madman!"—here he sprang furiously to his feet, and shrieked out his syllables, as if in the effort he were giving up his soul—*"Madman! I tell you that she now stands without the door!"*

As if in the superhuman energy of his utterance there had been found the potency of a spell, the huge antique panels to which the speaker pointed threw slowly back, upon the instant, their ponderous and ebony jaws. It was the work of the rushing gust—but then without those doors there *did* stand the lofty and enshrouded figure of the lady Madeline of Usher. There was blood upon her white robes, and the evidence of some bitter struggle upon every portion of her emaciated frame. For a moment she remained trembling and reeling to and fro upon the threshold—then, with a low moaning cry, fell heavily inward upon the person of her brother, and in her violent and now final death agonies, bore him to the floor a corpse, and a victim to the terrors he had anticipated.

From that chamber, and from that mansion, I fled aghast. The storm was still abroad in all its wrath as I found myself crossing the old causeway. Suddenly there shot along the path a wild light, and I turned to see whence a gleam so unusual could have issued; for the vast house and its shadows were alone behind me. The radiance

The Fall of the House of Usher 309

Literary Analysis
Gothic Literature and Single Effect What effect does the description of Usher trembling and rocking help to create?

. . . A SICKLY SMILE QUIVERED ABOUT HIS LIPS . . .

Literary Analysis
Gothic Literature
Which aspects of Gothic literature are apparent in this description of Madeline Usher?

Reading Check
What unusual sounds does the narrator hear as he reads aloud?

---

32 Literary Analysis
Gothic Literature

1. Read the bracketed two-sentence passage to students, noting that this is the second time in a short interval that the narrator has mentioned Usher's rocking motions.

2. **Ask** students the first Literary Analysis question: What effect does the description of Usher trembling and rocking help to create?
   Possible response: The descriptions of Usher's trembling and rocking makes his psychological stress visible. The rocking motions hint that Usher may be entering a disturbed, childlike state.

33 Literary Analysis
Gothic Literature

1. Read aloud the paragraph beginning "As if in the superhuman energy."

2. **Ask** students the second Literary Analysis question: Which aspects of Gothic literature are apparent in this description of Madeline Usher?
   Answer: This passage features Gothic elements such as macabre or violent plot details ("blood upon her white robes," "some bitter struggle," "violent and now final death agonies"), characters in physical or psychological torment (Madeline and Roderick), and the presence of a supernatural or otherworldly element ("superhuman energy").

34 Reading Check
Answer: During his reading, the narrator hears a cracking, ripping noise, a shriek, and a heavy metallic thud.

Differentiated
Instruction for Universal Access

Support for Less Proficient Readers
After a long, leisurely narrative, Poe packs the climax of his story into two dense paragraphs. Some students may have difficulty grasping the sequence of events or visualizing what is happening. As a class, build a timeline of the action, from the time the panels open, revealing Madeline, to the collapse of the mansion into the tarn. Be sure that students understand that Madeline is alive—not a ghost or vision—until the moment she and Usher die together.

Enrichment for Gifted/Talented Students
Roderick Usher's climactic words form one of the more vivid and theatrical speeches in literature. Invite a student with acting ability to memorize Usher's last words and prepare to perform them as a dramatic monologue for the entire class.

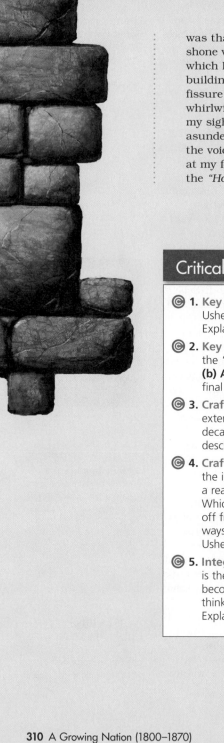

Before students respond, you may wish to have them write a brief objective summary of the selection. As they answer the questions below, remind them to support their answers with evidence from the text.

1. (a) The narrator arrives to help Usher, his boyhood friend, through an illness. (b) He is powerless to stop Usher's descent into madness and death.

2. (a) Usher believes that inanimate matter—in particular, the Usher house—is capable of feeling. He believes that the house has an organic connection to and influence on his family. (b) Usher's beliefs seem to be confirmed when the house "dies"—it completely collapses—after the deaths of Usher and his sister.

3. (a) Students might cite "excessive antiquity"; "discoloration of ages"; "minute fungi overspread the whole exterior"; "crumbling condition of individual stones"; "barely perceptible fissure . . . extending from the roof . . . down the wall in a zigzag fashion." (b) The detail of the fissure hints that the house may be vulnerable to collapse.

4. (a) Students might cite details such as "dark and intricate passages"; "phantasmagoric armorial trophies"; "feeble beams of encrimsoned light"; and "an air of stern, deep, and irredeemable gloom." (b) Possible responses include "overdone cordiality"; "cadaverousness of complexion, ghastly pallor of the skin, silken hair . . . suffered to grow all unheeded." (c) Like Usher's physical appearance, the house is in a state of decay; like his mind, the house is gloomy and full of sorrow.

5. (a) **Possible response:** Since mental illness is not contagious, the detail of the narrator being "infected" by Usher's condition may indicate a supernatural effect. (b) **Possible response:** Some students may feel that the narrator, though deeply stressed, remains reliable. Others may suggest that his overwrought narrative contains exaggerations and hallucinations.

310

was that of the full, setting, and bloodred moon, which now shone vividly through that once barely discernible fissure, of which I have before spoken as extending from the roof of the building, in a zigzag direction, to the base. While I gazed, this fissure rapidly widened—there came a fierce breath of the whirlwind—the entire orb of the satellite burst at once upon my sight—my brain reeled as I saw the mighty walls rushing asunder—there was a long tumultuous shouting sound like the voice of a thousand waters—and the deep and dank tarn at my feet closed sullenly and silently over the fragments of the *"House of Usher."*

Critical Reading

Ⓒ **1. Key Ideas and Details (a)** Why has the narrator gone to visit Usher? **(b) Assess:** Does the narrator succeed in his purpose? Explain.

Ⓒ **2. Key Ideas and Details (a) Interpret:** What beliefs about the "sentience" of matter does Usher express to the narrator? **(b) Analyze:** How are Usher's beliefs and fears borne out by the final events of the story?

Ⓒ **3. Craft and Structure (a) Analyze:** In the description of the exterior of the house, which words suggest the presence of decay in the structure itself? **(b) Connect:** In what ways does this description foreshadow, or hint at, the ending of the story?

Ⓒ **4. Craft and Structure (a) Interpret:** Which descriptive details of the interior of the house suggest that the narrator has entered a realm that is very different from the ordinary world? **(b) Infer:** Which details in Usher's appearance suggest that he has been cut off from the outside world for many years? **(c) Connect:** In what ways is the appearance of the interior of the house related to Usher's appearance and to the condition of his mind?

Ⓒ **5. Integration of Knowledge and Ideas (a) Analyze:** What is the significance of the detail that the narrator finds himself becoming affected by Usher's condition? **(b) Evaluate:** Do you think the narrator is a reliable witness of the events he describes? Explain your opinion.

Critical Commentary

On Writing "The Raven"
Edgar Allan Poe

Poe's most famous poem, "The Raven," was an instant popular and critical hit. Just as people today are interested in "behind-the-scenes" information about their favorite movies or songs, Poe's fans wanted to know how their favorite poem was written. Poe obliged with an essay explaining that he wrote "The Raven" with almost mathematical precision. First, Poe explains that he wanted to write a poem that was short enough to be read in one sitting, but long enough to have an impact:

> ... there is a distinct limit, as regards length, to all works of literary art—the limit of a single sitting.... Holding in view these consider-ations, as well as that degree of excitement which I deemed not above the popular, while not below the critical, taste, I reached at once what I conceived the proper length for my intended poem—a length of about one hundred lines. It is, in fact, a hundred and eight.

Poe goes on to tell how he chose both his subject matter and the mood of melancholy, or sadness, he wanted to convey:

> Beauty of whatever kind, in its supreme development, invariably excites the sensitive soul to tears. Melancholy is thus the most legitimate of all the poetical tones.

Poe then says that he wanted a **refrain,** or repeated set of phrases or lines, containing the *o* and *r* sounds, but he needed to find the right word:

> ... it became necessary to select a word embodying this sound, and at the same time in the fullest possible keeping with that melancholy which I had predetermined as the tone of the poem. In such a search it would have been absolutely impossible to overlook the word "Nevermore." In fact, it was the very first which presented itself.

Now Poe had a problem: what kind of creature would speak the refrain?

> Here, then, immediately arose the idea of a non-reasoning creature capable of speech; and, very naturally, a parrot, in the first instance, suggested itself, but was superseded forthwith by a Raven, as equally capable of speech, and infinitely more in keeping with the intended tone.

Ⓒ **Key Ideas and Details**

- What tone did Poe want to achieve in "The Raven"?
- What subject did Poe believe is the most suitable for poetry?
- Why did Poe choose a Raven and not a parrot to deliver the refrain "Nevermore"?

Extended Study: Edgar Allan Poe **311**

Critical Commentary

1. Before reading the Critical Commentary, poll students about what they already know about Poe's most famous poem. Even if they have never read the poem, many students may recognize the talking bird, the repetition of "Nevermore," and perhaps some phrases from the beginning of the poem.

2. Have students read the Commentary as a motivating introduction to the poem.

3. Encourage students to consider as they read other "behind-the-scenes" questions they wish Poe had answered.

4. After students have read the poem, you may wish to return to the Critical Commentary to discuss whether students find Poe's judgments (about length, subject, and the inappropriateness of parrots, for example) valid.

Key Ideas and Details
Answers

1. Poe wanted to achieve a tone of melancholy.

2. Poe believed that beauty is the subject most suitable for poetry.

3. Poe believed a raven would be more in keeping with the intended melancholy tone than would a parrot.

Enrichment: Investigating Career Connections

Literary Critics
A literary critic reads, analyzes, evaluates, and comments on literature for both general and specialized audiences. He or she does so online, in magazines or newspapers, on radio or television, or in professional journals. Have students read some literary criticism about Poe's "The Fall of the House of Usher" or "The Raven" to get a better grasp of a critic's objectives and style of writing. Tell students that literary critics usually support their opinions—whether positive or negative—about a literary work with citations from the text.

Activity: Discussion Have students find out more about literary criticism or reviewing as a career, recoding what they learn in the **Enrichment: Investigating Career Connections** work sheet, in *Professional Development Guidebook,* page 221. Then hold a group discussion in which students consider the qualities of a successful critic. Interested students may wish to submit their own literary reviews to a school newspaper.

About the Selection

On one level, "The Raven" tells of a man who grieves for his lost love, Lenore. A mysterious talking Raven appears at the speaker's door, prompting him to question the bird about Lenore. The Raven responds to each question—including the question of whether the speaker will ever see Lenore again—with the single word "Nevermore," leaving the speaker broken and devoid of hope. On another level, the poem explores how grief and loneliness can turn to madness. Poe depicts a mind going to pieces—and watching itself in the process.

Activating Prior Knowledge

The first words of "The Raven" tell the time: midnight. Ask students what feelings and events are typically linked with midnight. What associations do students themselves have with "the middle of the night"? After discussion, refer students to the poem, asking them as they read to consider the effect the time setting might have on the mood of the poem.

Literary Analysis

Gothic Literature

1. Have students practice saying the opening line aloud in a suitable tone.

2. **Ask** the Literary Analysis question: In the very first line of the poem, which words contribute to a dark, mysterious Gothic mood?
Answer: Words include "midnight," "dreary," "weak," and "weary."

The Raven
Edgar Allan Poe

Literary Analysis
Gothic Literature
In the very first line of the poem, which words contribute to a dark, mysterious Gothic mood?

Once upon a midnight dreary, while I pondered, weak and weary,
Over many a quaint and curious volume of forgotten lore—
While I nodded, nearly napping, suddenly there came a tapping,
As of some one gently rapping, rapping at my chamber door.
5 "'Tis some visitor," I muttered, "tapping at my chamber door—
            Only this, and nothing more."

312 A Growing Nation (1800–1870)

Differentiated Instruction   for Universal Access

Support for Special-Needs Students
Have students read the adapted version of *"The Raven"* in the *Reader's Notebook: Adapted Version*. This version provides basic-level instruction in an interactive format with questions and write-on lines. Completing these pages will prepare students to read the selection in the Student Edition.

Support for Less Proficient Readers
Have students read *"The Raven"* in the *Reader's Notebook*. This version provides basic-level instruction in an interactive format with questions and write-on lines. After students finish the selection in the *Reader's Notebook*, have them complete the questions and activities in the Student Edition.

EL Support for English Learners
Have students read *"The Raven"* in the *Reader's Notebook: English Learner's Version*. This version provides basic-level instruction in an interactive format with questions and write-on lines. Completing these pages will prepare students to read the selection in the Student Edition.

Ah, distinctly I remember it was in the bleak December;
And each separate dying ember wrought its ghost upon the floor.
Eagerly I wished the morrow;—vainly I had sought to borrow
10 From my books surcease[1] of sorrow—sorrow for the lost Lenore—
For the rare and radiant maiden whom the angels name Lenore—
     Nameless *here* for evermore.

And the silken, sad, uncertain rustling of each purple curtain
Thrilled me—filled me with fantastic terrors never felt before;
15 So that now, to still the beating of my heart, I stood repeating
"'Tis some visitor entreating entrance at my chamber door—
Some late visitor entreating entrance at my chamber door;—
     This it is and nothing more."

Presently my soul grew stronger; hesitating then no longer,
20 "Sir," said I, "or Madam, truly your forgiveness I implore;
But the fact is I was napping, and so gently you came rapping,
And so faintly you came tapping, tapping at my chamber door,
That I scarce was sure I heard you"—here I opened wide the door;—
     Darkness there and nothing more.

—————————————————

1. **surcease** (sŭr sēs') end.

Reading Strategy
**Breaking Down
Long Sentences**
Summarize the action of
the stanza-long sentence
beginning "Presently my
soul grew stronger. . ."

 39 **Reading
Check**
For whom is the
speaker grieving?

The Raven **313**

38 **Reading Strategy**
**Breaking Down Long
Sentences**
1. Have a volunteer read the fourth
   stanza to the class, or play the
   stanza from the *Hear It!* Audio
   CD.
2. **Ask** students to respond to
   the Reading Strategy prompt:
   Summarize the action of the
   stanza-long sentence beginning "Presently my soul grew
   stronger."
   Sample answer: The speaker
   feels bolder, stops hesitating, and
   speaks to his unknown visitor. He
   then opens the door and finds
   nothing but darkness.

39 **Reading Check**
Answer: He is grieving for his lost
love, Lenore.

Differentiated
Instruction   for Universal Access

Support for Less Proficient Readers
Many of Poe's poems demand to be heard and
performed as well as read, "The Raven" foremost among them. Play the professional reading
on the *Hear It!* Audio CD, or have dramatically
inclined students prepare an oral reading. Do
this twice. The first time, have students simply
listen to the performance. The second time,
have them follow along in the text as they listen
to the poem.

Strategy for Advanced Readers
Have students identify examples of Poe's use of
assonance, consonance, and alliteration in "The
Raven." Students might point out the repetition
of vowel sounds in "flung," "shutter," and "flutter" as examples of assonance; the repetition
of consonants in "shutter," "flirt," and "flutter"
as an example of consonance; and the repetitions of initial consonant sounds in "when" and
"with" and "flirt" and "flutter" as examples of
alliteration. These sound devices give the poem
its driving rhythm and musical flair.

1. Direct students to the stanza beginning "Then this ebony bird." **Ask** students: What is the speaker's first reaction to the bird that enters his room?
Answer: The speaker is charmed and amused by the bird and its very serious expression—so much so that he jokingly speaks to the Raven.

2. **Ask** the Literary Analysis question: What element of Gothic literature does the Raven's speaking introduce into the poem? Explain.
Possible response: A bird that speaks meaningful language introduces a supernatural or otherworldly element to the poem. Students may note that the word "Nevermore," even in its first utterance, has an ominous effect.

---

25 Deep into that darkness peering, long I stood there wondering, fearing,
    Doubting, dreaming dreams no mortal ever dared to dream before;
    But the silence was unbroken, and the stillness gave no token,
    And the only word there spoken was the whispered word, "Lenore?"
    This I whispered, and an echo murmured back the word, "Lenore!"
30   Merely this and nothing more.

    Back then into the chamber turning, all my soul within me burning,
    Soon again I heard a tapping somewhat louder than before.
    "Surely," said I, "surely that is something at my window lattice;
    Let me see, then, what thereat is, and this mystery explore—
35 Let my heart be still a moment and this mystery explore;—
                                    'Tis the wind and nothing more!"

    Open here I flung the shutter, when, with many a flirt and flutter,
    In there stepped a stately Raven of the saintly days of yore;
    Not the least obeisance made he; not a minute stopped or stayed he;
40 But, with mien of lord or lady, perched above my chamber door—
    Perched upon a bust of Pallas[2] just above my chamber door—
                                    Perched, and sat, and nothing more.

Literary Analysis
Gothic Literature What element of Gothic literature does the Raven's speaking introduce into the poem? Explain.

    Then this ebony bird beguiling[3] my sad fancy into smiling,
    By the grave and stern decorum of the countenance[4] it wore,
45 "Though thy crest be shorn and shaven, thou," I said, "art sure no craven,
40 Ghastly grim and ancient Raven wandering from the Nightly shore—
    Tell me what thy lordly name is on the Night's Plutonian[5] shore!"
                                    Quoth the Raven, "Nevermore."

    Much I marveled this ungainly fowl to hear discourse so plainly,
50 Though its answer little meaning—little relevancy bore;
    For we cannot help agreeing that no living human being
    Ever yet was blessed with seeing bird above his chamber door—
    Bird or beast upon the sculptured bust above his chamber door,
                                    With such name as "Nevermore."

55 But the Raven, sitting lonely on the placid bust, spoke only
    That one word, as if his soul in that one word he did outpour.
    Nothing farther than he uttered—not a feather then he fluttered—

---

2. **Pallas** (pal´ əs) Pallas Athena, the ancient Greek goddess of wisdom.
3. **beguiling** (bi gil´ iŋ) *part.* charming.
4. **countenance** (koun´ tə nəns) *n.* facial expression.
5. **Plutonian** (ploo tō´ nē ən) *adj.* like the underworld or infernal regions; refers to Pluto, Greek and Roman god of the underworld.

Enrichment: Analyzing Symbols

The Raven as Symbol

When Poe wrote this poem, he drew from a long tradition that viewed the raven as a bird of ill omen—a sign of bad luck. In some cultures, however, the raven enjoys a more positive image. For many Native Americans, the raven is a symbol of cleverness or cunning. In Christian art, ravens are often depicted as symbols of providence. When lost at sea, Vikings would release a raven and follow it to land. Vikings valued ravens and often featured them on their flags.

Discuss the symbolism of various birds, for example, the albatross, eagle, crow, owl, and vulture.

Activity: Research Ask individual students to research the symbolism of one bird across several cultures. Suggest that they record their findings in the **Enrichment: Analyzing Themes and Symbols** work sheet, in *Professional Development Guidebook*, page 243. Have volunteers report their findings to the class.

Till I scarcely more than muttered, "Other friends have flown
  before—
On the morrow *he* will leave me, as my Hopes have flown before."
60   Then the bird said, "Nevermore."

Startled at the stillness broken by reply so aptly spoken,
"Doubtless," said I, "what it utters is its only stock and store
Caught from some unhappy master whom unmerciful Disaster
Followed fast and followed faster till his songs one burden bore—
65 Till the dirges of his Hope that melancholy burden bore
    Of 'Never—nevermore.'"

But the Raven still beguiling my sad fancy into smiling,
Straight I wheeled a cushioned seat in front of bird, and bust
  and door;
41 Then, upon the velvet sinking, I betook myself to linking
70 Fancy unto fancy, thinking what this ominous[6] bird of yore—
What this grim, ungainly, ghastly, gaunt, and ominous bird of yore
    Meant in croaking "Nevermore."

This I sat engaged in guessing, but no syllable expressing
To the fowl whose fiery eyes now burned into my bosom's core;
75 This and more I sat divining, with my head at ease reclining
On the cushion's velvet lining that the lamp-light gloated o'er,
But whose velvet-violet lining with the lamp-light gloating o'er,
    She shall press, ah, nevermore!

42 Then, methought, the air grew denser, perfumed from an unseen
  censer
80 Swung by seraphim whose foot-falls tinkled on the tufted floor.
"Wretch," I cried, "thy God hath lent thee—by these angels he hath
  sent thee
Respite—respite and nepenthe[7] from thy memories of Lenore;
Quaff, oh quaff this kind nepenthe and forget this lost Lenore!"
    Quoth the Raven, "Nevermore."

85 "Prophet!" said I, "thing of evil!—prophet still, if bird or devil!—
Whether Tempter sent, or whether tempest tossed thee here
  ashore,
Desolate yet all undaunted, on this desert land enchanted—
On this home by Horror haunted—tell me truly, I implore—
Is there—*is* there balm in Gilead?[8]—tell me—tell me, I implore!"

---

6. ominous (äm´ ə nəs) *adj.* threatening; sinister.
7. nepenthe (ni pen´ thē) *n.* drug that the ancient Greeks believed could relieve sorrow.
8. balm in Gilead (gil´ ē əd) in the Bible, a healing ointment made in Gilead, a region of ancient Palestine.

Literary Analysis
Gothic Literature
How is the speaker's psychological distress increasing?

43 Reading Check
What does the speaker want from the Raven?

The Raven **315**

44 Literary Analysis

Gothic Literature

1. **Ask** students to identify the questions that the speaker asks during the course of the poem.
   Answer: Though the speaker several times demands information from the Raven, he asks only two questions in the poem. Drawn to the door by mysterious tapping, he asks the empty darkness: "Lenore?" (l. 28). Later, he asks the Raven, "Is there—*is* there balm in Gilead?" (l. 89).

2. **Ask:** What do you think the speaker means by these questions?
   Possible response: Students may say that in his first question the speaker is asking if his lost love is actually present—suggesting that the speaker is hopeful that his lost love has returned or is signaling to him in some miraculous way. The second question is similar: The speaker is asking if there is some way that his grief might end—or that he might miraculously reunite with Lenore.

3. **Ask:** How do the Gothic elements in the last stanza suggest an answer to the speaker's questions?
   Possible response: Students may say that the looming presence of the Raven and the bird's dark shadow that covers the speaker's soul give a grim, hopeless answer to the speaker: He will never reunite with Lenore; his grief will never end.

316 A Growing Nation (1800–1870)

Vocabulary Development

Vocabulary Knowledge Rating
When students have completed reading and discussing both selections, have them take out the **Vocabulary Knowledge Rating** charts they worked on earlier. Read the words aloud and have students rate their knowledge of the words again in the After Reading column. Clarify any words that are still problematic. Have students write their own definitions and example or sentence in the appropriate column. Then have students complete the Vocabulary Lesson at the end of this selection. Encourage students to use the words in further discussion and written work about the selections. Remind them that they will be accountable for these words on the *Selection Test, Unit 21 Resources,* pages 81–83 or 84–86.

Quoth the Raven, "Nevermore."

"Prophet!" said I, "thing of evil!—prophet still, if bird or devil!
By that Heaven that bends above us—by that God we both adore—
Tell this soul with sorrow laden if, within the distant Aidenn,[9]
It shall clasp a sainted maiden whom the angels name Lenore—
95 Clasp a rare and radiant maiden whom the angels name Lenore."
Quoth the Raven, "Nevermore."

"Be that word our sign of parting, bird or fiend!" I shrieked,
upstarting—
"Get thee back into the tempest and the Night's Plutonian shore!
Leave no black plume as a token of that lie thy soul hath spoken!
100 Leave my loneliness unbroken!—quit the bust above my door!
Take thy beak from out my heart, and take thy form from off
my door!"
Quoth the Raven, "Nevermore."

And the Raven, never flitting, still is sitting, *still* is sitting
On the pallid bust of Pallas just above my chamber door;
105 And his eyes have all the seeming of a demon's that is dreaming;
And the lamp-light o'er him streaming throws his shadow on
the floor;
And my soul from out that shadow that lies floating on the floor
Shall be lifted—nevermore!

45 ◀ **Critical Viewing**
In this illustration of the poem's opening scene, how do the details in the setting and the angle of the image itself add to a sense of the speaker's fear and distress? **[Analyze]**

9. Aidenn (ā′ den) Arabic for *Eden* or *heaven*.

Critical Reading ©

© 1. Key Ideas and Details (a) With what emotion does the speaker first greet the Raven? **(b) Interpret:** As the poem progresses, how does the speaker's attitude toward the Raven change? **(c) Analyze Cause and Effect:** In what way is the word *nevermore* related to the emotional changes?

© 2. Key Ideas and Details (a) What does the speaker eventually order the Raven to do? **(b) Analyze:** At the end of the poem, what does the speaker mean when he says the Raven "still is sitting" above the door?

© 3. Craft and Structure (a) Interpret: What is the relationship between the Raven's shadow and the speaker's soul at the end of the poem? **(b) Analyze:** In your opinion, what does the Raven finally come to represent?

© 4. Craft and Structure Review your list of details that make Poe's settings seem dreamlike. Then, write a paragraph describing the power of Poe's landscapes. In your response, use at least two of these Essential Question words: *fantastic, personal, terrors, realistic.* [Connecting to the Essential Question: What is the relationship between literature and place?]

Cite textual evidence to support your responses.

The Raven **317**

Concept Connector

Reading Strategy Graphic Organizer
Ask students to review the graphic organizers in which they have broken down long sentences into more comprehensible parts. Then have students share their organizers and compare the details they identified.

Activating Prior Knowledge
Have students return to their expectations from the Activating Prior Knowledge discussion. Ask them to discuss how many of their expectations were fulfilled by the story.

Writing About the Essential Question
Have students compare their responses to the prompt before reading the selections with their thoughts after reading them. Have them work individually or in groups, writing or discussing their thoughts, to define their new responses. Then lead a class discussion, probing for what students have learned that confirms or invalidates their initial thoughts. Encourage students to cite specific textual details to support their responses.

---

45 Critical Viewing

Possible response: The skewed, tilted perspective of the painting, the gaping darkness of the open window, and the turbulent movement of fabrics all reflect the speaker's disorientation and fear.

ASSESS

Answers

Before students respond, you may wish to have them write a brief objective summary of the selection. As they answer the questions below, remind them to support their answers with evidence from the text.

1. (a) At first the speaker is amused by the creature. (b) The speaker marvels that the bird can speak; he tries to understand its meaning; he begins to believe that the bird is a messenger from heaven; then he thinks it is evil; finally he becomes angry. (c) The speaker grows more agitated each time the Raven says "Nevermore."

2. (a) He orders the Raven to leave. (b) Students might say that the Raven has, in fact, never left the chamber—or that the creature so disturbed the speaker's mind that now he is now haunted by the Raven's presence.

3. (a) The effect of the Raven's visit, symbolized by its shadow, has been to permanently darken the speaker's soul. (b) **Possible response:** The Raven comes to represent the speaker's permanent state of madness and despair.

4. **Sample response:** Poe's landscapes, true to his <u>personal</u> commitment to a single effect, are sometimes monotonous but always powerful. More <u>fantastic</u> than <u>realistic,</u> Poe's terrain reflects, not the real dangers of an actual wilderness, but the hidden <u>terrors</u> lurking in the human mind. Poe effectively uses the power of place to establish the literary effects of tone and mood.

Answers

1. **Setting:** "Usher": isolated, gloomy mansion; "Raven": midnight; midwinter; lonely chamber. **Violence:** "Usher": Madeline claws her way out of her tomb; mansion collapses; "Raven": shrieking questions of the narrator. **Characterization:** "Usher": Roderick's obsessions and mental anguish. "Raven": narrator's hopeless grief. **The Supernatural:** "Usher": Madeline's appearance after death; death of Roderick; collapse of mansion. "Raven": talking bird. A partially completed version of this chart, **Literary Analysis Graphic Organizer A**, is available at **www.PHLitOnline.com.**

2. (a) The description of the mansion establishes a mood of gloom and bleakness. (b) Madeline's entombment provides a sense of the ultimate horror for Roderick—the fear of being buried alive. (c) The storm reinforces the growing terror inside the mansion and eventually accompanies the story's climax.

3. (a) **Possible response:** The hysteria of the final two paragraphs leaves the reader unclear about Madeline's existence and Roderick's fate. (b) Some interpretations: The story is literally true; Madeline is a ghost or a hallucination; the collapse of the mansion is imaginary. (c) Be sure students explain their choices.

4. The tapping and the "fiery eyes" captivate the speaker, causing him to fix his attention and his hopes more and more upon the bird.

5. (a) Students who believe Madeline actually appears may cite the narrator's explicit description. Students who doubt her actuality may cite the implausibility of her escape and the narrator's possible derangement. (b) Students who believe in a literal Raven may cite lines 103–104. Other students may say that the final stanza is meant metaphorically.

6. The humor lies in the viewer's recognition that the caged bird is the Raven and the one word it knows is "Nevermore."

7. **Possible response:** "Sometimes I thought that everything was just the quirks of insanity, because I saw him looking at nothing for hours in rapt attention, as if listening to a nonexistent noise."

318

After You Read

The Fall of the House of Usher • The Raven

Literary Analysis

© 1. **Craft and Structure** Use a chart like the one shown to identify the **Gothic** elements in "The Fall of the House of Usher" and "The Raven."

Gothic Element	House of Usher	Raven
Setting		
Violence		
Characterization		
The Supernatural		

© 2. **Craft and Structure** Describe the ways in which the following elements contribute to the **single effect** of a sense of terror in "The Fall of the House of Usher": **(a)** description of the house, **(b)** Madeline's entombment, **(c)** the storm.

© 3. **Craft and Structure (a)** In what ways is the ending of the story intentionally *ambiguous*? What does Poe leave uncertain? **(b)** What are some possible interpretations of the ending? **(c)** Which do you support, and why?

© 4. **Craft and Structure** In "The Raven," how do both the tapping and the Raven's fiery eyes add to the speaker's deteriorating emotional state?

© 5. **Integration of Knowledge and Ideas (a)** When Madeline appears at the end of the story, is she actually there, or is she a hallucination? Explain. **(b)** At the end of "The Raven," do you think the bird is actually in the room? Why or why not?

6. **Analyzing Visual Text** Explain the cartoon.

Reading Strategy

7. **Break down this long sentence** from the story and restate it in your own words:

   At times, again, I was obliged to resolve all into the mere inexplicable vagaries of madness, for I beheld him gazing upon vacancy for long hours, in an attitude of the profoundest attention, as if listening to some imaginary sound.

8. Choose another long sentence from the story or poem. Break the sentence down and restate it in your own words.

Common Core State Standards

Language
4.c. Consult general and specialized reference materials, both print and digital, to find the pronunciation of a word or determine or clarify its precise meaning or its standard usage. *(p. 319)*

EDGAR ALLAN POE RETURNS A CHRISTMAS GIFT

He only knows one word.

8. Be sure students rephrase each clause of the long sentences they have chosen.

Integrated Language Skills

© Vocabulary Acquisition and Use

Word Analysis: Latin Root -voc-

The word *equivocal* contains the Latin root *-voc-*, which derives from the Latin word *vox*, meaning "voice." Combined with the Latin prefix *equi-*, meaning "equal," *equivocal* can be defined as "having two equal voices" or "having more than one possible interpretation." Consider the meaning of these words containing *-voc-*. Then, answer the questions.

advocate *v.* speak or argue in favor of

equivocate *v.* avoid making a clear statement

vociferous *adj.* noisy or aggressive in making one's feelings known

1. The council *advocates* banning parking near the bridge. Is the council for or against it? Explain.
2. When the reporter asked the mayor about the new law, the mayor *equivocated*. Did the reporter like the mayor's answer? Explain.
3. Several citizens were *vociferous* in their response to the law. Do you think the mayor heard them? Why or why not?

Using Resources to Build Vocabulary

Gothic Style: Words For a Character in Torment
In drawing a picture of his tormented friend, the narrator of "The Fall of the House of Usher" uses the following words:

agitation	leaden
feeble	tremulous
futile	trepidancy

Reread the last paragraph on page 298 to see these words in context. Then, *use a dictionary and a print or electronic thesaurus* to find synonyms for each word. On your own paper, rewrite the paragraph by replacing each of the words shown above with a duller, more ordinary word. Now, compare the original paragraph with your version. Write several sentences in which you describe the differences between the two versions.

Vocabulary: True or False?

Indicate which of the statements below are true and which are false. Explain your answers.

1. If historians decide that a document is *specious*, they will probably write a paper about its importance.
2. The quality of *sentience* is evident in rocks and other inanimate matter.
3. If a senator's position in a debate is *equivocal*, he probably believes strongly in his argument.
4. Misers are *munificent* and often give to the needy.
5. Someone who is in desperate need might be *importunate* about a request.
6. A professional's *anomalous* behavior will make others feel confident about using his or her services.

Extended Study: Integrated Language Skills **319**

Assessment Resources

Unit 2 Resources

L1 L2 EL Selection Test A, pp. 81–83.
Administer Test A to less advanced students.

L3 L4 EL Selection Test B, pp. 84–86.
Administer Text B to on-level or more advanced students.

Open-Book Test, pp.78–80. As an alternative, give the Open-Book Test.

All Customizable Test Bank

All Self-tests
Students may prepare for the **Selection Test** by taking the Self-test online.

PHLit Online! All assessment resources are available at **www.PHLitOnline.com.**

Vocabulary Acquisition and Use

1. Introduce the skill, using the instruction on the student page.
2. Have students complete the Word Analysis activity and the Vocabulary practice.

Word Analysis
Sample Answers

1. Since *to advocate* means "to speak in favor of," the council is for a ban on parking near the bridge.
2. Because the mayor *equivocated*, or avoided giving a clear response, the reporter probably disliked the mayor's answer.
3. A *vociferous* response is a loud one, so the mayor is certain to have heard the citizens.

Vocabulary
Sample Answers

1. False; a document that is false or counterfeit will not merit investigation by historians.
2. False; nonliving matter is not capable of feeling.
3. False; a senator who believed strongly in his own argument would not appear to offer more than one interpretation.
4. False; misers are by nature stingy, not generous.
5. True; a desperate person would urgently insist on a response.
6. False; odd behavior would cause people to be doubtful about using a professional's services.

Using Resources to Build Vocabulary
Sample Answer

". . . I soon found this to arise from a series of *weak* and *useless* struggles to overcome a habitual *trembling fear*—an excessive nervous *unrest*. . . . His voice changed quickly from a *quivering* indecision . . . to a *dull*, even, harsh speech . . . ."

The sentence revised with synonyms has a less formal tone and lacks the alliteration Poe produced with "feeble and futile."

Writing

You may use this writing lesson as timed-writing practice, or you may allow students to develop the explanatory text as a writing assignment over several days.

1. Before students begin to work independently on this assignment, review the Davidson and Lovecraft quotations as a class. Be sure that students understand both points of view and that they analyze why they themselves are drawn to one viewpoint over the other.

2. As students gather evidence in support of their chosen viewpoint, remind them to note any significant contrary evidence they find and to be prepared to engage this information. A strong argument overcomes opposing details; it does not ignore them.

3. Before drafting, students should evaluate their evidence and rank items in order of importance or persuasiveness. As they write, students should present their evidence in a meaningful order, rather than simply recording details as they appear in the story. Outlining will help students try out organizational options.

4. Use the model within the lesson to emphasize transitions as students revise their initial drafts.

5. Use the **Rubrics for Responses to Literature**, in *Professional Development Guidebook,* pages 250–251, to evaluate students' work.

PERFORMANCE TASKS
Integrated Language Skills

Writing

 **Explanatory Text** Since its original publication in 1839, "The Fall of the House of Usher" has prompted varied critical opinions. Some see the story as entirely symbolic, while others take it at face value as a tale of sheer horror. These passages represent two differing critical views:

> **Edward H. Davidson:** The three characters are unique people with distinct characters, but they are tied together by the same type of "mental disorder." All of them suffer from insanity....

> **H. P. Lovecraft:** "The Fall of the House of Usher"… displays an abnormally linked trinity of entities at the end of a long and isolated family history—a brother, his twin sister, and their incredibly ancient house all sharing a single soul …

While both critics note strong connections among the characters, they see different meanings in these connections. Do you agree with Davidson that all the characters are separate, insane personalities, or do you prefer Lovecraft's analysis, that the brother, sister, and house represent different aspects of a single personality? Write an **essay** in which you evaluate these views and state your own judgment about Poe's story.

Prewriting Review the story to develop your perspective. As you read, gather details that relate to the two critical views. Jot down details, looking for patterns among them. Then, determine which viewpoint—Davidson's or Lovecraft's—is more persuasive. Remember that *ambiguities, nuances, and complexities* are an integral part of Poe's writing. While you may not be able to fully explain them, assess the effect they have on the story's meaning.

Model: Using Transitions to Clarify Meaning

The idea that all the characters in the story are insane is intriguing. It would explain the story's strangeness. **After all,** if the narrator is mad, he would not be able to relate events clearly.

This idea is intriguing. **; however,** It is not convincing.

Use transitional words and phrases to make the flow of your ideas clear.

Punctuation Tip: The word "however" joins two complete sentences. When you combine sentences with a transitional word or phrase, use a semicolon.

Drafting Establish a logical organizational pattern for your essay. In your introduction, summarize the two critical viewpoints and state which one you support. Elaborate upon your reasoning in each body paragraph, citing details that are substantial, specific, and relevant to your position.

Revising Reread your essay, making sure you have established a logical flow of ideas. Improve the logic by adding transitional words and phrases at points where relationships among ideas are not perfectly clear.

320 A Growing Nation (1800–1870)

Common Core State Standards

Writing
2.c. Use appropriate and varied transitions and syntax to link the major sections of the text, create cohesion, and clarify the relationships among complex ideas and concepts.
9.a. Apply *grades 11-12 Reading standards* to literature.

Language
1. Demonstrate command of the conventions of standard English grammar and usage when writing or speaking. *(p. 321)*

Teaching Resources

Unit 2 Resources
- L3 L4 **Vocabulary Builder,** p. 74
- L3 L4 **Support for Writing Lesson,** p. 76
- L3 L4 **Grammar and Style,** p. 75
- L4 **Enrichment,** p. 77

- All **Interactive Grammar Lesson:** available under After You Read for this selection
- All **Enriched Online Student Edition Internet Research Activity:** available under After You Read for this selection
- **Professional Development Guidebook Rubrics for Self Assessment: Responses to Literature** pp. 250–251

PHLit Online! All resources are available at **www.PHLitOnline.com.**

Conventions and Style: Comparative and Superlative Adjectives and Adverbs

In academic writing, you will often be asked to explain how things are similar and different. To do so, use modifiers showing comparison and contrast correctly. Adjectives and adverbs can take three forms: **positive, comparative,** and **superlative.**

Positive	Comparative	Superlative
dark	darker	darkest
weary	wearier	weariest
nervous	more nervous	most nervous
painfully	more painfully	most painfully
bad	worse	worst
good	better	best

Using Comparative and Superlative Forms

Use the comparative degree to compare *two* persons, places, or things.

Comparative Adjective: Madeline is even *spookier* than her brother.
Comparative Adverb: The narrator describes Roderick *more fully* than he does Madeline.

Use the superlative degree to compare *three or more* persons, places, or things.

Superlative Adjective: The underground chamber is the *worst* place in the house.
Superlative Adverb: Usher's home is the *most elaborately* described mansion in all of literature.

© **Writing and Speaking Conventions**

A. Writing For each item listed, write two sentences. In one, use the comparative form, and in the other, use the superlative form.

1. damp 2. desperately 3. sick 4. gloomy 5. hesitantly

Example: cold
Comparative: The bedroom is colder than the kitchen.
Superlative: The attic is the coldest place in the house.

B. Speaking Write and recite an alternate ending to the story in which you use at least one comparative form and one superlative form.

Practice Complete each sentence below by supplying the correct form of the adjective or adverb shown in parentheses.

1. In your opinion, who is the _____ writer, Edgar Allan Poe or Stephen King? (*good*)
2. He got into trouble _____ than his friend did. (*frequently*)
3. Some scholars have criticized Poe's work _____ than others have. (*harshly*)
4. Of all the writers we have studied so far, I think Edgar Allan Poe had the _____ life. (*sad*)
5. Which deteriorated _____, the house or Usher's mental state? (*quick*)
6. He considers the narrator his _____ friend in the world. (*close*)
7. His last night at the mansion was by far the _____ one. (*bad*)
8. The second time he heard the tapping, it was _____ than before. (*loud*)
9. "The Raven" may be the _____ of Poe's poems. (*popular*)
10. Both selections are scary, but I think the poem is the _____ of the two. (*terrifying*)

Extended Study: Integrated Language Skills **321**

Practice

1. better
2. more frequently
3. more harshly
4. saddest
5. more quickly
6. closest
7. worst
8. louder
9. most popular
10. more terrifying

Writing and Speaking Conventions

A. Sample answers:

1. The leaky roof left my room <u>damper</u> than yours. My sister's room is <u>dampest</u> of all.
2. The trailing crew paddled <u>more desperately</u> than the leading canoeists. Who was <u>most desperately</u> anxious to get out of the water?
3. Madeline is <u>sicker</u> than Roderick. Perhaps the narrator is <u>sickest</u> of all.
4. The inside of the House of Usher was <u>gloomier</u> than its exterior. The family tomb was <u>gloomiest</u> of all.
5. She responded <u>more hesitantly</u> than I expected. Roderick, though, moved <u>most hesitantly</u> of the three.

B. Sample answer:

Madeline collapsed into Roderick's arms. Silence reigned. Then they began to giggle. I could not tell which sibling was <u>more amused.</u> "All this was a joke? A charade? A prank?" I sputtered. "My friend, we had to shock you out of your melancholy," Roderick explained. "All your friends—" I cut him off: "Usher, this is the <u>worst</u> trick you have ever played! You will see me again—nevermore!"

Extend the Lesson

Sentence Modeling

Write the following sentences on the chalkboard:

> The setting of "The Fall of the House of Usher" is far more gloomier than that of "The Raven." It among the most dreadfulest settings in all of Poe's work.

Ask students what they notice about the sentence. Elicit from them that the first sentence contains a comparative adjective; the second sentence contains a superlative adjective. Ask students if they notice any problems in the sentences. Students should see that both "more gloomier" and "most dreadfulest" are incorrect forms. Invite students to say how they would correct the problems. Students may offer "more gloomy" or "gloomier" to correct the first sentence and "most dreadful" to correct the second. Finally, ask students to write their own comparisons of Poe's story and poem, using at least one comparative and one superlative adjective.

321

❶ The Gothic Family Tree

1. Review the British and American branches of Gothic writers. Invite students to share their own knowledge of any of these writers or their literary creations. Students are likely to be familiar with the enduring literary creations of Mary Shelley and Bram Stoker (the Frankenstein monster and the vampire Dracula) and the novels of H. P. Lovecraft. Each of the "New Gothic" writers listed has enjoyed best-selling status.

2. Students may be familiar with these Gothic writers through films made of their works. Shelley's *Frankenstein* and Stoker's *Dracula* reappear in film versions for every new generation of moviegoers. The works of du Maurier, Poe, Lovecraft, Oates, Rice, Straub, and King have provided the plots for many Hollywood films and television programs. Have students briefly describe examples that they have seen.

3. **Ask** students why the movies might be such a successful medium for expressing the atmospheres, settings, and plots of Gothic fiction. **Possible response:** Movies can be very effective in capturing suspenseful or mysterious moods through the lighting, sets, and sound track (music and effects). Special visual effects allow films to realistically present Gothic inventions such as ghosts, monsters, and zombies that have no existence in the real world. The film industry has a long and lucrative experience in frightening and horrifying audiences.

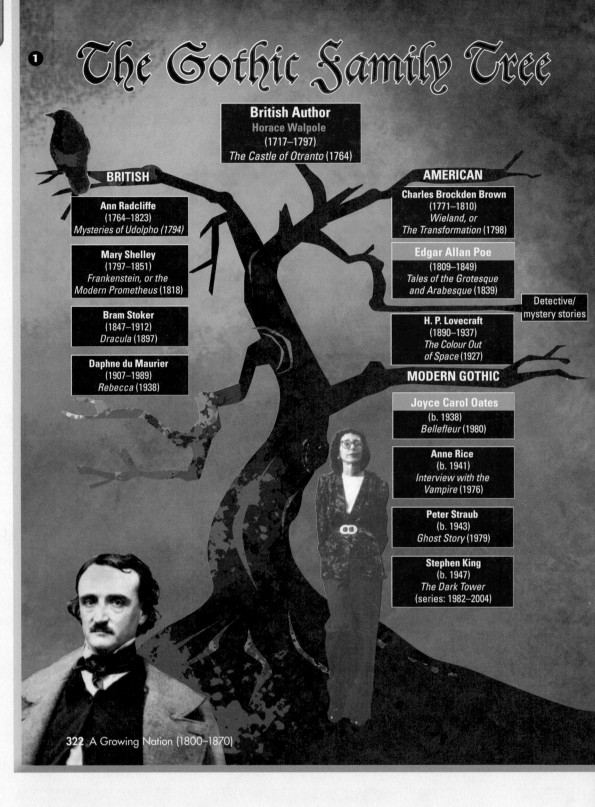

❶ The Gothic Family Tree

British Author
Horace Walpole
(1717–1797)
The Castle of Otranto (1764)

BRITISH

AMERICAN

Ann Radcliffe
(1764–1823)
Mysteries of Udolpho (1794)

Mary Shelley
(1797–1851)
Frankenstein, or the Modern Prometheus (1818)

Bram Stoker
(1847–1912)
Dracula (1897)

Daphne du Maurier
(1907–1989)
Rebecca (1938)

Charles Brockden Brown
(1771–1810)
Wieland, or The Transformation (1798)

Edgar Allan Poe
(1809–1849)
Tales of the Grotesque and Arabesque (1839)

Detective/ mystery stories

H. P. Lovecraft
(1890–1937)
The Colour Out of Space (1927)

MODERN GOTHIC

Joyce Carol Oates
(b. 1938)
Bellefleur (1980)

Anne Rice
(b. 1941)
Interview with the Vampire (1976)

Peter Straub
(b. 1943)
Ghost Story (1979)

Stephen King
(b. 1947)
The Dark Tower (series: 1982–2004)

322 A Growing Nation (1800–1870)

Comparing Literary Works

"The Fall of the House of Usher"
by Edgar Allan Poe ▪ **"Where Is Here?"**
by Joyce Carol Oates

 Common Core State Standards

- Reading Literature 3
- Writing 1.a, 10
- Language 4.c

❷ Comparing Gothic Literature Past and Present

Gothic Literature Edgar Allan Poe's work has roots deep in European Gothic literature. Horace Walpole's *The Castle of Otranto: A Gothic Tale* (1764) and Ann Radcliffe's *Mysteries of Udolpho* (1794) are just two of the books that probably influenced Poe (see the Gothic Family Tree on page 322). In a similar way, modern writers such as Joyce Carol Oates, author of "Where Is Here?," look back to Poe as the founding voice of an American Gothic tradition. The legacy of traditional Gothic literature cuts across genre classifications, and its elements can be found in poetry, drama, novels, and short stories. Regardless of the genre, traditional Gothic writing such as Poe's has these elements:

- A bleak or remote setting; often grand, such as a castle or mansion
- A gloomy atmosphere; a sense of impending doom
- Characters in physical or psychological torment
- Horrific or violent incidents
- Supernatural elements

Modern Gothic literature uses the same elements but does so with more subtlety or with details that reflect modern life. As you read "Where Is Here?," use a chart like the one shown to examine how Oates puts a new spin on traditional Gothic features.

Common Core State Standards

Reading Literature
3. Analyze the impact of the author's choices regarding how to develop and relate elements of a story.

Language
4.c. Consult general and specialized reference materials, both print and digital, to find the precise meaning of a word and its etymology.

	Traditional: Poe	Modern: Oates
Setting	a crumbling mansion	
Characters	Roderick Usher, who is ghostly and tormented	
Violence	Burying sister in vault	
The Supernatural	Link between house and Usher	

ⓒ Gather Vocabulary Knowledge

Joyce Carol Oates uses related forms of the words *perplex*, *disturb*, and *resent*. Use a **dictionary** to define each word. Then, employ other references to further explore these words:

- **History of Language:** Use a book on the history of English to research each word's origins. Write a paragraph about the word's emergence in English.
- **Glossary of Affixes:** Consult a print or online list of affixes. For each word, explain how the addition of a specific affix modifies its meaning.

Comparing References Compare and contrast what you learn about the words from each reference.

www.PHLitOnline.com

The Fall of the House of Usher ▪ Where Is Here? **323**

❷ Comparing Gothic Literature Past and Present

1. Introduce the Gothic tradition, using the instruction on the student page.

2. Encourage students to use a chart similar to the one shown to record Oates's modern equivalents to traditional Gothic features.

Think Aloud: Model the Skill

Say to students:

When I read a modern Gothic story, I expect to shiver with dread—but I also expect to ask questions. In most traditional Gothic stories, when a character sees a ghost, I assume that there really is a ghost. In a modern Gothic story, when a character sees a ghost, I wonder, Is it a trick? Is it a shadow? Is the character going insane? Or *is* it really a ghost? The uncertainty makes me want to read faster.

❸ Gather Vocabulary Knowledge

1. Pronounce each word, giving its definition, and have students say it aloud.

2. For more guidance, see the *Classroom Strategies and Teaching Routines* card for teaching vocabulary.

Have lists of common affixes and their meanings available for students. Encourage students to use their knowledge of affixes to discuss meanings of related forms of the words *perplex*, *disturb*, and *resent*, including *perplexing*, *disturbing*, *disturbance*, *resentment*.

Teaching Resources

- ⏹ *Unit 2 Resources,* pp. 87–91
- ⏹ *Enriched Online Student Edition*
- ⏹ *Common Core Companion,* pp. 28–35; 261–276; 324–331

 All resources are available at **www.PHLitOnline.com**

Daily Bellringer

As you teach the Comparing Literary Works selection, have students complete the Quick Write activities that remain for the appropriate week in the *Daily Bellringer Activities* booklet.

Multidraft Reading

To assist struggling readers and to enhance reading for all, assign the text in chunks as warranted by length and apply multidraft reading protocols. For each reading, have students set the purpose indicated:

- **First reading**—identifying key ideas and details and answering any Reading Checks.
- **Second reading**—analyzing craft and structure and responding to the side-column prompts.
- **Third reading**—integrating knowledge and ideas, connecting to other texts and the world, and answering the end-of-selection questions.

For more guidance, refer to the *Classroom Strategies and Teaching Routines* card, **Multidraft Reading**.

❹ Background

More About the Author

In his relatively brief career, Edgar Allan Poe produced a significant body of literature, including nearly seventy works of short fiction and several collections of poems, essays, and literary criticism. This output pales, however, in comparison to the productivity of Joyce Carol Oates, who has published more than thirty-four novels, twenty-nine story collections, eight poetry collections, and assorted collections of plays, essays, and literary criticism. In addition, Oates has maintained a full academic career; she has been a professor at Princeton University since 1978. When asked about her staggering workload, Oates has responded, "Writing and teaching have always been, for me, so richly rewarding that I don't think of them as work in the usual sense of the word."

❹ Joyce Carol Oates
(b. 1938)

Author of "Where Is Here?"

Joyce Carol Oates was born in 1938 in Lockport, New York, a small, rural town. Though she grew up without many books, she always had a strong attraction to storytelling and began drawing picture stories even before she knew how to write.

Oates's elementary school years were spent in a one-room schoolhouse. At age 14, she received a typewriter as a gift and began writing in earnest. She was soon producing one book after another. In her college days, she would write one novel using one side of the paper, then write another novel on the reverse side. Then, she would throw the papers away.

Early Success Oates won the *Mademoiselle* short story contest, an important national fiction prize, while still in college, and published her first book at the age of twenty-five. Today, she is renowned not just for the quality of her work, but for her immense literary output. She has averaged two books a year during the course of her career. Her many honors include the National Book Award and three separate nominations for the Pulitzer Prize.

A Taste for the Gothic Oates's discovery of the Gothic novels of Ann Radcliff, an English writer, and of Edgar Allan Poe's remarkable short stories sparked her interest in Gothic fiction. Though she has written fiction and nonfiction in a wide variety of styles, she always returns to the Gothic. "Horror," she says, "Is a fact of life. As a writer I'm fascinated by all facets of life." Over her desk she keeps a quote from Henry James, another American master, which reads: "We work in the dark—we do what we can—we give what we have. Our doubt is our passion, and our passion is our task. The rest is the madness of art."

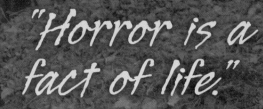

"Horror is a fact of life."

324 A Growing Nation (1800–1870)

Teaching From Technology

Preparing to Read
Go to **www.PHLitOnline**.com in class or in a lab and display the **Get Connected!** slide show for these selections. Have the class brainstorm for responses to the slide show writing prompt, entering ideas in the interactive journal. Then have students complete their written responses individually in a lab or as homework.

To build background, display the Background video and More About the Author features.

Where Is Here?

Joyce Carol Oates

For years they had lived without incident in their house in a quiet residential neighborhood when, one November evening at dusk, the doorbell rang, and the father went to answer it, and there on his doorstep stood a man he had never seen before. The stranger apologized for disturbing him at what was probably the dinner hour and explained that he'd once lived in the house— "I mean, I was a child in this house"—and since he was in the city on business he thought he would drop by. He had not seen the house since January 1949 when he'd been eleven years old and his widowed mother had sold it and moved away but, he said, he thought of it often, dreamt of it often, and never more powerfully than in recent months. The father said, "Would you like to come inside for a few minutes and look around?" The stranger hesitated, then said firmly, "I think I'll just poke around outside for a while, if you don't mind. That might be sufficient." He was in his late forties, the father's approximate age. He wore a dark suit, conservatively cut; he was hatless, with thin silver-tipped neatly combed hair; a plain, sober, intelligent face and frowning eyes. The father, reserved by nature, but genial and even *gregarious* when taken unaware, said amiably, "Of course we don't mind. But I'm afraid many things have changed since 1949."

So, in the chill, damp, deepening dusk, the stranger wandered around the property while the mother set the dining room table and the father peered covertly out the window. The children were upstairs in their rooms. "Where is he now?" the mother asked. "He just went into the garage," the father said. "The garage! What does he want in there!" the mother said uneasily. "Maybe you'd better go out there with him." "He wouldn't want anyone with him," the father said. He moved stealthily to another window, peering through the curtains. A moment passed in silence. The mother, paused in the act of setting down plates, neatly folded paper napkins, and stainless-steel cutlery, said impatiently, "And where is he now? I don't like this." The father said, "Now he's coming out of the garage," and stepped back hastily from the window. "Is he going now?" the mother asked. "I wish I'd answered the door." The father watched for a moment in silence then said, "He's headed into the backyard." "Doing what?" the mother asked. "Not doing anything, just walking," the father said. "He seems

Vocabulary
stealthily (stel´ thə lē) *adv.*
slowly so as to avoid notice

Who invites the stranger in to the house?

---

4 **Comparing Gothic Literature**

1. Direct students to the bracketed passage. Point out that the three characters introduce themselves but promptly forget one another's names. The writer, even after these introductions, never refers to any character in the story by personal name.

2. **Ask** students what Gothic effect the writer develops by referring to the three characters only as "father," "mother," and "stranger."
   Answers: By referring to the couple only as "father" and "mother," the writer keeps them at an impersonal distance from the reader. The constant repetition of "stranger" in the story has an even more alienating effect on readers, subtly adding to the gathering sense of his oddness and menace.

3. **Ask** the Comparing Gothic Literature question: Which details in the description of the stranger create a sense of his agitation or distress?
   Possible response: Students may cite the stranger's darting, blinking eyes, odd posture, halting speech, and lapses into silence as details that convey his distress.

Vocabulary
exasperation (eks äs pə rā´ shun) *n.* annoyance; frustration

Comparing Gothic Literature
Which details in the description of the stranger create a sense of his agitation or distress?

to have a slight limp." "Is he an older man?" the mother asked. "I didn't notice," the father confessed. "Isn't that just like you!" the mother said.

She went on worriedly, "He could be anyone, after all. Any kind of thief, or mentally disturbed person, or even a murderer. Ringing our doorbell like that with no warning and you don't even know what he looks like!"

The father had moved to another window and stood quietly watching, his cheek pressed against the glass. "He's gone down to the old swings. I hope he won't sit in one of them, for memory's sake, and try to swing—the posts are rotted almost through." The mother drew breath to speak but sighed instead, as if a powerful current of feeling had surged through her. The father was saying, "Is it possible he remembers those swings from his childhood? I can't believe they're actually that old." The mother said vaguely, "They were old when we bought the house." The father said, "But we're talking about forty years or more, and that's a long time." The mother sighed again, involuntarily. "Poor man!" she murmured. She was standing before her table but no longer seeing it. In her hand were objects—forks, knives, spoons—she could not have named. She said, "We can't bar the door against him. That would be cruel." The father said, "What? No one has barred any door against anyone." "Put yourself in his place," the mother said. "He told me he didn't *want* to come inside," the father said. "Oh—isn't that just like you!" the mother said in exasperation.

Without a further word she went to the back door and called out for the stranger to come inside, if he wanted, when he had finished looking around outside.

4 They introduced themselves rather shyly, giving names, and forgetting names, in the confusion of the moment. The stranger's handshake was cool and damp and tentative. He was smiling hard, blinking moisture from his eyes; it was clear that entering his childhood home was enormously exciting yet intimidating to him. Repeatedly he said, "It's so nice of you to invite me in—I truly hate to disturb you—I'm really so grateful, and so—" But the perfect word eluded him. As he spoke his eyes darted about the kitchen almost like eyes out of control. He stood in an odd stiff posture, hands gripping the lapels of his suit as if he meant to crush them. The mother, meaning to break the awkward silence, spoke warmly of their satisfaction with the house and with the neighborhood, and the father concurred, but the stranger listened only politely, and continued to stare, and stare hard. Finally he said that the kitchen had been so changed— "so modernized"—he almost didn't recognize it. The floor tile, the size of the windows, something about the position of the cupboards—all

326 A Growing Nation (1800–1870)

were different. But the sink was in the same place, of course; and the refrigerator and stove; and the door leading down to the basement— "That is the door leading down to the basement, isn't it?" He spoke strangely, staring at the door. For a moment it appeared he might ask to be shown the basement but the moment passed, fortunately—this was not a part of their house the father and mother would have been comfortable showing to a stranger.

Finally, making an effort to smile, the stranger said, "Your kitchen is so—pleasant." He paused. For a moment it seemed he had nothing further to say. Then, "A—controlled sort of place. My mother— When we lived here—" His words trailed off into a dreamy silence and the mother and father glanced at each other with carefully neutral expressions.

On the windowsill above the sink were several lushly blooming African violet plants in ceramic pots and these the stranger made a show of admiring. Impulsively he leaned over to sniff the flowers— "Lovely!"—though African violets have no smell. As if embarrassed he said, "Mother too had plants on this windowsill but I don't recall them ever blooming."

The mother said tactfully, "Oh they were probably the kind that don't bloom—like ivy."

In the next room, the dining room, the stranger appeared to be even more deeply moved. For some time he stood staring, wordless. With fastidious slowness he turned on his heel, blinking, and frowning, and tugging at his lower lip in a rough gesture that must have hurt. Finally, as if remembering the presence of his hosts, and the necessity for some display of civility, the stranger expressed his admiration for the attractiveness of the room, and its coziness. He'd remembered it as cavernous, with a ceiling twice as high. "And dark most of the time," he said wonderingly. "Dark by day, dark by night." The mother turned the lights of the little brass chandelier to their fullest: shadows were dispersed like ragged ghosts and the cut-glass fruit bowl at the center of the table glowed like an exquisite multi-faceted jewel. The stranger exclaimed in surprise. He'd extracted a handkerchief from his pocket and was dabbing carefully at his face, where beads of perspiration shone. He said, as if thinking aloud, still wonderingly, "My father was a unique man. Everyone who knew him admired him. He sat *here*," he said, gingerly touching the chair that was in fact the father's chair, at one end of the table. "And Mother sat *there*," he said, merely pointing. "I don't recall my own place or my sister's but I suppose it doesn't matter. . . . I see you have four place settings, Mrs. . . .? Two children, I suppose?" "A boy eleven, and a girl thirteen," the mother said. The stranger stared not at her but at the table, smiling. "And so too we were—I mean, there were two of us: my sister and me."

Comparing Gothic Literature

How do the stranger's halted, or unfinished, statements affect your reading of his character?

Vocabulary

impulsively (im puhl′ siv lē) *adv.* spontaneously

fastidious (fa stid′ ē əs) *adj.* careful; meticulous

cavernous (cav′ ərn nəs) *adj.* cavelike; vast

❼ Reading Check

What similarity does the stranger notice between his own family and that of the house's current occupants?

Where Is Here? **327**

TEACH

❺ Comparing Gothic Literature

1. Read or ask a prepared student to read the bracketed passage, taking care to emphasize the stranger's halting speech pattern.

2. **Ask** the Comparing Gothic Literature question: How do the stranger's halted, unfinished statements affect your reading of his character?
   Possible response: Students may say that the stranger's halting speech may indicate that he is struggling with childhood memories or stopping himself from divulging details of his family's life.

❻ Comparing Gothic Literature

1. Refer students to the bracketed paragraph describing the stranger's visit to the dining room.

2. Have students work through this paragraph line by line to identify details that contribute to a feeling of uncertainty or eeriness. Write these on the chalkboard as students point them out.
   Answer: The stranger blinks, frowns, and hurtfully tugs at his lip. He remembers the room as "dark by day, dark by night." When the mother turns on the light, shadows scatter "like ragged ghosts." The stranger is sweating. He makes the random statement that his father "was a unique man."

❼ Reading Check

Answer: The stranger notices that both families had four members: a father, mother, girl, and boy.

Differentiated Instruction   for Universal Access

Enrichment for Gifted/Talented Students
Challenge students to select a passage from this modern Gothic story and to rewrite it in traditional Gothic style, as Poe himself might have written the passage. For example, students might choose a description of one of the rooms in the house or a description of the stranger himself. Suggest that students begin by reviewing some of Poe's works in order to identify typical word choices that reflect his style. Invite students to share their Gothic passages with the class.

Strategy for Advanced Readers
Point out that Oates draws parallels between the stranger's family and the one currently occupying the house. For example, both families consist of father, mother, son, and daughter. The father and the stranger are approximately the same age. As they continue reading, ask students to identify other parallels between the families in order to analyze the overall effect of these similarities.

327

❽ Comparing Gothic Literature

1. Have students review how the stranger's mood and behavior change after entering the house.

2. Direct students' attention to the bracketed passage. **Ask** the Comparing Gothic Literature question: In this and the next two paragraphs, what is odd or upsetting in the stranger's responses? Explain.
   Possible response: The stranger acts like a distracted child. He speaks aloud, but as if to himself, posing strange, remembered riddles. When asked about his family, the stranger at first says, "We've all been dead" before correcting himself.

3. Draw students' attention to the riddles and odd questions the stranger poses in the first paragraph of this passage. (See the Enrichment note below for more information on the riddles.) **Ask:** What is significant about the last question?
   Answer: The last question, "Where *is* here?" is also the title of the story, a significant signal from the writer that the question is highly meaningful.

4. Point out that in this paragraph the stranger jarringly shifts from childhood reminiscence to posing profound questions of human existence. Ask students to watch for similar perplexing questions as they continue to read and to consider how they contribute to the Gothic effect of the story.

...Who was this man, and how could they tactfully get rid of him?

Comparing Gothic Literature
In this and the next two paragraphs, what is odd or unsettling in the stranger's responses? Explain.

❽

The mother said, as if not knowing what else to say, "Are you—close?"

The stranger shrugged, distractedly rather than rudely, and moved on to the living room.

This room, cozily lit as well, was the most carefully furnished room in the house. Deep-piled wall-to-wall carpeting in hunter green, cheerful chintz drapes, a sofa and matching chairs in nubby heather green, framed reproductions of classic works of art, a gleaming gilt-framed mirror over the fireplace: wasn't the living room impressive as a display in a furniture store? But the stranger said nothing at first. Indeed, his eyes narrowed sharply as if he were confronted with a disagreeable spectacle. He whispered, "Here too! Here too!"

He went to the fireplace, walking, now, with a decided limp; he drew his fingers with excruciating slowness along the mantel as if testing its materiality. For some time he merely stood, and stared, and listened. He tapped a section of wall with his knuckles—"There used to be a large water stain here, like a shadow.

"Was there!" murmured the father out of politeness, and "Was there!" murmured the mother. Of course, neither had ever seen a water stain there.

Then, noticing the window seat, the stranger uttered a soft surprised cry, and went to sit in it. He appeared delighted: hugging his knees like a child trying to make himself smaller. "This was one of my happy places! At least when Father wasn't home. I'd hide away here for hours, reading, daydreaming, staring out the window! Sometimes Mother would join me, if she was in the mood, and we'd plot together—oh, all sorts of fantastical things!" The stranger remained sitting in the window seat for so long, tears shining in his eyes, that the father and mother almost feared he'd forgotten them. He was stroking the velvet fabric of the cushioned seat, gropingly touching the leaded windowpanes. Wordlessly, the father and mother exchanged a glance: who was this man, and how could they tactfully get rid of him? The father made a face signaling impatience and the mother shook her head without seeming to move it. For they couldn't be rude to a guest in their house.

The stranger was saying in a slow, dazed voice, "It all comes back to me now. How could I have forgotten! Mother used to read to me, and tell me stories, and ask me riddles I couldn't answer. 'What creature walks on four legs in the morning, two legs at midday, three legs in the evening?' 'What is round, and flat, measuring mere inches in one direction, and infinity in the other?' 'Out of what does our life arise? Out of what does our consciousness arise? Why are we here? Where *is* here?' "

The father and mother were perplexed by these strange words and hardly knew how to respond. The mother said uncertainly, "Our daughter used to like to sit here too, when she was younger. It *is* a lovely place." The father said with surprising passion, "I hate

Enrichment: Analyzing Forms and Genres

Ambiguity in Modern Gothic Literature

An aura of uncertainty and perplexity is essential to modern Gothic fiction. Oates achieves confusing effects by seeding her story with riddles, deep questions, and notions of infinity. Students may recognize the stranger's first riddle from Greek mythology: The monstrous Sphinx plagued the city of Thebes by posing the "leg riddle" to travelers and killing those who answered incorrectly. When Oedipus gave the correct answer—man, who crawls on four legs as a baby, walks on two legs as an adult, and limps with the aid of a staff in old age—the Sphinx killed itself.

Activity: Analyzing Modern Gothic Literature Have students identify the riddles and unanswerable questions the stranger introduces into the story. How do these details reflect the nature of modern Gothic fiction? For their analysis, students may use the **Enrichment: Analyzing Forms and Genres** work sheet, in *Professional Development Guidebook,* page 227.

riddles—they're moronic some of the time and obscure the rest of the time." He spoke with such uncharacteristic rudeness, the mother looked at him in surprise.

Hurriedly she said, "Is your mother still living, Mr. . . .?" "Oh no. Not at all," the stranger said, rising abruptly from the window seat, and looking at the mother as if she had said something mildly preposterous. "I'm sorry," the mother said. "Please don't be," the stranger said. "We've all been dead—*they've* all been dead—a long time."

The stranger's cheeks were deeply flushed as if with anger and his breath was quickened and audible.

The visit might have ended at this point but so clearly did the stranger expect to continue on upstairs, so purposefully, indeed almost defiantly, did he limp his way to the stairs, neither the father nor the mother knew how to dissuade him. It was as if a force of nature, benign at the outset, now uncontrollable, had swept its way into their house! The mother followed after him saying nervously, "I'm not sure what condition the rooms are in, upstairs. The children's rooms especially—" The stranger muttered that he did not care in the slightest about the condition of the household and continued on up without a backward glance.

The father, his face burning with resentment and his heart accelerating as if in preparation for combat, had no choice but to follow the stranger and the mother up the stairs. He was flexing and unflexing his fingers as if to rid them of stiffness.

On the landing, the stranger halted abruptly to examine a stained-glass fanlight—"My God, I haven't thought of this in years!" He spoke excitedly of how, on tiptoe, he used to stand and peek out through the diamonds of colored glass, red, blue, green, golden yellow: seeing with amazement the world outside so *altered*. "After such a lesson it's hard to take the world on its own terms, isn't it?" he asked. The father asked, annoyed, "On what terms should it be taken, then?" The stranger replied, regarding him levelly, with a just perceptible degree of disdain, "Why, none at all."

It was the son's room—by coincidence, the stranger's old room—the stranger most wanted to see. Other rooms on the second floor, the "master" bedroom in particular, he decidedly did not want to see. As he spoke of it, his mouth twisted as if he had been offered something repulsive to eat.

10 Reading Check

Which room on the second floor does the stranger want to see and which does he "decidedly" not wish to see?

Where Is Here? **329**

❾ Comparing Gothic Literature

1. Direct students to the bracketed passage, noting that this is the second time the narrator focuses on the father's responses to the stranger.

2. **Ask** students: What physical reactions does the father show in this passage?
   Answer: The father's face burns; his heart beats faster; and he flexes his fingers.

3. Then **ask** students what these details indicate about the father's emotional state.
   Possible response: Students may say that the details express the father's growing anger and agitation.

4. Direct students to monitor the father's emotional reactions as they continue to read the story.

❿ Reading Check

Answer: The stranger is anxious to see the son's room. He does not want to see the master bedroom.

329

⓫ Comparing Gothic Literature

1. Have students review the bracketed passage. **Ask** students to
identify details that suggest the
stranger's struggle to understand
what is real and what is not.
Answer: The stranger sees his
"ghostly and insubstantial" reflection in the window, an unreal
detail. He taps the window and
gropes the bedroom wall as if to
confirm their reality and takes
notice of the ceiling and floor,
saying, "That is what *is*."

2. **Ask** the Comparing Gothic
Literature question: Which details
suggest that the stranger's psychological torment has continued
to intensify?
Possible response: His behavior becomes odder and more
self-involved. As noted above, he
seems to be testing the very existence of the bedroom. Physical
details show his distress: The
stranger is flushed, breathing
hard, and sweating. He nearly
faints when he stands up.

No one had expected a visitor this evening!

Comparing Gothic Literature
Which details suggest that
the stranger's psychological
torment has continued to
intensify?

The mother hurried on ahead to warn the boy and to straighten
up his room a bit. No one had expected a visitor this evening! "So
you have two children," the stranger murmured, looking at the father
with a small quizzical smile. "Why?" The father stared at him as if he
hadn't heard correctly. "'Why'?" he asked. "Yes. *Why?*" the stranger
repeated. They looked at each other for a long strained moment, then
the stranger said quickly, "But you love them—of course." The father
controlled his temper and said, biting off his words, "Of course."

"Of course, of course," the stranger murmured, tugging at his
necktie and loosening his collar, "otherwise it would all come to an
end." The two men were of approximately the same height but the
father was heavier in the shoulders and torso; his hair had thinned
more severely so that the scalp of the crown was exposed, flushed,
damp with perspiration, sullenly alight.

With a stiff avuncular formality the stranger shook the son's
hand. "So this is your room, now! So you live here, now!" he murmured, as if the fact were an astonishment. Not used to shaking
hands, the boy was stricken with shyness and cast his eyes down.
The stranger limped past him, staring. "The same!—the same!—
walls, ceiling, floor—window—" He drew his fingers slowly along the
windowsill; around the frame; rapped the glass, as if, again, testing
materiality; stooped to look outside—but it was night, and nothing
but his reflection bobbed in the glass, ghostly and insubstantial. He
groped against the walls, he opened the closet door before the mother
could protest, he sat heavily on the boy's bed, the springs creaking
beneath him. He was panting, red-faced, dazed. "And the ceiling overhead," he whispered. He nodded slowly and repeatedly, smiling. "And
the floor beneath. That is what *is*."

He took out his handkerchief again and fastidiously wiped his
face. He made a visible effort to compose himself.

The father, in the doorway, cleared his throat and said, "I'm afraid
it's getting late—it's almost six."

The mother said, "Oh yes I'm afraid— I'm afraid it *is* getting late.
There's dinner, and the children have their homework—"

The stranger got to his feet. At his full height he stood for a precarious moment swaying, as if the blood had drained from his head
and he was in danger of fainting. But he steadied himself with a
hand against the slanted dormer ceiling. He said, "Oh yes!—I know!—
I've disturbed you terribly! —you've been so kind." It seemed, surely,
as if the stranger *must* leave now, but, as chance had it, he happened
to spy, on the boy's desk, an opened mathematics textbook and several smudged sheets of paper, and impulsively offered to show the boy
a mathematical riddle—"You can take it to school tomorrow and surprise your teacher!"

So, out of dutiful politeness, the son sat down at his desk and
the stranger leaned familiarly over him, demonstrating adroitly
with a ruler and a pencil how "what we call 'infinity'" can be con-

Vocabulary Development

Vocabulary Knowledge Rating
When students have completed reading and
discussing the selection, have them take out
the **Vocabulary Knowledge Rating** charts
they worked on earlier. Read the words aloud
and have students rate their knowledge of
the words again in the After Reading column.
Clarify any words that are still problematic.
Have students write their own definitions
and example or sentence in the appropriate
column. Then have students complete the
Vocabulary practice at the end of this selection.
Encourage students to use the words in further
discussion and written work about the selection. Remind them that they will be accountable for these words on the **Selection Test,**
Unit 2 Resources, pages 90–91.

tained within a small geometrical figure on a sheet of paper. "First you draw a square; then you draw a triangle to fit inside the square; then you draw a second triangle, and a third, and a fourth, each to fit inside the square, but without their points coinciding, and as you continue—here, son, I'll show you—give me your hand, and I'll show you—the border of the triangles' common outline gets more complex and measures larger, and larger, and larger—and soon you'll need a magnifying glass to see the details, and then you'll need a microscope, and so on and so forth, forever, laying triangles neatly down to fit inside the original square *without their points coinciding*—!" The stranger spoke with increasing fervor; spittle gleamed in the corners of his mouth. The son stared at the geometrical shapes rapidly materializing on the sheet of paper before him with no seeming comprehension but with a rapt staring fascination as if he dared not look away.

After several minutes of this the father came abruptly forward and dropped his hand on the stranger's shoulder. "The visit is over," he said calmly. It was the first time since they'd shaken hands that the two men had touched, and the touch had a galvanic effect upon the stranger: he dropped ruler and pencil at once, froze in his stooped posture, burst into frightened tears.

Now the visit truly was over; the stranger, at last, *was* leaving, having wiped away his tears and made a stoical effort to compose himself; but on the doorstep, to the father's astonishment, he made a final, preposterous appeal—he wanted to see the basement. "Just to sit on the stairs? In the dark? For a few quiet minutes? And you could close the door and forget me, you and your family could have your dinner and—"

The stranger was begging but the father was resolute. Without raising his voice he said, "*No. The visit is over.*"

He shut the door, and locked it.

Locked it! His hands were shaking and his heart beat angrily.

He watched the stranger walk away—out to the sidewalk, out to the street, disappearing in the darkness. Had the streetlights gone out?

Behind the father the mother stood apologetic and defensive, wringing her hands in a classic stance. "Wasn't that *sad*! Wasn't that—*sad*! But we had no choice but to let him in, it was the only

Spiral Review
Characterization How does the stranger's behavior as he draws contribute to the development of his character?

⓭ ☑ Reading Check

Before he leaves, what request does the stranger make?

Where Is Here? **331**

Strategy for Less Proficient Readers
Literal-minded readers may be disappointed that the story never answers questions they had about the stranger and what might have happened during his childhood. Point out to students that possibly the writer wanted readers to imagine for themselves what might have happened. Divide the class into groups and ask them to discuss their own ideas about the following issues: Did a tragedy occur in the house? What really happened to the stranger's father, mother, and sister? Why does the stranger want to go into the basement?

Enrichment for Gifted/Talented Students
Invite students to imagine what might have happened in the house during the stranger's childhood and to put their ideas in the form of a newspaper story, police report, or television script about a haunted house. Have students respond to these questions: Was the stranger harmed in the house? Why did he want to go into the basement? Why did he avoid the master bedroom? What happened to the stranger's parents and sister? Is the stranger now alive or is he a ghost?

⓬ Comparing Gothic Literature

1. Have students read the bracketed passage in which the stranger draws a "mathematical riddle." Remind students that earlier in the story the stranger had quoted a riddle about infinity.

2. On the chalkboard, sketch the drawing that the stranger describes: a square and the descending series of triangles within it. (You may wish to prepare, or have a student volunteer prepare, a poster-sized version of the drawing in advance.) Some students may notice that the drawing produces an optical effect, creating the illusion of a tunnel spiraling into the surface.

3. **Ask** students what the stranger claims to be doing in the drawing. **Answer:** The stranger claims that "infinity" can be contained in a geometric drawing of nested triangles.

4. Point out that, whatever the drawing means, the father takes no chances. The sight of the drawing and the stranger's increasing fervor cause the father to bring the visit—and the story—to a climax by announcing that the visit is over.

Spiral Review

Characterization

1. Remind students that they studied the concept of characterization.

2. **Ask** students the Spiral Review question.

   Possible response: The stranger's obsession with the math riddle develops the intensity and mysteriousness of his character. The endless nature of the math riddle suggests hidden twists to his character.

⓭ Reading Check

Answer: The stranger asks permission to spend some time in the basement of the house.

⑭ Comparing Gothic Literature

1. Have students review the bracketed conclusion of the story. **Ask** them to list the eerie or strange events that mark the end of the story.
Possible response: Students may cite the unusual darkness into which the stranger disappears; the flickering lights and wallpaper stain in the living room; the dimmed lights and sour odor of the kitchen; the father's mysterious rage; the mother's mysterious bruise and loss of balance.

2. **Ask:** How do these details reflect the nature of modern Gothic literature?
Possible response: Students may say that the details reflect the ambiguity or uncertainty of modern Gothic fiction; the reader is left dangling between ordinary and supernatural explanations. Does the stranger disappear into a sinister darkness, or are the streetlights out? Is the living room haunted, or is it only an optical illusion? Does the kitchen reek of evil, or is something burning in the oven? Is the father possessed by an angry spirit, or is he merely overstressed? Oates sustains the ambiguities to the end of her story.

ASSESS
Answers

Before students respond, you may wish to have them write a brief objective summary of the selection. As they answer the questions below, remind them to support their answers with evidence from the text.

1. (a) The stranger arrives at dusk. (b) His arrival in darkness adds an aura of mystery to the stranger.

2. (a) The father initially invites the stranger inside; then he allows him to look around outside. (b) The mother is uneasy with a stranger on their property and blames the father for permitting it. (c) The stranger's visit leaves the father and mother deeply estranged from each other.

3. (a) The stranger is surprised and delighted by the window seat, describing it as one of his "happy places." (b) The stranger seems overcome with deep emotion in the boy's bedroom; perhaps it

---

Everywhere the father looked, a pulse beat mute with rage.

⑭ decent thing to do." The father pushed past her without comment. In the living room he saw that the lights were flickering as if on the brink of going out; the patterned wallpaper seemed drained of color; a shadow lay upon it shaped like a bulbous cloud or growth. Even the robust green of the carpeting looked faded. Or was it an optical illusion? Everywhere the father looked, a pulse beat mute with rage. "I wasn't the one who opened the door to that man in the first place," the mother said, coming up behind the father and touching his arm. Without seeming to know what he did the father violently jerked his arm and thrust her away.

"Shut up. We'll forget it," he said.

"But—"

"We'll forget it."

The mother entered the kitchen walking slowly as if she'd been struck a blow. In fact, a bruise the size of a pear would materialize on her forearm by morning. When she reached out to steady herself she misjudged the distance of the door frame—or did the door frame recede an inch or two—and nearly lost her balance.

In the kitchen the lights were dim and an odor of sourish smoke, subtle but unmistakable, made her nostrils pinch.

She slammed open the oven door. Grabbed a pair of pot holders with insulated linings. "I wasn't the one, . . ." she cried, panting, "and you know it."

Critical Reading ©

© 1. **Key Ideas and Details** **(a)** At what time of day does the stranger arrive at the house? **(b) Analyze:** In what ways does this choice add to the air of mystery surrounding the stranger?

© 2. **Key Ideas and Details** **(a) Describe:** How does the father react to the stranger's request to look around? **(b) Analyze Cause and Effect:** What conflict does this decision set up between the father and mother? **(c) Analyze Cause and Effect:** At the end of the story, how does the stranger's visit continue to affect the family?

© 3. **Integrate Knowledge and Ideas** **(a) Interpret:** How does the stranger react to the window seat? **(b) Interpret:** How does he react to the boy's bedroom? **(c) Speculate:** What do these details suggest about his relationship to his own father?

© 4. **Integrate Knowledge and Ideas** **(a) Deduce:** What apparent mistake does the stranger make when he responds to the mother's question about whether his family is still living? **(b) Make a Judgment:** Is this a ghost story? Explain your answer.

---

was once his own. (c) The stranger's comments about the house hint that he feared his own father and perhaps felt unloved. His frightened reaction when the father touches him suggests some past trauma.

4. (a) The stranger blurts out, "We've all been dead" before correcting himself. (b) Some students may believe that the apparent mistake is a clear signal that the speaker is a ghost, as are the facts that he seems to vanish into the night and leaves the mother and father evidently haunted by his visit. Students who disagree may point out that ghosts cannot shake hands.

After You Read

The Fall of the House of Usher • Where Is Here?

Comparing Gothic Literature

1. Craft and Structure (a) Which character in Poe's story is most tormented? Explain. **(b)** Which character in Oates's story is tormented? **(c)** In what ways does the tormented character affect other characters in each story?

2. Craft and Structure (a) Where do readers first encounter a hint of the supernatural in Oates's story? **(b)** What are some supernatural elements in "The Fall of the House of Usher?" **(c)** Explain how these elements are both similar and different in the two stories.

3. Craft and Structure (a) What violent acts occur in "The Fall of the House of Usher?" **(b)** In what more subtle ways does Oates's story suggest the occurrence of mysterious but equally awful events?

Timed Writing

Explanatory Text: Analytical Essay

The castles and mansions that provide the settings for traditional Gothic tales are full of grandeur, darkness, and decay. These settings are one of the most recognizable elements of traditional Gothic fiction. Is setting equally important in a modern Gothic story?

Assignment: Write an **analytical essay** in which you explore the importance of setting in these two stories. Prewrite by answering the questions listed below to generate ideas and focus your analysis. **[40 minutes]**

- How are the settings in each story described? Note specific words each author uses to paint a picture of the setting.
- What *mood*, or atmosphere, does each setting have? Does this mood or atmosphere change as the story progresses? Explain.
- Which details in "Where Is Here?" show the setting as ordinary and which give it a frightening quality?
- Are the settings of "The Fall of the House of Usher" and "Where Is Here?" equally important to the events of each story? Explain.

As you write, support your ideas with detailed references to the stories.

5-Minute Planner

Complete these steps before you begin to write:

1. Read the prompt carefully. Underline key words and phrases.
2. Skim the stories and jot down notes about elements that address the focus questions in the prompt.
3. Write an outline to structure your ideas. **TIP** As part of your outline, note specific textual details you will use in each paragraph.
4. Reread the prompt, and draft your essay.

Common Core State Standards

Writing

9.a. Apply *grades 11-12 Reading standards* to literature.

10. Write routinely over shorter time frames for a range of tasks, purposes, and audiences.

USE ACADEMIC VOCABULARY

As you write, use academic language, including the following words or their related forms:

quote
distinguish
illustrate
compare

For more on academic language, see the vocabulary charts in the introduction to this book.

Answers

Comparing Gothic Literature

1. **(a)** The most tormented character in Poe's story is Roderick Usher. **(b)** In Oates's story, the stranger is most tormented. **(c)** Roderick's friend barely escapes with his life and sanity. Feelings between the father and the mother are strained.

2. **(a)** The stranger says, "We've all been dead—*they've* all been dead—a long time." **(b)** Students may cite the uncanny connection between Roderick and Madeline, her reappearance after many days of entombment, their simultaneous deaths, and the collapse of the mansion. **(c)** In both stories, characters have an eerie connection to their homes.

3. **(a)** Students may cite Madeline's struggle to be free of her coffin, her death embrace of Roderick, and the collapse of the mansion. **(b)** The mother's worrying questions foreshadow the mysterious effects of the stranger's visit. The stranger's memories include dark hints about the past.

Timed Writing

Evaluate students' essays using the **Rubrics for Comparison Contrast Essays,** in *Professional Development Guidebook,* pages 260–261.

Assessment Resources

Unit 2 Resources

L3 L4 **Selection Test,** pp. 90–91.

All **Customizable Test Bank**

All **Self-tests**

Students may prepare for the **Selection Test** by taking the **Self-test** online.

All assessment resources are available at **www.PHLitOnline.com**.

• from Moby-Dick
Lesson Pacing Guide

DAY 1 Preteach

- Administer the Reading and Vocabulary Warm-ups (*Unit 2 Resources*, pp. 92–95) as necessary.
- Introduce the Literary Analysis concepts: Symbol and Theme
- Introduce the Reading Strategy: Identify relevant details.
- Build background with the author and Background features.
- Develop thematic thinking with Connecting to the Essential Question.
- Teach the selection vocabulary.

DAY 2 3 Preteach/Teach/Assess

- Distribute copies of the appropriate graphic organizer for Literary Analysis (*Graphic Organizer Transparencies*, pp. 74–75).
- Distribute copies of the appropriate graphic organizer for the Reading Strategy (*Graphic Organizer Transparencies*, pp. 76–77).
- Prepare students to read with the Activating Prior Knowledge activities (TE).
- Informally monitor comprehension while students read.
- Use the Reading Check question to confirm comprehension.
- Develop students' understanding of symbol and theme using the Literary Analysis prompts.
- Develop students' ability to identify relevant details using the Reading Strategy prompts.
- Reinforce vocabulary with the Vocabulary notes.
- Assess students' comprehension and mastery of the skills by having them answer the Critical Reading, Literary Analysis, and Reading Strategy questions.
- Have students complete the Vocabulary Lesson.

DAY 4 Extend/Assess

- Have students complete the Convention and Style Lesson.
- Have students complete the Writing lesson and write a character study. (You may assign as homework.)
- Administer Selection Test A or B (*Unit 2 Resources,* pp. 105–107 or 108–110).

© Common Core State Standards

Reading Literature 1. Cite strong and thorough textual evidence to support analysis of what the text says explicitly as well as inferences drawn from the text, including determining where the text leaves matters uncertain.

2. Determine two or more themes or central ideas of a text and analyze their development over the course of the text, including how they interact and build on one another to produce a complex account; provide an objective summary of the text.

Writing 1. Write arguments to support claims in an analysis of substantive topics or texts, using valid reasoning and relevant and sufficient evidence.

1.a. Introduce precise, knowledgeable claim(s), establish the significance of the claim(s), distinguish the claim(s) from alternate or opposing claims, and create an organization that logically sequences claim(s), counterclaims, reasons, and evidence.

Additional Standards Practice
Common Core Companion, pp. 2–9; 15–22; 185–195

Daily Block Scheduling
Each day in this Lesson Pacing Guide represents a 40–50 minute period. Teachers using block scheduling may combine days to revise pacing. In addition, teachers may differentiate and support core instruction by integrating components for extended and intensive support as students require. See the Guide to Selected Leveled Resources (facing page).

Guide to Selected Leveled Resources

R T I Tier 1 (students performing on level)

from **Moby-Dick**

<table>
<tr>
<td>Warm Up</td>
<td>Practice, model, and monitor fluency, working with the whole class or in groups.</td>
<td>Vocabulary and Reading Warm-ups B, Unit 2 Resources, pp. 92–93, 95</td>
</tr>
<tr>
<td>Comprehension/Skills</td>
<td>Support and monitor comprehension and skills development, having students complete the activities, graphic organizers, and interactive prompts independently or as a class.</td>
<td>• Reader's Notebook, adapted instruction and summary

EL Reader's Notebook: English Learner's Version, adapted instruction and summary
• Reading Strategy Graphic Organizer B, Graphic Organizer Transparencies, p. 77
• Literary Analysis Graphic Organizer B, Graphic Organizer Transparencies, p. 75</td>
</tr>
<tr>
<td>Monitor Progress
A</td>
<td>Monitor student progress with the differentiated curriculum-based assessment in the Unit Resources.</td>
<td>• Selection Test B, Unit 2 Resources, pp. 108–110
• Open-Book Test, Unit 2 Resources, pp. 102–104</td>
</tr>
</table>

R T I Tier 2 (students requiring intervention)

from **Moby-Dick**

<table>
<tr>
<td>Warm Up</td>
<td>Practice, model, and monitor fluency in groups or with individuals.</td>
<td>• Vocabulary and Reading Warm-ups A, Unit 2 Resources, pp. 92–94
• Hear It! Audio CD</td>
</tr>
<tr>
<td>Comprehension/Skills</td>
<td>• Support and monitor comprehension and skills development, working in small groups or with individuals.
• As students complete the selection in the appropriate version of the Reader's Notebook, monitor comprehension frequently with group questions and individual instruction.
• Model strategies while guiding students in completing the activities and prompts in the Reader's Notebook, as well as the graphic organizers.
• Practice skills and monitor mastery with the Reading Kit worksheets.</td>
<td>• Reader's Notebook: Adapted Version, adapted instruction and summary

EL Reader's Notebook: English Learner's Version, adapted instruction and summary
• Reading Strategy Graphic Organizer A, Graphic Organizer Transparencies, p. 76
• Literary Analysis Graphic Organizer A, Graphic Organizer Transparencies, p. 74
• Reading Kit, Practice worksheets</td>
</tr>
<tr>
<td>Monitor Progress
A</td>
<td>Monitor student progress with the differentiated curriculum-based assessment in the Unit Resources and in the Reading Kit.</td>
<td>• Selection Test A, Unit 2 Resources, pp. 105–107
• Reading Kit, Assess worksheets</td>
</tr>
</table>

TIER 3 Tier 3 intervention may require consultation with the student's special education or dyslexia specialist
For additional support, see the Tier 2 activities and resources listed above.

One-on-one teaching Group work Whole-class instruction Independent work A Assessment
For a complete guide to selection support, including support for Advanced students, see the Overview of Resources in the frontmatter.

• from Moby Dick

FROM
MOBY-DICK
HERMAN MELVILLE

BACKGROUND *Moby-Dick* is the story of a man's obsession with the dangerous and mysterious white whale that years before had taken off one of his legs. The man, Captain Ahab, guides the *Pequod*, a whaling ship, and its crew in relentless pursuit of the whale, Moby-Dick. Among the more important members of the crew are Starbuck, the first mate; Stubb, the second mate; Flask, the third mate; Queequeg, Tashtego, and Daggoo, the harpooners; and Ishmael, the young sailor who narrates the story. When the crew signed aboard the *Pequod*, they believed the voyage to be a business venture. However, in the following excerpt, Ahab makes clear that his real purpose is to seek revenge against Moby-Dick.

FROM THE QUARTER-DECK

One morning shortly after breakfast, Ahab, as was his wont, ascended the cabin gangway to the deck. There most sea captains usually walk at that hour, as country gentlemen, after the same meal, take a few turns in the garden.

Soon his steady, ivory stride was heard, as to and fro he paced his old rounds, upon planks so familiar to his tread, that they were all over dented, like geological stones, with the peculiar mark of his walk. Did you fixedly gaze, too, upon that ribbed and dented brow; there also, you would see still stranger footprints—the footprints of his one unsleeping, ever-pacing thought.

But on the occasion in question, those dents looked deeper, even as his nervous step that morning left a deeper mark. And, so full of his thought was Ahab, that at every uniform turn that he made, now

◀ Critical Viewing
Which elements of this illustration emphasize human weakness in the face of nature? [Analyze]

☑ Reading Check
Why are the *Pequod*'s planks dented?

from Moby-Dick 337

RESOURCES FOR:

- **L1** Special-Needs Students
- **L2** Below-Level Students (Tier 2)
- **L3** On-Level Students (Tier 1)
- **L4** Advanced Students (Tier 1)
- **EL** English Learners
- **All** All Students

Vocabulary/Fluency/Prior Knowledge

Name _____ Date _____

from Moby-Dick by Herman Melville
Reading Warm-up A

Read the following passage. Pay special attention to the underlined words. Then, read it again, and complete the activities. Use a separate sheet of paper for your written answers.

Ever since arriving on Cape Cod, Jason had been hounding his mother to go on a whale-watching trip. She worried about getting seasick, having spent a miserable day on a boat twenty years ago in a thunderstorm. Jason persisted, though, doing everything his mother asked. Eventually, he had <u>accumulated</u> such a record of good conduct that his mother couldn't refuse. When he finally got her <u>acquiescence</u>, they made reservations on the *Bayman* and set off the next morning to look for whales.

The sky, gray and ominous, filled the morning with <u>foreboding</u>, as if a violent storm might erupt and send the boat tossing over enormous waves. His mother watched her feet carefully as she climbed aboard, her <u>downcast</u> face showing her nervousness. She seemed terrified as the boat <u>dislodged</u> itself from the dock and set out for the open sea. After that, she sat gripping the edge of her seat, <u>cringing</u> with anxiety each time the boat went over even the smallest wave.

They cruised the waters outside Provincetown for almost two hours without seeing even the slightest trace of a whale. Jason abandoned his mother and stood at the front of the boat, growing ever more impatient for a sighting. It would be <u>outrageous</u> to go to all this trouble and not see even a tail or a fin in the water. Then, just as he was about to give up hope, the captain shouted. A sperm whale jumped out of the water once, then twice, then a third time. The huge whale dominated the entire ocean, an <u>imperial</u> shape of enormous power. Even Jason's mother stood up to watch him as he appeared once more above the surface.

1. Underline the words in this sentence that give a clue to the meaning of *accumulated*. Use the word *accumulated* in an original sentence.

2. Circle the words in the previous sentence that give a clue to the meaning of the word *acquiescence*. What is a synonym for *acquiescence*?

3. Underline the words that give a clue to the meaning of *foreboding*. Use the word *foreboding* in a sentence of your own.

4. Circle the words that offer a clue to the meaning of *downcast* here. What are two antonyms for the word *downcast*?

5. Circle the words in this sentence that offer clues to the meaning of *dislodged*. Use a word meaning the opposite of *dislodged* in a sentence.

6. Underline the words in this sentence that give a clue to the meaning of *cringing*. What is a synonym for *cringing*?

7. Circle the words that give a clue to the meaning of *outrageous*. Use the word *outrageous* in an original sentence.

8. Underline the words that hint at the meaning of *imperial*. Is this word used literally or figuratively here?

Unit 2 Resources: A Growing Nation
© Pearson Education, Inc. All rights reserved.
94

(vertical tab) Unit 2 Resources

EL L1 L2 Reading Warm-ups A and B,
pp. 94–95

Also available for these selections:
EL L1 L2 Vocabulary Warm-ups A and B,
pp. 92–93
All Vocabulary Builder, p. 98

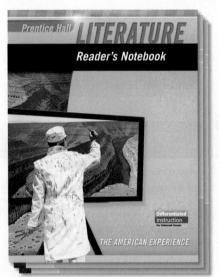

Prentice Hall
LITERATURE
Reader's Notebook

Differentiated Instruction for Universal Access
THE AMERICAN EXPERIENCE

Reader's Notebooks

Pre- and postreading pages for this selection appear in an interactive format in the *Reader's Notebooks*. Each *Notebook* is differentiated for a different group of learners.

The selections in the Adapted and English Learner's versions are abridged.

L2 L3 *Reader's Notebook*
L1 *Reader's Notebook: Adapted Version*
EL *Reader's Notebook: English Learner's Version*
EL *Reader's Notebook: Spanish Version*

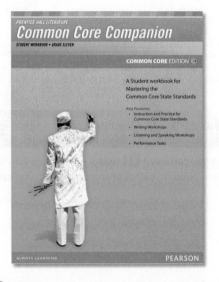

PRENTICE HALL LITERATURE
Common Core Companion
STUDENT WORKBOOK • GRADE ELEVEN

COMMON CORE EDITION ©

A Student workbook for Mastering the Common Core State Standards

Key Features
- Instruction and Practice for Common Core State Standards
- Writing Workshops
- Listening and Speaking Workshops
- Performance Tasks

ALWAYS LEARNING   PEARSON

© ***Common Core Companion***

Additional instruction and practice for each Common Core State Standard

Selection Support

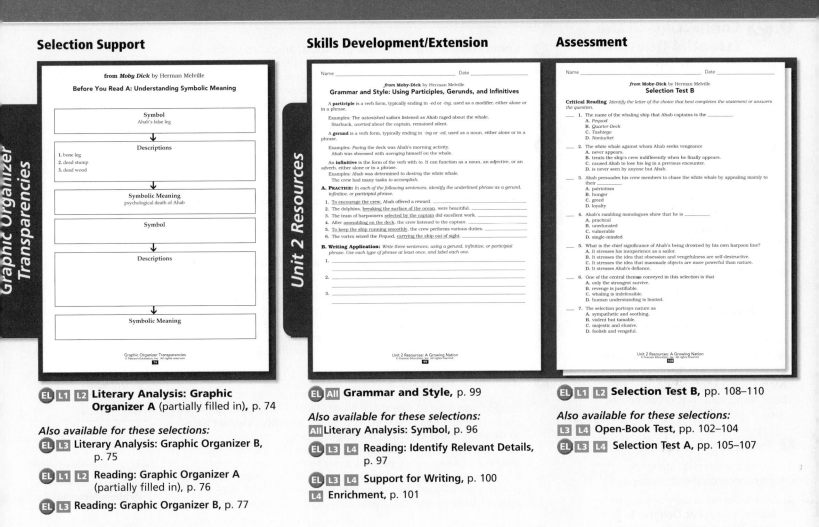

Graphic Organizer Transparencies

from Moby Dick by Herman Melville

Before You Read A: Understanding Symbolic Meaning

Symbol
Ahab's false leg

↓

Descriptions
1. bone leg
2. dead stump
3. dead wood

↓

Symbolic Meaning
psychological death of Ahab

Symbol

↓

Descriptions

↓

Symbolic Meaning

Graphic Organizer Transparencies
© Pearson Education, Inc. All rights reserved.
74

EL **L1** **L2** **Literary Analysis: Graphic Organizer A** (partially filled in), p. 74

Also available for these selections:

EL **L3** **Literary Analysis: Graphic Organizer B,** p. 75

EL **L1** **L2** **Reading: Graphic Organizer A** (partially filled in), p. 76

EL **L3** **Reading: Graphic Organizer B,** p. 77

Skills Development/Extension

Unit 2 Resources

Name _____ Date _____

from Moby-Dick by Herman Melville
Grammar and Style: Using Participles, Gerunds, and Infinitives

A **participle** is a verb form, typically ending in *-ed* or *-ing*, used as a modifier, either alone or in a phrase.

Examples: The *astonished* sailors listened as Ahab raged about the whale.
Starbuck, *worried* about the captain, remained silent.

A **gerund** is a verb form, typically ending in *-ing* or *-ed*, used as a noun, either alone or in a phrase.

Examples: *Pacing* the deck was Ahab's morning activity.
Ahab was obsessed with *avenging* himself on the whale.

An **infinitive** is the form of the verb with *to*. It can function as a noun, an adjective, or an adverb, either alone or in a phrase.

Examples: Ahab was determined *to destroy* the white whale.
The crew had many tasks *to accomplish*.

A. PRACTICE: *In each of the following sentences, identify the underlined phrase as a gerund, infinitive, or participial phrase.*

1. <u>To encourage the crew,</u> Ahab offered a reward. _____
2. The dolphins, <u>breaking the surface of the ocean,</u> were beautiful. _____
3. The team of harpooners <u>selected by the captain</u> did excellent work. _____
4. After <u>assembling on the deck,</u> the crew listened to the captain. _____
5. <u>To keep the ship running smoothly,</u> the crew performs various duties. _____
6. The vortex seized the *Pequod,* <u>carrying the ship out of sight.</u> _____

B. Writing Application: *Write three sentences, using a gerund, infinitive, or participial phrase. Use each type of phrase at least once, and label each one.*

1. _____
   _____

2. _____
   _____

3. _____
   _____

Unit 2 Resources: A Growing Nation
© Pearson Education, Inc. All rights reserved.
99

EL **All** **Grammar and Style,** p. 99

Also available for these selections:

All **Literary Analysis: Symbol,** p. 96

EL **L3** **L4** **Reading: Identify Relevant Details,** p. 97

EL **L3** **L4** **Support for Writing,** p. 100

L4 **Enrichment,** p. 101

Assessment

Name _____ Date _____

from Moby-Dick by Herman Melville
Selection Test B

Critical Reading *Identify the letter of the choice that best completes the statement or answers the question.*

___ 1. The name of the whaling ship that Ahab captains is the _____.
   A. Pequod
   B. Quarter-Deck
   C. Tashtego
   D. Nantucket

___ 2. The white whale against whom Ahab seeks vengeance
   A. never appears.
   B. treats the ship's crew indifferently when he finally appears.
   C. caused Ahab to lose his leg in a previous encounter.
   D. is never seen by anyone but Ahab.

___ 3. Ahab persuades his crew members to chase the white whale by appealing mainly to their _____.
   A. patriotism
   B. hunger
   C. greed
   D. loyalty

___ 4. Ahab's rambling monologues show that he is _____.
   A. practical
   B. uneducated
   C. vulnerable
   D. single-minded

___ 5. What is the chief significance of Ahab's being drowned by his own harpoon line?
   A. It stresses his inexperience as a sailor.
   B. It stresses the idea that obsession and vengefulness are self-destructive.
   C. It stresses the idea that manmade objects are more powerful than nature.
   D. It stresses Ahab's defiance.

___ 6. One of the central themes conveyed in this selection is that
   A. only the strongest survive.
   B. revenge is justifiable.
   C. whaling is indefensible.
   D. human understanding is limited.

___ 7. The selection portrays nature as
   A. sympathetic and soothing.
   B. violent but tamable.
   C. majestic and elusive.
   D. foolish and vengeful.

Unit 2 Resources: A Growing Nation
© Pearson Education, Inc. All rights reserved.
108

EL **L1** **L2** **Selection Test B,** pp. 108–110

Also available for these selections:

L3 **L4** **Open-Book Test,** pp. 102–104

EL **L3** **L4** **Selection Test A,** pp. 105–107

PHLit Online!
www.PHLitOnline.com

Online Resources: All print materials are also available online.

- complete narrated selection text
- a thematically related video with writing prompt
- an interactive graphic organizer
- highlighting feature
- access to all student print resources, adapted to individual student needs
- Spanish and English summaries
- adapted selection translations in Spanish

Background Video

Also available:

Get Connected! (thematic video with writing prompt)
All videos available in Spanish.

Vocabulary Central *(tools and activities for studying vocabulary)*

Also available:

Writer's Journal (with graphics feature)

❶ Connecting to the Essential Question

1. Review the assignment with the class.

2. Point out that students' responses to the assignment should include supporting details.

3. Suggest that students think about parallel examples in American history of persistence taken too far.

❷ Literary Analysis

Introduce the strategy, using the instruction on the student page.

Think Aloud: Model the Skill

Say to students:

A symbol can have several meanings. I know the color white represents cleanness, innocence, and peace—but it can also suggest emptiness, sterility, and death. In *Moby-Dick*, I know *white* is symbolic, but I must figure out which meaning applies.

❸ Reading Strategy

1. Introduce the skill, using the instruction on the student page.

2. Give students a copy of **Literary Analysis Graphic Organizer B,** page 75 in *Graphic Organizer Transparencies,* to fill out as they read.

Think Aloud

Say to students:

In Poe's "The Raven," the bird's species, behavior, and appearance are relevant details that show me that the raven is a symbol of doomed hope. Watch how Melville uses details about Moby-Dick as you read.

❹ Vocabulary

1. Pronounce each word, giving its definition, and have students say it aloud.

2. For more guidance, see the *Classroom Strategies and Teaching Routines* card for introducing vocabulary.

Before You Read | from *Moby-Dick*

❶ **Connecting to the Essential Question** Americans tend to admire persistence. However, Captain Ahab, Herman Melville's most famous character, is persistent to the point of obsession. As you read, notice details that suggest the dark side of Ahab's determination. This will help as you consider the Essential Question: **What makes American literature American?**

❷ Literary Analysis

A **symbol** is a person, place, or thing that has its own meaning and also represents something larger, usually an abstract idea. The main symbol in Melville's great novel—the whale that gives the book its title—is complex. To understand it as a symbol, reflect on all aspects of the whale's behavior and appearance, including the following qualities:

- Moby-Dick is enormous and powerful.
- Moby-Dick seems unpredictable but is controlled by natural laws.
- Moby-Dick seems immortal and indifferent to human suffering.

Analyzing the symbol of the whale will help you identify the novel's **theme,** its central message or comment on life. A writer develops theme through symbols, descriptions, characters, and imagery. A long and complex novel like *Moby-Dick* may have multiple themes. As you read, look for details related to concepts of good, evil, sacrifice, and revenge.

❸ Reading Strategy

© **Preparing to Read Complex Texts** Melville builds symbolic meaning and theme through details. As you read, **identify relevant details to determine the essential message.** Look for characters, settings, objects, and dialogue that suggest larger ideas. For example, Ahab's description of Moby-Dick provides a clue to the whale's essential meaning: "I see in him outrageous strength, with an inscrutable malice sinewing it." As you read, use a chart like the one shown to identify relevant details that will lead you to the novel's essential meanings.

❹ Vocabulary

pedestrian (pi des′ trē ən) *adj.* going on foot; walking (p. 338)

impulsive (im pul′ siv) *adj.* done without thinking (p. 338)

inarticulate (in′ är tik′ yōō lət) *adj.* unclearly spoken or expressed (p. 339)

inscrutable (in skrōōt′ ə bəl) *adj.* difficult to know or understand (p. 341)

maledictions (mal′ ə dik′ shənz) *n.* curses (p. 343)

prescient (presh′ ənt) *adj.* having foreknowledge (p. 348)

© **Common Core State Standards**

Reading Literature
2. Determine two or more themes or central ideas of a text and analyze their development over the course of the text, including how they interact and build on one another to produce a complex account; provide an objective summary of the text.

Symbol
Ahab's false leg

Descriptions
1.
2.
3.

Symbolic Meaning

334 A Growing Nation (1800–1870)

Vocabulary Development

Vocabulary Knowledge Rating

Create a **Vocabulary Knowledge Rating** chart (*Professional Development Guidebook,* p. 33) for the vocabulary words on the student page. Give each student a copy of the chart with the words on it. Read the words aloud and have students mark their rating in the Before Reading column. Urge students to attend to these words as they read and discuss the selection.

In order to gauge how much instruction you need to provide, tally how many students are confident in their knowledge of each word. As students read, point out the words and their context.

Vocabulary Central, featuring tools and activities for studying vocabulary, is available online at **www.PHLitOnline.com.**

HERMAN MELVILLE (1819–1891)

Author of *Moby-Dick*

One of America's greatest novelists, Herman Melville was born in New York City, the son of a wealthy merchant. His family's comfortable situation changed drastically in 1830, however, when his father's business failed. Two years later, Melville's father died, leaving the family in debt. Melville spent the rest of his childhood working as a clerk, a farmhand, and a teacher to help support his family.

Whaling in the South Pacific Melville became a sailor at the age of nineteen and spent several years working on whaling ships in the South Pacific. He returned to the United States in 1844, after a brief period of service in the navy. Soon thereafter, Melville began his writing career, using his adventures in the South Seas as material for his fiction. He produced two popular novels, *Typee* (1846) and *Omoo* (1847), both set in the Pacific islands. His third novel, *Mardi* (1849), was more abstract and symbolic. When readers rejected the book, Melville grew melancholy. He continued writing, however, turning out two more novels over the next two years.

Writing in the Berkshires Using the profits from his popular novels, Melville bought Arrowhead, a farm near Pittsfield, Massachusetts. There, he befriended the author Nathaniel Hawthorne, who lived nearby. Encouraged by Hawthorne's interest, Melville redoubled his creative efforts. In 1851, he published his masterpiece, *Moby-Dick*, under the title *The Whale*.

A Moment of Pride *Moby-Dick* is a complex novel with several layers of meaning. On the surface, it is the story of the fateful voyage of a whaling ship. On another level, it is the story of a bitter man's quest for vengeance. On still another level, it is a philosophical examination of humanity's relationship to the natural world. When he finished the book, Melville sensed the magnitude of his achievement. Unfortunately, nineteenth-century readers rejected the book. They also spurned his next two novels and Melville fell into debt. The job he took as an inspector at the New York customs house became another experience that would inform his fiction, especially the story "Bartleby, the Scrivener."

Rediscovered In the latter part of his life, Melville privately published several volumes of poetry, a handful of short stories, and the novella *Billy Budd*. He died in 1891, unappreciated and unnoticed. In the 1920s, however, his work was rediscovered, and he finally received the recognition he deserved. Today, *Moby-Dick* is widely regarded as one of the finest novels in all of American literature.

from Moby-Dick **335**

Daily Bellringer

For each class during which you will teach this selection, have students complete one of the five activities for the appropriate week in the *Daily Bellringer Activities* booklet.

Multidraft Reading

To assist struggling readers and to enhance reading for all, assign the text in chunks as warranted by length and apply multidraft reading protocols. For each reading, have students set the purpose indicated:

- **First reading**—identifying key ideas and details and answering any Reading Checks.
- **Second reading**—analyzing craft and structure and responding to the side-column prompts.
- **Third reading**—integrating knowledge and ideas, connecting to other texts and the world, and answering the end-of-selection questions.

For more guidance, refer to the *Classroom Strategies and Teaching Routines* card, **Multidraft Reading**.

More About the Author

After an unsuccessful job search and a brief stint as a teacher, Melville sailed on the whaler *Acushnet* to the South Seas in 1841, anchoring in the Marquesas Islands. On this voyage, he joined an uprising that landed him in a Tahitian jail. After escaping, Melville roamed throughout French Polynesia, during which time he became deeply embittered at the mistreatment of native Polynesian peoples by colonists and missionaries.

PHLit Online!
www.PHLitOnline.com

Teaching From Technology

Preparing to Read
Go to **www.PHLitOnline.com** and display the **Get Connected!** slide show for this selection. Have the class brainstorm for responses to the writing prompt, entering ideas in the interactive journal. Then have students complete their responses individually. You may also have students complete the assignment as homework.

To build background, display the Background video and More About the Author features.

Using the Interactive Student Edition
Go to **www.PHLitOnline.com** and display the **Enriched Online Student Edition**. As the class reads the selection or listens to the narration, record answers to side-column prompts using the graphic organizers accessible on the interactive page. Alternatively, have students use the online edition individually, answering the prompts as they read.

❶ About the Selection

Widely regarded as one of the finest American novels ever written, *Moby-Dick* expresses the view that despite people's desire to do so, they will never be able to control nature or understand it completely. In "The Quarter-Deck," one of the novel's key early chapters, Ahab becomes the novel's dominant character. Melville reveals Ahab's vengeful, obsessive personality and his conflict with Moby-Dick. At this turning point, the rest of the crew and readers alike learn the true purpose of the *Pequod*'s voyage. "The Chase—Third Day" is the book's last chapter. There, the novel reaches its climax in the final catastrophic contest with Moby-Dick.

❷ Activating Prior Knowledge

Ahab says, "Death to Moby-Dick! God hunt us all, if we do not hunt Moby-Dick to his death!" After reading this quotation, tell students that Ahab is a man obsessed. Invite students to think of people (or fictional characters) they know whose intense, single-minded efforts to reach a goal began at an early age. For example, students might think of athletes, actors, musicians, and other performers who fit that description. Ask students whether they see a distinction between concentrated effort and obsession. Suggest that they write a one-paragraph answer to this question: Does one need to be obsessed to reach lofty goals?

Concept Connector ➡

Tell students they will return to their ideas about obsession after reading the selection.

❸ Background

History

In Melville's day, the captain of a ship had unlimited authority—and all aboard ship knew this to be the case. Failing to follow orders brought harsh and perhaps arbitrary punishment, and most crew members were careful not to challenge the captain directly.

336 A Growing Nation (1800–1870)

ⓒ Text Complexity Rubric

from **Moby-Dick**	
Qualitative Measures	
Context/ Knowledge Demands	Nineteenth-century whaling voyage; technical knowledge demands 1 2 ③ 4 5
Structure/Language Conventionality and Clarity	Challenging (similes and metaphors; whaling/seamen's language and vocabulary; long compound and complex sentences) 1 2 3 ④ 5
Levels of Meaning/ Purpose/Concept Level	Challenging (Moby-Dick as a symbol of nature's beauty, power, and immortality) 1 2 3 4 ⑤
Quantitative Measures	
Lexile/Text Length	970L / 7,230 words
Overall Complexity	**More complex**

FROM
MOBY-DICK

1
2

HERMAN MELVILLE

3 BACKGROUND *Moby-Dick* is the story of a man's obsession with the dangerous and mysterious white whale that years before had taken off one of his legs. The man, Captain Ahab, guides the *Pequod*, a whaling ship, and its crew in relentless pursuit of the whale, Moby-Dick. Among the more important members of the crew are Starbuck, the first mate; Stubb, the second mate; Flask, the third mate; Queequeg, Tashtego, and Daggoo, the harpooners; and Ishmael, the young sailor who narrates the story. When the crew signed aboard the *Pequod*, they believed the voyage to be a business venture. However, in the following excerpt, Ahab makes clear that his real purpose is to seek revenge against Moby-Dick.

FROM THE QUARTER-DECK

One morning shortly after breakfast, Ahab, as was his wont, ascended the cabin gangway to the deck. There most sea captains usually walk at that hour, as country gentlemen, after the same meal, take a few turns in the garden.

5 Soon his steady, ivory stride was heard, as to and fro he paced his old rounds, upon planks so familiar to his tread, that they were all over dented, like geological stones, with the peculiar mark of his walk. Did you fixedly gaze, too, upon that ribbed and dented brow; there also, you would see still stranger footprints—the footprints of his one unsleeping, ever-pacing thought.

But on the occasion in question, those dents looked deeper, even as his nervous step that morning left a deeper mark. And, so full of his thought was Ahab, that at every uniform turn that he made, now

4 ◀ **Critical Viewing**
Which elements of this illustration emphasize human weakness in the face of nature? **[Analyze]**

6 ☑ Reading Check

Why are the *Pequod's* planks dented?

from Moby-Dick **337**

---

4 **Critical Viewing**

Answer: The fact that the human figures are being helplessly thrown from their boats emphasizes human weakness in the face of nature.

5 **Literary Analysis**
Symbol

1. Have a student volunteer read aloud the paragraph beginning "Soon his steady, ivory stride was heard." Make sure students understand the cause of the "dents" mentioned by Melville's narrator; these are the dents in the wooden planks of the ship's deck caused by Ahab's peg leg.

2. Point out that the repetition of the image of dents indicates the possible presence of a symbol. Draw students' attention to the language Melville uses—the footprints of his one unsleeping, ever-pacing thought—to describe the wrinkles in Ahab's brow.

3. In addition, point out the connection Melville draws between Ahab's dented brow and the deeper marks left by Ahab's "nervous" steps.

4. **Ask** students the following question: What might the "dents" on Ahab's furrowed brow symbolize? **Answer:** The "dents" might symbolize psychological injuries Ahab has suffered in his battle with the great whale.

6 **Reading Check**

Answer: Ahab has dented them walking back and forth with his artificial leg.

Ⓒ Text Complexity: Reader and Task Suggestions

from **Moby-Dick**

Preparing to Read the Text	Leveled Tasks
• Using the Background information on SE p. 335, discuss Melville's early career as a sailor. • Ask students how an object could have a literal meaning and a figurative meaning at the same time; for example, a star is a celestial object, but to many people it symbolizes hope, inspiration, eternity, and so on. Invite students to name other examples of objects with two levels of meaning. • Guide students to use Multidraft Reading strategies to deepen their comprehension (TE p. 335).	*Levels of Meaning* If students will have difficulty with the meaning, have them read to identify five literal details about Moby-Dick from the first excerpt. As they reread, have them add descriptive and narrative details from both excerpts to determine the symbolic meaning of the white whale. *Synthesizing* If students will not have difficulty with the meaning, ask them to state, in their own words, what Moby-Dick symbolizes to Ahab. Invite students to suggest literal objects from the modern-day world that, given certain circumstances, might have a similar symbolic meaning to someone today.

Identifying Details to Determine Essential Message

1. Have a student volunteer read the bracketed passage aloud. After the reading, **ask** the students to identify details about Ahab. Write the responses on the board.
   Answers: Ahab has a forbidding appearance; he looks quickly at the crew but seems to ignore them; he paces; he appears to ignore their whispering.

2. **Ask:** What do these details indicate about Ahab's state of mind during this scene?
   Answer: Ahab seems to be preoccupied with his own thoughts.

3. **Ask:** Based on the detailed description, how much time do you think passes from the time the ship's crew was assembled to Ahab's question about seeing a whale?
   Answer: Probably about three minutes pass.

4. **Ask:** What might Ahab's manner indicate about his attitude about the crew? Explain.
   Answer: Ahab considers himself superior to them, not just in rank but as a human being, as indicated by the way he makes them wait until he is ready to speak.

❽ Critical Viewing

Answer: Students may say that the illustration captures Ahab's implacable, obsessive nature very well.

❽ ▲ Critical Viewing
How does this portrait of Ahab compare with your mental image of him? **[Compare and Contrast]**

Vocabulary

pedestrian (pi des′ trē ən) *adj.* going on foot; walking

impulsive (im pul′ siv) *adj.* done without thinking

---

at the mainmast and now at the binnacle,[1] you could almost see that thought turn in him as he turned, and pace in him as he paced; so completely possessing him, indeed, that it all but seemed the inward mold of every outer movement.

"D'ye mark him, Flask?" whispered Stubb; "the chick that's in him pecks the shell. 'Twill soon be out."

The hours wore on—Ahab now shut up within his cabin; anon, pacing the deck, with the same intense bigotry of purpose[2] in his aspect.

It drew near the close of day. Suddenly he came to a halt by the bulwarks, and inserting his bone leg into the auger hole there, and with one hand grasping a shroud, he ordered Starbuck to send everybody aft.

"Sir!" said the mate, astonished at an order seldom or never given on shipboard except in some extraordinary case.

"Send everybody aft," repeated Ahab. "Mastheads, there! come down!"

When the entire ship's company were assembled, and with curious and not wholly unapprehensive faces, were eyeing him, for he looked not unlike the weather horizon when a storm is coming up, Ahab, after rapidly glancing over the bulwarks, and then darting his eyes among the crew, started from his standpoint; and as though not a soul were nigh him resumed his heavy turns upon the deck. With bent head and half-slouched hat he continued to pace, unmindful of the wondering whispering among the men; till Stubb cautiously whispered to Flask, that Ahab must have summoned them there for the purpose of witnessing a pedestrian feat. But this did not last long. Vehemently pausing, he cried:

"What do ye do when ye see a whale, men?"

"Sing out for him!" was the impulsive rejoinder from a score of clubbed voices.

"Good!" cried Ahab, with a wild approval in his tones; observing the hearty animation into which his unexpected question had so magnetically thrown them.

"And what do ye next, men?"

"Lower away, and after him!"

"And what tune is it ye pull to, men?"

"A dead whale or a stove[3] boat!"

More and more strangely and fiercely glad and approving, grew the countenance of the old man at every shout; while the mariners began to gaze curiously at each other, as if marveling how it was that they themselves became so excited at such seemingly purposeless questions.

❼

---

1. **binnacle** (bin′ ə kəl) *n.* case enclosing a ship's compass.
2. **bigotry of purpose** complete single-mindedness.
3. **stove** *v.* broken; smashed.

Enrichment: Investigating Geography

From Nantucket to the South Pacific

The *Pequod* sails from the island of Nantucket off the southern coast of Massachusetts. In the late 1700s and early 1800s, Nantucket was one of the world's major whaling centers. At one point more than a hundred whaling ships used Nantucket as their main port. Whalers were faced with long journeys that kept them at sea for months and years at a time

Activity: Map a Journey Invite students to research whaling in books or on the Internet.

Encyclopedias and museums, such as the New Bedford Whaling Museum, are helpful resources. Suggest that they map a typical whaling journey from Nantucket to the South Pacific, where the *Pequod* encountered Moby-Dick. They can record information in the **Enrichment: Investigating Geography** worksheet, in *Professional Development Guidebook,* page 228. Students can then present their maps to the class.

But, they were all eagerness again, as Ahab, now half-revolving in his pivot hole, with one hand reaching high up a shroud,[4] and tightly, almost convulsively grasping it, addressed them thus:

"All ye mastheaders have before now heard me give orders about a white whale. Look ye! d'ye see this Spanish ounce of gold?"—holding up a broad bright coin to the sun—"it is a sixteen-dollar piece, men. D'ye see it? Mr. Starbuck, hand me yon topmaul."

While the mate was getting the hammer, Ahab, without speaking, was slowly rubbing the gold piece against the skirts of his jacket, as if to heighten its luster, and without using any words was meanwhile lowly humming to himself, producing a sound so strangely muffled and inarticulate that it seemed the mechanical humming of the wheels of his vitality in him.

Receiving the topmaul from Starbuck, he advanced towards the mainmast with the hammer uplifted in one hand, exhibiting the gold with the other, and with a high raised voice exclaiming: "Whosoever of ye raises me a white-headed whale with a wrinkled brow and a crooked jaw; whosoever of ye raises me that white-headed whale, with three holes punctured in his starboard fluke[5]—look ye, whosoever of ye raises me that same white whale, he shall have this gold ounce, my boys!"

"Huzza! huzza!" cried the seamen, as with swinging tarpaulins they hailed the act of nailing the gold to the mast.

"It's a white whale, I say," resumed Ahab, as he threw down the topmaul: "a white whale. Skin your eyes for him, men; look sharp for white water; if ye see but a bubble, sing out."

All this while Tashtego, Daggoo, and Queequeg had looked on with even more intense interest and surprise than the rest, and at the mention of the wrinkled brow and crooked jaw they had started as if each was separately touched by some specific recollection.

"Captain Ahab," said Tashtego, "that white whale must be the same that some call Moby-Dick."

"Moby-Dick?" shouted Ahab. "Do ye know the white whale then, Tash?"

"Does he fantail[6] a little curious, sir, before he goes down?" said the Gay-Header deliberately.

"And has he a curious spout, too," said Daggoo, "very bushy, even for a parmacetty,[7] and mighty quick, Captain Ahab?"

"And he have one, two, tree—oh! good many iron in him hide, too, Captain," cried Queequeg disjointedly, "all twiske-tee betwisk, like him—him—" faltering hard for a word, and screwing his hand round and round as though uncorking a bottle—"like him—him—"

"Corkscrew!" cried Ahab, "aye, Queequeg, the harpoons lie all twisted and wrenched in him; aye, Daggoo, his spout is a big one, like

---

4. **shroud** *n.* set of ropes from a ship's side to the masthead.
5. **starboard fluke** (flōōk) *n.* right half of a whale's tail.
6. **fantail** *v.* to spread the tail like a fan.
7. **parmacetty** (pär′ mə set′ ē) *n.* dialect for sperm whale, from which spermaceti was derived. Spermaceti is a high quality oil that was once used to make candles and other products.

⑪ Reading Check

What reward does Ahab offer to the man who spots the white whale?

from Moby-Dick **339**

---

❾ Literary Analysis

Symbol

1. Point out that the narrator mentions several times a gold coin brandished by Ahab.

2. **Ask** students the following question: What does Ahab's treatment of the gold coin suggest about its presence as a symbol?
   Answer: Ahab's nailing of the coin to the mast of the *Pequod* ensures its central and continual presence throughout the voyage. The gold, worth a fortune to the sailors, thus symbolizes the value that the quest has for Ahab and the extreme nature of his desire for vengeance.

❿ Reading Strategy

Identifying Essential Details to Determine Message

1. Ask a volunteer to read the bracketed passage aloud. Invite listeners to focus on the details about Moby-Dick that are offered by each speaker.

2. **Ask** students the following question: What image of Moby-Dick is created in this discussion?
   Possible answer: The image of Moby-Dick as an almost supernatural being is created.

⑪ Reading Check

Answer: He offers a gold coin worth sixteen dollars.

Differentiated Instruction for Universal Access

Strategy for Less Proficient Readers

To help students comprehend the text, have them list and discuss the physical traits that Ahab and the crew members say distinguish Moby-Dick from other whales. These include his white color; his unique way of fanning his tail before submerging; his unusual, large, and "bushy" spout; his quickness; and his hide, which contains several iron harpoons.

EL Strategy for English Learners

Help improve students' comprehension by working with them to create a chart of the chain of events in the story. Each entry on the chart should name a character and briefly describe his action, as in the following example:

Ahab: Orders Starbuck to get the hammer.
Starbuck: Gives the hammer to Ahab.
Ahab: Nails the coin into the mast.

Use this technique to help students track and connect the events in the story.

⑫ ▲ **Critical Viewing**
What does this image suggest about the perils involved in whaling?
[Interpret]

a whole shock of wheat, and white as a pile of our Nantucket wool after the great annual sheepshearing; aye, Tashtego, and he fantails like a split jib in a squall. Death and devils! men, it is Moby-Dick ye have seen—Moby-Dick—Moby-Dick!"

"Captain Ahab," said Starbuck, who, with Stubb and Flask, had thus far been eyeing his superior with increasing surprise, but at last seemed struck with a thought which somewhat explained all the wonder. "Captain Ahab, I have heard of Moby-Dick—but it was not Moby-Dick that took off thy leg?"

"Who told thee that?" cried Ahab; then pausing, "Aye, Starbuck; aye, my hearties all round; it was Moby-Dick that dismasted me; Moby-Dick that brought me to this dead stump I stand on now. Aye, aye," he shouted with a terrific, loud, animal sob, like that of a heartstricken moose; "Aye, aye! it was that accursed white whale that razeed me; made a poor pegging lubber[8] for me forever and a day!" Then tossing both arms, with measureless imprecations he shouted out: "Aye, aye! and I'll chase him round Good Hope, and round the Horn, and round the Norway Maelstrom, and round perdition's flames before I give him up. And this is what ye have shipped for, men! to chase that white whale on both sides of land, and over all sides of earth, till he spouts black blood and rolls fin out. What say ye, men, will ye splice hands on it, now? I think ye do look brave."

"Aye, aye!" shouted the harpooneers and seamen, running closer to the excited old man: "A sharp eye for the white whale; a sharp lance for Moby-Dick!"

"God bless ye," he seemed to half sob and half shout. "God bless

---

8. **lubber** (lub´ ər) *n.* slow, clumsy person.

340 A Growing Nation (1800–1870)

Enrichment: Analyzing Themes and Symbols

Hunting Rituals

Ahab gathers his crew on the quarterdeck to begin the hunt for Moby-Dick. The gathering echoes the tradition of hunting rituals. Ever since the earliest humans drummed and sang to address the animal spirits before a hunt, many peoples have believed that a ritual will aid their success. For example, the Blackfeet and other Plains Indians prayed, danced, sang, smoked, and made offerings to ensure that their buffalo hunts would be successful.

Activity: Presentation Have students find out more about hunting rituals performed by two different peoples in North America or elsewhere. Focus on the similarities and differences between the use of symbolic objects and actions. Suggest that they record information in the **Enrichment: Analyzing Themes and Symbols** work sheet, in *Professional Development Guidebook,* page 243. Invite students to present their findings in class.

ye, men. Steward! go draw the great measure of grog. But what's this long face about, Mr. Starbuck; wilt thou not chase the white whale? art not game for Moby-Dick?"

"I am game for his crooked jaw, and for the jaws of Death too, Captain Ahab, if it fairly comes in the way of the business we follow; but I came here to hunt whales, not my commander's vengeance. How many barrels will thy vengeance yield thee even if thou gettest it, Captain Ahab? it will not fetch thee much in our Nantucket market."

"Nantucket market! Hoot! But come closer, Starbuck; thou requirest a little lower layer. If money's to be the measurer, man, and the accountants have computed their great countinghouse the globe, by girdling it with guineas, one to every three parts of an inch; then, let me tell thee, that my vengeance will fetch a great premium *here!*"

"He smites his chest," whispered Stubb, "what's that for? methinks it rings most vast, but hollow."

"Vengeance on a dumb brute!" cried Starbuck, "that simply smote thee from blindest instinct! Madness! To be enraged with a dumb thing, Captain Ahab, seems blasphemous."

"Hark ye yet again—the little lower layer. All visible objects, man, are but as pasteboard masks. But in each event—in the living act, the undoubted deed—there, some unknown but still reasoning thing puts forth the moldings of its features from behind the unreasoning mask. If man will strike, strike through the mask! How can the prisoner reach outside except by thrusting through the wall? To me, the white whale is that wall, shoved near to me. Sometimes I think there's naught beyond. But 'tis enough. He tasks me; he heaps me; I see in him outrageous strength, with an inscrutable malice sinewing it. That inscrutable thing is chiefly what I hate; and be the white whale agent, or be the white whale principal, I will wreak that hate upon him. Talk not to me of blasphemy, man; I'd strike the sun if it insulted me. For could the sun do that, then could I do the other; since there is ever a sort of fair play herein, jealousy presiding over all creations. But not my master, man, is even that fair play. Who's over me? Truth hath no confines. Take off thine eye! more intolerable than fiends' glarings is a doltish stare! So, so; thou reddenest and palest; my heat has melted thee to anger-glow. But look ye, Starbuck, what is said in heat, that thing unsays itself. There are men from whom warm words are small indignity. I meant not to incense thee. Let it go. Look! see yonder Turkish cheeks of spotted tawn—living, breathing pictures painted by the sun. The pagan leopards—the unrecking and unworshiping things, that live, and seek, and give no reasons for the torrid life they feel! The crew, man, the crew! Are they not one and all with Ahab, in this matter of the whale? See Stubb! he laughs! See yonder Chilean! he snorts to think of it. Stand up amid the general hurricane, thy one tossed sapling cannot, Starbuck! And what is it? Reckon it. 'Tis but to help strike a fin; no wondrous feat for Starbuck. What is it more? From this one poor hunt, then, the

from Moby-Dick **341**

Literary Analysis

Theme What do Ahab's comments suggest about the value of money compared with great desire?

Vocabulary

inscrutable (in skrōōt′ ə bəl) *adj.* difficult to know or understand

⑯ Reading Check

What is Starbuck's objection to Ahab's desire for vengeance on a "dumb brute"?

---

⑭ Literary Analysis

Theme

1. Have students read this passage and identify references to money and commerce ("Nantucket market," "money's," "accountants," "computed," "countinghouse," "guineas," "premium").

2. Then **ask** students how they know Ahab is using business metaphors to emphasize the strength of his desire to catch and kill Moby-Dick. If necessary, point out his explicit reference to "my vengeance" and his physical indication of his heart.

3. **Ask** students the Literary Analysis question: What do Ahab's comments say about the value of money compared with great desire?
   Answer: Ahab views desire—even if it is considered "vengeance"—as far more valuable than money.

⑮ Reading Strategy

Identifying Details to Determine Essential Message

1. Read aloud the bracketed passage more than once so that students can focus on Ahab's key ideas.

2. **Ask** students the following question: What insights into the whale's symbolic meaning can you gain from details in this passage?
   Answer: Ahab (and the reader) must view the whale on both real and symbolic levels. Ahab declares that he does not care whether the whale acts on its own out of malice or at the direction of another greater will ("Talk not to me of blasphemy, man; I'd strike the sun if it insulted me"). Indeed, the unknowability of the whale's—and by implication God's—motives are the very thing Ahab hates. Because it is hate that drives Ahab, his quest is cast symbolically in this passage as hubris, the placing of the self above the will of God as revealed in nature, which includes the white whale.

⑯ Reading Check

Answer: He objects that Ahab's desire for vengeance will not yield profits at market.

---

best lance out of all Nantucket, surely he will not hang back, when every foremasthand has clutched a whetstone. Ah! constrainings seize thee; I see! the billow lifts thee! Speak, but speak!—Aye, aye! thy silence, then, *that* voices thee. (*Aside*) Something shot from my dilated nostrils, he has inhaled it in his lungs. Starbuck now is mine; cannot oppose me now, without rebellion."

"God keep me!—keep us all!" murmured Starbuck, lowly.

But in his joy at the enchanted, tacit acquiescence of the mate, Ahab did not hear his foreboding invocation; nor yet the low laugh from the hold; nor yet the presaging vibrations of the winds in the cordage; nor yet the hollow flap of the sails against the masts, as for a moment their hearts sank in. For again Starbuck's downcast eyes lighted up with the stubbornness of life; the subterranean laugh died away; the winds blew on; the sails filled out; the ship heaved and rolled as before. Ah, ye admonitions and warnings! why stay ye not when ye come? But rather are ye predictions than warnings, ye shadows! Yet not so much predictions from without, as verifications of the fore-going things within. For with little external to constrain us, the innermost necessities in our being, these still drive us on.

"The measure! the measure!" cried Ahab.

Receiving the brimming pewter, and turning to the harpooneers, he ordered them to produce their weapons. Then ranging them before him near the capstan,[9] with their harpoons in their hands, while his three mates stood at his side with their lances, and the rest of the ship's company formed a circle round the group; he stood for an instant searchingly eyeing every man of his crew. But those wild eyes met his, as the bloodshot eyes of the prairie wolves meet the eye of their leader, ere he rushes on at their head in the trail of the bison; but, alas! only to fall into the hidden snare of the Indian.

"Drink and pass!" he cried, handing the heavy charged flagon to the nearest seamen. "The crew alone now drink. Round with it, round! Short drafts—long swallows, men; 'tis hot as Satan's hoof. So, so; it goes round excellently. It spiralizes in ye; forks out at the serpent-snapping eye. Well done; almost drained. That way it went, this way it comes. Hand it me—here's a hollow! Men, ye seem the years; so brimming life is gulped and gone. Steward, refill!

"Attend now, my braves. I have mustered ye all round this capstan; and ye mates, flank me with your lances; and ye harpooneers, stand there with your irons; and ye, stout mariners, ring me in, that I may in some sort revive a noble custom of my fishermen fathers before me. O men, you will yet see that—Ha! boy, come back? bad pennies come not sooner. Hand it me. Why, now, this pewter had run brimming again, wer't not thou St. Vitus' imp[10]—away, thou ague![11]

"Advance, ye mates! cross your lances full before me. Well done!

---

9. **capstan** (kap´ sten) *n.* large cylinder, turned by hand, around which cables are wound.
10. **St. Vitus' imp** offspring of St. Vitus, the patron saint of people stricken with the nervous disorder *chorea* which is characterized by irregular, jerking movements.
11. **ague** (ā´ gyo͞o) *n.* a chill or fit of shivering.

Let me touch the axis." So saying, with extended arm, he grasped the three level, radiating lances at their crossed center; while so doing, suddenly and nervously twitched them; meanwhile glancing intently from Starbuck to Stubb; from Stubb to Flask. It seemed as though, by some nameless, interior volition, he would fain have shocked into them the same fiery emotion accumulated within the Leyden jar[12] of his own magnetic life. The three mates quailed before his strong, sustained, and mystic aspect. Stubb and Flask looked sideways from him; the honest eye of Starbuck fell downright.

"In vain!" cried Ahab; "but, maybe, 'tis well. For did ye three but once take the full-forced shock, then mine own electric thing, *that* had perhaps expired from out me. Perchance, too, it would have dropped ye dead. Perchance ye need it not. Down lances! And now, ye mates, I do appoint ye three cupbearers to my three pagan kinsmen there—yon three most honorable gentlemen and noblemen, my valiant harpooneers. Disdain the task? What, when the great Pope washes the feet of beggars, using his tiara for ewer? Oh, my sweet cardinals! your own condescension, that shall bend ye to it. I do not order ye; ye will it. Cut your seizings and draw the poles, ye harpooneers!"

Silently obeying the order, the three harpooneers now stood with the detached iron part of their harpoons, some three feet long, held, barbs up, before him.

"Stab me not with that keen steel! Cant them; cant them over! know ye not the goblet end? Turn up the socket! So, so; now, ye cupbearers, advance. The irons! take them; hold them while I fill!" Forthwith, slowly going from one officer to the other, he brimmed the harpoon sockets with the fiery waters from the pewter.

"Now, three to three, ye stand. Commend the murderous chalices! Bestow them, ye who are now made parties to this indissoluble league. Ha! Starbuck! but the deed is done! Yon ratifying sun now waits to sit upon it. Drink, ye harpooneers! drink and swear, ye men that man the deathful whaleboat's bow—Death to Moby-Dick! God hunt us all, if we do not hunt Moby-Dick to his death!" The long, barbed steel goblets were lifted; and to cries and maledictions against the white whale, the spirits were simultaneously quaffed down with a hiss. Starbuck paled, and turned, and shivered. Once more, and finally, the replenished pewter went the rounds among the frantic crew; when, waving his free hand to them, they all dispersed; and Ahab retired within his cabin.

After Moby-Dick has been sighted in the Pacific Ocean, the Pequod's *boats pursue the whale for two days. One of the boats has been sunk, and Ahab's ivory leg has been broken off. However, as the next day dawns, the chase continues.*

---

12. **Leyden** (līd´ ən) **jar** *n.* glass jar coated inside and out with tinfoil and having a metal rod connected to the inner lining; used to condense static electricity.

Literary Analysis

Symbol What is Ahab's symbolic purpose in having his harpooners drink from their weapons?

Vocabulary

maledictions (mal´ ə dik´ shənz) *n.* curses

Reading Check

How do the three mates react to Ahab's gaze?

from Moby-Dick **343**

⑧

⑱ Literary Analysis

Symbol

1. Encourage students to visualize or model what the harpooners are doing, as well as what Ahab has in mind.

2. If necessary, help students understand that the harpooners are removing the iron part of their harpoons and upending the sockets to use as cups, which Ahab will fill with drink.

3. **Ask** students the Literary Analysis question: What is Ahab's symbolic purpose in having his harpooners drink from their weapons? **Answer:** Ahab may wish them to participate in a prehunt ritual that symbolizes a common mission and allegiance. The act of drinking from their weapons symbolically binds them together as extensions of Ahab's vision and vengeance. Students may mention that the drinking from the "chalices" is reminiscent of religious rituals.

⑲ Reading Check

Answer: The three mates look away from Ahab's gaze.

Differentiated Instruction for Universal Access

Support for Special-Needs Students
These students—and others—may benefit from seeing some or all of a dramatized version of Melville's sprawling story. *Moby-Dick* has all the elements of a blockbuster movie—compelling characters, exotic locations, and one of the largest movie "villains" imaginable—and filmmakers have tried a number of times to bring to the screen Melville's tale of the great white whale.

One of the best attempts was made by director John Huston, who cast Gregory Peck as Ahab in the 1956 film *Moby Dick.* Screen a DVD or video of this production for students. Have students view one or more scenes in order to help them appreciate the characterizations of Ahab, Starbuck, and Ishmael; the evocations of the whale as a symbol of nature's power and of the untamable; and the various conflicts that drive the story forward.

㉒ The American Experience

The Golden Age of Yankee Whaling

1. Have students review this page as homework. Have them imagine that they are about to embark on a voyage as a crew member of a whaling ship like the *Pequod*. **Ask** them to think about this question: Based on this information, what aspect of the experience ahead of you concerns or excites you the most?
Possible responses: Students may express fear about the possibility of dying at sea. Others may express excitement about traveling the world.

2. **Ask:** What occupations today might compare to whaling in terms of danger?
Answer: Students may suggest mining, construction, oil drilling, commercial fishing, and similar occupations.

3. Point out that the development of petroleum products such as kerosene was also a factor that, like electricity and spring steel, led to the decline in the need for whale products. **Ask:** What are examples of products that have become obsolete because of the development of new technologies in the past twenty-five years?
Possible responses: Students may mention vinyl recordings, rotary telephones, typewriters, and other examples.

㉑ Connect to the Literature

Ask the Connect to the Literature question: How do these facts about the business of whaling enhance your understanding of *Moby-Dick*?

Possible responses: Students may reply that they understand better why men would have been attracted to whaling as a job because it seems to have promised a good income despite the risks.

The Golden Age of ㉒ Yankee Whaling

During the nineteenth century, New England grew prosperous from whaling. Hundreds of ships set out from the ports of Nantucket, New Bedford, Boston, Sag Harbor, and New London and spread out across the world's seas in pursuit of whales. Whale oil and other by-products could make captains and ship owners rich, but whaling was a hard business. Voyages lasted as long as three years and many sailors died at sea. With the invention of the electric lamp (1879) and the development of spring steel (1906), whaling declined. However, during its heyday, whaling created fortunes.

CONNECT TO THE LITERATURE

㉑ How do these facts about the business of whaling enhance your understanding of *Moby-Dick*?

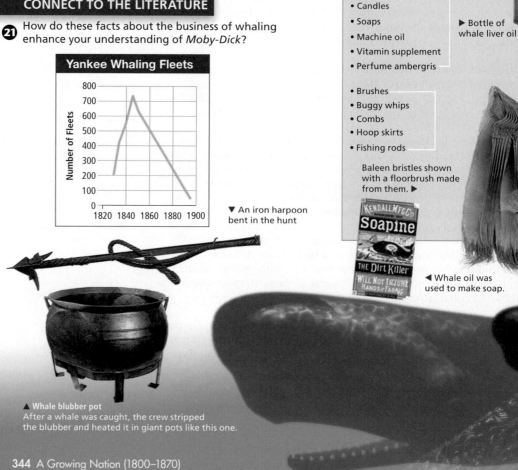

▲ Model of a British whaling s

WHALE PRODUCTS

- Corsets (from whale bone)
- Lamp oil
- Candles
- Soaps
- Machine oil
- Vitamin supplement
- Perfume ambergris

- Brushes
- Buggy whips
- Combs
- Hoop skirts
- Fishing rods

▶ Bottle of whale liver oil

Baleen bristles shown with a floorbrush made from them. ▶

Yankee Whaling Fleets

Number of Fleets (vertical axis): 0, 100, 200, 300, 400, 500, 600, 700, 800
Years (horizontal axis): 1820, 1840, 1860, 1880, 1900

▼ An iron harpoon bent in the hunt

KENDALL MFG CO

Soapine

THE DIRT KILLER
WILL NOT INJURE HANDS or FABRIC

◀ Whale oil was used to make soap.

▲ Whale blubber pot
After a whale was caught, the crew stripped the blubber and heated it in giant pots like this one.

344 A Growing Nation (1800–1870)

Enrichment: Investigating Science

Whales

In existence for over 10 million years, whales are among the world's most ancient and intelligent animals. They also are the largest: The blue whale is heavier and longer than any known dinosaur.

Activity: Presentation Invite students to find out more about these amazing mammals, using questions like these as starting points:

1. How do whales keep warm? How deep do they dive?
2. How do the swimming methods of whales

differ from those of fish? How far can whales swim?

3. What is the world's whale population today? Are whales in danger of extinction?
4. How do whales communicate with one another?

Suggest that they record information in the **Enrichment: Investigating Science** work sheet, in *Professional Development Guidebook*, page 241. Students can then present their findings to the class.

THE CHASE—THIRD DAY

The morning of the third day dawned fair and fresh, and once more the solitary night man at the foremasthead was relieved by crowds of the daylight lookouts, who dotted every mast and almost every spar.

"D'ye see him?" cried Ahab; but the whale was not yet in sight.

"In his infallible wake, though; but follow that wake, that's all. Helm there; steady, as thou goest, and hast been going. What a lovely day again! were it a new-made world, and made for a summerhouse to the angels, and this morning the first of its throwing open to them, a fairer day could not dawn upon that world. Here's food for thought, had Ahab time to think; but Ahab never thinks; he only feels, feels, feels; that's tingling enough for mortal man! to think's audacity. God only has that right and privilege. Thinking is, or ought to be, a coolness and a calmness; and our poor hearts throb, and our poor brains beat too much for that. And yet, I've sometimes thought my brain was very calm—frozen calm, this old skull cracks so, like a glass in which the contents turned to ice, and shiver it. And still this hair is growing now; this moment growing, and heat must breed it; but no, it's like that sort of common grass that will grow anywhere, between the earthy clefts of Greenland ice or in Vesuvius lava. How the wild winds blow it; they whip it about me as the torn shreds of split sails lash the tossed ship they cling to. A vile wind that has no doubt blown ere this through prison corridors and cells, and wards of hospitals, and ventilated them, and now comes blowing hither as innocent as fleeces.[13] Out upon it!—it's tainted. Were I the wind, I'd blow no more on such a wicked, miserable world. I'd crawl somewhere to a cave, and slink there. And yet, 'tis a noble and heroic thing, the wind! who ever conquered it? In every fight it has the last and bitterest blow. Run tilting at it, and you but run through it. Ha! a coward wind that strikes stark-naked men, but will not stand to receive a single blow. Even Ahab is a braver thing—a nobler thing than *that*. Would now the wind but had a body but all the things that most exasperate and outrage mortal man, all these things are bodiless, but only bodiless as objects, not as agents. There's a most special, a most cunning, oh, a most malicious difference! And yet, I say again, and swear it now, that there's something all glorious and gracious in the wind. These warm trade winds, at least, that in the clear heavens blow straight on, in strong and steadfast, vigorous mildness; and veer not from their mark, however the baser currents of the sea may turn and tack, and mightiest Mississippis of the land swift and swerve about, uncertain where to go at last. And by the eternal poles! these same trades that so directly blow my good ship on; these trades, or something like them—something so unchangeable, and

---

13. fleeces (flēs´ əz) *n.* sheep.

Literary Analysis
Symbol What does the wind symbolize to Ahab?

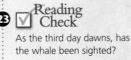
Reading Check
As the third day dawns, has the whale been sighted?

from Moby-Dick **345**

345

24 Literature in Context

Humanities Connection

The whale as archetype is not limited to the adversarial relationship seen in Melville's white whale and Ahab. In the biblical tale of Jonah, Jonah disobeys God's order to go to the city of Nineveh to prophesy against its wickedness. Jonah sails in the opposite direction, but when his ship is engulfed by a huge storm he admits his disobedience and asks the crew to throw him overboard. He is swallowed by a "great fish," stays inside it for three days and nights, prays for forgiveness, and is finally vomited onto dry land. When God again commands Jonah to go to Nineveh, Jonah obeys. The whale in this story is a vehicle of God's will. The ninth chapter of Melville's *Moby-Dick* addresses the story of Jonah directly.

The whale is not the only archetype in the pages of *Moby-Dick*. The journey, or quest, is itself an archetype that appears in works as old as Homer's *Odyssey* and as recent as *Cold Mountain*.

Students may benefit from being aware of other common archetypes that they might look for in their reading and movie- and television-watching. The trickster, the wise man or wise woman, and the healer are just three archetypes that occur not only in literature but also in comedy and drama seen on the stage, on television and at the movies.

Connect to the Literature Suggest that students compare images and impressions of Moby-Dick with recent news stories about whales.

Ask the Connect to the Literature question: Do you think modern readers react with fear and awe to the image of a whale? Explain.

Possible response: Today, some species of whales are threatened with extinction. While they still provoke awe, modern readers are less likely to fear them than they are to sympathize with them.

LITERATURE IN CONTEXT

24 Humanities Connection

The Whale as Archetype

An archetype is an image, a symbol, a character, or a plot that recurs so consistently across cultures and time that it is considered universal. The term comes from Swiss psychologist Carl Jung (1875–1961), who believed that certain human experiences have become a shared genetic memory. According to Jung, this "collective unconscious" explains why archetypes evoke strong feelings in people of all cultures.

The whale had made many appearances in myth, folklore, literature, and art well before Melville used it as a central symbol in *Moby-Dick*. Perhaps the most famous is the biblical tale in which Jonah is swallowed by a whale and then cast ashore. Because the whale is the largest of all animals, its image evokes fear and awe, as well as a sense of the power of nature. In *Moby-Dick*, Melville used these archetypal associations to create fiction of enduring power.

Connect to the Literature

Do you think modern readers react with fear and awe to the image of a whale? Explain.

---

full as strong, blow my keeled soul along! To it! Aloft there! What d'ye see?"

"Nothing, sir."

"Nothing! and noon at hand! The doubloon[14] goes a-begging! See the sun! Aye, aye, it must be so. I've over-sailed him. How, got the start? Aye, he's chasing me now; not I, him—that's bad; I might have known it, too. Fool! the lines—the harpoons he's towing.

Aye, aye, I have run him by last night. About! about! Come down, all of ye, but the regular lookouts! Man the braces!"

Steering as she had done, the wind had been somewhat on the Pequod's quarter, so that now being pointed in the reverse direction, the braced ship sailed hard upon the breeze as she rechurned the cream in her own white wake.

"Against the wind he now steers for the open jaw," murmured Starbuck to himself, as he coiled the new-hauled main brace upon the rail. "God keep us, but already my bones feel damp within me, and from the inside wet my flesh. I misdoubt me that I disobey my God in obeying him!"

"Stand by to sway me up!" cried Ahab, advancing to the hempen basket.[15] "We should meet him soon."

"Aye, aye, sir," and straightway Starbuck did Ahab's bidding, and once more Ahab swung on high.

A whole hour now passed; gold-beaten out to ages. Time itself now held long breaths with keen suspense. But at last, some three points off the weather bow, Ahab descried the spout again, and instantly from the three mastheads three shrieks went up as if the tongues of fire had voiced it.

"Forehead to forehead I meet thee, this third time, Moby-Dick! On deck there!—brace sharper up; crowd her into the wind's eye. He's too far off to lower yet, Mr. Starbuck. The sails shake! Stand over that helmsman with a top-maul! So, so; he travels fast, and I must down. But let me have one more good round look aloft here at the sea; there's time for that. An old, old sight, and yet somehow so young; aye, and not changed a wink since I first saw it, a boy, from the sand hills of Nantucket! The same!—the same!—the same to Noah as to me. There's a soft shower to leeward. Such lovely leewardings! They must lead somewhere—to something else than common land, more palmy than the palms. Leeward! the white whale goes that way; look to windward, then; the better if the bitterer quarter. But good-bye, good-bye, old masthead! What's this?—green? aye, tiny mosses in these warped cracks. No such green weather stains on Ahab's head! There's

25

---

14. **doubloon** (du blŌŌn´) *n.* old Spanish gold coin. (Ahab offered it as a reward to the first man to spot the whale.)

15. **hempen basket** rope basket. (The basket was constructed earlier by Ahab, so that he could be raised, by means of a pulley device, to the top of the mainmast.)

346 A Growing Nation (1800–1870)

Enrichment: Analyzing Music

Whale Songs

Scientists and musicians alike are fascinated by the mysterious, mournful, musical sounds whales make as they communicate with one another. Their groans, yips, and wails can carry many miles through and across the water. Humpback whales, in particular, are skillful performers: Each male sings its own unique song (lasting up to thirty-five minutes) over and over again.

Obtain recordings of whale songs to play for students. For example, on the Judy Collins album *The Very Best of Judy Collins*, the traditional sea song "Farewell to Tarwathie" incorporates recorded sounds of the humpback whale.

Activity: Discussion Encourage students to listen closely to a recording that incorporates whale songs and to analyze them, using as a guide the **Enrichment: Analyzing Music** worksheet, in *Professional Development Guidebook*, page 236. Students can then have a discussion about their responses to the music.

the difference now between man's old age and matter's. But aye, old mast, we both grow old together; sound in our hulls, though, are we not, my ship? Aye, minus a leg, that's all. By heaven this dead wood has the better of my live flesh every way. I can't compare with it; and I've known some ships made of dead trees outlast the lives of men made of the most vital stuff of vital fathers. What's that he said? he should still go before me, my pilot; and yet to be seen again? But where? Will I have eyes at the bottom of the sea, supposing I descend those endless stairs? and all night I've been sailing from him, wherever he did sink to. Aye, aye, like many more thou told'st direful truth as touching thyself, O Parsee; but, Ahab, there thy shot fell short. Good-bye, masthead—keep a good eye upon the whale, the while I'm gone. We'll talk tomorrow, nay, tonight, when the white whale lies down there, tied by head and tail."

He gave the word; and still gazing round him, was steadily lowered through the cloven blue air to the deck.

In due time the boats were lowered; but as standing in his shallop's stern, Ahab just hovered upon the point of the descent, he waved to the mate—who held one of the tackle ropes on deck—and bade him pause.

"Starbuck!"

"Sir?"

"For the third time my soul's ship starts upon this voyage, Starbuck."

"Aye, sir, thou wilt have it so."

"Some ships sail from their ports, and ever afterwards are missing, Starbuck!"

"Truth, sir: saddest truth."

"Some men die at ebb tide; some at low water; some at the full of the flood—and I feel now like a billow that's all one crested comb, Starbuck. I am old—shake hands with me, man."

Their hands met; their eyes fastened; Starbuck's tears the glue.

"Oh, my captain, my captain!—noble heart—go not—go not!—see, it's a brave man that weeps; how great the agony of the persuasion then!"

"Lower away!"—cried Ahab, tossing the mate's arm from him. "Stand by the crew!"

In an instant the boat was pulling round close under the stern.

"The sharks! the sharks!" cried a voice from the low cabin window there; "O master, my master, come back!"

But Ahab heard nothing; for his own voice was high-lifted then; and the boat leaped on.

Yet the voice spake true; for scarce had he pushed from the ship, when numbers of sharks, seemingly rising from out the dark waters beneath the hull, maliciously snapped at the blades of the oars, every time they dipped in the water; and in this way accompanied the boat with their bites. It is a thing not uncommonly happen-

Literary Analysis
Symbol What symbolic meaning do you find in the comparison between Ahab and the mast?

Reading Check ②⑧

What does Starbuck beg Ahab to do?

from Moby-Dick **347**

---

② **Literary Analysis**

Symbol

1. Have a student volunteer read the bracketed passage in which Ahab addresses the masthead and then begins to compare himself to it.

2. **Ask** students the Literary Analysis question: What symbolic meaning do you find in the comparison between Ahab and the mast? **Answer:** Students may say that to Ahab the mast represents his resolve in his quest for Moby-Dick. The mast stands alone, tall, strong, and long lasting, as Ahab does in his single-mindedness.

② **Background**

Literature

Parsee is a Persian sailor who disappeared in the previous chapter of the novel. Earlier in the book, a prediction was made that he would die before Ahab but that Ahab would see him once more before his own death.

② **Critical Thinking**

Analyze

1. Have three students—playing Ahab, Starbuck, and the narrator—read aloud the bracketed passage.

2. **Ask** students to explain what is happening in this exchange between Ahab and Starbuck. **Answer:** Students may respond that Ahab is expressing fear and apprehension prior to this (his next attempt to kill Moby-Dick) and that Starbuck is making one last futile effort to persuade Ahab to forgo the quest.

② **Reading Check**

Answer: Starbuck begs Ahab not to pursue Moby-Dick in a small harpooning boat.

Differentiated
Instruction   for Universal Access

Enrichment for Gifted/Talented Students
Students might enjoy acting out part of the exciting action of this chapter. Have students prepare a script, using correct conventions and style to indicate dialogue and stage directions. Guide students to rehearse lines and actions before performing their scenes for the class. If possible, have students include props to make their performances more realistic.

Support for Advanced Readers
Guide students to appreciate that the action is becoming increasingly kaleidoscopic. Have them notice that readers now catch only brief bits of the action, much as a sailor at the scene would do in the midst of the chaos of battle. Also help students note that Ahab's statements become increasingly disjointed. Aside from the frantic chase of the white whale, what do students think is causing Ahab's strange, sometimes incomprehensible statements?

Identifying Details to Determine Essential Message

1. As you read aloud this passage, **ask** students to think about the possible symbolic meaning of the sharks that surround Ahab and follow him in his small boat.

2. Help students understand that the sharks separate Ahab further from his crew. Moreover, they suggest in a symbolic way that Ahab's pursuit of the white whale is foolish and doomed. The sharks add an extra element of danger; they are harbingers of death.

30 **Reading Strategy**

Identifying Details to Determine Essential Message

1. Tell students that three is a traditional symbol echoing the trinity in Christian belief. The third number often represents finality.

2. **Ask** students to explain the significance of Starbuck's reference to the number three here.
Answer: Usually the voice of practicality, Starbuck now recognizes the grim meaning of the three-day chase. Ahab and the crew are now in the third day, and Starbuck seems to sense a mystical significance in the length of time the chase has taken.

31 **Critical Viewing**

Possible answer: Some students may find the illustration realistic. Others may suggest that it lacks the violent chaos that would have marked the actual situation.

Vocabulary
prescient (presh´ ənt) *adj.* having foreknowledge

31 ▼ **Critical Viewing**
Does this illustration seem like a realistic rendering of an actual situation? Explain. **[Evaluate]**

348 A Growing Nation (1800–1870)

ing to the whaleboats in those swarming seas; the sharks at times apparently following them in the same prescient way that vultures hover over the banners of marching regiments in the east. But these were the first sharks that had been observed by the *Pequod* since the White Whale had been first descried; and whether it was that Ahab's crew were all such tiger-yellow barbarians, and therefore their flesh more musky to the senses of the sharks—a matter sometimes well known to affect them—however it was, they seemed to follow that one boat without molesting the others.

"Heart of wrought steel!" murmured Starbuck gazing over the side, and following with his eyes the receding boat—"canst thou yet ring boldly to that sight?—lowering thy keel among ravening sharks, and followed by them, open-mouthed to the chase; and this the critical third day?—For when three days flow together in one continuous intense pursuit; be sure the first is the morning, the second the noon, and the third the evening and the end of that thing—be that end what it may. Oh! my God! what is this that shoots through me, and leaves me so deadly calm, yet expectant—fixed at the top of a shudder! Future things swim before me, as in empty outlines and skeletons; all the past is somehow grown dim. Mary, girl; thou fadest in pale glories behind me; boy! I seem to see but thy eyes grown wondrous blue.[16] Strangest problems of life seem clearing; but clouds sweep between—Is my journey's end coming? My legs feel faint; like his who has footed it all day. Feel thy heart—beats it yet? Stir thyself, Starbuck!— stave it off—move, move! speak aloud!— Masthead there! See ye my boy's hand on the hill?—Crazed—aloft there!—keep thy keenest eye upon the boats—mark well the whale!—Ho! again!—drive off that hawk! see! he pecks— he tears the vane"—pointing to the red flag flying at the maintruck—"Ha, he soars away with it!—Where's the old man now? see'st thou that sight, oh Ahab!—shudder, shudder!"

The boats had not gone very far, when by a signal from the mastheads—a downward pointed arm, Ahab knew that the whale had sounded; but intending to be near him at the next rising, he held on his way a little sideways from the vessel; the becharmed crew maintaining the profoundest silence, as the head-beat waves

16. **Mary . . . blue** reference to Starbuck's wife and son.

Enrichment: Investigating Science

Cetology

Cetology is the branch of zoology that deals with the study of cetaceans, a mammalian order that includes whales and dolphins. Oceanography is the study of the ocean environment, including analysis of the water, ocean depths, seabeds, animals, and plants.

Activity: Research and Report Invite interested students to research what kinds of work scientists in these fields are doing currently. Suggest that students get started on their research by talking with their science teachers about the best research paths to follow. They can use the Internet, books, scientific journals, or magazines such as *Nature* or *Natural History*, and might even interview a scientist. Suggest that they record information in the **Enrichment: Investigating Science** work sheet, in *Professional Development Guidebook,* page 241. Students can then report their findings to the class.

hammered and hammered against the opposing bow.

"Drive, drive in your nails, oh ye waves! to their uttermost heads drive them in! ye but strike a thing without a lid; and no coffin and no hearse can be mine:—and hemp only can kill me! Ha! ha!"

Suddenly the waters around them slowly swelled in broad circles; then quickly upheaved, as if sideways sliding from a submerged berg of ice, swiftly rising to the surface. A low rumbling sound was heard; a subterraneous hum; and then all held their breaths; as bedraggled with trailing ropes, and harpoons, and lances, a vast form shot lengthwise, but obliquely from the sea. Shrouded in a thin drooping veil of mist, it hovered for a moment in the rainbowed air; and then fell swamping back into the deep. Crushed thirty feet upwards, the waters flashed for an instant like heaps of fountains, then brokenly sank in a shower of flakes, leaving the circling surface creamed like new milk round the marble trunk of the whale.

Literary Analysis
Symbol What symbolic meaning is suggested by the description of the whale's behavior as he breaks the water's surface?

"Give way!" cried Ahab to the oarsmen, and the boats darted forward to the attack; but maddened by yesterday's fresh irons that corroded in him, Moby-Dick seemed combinedly possessed by all the angels that fell from heaven. The wide tiers of welded tendons overspreading his broad white forehead, beneath the transparent skin, looked knitted together; as head on, he came churning his tail among the boats; and once more flailed them apart; spilling out the irons and lances from the two mates' boats, and dashing in one side of the upper part of their bows, but leaving Ahab's almost without a scar.

While Daggoo and Queequeg were stopping the strained planks; and as the whale swimming out from them, turned, and showed one entire flank as he shot by them again; at that moment a quick cry went up. Lashed round and round to the fish's back; pinioned in the turns upon turns in which, during the past night, the whale had reeled the involutions of the lines around him, the half-torn body of the Parsee was seen; his sable raiment frayed to shreds; his distended eyes turned full upon old Ahab.

The harpoon dropped from his hand.

"Befooled, befooled!"—drawing in a long lean breath—"Aye, Parsee! I see thee again—Aye, and thou goest before; and this, this then is the hearse that thou didst promise. But I hold thee to the last letter of thy word. Where is the second hearse? Away, mates, to the ship! those boats are useless now; repair them if ye can in time, and return to me; if not, Ahab is enough to die—Down, men! the first thing that but offers to jump from this boat I stand in, that thing I harpoon. Ye are not other men, but my arms and my legs; and so obey me—Where's the whale? gone down again?"

Reading Strategy
Identifying Details to Determine Essential Message What does Ahab realize when he sees Parsee's body lashed to Moby-Dick?

But he looked too nigh the boat; for as if bent upon escaping with the corpse he bore, and as if the particular place of the last encounter had been but a stage in his leeward voyage, Moby-Dick was now again steadily swimming forward; and had almost passed the ship—which thus far had been sailing in the contrary direction to him,

34
Reading Check
What happens to Parsee?

from Moby-Dick **349**

㉟ Critical Viewing

The artist used the detail of the whale swimming away from the boat and the oarsmen rocking in a foundering boat.

㊱ Literary Analysis

Symbol and Theme

1. Remind students that every symbol functions on two levels—a literal meaning and a larger meaning—and that a theme is one of a literary work's central messages.

2. **Ask** students the following question: What does Melville mean when he describes Ahab as being tormented by "far other hammers"?
Possible response: He means that Ahab briefly feels a stab of regret and remorse when he passes the *Pequod* and sees his men working hard to repair damage Moby-Dick has done.

㊲ Critical Thinking

Speculate

1. Read this passage aloud and ask students to identify the surprising idea that the narrator seems to be suggesting. If necessary, point out that Ishmael is suggesting that Moby-Dick may be giving up the fight.

2. **Ask** students what they think will happen next.
Answer: Students might respond that because of what has happened up to this point, the fight with Moby-Dick is far from over. In fact, catastrophe may yet result.

㉟ ▼ Critical Viewing
Which details from the story did the artist use to create this illustration?
[Analyze]

though for the present her headway had been stopped. He seemed swimming with his utmost velocity, and now only intent upon pursuing his own straight path in the sea.

"Oh! Ahab," cried Starbuck, "not too late is it, even now, the third day, to desist. See! Moby-Dick seeks thee not. It is thou, thou, that madly seekest him!"

Setting sail to the rising wind, the lonely boat was swiftly impelled to leeward, by both oars and canvas. And at last when Ahab was sliding by the vessel, so near as plainly to distinguish Starbuck's face as he leaned over the rail, he hailed him to turn the vessel about, and follow him, not too swiftly, at a judicious interval. Glancing upwards he saw Tashtego, Queequeg, and Daggoo, eagerly mounting to the three mastheads; while the oarsmen were rocking in the two staved boats which had just been hoisted to the side, and were busily at work in repairing them, one after the other, through the portholes, as he sped, he also caught flying glimpses of Stubb and Flask, busying themselves on deck among bundles of new irons and lances. As he saw all this; as he heard the hammers in the broken boats; far other hammers seemed driving a nail into his heart. But he rallied. And now marking that the vane or flag was gone from the main masthead, he shouted to Tashtego, who had just gained that perch, to descend again for another flag, and a hammer and nails, and so nail it to the mast.

Whether fagged by the three days' running chase, and the resistance to his swimming in the knotted hamper he bore; or whether it was some latent deceitfulness and malice in him: whichever was true, the White Whale's way now began to abate, as it seemed, from the boat so rapidly nearing him once more; though indeed the whale's last start had not been so long a one as before. And still as Ahab glided over the waves the unpitying sharks accompanied him; and so pertinaciously stuck to the boat; and so continually bit at the plying oars, that the blades became jagged and crunched, and left small splinters in the sea, at almost every dip.

"Heed them not! those teeth but give new rowlocks to your oars. Pull on! 'tis the better rest, the sharks' jaw than the yielding water."

"But at every bite, sir, the thin blades grow smaller and smaller!"

"They will last long enough! pull on!—But who can tell"—he muttered—"whether these

350 A Growing Nation (1800–1870)

Enrichment: Analyzing Historical Patterns, Trends, and Periods

The Whale-Hunting Controversy
A decade after *Moby-Dick* was published, two inventions revolutionized whaling: harpoons tipped with explosives and faster, steam-powered whaling boats. More whales were killed in the first forty years of the twentieth century than in the previous four hundred years.

Many nations, including the United States, Canada, and most of those in Europe, have stopped hunting whales. Japan and Russia continue to hunt despite international pressure to stop.

Activity: Support an Opinion Encourage students to research the history of whaling and the whale products that drive people to hunt these animals. Suggest that they record information in the **Enrichment: Analyzing Historical Patterns, Trends, and Periods** work sheet, in *Professional Development Guidebook*, page 231. Students can then present and support their opinion on whether whaling should be prohibited internationally.

sharks swim to feast on the whale or on Ahab?—But pull on! Aye, all alive, now—we near him. The helm! take the helm! let me pass"—and so saying, two of the oarsmen helped him forward to the bows of the still flying boat.

At length as the craft was cast to one side, and ran ranging along with the White Whale's flank, he seemed strangely oblivious of its advance—as the whale sometimes will—and Ahab was fairly within the smoky mountain mist, which, thrown off from the whale's spout, curled round his great Monadnock[17] hump; he was even thus close to him; when, with body arched back, and both arms lengthwise high-lifted to the poise, he darted his fierce iron, and his far fiercer curse into the hated whale. As both steel and curse sank to the socket, as if sucked into a morass, Moby-Dick sidewise writhed; spasmodically rolled his nigh flank against the bow, and, without staving a hole in it, so suddenly canted the boat over, that had it not been for the elevated part of the gunwale to which he then clung, Ahab would once more have been tossed into the sea. As it was, three of the oarsmen—who foreknew not the precise instant of the dart, and were therefore unprepared for its effects—these were flung out; but so fell, that, in an instant two of them clutched the gunwale again, and rising to its level on a combing wave, hurled themselves bodily inboard again; the third man helplessly dropping astern, but still afloat and swimming.

Almost simultaneously, with a mighty volition of ungraduated, instantaneous swiftness, the White Whale darted through the weltering sea. But when Ahab cried out to the steersman to take new turns with the line, and hold it so; and commanded the crew to turn round on their seats, and tow the boat up to the mark; the moment the treacherous line felt that double strain and tug, it snapped in the empty air!

"What breaks in me? Some sinew cracks!—'tis whole again; oars! oars! Burst in upon him!"

Hearing the tremendous rush of the sea-crashing boat, the whale wheeled round to present his blank forehead at bay; but in that evolution, catching sight of the nearing black hull of the ship; seemingly seeing in it the source of all his persecutions; bethinking it—it may be—a larger and nobler foe; of a sudden, he bore down upon its advancing prow, smiting his jaws amid fiery showers of foam.

Ahab staggered; his hand smote his forehead. "I grow blind; hands! stretch out before me that I may yet grope my way. Is't night?"

"The whale! The ship!" cried the cringing oarsmen.

"Oars! oars! Slope downwards to thy depths. O sea that ere it be forever too late, Ahab may slide this last, last time upon his mark! I see: the ship! the ship! Dash on, my men! will ye not save my ship?"

But as the oarsmen violently forced their boat through the sledge-hammering seas, the before whale-smitten bow-ends of two planks burst through, and in an instant almost, the temporarily disabled

---

17. **Monadnock** (mə nad′ näk) mountain in New Hampshire.

Literary Analysis
Symbol What symbolic connection between his own body and the boat does Ahab seem to feel?

Reading Check
What happens to the boat carrying Ahab when it nears Moby-Dick?

from Moby-Dick **351**

38 Literary Analysis
Symbol

1. Have students note the rapid chain of events in the bracketed passage: Moby-Dick, having nearly turned the boat over, swims swiftly away. Ahab orders that the line connecting the boat to the whale be pulled taut in order to pull the boat closer to the whale. The rope snaps in two, and Ahab cries out.

2. Then **ask** students the Literary Analysis question: What symbolic connection between his own body and the boat does Ahab seem to feel?
   Answer: Ahab seems to feel as though the boat is an extension of his body.

39 Reading Check
Answer: The boat is nearly capsized by the whale's rolling motion.

Engaging the Essential Question

What makes American literature American?

1. Direct students to the last lines on page 353, where Ahab speaks of a "second hearse" made of American wood. Explain to students that Ahab is referring to a prediction Parsee (who has been killed by Moby-Dick) made that Ahab would follow him after he sees two hearses, the second made of American wood. Ahab realizes that the *Pequod* is second hearse, fulfilling Parsee's prophecy.

2. Use this reference to "American wood" as a lead-in to discuss *Moby-Dick* in terms of the essential question: What makes American literature American? Point out to students that many nations engaged in the whaling industry. **Ask:** What particularly "American" elements do you see in Melville's account of the quest for the white whale?

   Possible response: Students may note that the cultural diversity of the crew seems American, as does Ahab's driving ambition and the crew's responsiveness to offers of financial reward.

352 A Growing Nation (1800–1870)

boat lay nearly level with the waves; its half-wading, splashing crew, trying hard to stop the gap and bale out the pouring water.

Meantime, for that one beholding instant, Tashtego's masthead hammer remained suspended in his hand; and the red flag, half wrapping him as with a plaid, then streamed itself straight out from him, as his own forward-flowing heart; while Starbuck and Stubb, standing upon the bowsprit beneath, caught sight of the down-coming monster just as soon as he.

"The whale, the whale! Up helm, up helm! Oh, all ye sweet powers of air, now hug me close! Let not Starbuck die, if die he must, in a woman's fainting fit. Up helm I say—ye fools, the jaw! the jaw! Is this the end of all my bursting prayers? all my lifelong fidelities? Oh, Ahab, Ahab, lo, thy work. Steady! helmsman, steady. Nay, nay! Up helm again! He turns to meet us! Oh, his unappeasable brow drives on towards one, whose duty tells him he cannot depart. My God, stand by me now!"

"Stand not by me, but stand under me, whoever you are that will now help Stubb; for Stubb, too, sticks here. I grin at thee, thou grinning whale! Who ever helped Stubb, or kept Stubb awake, but Stubb's own unwinking eye? And now poor Stubb goes to bed upon a mattress that is all too soft; would it were stuffed with brushwood! I grin at thee, thou grinning whale! Look ye, sun, moon, and stars! I call ye assassins of as good a fellow as ever spouted up his ghost. For all that, I would yet ring glasses with thee, would ye but hand the cup! Oh, oh! oh, oh! thou grinning whale, but there'll be plenty of gulping soon! Why fly ye not, O Ahab! For me, off shoes and jacket to it; let Stubb die in his drawers! A most moldy and oversalted death, though—cherries! cherries! cherries! Oh, Flask, for one red cherry ere we die!"

"Cherries? I only wish that we were where they grow. Oh, Stubb, I hope my poor mother's drawn my part-pay ere this; if not, few coppers will now come to her, for the voyage is up."

From the ship's bows, nearly all the seamen now hung inactive; hammers, bits of plank, lances, and harpoons, mechanically retained in their hands, just as they had darted from their various employments; all their enchanted eyes intent upon the whale, which from side to side strangely vibrating his predestinating head, sent a broad band of overspreading semicircular foam before him as he rushed. Retribution, swift vengeance, eternal malice were in his whole aspect, and spite of all that mortal man could do, the solid white buttress of his forehead smote the ship's starboard bow, till men and timbers reeled. Some fell flat upon their faces. Like dislodged trucks, the heads of the harpooneers aloft shook on their bull-like necks. Through the breach, they heard the waters pour, as mountain torrents down a flume.

"The ship! The hearse!—the second hearse!" cried Ahab from the boat; "its wood could only be American!"

Literary Analysis
Symbol What is symbolized by the red flag streaming out from Tashtego?

42 ◀ Critical Viewing
How does this illustration emphasize the symbolic aspects of this story?
[Evaluate]

Reading Check
What does Moby-Dick finally do to the *Pequod*?

from Moby-Dick **353**

41 Literary Analysis
Symbol

1. Draw students' attention back to the passage on page 350 in which Ahab instructs Tashtego to nail another flag to the main masthead, because a hawk has torn down the other and flown away with it.

2. **Ask** students the Reading Strategy question: What is symbolized by the red flag streaming out from Tashtego?
   Answer: Students might say that the flag symbolizes the passionate desire of Tashtego, the crew, and Ahab to vanquish the white whale. Other students, noting that the blood-red flag is described as bursting from Tastego's heart, might say that it symbolizes the imminent deaths of Ahab and his crew.

42 Critical Viewing

Possible answer: The breaching whale may symbolize untamed nature, while the ship floating placidly at sea may symbolize humanity's presumed power over nature.

43 Literary Analysis
Symbol and Theme

1. After reviewing the material on symbols, read aloud with students the bracketed passage and **ask** students the following question: What details in this paragraph suggest that the whale has become a symbol of retribution?
   Answer: Students may point to details such as the whale's "swift vengeance" and the "eternal malice. . . in his whole aspect."

2. **Ask** students what is suggested by Ishmael's description of the whale as malicious and vengeful.
   Possible response: Students may point out that Ishmael's account suggests that he has joined Ahab in his view of the whale as a deliberate agent of destruction.

44 Reading Check

Answer: Moby-Dick causes the *Pequod* to sink in a vortex of swirling water.

Differentiated Instruction   for Universal Access

Strategy for Less Proficient Readers
Using repeated oral readings, help students understand how Ahab dies (see the paragraph beginning "The harpoon was darted," p. 354). Guide them to see that he is caught around the neck by the harpoon line and jerked from the boat. He dies throwing a harpoon into a fleeing Moby-Dick and declaring his eternal hatred of the animal. Have students use the same technique to recognize the fate of the *Pequod* in the next paragraph.

Vocabulary for Gifted/Talented Students
Invite students to review the text in order to create an illustrated glossary of nautical and other technical terms for readers of *Moby-Dick*. Students' entries might include such terms as *capstan, harpoon,* and *keel* and employ drawings and diagrams as well as definitions.

353

1. Read aloud this stirring speech, or play the recording of it on the *Hear It!* Audio CD.

2. **Ask** students the Literary Analysis question: What thematic elements come together in Ahab's climactic speech?
Possible response: In Ahab's speech, Melville touches on thematic elements such as personal loyalty, death, humanity's search for meaning in life, the mysteries of nature, and good and evil.

Diving beneath the settling ship, the whale ran quivering along its keel; but turning under water, swiftly shot to the surface again, far off the other bow, but within a few yards of Ahab's boat, where, for a time, he lay quiescent.

Literary Analysis
Symbol and Theme
What thematic elements come together in Ahab's climactic speech?

45 "I turn my body from the sun. What ho, Tashtego! let me hear thy hammer. Oh! ye three unsurrendered spires of mine; thou uncracked keel; and only god-bullied hull; thou firm deck, and haughty helm, and Pole-pointed prow—death-glorious ship! must ye then perish, and without me? Am I cut off from the last fond pride of meanest ship-wrecked captains? Oh, lonely death on lonely life! Oh, now I feel my topmost greatness lies in my topmost grief. Ho, ho! from all your furthest bounds, pour ye now in, ye bold billows of my whole foregone life, and top this one piled comber of my death! Towards thee I roll, thou all-destroying but unconquering whale; to the last I grapple with thee; from hell's heart I stab at thee; for hate's sake I spit my last breath at thee. Sink all coffins and all hearses to one common pool! and since neither can be mine, let me then tow to pieces, while still chasing thee, though tied to thee, thou damned whale! *Thus*, I give up the spear!"

The harpoon was darted; the stricken whale flew forward; with igniting velocity the line ran through the groove;—ran foul. Ahab stooped to clear it; he did clear it; but the flying turn caught him round the neck, and voicelessly as Turkish mutes bowstring their victim, he was shot out of the boat, ere the crew knew he was gone. Next instant, the heavy eye splice in the rope's final end flew out of the stark-empty tub, knocked down an oarsman, and smiting the sea, disappeared in its depths.

For an instant, the tranced boat's crew stood still; then turned. "The ship? Great God, where is the ship?" Soon they through dim, bewildering mediums saw her sidelong fading phantom, as in the gaseous fata morgana,[18] only the uppermost masts out of water: while fixed by infatuation, or fidelity, or fate, to their once lofty perches, the pagan harpooneers still maintained their sinking lookouts on the sea. And now, concentric circles seized the lone boat itself, and all its crew, and each floating oar, and every lance pole, and spinning, animate and inanimate, all round and round in one vortex, carried the smallest chip of the *Pequod* out of sight.

But as the last whelmings intermixingly poured themselves over the sunken head of the Indian at the mainmast, leaving a few inches of the erect spar yet visible, together with long streaming yards of the flag, which calmly undulated, with ironical coincidings, over the destroying billows they almost touched—at that instant, a red arm and a hammer hovered backwardly uplifted in the open air, in the act of nailing the flag faster and yet faster to the subsiding spar. A sky hawk that tauntingly had followed the main-truck downwards

---

18. **fata morgana** (fät´ə môr gän ə) *n.* mirage seen at sea.

Vocabulary Development

Vocabulary Knowledge Rating
When students have completed reading and discussing the selection, have them take out their **Vocabulary Knowledge Rating** charts for the story. Read the words aloud and have students rate their knowledge of words again in the After Reading column. Clarify any words that are still problematic. Have students write their own definitions and example or sentence in the appropriate column. Then have students complete the Vocabulary Lesson at the end of the selections. Encourage students to use the words in further discussion and written work about the selections. Remind them that they will be accountable for these words on the **Selection Test**, *Unit 2 Resources,* pages 105–107 or 108–110.

PHLit Online! **Vocabulary Central,** featuring tools and activities for studying vocabulary, is available online at **www.PHLitOnline.com.**

from its natural home among the stars, pecking at the flag, and incommoding Tashtego there: this bird now chanced to intercept its broad fluttering wing between the hammer and the wood: and simultaneously feeling that ethereal thrill, the submerged savage beneath, in his deathgasp, kept his hammer frozen there: and so the bird of heaven, with archangelic shrieks, and his imperial beak thrust upwards, and his whole captive form folded in the flag of Ahab, went down with his ship, which, like Satan, would not sink to hell till she had dragged a living part of heaven along with her, and helmeted herself with it.

Now small fowls flew screaming over the yet yawning gulf; a sullen white surf beat against its steep sides; then all collapsed, and the great shroud of the sea rolled on as it rolled five thousand years ago.

Critical Reading

Cite textual evidence to support your responses.

1. Key Ideas and Details (a) What happened to Ahab in his previous encounter with Moby-Dick? **(b) Interpret:** What does Ahab's obsession with Moby-Dick reveal about his character? **(c) Compare and Contrast:** In what ways is Starbuck different from Ahab?

2. Key Ideas and Details (a) How does Starbuck interpret Ahab's obsession with Moby-Dick? **(b) Analyze:** Why does Starbuck obey Ahab even though he disagrees with him?

3. Key Ideas and Details (a) What does Ahab believe exists "behind the unreasoning mask" of all visible things? **(b) Summarize:** Briefly, explain Ahab's beliefs about the nature of creation.

4. Key Ideas and Details (a) How does Moby-Dick react when the *Pequod* first approaches his flank? **(b) Compare and Contrast:** How does Moby-Dick's reaction illuminate the differences between the whale in reality and in Ahab's imagination?

5. Integration of Knowledge and Ideas Take a Position: This novel has been called a "voyage of the soul." Would you agree or disagree with that assessment? Explain.

6. Integration of Knowledge and Ideas (a) What happens to Ahab, Moby-Dick, and the *Pequod* at the story's end? **(b) Analyze:** What does the final paragraph indicate about the relationship between humanity and nature?

7. Integration of Knowledge and Ideas Does Ahab's persistence reflect aspects of a distinctly American character, or is it simply human? Explain. In your response, use at least two of these Essential Question words: *individualism, ambition, persistence, extreme.* *[Connecting to the Essential Question: What makes American literature American?]*

from Moby-Dick **355**

Concept Connector

Literary Analysis Graphic Organizer
Ask students to review the graphic organizers on which they have recorded symbols and analyzed their meaning. Then have students share their organizers and compare their interpretations.

Activating Prior Knowledge
Have students return to their responses to the Activating Prior Knowledge activity. Ask them to explain whether their thoughts have changed and if so, how.

Writing About the Essential Question
Have students compare their responses to the prompt before they completed reading *Moby-Dick* with their thoughts after reading it. Have them work individually or in groups, writing or discussing their thoughts, to define their new responses. Then lead a class discussion, probing for what students have learned that confirms or invalidates their initial thoughts. Encourage students to cite specific textual details to support their responses.

ASSESS

Answers

Before students respond, you may wish to have them write a brief objective summary of the selection. As they answer the questions below, remind them to support their answers with evidence from the text.

1. (a) He lost one of his legs. (b) It reveals that he is a stubborn, angry, and bitter man. (c) Starbuck is practical and realistic and is disturbed by Ahab's obsession.

2. (a) Starbuck sees the obsession as pointless vengeance against a dumb animal. (b) Starbuck obeys because he is loyal and has served Ahab a long time; he also cares about Ahab and may unwillingly admire his courage.

3. (a) Ahab believes that a mind and will exist behind the surface of things. (b) He believes that creation is ultimately unknowable.

4. (a) He surfaces and then disappears. (b) In his obsession, Ahab feels pursued and tormented by Moby-Dick; in reality, Moby-Dick is trying to escape his pursuers.

5. **Sample responses:** Yes, the novel is about a spiritual quest, the soul enduring danger and hardship on its journey. No, the novel is not a voyage but a fall, showing human pride brought low by the power of nature.

6. (a) Ahab is caught by the fouled, or tangled, harpoon line, is yanked out of the boat, and disappears; with the harpoon in him, Moby-Dick disappears; the *Pequod* sinks. (b) **Possible response:** Nature endures in the face of human mortality and is indifferent to human suffering.

7. **Possible response:** Ahab's persistence and his ambition to overcome challenges are aspects of the human condition in general. In *Moby-Dick*, striving individualism is taken to an extreme that seems particularly American.

Answers

1. (a) Sharks appear and surround his boat; Starbuck sees visions of his family. (b) Ahab sees the corpse of the Parsee. (c) Though he acknowledges each omen, he continues to pursue the whale.

2. **Sample answers:** The whale's color could symbolize the innocence of a creature simply following instinct. Or, the whale's whiteness represents inescapable death for Ahab and his crew.

3. The voyage may symbolize human efforts to control nature.

4. (a) Whereas Starbuck is practical, realistic, and thoughtful, Ahab is stubborn, angry, and bitter. (b) **Sample answer:** With these contrasting characters, Melville touches on themes such as good versus evil, loyalty, and sacrifice.

5. **Possible response:** The *Pequod*'s journey suggests that the most impassioned and determined human will is dwarfed and easily subdued by the vast, mysterious powers of nature.

6. An Ahab-like whaler uses a color swatch to find a whale of a particular hue, a joke on Ahab's pursuit of a white whale.

7. **Possible responses:** (a) "There's a soft shower to leeward. Such lovely leewardings! They must lead somewhere—to something else than common land, more palmy than the palms. Leeward! the white whale goes that way; look to windward, then . . . ." (b) "[I]t was Moby-Dick that dismasted me; Moby-Dick that brought me to this dead stump I stand on now . . . ." (c) Students may mention Moby-Dick's disappearance—but not death—at the end of the fight with Ahab.

8. (a) Ahab seems to believe that the human capacity for logic and reason is irrelevant. (b) **Possible response:** Ahab's worldview leads directly to the destruction of life and property, so his view is imbalanced.

9. **Sample answer:** Ishmael's comments suggest that humanity is itself responsible for much of what it sees as tragic or evil in the world.

356

Literary Analysis

© 1. **Key Ideas and Details** What omens appear **(a)** as Ahab's whaleboat pulls away from the *Pequod* and **(b)** when Moby-Dick surfaces? **(c)** What is Ahab's reaction to these omens?

© 2. **Craft and Structure** The color white is often used as a **symbol** for innocence, as well as for absence and death. What contradictory symbolic meanings does the whale's whiteness convey?

© 3. **Craft and Structure** If the *Pequod* crew symbolizes humanity and Moby-Dick symbolizes nature, what might the ship's voyage symbolize?

© 4. **Key Ideas and Details** **(a)** Use a chart like the one shown to compare and contrast the characters of Starbuck and Ahab. **(b)** What message, or **theme**, is Melville expressing through these contrasting characters?

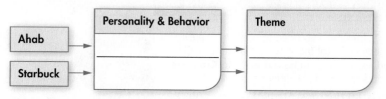

© 5. **Key Ideas and Details** Considering the journey's symbolic meaning and its terrible outcome, speculate about the novel's overall theme, or central idea.

6. **Analyze Visual Information** Explain the humor in this cartoon.

Reading Strategy

7. **Identify relevant details to determine the essential message.** Which events, dialogue, or descriptions in the excerpt lead you to recognize Moby-Dick as a symbol of **(a)** nature's beauty; **(b)** nature's power; and **(c)** nature's immortality. For each meaning, explain your reasoning.

8. **(a)** What does Ahab mean when he says "Ahab never thinks; he only feels, feel, feels; that's tingling enough for mortal man! to think's audacity." **(b)** Considering the events that occur as a result of Ahab's feelings, what message do you derive from that statement?

9. How does this statement by Ishmael suggest a way to look at the essential meaning of the events he narrates?

"Ah, ye admonitions and warnings! why stay ye not when ye come? But rather are ye predictions than warnings, ye shadows! Yet not so much predictions from without, as verifications of the foregoing things within."

"Have ye seen a whale that matches this swatch?"

Assessment Practice

Make Inferences and Generalizations For more practice, see *All-in-One Workbook.*

Many tests require students to make generalizations about a written passage. Use this sample test item:

. . . to and fro he paced his old rounds, upon planks so familiar to his tread, that they were all over dented, like geological stones, with the peculiar mark of his walk. Did you fixedly gaze, too, upon that ribbed and dented brow; there also, you would see still stranger footprints—the footprints of his one unsleeping, ever-pacing thought.

Which of the following best describes Ahab?
A rational and energetic
B calm and powerful
C reverent and self-effacing
D tormented and obsessed

A, B, and **C** are not supported by the text. Ahab's pacing shows his obsession. *D* is correct.

Vocabulary Acquisition and Use

Word Analysis: Latin Prefix *mal-*

The word "maledictions" combines the Latin prefix *mal-*, which means "bad" or "badly," with the root *-dic-*, which means "to speak." Hence, the word "maledictions" means "bad speech," or curses. Write a definition for each numbered word below. Explain how the meaning of the prefix or root contributes to the meaning of the word.

1. malevolent
2. malice
3. malignant
4. dictate
5. predict
6. diction

Vocabulary: Synonyms

For each vocabulary word, select the best synonym from the column on the right. Then, explain your reasoning.

1. maledictions
2. prescient
3. impulsive
4. inscrutable
5. pedestrian
6. inarticulate

a. thoughtless
b. curses
c. walking
d. prophetic
e. inexpressive
f. mysterious

Writing

Argument A **character study** is a type of *literary criticism* in which a writer analyzes a character and argues for a certain interpretation of that figure. Often, a character study focuses on a subject, like Ahab, whose behavior can be interpreted in varied ways. For example, some readers feel Ahab's obsession borders on madness, while others feel it borders on greatness. Write an essay in which you analyze Ahab's character and present a convincing argument for your ideas.

Prewriting Review the excerpt and gather details about Ahab's appearance, statements, and behavior. Note what other characters say and feel about him. Use a format like the one shown to assemble the details and look for patterns among them. Write one sentence—your thesis—that expresses your analysis.

Drafting In your introduction, state your thesis and provide background information readers may need to understand your ideas. Then, devote one body paragraph to each of your supporting points. Make sure to address alternative explanations of Ahab's character but show why yours is better. Summarize your ideas in your conclusion.

Revising Reread your draft and make sure you have developed your thesis thoroughly. If there are stray details that do not support your thesis, either delete them or strengthen their connections to your main idea.

Model: Gathering Details and Forming an Opinion

Details:
- Ahab becomes more consumed by his thoughts as the story progresses.
- The crew members notice Ahab's excitement and his wild appearance when he gathers them on the quarter-deck.
- Ahab continues to take greater risks with life and lives of crew members in an effort to kill Moby-Dick.

Thesis: Ahab's obsession with Moby-Dick eventually leads to his madness.

Details taken from the selection as a whole show a character's development.

Integrated Language Skills **357**

Answers

Vocabulary Acquisition and Use

1. Introduce the skill, using the instruction on the student page.
2. Have students complete the Word Analysis activity and the Vocabulary practice.

Word Analysis

1. displaying ill will; the prefix *mal-* indicates negativity.
2. intent to inflict pain or distress; the prefix *mal-* indicates a negativity.
3. likely to produce death or deterioration; the prefix *mal-* points toward a bad outcome.
4. to speak for transcription; the root *-dic-* indicates the spoken word.
5. to foretell; the root *-dic-* indicates that what is foretold is shared or spoken.
6. verbal expression; the root *-dic-* refers to speech.

Vocabulary

1. b
2. d
3. a
4. f
5. c
6. e

Writing

1. To guide students in writing this character study, give them the **Support for Writing** worksheet (*Unit 2 Resources,* p. 100).
2. Students' character studies should include a brief summary of the story as well as establish and explain their ideas and insights about Ahab's character.
3. As they develop their theses, remind students to take into account Ahab's position as the captain of the *Pequod*. Point out, also, that students should support their theses by citing Ahab's actions, behavior, and speech.
4. Assess students' character studies using the **Rubrics for Critiques,** in *Professional Development Guidebook,* pages 276–277.

Conventions and Style

Introduce and discuss the skill, using the instruction on the student page.

Think Aloud: Model the Skill

Model the skill of using participles. Say to students:

Using participles as adjectives helps me emphasize the key idea in the sentences. The combined sentence "Filled with vengeance, Ahab chases Moby-Dick" now emphasizes chasing Moby-Dick. As you combine sentences using participles, put the more important idea in the main clause.

Practice

1. infinitive phrase
2. gerund phrase
3. infinitive phrase
4. participial phrase
5. participial phrase
6. They use the basket <u>to lift Ahab to the top of the mainmast.</u>
7. Most of the crew were eager <u>to obey the captain's orders.</u>
8. Captain Ahab is obsessed with <u>getting revenge</u>.
9. <u>Motivated by their desire for the gold piece</u>, the sailor's follow Ahab's lead.
10. <u>Showing no aggression toward the men</u>, the whale initially swims away from the ship.

Writing and Speaking Conventions

A. Sample responses:

1. <u>Pacing the deck</u>, Ahab raged at the violent sea. Participial
2. Queequeg and the Parsee were anxious <u>to use their harpoons</u>. Infinitive
3. <u>Obeying orders</u> was natural for Starbuck. Gerund

B. Sample response: <u>Swimming toward the small boat</u>, I saw the man throw his harpoon. His sole intent was <u>to kill me</u>, but the rope caught his neck. <u>Diving below the boat</u> was my best chance at survival, so I dove deep, to <u>take the man with me</u>.

PH WRITING COACH   Grade 11

Students will find additional information about verbals in Chapters 15, 16, and 17.

Conventions and Style: Participles, Gerunds, and Infinitives (Verbals)

Your writing will be more interesting if you use varied sentences. Participles, gerunds, and infinitives, also called *verbals*, are good tools for creating sentence variety. A **participle** is a verb form, usually ending in *-ing* or *-ed*, that can be used as an adjective. A **gerund** is a verb form ending in *-ing* that acts as a noun. An **infinitive** is a verb form that appears with the word "to" and acts as a noun, an adjective, or an adverb. All of these verbals can be used with modifiers and complements to make a **phrase,** a group of words that lacks a subject or verb but adds detail to a sentence.

Varying Sentences with Verbals

Choppy: Ahab is filled with vengeance. Ahab chases Moby-Dick.
Combined Using Participial Phrase: *Filled with vengeance*, Ahab chases Moby-Dick.

Choppy: They are hunting whales. It is dangerous.
Combined Using Gerund Phrase: *Hunting whales* is dangerous.

Choppy: Their first task is clear. They must find the whale.
Combined Using Infinitive Phrase: Their first task is *to find the whale.*

Punctuation Tip: Always place a comma after an introductory participial phrase.

Ⓒ Writing and Speaking Conventions

A. Writing Use each phrase in a sentence and explain what type of phrase it is.

1. pacing the deck
2. to use their harpoons
3. obeying orders

Example: spying the whale
Sentence: Spying the whale, the men on watch shout out.
Type of Verbal: participial

B. Speaking Describe the final scene of the excerpt from Moby-Dick's point of view. As you speak, use at least one participial phrase, one gerund phrase, and one infinitive phrase.

Practice In items 1–5, identify the italicized phrase as a participial, gerund, or infinitive phrase. In items 6–10, use the type of phrase indicated in parentheses to combine the two sentences into a single more detailed sentence.

1. Captain Ahab wants *to kill Moby-Dick.*
2. *Angering a huge whale* is not a good idea.
3. *To hunt whales for profit* was the men's original plan.
4. *Damaged by the sharks' bites,* the oars were useless.
5. Starbuck, *doubting the wisdom of his captain,* quietly mutters a prayer.
6. They use the basket. They lift Ahab to the top of the mainmast. (infinitive)
7. Most of the crew were eager. They wanted to obey the captain's orders. (infinitive)
8. Captain Ahab is obsessed with one thing. He is obsessed with getting revenge. (gerund)
9. The sailors follow Ahab's lead. They are motivated by their desire for the gold piece. (participial)
10. The whale initially swims away from the ship. The whale shows no aggression toward the men. (participial)

PH WRITING COACH
Further instruction and practice are available in *Prentice Hall Writing Coach.*

Extend the Lesson

Example

Read this sentence from *Moby-Dick*:

Receiving the brimming pewter, and turning to the harpooners, he ordered them to produce their weapons.

Ask students what they notice about the sentence. Elicit from them that the sentence opens with two participial phrases.

Elicit further that the sentence ends with the infinitive phrase "to produce their weapons."

Ask the students to restate the sentence without participles or infinitives: "He received the pewter. The pewter was filled to the brim. He turned to the harpooners and ordered, 'Produce your weapons.'"

Have students write an original sentence that follows the same pattern as the one from *Moby-Dick*, matching each grammatical and stylistic feature discussed.

The Human Spirit and the Natural World

Text Complexity: At a Glance

This chart gives a general text complexity rating for the selections in this part of the unit to help guide instruction. For additional text complexity support, see the Text Complexity Rubric at point of use.			
from Nature	**More Accessible**	*from* Walden	**More Complex**
from Self-Reliance	**More Accessible**	*from* Civil Disobedience	**More Accessible**
Concord Hymn	**More Accessible**		

Selection Planning Guide

The section introduces students to two of the most influential writers of the nineteenth century. Ralph Waldo Emerson and Henry David Thoreau helped define the American character by inspiring people to turn to nature in order to better understand both themselves and the universal truths. Students may be surprised to find that they share many of the views on nature and individuality that Emerson expresses in *Nature* and "Self-Reliance." "Concord Hymn" reveals the poetic—and perhaps more accessible—side of Emerson's literary talent. Thoreau's views in *Walden* on how to live a productive life may intrigue students. Encourage them to assess the validity of his evaluation of government in "Civil Disobedience."

Visual Connection

1. Before you tell students that the photograph is titled "Aspens and Snow in Autumn, Vermont," **ask** them when they think the image was taken.
   Possible response: Students noting the snow cover may say winter; students noting the foliage on the trees may say autumn or spring.

2. **Ask:** Do you find these woods to be inviting or forbidding? Exhilarating or depressing? Explain.
   Possible response: Student responses may be contingent on their responses to the outdoors. Many may say that the brightness and airiness of the scene, magnified by the blue sky and yellow leaves of the aspens, is inviting and exhilarating.

Monitoring Progress

Before students read the poetry selections, refer to students' results on the **Vocabulary in Context** section of **Benchmark Test 2** (*Unit 4 Resources*, pp. 265–267). Use this diagnostic portion of the test to guide your choice of selections to teach as well as the depth of prereading preparation you will provide, based on students' readiness for the reading and vocabulary skills.

Common Core State Standards

• Reading Informational Text 4
• Language 5.a

Transcendentalism: The Seekers

1. Ask students what they think of when they hear the words *individual* or *individualism*. Discuss the role that strong individuals play in movies and television shows.

2. After students have discussed the role of individuals in popular media, have them read the article about the Transcendentalists.

Background

Meetings of Great Minds
Transcendentalism attracted many educated and intellectual women of the time. One of Margaret Fuller's closest friends was Elizabeth Palmer Peabody (1804–1894), the eldest of three remarkable sisters. A writer of an extraordinary collection of letters and a tireless correspondent with many of the foremost thinkers of her day, Elizabeth founded one of the first kindergartens in the United States. Mary Peabody Mann (1806–1887) worked with Elizabeth Peabody in the kindergarten movement. She married a man who became famous: Horace Mann, the educator. Sophia Peabody (1809–1871) married Nathaniel Hawthorne after a long courtship.

Critical Viewing

Answer: Students may say that Thoreau would be glad to see that people continued to be influenced by his ideas and wanted to see how he put them into practice.

Literary History: Transcendentalism

According to Ralph Waldo Emerson, the preeminent Transcendentalist of his day, the human mind is so powerful it can unlock any mystery, from the intricacies of nature to the wonder of God.

▲ **Critical Viewing**
How might Thoreau feel about this statue and replica of his cabin that stand today at Walden Pond State Reservation? **[Speculate]**

Transcendentalism: The Seekers

For the Transcendentalists, the loose-knit group of writers, artists, and reformers who flourished in the 1830s and 1840s, the individual was at the center of the universe, more powerful than any institution, whether political or religious. So it is fitting that the most influential literary and philosophical movement in American history began with the struggles of one man.

A Crisis of Confidence In the early 1830s, a young Boston pastor found himself wrestling with his faith. His beloved wife had died, and he began questioning his beliefs. At the time, many institutions downplayed the importance of the individual. The Industrial Revolution had shown that machines could actually replace people, that individuals did not matter.

The pastor was troubled by this notion. He believed, on the contrary, that the human mind was the most important force in the universe. The pastor was so passionate about his search for a new way of thinking that he resigned his position and traveled to Europe to visit with some of the great philosophers of the day.

That pastor was Ralph Waldo Emerson, and his crisis of confidence became a revolution in American thought. When Emerson returned to the United States in 1833, he helped forge the Transcendentalist movement.

The Individual Is the World The Transcendentalist movement lasted a mere ten years and produced only two major books—Emerson's *Nature* (1836) and Thoreau's *Walden* (1854). Yet its influence on American life and letters continues to this day. According to Emerson, the human mind is so powerful it can unlock any mystery, from the intricacies of nature to the wonder of God. To Emerson, "the individual is the world." This was a radical thought in an age that gave all authority to the organized institutions of government, religion, and education.

Emerson first proposed his ideas in 1833 in a speech at Harvard University. Then, he took his ideas further, proposing that every soul and all of nature was part of an "Over-Soul," a universal spirit to which all beings return after death. In other words, every being is part of God's mind.

Meetings of Great Minds Many people denounced Emerson as a heretic, but his supporters flocked to his home in Concord, Massachusetts. During the height of Transcendentalist activities, Concord attracted so many great minds that it was dubbed the "Athens of America."

Enrichment: Understanding a Literary Figure

Louisa May Alcott

The fame of Transcendentalist Amos Bronson Alcott was eclipsed by his daughter Louisa May. Louisa's novel *Little Women* and its sequels have never gone out of print. She actually preferred writing Gothic fiction, but because she was a woman, scandal would have resulted had she published her tales of mesmerism, murder, and the supernatural under her own name. Her stories appeared anonymously or under the pen name A. M. Barnard. Late in the twentieth century, scholars identified her as the author of *A Modern Mephistopheles* and a number of

Gothic tales by studying her journals and correspondence.

Activity: Discussion Have students conduct research on Louisa May Alcott. Tell them to look into the circumstances of her life and into the types of works she wrote. Suggest that they record information in the **Enrichment: Analyzing a Literary Figure** work sheet, in *Professional Development Guidebook*, page 235. Then have the class discuss whether Alcott should be considered a Transcendentalist.

Among Emerson's admirers was **Amos Bronson Alcott**, whose beliefs about education revolutionized American schools. Alcott insisted that students should not be taught through routine memorization, but should instead be challenged to think, debate, and discuss. Feminist author and editor **Margaret Fuller** was another eminent Transcendentalist. Along with Emerson, Fuller was the driving force behind the Transcendentalist journal *The Dial.*

Emerson's most famous protégé was **Henry David Thoreau.** As a twenty-year-old student, Thoreau heard Emerson speak at Harvard and was thrilled by his ideas. Not content merely to discuss Transcendentalist philosophy, Thoreau wanted to put it into action. In 1845, he built a rough cottage in the woods at Walden Pond and went there to live alone, in harmony with nature, untied to material things. Thoreau lived at Walden Pond for two years and wrote about his experiences in his collection of essays, *Walden.*

A Lasting Legacy Like other Transcendentalists, Thoreau was a fierce abolitionist. To protest slavery and the Mexican War, he refused to pay taxes and was imprisoned. Although Thoreau spent only one night in jail, the experience gave him insights into the relationship of individuals to government. The theory of nonviolent civil disobedience that he developed has had a profound effect on society throughout the world. During India's struggle for independence in the 1940s, **Mahatma Gandhi** adopted Thoreau's ideas. In America, nonviolent protest served as the guiding principle for **Martin Luther King, Jr.,** during the civil rights movement.

The influence of the Transcendentalists is so woven into the fabric of American culture that we take it for granted. Yet whenever we celebrate the individual, look to the natural world as a mirror of human lives, or state a belief in the power of intuition to grasp fundamental truths, we owe a debt to the great, brief meeting of minds in Concord.

Speaking and Listening: Small Group Discussion

© **Comprehension and Collaboration** The Transcendentalists believed that no institution should be as powerful as the individual. With a small group, discuss the role of the individual in our society today. Use these questions to guide your discussion:

- How much power do formal institutions have in our society? Support your position with examples.
- In what ways do individuals make a difference in our society?
- Should individuals have more power than they do? Why or why not?

Choose a point person to share your group's conclusions with the class.

Speaking and Listening: Small Group Discussion

1. Read The Power of One instructions with the class. Before they begin to discuss the questions, encourage students to clarify their ideas by tracking them in charts.

2. Tell them to create one chart for political, religious, and corporate institutions. In the first column, have them write how much power these institutions have; in the second, have them list examples; and, in the third, have them note how much power students think the institutions should have.

3. Have them create a second, similar chart tracking the power of individuals.

4. Point out that students' ideas may change as groups discuss the questions.

Differentiated Instruction   for Universal Access

EL Pronunciation for English Learners

When you introduce your class to Thoreau, you may notice some English learners have difficulty with the initial *th*, pronouncing it instead as an initial *d*. For such students, write the following pairs on the board, a large chart, or an overhead transparency for the students to view:

Pronounce each word in a pair in turn, and have students echo you. Then, station a volunteer at the board, chart or overhead, where the class will guide him or her to circle the correct word as you call out the words at random.

thank/dank	thigh/die
thrill/drill	thin/din
thinner/dinner	thug/dug

Themes Across Centuries

Charles Johnson

Tell students that Charles Johnson, a prize-winning novelist and teacher, was born in 1948 and so came of age during the civil rights movement of the 1960s. Johnson's novel *Middle Passage,* which won the prestigious National Book Award in 1990, treats the subject of slavery from the unconventional viewpoint of a freed slave who leaves his life in New Orleans and travels to Africa on a slave ship. In 1998 Johnson received a MacArthur Foundation "genius grant"—so-called because the grants are given to individuals with decidedly original minds—something of which Ralph Waldo Emerson would have approved.

Emerson Gave Me Permission to Question Everything

1. Have students read Johnson's comments about the influence of Emerson on his life.

2. Then **ask:** What might be the advantages and disadvantages in resisting, as Johnson and Emerson have done, "the pressure to conform to things that were unreasonable . . . and to value [their] own individual voice and vision"?
   Answer: The advantages of resisting social pressures and being true to one's "voice and vision" is having the personal satisfaction of doing what you think is right and of working for one's personal goals. The disadvantages might be that such an attitude is stressful and difficult to maintain, that others may perceive you as selfish or immature.

Challenging Us to Go Beyond the Ordinary

1. Have students read the last paragraph, focusing on Johnson's statement that Emerson transcended the ordinary.

2. **Ask:** What are Johnson and Emerson encouraging us to do when they tell us to go "beyond the ordinary"?
   Sample answer: They are encouraging us to believe in ourselves and try new things. We should not settle for mediocrity but constantly seek new knowledge and new challenges.

Themes Across Centuries: Scholar's Insights

Charles Johnson on Ralph Waldo Emerson

Emerson Gave Me Permission to Question Everything
At age sixteen, when I was an Illinois boy trying to figure out where my place might be in the tempestuous, rapidly changing decade of the 1960s, and long before I became a black American novelist and philosopher, my teachers at Evanston Township High School placed the essays of Ralph Waldo Emerson in front of me. I'm thankful they did.

In grand fashion, "Self-Reliance" gave me permission to be a free thinker and to rigorously question *every*thing around me—from the status quo to social cliques in my school, from neighborhood gangs to eighty-year-old social "conventions" that enshrined racial segregation in the South and in the North. Emerson gave me the courage to resist the pressure to conform to things that were unreasonable, to always trust myself, to dream "impossible dreams," and to value my own individual voice and vision, even if doing so resulted in disapproval and being unpopular with the hip "in crowd."

Challenging Us to Go Beyond the Ordinary Just as he served me well in my teens, Emerson's belief in "the infinitude of the private man," and his identification with all forms of life, proved to be reliable guides during my adult years. First, that's because he defined so beautifully the values that eight generations of Americans regard as the basis for our national character and core beliefs, particularly his devotion to what he called "the republic of Man." He condemned the institution of slavery, championed the right of women to vote, and spoke out against the "wicked Indian policy."

In his journal, Emerson dreamed of an America that would one day be an "asylum of all nations, the energy of Irish, Germans, Swedes, Poles & Cossacks, & all the European tribes—of the Africans, & of the Polynesians [who] will construct a new race, a new religion, a new State, a new literature, which will be as vigorous as the new Europe which came out of the smelting pot of the Dark Ages. . . ." He truly believed, and made *me* see, how "It is our duty to be discontented, with the measure we have of knowledge & virtue, to forget the things behind & press toward those before."

Meet the Author

Charles Johnson has published in a wide variety of genres, including cartoons, philosophical and literary criticism, screenplays, and novels. His novel *Middle Passage* won the National Book Award in 1990.

Critical Viewing

Possible response: Emerson must have been a captivating speaker because the audience is listening attentively. His stance, expression, and hand gesture show his ease in front of the crowd.

Secondly, Emerson has long inspired me—as he does anyone with an adventurous spirit—because he challenges us to be flexible and resourceful, like the "sturdy lad from New Hampshire or Vermont, who in turn tries all the professions, who *teams* it, *farms* it, *peddles*, keeps a school, preaches, edits a newspaper, goes to Congress, buys a township, and so forth, in successive years, and always, like a cat, falls on his feet" (from "Self-Reliance").

All those *are* our possibilities. There is nothing, Emerson says, that we cannot achieve if we believe in ourselves. As a Transcendentalist, he was a restless and superbly civilized man who went beyond (or transcended) the ordinary, the outdated, and the unoriginal, for, in his own words, he chose to "unsettle all things. No facts are to me sacred, none are profane; I simply experiment, an endless seeker, with no Past at my back" (from "Circles").

▲ **Critical Viewing**
This print shows Emerson delivering a lecture. What details reveal what he might have been like as a speaker? **[Analyze]**

Critical Reading

Ⓒ **1. Key Ideas and Details (a)** When Johnson was a teenager, what three important lessons did he learn from Emerson? **(b) Connect:** What important life lessons have you learned from a favorite author?

Ⓒ **2. Key Ideas and Details (a)** What two qualities does Emerson's "sturdy lad from New Hampshire or Vermont" display? **(b) Speculate:** Are these qualities still part of our "core beliefs" as Americans? Why or why not?

As You Read the Selections by Emerson . . .

Ⓒ **3. Integration of Knowledge and Ideas** Think about whether Emerson's work is still as relevant to today's high school students as it was to the young Charles Johnson.

Extended Study: Transcendentalism **363**

ASSESS

Answers

Before students respond, you may wish to have them write a brief objective summary of the selection. As they answer the questions below, remind them to support their answers with evidence from the text.

1. (a) As a teenager, Johnson learned to be a free-thinker and question everything around him, including high-school social cliques and societal norms such as segregation. He also learned to resist the pressure to conform; he learned to trust himself and "dream 'impossible dreams.'" (b) Students should cite a specific author whose writing has taught them something about living— for example, they might indicate how the *Diary of Anne Frank* shows the power and persistence of hope.

2. (a) Emerson's "sturdy lad from New Hampshire or Vermont" displays flexibility and resourcefulness. (b) Most students will probably feel that these qualities are still central to the American character, because Americans continue to show the ability to adapt to new circumstances and find solutions to new problems as they arise.

3. As they read Emerson, encourage students to look for the qualities that Johnson singles out in the author's writing and think of instances in their own lives when they resisted conforming and instead thought independently.

from Nature • from Self-Reliance • Concord Hymn
Lesson Pacing Guide

DAY 1 Preteach

- Administer the Reading and Vocabulary Warm-ups (*Unit 2 Resources*, pp. 111–114) as necessary.
- Introduce the Literary Analysis concepts: Figurative Language and Imagery.
- Introduce the Reading Strategy: Challenge or question the text.
- Build background with the author and Background features.
- Develop thematic thinking with Connecting to the Essential Question.
- Teach the selection vocabulary.

DAYS 2–3 Preteach/Teach/Assess

- Distribute copies of the appropriate graphic organizer for the Reading Strategy (*Graphic Organizer Transparencies*, pp. 78–79).
- Distribute copies of the appropriate graphic organizer for Literary Analysis (*Graphic Organizer Transparencies*, pp. 80–81).
- Prepare students to read with the Activating Prior Knowledge activities (TE).
- Informally monitor comprehension while students read.
- Use the Reading Check question to confirm comprehension.
- Develop students' understanding of figurative language using the Literary Analysis prompts.
- Develop students' ability to challenge or question the text using the Reading Strategy prompts.
- Reinforce vocabulary with the Vocabulary notes.
- Assess students' comprehension and mastery of the skills by having them answer the Critical Reading, Literary Analysis, and Reading Strategy questions.
- Have students complete the Vocabulary Lesson.

DAY 4 Extend/Assess

- Have students complete the Writing Lesson and write an evaluation of a philosophical essay. (You may assign as homework.)
- Administer Selection Test A or B (*Unit 2 Resources,* pp. 123–125 or 126–128).

Common Core State Standards

Reading Informational Text
4. Determine the meaning of words and phrases as they are used in the text, including figurative, connotative, and technical meanings.

Writing 2. Write explanatory texts to examine and convey complex ideas, concepts, and information clearly and accurately through the effective selection, organization, and analysis of content.
2.b. Develop the topic thoroughly by selecting the most significant and relevant facts, extended definitions, concrete details, quotations, or other information and examples appropriate to the audience's knowledge of the topic.

Language 5. Demonstrate understanding of word relationships.

Additional Standards Practice
Common Core Companion, *pp. 123–130; 196–207; 332–335*

Daily Block Scheduling
Each day in this Lesson Pacing Guide represents a 40–50 minute period. Teachers using block scheduling may combine days to revise pacing. In addition, teachers may differentiate and support core instruction by integrating components for extended and intensive support as students require. See the Guide to Selected Leveled Resources (facing page).

Guide to Selected Leveled Resources

R T I Tier 1 (students performing on level)

from Nature • from Self-Reliance • Concord Hymn

Warm Up		**Practice, model,** and **monitor** fluency, working **with the whole class** or **in groups.**	**Vocabulary and Reading Warm-ups B,** *Unit 2 Resources,* pp. 111–112, 114
Comprehension/Skills		**Support** and **monitor** comprehension and skills development, having students complete the activities, graphic organizers, and interactive prompts **independently** or **as a class.**	• *Reader's Notebook,* adapted instruction and summary **EL** *Reader's Notebook: English Learner's Version,* adapted instruction and summary • **Reading Strategy Graphic Organizer B,** *Graphic Organizer Transparencies,* p. 79 • **Literary Analysis Graphic Organizer B,** *Graphic Organizer Transparencies,* p. 81
Monitor Progress	**A**	**Monitor** student progress with the differentiated curriculum-based assessment in the *Unit Resources.*	• **Selection Test B,** *Unit 2 Resources,* pp. 126–128 • **Open-Book Test,** *Unit 2 Resources,* pp. 120–122

R T I Tier 2 (students requiring intervention)

from Nature • from Self-Reliance • Concord Hymn

Warm Up		**Practice, model,** and **monitor** fluency **in groups** or **with individuals.**	• **Vocabulary and Reading Warm-ups A,** *Unit 2 Resources,* pp. 111–113 • *Hear It!* **Audio CD**
Comprehension/Skills		• **Support** and **monitor** comprehension and skills development, working **in small groups** or **with individuals.** • As students complete the selection in the appropriate version of the *Reader's Notebook,* **monitor** comprehension frequently with group questions and individual instruction. • **Model** strategies while guiding students in completing the activities and prompts in the *Reader's Notebook,* as well as the graphic organizers. • **Practice** skills and **monitor** mastery with the *Reading Kit* worksheets.	• *Reader's Notebook: Adapted Version,* adapted instruction and summary **EL** *Reader's Notebook: English Learner's Version,* adapted instruction and summary • **Reading Strategy Graphic Organizer A,** *Graphic Organizer Transparencies,* p. 78 • **Literary Analysis Graphic Organizer A,** *Graphic Organizer Transparencies,* p. 80 • *Reading Kit,* Practice worksheets
Monitor Progress	**A**	**Monitor** student progress with the differentiated curriculum-based assessment in the *Unit Resources* and in the *Reading Kit.*	• **Selection Test A,** *Unit 2 Resources,* pp. 123–128 • *Reading Kit,* Assess worksheets

TIER 3 Tier 3 intervention may require consultation with the student's special-education or dyslexia specialist. For additional support, see the Tier 2 activities and resources listed above.

One-on-one teaching   Group work   Whole-class instruction   Independent work   **A** Assessment

For a complete guide to selection support, including support for Advanced students, see the Overview of Resources in the frontmatter.

from Nature • from Self-Reliance • Concord Hymn

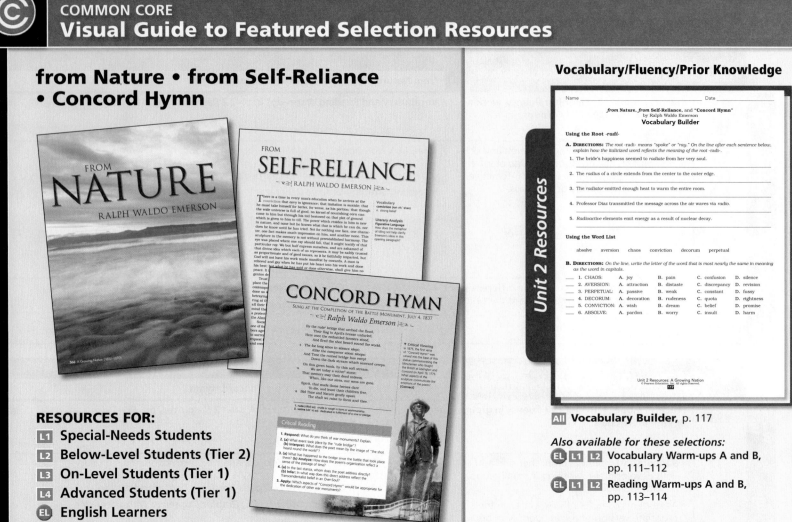

RESOURCES FOR:

- **L1** Special-Needs Students
- **L2** Below-Level Students (Tier 2)
- **L3** On-Level Students (Tier 1)
- **L4** Advanced Students (Tier 1)
- **EL** English Learners
- **All** All Students

Vocabulary/Fluency/Prior Knowledge

All Vocabulary Builder, p. 117

Also available for these selections:

EL **L1** **L2** Vocabulary Warm-ups A and B, pp. 111–112

EL **L1** **L2** Reading Warm-ups A and B, pp. 113–114

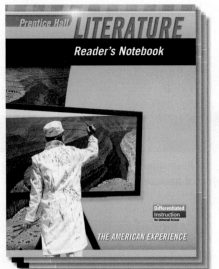

Reader's Notebooks

Pre- and postreading pages for these selections appear in an interactive format in the *Reader's Notebooks.* Each *Notebook* is differentiated for a different group of learners. The selections in the Adapted and English Learner's versions are abridged.

L2 **L3** *Reader's Notebook*

L1 *Reader's Notebook: Adapted Version*

EL *Reader's Notebook: English Learner's Version*

EL *Reader's Notebook: Spanish Version*

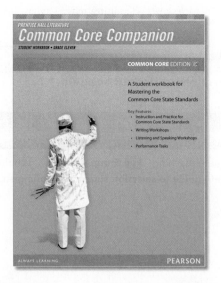

© *Common Core Companion*

Additional instruction and practice for each Common Core State Standard

Selection Support

from *Nature*, from *Self-Reliance*, and "Concord Hymn"
by Ralph Waldo Emerson

Before You Read B: Challenging the Text

Emerson's Statement

Evidence from the text

Your experiences

Your reaction

Graphic Organizer Transparencies

EL **L3** **Reading: Graphic Organizer B,** p. 79

Also available for these selections:

EL **L1** **L2** **Reading: Graphic Organizer A,** (partially filled in), p. 78

EL **L1** **L2** **Literary Analysis: Graphic Organizer A,** (partially filled in), p. 80

EL **L3** **Literary Analysis: Graphic Organizer B,** p. 81

Skills Development/Extension

Name _____ Date _____

from *Nature*, from *Self-Reliance*, and "Concord Hymn"
by Ralph Waldo Emerson

Reading Strategy: Challenging, or Questioning, the Text

One way to gain more understanding of a work is to **challenge the text**, or **question** the author's assertions. Here are some guidelines:

- Identify the author's opinions and restate them in your own words.
- Evaluate the examples, reasons, or other evidence the author provides to support his or her opinions.
- Consider other evidence that supports or refutes the author's opinions.
- On the basis of the evidence, decide if you agree or disagree with the author.

DIRECTIONS: Read the following passage from *Self-Reliance*. Then challenge the text by performing the numbered activities below. Write your responses on the lines provided.

Society everywhere is in conspiracy against the manhood of every one of its members. Society is a joint-stock company in which the members agree for the better securing of his bread to each shareholder, to surrender the liberty and culture of the eater. The virtue in most request is conformity. Self-reliance is its aversion. It loves not realities and creators, but names and customs.

1. Restate Emerson's basic opinion about society.

2. Identify and evaluate the evidence Emerson uses to support that opinion.

3. Provide examples from everyday life to support and refute Emerson's opinion of society.
   Support: _____

   Refute: _____

Unit 2 Resources

All **Reading: Challenging or Questioning the Text,** p. 116

Also available for these selections:

All **Literary Analysis: Figurative Language,** p. 115

EL **L3** **L4** **Support for Writing,** p. 118

L4 **Enrichment,** p. 119

Assessment

Name _____ Date _____

from *Nature*, from *Self-Reliance*, and "Concord Hymn" by Ralph Waldo Emerson

Open-Book Test

Short Answer *Write your responses to the questions in this section on the lines provided.*

1. What figurative language does Emerson use near the beginning of *Nature* to show that a person becomes younger in the presence of the natural world?

2. Read the sentence in the first paragraph of *Nature* that begins "There I feel that nothing can befall me in life-no disgrace . . . ." From this sentence, which of his senses is most important to Emerson in his experience of the natural world? Why do you think so?

3. When Emerson says in *Nature* that he becomes "a transparent eyeball," what is he communicating through this descriptive image?

4. Do you agree with Emerson's statement in *Nature* that "Nature is a setting that fits equally well a comic or mourning piece?" Explain what he means and state whether you agree or disagree.

5. In the sentence from *Nature*, "In good health, the air is a cordial of incredible virtue," what literary form does Emerson use? What two things does he compare?

L3 **L4** **Open-Book Test,** pp. 120–122

Also available for these selections:

EL **L1** **L2** **Selection Test A,** pp. 123–125

EL **L3** **L4** **Selection Test B,** pp. 126–128

PHLit Online!
www.PHLitOnline.com

Online Resources: All print materials are also available online.

- complete narrated selection text
- a thematically related video with writing prompt
- an interactive graphic organizer
- highlighting feature
- access to all student print resources, adapted to individual student needs
- Spanish and English summaries
- adapted selection translations in Spanish

Get Connected! (thematic video with writing prompt)

Also available:

Background Video
All videos are available in Spanish.

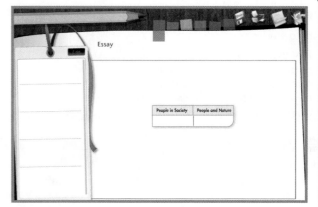

Writer's Journal (with graphics feature)

Also available:

Vocabulary Central (tools and activities for studying vocabulary)

❶ 🔲 Connecting to the Essential Question

1. Review the assignment with the class.

2. Invite students to think of ways in which school, jobs, family, and friends impose conformity on a person.

3. As students read, have them note passages about the difficulty of being true to oneself.

❷ Literary Analysis

Introduce the skills, using the instruction on the student page.

Think Aloud: Model the Skill

Say to students:

The sentence "As I rode past the orchard, I saw many hands plucking the juicy, golden balls off the branches" is describing a place with fruit trees. The phrase *juicy, golden balls* says what the fruit is like, so it's a metaphor, but it's also an image. The word *hands* refers to the workers, using a part to stand for the whole, an example of synecdoche.

❸ Reading Strategy

1. Introduce the strategy, using the instruction on the student page.

2. Give students a copy of **Reading Strategy Graphic Organizer B**, page 79 in *Graphic Organizer Transparencies,* to fill out as they read.

Think Aloud: Model the Skill

Say to students:

Emerson says that nature makes a person feel better. Some people don't like the country. Others don't have access to natural places. I'm going to reserve judgment.

❹ Vocabulary

1. Pronounce each word, giving its definition, and have students say it aloud.

2. For more guidance, see the *Classroom Strategies and Teaching Routines* card for introducing vocabulary.

© COMMON CORE ▪ EXTENDED STUDY: TRANSCENDENTALISM

Before You Read
from *Nature* • from *Self-Reliance* • *Concord Hymn*

❶ **Connecting to the Essential Question** Emerson's ideas about individualism were radical to many people during his lifetime and remain challenging to many people today. As you read, look for passages in which Emerson alludes to the difficulty of being true to oneself. This will help as you consider the Essential Question: **How does literature shape or reflect society?**

❷ ## Literary Analysis

Figurative language, which is also called **figures of speech,** is language that is used imaginatively instead of literally. Types of figurative language include the following:

- **Metaphor:** a stated similarity between two or more unlike things that does not use the words "*like*" or "*as*"
  Example: "Society is a joint-stock company."

- **Synecdoche:** the use of a part of something to stand for the whole
  Example: "the shot heard round the world" [The shot stands in for the whole of the Revolutionary War and the spread of American revolutionary ideals.]

In both his poetry and prose, Emerson uses metaphor and synecdoche to clarify ideas and stir readers' emotions. He also uses **imagery,** or word pictures, and is sensitive to the *sounds of words.* For example, the long *e* sounds in the phrase "the dark stream which seaward creeps" add to the beauty of the image. As you read, notice how figures of speech, images, and sound affect what you understand and feel about Emerson's ideas.

❸ ## Reading Strategy

© **Preparing to Read Complex Texts** As you read, check your understanding of Emerson's ideas by **challenging,** or **questioning,** the text. To do so, do not simply accept his arguments and evidence but evaluate them against your own experiences and other reading. As you read, use a chart like the one shown to record your challenges or questions and responses.

❹ ## Vocabulary

perpetual (pər pech′ ōō əl) *adj.* lasting forever (p. 367)

decorum (di kōr′ rəm) *n.* rightness; suitability (p. 367)

tranquil (traṇ′ kwəl) *adj.* calm, quiet, still (p. 368)

conviction (kən vik′ shən) *n.* strong belief (p. 369)

chaos (kā′ äs′) *n.* disorder of matter and space, supposed to have existed before the ordered universe (p. 369)

aversion (ə vʉr′ zhən) *n.* object arousing an intense dislike (p. 369)

absolve (ab zälv′) *v.* pardon; free from guilt (p. 370)

© **Common Core State Standards**

Reading Informational Text
4. Determine the meaning of words and phrases as they are used in the text, including figurative, connotative, and technical meanings.
Language
5.a. Interpret figures of speech in context and analyze their role in the text.

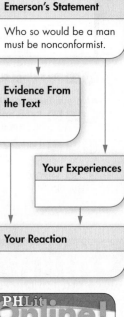

Emerson's Statement

Who so would be a man must be nonconformist.

Evidence From the Text

Your Experiences

Your Reaction

www.PHLitOnline.com

Vocabulary Development

Vocabulary Knowledge Rating
Create a **Vocabulary Knowledge Rating Chart** (in *Professional Development Guidebook,* p. 33) for the vocabulary words on the student page. Give each student a copy of the chart with the words on it. Read the words aloud and have students mark their rating in the Before Reading column. Urge students to attend to these words as they read and discuss the selections.

In order to gauge how much instruction you need to provide, tally how many students are confident in their knowledge of each word. As students read, point out the words and their context.

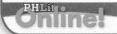 **Vocabulary Central,** featuring tools and activities for studying vocabulary, is available online at www.PHLitOnline.com.

⑤ RALPH WALDO EMERSON (1803–1882)

Author of "Nature" • "Self-Reliance" • "Concord Hymn"

Individuality, independence, and an appreciation for the wonders of nature are just a few of the principles that Ralph Waldo Emerson helped to instill in our nation's identity. Although his ideas were sometimes considered controversial, they continue to inspire people to this day. Throughout his life, Emerson's mind was constantly in motion, generating new ideas and defining and redefining his view of the world. His natural eloquence in expressing these ideas—in essays, lectures, and poetry—makes him one of the most quoted writers in American literature.

A New England Childhood The son of a Unitarian minister, Emerson was born in Boston. When Emerson was seven, his father died. The boy turned to a brilliant aunt, Mary Moody Emerson, who encouraged his independent thinking. At fourteen, Emerson entered Harvard, where he began the journal he was to keep all his life. After postgraduate studies at Harvard Divinity School, he became pastor of the Second Church of Boston.

Finding His Niche Emerson's career as a minister was short-lived. Grief-stricken at the death of his young wife, and dissatisfied with Unitarianism, Emerson resigned after three years. He then went to Europe, where he met the English writers Thomas Carlyle, Samuel Taylor Coleridge, and William Wordsworth. On his return to the United States, Emerson settled in Concord, Massachusetts. He married Lydia Jackson of Plymouth and began to write seriously. Slowly, the Emerson household began to welcome a widening circle of friends and admirers that included many of the country's most important thinkers. In time, Emerson became widely sought as a lecturer.

Emerson first achieved national fame in 1841, when he published *Essays*, a collection based on material from his journals and lectures. He went on to publish several more volumes of nonfiction, including *Essays, Second Volume* (1844), *Representative Men* (1849), and *The Conduct of Life* (1860).

Though Emerson was known mostly for his essays and lectures, he considered himself a poet. "I am born a poet," he once wrote, "of a low class without doubt, yet a poet. That is my nature and my vocation." He published two successful volumes of poetry, *Poems* (1847) and *May-Day and Other Pieces* (1867). Like his essays, Emerson's poems express his beliefs in individuality and in humanity's spiritual connection to nature.

from Nature • from Self-Reliance • Concord Hymn **365**

⟐ Daily Bellringer
For each class during which you will teach these selections, have students complete one of the five activities for the appropriate week in the *Daily Bellringer Activities* booklet.

● Multidraft Reading
To assist struggling readers and to enhance reading for all, assign the text in chunks as warranted by length and apply multidraft reading protocols. For each reading, have students set the purpose indicated:
- **First reading**—identifying key ideas and details and answering any Reading Checks.
- **Second reading**—analyzing craft and structure and responding to the side-column prompts.
- **Third reading**—integrating knowledge and ideas, connecting to other texts and the world, and answering the end-of-selection questions.

For more guidance, refer to the *Classroom Strategies and Teaching Routines* card, **Multidraft Reading.**

⑤ Background
More About the Author
Emerson published the ninety-five-page book *Nature* anonymously in Boston. It predates *The Dial*—the journal of the Transcendentalist Club—by four years. Almost everything Emerson wrote after *Nature* amplified or extended the ideas that appeared in it.

PHLit Online! www.PHLitOnline.com — Teaching From Technology

Preparing to Read
Go to **www.PHLitOnline.com** in class or in a lab and display the Get Connected! slide show for these selections. Have the class brainstorm for responses to the slide show writing prompt, entering ideas in the interactive journal. Then have students complete their written responses individually in a lab or as homework.

To build background, display the More About the Author feature.

Using the Interactive Student Edition
Go to **www.PHLitOnline.com** and display the **Enriched Online Student Edition.** As the class reads the selections or listens to the narration, record answers to side-column prompts using the graphic organizers accessible on the interactive page. Alternatively, have students use the online edition individually, answering the prompts as they read.

❶ About the Selection

In this excerpt from his book *Nature,* Emerson expresses his belief that the meaning of existence can be found by exploring the natural world. He describes how, through his exploration of nature, he has discovered that he is spiritually connected with the universe, with God, and with every living thing.

❷ Activating Prior Knowledge

Ask students about the different experiences they have had with nature, such as walking on the beach or in the woods, visiting a zoo, or listening to the wind and rain during a hurricane. Ask them what they thought or felt while in nature and what role human beings have in the natural world. Tell them that in "Nature," Emerson explains his view of the relationship individuals have with the natural world.

Concept Connector ➡

Tell students they will return to their responses after reading the selection.

❶ ❷ FROM

NATURE

RALPH WALDO EMERSON

366 A Growing Nation (1800–1870)

Ⓒ Text Complexity Rubric

	from Nature; Self-Reliance	Concord Hymn
Qualitative Measures		
Context/ Knowledge Demands	Nineteenth-century essays 1 ② 3 4 5	American Revolution 1 ② 3 4 5
Structure/Language Conventionality and Clarity	Formal diction 1 2 ③ 4 5	Poetic diction and syntax 1 2 ③ 4 5
Levels of Meaning/ Purpose/Concept Level	Transcendentalism; nonconformity 1 2 ③ 4 5	Accessible (bravery) 1 ② 3 4 5
Quantitative Measures		
Lexile/Text Length	960L; 980L / 487, 579 words	NP / 109 words
Overall Complexity	**More accessible**	**More accessible**

Reader and Task Suggestions

Preparing to Read the Text

- Use the Background information on SE pp. 365 and 367 to introduce Emerson's works.
- Ask students what they think it means to be "true to oneself." Ask: Is it easier or harder to be "true to oneself" in modern times?
- Guide students to use Multidraft Reading Strategies (TE p. 641).

Leveled Tasks

Structure/Language If students will have difficu[lty] with diction and vocabu[u]lary, have them jot dow[n] questions on first readin[g]. Then, have them reread [to] answer the questions.

Evaluating If students w[ill] not have difficulty with language, ask them whi[ch] essay had a greater imp[act] on their own thinking.

BACKGROUND *During the 1830s and 1840s, Emerson and a small group of like-minded friends gathered regularly in his study to discuss philosophy, religion, and literature. Among them were Emerson's protégé, Henry David Thoreau, as well as educator Bronson Alcott, feminist writer Margaret Fuller, and ex-clergyman and author George Ripley. The intimate group, known as the Transcendental Club, developed a philosophical system that stressed intuition, individuality, and self-reliance. In 1836, Emerson published Nature, the lengthy essay excerpted here that became the Transcendental Club's unofficial statement of belief.*

Nature is a setting that fits equally well a comic or a mourning piece. In good health, the air is a cordial of incredible virtue. Crossing a bare common,[1] in snow puddles, at twilight, under a clouded sky, without having in my thoughts any occurrence of special good fortune, I have enjoyed a perfect exhilaration. I am glad to the brink of fear. In the woods, too, a man casts off his years, as the snake his slough, and at what period soever of life is always a child. In the woods is perpetual youth. Within these plantations of God, a decorum and sanctity reign, a perennial festival is dressed, and the guest sees not how he should tire of them in a thousand years. In the woods, we return to reason and faith. There I feel that nothing can befall me in life—no disgrace, no calamity (leaving me my eyes), which nature cannot repair. Standing on the bare ground—my head bathed by the blithe air and uplifted into infinite space—all mean egotism vanishes. I become a transparent eyeball; I am nothing; I see all; the currents of the Universal Being circulate through me; I am part or parcel of God. The name of the nearest friend

---

1. **common** *n.* piece of open public land.

4 ◀ **Critical Viewing** What different emotions might the natural setting shown in this photograph evoke in people? Explain. **[Interpret]**

3  **Reading Check**
What effect does Emerson believe nature has on all people regardless of age?

from Nature **367**

Questioning the Text

1. Remind students not to take what a writer says at face value but to compare it with their own experience and what they have read elsewhere.

2. Read aloud the bracketed passage. Discuss the way in which a walk in nature is both a new experience and an old, familiar one.

3. Then **ask** students the Reading Strategy question: What question or challenge might you pose about Emerson's idea that one is not alone in nature?
Answer: Students may question whether plants can be companions in the same way other people or even animals are.

ASSESS

Answers

Before students respond, you may wish to have them write a brief objective summary of the selection. As they answer the questions below, remind them to support their answers with evidence from the text.

1. (a) It vanishes in the woods. (b) Students should identify it as petty narcissism. (c) It is replaced with divinity and delight.

2. (a) He becomes this after he sheds "mean egotism" amidst nature. (b) He feels connected to nature and to God. (c) Emerson, like everyone and everything, is connected to the Universal Being.

3. (a) It comes from a harmony of man and nature. (b) **Possible response:** He means that it is forever linked and intertwined but not necessarily that it is serene.

Vocabulary
tranquil (tran´ kwəl)
adj. calm, quiet, still

Reading Strategy
Questioning the Text ❺
What question or challenge might you pose to Emerson's idea that one is not alone in nature?

---

sounds then foreign and accidental: to be brothers, to be acquaintances, master or servant, is then a trifle and a disturbance. I am the lover of uncontained and immortal beauty. In the wilderness, I find something more dear and connate than in the streets or villages. In the tranquil landscape, and especially in the distant line of the horizon, man beholds somewhat as beautiful as his own nature.

The greatest delight which the fields and woods minister is the suggestion of an occult relation between man and the vegetable. I am not alone and unacknowledged. They nod to me, and I to them. The waving of the boughs in the storm is new to me and old. It takes me by surprise, and yet is not unknown. Its effect is like that of a higher thought or a better emotion coming over me, when I deemed I was thinking justly or doing right.

Yet it is certain that the power to produce this delight does not reside in nature, but in man, or in a harmony of both. It is necessary to use these pleasures with great temperance. For nature is not always tricked[2] in holiday attire, but the same scene which yesterday breathed perfume and glittered as for the frolic of the nymphs is overspread with melancholy today. Nature always wears the colors of the spirit. To a man laboring under calamity, the heat of his own fire hath sadness in it. Then there is a kind of contempt of the landscape felt by him who has just lost by death a dear friend. The sky is less grand as it shuts down over less worth in the population.

---

2. **tricked** *v.* dressed.

Cite textual evidence to support your responses.

Critical Reading

© **1. Key Ideas and Details** Under what circumstances, according to Emerson, does "mean egotism" vanish? **(b) Define:** How would you define Emerson's idea of "mean egotism"? **(c) Analyze Cause and Effect:** In nature, what emotion does Emerson believe replaces "mean egotism"?

© **2. Key Ideas and Details (a)** When does Emerson become a "transparent eyeball"? **(b) Analyze:** What are the characteristics of this experience? **(c) Connect:** In what ways does this description reflect Transcendentalist belief in an Over-Soul?

© **3. Integration of Knowledge and Ideas (a)** Where does the power to produce nature's delight come from? **(b) Define:** In describing a harmony between human beings and nature, do you think Emerson means the relationship is always serene? Explain.

---

368 A Growing Nation (1800–1870)

Enrichment: Analyzing a Historical Event

Emerson's Abolitionist Views

After the passage of the Fugitive Slave Act, which required people to return runaway slaves to their owners, Emerson became an active abolitionist. He remarked that anyone building a house should include space in it for fugitive slaves. Prompt students to discuss how Emerson's position relates to his statement in "Self-Reliance" that "nothing is at last sacred but the integrity of your own mind."
Activity: Group Roundtable Have students find out more about the details of the

Fugitive Slave Act and the Compromise of 1850. Suggest that they record information in the **Enrichment: Analyzing a Historical Event** work sheet, *Professional Development Guidebook,* page 230. Have small groups explain the views of those who supported slavery or cooperated with the law, and abolitionists. Then discuss why Emerson's Transcendentalist beliefs might have spurred him to become an abolitionist.

❻ FROM

SELF-RELIANCE

⌐⌐☙ RALPH WALDO EMERSON ☙⌐⌐

❼ There is a time in every man's education when he arrives at the conviction that envy is ignorance; that imitation is suicide; that he must take himself for better, for worse, as his portion; that though the wide universe is full of good, no kernel of nourishing corn can come to him but through his toil bestowed on that plot of ground which is given to him to till. The power which resides in him is new in nature, and none but he knows what that is which he can do, nor does he know until he has tried. Not for nothing one face, one character, one fact makes much impression on him, and another none. This sculpture in the memory is not without preestablished harmony. The eye was placed where one ray should fall, that it might testify of that particular ray. We but half express ourselves, and are ashamed of that divine idea which each of us represents. It may be safely trusted as proportionate and of good issues, so it be faithfully imparted, but God will not have his work made manifest by cowards. A man is relieved and gay when he has put his heart into his work and done his best; but what he has said or done otherwise, shall give him no peace. It is a deliverance which does not deliver. In the attempt his genius deserts him; no muse befriends; no invention, no hope.

Trust thyself: every heart vibrates to that iron string. Accept the place the divine providence has found for you; the society of your contemporaries, the connection of events. Great men have always done so and confided themselves childlike to the genius of their age, betraying their perception that the absolutely trustworthy was stirring at their heart, working through their hands, predominating in all their being. And we are now men, and must accept in the highest mind the same transcendent destiny; and not minors and invalids in a protected corner, but guides, redeemers, and benefactors. Obeying the Almighty effort and advancing on chaos and the Dark. . . .

Society everywhere is in conspiracy against the manhood of every one of its members. Society is a joint-stock company in which the members agree for the better securing of his bread to each shareholder, to surrender the liberty and culture of the eater. The virtue in most request is conformity. Self-reliance is its aversion. It loves not realities and creators, but names and customs.

Vocabulary
conviction (kən vik´ shən)
n. strong belief

Literary Analysis
Figurative Language
How does the metaphor of tilling soil help clarify Emerson's ideas in this opening paragraph?

Vocabulary
chaos (kā´ äs´) *n.* disorder of matter and space, supposed to have existed before the ordered universe

aversion (ə vur´ zhən) *n.* object arousing an intense dislike

❽ ☑ Reading Check

According to Emerson, what have great men always done?

from Self-Reliance **369**

---

❻ **About the Selection**
In his essay "Self-Reliance," which echoes a theme common to many of his works, Emerson exhorts readers to avoid blindly conforming to the ideas and behavior dictated by society or peers. Instead, he urges people to think and act independently.

In the poem "Concord Hymn," Emerson celebrates country and nature, praising the bravery of the minutemen who fought at Lexington and Concord. The poem conveys the message that people who make great sacrifices for noble causes such as freedom will never be forgotten.

❼ **Literary Analysis**
Figurative Language
1. Remind students that metaphors are comparisons that do not use *like* or *as* and that synecdoche is a figure of speech that uses a part to stand for the whole.

2. Read the paragraph with the class and discuss Emerson's ideas that every person has a God-given job to do that no one else can do, that doing that job brings happiness and satisfaction, and that a person receives no inspiration if he or she tries to do any other job.

3. **Ask** students the Literary Analysis question: How does the metaphor of tilling soil help clarify Emerson's ideas in this opening paragraph?
Answer: Tilling serves as an example of work in a field of endeavor (soil) that brings satisfaction or nourishment. Some students may say Emerson is using synecdoche.

❽ **Reading Check**
Answer: According to Emerson, great men have always trusted that God put them in the best possible time and place for them to realize their talents.

369

Answers

Before students respond, you may wish to have them write a brief objective summary of the selection. As they answer the questions below, remind them to support their answers with evidence from the text.

1. (a) He describes it as a joint-stock company. (b) Its purpose is to conspire against individual self-reliance. (c) People should not care how others perceive them.

2. (a) For Emerson, the divine is God's idea of what each of us might be if we had the courage to live up to our full creative potential. (b) **Possible response:** He would say that the reason for living is to seek out God's purpose for us and to pursue it without fear of society's pressures and opinions. Students' explanations should be supported with references from the text.

3. (a) It is important because it distinguishes between a rational consistency of thought and purpose and an unreasoning, compulsory conformity. (b) **Possible response:** Emerson clearly says that a foolish consistency is to be avoided. He would be unlikely to advocate inconsistency in scholarship, for example, or in friendships or family life.

4. **Possible response:** In the last paragraph excerpted from "Nature," Emerson points out that the power to experience God lies in the individual and in his or her <u>agreement</u> with nature, and that his or her experience is colored by his or her feelings. In the second paragraph from "Self-Reliance," Emerson affirms that all human beings have an individual purpose given to them by God. Students will probably say that Emerson is rejecting <u>conformity</u> to the ideas and behavior code of his <u>society</u> and attempting to reflect the <u>integrity</u> of the individual.

Vocabulary
absolve (ab zälv´) *v.* pardon; free from guilt

Whoso would be a man must be a nonconformist. He who would gather immortal palms must not be hindered by the name of goodness, but must explore if it be goodness. Nothing is at last sacred but the integrity of your own mind. Absolve you to yourself, and you shall have the suffrage of the world. . . .

A foolish consistency is the hobgoblin of little minds, adored by little statesmen and philosophers and divines. With consistency a great soul has simply nothing to do. He may as well concern himself with his shadow on the wall. Speak what you think now in hard words and tomorrow speak what tomorrow thinks in hard words again, though it contradict everything you said today. "Ah, so you shall be sure to be misunderstood?"—is it so bad, then, to be misunderstood? Pythagoras was misunderstood, and Socrates, and Jesus, and Luther, and Copernicus, and Galileo, and Newton,[1] and every pure and wise spirit that ever took flesh. To be great is to be misunderstood. . . .

1. **Pythagoras ... Newton** individuals who made major contributions to scientific, philosophical, or religious thinking.

Critical Reading

Cite textual evidence to support your responses.

1. **Key Ideas and Details (a)** What terms does Emerson use to describe society? **(b) Interpret:** According to Emerson, what is society's main purpose? **(c) Draw Conclusions:** In what ways does Emerson believe people should be affected by the way others perceive them?

2. **Key Ideas and Details (a) Interpret:** According to Emerson, what role does the "divine" have in determining each person's circumstances? **(b) Generalize:** What would Emerson say is each person's reason for living? Explain.

3. **Craft and Structure (a) Make a Judgment:** How important is Emerson's use of the adjective "foolish" in his discussion of consistency? **(b) Speculate:** Do you think there are any circumstances in which Emerson would advocate the benefits of consistency? Explain.

4. **Integration of Ideas and Knowledge** Which passage in these essays best expresses belief in the importance of the individual? Explain the reasons for your choice. In your response, use at least two of these Essential Question words: *conformity, integrity, society, agreement.* [Connecting to the Essential Question: *What makes American literature American?*]

370 A Growing Nation (1800–1870)

Vocabulary Development

Vocabulary Knowledge Rating
When students have completed reading and discussing these selections, have them take out the **Vocabulary Knowledge Rating** charts for the selections. Read the words aloud and have students rate their knowledge of the words again in the After Reading column. Clarify any words that are still problematic. Have students write their own definitions and example or sentence in the appropriate column. Then have students complete the Vocabulary Lesson at the end of the selections. Encourage them to use the words in further discussion and written work about the selections. Remind them that they will be accountable for these words on the **Selection Test,** *Unit 2 Resources,* pages 123–125 or 126–128.

CONCORD HYMN

SUNG AT THE COMPLETION OF THE BATTLE MONUMENT, JULY 4, 1837

Ralph Waldo Emerson

By the rude[1] bridge that arched the flood,
    Their flag to April's breeze unfurled,
Here once the embattled farmers stood,
    And fired the shot heard round the world.

The foe long since in silence slept;
    Alike the conqueror silent sleeps;
And Time the ruined bridge has swept
    Down the dark stream which seaward creeps.

On this green bank, by this soft stream,
    We set today a votive[2] stone;
That memory may their deed redeem,
    When, like our sires, our sons are gone.

Spirit, that made those heroes dare
    To die, and leave their children free,
Bid Time and Nature gently spare
    The shaft we raise to them and thee.

---

1. **rude** (rōōd) *adj.* crude or rough in form or workmanship.
2. **votive** (vōt´ iv) *adj.* dedicated in fulfillment of a vow or pledge.

Critical Reading ©

1. Key Ideas and Details (a) What event took place by the "rude bridge"? **(b) Interpret:** What does the poet mean by the image of "the shot heard round the world"?

2. Craft and Structure (a) What has happened to the bridge since the battle that took place there? **(b) Analyze:** How does the poem's organization reflect a sense of the passage of time?

3. Craft and Structure (a) In the last stanza, whom does the poet address directly? **(b) Infer:** In what way does this direct address reflect the Transcendentalist belief in an Over-Soul?

4. Integration of Knowledge and Ideas Apply: Which aspects of "Concord Hymn" would be appropriate for the dedication of other war monuments?

9 ▼ Critical Viewing
In 1875, the first verse of "Concord Hymn" was carved into the base of this statue commemorating the Minutemen who fought the British at Lexington and Concord on April 19, 1775. What aspects of the sculpture communicate the emotions of the poem? **[Connect]**

Cite textual evidence to support your responses.

Concord Hymn **371**

Answers

1. (a) **Possible responses:**
Students may suggest: from "Nature," "nature is not always tricked in holiday attire"; and from "Self-Reliance," "a foolish consistency is the hobgoblin of little minds." (b) Emerson means that nature does not always make people feel better and that only small-minded people are consistent; people with great minds may change them with time. (c) Students may say that Emerson wants to evoke a sense of personal power and responsibility.

2. (a) *Heart* stands for *person*. (b) Emerson is saying that in their hearts, all people feel a personal call.

3. The image suggests that the speaker not only sees all but also can blend with everything around him, merging into the universal Over-Soul.

4. Emerson is using a metaphor. A plantation is a large, carefully planted farm. Emerson is saying that Earth is God's farm, which he has carefully planted with trees and other plants.

5. Both phrases suggest that Emerson believed in a God who had some role in creating both humans and nature.

6. (a) **Possible responses:**
Students may suggest, for imagery, "Down the dark stream which seaward creeps"; for metaphor, "the conqueror silent sleeps"; and for synecdoche, "shot heard round the world." (b) The first two figures use the present tense, giving a sense of continuity. The "shot" resulted in the creation of the country where the reader lived.

7. (a) In nature, a person lets go of cares and worries as smoothly as a snake slides out of its old skin. (b) The repeated *s* sound focuses attention on the snake metaphor, emphasizing the meaning of the sentence.

After You Read

from *Nature* • from *Self-Reliance*
• *Concord Hymn*

Literary Analysis

1. **Craft and Structure (a)** Identify one **metaphor** in each essay. **(b)** Explain the abstract idea each metaphor helps Emerson express in concrete terms. **(c)** What emotion do you think Emerson hopes to evoke with each example? Explain.

2. **Craft and Structure (a)** Explain Emerson's use of **synecdoche** in this passage: "Trust thyself: every heart vibrates to that iron string." **(b)** How does this use of synecdoche help to clarify Emerson's point about belief in oneself?

3. **Craft and Structure** Does the **image** of the "transparent eyeball" effectively convey the Transcendentalist idea of a universal Over-Soul? Explain.

4. **Craft and Structure** In "Nature," Emerson describes the woods as the "plantations of God." What type of figurative language is he using? Explain your thinking.

5. **Key Ideas and Details** In "Self-Reliance," Emerson describes "that divine idea which each of us represents." How do that phrase and the one noted in question 4 represent similar ideas about the relationship of God to nature and people?

6. **Craft and Structure** "Concord Hymn" commemorates events that happened more than sixty years before the poem was written. **(a)** Note one example each of imagery, metaphor, and synecdoche in the poem. **(b)** Explain how each example helps bring the events of the past and the passage of time to life in the reader's mind.

7. **Craft and Structure (a)** Restate the meaning of this sentence: "In the woods, too, a man casts off his years, as the snake his slough." **(b)** How does the repeated *s* sound in the phrase "snake his slough" add to the meaning?

8. **Craft and Structure (a)** Use a chart like the one shown to compare and contrast Emerson's descriptions of the bonds between people in society and those between people and nature. **(b)** Which bonds would Emerson say are more important? Explain.

People in Society	People and Nature

Reading Strategy

9. **Challenge or question the text** by answering the questions below about this statement from "Self-Reliance": "Nature always wears the colors of the spirit."
   (a) What evidence does Emerson provide to support this statement?
   (b) Is this evidence convincing? Explain.
   (c) What argument can you make against this statement?
   (d) What argument can you make in support of this statement?

 **Common Core State Standards**

Writing
2. Write explanatory texts to examine and convey complex ideas, concepts, and information clearly and accurately through the effective selection, organization, and analysis of content. *(p. 373)*
2.b. Develop the topic thoroughly by selecting the most significant and relevant facts, extended definitions, concrete details, quotations, or other information and examples appropriate to the audience's knowledge of the topic. *(p. 373)*

Language
5. Demonstrate understanding of word relationships. *(p. 373)*

8. (a) Emerson suggests that social ties are largely expedients for material survival, whereas our relationship to nature binds us to the spiritual foundation of life.
(b) Emerson seems to think that our bonds to nature transcend personal relationships. Another sample answer can be found on **Literary Analysis Graphic Organizer A**, page 80 in *Graphic Organizer Transparencies.*

9. (a) Nature presents a different aspect to people in trouble or grief. **Sample answers:** (b) Emerson's evidence is too subjective to be convincing. (c) Some unhappy people find solace in nature. (d) Some people find their own moods reflected in nature.

Integrated Language Skills

© Vocabulary Acquisition and Use

Word Analysis: Latin Prefix *ab-*

The word *absolve* includes the Latin prefix *ab-* meaning "away" or "from." This prefix contributes to the meaning of *absolve,* which means to take guilt away from someone. When Emerson exhorts his readers to "Absolve you to yourself," he urges them to release themselves from their own guilt or shame.

Explain how the prefix *ab-* relates to the meaning of each of the words below. If any of the words are unfamiliar, refer to a dictionary to clarify their meanings.

1. abnormal   4. abrupt
2. absorb   5. abduct
3. abscond   6. abhor

Writing

© Explanatory Text Ever since they were first published, Emerson's essays have stirred argument and inspired admiration. Now, it is your turn to add your voice. Write a **critical evaluation** of "Self-Reliance." Include a summary of Emerson's points, an assessment of his uses of *stylistic devices,* such as imagery and figurative language, and a statement of your opinion.

Prewriting Reread the excerpt from "Self-Reliance," noting key ideas, images, and uses of figurative language from the beginning, middle, and end. Then, write one sentence that summarizes Emerson's argument and another sentence that states your opinion about his presentation.

Drafting State the goals of your essay in your introduction. Then, write your summary of Emerson's essay. Follow the summary with a statement of your opinion of his ideas and how he presents them. Support your ideas with accurate and detailed citations from the text.

> **Model: Using Relevant Citations**
> Emerson pays tribute to the value of being true to oneself. While most of us would agree with him in theory, how many of us withstand the pressures to conform? Emerson notes, "The virtue in most request is conformity."
>
> Citations specific to the argument keep the writing focused.

Revising As you revise, highlight any citations that do not effectively support your point. Replace weak citations with more relevant support.

Extended Study: Integrated Language Skills **373**

Vocabulary: Categorize Vocabulary

Review the vocabulary list on page 364. Then, study each item below to categorize each group of words as all synonyms or as a mixture of antonyms and synonyms. If necessary, consult a dictionary. Then, explain your reasoning.

1. chaos, order, clarity
2. conviction, principle, tenet
3. aversion, enticement, attraction
4. absolve, blame, castigate
5. decorum, propriety, politeness
6. perpetual, temporary, impermanent
7. tranquil, turbulent, moderate

Assessment Resources

Unit 2 Resources

L1 L2 EL **Selection Test A,** pp. 123–125. Administer Test A to less advanced students and English learners.

L3 L4 EL **Selection Test B,** pp. 126–128. Administer Test B to on-level or more advanced students.

L3 L4 **Open-Book Test,** pp. 120–122. As an alternative, administer the Open-Book Test

All **Customizable Test Bank**

All **Self-tests**
Students may prepare for the **Selection Test** by taking the **Self-test** online.

PHLit Online! All assessment resources are available at **www.PHLitOnline.com.**

Vocabulary Acquisition and Use

1. Introduce the skill, using the instruction on the student page.
2. Have students complete the Word Analysis activity and the Vocabulary practice.

Word Analysis

1. Something *abnormal* moves away from what is normal.
2. To *absorb* is to take away something from where it is.
3. To *abscond* is to run away.
4. An *abrupt* action or speech is sudden; it breaks away from what preceded it.
5. To *abduct* is to take away.
6. To *abhor* is to shrink away from something in disgust.

Vocabulary

1. antonyms and synonyms: *chaos* and *order* are opposites, and something chaotic lacks *clarity; order* is clear organization.
2. synonyms: a *conviction, principle,* or *tenet* is a rule one lives by.
3. antonyms and synonyms: an *aversion* is a strong dislike, the opposite of an *enticement* or *attraction,* which lures someone.
4. antonyms and synonyms: to *absolve* is to forgive, to *blame* or *castigate* is to accuse and scold.
5. synonyms: *decorum, propriety,* and *politeness* indicate good behavior.
6. antonyms and synonyms: *perpetual* is forever, but *temporary* and *impermanent* mean "short-lived."
7. antonyms and synonyms: *turbulent* means "violent," but *tranquil* and *moderate* mean "mild."

Writing

1. To guide students in writing this explanatory text, give them the Support for Writing page (*Unit 2 Resources,* p. 118).
2. Evaluate students' essays using the **Rubrics for Response to Literature,** in *Professional Development Guidebook,* pages 250–251.

from Walden • from Civil Disobedience
Lesson Pacing Guide

DAY 1 Preteach

- ⓒ Administer the Reading and Vocabulary Warm-ups (*Unit 2 Resources*, pp. 131–134) as necessary.
- ⓒ Introduce the Literary Analysis concepts: Author's Style and Metaphor.
- • Introduce the Reading Strategy: Analyze philisophical assumptions.
- ⓒ Build background with the author and Background features.
- • Develop thematic thinking with Connecting to the Essential Question.
- ⓒ Teach the selection vocabulary.

DAYS 2–3 Preteach/Teach/Assess

- • Distribute copies of the appropriate graphic organizer for the Reading Strategy (*Graphic Organizer Transparencies*, pp. 82–83).
- • Distribute copies of the appropriate graphic organizer for Literary Analysis (*Graphic Organizer Transparencies*, pp. 84–85).
- • Prepare students to read with the Activating Prior Knowledge activities (TE).
- • Informally monitor comprehension while students read.
- • Use the Reading Check question to confirm comprehension.
- ⓒ Develop students' understanding of author's style and metaphor using the Literary Analysis prompts.
- • Develop students' ability to analyze philosophical assumptions using the Reading Strategy prompts.
- ⓒ Reinforce vocabulary with the Vocabulary notes.
- • Assess students' comprehension and mastery of the skills by having them answer the Critical Reading, Literary Analysis, and Reading Strategy questions.
- ⓒ Have students complete the Vocabulary Lesson.

DAY 4 Extend/Assess

- ⓒ Have students complete the Writing Lesson and write an Editorial. (You may assign as homework.)
- ⓒ Have students read and respond to the Contemporary Commentary
- • Administer Selection Test A or B (*Unit 2 Resources*, pp. 143–145 or 146–148).

ⓒ Common Core State Standards

Reading Informational Text 1. Cite strong and thorough textual evidence to support analysis of what the text says explicitly as well as inferences drawn from the text, including determining where the text leaves matters uncertain.
4. Determine the meaning of words and phrases as they are used in the text, including figurative meanings; analyze how an author uses and refines the meaning of a key term or terms over the course of a text.

Writing 1. Write arguments to support claims in an analysis of substantive topics or texts, using valid reasoning.

Language 4.b. Identify and correctly use patterns of word changes that indicate different meanings.
5. Demonstrate understanding of figurative language, word relationships, and nuances in word meanings.
5.a. Interpret figures of speech in context and analyze their role in the text.

Additional Standards Practice
Common Core Companion, pp. 2–9, 41–48; 185–195; 324–335

Daily Block Scheduling
Each day in this Lesson Pacing Guide represents a 40–50 minute period. Teachers using block scheduling may combine days to revise pacing. In addition, teachers may differentiate and support core instruction by integrating components for extended and intensive support as students require. See the Guide to Selected Leveled Resources (facing page).

Guide to Selected Leveled Resources

R T I Tier 1 (students performing on level)

from Walden • *from* Civil Disobedience

Warm Up	Practice, model, and monitor fluency, working with the whole class or in groups.	Vocabulary and Reading Warm-ups B, *Unit 2 Resources*, pp. 131–132, 134
Comprehension/Skills	Support and monitor comprehension and skills development, having students complete the activities, graphic organizers, and interactive prompts independently or as a class.	• *Reader's Notebook,* adapted instruction and summary EL *Reader's Notebook: English Learner's Version,* adapted instruction and summary • Reading Strategy Graphic Organizer B, *Graphic Organizer Transparencies,* p. 83 • Literary Analysis Graphic Organizer B, *Graphic Organizer Transparencies,* p. 85
Monitor Progress	Monitor student progress with the differentiated curriculum-based assessment in the *Unit Resources.*	• Selection Test B, *Unit 2 Resources,* pp. 146–148 • Open-Book Test, *Unit 2 Resources,* pp. 140–142
Assess/ Screen	Assess student progress using Benchmark Test 3.	• Benchmark Test 3, *Unit 2 Resources,* pp. 149–154

R T I Tier 2 (students requiring intervention)

from Walden • *from* Civil Disobedience

Warm Up	Practice, model, and monitor fluency in groups or with individuals.	• Vocabulary and Reading Warm-ups A, *Unit 2 Resources,* pp. 131–133 • *Hear It!* Audio CD
Comprehension/Skills	• Support and monitor comprehension and skills development, working in small groups or with individuals. • As students complete the selection in the appropriate version of the *Reader's Notebook,* monitor comprehension frequently with group questions and individual instruction. • Model strategies while guiding students in completing the activities and prompts in the *Reader's Notebook,* as well as the graphic organizers. • Practice skills and monitor mastery with the *Reading Kit* worksheets.	• *Reader's Notebook: Adapted Version,* adapted instruction and summary EL *Reader's Notebook: English Learner's Version,* adapted instruction and summary • Reading Strategy Graphic Organizer A, *Graphic Organizer Transparencies,* p. 82 • Literary Analysis Graphic Organizer A, *Graphic Organizer Transparencies,* p. 84 • *Reading Kit,* Practice worksheets
Monitor Progress	Monitor student progress with the differentiated curriculum-based assessment in the *Unit Resources* and in the *Reading Kit.*	• Selection Test A, *Unit 2 Resources,* pp. 143–145 • *Reading Kit,* Assess worksheets
Assess/ Screen	Assess student progress using the Benchmark Test 1.	• Benchmark Test 4, *Unit 2 Resources,* pp. 149–154

TIER 3 Tier 3 intervention may require consultation with the student's special-education or dyslexia specialist. For additional support, see the Tier 2 activities and resources listed above.

One-on-one teaching   Group work   Whole-class instruction   Independent work   A Assessment

For a complete guide to selection support, including support for Advanced students, see the Overview of Resources in the frontmatter.

from Walden
• *from* Civil Disobedience

RESOURCES FOR:

L1 Special-Needs Students

L2 Below-Level Students (Tier 2)

L3 On-Level Students (Tier 1)

L4 Advanced Students (Tier 1)

EL English Learners

All All Students

Vocabulary/Fluency/Prior Knowledge

EL L1 L2 Vocabulary Warm-ups A and B, pp. 131–132

Also available for these selections:

EL L1 L2 Reading Warm-ups A and B, pp. 133–134

All Vocabulary Builder, p. 137

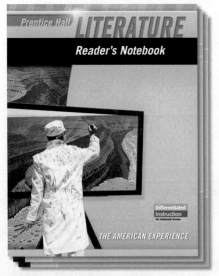

Reader's Notebooks

Pre- and postreading pages for these selections, as well as an excerpt from *Walden*, appear in an interactive format in the *Reader's Notebooks*. Each *Notebook* is differentiated for a different group of learners. The selections in the Adapted and English Learner's versions are abridged.

L2 L3 *Reader's Notebook*

L1 *Reader's Notebook: Adapted Version*

EL *Reader's Notebook: English Learner's Version*

EL *Reader's Notebook: Spanish Version*

© *Common Core Companion*

Additional instruction and practice for each Common Core State Standard

Selection Support

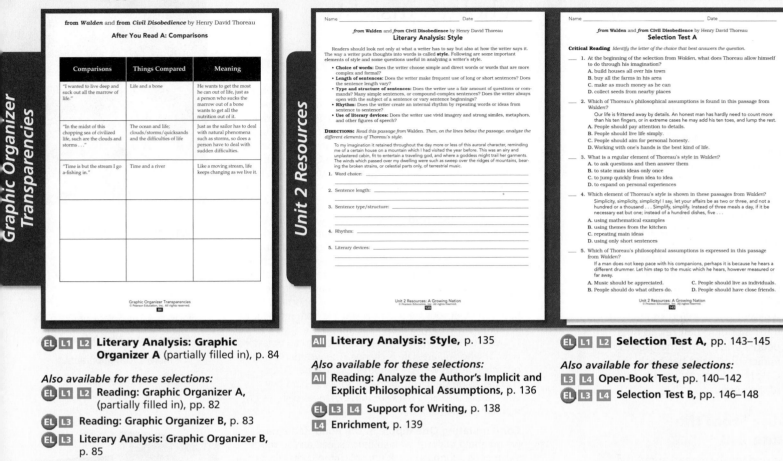

Graphic Organizer Transparencies

from Walden and *from Civil Disobedience* by Henry David Thoreau

After You Read A: Comparisons

Comparisons	Things Compared	Meaning
"I wanted to live deep and suck out all the marrow of life."	Life and a bone	He wants to get the most he can out of life, just as a person who sucks the marrow out of a bone wants to get all the nutrition out of it.
"In the midst of this chopping sea of civilized life, such as the clouds and storms . . ."	The ocean and life; clouds/storms/quicksands and the difficulties of life	Just as the sailor has to deal with natural phenomena such as storms, so does a person have to deal with sudden difficulties.
"Time is but the stream I go a-fishing in."	Time and a river	Like a moving stream, life keeps changing as we live it.

EL L1 L2 Literary Analysis: Graphic Organizer A (partially filled in), p. 84

Also available for these selections:

EL L1 L2 Reading: Graphic Organizer A, (partially filled in), pp. 82

EL L3 Reading: Graphic Organizer B, p. 83

EL L3 Literary Analysis: Graphic Organizer B, p. 85

Skills Development/Extension

Unit 2 Resources

Name _____ Date _____

from Walden and *from Civil Disobedience* by Henry David Thoreau
Literary Analysis: Style

Readers should look not only at what a writer has to say but also at how the writer says it. The way a writer puts thoughts into words is called **style.** Following are some important elements of style and some questions useful in analyzing a writer's style.

- **Choice of words:** Does the writer choose simple and direct words or words that are more complex and formal?
- **Length of sentences:** Does the writer make frequent use of long or short sentences? Does the sentence length vary?
- **Type and structure of sentences:** Does the writer use a fair amount of questions or commands? Many simple sentences, or compound-complex sentences? Does the writer always open with the subject of a sentence or vary sentence beginnings?
- **Rhythm:** Does the writer create an internal rhythm by repeating words or ideas from sentence to sentence?
- **Use of literary devices:** Does the writer use vivid imagery and strong similes, metaphors, and other figures of speech?

DIRECTIONS: *Read this passage from Walden. Then, on the lines below the passage, analyze the different elements of Thoreau's style.*

To my imagination it retained throughout the day more or less of this auroral character, reminding me of a certain house on a mountain which I had visited the year before. This was an airy and unplastered cabin, fit to entertain a traveling god, and where a goddess might trail her garments. The winds which passed over my dwelling were such as sweep over the ridges of mountains, bearing the broken strains, or celestial parts only, of terrestrial music.

1. Word choice: _____

2. Sentence length: _____

3. Sentence type/structure: _____

4. Rhythm: _____

5. Literary devices: _____

All Literary Analysis: Style, p. 135

Also available for these selections:

All Reading: Analyze the Author's Implicit and Explicit Philosophical Assumptions, p. 136

EL L3 L4 Support for Writing, p. 138

L4 Enrichment, p. 139

Assessment

Name _____ Date _____

from Walden and *from Civil Disobedience* by Henry David Thoreau
Selection Test A

Critical Reading *Identify the letter of the choice that best answers the question.*

_____ 1. At the beginning of the selection from *Walden,* what does Thoreau allow himself to do through his imagination?
A. build houses all over his town
B. buy all the farms in his area
C. make as much money as he can
D. collect seeds from nearby places

_____ 2. Which of Thoreau's philosophical assumptions is found in this passage from *Walden*?
Our life is frittered away by details. An honest man has hardly need to count more than his ten fingers, or in extreme cases he may add his ten toes, and lump the rest.
A. People should pay attention to details.
B. People should live life simply.
C. People should aim for personal honesty.
D. Working with one's hands is the best kind of life.

_____ 3. What is a regular element of Thoreau's style in *Walden*?
A. to ask questions and then answer them
B. to state main ideas only once
C. to jump quickly from idea to idea
D. to expand on personal experiences

_____ 4. Which element of Thoreau's style is shown in these passages from *Walden*?
Simplicity, simplicity, simplicity! I say, let your affairs be as two or three, and not a hundred or a thousand . . . Simplify, simplify. Instead of three meals a day, if it be necessary eat but one; instead of a hundred dishes, five . . .
A. using mathematical examples
B. using themes from the kitchen
C. repeating main ideas
D. using only short sentences

_____ 5. Which of Thoreau's philosophical assumptions is expressed in this passage from *Walden*?
If a man does not keep pace with his companions, perhaps it is because he hears a different drummer. Let him step to the music which he hears, however measured or far away.
A. Music should be appreciated.
B. People should do what others do.
C. People should live as individuals.
D. People should have close friends.

EL L1 L2 Selection Test A, pp. 143–145

Also available for these selections:

L3 L4 Open-Book Test, pp. 140–142

EL L3 L4 Selection Test B, pp. 146–148

PHLit Online!
www.PHLitOnline.com

Online Resources: All print materials are also available online.

- complete narrated selection text
- a thematically related video with writing prompt
- an interactive graphic organizer
- highlighting feature
- access to all student print resources, adapted to individual student needs
- Spanish and English summaries
- adapted selection translations in Spanish

Background Video

Also available:

Get Connected! (thematic video with writing prompt)
All videos are available in Spanish

Writer's Journal (with graphics feature)

Also available:

Vocabulary Central (tools and activities for studying vocabulary)

1. You might wish to have students reread Gretel Ehrlich's introduction to this unit on pages 223–224.

2. Ehrlich, an eloquent nature writer, comments on Henry David Thoreau's great and influential work, *Walden* (page 379).

3. Have students read the introductory paragraph about Ehrlich. She lived a number of years in Greenland, a place of great and desolate beauty. Living in such an environment was influential to her work; many of her books carry naturalistic themes.

4. Use the *See It!* DVD to introduce Ehrlich. Show Segment 2 to provide insight into her writing. After students have watched the segment, **ask:** What does the writing of Gretel Ehrlich reveal about her attitude toward nature?
   Answer: Her writing shows that understanding nature can help people understand themselves. Ehrlich organized her book *This Cold Heaven* according to seasons of the year.

Living From the Inside Out

After students have read about the effect of Thoreau's writing on Ehrlich, **ask:** What does Ehrlich mean when she talks about living "from the inside out"?
Answer: She means that people should focus their energies on taking in the world, thinking about it, and responding to it rather than being distracted by external forces, such as the quest for status or material goods.

Themes Across Centuries: Scholar's Insights

Gretel Ehrlich
Introduces *Walden* by Henry David Thoreau

When I was in high school, my parents took me to look at colleges on the East Coast, and on that trip, we visited Walden Pond. I'd bought a collection of Thoreau's essays at a bookstore in Boston, and standing at the edge of the pond, I read *Walden.* My parents had lived nearby before I was born, but I grew up on the central California coast. Thoreau's landscape was not familiar to me, and yet the ideas he expressed in his book-length essay *Walden* spoke to me as no others had.

Living From the Inside Out An essay is essentially a way of asking a question. It is an attempt to understand the nature of things: the human condition and the natural world. Thoreau's questions to me, the reader, asked me to think about where I lived and how I lived in that place. That "owning" land or a house is not as important as becoming friends with that place. That rich and poor are unimportant, but that how you meet your life and how you live from moment to moment, day to day, is most important of all.

Living comes from the inside out, not from an outsider's view of who you are. Life is change. The weather changes, our relationships with one another change; our bodies change. To be static is to be dead. To live in harmony with nature means to roll with those changes daily, yearly, moment by moment.

Contemplating One Ripple in the Pond These days we go about our lives with so much speed and so much extraneous information that it's difficult to contemplate just one thing, one sight, one evening or morning, one ripple in the pond. Thoreau would have us simplify, slow down, become quiet, and burrow into the heart of things with our minds. Not to "dumb down," but the opposite: to stop, listen, and see; to turn off the monologue in our minds; to erase our idea about how things are; to live in others' shoes.

Building a Fire in the Mind Thoreau would have us think like a river, a pond, a tree, another animal or human; to adopt their point of view instead of our own; to build a fire in the mind with real wood and a match that cannot be extinguished. Then, the fresh, dawnlike nature of things—what

Meet the Author

Gretel Ehrlich is the author of more than a dozen works of nonfiction, fiction, and poetry, including *The Solace of Open Spaces* and *A Match to the Heart.* For more information about Ehrlich, see page 222.

Teaching Resources

The following resources can be used to enrich or extend the instruction for Contemporary Commentary.

Unit 2 Resources
Contemporary Commentary, p. 129
Listening and Viewing, p. 130

See It! DVD
Gretel Ehrlich, Segment 2

PHLit Online!   All resources are available at www.PHLitOnline.com.

Thoreau calls "the auroral character"—will keep radiating, piercing the difficulties in our lives with new songs. A hut in the woods, a still pond, a fresh breeze: these morning winds carry poems, music, love, and loss into our days. Not a dreaminess, but the direct experience of life as it is.

Marching to a Different Drummer Thoreau encourages us to advance confidently in the direction of our dreams. He encourages each of us to be our own person—distinct, unique, thoughtful, precise, and passionate about what we love in the world. It is good to march to "a different drummer," if that's where our feet take us. To live fully, deeply, profoundly, unafraid to be ourselves—this is advice that travels forward for centuries, through all our lives.

▲ **Critical Viewing**
What details in this early hand-painted photograph of Walden Pond capture what Thoreau calls "the auroral character" of the setting? **[Connect]**

Critical Reading

1. Key Ideas and Details (a) What do Thoreau's questions ask Ehrlich—and all readers—to think about? **(b) Interpret:** In what way might Thoreau's questions help readers live "from the inside out"?

2. Key Ideas and Details (a) What would Thoreau have people do in a complex world? **(b) Speculate:** How might following Thoreau's advice change the way you live in the twenty-first century?

As You Read the excerpt from *Walden* . . .

3. Integration of Knowledge and Ideas Consider what relevance Thoreau's ideas have in today's world and in your own life.

4. Integration of Knowledge and Ideas Think about the ways in which Ehrlich's commentary enriches your understanding of specific passages in Thoreau's essays.

Cite textual evidence to support your responses.

Extended Study: Transcendentalism **375**

---

❶ Connecting to the Essential Question

1. Review the assignment with the class.

2. Invite students to explain what they consider a simple life. Then have them complete the assignment.

3. As students read, have them notice details that show Thoreau's goals and values.

❷ Literary Analysis

Introduce the skills, using the instruction on the student page.

Think Aloud: Model the Skill

Say to students:

When Thoreau says, "The life in us is like the water in the river. It may rise this year higher than man has ever known it, and flood the parched uplands," he seems to be saying that life is unpredictable. But he's talking about the "life *in* us," and that implies our thoughts and feelings. Thoreau is using figurative expressions to tell us that our inner life is what satisfies us.

❸ Reading Strategy

1. Introduce the strategy, using the instruction on the student page.

2. Give students a copy of **Reading Strategy Graphic Organizer B,** page 83 in *Graphic Organizer Transparencies,* to fill out as they read.

Think Aloud: Model the Skill

Say to students:

Thoreau says, "I heartily accept the motto that 'government is best which governs least'; and I should like to see it acted up to more rapidly and systematically." Thoreau is explicitly stating his philosophical position. I have to see how he supports that assumption to decide if he's right.

❹ Vocabulary

1. Pronounce each word, giving its definition, and have students say it aloud.

2. For more guidance, see the **Classroom Strategies and Teaching Routines** card for introducing vocabulary.

Before You Read
from *Walden* ●
from *Civil Disobedience*

❶ Connecting to the Essential Question In *Walden*, one of the most famous philosophical works in American literature, Thoreau explains his aim to live a simple life. As you read, look for details that demonstrate Thoreau's goals and values. This will help as you reflect on the Essential Question: **How does literature shape or reflect society?**

❷ Literary Analysis

An **author's style** is the unique manner in which he or she puts thoughts into words. Elements of style include an author's *diction*, or word choice, and *syntax*, or arrangement of words in sentences. Thoreau's style has a conversational **tone,** or attitude, as though he is talking to a friend. This aspect of his style serves his purpose of enlightening the reader without seeming to lecture or scold. Thoreau also "thinks" in images, often using a series of **figurative expressions** to develop ideas. For example, in *Walden,* Thoreau explains that modern life is too complex. He illustrates the point with a series of concrete examples:

- First, he uses a **metaphor,** a figure of speech that shows a similarity between two or more unlike things without using the words "like" or "as": *In the midst of this chopping sea of civilized life, such are the clouds and storms and quicksands . . .*

- Next, he uses an **analogy,** an extended comparison of relationships: *"Our life is like a German Confederacy, made up of petty states . . ."*

As you read, notice how these elements help to enhance Thoreau's ideas.

❸ Reading Strategy

Ⓒ **Preparing to Read Complex Texts** As a reader, you are not obligated to accept everything you see in print. When reading essays of opinion, **analyze the author's implicit and explicit philosophical assumptions**. Implicit ideas are only suggested, while explicit ideas are directly stated. First, ask yourself what fundamental beliefs the author holds about life. Then, identify the support the author provides. Decide if that support is convincing. As you read, use a chart like the one shown to analyze Thoreau's philosophical assumptions.

❹ Vocabulary

dilapidated (də lap′ ə dāt′ id) *adj.* in disrepair (p. 381)

sublime (sə blīm′) *adj.* noble; majestic (p. 383)

superfluous (sə pʉr′ flōō əs) *adj.* excessive; not necessary (p. 383)

magnanimity (mag′ nə nim′ ə tē) *n.* generosity (p. 386)

expedient (ek spē′ dē ənt) *n.* resource (p. 388)

alacrity (ə lak′ rə tē) *n.* speed (p. 389)

376 A Growing Nation (1800–1870)

Ⓒ Common Core State Standards

Reading Informational Text

1. Cite strong and thorough textual evidence to support analysis of what the text says explicitly as well as inferences drawn from the text, including determining where the text leaves matters uncertain.

4. Determine the meaning of words and phrases as they are used in the text, including figurative meanings; analyze how an author uses and refines the meaning of a key term or terms over the course of a text.

Language

5.a. Interpret figures of speech in context and analyze their role in the text.

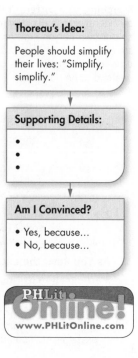

Thoreau's Idea:

People should simplify their lives: "Simplify, simplify."

Supporting Details:

- •
- •
- •

Am I Convinced?

- Yes, because…
- No, because…

PHLit Online!
www.PHLitOnline.com

Vocabulary Development

Vocabulary Knowledge Rating

Create a **Vocabulary Knowledge Rating Chart** (in *Professional Development Guidebook,* p. 33) for the vocabulary words on the student page. Give each student a copy of the chart with the words on it. Read the words aloud and have students mark their rating in the Before Reading column. Urge students to attend to these words as they read and discuss the selections.

In order to gauge how much instruction you need to provide, tally how many students are confident in their knowledge of each word. As students read, point out the words and their context.

 **Vocabulary Central,** featuring tools and activities for studying vocabulary, is available online at **www.PHLitOnline.com.**

❺ Henry David Thoreau

(1817–1862)

Author of *Walden* and "Civil Disobedience"

Henry David Thoreau was known by his Concord, Massachusetts, neighbors as an eccentric. As a child he rarely followed rules and was independent and strong-willed. He pursued a formal education at his mother's insistence. Thoreau attended Concord Academy, a college preparatory school, and later enrolled at Harvard University. Although Harvard's dress code required students to wear black coats, Thoreau wore a green one.

Questioning Authority When his objections to corporal punishment forced him to quit his first teaching job, Thoreau and his older brother John opened their own school in Concord. The school was successful, but they had to close it when John became ill.

In 1841, Thoreau moved into the house of another famous Concord resident, Ralph Waldo Emerson. He lived there for two years, performing odd jobs to pay for his room and board. Fascinated by Emerson's Transcendentalist ideas, Thoreau became Emerson's friend and disciple. Rather than return to teaching, he decided to devote his energies to exploring the spiritual relationship between humanity and nature and to living by his political and social beliefs.

On Walden Pond From 1845 to 1847, Thoreau lived alone in a one-room cabin he built at Walden Pond near Concord. This experience provided him with the material for his masterwork, *Walden* (1854). A blend of natural observation, social criticism, and philosophical insight, *Walden* is now generally regarded as the supreme work of Transcendentalist literature and one of the greatest examples of nature writing in American literature.

When he died of tuberculosis at the age of forty-four, Thoreau had received little public recognition. Only *A Week on the Concord and Merrimack Rivers* and some poems had been published—at his own expense—while he was alive. *The Maine Woods, Cape Cod,* and *A Yankee in Canada* were published posthumously. Nevertheless, Emerson knew that future generations would cherish Thoreau. Speaking at his funeral, Emerson said: "The country knows not yet, or in the least part, how great a son it has lost. . . . His soul was made for the noblest society; he had in a short life exhausted the capabilities of this world; wherever there is knowledge, wherever there is virtue, wherever there is beauty, he will find a home."

"Be true to your work, your word, and your friend."

from Walden **377**

Daily Bellringer

For each class during which you will teach these selections, have students complete one of the five activities for the appropriate week in the *Daily Bellringer Activities* booklet.

Multidraft Reading

To assist struggling readers and to enhance reading for all, assign the text in chunks as warranted by length and apply multidraft reading protocols. For each reading, have students set the purpose indicated:

- **First reading**—identifying key ideas and details and answering any Reading Checks.
- **Second reading**—analyzing craft and structure and responding to the side-column prompts.
- **Third reading**—integrating knowledge and ideas, connecting to other texts and the world, and answering the end-of-selection questions.

For more guidance, refer to the *Classroom Strategies and Teaching Routines* card, **Multidraft Reading.**

❺ Background

More About the Author

In "Civil Disobedience," Thoreau questions the government's right to tell him what to do. In life, he also questioned its right to tax him, especially when those taxes supported policies with which he disagreed. In 1846 Thoreau put his beliefs into practice by refusing to pay taxes that might in some way support policies to which he objected. For this passive resistance, Thoreau spent one night in jail.

PHLit Online!
www.PHLitOnline.com

Teaching From Technology

Preparing to Read
Go to **www.PHLitOnline.com** in class or in a lab and display the **Get Connected!** slide show for this grouping. Have the class brainstorm for responses to the slide show writing prompt, entering ideas in the interactive journal. Then have students complete their written responses individually in a lab or as homework.

To build background, display the More About the Author feature.

Using the Interactive Student Edition
Go to **www.PHLitOnline.com** and display the **Enriched Online Student Edition.** As the class reads the selections or listens to the narration, record answers to side-column prompts using the graphic organizers accessible on the interactive page. Alternatively, have students use the online edition individually, answering the prompts as they read.

❶ About the Selection

Walden was published in 1854, seven years after Thoreau's two-year residence at Walden Pond. During the intervening years, Thoreau reflected upon and revised the journals he had kept at Walden. A celebration of life and nature, *Walden* presents Thoreau's views on society and his philosophy of life. In the sections that follow, Thoreau expresses the belief that society has become too complex and fast paced and that people should do everything possible to simplify their lives. He also stresses the need to resist conformity and to follow our own inner voices.

❷ Activating Prior Knowledge

Remind students that Transcendentalism focuses on gaining spiritual knowledge through recognizing one's connection to God and nature. Transcendentalists tried to simplify their lives and live according to basic principles. Have students imagine that they are about to spend some time alone in the wilderness. Ask them to tell what essentials they would bring with them other than necessities such as food and shelter. Prompt them to predict what the experience would be like, physically, emotionally, and spiritually. Invite students who have spent any time in the wilderness to tell about it. Explain that the works they are about to read are drawn from the ideas and philosophy Thoreau developed while voluntarily living a life of rustic isolation.

Concept Connector ➡

Tell students they will return to their responses after reading the selection.

378 A Growing Nation (1800–1870)

Ⓒ Text Complexity Rubric

	from **Walden**	*from* **Civil Disobedience**
Qualitative Measures		
Context/ Knowledge Demands	Transcendentalism; literary knowledge demands **1 2 3 ④ 5**	Nineteenth-century individualism; historical knowledge demands **1 2 ③ 4 5**
Structure/Language Conventionality and Clarity	First-person narrative; formal language **1 2 ③ 4 5**	Some long sentences **1 2 ③ 4 5**
Levels of Meaning/ Purpose/Concept Level	Challenging (Transcendental philosophy) **1 2 3 ④ 5**	Accessible (political/social movements) **1 2 ③ 4 5**
Quantitative Measures		
Lexile/Text Length	1200L / 3,518 words	980L / 545 words
Overall Complexity	**More complex**	**More accessible**

❸ **Reading Check**

Answer: No, Thoreau was merely enjoying mental speculation about the land around him.

❹ **Critical Viewing**

Possible response: Students may respond that it must have been beautiful yet isolated. Others may say that it would be boring to live so far from society and modern conveniences.

❶ ❷ *from*

Walden

Henry David Thoreau

from **Where I Lived, and What I Lived For**

At a certain season of our life we are accustomed to consider every spot as the possible site of a house. I have thus surveyed the country on every side within a dozen miles of where I live. In imagination I have bought all the farms in succession, for all were to be bought, and I knew their price. I walked over each farmer's premises, tasted his wild apples, discoursed on husbandry[1] with him, took his farm at his price, at any price, mortgaging it to him in my mind; even put a higher price on it—took everything but a deed of it—took his word for his deed, for I dearly love to talk—cultivated it, and him too to some extent, I trust, and withdrew when I had enjoyed it long enough, leaving him to carry it on. This experience entitled me to be regarded as a sort of real-estate broker by my friends. Wherever I sat, there I might live, and the landscape radiated from me accordingly. What is a house but a *sedes*, a seat?—better if a country seat. I discovered many a site for a house not

❸ ✓ Reading Check

Did Thoreau truly intend to purchase a farm?

---

1. **husbandry** (huz´ bən drē) *n.* farming.

❹ ◀ **Critical Viewing** Based on this picture of Walden Pond, what do you think it would be like to live in such a place? **[Speculate]**

from Walden **379**

These selections are available in interactive format in the **Enriched Online Student Edition**, at **www.PHLitOnline.com**, which includes a thematically related video with writing prompt and an interactive graphic organizer.

Complexity: Reader and Task Suggestions

from Walden		*from* Civil Disobedience	
Read the Text	**Leveled Tasks**	**Preparing to Read the Text**	**Leveled Tasks**
nformation 77, discuss connection scendentalist . ts what they ans to live a e. ents to use Reading strate- pen their com- (TE p. 377).	*Levels of Meaning* If students will have difficulty with the meaning, have them recall the subtitle "Where I Lived, and What I Lived For" as they skim the excerpt. Then, have them reread to determine how "simple" living addresses both parts of that subtitle. *Synthesizing* If students will not have difficulty with the meaning, discuss whether a person today who attempted Thoreau's "simple" kind of life would reach the same conclusions.	• Using the Background information on TE p. 377, discuss the circumstances that inspired "Civil Disobedience." • Ask students how people today express disagreement with their governments. • Guide students to use Multidraft Reading strategies to deepen their comprehension (TE p. 377).	*Knowledge Demands* If students will have difficulty with context, have them review the headnote before they skim the excerpt. After students reread, have them explain why Thoreau disagreed with his government. *Analyzing* If students will not have difficulty with the context, discuss how Thoreau's confidence in the Amercian people, not the government, reflects his Transcendentalism.

Gretel Ehrlich
Scholar's Insight
Thoreau is saying that every rock is our home, every vista is ours to drink in. And as a result, the landscape comes into ❺ us, and pours out again as an image, a poem, a bit of music.

Literary Analysis
Author's Style and Metaphor Identify the metaphor Thoreau uses in ❻ this paragraph and the idea it helps him develop.

likely to be soon improved, which some might have thought too far from the village, but to my eyes the village was too far from it. Well, there might I live, I said; and there I did live, for an hour, a summer and a winter life; saw how I could let the years run off, buffet the winter through, and see the spring come in. The future inhabitants of this region, wherever they may place their houses, may be sure that they have been anticipated. An afternoon sufficed to lay out the land into orchard woodlot and pasture, and to decide what fine oaks or pines should be left to stand before the door, and whence each blasted tree could be seen to the best advantage; and then I let it lie, fallow[2] perchance, for a man is rich in proportion to the number of things which he can afford to let alone.

My imagination carried me so far that I even had the refusal of several farms—the refusal was all I wanted—but I never got my fingers burned by actual possession. The nearest that I came to actual possession was when I bought the Hollowell Place, and had begun to sort my seeds, and collected materials with which to make a wheelbarrow to carry it on or off with; but before the owner gave me a deed of it, his wife—every man has such a wife—changed her mind and wished to keep it, and he offered me ten dollars to release him. Now, to speak the truth, I had but ten cents in the world, and it surpassed my arithmetic to tell, if I was that man who had ten cents, or who had a farm, or ten dollars, or all together. However, I let him keep the ten dollars and the farm too, for I had carried it far enough; or rather, to be generous, I sold him the farm for just what I gave for it, and, as he was not a rich man, made him a present of ten dollars, and still had my ten cents, and seeds, and materials for a wheelbarrow left. I found thus that I had been a rich man without any damage to my poverty. But I retained the landscape, and I have since annually carried off what it yielded without a wheelbarrow. With respect to landscapes:

"I am monarch of all I *survey*,
My right there is none to dispute."[3]

I have frequently seen a poet withdraw, having enjoyed the most valuable part of a farm, while the crusty farmer supposed that he had got a few wild apples only. Why, the owner does not know it for many years when a poet has put his farm in rhyme, the most admirable kind of invisible fence, has fairly impounded it, milked it, skimmed it, and got all the cream, and left the farmer only the skimmed milk.

The real attractions of the Hollowell farm, to me, were: its complete retirement, being about two miles from the village, half a mile from the nearest neighbor, and separated from the highway by a broad field; its bounding on the river, which the owner said protected

---

2. **fallow** (fal´ ō) *adj.* left uncultivated or unplanted.
3. **"I . . . dispute"** from William Cowper's *Verses Supposed to Be Written by Alexander Selkirk.*

380 A Growing Nation (1800–1870)

Think Aloud

Reading Strategy: Analyzing the Author's Philosophical Assumptions

To model the process of using the strategy, use the following "think aloud." Say to students:

In the statement "a man is rich in proportion to the number of things which he can afford to let alone," Thoreau seems to be saying that the fewer things a person has to think about, the richer and freer that person's life will be. His underlying assumption seems to be that possessions and worldly concerns get in the way of true happiness.

But how many possessions and concerns are too many? Thoreau's examples so far are about how he imagined buying a farm and living in it but decided not to. He enjoys just taking in the landscape, but someone else might enjoy working the soil and growing living things. I'm not convinced by his idea yet; I have to see what else he says in support.

it by its fogs from frosts in the spring, though that was nothing to me; the gray color and ruinous state of the house and barn, and the dilapidated fences, which put such an interval between me and the last occupant; the hollow and lichen-covered apple trees, gnawed by rabbits, showing what kind of neighbors I should have; but above all, the recollection I had of it from my earliest voyages up the river, when the house was concealed behind a dense grove of red maples, through which I heard the house-dog bark. I was in haste to buy it, before the proprietor finished getting out some rocks, cutting down the hollow apple trees, and grubbing up some young birches which had sprung up in the pasture, or, in short, had made any more of his improvements. To enjoy these advantages I was ready to carry it on; like Atlas,[4] to take the world on my shoulders—I never heard what compensation he received for that—and do all those things which had no other motive or excuse but that I might pay for it and be unmolested in my possession of it; for I knew all the while that it would yield the most abundant crop of the kind I wanted if I could only afford to let it alone. But it turned out as I have said.

All that I could say, then, with respect to farming on a large scale (I have always cultivated a garden) was that I had had my seeds ready. Many think that seeds improve with age. I have no doubt that time discriminates between the good and the bad; and when at last I shall plant, I shall be less likely to be disappointed. But I would say to my fellows, once for all, As long as possible live free and uncommitted. It makes but little difference whether you are committed to a farm or the county jail.

Old Cato,[5] whose "De Re Rustica" is my "Cultivator," says, and the only translation I have seen makes sheer nonsense of the passage, "When you think of getting a farm, turn it thus in your mind, not to buy greedily; nor spare your pains to look at it, and do not think it enough to go round it once. The oftener you go there the more it will please you, if it is good." I think I shall not buy greedily, but go round and round it as long as I live, and be buried in it first, that it may please me the more at last. . . .

I do not propose to write an ode to dejection, but to brag as lustily as chanticleer[6] in the morning, standing on his roost, if only to wake my neighbors up.

When first I took up my abode in the woods, that is, began to spend my nights as well as days there, which, by accident, was on Independence Day, or the fourth of July, 1845, my house was not finished for winter, but was merely a defense against the rain, without plastering or chimney, the walls being of rough weatherstained boards, with wide chinks, which made it cool at night. The upright white hewn studs and freshly planed door and window casings gave

---

4. **Atlas** (at´ ləs) from Greek mythology, a Titan who supported the heavens on his shoulders.
5. **Old Cato** Roman statesman (234–149 B.C.). "De Re Rustica" is Latin for "Of Things Rustic."
6. **chanticleer** (chan´ tə klir´) n. rooster.

Vocabulary
dilapidated (də lap´ ə dāt´ id) *adj.* in disrepair

Reading Strategy
Analyzing the Author's Philosophical Assumptions
What do you think the idea of freedom means to Thoreau?

Reading Check
What were the "real attractions" of the Hollowell farm to Thoreau?

from Walden **381**

---

❼ Reading Strategy
Analyzing the Author's Philosophical Assumptions

1. Remind students they do not have to accept an author's philosophical assumptions at face value.

2. Have a volunteer read aloud the bracketed passage.

3. Then **ask** students the Reading Strategy question: What do you think the idea of freedom means to Thoreau?
   Possible response: Freedom for Thoreau means being able to come and go as he wishes.

4. **Ask:** What life appealed more to Thoreau, the life of a farmer or of a poet? Why?
   Answer: The life of a poet appealed more to Thoreau. As a poet, he could enjoy many farms, not just the one that he owned.

5. Encourage students to think about the underlying assumption behind the importance of freedom to Thoreau. Have them use a copy of the **Reading Strategy Graphic Organizer B,** page 83 in *Graphic Organizer Transparencies,* to analyze Thoreau's assumption. Charts should look like the following:

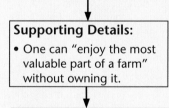

Thoreau's Ideas:
It makes but little difference whether you are committed to a farm or the county jail.

↓

Supporting Details:
• One can "enjoy the most valuable part of a farm" without owning it.

↓

Am I Convinced?
• Yes, because...

❽ Reading Check
Answer: Thoreau liked the farm because it was isolated and private.

Differentiated
Instruction for Universal Access

EL Pronunciation for English Learners

Write the words *found* and *pound* on the board. Tell students to listen carefully as you model the difference in pronunciation of the initial consonant. Then have them repeat the two words after you several times. Repeat the procedure with the words *few* and *pew*. Explain that students will read the words *found* and *few* on pages 380 and 381, along with the following words: *far, for, future, farm, fence, frequently, fairly, field, fog, from, frost, finished, free, fellows, first.* Pronounce each word and have students echo. Then go around in a circle, giving each student the opportunity to pronounce one of the words. Keep going around until all students have had the opportunity to practice pronouncing all the words.

381

1. Point out Ehrlich's comment on writers. **Ask** students if they agree with her idea that all writers must be students.
   Possible response: Students may agree with Ehrlich because writers must be open to all aspects of an experience. Better writing comes from those who let go of preconceptions.

2. After reading the excerpt from *Walden,* ask students if they feel Thoreau acted as a student of the world. Have them select passages that support their assertions.

❿ World Literature Connection

Mount Olympus

Elicit from students what they know about the Greek gods mentioned in the article. What symbols, traits, and roles are associated with each?

Connect to the Literature

After discussing the gods, **ask** the Connect to the Literature question: What attitude toward nature does Thoreau express with his metaphor about Olympus?
Possible response: Thoreau is expressing an almost reverent attitude toward nature, implying that the whole natural world is the home of the gods.

Gretel Ehrlich
Scholar's Insight
Thoreau comes to Walden Pond with a "beginner's mind." He allows the earth to instruct him in its ways, leaving preconceptions behind. That is how writers must approach all things, as a student of the world. **❾**

it a clean and airy look, especially in the morning, when its timbers were saturated with dew, so that I fancied that by noon some sweet gum would exude from them. To my imagination it retained throughout the day more or less of this auroral[7] character, reminding me of a certain house on a mountain which I had visited the year before. This was an airy and unplastered cabin, fit to entertain a traveling god, and where a goddess might trail her garments. The winds which passed over my dwelling were such as sweep over the ridges of mountains, bearing the broken strains, or celestial parts only, of terrestrial

---

7. **auroral** (ô rôr′ əl) *adj.* resembling the dawn.

---

❿ WORLD LITERATURE CONNECTION

MOUNT OLYMPUS

When Thoreau says, "Olympus is but the outside of the earth everywhere" he is referring to Mount Olympus, which is both a real mountain in northern Greece and the home of the gods and goddesses in Greek mythology. The ancient Greeks pictured their gods in human form with human flaws, so Olympus was not perfect. However, as a place of beauty, harmony, and enlightenment, it was more wonderful than anything mortals could achieve.

CONNECT TO THE LITERATURE

What attitude toward nature does Thoreau express with his metaphor about Olympus?

GREEK GODS

ZEUS:
KING OF THE GODS AND RULER OF HUMANITY ▶

APHRODITE:
GODDESS OF LOVE ▼

APOLLO:
GOD OF THE SUN AND MUSIC

ARES:
GOD OF WAR

HERMES:
GOD OF TRADE

POSEIDON:
GOD OF THE SEA

HADES:
GOD OF THE UNDERWORLD

382 A Growing Nation (1800–1870)

Enrichment: Investigating Popular Culture

Walden Pond Today

Today, tourists come from all over the world to visit Walden Pond. Some are drawn by its natural beauty, others by its literary significance. The pond and the surrounding forest are a public preserve, the Walden Pond State Reservation. There are guided walks along many paths, and visitors swim, boat, picnic, and hike. In summer, locals go to Walden to sunbathe on the beaches.

A re-creation of Thoreau's cabin stands a few dozen feet from the site of the original. In a tradition begun decades ago, visitors leave rocks and notes to Thoreau piled on the site.

Activity: Make a Brochure Have students gather information and images of Walden today. Suggest that they record the information in the **Enrichment: Investigating Popular Culture** work sheet, *Professional Development Guidebook*, page 238. Then have them prepare a brochure about Walden for distribution by tourist information centers.

music. The morning wind forever blows, the poem of creation is uninterrupted; but few are the ears that hear it. Olympus is but the outside of the earth everywhere. . . .

I went to the woods because I wished to live deliberately, to front only the essential facts of life, and see if I could not learn what it had to teach, and not, when I came to die, discover that I had not lived. I did not wish to live what was not life, living is so dear; nor did I wish to practice resignation, unless it was quite necessary. I wanted to live deep and suck out all the marrow of life, to live so sturdily and Spartanlike[8] as to put to rout all that was not life, to cut a broad swath and shave close, to drive life into a corner, and reduce it to its lowest terms, and, if it proved to be mean, why then to get the whole and genuine meanness of it, and publish its meanness to the world; or if it were sublime, to know it by experience, and be able to give a true account of it in my next excursion. For most men, it appears to me, are in a strange uncertainty about it, whether it is of the devil or of God, and have *somewhat hastily* concluded that it is the chief end of man here to "glorify God and enjoy him forever."[9]

Still we live meanly, like ants; though the fable tells us that we were long ago changed into men; like pygmies we fight with cranes:[10] it is error upon error, and clout upon clout, and our best virtue has for its occasion a superfluous and evitable wretchedness. Our life is frittered away by detail. An honest man has hardly need to count more than his ten fingers, or in extreme cases he may add his ten toes, and lump the rest. Simplicity, simplicity, simplicity! I say, let your affairs be as two or three, and not a hundred or a thousand; instead of a million count half a dozen, and keep your accounts on your thumbnail. In the midst of this chopping sea of civilized life, such are the clouds and storms and quicksands and thousand-and-one items to be allowed for, that a man has to live, if he would not founder and go to the bottom and not make his port at all, by dead reckoning,[11] and he must be a great calculator indeed who succeeds. Simplify, simplify. Instead of three meals a day, if it be necessary eat but one; instead of a hundred dishes, five; and reduce other things in proportion. Our life is like a German Confederacy,[12] made up of petty

---

8. **Spartanlike** like the people of Sparta, an ancient Greek state whose citizens were known to be hardy, stoical, simple, and highly disciplined.
9. **"glorify . . . forever"** the answer to the question "What is the chief end of man?" in the Westminster catechism.
10. **like . . . cranes** In the *Iliad*, the Trojans are compared to cranes fighting against pygmies.
11. **dead reckoning** navigating without the assistance of stars.
12. **German Confederacy** At the time, Germany was a loose union of thirty-nine independent states, with no common government.

from Walden **383**

Gretel Ehrlich
Scholar's Insight
Thoreau encourages us to face all that life brings to us, both its painful and beautiful sides. There cannot be one without the other.

Vocabulary
sublime (sə blīm´) *adj.* noble; majestic

superfluous (soo pur´ floo əs) *adj.* excessive; not necessary

Reading Check

Why did Thoreau go to the woods?

---

⑪ Scholar's Insight

1. Have a student read Ehrlich's note aloud to the class.
2. Discuss Thoreau's opinion that people should face the good and the bad in life. **Ask** students if they agree with this notion. **Possible response:** Students may feel that in order to appreciate the good, one must experience the bad.

⑫ Engaging the Essential Question

1. Remind students that Thoreau was testing Transcendentalist values by moving to Walden, stripping away the trappings of society, and living as close to nature as possible.
2. **Ask:** According to Thoreau, what is the "strange uncertainty" most people have? **Answer:** Most people are uncertain about the nature of life, whether it is essentially good or bad.
3. **Ask:** Why does Thoreau criticize these people, saying they have "somewhat hastily concluded" that the Westminster catechism is right about the "chief end of man"? **Possible response:** He criticizes these people because they parrot the catechism without having experienced life or given it much thought, thus lacking a sound basis for their conclusion. He would say these people live "shallow."
4. Discuss how Thoreau presents an unattractive reflection of society and urges people to change themselves. Have students look for other passages where Thoreau discusses how living "deeply" enriches life.

⑬ Reading Check

Answer: He went to the woods to live simply and deliberately, to try to understand the essential facts of life.

Possible Response: The cabin is extremely humble—plain, small, and unadorned. Such a cabin would provide only the most basic shelter and require little attention, leaving its inhabitant to focus on matters of the mind and spirit.

⓯ **Critical Thinking**

Infer

1. Direct students to the bracketed passage and read it aloud. Note that it is a highly developed metaphor.

2. **Ask:** Why does Thoreau call the intellect a "cleaver"?
   Answer: Like a cleaver that cuts things apart, the intellect is used for analyzing and sectioning ideas into parts.

3. **Ask:** In what sense is the head an organ for burrowing?
   Answer: It is an organ for digging into knowledge.

4. Encourage students to discuss the kinds of riches Thoreau hoped to dig up.

⓮ ▼ **Critical Viewing**
This picture shows a replica of Thoreau's cabin. How does it help you understand his point that people should work on the quality of their lives rather than the things they own? **[Interpret]**

states, with its boundary forever fluctuating, so that even a German cannot tell you how it is bounded at any moment. The nation itself, with all its so-called internal improvements, which, by the way, are all external and superficial, is just such an unwieldy and overgrown establishment, cluttered with furniture and tripped up by its own traps, ruined by luxury and heedless expense, by want of calculation and a worthy aim, as the million households in the land; and the only cure for it as for them is in a rigid economy, a stern and more than Spartan simplicity of life and elevation of purpose. It lives too fast. Men think that it is essential that the *Nation* have commerce, and export ice, and talk through a telegraph, and ride thirty miles an hour, without a doubt, whether *they* do or not; but whether we should live like baboons or like men, is a little uncertain. If we do not get out sleepers,[13] and forge rails, and devote days and nights to the work, but go to tinkering upon our *lives* to improve *them*, who will build railroads? And if railroads are not built, how shall we get to heaven in season? But if we stay at home and mind our business, who will want railroads? We do not ride on the railroad; it rides upon us. . . .

Time is but the stream I go a-fishing in. I drink at it; but while I drink I see the sandy bottom and detect how shallow it is. Its thin current slides away, but eternity remains. I would drink deeper; fish in the sky, whose bottom is pebbly with stars. I cannot count one. I know not the first letter of the alphabet. I have always been regretting that I was not as wise as the day I was born. The intellect is a cleaver; it discerns and rifts its way into the secret of things. I do not wish to be any more busy with my hands than is necessary. My head is hands and feet. I feel all my best faculties concentrated in it. My instinct tells me that my head is an organ for burrowing, as some creatures use their snout and forepaws, and with it I would mine and burrow my way through these hills. I think that the richest vein is somewhere hereabouts; so by the divining rod[14] and thin rising vapors I judge; and here I will begin to mine. . . .

⓯

13. **sleepers** (slē′ pərz) *n.* ties supporting railroad tracks.
14. **divining rod** a forked branch or stick alleged to reveal underground water or minerals.

Think Aloud

Vocabulary: Using Context
Direct students' attention to the word *impressible* near the top of page 385. Use the following "think aloud" to model the skill of using context to infer the meaning of the word. Say to students:

Thoreau compares the mind to the ground and says both are *impressible.* This word sounds like *impression,* which means "a mark or print on a surface." *Impression* can also mean "an effect someone makes on another person." He's saying that roads are impressible because they get worn out by the feet of many walkers. So *impressible* must describe something that's able to be marked or affected in some way.

from **The Conclusion**

I left the woods for as good a reason as I went there. Perhaps it seemed to me that I had several more lives to live, and could not spare any more time for that one. It is remarkable how easily and insensibly we fall into a particular route, and make a beaten track for ourselves. I had not lived there a week before my feet wore a path from my door to the pondside; and though it is five or six years since I trod it, it is still quite distinct. It is true, I fear that others may have fallen into it, and so helped to keep it open. The surface of the earth is soft and impressible by the feet of men; and so with the paths which the mind travels. How worn and dusty, then, must be the highways of the world, how deep the ruts of tradition and conformity! I did not wish to take a cabin passage, but rather to go before the mast and on the deck of the world, for there I could best see the moonlight amid the mountains. I do not wish to go below now.

I learned this, at least, by my experiment; that if one advances confidently in the direction of his dreams, and endeavors to live the life which he has imagined, he will meet with a success unexpected in common hours. He will put some things behind, will pass an invisible boundary; new, universal, and more liberal laws will begin to establish themselves around and within him; or the old laws be expanded, and interpreted in his favor in a more liberal sense, and he will live with the license of a higher order of beings. In proportion as he simplifies his life, the laws of the universe will appear less complex, and solitude will not be solitude, nor poverty poverty, nor weakness weakness. If you have built castles in the air, your work need not be lost; that is where they should be. Now put the foundations under them. . . .

Why should we be in such desperate haste to succeed, and in such desperate enterprises? If a man does not keep pace with his companions, perhaps it is because he hears a different drummer. Let him step to the music which he hears, however measured or far away. It is not important that he should mature as soon as an apple tree or an oak. Shall he turn his spring into summer? If the condition of things which we were made for is not yet, what were any reality which we can substitute? We will not be shipwrecked on a vain reality. Shall we with pains erect a heaven of blue glass over ourselves, though when it is done we shall be sure to gaze still at the true ethereal heaven far above, as if the former were not? . . .

However mean your life is, meet it and live it; do not shun it and call it hard names. It is not so bad as you are. It looks poorest when you are richest. The faultfinder will find faults even in paradise. Love your life, poor as it is. You may perhaps have some pleasant, thrilling, glorious hours, even in a poorhouse. The setting sun is reflected from the windows of the almshouse[15] as brightly as from the rich man's

---

15. **almshouse** *n.* home for people too poor to support themselves.

Literary Analysis
Author's Style and Metaphor What metaphor does Thoreau use in the sentence beginning "If a man does not keep pace with his companions . . .?" What idea does it help him develop?

☑ **Reading Check**
What does Thoreau claim to have learned from his experiment in living?

🔟 Literary Analysis
Author's Style and Metaphor

1. **Ask** students to define metaphor. **Answer:** A metaphor is a comparison of two unlike things that does not use the words *like* or *as*.

2. Direct students to read the bracketed passage.

3. **Ask** students the Literary Analysis question: What metaphor does Thoreau use in the sentence beginning, "If a man does not keep pace with his companions. . .," What idea does it help him develop? **Answer:** He speaks of life as though it were a march in time with music—as though people were soldiers marching in a parade. Thoreau is saying that people should not conform and do everything the same way others do. He is telling readers to be individuals.

🔟 Reading Check

Answer: Thoreau claims that if a person follows his or her dreams, the result will be unexpected success and greater freedom.

Differentiated Instruction *for Universal Access*

Support for Special-Needs Students
Read students the text beginning, "In proportion as he simplifies." Then focus on building an understanding of the metaphor "castles in the air." Guide students to understand that Thoreau is urging people to simplify their lives, to dream, and then to follow their dreams by building foundations for them.

Strategy for Advanced Readers
Have students read the last paragraph on this page through to the end on page 386. Tell them that, although not wealthy, Thoreau did have a Harvard education and a family business. Discuss with students how economic conditions today might lead Thoreau to change his advice about poverty. Ask students: How would living in a city affect one's ability to cope with poverty?

⑱ Scholar's Insight

1. Have a student read the bracketed passage.

2. Read Ehrlich's Insight note. Tell students that Thoreau is using this example to further explain his philosophy. **Ask** students if they feel readers of the time would be moved by Thoreau's explanation. **Possible response:** Students may suggest that the radical idea, no matter how it is expressed, would not affect people.

⑲ Reading Strategy

Analyzing the Author's Philosophical Assumptions

1. Remind students that they do not have to accept what an author claims to be true or correct.

2. Have a volunteer read aloud the bracketed passage and restate Thoreau's point.

3. Encourage students to analyze Thoreau's support for his ideas and then compare it with their own experience.

4. Then **ask** students the Reading Strategy question: Thoreau has strong opinions about how people should live, as shown in his advice to "cultivate poverty." Has he convinced you? **Possible answers:** Students may or may not be convinced that poverty is preferable to wealth.

Gretel Ehrlich
Scholar's Insight
To cultivate poverty is a radical thought and one that has been alive throughout history. Poverty in this sense means simplicity, like the "poverty" of an animal that wears only its own fur coat. The mind and the imagination are our true wealth. ⑱

Reading Strategy
Analyzing the Author's Philosophical Assumptions
Thoreau has strong opinions about how people should live, as shown in his advice to "cultivate poverty." Has he convinced you? Explain.

⑲

Vocabulary
magnanimity (mag′ nə nim′ ə tē) *n.* generosity

---

abode; the snow melts before its door as early in the spring. I do not see but a quiet mind may live as contentedly there, and have as cheering thoughts, as in a palace. The town's poor seem to me often to live the most independent lives of any. Maybe they are simply great enough to receive without misgiving. Most think that they are above being supported by the town; but it oftener happens that they are not above supporting themselves by dishonest means, which should be more disreputable. Cultivate poverty like a garden herb, like sage. Do not trouble yourself much to get new things, whether clothes or friends. Turn the old; return to them. Things do not change; we change. Sell your clothes and keep your thoughts. God will see that you do not want society. If I were confined to a corner of a garret[16] all my days, like a spider, the world would be just as large to me while I had my thoughts about me. The philosopher said: "From an army of three divisions one can take away its general, and put it in disorder; from the man the most abject and vulgar one cannot take away his thought." Do not seek so anxiously to be developed, to subject yourself to many influences to be played on; it is all dissipation. Humility like darkness reveals the heavenly lights. The shadows of poverty and meanness gather around us, "and lo! creation widens to our view."[17] We are often reminded that if there were bestowed on us the wealth of Croesus,[18] our aims must still be the same, and our means essentially the same. Moreover, if you are restricted in your range by poverty, if you cannot buy books and newspapers, for instance, you are but confined to the most significant and vital experiences; you are compelled to deal with the material which yields the most sugar and the most starch. It is life near the bone where it is sweetest. You are defended from being a trifler. No man loses ever on a lower level by magnanimity on a higher. Superfluous wealth can buy superfluities only. Money is not required to buy one necessary of the soul. . . .

The life in us is like the water in the river. It may rise this year higher than man has ever known it, and flood the parched uplands; even this may be the eventful year, which will drown out all our muskrats. It was not always dry land where we dwell. I see far inland the banks which the stream anciently washed, before science began to record its freshets. Everyone has heard the story which has gone the rounds of New England, of a strong and beautiful bug which came out of the dry leaf of an old table of apple-tree wood, which had stood in a farmer's kitchen for sixty years, first in Connecticut, and afterward in Massachusetts—from an egg deposited in the living tree many years earlier still, as appeared by counting the annual layers

---

16. **garret** (gar′ it) *n.* attic.
17. **"and . . . view"** from the sonnet "To Night" by British poet Joseph Blanco White (1775–1841).
18. **Croesus** (krē′ səs) King of Lydia (d. 546 B.C.), believed to be the wealthiest person of his time.

Enrichment: Investigating Science

Geology of Walden Pond

As the glacier that once covered New England melted, a huge block of ice remained on the site of Walden Pond. Streams of melted water ran off this block, leaving once-embedded sand and gravel around its base. When the block melted, a deep pond remained.

Walden's permeable sandbanks quickly absorb water when it rains. There are no streams feeding into the pond or shoreline development. For these reasons, the water remains pure and clear.

Activity: Pair Presentation Have students research how development along lakes affects the water and surrounding land. Suggest that they record information in the **Enrichment: Investigating Science** work sheet, *Professional Development Guidebook,* page 241. Have pairs of students prepare a presentation for the parks department arguing for or against development at Walden; the presentation should include an opinion about Thoreau's probable position on the issue.

beyond it; which was heard gnawing out for several weeks, hatched perchance by the heat of an urn. Who does not feel his faith in a resurrection and immortality strengthened by hearing of this? Who knows what beautiful and winged life, whose egg has been buried for ages under many concentric layers of woodenness in the dead dry life of society, deposited at first in the alburnum[19] of the green and living tree, which has been gradually converted into the semblance of its well-seasoned tomb—heard perchance gnawing out now for years by the astonished family of man, as they sat round the festive board— may unexpectedly come forth from amidst society's most trivial and handselled furniture, to enjoy its perfect summer life at last!

I do not say that John or Jonathan[20] will realize all this; but such is the character of that morrow which mere lapse of time can never make to dawn. The light which puts out our eyes is darkness to us. Only that day dawns to which we are awake. There is more day to dawn. The sun is but a morning star.

---

19. **alburnum** (al bǔr′ nəm) *n.* soft wood between the bark and the heartwood, where water is conducted.
20. **John or Jonathan** average person.

Critical Reading ©

1. **Key Ideas and Details (a)** What advice does Thoreau offer to his "fellows" about ownership of land or property? **(b) Interpret:** What does Thoreau mean by his comment, "It makes but little difference whether you are committed to a farm or the county jail"?

2. **Key Ideas and Details (a)** What advice does Thoreau offer to those who live in poverty? **(b) Analyze:** What does this advice suggest about Thoreau's definition of true wealth?

3. **Key Ideas and Details (a)** According to Thoreau, by what is our life "frittered away"? **(b) Interpret:** What does Thoreau mean by his advice to "simplify, simplify"?

4. **Key Ideas and Details (a) Deduce:** What did Thoreau hope to achieve by living at Walden Pond? **(b) Make a Judgment:** Do you believe Thoreau felt his time at Walden was well spent? Explain.

5. **Integration of Knowledge and Ideas (a) Apply:** How would you define those things that are necessary to the soul? **(b) Take a Position:** Do you agree with Thoreau that "money is not required to buy one necessary of the soul"? Explain.

Cite textual evidence to support your responses.

from Walden **387**

Differentiated Instruction   for Universal Access

Culturally Responsive Instruction

Culture Focus Tell students about Indian leader Mohandas Gandhi, who fought against British rule. Explain that Gandhi drew on Thoreau's ideas about civil disobedience when he formulated his philosophy of *satyagraha* ("devotion to truth"). Guided by this philosophy, Gandhi called for massive boycotts of British goods and British-run institutions in India that treated Indians unfairly. Thousands of Gandhi's supporters and Gandhi himself repeatedly went to prison without resistance. Point out that Gandhi gave up possessions and lived a simple life among the people he was trying to help. When India won its independence in 1947, it was largely due to his work. Invite students to discuss how Dr. Martin Luther King, Jr., also used nonviolent civil disobedience in the United States to fight racial segregation. Ask students if they know or have read about someone who took part in the protests of the 1950s and 1960s. Encourage students to draw parallels between the experiences of King and Gandhi and their followers.

This selection is excerpted from a long essay, about twenty pages in length, in which Thoreau advocates civil disobedience—the deliberate and public refusal to obey laws that violate one's personal principles. In the portions included here, Thoreau expresses his belief that government has been no more than an impediment to the productivity and achievements of the American people. Philosophically, he stands opposed to government. Practically, he urges readers to try to make a better government, one that commands respect.

Spiral Review

Rhetorical Techniques

1. Remind students that they studied the concept of rhetorical techniques.

2. **Ask** students the Spiral Review question.

   Possible response: Thoreau uses a rhetorical question to introduce his ideas about government.

21 **Literary Analysis**

Author's Style and Metaphor

1. Remind students of Thoreau's use of figurative expressions to develop his ideas. Direct their attention to the bracketed passage, and ask a volunteer to read it aloud.

2. Point out that Thoreau has already said that government is simply an "expedient." **Ask:** What metaphors does he use in this passage to describe government? How do they further explain how he sees government?
   Answer: Thoreau says government is a "tradition" that is not being kept properly, a "wooden gun" or toy weapon being held against the people, and a piece of "complicated machinery" that just makes a lot of noise. Each metaphor presents an additional way in which he sees government as ineffectual and even unethical.

20 from

CIVIL DISOBEDIENCE

Henry David Thoreau

BACKGROUND The Mexican War was a conflict between Mexico and the United States that took place from 1846 to 1848. The war was caused by a dispute over the boundary between Texas and Mexico, as well as by Mexico's refusal to discuss selling California and New Mexico to the United States. Believing that President Polk had intentionally provoked the conflict before gaining congressional approval, Thoreau and many other Americans strongly objected to the war. In protest, Thoreau refused to pay his taxes and was forced to spend a night in jail. After that experience, Thoreau wrote "Civil Disobedience," urging people to resist governmental policies with which they disagree.

I heartily accept the motto, "That government is best which governs least";[1] and I should like to see it acted up to more rapidly and systematically. Carried out, it finally amounts to this, which also I believe: "That government is best which governs not at all"; and when men are prepared for it, that will be the kind of government which they will have. Government is at best but an expedient; but most governments are usually, and all governments are sometimes, inexpedient. The objections which have been brought against a standing army, and they are many and weighty, and deserve to prevail, may also at last be brought against a standing government. The standing army is only an arm of the standing government. The government itself, which is only the mode which the people have chosen to execute their will, is equally liable to be abused and perverted before the people can act through it. Witness the present Mexican war, the work of comparatively a few individuals using the standing government as their tool; for in the outset, the people would not have consented to this measure.

This American government—what is it but a tradition, though a recent one, endeavoring to transmit itself unimpaired to posterity, but each instant losing some of its integrity? It has not the vitality and force of a single living man; for a single man can bend it to his will. It is a sort of wooden gun to the people themselves; and, if ever

Vocabulary
expedient
(ek spē´ dē ənt)
n. resource

Spiral Review
Rhetorical Techniques What rhetorical technique does Thoreau use in the sentence beginning "This American government…"? Explain. **21**

---

1. "That . . . least"
   the motto of the *United States Magazine and Democratic Review*, a literary-political journal.

Vocabulary Development

Vocabulary Knowledge Rating
When students have completed reading and discussing the selections, have them take out the **Vocabulary Knowledge Rating** charts for the essays. Read the words aloud and have students rate their knowledge of the words again in the After Reading column. Clarify any words that are still problematic. Have students write their own definitions and example or sentence in the appropriate column. Then have students complete the Vocabulary Lesson at the end of the selections. Encourage students to use the words in further discussion and written work about the selections. Remind them that they will be accountable for these words on the **Selection Test,** *Unit 2 Resources,* pages 143–145 or 146–148.

they should use it in earnest as a real one against each other, it will surely split. But it is not the less necessary for this; for the people must have some complicated machinery or other, and hear its din, to satisfy that idea of government which they have. Governments show thus how successfully men can be imposed on, even impose on themselves, for their own advantage. It is excellent, we must all allow; yet this government never of itself furthered any enterprise, but by the alacrity with which it got out of its way. *It* does not keep the country free. *It* does not settle the West. *It* does not educate. The character inherent in the American people has done all that has been accomplished; and it would have done somewhat more, if the government had not sometimes got in its way. For government is an expedient by which men would fain succeed in letting one another alone; and, as has been said, when it is most expedient, the governed are most let alone by it. Trade and commerce, if they were not made of India rubber,[2] would never manage to bounce over the obstacles which legislators are continually putting in their way; and, if one were to judge these men wholly by the effects of their actions, and not partly by their intentions, they would deserve to be classed and punished with those mischievous persons who put obstructions on the railroads.

But, to speak practically and as a citizen, unlike those who call themselves no government men, I ask for, not at once no government, but *at once* a better government. Let every man make known what kind of government would command his respect, and that will be one step toward obtaining it. . . .

2. **India rubber** a form of crude rubber.

Vocabulary
alacrity (ə lak′ rə tē) *n.*
speed

Critical Reading

1. Key Ideas and Details (a) How does Thoreau define the best possible kind of government? **(b) Draw Conclusions:** According to Thoreau, when will Americans get the best possible kind of government?

2. Key Ideas and Details (a) Summarize: What is Thoreau asking his readers to do? **(b) Evaluate:** Does Thoreau present a convincing argument for acting on one's principles?

3. Integration of Knowledge and Ideas (a) Criticize: What arguments might you use to counter Thoreau's objections to the idea of a standing government? **(b) Support:** What examples might support an argument that government benefits individuals?

4. Integration of Ideas and Knowledge Do you find it surprising that the goals Thoreau tried to achieve have influenced generations of people around the world? Explain. In your response, use at least two of these Essential Question words: *self-reliance, vision, freedom, principle. [Connecting to the Essential Question: How does literature shape or reflect society?]*

Cite textual evidence to support your responses.

from Civil Disobedience **389**

Before students respond, you may wish to have them write a brief objective summary of the selection. As they answer the questions below, remind them to support their answers with evidence from the text.

1. (a) A government that governs least is the best possible kind of government. (b) Thoreau says that when people are ready, they will dispense with government altogether.

2. (a) He is asking them to step forward and state what they want from government. (b) **Possible response:** Some students may be convinced by Thoreau's argument. Others may assert that if everyone acted on individual ideas, chaos might ensue.

3. **Possible responses:** (a) Without a standing government, the nation cannot prepare itself for war, cannot make plans for future needs, and cannot organize national elections. (b) Governments provide schools, military and civil defense, and transportation systems.

4. **Possible response:** It is not surprising that Thoreau's goals influenced people for generations. Today, in many parts of the world, people still long for freedom and for the right to live according to their principles. Others who are free but caught up in hurried modern lives have a personal vision of a more rural, peaceful existence.

Concept Connector

Reading Skill Graphic Organizer
Ask students to review the graphic organizers in which they have analyzed Thoreau's assumptions. Then have students share their organizers and compare their conclusions about Thoreau's implicit and explicit assumptions.

Activating Prior Knowledge
Have students return to their responses to the Activating Prior Knowledge activity. Ask them to explain whether their thoughts have changed and if so, how.

Writing About the Essential Question
Have students compare their responses to the prompt before they completed reading the selections with their thoughts after reading them. Have them work individually or in groups, writing or discussing their thoughts, to formulate their new responses. Then lead a class discussion, probing for what students have learned that confirms or invalidates their initial thoughts. Encourage students to cite specific textual details to support their responses.

Answers

1. (a) Thoreau addresses the reader directly as "you" and speaks of "our" common experience. He uses phrases such as "I say" and "lump it." (b) Thoreau describes modern life by means of four metaphors: people "live meanly, like ants"; people "fight with cranes," "like pygmies"; civilized life is a "chopping sea"; and "life is like a German Confederacy."

2. (a) Modern life is turbulent and shallow because people are concerned only with making money and having possessions, and people would be happier if they simplified their lives. (b) The passage on cultivating poverty also stresses the advantages of living a simple life.

3. (a) **Possible response:** The first paragraph from "The Conclusion" of *Walden* begins with an example. (b) Yes, it invites reader support with details before reaching "a larger truth."

4. Students should explain Thoreau's metaphors. A sample answer can be found in the **Literary Analysis Graphic Organizer A,** page 84, in *Graphic Organizer Transparencies.*

5. (a) The "wooden gun" is the government's authority over citizens. Civilized life is a "chopping sea" in the sense that it is turbulent, full of vicissitudes that people have no control over. (b) The "wooden gun" shows that the government has little true authority because it would break apart if people actually began to fight legal or legislative battles. The "chopping sea" metaphor serves to contrast civilized life with a simplified life.

6. (a) He makes more use of metaphor in *Walden.* (b) Metaphor is more suited to *Walden,* in which spiritual and physical journeys intertwine. "Civil Disobedience" is a persuasive essay about Thoreau's public views.

7. The cartoon ironically suggests that Thoreau calls enjoyable activities boring in order to discourage visitors.

8. (a) He claims that details distract us from real living. As evidence, he describes simplifying his life and experiencing greater freedom. (b) **Possible response:**

390

After You Read
from *Walden* •
from *Civil Disobedience*

Literary Analysis

1. **Craft and Structure** Explain how the paragraph on simplicity in *Walden* demonstrates the following elements of Thoreau's **style:** **(a)** a conversational **tone,** or attitude; **(b)** a tendency to use a series of **figurative expressions,** including **metaphor** and **analogy,** to develop a key idea.

2. **Key Ideas and Details (a)** What is the central idea Thoreau develops in the paragraph on simplicity? Summarize it in one sentence. **(b)** Note another section in *Walden* where Thoreau repeats the idea for emphasis.

3. **Craft and Structure** Thoreau often starts a paragraph with specific examples. He then applies them to a larger truth. **(a)** Identify one such paragraph. **(b)** Do you think this approach is effective? Explain.

4. **Craft and Structure** Choose two metaphors and one analogy from these essays. Use a chart like the one shown to examine the meanings of each one.

Metaphor/Analogy	Things Compared	Meaning
I wanted to live deep and suck out all the marrow of life		

5. **Craft and Structure** In "Civil Disobedience," Thoreau describes government as a "wooden gun." In *Walden,* he describes civilized life as a "chopping sea." **(a)** Explain the meaning of each metaphor. **(b)** Then, explain how the metaphor helps Thoreau develop the logic of his ideas.

6. **Craft and Structure (a)** In which essay does Thoreau spend more time translating abstract ideas into concrete metaphors and analogies? **(b)** How does this choice reflect the purpose of the essay and the nature of his topic?

7. **Analyze Visual Information** Explain the humor in the cartoon at right.

Reading Strategy

8. Thoreau expresses his **explicit philosophical assumption** that people should simplify their lives. **(a)** What support for this belief does he provide? **(b)** How might someone argue against this idea?

9. **(a)** What evidence does Thoreau use to support his point that "It makes but little difference whether you are committed to a farm or the county jail"? **(b)** What **implicit philosophical assumption** does this statement suggest? **(c)** Do you agree? Explain.

Common Core
State Standards

Writing
1. Write arguments to support claims in an analysis of substantive topics or texts, using valid reasoning. *(p. 391)*

Language
4.b. Identify and correctly use patterns of word changes that indicate different meanings. *(p. 391)*

5. Demonstrate understanding of figurative language, word relationships, and nuances in word meanings. *(p. 391)*

▼ *Text in Bubble: "Dear Ralph, Talk about boring!! Nothing to do but take stupid walks in the dreary woods! You'd hate it!! Best regards, Henry" Caption: By Strategic Use of Postcards, Thoreau Manages to Keep Walden Pond Unspoiled.*

© *The New Yorker* Collection 1988 J.B. Handelsman from cartoonbank.com. All Rights Reserved.

The details of living add richness to our lives. Students should defend their responses.

9. (a) Thoreau describes his enjoyment of the many farms around him, none of which he owned. (b) It is better to be free than to be rich. (c) People who are "free" often must rely on others for support.

PERFORMANCE TASKS
Integrated Language Skills

ⓒ Vocabulary Acquisition and Use

Word Analysis: Latin Root -flu-

The Latin root -flu-, found in words like *fluid*, means "flow." The word *superfluous* means "overflowing" or "exceeding what is sufficient." Consider the meanings of the -flu- words listed below. For each word, write an alternate explanation that contains the target word and the word *flow*. Follow the example shown here.

confluence *n.* a merging of two things
alternate definition: A confluence of two rivers occurs when they flow together.

1. affluence *n.* wealth; prosperity
2. fluent *adj.* effortlessly smooth
3. fluctuate *v.* change from high to low levels or change unpredictably
4. influx *n.* a sudden arrival of a large number of people or things
5. flue *n.* a shaft or tube used as an outlet for smoke or gas

Vocabulary: Synonyms

Synonyms are words that have the same or nearly the same meaning. Review the vocabulary list on page 376. Then, select the word below whose meaning is closest to that of the first word. For each answer, explain your reasoning.

1. **dilapidated: (a)** depressed **(b)** rundown **(c)** uneven
2. **sublime: (a)** lovely **(b)** enormous **(c)** awe-inspiring
3. **superfluous: (a)** toxic **(b)** extravagant **(c)** repetitive
4. **magnanimity: (a)** selflessness **(b)** tolerance **(c)** patience
5. **expedient: (a)** expense **(b)** instrument **(c)** barrier
6. **alacrity: (a)** awareness **(b)** preparedness **(c)** quickness

Writing

ⓒ Argument

In the century and a half since Thoreau wrote *Walden*, life for most Americans has become more complex rather than simpler. Write an **editorial**—a *persuasive article*—in which you argue for or against the relevance of Thoreau's ideas of simplicity in today's world. Refer to *Walden* and "Civil Disobedience" to support your ideas.

Prewriting Decide what you think of Thoreau's ideas, and brainstorm for examples that support your position. Plan to include specific *stylistic elements* to enhance meaning. Like Thoreau, develop *metaphors and analogies* that clarify your ideas.

Drafting Introduce Thoreau and his ideas. Write a statement either advocating or rejecting their relevance today. As you work, *use repetition* for emphasis; vary your wording, but drive home your key points. Conclude with a specific *call to action*.

Revising Reread your editorial, adding examples, anecdotes, or quotations as necessary to sharpen your argument. To complete your work, include photographs or illustrations that capture your ideas visually.

Model: Anticipating Reader's Concerns and Counterclaims
Today, Thoreau's ideas fall on deaf ears because everyone is glued to a cell phone. Instead of hearing his wisdom, people say, "But I can't live without my mobile GPS. It makes my life easier." Yet, people have less time with family, and less time for the simple pleasures of life than ever before.

Anticipating and answering opponents' arguments creates a more persuasive piece of writing.

Extended Study: Integrated Language Skills **391**

Assessment Resources

Answers

Vocabulary Acquisition and Use

1. Introduce the skill, using the instruction on the student page.
2. Have students complete the Word Analysis activity and the Vocabulary practice.

Word Analysis

1. a flow of wealth
2. flowing smoothly
3. to flow from one level to another or to flow from one state to another unpredictably
4. a sudden flow of people or things into a place
5. a shaft or tube through which smoke or gas flows out

Vocabulary

1. b; *rundown* means "not cared for," the same as *dilapidated*
2. c; *sublime* things are majestic and inspire awe
3. c; something repetitive is excessive or *superfluous*
4. a; *selflessness* is showing generosity or *magnanimity*
5. b; *instrument* and *expedient* both suggest tools
6. c; both *quickness* and *alacrity* describe speed

Writing

1. To guide students in writing this editorial, give them the Support for Writing worksheet (*Unit 2 Resources,* p. 138).
2. Tell students to clarify their own ideas and determine whether they wish to support or refute Thoreau. Have them list possible metaphors and analogies.
3. Encourage students to jot down opponents' arguments and their refutations. Point out that they may have to concede some opposing arguments.
4. Evaluate students' arguments using the **Rubrics for Editorials,** in *Professional Development Guidebook,* pages 289–290.

**Common Core
State Standards**

• Reading Informational Text 7
• Writing 1, 1.a, 10

About the Texts

1. Introduce the forms, using the instruction on the student page.

2. Tell students that they will apply their knowledge of consumer guides and government reports as they read the two documents.

Reading Strategy

1. Introduce the strategy, using the instruction on the student page.

2. Tell students that they will analyze and evaluate information from charts and diagrams as they read.

Think Aloud: Model the Skill

Say to students:

I always scan any charts, graphs, or other visual aids before I begin to read a document. Sometimes this saves me time: I may find the information I am looking for in the visual aids. Even when I plan to read the entire document, the visual aids serve as road signs that guide me through the flow of ideas. As I scan "Water on Tap," the diagram of a Water Treatment Plant highlights important information I expect to find in the document.

Content-Area Vocabulary

1. Pronounce each word, giving its definition; have students say it aloud.

2. Also see the *Classroom Strategies and Teaching Routines* card for vocabulary.

Reading for Information

Analyzing Functional and Expository Texts

Consumer Guide • Report

**Common Core
State Standards**

**Reading Informational Text
7.** Integrate and evaluate multiple sources of information presented in different media or formats as well as in words in order to address a question or solve a problem.

About the Texts

A **consumer guide** may be prepared by either a government agency or a private organization to educate the public about specific products or services. For a guide to be effective, it must be issued by a reliable source that does not stand to profit from the reporting. Most consumer guides contain basic facts about a product, service, or topic of interest; visual aids such as charts, graphs, or illustrations; and answers to frequently asked questions.

A **report** is a document written to inform officials and the public about issues such as environmental or health concerns. Reports are usually dated because they are often time sensitive. Most reports contain facts, statistics, and other data about an issue; dates and headings that organize the data; and a summary that omits all but the most essential information.

Reading Strategy

Many government and public documents use charts, graphs, and other visual aids to present complex data in an easy-to-read format. As you read, **evaluate the information from charts and graphs** and apply it to the information presented in the text. Notice the features listed in the chart below, and use a checklist like the one shown to identify, interpret, and evaluate the information each feature presents.

Content-Area Vocabulary

These words appear in the selections that follow. They may also appear in other content-area texts.

aquifer (ak´ wə fər) *n.* an underground rock formation in which water collects

contaminant (kən tam´ ə nənt) *n.* material that makes something impure or corrupt by contact or mixture

ecosystem (ē´ kō sis´ təm) *n.* a community of related organisms, together with their physical environment, considered as a unit

hydrologic (hī´ drə laj´ ik) *adj.* relating to the scientific study of water

Basic Elements			Purpose	Effectiveness
Titles and headings	Yes ☐	No ☐		
Charts or graphs	Yes ☐	No ☐		
Photos, maps, or illustrations	Yes ☐	No ☐		
Labels or captions	Yes ☐	No ☐		
Color-coding	Yes ☐	No ☐		
Issue dates	Yes ☐	No ☐		

Teaching Resources

Reading Support

L2 L3	*Reader's Notebook*
L1	*Reader's Notebook: Adapted Version*
EL	*Reader's Notebook: English Learner's Version*

WATER ON TAP
what you need to know

Where Does My Drinking Water Come From And How Is It Treated?

Your drinking water comes from **surface water** or **ground water**. The water that systems pump and treat from sources open to the atmosphere, such as rivers, lakes, and reservoirs is known as surface water. Water pumped from wells drilled into underground **aquifers**, geologic formations containing water, is called ground water. The quantity of water produced by a well depends on the nature of the rock, sand, or soil in the aquifer from which the water is drawn. Drinking water wells may be shallow (50 feet or less) or deep (more than 1,000 feet). More water systems have ground water than surface water as a source (approx. 147,000 v. 14,500), but more people drink from a surface water system (195 million v. 101,400). Large-scale water supply systems tend to rely on surface water resources, while smaller water systems tend to use ground water. Your water utility or public works department can tell you the source of your public water supply.

How Does Water Get To My Faucet?
An underground network of pipes typically delivers drinking water to the homes and businesses served by the water system. Small

systems serving just a handful of households may be relatively simple, while large metropolitan systems can be extremely complex—sometimes consisting of thousands of miles of pipes serving millions of people. Drinking water must meet required

health standards when it leaves the treatment plant. After treated water leaves the plant, it is monitored within the distribution system to identify and remedy any problems such as water main breaks, pressure variations, or growth of microorganisms.

> The headings anticipate questions readers may have.

How Is My Water Treated To Make It Safe?
Water utilities treat nearly 34 billion gallons of water every day.[1] The amount and type of treatment applied varies with the source and quality of the water. Generally, surface water systems require more treatment than ground water systems because they are directly exposed to the atmosphere and runoff from rain and melting snow. Water suppliers use a variety of treatment processes to remove **contaminants** from drinking water. These individual processes can be arranged in a "treatment train" (a series of processes applied in a sequence). The most commonly used processes include coagulation (flocculation and sedimentation), filtration, and disinfection. Some water systems also use ion exchange and adsorption. Water utilities select the treatment combination most appropriate to treat the contaminants found in the source water of that particular system.

Coagulation (Flocculation & Sedimentation):
Flocculation: This step removes dirt and other particles suspended in the water. Alum and iron salts or synthetic organic polymers are added to the water to form tiny sticky particles called "floc," which attract the dirt particles.

Informational Text: Consumer Guide **393**

TEACH

About Consumer Guides
1. Before students read the consumer guide, point out that such material is intended for the general public, an audience that may not have prior knowledge about the subject and its special terminology.
2. **Ask** students: If a document is intended for the average reader, how should its information be presented?
   Possible response: Students may say that the language in the document should be clear and direct, that new concepts should be introduced at a basic level, and that special terms should always be explained.

Reading Strategy
Evaluating Information From Titles and Headings
1. Have students scan the subheadings of "Water on Tap," noting that they are formulated as questions rather than statements or subtitles.
2. **Ask:** Does it make any difference to you that the headings are in question form? Explain.
   Possible response: Students may say that the questions stimulate their curiosity, making them more interested in reading the sections.

Differentiated Instruction   for Universal Access

Support for Less Proficient Readers
Before students read the guide, have them copy the diagram on page 394 in their notebooks. Tell them to add clarifying notes to the diagram to help them explain the process to a class of younger students. Then have them read the guide.

Reading Strategy

Evaluate Information From Diagrams

1. As a class, examine the Water Treatment Plant diagram. Clarify for students any details of the diagram that may be confusing.

2. **Ask:** How does the information in the diagram relate to the text of the consumer guide? In your opinion, are both forms of information essential to this consumer guide? Explain.
   Possible response: Students may note a close correlation between the text and the diagram. Key stages of treatment described in the text—coagulation, filtration, disinfection—are shown in the diagram. Most students will agree that text and diagram support each other and that both are essential to the effectiveness of the guide.

3. To help students evaluate the diagram, **ask:** Do you think this diagram is clear and complete, or would you prefer to see additional information? Explain.
   Possible response: Some students may find the diagram complete; others may wish to know what happens to the material that is removed during the treatment process or how long the treatment process takes.

All sources of drinking water contain some naturally occurring contaminants. At low levels, these contaminants generally are not harmful in our drinking water. Removing all contaminants would be extremely expensive, and in most cases, would not provide increased protection of public health. A few naturally occurring minerals may actually improve the taste of drinking water and may even have nutritional value at low levels.
Sedimentation: The flocculated particles then settle naturally out of the water.

Filtration:
Many water treatment facilities use filtration to remove all particles from the water. Those particles include clays and silts, natural organic matter, precipitates from other treatment processes in the facility, iron and manganese, and microorganisms. Filtration clarifies the water and enhances the effectiveness of disinfection.

Disinfection:
Disinfection of drinking water is considered to be one of the major public health advances of the 20th century. Water is often disinfected before it enters the distribution system to ensure that dangerous microbial contaminants are killed. Chlorine, chlorinates, or chlorine dioxides are most often used because they are very effective **disinfectants**, and residual concentrations can be maintained in the water system.

Water Treatment Plant

Follow a drop of water from the source through the treatment process. Water may be treated differently in different communities depending on the quality of the water which enters the plant. Groundwater is located underground and typically requires less treatment than water from lakes, rivers, and streams.

Lake or Reservoir

The diagram with commentary makes the water treatment process easier to understand.

Coagulation removes dirt and other particles suspended in water. Alum and other chemicals are added to water to form tiny sticky particles called "floc" which attract the dirt particles. The combined weight of the dirt and the alum (floc) become heavy enough to sink to the bottom during sedimentation.

Sedimentation: The heavy particles (floc) settle to the bottom and the clear water moves to filtration

Storage: Water is placed in a closed tank or reservoir for disinfection to take place. The water then flows through pipes to homes and businesses in the community.

Disinfection: A small amount of chlorine is added or some other disinfection method is used to kill any bacteria or microrganisms that may be in the water.

Filtration: The water passes through filters, some made of layers of sand, gravel, and charcoal that helps remove even smaller particles.

Source: AWWA Drinking Water Week Blue Thumb Kit

394 A Growing Nation (1800–1870)

Vocabulary Development

Cross-Curricular Vocabulary: Social Studies
Review the definitions of the cross-curricular vocabulary with students: *aquifer, contaminant, ecosystem,* and *hydrologic.* Then examine each word in its context in one of the documents. For example, in the "Water on Tap" guide, point out that a contaminant is something that must be removed from drinking water. The passage describes a number of methods used to make sure that the contaminants are taken out of the water. This emphasis tells the reader a contaminant is a substance that makes the water impure or unsafe to drink. In the government report, readers learn that draining a floodplain had a strong impact on the ecosystem. The article immediately explains the effects on waterfowl, wading birds, and fish, indicating that *ecosystem* refers to groups of living things and their habitat.

2007
SOUTH FLORIDA
ENVIRONMENTAL
REPORT

The heading indicates the topic covered in this section of the report.

The report is dated.

KISSIMMEE RIVER RESTORATION AND UPPER BASIN INITIATIVES

Covering approximately 3,000 square miles, the Kissimmee watershed forms the headwaters of the Kissimmee-Okeechobee-Everglades system. This watershed is comprised of a diverse group of wetland aquatic ecosystems within its Upper Basin—and Lower Basin, the Kissimmee River. The meandering Kissimmee River was channelized to prevent catastrophic flooding and much of the original floodplain was drained. However, there were pronounced impacts on the ecosystem—drastic declines in wintering waterfowl, wading bird, and fish populations and loss of ecosystem functions.

Another Year of Above-Average Rainfall In The Kissimmee Basin Poses Regional Water Management Challenges

During WY2006, hydrologic conditions in the Kissimmee watershed were quite variable, particularly due to extreme seasonal rainfall conditions. There were high levels of rainfall in June 2005, followed by a relatively dry spring and another surge of intense rainfall in October 2005 from Hurricane Wilma. The basin also experienced another year of above-average rainfall during WY2006, primarily due to Hurricane Wilma. The total rainfall during WY2006 in the Upper Basin (53 inches) and in the Lower Basin (49 inches) exceeded historical annual averages by about 3 to 4 inches, respectively. During this water year, discharges from the S-65 water control structure into the Kissimmee River peaked near 9,000 cubic feet per second and, were among the highest recorded in nearly 75 years.

The Next Phase of Kissimmee Basin Construction Was Launched In Water Year 2006

The District and the U.S. Army Corps of Engineers are collaborating in the Kissimmee River Restoration and the Kissimmee River Headwaters Revitalization projects.

Together, these large-scale restoration projects will **(1)** reestablish the river-floodplain system's ecological integrity by reconstructing the river's physical form, **(2)** provide the water storage and regulation

Informational Text: Report **395**

About Reports

1. Direct students to read the title and first paragraph of the government report. **Ask:** Based on this beginning, what do you infer about the intended audience of this report?
Possible response: Students may say that the report may be intended for government workers, managers, scientists, elected officials, and citizens with a prior awareness of the Kissimmee River restoration project.

2. **Ask:** How does the presentation of information in the government report differ from the presentation in the consumer guide? How do you account for the difference?
Possible response: The information in the government guide is more complex, with more technical language that is not defined or clarified. Students may explain the difference by noting that the report is intended for an informed readership that has prior knowledge about the subject and its terminology.

3. **Ask:** If the environmental report were to be presented to the general public in, for example, a newspaper, what modifications do you think should be made?
Possible response: Students may say that the information might be presented in simpler language, with more basic background information about the project and explanations of all technical terms.

Differentiated
Instruction   for Universal Access

Support for Less Proficient Readers
To help students better visualize the information in the government report, display a map of Florida in sufficient scale to point out the region and the specific sites mentioned. Ask students to find and trace the Kissimmee River, the location of Lake Okeechobee, and the Everglades. Discuss with students why this vast area might be so vital to humans as well as to wildlife.

EL Support for English Learners
The government report contains a number of words and concepts that may cause difficulty for students. Read the first paragraph aloud to the class, asking students to raise their hands when they need clarification. In addition to *ecosystem,* which is presented in Cross-Curricular Vocabulary, students may need explanations of *watershed, headwaters, aquatic,* and *channelized.* Have students complete the remaining text on their own.

Evaluating Information From Charts

1. Draw class attention to the chart on wading-bird densities. To familiarize students with extracting information from the chart, **ask:** According to the chart, in what year did wading-bird densities first exceed expectations? **Answer:** 2002.

2. **Ask:** How does the chart illustrate or emphasize information in the text of the report? **Answer:** The chart adds specific statistical information, in visual form, that supports the text's more general information about increasing densities of wading birds. The columns for the years 2004, 2005, and 2006 give visual emphasis to the dramatic improvement in wading-bird populations.

3. Based on the text of the report, what other statistical information could be presented in chart form? **Answer:** Data about increased fish populations and improved dissolved oxygen levels could be presented in chart form.

Government Report

schedule modifications needed to approximate the historical flow characteristics of the Kissimmee River system, and **(3)** increase the quantity and quality of shoreline habitat in lakes Kissimmee, Hatchineha, Tiger, and Cypress for the benefit of fish and wildlife.

The first of four major phases of canal backfilling was completed in early 2001, reclaiming almost 6,000 acres of floodplain habitat. Initiated in June 2006, the second phase of construction will backfill 1.9 miles of C-38 canal, remove three weirs, and excavate some portions of river channel. It is projected that all restoration-related construction will be completed by 2012. In total, this project will restore ecological integrity to approximately 20 square miles of river/floodplain habitat and 44 continuous miles of meandering river channel.

Kissimmee River Restoration Produces Promising Results

A key element of the Kissimmee River Restoration is a comprehensive, multi-phased evaluation program for tracking ecological responses to restoration. To address the goal of ecological integrity, the evaluation program has a broad scope encompassing hydrology, water quality, and major biological communities such as plants, invertebrates, fish, and birds. Although restoration efforts only have been under way for a few years and will continue through 2012, many positive responses to the first phase are already being observed. These responses include increases in dissolved oxygen levels, reductions in accumulated sediments, and increased populations of bass and sunfishes in river channels, as well as increased use of the river and floodplain by various birds. Remarkably, the highest densities of both waterfowl and long-legged wading birds, such as white ibis (*Eudocimus albus*), on the restored floodplain were recorded in 2006, almost two times those observed in 2005 (see figure below). Since completion of Phase I construction in 2001, wading bird densities have exceeded the projected restoration expectation in this area.

Wading Bird Densities Within The Kissimmee Phase I Restoration Area

The color-coded chart helps the reader interpret information.

MEAN DENSITY (# BIRDS PER SQUARE KILOMETER)

RESTORATION EXPECTATION

1997 | 1998 | 2002 | 2004 | 2005 | 2006

PRE-RESTORATION (BASELINE)

POST-RESTORATION

396 A Growing Nation (1800–1870)

Critical Reading

1. Key Ideas and Details (a) What public issue or issues does the consumer guide address? **(b)** Cite one fact presented in the guide that a citizen might find reassuring and one that might raise concerns. Explain your choices.

2. Key Ideas and Details (a) What environmental concern does the project discussed in the report seek to correct? Explain. **(b)** At the time the report was issued, is the project showing clear success? Cite specific details to support your response.

3. Integration of Knowledge and Ideas (a) Identify two visual elements in each text that clarify or organize information presented verbally. **(b)** For each, explain how the visual element helps you interpret and integrate the information contained in the text.

4. Content-Area Vocabulary (a) Explain how the Greek prefix *hydro-* ("water") contributes to the meaning of the word *hydrologic.*
(b) Determine the meaning of the following words that contain this Greek prefix: *hydraulic, hydrate, hydrant,* and *hydroplane.* Use a dictionary to verify the meanings.

Common Core State Standards

Writing

1. Write arguments to support claims in an analysis of substantive topics or texts, using valid reasoning and relevant and sufficient evidence.

1.a. Introduce precise, knowledgeable claim(s) and establish the significance of the claim(s).

10. Write routinely over shorter time frames for a range of tasks and purposes.

Timed Writing

Argument: Persuasive Essay [40 minutes]

Format

In an argument, or **persuasive essay,** you present a well-reasoned position or opinion. In an essay, you must explain and support your argument.

Refer to both the Consumer Guide and the Government Report to write a position statement, a **persuasive essay** in which you state and support an opinion, about the management of **natural resources** both today and in the future. Cite facts, statistics, and quotations from the documents to support your case and persuade readers to agree with your position.

Academic Vocabulary

The prompt asks you to discuss the management of **natural resources.** Focus your response on land, water, and air and ways in which to improve the management of these resources.

5-Minute Planner

Complete these steps before you begin to write:

1. Read the prompt carefully. List key words.

2. Review the texts. Make notes about details pertaining to the management of natural resources. Cite specific details to include in your essay.

3. Draft a rough outline. Note ideas with which to introduce and conclude your essay. **TIP** In your outline, include notes about how to transition smoothly between ideas and evidence to convey meaning clearly and logically.

4. Reread the prompt, and then draft your essay.

Extend the Lesson

Connecting to the Students' World
Invite students to create their own consumer guides. Divide the class into small groups. Ask students to develop a consumer guide that informs the general public about some project, process, or event in the school or community. Have students brainstorm for ideas about what information is essential, what terms must be explained, and what data could be expressed in a diagram, illustration, or chart. When the guides are completed, invite groups to share their project with the entire class.

Critical Reading

1. (a) **Answer:** The guide explains how tap water is treated.
   (b) **Possible responses:** It is reassuring that drinking water must meet certain health standards. Some citizens may be concerned about the chemicals used to disinfect water.

2. (a) **Answer:** The project was designed to help rebuild the river's ecosystem and to address water management challenges.
   (b) **Possible response:** The success of the first phase could be measured in positive changes such as increases in dissolved oxygen levels and fish populations.

3. (a) **Possible response:** Visual elements in the first text include an image of a glass of water and a diagram of a water treatment plant. The second text includes a color-coded chart.
   (b) **Possible response:** The water glass reinforces that the text is about drinking water, while the diagram helps break down the water-treatment process into steps. The chart in the second piece summarizes the information about bird populations. The color-coding helps emphasize the positive effects of the restoration.

4. (a) **Answer:** *Hydrologic* describes things that relate to the scientific study of water. The prefix "hydro" specifies the branch of science.
   (b) **Answer:** *Hydraulic* describes things that are moved by water. To *hydrate* is to absorb water. *Hydrant* is a receptacle that stores water. To *hydroplane* is to move across the surface of water.

Timed Writing

1. Before students begin the assignment, guide them in analyzing key words and phrases in the prompt, using the highlighted notes.

2. Work with students to draw up guidelines for their persuasive essays based on the key words they identified.

3. Have students use the 5-Minute Planner to structure their time.

4. Allow students 40 minutes to complete the assignment. Evaluate their work using the guidelines they have developed.

397

Contemporary Connection

"Embracing Wilderness" presents a photographer's response to a landscape explored by Henry David Thoreau. Introduce the photos by having students describe exactly what they see and suggesting how they might relate to Thoreau's life and writing. Then have students read the text to learn about the origin of the photos.

Embracing Wilderness Past and Present

1. Point out that Besaw's photographs focus on people in the wilderness. Have students consider how the focus of these photos would be different if they presented landscapes without evidence of human contact. **Ask** students to explain how the series connects to Thoreau's observations by including human subjects.

   Possible response: Landscapes without people might emphasize nature's power, but including people helps focus on the relationship between people and nature. Through scale, composition, and color, Besaw emphasizes the impression that nature makes on humans, just as it impressed Thoreau.

2. Review with students that living in harmony with nature and finding joy in the natural world is a key idea of Transcendentalism. In "Nature," Ralph Waldo Emerson states that the power of nature to produce delight "does not reside in nature, but in man, or in a harmony of both." Students might consider how these photographs illuminate Emerson's perspective.

Bridget Besaw

1. Review the information on Bridget Besaw with students.

2. **Ask:** How can photography be an effective tool for advocacy? **Answer:** Images can create a strong, lasting impression. People might be inspired by a photo to help preserve the regions shown.

Embracing WILDERNESS

Past and Present

In 1846, 1853, and 1857, Henry David Thoreau traveled through vast stretches of Maine wilderness, following ancient canoe routes used by the Wabanaki Indians. In the Maine woods, Thoreau hiked and scaled mountains, writing, "I looked with awe at the ground I trod on…This was the Earth of which we have heard, made out of Chaos and Old Night." These Maine expeditions, far more grueling than Thoreau's walks around Massachusetts, "left such an impression of stern, yet gentle, wildness on [his] memory as will not soon be effaced."

Today, the Thoreau-Wabanaki Trail, as it is now called, is still in use. In the spring of 2005, photographer Bridget Besaw shot a series of photographs featuring people hiking, fishing, canoeing, camping, and climbing on the Thoreau-Wabanaki Trail. The photographs, captioned with quotes from Thoreau's writings, became an exhibit and a book. In her striking images, Besaw shows people rising to the challenges of the wilderness, celebrating its beauty, and standing in awe of its power. Her images suggest that the wilderness remains as important for us today as it was for Thoreau and the Wabanaki before him.

Bridget Besaw / Photographer

Bridget Besaw's award-winning photographs appear in a full spectrum of media: magazines, newspapers, advertisements, documentaries, books, and exhibits. Her current focus is on creating images for use as an advocacy tool for environmental protection.

398 A Growing Nation (1800–1870)

Enrichment: Investigating Career Connections

Photographer

Professional photographers often specialize in a specific niche, such as Besaw's field of environmental photography. Other specializations include studio portraits of people or animals, wedding photography, celebrity or fashion shoots, advertising, or journalism.

With today's reliance on digital photography in most fields, another related career involves using computer software to improve and change raw photographic data. Experts in this field are employed by design and advertising firms, as well as periodicals and other media sources.

Activity: Research Have students choose a career in photography that interests them and find out what training, equipment, and experience are shared by most successful professionals.

Students can guide their exploration using **Enrichment: Investigating Career Connections** worksheet, *Professional Development Guidebook*, p. 221.

1. **Ask** students to compare Thoreau's response to the Maine wilderness with Besaw's response to the same region, as reflected in this photograph.

   Possible response: Thoreau was amazed by a wilderness that seemed "stern, yet gentle" and timelessly wild. Besaw's photograph emphasizes the timelessness of nature by showing a child's joyful response to the water. This picture seems to focus on the gentler side of nature that Thoreau encountered in Maine.

2. **Ask** students to identify what elements the composition of the photograph emphasizes and explain the effect of this emphasis.

   Possible response: By placing the child in the lower right corner, the photograph emphasizes the water and rocks, as well as the boy's path through them. This composition highlights the role of people in nature. If the photograph were cropped more tightly to focus on the boy, it might emphasize the free-spirited playfulness of youth.

Differentiated Instruction for Universal Access

Support for Less Proficient Readers

Students may need help interpreting Thoreau's quotation on page 400. Point out that Thoreau uses the noun *wildness* to describe his ideal wilderness, which he compares with civilization. Ask students whether Thoreau wants the wilderness or civilization to be more powerful. Help them understand that by saying that civilization cannot endure the glance, or sight, of this wilderness, the wilderness is much more powerful.

Strategy for Special-Needs Students

Suggest that students create a chart to compare Besaw's photographs with Thoreau's ideas. Label one column Thoreau and the other Besaw. Students can begin by summarizing Thoreau's quotations, using their own word to state the main ideas. Then students can note the main ideas communicated by each photograph.

1. **Possible response:** The photo of the rafters being nearly engulfed by the moving water suggests that the "wildness" of the water is much more powerful than "civilization."

2. (a) A contemporary view of the wilderness might be equally impressed by nature's power. However, a modern view might also acknowledge the increasing degree to which technology has replaced and damaged wilderness. (b) The differences between past and present perspectives reflect changing times. Industrialization in the 19th century and the growth of technology in the 20th and 21st centuries greatly changed the way we view the world.

3. **Possible response:** Any natural setting, from a local brook to the Grand Canyon, could celebrate the beauty of nature. Students should identify a specific setting and explain what elements they would highlight in a series of photographs. For example, photographs of Niagara Falls might emphasize the play of light on the water or the reactions of visitors to the falls' magnificence.

$\mathcal{G}$ive me a WILDNESS whose glance no CIVILIZATION can endure . . .

Henry David Thoreau

Critical Reading

1. **Describe:** Select one of these images and describe the relationship between Besaw's images and Thoreau's words.

2. **(a) Compare and Contrast:** In what ways might a contemporary person's view of the wilderness be both similar to and different from Thoreau's perspective? **(b) Assess:** What circumstances might account for these similarities and differences?

Use this question to focus a class discussion:

3. Bridget Besaw's subject in this series is the north woods of Maine. If your assignment were to celebrate the beauty of nature in photographs, what locale would you select? Explain your choices.

400 A Growing Nation (1800–1870)

American Masters

PART 4

This chart gives a general text complexity rating for the selections in this part of the unit to help guide instruction. For additional text complexity support, see the Text Complexity Rubric at point of use.

Because I could not stop for Death	**More Complex**	Water, is taught by thirst	**More Accessible**
I heard a Fly buzz when I died	**More Accessible**	*from* Preface to Leaves of Grass	**More Complex**
There's a certain Slant of light	**More Complex**	*from* Song of Myself	**More Accessible**
My life closed twice before its close	**More Complex**	When I Heard the Learn'd Astronomer	**More Accessible**
The Soul selects her own Society	**More Complex**	By the Bivouac's Fitful Flame	**More Accessible**
The Brain—is wider than the Sky	**More Accessible**	I Hear America Singing	**More Accessible**
There is a Solitude of Space	**More Accessible**	A Noiseless Patient Spider	**More Accessible**

Selection Planning Guide

The selections in this section reveal the range of two of the nation's most famous poets. Emily Dickinson's poetry explores the vast inner landscape. "The Brain—is wider than the Sky—" asserts that the human soul can encompass all things in the natural world and an individual identity. In "Because I could not stop for Death—" and "I heard a Fly buzz when I died—," the poet describes the somber journey from life to death. Rich in imagery and symbolism and innovative in its form, Dickinson's poetry has been celebrated and emulated long after the poet's death. Whitman's strong belief in the connection between humanity and nature as well as his unique catalog style are evident in the excerpt from "Song of Myself" and in "I Hear America Singing."

Humanities

Indian Summer, 1855, Règis Francois Gignoux

Born in Lyon, France, Règis Francois Gignoux studied landscape painting in Europe before coming to the United States in pursuit of the young woman who became his wife. In America, Gignoux became a prominent member of the Hudson River School of landscape painters. Paintings of the Hudson River School are often characterized by stately, formal notions of natural beauty, by highly detailed presentation of trees and foliage, and by deep-focus vistas of quiet water and distant mountains. People, when they appear, seem miniaturized in the vast landscape, suggesting both human humility and harmony with nature. Use the following question for discussion:

What details in this painting show the characteristics of the Hudson River School?
Answer: Students may find that the painting exemplifies many of the features of the school, including quiet water, distant mountains, detailed foliage, and small-scale human figures.

Benchmark

After students have completed the selections in Part 3, administer **Benchmark Test 3** (*Unit 2 Resources*, pp. 149–154). If the benchmark test reveals that some students need further work, use the **Interpretation Guide** to determine the appropriate reteaching page in the **Reading Kit**.

❶ Defining Poetry

1. Review with students the types of poetry listed on the student page. Point out that the categories of narrative and dramatic poetry have much in common with the major genres of prose and drama.

2. **Ask**: Aside from its appearance on the page, how would you distinguish a lyric poem about the sunrise from a prose description of the same scene?

   Sample responses: The lyric poem would probably describe the scene more succinctly than the prose version. It would use some combination of figurative language, rhyme, and rhythm to create a musical effect.

❷ Sound Devices

1. Point out that while meter is the regular pattern of beats, all poets consider the *rhythm* of words when writing. Explain that rhythm is the arrangement of stressed and unstressed syllables and exists in all spoken or written language. Write the phrase "the regular pattern of beats in a line" on the board. Invite volunteers to use accent marks to indicate the stressed syllables.

   Answer: The reg´ ular pat´ tern of beats´ in a line.´

2. Point out that Walt Whitman—like Billy Collins, whose poem is on page 403—often wrote in *free verse,* unrhymed poetry that lacks a regular rhythmical pattern.
   Ask: How would you recognize free verse as poetry if you heard it read?

   Sample response: You would notice the use of figurative language, imagery, and sound devices.

❸ Close Read: Poetic Elements

Review the chart with students. Point out the highlighted text in the model on page 403. Explain that in each case, the color of the highlighting matches the color of the category in the chart. Details that illustrate a given category are highlighted in the color of that category.

IF I FEEL PHYSICALLY AS IF THE TOP OF MY HEAD WERE TAKEN OFF, I KNOW THAT IS POETRY.

— EMILY DICKINSON

❶ Defining Poetry

Along with prose and drama, poetry is one of the three major genres, or forms, of literature. Poets usually employ highly charged language and arrange words in lines that form stanzas.

Types of Poetry Most poems fall into one of three categories:

- **Narrative poetry** tells a story and has the same literary elements as works of prose fiction. *Ballads* and *epics* are two types of narrative poem.
- **Dramatic poetry** uses the techniques of drama to present the speech of one or more characters in verse form.
- **Lyric poetry** expresses the thoughts and feelings of a single speaker.

❷ Sound Devices
Poets use the innate musical qualities of words to create patterns that emphasize meaning. **Meter,** the regular pattern of beats in a line, is one aspect of poetic sound. Other sound devices are

- **rhyme,** the repetition of sounds at the ends of words (*leaf* and *brief*);
- **consonance,** the repetition of final consonant sounds (*spea<u>k</u>* and *brea<u>k</u>*);
- **assonance,** repetition of similar vowel sounds (*sh<u>a</u>de* and *r<u>a</u>y*).

Alliteration, another sound device, is defined in the chart below.

Images and Figurative Language Images are words and phrases that appeal to the senses. Figurative language is language used imaginatively rather than literally. These, too, are hallmarks of poetry.

❸ Close Read: Poetic Elements
These poetic elements appear in the Model text at right.

Alliteration: repetition of initial identical consonant sounds in accented syllables *Example: "What <u>s</u>aint <u>s</u>trained <u>s</u>o much . . . ?"* (Theodore Roethke)	**Imagery:** language that appeals to the senses, creating word pictures that help to express meaning *Example: "a red wheelbarrow / glazed with rain water"* (William Carlos Williams)
Simile and Metaphor: figures of speech that compare two apparently unlike things. Similes use a connecting word (*like* or *as*); metaphors do not. Simile: *"The child's first step, / as awesome as an earthquake.* (Anne Sexton) Metaphor: *"...the fiery night that's in your eyes..."* (Edward Arlington Robinson)	**Precise Word Choice:** words that carry precise shades of meaning and express tone *Example: "Oh, but it is dirty!—this little filling station . . ."* (Elizabeth Bishop)

In This Section

- Defining Poetry (p. 402)
- Model: "Man Listening to Disc" (p. 403)
- Study: Emily Dickinson's Poetry (p. 406)
- Study: Walt Whitman's Poetry (p. 426)

For more practice analyzing poetry, see numerous pages throughout this textbook, including 82, 125, 256, 312, 428, 636, 643, 708, 722, 874 , 902, 1064, 1072, and 1366.

PROFESSIONAL DEVELOPMENT   Sharroky Hollie

APPLY THE STRATEGY:

The poetry of Emily Dickinson provides ample opportunities for culturally responsive read-alouds. Dickinson's prolific use of short stanzas and terse lines aligns well with read-alouds that involve call and response.

Choose one of Dickinson's poems. Read it aloud to the students, modeling the appropriate prosody. Then, have students reread the poem with you, using echo reading.

Have the students choose another Dickinson poem and, with a partner, read the poem aloud

and then do echo reading with the partner. Ask students to note their use of prosody and how it matches with their interpretation of the poem.

For more of Dr. Hollie's strategies, see the Professional Development essay, pp. 462a–462b.

Model

About the Text Billy Collins (born 1941) has written many poems about other art forms. This poem celebrates the musical qualities and artistry of jazz.

"Man Listening to Disc" by Billy Collins

This is not bad—
ambling along 44th Street
with Sonny Rollins for company,
his music flowing through the soft calipers
of these earphones,

❹ as if he were right beside me
on this clear day in March,
the pavement sparkling with sunlight,
pigeons fluttering off the curb,
nodding over a profusion of bread crumbs.

In fact, I would say
my delight at being suffused
❺ with phrases from his saxophone—
some like honey, some like vinegar—
is surpassed only by my gratitude

to Tommy Potter for taking the time
to join us on this breezy afternoon
with his most unwieldy bass
and to the esteemed Arthur Taylor
who is somehow managing to navigate

this crowd with his cumbersome drums.
And I bow deeply to Thelonious Monk
for figuring out a way
to motorize—or whatever—his huge piano
so he could be with us today.

This music is loud yet so confidential
I cannot help feeling even more
like the center of the universe
than usual as I walk along to a rapid
little version of "The Way You Look Tonight,"

❻ and all I can say to my fellow pedestrians,
to the woman in the white sweater,
the man in the tan raincoat and the heavy glasses,
who mistake themselves for the center of the universe—
all I can say is watch your step,

because the five of us, instruments and all,
are about to angle over
to the south side of the street
and then, in our own tightly knit way,
❼ turn the corner at Sixth Avenue.

And if any of you are curious
about where this aggregation,
this whole battery-powered crew,
is headed, let us just say
that the real center of the universe,

the only true point of view,
is full of the hope that he,
the hub of the cosmos
with his hair blown sideways,
will eventually make it all the way downtown.

---

❹ **Alliteration** Repetition of initial consonant *p* sounds mimics the popping rhythms of a jazz riff.

❺ **Simile** The comparisons suggest the changing textures of the sound from sweet and flowing to sharp and jagged.

❻ **Imagery** Word pictures appeal to the sense of sight. The speaker's head is filled with music, but he sees the world and its people clearly.

❼ **Precise Word Choice** Precise word choices suggest the speaker's physical movement as he walks, the reality of his listening on a portable CD-player, and the virtuoso precision of the musicians.

---

❹ **Alliteration**

Read aloud the bracketed passage and have students identify the alliteration (*pavement, pigeons,* and *profusion*). **Ask:** What other example of alliteration can you find in this stanza?

Answer: In line 8, the phrase "sparkling with sunlight" is an example of alliteration.

❺ **Simile**

Point out that this is a simile because it compares the music with honey, using the connecting word *like*. Remind students that a metaphor is a comparison that does not use *like* or *as*. **Ask:** How could you change this stanza so that the simile became a metaphor?

Sample response: In fact, I would say my delight at being suffused with the honey and vinegar from his saxophone is surpassed only by my gratitude.

❻ **Imagery**

Invite students to imagine that they are Billy Collins composing this poem. **Ask:** What other images of pedestrians can you think of that Billy Collins might have included in this stanza?

Sample responses: a girl with the Great Dane; a man in jeans eating a burrito

❼ **Precise Word Choice**

1. Point out that English gives the writer a wide choice of words to describe the act of walking. **Ask:** What are some other words that Billy Collins might have used in place of *angle*.

   Sample responses: *walk; amble; stride; march; jaywalk*

2. Invite students to experiment with their replacement words for *angle* and to vote on the one that seems most appropriate for the context.

Think Aloud

Vocabulary: Using Context

To model the skill of using context to infer the meaning of an unfamiliar word, use the following "think aloud." Say to students:

   I don't know what the word *suffused* means in line 2 of the third stanza, but I think I can figure it out by looking at its context—the words and phrases around it. The speaker is walking down the street, listening to jazz on a CD-player. He explains that he is delighted at "being suffused with phrases" from Sonny Rollins's saxophone.

   Then, he uses an interesting simile, comparing the music to honey and vinegar. Honey and vinegar are things you can pour out of a container, just the way music pours out of a saxophone. And when I look back to stanza 1, I get another clue: the music is "flowing" through the earphones. So it seems to me that the speaker feels that he is covered with music, like being covered, or spread, with honey. I'm going to guess that suffused means something like "covered all over."

403

• Emily Dickinson's Poetry
Lesson Pacing Guide

DAY 1 Preteach

- Administer the Reading and Vocabulary Warm-ups (*Unit 2 Resources*, pp. 155–158) as necessary.
- Introduce the Literary Analysis concepts: Exact Rhyme and Slant Rhyme and Paradox.
- Introduce the Reading Strategy: Reread.
- Build background with the author and Background features.
- Develop thematic thinking with Connecting to the Essential Question.
- Teach the selection vocabulary.

DAYS 2–3 Preteach/Teach/ Assess

- Distribute copies of the appropriate graphic organizer for the Reading Strategy (*Graphic Organizer Transparencies*, pp. 86–87).
- Distribute copies of the appropriate graphic organizer for Literary Analysis (*Graphic Organizer Transparencies*, pp. 88–89).
- Prepare students to read with the Activating Prior Knowledge activities (TE).
- Informally monitor comprehension while students read.
- Use the Reading Check question to confirm comprehension.
- Develop students' understanding of exact rhyme and slant rhyme and paradox using the Literary Analysis prompts.
- Develop students' ability to reread using the Reading Strategy prompts.
- Reinforce vocabulary with the Vocabulary notes.
- Assess students' comprehension and mastery of the skills by having them answer the Critical Reading, Literary Analysis, and Reading Strategy questions.
- Have students complete the Vocabulary Lesson.

DAY 4 Extend/Assess

- Have students complete the Writing Lesson and write a blog entry about poetry. (You may assign as homework.)
- Have students read and respond to the Critical Commentary.
- Administer Selection Test A or B (*Unit 2 Resources*, pp. 167–169 or 170–172).

Common Core State Standards

Reading Literature 4. Determine the meaning of words and phrases as they are used in the text, including figurative and connotative meanings; analyze the impact of specific word choices on meaning and tone.
5. Analyze how an author's choices concerning how to structure specific parts of a text contribute to its overall structure and meaning as well as its aesthetic impact.
6. Analyze a case in which grasping a point of view requires distinguishing what is directly stated in a text from what is really meant.

Writing 2. Write explanatory texts to examine and convey complex ideas, concepts, and information clearly and accurately through the effective selection, organization, and analysis of content.
2.b. Develop the topic thoroughly by selecting the most significant quotations or other information and examples appropriate to the audience's knowledge of the topic.

Language 4.b. Identify and correctly use patterns of word changes that indicate different meanings or parts of speech.
5. Demonstrate understanding of word relationships.
5.a. Interpret figures of speech in context and analyze their role in the text.

Additional Standards Practice
Common Core Companion, pp. 41–48; 54–55; 61–62; 196–207; 324–331; 332–335

Daily Block Scheduling
Each day in this Lesson Pacing Guide represents a 40–50 minute period. Teachers using block scheduling may combine days to revise pacing. In addition, teachers may differentiate and support core instruction by integrating components for extended and intensive support as students require. See the Guide to Selected Leveled Resources (facing page).

Guide to Selected Leveled Resources

R T I Tier 1 (students performing on level)

Emily Dickinson's Poetry

Warm Up	**Practice, model,** and **monitor** fluency, working **with the whole class** or **in groups.**	Vocabulary and Reading Warm-ups B, *Unit 2 Resources,* pp. 155–156, 158
Comprehension/Skills	**Support** and **monitor** comprehension and skills development, having students complete the activities, graphic organizers, and interactive prompts **independently** or **as a class.**	• *Reader's Notebook,* adapted instruction and summary **EL** *Reader's Notebook: English Learner's Version,* adapted instruction and summary • **Reading Strategy Graphic Organizer B,** *Graphic Organizer Transparencies,* p. 87 • **Literary Analysis Graphic Organizer B,** *Graphic Organizer Transparencies,* p. 89
Monitor Progress **A**	**Monitor** student progress with the differentiated curriculum-based assessment in the *Unit Resources.*	• **Selection Test B,** *Unit 2 Resources,* pp. 170–172 • **Open-Book Test,** *Unit 2 Resources,* pp. 164–166

R T I Tier 2 (students requiring intervention)

Emily Dickinson's Poetry

Warm Up	**Practice, model,** and **monitor** fluency **in groups** or **with individuals.**	• **Vocabulary and Reading Warm-ups A,** *Unit 2 Resources,* pp. 155–157 • *Hear It!* **Audio CD**
Comprehension/Skills	• **Support** and **monitor** comprehension and skills development, working **in small groups** or **with individuals.** • As students complete the selection in the appropriate version of the *Reader's Notebook,* **monitor** comprehension frequently with group questions and individual instruction. • **Model** strategies while guiding students in completing the activities and prompts in the *Reader's Notebook,* as well as the graphic organizers. • **Practice** skills and **monitor** mastery with the *Reading Kit* worksheets.	• *Reader's Notebook: Adapted Version,* adapted instruction and summary **EL** *Reader's Notebook: English Learner's Version,* adapted instruction and summary • **Reading Strategy Graphic Organizer A,** *Graphic Organizer Transparencies,* p. 86 • **Literary Analysis Graphic Organizer A,** *Graphic Organizer Transparencies,* p. 88 • *Reading Kit,* Practice worksheets
Monitor Progress **A**	**Monitor** student progress with the differentiated curriculum-based assessment in the *Unit Resources* and in the *Reading Kit.*	• **Selection Test A,** *Unit 2 Resources,* pp. 167–169 • *Reading Kit,* Assess worksheets

TIER 3 Tier 3 intervention may require consultation with the student's special education or dyslexia specialist. For additional support, see the Tier 2 activities and resources listed above.

One-on-one teaching   Group work   Whole-class instruction   Independent work   **A** Assessment

For a complete guide to selection support, including support for Advanced students, see the Overview of Resources in the frontmatter.

• Emily Dickinson's Poetry

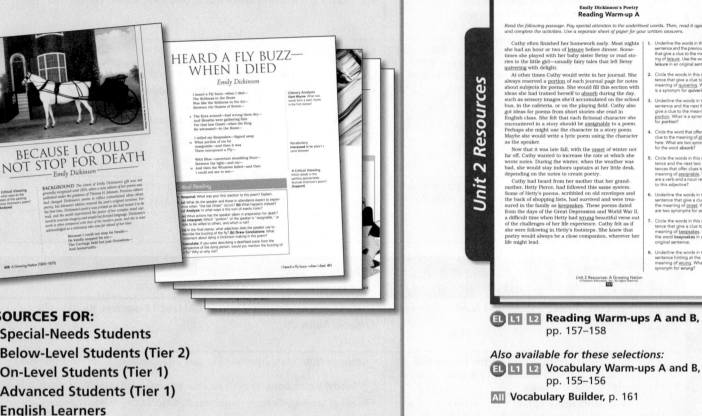

BECAUSE I COULD NOT STOP FOR DEATH
Emily Dickinson

HEARD A FLY BUZZ— WHEN I DIED
Emily Dickinson

RESOURCES FOR:

L1 Special-Needs Students

L2 Below-Level Students (Tier 2)

L3 On-Level Students (Tier 1)

L4 Advanced Students (Tier 1)

EL English Learners

All All Students

Vocabulary/Fluency/Prior Knowledge

Emily Dickinson's Poetry
Reading Warm-up A

EL L1 L2 Reading Warm-ups A and B, pp. 157–158

Also available for these selections:

EL L1 L2 Vocabulary Warm-ups A and B, pp. 155–156

All Vocabulary Builder, p. 161

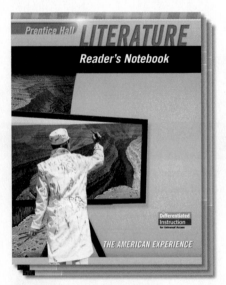

Reader's Notebooks

Pre- and postreading pages for these selections appear in an interactive format in the *Reader's Notebooks.* Each *Notebook* is differentiated for a different group of learners. The selections in the Adapted and English Learner's versions are abridged.

L2 L3 *Reader's Notebook*

L1 *Reader's Notebook: Adapted Version*

EL *Reader's Notebook: English Learner's Version*

EL *Reader's Notebook: Spanish Version*

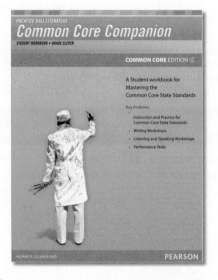

© *Common Core Companion*

Additional instruction and practice for each Common Core State Standard

Selection Support

Skills Development/Extension

Assessment

Selection Support

Emily Dickinson's Poetry

After You Read B: Analyzing Rhyme

Slant Rhyme	Lines	Exact Rhyme	Lines

Name _____ Date _____

Emily Dickinson's Poetry
Support for Writing

As you search Emily Dickinson's poetry for references to boundlessness, the infinite, and things without limit, keep track of your findings in the chart below.

Name of Poem	Detail referring to boundlessness, the infinite, or things without limit

On the lines below, write a general statement about Dickinson's views about the infinite. Put a check next to the details in your chart that best support this statement. Then, on a separate page, write a draft of your blog entry. Begin with your general statement, and support that statement with details from the poems. Be sure to punctuate each direct quotation correctly, and cite the poem in which it appears.

_____

_____

Name _____ Date _____

Emily Dickinson's Poetry
Selection Test B

Critical Reading *Identify the letter of the choice that best completes the statement or answers the question.*

___ 1. In "I heard a Fly buzz—when I died—," why is there a stillness in the room?
   A. The people in the room have stopped talking in order to listen to the fly.
   B. The people in the room are waiting for the speaker to make her will.
   C. The people in the room are waiting for the speaker's final moment.
   D. The storm outdoors has momentarily ceased its "heaves."

___ 2. In the following stanza from "I heard a Fly buzz—when I died—," which words create slant rhyme?
   I heard a Fly buzz—when I died— / The Stillness in the Room / Was like the Stillness in the Air— / Between the Heaves of Storm—
   A. *Air* and *Storm*
   B. *Room* and *Storm*
   C. *died* and *Room*
   D. *died* and *Air*

___ 3. Which of the following best clarifies these lines from "Because I could not stop for Death"?
   The Dews drew quivering and chill—/For only Gossamer, my Gown—/My Tippet—only Tule—
   A. The dews chilled me and caused shivering, because my gown was only gossamer and my tippet was only tule.
   B. The dews quivered and chilled my gossamer gown and my tule tippet.
   C. The dews caused quivering and chill, and I only wore Gossamer and Tule.
   D. The chill caused dews and made me quiver because of my gossamer gown and tule tippet.

___ 4. In "Because I could not stop for Death—," Death is personified as
   A. a polite gentleman.
   B. a rough and harried carriage driver.
   C. a weary gravedigger.
   D. a well-informed tour guide.

___ 5. Which of these statements best expresses the central message of "My life closed twice before its close—"?
   A. Our lives are divided into three parts, and death is the last one.
   B. Parting is heavenly when you are glad to be rid of someone but hellish when you know you will miss the person.
   C. Parting may be the closest we come in life to understanding death.
   D. Death is followed by immortality.

EL L3 **Literary Analysis: Graphic Organizer B,** p. 89

Also available for these selections:

EL L1 L2 **Reading: Graphic Organizer A,** (partially filled in), p. 86

EL L3 **Reading: Graphic Organizer B,** p. 87

EL L1 L2 **Literary Analysis: Graphic Organizer A,** (partially filled in), p. 88

EL L3 L4 **Support for Writing,** p. 162

Also available for these selections:

All **Literary Analysis: Rhyme and Paradox,** p. 159

All **Reading: Rereading to Monitor and Repair Comprehension,** p. 160

L4 **Enrichment,** p. 163

EL L3 L4 **Selection Test B,** pp. 170–172

Also available for these selections:

L3 L4 **Open-Book Test,** pp. 164–166

EL L1 L2 **Selection Test A,** pp. 167–169

PHLit Online!
www.PHLitOnline.com

Online Resources: All print materials are also available online.

- complete narrated selection text
- a thematically related video with writing prompt
- an interactive graphic organizer
- highlighting feature
- access to all student print resources, adapted to individual student needs
- Spanish and English summaries
- adapted selection translations in Spanish

Get Connected! (thematic video with writing prompt)

Also available:

Background Video
All videos are available in Spanish.

Writer's Journal (with graphics feature)

Also available:

Vocabulary Central (tools and activities for studying vocabulary)

Background

Overview: The Author's Work

Emily Dickinson was familiar with classic myths, the Bible, Shakespeare, and the English Romantics; some English contemporaries such as the Brontës, the Brownings, Tennyson, and George Eliot (Mary Anne Evans); and, among Americans, Thoreau and Emerson. Authorities, however, claim that these sources did not influence her highly inventive poems. While some of Dickinson's poems may strike readers as sweet and aphoristic, those that have elevated Dickinson to the highest ranks of American writers are darker and more sophisticated.

Once Dickinson's complete collection of poems was published, in chronological order, in 1955, scholars drew comparisons with some English Metaphysical poets, William Blake, and even the challenging Gerard Manley Hopkins (1844–1889).

The Writer in Her Time

Although Emily Dickinson's reclusive lifestyle was most likely of emotional origin, it also may have been encouraged by the social customs of the day. Unmarried, Dickinson had little choice but to live with her family. Her decision to isolate herself may have resulted from the trouble those around her had in understanding her. One eminent scholar has said, "The poet Emily Dickinson complained that everybody said: 'What?' to her, until finally she gave up trying to talk altogether and confined herself to writing notes." Such an explanation is supported by Dickinson's poem on page 414, "The soul selects her own Society."

Emily Dickinson
(1830–1886)

A unique voice of delicate intensity, Emily Dickinson is invariably named as one of our nation's greatest poets. Yet in her own lifetime, only a small circle of friends and relatives knew of Dickinson's poetic genius.

A Life Apart Born to a prominent family in Amherst, Massachusetts, Dickinson attended Amherst Academy and nearby Mount Holyoke Female Seminary. As a teenager she had an active social life, but over time she became increasingly reclusive, rarely venturing from her home after she was thirty. Devoting most of her time to writing poetry, she saw only the occasional visitor and communicated with friends and family mainly through letters.

Dickinson's Legacy Although she sometimes enclosed poetry in her letters, Dickinson published only a handful of her poems in her lifetime. When she died, her sister Lavinia found over a thousand poems in the drawers of her dresser, neatly tied in bundles known as **fascicles**. Dickinson left instructions that the poems be destroyed, but her family overrode that wish, recognizing that such a valuable legacy should be shared.

◄ This photograph shows the garden view of the Dickinson family homestead in Amherst, Massachusetts. The site is now a museum.

404 A Growing Nation (1800–1870)

Text Complexity Rubric

	Death, Fly, Slant, Life	Soul, Brain, Solitude, Thirst
Qualitative Measures		
Context/ Knowledge Demands	Innovative nineteenth-century works 1 2 ③ 4 5	Innovative nineteenth-century works 1 2 ③ 4 5
Structure/Language Conventionality and Clarity	Accessible (forceful, direct; concrete imagery) 1 2 3 ④ 5	Accessible (some unusual diction and syntax; concrete imagery) 1 2 ③ 4 5
Levels of Meaning/ Purpose/Concept Level	Challenging (abstract concepts translated into concrete imagery) 1 2 3 ④ 5	Accessible (concrete, familiar concepts) 1 2 ③ 4 5
Quantitative Measures		
Lexile/Text Length	NP / 120, 83, 70, 44 words	NP / 47, 61, 3, 23 words
Overall Complexity	**More complex**	**More accessible**

The Johnson Edition Unfortunately, Dickinson's early editors diminished the power of her verse by changing it to be more conventional in language and style. It was not until 1955 that Thomas H. Johnson published an edition of Dickinson's poetry that attempted to present the poems in their original form. With the appearance of the Johnson edition, Dickinson's poetic genius was more fully appreciated, and she is now acknowledged as a visionary who was far ahead of her time.

The Belle of Amherst In the years since the publication of her work, Dickinson has become the subject of plays, novels, and poems that have romanticized her life and celebrated her genius with varying levels of sentimentality and accuracy. In these works, she has been given a public personality that may or may not resemble the truth of who she was. However, in her work itself, the poets who have followed her find no peer.

FIND ECSTASY IN LIFE;
THE MERE SENSE OF
LIVING IS JOY ENOUGH.

— *Emily Dickinson*

Daily Bellringer

For each class during which you will teach these selections, have students complete one of the five activities for the appropriate week in the *Daily Bellringer Activities* booklet.

Multidraft Reading

To assist struggling readers and to enhance reading for all, apply multidraft reading protocols. For each reading, have students set the purpose indicated:

- **First reading**—identifying key ideas and details and answering any Reading Checks.
- **Second reading**—analyzing craft and structure and responding to the side-column prompts.
- **Third reading**—integrating knowledge and ideas, connecting to other texts and the world, and answering the end-of-selection questions.

For more guidance, refer to the *Classroom Strategies and Teaching Routines* card on multidraft reading.

Background
More About the Author

Biographers of Dickinson have noted that the poet developed strong emotional attachments to several men—to Benjamin Newton, her lawyer father's apprentice; Henry Vaughan Emmons, a student at Amherst College; Charles Wadsworth, a clergyman whom Dickinson met in Philadelphia; Thomas Wentworth Higginson, an editor to whom she sent some poems; and Otis P. Lord, a friend of her family's.

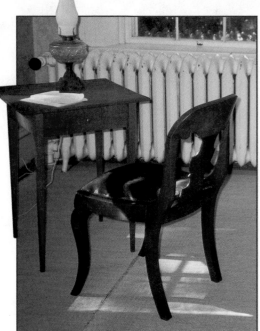

◄ This dress belonged to Emily Dickinson. It is now on display at the Emily Dickinson Homestead Museum.

◄ Emily Dickinson's writing desk and chair still stand in her bedroom at the Homestead.

Extended Study: Poetry **405**

Text Complexity: Reader and Task Suggestions

Death, Fly, Slant, Life		Soul, Brain, Solitude, Thirst	
Preparing to Read the Text	**Leveled Tasks**	**Preparing to Read the Text**	**Leveled Tasks**
• Using the Background on TE pp. 404–405, discuss Dickinson's place in American literary history. • Ask students how people's attitudes toward death differ (as something to be feared, welcomed, and so on). • Guide students to use Multidraft Reading strategies (TE p. 405).	*Levels of Meaning* If students will have difficulty with the meanings, have them skim the four poems and complete this statement for each one: "Here, Dickinson says that death _____." As students reread, have them verify or revise their statements. *Analyzing* If students will not have difficulty with the meanings, discuss the views that Dickinson presents about (1) death at the end of life and (2) circumstances in life that seem deathlike.	• Using the Background on TE pp. 404–405, discuss Dickinson's reputation for being a "reclusive" writer. • Ask students to describe what they see as the advantages and disadvantages of solitude. • Guide students to use Multidraft Reading strategies to deepen their comprehension (TE p. 405).	*Structure/Language* If students will have difficulty with the vocabulary or syntax, have them first read to identify words that signal the idea of solitude. Then, have them read the poems aloud to "hear" Dickinson describe her love for solitude. *Evaluating* If students will not have difficulty with the vocabulary or syntax, ask, "Do you think that these poems make a convincing case for living in solitude?"

405

❶ Dickinson's Style

1. Have students read the text about Dickinson's unconventional style.

2. Expand the information by explaining that in the original manuscripts the dashes varied in length. In addition, some angled upward and some downward rather than forming strict horizontals. The poet may—or may not—have intended these variations to signal more distinctions in sound.

3. After students have read and discussed a few of the poems, have them rewrite a Dickinson stanza with conventional punctuation and capitalization. **Ask** students what the stanza gains or loses with their edits.
Possible response: Students may find reading the stanza easier but perhaps lacking in musicality and emphasis.

4. Some students may have interest in exploring the order in which Dickinson composed the poems. The debate about their sequence is discussed in reference sources including the Web site associated with the Academy of American Poets, which also provides links to criticism of Dickinson and to information about the Dickinson home in Amherst.

❶ Dickinson's Style

Uncertain about her abilities, in 1862 Dickinson sent four poems to the influential literary critic Thomas Wentworth Higginson. With the poems she enclosed a card on which she had written her name and the following unsigned letter:

MR. HIGGINSON, — Are you too deeply occupied to say if my verse is alive? The mind is so near itself it cannot see distinctly, and I have none to ask. Should you think it breathed, and had you the leisure to tell me, I should feel quick gratitude. If I make the mistake, that you dared to tell me would give me sincerer honor toward you. I inclose my name, asking you, if you please, sir, to tell me what is true? That you will not betray me it is needless to ask, since honor is it's own pawn.

In his response to Dickinson, Higginson recognized Dickinson's talent and encouraged her to keep writing, but he also sought to change her unconventional style. He was especially concerned by her unorthodox use of dashes and capitalization. After Dickinson died, Higginson was one of the early editors of her verse. Along with other early editors, he failed to recognize that Dickinson crafted her poems with great precision and that her eccentric capitalization and punctuation were important elements in her poetry. When Thomas H. Johnson came out with his edition of Dickinson's poetry in 1955, he restored original elements including the dashes and capital letters, so that today we can read the poems as Dickinson meant them to be read.

This image shows Dickinson's original manuscript of her famous poem "Much Madness is Divinest Sense." Note her unconventional use of dashes throughout the poem.

406 A Growing Nation (1800–1870)

Vocabulary Development

Vocabulary Knowledge Rating
Create a **Vocabulary Knowledge Rating chart** (*Professional Development Guidebook*, p. 33) for the vocabulary words on the student page. Give each student a copy of the chart with the words on it. Read the words aloud, and have students mark their rating in the Before Reading column. Urge students to attend to these words as they read and discuss the selections.

In order to gauge how much instruction you need to provide, tally how many students are confident in their knowledge of each word. As students read, point out the words and their context.

PHLit Online! **Vocabulary Central**, featuring tools and activities for studying vocabulary, is available online at **www.PHLitOnline.com**.

Before You Read | *Emily Dickinson's Poetry*

❷ Connecting to the Essential Question Emily Dickinson's poems often express a preference for solitude, a value many people would not choose. As you read Dickinson's poems, notice references to the soul and society. This will help as you consider the Essential Question: **What makes American literature American?**

❸ Literary Analysis

Poets use rhyme to stress ideas, make poems musical, convey mood, and unify groups of lines. In **exact rhyme,** two or more words have identical sounds in their final stressed syllables, as in *one/begun.* In **slant rhyme** the final sounds are similar but not identical, as in *one/stone.* Dickinson's frequent use of slant rhyme at points where the reader expects an exact rhyme helps make her poetry surprising:

> *I've known her—from an ample nation—*
> *Choose One—*
> *Then—close the Valves of her attention—*
> *Like Stone—*

Another hallmark of Dickinson's style is her fondness for paradox. A **paradox** is a statement that seems contradictory but actually presents a truth. For example, the statement "The Brain—is wider than the Sky" is a paradox. It seems impossible but becomes true if you consider the brain's capacity to understand. As you read, analyze the effects of rhyme and notice examples of paradox in these poems.

❹ Reading Strategy

Ⓒ Preparing to Read Complex Texts Dickinson writes with great precision, using carefully chosen words in statements that are dense with meaning. Sometimes, she omits words that are expected to be understood. This is called *elliptical phrasing.* To clarify this language, it may be helpful to **reread.** As you reread, mentally fill in words that seem to be missing, and be alert to different possible meanings. Use a chart like the one shown to help as you reread.

❺ Vocabulary

surmised (sər mīzd´) *v.* guessed; concluded (p. 409)

eternity (ē tʉrn´ ə tē) *n.* time without beginning or end (p. 409)

interposed (in´ tər pōzd´) *v.* came between (p. 411)

affliction (ə flik´ shən) *n.* anything causing pain or distress (p. 412)

ample (am´ pəl) *adj.* large in size; more than enough (p. 414)

finite (fī´ nīt) *adj.* having measurable or definable limits (p. 416)

infinity (in fin´ i tē) *n.* endless or unlimited space, time, or distance (p. 416)

**Common Core
State Standards**

Reading Literature

4. Determine the meaning of words and phrases as they are used in the text, including figurative and connotative meanings; analyze the impact of specific word choices on meaning and tone.

5. Analyze how an author's choices concerning how to structure specific parts of a text contribute to its overall structure and meaning as well as its aesthetic impact.

6. Analyze a case in which grasping a point of view requires distinguishing what is directly stated in a text from what is really meant.

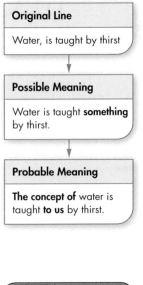

Original Line

Water, is taught by thirst

↓

Possible Meaning

Water is taught **something** by thirst.

↓

Probable Meaning

The concept of water is taught **to us** by thirst.

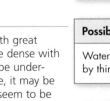
PHLit
Online!
www.PHLitOnline.com

Emily Dickinson's Poetry **407**

PHLit
Online!
www.PHLitOnline.com

Teaching From Technology

Preparing to Read
Go to **www.PHLitOnline.com** in class or in a lab and display the **Get Connected!** slide show for these selections. Have the class brainstorm for responses to the slide show writing prompt, entering ideas in the interactive journal. Then have students complete their written responses individually in a lab or as homework.
    To build background, display the Background and More About the Author features.

Using the Interactive Text
Go to **www.PHLitOnline.com** and display the **Enriched Online Student Edition.** As the class reads the selections or listens to the narration, record answers to side-column prompts using the graphic organizers accessible on the interactive page. Alternatively, have students use the online edition individually, answering the prompts as they read.

---

❷ ❓ Connecting to the Essential Question

1. Review the assignment with the class.

2. Ask students to distinguish *loneliness* from *aloneness.*

3. As students read, have them notice references to the soul and society.

❸ Literary Analysis

Introduce the skills, using the instruction on the student page.

Think Aloud: Model the Skill

Say to students:

Nursery rhymes use exact rhyme:

> Mary had a little lamb.
> Its fleece was white as *snow.*
> And everywhere that Mary went,
> The lamb was sure to *go.*

Exact rhymes can have a singsong effect. To make the four lines more interesting, I can introduce slant rhyme, keeping "Its fleece was white as *snow,*" but changing the fourth line to "The lamb did draw a *groan.*"

❹ Reading Strategy

1. Introduce the strategy, using the instruction on the student page.

2. Give students a copy of **Reading Strategy Graphic Organizer B,** page 87 in *Graphic Organizer Transparencies,* to fill out as they read.

Think Aloud: Model the Skill

Say to students:

Dickinson uses elliptical phrasing—she leaves out words. Will it be hard to figure out which words she omits? To understand phrasing, I often have to reread—slowly and imaginatively.

❺ Vocabulary

1. Pronounce each word, giving its definition, and have students say it aloud.

2. For more guidance, see the *Classroom Strategies and Teaching Routines* card for introducing vocabulary.

Waiting Outside No. 12, Anonymous, Crane Kalman Gallery

❶
❷

BECAUSE I COULD NOT STOP FOR DEATH

—*Emily Dickinson*—

❸ ▲ **Critical Viewing**
In what ways do the details of this painting mirror Dickinson's poem?
[Analyze]

BACKGROUND *The extent of Emily Dickinson's gift was not generally recognized until 1955, when a new edition of her poems was published under the guidance of Thomas H. Johnson. Previous editors had changed Dickinson's poems to reflect conventional ideas about poetry, but Johnson's edition restored the poet's original versions. For the first time, Dickinson's poetry was printed as she had meant it to be read, and the world experienced the power of her complex mind captured in concrete imagery and simple but forceful language. Dickinson's work is often compared with that of the modern poets, and she is now acknowledged as a visionary who was far ahead of her time.*

Because I could not stop for Death—
He kindly stopped for me—
The Carriage held but just Ourselves—
And Immortality.

408 A Growing Nation (1800–1870)

5 We slowly drove—He knew no haste
And I had put away
My labor and my leisure too,
For his Civility—

We passed the School, where Children strove
10 At Recess—in the Ring—
We passed the Fields of Gazing Grain—
We passed the Setting Sun—

 Or rather—He passed Us—
The Dews drew quivering and chill—
15 For only Gossamer,[1] my Gown—
My Tippet[2]—only Tulle[3]—

We paused before a House that seemed
A Swelling of the Ground—
The Roof was scarcely visible—
20 The Cornice—in the Ground—

Since then—'tis Centuries—and yet
Feels shorter than the Day
I first surmised the Horses' Heads
Were toward Eternity—

---

1. **Gossamer** *n.* very thin, soft, filmy cloth.
2. **Tippet** *n.* scarflike garment worn over the shoulders and hanging down in front.
3. **Tulle** (tool) *n.* thin, fine netting used for scarves.

Critical Reading

©

© 1. **Craft and Structure (a)** In the first two lines, what adverb defines Death's actions? **(b) Analyze:** In what sense is this depiction surprising or ironic?

© 2. **Key Ideas and Details (a)** What three scenes does the carriage pass in stanza three? **(b) Interpret:** What meaning do you attribute to these scenes?

© 3. **Key Ideas and Details (a)** How much time passes for the speaker in this poem? **(b) Speculate:** Why do you think the speaker notes that the time "feels shorter than the Day"? **(c) Compare and Contrast:** What does the speaker seem to feel about the experience of death in contrast with life?

© 4. **Integration of Knowledge and Ideas Take a Position:** Do you think this poem has a single meaning or message? Explain your reasoning.

Cite textual evidence to support your responses.

Reading Strategy
Reread Clarify the elliptical phrasing in lines 15
—16 and restate the poet's meaning.

Vocabulary
surmised (sər mīzd´) *v.* guessed; concluded

eternity (ē turn´ə tē) *n.* time without beginning or end

---

❹ **Reading Strategy**
Reread

1. To answer the question, have students read or reread not only lines 15–16 but also line 14, which notes that the speaker senses a chill; the reason for that sensation is then explained by lines 15–16.

2. **Ask** students the Reading Strategy question: Clarify the elliptical phrasing in lines 15–16 and restate the poet's meaning. **Answer:** Filling in the ellipses gives us "For only of gossamer was my gown made, and my tippet was made only of tulle." The poet means that the speaker felt a chill because her clothes were so thin (like the fragile fabrics that were used in making shrouds).

ASSESS

Answers

Before students respond, you may wish to have them write a brief objective summary of the selection. As they answer the questions below, remind them to support their answers with evidence from the text.

1. (a) The adverb "kindly" describes Death's actions. (b) **Possible response:** Death is usually personified in negative terms.

2. (a) It passes "the School," "the Fields," and "the Setting Sun." (b) These details could represent different times of day or the stages of life.

3. (a) It has been centuries since the speaker died. (b) The speaker depicts the timeless nature of eternity. (c) The speaker suggests that both life and death are journeys but that death's journey is free of the busy pace of life.

4. **Possible response:** Students may agree that the poem has a single meaning—that death comes as a friend who brings the dead to a new home. Students may come up with alternative interpretations as well.

Differentiated Instruction for Universal Access

Support for Special-Needs Students
Have students complete the **Before You Read** and the **Making Connections** pages for these selections in the *Reader's Notebook: Adapted Version.* These pages provide abbreviated skills instruction, a selection summary, the Before You Read graphic organizer, and a **Note-taking Guide.**

Support for Less Proficient Readers
Have students complete the **Before You Read** and the **Making Connections** pages for these selections in the *Reader's Notebook.* These pages provide abbreviated skills instruction, a selection summary, the Before You Read graphic organizer, and a **Note-taking Guide.**

EL Support for English Learners
Have students complete the **Before You Read** and the **Making Connections** pages for these selections in the *Reader's Notebook: English Learner's Version.* These pages provide additional vocabulary, vocabulary skills, and vocabulary practice, along with a **Getting Ready to Read** activity.

⑤ About the Selection

In this poem, Dickinson describes the final moments between life and death. A fly, an almost trivial symbol of life, is what the speaker is most aware of before death.

⑥ Humanities

Room With a Balcony, by Adolph von Menzel

Like von Menzel's other work, this painting is distinguished by its expressiveness, accurate details, and use of light and shade for subtle effects. It captures the contrasting ordinariness and extraordinariness of death. Use these questions for discussion:

1. How is the overall impression of the painting similar to that of the poem?
   Answer: Both the image and the poem convey stillness. There appears to be no life in the painted room. The chairs and lamps are placed symmetrically around the mirror. This detail reinforces the "Stillness" (line 2).

2. What might the image of an open window mean in a room in which someone has died?
   Possible answer: It suggests that something or someone may have just entered or left the room.

410 A Growing Nation (1800–1870)

I HEARD A FLY BUZZ— WHEN I DIED

Emily Dickinson

I heard a Fly buzz—when I died—
The Stillness in the Room
Was like the Stillness in the Air—
Between the Heaves of Storm—

5　The Eyes around—had wrung them dry—
And Breaths were gathering firm
For that last Onset—when the King
Be witnessed—in the Room—

I willed my Keepsakes—Signed away
10　What portion of me be
Assignable—and then it was
There interposed a Fly—

With Blue—uncertain stumbling Buzz—
Between the light—and me—
15　And then the Windows failed—and then
I could not see to see—

Literary Analysis
Slant Rhyme What two words form a slant rhyme in the first stanza?

Vocabulary
interposed (in′tər pōzd′) *v.* came between

❽ ◀ **Critical Viewing**
Which details in this painting appropriately illustrate Dickinson's poem? **[Support]**

Cite textual evidence to support your responses.

Critical Reading

1. **Key Ideas and Details (a)** What do the speaker and those in attendance expect to experience when "the last Onset" occurs? **(b)** What happens instead? **(c) Analyze:** In what ways is this turn of events ironic?

2. **Key Ideas and Details (a)** What actions has the speaker taken in preparation for death? **(b) Interpret:** Which "portion" of the speaker is "assignable," or able to be willed to others, and which is not?

3. **Craft and Structure (a)** In the final stanza, what adjectives does the speaker use to describe the buzzing of the fly? **(b) Draw Conclusions:** What statement about dying is Dickinson making in this poem?

4. **Integration of Knowledge and Ideas Speculate:** If you were describing a deathbed scene from the perspective of the dying person, would you mention the buzzing of a fly? Why or why not?

I heard a Fly buzz—when I died **411**

---

❼ **Literary Analysis**
Slant Rhyme
1. Have students read the bracketed passage.
2. **Ask** them the Literary Analysis question: What two words form a slant rhyme in the first stanza? **Answer:** "Room" and "Storm" form a slant rhyme.

❽ **Critical Viewing**
Answer: The mirrored image of a couch and painting, which are no longer in the room but are still suggested by shadows, reflects the poem's idea of death taking away life but leaving behind some mark of the departed.

ASSESS
Answers

Before students respond, you may wish to have them write a brief objective summary of the selection. As they answer the questions below, remind them to support their answers with evidence from the text.

1. (a) They expect to witness the speaker's death. (b) A fly begins to buzz. (c) It suggests that death is highly ordinary, even pedestrian.

2. (a) The speaker wills away keepsakes and other worldly goods. (b) **Possible response:** The material aspects are "assignable," but one's spirit is not.

3. (a) The speaker describes the fly with the terms "Blue," and "uncertain stumbling." (b) **Possible response:** She shows that death is an everyday event; she points out that the experience does not match people's expectations.

4. **Possible response:** Students might omit the fly as being trivial and inappropriate to the seriousness of the event or as being a gruesome omen of decomposition.

411

9 **About the Selections**

The first poem describes an unbearable hurt that fills the soul at winter, when the world is cold and still. The poet describes the hurt as a divine visitation, sent to teach the meaning of our own mortality. The second poem conveys the sense of pain that comes from parting from a loved one. The final poem is a meditation on the nature of the human soul. The poet depicts the soul as a feminine entity, separate from and indifferent to worldly claims on her attention. Dickinson portrays the soul as choosing, for unknowable reasons, a single person to share her society, and rejecting all others.

10 **Literary Analysis**

Slant Rhyme

1. After students read the entire poem "There's a certain Slant of light," direct them to reread the final bracketed stanza.

2. Then **ask** students to identify two words that form a slant rhyme in the stanza.
   Answer: The words "listens" and "Distance" form a slant rhyme.

9 THERE'S A CERTAIN SLANT OF LIGHT

EMILY DICKINSON

There's a certain Slant of light,
Winter Afternoons—
That oppresses, like the Heft
Of Cathedral Tunes—

5   Heavenly Hurt, it gives us—
We can find no scar,
But internal difference,
Where the Meanings, are—

None may teach it—Any—
10   'Tis the Seal Despair—
An imperial affliction
Sent us of the Air—

10 When it comes, the Landscape listens—
Shadows—hold their breath—
15   When it goes, 'tis like the Distance
On the look of Death—

Vocabulary
affliction (ə flik′ shən)
n. anything causing pain or distress

412 A Growing Nation (1800–1870)

Enrichment: Investigating Health and Medicine

Seasonal Affective Disorder

In "There's a certain Slant of light," Dickinson describes an emotional response to winter—depression—that people of her time might have referred to as "cabin fever." Only in the 1980s did doctors diagnose this depression as a mood disorder triggered by a lack of sunlight. Seasonal affective disorder (SAD) usually occurs from late fall through early winter.

Activity: Poster Have students conduct research on SAD. Suggest that they record information in the **Enrichment: Investigating Health and Medicine** work sheet, in *Professional Development Guidebook,* page 229. Have them use the results of their research to prepare an informative poster that might be displayed at school, in a health clinic, or at a senior citizens center.

MY LIFE CLOSED TWICE BEFORE ITS CLOSE—

—— EMILY DICKINSON ——

⑪ My life closed twice before its close—
It yet remains to see
If Immortality unveil
A third event to me.

5 So huge, so hopeless to conceive
As these that twice befell.
Parting is all we know of heaven.
And all we need of hell.

WORLD LITERATURE CONNECTION

⑫
Capturing the Moment

In her poems, Emily Dickinson often seems to capture a moment and hold it still. The tanka is a Japanese form of poetry that also captures the moment. In the original Japanese, tanka is a 31-syllable poem that usually contains at least one distinct pause. This pause is often represented by a dash in English translations. When translated into English, tanka are usually written in five lines, and the syllable count often changes. In Japan, tanka-writing has been popular for more than 1300 years and is still practiced today.

Renowned tanka writers include **Ki Tsurayuki** (died c. 945), an important figure in the Japanese imperial court and a leading poet of his time; **Ono Komachi** (833 – 857), a great beauty whose poems were noted for their passion and energy; and **Priest Jakuren** (1139? – 1202), a Buddhist priest whose poems are filled with beautiful, melancholy imagery.

CONNECT TO THE LITERATURE

What similarities do you see in this tanka and the Emily Dickinson poems you have read? In what ways are they different?

Tanka
Ki Tsurayuki
translated by Geoffrey Bownas

When I went to visit
The girl I love so much,
That winter night
The river blew so cold
That the plovers
were crying.

---

⑪ Literary Analysis
Paradox

1. After students have read the poem, **ask** them to identify the paradox in the first stanza.
   Answer: Line 1 presents a paradox: a life closing *before* its close.

2. Then **ask** students how the second stanza explicates the paradox.
   Answer: The stanza tells us that the two closings mentioned above were partings—ends of relationships.

▶ **Monitor Progress** Students may grasp the second stanza and, therefore, the poem more easily if they use **Reading Strategy Graphic Organizer B**, page 87 in *Graphic Organizer Transparencies,* to fill in the elliptical phrasing of lines 5–6.

▶ **Reteach:** Review the definition of *paradox:* "a statement that seems contradictory but actually presents a truth." You may jump to page 415, asking what is paradoxical about line 1; then return to "My life closed twice."

⑫ World Literature Connection

Capturing the Moment In Japanese, the thirty-one syllables (*onji*) of a tanka are divided into five sections of five, seven, five, seven, and seven syllables (which in the English example translate as lines of six, six, four, six, and seven syllables). Students may be familiar with the less ancient Japanese form of poetry called haiku, which presents three lines of five, seven, and five syllables, usually on a subject in nature. Neither tanka nor haiku rhyme.

Connect to the Literature Have students read the World Literature Connection feature; next, present the additional background information above. Then **ask** the Connect to the Literature question: What similarities do you see in this tanka and the Emily Dickinson poems you have read? In what ways are they different?
Answer: Similarities include brevity, sharp imagery, a contemplative mood, and touches of emotion. Some of Dickinson's poems involve more abrupt stops than the sample tanka.

413

Interpret

1. Read the poem aloud at least twice.

2. **Ask** students to state the central meaning of the poem in their own words.
   Possible response: The soul's role in our choice of friends is mysterious.

❹ **Literary Analysis**

Slant Rhyme

1. **Ask** a student to remind the class how a slant rhyme differs from an exact rhyme.
   Answer: Slant rhyme involves two words with close but not identical sounds in their final stressed syllables.

2. Ask a student to read the second stanza aloud to the class. Then **ask** the Literary Analysis question: What words create slant rhymes in the second stanza?
   Answer: The words are *gate* and *mat*.

ASSESS

Answers

Before students respond, you may wish to have them write a brief objective summary of the selection. As they answer the questions below, remind them to support their answers with evidence from the text.

1. (a) It oppresses people. (b) It seems to represent her own mortality.

2. (a) The third event is her death. (b) Each event is an ending.

3. (a) Chariots and emperors leave the soul unmoved. (b) The soul is indifferent to the world's attractions.

4. (a) The soul shuts the door. (b) **Possible response:** Students may suggest the adjectives *private, picky, detached,* and *divine.*

5. **Possible response:** The poems suggest that human relationships are complex, and that a single close friend may be more valuable than a whole group of less meaningful acquaintances.

The Soul Selects her own Society—

Emily Dickinson

❸
The Soul selects her own Society—
Then—shuts the Door—
To her divine Majority—
Present no more—

5 Unmoved—she notes the Chariots—pausing—
At her low Gate—
❹ Unmoved—an Emperor be kneeling
Upon her Mat—

I've known her—from an ample nation—
10 Choose One—
Then—close the Valves of her attention—
Like Stone—

Literary Analysis
Slant Rhyme What words create slant rhymes in the second stanza?

Vocabulary
ample (am′ pəl) *adj.* large in size; more than enough

Critical Reading

Cite textual evidence to support your responses.

© 1. **Key Ideas and Details (a)** According to the speaker of "There's a certain Slant of light," in what ways does the winter light affect people? **(b) Analyze:** What does this light seem to represent to the speaker?

© 2. **Key Ideas and Details (a) Interpret:** What is the third event to which the speaker of "My life closed twice before its close—" refers? **(b) Connect:** What is the relationship between the three events?

© 3. **Key Ideas and Details (a)** In "The Soul selects her own Society," what leaves the soul "unmoved"? **(b) Analyze:** How would you describe the soul's attitude toward the world's attractions?

© 4. **Key Ideas and Details (a)** What happens after the soul makes her choice? **(b) Assess:** What adjectives would you use to characterize the speaker based on this choice?

© 5. **Integration of Knowledge and Ideas Relate:** Our culture places a premium on popularity for its own sake. What do Dickinson's poems suggest about other ways to view human relationships?

Enrichment: Investigating Science

The Human Brain
On page 415, Dickinson compares the dimensions of the brain to those of the sky and sea. In fact, the average adult human brain weighs about three pounds. Even though a brain is just 2 percent of an adult's average total weight, it requires 20 percent of the oxygen a human takes in and can suffer serious damage in three to five minutes without sufficient oxygen.

Activity: Oral Report Have students conduct research on the cerebral cortex—the part of the brain that controls sensory perceptions, which are what Dickinson explores in this poem. Suggest that students record information in the **Enrichment: Investigating Science** work sheet, in *Professional Development Guidebook,* page 241. Have them use the results of their research to prepare an oral report that could be understood by middle-school students.

15

The Brain—
IS WIDER
THAN THE SKY—
Emily Dickinson

The Brain—is wider than the Sky—
For—put them side by side—
The one the other will contain
With ease—and You—beside—

5   The Brain is deeper than the sea—
For—hold them—Blue to Blue—
The one the other will absorb—
As Sponges—Buckets—do—

The Brain is just the weight of God—
10 For—Heft them—Pound for Pound—
And they will differ—if they do—
As Syllable from Sound—

Literary Analysis
Paradox What paradoxes
do you find in all three
stanzas of this poem?

16

---

15 **About the Selection**

The first poem contrasts the brain, as
a metaphor for the soul, with the sky
and the sea to arrive at the notion
that the human soul is infinite, like
God, and that, by implication, it is
of God. The second poem says that
the strongest solitude is the inner
solitude of aloneness. The third poem
suggests that some things can be
learned only by contrasting them
with their opposites.

16 **Literary Analysis**
Paradox

1. Have a volunteer read the first
   line. **Ask** the class what seems
   untrue about the line.
   Possible response: A human
   brain measures only a few inches
   in diameter, so it seems untrue
   to say that a brain is wider than
   the sky.

2. Have the volunteer now read the
   first four lines. **Ask** students how
   lines 2–4 make the claim in line 1
   less strange.
   Possible response: The brain
   can hold the idea of an enormous
   sky as well as many other ideas.

3. Follow the first two steps with
   Stanzas 2 and 3.

1. Following up on the Look for It task on page 407, draw students' attention to this poem's references to both society and the soul. You may need to help students with line 4, which places the subject complement ("Society") ahead of the verb phrase ("shall be").

2. Once students understand Dickinson's observation that the solitude of space, sea, and death is not the same as the solitude of one's own soul, **ask** students whether they think a person can fit both society and solitude into his or her life.
   Possible response: Students may say that much practice and patience are required to become someone who, on the one hand, is a social being and, on the other, is a person who is comfortable alone with himself or herself.

THERE IS A SOLITUDE OF SPACE

EMILY DICKINSON

Vocabulary
finite (fī´ nīt´) *adj.* having measurable or definable limits

infinity (in fin´ i tē) *n.* endless or unlimited space, time, or distance

17

There is a solitude of space
A solitude of sea
A solitude of death, but these
Society shall be
5 Compared with that profounder site
That polar privacy
A soul admitted to itself—
Finite Infinity.

416 A Growing Nation (1800–1870)

Vocabulary Development

Vocabulary Knowledge Rating
When students have completed reading and discussing the selections, have them take out their **Vocabulary Knowledge Rating** charts for the selections. Read the words aloud, and have students rate their knowledge of the words again in the After Reading column. Clarify any words that are still problematic. Have students write their own definitions and example or sentence in the appropriate column. Then have students complete the Vocabulary Lesson at the end of the selections. Encourage students to use the words in further discussion and written work about the selections. Remind them that they will be accountable for these words on the **Selection Test**, *Unit 2 Resources*, pages 167–169 or 170–172.

Water, is taught by thirst

EMILY DICKINSON

18

Water, is taught by thirst.
Land—by the Oceans passed.
Transport[1]—by throe[2]—
Peace—by its battles told—
5 Love, by Memorial Mold[3]—
Birds, by the Snow.

---

1. **Transport** ecstasy; rapture.
2. **throe** spasm or pang of pain.
3. **Memorial Mold** memorial grounds or cemetery.

Critical Reading

© 1. **Craft and Structure (a)** What comparisons does the speaker make in "The Brain—is wider than the Sky—"? **(b) Interpret:** What role does a surprising use of scale and size play in these comparisons?

© 2. **Key Ideas and Details (a)** In "There is a solitude of space," what three things does the speaker compare to "polar privacy"? **(b) Contrast:** How does the solitude of "a soul admitted to itself" differ from other types of solitude?

© 3. **Craft and Structure (a)** In "Water, is taught by thirst," what is the relationship between each line's first word and the words that follow? **(b) Interpret:** What is the theme or message of this poem?

© 4. **Integration of Ideas and Knowledge** Is the tension Dickinson sees between individuality and society true for most people, or is it simply the poet's view of her own life? In your response, use at least two of these Essential Question words: *unlimited, limited, social, private, public. [Connecting to the Essential Question: What makes American literature American?]*

Cite textual evidence to support your responses.

Water, is taught by thirst **417**

18 Critical Thinking

Analyze

1. Direct students to read the entire poem.

2. **Ask** students to explain the meaning of the last line.
Possible answer: Fallen snow is cold, still, and lifeless, while birds are vibrant and contrast starkly with snow.

ASSESS

Answers

Before students respond, you may wish to have them write a brief objective summary of the selection. As they answer the questions below, remind them to support their answers with evidence from the text.

1. (a) The speaker compares the brain to the sky, to the sea, and to God. (b) The speaker compares the brain to things that seem at first to be much larger, but she succeeds in establishing the immeasurability of the brain.

2. (a) Privacy is compared to the solitude of space, sea, and death. (b) "A soul admitted to itself" feels a greater solitude than the solitude of space, sea, and death.

3. (a) In each line, the speaker states that the first word is understood only from the words that follow, words that name the absence of the first word. (b) **Possible response:** We gain real understanding through loss and need.

4. **Possible response:** Many adolescents—but perhaps not all—will acknowledge a tension between being an individual with <u>private</u> feelings, thoughts, and fears and belonging to society, where one must present a <u>public</u> face in <u>social</u> interactions.

Concept Connector

Reading Strategy Graphic Organizer
Ask students to review the graphic organizers in which they have filled in missing words because of elliptical phrasing and have figured out likely meanings of lines. Then have students share their organizers and compare the meanings they have proposed.

Activating Prior Knowledge
Have students return to their responses to the Activating Prior Knowledge activity. Ask them to explain whether their thoughts have changed and if so, how.

Connecting to the Essential Question
Have students compare the responses they gave to the prompt before reading the selections with their thoughts afterwards. Have them work individually or in groups, writing or discussing their thoughts, to formulate their new responses. Then, lead a class discussion, probing for what students have learned that confirms or invalidates their initial thoughts. Encourage students to cite specific textual details to support their responses.

Critical Commentary
Galway Kinnell

1. Expand the description of Galway Kinnell as a prize-winning poet (the Pulitzer Prize and the National Book Award in 1980) by filling in his biography: He was born in Rhode Island in 1927 and has spent a lifetime writing poems (as well as prose, including criticism such as this piece), translating, teaching, and participating in social activism, such as the civil rights movement.

2. **Ask** students what Kinnell means by applying the term "reckless genius" to Dickinson.
   Possible response: While *reckless* can mean "careless," Kinnell suggests the meaning "not regarding consequences"—that is, "willing to take chances, try new things." Perhaps Dickinson was able to be a reckless genius because, showing her poetry to so few people, she did not have to worry about readers' comments.

3. **Ask** students to identify an example of Dickinson's "heart-stopping recklessness" (paragraph 1) or her "craving for a kind of forbidden knowledge of the unknowable" (paragraph 2).
   Possible responses: Students may cite the speaker's comparison of entering a carriage with immortality, personified; her willingness to imagine the moment of death; her daring to equate humans and God; and so on.

4. Point out that Kinnell's mention, in the second paragraph, of Dickinson's focus on a particular moment reinforces the **World Literature Connection** feature on page 413.

5. Encourage students to write essays agreeing with, modifying, or arguing against Kinnell's statement (paragraph 4): "Relative to their small surface, her poems have large inner bulk." Students must support their thesis with examples from Dickinson's poems.

(continued on p. 419)

418

Critical Commentary

Reckless Genius
Galway Kinnell

A Pulitzer Prize-winning Poet Pays Tribute to the Belle of Amherst.

Emily Dickinson wrote about the kinds of experience few poets have the daring to explore or the genius to sing. She is one of the most intelligent of poets and also one of the most fearless. If the fearlessness ran out, she had her courage, and after that her heart-stopping recklessness.

More fully than most poets, Dickinson tells how it is to be a human being in a particular moment, in compressed, hard, blazingly vivid poems—which have duende![1] Her greatest seem not sung but forced into being by a craving for a kind of forbidden knowledge of the unknowable.

Being thoroughly conventional, the few literary men of the time who saw Dickinson's poems found nothing very special about them and attributed her experiments in rhyme and rhythm to the naiveté of an untaught lady poet with a tin ear.

Similar figures today think she cannot be considered a major poet because she writes tiny poems. Of course there is nothing inherently minor in smallish poems, and in any case, many of Dickinson's poems are little because she omits the warming-up, preface and situation—and begins where a more discursive poet might be preparing to end. Relative to their small surface, her poems have large inner bulk. And since her themes obsessively reappear, a group of the poems, when read together, sweeps one along inside another's consciousness much as a long poem does.

In my opinion, she could not have accomplished her great work without making two technical innovations.

Dickinson's chosen form requires rhymes, which are scarce in English, at frequent intervals. To avoid using an imprecise word for the sake of rhyme, she made a simple revolutionary innovation: expanding the kinds of echoes that qualify as rhyme. To exact rhyme *(room/broom)* and slant rhyme *(room/brim)* she added assonant rhyme *(room/bruise)*, thus multiplying the supply of rhyme words many times over. Sometimes, perhaps shocked by the rightness of an unrhymable word, she resorted to rhyme by vague resemblance *(freeze/privilege)* or skipped the rhyme entirely.

---

1. **duende** (dwen´ da) intensity; burning within.

▲ Poet and translator Galway Kinnell is the recipient of the MacArthur Foundation "Genius" Grant and many other honors.

> She is one of the most intelligent of poets and also one of the most fearless.

Think Aloud

Vocabulary: Using Context

Point out "syncopated" in the second paragraph on page 419. Use the following "think aloud" to model how to use context to infer meaning. Say to students:

Kinnell says Dickinson's poetry presents "two rhythmic systems clashing and twining." He says one system uses the iambic beat. I know that means a regular progression of unaccented syllable followed by accented syllable, as in "My life closed twice before its close— / It yet remains to see."

Kinnell describes the other rhythm system as "syncopated," which must mean the *opposite* of a regular beat. I'll guess that *syncopated* means "irregular, with an unexpected beat." Looking at the third line of "My life closed twice," I find "If Immortality unveil." That line breaks the weak-strong regularity, so indeed *syncopated* has something to do with breaking or changing a beat.

Her other innovation protects the density and dissonance of her poems from the singsong latent in common meter's de dum, de dum, de dum, de dum / de dum, de dum, de dum / de dum, de dum, de dum, de dum / de dum, de dum, de dum. Using wee dashes, she divides lines into clusters of syllables (sometimes a single syllable) that are not unlike William Carlos Williams'[2] "variable feet"—rhythmic units of varying length that are all spoken in approximately the same amount of time.

Saying her poems aloud, we hear two rhythmic systems clashing and twining: the iambic beat, and superimposed upon it, Dickinson's own inner, speech-like, sliding, syncopated rhythm. The latter suggests an urge in her toward some kind of Creeley-like[3] free verse, and it is also what allows her to write in formal verse using all her passion and intelligence.

A poem by Dickinson that I particularly like is the widely admired "I heard a Fly buzz — when I died." Here, through what Keats[4] called "negative capability," Dickinson enters, imaginatively, a dying person and goes with her into death. To write this poem with authority, Dickinson had to "die" a moment in imagination, which may be to say that she had actually to die a little in reality. … The brilliance of Emily Dickinson's greatest poems may have exacted a high price in emotional stamina and stability, and foreshortened by years that amazingly prolific period (in one year, she wrote 364 poems) when she was writing with her full powers…

> To write this poem with authority, Dickinson had to "die" a moment in imagination...

---

2. **William Carlos Williams** (1883-1963) American poet and physician; one of the original Imagist poets, a group whose work stressed simplicity and the use of imagery.
3. **Creeley-like** The work of American poet Robert Creeley (1926-2005) was notable for its very short lines and simple language.
4. **Keats** John Keats (1795-1821), famous British poet whose work centered on the beauty found in ordinary things.

Check Your Comprehension

- According to Kinnell, what does Emily Dickinson do more fully than most other poets?
- What did Dickinson's contemporaries think of her work?
- With what two innovations does Kinnell credit Dickinson?

Reckless Genius

(continued)

6. **Ask** students what impression they form of Kinnell based on his citing the poets William Carlos Williams, Robert Creeley, and John Keats.
   Possible answer: Kinnell seems very well read and committed to a broad range of poets.

7. Students taken by Dickinson's poems and Kinnell's praise of them may enjoy learning that in his youth Kinnell was drawn not only to Dickinson but also to Edgar Allan Poe. They may want to revisit Poe's poem "The Raven" on pages 312–317.

ASSESS

Answers

1. According to Kinnell, Dickinson, more fully than other poets, captures a moment and compresses it into a brief but intense poem.

2. Dickinson's contemporaries thought the poet not only too unconventional but also unsophisticated.

3. Kinnell credits Dickinson with going beyond not only exact rhyme but also slant rhyme to experiment with assonant rhyme. He also credits her with her introduction of "wee dashes" to eliminate a singsong quality and replace it with more original meters.

Answers

1. (a) Slant rhymes: "room" and "storm" (lines 2 and 4); "firm" and "room" (lines 6 and 8). Exact rhyme: "me" and "see" (lines 14 and 6). (b) **Possible response:** The exact rhyme declares a definitive end to the poem.

2. (a) **Possible response:** Both "Because I could not stop" and "The Soul selects" deal with mysteries for which exact rhyme would seem simplistic. (b) The exact rhymes in "The Brain—is wider than the Sky" reflect the poem's figures of speech about measurement.

3. The paradox is that we can learn about things only by contrasting them with very different things. It is true in that the best way to grasp something is to feel its absence.

4. (a) The first line of "I heard a Fly buzz—" is a paradox in that one who has died cannot report the experience of dying. (b) Another poem built around a similar paradox is "My life closed twice." (c) **Possible response:** The paradox is possible if one has a belief in an afterlife.

5. An oxymoron is "Finite Infinity," a limited endlessness.

6. In "My life closed twice," the speaker is devastated by the end of relationships; in "The Soul selects," the speaker chooses to end relationships; in "There is a solitude," the speaker knows true loneliness.

7. (a) Human understanding is boundless in "There is a solitude," "The Soul selects," and "The Brain—is wider than the Sky."(b) Human understanding is limited in "There's a certain Slant of light" and "I heard a Fly buzz—." (c) The self is engaged with the world but aware of eternity and mortality.

8. (a) Lines 5–6 might say, "The anticipation of my death had wrung dry the tearful eyes of those by my bedside and caused those people to steel themselves." (b) The final line may mean that the speaker has died, so she can no longer perceive the world.

9. The last two lines may mean that the speaker is pained to learn of her mortality or that she is relieved and accepting.

420

After You Read *Emily Dickinson's Poetry*

Literary Analysis

1. **Craft and Structure (a)** Use a chart like the one shown to examine the use of **slant rhyme** and **exact rhyme** in "I heard a Fly buzz—when I died." **(b)** What is the effect of the exact rhyme after so many slant rhymes?

Slant Rhyme	Lines	Exact Rhyme	Lines

2. **Craft and Structure (a)** How do the many slant rhymes in "Because I could not stop for Death" and "The Soul selects her own Society—" reflect the content of those poems? **(b)** How do the many exact rhymes in "The Brain—is wider than the Sky—" suit the content of that poem?

3. **Craft and Structure** Each line of "Water, is taught by thirst" expresses the same basic **paradox.** What is that paradox, and how can it be true?

4. **Craft and Structure (a)** Explain how the first line of "I heard a Fly buzz—when I died" is a paradox. **(b)** Which of the other poems presented here is built around a similar paradox? **(c)** For both poems, what explanation might make the situation possible, even though it seems impossible?

5. **Craft and Structure** A two-word paradox, such as *cruel kindness*, is called an *oxymoron*. Identify an oxymoron in "There is a solitude of space," and explain the apparent contradiction.

6. **Integration of Knowledge and Ideas** What is similar and different about the speaker's attitude toward the self and other people in "My life closed twice before its close—," "The Soul selects her own Society—," and "There is a solitude of space"?

7. **Integration of Knowledge and Ideas (a)** Which poems present human understanding as something boundless or unlimited? **(b)** Which present it as something small and limited? **(c)** How would you define Dickinson's view of the individual self?

Reading Strategy

8. **Reread** "I heard a Fly buzz—when I died." **(a)** In Dickinson's elliptical style, what words do you understand to be missing from lines 5 and 6? **(b)** Explain your interpretation of the poem's final line.

9. Reread "There's a certain Slant of light." What are two possible meanings of the last two lines?

Common Core State Standards

Writing

2. Write explanatory texts to examine and convey complex ideas, concepts, and information clearly and accurately through the effective selection, organization, and analysis of content.

2.b. Develop the topic thoroughly by selecting the most significant quotations or other information and examples appropriate to the audience's knowledge of the topic.

Language

5.a. Interpret figures of speech in context and analyze their role in the text.

Assessment Practice

Make Inferences (For more practice, see *All-in-One Workbook*.)

The reading sections of many tests require students to make inferences. Explain to students that making inferences will help them understand poetry because poets often leave much of their message unstated. Use the following example to help students make inferences about "There's a certain Slant of light" on page 412:

Which of the following best describes the effect of the light?

A overwhelming

B uplifting

C encouraging

D energizing

Choices ***B***, ***C***, and ***D*** cannot be supported by details from the text. The light is oppressive and feels heavy, so ***A*** is the best choice.

PERFORMANCE TASKS
Integrated Language Skills

Vocabulary Acquisition and Use

Word Analysis: Latin Root -fin-

The Latin root -fin- means "end." In the word *finite* it combines with the suffix -ite to create an adjective meaning "having a definite end." In the word *infinite*, it combines with the suffix -ite and the prefix in-, meaning "not," to create an adjective meaning "without end." Use your knowledge of the root to explain the meaning of each italicized word below. Make clear how the word's meaning reflects the meaning of the root.

1. Perhaps you can count the stars, but to me they seem *infinite* in number.

2. The musical composition had an introduction, a long middle section, and a grand *finale*.

3. Stop being vague and give me a *definite* answer.

4. The contest began with fifty competitors, but I was one of only three *finalists*.

5. The coarse lad attended a special school, so his manners are now quite *refined*.

Vocabulary: Antonyms

For each numbered item, choose the letter of its antonym, or word that expresses an opposite meaning. Explain your choices.

1. **surmised:** **(a)** concluded **(b)** focused **(c)** asked **(d)** stated

2. **interposed:** **(a)** continuous **(b)** scattered **(c)** between **(d)** above

3. **affliction:** **(a)** poverty **(b)** passion **(c)** warfare **(d)** balm

4. **ample:** **(a)** smooth **(b)** huge **(c)** inhospitable **(d)** insufficient

5. **finite:** **(a)** countless **(b)** meaningless **(c)** worthwhile **(d)** thick

6. **infinity:** **(a)** trivia **(b)** limitation **(c)** confusion **(d)** endlessness

Writing

© Explanatory Text A **blog** is a forum for writing that is part of a web site. Most blogs contain a series of postings on related topics and many have rules for content and posting. Write a blog entry for a poetry site in which you analyze Dickinson's sense of infinity. Plan your work to meet the site's deadlines and other requirements.

Prewriting Reread Dickinson's poems, looking for references to infinity. List details and the poems in which they appear. Study the details, and write a statement in which you interpret patterns. This will serve as your controlling idea.

Drafting Develop your ideas in a logical sequence and support them with details from the poems. Follow correct requirements for citation.

Revising Make sure all the elements of your entry work to develop or support your controlling idea. Delete any stray ideas or unrelated details.

Model: Following Manuscript Requirements

In the "The Brain—is wider than the Sky—," Dickinson suggests that there is no limit to the amount of knowledge the human brain can take in. She compares the brain with the sky, writing, "For—put them side by side— / The one the other will contain."

A short quotation should be set off with quotation marks. If longer than four lines, a quotation should be set off and indented.

Extended Study: Integrated Language Skills **421**

Assessment Resources

Unit 2 Resources

[L1] [L2] [EL] **Selection Test A,** pp. 167–169
Administer Test A to less advanced students.

[L3] [L4] [EL] **Selection Test B,** pp. 170–172
Administer Test B to on-level and more advanced students.

[L3] [L4] **Open-Book Test,** pp. 164–166 As an alternative, give the Open-Book Test.

[All] **Customizable Test Bank**

[All] **Self-tests**
Students may prepare for the **Selection Test** by taking the **Self-test** online.

All assessment resources are available at **www.PHLitOnline.com**.

Vocabulary Acquisition and Use

1. Introduce the skill, using the instruction on the student page.

2. Have students complete the two vocabulary activities here.

Word Analysis

1. In *infinite*, -fin- means "end," the prefix in- means "not," and the suffix -ite signifies an adjective; they yield "without end."

2. In *finale*, fin- means "end" and *finale* means "end of a musical composition."

3. In *definite*, -fin- means "end," de- means "from," and -ite signals an adjective, so *definite* means "from something bounded," or "precise."

4. In *finalists*, the root fin- means "end," -al makes fin- into an adjective, and -ist makes the adjective a noun—*finalist*—which means "one who has made it to the end."

5. *Refin-* comes from the French *raffiner*, meaning "to make an end product free of impurities," and the -ed signals an adjective, leading to "polished."

Vocabulary

1. *Surmised* means "formed a conclusion"; antonym is (c) *asked*.

2. *Interposed* means "came between"; antonym is (a) *continuous*, "uninterrupted."

3. *Affliction* means "something that causes pain"; antonym is (d) *balm*, "something that soothes."

4. *Ample* means "more than enough"; antonym is (d) *insufficient*, "not enough."

5. *Finite* means "having measurable limits"; antonym is (a) *countless*, "without limit."

6. *Infinity* means "endlessness"; antonym is (b) *limitation*, or "end."

Writing

Use the **Rubrics for Explanatory Text**, in *Professional Development Guidebook*, pages 250–251 to evaluate students' work.

• Walt Whitman's Poetry
Lesson Pacing Guide

DAY 1 Preteach

- ⓒ Administer the Reading and Vocabulary Warm-ups (*Unit 2 Resources,* pp. 173–176) as necessary.
- ⓒ Introduce the Literary Analysis concepts: Epic theme and style.
- • Introduce the Reading Strategy: Adjust Your Reading Rate.
- ⓒ Build background with the author and Background features.
- • Develop thematic thinking with Connecting to the Essential Question.
- ⓒ Teach the selection vocabulary.

DAYS 2–3 Preteach/Teach/Assess

- • Distribute copies of the appropriate graphic organizer for the Reading Strategy (*Graphic Organizer Transparencies*, pp. 90–91).
- • Distribute copies of the appropriate graphic organizer for Literary Analysis (*Graphic Organizer Transparencies*, pp.92–93).
- • Prepare students to read with the Activating Prior Knowledge activities (TE).
- • Informally monitor comprehension while students read.
- • Use the Reading Check question to confirm comprehension.
- ⓒ Develop students' understanding of epic theme and style using the Literary Analysis prompts.
- • Develop students' ability to adjust their reading rate using the Reading Strategy prompts.
- ⓒ Reinforce vocabulary with the Vocabulary notes.
- • Assess students' comprehension and mastery of the skills by having them answer the Critical Reading, Literary Analysis, and Reading Strategy questions.

DAY 4 Extend/Assess

- ⓒ Have students complete the Vocabulary Lesson.
- ⓒ Have students complete the Writing lesson and write a free verse poem in honor of Whitman (You may assign as homework.)
- • Have students real and respond to the Critical Commentary.
- • Administer Selection Test A or B (*Unit 2 Resources,* pp. 185–187 or 188–190).

ⓒ Common Core State Standards

Reading Literature 4. Determine the meaning of words and phrases as they are used in the text, including figurative and connotative meanings; analyze the impact of specific word choices on meaning and tone, including words with multiple meanings or language that is particularly fresh, engaging, or beautiful.
5. Analyze how an author's choices concerning how to structure specific parts of a text contribute to its overall structure and meaning as well as its aesthetic impact.
9. Demonstrate knowledge of nineteenth-century foundational works of American literature, including how two or more texts from the same period treat similar themes or topics.

Writing 3.d. Use precise words and phrases, telling details, and sensory language to convey a vivid picture of the experiences, events, setting, and/or characters.
4. Produce clear and coherent writing in which the development, organization, and style are appropriate to task, purpose, and audience.

Language 4. Determine or clarify the meaning of unknown and multiple-meaning words and phrases based on grades 11–12 reading and content, choosing flexibly from a range of strategies.
4.d. Verify the preliminary determination of the meaning of a word or phrase.

5.a. Interpret figures of speech in context and analyze their role in the text.

Additional Standards Practice
Common Core Companion, pp. 41–55, 75–76; 208–220; 324–335

Daily Block Scheduling
Each day in this Lesson Pacing Guide represents a 40–50 minute period. Teachers using block scheduling may combine days to revise pacing. In addition, teachers may differentiate and support core instruction by integrating components for extended and intensive support as students require. See the Guide to Selected Leveled Resources (facing page).

Guide to Selected Leveled Resources

R T I Tier 1 (students performing on level)

Walt Whitman's Poetry

Warm Up	Practice, **model,** and **monitor** fluency, working **with the whole class** or **in groups.**	**Vocabulary and Reading Warm-ups B,** *Unit 2 Resources,* pp. 173–174, 176
Comprehension/Skills	**Support** and **monitor** comprehension and skills development, having students complete the activities, graphic organizers, and interactive prompts **independently** or **as a class.**	• *Reader's Notebook,* adapted instruction and summary **EL** *Reader's Notebook: English Learner's Version,* adapted instruction and summary • **Reading Strategy Graphic Organizer B,** *Graphic Organizer Transparencies,* p. 91 • **Literary Analysis Graphic Organizer B,** *Graphic Organizer Transparencies,* p. 93
Monitor Progress [A]	**Monitor** student progress with the differentiated curriculum-based assessment in the *Unit Resources.*	• **Selection Test B,** *Unit 2 Resources,* pp. 188–190 • **Open-Book Test,** *Unit 2 Resources,* pp. 182–184

R T I Tier 2 (students requiring intervention)

Walt Whitman's Poetry

Warm Up	Practice, **model,** and **monitor** fluency **in groups** or **with individuals.**	• **Vocabulary and Reading Warm-ups A,** *Unit 1 Resources,* pp. 173–175 • *Hear It!* Audio CD
Comprehension/Skills	• **Support** and **monitor** comprehension and skills development, working **in small groups** or **with individuals.** • As students complete the selection in the appropriate version of the *Reader's Notebook,* **monitor** comprehension frequently with group questions and individual instruction. • **Model** strategies while guiding students in completing the activities and prompts in the *Reader's Notebook,* as well as the graphic organizers. • **Practice** skills and **monitor** mastery with the *Reading Kit* worksheets.	• *Reader's Notebook: Adapted Version,* adapted instruction and summary **EL** *Reader's Notebook: English Learner's Version,* adapted instruction and summary • **Reading Strategy Graphic Organizer A,** *Graphic Organizer Transparencies,* p. 90 • **Literary Analysis Graphic Organizer A,** *Graphic Organizer Transparencies,* p. 92 • *Reading Kit,* Practice worksheets
Monitor Progress [A]	**Monitor** student progress with the differentiated curriculum-based assessment in the *Unit Resources* and in the *Reading Kit.*	• **Selection Test A,** *Unit 2 Resources,* pp. 185–187 • *Reading Kit,* Assess worksheets

TIER 3 Tier 3 intervention may require consultation with the student's special-education or dyslexia specialist. For additional support, see the Tier 2 activities and resources listed above.

One-on-one teaching   Group work   Whole-class instruction   Independent work   [A] Assessment

For a complete guide to selection support, including support for Advanced students, see the Overview of Resources in the frontmatter.

• Walt Whitman's Poetry

RESOURCES FOR:

- **L1** Special-Needs Students
- **L2** Below-Level Students (Tier 2)
- **L3** On-Level Students (Tier 1)
- **L4** Advanced Students (Tier 1)
- **EL** English Learners
- **All** All Students

Vocabulary/Fluency/Prior Knowledge

All **Vocabulary Builder,** p. 179

Also available for these selections:

EL **L1** **L2** Vocabulary Warm-ups A and B, pp. 173–174

EL **L1** **L2** Reading Warm-ups A and B, pp. 175–176

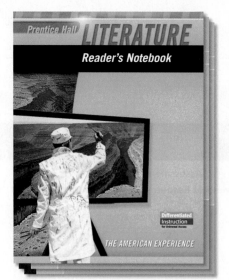

Reader's Notebooks

Pre- and postreading pages for these selections appear in an interactive format in the *Reader's Notebooks*. Each *Notebook* is differentiated for a different group of learners. The selections in the Adapted and English Learner's versions are abridged.

- **L2** **L3** *Reader's Notebook*
- **L1** *Reader's Notebook: Adapted Version*
- **EL** *Reader's Notebook: English Learner's Version*
- **EL** *Reader's Notebook: Spanish Version*

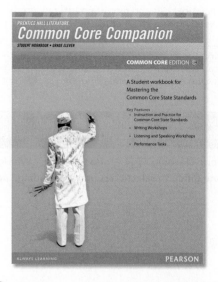

© *Common Core Companion*

Additional instruction and practice for each Common Core State Standard

Selection Support

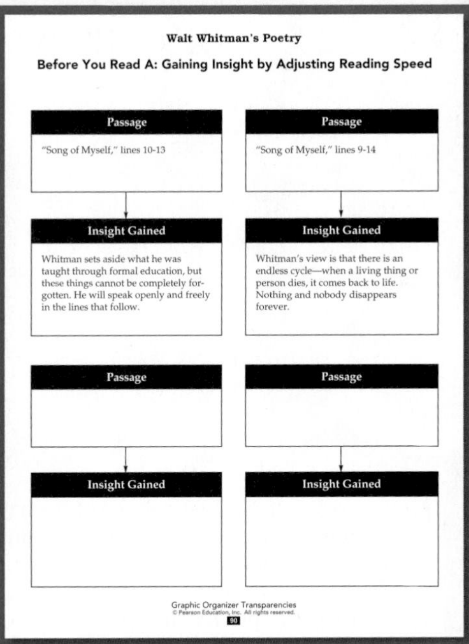

Walt Whitman's Poetry

Before You Read A: Gaining Insight by Adjusting Reading Speed

Passage
"Song of Myself," lines 10-13

↓

Insight Gained
Whitman sets aside what he was taught through formal education, but these things cannot be completely forgotten. He will speak openly and freely in the lines that follow.

Passage
"Song of Myself," lines 9-14

↓

Insight Gained
Whitman's view is that there is an endless cycle—when a living thing or person dies, it comes back to life. Nothing and nobody disappears forever.

Passage

↓

Insight Gained

Passage

↓

Insight Gained

Graphic Organizer Transparencies
© Pearson Education, Inc. All rights reserved.

Graphic Organizer Transparencies (side tab)

EL L1 L2 Reading: Graphic Organizer A
(partially filled in), p. 90

Also available for these selections:

EL L3 Reading: Graphic Organizer B, p. 91

EL L1 L2 Literary Analysis: Graphic Organizer A
(partially filled in), p. 92

EL L3 Literary Analysis: Graphic Organizer B,
p. 93

Skills Development/Extension

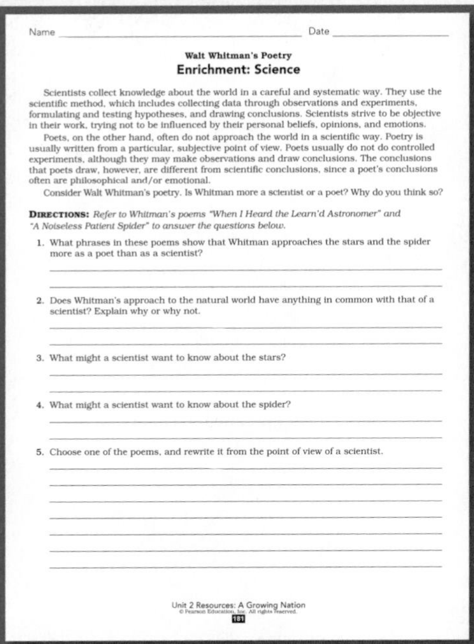

Unit 2 Resources (side tab)

Name _____ Date _____

Walt Whitman's Poetry
Enrichment: Science

Scientists collect knowledge about the world in a careful and systematic way. They use the scientific method, which includes collecting data through observations and experiments, formulating and testing hypotheses, and drawing conclusions. Scientists strive to be objective in their work, trying not to be influenced by their personal beliefs, opinions, and emotions.

Poets, on the other hand, often do not approach the world in a scientific way. Poetry is usually written from a particular, subjective point of view. Poets usually do not do controlled experiments, although they may make observations and draw conclusions. The conclusions that poets draw, however, are different from scientific conclusions, since a poet's conclusions often are philosophical and/or emotional.

Consider Walt Whitman's poetry. Is Whitman more a scientist or a poet? Why do you think so?

DIRECTIONS: *Refer to Whitman's poems "When I Heard the Learn'd Astronomer" and "A Noiseless Patient Spider" to answer the questions below.*

1. What phrases in these poems show that Whitman approaches the stars and the spider more as a poet than as a scientist?

2. Does Whitman's approach to the natural world have anything in common with that of a scientist? Explain why or why not.

3. What might a scientist want to know about the stars?

4. What might a scientist want to know about the spider?

5. Choose one of the poems, and rewrite it from the point of view of a scientist.

Unit 2 Resources: A Growing Nation
© Pearson Education, Inc. All rights Reserved.
181

L4 Enrichment, p. 181

Also available for these selections:

All Literary Analysis: American Epic Poetry,
p. 177

All Reading: Adjust Reading Rate, p. 178

EL L3 L4 Support for Writing, p. 180

Assessment

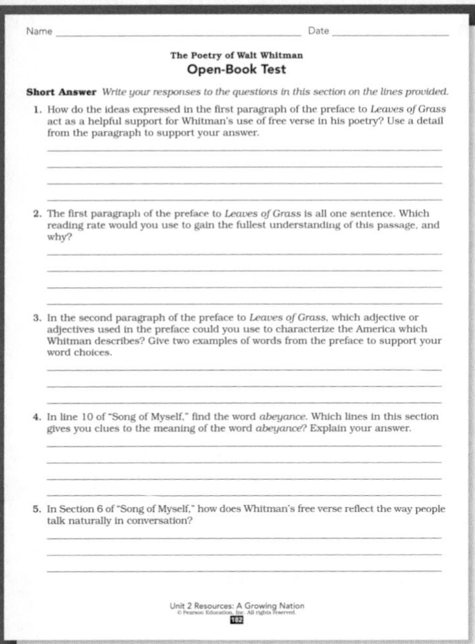

Name _____ Date _____

The Poetry of Walt Whitman
Open-Book Test

Short Answer *Write your responses to the questions in this section on the lines provided.*

1. How do the ideas expressed in the first paragraph of the preface to *Leaves of Grass* act as a helpful support for Whitman's use of free verse in his poetry? Use a detail from the paragraph to support your answer.

2. The first paragraph of the preface to *Leaves of Grass* is all one sentence. Which reading rate would you use to gain the fullest understanding of this passage, and why?

3. In the second paragraph of the preface to *Leaves of Grass*, which adjective or adjectives used in the preface could you use to characterize the America which Whitman describes? Give two examples of words from the preface to support your word choices.

4. In line 10 of "Song of Myself," find the word *abeyance*. Which lines in this section gives you clues to the meaning of the word *abeyance*? Explain your answer.

5. In Section 6 of "Song of Myself," how does Whitman's free verse reflect the way people talk naturally in conversation?

Unit 2 Resources: A Growing Nation
© Pearson Education, Inc. All rights Reserved.
182

L3 L4 Open-Book Test, pp. 182–184

Also available for these selections:

EL L1 L2 Selection Test A, pp. 185–187

EL L3 L4 Selection Test B, pp. 188–190

PHLit Online!
www.PHLitOnline.com

Online Resources: All print materials are also available online.

- complete narrated selection text
- a thematically related video with writing prompt
- an interactive graphic organizer
- highlighting feature
- access to all student print resources, adapted to individual student needs
- Spanish and English summaries
- adapted selection translations in Spanish

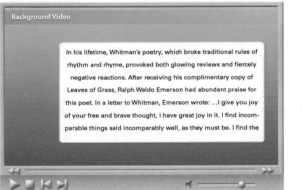

Background Video

In his lifetime, Whitman's poetry, which broke traditional rules of rhythm and rhyme, provoked both glowing reviews and fiercely negative reactions. After receiving his complimentary copy of Leaves of Grass, Ralph Waldo Emerson had abundant praise for this poet. In a letter to Whitman, Emerson wrote: ...I give you joy of your free and brave thought, I have great joy in it. I find incomparable things said incomparably well, as they must be. I find the

Background Video

Also available:

Get Connected! (thematic video with writing prompt)
All videos are available in Spanish.

Vocabulary Central

Vocabulary Central (tools and activities for studying vocabulary)

Also available:

Writer's Journal (with graphics feature

Background

Overview: The Author's Work

Walt Whitman sometimes uses a form similar to the poetry of the Hebrew Bible (also called the Old Testament). This form is also reminiscent of the *Bhagavad-Gita* (one of India's sacred texts), which Whitman may have read. The undulating rhythm of this form well suits Whitman's lyrical and emotional poems.

Whitman's powers of observation were honed by his work as a newspaper writer. Not surprisingly, Ralph Waldo Emerson remarked that Whitman's poetry was like a combination of the *Bhagavad-Gita* and a daily newspaper. This quality can be seen in "I Hear America Singing" and many of Whitman's other poems.

The Writer in His Time

After meeting Walt Whitman in Brooklyn in 1856, Henry David Thoreau wrote to a friend, "We ought to rejoice in him greatly. . . . He is awfully good." He remarked that Whitman's poetry "sounds to me very brave & American," and he carried a copy of Whitman's controversial *Leaves of Grass* around his hometown of Concord, Massachusetts, as if to dare anyone to challenge him for reading it.

Whitman was a spirited observer of humanity and nature but also made his living as a carpenter, a printer, a newspaper writer, a government clerk, and a volunteer in Civil War hospitals. Despite influential admirers, Whitman achieved only modest public acclaim during his lifetime.

Walt Whitman (1819–1892)

In the preface to his first volume of poetry, the 1855 edition of *Leaves of Grass,* Walt Whitman wrote: "The proof of a poet is that his country absorbs him as affectionately as he absorbed it." Whitman's hopes for such proof of his own merit as a poet were deferred: He was harshly denounced for his first volume of poetry, but in the following decades, his poems gained popularity, and he became famous as "the Good Gray Poet" and "the Bard of Democracy." In his later years, Whitman was admired by writers and intellectuals on both sides of the Atlantic. Today, he is widely recognized as one of the greatest and most influential poets the United States has ever produced.

The Poet at Work Whitman was born on Long Island and raised in Brooklyn, New York. His education was not formal, but he read widely, including the works of Sir Walter Scott, Shakespeare, Homer, and Dante. Trained to be a printer, Whitman spent his early years alternating between printing jobs and newspaper writing. When he was twenty-seven, he became the editor of the *Brooklyn Eagle,*

422 A Growing Nation (1800–1870)

Text Complexity Rubric

	from Leaves of Grass	*from* Song of Myself; I Hear America Singing	Bivouac	Learn'd Astronomer, Spider
Qualitative Measures				
Context/ Knowledge Demands	Poetic credo 1 2 ③ 4 5	American life 1 ② 3 4 5	Civil War poem 1 ② 3 4 5	Science and nature 1 2 ③ 4 5
Structure/Language and Clarity	Metaphors; above-level vocabulary 1 2 3 ④ 5	Easily read free verse 1 ② 3 4 5	Long sentences; free verse 1 2 ③ 4 5	Accessible free verse 1 ② 3 4 5
Levels of Meaning/ Purpose/Concept Level	Challenging (description of soul) 1 2 3 ④ 5	Accessible (American spirit) 1 2 ③ 4 5	Accessible (thoughts at a military encampment) 1 2 ③ 4 5	Accessible (contemplation of nature) 1 2 ③ 4 5
Quantitative Measures				
Lexile/Text Length	1900L / 322 words	NP / 958, 153 words	NP / 111 words	NP / 84, 87 words
Overall Complexity	**More complex**	**More accessible**	**More accessible**	**More accessible**

a respected newspaper, but the paper fired him in 1848 because of his opposition to slavery. After accepting a position on a paper in New Orleans, Whitman traveled across the country for the first time, observing the diversity of America's landscapes and people.

Whitman soon returned to New York City, however, and in 1850 quit journalism to devote his energy to writing poetry. Impressed by Ralph Waldo Emerson's prophetic description of a new kind of American poet, Whitman had been jotting down ideas and fragments of verse in a notebook for years. His work broke every poetic tradition of rhyme and meter as it celebrated America and the common man. When the first edition of *Leaves of Grass* was published in 1855, critics attacked Whitman's subject matter and abandonment of traditional poetic devices and forms. Noted poet John Greenleaf Whittier hated Whitman's poems so much that he hurled his copy of *Leaves of Grass* into the fireplace. Emerson, on the other hand, responded with great enthusiasm, remarking that the collection was "the most extraordinary piece of wit and wisdom that America has yet contributed."

The Bard of Democracy Though Whitman did publish other works in the course of his career, his life's work proved to be *Leaves of Grass,* which he continually revised, reshaped, and expanded until his death in 1892. The poems in later editions became less confusing, repetitious, and raucous, and more symbolic, expressive, and universal. He viewed the volume as a single long poem that expressed his evolving vision of the world. Using his poetry to convey his passionate belief in democracy, equality, and the spiritual unity of all forms of life, he celebrated the potential of the human spirit. Though Whitman's philosophy grew out of the ideas of the Transcendentalists, his poetry was mainly shaped by his ability to absorb and comprehend everything he observed. From its first appearance as twelve unsigned and untitled poems, *Leaves of Grass* grew to include 383 poems in its final, "death-bed" edition (1892). The collection captures the diversity of the American people and conveys the energy and intensity of all forms of life. In the century since Whitman's death, *Leaves of Grass* has become one of the most highly regarded collections of poetry ever written. There is little doubt that, according to his own definition, Whitman has proven himself as a poet.

> ## "THE UNITED STATES THEMSELVES ARE ESSENTIALLY THE GREATEST POEM."

Walt Whitman's Poetry **423**

Daily Bellringer

For each class during which you will teach these selections, have students complete one of the five activities for the appropriate week in the *Daily Bellringer Activities* booklet.

Multidraft Reading

To assist struggling readers and to enhance reading for all, assign the text in chunks as warranted by length and apply multidraft reading protocols. For each reading, have students set the purpose indicated:

- **First reading**—identifying key ideas and details and answering any Reading Checks.
- **Second reading**—analyzing craft and structure and responding to the side-column prompts.
- **Third reading**—integrating knowledge and ideas, connecting to other texts and the world, and answering the end-of-selection questions.

For more guidance, refer to the *Classroom Strategies and Teaching Routines* card, **Multidraft Reading**.

Background
More About the Author

In addition to his lifework, *Leaves of Grass,* Whitman wrote volumes of prose. Of particular note is *Specimen Days* (1882), in which Whitman gathered pieces of autobiography, memories of the Civil War, and reflections on nature, poets, and poetry. Many of the pieces that comprise *Specimen Days* were first published in *The New York Times* and other newspapers. The book has recently garnered more attention from scholars and critics, who see it as an experimental prose work that serves as a counterpart to Whitman's experiments in poetry.

Ⓒ Text Complexity: Reader and Task Suggestions

Preparing to Read the Text	Astronomer Leveled Tasks	Song of Myself Leveled Tasks	Leaves of Grass Leveled Tasks
• Using the Background information on TE pp. 422–423, discuss American poets from the 19th Century. • Ask students how science helps us understand nature. • Guide students to use Multidraft reading strategies (TE p. 423) to deepen their comprehension.	*Levels of Meaning* If students will have difficulty understanding the poem's meaning, have them identify details about science. Then, have them explain how the narrator feels about science. *Synthesizing* If students will not have difficulty with the poem's meaning, have them research astronomy during Whitman's time. Then, have them describe Whitman's reasoning.	*Levels of Meaning* If students will have difficulty understanding the poem's meaning, have them read to identify information about life cycles. Then, have them reread to explain Whitman's observations on life. *Evaluating* If students will not have difficulty understanding the poem's meaning, have them paraphrase Whitman's outlook on the cycle of life.	*Structure/Language* If students will have difficulty with the poem's vocabulary or syntax, have them first read to identify and define unfamiliar words. Then, have them read the text aloud. *Synthesizing* If students will not have difficulty with the poem's vocabulary or syntax, have students locate challenging words in the text and then use each one in a sentence.

423

PRETEACH block

PRETEACH

❶ Connecting to the Essential Question

1. Review the assignment with the class.

2. Share an example of a writer, performer, or artist with whom students might be familiar, and whose work, like Whitman's, can be characterized as bold, adventurous, generous, and optimistic. Include examples of the person's work. Then have the students complete the assignment.

3. As students read, have them make a list of words and phrases that embody Whitman's character and outlook.

❷ Literary Analysis

Introduce the skills, using the instruction on the student page.

Think Aloud: Model the Skill

Say to students:

The best way to appreciate Whitman's free verse is to read his poems aloud. Take, for example, the opening lines of "Song of Myself" on page 428. When I read aloud, I find myself emphasizing the words "celebrate" and "sing" in the first line, in part because of the aliteration of the syllables *cel* and *sing*. The line does not have a regular beat, but the repetition of "myself" gives the line its own rhythm.

That same pattern holds in the second line: I want to stress the words "I" and "you," and the repetition of "assume" gives me all the rhythm I need. Now I am sensing a pattern: The first half of each line is balanced by repetition in the second half. That pattern holds through the third line: Notice how "belonging to me" is balanced by "belongs to you."

Whitman drops this pattern after only three lines—any more would risk monotony—and freely uses new rhythms and patterns. It is free verse, after all.

Before You Read — *Walt Whitman's Poetry*

❶ **Connecting to the Essential Question** The poetry of Walt Whitman is bold, adventurous, generous, and optimistic. As you read Whitman's poems, note word choices that signal a sense of boldness, adventure, and optimism. This will help as you consider the Essential Question: **What makes American literature American?**

❷ Literary Analysis

Traditional **epic poetry** tells a long story about a hero whose adventures embody the values of a nation. Although many of his first readers were shocked by Whitman's *Leaves of Grass*, today the poem is considered a type of *American epic* that expresses national ideals. A true "poet of democracy," Whitman is broadly inclusive in his topics, which range from slavery and the Civil War to romantic love and immortality. Thrumming through these diverse subjects, though, is the constant echo of Whitman's **epic theme**— that all people of all times are connected by their shared experience of life. Whitman's **style** is marked by specific *structural and poetic elements* that contribute to a sense of epic sweep:

- **Free Verse:** Unlike formal verse, which has strict rules, free verse has irregular meter and line length and sounds like natural speech. Although free verse is as old as the Psalms in the Bible, Whitman was the first American poet to use it. It allows him to shape every line and stanza to suit his meaning, rather than fitting his message to a form:

  Do I contradict myself?
  Very well then I contradict myself. . . .

- **Long Lines:** Whitman uses long, sprawling lines for various effects. They may reflect the idea being expressed, capture a broad scene, develop a complex idea, or string together a list of objects:

  I lean and loaf at my ease observing a spear of
  summer grass.

- **Catalogues,** or **lists:** Whitman's use of catalogues, or lists, of people, objects, or situations, evokes the infinite range of elements that make up human experience. His catalogs create a colorful, inclusive parade of images while simultaneously suggesting that each element is of equal weight and worth. "I am enamor'd," he writes,

  Of men that live among cattle . . .
  Of the builders and steerers of ships and the wielders of
  axes and mauls, and the drivers of horses…

 **Common Core State Standards**

Reading Literature
4. Determine the meaning of words and phrases as they are used in the text, including figurative and connotative meanings; analyze the impact of specific word choices on meaning and tone, including words with multiple meanings or language that is particularly fresh, engaging, or beautiful. *(p. 425)*
5. Analyze how an author's choices concerning how to structure specific parts of a text contribute to its overall structure and meaning as well as its aesthetic impact.
9. Demonstrate knowledge of nineteenth-century foundational works of American literature, including how two or more texts from the same period treat similar themes or topics.
Language
5.a. Interpret figures of speech in context and analyze their role in the text.

www.PHLitOnline.com

Vocabulary Development

Vocabulary Knowledge Rating

Create a **Vocabulary Knowledge Rating** chart (*Professional Development Guidebook*, p. 33) for the vocabulary words on the student page. Give each student a copy of the chart with the words on it. Read the words aloud, and have students mark their rating in the Before Reading column. Urge students to attend to these words as they read and discuss the selections.

In order to gauge how much instruction you need to provide, tally how many students are confident in their knowledge of each word. As students read, point out the words and their context.

Vocabulary Central, featuring tools and activities for studying vocabulary, is available online at **www.PHLitOnline.com.**

- **Anaphora,** or the repetition of phrases or sentences with similar structures or meanings: In the preface to *Leaves of Grass,* Whitman writes that America "perceives that the corpse" of old ideas is being moved out of the "house" of the national literature. His use of anaphora in this paragraph creates a tone and rhythm that is almost biblical, even as it delivers a message that is revolutionary:

    ... perceives that it waits a little while in the door ...
    that it was fittest for its days ... that its action has
    descended to the stalwart and well-shaped heir who
    approaches ... and that he shall be fittest for his days.

- **Diction,** or **word choice:** In the example used to illustrate anaphora above, the words *fittest* and *heir* enhance the passage's biblical quality. Whitman chooses other words for their clarity, precision, or sound quality.

- **Onomatopoeia,** or words whose sounds imitate their meanings: Whitman's use of words like *grunting, gab,* and *yawp* give his poetry an earthy quality, while also suggesting that his ideas transcend language itself.

Comparing Literary Works As you read, notice Whitman's use of these structural and poetic elements, and compare their effects in different poems. Think about the ideas or emotions individual elements help to emphasize.

❸ Reading Strategy

ⓒ **Preparing to Read Complex Texts** To increase your understanding of Whitman's ideas, **adjust your reading rate.** When a poem's lines are long and dense, read slowly, and when you feel pulled by the rhythm of the verse, read more rapidly. *Read aloud* to hear the flow of Whitman's language and to better appreciate his sprawling lines, evocative sounds, and rhythmic repetitions. As you read, use a chart like the one shown to record passages you read slowly and to note how this strategy enhances your understanding.

Passage
"Song of Myself," lines 10–13

↓

Meaning
Whitman sets aside what he was taught through formal education, but these things cannot be completely forgotten. He will speak openly and freely in the lines to follow.

❹ Vocabulary

stirring (stur´ iŋ) *adj.* busy; full of energy (p. 427)

abeyance (ə bā´ əns) *n.* temporary suspension (p. 428)

effuse (e fyo͞oz´) *v.* pour out (p. 431)

bequeath (bē kwēth´) *v.* hand down or pass on (p. 431)

stealthily (stelth´ ə lē) *adv.* slyly or secretively (p. 433)

robust (rō bust´) *adj.* strong and healthy; full of life (p. 435)

Walt Whitman's Poetry **425**

❸ Reading Strategy

1. Introduce the skill, using the instruction on the student page.

2. Give students a copy of **Reading Strategy Graphic Organizer B,** page 97 in *Graphic Organizer Transparencies,* to fill out as they read.

Think Aloud: Model the Skill

Say to students:

Reading is a bit like driving a car. With a clear day and an open road, you can drive at the speed limit. Other times, when the route is uncertain and signs warn of trouble, it is wise to slow down.

I can read through many of Whitman's lines quickly—his famous lists for example. In Section 14 of "Song of Myself," Whitman starts off with a reference to geese, and by line 5 he is cataloging the rest of the animal kingdom, from moose to turkeys. As a reader, I am hitting about fifty-five miles an hour in these lines. Then I come to "The press of my foot to the earth springs a hundred affections, / They scorn the best I can do to relate them." I hit the brakes. What does that mean? I back up and read the lines again. And again.

As you read Whitman's poems, read at the rate that allows you to enjoy the flow of his language and his ideas—and be prepared to stop.

❹ Vocabulary

1. Pronounce each word, giving its definition, and have students say it aloud.

2. For more guidance, see the *Classroom Strategies and Teaching Routines* card for introducing vocabulary.

PHLit Online!
www.PHLitOnline.com

Teaching From Technology

Preparing to Read
Go to **www.PHLitOnline.com** and display the **Get Connected!** slide show for these selections. Have the class brainstorm for responses to the writing prompt, entering ideas in the interactive journal. Then have students complete their responses individually. You may also have students complete the assignment as homework.

To build background, display the Background video and More About the Author features.

Using the Interactive Student Edition
Go to **www.PHLitOnline.com** and display the **Enriched Online Student Edition.** As the class reads the selections or listens to the narration, record answers to side-column prompts using the graphic organizer accessible on the interactive page. Alternatively, have students use the online edition individually, answering the prompts as they read.

❶ About the Selection

In this preface to his historic 1855 edition of *Leaves of Grass,* Whitman says that America has never been static. It is an ever-growing nation of people, ideas, and beliefs that evolve as the nation itself changes. Americans perceive that old ways are passing and strong new ways approaching. Whitman comments that the United States is a great poem, a nation characterized by activity, diversity, and the gifts of its rich natural bounties.

❷ Activating Prior Knowledge

Walt Whitman's poetry celebrates his vision of the United States. Brainstorm with students to come up with images or metaphors for a poem about America by completing this line: "America is _____."

Students may suggest ideas such as "America is energy," "America is a struggle for freedom," "America is another chance," and so forth. List the variety of responses on the board. Then examine them for both positive and negative images and examples of the dignity, inten-sity, diversity, and democracy that Whitman evokes in his poetry.

Concept Connector ➡

Tell students they will return to their responses after reading the selection.

❸ Literary Analysis

Free Verse and Diction

1. **Invite** volunteers to read each of the phrases in the bracketed text in turn, then read all the phrases aloud yourself. Help students identify repeated words in the phrases. **Answer:** The words "perceives," "that it," or "that its" are repeated.

2. **Ask** students the following ques-tion: How does Whitman's use of parallel phrases beginning with "perceives" help establish an uplifting tone?
   Possible answer: The parallel structure and repetition create a crescendo in which each phrase adds to those previous. This rhythmic crescendo creates an uplifting tone.

426

FROM PREFACE TO
THE 1855 EDITION OF
❶
❷ LEAVES
OF
GRASS
WALT WHITMAN

BACKGROUND The 1855 edition of was the first edition of Whitman's opus. In the preface to his work, Whitman's prose sings much as his poetry does, full of poetic language, enthusiasm, and energy.

❸ America does not repel the past or what it has produced under its forms or amid other politics or the idea of castes or the old religions. . . . accepts the lesson with calmness . . . is not so impatient as has been supposed that the slough still sticks to opinions and manners and literature while the life which served its requirements has passed into the new life of the new forms . . . perceives that the corpse is slowly borne from the eating and sleeping rooms of the house . . . perceives that it waits a little while in the door . . . that it was fittest for its days . . . that its action has descended to the stalwart and well-shaped heir who approaches . . . and that he shall be fittest for his days.

426 A Growing Nation (1800–1870)

Differentiated Instruction for Universal Access

Support for Special-Needs Students
Have students complete the Before You Read and the Making Connections pages for these selections in the *Reader's Notebook: Adapted Version.* These pages provide abbreviated skills instruction, a selection summary, the Before You Read graphic organizer, and a Note-taking Guide.

Support for Less Proficient Readers
Have students complete the Before You Read and the Making Connections pages for these selections in the *Reader's Notebook.* These pages provide abbreviated skills instruction, a selection summary, the Before You Read graphic organizer, and a Note-taking Guide.

EL Support for English Learners
Have students complete the Before You Read and the Making Connections pages for these selections in the *Reader's Notebook: English Learner's Version.* These pages provide additional vocabu-lary, vocabulary skills, and vocabulary practice, along with a Getting Ready to Read activity.

The Americans of all nations at any time upon the earth have probably the fullest poetical nature. The United States themselves are essentially the greatest poem. In the history of the earth hitherto the largest and most *stirring* appear tame and orderly to their ampler largeness and stir. Here at last is something in the doings of man that corresponds with the broadcast doings of the day and night. Here is not merely a nation but a teeming nation of nations. Here is action untied from strings necessarily blind to particulars and details magnificently moving in vast masses. Here is the hospitality which forever indicates heroes. . . . Here are the roughs and beards and space and ruggedness and nonchalance that the soul loves. Here the performance disdaining the trivial unapproached in the tremendous audacity of its crowds and groupings and the push of its perspective spreads with crampless and flowing breadth and showers its prolific and splendid extravagance. One sees it must indeed own the riches of the summer and winter, and need never be bankrupt while corn grows from the ground or the orchards drop apples or the bays contain fish or men beget children upon women. . . .

Vocabulary
stirring (stur´ iŋ) *adj.* busy; full of energy

Literary Analysis
Epic Theme What portrait of America does Whitman paint in his references to "roughs and beards and space and ruggedness"?

Critical Reading

1. **Key Ideas and Details (a)** What subject does Whitman address in the first paragraph? **(b) Interpret:** What does Whitman mean when he says "the corpse is slowly borne from the eating and sleeping rooms of the house"?

2. **Key Ideas and Details (a)** According to Whitman, what makes America different from all other nations? **(b) Interpret:** What is the meaning of Whitman's notion that the United States is "a teeming nation of nations"?

3. **Key Ideas and Details (a)** According to Whitman, what is the greatest of all poems? **(b) Analyze:** Based on this statement, how is Whitman redefining the idea of a poem?

Cite textual evidence to support your responses.

from Leaves of Grass 427

Differentiated Instruction for Universal Access

Support for Less Proficient Readers
Help students access Whitman's ideas by providing support in understanding his style. For example, demonstrate how to interpret the ideas separated by ellipses by inserting a missing subject or verb to clarify meaning: "America accepts the lesson with calmness . . ." or "America perceives that it was fittest for its days."

EL Support for English Learners
Point out to students that Whitman sometimes implies, rather than states, ideas. Words may be missing or simply suggested by the surrounding context. For example, when Whitman repeats "Here" in the second paragraph, he means here in the United States.

---

④ Literary Analysis
Epic Theme

1. Direct students to read the bracketed text alone and then in the context of the surrounding paragraph. Guide them to understand the literal meanings of Whitman's images.
   Answer: "Roughs" and "beards" might be Americans, living in rough conditions, probably off the land and on the move, and perhaps wearing beards, as did Whitman.

2. **Ask** students the Literary Analysis question: What portrait of America does Whitman paint in his references to "roughs and beards and space and ruggedness"?
   Possible answer: He portrays America as rough but vital.

ASSESS

Answers

Before students respond, you may wish to have them write a brief objective summary of the selection. As they answer the questions below, remind them to support their answers with evidence from the text.

1. (a) **Possible response:** Whitman addresses the subject of America's attitude toward the past. (b) **Possible response:** He means that old habits die hard and that history is not quickly forgotten.

2. (a) It has the fullest poetical nature. (b) In this line, Whitman refers to the cultural diversity of the American people.

3. (a) According to Whitman, "the United States themselves are essentially the greatest poem." (b) Usually a poem is a highly organized group of words on a page. Whitman's metaphor seems to replace lines with land and words with human beings.

⑤ About the Selection

In these sections from "Song of Myself," the poet gives his evolving vision of life through the perspective of a vast set of encounters and observations. Its tone is optimistic, exuberant, and energetic; its subject, the poet himself. Yet the poem reaches beyond individual experience to all humankind. Whitman conveys his belief in the limitless potential of the human spirit to embrace the world and to grow from everything it experiences.

⑥ Literary Analysis

Free Verse

1. Call on a volunteer to read aloud Section 6. Point out the question-and-answer pattern in the text.

2. **Ask** students the following question: In Section 6, how does Whitman's rhythm reflect the natural cadences of speech?
Answer: The question-and-answer pattern makes Section 6 sound like a conversation, in this case, between the poet and himself.

from
⑤ Song of Myself
WALT WHITMAN

1

I celebrate myself, and sing myself,
And what I assume you shall assume,
For every atom belonging to me as good belongs to you.

I loaf and invite my soul,
5 I lean and loaf at my ease observing a spear of summer grass.

My tongue, every atom of my blood, formed from this soil, this air,
Born here of parents born here from parents the same, and
      their parents the same,
I, now thirty-seven years old in perfect health begin,
Hoping to cease not till death.

10 Creeds and schools in abeyance,
Retiring back a while sufficed at what they are, but never
      forgotten,
I harbor for good or bad, I permit to speak at every hazard,
Nature without check with original energy.

6

A child said *What is the grass?* fetching it to me with full hands,
⑥ How could I answer the child? I do not know what it is any
      more than he.

Vocabulary
abeyance (ə bāˊ əns) *n.*
temporary suspension

428 A Growing Nation (1800–1870)

Enrichment: Investigating Geography

Farming in America

The largely agrarian society in which Walt Whitman lived has almost disappeared from today's America. Although some Americans still live in rural areas, few still operate farms; those who do work in vastly different ways from farmers of the nineteenth century.

Farming—the sowing, tending, and harvesting of crops—is now largely mechanized. In 1992, one hundred years after Whitman's death, only 7 percent of rural residents lived on farms.

Activity: Mapmaking Have students research current urban, suburban, and rural population distribution in your state. Suggest that they record their findings in the **Enrichment: Investigating Geography** work sheet, in *Professional Development Guidebook,* page 228. Students should create a map of the state that graphically illustrates population distribution and present it to the class.

I guess it must be the flag of my disposition, out of hopeful
    green stuff woven.

Or I guess it is the handkerchief of the Lord,
5 A scented gift and remembrancer[1] designedly dropped,
Bearing the owner's name someway in the corners, that we may see
    and remark, and say *Whose?*

. . .

What do you think has become of the young and old men?
And what do you think has become of the women and children?

They are alive and well somewhere,
10 The smallest sprout shows there is really no death,
And if ever there was it led forward life, and does not wait at the
    end to arrest it,
And ceas'd the moment life appear'd.
All goes onward and outward, nothing collapses,
And to die is different from what anyone supposed, and luckier.

9

The big doors of the country barn stand open and ready,
The dried grass of the harvest-time loads the slow-drawn wagon.
The clear light plays on the brown gray and green intertinged,
The armfuls are pack'd to the sagging mow.

5 I am there, I help, I came stretch'd atop of the load,
I felt its soft jolts, one leg reclined on the other,
I jump from the crossbeams and seize the clover and timothy,
And roll head over heels and tangle my hair full of wisps.

14

The wild gander leads his flock through the cool night,
Ya-honk he says, and sounds it down to me like an invitation,
The pert may suppose it meaningless, but I listening close,
Find its purpose and place up there toward the wintry sky.

5 The sharp-hoof'd moose of the north, the cat on the house-sill,
    the chickadee, the prairie dog,
The litter of the grunting sow as they tug at her teats,
The brood of the turkey hen and she with her half-spread wings,
I see in them and myself the same old law.

The press of my foot to the earth springs a hundred affections,
10 They scorn the best I can do to relate them.

---

1. **remembrancer** reminder.

7 ◄ **Critical Viewing**
This drawing is based on a photograph of Whitman as a young man. What can you conclude about his attitudes and personality from this picture? How are they reflected in this poem?
[Infer; Support]

Literary Analysis
Epic Theme and Diction
What attitude toward the cycle of life is suggested by Whitman's use of the words "onward," "outward," and "luckier"? Explain.

9 ☑ Reading Check
What aspects of life does the poet celebrate in this poem?

from Song of Myself **429**

7 **Critical Viewing**
Answer: Students may respond that Whitman's clothing and casual pose suggest that he might be a rugged free spirit who shuns formality. He paints a similar portrait of himself in Section 14, lines 11–19, and elsewhere throughout the poem.

8 **Literary Analysis**
Epic Theme and Diction
1. Have students pause in their reading to study the bracketed passage.
2. Elicit from students their ideas about the connotations of "onward," "outward," and "luckier."
3. Then **ask** students the Literary Analysis question: What attitude toward the cycle of life is suggested by Whitman's use of the words "onward," "outward," and "luckier"?
   Answer: The words have positive, hopeful connotations. His attitude toward the life cycle is that it is natural and that it moves us ever forward.

9 **Reading Check**
Answer: He celebrates the natural aspects of life, those found in outdoor activities, in life's natural cycles, in animals, and in agriculture.

These selections are available in interactive format in the **Enriched Online Student Edition** at **www. PHLitOnline.com** which includes a thematically related video with writing prompt and an interactive graphic organizer.

❿ Literary Analysis

Epic Theme and Anaphora

1. Call on a volunteer to read aloud the bracketed passage. Have students identify the anaphora in Section 17.
   Answer: Lines 1–4 contain the phrase "they are not." Lines 5–6 begin with "This is the."

2. **Ask** students the Literary Analysis question: How does Whitman's use of anaphora in Section 17 emphasize the ideas he is expressing?
   Answer: The use of anaphora confronts the reader again and again with Whitman's ideas and drives them home.

⓫ Reading Strategy

Read Aloud

1. Direct students to Section 51 of "Song of Myself" and have them read it silently. Then ask a volunteer to read it aloud.

2. **Ask:** What type of sentence does the speaker use seven times in this section?
   Answer: The speaker asks questions.

3. **Ask:** Whom do you think the speaker is addressing?
   Possible responses: The speaker may be addressing nature or God.

▶ **Monitor Progress:** Have another volunteer read the section aloud again. Then **ask:** What is the speaker's attitude about time?
   Answer: The speaker seems dismissive of the past and present and eager to move into the future.

I am enamor'd of growing outdoors,
Of men that live among cattle or taste of the ocean or woods,
Of the builders and steerers of ships and the wielders of axes and mauls, and the drivers of horses,
I can eat and sleep with them week in and week out.

15 What is commonest, cheapest, nearest, easiest, is Me,
Me going in for my chances, spending for vast returns,
Adorning myself to bestow myself on the first that will take me,
Not asking the sky to come down to my good will,
Scattering it freely forever.

17

Literary Analysis
Epic Theme and Anaphora
How does Whitman's use of anaphora in Section 17 emphasize the ideas he is expressing?

These are really the thoughts of all men in all ages and lands, they are not original with me,
If they are not yours as much as mine they are nothing, or next to nothing,
 If they are not the riddle and the untying of the riddle they are nothing,
If they are not just as close as they are distant they are nothing.
5 This is the grass that grows wherever the land is and the water is,
This is the common air that bathes the globe.

51

The past and present wilt—I have fill'd them, emptied them,
And proceed to fill my next fold of the future.

Listener up there! what have you to confide to me?
Look in my face while I snuff the sidle of evening,[2]
5 (Talk honestly, no one else hears you, and I stay only a minute longer.)

⓫ Do I contradict myself?
Very well then I contradict myself,
(I am large, I contain multitudes.)
I concentrate toward them that are nigh,[3] I wait on the door-slab.

10 Who has done his day's work? who will soonest be through with his supper?
Who wishes to walk with me?

Will you speak before I am gone? will you prove already too late?

---

2. **snuff . . . evening** put out the hesitant last light of day, which is moving sideways across the sky.
3. **nigh** near.

430 A Growing Nation (1800–1870)

Enrichment: Investigating Religion and Myth

Taoism

Walt Whitman was inspired by Asian philosophy and thought. Whitman believed in the sacredness of the self and in placing the individual above society, ideas that echo the beliefs of the Chinese philosophy of Taoism. Tao, or the Way, is the central force that makes each thing in the universe unique but also brings everything together. The influence of Taoism is evident in Whitman's love of nature and the importance of living in harmony with it. Whitman also espoused the belief in a spiritual unity that connects all things. Such a universal philosophy gives Whitman's poetry broad appeal.

Activity: Presentation Invite interested students to learn more about the principles of Taoism. Suggest that they record their findings in the **Enrichment: Investigating Religion and Myth** work sheet, in *Professional Development Guidebook,* page 240. They can then create a presentation comparing Taoist philosophy and Whitman's ideas.

52

The spotted hawk swoops by and accuses me, he complains of
    my gab and my loitering.

I too am not a bit tamed, I too am untranslatable,
I sound my barbaric yawp over the roofs of the world.
The last scud⁴ of day holds back for me,
5 It flings my likeness after the rest and true as any on the
    shadow'd wilds,
It coaxes me to the vapor and the dusk.

I depart as air, I shake my white locks at the runaway sun,
I effuse my flesh in eddies, and drift it in lacy jags.

I bequeath myself to the dirt to grow from the grass I love,
10 If you want me again look for me under your boot soles.

You will hardly know who I am or what I mean,
But I shall be good health to you nevertheless,
And filter and fiber your blood.

Failing to fetch me at first keep encouraged,
15 Missing me one place search another,
I stop somewhere waiting for you.

---

4. **scud** low, dark, wind-driven clouds.

Vocabulary

effuse (e fyo͞oz′) v. to pour out

bequeath (bē kwēth′) v. to hand down or pass on

Critical Reading

© 1. Key Ideas and Details (a) From what does Whitman say his tongue and blood are formed? **(b) Analyze:** How does he view his relationship with nature? **(c) Analyze:** How does he view his relationship with other people?

© 2. Key Ideas and Details (a) In Section 17, what natural images does Whitman use to communicate the idea that his thoughts belong to everyone? **(b) Generalize:** Which elements of these images convey a belief in the spiritual unity of all natural forms?

© 3. Key Ideas and Details (a) In Section 52, where does the speaker say readers can find him? **(b) Infer:** What does he suggest will happen to his spirit and message after he is gone?

© 4. Integration of Knowledge and Ideas Evaluate: In Section 52, Whitman proudly characterizes his poetry as "barbaric yawp." What terms would you use to evaluate his work?

Cite textual evidence to support your responses.

from Song of Myself **431**

Differentiated Instruction   for Universal Access

Strategy for Special-Needs Students
Students may be confused about who is who as they read Whitman's many pronouns. To help these students form a clear picture of the narrative, have them perform a choral reading of the poem. Each time a new pronoun appears, such as "I" or "you," introduce a new reader. Help students understand to whom Whitman refers in each line.

Strategy for Less Proficient Readers
Clarify Whitman's use of pronouns by helping students identify antecedents. Point out the words "These," "they," and "this is" in Section 17. Remind students of Whitman's personal connections to nature—his belief in its power. Explain that Whitman's pronouns refer to spiritual bonds that link humanity and nature.

---

⑫ Literary Analysis
Free Verse

1. Ask students to paraphrase lines 2–3 of Section 52.
   Answer: I will not be tamed or made to follow rules in expressing my ideas.

2. **Ask** the following question: In what ways does Whitman's use of free verse in these lines emphasize the ideas he is expressing?
   Answer: Both the meaning and the form of these lines express Whitman's unwillingness to conform or be "tamed."

⑬ Critical Thinking
Synthesize

1. Point out in the bracketed lines that the speaker bequeaths himself "to the dirt."

2. Then **ask:** How does this statement take the grass and the speaker full circle?
   Possible response: The speaker begins by speculating about the meaning of the grass; by bequeathing himself to it—in the eternal circle of life, he will become one with the earth.

ASSESS
Answers

Before students respond, you may wish to have them write a brief objective summary of the selection. As they answer the questions below, remind them to support their answers with evidence from the text.

1. (a) He says they are formed from American soil and air. (b) He views himself as part of nature. (c) He views all people as being part of the same life cycle.

2. (a) He refers to the grass that grows everywhere and the air that everyone breathes. (b) **Possible response:** Whitman links these images to the "thoughts of all men in all ages and lands."

3. (a) He says they can find him under their boot soles in the earth. (b) He suggests that he will be "somewhere waiting."

4. **Possible response:** Students may describe Whitman's poetry as original, rambunctious, sweeping, conversational, or self-centered.

431

The Lawrence Tree, 1929, Georgia O'Keeffe, Wadsworth Atheneum, Hartford

15

WHEN I HEARD THE LEARN'D ASTRONOMER
14

WALT WHITMAN

When I heard the learn'd astronomer,
When the proofs, the figures, were ranged in columns before me,
When I was shown the charts and diagrams, to add, divide and
    measure them,
When I sitting heard the astronomer where he lectured with
    much applause in the lecture room,
5 How soon unaccountable I became tired and sick,
Till rising and gliding out I wander'd off by myself,
In the mystical moist night air, and from time to time,
Look'd up in perfect silence at the stars.

432 A Growing Nation (1800–1870)

BY THE BIVOUAC'S
fitful flame

WALT WHITMAN

By the bivouac's[1] fitful flame,
A procession winding around me, solemn and sweet and slow—but
    first I note,
The tents of the sleeping army, the fields' and woods' dim outline,
The darkness lit by spots of kindled fire, the silence,

5 Like a phantom far or near an occasional figure moving,
The shrubs and trees, (as I lift my eyes they seem to be stealthily
    watching me,)
While wind in procession thoughts, O tender and wondrous
    thoughts,
Of life and death, of home and the past and loved, and of those that
    are far away;
A solemn and slow procession there as I sit on the ground,

10 By the bivouac's fitful flame.

---

1. bivouac (biv´ wak´) *n.* night guard to prevent surprise attacks.

Vocabulary
stealthily (stelth´ ə lē)
adv. slyly or secretively

Critical Reading

Cite textual evidence to support your responses.

1. **Key Ideas and Details (a)** In "When I Heard the Learn'd Astronomer," what does the speaker do in reaction to the lecture? **(b) Connect:** What do his actions reveal about his character?

2. **Key Ideas and Details (a) Compare and Contrast:** In what ways does the "perfect silence" in the last line contrast with the lecture? **(b) Draw Conclusions:** What is the speaker saying about the value of science versus a personal experience with nature?

3. **Key Ideas and Details (a)** In lines 3–4 of "By the Bivouac's Fitful Flame," what sights does the speaker look upon? **(b) Infer:** What is the procession to which he refers in line 2?

4. **Key Ideas and Details (a)** Where does the speaker's mind go as he gazes upon the scene before him? **(b) Analyze:** Is the procession he refers to in line 9 the same one referred to earlier? Explain.

5. **Integration of Knowledge and Ideas Make a Judgment:** Whitman is known as a poet who celebrated life. Are these poems celebratory? If so, of what?

By the Bivouac's Fitful Flame **433**

ASSESS

Answers

Before students respond, you may wish to have them write a brief objective summary of the selection. As they answer the questions below, remind them to support their answers with evidence from the text.

1. (a) He leaves the lecture hall to look at the stars himself. (b) It suggests that he wants to experience things personally.

2. (a) One is silent, while the other is filled with numbers and words. (b) He is saying that personal experience with nature is more important than science.

3. (a) He looks upon an army camp, the camp's fire, and the darkness around him. (b) At line 2, the reader cannot know what the procession is—perhaps it is a unit of soldiers.

4. (a) It goes to his friends and family at home. (b) Yes, it is revealed that the procession is composed of the speaker's thoughts.

5. **Possible response:** Yes. "When I Heard the Learn'd Astronomer" celebrates nature's wonder, while "By the Bivouac's Fitful Flame" celebrates the human capacity for memory and love.

Differentiated
Instruction   for Universal Access

Support for Advanced Readers
Suggest that students read additional works by Walt Whitman. Provide students with the following titles: *Leaves of Grass, Drum Taps* and *Good-Bye, My Fancy.* You may also wish to refer students to *Authors in Depth: The American Experience,* which contains the following selections:
• "As I Ebb'd with the Ocean of Life"
• "Broadway"
• "Beat! Beat! Drums!"

• "As Toilsome I Wander'd Virginia's Woods"
• "Death of President Lincoln"
Before students read, have them choose particular issues or literary elements on which to focus. They might, for example, wish to study Whitman's use of free verse and diction, as well as his attitudes in the additional works they read. Lead a round-table discussion in which students can share their analysis of Whitman's other works.

⑰ Humanities

Haystack, 1938, Thomas Hart Benton

Born in 1889 in Missouri, Thomas Hart Benton painted in a realistic style when realism was out of fashion. He believed that as an American artist he should seek his subjects in the American heartland, and was a leader of the regionalist movement in painting. His paintings and murals celebrate American history, landscapes, and working men and women in both rural and urban settings. In *Haystack,* farm workers labor in a rhythmic, swirling landscape that is simultaneously local and vast. One senses that the painter, like Walt Whitman, can "hear America singing" as he observes and chronicles her people. Use this question for discussion:

What parallels can you draw between the artist's and the poet's attitude toward their subjects?

Answer: Both men seem to have admired and respected those who earn their living through manual labor.

⑱ About the Selection

"I Hear America Singing" celebrates Whitman's joyous view of the indomitable American spirit. People distinguish themselves by their work, perform tasks that build the future, and demonstrate an exuberance of skill and purpose that makes each of them a vibrant contributor to the spirit of a proud nation.

Haystack, 1938, Thomas Hart Benton, Museum of Fine Arts, Houston, Texas, USA, © DACS /Gift of Mr. Frank J. Hevrdejs / The Bridgeman Art Library International/©T.H. Benton and R.P. Benton Testamentary Trusts/Licensed by VAGA, New York, NY

434 A Growing Nation (1800–1870)

Enrichment: Analyzing a Literary Figure

A Man of the People

Whitman loved and admired the American people. He attended events just for the pleasure of being with others. He even rode on stage-coaches and ferries just to talk with ordinary people.

Whitman tried to imbue his poetry with America's diversity. In a letter to Ralph Waldo Emerson, he stated his poetic goal: "Every day I go among the people of Manhattan Island, Brooklyn, and other cities, and among the young men, to discover the spirit of them, and to refresh myself . . . . In poems, the young men of The States shall be represented, for they out-rival the best of the rest of the earth."

Activity: Literary Criticism Direct students to critique three poems by Whitman in light of his statement to Emerson. Suggest that they record their findings in the **Enrichment: Analyzing a Literary Figure** work sheet, in *Professional Development Guidebook,* page 235. Students should prepare a written critique to hand in.

I HEAR AMERICA SINGING

Walt Whitman

I hear America singing, the varied carols I hear,
Those of mechanics, each one singing his as it should be blithe
   and strong,
The carpenter singing his as he measures his plank or beam,
The mason singing his as he makes ready for work, or leaves
   off work,
5 The boatman singing what belongs to him in his boat, the
   deckhand singing on the steamboat deck,
The shoemaker singing as he sits on his bench, the hatter[1]
   singing as he stands,
The wood-cutter's song, the ploughboy's on his way in the
   morning, or at noon intermission or at sundown,
The delicious singing of the mother, or of the young wife at work,
   or of the girl sewing or washing,
Each singing what belongs to him or her and to none else,
10 The day what belongs to the day—at night the party of young
   fellows, robust, friendly,
Singing with open mouths their strong melodious songs.

Vocabulary
robust (rō bust´) *adj.*
strong and healthy;
full of life

☑ Reading
Check
Who sings at night?

---

1. **hatter** person who makes, sells, or cleans hats.

◀ **Critical Viewing** In this painting of farmwork, does the artist's style have qualities in common with Whitman's style? Explain. **[Compare and Contrast]**

Literary Analysis
Whitman's Style

1. Read or have a prepared volunteer read the poem to the class.

2. **Ask** students: What aspects of Whitman's style are most evident in this poem?
   Answer: Whitman uses cataloging in lines 2–9 to list various workers in America. Lines 3–6 use anaphora, each line beginning with the same phrasing: "The carpenter singing"; "The mason singing"; "The boatman singing"; "The shoemaker singing."

3. **Ask:** How does Whitman's style here reflect the meaning of the poem?
   Possible response: In the first line, Whitman describes America's music as "varied carols." The listing style that follows expresses and reinforces the broad range and variety of those "carols" in concrete, specific terms.

Critical Viewing

Possible response: The artist's style depicts a sense of harmony with nature, which is also apparent in Whitman's work.

Reading Check

Answer: A party of young fellows sings at night.

Differentiated
Instruction   for Universal Access

EL Vocabulary for English Learners
Students may be unfamiliar with the words Whitman uses to label various workers. List some of these on the chalkboard: "mechanic," "mason," "deckhand," "wood-cutter," "plough-boy." Use visual images, such as the painting on page 434, to convey information about the kind of work each laborer undertakes.

Strategy for Gifted/Talented Students
After students have read "I Hear America Singing," challenge them to list as many "singing" references in the poem as they can. Emphasize that Whitman referred to everyday people pursuing everyday activities. Then discuss the painting on page 434, pointing out the "everyday" look of the scene, the "slice-of-life" character of these artworks. Remind students that according to Whitman, everyone has "strong melodious songs" that belong "to him or her and to none else." Ask students to speculate what song the workers could be singing.

㉒ A NOISELESS PATIENT SPIDER

Walt Whitman

A noiseless patient spider,
I mark'd where on a little promontory it stood isolated,
Mark'd how to explore the vacant vast surrounding,
It launch'd forth filament, filament, filament, out of itself,
5   Ever unreeling them, ever tirelessly speeding them.

And you O my soul where you stand,
Surrounded, detached, in measureless oceans of space,
Ceaselessly musing, venturing, throwing, seeking the spheres
    to connect them,
Till the bridge you will need be form'd, till the ductile anchor hold,
10 Till the gossamer thread you fling catch somewhere, O my soul.

Critical Reading ©

Cite textual evidence to support your responses.

© 1. **Key Ideas and Details (a)** In "I Hear America Singing," what occupations does Whitman attribute to Americans? **(b) Draw Conclusions:** What does his catalog of occupations suggest about his vision of America?

© 2. **Key Ideas and Details (a)** What does Whitman describe the laborers doing at night? **(b) Analyze:** Why do you think the poem ends as it does?

© 3. **Key Ideas and Details (a)** In line three of "A Noiseless Patient Spider," what surrounds the spider? **(b) Interpret:** In line 7, what are the "measureless oceans of space" with which the speaker's soul is surrounded?

© 4. **Craft and Structure (a)** What verbs does Whitman use to describe the spider's actions? **(b)** What verbs does he use to describe the activities of his soul? **(c) Compare and Contrast:** How are the two explorations the same, and how are they different?

© 5. **Integration of Knowledge and ideas** What characteristics of America and the American spirit can you find in all the poems presented here? Use at least two of these Essential Question words in your response: *perseverance, bravery, spirit, unknown.* *[Connecting to the Essential Question: What makes American literature American?]*

Critical Commentary

America's Epic
James E. Miller, Jr.

James E. Miller, Jr. is the Helen A. Regenstein Professor Emeritus of English at the University of Chicago. He is the author of two important critical studies of Walt Whitman and another focusing on T. S. Eliot.

Did Whitman write the epic for modern America? There have been many who contend that *Leaves of Grass* is merely a collection of lyric poetry, some good, some bad, all of it of a peculiarly personal nature that disqualifies its attitudes and philosophy generally. There have been others who have defended Whitman's book as the embodiment of the American reality and ideal, as superb fulfillment of all the genuine requirements of the national epic.

What did Whitman believe? The answer may be found in a number of prose works, beginning with the 1855 Preface. It is clear in this early work that Whitman desired *Leaves of Grass* to bear a unique relationship with America: "Here [in America] at last is something in the doings of man that corresponds with the broadcast doings of the day and night… It awaits the gigantic and generous treatment worthy of it." It is generally recognized that the entire Preface is a veiled account of Whitman's concept of his own role as a poet. Certainly he includes himself in the category when he asserts: "The poets of the kosmos advance through all interpositions and coverings and turmoils and stratagems to first principles." Although Whitman does not use the term, it is clear throughout the 1855 Preface that he believes his book to have the basic nature and general scope of the traditional national epic.

In *Democratic Vistas*, in the same indirect manner, Whitman again reveals his concept of the nature of his poetry: "Never was anything more wanted than, to-day, and here in the States, the poet of the modern is wanted, or the great literatus of the modern. At all times, perhaps, the central point in any nation, and that whence it is itself really sway'd the most and whence it sways others, is its national literature, especially its archetypal poems" (V, 54–55). Whitman was by this time (1871) acutely aware that America had not accepted his book as he had planned and hoped. There can be little doubt that he conceived *Leaves of Grass* as an "archetypal" poem produced and offered to America at its "central point"—a book "sway'd" by the nation and written to sway others. Such a work as Whitman calls for in *Democratic Vistas* is surely the epic of America. And, basically, it is his own work which he desires to be recognized as such.

Ⓒ Key Ideas and Details What question about Whitman's work does Miller pose? According to Miller, how does Whitman himself answer that question? What evidence does Miller provide to support this answer?

---

23 Critical Commentary

1. Prepare to discuss this commentary by assigning it as homework. Give students the following definitions to assist in their reading:

   first principle: a fundamental rule that cannot be deduced from any other, for example, the shortest distance between two points is a straight line.
   archetypal: in the original pattern of which all things of the same type are based.

2. Invite students to discuss the concept Miller calls "the American reality and ideal." **Ask:** What does "the American reality and ideal" mean to you?
   Possible answers: Students may mention freedom, diversity, opportunity, democracy, power, land, and so on.

3. Refer students to the quotation from Whitman in which he refers to "first principles." **Ask:** What first principles do you think Whitman may have arrived at?
   Possible responses: Students may refer to the connectedness of humanity, the beauty of nature, the necessity of freedom, and so on.

24 Key Ideas and Details
Answers

1. Miller poses the question of whether Whitman wrote the epic for modern America.

2. Whitman believes that *Leaves of Grass* fulfills the requirements of the national epic.

3. Miller quotes Whitman's statements in the 1855 Preface to *Leaves of Grass* and in the 1871 *Democratic Vistas*. Miller contends that these statements reveal Whitman's belief that his work is epic in scope.

Answers

1. The use of catalog shows the inclusive quality of Whitman's vision, conveying the epic theme of connectedness.

2. (a) The use of free verse emphasizes Whitman's free, unconventional, and unconfined approach to the wonders of nature. (b) **Possible response:** In Section 51, lines 6–8, Whitman's use of free verse allows him to make a large point in a few words.

3. (a) He asks the listener to confide in him. (b) Whitman does not mean exactly what he says. The next two lines indicate that the speaker has multiple meanings. (c) The long line allows the speaker to express a complex idea.

4. Repeated use of the opening words "When I" sets up the reader's expectation of the speaker's bored response to the astronomer.

5. **Possible response:** Whitman's use of "fitful flame" creates the image and feeling of a fire that is dying out late at night. His description of a moving figure as a "phantom" gives the image a dreamlike feeling.

6. **Sample answers:** (a) "I Hear America Singing"; What is shared: Songs; By whom: Working people. (b) He believes that all human beings are connected.

7. **Sample answers:** (a) I slowed my reading rate for longer, complex lines in "Song of Myself." I read Section 9 slowly in order to have a clear understanding of both the setting and the action. (b) I perceived that the speaker takes joy in physical work.

8. **Sample answers:** (a) I read slowly because of the long lines. (b) My rate became slightly faster as I grew accustomed to the speaker's syntax.

9. **Sample answer:** I read "When I Heard the Learn'd Astronomer" aloud. Doing so helped me picture the images and follow the action within the poem.

438

After You Read | *Walt Whitman's Poetry*

Literary Analysis

1. **Craft and Structure** How does Whitman's use of **catalog**, or **list**, in the following line from the preface to *Leaves of Grass* help convey his **epic theme**:

   Here are the roughs and beards and space and ruggedness and nonchalance that the soul loves.

2. **Craft and Structure** (a) Note two ways in which his use of **free verse** in "Song of Myself" allows Whitman to express his ideas more effectively than would a formal structure. (b) Cite a passage that you think is a strong example of the relationship between free verse and meaning. Explain your choice.

3. **Craft and Structure** (a) In Section 51 of "Song of Myself," what does the speaker ask of the listener? (b) In line 5 of that section, do you think Whitman means exactly what he says? Why or why not? (c) In what ways does the **long line** enhance the poet's meaning?

4. **Craft and Structure** How does the use of **anaphora** in lines 1–4 of "When I Heard the Learn'd Astronomer" reinforce the speaker's idea of the astronomer?

5. **Craft and Structure** Note two examples of **word choice**, or **diction**, that add to the dreamlike quality of "By the Bivouac's Fitful Flame." Explain your choices.

6. **Comparing Literary Works** (a) Use a chart like the one shown to analyze and compare Whitman's epic theme of shared human experience in "Song of Myself" and at least two other poems in this grouping. (b) Based on your analysis, explain your understanding of Whitman's overall message or view of life.

Title	What Is Shared	Shared by Whom
"Song of Myself"	Atom	All, shared by everyone

Reading Strategy

7. Explain how you **adjusted your reading rate** as you read "Song of Myself." (a) Which stanzas or sections did you read more slowly? Why? (b) What new insight did slower reading help you gain?

8. (a) What reading rate did you use to read "I Hear America Singing"? Why? (b) Did your reading rate change over the course of the poem? Explain.

9. Which poems or sections of a poem did you *read aloud* slowly? How did doing so help you better understand the poet's meaning?

Common Core State Standards

Writing
3.d. Use precise words and phrases, telling details, and sensory language to convey a vivid picture of the experiences, events, setting, and/or characters. (p. 439)
4. Produce clear and coherent writing in which the development, organization, and style are appropriate to task, purpose, and audience. (p. 439)

Language
4. Determine or clarify the meaning of unknown and multiple-meaning words and phrases based on *grades 11–12 reading and content*, choosing flexibly from a range of strategies. (p. 439)
4.d. Verify the preliminary determination of the meaning of a word or phrase. (p. 439)

Assessment Practice

Make Inferences and Generalizations For more practice, see *All-in-One Workbook.*

Many tests require students to make inferences about a written passage. Explain that sometimes inferences need to be drawn concerning an author's point of view, opinions, or attitudes. Have students read "I Hear America Singing" on page 435 and then ask them the following question:

What is the poet's attitude toward the American workers about whom he writes?

A uncertain
B celebratory
C dismissive
D somber

The poet emphatically proclaims his admiration for the laborers; *A*, *C*, and *D* cannot be correct. The best choice is *B*.

438

PERFORMANCE TASKS
Integrated Language Skills

© Vocabulary Acquisition and Use

Multiple Meaning Words

Many words in English have more than one meaning. Usually, the meaning of a word changes according to its part of speech. For example, the word *bow* as a noun refers to a tied ribbon, to the implement that is drawn across a violin's strings, or to the front section of a boat. As a verb, it means "to bend one's head or body as a sign of respect." Explain the multiple meanings of each of the numbered words below. Use a dictionary to check your work.

1. stirring   3. figures
2. note   4. check

Then, choose two of the words, and use more than one meaning of both words in a brief paragraph describing the daily work of different kinds of Americans.

Writing

Poem Write a poem to be read aloud as part of a group poetry reading honoring Walt Whitman. In addition to the use of free verse, choose several key elements of Whitman's unique style—his use of long lines, catalogs, anaphora, and onomatopoeia—and use them to enhance your own individual voice. Your poem should be your own while also demonstrating your understanding of Whitman's literary achievement.

Prewriting Decide on a "Whitmanesque" topic, and review the traits of free verse. Use a format like the one shown here to list or diagram sensory details and images related to your topic.

Drafting As you write, let your meaning determine the lengths of lines and stanzas. Be aware of your *tone*, or attitude toward your subject, and make sure your *diction*, or word choice, reflects that tone. Choose vivid words that contribute to the mood you want to evoke.

Revising Read your draft aloud. Listen for natural rhythms of speech rather than formal grammatical structures. Make any changes necessary to maintain natural rhythms and to enhance your meaning. If your word choices could be more precise, use a dictionary or thesaurus to select more effective language.

Idea/Topic
Celebrate the Girls' Soccer Team

The sound of their cleats on pavement

Their life and energy after a win

Their white uniforms against the green field

Extended Study: Integrated Language Skills **439**

Vocabulary: Denotations

Denotations are the literal meanings of words, as opposed to their *connotative* meanings, which are the emotional associations the words bring forth. Answer each of the following questions. Then, explain your answers.

1. If a judge hands down a ruling in *abeyance* of a particular law, is she enforcing that law?
2. Does light that *effuses* from a lamp spread softly or shine in a sharply focused beam?
3. If you *bequeath* your bedroom to your little sister, could she use it?
4. If someone gave you a *robust* greeting, would you be likely to hear it?
5. Does a person typically move *stealthily* through a library?
6. If a town is *stirring*, is it peaceful and quiet?

Vocabulary Acquisition and Use

1. Introduce the skill, using the instruction on the student page.
2. Have students complete the Multiple Meaning Words activity and the Vocabulary practice.

Multiple Meaning Words

1. As a verb, *stirring* refers to making a slight movement. As an adjective, it describes something as being in motion or inspiring.
2. As a verb, *to note* is to observe. As a noun, a *note* is a written comment or a musical symbol.
3. As a verb, *figures* means "calculates" or "evaluates." As a noun, *figures* can refer to numerals, diagrams, shapes, or well-known persons.
4. As a verb, *to check* can mean "to verify or examine something or to stop something." As a noun, it can be a sudden stop, a mark, or a document used to transfer money.

Sample paragraph: The leaves are barely <u>stirring</u> as the farmer begins his day. His first job is to <u>check</u> on the animals. His hired hand is already in the barn <u>stirring</u> up the feed. At the end of the day he must write a <u>check</u> to pay his helper.

Vocabulary

1. No, because her ruling temporarily overturns the law.
2. Light that effuses spreads softly through the room.
3. She could, because I have given the room to her.
4. Yes, because the greeting would be energetic.
5. No, people in a library move quietly, but not secretively.
6. No, the town is bustling and energetic.

Writing

1. To guide students in writing this poem, give them the **Support for Writing** work sheet, in *Unit 2 Resources,* page 180.
2. Assess students' evaluations using the **Rubrics for Poems,** in *Professional Development Guidebook,* pages 274–275.

Assessment Resources

439

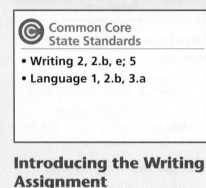

Common Core
State Standards

• Writing 2, 2.b, e; 5
• Language 1, 2.b, 3.a

Introducing the Writing Assignment

Review the assignment and the criteria, using the instruction on the student page.

What Do You Notice?

1. Draw class attention to the passage from *Walden*. Have a student read the highlighted sentence aloud. **Ask** students what makes the writing special.
   Possible responses: Students may cite words such as *impressible* and the strong imagery.

2. **Ask** students what punctuation mark joins the two clauses in the sentence.
   Answer: A semicolon joins the clauses. Point out that the semicolon is also joining two halves of an analogy or an explicit comparison. Guide students to see that the semicolon, too, gently guides the reader along the "path" of the sentence.

3. Suggest that students use semicolons to structure analogies in their own reflective essays.

Gretel Ehrlich on Essays

Show students Segment 3 on Gretel Ehrlich on the *See It!* DVD or via the link in the **Enriched Online Student Edition** at www.PHLitOnline.com.

A writing prompt for this mode of writing can be found on the *PH Online Essay Scorer* at www.PHLitOnline.com.

Write a Reflective Essay

Reflective Essay Ralph Waldo Emerson and Henry David Thoreau wrote essays that do not just report on events but also interpret them and consider their deeper meanings. Their **reflective essays** make connections between each writer's personal life experiences and the larger world. Follow the steps outlined in this workshop to write your own reflective essay.

Assignment Write a reflective essay in which you explore a personal experience or an event and reflect on its deeper meaning.

What to Include Your reflective essay should have these elements:
- You, the writer, as the main speaker or character
- Your personal feelings and thoughts about a clearly defined topic
- Insights presented in a logical organization
- A balanced approach that presents incidents from your life and connects them to more general or abstract ideas
- Illlustration of your important beliefs
- An appropriate and consistent tone

To preview the criteria on which your reflective essay may be assessed, see the rubric on page 447.

To get a feel for reflective essays, read this mentor text. Note how Thoreau connects his personal experiences to a larger theme.

from: Walden by Henry David Thoreau

It is remarkable how easily and insensibly we fall into a particular route, and make a beaten track for ourselves. I had not lived there a week before my feet wore a path from my door to the pondside; and though it is five or six years since I trod it, it is still quite distinct. It is true, I fear that others may have fallen into it, and so helped to keep it open. The surface of the earth is soft and impressible by the feet of men; and so with the paths which the mind travels.

Common Core
State Standards

Writing
2. Write informative texts to examine and convey complex ideas, concepts, and information clearly and accurately through the effective selection, organization, and analysis of content.
2.b. Develop the topic thoroughly by selecting the most significant and relevant facts, extended definitions, concrete details, quotations, or other information and examples appropriate to the audience's knowledge of the topic.

WRITE GUY
Jeff Anderson, M.Ed.

What Do You Notice?

Read the highlighted sentence several times. Then, with a partner, discuss the qualities that make it special. You might consider the following elements:
- Word choice
- Sentence length
- Vivid details
- Ideas or content

Share your group's observations with the class.

440 A Growing Nation (1800–1870)

Teaching Resources

The following resources can be used to enrich or extend the instruction.
Unit 2 Resources

- **All** **Writing Workshop, pp.** 191–192.

- **All** *Common Core Companion,*
  pp. 196–207, 226–227; 318–323

- **All** *Professional Development Guidebook*
  Rubric for Self-Assessment: Reflective Essay, pp. 293–294

- **All** *Graphic Organizer Transparencies*
  Rubric for Self-Assessment: Reflective Essay p. 94

- **All** *See It!* DVD
  Gretel Ehrlich, Segments 3 and 4

All resources are available at **www.PHLitOnline.com**.

Prewriting and Planning

Choosing Your Topic

To choose an event for your essay, use one of these strategies:

- **Listing** List the activities that fill your week, paying attention to any incidents that made you pause or that seemed special. Choose one to explore in your essay.

- **Freewriting** Consider the important moments in your life, such as meeting your best friend, or making a tough choice. As you free-write, ask yourself how this moment changed your life. Choose one moment to explore further.

Narrowing Your Topic

Write a topic sentence. Narrow your focus by identifying a lesson you learned, or the instant you suddenly saw yourself or the world in a new light. Write one sentence about the event and the lesson it taught you.

> **Model: Expressing an Insight**
>
> When I saw how long it took me to walk home, I marveled at
>
　　　　　　　　　　　 Event
> my ancestors who had cleared the land by themselves.
> 　　　　　　　　　　 **Insight**

Gathering Details

Make connections. Consider how your experience relates to themes in the world at large. Organize your thoughts in a diagram like the one shown below. You might also want to do some research to strengthen your knowledge about your subject. Talk with friends and family, or use the library or the Internet to gather details about past events or issues that relate to your personal experience.

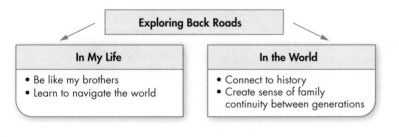

Exploring Back Roads

In My Life	**In the World**
• Be like my brothers • Learn to navigate the world	• Connect to history • Create sense of family continuity between generations

Applying Understanding by Design Principles

Clarifying Expected Outcomes: Using Rubrics

- Before students begin work on this assignment, have them preview the Rubric for Self-Assessment on page 447 to learn what qualities their reflective essays must have. A copy of this rubric appears in the *Professional Development Guidebook*, page 293.

- Review the criteria in the rubric with the class. Before students use the rubric to assess their own writing, work with them to rate the Student Model (p. 446) using the rubric.

- If you wish to assess students' reflective essays with either a four-point or a six-point scoring rubric, see the *Professional Development Guidebook*, pages 293–294.

Prewriting and Planning

1. Introduce the prewriting strategies, using the instruction on the student page.

2. Have students apply the strategies to choose and narrow their topics and gather details by using the strategies listed.

Teaching the Strategies

1. If students are using a list to generate writing ideas, guide them by mentioning areas of life that may yield memorable events—for example, family life, school, sports, competitions, jobs, or travel.

2. If students are freewriting about important moments in their lives in order to generate ideas, suggest that they use the Timeline work sheet in *Professional Development Guidebook*, page 101, to help them remember important childhood events.

Think Aloud: Model the Listing Strategy

Model the listing strategy, using the following "think aloud." Say to students:

> My listing strategy is very similar to my freewriting technique: I jot down ideas as quickly as I can without looking back, checking my spelling, or worrying about penmanship. Sometimes I set a timer, giving myself two minutes to write the list. Racing against time seems to speed up the flow of ideas.

Six Traits Focus

✔	Ideas		Word Choice
✔	Organization		Sentence Fluency
	Voice		Conventions

PH WRITING COACH | Grade 11

Students will find additional information on essays and reflections in Chapters 2, 7, and 10.

Drafting

1. Introduce the drafting strategies, using the instruction on the student page.

2. Have students apply the strategies as they draft.

Teaching the Strategies

1. Encourage students to adapt the organizational model on the student page to their own work, if the structure is a good fit for their essays.

2. Suggest other organizational approaches, such as beginning with the insight and then describing the experience that produced it. Mention the option of presenting several different experiences that, taken together, had a significant impact.

3. Help students extend and elaborate ideas by giving them more practice in using the SEE process. For instance, ask students to provide personal observations that elaborate on the idea that members of their class view their school in a way quite different from the way ninth graders see it.

4. Encourage students to use concrete sensory details and dialogue to enliven the narrative portions of their essays.

5. Tell students to use language that is natural to them so that their personalities come through to the reader and their writing sounds sincere.

Six Traits Focus

✔	Ideas		Word Choice
✔	Organization		Sentence Fluency
	Voice		Conventions

Drafting

Shaping Your Writing

Organize your ideas. Choose an organization that places the incident you are describing in a larger context. The format shown here is one effective way to build a reflective essay.

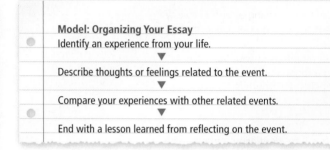

Model: Organizing Your Essay

Identify an experience from your life.

▼

Describe thoughts or feelings related to the event.

▼

Compare your experiences with other related events.

▼

End with a lesson learned from reflecting on the event.

Start with a strong lead. A simple, compelling lead, or opening sentence, provides enough information to activate readers' curiosity and make them want to read your essay. Notice how both of these leads raise questions in your mind:

- *Whenever I hear the song "Memory," I burst into laughter.*
- *My sister refuses to wear the color purple.*

Providing Elaboration

Use the SEE technique. The step-by-step approach of the SEE method can help you add details and develop your ideas. This is what the initials mean:

S **Statement:** Write a sentence to express a main idea.

E **Extension:** Restate or develop the main idea.

E **Elaboration:** Provide further information that amplifies or expands on the main idea.

Be generous as you extend and elaborate. Include sensory details, images, and personal thoughts that will make your writing vivid and interesting.

Model: Extending and Elaborating to Add Details

[*Statement*] They are small country roads [*Extension*] —the ones that change color [*Extension*] and ride when you cross a simple parish line. [*Extension*] They have four-ton limits...

Extending and elaborating on the definition with personal observations provides a more vivid picture of the topic.

Writers on Writing

Gretel Ehrlich On Using Layers of Meaning

Gretel Ehrlich is the author of "Inspired by Nature" (p. 222).

These are the closing paragraphs of the title essay of my book *The Solace of Open Spaces*. Here, I stepped back from the details in the essay—those of anecdote and description—to contemplate the larger meaning of "space" and the way it shapes our minds and our experience of the world—the "internal weather" of our lives.

"Writing is an act of seeing through to the other side of our lives, then coming back and putting an expression of that otherness on the page."

—Gretel Ehrlich

from *The Solace of Open Spaces*

At night, by moonlight, the land is whittled to slivers—a ridge, a river, a strip of grassland stretching to the mountains, then the huge sky. One morning a full moon was setting in the west just as the sun was rising. I felt precariously balanced between the two as I loped across a meadow. For a moment, I could believe that the stars, which were still visible, work like cooper's bands, holding together everything above Wyoming.

Space has a spiritual equivalent and can heal what is divided and burdensome in us. My grandchildren will probably use space shuttles for a honeymoon trip or to recover from heart attacks, but closer to home we might also learn how to carry space inside ourselves in the effortless way we carry our skins. Space represents sanity, not a life purified or dull, or "spaced out," but one that might accommodate intelligently any idea or situation.

From the clayey soil of northern Wyoming is mined bentonite, which is used as a filler in candy, gum, and lipstick. We Americans are great on fillers, as if what we have, what we are, is not enough. We have a cultural tendency toward denial, but, being affluent, we strangle ourselves with what we can buy. . . . We fill up space as if it were a pie shell, with things whose opacity further obstructs our ability to see what is already there.

> In this paragraph, I turn the concept of "space" in four directions: as a spiritual guide, as a healer of physical maladies, as an actual component of our body's makeup, and as a state of mind.

> Here I take an actual geological substance—bentonite, which is a kind of clay—and use it metaphorically: to indicate the way we pack our heads, hearts, and homes with things we don't need.

> Here I am reminding the reader that "space" does not represent an "absence" but something positive.

Writing Workshop **443**

Gretel Ehrlich on Using Layers of Meaning

Review the passage on the student page with the class, using Gretel Ehrlich's comments to deepen students' understanding of the process of writing a reflective essay.

Teaching From the Professional Model

1. Explain to students that Gretel Ehrlich has been a ranch hand and a documentary filmmaker. As a professional writer, she is best known for her studies of nature. Show students Segment 4 on Gretel Ehrlich on the *See It!* **DVD** or from this page in the **Enriched Online Student Edition.** Discuss her comments about how she elaborated on the concept of space as both a physical and mental entity.

2. Draw students' attention to Ehrlich's striking use of the information about bentonite in the passage on the student page. She provides an interesting detail about a little-known substance to create a clever analogy illustrating how people compulsively fill up their lives with trivia. Encourage students to make their ideas easier to grasp and more memorable by elaborating on them with extended details and creative figures of speech, just as Ehrlich uses this detail to comment on our waste of physical and mental space.

3. Review Ehrlich's comments about treating space as if it were a pie shell, to be filled with things "whose opacity further obstructs our ability to see what is already there." **Ask** students to give other examples of things that interfere with clear perception and thought.
   Possible response: Students might mention the frenzy to buy the latest fashions and consumer items or the hours spent watching television, chatting online, or playing video games.

Differentiated Instruction for Universal Access

Strategy for Less Proficient Writers

Have students choose partners to whom they will tell the stories they are using as the basis for their reflective essays. Telling their stories as part of the prewriting activity will help students organize and focus their ideas, eliminate less relevant details, shape the plots of their narratives, and express their insights and reflections more coherently.

Have each student prepare to tell his or her story by making a timeline to use as a guide when writing. Tell partners to help each other make certain that their timelines show events in the proper order. Partners can ask each other questions to make sure of accurate chronology and to draw out meaningful information.

PHLit Online!

Enriched Online Student Edition
Show or assign the video online at
www.PHLitOnline.com.

Revising

1. Introduce the revising strategies, using the instruction on the student page.
2. Have students apply the strategies as they revise their reflective essays.

Teaching the Strategies

1. Arrange deadlines for the assignment to allow students at least twenty-four hours before they reread their drafts with an eye toward revision. Time away from a piece of writing helps the writer see his or her work with fresh eyes and new energy.
2. Remind students that the more concrete and specific their writing is, the more lifelike and appealing it will seem to their readers. Urge students to find places to add details and specific observations.
3. Before students engage in peer review, remind them of the importance of fairness and tact in discussing another writer's work. The emphasis in comments must not be on what is "wrong" with the writing, but on how to make the draft clearer and more interesting to the reader.
4. Suggest that students practice varying sentence beginnings; remind them of alternative ways of starting a sentence. You may wish to look at the Student Model (p. 446) as a class to glean ideas for sentence starters.

Six Traits Focus

✔	Ideas	✔	Word Choice
✔	Organization		Sentence Fluency
	Voice		Conventions

Revising

Revising Your Overall Structure

Take a balanced approach. Your reflective essay will have more meaning for readers if you achieve a subtle balance between your personal experiences and broader themes or ideas about life. Use the following strategy to evaluate your draft:

★ Place a blue star next to sentences that describe your personal experiences.

✔ Place a red check next to sentences that refer to outside events or to reflections about the meaning of your experiences.

Check that your draft balances information about your personal experiences with reflections on larger, related themes. If you have too few red checks, revise to include statements that broaden your focus.

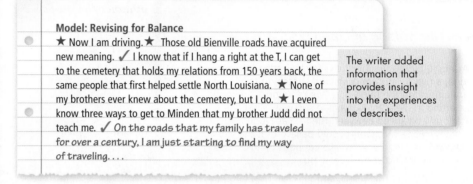

Model: Revising for Balance

★ Now I am driving. ★ Those old Bienville roads have acquired new meaning. ✔ I know that if I hang a right at the T, I can get to the cemetery that holds my relations from 150 years back, the same people that first helped settle North Louisiana. ★ None of my brothers ever knew about the cemetery, but I do. ★ I even know three ways to get to Minden that my brother Judd did not teach me. ✔ On the roads that my family has traveled for over a century, I am just starting to find my way of traveling. . . .

The writer added information that provides insight into the experiences he describes.

Revising Your Sentences

Vary your sentences. Even though your essay is about you, avoid beginning every sentence with *I*. Go through your draft and highlight the first word in every sentence. Make sure you are using a variety of sentence openers. If all or a majority of your sentences begin in the same way, combine or rewrite them to create more interest and variety.

Examples:

Monotonous: I remember the door. I remember it was locked. I wanted to get inside. I was nervous about what I might find. I was very curious.

Varied: The door was locked, and I wanted to get in there. While I was nervous about what I might find, I was also curious.

Peer Review: Exchange drafts with a partner. After you have read each other's essays, meet to discuss them. Focus on the clarity of the events and insights you present throughout your essay. Ask for specific suggestions, such as modifying sentences, omitting or adding transitions, or reordering paragraphs, to improve the logical flow of your ideas.

444 A Growing Nation (1800–1870)

Common Core State Standards

Writing

2.d. Use precise language to manage the complexity of the topic.

2.e Establish and maintain a formal style and objective tone while attending to the norms and conventions of the discipline in which they are writing.

5. Develop and strengthen writing as needed by revising, rewriting, or trying a new approach.

Language

3.a. Vary syntax for effect.

Strategies for
Using Technology in Writing

At the revision stage, students using word processors can use an online thesaurus to expand their word-choice options. In particular, if they discover repetition of words or phrases within the space of a sentence or two, they can find a replacement. In addition, students can use the word-count feature of many word-processing programs to determine whether their essays meet length requirements. If they are more than one hundred words over or under the requirement, they can review their essays, looking for ways to shorten or expand certain sections. Students can also use the organizing tools and revision checkers in the **Writing and Grammar Interactive Textbook** online at **www.PHLitOnLine.com.**

| **Voice** | Organization | Word Choice | Ideas | Conventions | Sentence Fluency |

Developing Your Style

Voice: Controlling Your Tone and Diction

Voice is a writer's distinctive "sound" on the page. Voice is partly based on **tone,** the attitude you express toward your subject; and **diction,** your choice and arrangement of words. Your tone may be described as serious, lighthearted, humorous, insincere, soulful, and so on. Your diction may be casual, formal, technical, simple, or complex.

Serious Tone/Formal Diction
To my horror, I realized that I had absentmindedly mailed the urgent letter without a stamp.

Lighthearted Tone/Casual Diction
Oops, I must have goofed and forgotten to put a stamp on that!

Find It in Your Reading

Read the selection from *Walden* by Henry David Thoreau.

1. Describe Thoreau's tone. Note key passages that convey that tone.

2. For each passage you choose, list two words that help express Thoreau's attitude toward his subject or audience.

3. **Discuss:** Choose three of your key words, and replace them with words that have a different tone. With a partner, discuss how these changes in diction affect the overall tone of the writing and create a different sense of voice.

Apply It to Your Writing

For each paragraph in your draft reflective essay, follow these steps:

1. Read your essay aloud, paying attention to specific words that convey your attitude toward your reader or subject. Be sure that the overall tone of your essay is consistent throughout the essay. In addition, make sure your tone is appropriate to both personal reflection and the larger themes you discuss.

2. If your tone seems inappropriate, change it. Informal and friendly tones usually work best with personal observations, whereas formal or distant tones keep your far-reaching comments from sounding flippant or insincere.

3. Identify any words that do not support the tone you would like to have. Replace these words with ones that better express your attitudes. The voice of your essay will shift as a result.

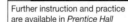

PH WRITING COACH

Further instruction and practice are available in *Prentice Hall Writing Coach.*

Differentiated Instruction for Universal Access

EL Strategy for English Learners
Encourage students to use vocabulary words with which they are comfortable rather than trying to include new and unfamiliar words. However, use this assignment as an opportunity for English learners to add a few words to their vocabularies. Help them by having them tell you their stories. Identify points in the narrative that could be made clearer with a synonym. Ask students to consult a thesaurus or a dictionary to find useful synonyms. Assist them with nuances in meaning and usage.

Developing Your Style

1. Introduce the style points to students, using the instruction on the student page.

2. Have students complete the Find It in Your Reading and Apply It to Your Writing activities.

Teaching the Strategies

1. Organize students into pairs and have partners read their essays to each other. Have students define the tone of their partners' essays.

2. Have partners read their essays aloud again, with each partner listening for passages that do not fit the overall tone.

3. Discuss with students how sentence structure and variety contribute to the pace, tone, and mood of a piece of writing. Have students read one another's essays aloud to listen for monotonous or awkward sentence structure.

Think Aloud: Model Word Choice

Model the strategy of choosing better words, using the following "think aloud." Say to students:

When I "walk down memory lane" as I write a reflective essay, I often include too many experience details. It is natural to do this: These things really happened, and they must be important because, after all, I remember them. Tagging all the personal-experience sentences in my draft with a blue star is a useful exercise for me. Once I have identified these sentences, I can filter out the unnecessary ones by asking, "Is this detail merely pleasant for me to recall, or is it interesting to the reader and vital to my meaning?"

Six Traits Focus

Ideas		✔	Word Choice
Organization			Sentence Fluency
✔	Voice		Conventions

Student Model

Review the Student Model with the class, using the annotations to analyze the writer's incorporation of the elements of a reflective essay.

Teaching the Strategies

1. Explain that the Student Model is a sample and that many reflective essays may be longer.

2. Note that the author does not focus on any one particular event in this reflective essay. **Ask** students to summarize the experiences the author relates in this essay.

   Possible response: The essay describes the back roads that Graham Walker rode with his brothers and explains how learning the roads was part of a passage to adulthood, beginning with his emulation of his brothers.

3. **Ask** students to explain the insight that Walker expresses by describing the back roads.

   Possible response: Walker's insight has to do with a stronger sense of his own identity and his roots: a journey to who he is, where he has come from, and, eventually, where he is headed.

Connecting to Real-life Writing

Tell students that professional writers often include reflective passages in personal essays, memoirs, and travel writing. Reflective essays often are published in magazines or on the opinion pages of newspapers. Journals and diaries are also enlivened and enriched by short reflective essays.

Student Model: Graham Walker, Ruston, Louisiana

Back Roads to Tomorrow

They are small country roads—the ones that change color and ride when you cross a simple parish line. They have four-ton limits assigned to small bridges that hop over waters like Bear Creek and Black Lake Bayou. Their ragged shoulders are missing chunks of pavement and rise three inches above the packed red clay that supports the asphalt. Bright ribbons of tape hang from the lower limbs of pine trees to escort log trucks to jobs. Now and again a color will halt at a worn path entering a clean-bottomed plot of trees, but the others remain loyal to the country road.

These are the roads I grew up on.

It was usually just my oldest brother, Judd, and me. In a blue and gray Ford truck, we would branch out from our home in Taylor, Louisiana, with the windows down. Whether we went and looked at natural gas wells or whether we shot big turtles sunning themselves on logs in a bayou, it never took too much to keep us rolling along on those old Bienville back roads.

But it was not pure riding experience that I enjoyed so much. It was the infinite knowledge of the roads that I believed I gained from those trips. I was in Back Roads 101: Knowing the Road. I made sure that I asked my brother whether we would take a right here or keep straight at the intersections. I felt that I had to know three different ways to get to Minden, ten miles away, or which way the T below our house would take me in case I wanted to slip off for a spin in my pre–double digit years.

Looking back, I realize it was not my concern for my future driving years that led me to study those roads so intently and to map them in my memory. It was one of the lengths I went to so I could be like my three older brothers. All three of them knew the lay of the pavement throughout the Bienville Parish. They could tell me how to get wherever I wished by a backroad route—even to Shreveport, I am sure. And more than I wanted to get to Shreveport, I wanted to be like them.

So I soon knew most of the roads they knew. I could tell anyone three different ways to get to Minden, or which way the T would take me. But I was mapping more than Bienville Parish.

Now I am driving. Those old Bienville roads have acquired new meaning. I know that if I hang a right at the T, I can get to the cemetery that holds my relations from 150 years back, the same people who first helped settle North Louisiana. None of my brothers ever knew about the cemetery, but I do. I even know three ways to get to Minden that my brother Judd did not teach me. On the roads that my family has traveled for over a century, I am just starting to find my way of traveling. That journey, I now understand, is what all my rides with my brothers were really about.

This descriptive language creates a strong sense of place and establishes a personal tone.

Graham uses sensory details to convey a vivid picture of his experience.

Graham begins to draw connections between the specific experience and a deeper meaning.

Graham extends his personal experience into the abstract realm of family, identity, and history.

Strategies for Test Taking

Explain to students that they may be called to write a reflective essay on a timed writing test. Remind students to budget their time when they take a timed test. They should not spend too much time on any one stage of the writing process. They should choose a topic quickly and elaborate on a first instinct. Students should allow about two-thirds of the allotted time for prewriting and drafting and the balance of the time for rereading, revising, and proofreading their essays.

Editing and Proofreading

Check your essay to eliminate errors in grammar, spelling, or punctuation.

Focus on fragments. Look for sentence fragments and correct them.

    Fragment: *Because I wanted to avoid traffic.*
    Complete: *We took the back road because I wanted to avoid traffic.*

    Fragment: *The orchestra uses many types of strings. Cellos, violins, and violas.*
    Complete: *The orchestra uses many types of strings, including cellos, violins, and violas.*

Focus on spelling. In general, use *–tion* to spell the sound of *shun,* as in *exploration* and *portion.* Use *–sion* to spell the sound of *zhun,* as in *vision* and *incision.* Check your spelling of any words that end with these suffixes.

Spiral Review: Conventions Earlier in this unit, you learned about adjective and adverb clauses (p. 287) and comparative and superlative adjectives and adverbs (p. 321). Check your reflective essay to be sure you have used those conventions correctly.

Publishing, Presenting, and Reflecting

Consider one of the following ways to share your writing:

Deliver a reflective presentation. Use your reflective essay as the basis for an oral presentation. Select photographs, drawings, or other images to share with your audience, as well as music or sound effects.

Publish a literary magazine. Gather a variety of reflective essays to create a classroom magazine. Assign committees the tasks of designing the format, creating illustrations, proofreading, and distributing copies to other classes.

Reflect on your writing. Jot down your thoughts about the experience of writing a reflective essay. Begin by answering these questions: What new insights into your own life did you have? What did you learn about the effect of diction on your tone?

Rubric for Self-Assessment

Evaluate your reflective essay using the following criteria and rating scale.

Criteria	Rating Scale
	not very *very*
Focus: How well do you establish yourself as the main character?	1 2 3 4 5
Organization: How well have you organized your feelings, thoughts, and views?	1 2 3 4 5
Support/Elaboration: How effectively do you use specific incidents to connect to broader themes?	1 2 3 4 5
Style: How well do you describe the insights you gained?	1 2 3 4 5
Conventions: How correct is your use of grammar, especially your use of complete sentences?	1 2 3 4 5

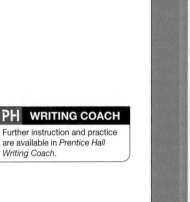

Common Core State Standards

Writing
5. Develop and strengthen writing as needed by editing, focusing on addressing what is most significant for a specific purpose and audience.

Language
1. Demonstrate command of the conventions of standard English grammar and usage when writing.
2.b. Spell correctly.

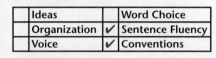

PH WRITING COACH

Further instruction and practice are available in *Prentice Hall Writing Coach.*

Editing and Proofreading

1. Introduce the editing and proofreading focuses, using the instruction on the student page.
2. Have students read their reflective essays carefully, marking them for line edits, including changes in word choice and corrections in grammar, spelling, and punctuation. Make sure they check for errors of the type noted in the lesson focus and the Spiral Review.

Teaching the Strategies

1. Ask students to exchange papers so a more objective reader can proofread them.
2. Have students read essays aloud to one another to listen for coherence.

Six Traits Focus

Ideas		Word Choice	
Organization		Sentence Fluency	✔
Voice		Conventions	✔

ASSESS

Publishing, Presenting, and Reflecting

1. Budget time for students to deliver their reflective essays as oral presentations to the class.
2. Set aside a reading area so that students may browse the classroom magazine of reflective essays.
3. Ask students which writing strategy was most useful in completing this assignment. How will they incorporate this technique when writing on another topic?

Strategies for Test Taking

A writing prompt on a standardized test may ask the student to write a reflective essay, communicating an insight gained from a past experience. Help students develop a method for writing a strong reflective essay in a relatively short time period by reviewing the process they followed in writing this essay. Remind them of the important steps in this process and suggest that they remember particularly effective methods they used to choose a subject and to organize their reflective essays. Suggest that, when possible, they choose a topic they have written about once before, adapting their previous treatment to the requirements of the test prompt.

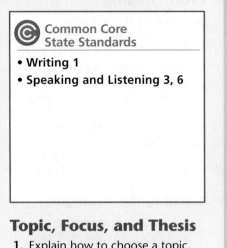

Common Core State Standards

- Writing 1
- Speaking and Listening 3, 6

Topic, Focus, and Thesis

1. Explain how to choose a topic, narrow the focus, and determine a thesis, using the instruction on the student page.

2. As students consider what makes an effective thesis, **ask** them to give both strong and weak examples. Emphasize that strong examples should reflect ideas about which people might reasonably disagree; weak examples might be obvious or unlikely to provoke disagreement.
Possible response: Strong thesis: Standardized testing is the fairest way to assess student progress. Weak thesis: Tests should be administered in a quiet, comfortable location.

Appeals and Rhetorical Devices

1. Present the types of persuasive appeals, language techniques, and persuasive techniques. To illustrate the types of persuasive appeals, provide the following examples. Logical argument: "Our town's population has increased by 80 percent, therefore we need a new playing field to accommodate new players." Ethical argument: "It is only fair that we provide fields for all players, not just the most experienced." Emotional argument: "Imagine how disappointed little kids will be when they find out there's no field for them."

(continued on p. 449)

Write and Deliver a Persuasive Speech

Persuasive speech is language designed to influence the way other people think or act. You use persuasive speech often. Perhaps you want to convince a friend to see a certain movie, or a prospective employer to hire you. Both situations require you to speak persuasively. In daily life, persuasive speech is usually spontaneous. However, in formal speaking situations, you must develop persuasion with forethought and organization.

Topic, Focus, and Thesis

To write and deliver a formal persuasive speech, choose a topic that means something to you. Ask yourself, "What do people argue about when they discuss this topic?" The answer will help you narrow your focus. Then, determine your **thesis**—your specific position or claim. This should be a statement with which reasonable people could agree or disagree. *Example thesis:* "The Hillsboro Library is inadequate because it does not have enough computer workstations."

Appeals and Rhetorical Devices

Consider your audience. After defining your topic and thesis, think about your audience and what they may know or feel about your topic. This will help you choose effective *persuasive appeals* to reach them.

- To prove a position, use a **logical argument** that relies on *facts* and sound *reasoning*. Draw facts from credible sources, such as newspapers, journals, encyclopedias, and government Web sites.

- To gain your audience's trust, use an **ethical argument** that establishes your credibility as a speaker. Cite trusted sources and demonstrate knowledge of your topic.

- To move your audience, use an **emotional argument** that evokes sympathy or humor. Relate affecting stories and use vivid language that sets a specific *tone*, or attitude, toward the subject.

Structure your speech. Like an essay, a strong speech has a logical structure. In your **introduction,** engage your audience and show why your topic matters. In the **body** of your speech, develop your ideas point by point. In your **conclusion,** restate your thesis and issue a call to action, or urgent request that your audience do something or think in a new way.

Select language techniques. Make deliberate choices about the *diction*, or word choice, and *syntax*, or grammar and sentence structure, you use. To ensure your ideas are clear, use *formal English*, the version of English taught in school. Use *informal expressions*, such as slang, sparingly to connect to your audience. If your topic is scientific or technical, use *technical language*, such as the specific names of devices or processes.

Common Core State Standards

Writing
1. Write arguments to support claims in an analysis of substantive topics or texts, using valid reasoning and relevant and sufficient evidence.

Speaking and Listening
3. Evaluate a speaker's point of view, reasoning, and use of evidence and rhetoric, assessing the stance, premises, links among ideas, word choice, points of emphasis, and tone used.

6. Adapt speech to a variety of contexts and tasks, demonstrating a command of formal English when indicated or appropriate.

There is also a rich variety of rhetorical devices and expressive language that can help you convince your audience in a clear and forceful way:

- **Rhetorical Questions:** questions asked for effect, not to get information. "Shouldn't the library be a valuable resource for students?"
- **Parallel Structure:** repeated grammatical patterns that create balance and emphasis. "The books are ancient, the computers are slow, and the lighting is terrible."
- **Concrete Images:** vividly described situations, places, or people
- **Figurative Language:** symbolic or non-literal language, such as similes and metaphors, used to make ideas memorable

Select appropriate persuasive techniques. To support your thesis and keep your audience interested, use a variety of supporting arguments:

- **Characterization:** using evaluative language, such as "essential" or "unfair" to classify a position or a situation
- **Irony:** pointing out incongruities. "The library has more computers for its staff than for the public."
- **Dialogue:** relating conversations or quoting directly from sources

Activities: Deliver and Evaluate Persuasive Speech

© **Comprehension and Collaboration** For both activities, use an evaluation form like the one shown below.

A. Write and deliver a persuasive speech to the class. Have your audience assess your argument.

B. Using your class's responses, develop additional arguments and then present an *impromptu speech* to further defend your thesis.

Peer Evaluation Form for Persuasive Speech

Title of Speech _____

Thesis _____

    Exhibits a Logical Structure: Yes ☐ No ☐

    Explain _____

Diction and Syntax:

    Standard English ☐ Rhetorical Questions ☐ Figurative Language ☐

    Informal Language ☐ Parallel Structure ☐

    Technical Language ☐ Concrete Images ☐

    Examples _____

What would the speaker's opponents say in response to this argument?

_____

What did the speaker do well? What could be improved? _____

_____

---

2. To illustrate rhetorical questions, parallel structure, concrete images, and figurative language, ask students to review the selection from Ralph Waldo Emerson's essay "Self-Reliance" on page 369 and find examples of each technique.

3. Help students understand the persuasive techniques of characterization, irony, and dialogue by providing the following examples. To persuade an audience to support a new highway, a speaker might characterize the plan as necessary, essential, or overdue. The speaker could also use irony by pointing out that pedestrians are likely to benefit the most because the highway will route traffic away from city streets. A speaker might cite overheard dialogue, such as "Traffic is worse than ever and no one ever does anything about it."

Activities: Deliver and Evaluate Persuasive Speech

1. Remind students to practice their speech several times in front of a mirror, making decisions about which words to emphasize, how to vary pacing, and how to use gestures to highlight ideas. Review strong communication strategies, including speaking slowly and clearly, maintaining eye contact, and adjusting delivery for audience response.

2. Review the Peer Evaluation Forms prior to asking students to deliver their speeches. Ask student volunteers to define each of the terms on the form and give an example they might hear in a speech.

3. Allow time for students to present their speeches to the class and then for students to complete the evaluation forms.

4. Suggest that students who accept the Challenge activity respond with a one-minute extemporaneous speech. Setting a time limit can help students stay on-topic and focus their defense.

Differentiated Instruction for Universal Access

Support for Special-Needs Students

Students who have difficulty using the Peer Evaluation Form to evaluate a persuasive speech may provide more useful feedback if they concentrate on a single listening objective. Suggest that students choose one element listed on the Evaluation Form, such as Analogies or Parallel Structure, and listen for examples. During class responses, ask students to identify effective examples of their focus element.

EL Support for English Learners

Encourage students to practice their speeches for a partner, using notecards or an outline to guide their delivery. If audio recorders are available, suggest that students make and review their own recordings, focusing on both persuasive techniques and pronunciation. Students can also sharpen listening skills by recording and replaying speeches given by other students.

EXTEND

Common Core State Standards

- Language 1.a, 4.a, c; 6

Etymology: Political Science/History Terms

1. Teach the skills, using the instruction, timeline, and chart on the student page.

2. If possible, demonstrate the use of an electronic dictionary on computers in a lab or the classroom.

Think Aloud: Model the Skills

Say to students:

When I read works that deal with history or politics, I notice some words that are unfamiliar or seem to have specific meanings. A dictionary will tell me the word's meaning, but it will also tell me the word's etymology—how it developed as an English word. Taking the time to think about etymologies helps me remember what a word means. When I look up *demographics,* I learn that it comes from the Greek roots meaning "people" and "writing," which helps me recall that demographics are the characteristics of a population.

Practice

Answers:

1. *Autocracy* comes from Greek roots meaning "self-rule" and refers to a government in which one person holds unlimited power. *Democracy* comes from Greek roots meaning "rule of the people" and refers to a government in which all people have a right to participate equally, often by electing representatives.

2. *Bellicose* means "warlike" or "inclined to fight or go to war." A *constitution* is a formal written statement outlining the laws and principles by which a country is governed.

450

Vocabulary Workshop

Etymology: Political Science/History Terms

Many events have shaped the development of the English language. The timeline shown here identifies events that brought critical changes:

5th century
Angles and Saxons invade the British Isles. Anglo-Saxon becomes the dominant culture and language.

6th century
Christianity spreads into England, adding Latin and Greek words to Anglo-Saxon.

11th century
Normans invade from France, bringing thousands of French and Latin words.

The Romans and Greeks introduced numerous political ideas to the world, and English reflects those influences. The Normans became the ruling class of England, and many of their word contributions relate to politics, history, and law. Knowing key affixes and roots will help you define unfamiliar terms you encounter as you study political science and history.

	Word Part	Meaning	Example Words
Prefixes	con- (Latin)	with; together	constitution, congress
	auto- (Greek)	self	autocracy, autonomy
	dom- (Latin)	rule	dominion, dominant
Roots	-belli- (Latin)	war	bellicose, belligerent
	-dem- (Greek)	people	demographics, democracy
	-polis- (Greek)	city	politician, politics
Suffixes	-cracy (Greek)	government; rule	meritocracy, aristocracy
	-hood (Anglo-Saxon)	sharing a condition	statehood, knighthood
	-ism (Greek)	quality or practice of	nationalism, colonialism

Practice

1. Refer to the chart above to define **(a)** autocracy; **(b)** democracy.

2. Write definitions for each italicized word: **(a)** *Bellicose* acts caused greater conflict. **(b)** Members of the convention wrote a *constitution*.

3. Choose a word from the chart above and create a timeline *tracing its etymology,* or development as an English word. Include its language of origin, its movement from one language to another, changes in its meaning, and a discussion of any points at which its usage may have been contested. Consult reference materials, both print and digital, to aid your work.

450 A Growing Nation (1800–1870)

Common Core State Standards

Language

1.a. Apply the understanding that usage is a matter of convention, can change over time, and is sometimes contested.

4.a. Use context as a clue to the meaning of a word or phrase.

4.c. Consult general and specialized reference materials, both print and digital, to find the pronunciation of a word or determine or clarify its precise meaning, its part of speech, its etymology, or its standard usage.

6. Acquire and use accurately general academic and domain-specific words and phrases.

3. **Sample response:** *Meritocracy* comes from the Latin root *-meritum-,* meaning "reward" or "merit," and the suffix *-cracy,* meaning "government." Although its origins are Latin, the word was coined by Michael Young in 1958. It refers to a social system that gives opportunities based on ability rather than on other criteria, such as wealth, age, or popularity.

Vocabulary Acquisition and Use: Context Clues

Sentence Completion questions appear in most standardized tests. One skill that Sentence Completions test is your ability to figure out what a word means by examining its context, or the surrounding words or sentences. In these types of questions, you are given sentences with one or more missing words. Your task is to choose the correct word or words to complete each sentence logically. Try using the following strategy: (1) Read the entire sentence and anticipate a word that would logically complete it. (2) Scan the answer choices for that word. (3) If the word you anticipated is not there, look for a synonym.

Practice

This exercise is modeled after the Sentence Completions exercises that appear in the Critical Reading section of the SAT.

Directions: Each of the following sentences is missing one or two words. Choose the word or set of words that best completes each sentence.

> **Test-Taking Tip**
> Before you mark an answer, carefully read the complete sentence to confirm that it makes sense.

1. Both his vengefulness and his __?__ prevent Captain Ahab from surrendering to the white whale.
   A. parsimony
   B. alacrity
   C. obstinacy
   D. magnanimity
   E. flexibility

2. Those who celebrate the beauty of nature sometimes have an __?__ to industrialization.
   A. eloquence
   B. aversion
   C. expedience
   D. attraction
   E. affinity

3. In the staid congregations of New England, __?__ was considered not only __?__, but sinful.
   A. ostentation . . . indecorous
   B. pathos . . . prevalent
   C. discord . . . impulsive
   D. avarice . . . superfluous
   E. obstinacy . . . vengeful

4. Mr. Hooper's reasons for wearing the mysterious veil are __?__ to his parishioners.
   A. impertinent
   B. ample
   C. inscrutable
   D. stirring
   E. sublime

5. In *Walden*, Thoreau voices his desire to lead a simple life and rid himself of __?__ concerns.
   A. ominous
   B. venerable
   C. imperceptible
   D. superfluous
   E. essential

6. Though the human mind is limited and __?__, it is able to contemplate __?__.
   A. tremulous . . . maledictions
   B. finite . . . infinity
   C. infinite . . . chaos
   D. prescient . . . posterity
   E. radiant . . . iniquity

Practice

1. Introduce the skill, using the instruction on the student page. Be sure students understand how context clues can reveal the meaning of an unknown word.

2. You may wish to go over the first item with students, helping them anticipate missing words. Read the first item to the class. Before reading the choices, have students suggest words that can complete the sentence sensibly. Students might suggest *stubbornness* or *persistence*. Then, read the answer choices that follow. Because these words do not appear in the answer choices, have students look for a word that is a synonym for the words they provided. Students should recognize that *stubbornness* and *obstinacy* are synonyms. Choice C is the correct answer.

3. Assign the remaining items in the Practice Test. Point out that some questions require pairs of words, rather than a single word, for completion. Allow students 6 minutes to complete the questions.

Answers:
1. C
2. B
3. A
4. C
5. D
6. B

Differentiated
Instruction   for Universal Access

Support for Special-Needs Students
Point out that vocabulary tests do not require students to remember details from selections or works they have read. Each item includes context clues that help students identify the necessary relationship between words. For example, students may think that they need to recall details about *Walden* to answer item 5. Point out that the sentence itself contains all of the information they need. The missing word relates to the idea of leading "a simple life" and can modify the noun *concerns*.

Test-Taking Practice

In this Assessment Workshop (pp. 452–455), students apply the skills in Unit 2. The practice is divided into three sections.

1. Before assigning each section, review the relevant unit skills with students. Discuss the characteristics of each type of test and specific strategies for test questions, using the instruction that precedes each practice.

2. Set a time limit for the multiple-choice items in each practice, allowing a little over 1 minute per question. Use the designated time allowance set for the Timed Writing section.

3. Administer each section. Have students write the starting time at the top of their papers. When half of the time for the multiple-choice items has run out, ask students to write the time next to the answer on which they are working. Have them make similar notes when three-quarters of the time has expired and again when time is up. Follow a similar procedure for the Timed Writing assignment.

4. Review with students the pacing reflected in their notes.

Test-Taking Practice

Reading Test: Paired Passages

Paired reading passages are one type of critical reading passage used on standardized tests. Paired passages may be fiction or nonfiction, prose or poetry, and may vary in length. As you read, keep in mind that the passages will be **compared and contrasted.** Questions following paired passages will refer to each passage individually and to both passages as a unit. Note similarities and differences between the passages, especially the author's attitudes, word choices, and styles.

© Common Core
State Standards

RI.11-12.1, RI.11-12.2, RI.11-12.3, RI.11-12.4; L.11-12.4, L.11-12.5.a, L.11-12.6

[For the full wording of the standards, see the standards chart in the front of your textbook.]

Practice

The following exercise is modeled after the SAT Paired Passages Critical Reading section. This section usually includes 48 questions.

Directions: Read both passages. Then, answer the questions. Passage 1 is from *Walden* by Henry David Thoreau. Passage 2 is by Gretel Ehrlich.

PASSAGE 1

The life in us is like the water in the river. It may rise this year higher than man has ever known it, and flood the parched uplands. . . . It was not always dry land where we dwell. I see far inland the banks which the stream anciently washed, before science began to record its
5　freshets. Everyone has heard the story which has gone the rounds of New England, of a strong and beautiful bug which came out of the dry leaf of an old table of apple-tree wood, which had stood in the farmer's kitchen for sixty years. . . . From an egg deposited in the living tree many years earlier still, as appeared by counting the annual layers beyond it;
10　which was heard gnawing out for several weeks, hatched perchance by the heat of an urn. . . . Who knows what beautiful and winged life, whose egg has been buried for ages under many concentric layers of woodenness in the dead dry life of society . . . may unexpectedly come forth . . . to enjoy its perfect summer life at last.

PASSAGE 2

These days we go about our lives with so much speed and so much extraneous information that it's difficult to contemplate just one thing, one sight, one ripple in the pond. Thoreau would have us simplify, slow down, become quiet, and burrow into the heart of things without
5　minds. Not to "dumb down," but the opposite: to stop, to listen, and see; to turn off the monologue in our minds; to erase our idea about how things are; to live in others' shoes. Thoreau would have us think like a river, a pond, a tree, another animal or human; to adopt their point of view instead of our own. Then, the fresh, dawnlike nature of
10　things . . . will keep radiating, piercing the difficulties in our lives with new songs.

Strategy

Break the task into parts.

- **Read Passage 1,** and answer the questions that refer only to the first passage.

- **Read Passage 2,** and answer the questions that refer only to the second passage.

- Finally, answer the compare-and-contrast questions.

Strategies for
Test Taking

Tell students to be alert for incorrect answers that use exact words from the selection. Many incorrect answers include selection words in order to appear correct at first glance. These selection words may identify unimportant details or ideas that are not related to the question.

1. What is the best statement of the main idea of Passage 1?
   - **A.** It is unusual that a large bug should hatch from old wood.
   - **B.** One can determine the age of a tree by counting its rings.
   - **C.** Life ebbs and flows, sometimes surprisingly.
   - **D.** Science cannot measure life's force.
   - **E.** Summer is the best season.

2. In Passage 1, the hatched bug is used as a symbol for
   - **A.** life's irrepressibility.
   - **B.** unexpected beauty.
   - **C.** rebelliousness.
   - **D.** the act of writing.
   - **E.** a nightmare.

3. The main idea of Passage 2 is that
   - **A.** people should use less technology.
   - **B.** Americans should be less materialistic.
   - **C.** people are like bodies of water.
   - **D.** the truth can be found only in our minds.
   - **E.** serenity will bring us new understanding.

4. It would be most accurate to say that
   - **A.** Passage 2 is a commentary on Passage 1.
   - **B.** Passage 1 is a commentary on Passage 2.
   - **C.** Passage 1 is an excerpt of Passage 2.
   - **D.** Passage 2 is an unfavorable review of Passage 1.
   - **E.** Passage 1 was written after Passage 2.

5. In Passage 1, Thoreau uses a metaphor to compare
   - **A.** life to water in the river.
   - **B.** New England to a strong, beautiful bug.
   - **C.** the heat of an urn to the heat of the sun.
   - **D.** society to concentric layers of woodenness.
   - **E.** an egg to summer.

6. It can be inferred that the author of Passage 2
   - **A.** struggles to understand aspects of Thoreau's thinking.
   - **B.** embraces some of Thoreau's views, but rejects others.
   - **C.** thinks that Thoreau's philosophy is too simplistic.
   - **D.** has read all of Thoreau's writings.
   - **E.** respects Thoreau's philosophy.

7. In Passage 1, Thoreau's reference to the "parched uplands" (line 2) is
   - **A.** a description of the landscape he is viewing as he writes.
   - **B.** an image that evokes a sense of dryness and thirst.
   - **C.** a metaphor for the story that follows.
   - **D.** an example of synecdoche.
   - **E.** a symbol of summer.

8. Why does Thoreau mention the "dry leaf" (line 7) of the kitchen table?
   - **A.** to remind readers that the table was once a living tree
   - **B.** to create suspense
   - **C.** to create an atmosphere of dry lifelessness
   - **D.** to urge people not to abuse nature
   - **E.** as a metaphor for the page of a book

9. It can be inferred from the phrase "piercing the difficulties in our lives with new songs" that the author of Passage 2
   - **A.** uses straightforward language.
   - **B.** is not in tune with Thoreau's philosophy.
   - **C.** appreciates Thoreau, but does not echo his voice.
   - **D.** is attuned with Thoreau in both thought and writing style.
   - **E.** believes that problem solving is painful.

GO ON

Test-Taking Practice **453**

Answers

Reading Test
Paired Passages

1. Introduce the skill, using the instruction on page 452. Be sure students understand the strategy set off in the boxed section.

2. Assign the practice exercise. Have students read the passages and answer the questions on their own. Allow 15 minutes for this process, and announce to students when they have 5 minutes and 1 minute remaining.

Answers
1. C
2. A
3. E
4. A
5. D
6. E
7. B
8. C
9. D

Reteaching
Use the Reteach charts to determine which skills require reteaching, based on the items students answer incorrectly. Reteach these skills prior to assigning **Benchmark Test 3** (*Unit 2 Resources,* pp. 149–154).

Reteach

Question	Pages to Reteach
1	334
2	334
3	334
4	242
5	364
6	270
7	364
8	334, 376
9	270

Differentiated
Instruction   for Universal Access

**Support for
Less Proficient Readers**
Emphasize that questions are designed to test student's knowledge of specific literary elements they have studied. Have students scan questions to find words that name specific literary elements. For example, students should be able to identify these terms: "main idea" (items 1 and 3), "symbol" (item 2), and "metaphor" (item 5).

**EL Support for
English Learners**
Review the nine questions, making sure that students understand "inferred" (items 6 and 9), and "reference" (item 7). Allow students to ask clarifying questions about any of the question choices, being careful not to reveal correct answers.

Grammar and Writing
Editing in Context

1. Introduce the skill, using the instruction on the student page. Be sure students understand the strategy set off in the boxed section.

2. Read the direction line. Then go over the first test item with students, modeling the strategy "listen" for errors.

3. Read the sentence aloud. Then read the sentence a second time, asking students to raise their hands when they think they hear an error. Have students explain why they think part of the sentence is incorrect. Students should hear that the phrase "greater of all sea mammals" does not sound correct. It uses a comparative adjective when a superlative is necessary. Choice C is correct.

4. Have students complete questions 2–8 on their own. Allow students 9 minutes to complete the questions.

Strategies for Test Taking

When completing these tests, students may find it useful to provide the word that correctly completes the sentence, although this step is not required by the test. For example, in item 1, "greater" should be replaced by "greatest." Point out that students are allowed to write in the SAT test booklet, so quickly making necessary revisions may help them identify specific errors. Marking the correct words can also help students identify which questions they are most certain of and do not need to review if time permits.

Grammar and Writing: Editing in Context

Editing in Context segments often appear in the writing sections of standardized tests. The passages or sample sentences used are usually drafts of student essays that may or may not contain errors in grammar, style, and usage. For each question, you must first decide if there is an error and then determine which of four possible answers will best correct a given sentence.

Practice

This exercise is modeled after the Identifying Sentence Errors portion of the SAT Writing test.

Directions: Each of the following sentences contains either a single error or no error at all. The error, if there is one, is underlined and lettered. If a sentence contains an error, select the letter of that underlined part. If the sentence is correct, select choice E.

Strategy

"Listen" for errors.
Read the sentence straight through. If you mentally "trip" over one of the underlined portions, it is probably wrong.

1. Humankind <u>has been fascinated</u> with
        A   B
   whales, the <u>greater</u> of all sea mammals,
            C
   <u>for</u> the entire span of recorded history.
    D
   <u>No error</u>
     E
   A.
   B.
   C.
   D.
   E.

2. Byzantine <u>scholar and historian</u>
             A
   Procopius wrote of a whale <u>who</u> made
               B
   its way into the inland <u>Sea of Marmara</u>,
              C
   where it happily consumed the fisheries
   <u>that</u> were maintained there. <u>No error</u>
    D   E
   A.
   B.
   C.
   D.
   E.

3. The whale is <u>an</u> archetype <u>that</u> appears
            A   B
   <u>repeatedly</u> throughout world religions,
      C
   <u>cultures, and literature</u>. <u>No error</u>
        D   E
   A.
   B.
   C.
   D.
   E.

4. The King James Version <u>of</u> the Bible
                 A
   <u>makes</u> several <u>mention</u> of <u>whales</u>.
    B   C   D
   <u>No error</u>
     E
   A.
   B.
   C.
   D.
   E.

Differentiated
Instruction   for Universal Access

Support for Special-Needs Students
Point out that vocabulary tests do not require students to remember details from selections or works they have read. Each item includes context clues that help students identify the necessary relationship between words. For example, students may think that they need to recall details about *Walden* to answer item 5. Point out that the sentence itself contains all of the information they need. The missing word relates to the idea of leading "a simple life" and can modify the noun *concerns*.

5. The <u>more</u> famous <u>one</u> is the story of Jonah,
_A   _B
<u>who is said</u> to have survived three
_C
days and nights in the belly of a <u>great</u> whale.
_D
<u>No error</u>
_E

A.
B.
C.
D.
E.

6. <u>Because</u> <u>whaling</u> was a lucrative <u>and</u>
_A   _B   _C
dangerous industry in nineteenth-century
America, it is no surprise <u>so that</u> a whale
_D
would become the centerpiece of an
American novel. <u>No error</u>
_E

A.
B.
C.
D.
E.

7. Herman Melville's masterwork, *Moby-Dick,*
<u>widely regarded</u> as one of the <u>finer</u> novels
_A   _B
ever written, <u>uses</u> the whale <u>as a character</u>,
_C   _D
a symbol, and a force of nature. <u>No error</u>
_E

A.
B.
C.
D.
E.

8. *Moby-Dick* is a <u>rich</u>, complex, <u>and</u> entirely
_A   _B
American <u>rendition of</u> the <u>archetypal</u> whale.
_C   _D
<u>No error</u>
_E

A.
B.
C.
D.
E.

⏱ Timed Writing: Position Statement [25 minutes]

Ralph Waldo Emerson wrote, "There is a time in every man's education when he arrives at the conviction that envy is ignorance; that imitation is suicide; that he must take himself for better, for worse, as his portion. . . ."

Write a position statement—an essay in which you express and support an opinion—in response to Emerson's statement. First, explain what the statement means. Then, explain your views: Do you believe the type of individualism he describes is an important value that people should try to develop? This assigment is similar to the essay portion of the SAT Writing Section.

> **Academic Vocabulary**
>
> The prompt asks you to *express*, or state, and *support*, or defend, your opinion.

STOP

Benchmark

Reteach skills as indicated by students' performance, following the Reteach charts on pages 452 and 455. Then administer the end-of-unit **Benchmark Test 3** (*Unit 2 Resources,* pp. 149–154). Follow the **Interpretation Guide** for the test (*Unit 2 Resources,* pp. 196–201) to assign reteaching pages as necessary in the *Reading Kit.* Use the built-in tracking software at www.PHLitOnline.com to automatically assign these pages.

Reteach

Question	Pages to Reteach
1	321
2	287
3	287
4	358
5	321
6	287
7	321
8	287

Answers

1. C
2. B
3. E
4. C
5. A
6. D
7. B
8. E

⏱ Timed Writing
Position Statement

1. Go over the two paragraphs of the timed writing assignment on the student page.

2. Tell students that they can quickly formulate a thesis statement for their position by completing one of the following sentence starters: "I agree with Emerson's idea of individualism because . . . ." or "I disagree with Emerson's idea of individualism because . . . ." Emphasize that the language of their opening thesis comes directly from the prompt.

3. Encourage students to budget adequate time for prewriting and revising/editing. Students should spend about 8 minutes in the prewriting stage, 12 minutes drafting, and 5 minutes revising and editing. Reinforce this by announcing elapsed time at the 8-, 12-, and 20-minute marks as students respond to the assignment.

4. Use the **Rubrics for Writing for Assessment Essays,** in *Professional Development Guidebook,* pages 258–259, to evaluate students' work.

The **Benchmark Tests** are available online at www.PHLitOnline.com.

455

Performance Tasks

Assigning Tasks/Reteaching Skills

Use the chart below to choose appropriate Performance Tasks by identifying which tasks assess lessons in the textbook that you have taught. Use the same lessons for reteaching when students' performance indicates a failure to fully master a standard. For additional instruction and practice, assign the *Common Core Companion* pages indicated for each task.

Task	Where Taught/ Pages to Reteach	Common Core Companion Pages
1	226, 242, 291, 323, 357	28–40, 196–207
2	241, 242, 319, 321, 407, 424	41–53, 261–268
3	364, 392–396, 424, 440, 444	54–60, 196–207
4	212–221, 226, 291, 323, 334, 437	75–81, 306–312
5	242, 376, 381, 418–419	123–135, 306–312
6	213, 320, 334, 362–363	15–27, 306–312

Assessment Pacing

In assigning the Writing Tasks on this student page, allow a class period for the completion of a task. As an alternative, assign tasks as homework. In assigning the Speaking and Listening Tasks on the facing page, consider having students do any required preparation as a homework assignment. Then, allow a class period for the presentations themselves.

Evaluating Performance Tasks

Use the rubric at the bottom of this Teacher Edition page to evaluate students' mastery of the standards as demonstrated in their Performance Task responses. Review the rubric with students before they begin work so they know the criteria by which their work will be evaluated.

Performance Tasks

Follow the instructions to complete the tasks below as required by your teacher. As you work on each task, incorporate both general academic vocabulary and literary terms you learned in this unit.

Common Core State Standards

RL.11-12.2, RL.11-12.3, RL.11-12.4, RL.11-12.5, RL.11-12.9; RI.11-12.4; W.11-12.2, W.11-12.9; SL.11-12.6; L.11-12.4, L.11-12.5

[For the full wording of the standards, see the standards chart in the front of your textbook.]

Writing

Task 1: Literature [RL.11-12.3; W.11-12.2]
Analyze the Development of a Story

*Write an **essay** in which you analyze and evaluate the development of a story from this unit.*

- Explain which story you chose and briefly summarize the plot.
- Identify key choices the author made in writing the story. For example, consider where the story is set, how the action is ordered, or how the characters are introduced and developed.
- Analyze the impact of the author's choices, discussing how these decisions affect both the story's meaning and the reader's experience.
- Organize your ideas so that each new idea builds on the one it follows to create a unified whole.
- Provide a concluding section that follows from the explanation presented.

Task 2: Literature [RL.11-12.4; W.11-12.9; L.11-12.4, L.11-12.5]
Analyze Word Choice

*Write an **essay** in which you analyze the word choice in a poem from this unit.*

- Explain which poem you chose and why you chose it.
- Identify specific examples of language in the poem that you find especially effective. Consider the following elements: figures of speech, such as similes or metaphors; specific words that are particularly interesting or beautiful; connotative meanings that are especially rich or striking. Explain your choices and the reasons for them.

- Identify any words in the poem that readers may not understand. Explain the meanings of these words. If any have multiple meanings, explain which ones are most important in this work.
- Consider how the combined word choices in the poem develop the author's tone.
- Cite specific examples from the poems to support your ideas. Quote precisely and accurately.

Task 3: Literature [RL.11-12.5; W.11-12.2]
Analyze Text Structure

*Write an **essay** in which you analyze the structure of a story in this unit.*

- Introduce your essay by discussing the overall structure of your chosen story. For example, does it follow simple chronological order or does it move about in time?
- Identify a specific section or aspect of the story you will analyze in depth. For example, you may discuss how the story begins, how events are ordered, or how it ends (happily, tragically, or inconclusively). Discuss how the specific section or aspect of the story contributes to the overall structure.
- Discuss the aesthetic, or artistic, impact of the author's structural choices. For example, consider how the structure affects the story's overall meaning.
- Choose varied transitional words and phrases to connect your ideas and clearly express the relationships you are analyzing.

456 A Growing Nation (1800–1870)

Performance Task Rubric: Standards Mastery	Rating Scale				
	not very				*very*
Critical Thinking: How clearly and consistently does the student pursue the specific mode of reasoning or discourse required by the standard, as specified in the prompt (e.g., comparing and contrasting, analyzing, explaining)?	1	2	3	4	5
Focus: How well does the student understand and apply the focus concepts of the standard, as specified in the prompt (e.g., development of theme or of complex characters, effects of structure, and so on)?	1	2	3	4	5
Support/Elaboration: How well does the student support points with textual or other evidence? How relevant, sufficient, and varied is the evidence provided?	1	2	3	4	5
Insight: How original, sophisticated, or compelling are the insights the student achieves by applying the standard to the text(s)?	1	2	3	4	5
Expression of Ideas: How well does the student organize and support ideas? How well does the student use language, including word choice and conventions, in the expression of ideas?	1	2	3	4	5

Speaking and Listening

Ⓒ Task 4: Literature [RL.11-12.9; SL.11-12.6]
Demonstrate Knowledge of Foundational Works of American Literature

*Deliver a **speech** in which you analyze how two or more foundational literary works in this unit treat similar themes or topics.*

- Identify the works you will discuss and explain why you chose them. Discuss why these works are examples of foundational American literature.

- Identify the topic each work addresses and describe how each one presents characters, settings, or ideas.

- Explain the theme, or themes, the two works explore. Discuss similarities and differences—and the reasons for them—in these presentations or portrayals.

- Cite specific details to support your ideas.

- Include graphics or notes to support your analysis and clarify your ideas.

- Adapt your speech as you present. For example, you might slow your pace as you explain complex ideas.

Ⓒ Task 5: Informational Text [RI.11-12.4; SL.11-12.6]
Determine Author's Point of View

*Deliver an **oral presentation** in which you analyze the use of language in a nonfiction work from this unit.*

- Introduce the work you chose. Explain the historical context for the work and briefly summarize its central ideas.

- Identify specific word choices that are particularly critical to the writer's overall purpose and expression of ideas. State why you chose these words and phrases, and explain their figurative, technical, or connotative meanings.

- Speak clearly and precisely so that listeners can follow your line of reasoning, including your use of examples to illustrate your ideas.

Ⓒ Task 6: Literature [RL.11-12.2; SL.11-12.6]
Analyze Development of Theme

*Deliver an **oral presentation** in which you analyze the development of two or more themes in a work from this unit.*

- Explain which work you chose. Introduce your analysis by summarizing the work and identifying two distinct themes it conveys.

- Explain how the author develops the themes over the course of the work. For example, consider descriptions of the setting, characters' actions and reactions, and specific events. Also, consider symbols, imagery, or other literary elements that add to the development of two or more themes.

- Explain how the two themes interact and build on one another throughout the work.

- As you speak, use both general academic language and literary terms accurately. Employ formal English appropriate to an academic setting.

How does literature shape or reflect society?

A Growing Nation Some writers in the 1800s celebrated the growing American nation and contributed to the sense of the country's unlimited potential. Others viewed the growing American culture less positively.

Assignment Choose two or more literary works from this unit that portray distinctly American settings and characters. Write a **comparison-and-contrast essay** in which you analyze these portrayals and characterize their perspective on American culture.

Supporting Speaking and Listening

1. Consider having students work with partners or in groups to complete Performance Tasks involving listening and speaking. For tasks that you assign for individual work, you may still wish to have students rehearse with partners, who can provide constructive feedback.

2. As students rehearse, have them keep in mind these tips:

   - Present findings and evidence clearly and concisely.

   - Observe conventions of standard English grammar and usage.

   - Be relaxed and friendly but maintain a formal tone.

   - Make eye contact with the audience, pronounce words clearly, and vary your pace.

   - When working with a group, respond thoughtfully to others' positions, modifying your own in response to new evidence.

Linking Performance Tasks to Independent Reading

If you wish to cover the standards with students' independent reading, adapt Performance Tasks of your choice to the works they have selected. (Independent reading suggestions appear on the next page.)

How does literature shape or reflect society?

1. Remind students of the Essential Question, "How does literature shape or reflect society?"

2. Have students complete their responses to the prompt on the student page. Point out that they have read selections in this unit from the American Renaissance and that they should draw on these selections in their responses. Remind them that they can also draw on their own experiences and what they have learned in other subject areas in formulating their answers.

Differentiated Instruction for Universal Access

Strategy for Less Proficient Readers

Assign a Performance Task, and then have students meet in groups to review the standard assessed in that task. Remind students of the selections or independent readings to which they have previously applied the standard. Have groups summarize what they learned in applying the standard and then present their summaries. Discuss, clarifying any points of confusion. After students have completed their tasks, have groups meet again to evaluate members' work. Encourage members to revise their work based on the feedback they receive.

EL Strategy for English Learners

For each assigned Performance Task, review the instructions with students. Clarify the meaning of any unfamiliar vocabulary, emphasizing routine classroom words such as *essay, present,* and *unit* and academic vocabulary such as *analyze.*

Next, have students note ideas for their responses. Pair students, and have them review each other's notes, asking questions to clarify meaning and suggesting improvements. Encourage students to ask for your assistance in supplying English words or expressions they may require.

457

Independent Reading

Titles featured on the Independent Reading pages at the end of each unit represent a range of reading, including stories, dramas, and poetry, as well as literary nonfiction and other types of informational text. Throughout, labels indicate the works that are CCSS Exemplar Texts. Choosing from among these featured titles will help students read works at increasing levels of text complexity in the grades 11–12 text complexity band.

Using Literature Circles

A literature circle is a temporary group in which students independently discuss a book.

Use the guidance in the *Professional Development Guidebook*, pp. 47–49, as well as the teaching notes on the facing page, for additional suggestions for literature circles.

© Meeting Unit 2 CCS Standards

Students can use books listed on this page to apply and reinforce their mastery of the CCS Standards covered in this unit.

Introducing Featured Titles

Have students choose a book or books for independent reading. Assist them by previewing the titles, noting their subject matter and level of difficulty. **Note:** Before recommending a work to students, preview it, taking into account the values of your community as well as the maturity of your students.

Featured Titles

In this unit, you have read a variety of literature from the American Renaissance. Continue to read works related to this era on your own. Select books that you enjoy, but challenge yourself to explore new topics, new authors, and works offering varied perspectives or approaches. The titles suggested below will help you get started.

LITERATURE

The Scarlet Letter
Nathaniel Hawthorne   EXEMPLAR TEXT ©

Novel Set in Puritan Boston in the early 1600s, *The Scarlet Letter* tells the story of Hester Prynne, a woman who is branded as an outcast for her sins and must struggle to create her own redemption.

["The Minister's Black Veil" by Hawthorne appears on page 272. Build knowledge by reading a longer work by this author.]

Leaves of Grass
Walt Whitman   EXEMPLAR TEXT ©

Poetry A landmark collection of free verse poetry that includes "Song of Myself," *Leaves of Grass* combines heroic and historical themes with deeply personal observations.

[Excerpts from Leaves of Grass begin on page 426 in this book. Build knowledge by reading the full text.]

Complete Stories and Poems of Edgar Allan Poe
Edgar Allan Poe
Doubleday, 1984   EXEMPLAR TEXT ©

Short Story/Poetry This collection of Poe's short stories and poems reveals his talent for developing mysterious, macabre characters and plots. The collection includes his famous story "The Cask of Amontillado."

[Two of Edgar Allan Poe's works begin on pages 292 and 312 in this book. Build knowledge by reading Poe's complete works.]

The Complete Poems of Emily Dickinson
Emily Dickinson
Back Bay Books, 1976   EXEMPLAR TEXT ©

Poetry Emily Dickinson's small, precise poems describe enormous topics, such as mortality and the nature of the imagination. She is one of the great poets of American literature. This volume, which includes "Because I Could Not Stop for Death," presents her collected works.

[Poems by Emily Dickinson appear on pages 408–417 of this book. Build knowledge by reading her complete works.]

INFORMATIONAL TEXTS

Historical Texts

Selected Writings of Ralph Waldo Emerson
Ralph Waldo Emerson
edited by William H. Gilman

Essay One of the great essayists in American letters, Ralph Waldo Emerson addressed subjects ranging from everyday experiences to the meaning of life.

[Excerpts from Emerson's essays begin on page 366 in this book. Build knowledge by reading the full texts.]

Walden and Civil Disobedience
Henry David Thoreau

Essay These essays by poet and philosopher Henry David Thoreau are among the most influential works of nonfiction in American literature.

[Excerpts from Thoreau's essays begin on page 378 of this book. Build knowledge by reading the full text.]

Eyewitness to America: 500 Years of American History in the Words of Those Who Saw It Happen
edited by David Colbert   EXEMPLAR TEXT ©

Primary Source Read first-hand accounts of 500 years of the American experience in this extraordinary book. Subjects range from Horace Porter's description of Robert E. Lee's surrender to Grant to Hunter S. Thompson's discussion of a Super Bowl game.

Contemporary Scholarship

An American Primer
edited by Daniel Boorstin   EXEMPLAR TEXT ©

Primary Source and Commentary This collection presents the most important documents in American history, accompanied by commentary from celebrated historians.

458 A Growing Nation (1800–1870)

© Text Complexity: Aligning Texts With Readers and Tasks

TEXTS	READERS AND TASKS
• *Eyewitness to America* • *An American Primer*	**Below-Level Readers** Allow students to focus on reading for content, and challenge them to interpret multiple perspectives.
• *Leaves of Grass* • *Complete Stories and Poems of Edgar Allan Poe* • *The Complete Poems of Emily Dickinson* • *Selected Writings of Ralph Waldo Emerson*	**Below-Level Readers** Challenge students as they read for content. **On-Level Readers** Allow students to focus on reading for content, and challenge them to interpret multiple perspectives. **Advanced Readers** Allow students to focus on interpreting multiple perspectives.
• *The Scarlet Letter* (Lexile: 1340L) • *Walden and Civil Disobedience* (Lexile: 1340L)	**On-Level Readers** Challenge students as they read for content. **Advanced Readers** Allow students to focus on reading for content, and challenge them to interpret multiple perspectives.

Preparing to Read Complex Texts

Reading for College and Career In both college and the workplace, readers must analyze texts independently, draw connections among works that offer varied perspectives, and develop their own ideas and informed opinions. The questions shown below, and others that you generate on your own, will help you more effectively read and analyze complex college-level texts.

© Common Core State Standards

Reading Literature/Informational Text
10. By the end of grade 11, read and comprehend literature, including stories, dramas, and poems, and literary nonfiction, in the grades 11-CCR text complexity band proficiently, with scaffolding as needed at the high end of the range.

When reading complex texts, ask yourself...

- What idea, experience, or story seems to have compelled the author to write? Has the author presented that idea, experience, or story in a way that I, too, find compelling?

- How might the author's era, social status, belief system, or personal experiences have affected the point of view he or she expresses in the text?

- How do my circumstances affect what I understand and feel about this text?

- What key idea does the author state explicitly? What key idea does he or she suggest or imply? Which details in the text help me to perceive implied ideas?

- Do I find multiple layers of meaning in the text? If so, what relationships do I see among these layers of meaning?

- How do details in the text connect or relate to one another? Do I find any details unconvincing, unrelated, or out of place?

- Do I find the text believable and convincing?

© Key Ideas and Details

- What patterns of organization or sequences do I find in the text? Do these patterns help me understand the ideas better?

- What do I notice about the author's style, including his or her diction, use of imagery and figurative language, and syntax?

- Do I like the author's style? Is the author's style memorable?

- What emotional attitude does the author express toward the topic, the story, or the characters? Does this attitude seem appropriate?

- What emotional attitude does the author express toward me, the reader? Does this attitude seem appropriate?

- What do I notice about the author's voice—his or her personality on the page? Do I like this voice? Does it make me want to read on?

© Craft and Structure

- Is the work fresh and original?

- Do I agree with the author's ideas entirely, or are there elements I find unconvincing?

- Do I disagree with the author's ideas entirely, or are there elements I can accept as true?

- Based on my knowledge of American literature, history, and culture, does this work reflect the American tradition? Why or why not?

© Integration of Ideas

Independent Reading **459**

© Text Complexity: Reader and Task Support Suggestions

INDEPENDENT READING

Increased Support Suggest that students choose a book that they feel comfortable reading and one that is a bit more challenging. Pair a more proficient reader with a less proficient reader and have them work together on the more challenging text. Partners can prepare to read the book by reviewing questions on this student page. They can also read difficult passages together, sharing questions and insights. They can use the questions on the student page to guide after-reading discussion.	*Increased Challenge* Encourage students to integrate knowledge and ideas by combining the Essential Questions and the unit concepts in their approach to two or more featured titles. For example, students might consider how *The Scarlet Letter* and *Leaves of Grass* reflect American culture in the time in which they were written. Students can focus on the similarities and differences in the ideas, values, and attitudes of different authors working in the same time period.

Preparing to Read Complex Texts

1. Tell students they can be attentive readers by bringing their experience and imagination to the texts they read and by actively questioning those texts. Explain that the questions they see on the student page are examples of types of questions to ask about works of fiction and nonfiction.

2. Point out that, like writing, reading is a "multidraft" process, involving several readings of complete works or passages, revising and refining one's understanding each time.

© Key Ideas and Details

3. Review and amplify the first bulleted point in the Key Ideas and Details box. **Ask:** What details in the text lead you to conclude that this idea or experience compelled the author to write?

   Possible response: Students may point out that the cited idea is the central idea of the text, or that it is the idea that is treated with the most passion.

© Craft and Structure

4. **Ask:** In what ways does the author express an attitude toward the reader?

   Possible response: The author forgoes background information about his or her subject, assuming that the reader has this knowledge already or is intelligent enough to make accurate assumptions.

© Integration of Ideas

5. Focus on the first bulleted point in the Integration of Ideas box. **Ask:** Do the ideas in this work seem original today? Might they have been more original when first published?

   Possible response: The ideas in the work do not seem original today. However, most of the works suggested were written between 1800 and 1870. It is possible that these ideas were very original in their time.

6. Finally, explain to students that they should cite key ideas and details, examples of craft and structure, or instances of the integration of ideas as evidence to support their points during a discussion of fiction, nonfiction, or poetry. After hearing the evidence, the group might reach a consensus or might agree to disagree.

Division, Reconciliation, and Expansion

Literature of the Civil War and the Frontier

PHLit Online!
www.PHLitOnline.com

Teaching From Technology

Enriched Online Student Edition
- full narration of selections
- interactive graphic organizers
- linked **Get Connected!** and **Background** videos
- all work sheets and other student resources

Professional Development
- the *Professional Development Guidebook* online
- additional professional-development essays by program authors

Planning, Assigning, and Monitoring
- software for online assignment of work to students, individually or to the whole class
- a system for tracking and grading student work

PHLit
Online!
www.PHLitOnline.com

Hear It!
• Selection summary audio
• Selection audio

See It!
• Author videos
• Essential Question video
• Get Connected videos
• Background videos
• More about the authors
• Illustrated vocabulary words
• Vocabulary flashcards

Do It!
• Interactive journals
• Interactive graphic organizers
• Grammar tutorials
• Interactive vocabulary games
• Test practice

461

Fondly do we hope—fervently do we pray—that this mighty scourge of war may speedily pass away.

– *Abraham Lincoln*
Second Inaugural
Address, 1865

Introduce Unit 3

1. Direct students' attention to the title of the unit, including the time period covered. Have a volunteer read the quotation. **Ask:** What does the quotation suggest about the period?
   Possible response: The period is likely to be dominated by the Civil War.

2. Discuss the artwork, *The Fall of Richmond,* 1865, Currier and Ives lithograph. Tell students that the painting depicts one of the climactic events of the Civil War. **Ask:** What details of the scene suggest the broad extent of the war's devastation?
   Possible response: The painting shows the heart of an American city ravaged by explosions and fire, with civilians fleeing for their lives.

3. Have students speculate about the literature of the period, given the quotation and the art.
   Possible response: The literature of the period will likely grapple with the divisive reality and lingering effects of the Civil War.

Unit Resources

Unit 3 Resources includes these pages:

▶ **Benchmark Tests** assess and monitor student progress.

▶ **Vocabulary and Reading Warm-ups** provide additional vocabulary support, based on Lexile rankings, for each selection. **"A" Warm-ups** are for students reading two grades below level. **"B" Warm-ups** are for students reading one grade below level.

▶ **Selection Support**
   • **Reading Strategy**
   • **Literary Analysis**
   • **Vocabulary Builder**
   • **Support for Writing**
   • **Enrichment**

Unit Features

Unit Author
Nell Irvin Painter helps introduce the period in the unit introduction, provides Recent Scholarship on literature in the unit, and offers insight in the Writing Workshop.

Extended Study
Students explore in depth the works of Mark Twain, accompanied by links to contemporary culture, a Critical Commentary, and a Comparing Literary Works feature.

Comparing Literary Works
Students compare classic and contemporary literary works.

Primary Sources
Students engage the documents that recorded history as it was made.

Informational Texts
Students learn to use and evaluate various types of informational text.

Themes Across Centuries
Students discover links between canonical literature and the contemporary world.

All worksheets and other student resources are also available online at **www.PHLitOnline.com.**

The Added Value of Culturally Responsive Literature **Sharroky Hollie Ph.D.**

" Jump-in reading validates and affirms the home culture of our students, and provides a bridge that transitions them to the culture of school. "

Culturally responsive literature is defined as literature that validates and affirms the culture and the language of a community or an identified group of people. These texts speak to the history, tradition, mores, struggles, and indigenous heritage of that group. It is safe to say that most cultures have seminal pieces of literature that have become the voices for the people. Whether it is James Baldwin for African Americans or Louise Erdrich for Native Americans, the commonality is that the literature illuminates the experiences of these communities in a positive way. For students who are from cultural groups that have been traditionally underserved and discriminated against, culturally responsive literature provides legitimacy and responsiveness.

Culturally Responsive Read-Alouds

Using Read-Alouds to Validate and Affirm When looking through the lens of culture and language, the definition of literacy has to be broadened beyond the traditional window. For Standard English Learners (SELs), we not only want to teach reading skills; we also want to inspire students with the desire to read. It's critical to engage these students who might be otherwise disengaged and unmotivated— students who are turned off to the idea of reading as a source of pleasure and entertainment, as well as information and knowledge. Engaging read alouds can reach out to these students and cultivate a desire to read.

Select Culturally Responsive Literature Not all literature with characters of color is authentic culturally responsive literature. Sometimes other types of literature can be mistaken for authentic culturally responsive literature. For example, some literature is culturally generic, meaning that the images and characters are of color but the storyline or theme is not central to a community or culture, like a version of a popular fairy tale that is written with an African American main character instead of the mainstream character. Teachers have to know what type of literature they are using with their students, not for the purpose of screening out, but for the purpose of being strategically selective in their choices to lead to enhanced learning for students.

The Research on Read Alouds Reading aloud to students helps to develop and improve literacy skills such as reading, writing, speaking, and listening (Trelease 2006). Research indicates that when students listen to others read their growth and understanding of vocabulary and language patterns increases.

Two Culturally Responsive Read-Aloud Strategies

Jump In Reading

Description: Students have the autonomy to choose when they participate and read aloud by "jumping-in."

How-To Steps: While one student reads (Reader 1), another student (Reader 2) can jump in, as long as it is at a time when Reader 1 has come to a period stop. A few guidelines:

- Each student must read at least one sentence.
- Readers can read for as long as they want or until someone jumps in.
- Moments of silence are fine—they allow students time to think and to reflect about what was just read.
- If two or more students jump in at the same time, one shall defer to the other.
- Encourage students not to compete against one another but to collaborate
- The teacher may jump in at any time.
- Establish equitable rules for how many times students can jump in during a reading or give fun parameters, such as "only the boys today," "students on the left side of the room" or "those folks wearing black shoes"

Pros: Highly engaging; decreases anxiety and pressure on the student to read; student-centered,

Cons: Struggling readers will not want to read; lacks equitable participation if not structured appropriately.

What Makes It Culturally Responsive: The appropriate time to jump in during a conversation is different for various cultures. Jump-in reading simulates the natural rhythm of conversations in some cultures. In the culture of school and mainstream culture, jumping in is considered rude and interruptive. Jump-in reading validates and affirms the home culture of our students, and provides a bridge that transitions them to the culture of school.

Strategy: Echo Read

Description: Teacher reads and students echo.

How-To Steps: Teacher reads one sentence, paragraph, or section then stops. Students echo the teacher by reading the same sentence in the same way.

Pros: Great for modeling prosody; builds a sense of cooperation and community.

Cons: Making sure that all students participate can be challenging.

What Makes It Culturally Responsive: Call and response, the verbal interplay between audience and speaker or students and teacher, is an important cultural element for many cultures. In mainstream society, call and response plays a key role in an experience such as sports events or worship services. For some cultures, such as Black culture, call and response is an almost mandatory aspect of the events, activities, and gatherings. Bringing that interplay into the classroom through echo reading not only can be fun, it also provides a positive cultural resonance for many students.

Modeled Strategy

See p. 403 for a point-of-use note modeling these strategies.

Teacher Resources

- *Professional Development Guideboook*
- *Classroom Strategies and Teaching Routines cards*

Log on as a teacher at **www.PHLitOnline.com** to access a library of all Professional Development articles by the Contributing Authors of Pearson Prentice Hall *Literature.*

Sharroky Hollie, Ph.D

Sharroky Hollie is a professor in Teacher Education at Cal State Dominguez Hills. He is also the co-founder and co-director of a laboratory school in culturally and linguistically responsive teaching. Dr. Hollie's research interests are language and literacy development for Standard English Learners, culturally responsive teaching, professional development design, and teacher development. He consults nationally on the topic of culturally responsive instruction.

Supporting Research

Jim Trelease, *The read aloud handbook,* Penguin, 2001

Violet Harris, *Culturally responsive literature,* Heinemann, 1999

Reading the Unit Introduction

Division, Reconciliation, and Expansion

Explain to students that this unit covers American literature from 1850 to 1914, a period during which the nation suffered through a Civil War and became an industrial world power. The Unit Introduction includes these components:

- a **Snapshot** offering a quick glimpse at the period;
- a **Historical Background** section discussing major events;
- a **Timeline** that covers the period from 1850 to 1914 over a span of ten pages.
- a **Unit Essay** examining the literature of the period through the lens of three Essential Questions;
- **Following-through** activities;
- a **Contemporary Commentary**.

Introducing the Essential Questions

1. Introduce each of the Essential Questions on the student page.

2. Show the **Essential Question** video on the *See It!* DVD. Help students relate the Essential Questions to the unit and their own experiences by asking the following:
Place and Literature How would you feel about the prospect of change in your community? Do you like things the way they are, or would you prefer change?
Literature and Society Name a newspaper, book, movie, or television show that made you change your mind about an issue.
American Literature What contemporary American would you like to see as the main character in a novel, play, or movie? Why?

3. Tell students that the ideas they have discussed also apply to the history of the period leading up to and following the Civil War. Have them begin reading the Unit Introduction, looking for these ideas.

Snapshot of the Period

The years between 1850 and 1914 witnessed a transformation of the United States. During those years, America came of age—the country changed from a decentralized, mostly agricultural nation to the modern industrial power that we know today. This transformation began in the period leading up to the Civil War. In that war, Americans took up arms against one another to determine which should prevail: The Union of the North or the Confederacy of the South? The federal Union or states' rights? Freedom or slavery? As the Civil War began, each side possessed significant strengths and notable weaknesses. The North had a tremendous advantage in population and was far more industrialized and thus better prepared to wage war than the agrarian South. However, the Confederacy had the psychological advantage of greater motivation: it was fighting for its very survival. The South also had a strong military tradition and notably fine leaders. When the struggle was over, the North won, the Union held, and slavery was abolished—but all at a devastating cost to the nation.

▲ Abraham Lincoln signed the Emancipation Proclamation in 1863, as the nation approached the third year of Civil War.

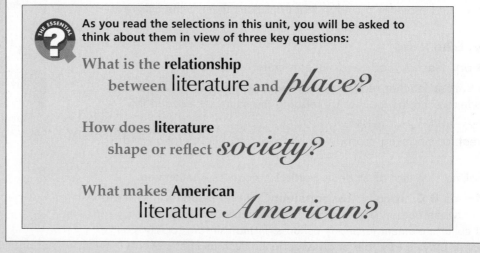

Twain   Douglass   Chopin   Crane   Cather   Chief Joseph

As you read the selections in this unit, you will be asked to think about them in view of three key questions:

What is the **relationship** between literature and *place?*

How does **literature** shape or reflect *society?*

What makes **American** literature *American?*

462 Division, Reconciliation, and Expansion (1850–1914)

Teaching Resources

The following resources can be used to support, enrich, or extend the instruction for the Unit 3 Introduction.

Unit 3 Resources
Names and Terms to Know, p. 5
Essential Question, pp. 2–4
Follow-Through Activities, p. 6

Common Core Companion,
pp. 10–16; 33–38;

Professional Development Guidebook
Cross-Curricular Enrichment, pp. 225, 235, 242

See It! DVD
Essential Question Video: Unit 3
Nell Irvin Painter, Segment 1

PHLit Online! All resources are available at **www.PHLitOnline.com.**

Integration of Knowledge and Ideas What does the information shown in the charts below help you understand about differences between the North and South in their economies, population densities, and overall lifestyles? How do you think these differences affected the outcome of the Civil War?

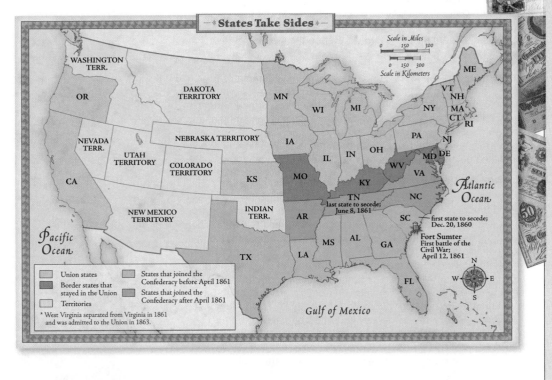

◆ States Take Sides ◆

Scale in Miles
0   150   300

Scale in Kilometers
0   150   300

WASHINGTON TERR.
OR
DAKOTA TERRITORY
MN
WI   MI
NY
ME
VT   NH
MA
CT   RI
NEVADA TERR.
NEBRASKA TERRITORY
IA
PA
NJ
UTAH TERRITORY
COLORADO TERRITORY
KS
IL   IN   OH
WV   MD   DE
VA
CA
MO   KY
NEW MEXICO TERRITORY
INDIAN TERR.
AR
TN
last state to secede;
June 8, 1861
NC
SC
first state to secede;
Dec. 20, 1860
TX
MS   AL   GA
LA
Fort Sumter
First battle of the Civil War;
April 12, 1861
FL

Atlantic Ocean

Pacific Ocean

Gulf of Mexico

N   W   E   S

Union states
Border states that stayed in the Union
Territories
States that joined the Confederacy before April 1861
States that joined the Confederacy after April 1861

* West Virginia separated from Virginia in 1861 and was admitted to the Union in 1863.

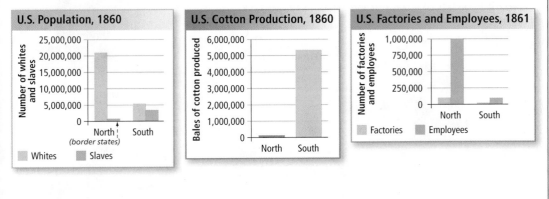

U.S. Population, 1860

Number of whites and slaves
25,000,000
20,000,000
15,000,000
10,000,000
5,000,000
0
North (border states)   South

Whites   Slaves

U.S. Cotton Production, 1860

Bales of cotton produced
6,000,000
5,000,000
4,000,000
3,000,000
2,000,000
1,000,000
0
North   South

U.S. Factories and Employees, 1861

Number of factories and employees
1,000,000
750,000
500,000
250,000
0
North   South

Factories   Employees

Snapshot of the Period **463**

The Historical Background section discusses the most significant events of this period: the Civil War that emancipated enslaved African-Americans, cost 600,000 lives, and left the South in ruins; the postwar era of dramatic change; the Homestead Act that accelerated the movement west and the disappearance of the frontier; the "Second Industrial Revolution" that brought electricity, automobiles, and airplanes into Americans' lives and made American cities much larger—and considerably dirtier.

1. Point out that the story of this period is a story of conflict and rapid change.

2. Have students read the Background. Then **ask** them to show a cause-effect relationship between at least two (if possible more) of the following events: the Civil War; emancipation; the Homestead Act; railroads; the frontier's disappearance; the Second Industrial Revolution; the Gilded Age.
   Possible response: The Civil War led to the emancipation of enslaved African Americans, who, like other Americans, were encouraged to settle the West by the Homestead Act, leading to the frontier's disappearance.

Teaching the Timeline

Tell students that the Timeline for 1850 to 1914 appears on pages 464–473 of this Unit Introduction. Each portion of the Timeline identifies and illustrates several major events in the United States and the world for that period.

© COMMON CORE • MULTIPLE PERSPECTIVES ON THE ERA

Historical Background

The Civil War Era (1850–1914)

Between the Civil War and World War I, America changed dramatically. The period began with cotton plantations and the Pony Express, and it ended with cars, airplanes, telephones, and movies. The Civil War scarred everyone—soldier, civilian, slave—and the shift from agriculture to industry accelerated. No American's life would ever be the same.

Prelude to War

The North and the South had developed differently. Commerce ruled the North and King Cotton ruled the South. The Industrial Revolution, advances in transportation, and a tide of immigration turned northern cities into centers of bustling activity. By contrast, cotton plantations and the system of slavery defined the South. Issues such as what to do about fugitive slaves and whether new states should be slave states or free states dominated politics. Rage and resentment grew. War was waiting.

Brother Against Brother

When Abraham Lincoln, dedicated to halting the spread of slavery, was elected president in 1860, South Carolina and five other states left the Union and established the Confederate States of America. Fighting began at Fort Sumter, in Charleston Harbor. Many on both sides anticipated a short war. No one could know what lay ahead: the carnage of Antietam, where more than 26,000 men fell in a single day; the deprivation of the siege of Vicksburg, where people survived only by eating dogs and rats; the destruction of Georgia, when Union troops marched to the coast. The devastating civil war lasted four long years.

By the time Confederate general Robert E. Lee surrendered to Union general Ulysses S. Grant in the spring of 1865, over 600,000 American soldiers had lost their lives. The South lay in ruins, its cities, farms, and plantations destroyed. The future looked grim. Just after the surrender, Abraham Lincoln was assassinated, and the exhausted, war-torn nation faced the huge task of reconstruction without him.

TIMELINE

1850

1850: **China** Taiping rebellion begins against the authority of the Qing government.

◀ 1856: **France** Gustave Flaubert publishes *Madame Bovary*, a classic novel of realism.

1857: **Dred Scott** decision by the U.S. Supreme Court rules that people of African descent cannot become U.S. citizens.

▶ 1859: John Brown, an abolitionist, leads a raid on the federal arsenal at Harpers Ferry, Virginia; he is hanged for treason.

1859: **England** Charles Darwin introduces theory of evolution in *The Origin of the Species*.

Enrichment: Investigating Technology

The *Monitor* and the *Merrimack*

To break the Union blockade of Southern ports, the South built the ironclad *Merrimack*. The sloping sides of the vessel were plated with iron sheets, and its bow was tipped with a deadly iron ram. When it attacked at Hampton Roads, Virginia, on March 8, 1862, the *Merrimack* wreaked havoc on the Union's wooden warships. The Union fleet was helpless until the next day, when a Union ironclad, the *Monitor,* appeared. The smaller *Monitor* carried only two cannons, but these were housed in an innovative rotating armored turret. The two ships fought an extended duel with no decisive result—except that the Union blockade continued and naval warfare changed forever.

Activity: Report Have students use the **Investigating Technology** work sheet, in *Professional Development Guidebook,* page 242, to record further details about ironclad ships and to report their findings to the class.

Americans Go West

After the Civil War, physical expansion and industrialization transformed the American landscape, economy, and society. The Homestead Act of 1862 promised 160 acres to anyone who would live on the land for a certain period and improve it. This shifted the westward movement into high gear. Half a million farmers, including tens of thousands of emancipated African Americans, staked their claims on the Great Plains. Miners went west, with dreams of gold sparkling in their eyes. In 1869, workers drove the last spike in the transcontinental railroad.

The Frontier Disappears

By 1890, the frontier had ceased to exist. Settlers, railroads, mines, ranches, and the slaughter of the buffalo had transformed the West. In place of open range were ploughed fields, grazing lands, and miles of fences. Gone, too, were the Indian nations; by 1890, almost all Native Americans in the West had been forced from their lands.

The "Electric" Society

When electricity entered the scene in the 1880s, the second Industrial Revolution began. Americans began to enjoy electric lights, telephones, automobiles, motion pictures, and skyscrapers, along with noise, traffic, and air pollution. Urban populations exploded; millions of immigrants provided cheap labor. Low wages, child labor, and disease were the norm for the working class, while a handful of industrial giants lived like kings. Mark Twain perfectly summarized the contradictions of this era when he called it "The Gilded Age."

Key Historical Theme: Painful Growth and Electric Change

- The Civil War left the nation physically, economically, and emotionally devastated as reconstruction began.
- Riding the railroad, Americans moved West and annihilated the frontier.
- The Age of Electricity transformed everyday life. Cities, with all their pleasures and problems, expanded rapidly.

1860: Abraham Lincoln is elected United States president. ▼

1862: Emily Dickinson's poem "Safe in their Alabaster Chambers" is published in the Massachusetts newspaper *The Republican*.

1865

▲ 1861: Civil War begins in April with firing on Fort Sumter.

▼ 1862: **France** Louis Pasteur proposes modern germ theory of disease.

1863: Lincoln issues the Emancipation Proclamation.

Historical Background **465**

Teaching the Essential Questions

As students read The Civil War and the Frontier, they will examine its information through the lens of three Essential Questions. Each Essential Question is broken down into "stepping-pingstone" questions. Work through each steppingstone question with the class. Then have students pose answers to each Essential Question as it applies to the period.

How does literature shape or reflect society?

1. Before they read this section of the essay, tell students that from 1850 to 1914, American society was being reshaped at a rapid rate.

2. Have students read this section of the essay. Then pose the first steppingstone question. **Ask:** What literary forms did writers use to discuss social and political issues during this period? **Possible response:** Spirituals expressed the woes of slavery and the hope for freedom. Real-life stories like the autobiography of Frederick Douglass and Mary Chesnut's journal put a personal face on the time's significant events. After the Civil War, investigative writers exposed economic and industrial failings.

(continued on p. 467)

Critical Viewing

Connect

1. Direct students to the image on the Timeline of the Northern Lights over a mountain range, illustrating the purchase of Alaska from Russia in 1867. Explain that the purchase of Alaska added millions of square miles to American territory.

2. **Ask** students to describe the impression of Alaska created by the image. Do they think this image would be likely to attract people to settle in Alaska? **Possible response:** The image of Alaska is exotic and beautiful but also rather forbidding. The image might attract very adventurous people to move to Alaska.

466

Essential Questions Across Time

The Civil War and the Frontier (1850–1914)

How does **literature** shape or reflect *society?*

What literary forms did writers use to discuss social and political issues during this period?

Spirituals Although spirituals were sung, not written down, they were the form of literature that grew directly out of the major social and political issue of the time—slavery. Born in the rhythms of work and based on biblical imagery, spirituals were lyrical expressions of lamentation, comfort, and hope. Songs like "Go Down, Moses" and "Swing Low, Sweet Chariot" made it possible for slaves to at least imagine release into a better life.

Life Stories Nonfiction in which men and women related the dramatic events of their lives also gave literary form to the issues of the era. Sojourner Truth's first-person account of her life and Frederick Douglass's autobiography were true-life narratives of bondage and freedom. Richly detailed diaries, such as the one kept by Confederate wife Mary Chesnut, as well as the journals and letters of countless Civil War soldiers remain valuable and moving literary resources that turn abstract issues into the daily realities of actual human beings.

Fiction and Journalism With Harriet Beecher Stowe's *Uncle Tom's Cabin*, fiction stepped up to play a major role in the politics of the era. Newspapers, too, took stands on a wide variety of issues and provided forums for editorials, essays, and public letters. After the Civil War, investigative journalists called muckrakers wrote blistering exposés of corruption, scandal, and incompetence in American industries.

> **ESSENTIAL QUESTION VOCABULARY**
>
> These Essential Question words will help you think and write about literature and society:
>
> **lamentation** (lam´ən tā´ shən) *n.* outward expression of grief; wail or cry
>
> **forum** (fôr´əm) *n.* place for the discussion of public matters
>
> **unflinching** (un flin´chiṇ) *adj.* steadfast; resolute

TIMELINE

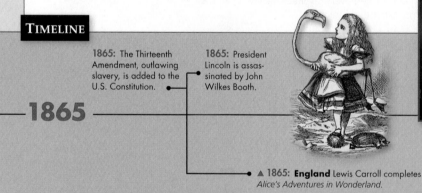

1865

1865: The Thirteenth Amendment, outlawing slavery, is added to the U.S. Constitution.

1865: President Lincoln is assassinated by John Wilkes Booth.

▲ **1865: England** Lewis Carroll completes *Alice's Adventures in Wonderland.*

▲ **1867:** The United States buys the state of Alaska from Russia.

466 Division, Reconciliation, and Expansion (1850–1914)

Vocabulary Development

Essential Question Vocabulary

Students will be expected to use Essential Question Vocabulary (introduced on pp. 466, 470, and 473) when they talk and write about the Essential Questions. Introduce the vocabulary as students complete each section of this Unit Introduction. Then, have students complete sentence starters like the following to help them internalize this vocabulary.

The settlers held a **forum** in which they discussed _____. (**Sample answer:** rules of the community, property rights)

People traveling westward used many kinds of **transportation,** such as _____. (**Sample answer:** boats and wagons)

An **objective** description of life for the settlers might be found in _____. (**Sample answer:** a book written by an expert about the time.)

How did popular literature reflect the era's social and political issues?

Rags to Riches As America's cities grew, the struggle against crushing urban poverty became a fact of life for more and more people. Many readers turned to the young adult novels of Horatio Alger to find inspiration on the hard road to success. Alger's rags-to-riches stories of young men finding fame and fortune through right-thinking and moral actions were immensely popular, selling more than twenty million copies.

Twists and Turns William Sydney Porter started out as a journalist, worked in a bank, went to prison for embezzlement, and became a short story writer. Under the name "O. Henry," he published hundreds of tales of ordinary city dwellers and became one of the most popular writers in America. His stories are often humorous episodes that include twists of fate. Beneath the light-hearted surface, however, his ironic surprise endings suggest how much people felt their lives were subject to coincidence and chance.

The West and the Wizard Millions of Americans who never set foot on a prairie or an open range loved the Western novels of Zane Grey. The closing of the frontier encouraged a romantic view of the lost West, and Grey capitalized on that vision with exciting tales of self-reliant cowboys, many of which were later turned into movies. Industrial-age Americans found escapism of a different kind in L. Frank Baum's *The Wonderful Wizard of Oz* (1900), a fantasy so popular it led to thirteen sequels.

The American EXPERIENCE

ART IN THE HISTORICAL CONTEXT

Realism in Painting: The Ashcan School

At the turn of the twentieth century, a group of artists working in Philadelphia and New York realized that city life was fertile ground for a new kind of imagery. They shared the basic principles and attitudes of Realism, and they developed ways of conveying Realism visually. These painters were aware that America was becoming increasingly urban, and they wanted to depict this new steel-and-concrete reality. They painted the grubby and the drab as well as the hectic and the colorful. These frank and honest painters included Robert Henri, William Glackens, and George Luks. Some critics insultingly called them the Ashcan ("garbage can") School, a label that has endured but is no longer an insult.

One prominent Ashcan painter was John Sloan (1871–1951). Sloan said that he saw the city as a "vast stage set where all sorts of lively business was in progress." His painting *Six O'Clock, Winter* (c. 1912) shows the "lively business" of a New York City rush hour.

SIX O'CLOCK, WINTER, 1912, JOHN SLOAN, THE PHILLIPS COLLECTION

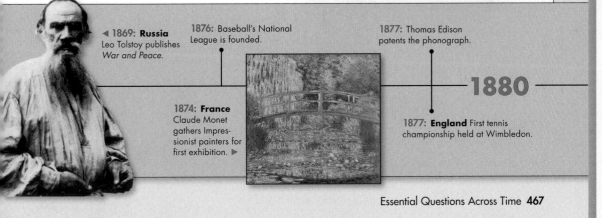

◀ **1869: Russia** Leo Tolstoy publishes *War and Peace*.

1876: Baseball's National League is founded.

1874: France Claude Monet gathers Impressionist painters for first exhibition. ▶

1877: Thomas Edison patents the phonograph.

1877: England First tennis championship held at Wimbledon.

1880

Essential Questions Across Time **467**

Teaching the Essential Question (cont.)

3. Then **ask** the second stepping-stone question: How did popular literature reflect the era's social and political issues?
   Possible response: "Rags to riches" tales like the Horatio Alger stories reflected the economic growth of the time. O. Henry's surprise endings emphasized the powerful element of chance. The novels of Zane Grey romanticized the now-closed frontier, and L. Frank Baum's *The Wonderful Wizard of Oz* provided another kind of escapism, the flight into fantasy.

(continued on p. 469)

The American Experience
Art in the Historical Context

1. Have students read the sidebar feature on the Ashcan School.

2. Explain to students that the realism of the Ashcan School represented a dramatic break from the mainstream art of the day, which was still heavily influenced by Europe. By refusing to portray unrealistic, popular subjects such as mythology and idealized landscapes, Sloan and the other members of his group, The Eight, challenged audiences to find beauty and artistic inspiration in their own country and in their own lives.

3. **Ask** students to consider how the urban realism first popularized by the Ashcan School continues to shape American culture today.
   Possible response: Urban realism remains a popular subject for contemporary music (such as rap), music videos, and movies. It also influences fashion.

Enrichment: Understanding Economics

Economies of the North and the South

The North and the South had developed along different economic lines. In the North, commerce was king. The Industrial Revolution and cheap transportation had caused explosive urban growth. Immigration, too, was changing the face of the North. A rising ride of Irish and German immigrants, among others, were seeking new lives in Northern cities and often finding work in factories.

The South was a slower-paced region of plantations and small farms. There were cities, but the area was most truly defined by its cotton plantations. Sugar, rice, and tobacco were also important crops. Technological progress, with its social issues and problems, had little impact on the prewar South.

Activity: Have students use the **Understanding Economics** work sheet, in *Professional Development Guidebook,* page 225, to help them list the factors in the North's economy that would be beneficial in mobilizing for war.

467

The American Experience

Contemporary Connection

1. Have students read the Contemporary Connection.

2. Explain that Mark Twain's (1835–1910) *A Connecticut Yankee in King Arthur's Court* spins the tale of a nineteenth-century American who accidentally time-travels to medieval England. He introduces electricity, bicycles, and other modern marvels to the Middle Ages. The novel also has a dark, ironic side. Applying modern technology to warfare, Twain's hero creates fences that electrocute his enemies but also trap his own knights within a ring of death.

3. Have students imagine what Mark Twain might think if he could time-travel one century forward to our time. **Ask:** What would he recognize? What would he admire? What would distress him?
   Possible response: Twain would probably recognize many things—telephones, electricity, trains, automobiles, perhaps airplanes. He might admire television, computers, and the Internet. He would probably be distressed by the destructive power of modern warfare and might have concerns about technology.

Critical Viewing

Draw Conclusions

1. Draw students' attention to the photograph of the Statue of Liberty map on the Timeline on this page.

2. Tell students that the statue was a birthday present from France for America's 1876 Centennial. **Ask** students: What elements in the Statue of Liberty make it an effective symbol for the nation?
   Possible response: The statue is large and majestic. The woman's figure wears a crown, but not the crown of an earthly ruler—the crown looks more like a halo or star, creating a spiritual aura. She lifts a torch that suggests the bright and enduring nature of liberty.

The American EXPERIENCE

CONTEMPORARY CONNECTION

Mark Twain, the Original Time Traveler

In his novel, *A Connecticut Yankee in King Arthur's Court*, Mark Twain places a present-day hero in the distant past. Twain said the idea was inspired by a dream in which he was "a knight errant in armor in the Middle Ages." When the book was published in 1889, *The Boston Herald* raved, "Of all the extraordinary conceits that have germinated in his fruitful imagination, nothing more delicious has ever occurred to Mark Twain than that of running riot among the legendary times of our ancestral race. . . .'"

While he must have enjoyed the book's success, Twain probably never imagined its long-term effect. Indeed, the time travel tale—now a familiar device in science fiction—is widely regarded to have begun with Twain's book. Perhaps because of this, many science fiction writers have a fondness for Twain. He often appears as a character in sci-fi books, films, television shows, and comics, including the following brief list of examples:

• *The Riverworld* series by Philip José Farmer

• *To Sail Beyond the Sunset* by Robert A. Heinlein

• *Star Trek: The Next Generation,* "Time's Arrow" episode

• *The Sandman* graphic novel series by Neil Gaiman

• *The Transformers: Evolutions* "Hearts of Steel" comic book series

TIMELINE

1880

1883: Railroads adopt standard time zones.

1883: The Brooklyn Bridge is opened. ▶

◀ **1884:** Mark Twain publishes *The Adventures of Huckleberry Finn.*

1886: Statue of Liberty dedicated in New York Harbor. ▶

1888: Great mid-March blizzard in eastern United States piles 30-foot drifts in New York's Herald Square.

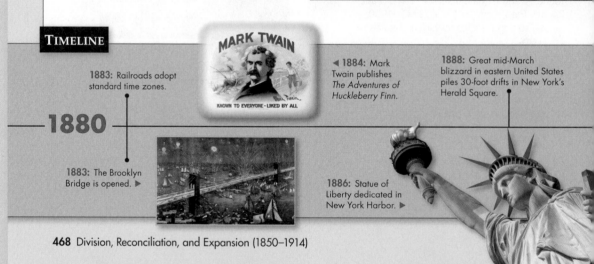

MARK TWAIN

KNOWN TO EVERYONE · LIKED BY ALL

Think Aloud

Vocabulary: Using Context
Direct students' attention to the word *germinated* on this page. Use the following "think aloud" to model the skill of using context to infer the meaning of the word *germinated.* Say to students:

I may not know the meaning of the word *germinated.* When I read the sentence, however, I realize that the writer is using *germinated* to describe something that happened in Mark Twain's "fruitful" imagination, and that what Twain's imagination "germi-nated" seems to have been a "delicious" idea for a story. The word *fruitful* makes Twain's imagination seem like a kind of plant or tree, and *delicious* makes the novel sound like a tasty fruit. So I think *germinated* refers to a process of creating something. The literal meaning probably relates to a plant producing a fruit. In this nonliteral sense, it means growing or developing a creative idea.

How did social and political issues lead to Realism and Naturalism?

The war was over. The unthinkable had happened: Americans had tried to slaughter each other. Although the outcome of the war had given the nation a hard-won sense of unity, the enormous cost in human life had shattered the nation's idealism. Like the hero of Stephen Crane's *Red Badge of Courage*, Americans had lost their innocence. The youthful sense of enthusiastic optimism that had built the country had faded away. Frustrated, unfulfilled, young writers turned away from the Romanticism that was popular before the war. They threw away their rose-colored glasses and saw the world for what it was. They became Realists.

The Common Life American writers began to focus on creating portrayals of "real life" as ordinary people lived it. They attempted to show characters and events in an honest, objective, almost factual way. In prose, Willa Cather wrote unflinchingly of the loneliness and cultural isolation of life on the prairie. In poetry, Edwin Arlington Robinson created unsparing psychological portraits of a variety of small-town characters. In *Spoon River Anthology*, Edgar Lee Masters presented a disturbingly candid portrait of small-town life in the form of epitaphs spoken by the dead themselves.

Naturalism Like Realists, Naturalists also depicted ordinary people in real-life situations, but they took it a step further. They believed that forces far more powerful than any individual shaped human destinies. Indifferent Nature, blind fate, heredity, pure chance—these determined the lives of men and women. Even fierce self-interest was not enough to guarantee success or survival. Jack London, for example, set much of his fiction in the Alaskan wilderness, where the frigid environment was unforgiving. The Naturalist theme of human endurance in the face of overwhelming natural forces pervades his fiction. The atmosphere of urban life fed Naturalism too, as people recognized that industrialization, mechanization, and anonymity were forces against which individuals were increasingly powerless.

◀ **1889: France** Eiffel Tower is completed in Paris, becoming the world's tallest structure.

1891: England Thomas Hardy publishes *Tess of the D'Urbervilles.* ▶

1894: Korea Sino-Japanese War begins; Japanese army defeats Chinese.

1890: Last major battle between U.S. troops and Native Americans fought at Wounded Knee, South Dakota.

1892: Ellis Island opens as a receiving center for immigrants.

1895

Teaching the Essential Question (cont.)

3. Have students read this section of the essay. Then **ask** the third stepping-stone question: How did social and political issues lead to Realism and Naturalism?
Possible response: The Civil War had led many Americans to lose their idealism. Writers turned from Romanticism to the harsher Realism. Realists like Stephen Crane, Willa Cather, Edwin Arlington Robinson, and Edgar Lee Masters portrayed the lonely, hard realities of frontier settlers, small-town dwellers, and inhabitants of cities. Naturalistic writers like Jack London were even more pessimistic, describing the helplessness of humans in the face of a hostile universe.

Applying the Essential Question

1. Summarize the class discussion of the three stepping-stone questions on pages 466–469.

2. Then **ask** students to speculate about the effects of the instant communications of our own time, and to compare the power of today's writers to the power of writers a century ago in their ability to reflect and shape their societies.
Possible response: Americans a century ago probably read relatively more printed works than we do today. It is possible that such reading created a deeper impression than our exposure to constantly changing waves of television and Internet sensations. In our day, however, writers are more likely to produce a quicker effect and, as a result, to both reflect and shape their social realities more rapidly.

Enrichment: Analyzing a Literary Figure

Naturalism Around the World
Naturalism flourished in Europe during the late nineteenth and early twentieth centuries. The writer Emile Zola (1840–1902) was its leading practitioner. His approach to literature was similar to a scientist's approach to an experiment. Naturalism imported scientific principles into literature, and writers created characters whose lives were shaped and whose actions were dictated by powerful forces—heredity and nature, but also social and economic pressures—entirely beyond their control. Major American Naturalist authors included Jack London, Stephen Crane, Frank Norris, and Theodore Dreiser.

Activity: Analyzing a Literary Figure Have students use the **Analyzing a Literary Figure** work sheet, in *Professional Development Guidebook*, page 235, to help them learn more about Emile Zola and his possible influence on American Naturalist writers.

469

What is the relationship between literature and place?

1. Before they read this section of the essay, tell students that from 1850 to 1914, the various regions of the country defined themselves more sharply, focusing more on the differences that made each area distinct.

2. Have students read this section of the essay. Then pose the first stepping-stone question. **Ask:** What elements of their physical environment affected Northern writers' attitudes?
   Possible response: The North was becoming highly industrialized and more urban. Waves of immigrants entered Northern cities. The problems of city life weighed heavily on writers from this region.

3. Then **ask** the second stepping-stone question: What elements of the physical environment affected Southern writers' attitudes?
   Possible response: The South remained more rural, but its plantation system had been destroyed by the Civil War. Southern writers reacted to the loss of the old order and also focused on "local color" that made their various locales unique and memorable.

4. Then **ask** the third stepping-stone question: How did expressions of place show up in literature?
   Possible response: Writers from every region expressed a strong sense of the uniqueness of place. "Local color" writers included Mark Twain, southerner Kate Chopin, westerner Bret Harte, Sarah Orne Jewett from Maine, and Willa Cather and Hamlin Garland from the Midwest. Urban sophistication was explored in the writings of easterners Henry James, Edith Wharton, and William Dean Howells.

What is the relationship between literature and *place?*

What elements of the physical environment affected Northern writers' attitudes?

Industry The growth of industry in the North radically changed the landscape, and the landscape profoundly affected the thoughts, attitudes, and values of the people. In fact, change itself became a significant value. Technological advances in manufacturing, transportation, and the conveniences of daily life encouraged Northerners to believe that anything bigger, stronger, faster, and newer was necessarily better.

Urban Life On the other hand, the increased sizes and populations of Northern cities led to a host of urban problems and discontents. Conflicts arose over the treatment of immigrants, the role of organized labor, and the causes and effects of poverty. Writers were particularly sensitive to what was happening to the spirits—the emotions and values—of people crowded into cities and working at mind-numbing jobs in factories.

What elements of the physical environment affected Southern writers' attitudes?

Regionalism The South of course had cities too, but overall it remained a predominantly rural environment. Agriculture had always been at the heart of the economy, but the war had devastated the plantation system and abolished slavery, radically altering the Southern way of life. Nevertheless, Southern writers focused on the distinctive qualities of their geographical setting. Like writers in other parts of the country, Southern regionalists used the features and color of their local landscapes to tell stories that seemed to grow out of the land itself.

How did expressions of place show up in literature?

Local Color Almost as a conscious national reaction to the Civil War, writers all over the country seemed to realize how precious each separate part of the country could be. In the Northeast, South, Midwest, and West,

ESSENTIAL QUESTION VOCABULARY

These Essential Question words will help you think and write about literature and place:

industry (in´dəs trē) *n.* the production of goods; manufacturing enterprises collectively

transportation (trans´pər tā´shən) *n.* system for carrying passengers or goods from one place to another

rural (roor´əl) *adj.* characteristic of the country or farm rather than the city

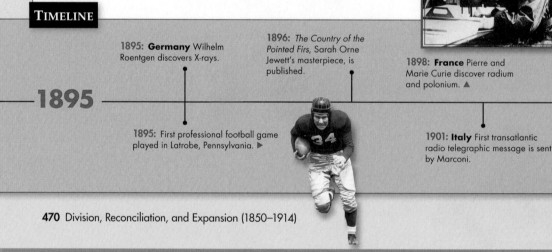

TIMELINE

1895: Germany Wilhelm Roentgen discovers X-rays.

1896: *The Country of the Pointed Firs,* Sarah Orne Jewett's masterpiece, is published.

1898: France Pierre and Marie Curie discover radium and polonium. ▲

1895

1895: First professional football game played in Latrobe, Pennsylvania. ▶

1901: Italy First transatlantic radio telegraphic message is sent by Marconi.

470 Division, Reconciliation, and Expansion (1850–1914)

writers began to feature characters and details that were unique to a particular geographic area. Characters spoke in dialect, linking themselves to a specific locale. Landscapes were so fully integrated into stories that they virtually became characters. Descriptions of customs, clothing, manners, and attitudes all contributed to a literature of local color.

The mining-camp sketches and stories of Bret Harte made the West, especially California, a lively locale in the American literary imagination. Hamlin Garland and Willa Cather found hardship and tragedy, sometimes touched with romance, on the farms of the Midwest. Mark Twain told stories, like *The Adventures of Huckleberry Finn*, that are so deeply entwined with the landscape of the Mississippi River we cannot imagine them happening in any other place. In Maine, Sarah Orne Jewett created delicate and unforgettable New England idylls, and in Louisiana Kate Chopin told wrenchingly realistic stories of life in the bayous.

Urban Sophistication Not all realism, however, was set on farms, in small towns, and on riverboats. Some American writers were also comfortable in elegant drawing rooms. Edith Wharton wrote novels and stories about repressive customs in the Eastern high society into which she had been born. William Dean Howells applied his brand of realism to New England novels of manners and class. Urban subtlety and sophistication found its greatest American analyst in Henry James. Often placing his Americans back in Europe, James probed deeply into characters motivated by complex mixes of desire, honor, ambition, and guilt.

The American EXPERIENCE

DEVELOPING AMERICAN ENGLISH

Mark Twain and the American Language by Richard Lederer

On February 18, 1885, thirty thousand copies of *The Adventures of Huckleberry Finn* were released, and the novel changed the direction of American letters. Twain used everyday speech instead of formal, standard English. He used seven distinct dialects to reflect the speech patterns of his characters, and he showed the vitality of the American idiom in narrative as well as in dialogue. *Huckleberry Finn* is the first novel of world rank written entirely in American.

Readin', Writin', and Twain
Twain held strong opinions about a passel of subjects. Here are a few things he had to say about the American language that he helped to shape.

- *On dialects*: I have traveled more than anyone else, and I have noticed that even the angels speak English with an accent.
- *On choosing words*: The difference between the almost right word and the right word is really a large matter—'tis the difference between the lightning-bug and the lightning.
- *On style* (in a letter to a twelve-year-old): I notice that you use plain, simple language, short words, and brief sentences. That is the way to write English—it is the modern way and the best way. Stick to it; and don't let fluff and flowers and verbosity creep in.

1903: Jack London publishes *The Call of the Wild*.

1903: **Spain** Pablo Picasso paints *The Old Guitarist.* ▶

1903: Wright Brothers fly 852 feet in their airplane at Kitty Hawk, North Carolina. ▼

1903: W.E.B. DuBois publishes *The Souls of Black Folk,* a collection of essays.

1904: Russo-Japanese War begins.

1905

The Old Guitarist, 1903, Pablo Picasso, The Art Institute of Chicago, ©2004 Estate of Pablo Picasso/Artists Rights Society (ARS), New York

---

Differentiated Instruction for Universal Access

Culturally Responsive Instruction
Language Focus Have students discuss Twain's statement about dialects. Then ask each student to list characteristics of the dialect he or she speaks, and contrast the dialect with standard American English. Finally, have students list two situations in which dialect is more appropriate to use than standard American English, and two situations in which standard American English is more appropriate, along with reasons why.

Applying the Essential Question

1. Summarize discussion of the three stepping-stone questions on page 470.

2. Then **ask** students what special aspect of their own region they would focus on if they wrote of "local color."
   Possible response: Students may focus on interesting local landmarks, indigenous groups, impressive landscape or geographic features, or historical figures.

The American Experience
Developing American English

1. Have students read the sidebar about Mark Twain.

2. **Ask** why Twain favored short words over long ones.
   Possible response: He seems to have felt that longer words were more pretentious or flowery than shorter words.

3. **Activity:** Have students replace the words below with simpler ones (they can check meanings in a dictionary):
   affluent ornate elderly
   chronicle locution puissant
   Sample answers: rich, fancy, old, story, speech, strong

Critical Viewing
Draw Conclusions

1. Draw students' attention to the Timeline image of the Wright brothers' flight in 1903.

2. **Ask** students: What do you think the spectators felt as they watched the flight?
   Possible response: They probably wondered how long the plane would stay up and what would happen when it came down. They must have been excited at the first successful flight.

471

What makes American literature American?

1. Before students read this section of the essay, point out that the nation's "story" and "character," though changing in this period, remained unique in the world.

2. **Ask** the first stepping-stone question on this page: What literary elements contributed to an American style?
   Possible response: Realistic portrayals of American plots and settings gave American literature its special identity. Humor and informal language created a unique American style.

3. **Ask** the second stepping-stone question: What roles did writers play in shaping American identity?
   Possible response: American writers tried to reflect their world objectively. Realistic details from local colorists replaced Transcendentalist philosophy. Naturalist writers expressed more pessimistic views of life.

(continued on p. 473)

Background

Literature

1. Tell students that on the southwestern frontier during this period, immigrants from Mexico developed a rich tradition of folklore. The tales and legends—or *cuentos*—of the Mexican-American Southwest include both stories with complex religious and social morals and fantasies filled with magic and the supernatural. This folk culture had its roots in the Old World, but the tales had developed their own flavor in the physical and social landscape of Mexico and the Southwest.

2. **Ask** students to give examples of stories that they were told but have never actually read.
   Possible answer: Students might mention fairy tales or even family stories that have been passed down by word of mouth.

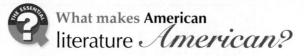

What makes American literature *American?*

What literary elements contributed to an American style?

Settings and Plots Unique local settings were essential in creating the "Americanness" of literature during this period. A Civil War battlefield, a Mississippi riverboat, a Western mining town, a Yukon wilderness—these and other sites grounded American literature in truly American places.

Dialogue and Style Common speech and dialects contributed to an American style. The way characters talked linked them to specific parts of the country and gave them distinct identities. Straightforward, deliberately "unliterary" speech defined a plain and powerful American style.

Humor Mark Twain said, "The humorous story is American." He felt that a good comic story depended on *how* it was told. Twain and other American writers often used humor to expose corruption and dissect human foibles.

What roles did writers play in shaping American identity?

Writer as Realist During the first half of the nineteenth century, Romantic subjectivity dominated American writing. The adventure tales of Irving and Cooper, the romances and fantasies of Hawthorne and Poe, and the otherworldly quests of Emerson and Melville defined American literature. However, after the horrors of the Civil War, the second half of the century saw the rise of a more objective attitude toward the world and human affairs. Hard fact took on more value than the search for the Transcendentalist Oversoul.

Local color writers such as Bret Harte, Sarah Orne Jewett, and Kate Chopin took great pains to depict details of the places they loved. As a result, their readers came to love those places as well. Local colorists were storytellers—Mark Twain the finest of them all—but they were also documentarians, recording life as it was lived.

TIMELINE

1905

1905: Germany Albert Einstein proposes his relativity theory. ▼

▲ **1906:** The San Francisco earthquake results in the deaths of at least 3,000 people.

1906: Finland Women's suffrage is granted.

1907: Frank Lloyd Wright hosts his first solo exhibition at the Art Institute of Chicago.

1908: Henry Ford builds the first Model T. ▲

1908: The electric washing machine is invented.

These were also the years when a new invention, photography, began to flourish, further feeding the demand for realistic images of life.

Writer as Naturalist The writers associated with Naturalism, including Stephen Crane, Frank Norris, and Jack London, were even more detached. They were deeply influenced by the writings of British naturalist Charles Darwin, German political economist Karl Marx, and French novelist Emile Zola, who believed that heredity, environment, and social conditions determined people's actions. To the American Naturalists, Emerson's self-reliance was an illusion, and the role of the writer was to make that clear.

At the dawn of the twentieth century, what did literature reveal about American attitudes?

Pragmatism The American Romantic impulse had faded. The dream-life expressed by Hawthorne and Poe had given way to a hard-edged pragmatism. Melville's Captain Ahab, an obsessive, tragic figure on a doomed whaling ship, was succeeded by Twain's Huck Finn, a clear-eyed and clear-headed boy on a raft.

Loss of Idealism The Civil War tarnished many of the ideals that had characterized the pre-war nation. In the face of Civil War deaths, postwar poverty, urban crowding, and mass production, Emersonian self-reliance lost its relevance. Henry David Thoreau, living alone at Walden and becoming one with nature, was succeeded by Jack London's doomed Yukon camper in "To Build a Fire."

Democracy Americans continued to put their faith in democracy. Realism emphasized the common person. It praised the everyday and the ordinary, even at the risk of glorifying mediocrity. Hawthorne's Hester Prynne, an exceptional woman reviled by her community, was succeeded by Edgar Lee Masters' Lucinda Matlock, an ordinary woman in small-town America.

Science As the nation entered the twentieth century, science and technology took on ever greater importance. Americans believed in progress and measured it in concrete ways. Over 27 million people visited the 1893 World's Columbian Exposition in Chicago, a massive world's fair that celebrated culture, craft, and commerce. The fair symbolized America's future as a leader in the practical industries that would continue to transform the world and create the Modern Age.

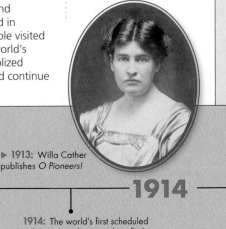

> **ESSENTIAL QUESTION VOCABULARY**
>
> These Essential Question words will help you think and write about American literature:
>
> **objective** (əb jek´tiv) *adj.* real; actual
>
> **realistic** (rē ə lis´tik) *adj.* practical or concrete rather than visionary
>
> **pragmatism** (prag´mə tiz´əm) *n.* quality of being practical, sensible

1909: A multi-racial group of activists founds the National Association for the Advancement of Colored People.

TITANIC
WHITE STAR LINE
The World's Largest Liner
SOUTHAMPTON ~ NEW YORK
VIA CHERBOURG & QUEENSTOWN

1912: Over 1,500 people die in the sinking of the *Titanic.* ▶

▶ **1913:** Willa Cather publishes *O Pioneers!*

1914: The world's first scheduled airline service begins taking flight from St. Petersburg to Tampa.

1914

Essential Questions Across Time **473**

Differentiated Instruction for Universal Access

Strategies for Special-Needs Students
Ask students to make a chronological list of only the American events shown on the Timeline for 1850–1914. Have students mark each decade. Encourage them to draw arrows between related events and to star the Timeline listings that feature American writers.

Enrichment for Gifted/Talented Students
Have verbally talented students create an eye-witness account for one of the events on the Timeline. Encourage the students to do research to find additional information about the event and to create a character who could have been present at the event and who expresses a clear attitude toward it.

Teaching the Essential Question (cont.)

4. Have students read this section of the essay. Then **ask** the third stepping-stone question: At the dawn of the twentieth century, what did literature reveal about American attitudes?
   Possible response: Pragmatism had replaced Romanticism; the obsession of Melville's Ahab was replaced by the clear-headedness of Twain's Huck Finn. The horrors of the Civil War and the hardships of life described by the Naturalists put an end to Emersonian self-reliance and idealism.

Applying the Essential Question

1. Summarize the discussion of the Essential Question on pages 472–473.

2. Then **ask:** To what extent do Americans today share the disillusionment expressed by the writers of the late nineteenth and early twentieth centuries? To what extent have our values changed?
   Sample answer: Americans today have new reasons to be disillusioned after the wars of the twentieth century and the threat of massive nuclear war and smaller-scale terrorism. However, advances in knowledge and science as well as in international diplomacy also provide much reason for hope.

Critical Viewing
Apply Science Skills

1. Call students' attention to the image on the Timeline of the 1906 San Francisco earthquake (page 472).

2. Point out that the 1989 Loma Prieta earthquake in the San Francisco Bay area took fewer than 60 lives (compared with 3,000 deaths in 1906). **Ask** students to suggest reasons for the reduction in the death toll.
   Possible answer: Buildings today are built to withstand earthquakes; more fireproof materials are used. Improved communication spreads news quickly and so saves lives.

473

Recent Scholarship

Introduce Nell Irvin Painter

1. Nell Irvin Painter, a well-known historian, introduces the unit and provides insights into thoughts of historians as they organize history into periods. Later in this unit, on pages 550–551, Painter introduces Sojourner Truth's "Account of an Experience with Discrimination."

2. Have students read the Meet the Author feature about Nell Irvin Painter. Tell students that Painter is a noted historian with wide-ranging interests that include late-nineteenth-century American social patterns, ideas of race and ethnicity, and the life and times of Sojourner Truth.

3. Use the *See It!* DVD to introduce Nell Irvin Painter. Show Segment 1 to provide insights into her career as a historian and teacher. After students have watched the segment, **ask:** What events and circumstances in Nell Irvin Painter's youth might have contributed to her scholarly interests as an adult?
   Possible answer: Her family had a history of scholarship; her grandfather had been a professor. She grew up in an environment that fostered learning—the neighborhood around the University of California at Berkeley.

Recent Scholarship

Defining an Era

Nell Irvin Painter

O ne of my most-read books, *Standing at Armageddon: The United States, 1877–1919*, showed me how politics changes as the times change. (The word *Armageddon* in the title refers to the end of the world, and the phrase *Standing at Armageddon* comes from a statement Theodore Roosevelt made in 1912.)

Historians, of course, know that timing is everything. We call one of our specialties "periodization," meaning the breaking up of the past into meaningful chunks of time. Historians decided that certain dates—in this textbook, for example, 1750, 1800, 1850, 1870, 1914, and 1946—carried special meaning, that what came before was different from what came afterward. The periodization in this unit (1850–1914) generally corresponds to the periodization of my book (1877–1919), although this unit includes the Civil War and Reconstruction and my book does not.

I made my own discoveries as I was just starting to work on *Standing at Armageddon*. I had to decide where to start and end a book on the period that covered roughly 1885 to 1915. The years 1885 and 1915 had no particular resonance: Nothing earthshaking occurred in either of those years to change the course of United States history. So I set about finding meaningful years by reading newspapers and news magazines, where I could follow the news of the day as it unfolded, day by day and week by week.

Meet the Author

Introducing Nell Irvin Painter (b. 1942)

Nell Irvin Painter served as the director of Princeton University's Program in African American Studies from 1997 to 2000. She is the author of numerous books, including *Standing at Armageddon: The United States, 1877–1919; Southern History Across the Color Line;* and *Sojourner Truth: A Life, A Symbol.*

474 Division, Reconciliation, and Expansion (1850–1914)

A Shift from Land to Labor Issues

At the beginning of the 1870s, the news still bristled with violence related to the politics of the Civil War, as Democrats attacked Republicans and killed off the people associated with Reconstruction. Reconstruction—the reorganization of Southern states from 1867 to 1877—was dying a bloody death in the South, as Democrats took back by force the power they had held before the war. In 1877, however, new conflicts eclipsed the focus on Southern political terrorism. The news also revealed a great deal of labor conflict outside the South. A nationwide strike of railroad workers occurred in 1877 that began a whole new era in which politics revolved around working people and strikes. Before the Civil War, politics had been about land and access to land. After Reconstruction, postwar politics focused on industries and workers; 1877—the year national attention shifted from land to labor—became the starting point for *Standing at Armageddon*.

What about the end? Where should my period and my book end? Still reading the newspapers and news magazines, I found an echo of 1877's strikes and riots in 1919, the year contemporaries called the "Great Upheaval." There was the end of my period, a time in which working people and their issues once again dominated American politics.

Organized Labor Becomes a Force

Before 1877, American politics revolved around questions of land. But after 1877, politics revolved around industry and the people who worked in it. Organized labor became a force in U.S. politics between 1877 and 1919 and, building on this foundation, labor unions would surge to the fore in the 1930s. My periodization of 1877–1919 reflects my belief that working people and their concerns lie at the heart of the politics of the era. I begin and end *Standing at Armageddon* at moments in which workers attract the attention of Americans as a whole.

©Speaking and Listening: Collaboration

Nell Irvin Painter discusses "periodization," the breaking up of the past into meaningful time periods. Some periods begin or end with major dramatic events, such as a war or an economic change. The beginning or ending of other periods, such as a "renaissance," are more difficult to pinpoint.

Hold a **small group discussion** about your own time period. What event or events define it? When would you say it started? What name or label would you give it? As a group, arrive at a consensus and then share your ideas with the class.

◀ **Critical Viewing**
Explain how this photograph of a railroad strike reflects Painter's discussion of American workers.
[Connect]

Speaking and Listening: Collaboration
Small Group Discussion

1. Review the assignment with students.

2. Divide the class into small groups and have students discuss the idea of how historians divide the past into meaningful time periods. Have a representative from each group present the group's ideas to the class.

3. Open up the discussion to the whole class. Write on the board the sentences "What are the benefits of organizing the past into 'meaningful units'? What are the drawbacks?" Then invite students to respond, and list their comments on the board.

4. To help conduct the discussion, use the **Discussion Guide** in the *Professional Development Guidebook,* page 65

Critical Viewing

Possible response: Though the scene is peaceful, the large number of workers present and the size of the arriving troop contingent show that the strike is a very serious event with the potential for violence.

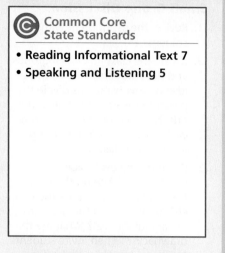

Common Core State Standards

- **Reading Informational Text 7**
- **Speaking and Listening 5**

Integrate and Evaluate Information

1. Review the chart assignment with the class. Then, ask students to use the Activity A chart in the Follow-Through worksheet (p. 6 in *Unit 3 Resources*) to complete this activity.

   Possible response: *Literature and Place: Key Concept—urbanization of the North; Key Author—Edith Wharton; Literature and Society: Key Concept:—popular nonfiction writing portrayed the issues and events of the day; Key Author—Frederick Douglass*

2. **Possible response:** The map and graphs on p. 463 show the Union and Confederate states and contrast these regions at the start of the war. The photograph on p. 471 of the Wright Brothers' flight adds to the understanding of the development of science and industry after the war.

3. **Possible response:** Writers around the country incorporated characters, dialect, and details of the land in their writing to express and preserve the perspectives of people in their regions. Writers in the North wrote novels about life in the cities, while Southern writers depicted the features of the local landscapes. Some writers described life on the Midwestern prairies, and others wrote novels expressing a romantic view of the West.

Integrate and Evaluate Information

1. Use a chart like the one shown to determine the key ideas expressed in the Essential Question essays on pages 466–473. Fill in two ideas related to each Essential Question and note the authors most closely associated with each concept. One example has been done for you.

Essential Question	Key Concept	Key Author
Literature and Place		
American Literature	Influence of heredity and environment	Crane
Literature and Society		

2. How do the visual sources in this section—map, charts, paintings, and photographs—add to your understanding of the ideas expressed in words? Cite specific examples.

3. After the Civil War, Americans were more conscious than ever of their regional identities. How did writers of this era express and preserve the distinct perspectives of Americans across the land? Cite evidence from the various sources presented on pages 462–473 in your answer.

4. **Address a Question:** In her essay "Defining an Era," Nell Irvin Painter states her contention that politics before the Civil War dealt with issues related to land, while politics after the Civil War dealt with issues related to labor. In what ways does her point echo other societal changes occurring during this era? Consider information presented in this textbook about urbanization and industrialization. In addition, integrate information from other sources to support your ideas.

Speaking and Listening: Oral Presentation

During the Civil War era, speeches and debates played an important role in American life. Research and develop an **oral presentation** about the public-speaking style of one of these famous American orators:

- Abraham Lincoln
- Sojourner Truth
- Henry Ward Beecher
- Mark Twain

Solve a Research Problem: To complete this assignment, you will need to locate examples of and commentaries about the public speaking of a person who lived before the age of sophisticated recording devices. Formulate a plan to meet this research challenge. Consider primary and secondary sources such as:

- Journal and newspaper articles written during the speaker's life
- Writings of later scholars familiar with the speaker's works
- Recordings of other people reenacting the speaker's speeches

As part of your presentation, explain the process you used to identify and evaluate information and solve the research problem. To add interest and evidence to your presentation, use a digital recording of a reenactment of the speaker's words or of an expert discussing the speaker's abilities and ideas.

476 Division, Reconciliation, and Expansion (1850–1914)

Common Core State Standards

Reading Informational Text
7. Integrate and evaluate multiple sources of information presented in different media or formats as well as in words in order to address a question or solve a problem.

Speaking and Listening
5. Make strategic use of digital media in presentations to enhance understanding of findings, reasoning, and evidence and to add interest.

ESSENTIAL QUESTION VOCABULARY

Use these words in your responses:

Literature and Place
industry
transportation
rural

American Literature
objective
realistic
pragmatism

Literature and Society
lamentation
forum
unflinching

4. **Possible response:** With the second industrial revolution, the growth of cities and cheap immigrant labor created a working class that experienced low wages, child labor, and disease. At the same time, a few industrial owners were extremely wealthy. The role of organized labor, poverty, and the treatment of immigrants were sources of conflict during this period.

Speaking and Listening

1. Point out that students will be researching commentary about public speakers.

2. Have students analyze the activity and identify its key terms: *Civil War era; speeches and debates; primary and secondary sources.*

3. Then, have students choose a speaker to analyze and complete the chart in Activity B in the **Follow-Through** worksheet (p. 6) in the *Unit 3 Resources.*

A Nation Divided

PART 1

Text Complexity: At a Glance

This chart gives a general text complexity rating for the selections in this part of the unit to help guide instruction. For additional text complexity support, see the Text Complexity Rubric at point of use.

An Occurrence at Owl Creek Bridge	**More Complex**	Swing Low, Sweet Chariot	**More Accessible**
An Episode of War	**More Accessible**	The Gettysburg Address	**More Accessible**
from My Bondage, and My Freedom	**More Complex**	Letter to His Son	**More Complex**
Go Down, Moses	**More Accessible**	An Account of an Experience With Discrimination	**More Accessible**

Selection Planning Guide

The selections in this section show the many faces of a nation divided. "An Occurrence at Owl Creek Bridge" will have students debating whether all is really fair in love and war. Stephen Crane's "An Episode of War" portrays the battlefront. The spirituals and the Frederick Douglass excerpt provide a candid look at the divisive issue of slavery; Sojourner Truth's account shows that the effects of slavery did not end with emancipation. Two of the war's greatest figures—Abraham Lincoln and Robert E. Lee—reveal in their own words the issues at the heart of the Civil War.

Humanities

Photograph, 1862, Alexander Gardner

This photograph was taken on October 3, 1862, about two weeks after the narrow Union victory at Antietam. This is one of the few photographs to show Abraham Lincoln wearing his famous top hat. The officer is General John McClernand; the civilian is detective Alan Pinkerton, who at the time was running the Union Intelligence Service.

1. Point out to students that cameras of the time needed several seconds of exposure to produce an image; any movement during the process resulted in a blur. That explains the slight blurring of Lincoln's face in the photograph.

2. **Ask:** What impression of Lincoln do you get from this photograph?
   Possible response: Students are likely to comment on Lincoln's stature, formality, and dignity in this photograph.

Monitoring Progress

Before students read the selections in Part 1, refer to the results for the Vocabulary in Context items on **Benchmark Test 2** (*Unit 1 Resources,* pp. 265–267). Use this diagnostic portion of the test to guide your choice of selections to teach, as well as the depth of prereading preparation you will provide, based on students' readiness for the reading and vocabulary skills.

477

• An Occurrence at Owl Creek Bridge
Lesson Pacing Guide

DAY 1 Preteach

- Ⓒ Administer the Reading and Vocabulary Warm-ups *(Unit 3 Resources,* pp. 7–10*)* as necessary.
- Introduce the Literary Analysis concept: Point of View and Stream of Consciousness.
- Ⓒ Introduce the Reading Strategy: Analyzing the Story's Pattern of Organization.
- Ⓒ Build background with the author and Background features.
- Develop thematic thinking with Connecting to the Essential Question.
- Ⓒ Teach the selection vocabulary.

DAYS 2–3 Preteach/Teach/Assess

- Distribute copies of the appropriate graphic organizer for the Reading Strategy *(Graphic Organizer Transparencies,* pp. 95–96*)*.
- Distribute copies of the appropriate graphic organizer for Literary Analysis *(Graphic Organizer Transparencies,* pp. 97–98*)*.
- Prepare students to read with the Activating Prior Knowledge activities (TE).
- Informally monitor comprehension while students read.
- Use the Reading Check question to confirm comprehension.
- Develop students' understanding of point of view and stream of consciousness using the Literary Analysis prompts.
- Develop students' ability to analyze the story's pattern of organization using the Reading Strategy prompt.
- Ⓒ Reinforce vocabulary with the Vocabulary notes.
- Assess students' comprehension and mastery of the skills by having them answer the Critical Reading, Literary Analysis, and Reading Strategy questions.
- Have students complete the Vocabulary Lesson.

DAY 4 Extend/Assess

- Ⓒ Have students complete the Writing Lesson and write a critical essay on a stylistic device. (You may assign as homework.)
- Administer Selection Test A or B *(Unit 3 Resources,* pp. 19–21 or 22–24*)*.

Ⓒ Common Core State Standards

Reading Literature 3. Analyze the impact of the author's choices regarding how to develop and relate elements of a story (e.g., how the characters are introduced and developed).
5. Analyze how an author's choices concerning how to structure specific parts of a text contribute to its overall structure and meaning as well as its aesthetic impact.

Writing 2. Write explanatory texts to examine and convey complex ideas, concepts, and information clearly and accurately through the effective selection, organization, and analysis of content.
2.b. Develop the topic thoroughly by selecting the most significant quotations or other information and examples appropriate to the audience's knowledge of the topic.

Language 3. Apply knowledge of language to make effective choices for meaning.

Additional Standards Practice
Common Core Companion, pp. 28–35; 54–55; 196–207; 322–323

Daily Block Scheduling
Each day in this Lesson Pacing Guide represents a 40–50 minute period. Teachers using block scheduling may combine days to revise pacing. In addition, teachers may differentiate and support core instruction by integrating components for extended and intensive support as students require. See the Guide to Selected Leveled Resources (facing page).

Guide to Selected Leveled Resources

R T I Tier 1 (students performing on level)

An Occurrence at Owl Creek Bridge

Warm Up	**Practice, model,** and **monitor** fluency, working **with the whole class** or **in groups**.	Vocabulary and Reading Warm-ups B, *Unit 3 Resources,* pp. 7–8, 10
Comprehension/Skills	**Support** and **monitor** comprehension and skills development, having students complete the activities, graphic organizers, and interactive prompts **independently** or **as a class**.	• *Reader's Notebook,* adapted instruction and summary **EL** *Reader's Notebook: English Learner's Version,* adapted instruction and summary • **Reading Strategy Graphic Organizer B,** *Graphic Organizer Transparencies,* p. 96 • **Literary Analysis Graphic Organizer B,** *Graphic Organizer Transparencies,* p. 98
Monitor Progress	**Monitor** student progress with the differentiated curriculum-based assessment in the *Unit Resources.*	• **Selection Test B,** *Unit 3 Resources,* pp. 22–24 • **Open-Book Test,** *Unit 3 Resources,* pp. 16–18

R T I Tier 2 (students requiring intervention)

An Occurrence at Owl Creek Bridge

Warm Up	**Practice, model,** and **monitor** fluency **in groups** or **with individuals**.	• **Vocabulary and Reading Warm-ups A,** *Unit 3 Resources,* pp. 7–9 • *Hear It!* **Audio CD**
Comprehension/Skills	• **Support** and **monitor** comprehension and skills development, working **in small groups** or **with individuals**. • As students complete the selection in the appropriate version of the *Reader's Notebook,* **monitor** comprehension frequently with group questions and individual instruction. • **Model** strategies while guiding students in completing the activities and prompts in the *Reader's Notebook,* as well as the graphic organizers. • **Practice** skills and **monitor** mastery with the *Reading Kit* worksheets.	• *Reader's Notebook: Adapted Version,* adapted instruction and summary **EL** *Reader's Notebook: English Learner's Version,* adapted instruction and summary • **Reading Strategy Graphic Organizer A,** *Graphic Organizer Transparencies,* p. 95 • **Literary Analysis Graphic Organizer A,** *Graphic Organizer Transparencies,* p. 97 • *Reading Kit,* Practice worksheets
Monitor Progress	**Monitor** student progress with the differentiated curriculum-based assessment in the *Unit Resources* and in the *Reading Kit.*	• **Selection Test A,** *Unit 3 Resources,* pp. 19–21 • *Reading Kit,* Assess worksheets

TIER 3 Tier 3 intervention may require consultation with the student's special-education or dyslexia specialist. For additional support, see the Tier 2 activities and resources listed above.

One-on-one teaching   Group work   Whole-class instruction   Independent work   **A** Assessment

For a complete guide to selection support, including support for Advanced students, see the Overview of Resources in the frontmatter.

• An Occurrence at Owl Creek Bridge

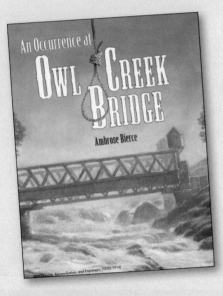

An Occurrence at
OWL CREEK BRIDGE
Ambrose Bierce

Vocabulary/Fluency/Prior Knowledge

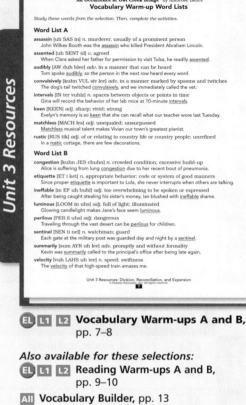

Unit 3 Resources

"An Occurrence at Owl Creek Bridge" by Ambrose Bierce
Vocabulary Warm-up Word Lists

Study these words from the selection. Then, complete the activities.

Word List A

assassin [uh SAS in] *n.* murderer, usually of a prominent person
John Wilkes Booth was the assassin who killed President Abraham Lincoln.

assented [uh SENT id] *v.* agreed
When Clara asked her father for permission to visit Tulsa, he readily assented.

audibly [AW duh blee] *adv.* in a manner that can be heard
Tom spoke audibly, so the person in the next row heard every word.

convulsively [kuhn VUL siv lee] *adv.* in a manner marked by spasms and twitches
The dog's tail twitched convulsively, and we immediately called the vet.

intervals [IN ter vuhlz] *n.* spaces between objects or points in time
Gina will record the behavior of her lab mice at 10-minute intervals.

keen [KEEN] *adj.* sharp; vivid; strong
Evelyn's memory is so keen that she can recall what our teacher wore last Tuesday.

matchless [MACH les] *adj.* unequaled; unsurpassed
Matchless musical talent makes Vivian our town's greatest pianist.

rustic [RUS tik] *adj.* of or relating to country life or country people; unrefined
In a rustic cottage, there are few decorations.

Word List B

congestion [kuhn JES chuhn] *n.* crowded condition; excessive build-up
Alice is suffering from lung congestion due to her recent bout of pneumonia.

etiquette [ET i ket] *n.* appropriate behavior; code or system of good manners
Since proper etiquette is important to Lola, she never interrupts when others are talking.

ineffable [in EF uh buhl] *adj.* too overwhelming to be spoken or expressed
After being caught stealing his sister's money, Ian blushed with ineffable shame.

luminous [LOOM in uhs] *adj.* full of light; illuminated
Glowing candlelight makes Jane's face seem luminous.

perilous [PER il uhs] *adj.* dangerous
Traveling through the vast desert can be perilous for children.

sentinel [SEN ti nel] *n.* watchman; guard
Each gate at the military post was guarded day and night by a sentinel.

summarily [sum AYR uh lee] *adv.* promptly and without formality
Kevin was summarily called to the principal's office after being late again.

velocity [vuh LAHS uh tee] *n.* speed; swiftness
The velocity of that high-speed train amazes me.

Unit 3 Resources: Division, Reconciliation, and Expansion
© Pearson Education, Inc. All rights reserved.
7

RESOURCES FOR:

L1 Special-Needs Students

L2 Below-Level Students (Tier 2)

L3 On-Level Students (Tier 1)

L4 Advanced Students (Tier 1)

EL English Learners

All All Students

EL **L1** **L2** **Vocabulary Warm-ups A and B,** pp. 7–8

Also available for these selections:

EL **L1** **L2** **Reading Warm-ups A and B,** pp. 9–10

All **Vocabulary Builder,** pp. 13

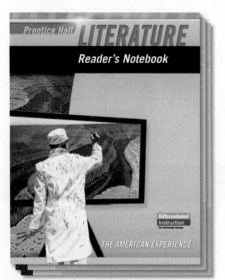

Prentice Hall LITERATURE
Reader's Notebook

Differentiated Instruction for Universal Access

THE AMERICAN EXPERIENCE

Reader's Notebooks

Pre- and postreading pages for this selection, as well as "An Occurrence at Owl Creek Bridge," appear in an interactive format in the *Reader's Notebooks.* Each *Notebook* is differentiated for a different group of learners.
The selections in the Adapted and English Learner's versions are abridged.

L2 **L3** *Reader's Notebook*

L1 *Reader's Notebook: Adapted Version*

EL *Reader's Notebook: English Learner's Version*

EL *Reader's Notebook: Spanish Version*

PRENTICE HALL LITERATURE
Common Core Companion
STUDENT WORKBOOK • GRADE ELEVEN

COMMON CORE EDITION ©

A Student workbook for Mastering the Common Core State Standards

Key Features
• Instruction and Practice for Common Core State Standards
• Writing Workshops
• Listening and Speaking Workshops
• Performance Tasks

ALWAYS LEARNING   PEARSON

© *Common Core Companion*

Additional instruction and practice for each Common Core State Standard

Selection Support

Graphic Organizer Transparencies *(side tab)*

EL L3 Reading: Graphic Organizer B, pp. 96

Also available for these selections:

EL L1 L2 Reading: Graphic Organizer A, (partially filled in), p. 95

EL L1 L2 Literary Analysis: Graphic Organizer A, (partially filled in), pp. 97

EL L3 Literary Analysis: Graphic Organizer B, p. 98

Skills Development/Extension

Unit 3 Resources *(side tab)*

All Reading: Identify Chronological Order, pp. 12

Also available for these selections:

All Literary Analysis: Point of View, pp. 11

EL L3 L4 Support for Writing, p. 14

L4 Enrichment, p. 15

Assessment

EL L1 L2 Selection Test A, pp. 19–21

Also available for these selections:

L3 L4 Open-Book Test, pp. 16–18

EL L3 L4 Selection Test B, pp. 22–24

PHLit Online!
www.PHLitOnline.com

Online Resources: All print materials are also available online.

- complete narrated selection text
- a thematically related video with writing prompt
- an interactive graphic organizer
- highlighting feature
- access to all student print resources, adapted to individual student needs
- Spanish and English summaries
- adapted selection translations in Spanish

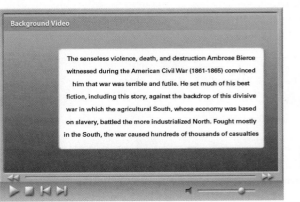

The senseless violence, death, and destruction Ambrose Bierce witnessed during the American Civil War (1861-1865) convinced him that war was terrible and futile. He set much of his best fiction, including this story, against the backdrop of this divisive war in which the agricultural South, whose economy was based on slavery, battled the more industrialized North. Fought mostly in the South, the war caused hundreds of thousands of casualties

Background Video

Also available:

Get Connected! (thematic video with writing prompt)
All videos are available in Spanish.

Vocabulary Central (tools and activities for studying vocabulary)

Also available:

Writer's Journal (with graphics feature)

❶ Connecting to the Essential Question

1. Review the assignment.

2. Mention that a place can be charged by an event—say, a car accident. Have students complete the assignment.

3. Ominous details are more noticeable on rereading; tell students to read the story twice.

❷ Literary Analysis

Introduce the strategy, using the instruction on the student page.

Think Aloud: Model the Skill

Say to students:

Freewriting can be done in a first-person stream-of-consciousness style:

Write what you know. Know? I know I had a good weekend. Did snowshoeing.

Here's an example of the third-person stream-of-consciousness technique:

The man in the water saw the eye of the man on the bridge. . . . He observed that it was a gray eye. . . .

❸ Reading Strategy

1. Introduce the strategy, using the instruction on the student page.

2. Give students a copy of **Reading Strategy Graphic Organizer B,** page 96 in *Graphic Organizer Transparencies,* to fill out as they read.

Think Aloud: Model the Skill

Say to students:

"An Occurrence at Owl Creek Bridge" is presented in chronological order, but with major shifts in time at key points. I sense the writer is carefully controlling the information he gives the reader.

❹ Vocabulary

1. Pronounce each word. Give its definition; have students say the word.

2. For more guidance, see the *Classroom Strategies and Teaching Routines* card for introducing vocabulary.

Before You Read

An Occurrence at Owl Creek Bridge

❶ **Connecting to the Essential Question** Everyday locations become charged with strategic importance and danger during times of war. As you read this story, which takes place during the Civil War, notice ominous details about the setting. This will help as you reflect on the Essential Question: **What is the relationship between literature and place?**

❷ Literary Analysis

Point of view is the perspective, or vantage point, from which a story is told. An author's choice of point of view affects every aspect of a story. For example, different points of view convey different types of information to the reader.

- In stories told from an **omniscient point of view,** the narrator is an observer who can relate everything that happens, as well as the private thoughts and feelings of all the characters. The opening scene of this story is related from an omniscient, "bird's eye" perspective: "A man stood on a railroad bridge in northern Alabama . . ."

- In stories told from a **limited third-person point of view,** readers' information is limited to what a single character feels, thinks, and observes: "A piece of dancing driftwood caught his attention . . ."

The point of view in this story shifts from omniscient to limited third-person. As the point of view shifts, so do the emotional tone and sense of time. To emphasize this change, Bierce introduces yet another narrative approach. He uses **stream of consciousness,** a technique in which a character's thoughts are presented as the mind experiences them—in short bursts without obvious logic. As you read, consider which events spark the thoughts and feelings the main character experiences.

❸ Reading Strategy

Preparing to Read Complex Texts Bierce chooses to structure this story in three sections, each representing a shift in time and in chronological order. Clarify meaning by **analyzing the story's pattern of organization,** or *text structure.* Use a chart like the one shown to identify the time frame and events for each section. Then, analyze how this pattern of organization contributes to the story's meaning and impact.

❹ Vocabulary

etiquette (et´ i kit) *n.* appropriate behavior and ceremonies (p. 482)

deference (def´ ər əns) *n.* respect; courtesy; regard (p. 482)

dictum (dik´ təm) *n.* formal statement of fact or opinion (p. 483)

summarily (sə mer´ ə lē) *adv.* without formality; hastily (p. 484)

apprised (ə prizd´) *v.* informed; notified (p. 485)

ineffable (in ef´ ə bəl) *adj.* too overwhelming to be spoken (p. 489)

Common Core State Standards

Reading Literature
3. Analyze the impact of the author's choices regarding how to develop and relate elements of a story.
5. Analyze how an author's choices concerning how to structure specific parts of a text contribute to its overall structure and meaning as well as its aesthetic impact.

Section I
Time:
Key Events:

Section II
Time:
Key Events:

Section III
Time:
Key Events:

www.PHLitOnline.com

478 Division, Reconciliation, and Expansion (1850–1914)

Vocabulary Development

Vocabulary Knowledge Rating

Create a **Vocabulary Knowledge Rating Chart** (*Professional Development Guidebook,* p. 33) for the vocabulary words on the student page. Give each student a copy of the chart with the words on it. Read the words aloud, and have students mark their rating in the Before Reading column. Urge students to attend to these words as they read and discuss the selection.

In order to gauge how much instruction you need to provide, tally how many students are confident in their knowledge of each word. As students read, point out the words and their context.

 **Vocabulary Central,** featuring student tools and activities for studying vocabulary, is available online at **www.PHLitOnline.com.**

⑤ AMBROSE BIERCE *(1842–1914?)*

Author of **"An Occurrence at Owl Creek Bridge"**

Ambrose Bierce's writing and worldview were shaped by his career as a Union officer in the Civil War. The poverty in which he was raised helped to foster Bierce's unsentimental outlook; the brutality he saw during the war cemented his cynicism. Bierce explored themes of cruelty and death in his writing, earning himself the nickname "Bitter Bierce."

A Civil War Soldier Bierce was born in Ohio and raised on a farm in Indiana. Having educated himself by reading his father's books, he left the farm while in his teens to attend a military academy in Kentucky. When the Civil War broke out, he enlisted in the Union army. Bierce fought in several important battles, rose from private to lieutenant, and won many awards for bravery. Toward the end of the war he was seriously wounded, but he returned to battle a few months later.

Poisoned Pen After the war, Bierce settled in San Francisco as a journalist. His "Prattler" column, which appeared in *The Argonaut* (1877–1879), the *Wasp* (1881–1886), and the *San Francisco Sunday Examiner* (1887–1896), mixed political and social satire, literary reviews, and gossip. The broodingly handsome writer was dubbed "the wickedest man in San Francisco" for his cynical and often malicious commentary. Yet Bierce's dark reputation only added to his personal popularity. He was a magnetic figure who charmed those around him despite the malice of his words.

Establishing His Legacy Although Bierce published many of his finest short stories in his column, he decided in the early 1890s to publish his collected short stories in two volumes entitled *Tales of Soldiers and Civilians* (1891) and *Can Such Things Be?* (1893). The concise, carefully plotted stories in these collections, set for the most part during the Civil War, capture the cruelty and futility of war and the indifference of death.

The Perfect Cynic Writer George Sterling wrote of Bierce, his longtime friend, that he "never troubled to conceal his justifiable contempt of humanity. . . . Bierce was a 'perfectionist,' a quality that in his case led to an intolerance involving merciless cruelty."

While he was successful professionally, Bierce found little happiness in a world where so few people met his expectations. His marriage ended in divorce, and both of his sons died at an early age. In 1913, at age 71, Bierce traveled to Mexico, a country in the midst of a bloody civil war. To this day, his fate is unknown, although a reasonable speculation is that he was killed during the siege of Ojinaga in 1914.

An Occurrence at Owl Creek Bridge **479**

⚡ Daily Bellringer

For each class during which you will teach this selection, have students complete one of the five activities for the appropriate week in the *Daily Bellringer Activities* booklet.

◗ Multidraft Reading

To assist struggling readers and to enhance reading for all, assign the text in chunks as warranted by length and apply multidraft reading protocols. For each reading, have students set the purpose indicated:

- **First reading**—identifying key ideas and details and answering any Reading Checks.
- **Second reading**—analyzing craft and structure and responding to the side-column prompts.
- **Third reading**—integrating knowledge and ideas, connecting to other texts and the world, and answering the end-of-selection questions.

For more guidance, refer to the *Classroom Strategies and Teaching Routines* card on multidraft reading.

⑤ Background
More About the Author

Ernest Hopkins, an editor and author who has specialized in the work of Ambrose Bierce, claims that Bierce's general philosophy was a "realistic, pessimistic, hard-boiled attitude toward life. This first-handed approach made him rather difficult to work with, no doubt, but it did make his writings refreshingly original and does so today—to read Bierce is to enter a different world."

PHLit Online!
www.PHLitOnline.com

Teaching From Technology

Preparing to Read
Go to **www.PHLitOnline.com** in class or in a lab and display the Get Connected! slide show for this selection. Have the class brainstorm for responses to the slide show writing prompt, entering ideas in the interactive journal. Then have students complete their responses individually in a lab or as homework.

To build background, display the Background and More About the Author features.

Using the Interactive Student Edition, go to **www.PHLitOnline.com** and display the **Enriched Online Student Edition.** As the class reads the selection or listens to the narration, record answers to side-column prompts using the graphic organizers accessible on the interactive page. Alternatively, have students use the online edition individually, answering the prompts as they read.

❶ About the Selection

Ambrose Bierce creates a compelling depiction of the Civil War hanging of a Southern planter, Peyton Farquhar, who has attempted, and failed, to commit sabotage. Bierce explores the rapid movement of Farquhar's thoughts in the moments before death and the way in which the perception of time can become distorted in traumatic situations. As Farquhar falls to his death by hanging, he imagines that the rope breaks. Farquhar plunges into the stream below, swims to safety, returns home to his family—only to be snapped back to a horrifying reality.

❷ Activating Prior Knowledge

Have a student read aloud the first four sentences of this story. Then elicit from the students their understanding that the man on the bridge is about to be hanged. Ask what they imagine is going through the man's mind at this moment. After students have shared responses, tell them to read the story to discover the man's thoughts as well as his fate.

Concept Connector ➡

Tell students they will return to their responses after reading the selection.

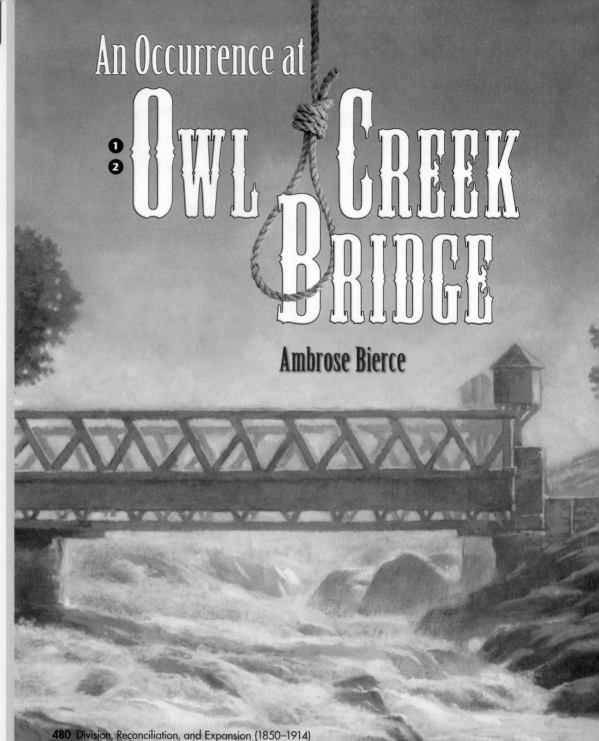

An Occurrence at

❶ ❷ Owl Creek Bridge

Ambrose Bierce

480 Division, Reconciliation, and Expansion (1850–1914)

© Text Complexity Rubric

An Occurrence at Owl Creek Bridge

Qualitative Measures			
Context/Knowledge Demands	Civil War setting; historical knowledge demands 1 2 ③ 4 5		
Structure/Language Conventionality and Clarity	Stream of consciousness 1 2 3 ④ 5		
Levels of Meaning/ Purpose/Concepts	Abstract (death) 1 2 ③ 4 5		
Quantitative Measures			
Lexile	1000L	Text Length	3,723 words
Overall Complexity	**More complex**		

Reader and Task Suggestions

Preparing to Read the Text
- Using the Background information on TE p. 479, discuss how Bierce's grim philosophy might affect the kinds of stories that he would write.
- Ask students when or why it might be important to know a story character's thoughts.
- Guide students to use Multidraft Reading strategies (TE p. 479).

Leveled Tasks

Structure/Language If students will have difficulty with structure, have them read to grasp the setting of the railroad bridge. Then, have students reread to distinguish that setting from Farquhar's thoughts.

Analyzing If students will not have difficulty with structure, discuss how the narrative mixes Farquhar's thoughts with realistic plot details.

③ BACKGROUND *The senseless violence, death, and destruction Ambrose Bierce witnessed during the American Civil War (1861–1865) convinced him that war was terrible and futile. He set much of his best fiction, including this story, against the backdrop of this divisive war in which the agricultural South, whose economy was based on slavery, battled the more industrialized North. Fought mostly in the South, the war caused hundreds of thousands of casualties on both sides.*

I

A man stood upon a railroad bridge in northern Alabama, looking down into the swift water twenty feet below. The man's hands were behind his back, the wrists bound with a cord. A rope closely encircled his neck. It was attached to a stout cross timber above his head and the slack fell to the level of his knees. Some loose boards laid upon the sleepers supporting the metals of the railway supplied a footing for him and his executioners—two private soldiers of the Federal army, directed by a sergeant who in civil life may have been a deputy sheriff. At a short remove upon the same temporary platform was an officer in the uniform of his rank, armed. He was a captain. A sentinel at each end of the bridge stood with his rifle in the position known as "support," that is to say, vertical in front of the left shoulder, the hammer resting on the forearm thrown straight across the chest—a formal and unnatural position, enforcing an erect carriage of the body. It did not appear to be the duty of these two men to know what was occurring at the center of the bridge; they merely blockaded the two ends of the foot planking that traversed it.

Beyond one of the sentinels nobody was in sight; the railroad ran straight away into a forest for a hundred yards, then, curving, was lost to view. Doubtless there was an out-post farther along. The other bank of the stream was open ground—a gentle acclivity[1] topped with a stockade of vertical tree trunks, loopholed for rifles, with a single embrasure through which protruded the muzzle of a brass cannon commanding the bridge. Midway of the slope between bridge and fort were the spectators—a single company of infantry in line, at "parade rest," the butts of the rifles on the ground, the barrels inclining slightly backward against the right shoulder, the hands crossed upon the stock. A lieutenant stood at the right of the line, the point of his sword upon the ground, his left hand resting upon his right. Excepting the group of four at the center of the bridge, not a man moved. The company faced the bridge, staring stonily, motionless. The sentinels, facing the banks of the stream, might have been statues to adorn the

---

Literary Analysis
Point of View Which details in the first paragraph show the use of the omniscient point of view? Explain.

Reading Check ⑤

What event is about to take place on the bridge?

---

1. **acclivity** (ə klivʹ ə tē) *n.* upward slope.

---

③ Background
For a nineteenth-century story about the Civil War, "An Occurrence at Owk Creek Bridge" is far ahead of its time. The clinical detachment of Bierce's narrative, its pyschological realism, the use of stream-of-consciousness, and, most of all, the shocking twist of its ending give the story a very modern sensibility. A number of modern stories and films have imitated Bierce's climatic ending.

④ Literary Analysis
Point of View

1. Review with students the definition of the omniscient point of view. (An omniscient narrator objectively describes everything that happens.)

2. Ask a student to read aloud the first paragraph of the story. Then **ask** the Literary Analysis question. **Answer:** Details that show the omniscient point of view include the descriptions of the man who is about to be hanged and the identities, responsibilities, and ranks of the soldiers on the bridge.

⑤ Reading Check

Answer: A man is about to be hanged by members of the Federal army.

This selection is available in an interactive format in the **Enriched Online Student Edition,** at **www.PHLitOnline.com,** which includes a thematically related video with writing prompt and an interactive graphic organizer.

History

During the Civil War, executions were always carried out according to strict military code. In that war, as in most others, civilian attempts at sabotage were treated harshly; the culprits were immediately hanged or shot. Military personnel taken in such attempts, on the other hand, were not subject to execution but became prisoners of war. Civilian saboteurs such as Bierce's Peyton Farquhar knew their deeds warranted an extreme penalty but nonetheless took great risks.

Point of View

1. **Ask** a student volunteer to explain the difference between the omniscient and the limited third-person points of view. Then ask students which point of view Bierce has employed in the story so far. **Answer:** He has employed the omniscient point of view.

2. **Ask** students: What phrase indicates that the point of view has shifted from omniscient to limited third-person? Explain.
   Answer: Students may point to the phrase "fix his last thoughts upon his wife and children" as an indication that the point of view has shifted. This shift changes the story's focus to the observations and feelings of a single character.

Vocabulary
etiquette (et′ i kit) *n.* appropriate behavior and ceremonies

deference (def′ ər əns) *n.* respect; courtesy; regard

bridge. The captain stood with folded arms, silent, observing the work of his subordinates, but making no sign. Death is a dignitary who when he comes announced is to be received with formal manifestations of respect, even by those most familiar with him. In the code of military **etiquette** silence and fixity are forms of **deference**.

The man who was engaged in being hanged was apparently about thirty-five years of age. He was a civilian, if one might judge from his habit, which was that of a planter. His features were good—a straight nose, firm mouth, broad forehead, from which his long, dark hair was combed straight back, falling behind his ears to the collar of his well-fitting frock coat. He wore a mustache and pointed beard, but no whiskers; his eyes were large and dark gray, and had a kindly expression which one would hardly have expected in one whose neck was in the hemp. Evidently this was no vulgar assassin. The liberal military code makes provision for hanging many kinds of persons, and gentlemen are not excluded.

The preparations being complete, the two private soldiers stepped aside and each drew away the plank upon which he had been standing. The sergeant turned to the captain, saluted and placed himself immediately behind that officer, who in turn moved apart one pace. These movements left the condemned man and the sergeant standing on the two ends of the same plank, which spanned three of the crossties of the bridge. The end upon which the civilian stood almost, but not quite, reached a fourth. This plank had been held in place by the weight of the captain; it was now held by that of the sergeant. At a signal from the former the latter would step aside, the plank would tilt and the condemned man go down between two ties. The arrangement commended itself to his judgment as simple and effective. His face had not been covered nor his eyes bandaged. He looked a moment at his "unsteadfast footing," then let his gaze wander to the swirling water of the stream racing madly beneath his feet. A piece of dancing driftwood caught his attention and his eyes followed it down the current. How slowly it appeared to move! What a sluggish stream!

He closed his eyes in order to fix his last thoughts upon his wife and children. The water, touched to gold by the early sun, the brooding mists under the banks at some distance down the stream, the fort, the soldiers, the piece of drift—all had distracted him. And now he became conscious of a new disturbance. Striking through the thought of his dear ones was a sound which he could neither ignore nor understand, a sharp, distinct, metallic percussion like the stroke of a blacksmith's hammer upon the anvil; it had the same ringing quality. He wondered what it was, and whether immeasurably distant or near by—it seemed both. Its recurrence was regular, but as slow as the tolling of a death knell. He awaited each stroke with

482 Division, Reconciliation, and Expansion (1850–1914)

Multiple Lens Reading When reading "An Occurence at Owl Creek Bridge," divide your students into three groups. As the text is being read, give each group a different purpose for reading.
- Group 1: Track the author's use of sensory detail. How does this use of detail enrich the story?
- Group 2: Focus on the author's use of point of view (and how it shifts). Be prepared to discuss why he employs different

points of view.
- Group 3: Examine how the author employs time shifts in the story. What effect is achieved through these shifts in time?

After some collaborative time, have each group share their findings with the entire class.

For more of Kelly Gallagher's strategies, see his Professional Development essay , p. 690a.

impatience and—he knew not why—apprehension. The intervals of silence grew progressively longer; the delays became maddening. With their greater infrequency the sounds increased in strength and sharpness. They hurt his ear like the thrust of a knife; he feared he would shriek. What he heard was the ticking of his watch.

He unclosed his eyes and saw again the water below him. "If I could free my hands," he thought, "I might throw off the noose and spring into the stream. By diving I could evade the bullets and, swimming vigorously, reach the bank, take to the woods and get away home. My home, thank God, is as yet outside their lines; my wife and little ones are still beyond the invader's farthest advance."

As these thoughts, which have here to be set down in words, were flashed into the doomed man's brain rather than evolved from it the captain nodded to the sergeant. The sergeant stepped aside.

II

Peyton Farquhar was a well-to-do planter, of an old and highly respected Alabama family. Being a slave owner and like other slave owners a politician he was naturally an original secessionist and ardently devoted to the Southern cause. Circumstances of an imperious nature, which it is unnecessary to relate here, had prevented him from taking service with the gallant army that had fought the disastrous campaigns ending with the fall of Corinth,[2] and he chafed under the inglorious restraint, longing for the release of his energies, the larger life of the soldier, the opportunity for distinction. That opportunity, he felt, would come, as it comes to all in war time. Meanwhile he did what he could. No service was too humble for him to perform in aid of the South, no adventure too perilous for him to undertake if consistent with the character of a civilian who was at heart a soldier, and who in good faith and without too much qualification assented to at least a part of the frankly villainous dictum that all is fair in love and war.

One evening while Farquhar and his wife were sitting on a rustic bench near the entrance to his grounds, a gray-clad soldier rode up to the gate and asked for a drink of water. Mrs. Farquhar was only too happy to serve him with her own white hands. While she was fetching the water her husband approached the dusty horseman and inquired eagerly for news from the front.

"The Yanks are repairing the railroads," said the man, "and are getting ready for another advance. They have reached the Owl Creek bridge, put it in order and built a stockade on the north

---

2. **Corinth** Mississippi town that was the site of an 1862 Civil War battle.

Spiral Review
Characterization
Identify one example of direct and one example of indirect characterization in this paragraph. Explain what you learn about Farquhar from each example.

Vocabulary
dictum (dik ´ təm) n. formal statement of fact or opinion

Reading
Check
In the war that divides his nation, which side does Farquhar support?

An Occurrence at Owl Creek Bridge **483**

❽ Critical Thinking
Make Connections
1. Guide students to notice the man's overly acute senses: A watch's ticking sounds to him like the stroke of a blacksmith's hammer on an anvil. Invite students to explain what this description indicates about Farquhar.
   Answer: Students may say that Farquhar's perceptions are compromised by the trauma he is experiencing.
2. **Ask** students to compare the man's heightened senses with those of other characters they may have encountered.
   Answer: Students may recall Roderick's ability to hear his sister in Poe's "Fall of the House of Usher."

❾ Reading Strategy
Analyzing the Story's Pattern of Organization
1. Read the bracketed sentences for the class. Then help students clarify the action described.
2. Point out that the first sentence contains information about the first "action" (the condemned man's thinking) and the second action (the captain's nod). The third action occurs when the sergeant steps off the plank.
3. Help students visualize the effect of this third action.

Spiral Review
Characterization
Ask students the Spiral Review question.

Sample answer: The author directly states that Farquhar is a well-to-do planter and ardently devoted to the Southern cause. By indicating that no task is too humble or dangerous if it is helpful to the South, the author uses indirect characterization to communicate to readers Farquhar's devotion to the Southern cause. Readers learn that Farquhar is a man of action.

❿ Reading Check
Answer: Farquhar supports the Confederacy.

Differentiated
Instruction   for Universal Access

Strategy for Less Proficient Readers
Suggest that students not give up on the story but rather use self-sticking notes to mark any passages that confuse them. Sustained reading may clarify many ambiguous points. If students remain confused about certain passages, they can return to these pages to ask questions during a class discussion.

Support for Special-Needs Students
Help students understand that the Federal scout plants an idea in Farquhar's mind. The reader is expected to infer that Farquhar then set about to burn the bridge and that the scout reported this possibility to Federal officers. Guide students to understand that Farquhar's capture is the result of the scout's trickery.

Support for Gifted/Talented Students
Students should note that Bierce describes the waters of Owl Creek as "swirling" and "racing" and then as "sluggish." This contradiction hints that things may not be what they seem and that the man's perceptions of the environment and the events taking place may not be altogether reliable.

Analyzing Patterns of Organization

1. Discuss with students how the second section of the story differs from the first section.

2. If necessary, explain that here, for the first time, Bierce provides background information on Peyton Farquhar.

3. **Ask** students: Does the encounter with the "gray-clad soldier" take place before or after the opening scene on the bridge?
   Answer: This scene occurs before the story's opening events. Here the reader learns what generated Farquhar's interest in the bridge and can infer the reason for his execution.

⓬ **Reading Strategy**

Analyzing Patterns of Organization

1. **Ask** a student volunteer to summarize the information Bierce conveys in Section II of the story.

2. Then have students **respond** to the Reading Strategy question.
   Answer: Students may respond that the scene shifts back abruptly to the "present," when Farquhar stands with a noose around his neck in the middle of Owl Creek Bridge and is about to be hanged.

Vocabulary
summarily (sə mer′ ə lē) *adv.* without formality; hastily

Reading Strategy
Analyzing Patterns of Organization
Describe the shift in time that occurs between sections II and III. ⓬

bank. The commandant has issued an order, which is posted everywhere, declaring that any civilian caught interfering with the railroad, its bridges, tunnels or trains will be summarily hanged. I saw the order."

"How far is it to the Owl Creek bridge?" Farquhar asked.

"About thirty miles."

"Is there no force on this side the creek?"

"Only a picket post[3] half a mile out, on the railroad, and a single sentinel at this end of the bridge."

"Suppose a man—a civilian and student of hanging—should elude the picket post and perhaps get the better of the sentinel," said Farquhar, smiling, "what could he accomplish?"

The soldier reflected. "I was there a month ago," he replied. "I observed that the flood of last winter had lodged a great quantity of driftwood against the wooden pier at this end of the bridge. It is now dry and would burn like tow."[4]

The lady had now brought the water, which the soldier drank. He thanked her ceremoniously, bowed to her husband and rode away. An hour later, after nightfall, he repassed the plantation, going northward in the direction from which he had come. He was a Federal scout.

III

As Peyton Farquhar fell straight downward through the bridge he lost consciousness and was as one already dead. From this state he was awakened—ages later, it seemed to him—by the pain of a sharp pressure upon his throat, followed by a sense of suffocation. Keen, poignant agonies seemed to shoot from his neck downward through every fiber of his body and limbs. These pains appeared to flash along well-defined lines of ramification[5] and to beat with an inconceivably rapid periodicity. They seemed like streams of pulsating fire heating him to an intolerable temperature. As to his head, he was conscious of nothing but a feeling of fullness—of congestion. These sensations were unaccompanied by thought. The intellectual part of his nature was already effaced: he had power only to feel, and feeling was torment. He was conscious of motion. Encompassed in a luminous cloud, of which he was now merely the fiery heart, without material substance, he swung through unthinkable arcs of oscillation, like a vast pendulum. Then all at once, with terrible suddenness, the light about him shot upward with the noise of a loud plash; a frightful roaring was in his ears, and all was cold and dark. The power of thought was restored; he knew that the rope had broken and he had fallen into the stream. There was no additional strangulation; the

---

3. **picket post** troops sent ahead with news of a surprise attack.
4. **tow** (tō) *n.* coarse, broken fibers of hemp or flax before spinning.
5. **flash along well-defined lines of ramification** spread out quickly along branches from a central point.

noose about his neck was already suffocating him and kept the water from his lungs. To die of hanging at the bottom of a river!—the idea seemed to him ludicrous. He opened his eyes in the darkness and saw above him a gleam of light, but how distant, how inaccessible! He was still sinking, for the light became fainter and fainter until it was a mere glimmer. Then it began to grow and brighten, and he knew that he was rising toward the surface—knew it with reluctance, for he was now very comfortable. "To be hanged and drowned," he thought, "that is not so bad; but I do not wish to be shot. No; I will not be shot; that is not fair."

He was not conscious of an effort, but a sharp pain in his wrist apprised him that he was trying to free his hands. He gave the struggle his attention, as an idler might observe the feat of a juggler, without interest in the outcome. What splendid effort!—what magnificent, what superhuman strength! Ah, that was a fine endeavor! Bravo! The cord fell away; his arms parted and floated upward, the hands dimly seen on each side in the growing light. He watched them with a new interest as first one and then the other pounced upon the noose at his neck. They tore it away and thrust it fiercely aside, its undulations resembling those of a water-snake. "Put it back, put it back!" He thought he shouted these words to his hands, for the undoing of the noose had been succeeded by the direst pang that he had yet experienced. His neck ached horribly; his brain was on fire; his heart, which had been fluttering faintly, gave a great leap, trying to force itself out at his mouth. His whole body was racked and wrenched with an insupportable anguish! But his disobedient hands gave no heed to the command. They beat the water vigorously with quick, downward strokes, forcing him to the surface. He felt his head emerge; his eyes were blinded by the sunlight; his chest expanded convulsively, and with a supreme and crowning agony his lungs engulfed a great draft of air, which instantly he expelled in a shriek!

He was now in full possession of his physical senses. They were, indeed, preternaturally[6] keen and alert. Something in the awful disturbance of his organic system had so exalted and refined them that they made record of things never before perceived. He felt the ripples upon his face and heard their separate sounds as they struck. He looked at the forest on the bank of the stream, saw the individual trees, the leaves and the veining of each leaf—saw the very insects upon them: the locusts, the brilliant-bodied flies, the gray spiders

---

6. **preternaturally** (prēt′ ər nach′ ər əl ē) *adv.* abnormally; extraordinarily.

13
LITERATURE IN CONTEXT

History Connection

The Battle of Shiloh
Owl Creek is the stream that runs through Tennessee at the site of one of the bloodiest battles of the Civil War—the Battle of Shiloh—where more than 20,000 soldiers died. Railroad bridges like Owl Creek Bridge were important because they gave the armies access over bodies of water.

Connect to the Literature

Why does Farquhar ask so many questions about the bridge?

Vocabulary
apprised (ə prizd′) *v.* informed; notified

14
Reading Check
What surprising event happens after Farquhar first loses consciousness?

13 Literature in Context
History Connection
In early April 1862, Union troops were headed toward Corinth—an Alabama town that was strategically important because two key railroads crossed at that point. On their journey, the soldiers collided with Confederate troops at Shiloh. Soon after the Battle of Shiloh, a Union army occupied and then defended Corinth. The troops held the town until it was no longer strategically important.

Connect to the Literature
Encourage students to find information in the story about Farquhar's situation that supports their answers.
Possible response: Farquhar wants to help the Confederate cause and is trying to determine whether he can sabotage the bridge. This view is supported by the fact that he is a well-to-do Southern planter, and it is in his interest to support the Confederate cause.

14 Reading Check
Answer: The rope apparently breaks, and he falls into the water.

Differentiated Instruction for Universal Access

EL Vocabulary for English Learners
The term "report" is one of several examples in this story of a familiar word used in an unfamiliar way. "Habit," "smartly," "sleepers," and "bank" are others. Guide students to use context clues or to consult a dictionary to ascertain the meanings of these words as Bierce uses them.

Enrichment for Advanced Readers
Students may enjoy reading or rereading Edgar Allan Poe's short story "The Tell-Tale Heart" to appreciate another striking example of a character who is "preternaturally keen and alert." As his mental condition deteriorates, the narrator of Poe's famous story hears "all things in heaven and hell." Invite students to compare and contrast the reasons for these heightened senses in the characters.

⑮ ? Engaging the Essential Question

⑮ Engaging the Essential Question

1. Read the bracketed text aloud. Point out to students that as Farquhar surfaces, the world he sees is not only completely unexpected—he had thought he was about to die—but also fraught with danger. The narrator makes a point of describing these dangers objectively but also helps us see them from Farquhar's perspective.

2. **Ask** students to identify the objective descriptions of danger and Farquhar's subjective view of what he sees.
   Answer: Objectively, the narrator says that the soldiers on the bridge are pointing at Farquhar and shouting and that one has drawn his pistol. To Farquhar they appear "grotesque," "horrible," and "gigantic."

3. Point out that the story takes place in Farquhar's home region. **Ask** students: What do you make of Farquhar's perceptions of things near his home as "grotesque," "horrible," and "gigantic"?
   Possible response: Farquhar can no longer think of his home region as a haven; it has become hostile territory.

4. Tell students to look as they read for other descriptions of place from Farquhar's perspective rather than from an objective perspective.

⑯ Critical Viewing

Possible response: The illustrations show the Federal soldiers on the bridge watching as Farquhar, on the facing page, falls from the bridge after the rope breaks. The soldier on the left appears to be calling for help or perhaps reaching for his weapon.

⑯ ▲ Critical Viewing
Explain the connection between the illustrations on this and the facing page and their relationship to the story. **[Connect]**

⑮ stretching their webs from twig to twig. He noted the prismatic colors in all the dewdrops upon a million blades of grass. The humming of the gnats that danced above the eddies of the stream, the beating of the dragonflies' wings, the strokes of the water spiders' legs, like oars which had lifted their boat—all these made audible music. A fish slid along beneath his eyes and he heard the rush of its body parting the water.

He had come to the surface facing down the stream; in a moment the visible world seemed to wheel slowly round, himself the pivotal point, and he saw the bridge, the fort, the soldiers upon the bridge, the captain, the sergeant, the two privates, his executioners. They were in silhouette against the blue sky. They shouted and gesticulated, pointing at him. The captain had drawn his pistol, but did not fire; the others were unarmed. Their movements were grotesque and horrible, their forms gigantic.

Suddenly he heard a sharp report and something struck the water smartly within a few inches of his head, spattering his face with spray. He heard a second report, and saw one of the sentinels with his rifle at his shoulder, a light cloud of blue smoke rising from the muzzle. The man in the water saw the eye of the man on the bridge gazing into his own through the sights of the rifle. He observed that it was a gray eye and remembered having read that gray eyes were keenest, and that all famous marksmen had them. Nevertheless, this one had missed.

A counterswirl had caught Farquhar and turned him half round; he was again looking into the forest on the bank opposite the fort. The sound of a clear, high voice in a monotonous singsong now rang out behind him and came across the water with a distinctness that pierced and subdued all other sounds, even the beating of the ripples in his ears. Although no soldier, he had frequented camps enough to know the dread significance of that deliberate, drawling, aspirated

---

Enrichment: Investigating Career Connections

Engineers
During the Civil War, armies regularly destroyed bridges and railroad tracks to deter the enemy. Civil engineers put these structures together again.
Activity: Career Day Have students find out more about the work engineers do. Start them off with the following distinctions:
- Civil engineers focus on municipal projects such as highways.
- Mechanical engineers plan the design of engines and machinery, such as elevators.

- Electrical engineers design power and lighting systems.
- Aeronautical engineers design aircraft, helicopters, and spacecraft.

Suggest that students record information in the **Enrichment: Investigating Career Connections** work sheet, in *Professional Development Guidebook*, page 221. Have students make brief "career day" presentations to the class.

chant; the lieutenant on shore was taking a part in the morning's work. How coldly and pitilessly—with what an even, calm intonation, presaging,[7] and enforcing tranquillity in the men—with what accurately measured intervals fell those cruel words:

"Attention, company! . . . Shoulder arms! . . . Ready! . . . Aim! . . . Fire!"

Farquhar dived—dived as deeply as he could. The water roared in his ears like the voice of Niagara, yet he heard the dulled thunder of the volley and, rising again toward the surface, met shining bits of metal, singularly flattened, oscillating slowly downward. Some of them touched him on the face and hands, then fell away, continuing their descent. One lodged between his collar and neck; it was uncomfortably warm and he snatched it out.

As he rose to the surface, gasping for breath, he saw that he had been a long time under water; he was perceptibly farther down stream—nearer to safety. The soldiers had almost finished reloading; the metal ramrods flashed all at once in the sunshine as they were drawn from the barrels, turned in the air, and thrust into their sockets. The two sentinels fired again, independently and ineffectually.

The hunted man saw all this over his shoulder; he was now swimming vigorously with the current. His brain was as energetic as his arms and legs; he thought with the rapidity of lightning.

"The officer," he reasoned, "will not make that martinet's[8] error a second time. It is as easy to dodge a volley as a single shot. He has probably already given the command to fire at will. God help me, I cannot dodge them all!"

An appalling plash within two yards of him was followed by a loud, rushing sound, *diminuendo*,[9] which seemed to travel back through the air to the fort and died in an explosion which stirred the very river to its deeps! A rising sheet of water curved over him, fell down upon him, blinded him, strangled him! The cannon had taken a hand in the game. As he shook his head free from the commotion of the smitten water he heard the deflected shot humming through the air ahead, and in an instant it was cracking and smashing the branches in the forest beyond.

"They will not do that again," he thought; "the next time they

---

7. **presaging** (prē sāj´ iŋ) *v.* predicting; warning.
8. **martinet** (märt´ 'n et´) *n.* strict military disciplinarian.
9. **diminuendo** (də min´ yoo en´ dō) *adj.* musical term used to describe a gradual reduction in volume.

An Occurrence at Owl Creek Bridge **487**

Reading Check ☑
How do the soldiers try to stop Farquhar after he dives?

20

Literary Analysis

Point of View and Stream of Consciousness

1. Read aloud the bracketed text beginning on page 487.

2. **Ask:** What is the narrator describing, and what point of view does this passage use?

   Answer: The narrator is describing Farquhar's perceptions of and reactions to various physical phenomena. He is using a limited third-person point of view in this passage.

3. Instruct students to evaluate the reliability of the text as you read the bracketed section again. Then **ask** students the Literary Analysis question.

   Answer: Students may note details such as the narrator's use of exclamation points and presentation of patently absurd information ("heard the deflected shot humming through the air ahead, and in an instant it was cracking and smashing . . . in the forest beyond").

21 Critical Thinking

Interpret

1. Draw students' attention to language in the bracketed text that indicates the foreignness of Farquhar's surroundings. Invite students to speculate about why everything seems so unfamiliar to him even though he is not far from home.

2. Have students identify examples of sensory details that convey the idea that Farquhar's flight is marked by strangeness.

   Possible responses: Touch: throwing sand; Sight: trees as giant garden plants; Smell: fragrance of blooms; Sound: wind like harps

3. **Ask** students to explain what these details may indicate (or have them refer back to this passage after they have finished reading).

   Answer: Students may say that Farquhar's journey is more dreamlike than real. That quality is suggested by the fact that the surroundings seem unfamiliar, the journey seems endless, and the path seems untraveled.

488

20

Literary Analysis
Point of View and Stream of Consciousness
What clues suggest Farquhar may not be totally reliable as a witness?

> Suddenly he felt himself whirled round and round—spinning like a top. **21**

---

will use a charge of grape.[10] I must keep my eye upon the gun; the smoke will apprise me—the report arrives too late; it lags behind the missile. That is a good gun."

Suddenly he felt himself whirled round and round—spinning like a top. The water, the banks, the forests, the now distant bridge, fort and men—all were commingled and blurred. Objects were represented by their colors only; circular horizontal streaks of color—that was all he saw. He had been caught in a vortex and was being whirled on with a velocity of advance and gyration that made him giddy and sick. In a few moments he was flung upon the gravel at the foot of the left bank of the stream—the southern bank—and behind a projecting point which concealed him from his enemies. The sudden arrest of his motion, the abrasion of one of his hands on the gravel, restored him, and he wept with delight. He dug his fingers into the sand, threw it over himself in handfuls and audibly blessed it. It looked like diamonds, rubies, emeralds; he could think of nothing beautiful which it did not resemble. The trees upon the bank were giant garden plants; he noted a definite order in their arrangement, inhaled the fragrance of their blooms. A strange, roseate[11] light shone through the spaces among their trunks and the wind made in their branches the music of aeolian harps.[12] He had no wish to perfect his escape—was content to remain in that enchanting spot until retaken.

A whiz and rattle of grapeshot among the branches high above his head roused him from his dream. The baffled cannoneer had fired him a random farewell. He sprang to his feet, rushed up the sloping bank, and plunged into the forest.

All that day he traveled, laying his course by the rounding sun. The forest seemed interminable; nowhere did he discover a break in it, not even a woodman's road. He had not known that he lived in so wild a region. There was something uncanny in the revelation.

By night fall he was fatigued, footsore, famishing. The thought of his wife and children urged him on. At last he found a road which led him in what he knew to be the right direction. It was as wide and straight as a city street, yet it seemed untraveled. No fields bordered it, no dwelling anywhere. Not so much as the barking of a dog suggested human habitation. The black bodies of the trees formed a straight wall on both sides, terminating on the horizon in a point, like a diagram in a lesson in perspective. Overhead, as he looked up through this rift in the wood, shone great golden stars looking unfamiliar and grouped in strange constellations. He was sure they were arranged in some order which had a secret and malign significance. The wood on either side was full of singular noises, among which—once, twice, and again, he distinctly heard whispers in an unknown tongue.

10. **charge of grape** cluster of small iron balls—"grape shot"—that disperse once fired from a cannon.
11. **roseate** (rō′ zē it) *adj.* rose-colored.
12. **aeolian** (ē ō′ lē ǝwn) **harps** stringed instruments that produce music when played by the wind. In Greek mythology, Aeolus is the god of the winds.

488 Division, Reconciliation, and Expansion (1850–1914)

Vocabulary Development

Vocabulary Knowledge Rating

When students have completed reading and discussing the selection, have them take out their **Vocabulary Knowledge Rating Charts** for the story. Read the words aloud, and have students rate their knowledge of words again in the After Reading column. Clarify any words that are still problematic. Have students write their own definitions and example or sentence in the appropriate column. Then have students complete the Vocabulary Lesson at the end of the selection. Encourage students to use the words in further discussion and written work about the selection. Remind them that they will be accountable for these words on the **Selection Test,** *Unit 3 Resources,* pages 19–21 or 22–24.

His neck was in pain and lifting his hand to it he found it horribly swollen. He knew that it had a circle of black where the rope had bruised it. His eyes felt congested: he could no longer close them. His tongue was swollen with thirst; he relieved its fever by thrusting it forward from between his teeth into the cold air. How softly the turf had carpeted the untraveled avenue—he could no longer feel the roadway beneath his feet!

Doubtless, despite his suffering, he had fallen asleep while walking, for now he sees another scene—perhaps he has merely recovered from a delirium. He stands at the gate of his own home. All is as he left it, and all bright and beautiful in the morning sunshine. He must have traveled the entire night. As he pushes open the gate and passes up the wide white walk, he sees a flutter of female garments: his wife, looking fresh and cool and sweet, steps down from the veranda to meet him. At the bottom of the steps she stands waiting, with a smile of ineffable joy, an attitude of matchless grace and dignity. Ah, how beautiful she is! He springs forward with extended arms. As he is about to clasp her he feels a stunning blow upon the back of the neck; a blinding white light blazes all about him with a sound like the shock of a cannon—then all is darkness and silence!

Peyton Farquhar was dead; his body, with a broken neck, swung gently from side to side beneath the timbers of the Owl Creek bridge.

Vocabulary
ineffable (in ef´ ə bəl) *adj.*
too overwhelming to be spoken

Critical Reading

Ⓒ Cite textual evidence to support your responses.

Ⓒ 1. **Key Ideas and Details (a)** Identify one example of Farquhar's distorted perceptions. **(b) Interpret:** What causes this distortion?

Ⓒ 2. **Key Ideas and Details (a)** What does Farquhar visualize moments before he is hanged? **(b) Connect:** How is his journey connected with this earlier vision?

Ⓒ 3. **Craft and Structure (a)** What sensation does Farquhar experience "with terrible suddenness"? **(b) Distinguish:** Which details suggest that Farquhar's escape occurs in his mind?

Ⓒ 4. **Key Ideas and Details (a)** What does this story suggest about the psychology of a person facing a life or death situation? **(b) Speculate:** Are such insights applicable in daily life, or merely in extreme circumstances, like those of war? Explain.

Ⓒ 5. **Integration of Knowledge and Ideas** How does the contrast between the ordinary settings and the awful events of this story add to its power? Explain. In your response, use at least two of these Essential Question words: *heighten, conflict, tension, perspective.* *[Connecting to the Essential Question: What is the relationship between literature and place?]*

An Occurrence at Owl Creek Bridge **489**

Concept Connector

Reading Strategy Graphic Organizer
Ask students to review the graphic organizers in which they have kept track of the story's time frame and events. Then have students share their organizers and compare conclusions about the work's pattern of organization.

Activating Prior Knowledge
Have students return to their responses to the Activating Prior Knowledge activity. Ask them to explain whether their thoughts have changed and if so, how.

Writing About the Essential Question
Have students compare the responses to the prompt before they completed reading with their thoughts afterward. Have them work individually or in groups, writing or discussing their thoughts, to formulate their new responses. Then lead a class discussion, probing for what students have learned that confirms or invalidates their initial thoughts. Encourage students to cite specific textural details to support their responses.

Answers

490

After You Read
An Occurrence at Owl Creek Bridge

Literary Analysis

1. **Craft and Structure** Reread the story to find examples of the two different **points of view** Bierce uses. Then, using a chart like the one shown, analyze the effects of these choices.

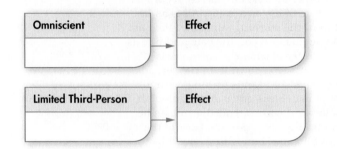

2. **Craft and Structure (a)** What point of view does Bierce use in Section III? **(b)** Explain why this choice of point of view is essential to the story's overall impact.

3. **Craft and Structure** What is the effect of the shift in point of view in the last paragraph of the story? Explain.

4. **Craft and Structure (a)** Which details in the second paragraph of Section III are revealed through the use of **stream of consciousness? (b)** What is the "sharp pain" that sparks Farquhar's thoughts? **(c)** In what ways does this passage mimic the natural, jumbled flow of thought?

5. **Craft and Structure** Why is the stream-of-consciousness technique particularly appropriate for this story?

Reading Strategy

6. Clarify meaning by **analyzing the story's pattern of organization. (a)** Explain how the time frame of the story shifts from Section I to Section II and from Section II to Section III. **(b)** How does the style of writing shift from section to section?

7. **(a)** What do you learn in Section II about the main character's home life, political loyalties, and motivations? **(b)** How does this detailed information shed light on the scene described in Section I? Explain.

8. At the end of the story, what do you suddenly understand about both the scene described in Section I and the incident described in Section II?

9. How important do you think the structure of this story is to its overall power and effect on the reader? Explain, citing specific story details in your response.

Common Core State Standards

Writing
2. Write explanatory texts to examine and convey complex ideas, concepts, and information clearly and accurately through the effective selection, organization, and analysis of content. *(p. 491)*
2.b. Develop the topic thoroughly by selecting the most significant quotations or other information and examples appropriate to the audience's knowledge of the topic. *(p. 491)*
9.a. Apply *grades 11–12 Reading* standards to literature. *(p. 491)*

Language
3. Apply knowledge of language to make effective choices for meaning. *(p. 491)*

Assessment Practice

Context (For more practice, see *All-in-One Workbook*.)

Use the following sample item to teach students how to use context clues to determine the meanings of specialized terms.

> The two private soldiers stepped aside and each drew away the plank upon which he had been standing. The sergeant turned to the captain, saluted and placed himself immediately behind that officer.

Which answer lists the soldiers in order from lowest to highest in rank?
  A captain, sergeant, private
  B sergeant, private, captain
  C private, sergeant, captain
  D private, captain, sergeant

The privates perform duties, the sergeant salutes the captain, and the captain is an officer. The correct answer is **C.**

Integrated Language Skills

Vocabulary Acquisition and Use

Word Analysis: Latin Root -dict-

The noun *dictum* derives from the Latin root *-dict-*, meaning "saying; expression; word." Words that share this root include *verdict* and *dictionary*. Decide whether each of the following statements is true or false and explain each answer. In your explanation, demonstrate your understanding of the meaning of the root *-dict-* in words with different meanings and parts of speech.

1. If two arguments are nearly identical, there is a *contradiction* of terms.
2. An *unpredictable* disaster is one that cannot be avoided.
3. A governmental *edict* is usually written in a formal style.
4. A school board often has *jurisdiction* to establish regulations relating to school safety.
5. Writers who prefer not to type might *dictate* their stories for someone to transcribe.
6. Radio announcers do not need clear *diction* in order to do their jobs well.

Vocabulary: Revising Sentences for Logic

Revise each sentence below so that the underlined vocabulary word is used logically and effectively. Do not change the word.

Example: His <u>preparation</u> for the exam gave him a feeling of apprehension.

Corrected Sentence: His lack of preparation for the exam gave him a feeling of apprehension.

1. He followed proper <u>etiquette</u> and offended nearly everyone in attendance.
2. The judge acted so <u>summarily</u> that we were certain her decision was just.
3. A <u>dictum</u> is likely to use slang or dialect in order to keep an informal tone.
4. In <u>deference</u> to the elders' frailty, we asked them to walk to the reunion.
5. The moment had an <u>ineffable</u> quality that was perfectly described by the soldier.
6. The reporter had not been <u>apprised</u> of the breaking news, so she scooped the story.

Writing

Explanatory Text Bierce was among the first writers to use stream of consciousness, a *stylistic device* that imitates the natural flow of thoughts and feelings. In an **essay,** explain how Bierce's use of this technique adds to the story's drama.

Prewriting Reread the story and generate a list of selected passages in which the use of stream of consciousness helps you understand Farquhar's thoughts and feelings. Then, select the two or three most significant passages to discuss.

Drafting Focus on one passage at a time. Explain why the use of stream-of-consciousness narration reveals the character's thoughts with heightened realism and drama.

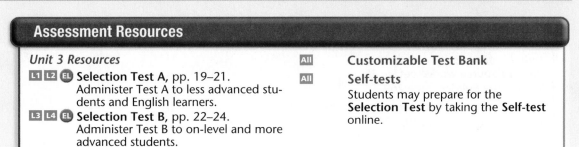

Model: Incorporating Quotations From the Story
Through stream of consciousness, Bierce enables readers to empathize with Farquhar as he desperately imagines a struggle to save his life. The moment of full peace when he reunites with his wife is especially powerful. In his own words, Farquhar thinks he "must have traveled the entire night."

Appropriate quotations from the story create strong connections between the writer's opinions and the text.

Revising As you review your draft, note points where quotations from the story will help support your opinions and analysis. To assure effective organization, make strong connections between your opinions and each passage you are quoting.

Integrated Language Skills **491**

Assessment Resources

Unit 3 Resources

L1 L2 EL Selection Test A, pp. 19–21. Administer Test A to less advanced students and English learners.

L3 L4 EL Selection Test B, pp. 22–24. Administer Test B to on-level and more advanced students.

L3 L4 Open-Book Test, pages 16–18. As an alternative, give the Open-Book Test.

All **Customizable Test Bank**

All **Self-tests**
Students may prepare for the **Selection Test** by taking the **Self-test** online.

All assessment resources are available at **www.PHLitOnline.com.**

Vocabulary Acquisition and Use

1. Introduce the skill, using the instruction on the student page.
2. Have students complete the Word Analysis activity and the Vocabulary practice.

Word Analysis

1. False. A contradiction expresses an idea that is not compatible with another idea.
2. True. A disaster that is unpredictable cannot be discussed or prepared for.
3. True. An edict expresses official ideas.
4. True. The school board articulates the rules.
5. True. Writers would speak their words aloud for transcription.
6. False. Speaking clearly is a key factor for success in radio.

Vocabulary

1. He did not follow proper <u>etiquette</u>, so he offended everyone in attendance.
2. The judge acted so <u>summarily</u> that we were not certain her decision was just.
3. In order to keep a formal tone, a <u>dictum</u> is unlikely to use slang or dialect.
4. In <u>deference</u> to the elders' frailty, we drove them to the reunion.
5. The moment had an <u>ineffable</u> quality that could not be described by the soldier.
6. The reporter had not been <u>apprised</u> of the breaking news, so she missed the story.

Writing

1. To guide students in writing this essay, give them the **Support for Writing** worksheet (*Unit 3 Resources,* p. 14).
2. Encourage students to scour the story for passages that show how the use of stream of consciousness captures Peyton Farquhar's experience better than a conventional narrative approach would.
3. Use the **Rubrics for Critiques,** in *Professional Development Guidebook,* pages 276–277, to evaluate students' work.

491

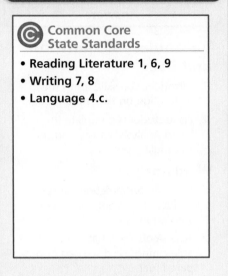

Common Core State Standards

- Reading Literature 1, 6, 9
- Writing 7, 8
- Language 4.c.

❶ About the Forms

Introduce the forms, using the instruction on the student page.

Think Aloud: Model the Skill

Say to students:

A sure-fire way to identify a diary or journal is to look for interspersed dates. I see three examples of dates in the work that begins on page 495. I see that each piece is told in the first person, and each writer admits defeat or naïveté. That personal admission makes me think that each piece is from a diary or journal.

❷ Reading Strategy

Introduce the skill, using the instruction on the student page.

Think Aloud: Model the Skill

Say to students:

As an active reader of diaries and journals, I can ask questions about not only what the writer reveals but also what he or she conceals. So when Chesnut writes, "Lincoln or Seward has made such silly advances," I can ask, "What was so silly about the advances?"

❸ ❓ What is the relationship between literature and place?

As students read, tell them to look for details that will help them answer the Essential Question.

 WRITING COACH | Grade 11

Students will find additional information on research writing in Chapter 11.

492

Primary Sources

Civil War Diaries and Journals

| Mary Chesnut's Civil War | A Confederate Account of the Battle of Gettysburg | Recollections of a Private |

❶ About the Text Forms

Diaries and **journals** are personal records of events, thoughts, feelings, and observations. These texts are written informally in a series of dated entries, express the writer's immediate responses to events, and use the first-person pronouns *I* and *we*.

Diaries and journals tell us a great deal about each writer's beliefs, political leanings, values, and experience of life. While most remain unpublished, some that are especially powerful or shed light on historical events, such as these Civil War writings, may be published after the writer's death.

❷ Reading Strategy

Generating questions, or asking questions about a text as you read, can help you focus your reading and better understand the *authors' purposes and perspectives* in historical documents. As you read these diaries and journals, pose questions such as the following:

- *What main purpose prompts the writer to record these experiences?*
- *What does the writer's use of language suggest about his or her position in life?*
- *What does the writer feel or believe about the Civil War? Why? Does the writer express a thematic insight about war in general? If so, how does it relate to those expressed in similar texts?*
- *Does the writer state opinions, feelings, and beliefs directly or implicitly through observation and descriptions?*
- *What clues suggest an opinion or belief is being stated?*

As you read, generate questions to help you better understand each author's position on the Civil War and other aspects of life during that era.

❸ ❓ What is the **relationship** between literature and *place?*

The Civil War was fought on American soil and in American waters. Reading these diary and journal entries will help you see how the war caused people to view their own towns, hillsides, and harbors differently. As you read, note details that describe various locations as being unfamiliar, comforting, strange, or frightening.

492 Division, Reconciliation, and Expansion (1850–1914)

 **Common Core State Standards**

Reading Informational Text

1. Cite strong and thorough textual evidence to support analysis of what the text says explicitly as well as inferences drawn from the text, including determining where the text leaves matters uncertain.

6. Determine an author's point of view or purpose in a text.

9. Analyze nineteenth-century foundational U.S. documents of historical and literary significance for their themes, purposes, and rhetorical features.

Teaching Resources

Unit 3 Resources
Primary Source worksheet, p. 25
Vocabulary Builder, page 26

Professional Development Guidebook
Enrichment, pp. 224, 230, 236

All resources are available at
www.PHLitOnline.com.

④ Note-Taking Guide

Primary-source documents are a rich source of information for researchers. As you read these documents, use a note-taking guide like the one shown to organize relevant and accurate information.

1 Type of Document (check one)
☐ Newspaper   ☐ Advertisement   ☐ Telegram   ☐ Letter
☐ Press Release   ☐ Diary or Journal   ☐ E-mail   ☐ Report

2 Date(s) of Document _____

3 Author of Document _____
Author's Position, Title, or Circumstances _____

4 Purpose and Audience: Why and for whom was the document written?_____
_____

5 Document Information

　a List two observations or pieces of information given near the beginning of the document that strike you as important. _____
_____

　b Ask a question about each piece of information. _____
_____
_____

　c Identify answers. _____
_____

　d If answers are not clear, explain how you might find them. _____
_____
_____

Reading Strategy
Generating Questions
A primary source document may raise questions in your mind about a historical event. Pay attention to these questions and use them to focus your reading.

This guide was adapted from the **U.S. National Archives** Document Analysis Worksheets.

⑤ Vocabulary

adjourned (ə jʉrnd´) *v.* closed for a time (p. 495)

convention (kən ven´ shən) *n.* a meeting attended by members or delegates (p. 495)

intercepted (in´ tər sept´ əd) *v.* seized or stopped something on its way from one place to another (p. 496)

obstinate (äb´ stə nət) *adj.* stubborn (p. 497)

recruits (ri kro͞ots´) *n.* newly drafted soldiers (p. 500)

fluctuation (fluk´ cho͞o ā´ shən) *n.* a change in level or intensity (p. 500)

spectator (spek´ tāt´ ər) *n.* a person who watches something without taking part in it (p. 501)

offensive (ô´ fen´ siv) *n.* an attitude or position of attack (p. 502)

brigade (bri gād´) *n.* a unit of soldiers (p. 502)

entrenchments (en trench´ mənts) *n.* long, deep holes with steep sides, used as defense against enemy fire (p. 503)

Primary Sources: Diaries and Journals **493**

④ Note-Taking Guide

1. As a class, review the instruction on the student page about the note-taking guide.

2. Emphasize question 5b on the guide by having a student read the Reading Strategy note in the margin of the student page.

3. Encourage students to use a similar guide as they read the primary sources in this set. Point out that they may customize their note-taking guides to fit the particular needs of the reading assignment.

⑤ Vocabulary

1. Have students preview the vocabulary for these selections, pronouncing the words and reading their definitions. Have students identify any words with which they are already familiar.

2. Use each word in a sentence with sufficient context to define the word. Then repeat your definitional sentence or a similar sentence with the vocabulary word missing, requiring the class to "fill in the blank" orally. Here is an example:

   As many as five thousand English teachers meet once a year for workshops and exhibits at a national <u>convention</u>.

   If not before, the presidential nominee of each U.S. political party is chosen the summer before the election at a _____.

6 Background

The Story Behind the Documents

Mary Chesnut's circle of friends included Jefferson Davis and others in the highest ranks of the Confederacy. Chesnut started keeping a diary as the tension mounted in Charleston.

Along with several generals and other officers, Warren Lee Goss was one of 230 contributors to *Battles and Leaders of the Civil War,* a four-volume compilation of essays published in the 1880s. His writing also appeared in the 1880s in *The Century Illustrated Monthly Magazine.*

Later in the war, Randolph McKim became the chaplain for a Virginia cavalry regiment. In 1910, years after the war, McKim published his diaries as *A Soldier's Recollections.*

6 THE STORY BEHIND THE DOCUMENTS

Mary Chesnut

Randolph McKim

In the early days of April 1861, the nation held its collective breath. South Carolina and six other Southern states had recently seceded, or split away; formed their own government; and elected Jefferson Davis as the president of their new Confederacy. Meanwhile, Abraham Lincoln had been inaugurated as president of the United States. When he refused to acknowledge the Confederacy as a separate entity, an armed conflict between the two regions seemed inevitable.

The drama was centered on a massive fort that stood in the harbor of Charleston, South Carolina. Since December 26, 1860, Fort Sumter had housed 85 unwelcome Union soldiers and their commander. In spite of stern warnings from the Confederate army, the Union troops refused to budge. Meanwhile, their food supplies began to dwindle.

It was an uneasy stalemate: neither the North nor the South wanted to fire the first shot. On April 6, President Lincoln ordered supplies sent to Fort Sumter. The gesture was seen as a threat. Southern leaders decided to attack the fort before the shipment arrived.

As the attack began at 4:30 A.M. on April 12, 1861, citizens of Charleston clambered to their rooftops to watch the action. **Mary Boykin Chesnut** (1823–1886) was one of these spectators. Raised in a wealthy aristocratic family, Boykin married James Chesnut, Jr., a senator and a Confederate officer. While her diary provides a detailed account of the events at Fort Sumter, it also conveys the mixture of optimism and dread felt by most Southern aristocrats during the opening days of the war.

Once the war was underway, men hurried to enlist in what most believed would be a swift and glorious conflict. Some saw the military as an opportunity for adventure and advancement, as we learn from the journal of Union soldier **Warren Lee Goss.** Like Goss, most soldiers were young—21 on average—and had no military experience. These naive young men quickly learned that war meant misery, not glory.

Perhaps no other Civil War battle was as painful as the Battle of Gettysburg, in which 51,000 men were either wounded or killed. From July 1 to July 3, 1863, Union and Confederate troops fought near the small town of Gettysburg, Pennsylvania. After Union troops gained control of the nearby hills, the Confederate troops launched a risky attack on the strongest Union position. The attack—described as both "gallant" and "terrible" in the diary of Confederate soldier **Randolph McKim**—was a bitter failure.

Although Chesnut, Goss, and McKim experienced the Civil War in different ways, their diaries and journals reveal profound similarities. They all try to make sense of a fearful unknown, and to contribute, in some way, to the safety and well-being of their loved ones, their companions, and the country and ideals they cherish.

Fort Sumter

South Carolina had seceded from the Union on December 20, 1860, and demanded federal property within the state, including Fort Sumter, a fortification on an island in Charleston Harbor. In April 1861, after 34 hours of attack on the fort, the Union surrendered it to the Confederates.

Activity: Comparing Primary and Secondary Sources Chesnut's account gives us a "you are there" perspective of life in Charleston during the attack on and surrender of the fort. Have

students conduct research on historians' analyses of the meaning of the event in the history of the country. Suggest that they record information in the **Enrichment: Analyzing a Historical Event** work sheet, in *Professional Development Guidebook,* page 230. Students should discuss what the historians offer that Chesnut could not and vice versa.

from Mary Chesnut's
CIVIL WAR
Mary Chesnut

❶ BACKGROUND *As Mary Chesnut notes in the first diary entry below, plans for an attack on Fort Sumter have been made, and the citizens of Charleston wait with both excitement and anxiety for something—or nothing—to happen.*

⬥

APRIL 7, 1861. Today things seem to have settled down a little.

One can but hope still. Lincoln or Seward[1] have made such silly advances and then far sillier drawings back. There may be a chance for peace, after all.

Things are happening so fast.

My husband has been made an aide-de-camp[2] of General Beauregard.

Three hours ago we were quietly packing to go home. The convention has adjourned.

Now he tells me the attack upon Fort Sumter[3] may begin tonight. Depends upon Anderson and the fleet outside. The *Herald* says that this show of war outside of the bar is intended for Texas.

John Manning came in with his sword and red sash. Pleased as a boy to be on Beauregard's staff while the row goes on. He has gone with Wigfall to Captain Hartstene with instructions.

Mr. Chesnut is finishing a report he had to make to the convention.

Mrs. Hayne called. She had, she said, "but one feeling, pity for those who are not here."

Jack Preston, Willie Alston—"the take-life-easys," as they are called—with John Green, "the big brave," have gone down to the island—volunteered as privates.

Seven hundred men were sent over. Ammunition wagons rumbling along the streets all night. Anderson burning blue lights—signs and signals for the fleet outside, I suppose.

---

1. **Seward** William Henry Seward (1801–1872), U.S. Secretary of State from 1861 through 1869.
2. **aide-de-camp** (ād' də kamp') *n.* officer serving as assistant and confidential secretary to a superior.
3. **Fort Sumter** fort in Charleston Harbor, South Carolina. At the time, the fort was occupied by Union troops commanded by Major Robert Anderson.

Primary Sources
Diaries and Journals What details of style and form tell you that you are reading a diary or journal entry?

Vocabulary
adjourned (ə jurnd')
v. closed for a time

convention (kən ven' shən)
n. a meeting attended by members or delegates

❸ ☑ **Reading Check**
What event might happen on the night of April 7, 1861?

---

❶ **Background**
History
After the war, friends encouraged Chesnut to publish the forty-eight volumes of diary she had amassed, and she spent four years preparing them but died before completing the project. In the years since her death in 1886, at least three versions of her edited diary have appeared.

❷ **Primary Sources**
Diaries and Journals
After reading the bracketed passage, **ask** the Primary Sources question: What details of style and form tell you that you are reading a diary or journal entry?
Answer: The date at the beginning of the passage, the first-person point of view, and the informal paragraphing indicate that this is a diary or journal entry.

❸ **Reading Check**
Answer: Confederate troops may attack Fort Sumter, held by Union forces.

Differentiated Instruction
for Universal Access

**Strategy for
Less Proficient Readers**
To help less proficient students through these diary and journal entries, suggest that more proficient partners paraphrase complex passages for them. Have the partners focus on passages filled with terminology peculiar to the Civil War era or on passages that contain military terms.

**Enrichment for
Gifted/Talented Students**
Explain to students that while we see Chesnut at home only as an observer, some women from both the North and the South single-handedly ran family businesses, farms, and plantations while husbands and sons were at war or worked in factories, hospitals, and in relief efforts. Suggest that students research the humanitarian work of Dorothea Dix and Clara Barton or look into the espionage work of Belle Boyd, Elizabeth Van Lew, or Rose Greenhow.

❹ Humanities

Bombardment of Fort Sumter, 1861
This wood engraving was done by an unknown artist for the May 4, 1861, edition of *Harper's Weekly.* Correspondents and artists were dispatched by the magazine to war zones in order to provide a steady flow of reportage. Although photography had recently been invented, there was as yet no method for reproducing photographs in printed matter. On-the-scene drawings were the means by which events of the war were visually recorded for the public. These drawings were sent to the publication, where a skilled artisan engraved the image into a block of wood that was then inked and pressed onto paper. Use these questions for discussion.

1. What details correspond to those in Chesnut's account?
   Possible response: Chesnut describes the women as "wild" as they watched from the rooftops.

2. Do you think a photograph of the same scene would have been more or less effective than the engraving? Why?
   Possible response: Students may note that a photograph captures only a single moment, whereas an artist may combine two or more moments into one drawing.

❺ Primary Source: Art

Answer: Most of the women seem upset and appear to be comforting one another as they watch the shelling.

❻ Primary Sources

Diaries and Journals

1. Read the bracketed passage to the class.

2. **Ask** the Primary Sources question: Judging from her list of dinner guests, what do you understand about Mary Chesnut's social circumstances?
   Answer: Chesnut moves in an elite social circle. She counts a judge and governors among her acquaintances.

Bombardment of Sumter, Harper's Weekly, 1861

❺ ▶ **Primary Source: Art**
Describe the spectators' differing reactions to the attack on Fort Sumter as shown in this illustration. **[Distinguish]**

Primary Sources
Diaries and Journals
Judging from her list of dinner guests, what do you understand about Mary Chesnut's social circumstances?

Vocabulary
intercepted (in′ tər sept′ əd) *v.* seized or stopped something on its way from one place to another

Today at dinner there was no allusion to things as they stand in Charleston Harbor. There was an undercurrent of intense excitement. There could not have been a more brilliant circle. In addition to our usual quartet (Judge Withers, Langdon Cheves, and Trescot) our two governors dined with us, Means and Manning.

These men all talked so delightfully. For once in my life I listened.

That over, business began. In earnest, Governor Means rummaged a sword and red sash from somewhere and brought it for Colonel Chesnut, who has gone to demand the surrender of Fort Sumter.

And now, patience—we must wait.

Why did that green goose Anderson go into Fort Sumter? Then everything began to go wrong.

Now they have intercepted a letter from him, urging them to let him surrender. He paints the horrors likely to ensue if they will not.

He ought to have thought of all that before he put his head in the hole.

496 Division, Reconciliation, and Expansion (1850–1914)

APRIL 12, 1861. Anderson will not capitulate.

Yesterday was the merriest, maddest dinner we have had yet. Men were more audaciously wise and witty. We had an unspoken foreboding it was to be our last pleasant meeting. Mr. Miles dined with us today. Mrs. Henry King rushed in: "The news, I come for the latest news—all of the men of the King family are on the island"—of which fact she seemed proud.

While she was here, our peace negotiator—or envoy—came in. That is, Mr. Chesnut returned—his interview with Colonel Anderson had been deeply interesting—but was not inclined to be communicative, wanted his dinner. Felt for Anderson. Had telegraphed to President Davis[4] for instructions.

What answer to give Anderson, etc., etc. He has gone back to Fort Sumter with additional instructions.

When they were about to leave the wharf, A. H. Boykin sprang into the boat, in great excitement; thought himself ill-used. A likelihood of fighting—and he to be left behind!

I do not pretend to go to sleep. How can I? If Anderson does not accept terms—at four—the orders are—he shall be fired upon.

I count four—St. Michael chimes. I begin to hope. At half-past four, the heavy booming of a cannon.

I sprang out of bed. And on my knees—prostrate—I prayed as I never prayed before.

There was a sound of stir all over the house—pattering of feet in the corridor—all seemed hurrying one way. I put on my double gown and a shawl and went, too. It was to the housetop.

The shells were bursting. In the dark I heard a man say "waste of ammunition."

I knew my husband was rowing about in a boat somewhere in that dark bay. And that the shells were roofing it over—bursting toward the fort. If Anderson was *obstinate*—he was to order the forts on our side to open fire. Certainly fire had begun. The regular roar of the cannon—there it was. And who could tell what each volley accomplished of death and destruction.

The women were wild, there on the housetop. Prayers from the women and imprecations from the men, and then a shell would light up the scene. Tonight, they say, the forces are to attempt to land.

The *Harriet Lane*[5] had her wheelhouse[6] smashed and put back to sea.

---

4. **President Davis**
       Jefferson Davis (1808–1889), president of the Confederacy (1861–1865).
5. **The *Harriet Lane***
       federal steamer that had brought provisions to Fort Sumter.
6. **wheelhouse**
       n. enclosed place on the upper deck of a ship, in which the helmsman stands while steering.

from Mary Chesnut's Civil War **497**

Reading Strategy
Generating Questions
What questions might you ask about Chesnut's daily life?

Vocabulary
obstinate (äb′ stə nət)
adj. stubborn

8 ☑ Reading Check

What happens at half past four on April 12, 1861?

Differentiated
Instruction   **for Universal Access**

Culturally Responsive Instruction
Culture Focus On the next page, point out to students the line that Mary Chesnut quotes from Shakespeare's *Macbeth*. Explain that educated English speakers often allude, in everyday life, to classic English-language works, such as those by Shakespeare, that seem to have universal meaning. Encourage students to suggest writings, writers, and real or literary figures that speakers of other languages refer to in order to underscore a point they are making. For example, it is not unusual in India to hear children and adults in the course of a day citing a hero or god from the long series of Sanskrit poems, written between 200 B.C. and A.D. 200, called the *Mahabharata*.

❾ Critical Thinking

Evaluate

1. Request students review the bracketed passage.

2. **Ask** students to comment on the relationship, if any, between the content of the first paragraph and the subsequent two paragraphs. **Possible response:** The first paragraph mentions guests; the second paragraph moves on to an incident about clothes catching fire. The topics of the two paragraphs are unrelated. Disconnected paragraphs are not uncommon in diaries and journals.

❿ Primary Sources

Diaries and Journals

1. Have students read the complete entry for April 13, 1861.

2. **Ask** students the Primary Sources question: What do you learn from the entry of April 13, 1861, that you would probably not learn from a textbook? **Answers:** The diarist describes the way aides are dressed, what and where she and others eat, and the anxiety and faith of some women.

We watched up there—everybody wondered. Fort Sumter did not fire a shot.

Today Miles and Manning, colonels now—aides to Beauregard—dined with us. The latter hoped I would keep the peace. I give him only good words, for he was to be under fire all day and night, in the bay carrying orders, etc.

❾ Last night—or this morning truly—up on the housetop I was so weak and weary I sat down on something that looked like a black stool.

"Get up, you foolish woman—your dress is on fire," cried a man. And he put me out.

It was a chimney, and the sparks caught my clothes. Susan Preston and Mr. Venable then came up. But my fire had been extinguished before it broke out into a regular blaze.

Do you know, after all that noise and our tears and prayers, nobody has been hurt. Sound and fury, signifying nothing.[7] A delusion and a snare. . . .

Somebody came in just now and reported Colonel Chesnut asleep on the sofa in General Beauregard's room. After two such nights he must be so tired as to be able to sleep anywhere. . . .

Primary Sources
Diaries and Journals
What do you learn from the entry of April 13, 1861, that you would probably not learn from a textbook?

APRIL 13, 1861. Nobody hurt, after all. How gay we were last night.

Reaction after the dread of all the slaughter we thought those dreadful cannons were making such a noise in doing.

Not even a battery[8] the worse for wear.

Fort Sumter has been on fire. He has not yet silenced any of our ❿ guns. So the aides—still with swords and red sashes by way of uniform—tell us.

But the sound of those guns makes regular meals impossible. None of us go to table. But tea trays pervade the corridors, going everywhere.

Some of the anxious hearts lie on their beds and moan in solitary misery. Mrs. Wigfall and I solace ourselves with tea in my room.

These women have all a satisfying faith.

APRIL 15, 1861. I did not know that one could live such days of excitement.

---

7. **Sound . . . nothing** from Shakespeare's *Macbeth*, Act V, Scene v, lines 27–28. Macbeth is contemplating the significance of life and death after learning of his wife's death.
8. **battery** *n.* artillery unit.

Enrichment: Investigating Daily Life

Women's Clothing
Explain to students that in past eras it was not uncommon for women's skirts to catch fire, as Chesnut describes on this page. Long, flowing skirts, flammable fabrics, and open hearths were a deadly combination that left thousands of women badly—even fatally—injured.

Activity: Sketching Encourage students to conduct research on the clothes worn by women during the Civil War period in the United States. Interested students may also research the dress-reform movement, led by such figures as Amelia Bloomer, that emerged in the United States shortly after the Civil War. Suggest that students record their findings in the **Enrichment: Investigating Daily Life** work sheet, in *Professional Development Guidebook*, page 224. Have students produce sketches of clothing styles to share with the class.

They called, "Come out—there is a crowd coming."

A mob indeed, but it was headed by Colonels Chesnut and Manning.

The crowd was shouting and showing these two as messengers of good news. They were escorted to Beauregard's headquarters. Fort Sumter had surrendered.

Those up on the housetop shouted to us, "The fort is on fire." That had been the story once or twice before.

When we had calmed down, Colonel Chesnut, who had taken it all quietly enough—if anything, more unruffled than usual in his serenity—told us how the surrender came about.

Wigfall was with them on Morris Island when he saw the fire in the fort, jumped in a little boat and, with his handkerchief as a white flag, rowed over to Fort Sumter. Wigfall went in through a porthole.

When Colonel Chesnut arrived shortly after and was received by the regular entrance, Colonel Anderson told him he had need to pick his way warily, for it was all mined.

As far as I can make out, the fort surrendered to Wigfall.

But it is all confusion. Our flag is flying there. Fire engines have been sent to put out the fire.

Everybody tells you half of something and then rushes off to tell something else or to hear the last news. . . .

Critical Reading ©

© 1. **Key Ideas and Details** **(a)** What significant events does Chesnut describe in her diary? **(b) Interpret:** What does her diary reveal about daily life during these historical events? **(c) Evaluate:** Do you find anything surprising about Chesnut's depiction of the events themselves or of people's reactions to them? Explain.

© 2. **Key Ideas and Details** **(a)** What role does Chesnut's husband play in the events at Fort Sumter? **(b) Infer:** What does his response to the events and the people involved tell you about him? **(c) Hypothesize:** Do you think the Chesnuts' feelings about the events mirror those of most other Southerners? Explain.

© 3. **Key Ideas and Details** **(a)** Does Chesnut seem worried about the fate of her hometown, or does she seem to feel safe even in the face of battle? Cite details to support your answer. **(b)** What do you think explains Chesnut's attitude?

from Mary Chesnut's Civil War **499**

Answers

1. (a) She describes the events surrounding the firing on Fort Sumter by Confederate troops. (b) Her diary reveals that the home was visited by principals in the battle and that some routines—such as eating in the dining room—were modified. (c) **Possible response:** Some students may be surprised that civilians were close enough to witness an attack.

2. (a) Colonel Chesnut, who was in Charleston for a Confederate convention, becomes an assistant to a general, goes to the fort to demand surrender by the Union troops, rows a boat as the bombardment begins, falls asleep on a sofa. That is, he plays an active role. (b) His response indicates that he is quite important. (c) **Possible response:** Yes, probably other Southerners also feel they have no choice but to fight but feel anxious about a war's consequences.

3. (a) **Possible response:** Chesnut is excited about unfolding events and concerned for her husband, but she shows no worries about her hometown. She watches the bombardment with others, dining and taking tea. (b) Chesnut seems to have great confidence in Confederate leadership and military force. Her close contact with key participants in the attack, including her husband, probably increases her assurance.

Differentiated
Instruction   for Universal Access

EL **Pronunciation for English Learners**

The end of the excerpt by Chesnut is loaded with words beginning with the voiced initial *th*, a sound absent in many languages, leading some English learners to substitute an additional *t*.

Write the following word pairs for students to view:

that/tat	then/ten
there/tear	these/tease
those/toes	though/toe

Pronounce each word in a pair in turn and have students echo you. Then, let the class guide a volunteer to circle the correct word as you call out the words at random. (As appropriate, mention the word *thyme*, an exception; it is pronounced not with either a voiced or unvoiced *th* but, rather, with a *t: tyme.*)

499

⓫ Background
Army Life

Enlisted men on both sides—like this recent Union recruit—faced the drudgery of camp life—mud, drill, and more drill.

⓬ Primary Source: Art

Possible response: In the painting, the soldier's downward glance and tired-looking stance suggest some lack of enthusiasm, perhaps fatigue.

Recollections of
A PRIVATE
Warren Lee Goss

⓫ *In the weeks that followed the attack on Fort Sumter, thousands of men on both sides volunteered to fight. Among the early enlistees was young Warren Lee Goss of Massachusetts.*

"Cold chills" ran up and down my back as I got out of bed after the sleepless night, and shaved preparatory to other desperate deeds of valor. I was twenty years of age, and when anything unusual was to be done, like fighting or courting, I shaved.

With a nervous tremor convulsing my system, and my heart thumping like muffled drumbeats, I stood before the door of the recruiting office, and before turning the knob to enter read and reread the advertisement for recruits posted thereon, until I knew all its peculiarities. The promised chances for "travel and promotion" seemed good, and I thought I might have made a mistake in considering war so serious after all. "Chances for travel!" I must confess now, after four years of soldiering, that the "chances for travel" were no myth; but "promotion" was a little uncertain and slow.

I was in no hurry to open the door. Though determined to enlist, I was half inclined to put it off awhile; I had a fluctuation of desires; I was fainthearted and brave; I wanted to enlist, and yet— Here I turned the knob, and was relieved. . . .

My first uniform was a bad fit: My trousers were too long by three or four inches; the flannel shirt was coarse and unpleasant, too large at the neck and too short elsewhere. The forage cap[1] was an ungainly bag with pasteboard top and leather visor; the blouse was the only part which seemed decent; while the overcoat made me feel like a little nubbin of corn in a large preponderance of husk. Nothing except "Virginia mud" ever took down my ideas of military pomp quite so low.

---

1. forage cap

cap worn by infantry soldiers.

⓬ ▲ **Primary Source: Art**
What attitude toward war does this 1861 painting of a young Civil War soldier convey? Explain. **[Analyze]**

Vocabulary
recruits (ri krōōts) *n.* newly drafted soldiers

fluctuation (fluk´ chōō ā´ shən) *n.* a change in level or intensity

---

Enrichment: Analyzing Music

Civil War Music
Goss writes, "my heart thumping like muffled drumbeats." Although Goss refers to music metaphorically, music played a role in the Civil War. In 1862, abolitionist Julia Ward Howe wrote "The Battle Hymn of the Republic." Reportedly, Union soldiers sang this song over and over. Robert E. Lee said that there could not be an army without music. Drumbeats spurred soldiers into battle, and regimental bands raised the spirits of marching soldiers.

Activity: Presenting Songs Have students research the songs the Union and Confederate armies sang, some of which they can listen to themselves. Direct them to learn more about the origins of the songs. Suggest that they record information in the **Enrichment: Analyzing Music** work sheet, in *Professional Development Guidebook,* page 236. Then invite them to present the songs and their findings to the class.

After enlisting I did not seem of so much consequence as I had expected. There was not so much excitement on account of my military appearance as I deemed justly my due. I was taught my facings, and at the time I thought the drillmaster needlessly fussy about shouldering, ordering, and presenting arms. At this time men were often drilled in company and regimental evolutions long before they learned the manual of arms, because of the difficulty of obtaining muskets. These we obtained at an early day, but we would willingly have resigned them after carrying them a few hours. The musket, after an hour's drill, seemed heavier and less ornamental than it had looked to be.

The first day I went out to drill, getting tired of doing the same things over and over, I said to the drill sergeant: "Let's stop this fooling and go over to the grocery." His only reply was addressed to a corporal: "Corporal, take this man out and drill him"; and the corporal did! I found that suggestions were not so well appreciated in the army as in private life, and that no wisdom was equal to a drillmaster's "Right face," "Left wheel," and "Right, oblique, march." It takes a raw recruit some time to learn that he is not to think or suggest, but obey. Some never do learn. I acquired it at last, in humility and mud, but it was tough. Yet I doubt if my patriotism, during my first three weeks' drill, was quite knee high. Drilling looks easy to a spectator, but it isn't. After a time I had cut down my uniform so that I could see out of it, and had conquered the drill sufficiently to see through it. Then the word came: on to Washington! . . .

Reading Strategy
Generating Questions
What question might you ask about Goss's future as a soldier?

Vocabulary
spectator (spek´ tāt´ ər) *n.* a person who watches something without taking part in it

---

Critical Reading

© 1. **Key Ideas and Details (a) Summarize:** Describe Warren Lee Goss's feelings on the day he was to enlist in the army. **(b) Analyze:** How did Private Goss's attitudes and expectations change after he enlisted?

© 2. **Key Ideas and Details (a)** According to Goss, what takes a long time for a recruit to learn? **(b) Infer:** What do you think happened to cause him to say, "I acquired it at last, in humility and in mud, but it was tough"?

© 3. **Integration of Knowledge and Ideas (a) Make a Judgment:** In your view, how well suited is Goss for military life? **(b) Generalize:** How similar or different do you think Goss might be to other young men in his situation? Explain.

---

⑬ Reading Strategy
Generating Questions

1. After reviewing the final two paragraphs, what is your opinion of Goss as a soldier in training? **Possible response:** Students may say that Goss seems comically unaware of the purposes of military training, with little aptitude for the work.

2. **Ask** the Reading Strategy question: What question might you ask about Goss's future as a soldier? **Sample answers:** Did Goss continue to focus on his appearance, or did he give up that concern as time went on? How well did Goss learn his drill as time went on? What does he mean by learning "to see through"? How did he perform in his first battle?

ASSESS

Answers

1. (a) He is nervous and excited and feels "a fluctuation of desires." (b) Before enlisting, he imagines himself looking impressive and exciting in uniform; after enlisting, he develops a more realistic and humble image of himself

2. (a) It takes a long time for a recruit to learn to obey without thinking or making suggestions. (b) Students may say that Goss was "drilled," or vigorously trained, until he responded instinctively with obedience.

3. (a) Students may suggest that, although ill suited initially, Goss may have learned how to adjust to military life. (b) Students will probably think Goss's mind-set was similar to that of other young men new to military life. The transition from independent living to living as part of a machine must be difficult.

History

From July 1 to July 3, 1863, Union and Confederate troops fought near the small town of Gettysburg, Pennsylvania. After Union troops gained control of the hills surrounding the town, the Confederate troops commanded by Robert E. Lee launched a risky attack on the strongest Union position. When the attack failed, the Confederate troops were forced to retreat. The battle was the last that Lee would fight on Union soil. This entry by McKim describes his unit's attack on the final day, a day that ended with the famous failure of Pickett's charge.

⒂ Primary Sources

Diaries and Journals

1. Direct students to read particularly closely the second paragraph on page 502 to "early morning" on page 503.

2. **Ask** the Primary Sources question: Which words in this description of the battle show McKim's political leanings?
Answer: Twice, McKim uses the adjective "gallant" to describe the brigade. McKim goes on to say that "its nerve and spirit were undiminished." He continues with "on they pressed," then describes some of the men, followed by "heroes daring to attempt what could not be done by flesh and blood." The next paragraph relates "the strenuous efforts of the officers." These descriptions all reflect McKim's commitment to the Confederate army.

A Confederate Account of the
BATTLE OF GETTYSBURG

Randolph McKim

⒁ *The Battle of Gettysburg is often referred to as the "turning point" in the Civil War—the point at which the North gained the upper hand. In his diary, Confederate soldier Randolph McKim recounts the bravery of his companions, many of whom were killed or wounded during the advance on Culp's Hill. The advance was led by McKim himself.*

Vocabulary
offensive (ô´ fen´ siv) *n.* an attitude or position of attack

brigade (bri gād´) *n.* a unit of soldiers

Primary Sources
Diaries and Journals
Which words in this description of the battle show McKim's political leanings?

Then came General Ewell's order to assume the offensive and assail the crest of Culp's Hill, on our right. . . . The works to be stormed ran almost at right angles to those we occupied. Moreover, there was a double line of entrenchments, one above the other, and each filled with troops. In moving to the attack we were exposed to enfilading fire[1] from the woods on our left flank, besides the double line of fire which we had to face in front, and a battery of artillery posted on a hill to our left rear opened upon us at short range. . . .

On swept the gallant little brigade, the Third North Carolina on the right of the line, next the Second Maryland, then the three Virginia regiments (10th, 23d, and 37th), with the First North Carolina on the extreme left. Its ranks had been sadly thinned, and its energies greatly depleted by those six fearful hours of battle that morning; but its nerve and spirit were undiminished. Soon, however, the left and center were checked and then repulsed, probably by the severe flank fire from the woods; and the small remnant of the Third North Carolina, with the stronger Second Maryland (I do not recall the banners of any other regiment), were far in advance of the rest of the line. On they pressed to within about twenty or thirty paces of the works—a small but gallant band of heroes daring to attempt what could not be done by flesh and blood.

The end soon came. We were beaten back to the line from which we had advanced with terrible loss, and in much confusion, but the enemy did not make a countercharge. By the strenuous efforts of the officers of the line and of the staff, order was restored, and we re-formed in the breastworks[2] from which we had emerged, there to be again exposed to an artillery fire exceeding in violence that of the

---

1. enfilading (en´ fə lād´ in) **fire** gunfire directed along the length of a column or line of troops.
2. breastworks low walls put up quickly as a defense in battle.

16

17 ◀ **Primary Source: Art** Does this painting of the Battle of Gettysburg help you understand McKim's pride in his brigade? Explain. **[Connect]**

early morning. It remains only to say that, like Pickett's men[3] later in the day, this single brigade was hurled unsupported against the enemy's works. Daniel's brigade remained in the breastworks during and after the charge, and neither from that command nor from any other had we any support. Of course it is to be presumed that General Daniel acted in obedience to orders. We remained in this breastwork after the charge about an hour before we finally abandoned the Federal entrenchments and retired to the foot of the hill.

Vocabulary
entrenchments (en trench´ mənts) *n.* long, deep holes with steep sides, used as defense against enemy fire

---

3. **Pickett's men** General George Pickett was a Confederate officer who led the unsuccessful attack on the Union position.

Critical Reading

© 1. **Integration of Knowledge and Ideas (a) Summarize:** Describe in your own words the attack on Culp's Hill. **(b) Speculate:** In your view, who or what was responsible for the Confederates' defeat?

© 2. **Key Ideas and Details (a)** According to McKim, how was the attack like Pickett's charge later in the day? **(b) Infer:** How do you think McKim felt about his superiors' decisions and orders during the battle? Support your inference with a quotation from the text.

© 3. **Integration of Knowledge and Ideas Make a Judgment:** Is McKim's account trustworthy? Explain.

A Confederate Account of the Battle of Gettysburg **503**

---

16 **Visual Connection**

1. Direct students to a detailed examination of the painting.

2. **Ask** students how they would go about determining which side in the battle—Confederate or Union—is in the foreground and which in the background.
   Possible response: Students may suggest that with a magnifying glass they might be able to see more clearly soldiers' uniforms and battle flags, both of which identify sides in a battle.

17 **Primary Source: Art**

Possible response: While the open battle scene looks fierce, the painting does not let viewers isolate individual actions, particularly heroic ones.

ASSESS
Answers

1. (a) Students should capture McKim's observation that the Confederate soldiers lacked support. (b) Some students may argue that in this case the Confederates were responsible for their own defeat. Students may say that the Confederates should have accepted the defeats of the first two days of the battle and should not have brought even greater losses on themselves.

2. (a) The attack was like Pickett's charge that occurred later in the day, because in both cases the brigades had insufficient support as they faced the enemy. (b) It is likely that McKim was displeased with his superiors' decision; he criticizes with faint praise when he says, "Of course it is to be presumed that General Daniel acted in obedience to orders."

3. Although writing a diary, McKim may have assumed that his writing might find its way to publication some day, and he would have wanted to present his men in the best possible light.

Comparing Primary Sources

1. (a) These writers felt compelled to write because they were living in a momentous time. (b) All three would want descendants to think positively about them; Chesnut and Goss include details that might elicit a laugh at their expense, but McKim does not.

2. (a) Chesnut provides lists of who dined with her, showing that she was in the center of things; Goss describes how bad he looked in his uniform, revealing that he could laugh at himself; McKim mentions that Daniel's brigade did not help McKim's men, suggesting that failure was not solely McKim's fault. (b) Chesnut and Goss state their beliefs explicitly. (c) McKim's criticism is carefully implied.

3. Students' paragraphs should acknowledge Chesnut's high social rank and commitment to the Confederacy, Goss's status as an uncertain soldier, and McKim's role as an officer who would be expected to perform well.

Vocabulary Acquisition and Use

1. True; if police intercepted, or seized, stolen goods, they would foil a crime.

2. False; an obstinate, or stubborn, person is not a good negotiator.

3. True; a sudden rainstorm can cause a fluctuation or change in temperature.

4. False; while a spectator can offer a team emotional support, he or she is a viewer and is not often responsible for a win.

5. a; words about political process.

6. c; words about armed forces.

7. c; words about armed forces.

8. b; words about maneuvers.

9. a; words about political process.

10. b; words about maneuvers.

Etymology Study

Journal comes from diurnalis, which comes from dies, which means "day." Diary also comes from dies. Related words: journalism and journeyman.

 COMMON CORE ▪ RESEARCH PROJECT

Diaries and Journals

Comparing Primary Sources

Refer to your Note-Taking Guide to answer these questions.

1. (a) Why do you think each of these writers felt compelled to write a diary or journal? (b) What connection do you see between each writer's purpose and the details he or she includes in a diary entry?

2. (a) Using a chart like the one shown below, identify one detail or observation from each diary or journal that reveals something important about the writer's beliefs. (b) Which writers state their beliefs explicitly? (c) Which express their beliefs implicitly? Explain.

Writer	Detail or Observation	What It Reveals
Chesnut		
Goss		
McKim		

3. Write several paragraphs in which you compare and contrast these writers' stations in life and the perspectives they bring to their descriptions of the war. Consider each writer's objectivity, political feelings, and philosophical beliefs.

Ⓒ Vocabulary Acquisition and Use

True or False Indicate whether each sentence below is true or false. Explain your answer.

1. The police would foil a crime if they *intercepted* stolen goods.

2. An *obstinate* person makes a good negotiator.

3. A sudden summer rainstorm can cause a *fluctuation* in temperature.

4. At a sports event, a *spectator* is often responsible for a team's win.

Content-Area Vocabulary Link each word on the left with a set of words on the right. Explain why the word belongs to that set.

5. adjourned

6. recruits **a.** delegates, capitol, elect, legislature

7. brigade **b.** combat, campaign, tactic, siege

8. offensive **c.** soldiers, enlist, drill, military

9. convention

10. entrenchments

Etymology Study The word *adjourned* comes from the Latin word *diurnus*, which means "day" or "daily." Use a dictionary to determine how the words *journal* and *diary* are also related to this Latin root. Then, locate other words that share the same root.

Ⓒ Common Core
State Standards

Writing
7. Conduct short as well as more sustained research projects to answer a question or solve a problem; narrow or broaden the inquiry when appropriate; synthesize multiple sources on the subject, demonstrating understanding of the subject under investigation.

8. Gather relevant information from multiple authoritative print and digital sources, using advanced searches effectively; assess the strengths and limitations of each source in terms of the task, purpose, and audience; integrate information into the text selectively to maintain the flow of ideas, avoiding plagiarism and overreliance on any one source.

Language
4.c. Consult general and specialized reference materials to find the etymology of a word.

Extend the Lesson

Connecting to the Students' World

- Encourage students to find in the library or on the Internet diaries or journals by twentieth- or twenty-first–century observers (like Mary Chesnut) or participants in an armed battle (like Goss and McKim). Direct students to read a few entries and then to compare and contrast those entries to the ones they have read from the Civil War period. In doing so, they should consider the following questions. What, if any, of the writer's political or philosophical beliefs are clear from what he or she wrote?

- Is the writer strictly serious, or does the writer have a sense of humor about himself or herself?

- What did you learn about the battle from the diary or journal that, most likely, was not reported in an article in a more formal publication, such as a newspaper or magazine?

Research Task

Topic: Women and the Civil War

Waiting wives and mourning mothers, fighters and farmers, abolitionists and slaves, nurses and spies—American women during the Civil War played many roles. Before, during, and after the war, women's lives told a vital and often heartrending part of the tragic American story.

Assignment: Write a **research report** on women and the Civil War. Do not rely strictly on texts written for students; instead, include evidence from texts written by experts for informed, scholarly audiences.

Formulate your research plan. "Women and the Civil War" is a huge topic that cannot be covered adequately in a brief research report. Therefore, narrow the topic to make it manageable and interesting. Alone or in a group, brainstorm for a list of focused topics such as the following:

- women who participated in military action
- the domestic lives of women during the war
- women who worked as spies during the war
- wartime for Northern women vs. Southern women
- one particular woman, such as Mary Chesnut

Choose a focused topic that grabs your interest. Then, formulate a brief list of major questions to answer through research.

Gather sources. Answer your questions using online and library materials. To avoid overreliance on one source, create a chart of the different kinds of information you acquire from a variety of sources.

Model: Researching Using Multiple Sources

Source	Type of Source	Type of Information
"Belle Boyd"	encyclopedia	biographical facts
"Belle Boyd"	history Web site	other women spies
Belle Boyd	2007 biography	details of spy missions

Synthesize information. As you synthesize details from different sources, flexibility is key. You may need to further refine the topic, shift the focus of your research, or add or discard sources. Be prepared to pursue new thoughts and new directions.

Organize and present your ideas. Organize your report into sections identified by subheads. This will clarify the flow of your ideas and information and make the job of writing easier. Add summary statements at the end of each section to make the final report clearer.

▲ Clara Barton traveled behind enemy lines to bring medical care to wounded Union soldiers.

RESEARCH TIP

Read author information, often on a jacket flap or back page, to evaluate a writer's authority. On a Web site, read the "About Me" section to evaluate credentials.

Use a checklist like the one shown to ensure the reliability of your research report.

Research Checklist

- ☐ Have I answered all my research questions?
- ☐ Does my evidence come from experts and texts written for informed audiences in the field?
- ☐ Have I avoided relying too much on one source?
- ☐ Is my report clearly organized, with sections, subheads, and summary statements?

Research Task **505**

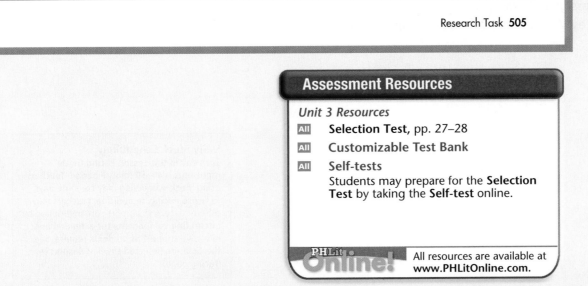

Women and the Civil War

Introduce the Assignment

1. Review the assignment. Explain that a research report of any kind should be based on different types of resources.

2. Using the list on the student page, students should formulate a research plan. To aid students, help them to ask open-ended research questions, such as "What was life like for women who stayed at home in the North?"

Guide Student Research

1. Students should explore a range of relevant sources. Point out that encyclopedia articles give an overview of a topic and that accounts written for experts give more detail.

2. Have students use a chart like the one on the student page to keep track of their sources.

Think Aloud: Model Synthesizing Information

Say to students:

To keep from relying too much on one source, I ask: "How does this source answer the research question?" For example, if the question is, "What was life like for women in the North who stayed at home during the Civil War?" and I read a general account of the Civil War, there may be a lot of information that I do not need. Look for sources for informed readers that give more specific information.

Guide Student Writing

1. Students should use subheads and summary statements to organize their work.

2. Encourage students to make sure that the ideas and details from their research sources are presented clearly.

• An Episode of War
Lesson Pacing Guide

DAY 1 Preteach

- Administer the Reading and Vocabulary Warm-ups (*Unit 3 Resources,* pp. 29–32) as necessary.
- Introduce the Literary Analysis concept: Naturalism.
- Introduce the Reading Strategy: Apply Background Knowledge.
- Build background with the author and Background features.
- Develop thematic thinking with Connecting to the Essential Question.
- Teach the selection vocabulary.

DAYS 2–3 Preteach/Teach/Assess

- Distribute copies of the appropriate graphic organizer for the Reading Strategy (*Graphic Organizer Transparencies,* pp. 101–102).
- Distribute copies of the appropriate graphic organizer for Literary Analysis (*Graphic Organizer Transparencies*, pp. 103–104).
- Prepare students to read with the Activating Prior Knowledge activities (TE).
- Informally monitor comprehension while students read.
- Use the Reading Check question to confirm comprehension.
- Develop students' understanding of naturalism using the Literary Analysis prompt.
- Develop students' ability to apply background knowledge using the Reading Strategy prompt.
- Reinforce vocabulary with the Vocabulary notes.
- Assess students' comprehension and mastery of the skills by having them answer the Critical Reading, Literary Analysis, and Reading Strategy questions.
- Have students complete the Vocabulary Lesson.

DAY 4 Extend/Assess

- Have students complete the Writing Lesson and write an essay in response to criticism. (You may assign as homework.)
- Administer Selection Test A or B (*Unit 3 Resources,* pp. 41–43 or 44–46).

© Common Core State Standards

Reading Literature 1. Cite strong and thorough textual evidence to support analysis of what the text says explicitly as well as inferences drawn from the text, including determining where the text leaves matters uncertain.

3. Analyze the impact of the author's choices regarding how to develop and relate elements of a story (e.g., how the characters are introduced and developed).

9. Demonstrate knowledge of nineteenth-century foundational works of American literature, including how two or more texts from the same period treat similar themes or topics.

Writing 2. Write informative/explanatory texts to examine and convey complex ideas, concepts, and information clearly and accurately through the effective selection, organization, and analysis of content. *(p. 515)*
2.a. Introduce a topic; organize complex ideas, concepts, and information so that each new element builds on that which precedes it to create a unified whole. *(p. 515)*

Language 4.b. Identify and correctly use patterns of word changes that indicate different meanings or parts of speech. *(p. 515)*

Additional Standards Practice
Common Core Companion, pp. 2–9; 28–35; 75–76; 196–207; 324–331

Daily Block Scheduling
Each day in this Lesson Pacing Guide represents a 40–50 minute period. Teachers using block scheduling may combine days to revise pacing. In addition, teachers may differentiate and support core instruction by integrating components for extended and intensive support as students require. See the Guide to Selected Leveled Resources (facing page).

Guide to Selected Leveled Resources

R T 1 Tier 1 (students performing on level)

An Episode of War

Warm Up	Practice, model, and **monitor** fluency, working **with the whole class** or **in groups**.	Vocabulary and Reading Warm-ups B, *Unit 3 Resources*, pp. 29–30, 32
Comprehension/Skills	**Support** and **monitor** comprehension and skills development, having students complete the activities, graphic organizers, and interactive prompts **independently** or **as a class**.	• *Reader's Notebook*, adapted instruction and full selection **EL** *Reader's Notebook: English Learner's Version*, adapted instruction and adapted selection • **Reading Strategy Graphic Organizer B**, *Graphic Organizer Transparencies*, p. 102 • **Literary Analysis Graphic Organizer B**, *Graphic Organizer Transparencies*, p. 104
Monitor Progress	**Monitor** student progress with the differentiated curriculum-based assessment in the *Unit Resources*.	• **Selection Test B**, *Unit 3 Resources*, pp. 44–46 • **Open-Book Test**, *Unit 3 Resources*, pp. 38–40

R T 1 Tier 2 (students requiring intervention)

An Episode of War

Warm Up	Practice, model, and **monitor** fluency **in groups** or **with individuals**.	• **Vocabulary and Reading Warm-ups A**, *Unit 3 Resources*, pp. 29–31 • *Hear It!* Audio CD
Comprehension/Skills	• **Support** and **monitor** comprehension and skills development, working **in small groups** or **with individuals**. • As students complete the selection in the appropriate version of the *Reader's Notebook*, **monitor** comprehension frequently with group questions and individual instruction. • **Model** strategies while guiding students in completing the activities and prompts in the *Reader's Notebook*, as well as the graphic organizers. • **Practice** skills and **monitor** mastery with the *Reading Kit* worksheets.	• *Reader's Notebook: Adapted Version*, adapted instruction adapted selection **EL** *Reader's Notebook: English Learner's Version*, adapted instruction and adapted selection • **Reading Strategy Graphic Organizer A**, *Graphic Organizer Transparencies*, p. 101 • **Literary Analysis Graphic Organizer A**, *Graphic Organizer Transparencies*, p. 103 • *Reading Kit*, Practice worksheets
Monitor Progress	**Monitor** student progress with the differentiated curriculum-based assessment in the *Unit Resources* and in the *Reading Kit*.	• **Selection Test A**, *Unit 3 Resources*, pp. 41–43 • *Reading Kit*, Assess worksheets

TIER 3 Tier 3 intervention may require consultation with the student's special-education or dyslexia specialist. For additional support, see the Tier 2 activities and resources listed above.

One-on-one teaching   Group work   Whole-class instruction   Independent work   **A** Assessment

For a complete guide to selection support, including support for Advanced students, see the Overview of Resources in the frontmatter.

• An Episode of War

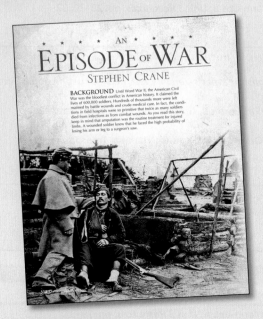

RESOURCES FOR:
- **L1** Special-Needs Students
- **L2** Below-Level Students (Tier 2)
- **L3** On-Level Students (Tier 1)
- **L4** Advanced Students (Tier 1)
- **EL** English Learners
- **All** All Students

Vocabulary/Fluency/Prior Knowledge

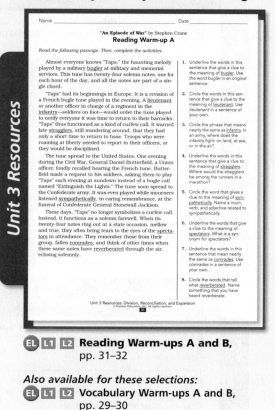

EL L1 L2 Reading Warm-ups A and B, pp. 31–32

Also available for these selections:

EL L1 L2 Vocabulary Warm-ups A and B, pp. 29–30

All Vocabulary Builder, p. 35

Reader's Notebooks

Pre- and postreading pages for this selection, as well as "An Episode of War," appear in an interactive format in the *Reader's Notebooks*. Each *Notebook* is differentiated for a different group of learners. The selections in the Adapted and English Learner's versions are abridged.

- **L2 L3** *Reader's Notebook*
- **L1** *Reader's Notebook: Adapted Version*
- **EL** *Reader's Notebook: English Learner's Version*
- **EL** *Reader's Notebook: Spanish Version*

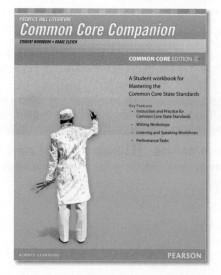

© Common Core Companion

Additional instruction and practice for each Common Core State Standard

Selection Support

Graphic Organizer Transparencies

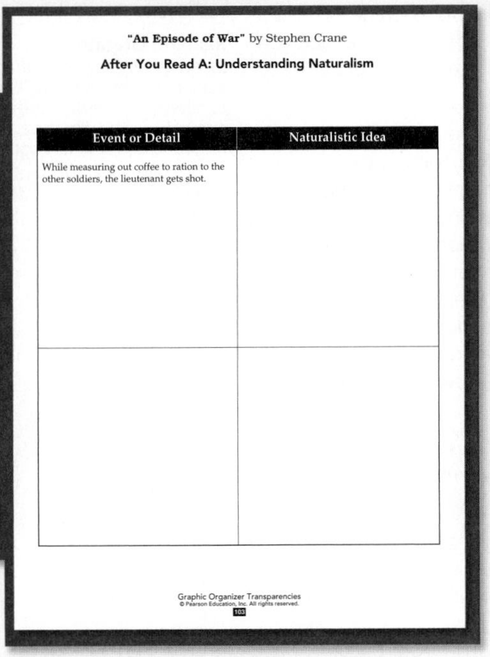
"An Episode of War" by Stephen Crane

After You Read A: Understanding Naturalism

Event or Detail	Naturalistic Idea
While measuring out coffee to ration to the other soldiers, the lieutenant gets shot.	

Graphic Organizer Transparencies
© Pearson Education, Inc. All rights reserved.
103

EL L1 L2 Literary Analysis: Graphic Organizer A, (partially filled in), p. 103

Also available for these selections:

EL L1 L2 Reading: Graphic Organizer A, (partially filled in), p. 101

EL L3 Reading: Graphic Organizer B, p. 102

EL L3 Literary Analysis: Graphic Organizer B, p. 104

Skills Development/Extension

Unit 3 Resources

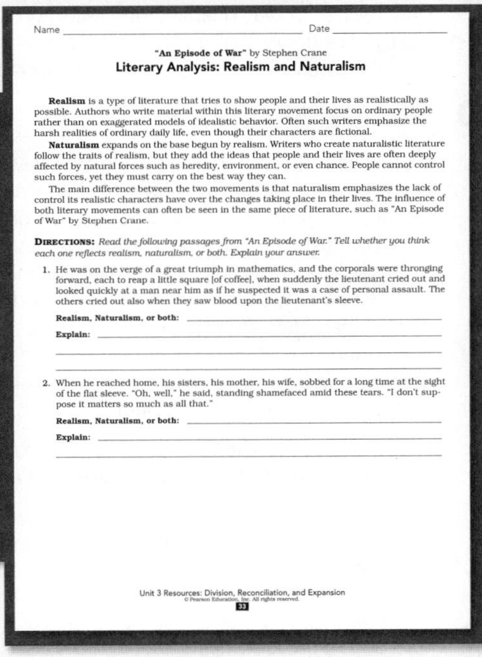
Name ______________________ Date __________

"An Episode of War" by Stephen Crane

Literary Analysis: Realism and Naturalism

Realism is a type of literature that tries to show people and their lives as realistically as possible. Authors who write material within this literary movement focus on ordinary people rather than on exaggerated models of idealistic behavior. Often such writers emphasize the harsh realities of ordinary daily life, even though their characters are fictional.

Naturalism expands on the base begun by realism. Writers who create naturalistic literature follow the traits of realism, but they add the ideas that people and their lives are often deeply affected by natural forces such as heredity, environment, or even chance. People cannot control such forces, yet they must carry on the best way they can.

The main difference between the two movements is that naturalism emphasizes the lack of control its realistic characters have over the changes taking place in their lives. The influence of both literary movements can often be seen in the same piece of literature, such as "An Episode of War" by Stephen Crane.

Directions: *Read the following passages from "An Episode of War." Tell whether you think each one reflects realism, naturalism, or both. Explain your answer.*

1. He was on the verge of a great triumph in mathematics, and the corporals were thronging forward, each to reap a little square [of coffee], when suddenly the lieutenant cried out and looked quickly at a man near him as if he suspected it was a case of personal assault. The others cried out also when they saw blood upon the lieutenant's sleeve.

Realism, Naturalism, or both: ______________________

Explain: ______________________

2. When he reached home, his sisters, his mother, his wife, sobbed for a long time at the sight of the flat sleeve. "Oh, well," he said, standing shamefaced amid these tears. "I don't suppose it matters so much as all that."

Realism, Naturalism, or both: ______________________

Explain: ______________________

Unit 3 Resources: Division, Reconciliation, and Expansion
© Pearson Education, Inc. All rights reserved.
33

All Literary Analysis: Realism and Naturalism, p. 33

Also available for these selections:

All Reading: Clarify Historical Details, p. 34

EL L3 L4 Support for Writing, p. 36

L4 Enrichment, p. 37

Assessment

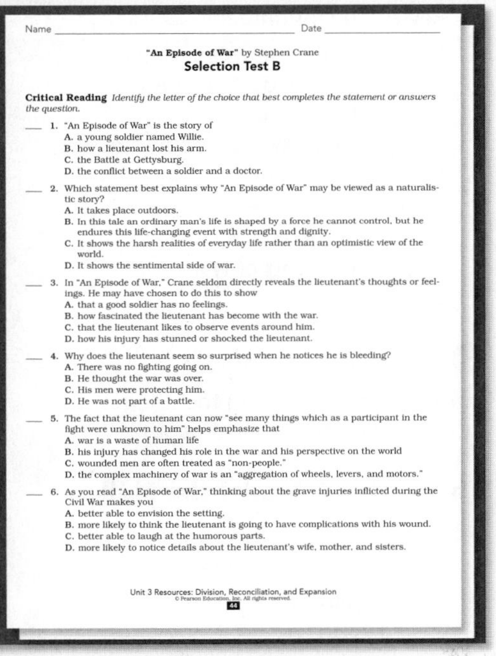
Name ______________________ Date __________

"An Episode of War" by Stephen Crane

Selection Test B

Critical Reading *Identify the letter of the choice that best completes the statement or answers the question.*

___ 1. "An Episode of War" is the story of
A. a young soldier named Willie.
B. how a lieutenant lost his arm.
C. the Battle at Gettysburg.
D. the conflict between a soldier and a doctor.

___ 2. Which statement best explains why "An Episode of War" may be viewed as a naturalistic story?
A. It takes place outdoors.
B. In this tale an ordinary man's life is shaped by a force he cannot control, but he endures this life-changing event with strength and dignity.
C. It shows the harsh realities of everyday life rather than an optimistic view of the world.
D. It shows the sentimental side of war.

___ 3. In "An Episode of War," Crane seldom directly reveals the lieutenant's thoughts or feelings. He may have chosen to do this to show
A. that a good soldier has no feelings.
B. how fascinated the lieutenant has become with the war.
C. that the lieutenant likes to observe events around him.
D. how his injury has stunned or shocked the lieutenant.

___ 4. Why does the lieutenant seem so surprised when he notices he is bleeding?
A. There was no fighting going on.
B. He thought the war was over.
C. His men were protecting him.
D. He was not part of a battle.

___ 5. The fact that the lieutenant can now "see many things which as a participant in the fight were unknown to him" helps emphasize that
A. war is a waste of human life
B. his injury has changed his role in the war and his perspective on the world
C. wounded men are often treated as "non-people."
D. the complex machinery of war is an "aggregation of wheels, levers, and motors."

___ 6. As you read "An Episode of War," thinking about the grave injuries inflicted during the Civil War makes you
A. better able to envision the setting.
B. more likely to think the lieutenant is going to have complications with his wound.
C. better able to laugh at the humorous parts.
D. more likely to notice details about the lieutenant's wife, mother, and sisters.

Unit 3 Resources: Division, Reconciliation, and Expansion
© Pearson Education, Inc. All rights reserved.
44

EL L3 L4 Selection Test B, pp. 44–46

Also available for these selections:

L3 L4 Open-Book Test, pp. 38–40

EL L3 L4 Selection Test A, pp. 41–43

PHLit Online!
www.PHLitOnline.com

- complete narrated selection text
- a thematically related video with writing prompt
- an interactive graphic organizer
- highlighting feature
- access to all student print resources, adapted to individual student needs
- Spanish, Haitian Creole, and English summaries
- adapted selection translations in Spanish

Online Resources: All print materials are also available online.

Get Connected! (thematic video with writing prompt)

Also available:

Background Video
All videos are available in Spanish.

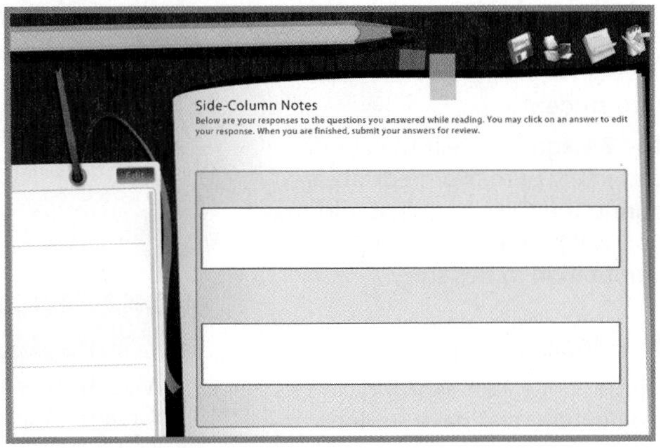

Writer's Journal (with graphics feature)

Also available:

Vocabulary Central (tools and activities for studying vocabulary)

❶ 🔑 Connecting to the Essential Question

1. Review the assignment.

2. Explain that some writers strive to confirm a reader's worldview while others hope to change minds. Then have students complete the assignment.

3. As students read, have them notice ways in which Crane makes the events of war seem undramatic.

❷ Literary Analysis

Introduce the skill, using the instruction on the student page.

Think Aloud: Model the Skill

Say to students:

Here's a poem by Stephen Crane:

A man said to the universe:
"Sir, I exist!"
"However," replied the universe,
"The fact has not created in me
A sense of obligation."

The poem is an example of Naturalism. It shows the universe disinterested in humans.

❸ Reading Strategy

1. Introduce the strategy, using the instruction on the student page.

2. Give students a copy of **Reading Strategy Graphic Organizer B,** page 102 in *Graphic Organizer Transparencies,* to fill out as they read.

Think Aloud: Model the Skill

Say to students:

The Background tells me about extremely primitive medical care during the Civil War. That information will prepare me for a possible amputation in this story.

❹ Vocabulary

1. Pronounce each word, giving its definition, and have students say it aloud.

2. For more guidance, see the *Classroom Strategies and Teaching Routines* card for introducing vocabulary.

Before You Read *An Episode of War*

❶ Connecting to the Essential Question Stephen Crane presents the stark realities of war, omitting lofty reflections on honor or courage. As you read, notice details that downplay the drama of war. This will help as you consider the Essential Question: **How does literature shape or reflect society?**

❷ Literary Analysis

Naturalism is a literary movement that developed in reaction to *Romanticism.* The horrors of the Civil War caused many American writers to question Romantic ideas about human goodness and nature's beauty. In stark contrast to the Romantic view, Naturalists felt that people's lives are controlled by forces beyond their understanding or control. These forces include heredity, people's surroundings, and sheer chance. In Naturalistic works, characters are often victims of their own instincts or of a violent world, and they endure their suffering with a quiet dignity. For example, the wounded main character in "An Episode of War" wanders aimlessly through a Civil War encampment:

> *He wore the look of one who knows he is the victim of a terrible disease and understands his helplessness.*

Like other Naturalistic writers, Crane presents a bleak reality without explaining it. Instead, he allows the reader to draw his or her own conclusions. As you read, look for these Naturalistic elements in Crane's story.

❸ Reading Strategy

ⓒ **Preparing to Read Complex Texts** Knowledge of the Civil War era can clarify your understanding of the characters and action in this story. The diaries and journals that appear on pages 494–503, as well as the unit introduction, background note, and other features in this textbook offer valuable insights into the realities of the Civil War experience. As you read, **apply background knowledge** you gain from these texts to clarify details. Doing so will also help you *predict* the story's events. Use a chart like the one shown to record your observations.

❹ Vocabulary

precipitate (prē sip´ ə tāt´) *v.* cause to happen before expected or desired (p. 510)

aggregation (ag´ rə gā´ shən) *n.* group of distinct objects or individuals (p. 511)

commotion (kə mō´ shən) *n.* noisy confusion (p. 512)

disdainfully (dis dān´ fəl ē) *adv.* showing scorn or contempt (p. 513)

sinister (si´ nəs tər) *adj.* threatening harm, evil, or misfortune (p. 513)

Background Knowledge	Story Details

ⓒ **Common Core State Standards**

Reading Literature
3. Analyze the impact of the author's choices regarding how to develop and relate elements of a story (e.g., how the characters are introduced and developed).
9. Demonstrate knowledge of nineteenth-century foundational works of American literature, including how two or more texts from the same period treat similar themes or topics.

Vocabulary Development

Vocabulary Knowledge Rating

Create a **Vocabulary Knowledge Rating Chart** (*Professional Development Guidebook,* p. 33) for the vocabulary words on the student page. Give each student a copy of the chart with the words on it. Read the words aloud, and have students mark their rating in the Before Reading column. Urge students to attend to these words as they read and discuss the selection.

In order to gauge how much instruction is needed, tally how many students are confident in their knowledge of each word. As students read, point out the words and their context.

Vocabulary Central, featuring tools activities and for vocabulary, is available at www.PHLitOnline.com.

⑤ STEPHEN CRANE *(1871–1900)*

Author of "An Episode of War"

Stephen Crane had not been born when the last battle of the American Civil War was fought, yet he is best remembered for his compelling depiction of the conflict. During his brief life, Crane established himself as both a leader of the Naturalist movement and one of the greatest writers of his time.

Early in his career, Crane worked as a journalist in New York City. His experiences there inspired his first novel, *Maggie: A Girl of the Streets* (1893). Its grimly realistic portrayal of life in the city's slums was so frank and shocking that Crane was unable to find a publisher, and he printed the book at his own expense.

The Red Badge of Courage Crane's second novel, published in 1895, was *The Red Badge of Courage: An Episode of the American Civil War*. A psychological exploration of a young soldier's mental and emotional reactions under enemy fire, the wildly successful novel earned international acclaim for the twenty-four-year-old writer. Crane had never experienced military combat, but he interviewed Civil War veterans and studied photographs, battle plans, and biographical accounts before writing the realistic battle scenes.

Crane later viewed war firsthand when he served as a newspaper correspondent during the Greco-Turkish War in 1897 and the Spanish-American War in 1898. His war experiences provided material for a collection of poetry, *War Is Kind* (1899), but they took their toll on his health. He died of tuberculosis at the age of twenty-eight.

A Short, Passionate Life Like other Naturalists, Crane depicts characters who are manipulated by forces that are beyond their understanding or control. His most common themes include the harsh reality of war, the degradation of humanity, social rebellion, betrayal, and guilt. Knowing he would not live long, Crane worked intensely in the last years of his life. His novels, short stories, poems, and other writings fill twelve volumes. He is considered a literary prodigy who wrote as quickly and passionately as he lived.

✎ Daily Bellringer

For each class during which you will teach this selection, have students complete one of the five activities for the appropriate week in the *Daily Bellringer Activities* booklet.

● Multidraft Reading

To assist struggling readers and to enhance reading for all, assign the text in chunks as warranted by length and apply multidraft reading protocols. For each reading, have students set the purpose indicated:

- **First reading**—identifying key ideas and details and answering any Reading Checks.
- **Second reading**—analyzing craft and structure and responding to the side-column prompts.
- **Third reading**—integrating knowledge and ideas, connecting to other texts and the world, and answering the end-of-selection questions.

For more guidance, refer to the *Classroom Strategies and Teaching Routines* card on multidraft reading.

⑤ Background
More About the Author

Crane received firsthand experience fighting natural forces beyond his control when a boat on which he was traveling sank off the Florida coast. He and three other passengers spent nearly thirty hours afloat in a dinghy before landing safely at Daytona.

An Episode of War **507**

PHLit Online!
www.PHLitOnline.com

Teaching From Technology

Preparing to Read
Go to **www.PHLitOnline.com** in class or in a lab and display the **Get Connected!** slide show for this selection. Have the class brainstorm for responses to the slide show writing prompt, entering ideas in the interactive journal. Then have students complete their written responses individually in a lab or as homework.

To build background, display the Background and More About the Author features.

Using the Interactive Text
Go to **www.PHLitOnline.com** and display the **Enriched Online Student Edition.** As the class reads the selection or listens to the narration, record answers to side-column prompts using the graphic organizers accessible on the interactive page. Alternatively, have students use the online edition individually, answering the prompts as they read.

❶ About the Selection

This stark account of how a Civil War lieutenant loses his arm to amputation is detached and impersonal, yet hauntingly moving. The lieutenant is rationing coffee when a stray bullet hits his arm and changes his life forever. So begins his dreamlike journey toward the field hospital. Although the nameless lieutenant appears numb, the reader can imagine his dread as he anticipates the medical attention he will receive. Despite his protests and the doctor's false assurances, the lieutenant loses his arm in just another "episode of war." Through his depiction of this gripping series of events, Crane conveys an important message about the tragedy of war and the helplessness of those caught up in the fighting.

❷ Activating Prior Knowledge

Have students discuss the differences between photography and other forms of art, such as painting or drawing. Students should understand that the photographs in this story depict real soldiers who fought in the Civil War. Ask students to tell which records of historical events they find more powerful—written or visual.

Concept Connector ➡

Tell students they will revisit the ways in which both fiction and visual records can enhance our understanding of historical events.

An ❶ ❷ EPISODE OF WAR
STEPHEN CRANE

BACKGROUND Until World War II, the American Civil War was the bloodiest conflict in American history. It claimed the lives of 600,000 soldiers. Hundreds of thousands more were left maimed by battle wounds and crude medical care. In fact, the conditions in field hospitals were so primitive that twice as many soldiers died from infections as from combat wounds. As you read this story, keep in mind that amputation was the routine treatment for injured limbs. A wounded soldier knew that he faced the high probability of losing his arm or leg to a surgeon's saw.

508 Division, Reconciliation, and Expansion (1850–1914)

Ⓒ Text Complexity Rubric

An Episode of War		
Qualitative Measures		
Context/Knowledge Demands	U. S. Civil War; historical knowledge demands 1 2 ③ 4 5	
Structure/Language Conventionality and Clarity	Some long sentences and historical vocabulary 1 2 3 ④ 5	
Levels of Meaning/ Purpose/Concept Level	Accessible (realistic description) 1 2 ③ 4 5	
Quantitative Measures		
Lexile	1090L	Text Length	1,599 words
Overall Complexity	More accessible	

Reader and Task Suggestions

Preparing to Read the Text
- Using the information on SE p. 507, discuss Crane's fascination with war, especially the Civil War.
- Ask students what they might learn about people or about life by reading a story set on a battlefield.
- Guide students to use Multidraft Reading strategies (TE p. 507).

Leveled Tasks

Structure/Language If students will have difficulty with syntax, have them focus on the lieutenant's actions during a first read. As students reread, have them add details about others on the battlefield.

Evaluating If students will not have difficulty with syntax, have them judge the effectiveness of Crane's omission of battlefield details just before the final paragraph.

The lieutenant's rubber blanket lay on the ground, and upon it he had poured the company's supply of coffee. Corporals and other representatives of the grimy and hot-throated men who lined the breast-work[1] had come for each squad's portion.

The lieutenant was frowning and serious at this task of division. His lips pursed as he drew with his sword various crevices in the heap, until brown squares of coffee, astoundingly equal in size, appeared on the blanket. He was on the verge of a great triumph in mathematics, and the corporals were thronging forward, each to reap a little square, when suddenly the lieutenant cried out and looked quickly at a man near him as if he suspected it was a case of personal assault. The others cried out also when they saw blood upon the lieutenant's sleeve.

He had winced like a man stung, swayed dangerously, and then straightened. The sound of his hoarse breathing was plainly audible. He looked sadly, mystically, over the breast-work at the green face of a wood, where now were many little puffs of white smoke. During this moment the men about him gazed statuelike and silent, astonished and awed by this catastrophe which happened when catastrophes were not expected—when they had leisure to observe it.

As the lieutenant stared at the wood, they too swung their heads, so that for another instant all hands, still silent, contemplated the distant forest as if their minds were fixed upon the mystery of a bullet's journey.

The officer had, of course, been compelled to take his sword into his left hand. He did not hold it by the hilt. He gripped it at the middle of the blade, awkwardly. Turning his eyes from the hostile wood, he looked at the sword as he held it there, and seemed puzzled as to what to do with it, where to put it. In short, this weapon had of a sudden become a strange thing to him. He looked at it in a kind of stupefaction, as if he had been endowed with a trident, a sceptre,[2] or a spade.

Finally he tried to sheathe it. To sheathe a sword held by the left hand, at the middle of the blade, in a scabbard hung at the left hip, is a feat worthy of a sawdust ring.[3] This

---

1. **breast-work** low wall put up quickly as a defense in battle.
2. **a trident, a sceptre** (trīd′ ənt; sep′ tər) three-pronged spear; decorated ornamental rod or staff symbolizing royal authority.
3. **sawdust ring** ring in which circus acts are performed.

❹ ◀ **Critical Viewing** What similarities do you see between this photograph and Crane's description of the wounded lieutenant being helped by his men? **[Connect]**

---

❸ The American EXPERIENCE

Humanities Connection

Photographer Mathew Brady
Thanks to photography pioneer Mathew Brady (1823?–1896), the Civil War was the first war to be captured on film. As a young man, Brady met Samuel Morse, the inventor of the telegraph. Morse taught Brady how to make daguerreotypes, the forerunners of photographs. By the 1850s, Brady owned a thriving studio in New York City and was known for his portraits of distinguished Americans. When the Civil War broke out, Brady hired twenty photographers and sent them out to document the conflict. Due to the limitations of their technology, the photographers rarely captured battlefield action. Instead, they took pictures of events behind the scenes and of the carnage after battles. **The photographs that illustrate this story were taken by Brady and his team.** Their images, often horrific, forced viewers to face the realities of war more directly than ever before.

Connect to the Literature

How is documentary photography, like the images on these pages, similar to Naturalism?

An Episode of War **509**

---

❸ The American Experience: Humanities Connection

Photographer Mathew Brady

The camera was a relatively new invention when Brady and his team began documenting the Civil War with photographs. One of the key limitations of early cameras was the slow shutter speed. In order to capture a focused image, the subject had to be completely still. As a result, Brady could not capture scenes of battles in progress. Instead, he documented events before and after the fighting. When Brady exhibited photographs of battlefield corpses at Antietam in 1862, a newspaper noted that Brady brought "home to us the terrible reality and earnestness of war."

Connect to the Literature

Have students read The American Experience feature; next present the additional background information above. Then **ask** the Connect to the Literature question.
Answer: Both documentary photography and Naturalism present an uncensored view of the harsh realities of life.

❹ Critical Viewing

Possible response: Like the men in the story, this soldier expresses aloofness in his body language, as though proximity to the wounded man will cause his own doom. Nevertheless, he still attempts to help his fallen comrade by giving him water from a canteen, much as the soldiers in the story offer timid assistance to their lieutenant.

Differentiated Instruction for Universal Access

Support for Special Needs Students
Have students read the adapted version of "An Episode of War" in the *Reader's Notebook: Adapted Version.* This version provides basic instruction in an interactive format with questions and write-on lines. Completing these pages will prepare students to read the selections in the Student Edition.

Support for Less Proficient Readers
Have students read the "An Episode of War" in the *Reader's Notebook.* This version provides basic instruction in an interactive format with questions and write-on lines. After students finish reading the selection in the *Reader's Notebook,* have them complete the questions and activities in the Student Edition.

EL Support for English Learners
Have students read the adapted version of the story in the *Reader's Notebook: English Learner's Version.* This version provides basic instruction in an interactive format with questions and write-on lines. Completing these pages will prepare students to read the selections in the Student Edition.

PHLit Online!
This selection is available in interactive format in the **Enriched Online Student Edition**, at **www.PHLitOnline.com**, which includes a thematically related video with writing prompt and an interactive graphic organizer.

❺ Literary Analysis

Naturalism

1. Have students read the brack-eted passage. Remind them that Naturalists focused on the digni-fied suffering of people who face fates that they cannot control.

2. **Ask** students the Literary Analysis question.
Possible response: The orderly-sergeant's careful but distant reaction suggests that the lieuten-ant is isolated and must face his tragedy alone.

▶ **Monitor Progress: Ask** how the list of "revelations of all exis-tence" reflects a Naturalist point of view.
Answer: The list equates sub-jects large and small, from ants to potentates, and suggests that they are all subject to chance.

▶ **Reteach:** If students do not rec-ognize the ideas of Naturalism, emphasize that this move-ment was a reaction against Romanticism. Have students list traits of both movements, and check their understanding that Naturalists tried to present a realistic, unromantic view of the world.

❻ Reading Strategy

Applying Background Knowledge

1. Have students use the **Reading Strategy Graphic Organizer B,** page 102 in *Graphic Organizer Transparencies.*

2. **Ask** students the Reading Strategy question.
Possible response: Knowing that the Civil War was the bloodi-est conflict in American history clarifies the contrast between the chaos of battle and the calm the lieutenant feels when wounded and withdrawn from that chaos.

510

Literary Analysis
Naturalism What Naturalist ideas are evident in this passage about the orderly-sergeant's reaction to the lieutenant's wound?

❺

Vocabulary
precipitate (prē sip´ ə tāt´)
v. cause to happen before expected or desired

Reading Strategy ❻
Applying Background Knowledge How does your knowledge of the Civil War clarify your understanding of these battlefield details?

wounded officer engaged in a desperate struggle with the sword and the wobbling scabbard, and during the time of it breathed like a wrestler.

But at this instant the men, the spectators, awoke from their stone-like poses and crowded forward sympathetically. The orderly-sergeant took the sword and tenderly placed it in the scabbard. At the time, he leaned nervously backward, and did not allow even his finger to brush the body of the lieutenant. A wound gives strange dignity to him who bears it. Well men shy from his new and terrible majesty. It is as if the wounded man's hand is upon the curtain which hangs before the revelations of all existence—the meaning of ants, poten-tates,[4] wars, cities, sunshine, snow, a feather dropped from a bird's wing; and the power of it sheds radiance upon a bloody form, and makes the other men understand sometimes that they are little. His comrades look at him with large eyes thoughtfully. Moreover, they fear vaguely that the weight of a finger upon him might send him headlong, precipitate the tragedy, hurl him at once into the dim, grey unknown. And so the orderly-sergeant, while sheathing the sword, leaned nervously backward.

There were others who proffered assistance. One timidly presented his shoulder and asked the lieutenant if he cared to lean upon it, but the latter waved him away mournfully. He wore the look of one who knows he is the victim of a terrible disease and understands his help-lessness. He again stared over the breast-work at the forest, and then, turning, went slowly rearward. He held his right wrist tenderly in his left hand as if the wounded arm was made of very brittle glass.

And the men in silence stared at the wood, then at the departing lieutenant; then at the wood, then at the lieutenant.

As the wounded officer passed from the line of battle, he was enabled to see many things which as a participant in the fight were unknown to him. He saw a general on a black horse gazing over the lines of blue infantry at the green woods which veiled his problems. An aide galloped furiously, dragged his horse suddenly to a halt, saluted, and presented a paper. It was, for a wonder, precisely like a historical painting.

To the rear of the general and his staff a group, composed of a bugler, two or three orderlies, and the bearer of the corps standard,[5] all upon maniacal horses, were working like slaves to hold their ground, preserve their respectful interval, while the shells boomed in the air about them, and caused their chargers to make furious quiv-ering leaps.

A battery, a tumultuous and shining mass, was swirling toward the right. The wild thud of hoofs, the cries of the riders shouting

---

4. potentates (pōt´ ən tāts) *n.* rulers; powerful people.
5. corps standard (kôr) flag or banner representing a military unit.

Enrichment: Investigating Career Connections

Photojournalism

The work of photographers such as Mathew Brady (see pp. 508, 509, and 511) brought the horrors of the Civil War into homes across the country. Like their earlier counterparts, today's photojournalists capture news events and explore timely issues through images rather than words. Although some work as staff photographers for newspapers and magazines, most work as freelancers.

Activity: Research Invite students to investigate work as a photojournalist. Suggest that they use

Internet and library resources to gather information. Students might also contact modern-day photojournalists to learn more about the nature and history of this career. Students can guide their research using the **Enrichment: Investigating Career Connections** work sheet, in *Professional Development Guidebook,* page 221.

blame and praise, menace and encouragement, and, last, the roar of the wheels, the slant of the glistening guns, brought the lieutenant to an intent pause. The battery swept in curves that stirred the heart; it made halts as dramatic as the crash of a wave on the rocks, and when it fled onward this aggregation of wheels, levers, motors had a beautiful unity, as if it were a missile. The sound of it was a war-chorus that reached into the depths of man's emotion.

The lieutenant, still holding his arm as if it were of glass, stood watching this battery until all detail of it was lost, save the figures of the riders, which rose and fell and waved lashes over the black mass.

Later, he turned his eyes toward the battle, where the shooting sometimes crackled like bush-fires, sometimes sputtered with exasperating irregularity, and sometimes reverberated like the thunder. He saw the smoke rolling upward and saw crowds of men who ran and cheered, or stood and blazed away at the inscrutable distance.

He came upon some stragglers, and they told him how to find the field hospital. They described its exact location. In fact, these men, no longer having part in the battle, knew more of it than others. They told the performance of every corps, every division, the opinion of every general. The lieutenant, carrying his wounded arm rearward, looked upon them with wonder.

At the roadside a brigade was making coffee and buzzing with talk like a girls' boarding school. Several officers came out to him

7 ▲ Critical Viewing
What mood do the expressions and body language of these Civil War officers convey? Explain. **[Analyze]**

Vocabulary
aggregation (ag′ rə gā′ shən) *n.* group of distinct objects or individuals

9

Reading Check 10

What does the lieutenant stop to watch on his way to the field hospital?

An Episode of War **511**

---

7 Critical Viewing

Answer: Students might point out that the mood is relaxed and somewhat detached; these officers do not show signs of great stress or tension.

8 Critical Thinking
Analyze Causes and Effects

1. Have a student volunteer read this page aloud, beginning with "The wild thud of hoofs" and ending with "looked upon them with wonder." Guide students to recognize that the lieutenant makes a variety of observations as he is walking.

2. **Ask** students to explain why the stragglers might know more about the battle than the lieutenant does. Is their information reliable?
Answer: Students may say that the stragglers, removed as they are from the thick of battle, have seen more of the larger conflict than the lieutenant has. Others may suggest that these men may not have accurate information and know little of what the generals are thinking.

9 Background

During the Civil War, field hospitals would not have met the standards in place at present-day hospitals, Most field amputations were performed without anesthetic. Doctors worked at top speed to minimize the agony and shock. Antiseptics were unknown and doctors did not sterilize their hands or their instruments between operations.

10 Reading Check

Answer: He stops to watch the battle in progress, including the actions of a general, his aide, and other soldiers.

Differentiated
Instruction for Universal Access

Support for Less Proficient Readers
Guide students through the description of the effect of the wound on page 510—particularly the sentence beginning with "It is as if the wounded man's hand." Point out the "as if" and explain that the author uses an imaginative word picture (a hand on a curtain hanging in front of the answers to life's questions) to convey an important idea. Guide students through the list of nouns— "ants," "wars," and so on—

and invite them to suggest what the "meaning" of each might be.

Make sure students understand Crane's essential point: a wound carries a strange power: Other people believe that the wounded stands closer to the essence of life itself. Moreover, Crane is also suggesting that in the final analysis, humans may not "mean" more than an insect or an inanimate object.

511

⑪ Critical Viewing

Answer: Students may say that the conditions in this medical tent appear rough and basic; they may conclude that the care given to wounded soldiers was probably poor because of limited resources and unsanitary surroundings.

⑫ Critical Viewing

Answer: This set of surgical instruments highlights the brutality and crudeness of Civil War medical practices. In particular, both the small hatchet and the saw suggest the frequency with which amputations were performed. The instruments suggest that the lieutenant's treatment will be painful.

⑬ Engaging the Essential Question

How does literature shape or reflect society?

1. Point out that Naturalist writers tried to reflect society by presenting a realistic, human view of all events, even large-scale conflicts like war.

2. **Ask** students to explain how the doctor's reaction, beginning in the last paragraph of this page, downplays the lieutenant's situation.
   Answer: The doctor's attitude is impatient and dismissive; he does not treat the lieutenant's wound as an emergency or cause for urgent action. Instead he treats it as a dull daily routine and thinks little of lying to the lieutenant about the likely outcome of the surgery.

3. **Ask:** What view of society does Crane present with this depiction?
   Possible response: He presents a view of a society that is often indifferent to people's suffering. He reveals a dignity in the victim, but that dignity is ignored or unrecognized by others.

⑪ ▶ **Critical Viewing**
This is a photograph of a Civil War field hospital. Do you think that soldiers received quality treatment in this setting? Explain. **[Deduce]**

Vocabulary
commotion (kə mō′ shən)
n. noisy confusion

⑫ ▶ **Critical Viewing**
What do the Civil War era surgical instruments shown on the next page suggest about the care the lieutenant will receive? **[Infer]**

and inquired concerning things of which he knew nothing. One, seeing his arm, began to scold. "Why, man, that's no way to do. You want to fix that thing." He appropriated the lieutenant and the lieutenant's wound. He cut the sleeve and laid bare the arm, every nerve of which softly fluttered under his touch. He bound his handkerchief over the wound, scolding away in the meantime. His tone allowed one to think that he was in the habit of being wounded every day. The lieutenant hung his head, feeling, in this presence, that he did not know how to be correctly wounded.

The low white tents of the hospital were grouped around an old schoolhouse. There was here a singular commotion. In the foreground two ambulances interlocked wheels in the deep mud. The drivers were tossing the blame of it back and forth, gesticulating and berating, while from the ambulances, both crammed with wounded, there came an occasional groan. An interminable crowd of bandaged men were coming and going. Great numbers sat under the trees nursing heads or arms or legs. There was a dispute of some kind raging on the steps of the schoolhouse. Sitting with his back against a tree a man with a face as grey as a new army blanket was serenely smoking a corncob pipe. The lieutenant wished to rush forward and inform him that he was dying.

⑬ ↓ A busy surgeon was passing near the lieutenant. "Good-morning," he said, with a friendly smile. Then he caught sight of the

512 Division, Reconciliation, and Expansion (1850–1914)

Vocabulary Development

Vocabulary Knowledge Rating
When students have completed reading and discussing the selection have them take out their **Vocabulary Knowledge Rating Charts** for the story. Read the words aloud, and have students rate their knowledge of words again in the After Reading column. Clarify any words that are still problematic. Have students write their own definitions and example or sentence in the appropriate column. Then have students complete the Vocabulary Lesson at the end of the selection. Encourage students to use the words in further discussion and written work about the selection. Remind them that they will be accountable for these words on the **Selection Test,** *Unit 3 Resources,* pages 41–43 or 44–46.

lieutenant's arm, and his face at once changed. "Well, let's have a look at it." He seemed possessed suddenly of a great contempt for the lieutenant. This wound evidently placed the latter on a very low social plane. The doctor cried out impatiently, "What mutton-head had tied it up that way anyhow?" The lieutenant answered, "Oh, a man."

When the wound was disclosed the doctor fingered it disdainfully. "Humph," he said. "You come along with me and I'll 'tend to you." His voice contained the same scorn as if he were saying: "You will have to go to jail."

The lieutenant had been very meek, but now his face flushed, and he looked into the doctor's eyes. "I guess I won't have it amputated," he said.

"Nonsense, man! Nonsense! Nonsense!" cried the doctor. "Come along, now. I won't amputate it. Come along. Don't be a baby."

"Let go of me," said the lieutenant, holding back wrathfully, his glance fixed upon the door of the old schoolhouse, as sinister to him as the portals of death.

And this is the story of how the lieutenant lost his arm. When he reached home, his sisters, his mother, his wife, sobbed for a long time at the sight of the flat sleeve. "Oh, well," he said, standing shamefaced amid these tears, "I don't suppose it matters so much as all that."

Vocabulary

disdainfully (dis dān′ fəl ē) *adv.* showing scorn or contempt

sinister (si′ nəs tər) *adj.* threatening harm, evil, or misfortune

© Museum of the Confederacy, Richmond, Virginia

Critical Reading

©

1. **Key Ideas and Details (a)** What happens to cause the lieutenant's injury? **(b) Analyze:** How do the details of his injury make him a sympathetic character?

©

2. **Key Ideas and Details (a)** What is the lieutenant's reaction when a soldier offers a helpful shoulder? **(b) Infer:** Why does he react this way?

©

3. **Integration of Knowledge and Ideas (a)** Note three examples of the lieutenant's distance from the uninjured people around him. **(b) Interpret:** What do these examples suggest about the way others see him and the way he sees himself?

©

4. **Integration of Knowledge and Ideas** In your view, does society benefit from frank portrayals of suffering? In your response, use at least two of these Essential Question words: *awareness, assumption, reality, despair.* [*Connecting to the Essential Question: How does literature shape or reflect society?*]

Cite textual evidence to support your responses.

An Episode of War **513**

Concept Connector

Reading Strategy Graphic Organizer
Ask students to review the graphic organizers in which they have connected background knowledge with story details. Then have students compare their filled-in organizers.

Activating Prior Knowledge
Remind students of their opinions about the relative power of written and visual records of events. Ask how reading Crane's work may have changed their thoughts about the power of a story.

Writing About the Essential Question
Have students compare responses to the prompt before they completed reading with their thoughts afterward. Have them work individually or in groups, writing or discussing their thoughts, to formulate their new responses. Then probe for what students have learned that confirms or invalidates their initial thoughts. Encourage students to cite specific textual details to support their responses.

Answers

1. **(a)** He is rationing coffee. **(b)** During a daily routine, he is struck by a random bullet.

2. **(a)** Leaving the lieutenant nameless makes him more anonymous, an unfortunate Everyman. **(b) Possible response:** This anonymity heightens the story's impact by making the lieutenant seem more detached from the other soldiers once he is wounded.

3. He submits to the doctor when he suspects his worst fear may become real. He downplays the trauma to spare his family.

4. **Possible responses: (a)** "The sound of his hoarse breathing was plainly audible"; "they, too, swung their heads"; "He again stared over the breast-work at the forest, and then, turning, went slowly rearward." **(b)** The descriptions depict the men as helpless animals, reacting to incidents instinctively.

5. **Possible answers: (a)** The orderly-sergeant places the lieutenant's sword in his scabbard but is unwilling to touch the wounded man. One officer helps the lieutenant by redressing his wound, but the doctor criticizes the job. **(b)** The details suggest that kindness cannot help people endure suffering caused by fate.

6. **Possible response:** If this story were written by a Romantic writer, the soldiers, through camaraderie, might have helped the lieutenant.

7. **Possible responses: (a)** Because of limited resources, he lies to persuade the lieutenant to be treated. **(b)** Knowing that amputation was common may help readers predict the outcome.

8. **Possible responses: (a)** Chesnut's reference to a telegraph; Goss's explanation of his motivations for volunteering; McKim's mention of gunfire from the woods. **(b)** The use of telegraphs indicates that communication was limited so obtaining medical supplies would have been difficult; Goss's motives suggest that many soldiers were not prepared for the harsh realities of war; gunfire from the woods at Gettysburg indicates that this was a common tactic.

Literary Analysis

1. **Key Ideas and Details (a)** What is the lieutenant doing when he is injured? **(b)** How does this detail reflect the **Naturalist** idea that people are victims of chance?

2. **Key Ideas and Details (a)** Why do you think Crane chooses to have the lieutenant remain nameless? **(b)** Does the lieutenant's namelessness heighten or lessen the emotional impact of the story? Explain.

3. **Key Ideas and Details** Note two details that show how the lieutenant exhibits a quiet endurance typical of characters in Naturalist works. Explain your choices.

4. **Key Ideas and Details (a)** Identify three descriptions of human actions in the story that could also describe the actions of animals. **(b)** How do these descriptions reflect Naturalist ideas about people's helplessness in the face of nature and circumstance?

5. **Key Ideas and Details (a)** At various points in the story, people make gestures of kindness toward the lieutenant. Use a chart like the one shown to record these details and explain why they fail. **(b)** What Naturalist ideas about the possibility of kindness does this series of details imply?

Event or Detail	Why It Fails	Naturalist Idea

6. **Integration of Knowledge and Ideas** What differences might exist in the mood, events, or outcome of this story if it had been written by a *Romantic* writer who believed in the harmony of humanity and nature? Explain.

Reading Strategy

7. **(a) Apply your background knowledge** of Civil War medical practices to explain why the doctor promises the lieutenant he will not amputate. **(b)** How did your background knowledge help you anticipate, or *predict,* the type of medical treatment the lieutenant would receive?

8. Apply the background knowledge you gain from reading the Civil War documents on pages 494–503. **(a)** List at least three details from the primary sources that relate to the setting, characters, and events in *An Episode of War.* **(b)** For each detail you cite, explain how it adds to your understanding of the story.

Common Core State Standards

Writing
2. Write informative/explanatory texts to examine and convey complex ideas, concepts, and information clearly and accurately through the effective selection, organization, and analysis of content. *(p. 515)*

2.a. Introduce a topic; organize complex ideas, concepts, and information so that each new element builds on that which precedes it to create a unified whole. *(p. 515)*

Language
4.b. Identify and correctly use patterns of word changes that indicate different meanings or parts of speech. *(p. 515)*

Assessment Practice

Context (For more practice, see *All-in-One Workbook*.)

The reading sections of some tests require students to use context to determine the meaning of figurative language. Remind students that the words surrounding the targeted expression can provide clues to its meaning. Use the following sample test item to demonstrate.

> But at this instant the men, the spectators, awoke from their stone-like poses and crowded forward sympathetically.

In this passage, "awoke from their stone-like poses" most nearly means

A got off their stone beds.

B moved suddenly after being still.

C got up to look at statues.

D posed for a sculpture.

The men, referred to as impassive "spectators," were like "stone" until they "awoke" and roused themselves from their stupor. Context clues support answer **B.**

514

Integrated Language Skills

Vocabulary Acquisition and Use

Word Analysis: Latin Root -greg-

The word *aggregation* contains the Latin root -*greg-*, meaning "herd" or "flock." An *aggregation* is a group of people or things taken as a whole. A *congregation* is a group, and a *gregarious* person is someone who enjoys being part of a crowd. Copy the paragraph below, filling in each blank with the appropriate -*greg-* word from the list. Be sure to fill in each blank with a word that is appropriate in meaning and part of speech.

aggregate   gregarious   congregated

The wounded soldiers _____ on the steps, waiting to see the doctor. They were silent, except for one _____ private who described his injury in great detail to the rest of the group. In the _____, an orderly reflected, wounded men are a quiet bunch.

Vocabulary: Analogies

Analogies show the relationships between pairs of words. Complete each analogy using a word from the vocabulary list on page 506. In each, your choice should create a word pair that matches the relationship between the first two words given. Then, explain your answer.

1. *Quickly* is to *rapidly* as _____ is to *scornfully*.
2. *Hidden* is to *revealed* as _____ is to *harmless*.
3. *Storm* is to *peace* as _____ is to *serenity*.
4. *Laugh* is to *cry* as _____ is to *delay*.
5. *Sum* is to *parts* as _____ is to *individual*.

Writing

Explanatory Text
Many critics have observed that Crane's fiction asks questions but does not provide answers, challenging readers to evaluate their ideas about people's behavior, feelings, and thoughts. Write an **essay** in which you respond to this assessment of Crane's work. Determine whether "An Episode of War" provides strong support for this critical view.

Prewriting Use a format like the one shown to list assumptions about war that people commonly hold. Then, reread the story. Note details that relate to your list of assumptions. Decide if you think this story poses challenges to those assumptions and whether it provides support for the critical view. Write a statement that summarizes your observations.

Drafting Clearly state the critical assessment of Crane's work. Then, state your position. Using your prewriting notes, devote one paragraph to each assumption and its expression in the story.

Revising Reread your essay to make sure that your ideas are fully developed, that your ideas flow in a logical order, and that each idea builds on the one that comes before. If necessary, reorder your paragraphs to improve the flow of ideas.

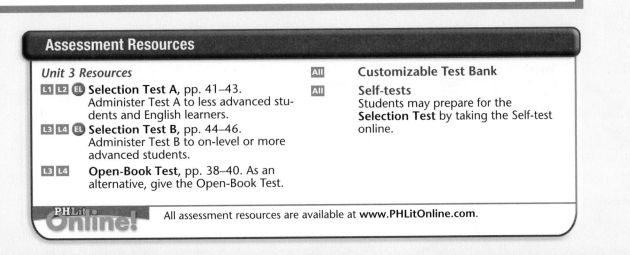

Model: Questioning Assumptions

Assumption: Soldiers have what they need to do their job well.
Challenge question: Do soldiers always have what they need?
Related detail: The soldiers are each being rationed a small bit of coffee.

To challenge an assumption, ask, "Is this always true?"

Vocabulary Acquisition and Use

1. Introduce the skill, using the instruction on the student page.
2. Have students complete the Word Analysis activity and the Vocabulary practice.

Word Analysis:
congregated; gregarious; aggregate

Vocabulary: Analogies
1. disdainfully
2. sinister
3. commotion
4. precipitate
5. aggregation

Writing

1. To guide students in writing the essay, give them the Support for Writing worksheet (*Unit 3 Resources,* p. 36).
2. Point out that students must be clear about the critical assessment—that Crane asks questions and challenges readers rather than providing answers.
3. Help students think of other assumptions about war based on what they know about contemporary conflicts around the world.
4. Use the **Rubrics for Response to Literature,** in *Professional Development Guidebook,* pages 250–251, to evaluate students' work.

Assessment Resources

Unit 3 Resources

L1 L2 EL Selection Test A, pp. 41–43.
Administer Test A to less advanced students and English learners.

L3 L4 EL Selection Test B, pp. 44–46.
Administer Test B to on-level or more advanced students.

L3 L4 Open-Book Test, pp. 38–40. As an alternative, give the Open-Book Test.

All Customizable Test Bank

All Self-tests
Students may prepare for the **Selection Test** by taking the Self-test online.

PHLit Online! All assessment resources are available at **www.PHLitOnline.com**.

❶ Defining Narrative Nonfiction

Introduce the concept of narrative nonfiction, using the description on the student page. Point out narrative nonfiction's similarities to fiction and explain that the line between these two genres is not always clear.
Ask: Under what circumstances might an author introduce fiction to a nonfiction narrative?
Sample response: The author of an autobiography might invent details to make his or her life story more exciting.

❷ Types of Narrative Nonfiction

Explain that the types of narrative nonfiction defined on the student page are rarely mutually exclusive. A narrative can belong to more than one type. Invite students to speculate how two or more of these forms could exist in the same work.
Ask: How could an autobiography and a journal overlap? How could a memoir also be a historical narrative?
Possible responses: The writer of an autobiography might include excerpts from his or her journal. An author of a memoir might focus on his or her experiences during a period of historical importance.

❸ Style and Tone

Point out that many narrative accounts are written in a distinctive style and tone. For example, in the excerpt from *My Bondage and My Freedom*, p. 520, Frederick Douglass's style is masterful, authoritative, and persuasive. **Ask:** Why might Frederick Douglass have used vivid details and well-drawn observations of the experience of slavery?
Possible response: He wanted to shed light on the entire institution of slavery, not just on his own life.

❹ Close Read: Style and Tone

Review the chart with students. Point out the highlighted text in the model on page 517. Explain that in each case, the color of the highlighting matches the color of the category in the chart. Details that illustrate a given category are highlighted in the color of that category.

516

There are events which are so great that if a writer has participated in them his obligation is to write truly rather than assume the presumption of altering them with invention.

~ Ernest Hemingway

❶ Defining Narrative Nonfiction

Narrative nonfiction is prose writing that tells the stories of real people, places, objects, or events. It features many of the same elements as fiction—including characters, setting, and a sequence of events—but these are based on actual, lived experiences, rather than imagination.

❷ Types of Narrative Nonfiction
These are the most common forms of narrative nonfiction:

- **Biography and Autobiography:** works that tell life stories. A biography is a life story written by another person, while an autobiography is an account of the writer's own life.
- **Historical Narrative:** a work that relates historical events that the writer may or may not have experienced firsthand
- **Memoir:** an autobiographical work that focuses on a particular time period or aspect of the writer's life
- **Diary and Journal:** an informal account of the writer's daily experiences
- **Narrative Essay:** a short work that explores ideas while relating a story

❸ Style and Tone
Style is a writer's particular way of using language, and tone is his or her attitude toward the audience and subject. Both are key ingredients in narrative nonfiction.

❹ Close Read: Style and Tone
Many literary elements contribute to a writer's style and tone. The following elements appear in the Model Text.

Diction: the types of words a writer favors. Diction may be ornate, plain, familiar, formal, technical, or any combination thereof. *Example: "Why did that green goose Anderson go into Fort Sumter?" (Mary Chesnut)*	**Rhetorical Devices:** meaningful patterns of words and ideas. *Parallelism* is the repetition of the same grammatical structure. *Rhetorical questions* are asked for effect. *Example (parallelism): "She had bread for the hungry, clothes for the naked, and comfort for every mourner. . . ." (Frederick Douglass)*
Syntax: sentence length and complexity. Syntax may involve any combination of long, short, complex, or simple sentences. *Example: "When I was a boy, there was but one permanent ambition among my comrades in our village on the west bank of the Mississippi River. That was, to be a steamboatman." (Mark Twain)*	**Telling Details:** precise details that reveal important information about the characters, setting, or situation. *Example: ". . . she had two shopping bags full of canned peaches, real peaches, beans wrapped in taro leaves, cookies, Thermos bottles, enough food for everybody . . ." (Maxine Hong Kingston)*

516 Division, Reconciliation, and Expansion (1850–1914)

Think Aloud

Vocabulary: Word Origins
Direct students' attention to the word *narrative*. Use the following "think aloud" to model the skill of using word origins to understand related words. Say to students:

> I know that a narrative tells a story. When I look up the word *narrative* in a dictionary, I find out that it comes from the Latin root that means "to tell, relate, or explain."

Nearby, I find several other words that share the same Latin root. A *narrator* is someone who tells a story. To *narrate* is to tell a story, and *narration* is the act of telling or giving an account. All of these words will be useful when I want to talk about narrative nonfiction.

Model

About the Text Richard Wright (1908–1960) was one of the first African American writers to achieve international fame. His autobiography, *Black Boy,* was published in 1945, five years after the appearance of his acclaimed first novel, *Native Son.* In this excerpt, he refers to *A Book of Prefaces* by journalist and social critic H. L. Mencken.

from *Black Boy*
by Richard Wright

⑤ That night in my rented room, while letting the hot water run over my can of pork and beans in the sink, I opened *A Book of Prefaces* and began to read. I was jarred and shocked by the style, the clear, clean, sweeping sentences. Why did he write like that? And how did one write like that? I pictured the man as a **⑥** raging demon, slashing with his pen, consumed with hate, denouncing everything American, extolling everything European or German, laughing at the weakness of people, mocking God, authority. What was this? I stood up, trying to realize what reality lay behind the meaning of the words. Yes, this man was fighting, fighting with words. He was using words as a weapon, using them as one would use a club. **⑦** Could words be weapons? Well, yes, for here they were. Then maybe, perhaps, I could use them as a weapon? No. It frightened me. I read on and what amazed me **⑧** was not what he said, but how on earth anybody had the courage to say it.

Occasionally I glanced up to reassure myself that I was alone in the room. Who were these men about whom Mencken was talking so passionately? Who was Anatole France? Joseph Conrad? Sinclair Lewis, Sherwood Anderson, Dostoevski, George Moore, Gustave Flaubert, Maupassant, Tolstoy, Frank Harris, Mark Twain, Thomas Hardy, Arnold Bennett, Stephen Crane, Zola, Norris, Gorky, Bergson, Ibsen, Balzac, Bernard Shaw, Dumas, Poe, Thomas Mann, O. Henry, Dreiser, H. G. Wells, Gogol, T. S. Eliot, Gide, Baudelaire, Edgar Lee Masters, Stendhal, Turgenev, Huneker, Nietzsche,[1] and scores of others? Were these men real? Did they exist or had they existed? And how did one pronounce their names?

⑤ Telling Details
Specific details, such as "rented room," and "can of pork and beans" clearly establish both the setting and Wright's less than affluent circumstances.

⑥ Rhetorical Devices
Note the use of parallel structure in Wright's description of Mencken's prose: "slashing," "denouncing," "extolling," and "mocking."

⑦ Syntax Wright's syntax—featuring short, staccato sentences—reflects the intensity and speed of his thoughts. It is as though the reader is allowed to experience Wright's internal, highly charged conversation.

⑧ Diction Wright uses an idiomatic expression: "how on earth." This strengthens the sense of authenticity in his impassioned, emotional reaction to Mencken's words.

[1]**Anatole France...Nietzsche** This list identifies some of the most celebrated European and American philosophers, poets, playwrights, and fiction writers of the 19th and 20th centuries.

Extended Study: Narrative Nonfiction **517**

⑤ Telling Details

Point out how Wright painstakingly adds a detail such as "letting the hot water run over my can of pork and beans." **Ask:** How might such a detail affect the reader?

Sample response: The detail pulls the reader into the narrative and makes him or her more attentive to Wright's ideas.

⑥ Rhetorical Devices

Point out that Wright uses the rhetorical device of parallel structure to create emphasis and stir the reader's emotions. **Ask:** How does Wright's use of parallel structure help confirm his description of Mencken as a "raging demon"?

Sample response: The parallel structure emphasizes the harsh, scandalous actions of this "raging demon."

⑦ Syntax

Read the bracketed text aloud and refer students to the Syntax callout box in their books. **Ask:** Based on his syntax, how would you describe Wright's state of mind?

Sample response: He is amazed, confused, and excited.

⑧ Diction

Point out that the idiom "how on earth" has a meaning that is different from its literal meaning. **Ask:** How else might you write this sentence to express the meaning of the idiom "how on earth"?

Sample response: I read on and what amazed me was not what he said, but how anybody could *possibly* have the courage to say it.

Extend the Lesson

Exploring Narrative Nonfiction
Students may have difficulty identifying the style and tone of narrative nonfiction. Help them focus on those features by distributing copies of the three-column chart on page 345 in *Graphic Organizer Transparencies.* Have students write the title of the selection in the left column. In the center column, ask them to note the style of the selection and examples from the text that demonstrate the style. Ask students to use the right column to identify the tone and list their reasons for identifying it as such. After reading a piece of narrative nonfiction, have students compare their charts.

• *from* My Bondage and My Freedom
Lesson Pacing Guide

DAY 1 Preteach

- Ⓒ Administer the Reading and Vocabulary Warm-ups (*Unit 3 Resources*, pp. 47–50) as necessary.
- Ⓒ Introduce the Literary Analysis concept: Autobiography.
- • Introduce the Reading Strategy: Setting a Purpose.
- Ⓒ Build background with the author and Background features.
- • Develop thematic thinking with Connecting to the Essential Question.
- Ⓒ Teach the selection vocabulary.

DAY 2–3 Preteach/Teach/Assess

- • Distribute copies of the appropriate graphic organizer for the Reading Strategy (*Graphic Organizer Transparencies*, pp. 105–106).
- • Distribute copies of the appropriate graphic organizer for Literary Analysis (*Graphic Organizer Transparencies*, pp. 107–108).
- • Prepare students to read with the Activating Prior Knowledge activities (TE).
- • Informally monitor comprehension while students read.
- • Use the Reading Check question to confirm comprehension.
- • Develop students' ability to set a purpose using the Reading Strategy prompts.
- Ⓒ Reinforce vocabulary with the Vocabulary notes.
- • Assess students' comprehension and mastery of the skills by having them answer the Critical Reading, Literary Analysis, and Reading Strategy questions.
- Ⓒ Have students complete the Vocabulary Lesson.

DAY 4 Extend/Assess

- Ⓒ Have students complete the Writing Lesson and write a college application essay. (You may assign as homework.)
- • Administer Selection Test A or B (*Unit 3 Resources*, pp. 59–61 or 62–64).

Ⓒ Common Core State Standards

Reading Informational Text
6. Determine an author's point of view or purpose in a text in which the rhetoric is particularly effective, analyzing how style and content contribute to the power, persuasiveness, or beauty of the text.

Writing 2. Write informative/explanatory texts to examine and convey complex ideas, concepts, and information clearly and accurately through the effective selection, organization, and analysis of content.
2.a. Introduce a topic; organize complex ideas, concepts, and information so that each new element builds on that which precedes it to create a unified whole.
2.b. Develop the topic thoroughly by selecting the most significant and relevant facts, concrete details, quotations, or other information and examples.
2.c. Use appropriate and varied transitions and syntax to link the major sections of the text, create cohesion, and clarify the relationships among complex ideas and concepts.

Language 4.b. Identify and correctly use patterns of word changes that indicate different meanings or parts of speech.
4.d. Verify the preliminary determination of the meaning of a word or phrase.

Additional Standards Practice
Common Core Companion, pp. 143–150; 196–207; 324–331

Daily Block Scheduling
Each day in this Lesson Pacing Guide represents a 40–50 minute period. Teachers using block scheduling may combine days to revise pacing. In addition, teachers may differentiate and support core instruction by integrating components for extended and intensive support as students require. See the Guide to Selected Leveled Resources (facing page).

Guide to Selected Leveled Resources

RTI Tier 1 (students performing on level)

from My Bondage and My Freedom

Warm Up	Practice, **model,** and **monitor** fluency, working **with the whole class** or **in groups.**	Vocabulary and Reading Warm-ups B, *Unit 3 Resources,* pp. 47–48, 50
Comprehension/Skills	**Support** and **monitor** comprehension and skills development, having students complete the activities, graphic organizers, and interactive prompts **independently** or **as a class.**	• *Reader's Notebook,* adapted instruction and full selection **EL** *Reader's Notebook: English Learner's Version,* adapted instruction and adapted selection • **Reading Strategy Graphic Organizer B,** *Graphic Organizer Transparencies,* p. 106 • **Literary Analysis Graphic Organizer B,** *Graphic Organizer Transparencies,* p. 108
Monitor Progress	**A** Monitor student progress with the differentiated curriculum-based assessment in the *Unit Resources.*	• **Selection Test B,** *Unit 3 Resources,* pp. 62–64 • **Open-Book Test,** *Unit 3 Resources,* pp. 56–58

RTI Tier 2 (students requiring intervention)

from My Bondage and My Freedom

Warm Up	Practice, **model,** and **monitor** fluency **in groups** or **with individuals.**	• **Vocabulary and Reading Warm-ups A,** *Unit 3 Resources,* pp. 47–49 • *Hear It!* Audio CD
Comprehension/Skills	• **Support** and **monitor** comprehension and skills development, working **in small groups** or **with individuals.** • As students complete the selection in the appropriate version of the *Reader's Notebook,* **monitor** comprehension frequently with group questions and individual instruction. • **Model** strategies while guiding students in completing the activities and prompts in the *Reader's Notebook,* as well as the graphic organizers. • **Practice** skills and **monitor** mastery with the *Reading Kit* worksheets.	• *Reader's Notebook: Adapted Version,* adapted instruction and adapted selection **EL** *Reader's Notebook: English Learner's Version,* adapted instruction and adapted selection • **Reading Strategy Graphic Organizer A,** *Graphic Organizer Transparencies,* p. 105 • **Literary Analysis Graphic Organizer A,** *Graphic Organizer Transparencies,* p. 107 • *Reading Kit,* Practice worksheets
Monitor Progress	**A** Monitor student progress with the differentiated curriculum-based assessment in the *Unit Resources* and in the *Reading Kit.*	• **Selection Test A,** *Unit 3 Resources,* pp. 59–61 • *Reading Kit,* Assess worksheets

TIER 3 Tier 3 intervention may require consultation with the student's special-education or dyslexia specialist. For additional support, see the Tier 2 activities and resources listed above.

One-on-one teaching   Group work   Whole-class instruction   Independent work   **A** Assessment

For a complete guide to selection support, including support for Advanced students, see the Overview of Resources in the frontmatter.

• *from* My Bondage and My Freedom

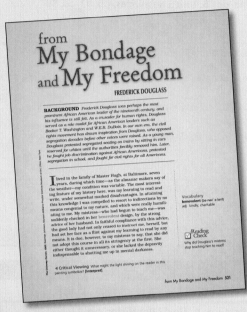

RESOURCES FOR:
- **L1** Special-Needs Students
- **L2** Below-Level Students (Tier 2)
- **L3** On-Level Students (Tier 1)
- **L4** Advanced Students (Tier 1)
- **EL** English Learners
- **All** All Students

Vocabulary/Fluency/Prior Knowledge

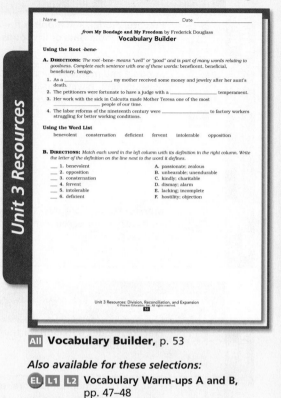

All **Vocabulary Builder,** p. 53

Also available for these selections:

EL **L1** **L2** Vocabulary Warm-ups A and B, pp. 47–48

EL **L1** **L2** Vocabulary Warm-ups A and B, pp. 49–50

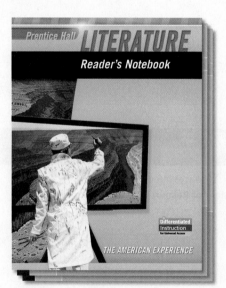

- **L2** **L3** *Reader's Notebook*
- **L1** *Reader's Notebook: Adapted Version*
- **EL** *Reader's Notebook: English Learner's Version*
- **EL** *Reader's Notebook: Spanish Version*

Reader's Notebooks

Pre- and postreading pages for this selection, as well as an excerpt from *My Bondage and My Freedom*, appear in an interactive format in the *Reader's Notebooks*. Each *Notebook* is differentiated for a different group of learners. The selections in the Adapted and English Learner's versions are abridged.

© *Common Core Companion*

Additional instruction and practice for each Common Core State Standard

Selection Support

Skills Development/Extension

Assessment

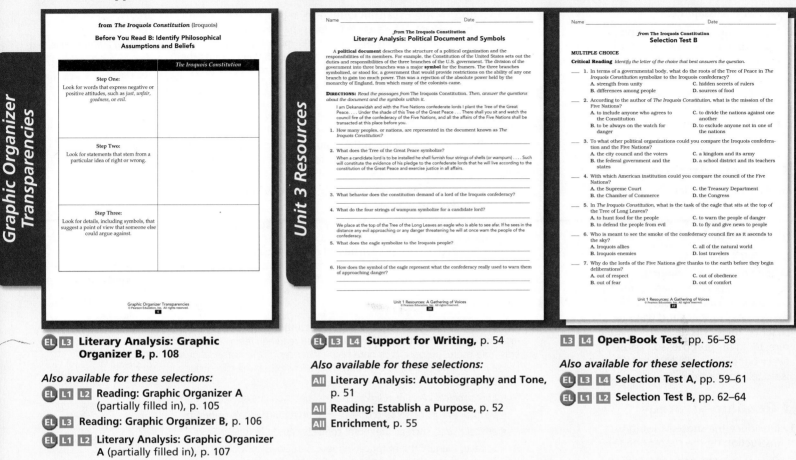

from The Iroquois Constitution (Iroquois)

Before You Read B: Identify Philosophical Assumptions and Beliefs

	The Iroquois Constitution
Step One: Look for words that express negative or positive attitudes, such as *just, unfair, goodness,* or *evil.*	
Step Two: Look for statements that stem from a particular idea of right or wrong.	
Step Three: Look for details, including symbols, that suggest a point of view that someone else could argue against.	

Graphic Organizer Transparencies
© Pearson Education, Inc. All rights reserved.

Name _____ Date _____

from **The Iroquois Constitution**
Literary Analysis: Political Document and Symbols

A **political document** describes the structure of a political organization and the responsibilities of its members. For example, the Constitution of the United States sets out the duties and responsibilities of the three branches of the U.S. government. The division of the government into three branches was a major **symbol** for the framers. The three branches symbolized, or stood for, a government that would restrict the ability of any one branch to gain too much power. This was a rejection of the absolute power held by the monarchy of England, from which many of the colonists came.

DIRECTIONS: *Read the passages from* The Iroquois Constitution. *Then, answer the questions about the document and the symbols within it.*

I am Dekanawidah and with the Five Nations confederate lords I plant the Tree of the Great Peace. . . . Under the shade of this Tree of the Great Peace . . . There shall you sit and watch the council fire of the confederacy of the Five Nations, and all the affairs of the Five Nations shall be transacted at this place before you.

1. How many peoples, or nations, are represented in the document known as *The Iroquois Constitution?*

2. What does the Tree of the Great Peace symbolize?

When a candidate lord is to be installed he shall furnish four strings of shells (or wampum) . . . . Such will constitute the evidence of his pledge to the confederate lords that he will live according to the constitution of the Great Peace and exercise justice in all affairs.

3. What behavior does the constitution demand of a lord of the Iroquois confederacy?

4. What do the four strings of wampum symbolize for a candidate lord?

We place at the top of the Tree of the Long Leaves an eagle who is able to see afar. If he sees in the distance any evil approaching or any danger threatening he will at once warn the people of the confederacy.

5. What does the eagle symbolize to the Iroquois people?

6. How does the symbol of the eagle represent what the confederacy really used to warn them of approaching danger?

Unit 1 Resources: A Gathering of Voices
© Pearson Education, Inc. All rights reserved.

Name _____ Date _____

from **The Iroquois Constitution**
Selection Test B

MULTIPLE CHOICE

Critical Reading *Identify the letter of the choice that best answers the question.*

___ 1. In terms of a governmental body, what do the roots of the Tree of Peace in *The Iroquois Constitution* symbolize to the Iroquois confederacy?
A. strength from unity
B. differences among people
C. hidden secrets of rulers
D. sources of food

___ 2. According to the author of *The Iroquois Constitution,* what is the mission of the Five Nations?
A. to include anyone who agrees to the Constitution
B. to be always on the watch for danger
C. to divide the nations against one another
D. to exclude anyone not in one of the nations

___ 3. To what other political organizations could you compare the Iroquois confederation and the Five Nations?
A. the city council and the voters
B. the federal government and the states
C. a kingdom and its army
D. a school district and its teachers

___ 4. With which American institution could you compare the council of the Five Nations?
A. the Supreme Court
B. the Chamber of Commerce
C. the Treasury Department
D. the Congress

___ 5. In *The Iroquois Constitution,* what is the task of the eagle that sits at the top of the Tree of Long Leaves?
A. to hunt food for the people
B. to defend the people from evil
C. to warn the people of danger
D. to fly and give news to people

___ 6. Who is meant to see the smoke of the confederacy council fire as it ascends to the sky?
A. Iroquois allies
B. Iroquois enemies
C. all of the natural world
D. lost travelers

___ 7. Why do the lords of the Five Nations give thanks to the earth before they begin deliberations?
A. out of respect
B. out of fear
C. out of obedience
D. out of comfort

Unit 1 Resources: A Gathering of Voices
© Pearson Education, Inc. All rights reserved.

EL L3 **Literary Analysis: Graphic Organizer B,** p. 108

Also available for these selections:

EL L1 L2 Reading: Graphic Organizer A (partially filled in), p. 105

EL L3 Reading: Graphic Organizer B, p. 106

EL L1 L2 Literary Analysis: Graphic Organizer A (partially filled in), p. 107

EL L3 L4 **Support for Writing,** p. 54

Also available for these selections:

All Literary Analysis: Autobiography and Tone, p. 51

All Reading: Establish a Purpose, p. 52

All Enrichment, p. 55

L3 L4 **Open-Book Test,** pp. 56–58

Also available for these selections:

EL L3 L4 Selection Test A, pp. 59–61

EL L1 L2 Selection Test B, pp. 62–64

PHLit Online!
www.PHLitOnline.com

Online Resources: All print materials are also available online.

- complete narrated selection text
- a thematically related video with writing prompt
- an interactive graphic organizer
- highlighting feature
- access to all student print resources, adapted to individual student needs
- Spanish and English summaries
- adapted selection translations in Spanish

Background Video

Also available:

Get Connected! (thematic video with writing prompt)
All videos are available in Spanish.

Writer's Journal (with graphics feature)

Also available:

Vocabulary Central (tools and activities for studying vocabulary)

❶ 🎯 Connecting to the Essential Question

1. Review the assignment.

2. Describe one leader you respect, and explain why. Then have students complete the assignment, identifying qualities of a compelling advocate.

3. As students read, have them look for clues about Douglass's ability to lead others.

❷ Literary Analysis

Introduce the skill, using the instruction on the student page.

Think Aloud: Model the Skill

Say to students:

> When I read an autobiography, I know that the writer made numerous choices. Douglass had to select experiences to share and ways to describe them. His decisions relate directly to his purpose, so I pause every once in a while to ask, "*Why is he telling me this?*"

❸ Reading Strategy

1. Introduce the strategy, using the instruction on the student page.

2. Give students a copy of **Reading Strategy Graphic Organizer B,** page 106 in *Graphic Organizer Transparencies,* to fill out as they read.

Think Aloud: Model the Skill

Say to students:

> When I read a text from history, my purpose can be to understand the ideas that influenced people then. So with slavery, I ask, "How did the moral standards of the time allow slavery to exist?"

❹ Vocabulary

1. Pronounce each word, giving its definition, and have students say it aloud.

2. For more guidance, see the *Classroom Strategies and Teaching Routines* card for introducing vocabulary.

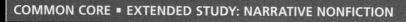

COMMON CORE • EXTENDED STUDY: NARRATIVE NONFICTION

Before You Read

from *My Bondage and My Freedom*

Common Core State Standards

Reading Informational Text
6. Determine an author's point of view or purpose in a text in which the rhetoric is particularly effective, analyzing how style and content contribute to the power, persuasiveness, or beauty of the text.
9. Analyze nineteenth-century foundational U.S. documents for their themes, purposes, and rhetorical features.

❶ **Connecting to the Essential Question** In both his writing and, implicitly, in the example he provided through his own life, Frederick Douglass argued for freedom and equality. As you read, notice details that reveal Douglass's character. Doing so will help as you consider the Essential Question: **How does literature shape or reflect society?**

❷ Literary Analysis

An **autobiography** is a person's account of his or her own life. Most autobiographers feel their lives are noteworthy and can somehow help others. This belief is part of the **author's purpose,** or reason for writing. Douglass's purpose was to show through his own life that African Americans are as intelligent, capable, and feeling as whites:

> *I could talk and sing; I could laugh and weep;*
> *I could reason and remember . . .*

Douglass's formal and dignified writing style, or specific way of using language, contributes to his purpose. It also helps to expresses his *tone,* or attitude, which is both passionate and compassionate. As you read, think about Douglass's purpose for relating the events in this excerpt and analyze how his style contributes to that purpose.

❸ Reading Strategy

© **Preparing to Read Complex Texts** **Setting a purpose** for reading gives you a concept on which to focus. When reading literature from other eras, one useful purpose is to note how *influences of the historical period shape characters, events, and settings*. Historical influences may include the following broad areas:

- *philosophical ideas* or *religious beliefs* that motivate specific actions
- *political events* or *social problems* that affect individuals or groups
- *ethical issues,* such as the moral conflicts caused by slavery

As you read, identify the historical influences in Douglass's narrative. Record your observations in a chart like the one shown.

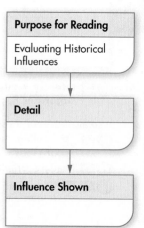

Purpose for Reading
Evaluating Historical Influences

Detail

Influence Shown

❹ Vocabulary

benevolent (bə nev′ ə lənt) *adj.* kindly; charitable (p. 521)

deficient (di fi′ shənt) *adj.* incomplete; defective (p. 522)

fervent (fer′ vənt) *adj.* intensely devoted or earnest (p. 523)

opposition (ä pə zi′ shən) *n.* resistance; hostility (p. 523)

consternation (kän′ stər nā′ shən) *n.* fear or shock that makes one feel helpless or bewildered (p. 523)

intolerable (in täl′ ər ə bəl) *adj.* unbearable; too severe (p. 525)

www.PHLitOnline.com

518 Division, Reconciliation, and Expansion (1850–1914)

Vocabulary Development

Vocabulary Knowledge Rating

Create a **Vocabulary Knowledge Rating Chart** (*Professional Development Guidebook,* p. 33) for the vocabulary words on the student page. Give each student a copy of the chart with the words on it. Read the words aloud, and have students mark their rating in the Before Reading column. Urge students to attend to these words as they read and discuss the selection.

In order to gauge how much instruction is needed, tally how many students are confident in their knowledge of each word. As students read, point out the words and their context.

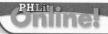
Vocabulary Central, featuring tools and activities for vocabulary, is available at www.PHLitOnline.com.

FREDERICK DOUGLASS (1817–1895)

Author of *My Bondage and My Freedom*

Frederick Douglass rose out of slavery to become one of the most gifted writers and orators of his time. He used his talents to fight for the abolition of slavery and for civil rights. His life served as an inspiration and example for all Americans, both black and white throughout the country.

Early Years Douglass was born on a Maryland plantation. Historians believe that his name at birth was Frederick Augustus Bailey. At the age of eight, he was sent as a slave to the Baltimore home of the Auld family, where he learned to read and write. Learning became an unquenchable thirst for Douglass. As his knowledge grew, so did his desire for freedom. At age twenty, he escaped to Massachusetts, a free state, and took the surname Douglass to avoid arrest as a fugitive.

A Public Life In 1841, despite the fear of being arrested, Douglass began lecturing against slavery and for civil rights for all people. Rumors spread that a man of such eloquence could not possibly have been a slave. In response, Douglass published his first autobiography, *Narrative of the Life of Frederick Douglass, an American Slave, Written By Himself* (1845). Fearing re-enslavement, Douglass then fled to England, where he worked to gain British support for the abolitionist movement in the United States.

Freedom at Last After English friends raised money to buy his freedom, Douglass returned to the United States, founded a newspaper for African Americans, and resumed lecturing. In 1855, he published *My Bondage and My Freedom,* an updated version of his autobiography.

After slavery was abolished, Douglass fought vigorously for civil rights for African Americans. He became a consultant to President Lincoln and held several government positions, including United States minister to Haiti.

A Vision for the Future In 1883, Douglass said "I expect to see the colored people of this country enjoying the same freedom, voting at the same ballot-box, . . . going to the same schools, attending the same churches, . . . proud of the same country, fighting the same foe, and enjoying the same peace and all its advantages. . . ."

from My Bondage and My Freedom **519**

❶ Humanities

The Chimney Corner, by Eastman Johnson, 1863

Johnson (1824–1906) painted portraits of notable Americans of his time. Use these questions for discussion:

1. Do you think this man is a slave?
   Possible response: Because of the date of the work, the man may be a slave, shown in a moment of privacy. If not a slave, he may be a house servant who was literate.

2. How would you describe the mood of the work?
   Possible response: The corner may provide privacy. The man is engrossed in the book despite the mean surroundings.

❷ About the Selection

In this excerpt from his second autobiography, Douglass shows that slavery victimized everyone—including slaveholders. The passage describes how his master's wife abandons her efforts to educate young Frederick. Douglass continues to learn from his white playmates, trading biscuits for lessons.

❸ Activating Prior Knowledge

Have students discuss this seemingly paradoxical statement: "Both slaves and slaveholders were victims of slavery."

Concept Connector ➡

Tell students they will revisit the idea that slaveholders could be perceived as victims of a system from which they nonetheless benefited.

520 Division, Reconciliation, and Expansion (1850–1914)

ⓒ Text Complexity Rubric

from My Bondage and My Freedom		
Qualitative Measures		
Context/Knowledge Demands	Chronicle of slavery; historical knowledge demands	
	1 2 3 ④ 5	
Structure/Language Conventionality and Clarity	Complicated sentence structure; challenging vocabulary	
	1 2 3 ④ 5	
Levels of Meaning/ Purpose/Concept Level	Challenging (social philosophy)	
	1 2 3 ④ 5	
Quantitative Measures		
Lexile	1110L	**Text Length**	2,302 words
Overall Complexity	**More complex**	

Reader and Task Suggestions

Preparing to Read the Text

- Using the Background information on TE p. 519, discuss the setting for Douglass's account.
- Ask students to review an event from early childhood. How has their thinking about that past event changed over time?
- Guide students to use Multidraft Reading strategies (TE p. 519).

Leveled Tasks

Levels of Meaning If students will have difficulty with levels of meaning, have them list (1) past facts and (2) Douglass's comments as he reviews them. Then have students reread the text.

Synthesizing If students will have difficulty with levels of meaning, have them explain how they would adapt into a play the reviewing "voice" of Douglass.

from My Bondage and My Freedom

❷ ❸

FREDERICK DOUGLASS

BACKGROUND *Frederick Douglass was perhaps the most prominent African American leader of the nineteenth century, and his influence is still felt. As a crusader for human rights, Douglass served as a role model for African American leaders such as Booker T. Washington and W.E.B. DuBois. In our own era, the civil rights movement has drawn inspiration from Douglass, who opposed segregation decades before other voices were raised. As a young man, Douglass protested segregated seating on trains by sitting in cars reserved for whites until the authorities forcibly removed him. Later, he fought job discrimination against African Americans, protested segregation in school, and fought for civil rights for all Americans.*

I lived in the family of Master Hugh, at Baltimore, seven years, during which time—as the almanac makers say of the weather—my condition was variable. The most interesting feature of my history here, was my learning to read and write, under somewhat marked disadvantages. In attaining this knowledge I was compelled to resort to indirections by no means congenial to my nature, and which were really humiliating to me. My mistress—who had begun to teach me—was suddenly checked in her benevolent design, by the strong advice of her husband. In faithful compliance with this advice, the good lady had not only ceased to instruct me, herself, but had set her face as a flint against my learning to read by any means. It is due, however, to my mistress to say, that she did not adopt this course in all its stringency at the first. She either thought it unnecessary, or she lacked the depravity indispensable to shutting me up in mental darkness.

❹

Vocabulary
benevolent (bə nev′ ə lənt)
adj. kindly; charitable

❻ **Reading Check**
Why did Douglass's mistress stop teaching him to read?

❺ ◄ **Critical Viewing** What might the light shining on the reader in this painting symbolize? **[Interpret]**

The Chimney Corner, 1863, Eastman Johnson, Munson–Williams–Proctor Institute Museum of Art, Utica, New York

from My Bondage and My Freedom **521**

521

How does literature shape or reflect society?

1. Point out that writers who seek to shape society need to be able to connect with their readers. A writer's personality often comes through in writing, and readers are much more likely to be affected by a writer they respect and appreciate.

2. **Ask** students to tell how Douglass's description of Mrs. Auld reflects his attitude toward human nature.
Answer: Douglass's description shows that he believes people are naturally good; Mrs. Auld's "noble soul" was overthrown.

3. **Ask:** How might Douglass's attitude toward human nature have helped him make a change in society?
Possible response: A positive attitude that respects people as naturally good is generally more attractive to readers than one that views human nature as indifferent or immoral.

8 Critical Viewing

Answer: The image shows a white woman teaching a black child, as Douglass's mistress once taught him before her husband insisted that she stop.

It was, at least, necessary for her to have some training, and some hardening, in the exercise of the slaveholder's prerogative, to make her equal to forgetting my human nature and character, and to treating me as a thing destitute of a moral or an intellectual nature. Mrs. Auld—my mistress—was, as I have said, a most kind and tender-hearted woman; and, in the humanity of her heart, and the simplicity of her mind, she set out, when I first went to live with her, to treat me as she supposed one human being ought to treat another.

It is easy to see, that, in entering upon the duties of a slaveholder, some little experience is needed. Nature has done almost nothing to prepare men and women to be either slaves or slaveholders. Nothing but rigid training, long persisted in, can perfect the character of the one or the other. One cannot easily forget to love freedom; and it is as hard to cease to respect that natural love in our fellow creatures. On entering upon the career of a slaveholding mistress, Mrs. Auld was singularly deficient; nature, which fits

7

Vocabulary
deficient (di fi′ shənt)
adj. incomplete; defective

8 ▲ Critical Viewing
Is the situation and relationship shown in this image similar to Douglass's? Explain. [**Distinguish**]

522 Division, Reconciliation, and Expansion (1850–1914)

Enrichment: Analyzing Historical Trends, Patterns, and Periods

Slavery

Slavery neither began nor ended with Southern plantation owners. A common practice since ancient times, slavery has been the fate that has awaited many conquered people. Sadly, slavery continues to exist in the world.
Activity: Compare Slave Narratives Invite students to find out how other slaves responded to their bondage. They might read in a Haggadah (the narrative of the Exodus from Egypt that is read at the Jewish festival of Passover) about how the slave Nachshon obtained freedom. They can research the 1831 sustained slave rebellion led by Nat Turner. Students can take notes about the period they research on the **Enrichment: Analyzing Historical Trends, Patterns, and Periods** work sheet, in *Professional Development Guidebook,* page 231. Then they should compare findings.

nobody for such an office, had done less for her than any lady I had known. It was no easy matter to induce her to think and to feel that the curly-headed boy, who stood by her side, and even leaned on her lap; who was loved by little Tommy, and who loved little Tommy in turn; sustained to her only the relation of a chattel.[1] I was *more* than that, and she felt me to be more than that. I could talk and sing; I could laugh and weep; I could reason and remember; I could love and hate. I was human, and she, dear lady, knew and felt me to be so. How could she, then, treat me as a brute, without a mighty struggle with all the noble powers of her own soul. That struggle came, and the will and power of the husband was victorious. Her noble soul was overthrown; but, he that overthrew it did not, himself, escape the consequences. He, not less than the other parties, was injured in his domestic peace by the fall.

When I went into their family, it was the abode of happiness and contentment. The mistress of the house was a model of affection and tenderness. Her fervent piety and watchful uprightness made it impossible to see her without thinking and feeling—"that woman is a Christian." There was no sorrow nor suffering for which she had not a tear, and there was no innocent joy for which she did not [have] a smile. She had bread for the hungry, clothes for the naked, and comfort for every mourner that came within her reach. Slavery soon proved its ability to divest her of these excellent qualities, and her home of its early happiness. Conscience cannot stand much violence. Once thoroughly broken down, *who* is he that can repair the damage? It may be broken toward the slave, on Sunday, and toward the master on Monday. It cannot endure such shocks. It must stand entire, or it does not stand at all. If my condition waxed bad, that of the family waxed not better. The first step, in the wrong direction, was the violence done to nature and to conscience, in arresting the benevolence that would have enlightened my young mind. In ceasing to instruct me, she must begin to justify herself *to* herself; and, once consenting to take sides in such a debate, she was riveted to her position. One needs very little knowledge of moral philosophy, to see *where* my mistress now landed. She finally became even more violent in her opposition to my learning to read, than was her husband himself. She was not satisfied with simply doing as *well* as her husband had commanded her, but seemed resolved to better his instruction. Nothing appeared to make my poor mistress—after her turning toward the downward path—more angry, than seeing me, seated in some nook or corner, quietly reading a book or a newspaper. I have had her rush at me, with the utmost fury, and snatch from my hand such newspaper or book, with something of the wrath and consternation which a traitor might be supposed to feel on being discovered in a plot by some dangerous spy.

---

1. **chattel** (chat´ ´l) *n.* a movable item of personal property, as a piece of furniture or a head of livestock.

from My Bondage and My Freedom **523**

Reading Strategy
Purpose for Reading: Historical Influences How do the ethical conflicts of slavery affect everyone in the Auld household?

Vocabulary
fervent (fər´ vənt) *adj.* intensely devoted or earnest

Vocabulary
opposition (ä pə zi´ shən) *n.* resistance; hostility

consternation (kän´ stər nā´ shən) *n.* fear or shock that makes one feel helpless or bewildered

10 ☑ **Reading Check**

What extreme measure does Mrs. Auld take?

9 Reading Strategy

Purpose for Reading: Historical Influences

1. Give students a copy of **Reading Strategy Graphic Organizer B**, page 106 in *Graphic Organizer Transparencies,* to fill out as they read.

2. **Ask** students the Reading Strategy question.
Answer: Douglass is enslaved; Mrs. Auld must give up her desire to help him; Mr. Auld must assert his dominance in the family to make a change he sees as necessary. Slavery causes tension not only between Douglass and the Aulds but between husband and wife as well.

10 Reading Check

Answer: Mrs. Auld becomes "even more violent [than Mr. Auld] in her opposition" to Douglass's reading.

Differentiated Instruction for Universal Access

Support for Special-Needs Students
Douglass writes challengingly long sentences. Help students break down the sentences by identifying the core of each one—its subject and verb. Then have students look at how the other groups of words in the sentence relate to the subject and the verb.

Enrichment for Gifted/Talented Students
Guide students to appreciate Douglass's views concerning the right to acquire knowledge and on the effects of denying a person that right. Invite students to discuss why the decision about Douglass's education places the Aulds in a "condition" Douglass views as worse than his. Encourage students to create a visual that captures the power of knowledge and the relationship between the Aulds and Douglass.

11 Reading Strategy

Purpose for Reading: Historical Influences

1. Point out that "apt" here means "well suited to the circumstances." **Ask** students to explain what Douglass means when he says that Mrs. Auld was "an apt woman."
Answer: She was able to adapt herself to her new circumstances; in other words, she changed her natural helpfulness in order to fall in line with her husband's views.

2. **Ask** students the Reading Strategy question.
Answer: Mr. Auld's belief that slaves should not be taught to read reflects the slaveholder's need to limit slaves' access to culture. The Aulds' attitudes are heavily influenced by their society and their conception of family roles. Douglass is himself influenced by the ability to read and by connecting with the authors whose works he reads.

12 Critical Thinking

Interpret/Support

1. Point out that Douglass presents another version of the expression "Give him an inch, and he'll take a mile." **Ask** students to explain the meaning of this expression.
Answer: The expression means that if you give someone a small bit of freedom or leeway, he or she will want to take more.

2. Point out that this saying summarizes Mr. Auld's fears regarding Douglass's education. Douglass's autobiography is itself an example of how someone capitalized on receiving an inch (from Mrs. Auld) but went much farther.

Reading Strategy
Purpose for Reading:
Historical Influences What multiple influences of the period are evident in this paragraph? Explain. **11**

12

For a single biscuit, any of my hungry little comrades would give me a lesson more valuable to me than bread.

Mrs. Auld was an apt woman, and the advice of her husband, and her own experience, soon demonstrated, to her entire satisfaction, that education and slavery are incompatible with each other. When this conviction was thoroughly established, I was most narrowly watched in all my movements. If I remained in a separate room from the family for any considerable length of time, I was sure to be suspected of having a book, and was at once called upon to give an account of myself. All this, however, was entirely *too late*. The first, and never to be retraced, step had been taken. In teaching me the alphabet, in the days of her simplicity and kindness, my mistress had given me the "inch," and now, no ordinary precaution could prevent me from taking the "ell."[2]

Seized with a determination to learn to read, at any cost, I hit upon many expedients to accomplish the desired end. The plea which I mainly adopted, and the one by which I was most successful, was that of using my young white playmates, with whom I met in the street, as teachers. I used to carry, almost constantly, a copy of Webster's spelling book in my pocket; and, when sent on errands, or when play time was allowed me, I would step, with my young friends, aside, and take a lesson in spelling. I generally paid my *tuition fee* to the boys, with bread, which I also carried in my pocket. For a single biscuit, any of my hungry little comrades would give me a lesson more valuable to me than bread. Not everyone, however, demanded this consideration, for there were those who took pleasure in teaching me, whenever I had a chance to be taught by them. I am strongly tempted to give the names of two or three of those little boys, as a slight testimonial of the gratitude and affection I bear them, but prudence forbids; not that it would injure me, but it might, possibly, embarrass them; for it is almost an unpardonable offense to do anything, directly or indirectly, to promote a slave's freedom, in a slave state. It is enough to say, of my warm-hearted little play fellows, that they lived on Philpot Street, very near Durgin & Bailey's shipyard.

Although slavery was a delicate subject, and very cautiously talked about among grownup people in Maryland, I frequently talked about it—and that very freely—with the white boys. I would, sometimes, say to them, while seated on a curbstone or a cellar door, "I wish I could be free, as you will be when you get to be men." "You will be free, you know, as soon as you are twenty-one, and can go where you like, but I am a slave for life. Have I not as good a right to be free as you have?" Words like these, I observed, always troubled them; and I had no small satisfaction in wringing from the boys, occasionally, that fresh and bitter condemnation of slavery, that springs from nature, unseared and unperverted.[3] Of all consciences let me have those to deal with which have not been bewildered by the cares of

---

2. **ell** *n.* former English measure of length, equal to forty-five inches.
3. **unperverted** (un´ pər vurt´ id) *adj.* uncorrupted; pure.

Think Aloud

Reading Strategy: Setting a Purpose for Reading: Historical Influences
To model the process of working out the answer to the Reading Strategy question on the student page, use the following "think aloud." Say to students:

When my purpose for reading is to understand historical influences, I have to make a lot of inferences. Writers seldom state influences directly. Instead, I have to think about what happens and figure out what historical situation influences the outcome. One of the unspoken historical influences here is the roles of men and women. Men were expected to govern the household and women to obey. Mrs. Auld gives up her own independence and follows Mr. Auld's insistent advice because it was expected that wives follow their husbands. This is a key historical influence on the events.

A Home on the Mississippi, Currier & Ives, The Museum of the City of New York

life. I do not remember ever to have met with a *boy*, while I was in slavery, who defended the slave system; but I have often had boys to console me, with the hope that something would yet occur, by which I might be made free. Over and over again, they have told me, that "they believed *I* had as good a right to be free as *they* had"; and that "they did not believe God ever made anyone to be a slave." The reader will easily see, that such little conversations with my play fellows, had no tendency to weaken my love of liberty, nor to render me contented with my condition as a slave.

When I was about thirteen years old, and had succeeded in learning to read, every increase of knowledge, especially respecting the free states, added something to the almost intolerable burden of the thought—"I am a slave for life." To my bondage I saw no end. It was a terrible reality, and I shall never be able to tell how sadly that thought chafed my young spirit. Fortunately, or unfortunately, about this time in my life, I had made enough money to buy what was then a very popular schoolbook, the *Columbian Orator*. I bought this addition to my library, of Mr. Knight, on Thames street, Fell's Point, Baltimore, and paid him fifty cents for it. I was first led to buy this book, by hearing some little boys say they were going to learn some little pieces out of it for the exhibition. This volume was, indeed, a rich treasure, and every opportunity afforded me, for a time, was spent in diligently perusing it. . . . The dialogue and the

14

13 ▲ Critical Viewing
How does this idealized picture of plantation life contrast with Douglass's experiences as an enslaved African American? **[Contrast]**

Vocabulary
intolerable (in ′täl ər ə bəl)
adj. unbearable; too severe

15 ☑ Reading Check
What beliefs do Douglass's playmates express about slavery?

from My Bondage and My Freedom **525**

Differentiated Instruction for Universal Access

Culturally Responsive Instruction
Culture Focus Students may lack the background knowledge or context-building experiences necessary to fully comprehend Douglass's interactions with boys from a variety of backgrounds. Point out that Maryland was not one of the states that seceded from the United States to join the Confederacy. Although slavery was present in Maryland, it was not as prevalent as it was in the states of the Deep South.

Discuss how growing up in this mixed society may have shaped Douglass's views of society and humanity. Guide students to recognize that Douglass's deep faith in the goodness of human nature might have been partly based on his experiences with white youths, who did not defend the slave system.

Slave Narratives

The first known slave narrative—*A Narrative of the Uncommon Sufferings and Surprising Deliverance of Briton Hammon, a Negro Man*—appeared in 1760 in Boston. Other notable examples of this subgenre of autobiography include *A Narrative of the Lord's Wonderful Dealings with J. Murrant, a Black, Taken Down from His Own Relation* (1784); *Incidents in the Life of a Slave Girl, Written by Herself* (1861), by Harriet Jacobs; and *Scenes in the Life of Harriet Tubman* (1869).

Connect to the Literature

Have students read The American Experience feature; next present the additional background information above. Encourage students to consider why children whose parents were slaveholders did not support keeping people in bondage. Then **ask** the Connect to the Literature question.

Possible response: By showing the children's opposition to slavery, Douglass may have intended readers to observe that proslavery attitudes were learned, not natural. The example supports Douglass's view that slavery goes against human nature.

---

❶⑥ *The* **American EXPERIENCE**

Slave Narratives

Between 1760 and the end of the Civil War, when slavery was officially abolished, testimonies of hundreds of fugitives and former slaves appeared in the form of slave narratives. These narratives exposed the inhumanities of the slave system as former slaves recorded the harsh conditions they suffered at the hands of their owners. Their writings did more than document their personal experiences for the enlightenment of others. They also served to create permanent reminders that could not be easily ignored by the reunified nation. In the 1920s and 1930s, The Federal Writers Project created an archive of these narratives, preserving the memory of the painful realities of American slavery.

Connect to the Literature

Douglass intended his narrative to be read by both black and white audiences. What do you think his purpose was in describing his white playmates' attitudes toward slavery?

LADIES' DEPARTMENT.

'Am I not a Woman and a Sister?'

White Lady, happy, proud and free,
Lend awhile thine ear to me ;
Let the Negro Mother's wail
Turn thy pale cheek still more pale.
Can the Negro Mother joy
Over this her captive boy,
Which in bondage and in tears,
For a life of wo she rears?
Though she bears a Mother's name,
A Mother's rights she may not claim ;
For the white man's will can part,
Her darling from her bursting heart.

---

speeches were all redolent of the principles of liberty, and poured floods of light on the nature and character of slavery. As I read, behold! the very discontent so graphically predicted by Master Hugh, had already come upon me. I was no longer the light-hearted, gleesome boy, full of mirth and play, as when I landed first at Baltimore. Knowledge had come. . . . This knowledge opened my eyes to the horrible pit, and revealed the teeth of the frightful dragon that was ready to pounce upon me, but it opened no way for my escape. I have often wished myself a beast, or a bird—anything, rather than a slave. I was wretched and gloomy, beyond my ability to describe. I was too thoughtful to be happy. It was this everlasting thinking which distressed and tormented me; and yet there was no getting rid of the subject of my thoughts. All nature was redolent of it. Once awakened by the silver trump[4] of knowledge, my spirit was roused to eternal wakefulness. Liberty! the inestimable birthright of every man, had, for me, converted every object into an asserter of this great right. It was heard in every sound, and beheld in every object. It was ever present, to torment me with a sense of my wretched condition. The more beautiful and charming were the smiles of nature, the more horrible and desolate was my condition. I saw nothing without seeing it, and I heard nothing without hearing it. I do not exaggerate, when I say, that it looked from every star, smiled in every calm, breathed in every wind, and moved in every storm.

I have no doubt that my state of mind had something to do with the change in the treatment adopted, by my once kind mistress toward me. I can easily believe, that my leaden, downcast, and discontented look, was very offensive to her. Poor lady! She did not know my trouble, and I dared not tell her. Could I have freely made her acquainted with the real state of my mind, and given her the reasons therefor, it might have been well for both of us. Her abuse of me fell upon me like the blows of the false prophet upon his ass; she did not know that an *angel* stood in the way;[5] and—such is the relation of master and slave—I could not tell her. Nature had made us *friends*; slavery made us *enemies*. My interests were in a direction opposite to hers, and we both had our private thoughts and plans. She aimed to keep me ignorant; and I resolved to know, although knowledge only increased my discontent. My feelings were

---

4. **trump** trumpet.
5. **blows . . . the way** allusion to a biblical tale (Numbers 22:21–35) about an ass that cannot move, though she is beaten by her master, because her path is blocked by an angel.

Vocabulary Development

Vocabulary Knowledge Rating
When students have completed reading and discussing the selection have them take out their **Vocabulary Knowledge Rating Charts** for the selection. Read the words aloud and have students rate their knowledge of words again in the After Reading column. Clarify any words that are still problematic. Have students write their own definitions and example or sentence in the appropriate column. Then have students complete the Vocabulary Lesson at the end of the selection. Encourage students to use the words in further discussion and written work about the selection. Remind them that they will be accountable for these words on the **Selection Test,** *Unit 3 Resources,* pages 59–61 or 62–64.

not the result of any marked cruelty in the treatment I received; they sprung from the consideration of my being a slave at all. It was *slavery*—not its mere *incidents*—that I hated. I had been cheated. I saw through the attempt to keep me in ignorance. . . . The feeding and clothing me well, could not atone for taking my liberty from me. The smiles of my mistress could not remove the deep sorrow that dwelt in my young bosom. Indeed, these, in time, came only to deepen my sorrow. She had changed; and the reader will see that I had changed, too. We were both victims to the same overshadowing evil—*she*, as mistress, *I*, as slave. I will not censure her harshly; she cannot censure me, for she knows I speak but the truth, and have acted in my opposition to slavery, just as she herself would have acted, in a reverse of circumstances.

> I have often wished myself a beast, or a bird—anything, rather than a slave.

Critical Reading

Cite textual evidence to support your responses.

1. **Key Ideas and Details** (a) What does Mrs. Auld initially think about Douglass's reading? (b) **Draw Conclusions:** Why do you think she is later "violent in her opposition" to Douglass's reading?

2. **Key Ideas and Details** (a) What book does Douglass buy when he is about thirteen years old? (b) **Analyze Causes and Effects:** How does reading this transform Douglass from "light-hearted" to "wretched and gloomy"?

3. **Key Ideas and Details** (a) What consumed Douglass once he obtained knowledge? (b) **Support:** How does his experience prove his mistress's belief that education and slavery are incompatible?

4. **Integration of Knowledge and Ideas** What personal qualities do you think helped Douglass become an effective champion of human rights? Use at least two of these Essential Question words in your response: *conviction, determination, goal, justice, humanity.* [*Connecting to the Essential Question: How does literature shape or reflect society?*]

from My Bondage and My Freedom **527**

Before students respond, you may wish to have them write a brief objective summary of the selection. As they answer the questions below, remind them to support their answers with evidence from the text.

1. (a) At first, she approves of it and actively supports it. (b) **Possible response:** In order to compensate for her initial, natural reaction of support, Mrs. Auld adopts an attitude even more extreme than her husband's. In this way she may hope to fool herself into thinking that she is comfortable with suppressing the intellectual curiosity of a boy.

2. (a) He buys the *Columbian Orator,* a popular schoolbook. (b) Reading the book opens his eyes to the pain and evil of slavery but gives him few tools—at least initially—with which to escape it.

3. (a) He is consumed by his desire for freedom. (b) The ability to read gives Douglass access to voices and ideas that challenge and condemn the institution of slavery. Without education, he would have remained ignorant of these ideas and received no validation for his innate desire to be free.

4. **Sample response:** The excerpt makes it clear that Douglass was a man of conviction and determination. He was a keen observer of people's behaviors and motivations. His strong commitment to communication and clear self-expression helped him connect with his readers. His faith in justice and humanity, might have also appealed to readers who shared a similar perspective.

Concept Connector

Reading Strategy Graphic Organizer
Ask students to review the graphic organizers in which they identified historical influences and effects on characters, events, and settings. Have students compare the influences they identified.

Activating Prior Knowledge
Remind students of the idea that slaves and slaveholders alike were victims. Ask how reading the selection helped them understand this paradox.

Writing About the Essential Question
Have students compare the responses to the prompt before they completed reading with their thoughts afterward. Have them work individually or in groups, writing or discussing their thoughts, to formulate their new responses. Then lead a class discussion, probing for what students have learned that confirms or invalidates their initial thoughts. Encourage students to cite specific textual details to support their responses.

Answers

1. (a) His basic needs are met, but he is not given access to education. (b) He uses his relationship with his mistress as an example of the many ways in which slavery forces people to betray their natural tendencies.

2. **Possible answers:** (a) *Event:* Mrs. Auld teaches Douglass to read. *Author's Purpose:* His learning proves that blacks are equal to whites in ability. *Event:* Mr. Auld insists that Mrs. Auld stop the lessons. *Author's Purpose:* This incident shows how slaves' natural abilities were curtailed. *Event:* Douglass buys the *Columbian Orator. Author's Purpose:* Douglass shows more evidence of the intolerable situation of a slave. (b) All three events help the author communicate the intolerableness of the institution.

3. **Possible answers:** (a) He uses *benevolent, kind, tender hearted, apt.* (b) He seems sympathetic with her struggle.

4. **Possible answers:** (a) Douglass describes her with respect. (b) His purpose is to show the effects of slavery without disrespecting his audience.

5. **Possible answer:** She may have denied that any change occurred in her personality and would have seen her actions as proper.

6. **Possible answers:** Students may observe that slaveholders were afraid that slaves might become too powerful through education and that women were expected to follow men's rules.

7. **Possible answers:** Douglass is a slave; his master believes it is wrong to teach him to read; his mistress stops teaching him in obedience to her husband.

8. **Possible answer:** Mrs. Auld changes her ethical position about blacks reading; she is socially compelled to obey her husband; slavery is a political system she cannot reform.

9. (a) It makes him gloomy. (b) It highlights philosophies of liberty.

10. **Possible answer:** Influences, like the *Columbian Orator,* strengthened his commitment.

11. Some people felt that slaves were not fully human, so they were not entitled to human rights.

528

After You Read
from *My Bondage and My Freedom*

Literary Analysis

1. **Key Ideas and Details (a)** Describe the treatment Douglass receives as a slave in the Auld household. **(b)** In what ways does his **autobiography** make a powerful case against slavery?

2. **Craft and Structure (a)** Using a chart like the one shown, select three events from this excerpt, and explain the **purpose,** or reason, Douglass includes each one in his narrative. **(b)** How does each event advance his overall purpose for writing?

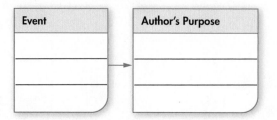

Event		Author's Purpose
	→	

3. **Craft and Structure (a)** Note at least three positive words or phrases Douglass uses to describe Mrs. Auld. **(b)** How does he seem to feel about her? Explain.

4. **Craft and Structure (a)** Considering their relationship as owner and slave, what is remarkable about Douglass's **tone** in his discussion of Mrs. Auld? **(b)** What does this suggest about Douglass's purpose in writing his life story?

5. **Integration of Knowledge and Ideas** In what ways would this account be different if it had been written by another member of the Auld household, such as Mrs. Auld? Explain.

Reading Strategy

6. In approaching this selection, you **set a purpose for reading**—to *evaluate the historical influences that shape the narrative.* Note two specific observations you made as a result of setting this focus. Explain.

7. Note three specific ways in which Douglass's narrative—indeed, his life itself—is shaped by historical influences of the period.

8. What *ethical, political, and social* conflicts are evident in Mrs. Auld's changing behavior toward Douglass? Explain.

9. **(a)** How does his reading of the *Columbian Orator* affect Douglass? **(b)** To what *philosophical* ideas does it awaken him?

10. As an adult, Douglass was a staunch advocate of human rights. How do you think the philosophical influences he encountered as a child affected his adult decisions? Explain.

11. Based on this account, how did some people of Douglass's era justify owning slaves?

Common Core State Standards

Writing

2. Write informative/ explanatory texts to examine and convey complex ideas, concepts, and information clearly and accurately through the effective selection, organization, and analysis of content. *(p. 529)*

2.a. Introduce a topic; organize complex ideas, concepts, and information so that each new element builds on that which precedes it to create a unified whole. *(p. 529)*

2.b. Develop the topic thoroughly by selecting the most significant and relevant facts, concrete details, quotations, or other information and examples. *(p. 529)*

2.c. Use appropriate and varied transitions and syntax to link the major sections of the text, create cohesion, and clarify the relationships among complex ideas and concepts. *(p. 529)*

Language

4.b. Identify and correctly use patterns of word changes that indicate different meanings or parts of speech. *(p. 529)*

4.d. Verify the preliminary determination of the meaning of a word or phrase. *(p. 529)*

Assessment Practice

Context (For more practice, see *All-in-One Workbook.*)

Many tests require students to use context to determine the appropriate meaning of a multiple-meaning word. Use the following sample test item to give students practice in this skill.

> I was compelled to resort to indirections by no means <u>congenial</u> to my nature, and which were really humiliating to me.

In this passage, "congenial" most nearly means

A outgoing

B warm

C kindred

D suited

The word *humiliating* provides a context clue that the indirections are not suited to the speaker's nature or temperament. Although the other choices are also definitions of *congenial,* **D** is the appropriate meaning in the context of this passage.

Integrated Language Skills

Vocabulary Acquisition and Use

Word Analysis: Latin Root -bene-

The Latin root -bene- means "well" or "good." In the word *benevolent*, it combines with a form of the Latin word *velle*, which means "to want," or "to wish." Thus, *benevolent* literally means "a disposition to do good," or "with good wishes." Define each of the numbered words, incorporating the meaning of the root –bene- into your definition. If necessary, consult a dictionary to check your work.

1. benefit
2. benefactor
3. benediction
4. beneficence
5. benign

Vocabulary: Sentence Completions

Fill in the blanks in each sentence below with the appropriate vocabulary word from the list on page 518. Then, explain your reasoning.

1. Douglass holds a _____ belief that slavery is morally wrong.
2. His eloquent prose proves that slaves are not _____ in intellect.
3. Douglass argues that slavery is an _____ institution that must be eliminated.
4. His _____ to slavery could not be more firm.
5. Douglass's _____ attitude toward Mrs. Auld suggests his greatness of spirit.
6. The conflicts and _____ of violating her own good nature changes Mrs. Auld's personality.

Writing

Informative Text College applications often require a **reflective essay** about an experience that helped shape you as a person. Just as Douglass described how knowledge freed him, identify a key event in your life, and write an essay communicating its significance. Follow the model Douglass set of combining *narration*, or storytelling, with other rhetorical strategies, such as *description, exposition,* or *explanation,* and—if appropriate—*persuasion.*

Prewriting Outline the details of the event and its effect on you. List details in chronological order to establish organization. Identify points at which your essay will benefit from description, explanation, or persuasion.

Drafting Introduce the experience and explain why it is important. Then, write the body paragraphs to follow your outline. Conclude with a paragraph that insightfully sums up the meaning of the experience in your life.

Revising Review your essay and make sure you have balanced the narrative, or storytelling aspect, with a discussion of its meaning. If necessary, add transitional words, concrete sensory details, or more in-depth explanation to clarify that balance.

> **Model: Planning a Clear and Logical Organization**
>
> A. **Experience:** I worked in a local campaign office.
> B. **What happened:**
> 1. met the candidate; was inspired to join her campaign
> 2. distributed flyers; polled voters
> 3. phoned residents to encourage voting
> C. **Outcome:** I learned teamwork and the power of democracy.

Chronological order makes it easy for readers to follow events.

Integrated Language Skills **529**

Assessment Resources

Unit 3 Resources

L1 L2 EL **Selection Test A,** pp. 59–61. Administer Test A to less advanced students and English learners.

L3 L4 EL **Selection Test B,** pp. 62–64. Administer Test B to on-level or more advanced students.

L3 L4 **Open-Book Test,** pp. 56–58. As an alternative, give the Open-Book Test.

All **Customizable Test Bank**

All **Self-tests**
Students may prepare for the **Selection Test** by taking the Self-test online.

PHLit Online! All assessment resources are available at **www.PHLitOnline.com.**

Vocabulary Acquisition and Use

1. Introduce the skill, using the instruction on the student page.
2. Have students complete the Word Analysis activity and the Vocabulary practice.

Word Analysis

1. "a good effect"
2. "someone who makes good things happen for someone or something"
3. "a spoken request for goodness, or blessing, for someone or something"
4. "an act of doing good for someone or something"; "charity"
5. "of a good nature"

Vocabulary

1. fervent
2. deficient
3. intolerable
4. opposition
5. benevolent
6. consternation

Writing

1. To guide students in writing about experiences that shaped them, provide the **Support for Writing** worksheet (*Unit 3 Resources,* p. 54).
2. Point out that students should write about an event that had great significance for them and should explain in detail the impact of the event on their lives.
3. Remind students that their audience knows nothing about the context in which this key event occurred. Therefore, early in their essays, students must describe what their lives and viewpoints were like *before* the event. Readers will then understand both the nature of the event and its significance in the writer's life.
4. Use the **Rubrics for Reflective Essays,** in *Professional Development Guidebook,* pages 293–294, to evaluate students' work.

529

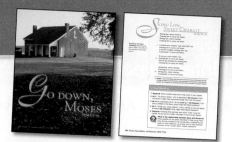

Go Down Moses • Swing Low, Sweet Chariot
Lesson Pacing Guide

DAY 1 Preteach

- Ⓒ Administer the Reading and Vocabulary Warm-ups (*Unit 3 Resources*, pp. 65–68) as necessary.
- Ⓒ Introduce the Literary Analysis concepts: Spirituals.
- • Introduce the Reading Strategy: Listening.
- Ⓒ Build background with the author and Background features.
- • Develop thematic thinking with Connecting to the Essential Question.
- Ⓒ Teach the selection vocabulary.

DAY 2 Preteach/Teach/Extend

- • Distribute copies of the appropriate graphic organizer for the Reading Strategy (*Graphic Organizer Transparencies*, pp. 109–110).
- • Distribute copies of the appropriate graphic organizer for Literary Analysis (*Graphic Organizer Transparencies*, pp. 111–112).
- • Prepare students to read with the Activating Prior Knowledge activities (TE).
- • Informally monitor comprehension while students read.
- • Develop students' ability to listen using the Reading Strategy prompt.
- Ⓒ Reinforce vocabulary with the Vocabulary notes.
- • Assess students' comprehension and mastery of the skills by having them answer the Critical Reading, Literary Analysis, and Reading Strategy questions.

DAY 3 Assess

- Ⓒ Have students complete the Vocabulary Lesson.
- Ⓒ Have students complete the Writing lesson and write an electronic slide presentation. (You may assign as homework.)
- • Administer Selection Test A or B (*Unit 3 Resources*, pp. 77–79 or 80–82).

Ⓒ Common Core State Standards

Reading Literature 4. Determine the meaning of words and phrases as they are used in the text, including figurative meanings; analyze the impact of specific word choices on meaning and tone, including language that is particularly fresh, engaging, or beautiful.
5. Analyze how an author's choices concerning how to structure specific parts of a text contribute to its overall structure and meaning as well as its aesthetic impact.

Writing 6. Use technology, including the Internet, to produce, publish, and update individual or shared writing products in response to ongoing feedback, including new arguments or information.

Language 5. Demonstrate understanding of word relationships.

Additional Standards Practice
Common Core Companion, pp. 41–48; 233–234; 332–335

Daily Block Scheduling
Each day in this Lesson Pacing Guide represents a 40–50 minute period. Teachers using block scheduling may combine days to revise pacing. In addition, teachers may differentiate and support core instruction by integrating components for extended and intensive support as students require. See the Guide to Selected Leveled Resources (facing page).

Guide to Selected Leveled Resources

R T I Tier 1 (students performing on level)

Go Down Moses • Swing Low, Sweet Chariot

Warm Up	**Practice, model,** and **monitor** fluency, working **with the whole class** or **in groups.**	**Vocabulary and Reading Warm-ups B,** *Unit 3 Resources,* pp. 65–66, 68
Comprehension/Skills	**Support** and **monitor** comprehension and skills development, having students complete the activities, graphic organizers, and interactive prompts **independently** or **as a class.**	• *Reader's Notebook,* adapted instruction and summary **EL** *Reader's Notebook: English Learner's Version,* adapted instruction and summary • **Reading Strategy Graphic Organizer B,** *Graphic Organizer Transparencies,* p. 110 • **Literary Analysis Graphic Organizer B,** *Graphic Organizer Transparencies,* p. 112
Monitor Progress	**Monitor** student progress with the differentiated curriculum-based assessment in the *Unit Resources.*	• **Selection Test B,** *Unit 3 Resources,* pp. 80–82 • **Open-Book Test,** *Unit 3 Resources,* pp. 74–76
Assess/ Screen	**Assess** student progress using Benchmark Test 4.	• **Benchmark Test 4,** *Unit 3 Resources,* pp. 83–88

R T I Tier 2 (students requiring intervention)

Go Down Moses • Swing Low, Sweet Chariot

Warm Up	**Practice, model,** and **monitor** fluency **in groups** or **with individuals.**	• **Vocabulary and Reading Warm-ups A,** *Unit 1 Resources,* pp. 65–67 • *Hear It!* **Audio CD**
Comprehension/Skills	• **Support** and **monitor** comprehension and skills development, working **in small groups** or **with individuals.** • As students complete the selection in the appropriate version of the *Reader's Notebook,* **monitor** comprehension frequently with group questions and individual instruction. • **Model** strategies while guiding students in completing the activities and prompts in the *Reader's Notebook,* as well as the graphic organizers. • **Practice** skills and **monitor** mastery with the *Reading Kit* worksheets.	• *Reader's Notebook: Adapted Version,* adapted instruction and summary **EL** *Reader's Notebook: English Learner's Version,* adapted instruction and summary • **Reading Strategy Graphic Organizer A,** *Graphic Organizer Transparencies,* p. 109 • **Literary Analysis Graphic Organizer A,** *Graphic Organizer Transparencies,* p. 111 • *Reading Kit,* Practice worksheets
Monitor Progress	**Monitor** student progress with the differentiated curriculum-based assessment in the *Unit Resources* and in the *Reading Kit.*	• **Selection Test A,** *Unit 1 Resources,* pp. 77–79 • *Reading Kit,* Assess worksheets
Assess/ Screen	**Assess** student progress using the Benchmark Test 1.	**Benchmark Test 4,** *Unit 3 Resources,* pp. 83–88

TIER 3 Tier 3 intervention may require consultation with the student's special-education or dyslexia specialist. For additional support, see the Tier 2 activities and resources listed above.

One-on-one teaching   Group work   Whole-class instruction   Independent work   A Assessment

For a complete guide to selection support, including support for Advanced students, see the Overview of Resources in the frontmatter.

Go Down, Moses
• Swing Low, Sweet Chariot

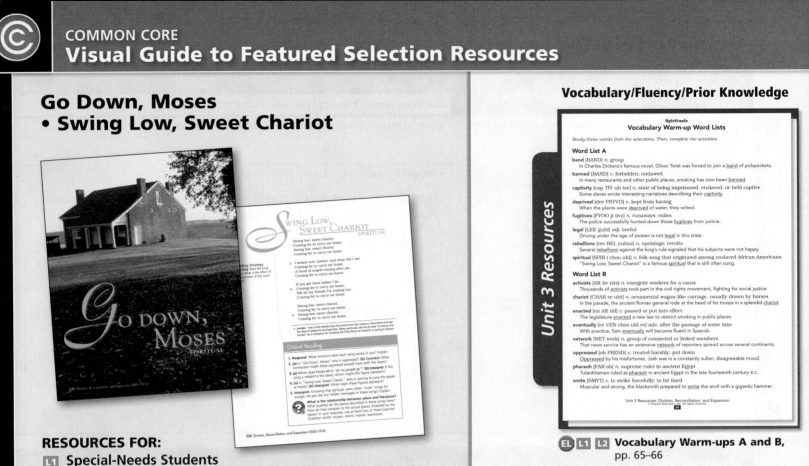

Vocabulary/Fluency/Prior Knowledge

Spirituals
Vocabulary Warm-up Word Lists

Study these words from the selections. Then, complete the activities.

Word List A

band [BAND] *n.* group
In Charles Dickens's famous novel, Oliver Twist was forced to join a <u>band</u> of pickpockets.

banned [BAND] *v.* forbidden; outlawed
In many restaurants and other public places, smoking has now been <u>banned</u>.

captivity [cap TIV uh tee] *n.* state of being imprisoned, enslaved, or held captive
Some slaves wrote interesting narratives describing their <u>captivity</u>.

deprived [dee PRYVD] *v.* kept from having
When the plants were <u>deprived</u> of water, they wilted.

fugitives [FYOO ji tivz] *n.* runaways; exiles
The police successfully hunted down those <u>fugitives</u> from justice.

legal [LEE guhl] *adj.* lawful
Driving under the age of sixteen is not <u>legal</u> in this state.

rebellions [ree BEL yuhnz] *n.* uprisings; revolts
Several <u>rebellions</u> against the king's rule signaled that his subjects were not happy.

spiritual [SPIR i choo uhl] *n.* folk song that originated among enslaved African Americans
"Swing Low, Sweet Chariot" is a famous <u>spiritual</u> that is still often sung.

Word List B

activists [AK tiv ists] *n.* energetic workers for a cause
Thousands of <u>activists</u> took part in the civil rights movement, fighting for social justice.

chariot [CHAR ee uht] *n.* ornamental wagon-like carriage, usually drawn by horses
In the parade, the ancient Roman general rode at the head of his troops in a splendid <u>chariot</u>.

enacted [en AK tid] *v.* passed or put into effect
The legislature <u>enacted</u> a new law to restrict smoking in public places.

eventually [ee VEN choo uhl ee] *adv.* after the passage of some time
With practice, Sam <u>eventually</u> will become fluent in Spanish.

network [NET werk] *n.* group of connected or linked members
That news service has an extensive <u>network</u> of reporters spread across several continents.

oppressed [oh PRESD] *v.* treated harshly; put down
<u>Oppressed</u> by his misfortunes, Josh was in a constantly sullen, disagreeable mood.

pharaoh [FAR oh] *n.* supreme ruler in ancient Egypt
Tutankhamen ruled as <u>pharaoh</u> in ancient Egypt in the late fourteenth century B.C.

smite [SMYT] *v.* to strike forcefully; to hit hard
Muscular and strong, the blacksmith prepared to <u>smite</u> the anvil with a gigantic hammer.

Unit 3 Resources

RESOURCES FOR:

L1 Special-Needs Students

L2 Below-Level Students (Tier 2)

L3 On-Level Students (Tier 1)

L4 Advanced Students (Tier 1)

EL English Learners

All All Students

EL L1 L2 Vocabulary Warm-ups A and B, pp. 65–66

Also available for these selections:

EL L1 L2 Reading Warm-ups A and B, pp. 67–68

All Vocabulary Builder, p. 71

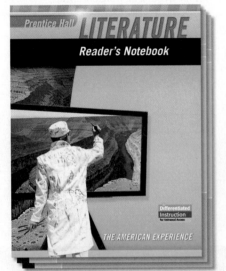

Reader's Notebooks

Pre- and postreading pages for these selections appear in an interactive format in the *Reader's Notebooks*. Each *Notebook* is differentiated for a different group of learners. The selections in the Adapted and English Learner's versions are abridged.

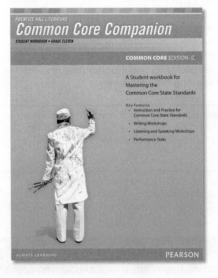

L2 L3 *Reader's Notebook*

L1 *Reader's Notebook: Adapted Version*

EL *Reader's Notebook: English Learner's Version*

EL *Reader's Notebook: Spanish Version*

© *Common Core Companion*

Additional instruction and practice for each Common Core State Standard

Selection Support

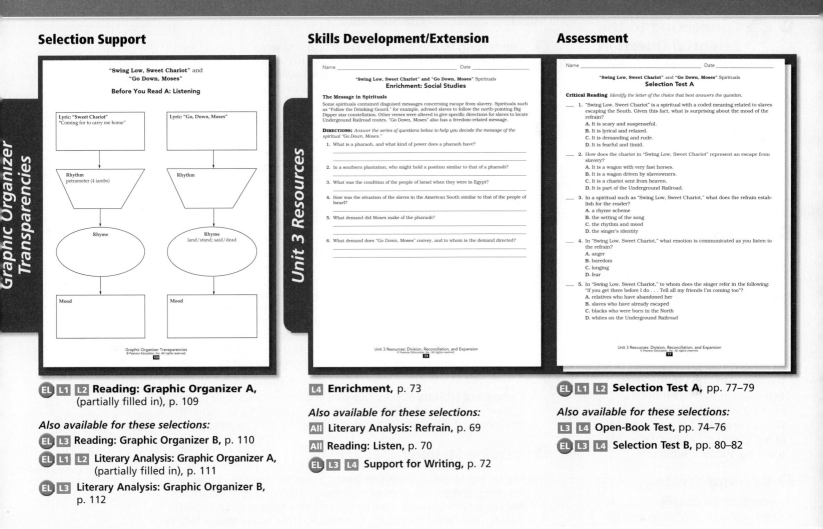

"Swing Low, Sweet Chariot" and
"Go Down, Moses"

Before You Read A: Listening

Lyric: "Sweet Chariot"	Lyric: "Go, Down, Moses"
"Coming for to carry me home"	

Rhythm
petrameter (4 iambs)

Rhythm

Rhyme

Rhyme
land/stand; said/dead

Mood

Mood

Graphic Organizer Transparencies
© Pearson Education, Inc. All rights reserved.
109

Graphic Organizer Transparencies

EL **L1** **L2** **Reading: Graphic Organizer A,**
(partially filled in), p. 109

Also available for these selections:

EL **L3** **Reading: Graphic Organizer B,** p. 110

EL **L1** **L2** **Literary Analysis: Graphic Organizer A,**
(partially filled in), p. 111

EL **L3** **Literary Analysis: Graphic Organizer B,**
p. 112

Skills Development/Extension

Name _____ Date _____

"Swing Low, Sweet Chariot" and "Go Down, Moses" Spirituals
Enrichment: Social Studies

The Message in Spirituals
Some spirituals contained disguised messages concerning escape from slavery. Spirituals such as "Follow the Drinking Gourd," for example, advised slaves to follow the north-pointing Big Dipper star constellation. Other verses were altered to give specific directions for slaves to locate Underground Railroad routes. "Go Down, Moses" also has a freedom-related message.

DIRECTIONS: *Answer the series of questions below to help you decode the message of the spiritual "Go Down, Moses."*

1. What is a pharaoh, and what kind of power does a pharaoh have?

   _____

2. In a southern plantation, who might hold a position similar to that of a pharaoh?

   _____

3. What was the condition of the people of Israel when they were in Egypt?

   _____

4. How was the situation of the slaves in the American South similar to that of the people of Israel?

   _____

5. What demand did Moses make of the pharaoh?

   _____

6. What demand does "Go Down, Moses" convey, and to whom is the demand directed?

   _____

Unit 3 Resources: Division, Reconciliation, and Expansion
© Pearson Education, Inc. All rights reserved.
73

Unit 3 Resources

L4 **Enrichment,** p. 73

Also available for these selections:

All **Literary Analysis: Refrain,** p. 69

All **Reading: Listen,** p. 70

EL **L3** **L4** **Support for Writing,** p. 72

Assessment

Name _____ Date _____

"Swing Low, Sweet Chariot" and "Go Down, Moses" Spirituals
Selection Test A

Critical Reading *Identify the letter of the choice that best answers the question.*

____ 1. "Swing Low, Sweet Chariot" is a spiritual with a coded meaning related to slaves escaping the South. Given this fact, what is surprising about the mood of the refrain?
   A. It is scary and suspenseful.
   B. It is lyrical and relaxed.
   C. It is demanding and rude.
   D. It is fearful and timid.

____ 2. How does the chariot in "Swing Low, Sweet Chariot" represent an escape from slavery?
   A. It is a wagon with very fast horses.
   B. It is a wagon driven by slaveowners.
   C. It is a chariot sent from heaven.
   D. It is part of the Underground Railroad.

____ 3. In a spiritual such as "Swing Low, Sweet Chariot," what does the refrain establish for the reader?
   A. a rhyme scheme
   B. the setting of the song
   C. the rhythm and mood
   D. the singer's identity

____ 4. In "Swing Low, Sweet Chariot," what emotion is communicated as you listen to the refrain?
   A. anger
   B. boredom
   C. longing
   D. fear

____ 5. In "Swing Low, Sweet Chariot," to whom does the singer refer in the following: "If you get there before I do . . . Tell all my friends I'm coming too"?
   A. relatives who have abandoned her
   B. slaves who have already escaped
   C. blacks who were born in the North
   D. whites on the Underground Railroad

Unit 3 Resources: Division, Reconciliation, and Expansion
© Pearson Education, Inc. All rights reserved.
77

EL **L1** **L2** **Selection Test A,** pp. 77–79

Also available for these selections:

L3 **L4** **Open-Book Test,** pp. 74–76

EL **L3** **L4** **Selection Test B,** pp. 80–82

PHLit Online!
www.PHLitOnline.com

Online Resources: All print materials are also available online.

- complete narrated selection text
- a thematically related video with writing prompt
- an interactive graphic organizer
- highlighting feature
- access to all student print resources, adapted to individual student needs
- Spanish and English summaries
- adapted selection translations in Spanish

Get Connected! (thematic video with writing prompt)

Also available:

Background Video
All videos are available in Spanish.

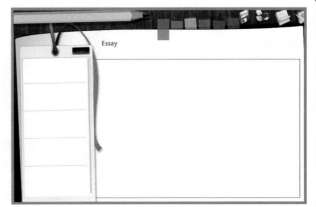

Writer's Journal (with graphics feature)

Also available:

Vocabulary Central (tools and activities for studying vocabulary)

❶  Connecting to the Essential Question

1. Review the assignment with the class.

2. Focus student attention on the idea that visualizing an ideal place may help relieve suffering in a difficult setting. Then have them complete the assignment.

3. As students read, have them look for and analyze specific images that describe settings.

❷ Literary Analysis

Introduce the skill, using the instruction on the student page.

Think Aloud: Model the Skill

Say to students:

When I come to lines in a song that are repeated at regular intervals, I know I've found the refrain. I'll pay close attention to the ideas expressed in the refrain because I know they must be important. Often the refrain becomes locked in my memory, helping me recall the song and its emotions.

❸ Reading Strategy

1. Introduce the strategy, using the instruction on the student page.

2. Give students a copy of **Reading Strategy Graphic Organizer B,** page 110 in *Graphic Organizer Transparencies,* to fill out as they read.

Think Aloud: Model the Skill

Say to students:

Of course, the best way to appreciate a song lyric is to hear it sung. When that is not possible, I read the song aloud—not whispering or murmuring. Changes in rhythm and emotion become more obvious. I notice that in many songs the refrain may have its own distinct rhythm.

❹ Vocabulary

1. Pronounce each word, giving its definition, and have students say it aloud.

2. For more guidance, see the *Classroom Strategies and Teaching Routines* card for intro-card for introducing vocabulary.

530

Before You Read | *Go Down, Moses • Swing Low, Sweet Chariot*

❶ **Connecting to the Essential Question** The sense of place in spirituals is often a longed-for promised land that offers delivery from pain. As you read, noticing how settings are described will help as you consider the Essential Question: **What is the relationship between literature and place?**

❷ **Literary Analysis**

Spirituals are folk songs that were often sung by enslaved African Americans. The following structures are shared by virtually all spirituals:

- A **refrain** is a word, phrase, line, or group of lines repeated at regular intervals. A refrain emphasizes key ideas, sets a rhythm, and makes a song easier to remember. Refrains also allowed spirituals to have a call-and-response format in which a leader sang the verses and the rest of the group acted like a chorus and sang the refrain.

- **Biblical allusions** and **allegory:** Spirituals are full of allusions, or references, to people, places, and events from the Bible. These allusions often have allegorical meaning. An allegory is a story in which all the literal elements are also symbols. For example, in the Old Testament story, Moses led the ancient Israelites out of slavery. References to Moses in the spirituals are allegorical; the slaves are referring to both the Biblical story and to their own yearning for a guide who will lead them to freedom. As you read, analyze the meaning of Biblical allusions in specific passages as well as in each spiritual as a whole.

Comparing Literary Works Compare and contrast the messages of freedom expressed in the refrains to these songs. In particular, consider similarities and differences in the emotional quality of those messages.

❸ **Reading Strategy**

ⓒ **Preparing to Read Complex Texts** Songs are created to be heard; **listening,** therefore, is an especially important skill for appreciating lyrics. Read each spiritual aloud, listening to its *rhythm, rhymes,* and *repeated sounds.* Think about the *moods,* or emotions, these sound devices help to express. Record your observations in a chart like the one shown.

❹ **Vocabulary**

oppressed (ə prest´) *v.* kept down by cruel or unjust power (p. 533)

smite (smīt) *v.* kill by a powerful blow (p. 533)

ⓒ **Common Core State Standards**

Reading Literature
4. Determine the meaning of words and phrases as they are used in the text, including figurative meanings; analyze the impact of specific word choices on meaning and tone, including language that is particularly fresh, engaging, or beautiful.
5. Analyze how an author's choices concerning how to structure specific parts of a text contribute to its overall structure and meaning as well as its aesthetic impact.

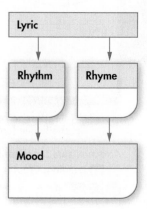

www.PHLitOnline.com

Vocabulary Development

Vocabulary Knowledge Rating

Create a **Vocabulary Knowledge Rating Chart** (*Professional Development Guidebook,* p. 33) for the vocabulary words on the next student page. Give each student a copy of the chart with the words on it. Read the words aloud, and have students mark their rating in the Before Reading column. When students have completed reading and discussing the selections, have them take out their **Vocabulary Knowledge Rating Charts** for each. Read the words aloud and have students rate their knowledge again in the After Reading column. Clarify any words that are still problematic. Then have students complete the Vocabulary practice at the end of the selections.

 **Vocabulary Central,** featuring tools and activities for studying vocabulary, is available online at **www.PHLitOnline.com.**

⑤ SPIRITUALS

Spirituals are folk songs that originated among enslaved and oppressed African Americans. Spirituals took the forms of anthems, ballads, shouts, and jubilees to reflect different moods and circumstances. Containing both social and religious content, spirituals helped to shape the conscious identity of an enslaved people. They also helped slaves persevere under the physical and psychological pressures of their daily lives. These songs conveyed the singers' pain, their yearning for freedom, and their rage against slavery. In doing so, they brought to life the emotional impact of slavery, which divided our nation for decades and played a key role in causing the Civil War. Frederick Douglass, a slave who became one of the most important writers of his time, wrote of the spirituals, "Every tone was a testimony against slavery and a prayer to God for deliverance from chains."

Song of the Fields Plantation owners encouraged field hands to sing, reasoning that people who were busy singing could not plot escape or rebellion. They generally accepted spirituals because of their religious content. The slaves, however, found ways to benefit from singing. These songs provided an outlet for the grief and frustration they often kept bottled up inside. Spirituals also communicated messages of hope and encouragement. Likewise, their traditional African sounds and rhythms helped slaves maintain a connection to their homelands and heritages. In addition, the language in some spirituals provided a means to communicate forbidden thoughts and feelings. For example, songs that referred to the escape of Biblical slaves expressed the slaves' own hope that they would someday escape to a "promised land." Other songs did more than express feelings; they actually provided specific directions for escape. In "Follow the Drinking Gourd," fugitive slaves were advised to follow the Big Dipper north to freedom.

Path to Popularity Spirituals were almost unknown outside the South until after the Civil War. In 1867, a collection of African American music called *Slave Songs of the United States* was published. In 1871, a black choral group, The Jubilee Singers from Fisk University, traveled throughout the United States and to England and Germany singing spirituals to raise money for their school. The Jubilee Singers were extremely gifted and became highly successful, even singing for Queen Victoria in England. Students from other schools followed their example and helped popularize the spiritual. Today, spirituals are performed by singers of all types, and their influence is apparent in contemporary music forms such as blues and jazz.

> "Every tone was a testimony against slavery and a prayer to God for deliverance from chains."
>
> —Frederick Douglass

Go Down, Moses • Swing Low, Sweet Chariot **531**

🔔 Daily Bellringer

For each class during which you will teach these selections, have students complete one of the five activities for the appropriate week in the *Daily Bellringer Activities* booklet.

Multidraft Reading

To assist struggling readers and to enhance reading for all, assign the text in chunks as warranted by length and apply multidraft reading protocols. For each reading, have students set the purpose indicated:

- **First reading**—identifying key ideas and details and answering any Reading Checks.
- **Second reading**—analyzing craft and structure and responding to the side-column prompts.
- **Third reading**—integrating knowledge and ideas, connecting to other texts and the world, and answering the end-of-selection questions.

For more guidance, refer to the *Classroom Strategies and Teaching Routines* card on multidraft reading.

⑤ Background
More About the Literature

In his autobiography, former slave Frederick Douglass discusses why enslaved Africans sang spirituals as they worked: "Slaves are generally expected to sing as well as to work. A silent slave is not liked by masters or overseers. . . . The remark is not unfrequently made, that slaves are the most contented and happy laborers in the world. They dance and sing, and make all manner of joyful noise—so they do; but it is a great mistake to suppose them happy because they sing. The songs of the slave represent the sorrows rather than the joys, of his heart; and he is relieved by them, only as an aching heart is relieved by its tears."

PHLit Online!
www.PHLitOnline.com

Teaching From Technology

Preparing to Read
Go to **www.PHLitOnline.com** in class or in a lab and display the **Get Connected!** slideshow for these selections. Have the class brainstorm for responses to the slideshow writing prompt, entering ideas in the interactive journal. Then, have students complete their written responses individually, in a lab or as homework.
To build background, display the Background and More About the Author features.

Using the Interactive Text
Go to **www.PHLitOnline.com** and display the **Enriched Online Student Edition**. As the class reads the selections or listens to the narration, record answers to side column prompts using the graphic organizers accessible on the interactive page. Alternatively, have students use the online edition individually, answering the prompts as they read.

❶ About the Selection

This lyric refers to the biblical account of Moses leading the Hebrews out of bondage. In this song, the Pharaoh is a metaphor for any slaveholder; the Israelites are the slaves; Moses is a redeemer or savior; and Egypt represents the American South.

❷ Activating Prior Knowledge

Ask students to identify ways in which people listen to today's rhythm and blues, gospel, jazz, or hip-hop music to escape their current surroundings. Have them suggest ways that each musical genre reflects the influence of spirituals and challenge them to identify specific musical elements that are common to all these styles.

Concept Connector ➡

Tell students they will revisit the ways in which spirituals provided an emotional escape from suffering and how this idea relates to the way we use music today.

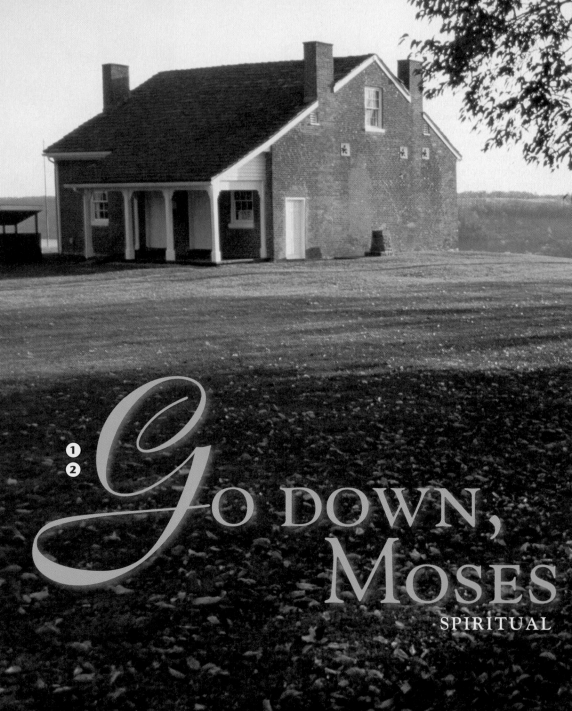

❶
❷

Go down, Moses
SPIRITUAL

532 Division, Reconciliation, and Expansion (1850–1914)

© Text Complexity Rubric

Go Down, Moses; Swing Low, Sweet Chariot

Qualitative Measures	
Context/Knowledge Demands	Song of slavery 1 2 ③ 4 5
Structure/Language Conventionality and Clarity	Poetic diction; allegory 1 2 ③ 4 5
Levels of Meaning/ Purpose/Concept Level	Accessible (allegory) 1 2 ③ 4 5
Quantitative Measures	
Lexile	NP	Text Length	89; 94 words
Overall Complexity	**More accessible**

Reader and Task Suggestions

Preparing to Read the Text

- Using the Background information on TE p. 531, discuss Douglass's comment about why enslaved Africans sang.
- Ask students why they think that Bible stories continue to be powerful, long after they were written.
- Guide students to use Multidraft Reading strategies (TE p. 531).

Leveled Tasks

Knowledge Demands If students will have difficulty with knowledge demands, share the "About the Selection" notes before a first reading. Have students reread aloud to hear the rhythms of the songs.

Analyzing If students will not have difficulty with knowledge demands, have them explain how the refrains emphasize meaning.

BACKGROUND Africans were first brought to this country as slaves in 1619. Although the slave trade was banned in 1808, slavery itself remained legal. In the years before the Civil War, many enslaved Africans fled captivity. They were hidden and transported by the Underground Railroad, a secret network of activists dedicated to helping fugitives reach freedom in the North and in Canada. One of these activists was Harriet Tubman, who was born a slave around 1820. Tubman's remarkable efforts earned her the name "Moses." In the Bible, Moses led the Israelites out of captivity in Egypt. Tubman escaped slavery via the Underground Railroad and then risked her life to return for her family. She returned to the South repeatedly to rescue other enslaved Africans, eventually leading more than 300 people to freedom.

▲ Portrait of Harriet Tubman, also known as "Moses"

Go down, Moses,
Way down in Egypt land
❸ Tell old Pharaoh
To let my people go.

5 When Israel was in Egypt land
Let my people go
❹ Oppressed so hard they could not stand
Let my people go.

Go down, Moses,
10 Way down in Egypt land
Tell old Pharaoh
"Let my people go."

"Thus saith the Lord," bold Moses said,
"Let my people go;
15 If not I'll smite your first-born dead
Let my people go."

Go down, Moses,
Way down in Egypt land,
Tell old Pharaoh,
20 "Let my people go!"

❺ ◀ **Critical Viewing** The Rankin House, shown here, was a stop on the Underground Railroad. How does the mood of this picture reflect the role the home played? **[Connect]**

Vocabulary
oppressed (ə prest′) v. kept down by cruel or unjust power

smite (smīt) v. kill by a powerful blow

Go Down, Moses **533**

---

❸ Literary Analysis
Spirituals

1. Have students listen to the spiritual as it is read aloud.

2. **Ask** students to identify the refrain and to explain how they can recognize it.
   Answer: The refrain is found in the first four lines and again in lines 9–12 and 17–20.

▶ **Monitor Progress Ask** students to name and explain the biblical allusions in the refrain.
   Answer: Moses, Egypt, Pharaoh, "Let my people go." Moses led the Israelites out of slavery under Pharaoh in Egypt.

▶ **Reteach:** If students do not recognize allusions to the Bible in the refrain, emphasize that an allusion is a reference. An allusion to the Bible is a reference to a biblical person, place, or event. **Ask** them to classify the allusions in each category.
   Answer: *People:* Moses, Pharaoh; *Place:* Egypt; *Event:* Moses demanding freedom for his people.

❹ Vocabulary Builder

1. Draw students' attention to the use of the word "oppressed," and read its definition. Then tell students that the root -*press*- derives from the Latin word *premere,* meaning "to press."

2. In small groups, have students brainstorm for a list of other words that share the root -*press*-.
   Possible response: Students may cite *pressure, depression, suppress, repress, impress.*

❺ Critical Viewing

Possible response: The mood of the picture is peaceful and calm, comfortable and free from conflict. It suggests that home was a tranquil oasis.

These selections are available in an interactive format in the **Enriched Online Student Edition,** at www.PHLitOnline.com, which includes a thematically related video with writing prompt and an interactive graphic organizer.

❻ About the Selection

This spiritual, constructed around the refrain "Coming for to carry me home," expresses both a desire for eternal salvation in heaven and a longing for freedom from slavery. The "sweet chariot" and the "band of angels" can be viewed as symbols for the Underground Railroad. This song is based on an Old Testament story in which the prophet Elijah is taken to heaven in a fiery chariot.

❼ Reading Strategy

Listening

1. Have students read aloud the spiritual, emphasizing the rhythm and rhymes.

2. **Ask** students the Reading Strategy question.
   Answer: Repeating the word "home" emphasizes the emotional importance of this idea.

ASSESS

Answers

Before students respond, you may wish to have them write a brief objective summary of the selection. As they answer the questions below, remind them to support their answers with evidence from the text.

1. (a) The people of Israel are oppressed. (b) The two groups share the experience of being enslaved.

2. (a) Moses issues his demand to Pharaoh. (b) Pharaoh represents slave owners.

3. (a) "A band of angels" is coming across the Jordan River to carry the speaker home. (b) These figures might represent abolitionists or those helping fugitives.

4. **Sample answer:** "Swing Low, Sweet Chariot" seems to contain a secret message that help and safety are on the other side of a river.

5. **Sample answer:** The longed-for home in "Swing Low, Sweet Chariot" represents the heartfelt <u>desire</u> of all slaves: to <u>escape</u> from slavery into freedom. The image of a free paradise offered a <u>respite</u> from the harsh conditions of their actual lives. "Go Down, Moses" is also an <u>expression</u> of that <u>desire</u>.

---

❻

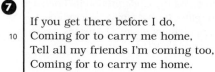

Swing Low, Sweet Chariot
SPIRITUAL

Swing low, sweet chariot,
Coming for to carry me home,
Swing low, sweet chariot,
Coming for to carry me home.

5 I looked over Jordan[1] and what did I see
Coming for to carry me home,
A band of angels coming after me,
Coming for to carry me home.

❼ If you get there before I do,
10 Coming for to carry me home,
Tell all my friends I'm coming too,
Coming for to carry me home.

Swing low, sweet chariot,
Coming for to carry me home,
15 Swing low, sweet chariot,
Coming for to carry me home.

Reading Strategy
Listening Read the song aloud. What is the effect of the repetition of the word *home*?

---

1. **Jordan** river of the Middle East that flows from the Lebanon Mountains through the Sea of Galilee to the Dead Sea. Many spirituals use the phrase "crossing over Jordan" as a metaphor for crossing the Ohio River to freedom or going to heaven.

Critical Reading

Cite textual evidence to support your responses.

1. **Key Ideas and Details (a)** In "Go Down, Moses," who is oppressed? **(b) Connect:** What connection might these oppressed people have with the slaves?

2. **Key Ideas and Details (a)** Whom does Moses tell to "let my people go"? **(b) Interpret:** If this song is related to the slaves, whom might this figure represent?

3. **Key Ideas and Details (a)** In "Swing Low, Sweet Chariot," who is coming to carry the speaker home? **(b) Interpret:** What might these figures represent?

4. **Key Ideas and Details Interpret:** Knowing that spirituals were often "code" songs for escape, do you see any hidden messages in these songs? Explain.

5. **Integration of Knowledge and Ideas** What qualities do the places described in these songs have? How do they compare to the actual places inhabited by the slaves? In your response, use at least two of these Essential Question words: *escape, desire, respite, expression. [Connecting to the Essential Question: What is the relationship between literature and place?]*

Concept Connector

Reading Strategy Graphic Organizer
Ask students to review the graphic organizers in which they have collected examples of song rhythms and moods. Then have students share their organizers and compare the rhythms and moods they identified.

Activating Prior Knowledge
Have students review their earlier opinions about how people today use music to escape. Ask them to explain whether reading these songs changed their thoughts about the power of music or the importance of positive visualization.

Writing About the Essential Question
Have students compare the responses to the prompt before they completed their reading with their thoughts afterward. Have them work individually or in groups, writing or discussing their thoughts, to formulate their new responses. Then lead a class discussion, probing for what students have learned that confirms or invalidates their initial thoughts. Encourage students to cite specific textual details to support their responses.

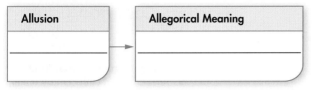

Literary Analysis

1. **Craft and Structure** What **refrains**, both lines and entire stanzas, appear in each **spiritual?**

2. **Key Ideas and Details** **(a)** Using a chart like the one shown, identify one **Biblical allusion** in each spiritual. **(b)** Explain how each allusion functions as an **allegory.**

Allusion		Allegorical Meaning
	→	

3. **Comparing Literary Works (a)** In what ways are the messages about freedom in each song similar and different? **(b)** How are the moods or emotional qualities of each song similar and different? Explain.

Reading Strategy

4. Read the spirituals aloud, **listening** to their sound elements. **(a)** Identify the uses of *rhythm, rhyme, and repetition* in both songs. **(b)** Explain how these musical elements help reinforce each song's meaning.

PERFORMANCE TASKS
Integrated Language Skills

Vocabulary Acquisition and Use

Antonyms For each numbered word, select the letter of the answer that is the best antonym, or word of opposite meaning. Explain your choices.

1. oppressed   **(a)** crushed   **(b)** assisted   **(c)** punished
2. smite   **(a)** hit   **(b)** question   **(c)** caress

Writing

Informative Text Using the Internet and library resources, find recordings of several spirituals and related art or illustrations from the historical period discussed in this unit. Incorporate the recordings and images into a **slide presentation** about spirituals in their historical context. Write a brief introduction for each song and a general introduction to the presentation as a whole. Consider including quotations from the following types of writers or speakers:

- scholars who have written about this genre of music
- important African American figures, such as Harriet Tubman or Frederick Douglass

If possible, post your presentation to an approved Internet site, such as a class or school Web site. Invite constructive comments and incorporate feedback into a revised presentation.

Common Core State Standards

Writing
6. Use technology, including the Internet, to produce, publish, and update individual or shared writing products in response to ongoing feedback, including new arguments or information.

Language
5. Demonstrate understanding of word relationships.

Answers

1. The refrain in "Go Down, Moses" is found in lines 1–4, 9–12, and 17–20. In "Swing Low, Sweet Chariot," a refrain is found in lines 1–4 and 13–16. The line "Coming for to carry me home" is also used as a refrain in lines 8 and 12.

2. **Possible responses:** (a) Moses in "Go Down, Moses" and the Jordan River in "Swing Low, Sweet Chariot" (b) Moses is an allegorical figure who represents Harriet Tubman, a leading abolitionist who led many of her people to freedom. The Jordan River represents the Ohio River, the boundary between slavery and freedom.

3. (a) Both spirituals focus on the glory of liberation. "Go Down, Moses" emphasizes the role that one powerful leader can have in achieving freedom. "Swing Low, Sweet Chariot" emphasizes the necessity of endurance and persistence in the face of adversity. (b) "Go Down, Moses" is dignified and defiant in mood, while "Swing Low, Sweet Chariot" is calmer and more melancholy.

4. (a) Both spirituals repeat single lines and entire stanzas; both use end rhymes extensively; both feature strong, regular rhythms. The rhythm of "Swing Low, Sweet Chariot" is smoother and gentler. (b) The gentler rhythms emphasize the melancholy mood of "Swing Low, Sweet Chariot," while the blunt, direct rhythms of "Go Down, Moses" emphasize its defiant message.

Vocabulary Acquisition and Use

1. b. If people are <u>oppressed</u>, they are kept down; if they are assisted, they are helped.

2. c. To <u>smite</u> is to attack with a powerful blow; to caress is to stroke gently and affectionately.

Writing

Evaluate students' presentations using the **Rubrics for Multimedia Presentation**, in *Professional Development Guidebook,* pages 266–267.

Assessment Resources

Unit 3 Resources

- **L1 L2 EL** **Selection Test A**, pp. 77–79. Administer Test A to less advanced readers.
- **L3 L4 EL** **Selection Test B**, pp. 80–82. Administer Text B to on-level or more advanced students.
- **L3 L4** **Open-Book Test**, pp. 74–76. As an alternative, give the Open-Book Test.

All **Customizable Test Bank**

All **Self-tests**
Students may prepare for the **Selection Test** by taking the **Self-test** online.

All assessment resources are available at **www.PHLitOnline.com.**

535

A Few Don'ts • In a Station of the Metro
Lesson Pacing Guide

DAY 1 Preteach

- Administer the Reading and Vocabulary Warm-ups (*Unit 3 Resources*, pp. 92–95) as necessary.
- Introduce the Literary Analysis concept: Diction.
- Introduce the Reading Strategy: Use Your Background Knowledge.
- Build background with the author and Background features.
- Develop thematic thinking with Connecting to the Essential Question.
- Teach the selection vocabulary.

DAY 2 Preteach/Teach/Extend

- Distribute copies of the appropriate graphic organizer for the Reading Strategy (*Graphic Organizer Transparencies*, pp. 113–114).
- Distribute copies of the appropriate graphic organizer for Literary Analysis (*Graphic Organizer Transparencies*, pp. 115–116).
- Prepare students to read with the Activating Prior Knowledge activities (TE).
- Informally monitor comprehension while students read.
- Use the Reading Check question to confirm comprehension.
- Develop students' understanding of diction using the Literary Analysis prompt.
- Develop students' ability to use their background knowledge using the Reading Strategy prompt.
- Reinforce vocabulary with the Vocabulary notes.
- Assess students' comprehension and mastery of the skills by having them answer the Critical Reading, Literary Analysis, and Reading Strategy questions.

DAY 3 Assess

- Have students complete the Vocabulary Lesson.
- Have students complete the Writing Lesson and write a compare–and–contrast essay. (You may assign as homework.)
- Administer Selection Test A or B (*Unit 3 Resources*, pp. 104–106 or 107–109).

Common Core State Standards

Reading Informational Text
9. Analyze nineteenth-century foundational U.S. documents of historical and literary significance for their themes, purposes, and rhetorical features.

Writing 2. Write informative/explanatory texts to examine and convey complex ideas, concepts, and information clearly and accurately through the effective selection, organization, and analysis of content.
2.c. Use appropriate and varied transitions and syntax to link the major sections of the text, create cohesion, and clarify the relationships among complex ideas and concepts.

Language 4.c. Consult reference materials, both print and digital, to find the pronunciation of a word or determine or clarify its precise meaning, its part of speech, its etymology, or its standard usage.

Additional Standards Practice
***Common Core Companion**, pp. 170–171; 196–207; 324–331*

Daily Block Scheduling
Each day in this Lesson Pacing Guide represents a 40–50 minute period. Teachers using block scheduling may combine days to revise pacing. In addition, teachers may differentiate and support core instruction by integrating components for extended and intensive support as students require. See the Guide to Selected Leveled Resources (facing page).

Guide to Selected Leveled Resources

R T I Tier 1 (students performing on level)

The Gettysburg Address • Letter to His Son

Warm Up	Practice, **model,** and **monitor** fluency, working **with the whole class** or **in groups.**	Vocabulary and Reading Warm-ups B, *Unit 3 Resources,* pp. 92–93, 95
Comprehension/Skills	**Support** and **monitor** comprehension and skills development, having students complete the activities, graphic organizers, and interactive prompts **independently** or **as a class.**	• *Reader's Notebook,* adapted instruction and summary **EL** *Reader's Notebook: English Learner's Version,* adapted instruction and summary • **Reading Strategy Graphic Organizer B,** *Graphic Organizer Transparencies,* p. 114 • **Literary Analysis Graphic Organizer B,** *Graphic Organizer Transparencies,* p. 116
Monitor Progress	**A** Monitor student progress with the differentiated curriculum-based assessment in the *Unit Resources.*	• **Selection Test B,** *Unit 3 Resources,* pp. 107–109 • **Open-Book Test,** *Unit 3 Resources,* pp. 101–103

R T I Tier 2 (students requiring intervention)

The Gettysburg Address • Letter to His Son

Warm Up	Practice, **model,** and **monitor** fluency **in groups** or **with individuals.**	• Vocabulary and Reading Warm-ups A, *Unit 3 Resources,* pp. 92–94 • *Hear It!* Audio CD
Comprehension/Skills	• **Support** and **monitor** comprehension and skills development, working **in small groups** or **with individuals.** • As students complete the selection in the appropriate version of the *Reader's Notebook,* **monitor** comprehension frequently with group questions and individual instruction. • **Model** strategies while guiding students in completing the activities and prompts in the *Reader's Notebook,* as well as the graphic organizers. • **Practice** skills and **monitor** mastery with the *Reading Kit* worksheets.	• *Reader's Notebook: Adapted Version,* adapted instruction and summary **EL** *Reader's Notebook: English Learner's Version,* adapted instruction and summary • **Reading Strategy Graphic Organizer A,** *Graphic Organizer Transparencies,* p. 113 • **Literary Analysis Graphic Organizer A,** *Graphic Organizer Transparencies,* p. 115 • *Reading Kit,* Practice worksheets
Monitor Progress	**A** Monitor student progress with the differentiated curriculum-based assessment in the *Unit Resources* and in the *Reading Kit.*	• **Selection Test A,** *Unit 3 Resources,* pp. 104–106 • *Reading Kit,* Assess worksheets

TIER 3 Tier 3 intervention may require consultation with the student's special-education or dyslexia specialist. For additional support, see the Tier 2 activities and resources listed above.

One-on-one teaching   **Group work**   **Whole-class instruction**   **Independent work**   **A** Assessment
For a complete guide to selection support, including support for Advanced students, see the Overview of Resources in the frontmatter.

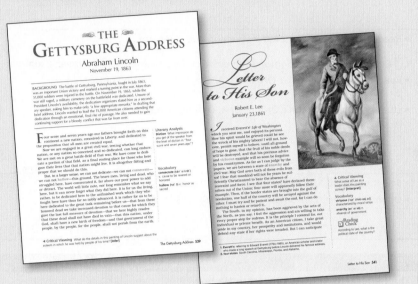

The Gettysburg Address
• Letter to His Son

RESOURCES FOR:

- **L1** Special-Needs Students
- **L2** Below-Level Students (Tier 2)
- **L3** On-Level Students (Tier 1)
- **L4** Advanced Students (Tier 1)
- **EL** English Learners
- **All** All Students

Vocabulary/Fluency/Prior Knowledge

EL **L1** **L2** Reading Warm-ups A and B, pp. 94–95

Also available for these selections:

EL **L1** **L2** Vocabulary Warm-ups A and B, pp. 92–93

All Vocabulary Builder, p. 98

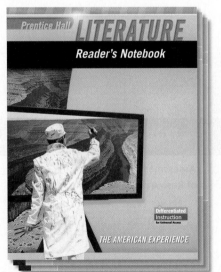

Reader's Notebooks

Pre- and postreading pages for these selections appear in an interactive format in the *Reader's Notebooks*. Each *Notebook* is differentiated for a different group of learners. The selections in the Adapted and English Learner's versions are abridged.

- **L2** **L3** *Reader's Notebook*
- **L1** *Reader's Notebook: Adapted Version*
- **EL** *Reader's Notebook: English Learner's Version*
- **EL** *Reader's Notebook: Spanish Version*

© *Common Core Companion*

Additional instruction and practice for each Common Core State Standard

Selection Support

Skills Development/Extension

Assessment

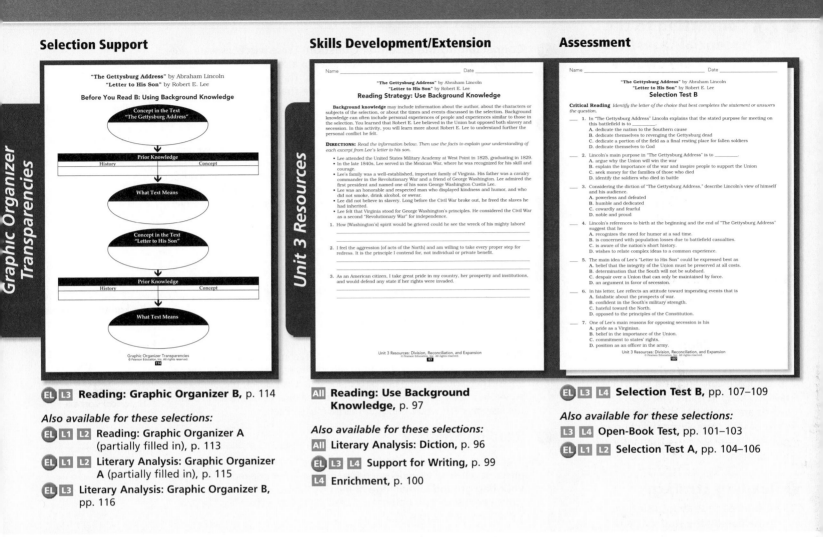

EL L3 Reading: Graphic Organizer B, p. 114

Also available for these selections:

EL L1 L2 Reading: Graphic Organizer A (partially filled in), p. 113

EL L1 L2 Literary Analysis: Graphic Organizer A (partially filled in), p. 115

EL L3 Literary Analysis: Graphic Organizer B, pp. 116

All Reading: Use Background Knowledge, p. 97

Also available for these selections:

All Literary Analysis: Diction, p. 96

EL L3 L4 Support for Writing, p. 99

L4 Enrichment, p. 100

EL L3 L4 Selection Test B, pp. 107–109

Also available for these selections:

L3 L4 Open-Book Test, pp. 101–103

EL L1 L2 Selection Test A, pp. 104–106

PHLit Online!
www.PHLitOnline.com

Online Resources: All print materials are also available online.

- complete narrated selection text
- a thematically related video with writing prompt
- an interactive graphic organizer
- highlighting feature
- access to all student print resources, adapted to individual student needs
- Spanish and English summaries
- adapted selection translations in Spanish

Background Video

Also available:

Get Connected! (thematic video with writing prompt)
All videos are available in Spanish.

Vocabulary Central (tools and activities for studying vocabulary)

Also available:

Writer's Journal (with graphics feature)

❶ Connecting to the Essential Question

1. Review the assignment with the class.

2. Point out that someone who is patriotic is devoted to his or her country. Have students discuss whether all patriotic people share similar opinions about their country. Then have them complete the assignment.

3. As students read, have them notice how Lincoln and Lee express their devotion to their country.

❷ Literary Analysis

Introduce the skill, using the instruction on the student page.

Think Aloud: Model the Skill

Say to students:

> To compare Lincoln's and Lee's diction, I'll keep in mind that abstract words are not better than concrete ones or vice versa. Formal diction is not better—or worse— than informal diction.

❸ Reading Strategy

1. Introduce the strategy, using the instruction on the student page.

2. Give students a copy of **Reading Strategy Graphic Organizer B**, page 114 in *Graphic Organizer Transparencies*, to fill out as they read.

Think Aloud: Model the Skill

Say to students:

> I will apply what I know about the period as I read. My background knowledge includes not only facts but also thoughts and feelings about the division between the states. I know that the split reflected both geography and strongly conflicting ideas.

❹ Vocabulary

1. Pronounce each word, giving its definition, and have students say it aloud.

2. For more guidance, see the *Classroom Strategies and Teaching Routines* card for introducing vocabulary.

Before You Read | **The Gettysburg Address • Letter to His Son**

❶ **Connecting to the Essential Question** These selections were written by two patriotic men on opposite sides of a conflict. As you read, look for ideas that express each writer's patriotism. This will help as you consider the Essential Question: **How does literature shape or reflect society?**

❷ Literary Analysis

Diction, the choice and arrangement of words, gives a piece of writing its unique quality and helps the writer express ideas clearly and precisely. Diction may be formal or informal, technical or plain, elevated or simple. Diction is influenced by the *audience, purpose,* and *occasion* for a given text. For example, in this public speech, Lincoln's diction has a formality that suits the occasion and purpose of the event:

> Four score and seven years ago, our fathers brought
> forth on this continent a new nation . . .

In this private letter to his son, Lee's informal diction suits his audience:

> As far as I can judge by the papers, we are between
> a state of anarchy and civil war . . .

As you read, note how each writer's diction reflects the audience, purpose, and occasion of his writing.

Comparing Literary Works Each selection communicates a writer's views about the Civil War, but from very different vantage points. Lee, a Southerner, wrote on the eve of conflict, whereas Lincoln, the Union leader, wrote from a battlefield two years into the war. Compare and contrast the insights each writer brings to this painful conflict.

❸ Reading Strategy

Preparing to Read Complex Texts When reading historical documents, it is helpful to understand the situations that inspired them. **Use your background knowledge** of the Civil War to analyze the ideas these writers express in their historical context. Complete a chart like the one shown to organize your ideas.

❹ Vocabulary

consecrate (kän′ si krāt′) *v.* cause to be revered or honored (p. 539)

hallow (hal′ ō) *v.* honor as sacred (p. 539)

virtuous (vʉr′ choo əs) *adj.* characterized by moral virtue (p. 541)

anarchy (an′ ər kē) *n.* absence of government (p. 541)

Common Core State Standards

Reading Informational Text
9. Analyze nineteenth-century foundational U.S. documents of historical and literary significance for their themes, purposes, and rhetorical features.

Background Knowledge

↓

Meaning of Text in Historical Context

Vocabulary Development

Vocabulary Knowledge Rating

Create a **Vocabulary Knowledge Rating Chart** (*Professional Development Guidebook,* p. 33) for the vocabulary words on the student page. Give each student a copy of the chart with the words on it. Read the words aloud, and have students mark their rating of each in the Before Reading column. When students have completed reading and discussing the selections, have them take out their **Vocabulary Knowledge Rating Charts** for each. Read the words aloud, and have students rate their knowledge again in the After Reading column. Clarify any words that are still problematic. Then have students complete the Vocabulary practice at the end of the selections.

Vocabulary Central, featuring tools and activities for studying vocabulary, is available online at www.PHLitOnline.com.

⑤ ABRAHAM LINCOLN
(1809–1865)

Author of the Gettysburg Address

Serving as president during one of the most tragic periods in American history, Abraham Lincoln fought to reunite a nation torn apart by war. His courage, strength, and dedication in the face of an overwhelming national crisis have made him one of the most admired and respected American presidents.

Lincoln was born into a family of humble means. As a child, his duties on his parents' farm limited his opportunities to receive a formal education. Still, he was an avid reader and developed an early interest in politics. He served in the Illinois state legislature and the United States Congress, where he earned a reputation as a champion of emancipation. In 1858, he ran for the United States Senate against Stephen Douglas. Lincoln lost the election, but his heated debates with Douglas brought him national recognition and helped him win the presidency in 1860.

Troubled Times Shortly after his election, the Civil War erupted. Throughout the war, Lincoln showed great strength and courage. He also demonstrated his gift for oratory. He was invited to make "a few appropriate remarks" in November 1863 for a dedication of the Gettysburg battlefield as a national cemetery. The world has long remembered what he said there.

Lincoln's great care as a writer shows in the Gettysburg Address, as it does in many of his other speeches. He worked diligently and thoughtfully to prepare messages that would have the effect he desired. Two important aspects of the Gettysburg speech are its brevity—just 272 words—and its reaffirmation of the democratic principles at the heart of American government. Lincoln was killed by an assassin's bullet in 1865 while attending the theater with his wife.

" *As* I would not be a slave, so I would not be a master. This expresses my idea of democracy. Whatever differs from this, to the extent of the difference, is no democracy."

The Gettysburg Address **537**

◆ Multidraft Reading

To assist struggling readers and to enhance reading for all, apply multidraft reading protocols. For each reading, have students set the purpose indicated:

- **First reading**—identifying key ideas and details and answering any Reading Checks.
- **Second reading**—analyzing craft and structure and responding to the side-column prompts.
- **Third reading**—integrating knowledge and ideas, connecting to other texts and the world, and answering the end-of-selection questions.

For more guidance, refer to the *Classroom Strategies and Teaching Routines* card on multidraft reading.

⑤ Background
More About the Author

Stories abound regarding Lincoln's drafting of the Gettysburg Address: He wrote it the week before; he wrote it the night before; he wrote it on the train; he wrote it on a piece of scrap paper. Certainly, we know that he was still revising it even as he spoke, adding the phrase "under God" to describe the nation. An experienced orator, Lincoln probably anticipated the positive effect this suggestion of divine approval of the United States and its goals of freedom would have on the audience.

It has been computed that Lincoln's printed speeches and writings contain 1,078,365 words. This figure is even more impressive when one considers that his writing style is admired especially for its precision and conciseness.

PHLit Online!
www.PHLitOnline.com

Teaching From Technology

Preparing to Read
Go to **www.PHLitOnline.com** in class or in a lab and display the **Get Connected!** slide show for these selections. Have the class brainstorm for responses to the slide show writing prompt, entering ideas in the interactive journal. Then have students complete their written responses individually in a lab or as homework.

To build background, display the Background and More About the Author features.

Using the Interactive Text
Go to **www.PHLitOnline.com** and display the **Enriched Online Student Edition.** As the class reads these selections or listens to the narration, record answers to side-column prompts using the graphic organizers accessible on the interactive page. Alternatively, have students use the online edition individually, answering the prompts as they read.

❶ About the Selection

Lincoln's short but powerful Gettysburg Address places the Civil War into the historical context of the American fight for freedom. Lincoln asserts that the war is a test of the ideals for which colonials fought in 1776—in a sense, it is a continuation of the American Revolution. In an attempt to give direction to his divided country, Lincoln urges Americans to devote themselves to the task begun but not completed—to preserve freedom for all Americans.

❷ Activating Prior Knowledge

Have students discuss how reading primary sources, such as speeches and letters, can help us understand a historical period. Ask students to share their experiences with such primary sources. For example, students might discuss what they learned about a time period by listening to a famous speech, such as Dr. Martin Luther King Jr.'s "I have a dream," delivered on August 28, 1963, in Washington, D.C.

Concept Connector ➡

Tell students they will revisit the ways in which primary resources can enhance our understanding of historical events, such as the Civil War.

538 Division, Reconciliation, and Expansion (1850–1914)

© Text Complexity Rubric: Leveled Texts

	The Gettysburg Address	Letter to His Son
Qualitative Measures		
Context/ Knowledge Demands	U.S. Civil War; historical knowledge demands 1 2 ③ 4 5	U.S Civil War; historical knowledge demands 1 2 ③ 4 5
Structure/Language Conventionality and Clarity	Formal diction; use of parallelism 1 2 3 ④ 5	Mix of formal and informal diction 1 2 3 ④ 5
Levels of Meaning/ Purpose/Concept Level	Accessible (war) 1 2 ③ 4 5	Challenging (war) 1 2 3 ④ 5
Quantitative Measures		
Lexile/Text Length	1490L / 264 words	1110L / 496 words
Overall Complexity	**More accessible**	**More complex**

❶ ❷

THE GETTYSBURG ADDRESS

Abraham Lincoln
November 19, 1863

BACKGROUND The battle of Gettysburg, Pennsylvania, fought in July 1863, was an important Union victory and marked a turning point in the war. More than 51,000 soldiers were injured in the battle. On November 19, 1863, while the war still raged, a military cemetery on the battlefield was dedicated. Unsure of President Lincoln's availability, the dedication organizers slated him as a secondary speaker, asking him to make only "a few appropriate remarks." In drafting that brief address, Lincoln wanted to lead the 15,000 American citizens attending the dedication through an emotional, final rite of passage. He also needed to gain continuing support for a bloody conflict that was far from over.

---

❸

Four score and seven years ago our fathers brought forth on this continent a new nation, conceived in Liberty, and dedicated to the proposition that all men are created equal.

Now we are engaged in a great civil war, testing whether that nation, or any nation so conceived and so dedicated, can long endure. We are met on a great battle-field of that war. We have come to dedicate a portion of that field, as a final resting place for those who here gave their lives that that nation might live. It is altogether fitting and proper that we should do this.

But, in a larger sense, we can not dedicate—we can not consecrate—we can not hallow—this ground. The brave men, living and dead, who struggled here, have consecrated it, far above our poor power to add or detract. The world will little note, nor long remember what we say here, but it can never forget what they did here. It is for us the living, rather, to be dedicated here to the unfinished work which they who fought here have thus far so nobly advanced. It is rather for us to be here dedicated to the great task remaining before us—that from these honored dead we take increased devotion to that cause for which they gave the last full measure of devotion—that we here highly resolve that these dead shall not have died in vain—that this nation, under God, shall have a new birth of freedom—and that government of the people, by the people, for the people, shall not perish from the earth.

Literary Analysis
Diction What impression do you get of the speaker from the level of diction in "four score and seven years ago"?

Vocabulary
consecrate (kän′ si krāt′) *v.* cause to be revered or honored

hallow (hal′ ō) *v.* honor as sacred

❹ ◄ Critical Viewing What do the details in this painting of Lincoln suggest about the esteem in which he was held by people of his time? **[Infer]**

The Gettysburg Address **539**

---

❸ Literary Analysis
Diction

1. Have students read the opening sentence aloud.

2. **Ask** students the Literary Analysis question.
   Answer: Students should note that this formal, eloquent diction suggests that the speaker, Lincoln, is dignified, serious, and respectful.

▶ **Monitor progress: Ask:** Which other word choices in the opening sentence do you think best reflect Lincoln's diction?
   Sample response: "brought forth," "conceived in Liberty," "dedicated to the proposition"

▶ **Reteach:** If students have difficulty identifying formal diction, suggest that they consider other words the writer might have chosen. For example, Lincoln might have begun his speech with "Eighty-seven years ago." **Ask** students to compare both versions and consider why Lincoln chose "Four score and seven years ago."
   Possible response: The longer version is more formal, giving a greater sense of importance to the occasion.

❹ Critical Viewing

Answer: The crowd's rapt attention and emotional response suggest that Lincoln was greatly admired and respected.

These selections are available in an interactive format in the **Enriched Online Student Edition**, at **www.PHLitOnline.com**, which includes a thematically related video with writing prompt and an interactive graphic organizer.

© Text Complexity: Reader and Task Suggestions

The Gettysburg Address		Letter to His Son	
Preparing to Read the Text	**Leveled Tasks**	**Preparing to Read the Text**	**Leveled Tasks**
• Using the Background information on TE p. 537, discuss Lincoln's legacy as a skilled speechwriter. • Ask students to name recent news events involving fatalities. Discuss how students would pay tribute to those who died. • Guide students to use Multidraft Reading strategies (TE p. 537).	*Structure/Language* If students will have difficulty with Lincoln's parallelism, guide them in deconstructing the first sentence. As students reread, have them apply that technique to the rest of the speech. *Synthesizing* If students will not have difficulty with Lincoln's parallelism, invite them to create a formal tribute to a historical figure whom they admire, following the progression of ideas in the Gettysburg Address.	• Using the Background information on SE p. 540, discuss the circumstances that led Lee to write. • Ask students to give examples of situations in which people disagree. Discuss how each side may have valid ideas. • Guide students to use Multidraft Reading strategies (TE p. 537).	*Levels of Meaning* If students will have difficulty following Lee's ideas, have them keep "pro" and "con" lists of arguments during a first reading. After students reread, have them summarize the sense of conflict that Lee describes. *Analyzing* If students will not have difficulty following Lee's ideas, have them explain what *Union* means to Lee and why the conflict that threatens that union grieves him so much.

More About the Author

Robert E. Lee may have been the most respected and admired Southerner of his time. Even Ulysses S. Grant remarked, "There was not a man in the Confederacy whose influence with the whole people was as great as his."

⑤ Robert E. Lee (1807–1870)

Author of "Letter to His Son"

Robert E. Lee was born into a respected Virginia family with a strong military tradition and graduated with high honors from the United States Military Academy at West Point. During the Mexican War, he established a reputation as one of the finest leaders in the United States Army.

Divided Loyalties Despite his military training and talent, the job of commanding the Confederate army during the Civil War was not one that Robert E. Lee wanted. As the dispute over slavery grew, Lee was torn. A descendant of a number of distinguished patriots and statesmen, he believed in the Union and opposed both slavery and secession. Still, when President Lincoln offered him command of the Union forces, Lee refused to lead an army against his native state and resigned from the army, vowing to fight only in defense of Virginia.

A Difficult Task Unlike many Confederate leaders, Lee had no illusions about the South's power. Serving initially as commander of the army of northern Virginia and later of all the Confederate armies, he expected the widespread bloodshed and destruction caused by the war. He was an extraordinary military leader whose accomplishments and personal integrity in the face of overwhelming odds inspired great loyalty in both soldiers and civilians.

An avid letter writer, Lee wrote frequently to family members explaining his actions and expressing his feelings. On the eve of resigning his U.S. Army commission, Lee explored his divided loyalties in "Letter to His Son." After the war, Lee served as president of Washington College (now Washington and Lee) until his death.

"Do your duty in all things. You cannot do more, you should never wish to do less. "

Enrichment: Analyzing Music

Aaron Copland

Commissioned to write a musical portrait of a great American, Aaron Copland (1900–1990) chose Lincoln. "A Lincoln Portrait" blends original music with folk tunes to accompany a script of Lincoln's words. Copland explained, "In the opening section I wanted to suggest something of the mysterious sense of fatality that surrounds Lincoln's personality. . . . The quick middle section briefly sketches in the background of the times. . . . This merges into the concluding section where my sole purpose was to draw a simple but impressive frame about the words of Lincoln himself."

Activity: Musical Evaluation Invite students to listen to the piece and determine whether Copland succeeded in creating the effects he intended. Students can guide their analysis by using the **Enrichment: Analyzing Music** work sheet, in *Professional Development Guidebook,* page 236.

❻ Letter to His Son

Robert E. Lee
January 23, 1861

I received Everett's[1] *Life of Washington* which you sent me, and enjoyed its perusal. How his spirit would be grieved could he see the wreck of his mighty labors! I will not, however, permit myself to believe, until all ground of hope is gone, that the fruit of his noble deeds will be destroyed, and that his precious advice and *virtuous* example will so soon be forgotten by his countrymen. As far as I can judge by the papers, we are between a state of *anarchy* and civil war. May God avert both of these evils from us! I fear that mankind will not for years be sufficiently Christianized to bear the absence of restraint and force. I see that four states[2] have declared themselves out of the Union; four more will apparently follow their example. Then, if the border states are brought into the gulf of revolution, one half of the country will be arrayed against the other. I must try and be patient and await the end, for I can do nothing to hasten or retard it.

The South, in my opinion, has been aggrieved by the acts of the North, as you say. I feel the aggression and am willing to take every proper step for redress. It is the principle I contend for, not individual or private benefit. As an American citizen, I take great pride in my country, her prosperity and institutions, and would defend any state if her rights were invaded. But I can anticipate

---

1. **Everett's** referring to Edward Everett (1794–1865), an American scholar and orator who made a long speech at Gettysburg before Lincoln delivered his famous address.
2. **four states** South Carolina, Mississippi, Florida, and Alabama.

❽ ▲ Critical Viewing
What sense of Lee as a leader does this painting convey? **[Interpret]**

Vocabulary
virtuous (vur´ chŏŏ əs) *adj.* characterized by moral virtue

anarchy (an´ ər kē) *n.* absence of government

❾ ☑ Reading Check

According to Lee, what is the political state of the country?

Letter to His Son **541**

Using Background Knowledge

1. Help students understand the dense final paragraph (which begins on p. 541) by having them focus on Lee's conflicting impulses: loyalty to both his nation and home state.

2. **Ask** students the Reading Strategy question.
   Answer: Lee was trained for the military in the North and served the Union Army as an officer in Mexico. Many of his ancestors were statesmen and patriots. Yet, Lee was a proud native of Virginia, a "simple" fact that led him to defend the Confederacy rather than the Union.

ASSESS

Answers

Remind students to support their answers with evidence from the text.

1. (a) He describes a vision of the nation as healthy, peaceful, and free. (b) This vision helps him achieve his goal of inspiring people to fight to regain national unity

2. (a) He has given Lee a biography of Washington. (b) Lee asserts that Washington would be upset if he knew that the Union, which Washington worked so hard to create, might soon fall apart.

3. (a) Lee believes the Union is a permanent government that can be ended only by revolution or universal agreement. (b) A Union maintained only by force has no value to Lee. (c) He argues that secession conflicts with the goals of the Constitution.

4. **Sample response:** For both men, American patriotism includes a <u>devotion</u> to the principles established by the country's founders and a <u>conviction</u> that they are supporting freedom. Lincoln's <u>aspiration</u> is to maintain the <u>unity</u> of all states. Lee shares this desire but pledges his ultimate allegiance to his state.

Reading Strategy
Using Background Knowledge Given what you know about Lee, why was he so committed to both the Union and to Virginia?

> *I* shall mourn for my country and for the welfare and progress of mankind.

⑩

no greater calamity for the country than a dissolution of the Union. It would be an accumulation of all the evils we complain of, and I am willing to sacrifice everything but honor for its preservation. I hope, therefore, that all constitutional means will be exhausted before there is a resort to force. Secession is nothing but revolution. The framers of our Constitution never exhausted so much labor, wisdom, and forbearance in its formation, and surrounded it with so many guards and securities, if it was intended to be broken by every member of the Confederacy at will. It was intended for "perpetual union," so expressed in the preamble, and for the establishment of a government, not a compact, which can only be dissolved by revolution or the consent of all the people in convention assembled. It is idle to talk of secession. Anarchy would have been established, and not a government, by Washington, Hamilton, Jefferson, Madison, and the other patriots of the Revolution. . . . Still, a Union that can only be maintained by swords and bayonets, and in which strife and civil war are to take the place of brotherly love and kindness, has no charm for me. I shall mourn for my country and for the welfare and progress of mankind. If the Union is dissolved, and the government disrupted, I shall return to my native state and share the miseries of my people; and, save in defense, will draw my sword on none.

Critical Reading

Ⓒ

Cite textual evidence to support your responses.

Ⓒ 1. **Key Ideas and Details (a)** What vision of the nation does Lincoln describe at the close of his speech? **(b) Connect:** In what way does an expression of this vision further his purpose for speaking?

Ⓒ 2. **Key Ideas and Details (a)** What gift has Lee's son given him? **(b) Connect:** How is Lee's recognition of this gift linked to his feelings about secession? Explain.

Ⓒ 3. **Key Ideas and Details (a)** How would you explain Lee's use of the word *Union*? **(b)** In what ways does he clarify or refine the meaning of the word *Union*? **(c) Summarize:** In your own words, explain Lee's argument against secession.

Ⓒ 4. **Integration of Knowledge and Ideas** Based on these selections, how do you think both Lincoln and Lee define American patriotism? In your response, use at least two of these Essential Question words: *devotion, unity, conviction, aspiration.* *[Connecting to the Essential Question: How does literature shape or reflect society?]*

542 Division, Reconciliation, and Expansion (1850–1914)

Assessment Practice

Context (For more practice, see *All-in-One Workbook*.)

Many tests require students to use context clues such as synonyms and antonyms to determine the meanings of unfamiliar words. Write the following passage on the chalkboard. Then ask students the question that follows.

> Both parties deprecated war; but one of them would *make* war rather than let the nation survive; and the other would *accept* war rather than let it <u>perish</u>.

In this passage, the word "perish" means

A flourish
B compromise
C expand
D die

The parallel construction of the sentence—"let the nation *survive* . . . let it *perish*"—combined with the use of "rather," which means "to the contrary," or "instead," suggests that *perish* means the opposite of *survive*. D is the correct answer.

Literary Analysis

© 1. Craft and Structure Using a chart like the one shown, analyze how the **diction** used by each writer is appropriate to the audience, occasion, and purpose of the text.

	Examples of Diction	Audience	Occasion	Purpose
Lincoln				
Lee				

© 2. Craft and Structure Choose one passage from each selection in which the diction seems especially effective in expressing and clarifying the writer's meaning. Explain your choices.

3. Comparing Literary Works (a) What words does Lincoln use to describe the war? **(b)** What words does Lee use to describe it? **(c)** What personal views about the war do you think the two men share?

© 4. Craft and Structure Which voice do you find more engaging, Lincoln's or Lee's? Why?

Reading Strategy

5. Using background knowledge, explain why President Lincoln wrote such a short speech for his address at Gettysburg.

6. Why did Lincoln connect the honoring of those who died at Gettysburg with the goal of continuing the war toward a Union victory?

7. Why was Lee so opposed to secession?

PERFORMANCE TASKS
Integrated Language Skills

© Vocabulary Acquisition and Use

Use New Words in Sentences For each word pair, write one sentence using both words correctly.

    1. consecrate/hallow

    2. anarchy/virtuous

Writing

© Explanatory Text Abraham Lincoln and Robert E. Lee wrote from different sides of the Civil War conflict, yet both take a historical view about the founding principles of the United States. Write a **compare-and-contrast essay** in which you describe each writer's understanding of the relationship between the Civil War strife of their own generation and the ideas on which the United States was founded. To clarify the flow of your ideas, *use transitional words and phrases* that show contrast or similarity, such as "alternatively," "on the other hand," and "in a similar way."

© Common Core State Standards

Writing

2. Write informative/explanatory texts to examine and convey complex ideas, concepts, and information clearly and accurately through the effective selection, organization, and analysis of content.

2.c. Use appropriate and varied transitions and syntax to link the major sections of the text, create cohesion, and clarify the relationships among complex ideas and concepts.

The Gettysburg Address • Letter to His Son **543**

Answers

1. **Sample answers:** Lincoln— *Diction:* we cannot consecrate— we cannot hallow this ground; we here highly resolve that these dead shall not have died in vain; *Audience:* Union supporters; *Purpose:* to help pay tribute to the slain and to gain support for the war. Lee—*Diction:* It is the principle I contend for, not individual or private benefit; *Audience:* his son; *Purpose:* to explain his support of the Confederacy

2. **Sample answers:** Lincoln's opening marks the occasion with a respectful formality. Lee's description of the country as torn between "anarchy and civil war" suggests his deep personal feelings about the events.

3. (a) Lincoln describes the war as "a great civil war," "the great task remaining before us." (b) Lee describes the war and anarchy as "these evils." (c) **Possible response:** Perhaps because of his military background, Lee seems to revile war more deeply than does Lincoln, but both realize the price of war.

4. **Possible response:** Some students may respond to Lincoln's direct, formal voice. Others will respond to Lee's less rhetorical diction.

5. He was asked to "make a few appropriate remarks."

6. As president, he wanted to see the nation survive. He did not want the loss of life to have been in vain.

7. Having served in the United States military, Lee felt strong ties to the Union.

Vocabulary Acquisition and Use

1. **Sample response:** We <u>hallow</u> many battle sites in order to <u>consecrate</u> the memory of soldiers who died there.

2. **Sample answer:** Most politicians agree that it is <u>virtuous</u> to fight <u>anarchy</u> and to maintain order.

Writing

Evaluate students' work using the **Rubrics for Comparison-and-Contrast Essay,** in *Professional Development Guidebook,* pages 260–261.

Assessment Resources

Unit 3 Resources

L1 L2 EL **Selection Test A,** pp. 104–106. Administer Test A to less advanced readers.

L3 L4 EL **Selection Test B,** pp. 107–109. Administer Test B to on-level and more advanced students.

L3 L4 **Open-Book Test,** pp. 101–103. As an alternative, give the Open-Book Test.

All **Customizable Test Bank**

All **Self-tests** Students may prepare for the **Selection Test** by taking the Self-test online.

 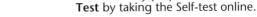

Contemporary Connection

Present the following overview. The film *Cold Mountain,* based on Charles Frazier's 1997 novel, is set in the rural South in the 1860s. It focuses on three characters—Inman, who loves Ada but leaves for the war; wealthy Ada, who must deal with Inman's departure and crises on the farm she inherits; and brazen Ruby, who teaches Ada how to survive and learns the value of human contact. All three experience difficult journeys.

Civil War Writings Past and Present

1. Much writing about war spotlights battles and generals. **Ask** students for examples from this unit.
   Possible response: "An Episode of War" presents the aftermath of battle; Mary Chesnut's diary mentions the home front but only in relation to the doings of officers.

2. *Cold Mountain* deals with ordinary Americans in the 1860s. **Ask** students what a writer or filmmaker could show about a war besides battlefields.
   Possible response: A writer or filmmaker could show those left behind—women, children, older men, men who avoid conscription.

Anthony Minghella

1. After students read about the screenwriter and skim pages 546–549, **ask** them to explain what Minghella means by saying a screenplay is "not beautiful in the way a book is beautiful."
   Possible response: A screenplay presents dialogue and stage directions—not crafted passages.

2. According to the bio, after Minghella read Frazier's novel, "he knew the journey to his next movie had already begun." **Ask** students how making a movie is a journey.
   Possible response: A filmmaker goes through stages—getting an idea, raising funds, writing a script, casting actors, identifying crew, finding locations, and so on until the release of the film and reviews.

CONTEMPORARY CONNECTION

Civil War Writings Past and Present

A turbulent and tragic stage in America's story, the Civil War has captured the imaginations of generations of American writers. Ambrose Bierce wrote about the war from firsthand experience as a Union soldier. Stephen Crane steeped himself in knowledge about the war in order to write his vivid stories. Margaret Mitchell set her sweeping 1936 bestseller *Gone With the Wind* during the Civil War. Ken Burns's documentary series, *Civil War,* debuted on public television stations in 1990. With 40 million viewers, it was the most-watched PBS series ever aired.

Charles Frazier's novel *Cold Mountain* continues this tradition. The story of a man's quest to return from the battlefield to his home in the Carolina mountains, the book stormed onto bestseller lists when it was published in 1997. In 2003, Nicole Kidman, Jude Law, and Renée Zellwegger starred in the feature film based on the book.

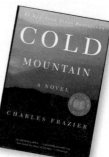

ANTHONY MINGHELLA Screenwriter/Director

British director and screenwriter Anthony Minghella's film career took off in 1990 with the release of *Truly, Madly, Deeply,* a drama he wrote and directed for Britain's BBC. He later wrote the screenplay adaptation of Patricia Highsmith's novel *The Talented Mr. Ripley* and directed the 1999 film starring Matt Damon. In 1996, Minghella won the Academy Award for Best Director for his work on *The English Patient,* a film he adapted from his friend Michael Ondaatje's novel. Minghella once described a screenplay as "not beautiful in the way a book is beautiful . . . It's much more sort of a plan. So I tried not to even think of the screenplay as a defining document, as a piece of work in itself, but only as a route." Minghella was in Toronto, Canada, when Ondaatje gave him a copy of *Cold Mountain.* Upon his return home to London, he discovered two other people had sent him copies of the novel. He said, "I felt there must be some augury," or prophecy, in the coincidence. The film he wrote and directed was a critical and box office success and received seven Academy Award nominations. Sadly, Minghella's thriving career was cut short by his death in 2008.

544 Division, Reconciliation, and Expansion (1850–1914)

JUDE LAW   NICOLE KIDMAN   RENÉE ZELLWEGER

FIND YOUR WAY HOME

from COLD MOUNTAIN

Cold Mountain

1. Have students look at the illustration promoting the movie. Draw their attention to the tagline "Find your way home." Tell students that the movie's marketing campaign included another, longer version: "Find the strength. Find the courage. No matter what it takes . . . find the way home." **Ask** students to put into their own words the theme of the movie based on these taglines.
   Possible response: Home and what it represents—family, acceptance, love, continuity—are the most important things in life.

2. Based either on the film *Cold Mountain* or on other works that Jude Law, Nicole Kidman, and Renée Zellweger have appeared in, give students the opportunity to discuss what they see as the strengths and weaknesses of these actors.
   Possible response: Students might comment on Law's performances in *The Aviator* (2004), *Blueberry Nights* (2007), and *Sleuth* (2007); Kidman's performances in *The Hours* (2003) and *Bewitched* (2005); and Renée Zellweger's performances in *Cinderella Man* (2005) and *Miss Potter* (2006).

Cold Mountain

1. Point out to students that this excerpt shows Ada and Ruby at the very start of a joint journey to protect and preserve Ada's farm.

2. **Ask** students to use only the material in scenes 79–81 to describe the differences between Ada and Ruby here at the beginning of their relationship.
Possible response: Compared with Ada, Ruby rises earlier, gets to work more quickly, and is more concerned with the farm than with her own comfort.

▲ Nicole Kidman plays Ada Monroe, a cultured young woman struggling to survive during the Civil War in the film version of *Cold Mountain*.

from COLD MOUNTAIN

a screenplay by
Anthony Minghella

based on the novel by
Charles Frazier

BACKGROUND The following scenes are set at Black Cove Farm, the home of Ada Monroe. Ada is a privileged young woman who has never had to work the land before. With the Civil War in full force, she has fallen on desperate times. The arrival of capable and tough Ruby Thewes saves both Ada's farm and her life.

79.[1] INT.[2] ADA'S BEDROOM, BLACK COVE FARM. PREDAWN. SUMMER 1864.

Ada wakes up to persistent knocking.

RUBY. (O.S.[3]) Ada? Ada? You up?

---

1. Numbers indicate scene numbers.
2. **INT.** abbreviation for "interior" or a scene shot indoors.
3. **O.S.** off screen, a voice heard without the actor appearing on screen.

ADA. Yes. *(opening her eyes)* It's still dark.

RUBY. (O.S.) Tell the cows that. It's late.

80. INT. KITCHEN, BLACK COVE FARM. PREDAWN. SUMMER 1864.

Ada enters blearily, clutching her novel. Ruby is already busy.

ADA. I have to eat something.

RUBY. Then you have to get up earlier. *(at Ada's book)* What's that?

ADA. A novel.

RUBY. *(heading outside)* You want to carry a book, carry one you can write in—

81. EXT.[4] BLACK COVE FARM. DAWN. SUMMER 1864.

Ruby emerges, followed by Ada, chewing on a carrot.

RUBY. —we got our own story. Called Black Cove Farm : a catastrophe.

She looks back at Ada for a reaction.

RUBY. (CONT.[5]) I can spell it, too. Learned the same place you did, in the schoolhouse. That's one of the first words they taught me. Ruby Thewes, you are a c-a-t-a-s-t-r-o-p-h-e.

They're heading for the stable.

82. INT. STABLE, BLACK COVE FARM. DAY. SUMMER 1864.

Ruby's already pitching hay. Turns to Ada, hands her a rake. Ada, half asleep, accepts obediently, stunned by this energy.

RUBY. Three years I was in school before my daddy—saying God rest his soul is like wishing him what he had in life, 'cause he lived to rest, he was born tired—before my daddy decided there was better use for me than have me sat all day in front of a chalkboard.

83. EXT. A FIELD OF WEEDS, BLACK COVE FARM. DAY.

---

4. **EXT.** exterior, a scene shot outdoors.
5. **CONT.** continued, here dialogue that is interrupted for a moment, but begins again.

▲ Renée Zellweger plays the feisty and practical Ruby Thewes.

Cold Mountain

1. While Ruby is clearly in charge here, she seems a bit self-conscious. **Ask** students to find evidence in the dialogue and stage directions on this page of Ruby's self-consciousness.
   Answer: Not to be outdone by Ada's walking around with a novel, Ruby shows that she can spell correctly even though she admits to having had only three years of schooling.

2. Point out to students that the setting keeps changing on these first two pages of the excerpt. **Ask:** From where to where do the women move in the course of these two pages, and what do those moves accomplish for the film?
   Answer: We first see Ada in bed and hear Ruby outside Ada's bedroom. The scene shifts to the kitchen, outside the kitchen, then to the stable, and then to a field of weeds. These changes of setting show us that the day is moving on with Ruby leading and Ada following.

Differentiated Instruction   for Universal Access

Support for Special-Needs Students
Explain that each numbered shot contains (1) setting, in capital letters; (2) dialogue, with characters' names in boldface indented from the margin; and (3) stage directions, set at the left margin. Explain the abbreviations: INT. = "interior"; O.S. = "off-screen"—that is, not in the film frame; EXT. = "exterior."

Strategy for Less Proficient Readers
Put on a readers' theater version of the script. Assign a less proficient student to each of the two roles to read aloud only the dialogue, giving the setting and stage directions to more proficient students to read aloud.

EL Vocabulary for English Learners
Point out scene 83, in which Ada, who has inherited the farm from her father, does not recognize the words "maul" (a kind of hammer) and "froe" (a cleaver), which Ruby uses. This is an opportunity to stress that even native English speakers may not know terms that have gone out of use or pertain to a specific work.

1. Review the definitions of *Realism* and *Naturalism* as literary movements.
2. Encourage students to **identify** an instance of Realism or Naturalism on this page of the script.
   Answer: Instances include Ruby's getting her hands dirty and not hesitating to taste soil.

SUMMER 1864.

Ruby dictates a list to Ada as they bustle along.

> **RUBY.** Number one—lay out a winter garden for cool-season crops: turnips, onions, cabbage, greens.

Ada scribbles, walks, scribbles.

84. EXT. BARN, BLACK COVE FARM. DAY. SUMMER 1864.

Ruby up a ladder, inspecting the roof.

> **RUBY.** Number two: patch the shingles on the barn roof. Do we have a maul and froe?
>
> **ADA.** *(writing, holding the ladder)* Maul?
>
> **RUBY.** Maul. M-a-u-l.
>
> **ADA.** I have no idea.

85. INT. SPRINGHOUSE, BLACK COVE FARM. DAY. SUMMER 1864.

Ruby cleans out leaves and detritus from the stone channel, allowing the stream to flow free and cool.

> **RUBY.** Number three: clay crocks for preserves. Peppers. Beans. Jams.

86. EXT. BOTTOM FIELD, BLACK COVE FARM. DUSK. SUMMER 1864.

Ruby doing her version of soil analysis, scrunching the earth, tasting it, spitting it out. Ada makes a face.

> **RUBY.** Clear and turn this field. No harm done letting it go fallow, now we'll do well.

87. EXT. OUTBUILDINGS, BLACK COVE FARM. AFTERNOON. SUMMER 1864.

Ruby looks up. Ada catches up with her.

RUBY. Number fifteen—

ADA. Sixteen.

RUBY. Number sixteen: let's hang some gourds for a martin colony. Keep away crows. You got one thing in abundance on this farm, and that's crows. Shut the gate.

88. EXT. APPLE ORCHARD, BLACK COVE FARM. DUSK. SUMMER 1864.

Ruby, delighted, contemplates the bounty of apples.

RUBY. There's survival. On them trees. *(turns to an exhausted Ada)* You got a cider press or would that be wishing on a blessing?

ADA. Actually, yes, I think we do.

Ruby whoops, jogs away. Ada, exhausted, takes a bite of an apple, watching her.

Critical Reading

1. **(a)** When Ruby wakes Ada, what does each woman say about breakfast? **(b) Compare and Contrast:** Explain the similarities and differences in the two women's perceptions of morning. **(c)** What does this suggest about other differences in their characters?

2. **(a)** As Ada and Ruby walk, what does Ruby say about the farm? **(b) Describe:** How does Ada respond? **(c) Infer:** What does each woman know about farming?

Use these questions to focus a class discussion of *Cold Mountain*:

3. Why do you think writers and filmmakers are interested in characters who do not see battle but nevertheless struggle during a war?

4. In what ways are depictions of events in a screenplay different from their presentation in short stories or novels?

from Cold Mountain **549**

1. **Ask** students to explain what the screenwriter-director wants viewers to understand about what happens between the bottom of page 548 and the top of page 549.

   Answer: The last numbered command that Ruby makes on page 548 is "Number three: clay crocks for preserves. Peppers. Beans. Jams." Then on page 549, Ruby picks up with number fifteen or sixteen. The screenwriter-director wants us to imagine all the commands Ruby has been barking out between the bottom of page 548 and the top of page 549.

2. **Ask:** On what note does the scene end?

   Possible response: The scene ends on a positive, light-hearted note: After finding problems with one thing after another on the farm, Ruby is delighted by the "bounty of apples." She makes a kind joke.

ASSESS

Answers

1. (a) Ada says it is still dark out; Ruby says that the cows do not think so. (b) For Ada, it is time for more sleep and then some breakfast; for Ruby, it is time to get to work. (c) This suggests that Ada is more the child of privilege while Ruby is used to a harder life.

2. (a) Ruby identifies all the work that needs to be done on the farm. (b) Ada does not understand Ruby's questions or observations; she is "stunned" by Ruby's energy. (c) Ruby seems to know everything, and Ada seems to know nothing, about farming.

3. **Possible response:** Frazier and Minghella may have felt that soldiers had been featured enough in Civil War literature and that now it was time to focus on others.

4. In scripts, events are conveyed only by visuals (sometimes quickly changing) and by dialogue; in short stories or novels, events are described in much more detail.

• An Account of an Experience With Discrimination
Lesson Pacing Guide

DAY 1 Preteach

- Ⓒ Administer the Reading and Vocabulary Warm-ups (*Unit 3 Resources*, pp. 112–115) as necessary.
- Ⓒ Introduce the Literary Analysis concepts: Author's General Purpose for Writing and Tone.
- Introduce the Reading Strategys: Identify Relevant Facts and Details.
- Ⓒ Build background with the author and Background features.
- Develop thematic thinking with Connecting to the Essential Question.
- Ⓒ Teach the selection vocabulary.

DAY 2 Preteach/Teach/Extend

- Distribute copies of the appropriate graphic organizer for the Reading Strategy (*Graphic Organizer Transparencies*, pp. 117–118).
- Distribute copies of the appropriate graphic organizer for Literary Analysis (*Graphic Organizer Transparencies*, pp. 119–120).
- Prepare students to read with the Activating Prior Knowledge activities (TE).
- Informally monitor comprehension while students read.
- Use the Reading Check question to confirm comprehension.
- Ⓒ Reinforce vocabulary with the Vocabulary notes.
- Assess students' comprehension and mastery of the skills by having them answer the Critical Reading, Literary Analysis, and Reading Strategy questions.

DAY 3 Assess

- Ⓒ Have students complete the Vocabulary Lesson.
- Ⓒ Have students complete the Writing Lesson and write a newspaper article. (You may assign as homework.)
- Administer Selection Test A or B (*Unit 3 Resources*, pp. 124–126 or 127–129).
- Have students read and respond to the Contemporary Commentary.

Ⓒ Common Core
State Standards

Reading Informational Text
6. Determine an author's point of view or purpose in a text in which the rhetoric is particularly effective, analyzing how style and content contribute to the power, persuasiveness, or beauty of the text.

Writing 2. Write informative/explanatory texts to examine and convey complex ideas, concepts, and information clearly and accurately through the effective selection, organization, and analysis of content.
2.a. Introduce a topic; organize complex ideas, concepts, and information; include formatting when useful to aiding comprehension.
2.b. Develop the topic thoroughly by selecting the most significant and relevant facts, concrete details, quotations, or other information and examples appropriate to the audience's knowledge of the topic.
2.e. Establish and maintain a formal style and objective tone while attending to the norms and conventions of the discipline in which they are writing.

Language 4.d. Verify the preliminary determination of the meaning of a word.

Additional Standards Practice
Common Core Companion, pp. 143–150; 196–207; 324–331

Daily Block Scheduling
Each day in this Lesson Pacing Guide represents a 40–50 minute period. Teachers using block scheduling may combine days to revise pacing. In addition, teachers may differentiate and support core instruction by integrating components for extended and intensive support as students require. See the Guide to Selected Leveled Resources (facing page).

Guide to Selected Leveled Resources

R T I **Tier 1** (students performing on level)	An Account of an Experience With Discrimination
Warm Up — Practice, **model**, and **monitor** fluency, working with the **whole class** or **in groups**.	Vocabulary and Reading Warm-ups B, *Unit 3 Resources,* pp. 112–113, 115
Comprehension/Skills — **Support** and **monitor** comprehension and skills development, having students complete the activities, graphic organizers, and interactive prompts **independently** or **as a class**.	• *Reader's Notebook,* adapted instruction and summary **EL** *Reader's Notebook: English Learner's Version,* adapted instruction and summary • **Reading Strategy Graphic Organizer B,** *Graphic Organizer Transparencies,* p. 118 • **Literary Analysis Graphic Organizer B,** *Graphic Organizer Transparencies,* p. 120
Monitor Progress — A — **Monitor** student progress with the differentiated curriculum-based assessment in the *Unit Resources.*	• **Selection Test B,** *Unit 3 Resources,* pp. 127–129 • **Open-Book Test,** *Unit 3 Resources,* pp. 121–123

R T I **Tier 2** (students requiring intervention)	An Account of an Experience With Discrimination
Warm Up — Practice, **model**, and **monitor** fluency **in groups** or **with individuals**.	• **Vocabulary and Reading Warm-ups A,** *Unit 3 Resources,* pp. 112–114 • *Hear It!* Audio CD
Comprehension/Skills — • **Support** and **monitor** comprehension and skills development, working **in small groups** or **with individuals**. • As students complete the selection in the appropriate version of the *Reader's Notebook,* **monitor** comprehension frequently with group questions and individual instruction. • **Model** strategies while guiding students in completing the activities and prompts in the *Reader's Notebook,* as well as the graphic organizers. • **Practice** skills and **monitor** mastery with the *Reading Kit* worksheets.	• *Reader's Notebook: Adapted Version,* adapted instruction and summary **EL** *Reader's Notebook: English Learner's Version,* adapted instruction and summary • **Reading Strategy Graphic Organizer A,** *Graphic Organizer Transparencies,* p. 117 • **Literary Analysis Graphic Organizer A,** *Graphic Organizer Transparencies,* p. 119 • *Reading Kit,* Practice worksheets
Monitor Progress — A — **Monitor** student progress with the differentiated curriculum-based assessment in the *Unit Resources* and in the *Reading Kit.*	• **Selection Test A,** *Unit 3 Resources,* pp. 124–126 • *Reading Kit,* Assess worksheets

TIER 3 Tier 3 intervention may require consultation with the student's special-education or dyslexia specialist. For additional support, see the Tier 2 activities and resources listed above.

One-on-one teaching ▪ Group work ▪ Whole-class instruction ▪ Independent work ▪ Assessment

For a complete guide to selection support, including support for Advanced students, see the Overview of Resources in the frontmatter.

• An Account of an Experience With Discrimination

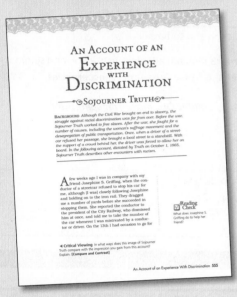

RESOURCES FOR:

L1 Special-Needs Students

L2 Below-Level Students (Tier 2)

L3 On-Level Students (Tier 1)

L4 Advanced Students (Tier 1)

EL English Learners

All All Students

Vocabulary/Fluency/Prior Knowledge

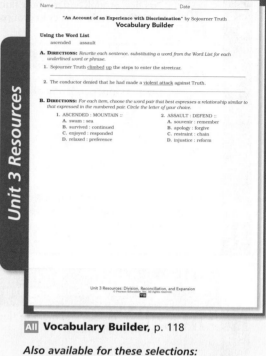

All Vocabulary Builder, p. 118

Also available for these selections:

EL **L1** **L2** Vocabulary Warm-ups A and B, pp. 112–113

EL **L1** **L2** Reading Warm-ups A and B, pp. 114–115

Reader's Notebooks

Pre- and postreading pages for this selection appear in an interactive format in the *Reader's Notebooks*. Each *Notebook* is differentiated for a different group of learners.

The selections in the Adapted and English Learner's versions are abridged.

L2 **L3** *Reader's Notebook*

L1 *Reader's Notebook: Adapted Version*

EL *Reader's Notebook: English Learner's Version*

EL *Reader's Notebook: Spanish Version*

Ⓒ *Common Core Companion*

Additional instruction and practice for each Common Core State Standard

Selection Support

Skills Development/Extension

Assessment

Graphic Organizer Transparencies

Unit 3 Resources

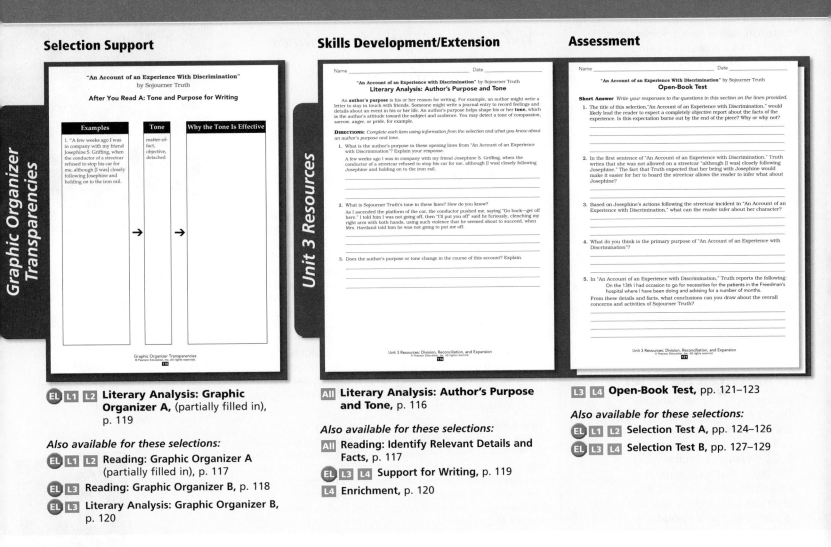

EL L1 L2 Literary Analysis: Graphic Organizer A, (partially filled in), p. 119

Also available for these selections:

EL L1 L2 Reading: Graphic Organizer A (partially filled in), p. 117

EL L3 Reading: Graphic Organizer B, p. 118

EL L3 Literary Analysis: Graphic Organizer B, p. 120

All Literary Analysis: Author's Purpose and Tone, p. 116

Also available for these selections:

All Reading: Identify Relevant Details and Facts, p. 117

EL L3 L4 Support for Writing, p. 119

L4 Enrichment, p. 120

L3 L4 Open-Book Test, pp. 121–123

Also available for these selections:

EL L1 L2 Selection Test A, pp. 124–126

EL L3 L4 Selection Test B, pp. 127–129

Online Resources: All print materials are also available online.

PHLit Online!
www.PHLitOnline.com

- complete narrated selection text
- a thematically related video with writing prompt
- an interactive graphic organizer
- highlighting feature
- access to all student print resources, adapted to individual student needs
- Spanish and English summaries
- adapted selection translations in Spanish

Get Connected! (thematic video with writing prompt)

Also available:

Background Video
All videos are available in Spanish.

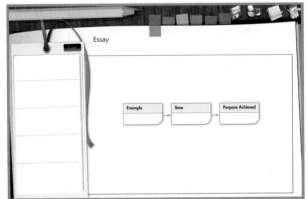

Writer's Journal (with graphics feature)

Also available:

Vocabulary Central (tools and activities for studying vocabulary)

550d

Themes Across Centuries

Nell Irvin Painter

1. Nell Irvin Painter, a well-known historian, writes about Sojourner Truth's 1865 account of being discriminated against on a streetcar in Washington, D.C. (page 555). You may wish to have students review Painter's previous Contemporary Commentary on pages 475–476.

2. Have students read the introductory paragraph about Nell Irvin Painter. Then show Segment 2 on Painter on the *See It!* DVD to provide insight into her thoughts about Sojourner Truth.

3. After students have watched the segment, **ask:** How does Painter dispel some misconceptions about Sojourner Truth?
   Answer: She offers a personal description of Sojourner Truth and mentions some surprising details about her life.

Two American Histories

1. Painter explains that Sojourner Truth's experience of discrimination arose in part because the nation's capital, Washington, D.C., began as a Southern city. She notes that discrimination against African Americans was common on the city's various modes of public transportation. Both the local situation and the national pattern it illustrates were not dealt with by the law until the mid-twentieth century.

2. **Ask** students: What point does Painter make by connecting Sojourner Truth's individual experience of discrimination with a larger national pattern?
   Possible response: Linking Truth's account with a national pattern of discrimination enables Painter to show in specific terms how racial discrimination hurt ordinary people and famous people alike. It also provides a reminder that this problem lasted long past the Civil War because it was embedded in America's early history.

Nell Irvin Painter Introduces

AN ACCOUNT OF AN EXPERIENCE WITH DISCRIMINATION

BY SOJOURNER TRUTH

A Public Figure Encounters Discrimination Sojourner Truth, an African American abolitionist born in upstate New York in 1797, belonged to a group of antislavery women volunteering with the ex-slave refugees in Washington, D.C., during the Civil War. Poor people from the battlefields of Virginia and from slaveholding Maryland sought protection and jobs in the nation's capital. Volunteers like Truth and her comrades, Josephine Griffing and Laura Haviland, helped them cope with their situation. Although Truth did not read or write, she dictated this account for publication in the anti-slavery press. In this way, people who cared about human rights would know that one Washington, D.C., streetcar conductor had not stopped for her and another had tried to push her from the platform of the car, even though she was a well-known public figure.

Two American Histories Truth's experience of discrimination in public transportation belongs to two American histories, both beginning in the early nineteenth century and both ending with the passage and enforcement of federal legislation against discrimination in public services in the 1950s and 1960s. The first history is that of Washington, D.C., a Southern city. The second history is that of discrimination against African Americans throughout the United States.

In 1791, President George Washington chose land on the border of Maryland and Virginia near his own home to serve as the nation's capital. In the 1790s, slavery existed in virtually the whole country. But during the early nineteenth century the Northern states abolished slavery, while the institution grew stronger in the South, of which Washington, D.C., was a part. The Washington slave market sat near the capitol building, and slavery flourished in the District until abolition in 1862. The discrimination Sojourner Truth experi-

Meet the Author

Nell Irvin Painter is an award-winning historian and professor. Her book *Sojourner Truth: A Life, A Symbol* was a choice of both the Book of the Month Club and the History Book Club.

Teaching Resources

The following resources can be used to enrich or extend the instruction for Contemporary Commentary.

Unit 3 Resources
   Contemporary Commentary: Nell Irvin Painter, pp. 110–111

See It! **DVD**
   Nell Irvin Painter, Segment 2

enced belonged partly to Washington, D.C.'s Southern traditions. However, even after the abolition of slavery, racial discrimination in transportation remained a national problem. The war between black people and American railroads was national in scope, because racial discrimination was national in scope.

Truth's Experience Was Not Unique Sojourner Truth's painful experience caused her psychic and physical pain—she was in her sixties at the time. However, the insult she suffered was one she shared with many other black people trying to get from one place to another before the middle of the twentieth century.

Before the Civil War, the black abolitionists Frederick Douglass and David Ruggles had traded blows with conductors pushing them out of their seats. During the war, Harriet Tubman, who had guided Union troops during the Civil War, suffered shoulder injuries in New Jersey, when a conductor and three other men dragged her out of her seat and threw her into the baggage car. After the war, Frances Ellen Watkins Harper, the most prominent black woman writer of the era, experienced humiliating and bruising conflicts on railroads and streetcars. George T. Downing, an African American businessman, encountered difficulties in railroad transportation during Reconstruction. The Civil War and Reconstruction ended slavery but not discrimination and exclusion.

Critical Reading

Ⓒ 1. **Key Ideas and Details (a)** Who was Sojourner Truth? **(b)** What was she doing in Washington, D.C., during and after the Civil War? **(c) Connect:** Was the act of making public her own experience with discrimination related to her purpose for being in Washington? Explain.

Ⓒ 2. **Key Ideas and Details (a)** According to Nell Irvin Painter, to what two American histories does Truth's experience of discrimination belong? **(b) Speculate:** Why do you think discrimination persisted in both the North and South even after slavery ended?

As You Read "An Account of an Experience With Discrimination" . . .

Ⓒ 3. **Integration of Knowledge and Ideas** Identify two ways in which Painter's commentary helps you better understand Sojourner Truth's experiences and reactions.

Ⓒ 4. **Integration of Knowledge and Ideas** Decide what an individual who experiences or witnesses discrimination should do.

Critical Thinking

Before students respond, you may wish to have them write a brief objective summary of the selection. As they answer the questions below, remind them to support their answers with evidence from the text.

1. (a) She was an African American who worked for the abolition of slavery. (b) She helped ex-slave refugees as they sought sanctuary in Washington, D.C. (c) By making her experience of discrimination public, Truth helped white people realize how such discrimination injured innocent individuals; she also helped prevent future incidents.

2. (a) Truth's experience of discrimination belongs to both the local history of Washington, D.C., which began as a Southern city where slaveholding was legal, and the national history of discrimination throughout the United States. (b) **Possible response:** Discrimination persisted because it was deeply embedded in American traditions and because slavery had to be ended forcibly rather than voluntarily. It is also part of the negative side of human nature for groups of people to set themselves above other groups.

3. **Possible response:** Painter's commentary shows how the incidents Truth relates are similar to events in our own time. By mentioning other examples, the commentary also shows how innocent people suffer the effects of racial prejudice.

4. **Possible response:** Individuals experiencing or witnessing discrimination should record the name of the person doing the discriminating and report the incident as soon as possible. Witnesses should also do their best to take care of the victims if there is physical injury. They should also make it clear that they saw what happened and that it will be reported.

① 🔍 Connecting to the Essential Question

1. Review the assignment with the class.

2. Invite students to define courage. Then have them complete the assignment.

3. As students read, have them notice details that show Truth's reactions to injustice.

② Literary Analysis

Introduce the skills, using the instruction on the student page.

Think Aloud: Model the Skill

Say to students:

Frederick Douglass wrote about slaves and slaveholders that "Nothing but rigid training, long persisted in, can perfect the character of the one or the other." His formal word choice and tone signal that he wants readers to take him seriously.

③ Reading Strategy

1. Introduce the strategy, using the instruction on the student page.

2. Give students a copy of **Reading Strategy Graphic Organizer B**, page 118 in *Graphic Organizer Transparencies,* to fill out as they read.

Think Aloud: Model the Skill

Say to students:

An article about Thomas Jefferson states that he founded the University of Virginia and that his personal library became the basis for the Library of Congress. The author concludes that Jefferson valued learning. The author's two relevant facts—founding a university and owning a huge library—make it easy for me to agree.

④ Vocabulary

1. Pronounce each word, giving its definition, and have students say it aloud.

2. For more guidance, see the *Classroom Strategies and Teaching Routines* card for introducing vocabulary.

Before You Read

An Account of an Experience With Discrimination

① Connecting to the Essential Question Sojourner Truth showed courage in the face of injustice—one aspect of the American ideal. As you read, notice details that show Truth's reactions to harsh treatment and injustice. Doing so will help as you consider the Essential Question: **What makes American literature American?**

② Literary Analysis

Every author has both a general and a specific purpose for writing. An **author's general purpose for writing** may be *to inform, to persuade, to entertain,* or *to describe.* Authors also have at least one **specific purpose for writing** any given literary work. For example, in this account Truth seeks to inform readers about a distressing experience. She also has an implicit, or unstated, persuasive purpose: by describing her experiences, she may move readers to put an end to prejudice and injustice.

An author's purpose affects all elements of a literary work, including the **tone,** or attitude, the writer assumes toward the subject and audience. Tone, a key aspect of a writer's style, may be formal or informal, personal or distant, modest or pretentious. For an account of a distressing experience, Truth chooses a surprisingly factual, unemotional tone:

A few weeks ago I was in company with my friend Josephine S. Griffing, when the conductor of a streetcar refused to stop his car for me . . . They dragged me a number of yards before she succeeded in stopping them.

As you read this account, think about why Truth adopted this even tone and how it helps her achieve her purpose for writing.

③ Reading Strategy

Ⓒ **Preparing to Read Complex Texts** In this account, Truth presents a series of factual events. Taken together, these facts build toward a powerful main idea or **essential message.** As you read, **identify relevant facts and details** to determine the essential message of Truth's account. Use a chart like the one shown to collect important details and identify the essential message of Truth's narrative.

④ Vocabulary

ascended (ə send′ əd) *v.* climbed up (p. 556)

assault (ə sôlt′) *n.* violent attack (p. 556)

Ⓒ Common Core State Standards

Reading Informational Text
6. Determine an author's point of view or purpose in a text in which the rhetoric is particularly effective, analyzing how style and content contribute to the power, persuasiveness, or beauty of the text.

Detail/Fact

↓

Detail/Fact

↓

Essential Message

---

552 Division, Reconciliation, and Expansion (1850–1914)

Vocabulary Development

Vocabulary Knowledge Rating
Create a **Vocabulary Knowledge Rating Chart** (*Professional Development Guidebook,* p. 33) for the vocabulary words on the student page. Give each student a copy of the chart with the words on it. Read the words aloud, and have students mark their rating of each in the Before Reading column. When students have completed reading and discussing the selection, have them take out their **Vocabulary Knowledge Rating** charts for the account. Read the words aloud, and have students rate their knowledge again in the After Reading column. Clarify any words that are still problematic. Then have students complete the Vocabulary practice at the end of the selection.

PHLit Online! **Vocabulary Central,** featuring tools and activities for studying vocabulary, is available online at **www.PHLitOnline.com.**

⑤ Sojourner Truth *(1797–1883)*

Author of "An Account of an Experience With Discrimination"

Sojourner Truth was born into slavery in Ulster County, New York. At the age of nine, she was separated from her family and sold several times, facing abuse at the hands of harsh masters. She was finally bought by John and Sally Dumont. As a slave in the Dumont household, she was forced into marriage with a fellow slave, Thomas, with whom she had at least four children. In 1826, one year before New York state emancipated slaves, Truth escaped from her master's household with her youngest son. She was later able to recover custody of another son, who was illegally sold as a slave in the South. In 1829, Truth and her two youngest children moved to New York City, where she found work as a domestic employee.

A Passion for Preaching Throughout her life, Truth felt a strong commitment to religion. In New York City, she became a missionary, preaching on the streets. Truth was a powerful speaker whose passion and charisma often drew large crowds. In 1843, she assumed the name Sojourner Truth and began preaching along the east coast. She began to travel through the Midwest in 1850, spreading her opinions and beliefs. She dictated her autobiography, *The Narrative of Sojourner Truth,* to Olive Gilbert and sold copies to support her tours.

A Voice for Justice Truth became a noted abolitionist, eloquently arguing against the horrifying injustices of slavery. After the Civil War ended in 1865, she continued to battle the lasting effects of slavery, including discrimination and racism. Working as a counselor, she helped former slaves find employment and build new lives. During her lifetime, Truth also earned fame as an advocate for women's rights and for workplace and prison reform.

> ❝*That man over there says that women need to be helped into carriages, and lifted over ditches, and to have the best place everywhere. Nobody ever helps me into carriages, or over mud-puddles, or gives me any best place! And ain't I a woman?*❞

An Account of an Experience With Discrimination **553**

📣 Daily Bellringer

For each class during which you will teach this selection, have students complete one of the five activities for the appropriate week in the *Daily Bellringer Activities* booklet.

Multidraft Reading

To assist struggling readers and to enhance reading for all, assign the text in chunks as warranted by length and apply multidraft reading protocols. For each reading, have students set the purpose indicated:

- **First reading**—identifying key ideas and details and answering any Reading Checks.
- **Second reading**—analyzing craft and structure and responding to the side-column prompts.
- **Third reading**—integrating knowledge and ideas, connecting to other texts and the world, and answering the end-of-selection questions.

For more guidance, refer to the *Classroom Strategies and Teaching Routines* card on multidraft reading.

⑤ Background
More About the Author

During the Civil War, Sojourner Truth gathered contributions of food and clothing for the African American regiments. She met with President Abraham Lincoln in the White House in 1864. Truth was a powerful speaker whose passion and charisma often drew large crowds to her informal talks. According to Frederick Douglass, she had a "strange compound of wit and wisdom, of wild enthusiasm, and flint-like common sense."

PHLit Online!
www.PHLitOnline.com

Teaching From Technology

Preparing to Read
Go to **www.PHLitOnline.com** in class or in a lab and display the **Get Connected!** slide show for this selection. Have the class brainstorm for responses to the slide show writing prompt, entering ideas in the interactive journal. Then have students complete their written responses individually in a lab or as homework.

To build background, display the More About the Author feature.

Using the Interactive Student Edition
Go to **www.PHLitOnline.com** and display the **Enriched Online Student Edition.** As the class reads the selection or listens to the narration, record answers to side-column prompts using the graphic organizers accessible on the interactive page. Alternatively, have students use the online edition individually, answering the prompts as they read.

❶ About the Selection

Sojourner Truth describes her proactive responses to acts of racial discrimination on a streetcar.

❷ Activating Prior Knowledge

Revisit with students what race relations were like under slavery. Review the way Olaudah Equiano and Frederick Douglass were treated by slave owners and other whites. Invite students to describe what they would expect relations between blacks and whites to be like after the Civil War. Tell them they will be reading about the way African Americans had to fight for their rights after emancipation.

Concept Connector ➡️

Tell students they will return to their responses after reading the selection.

❸ Visual Connection

1. Discuss the formal nature of the portrait of Sojourner Truth. Typically, she is seated at a table, sitting straight, with symbolic objects beside her. Her expression is both sensitive and alert, suggesting kindliness and, perhaps, a hard life.

2. **Ask:** How do the objects beside Truth create the impression that she is a proper, middle-class woman of her day?

   Possible response: The knitting suggests that she attends to domestic concerns; the book suggests that she is intelligent and possibly religious because the volume might be a prayer book

554 Division, Reconciliation, and Expansion (1850–1914)

© Text Complexity Rubric

An Account of an Experience With Discrimination	
Qualitative Measures	
Context/Knowledge Demands	Post-Civil War era; historical knowledge demands 1 ②　3　4　5
Structure/Language Conventionality and Clarity	Accessible 1　2　③　4　5
Levels of Meaning/ Purpose/Concept Level	Accessible 1　2　③　4　5
Quantitative Measures	
Lexile	1130L	**Text Length**	299 words
Overall Complexity	**More accessible**

Reader and Task Suggestions

Preparing to Read the Text
- Using the Background information on TE p. 553, discuss Sojourner Truth's character traits.
- Ask students how they would react if they felt that they were being discriminated against—by race, gender, age, and so on.
- Guide students to use Multidraft Reading strategies (TE p. 553).

Leveled Tasks

Structure/Language If students will have difficulty with structure, have them first read to locate phrases that signal the steps in the narrative. Then, have students reread to see how discrimination is shown or dealt with at each step.

Analyzing If students will not have difficulty with structure, have them reread and then explain the final two sentences.

① ② AN ACCOUNT OF AN EXPERIENCE WITH DISCRIMINATION

◦⟨ SOJOURNER TRUTH ⟩◦

BACKGROUND *Although the Civil War brought an end to slavery, the struggle against racial discrimination was far from over. Before the war, Sojourner Truth worked to free slaves. After the war, she fought for a number of causes, including the woman's suffrage movement and the desegregation of public transportation. Once, when a driver of a streetcar refused her passage, she brought a local street to a standstill. With the support of a crowd behind her, the driver was forced to allow her on board. In the following account, dictated by Truth on October 1, 1865, Sojourner Truth describes other encounters with racism.*

A few weeks ago I was in company with my friend Josephine S. Griffing, when the conductor of a streetcar refused to stop his car for me, although [I was] closely following Josephine and holding on to the iron rail. They dragged me a number of yards before she succeeded in stopping them. She reported the conductor to the president of the City Railway, who dismissed him at once, and told me to take the number of the car whenever I was mistreated by a conductor or driver. On the 13th I had occasion to go for

⑤ ☑ Reading Check
What does Josephine S. Griffing do to help her friend?

④ ◀ **Critical Viewing** In what ways does this image of Sojourner Truth compare with the impression you gain from this account? Explain. **[Compare and Contrast]**

An Account of an Experience With Discrimination **555**

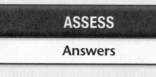

⑥ Scholar's Insight

1. Have a student read the bracketed passage. Then draw students' attention to Painter's note about Ida B. Wells.

2. **Ask:** How does Painter's note further exemplify Truth's remarks in the passage?
   Answer: It is another example of how the "slaveholding spirit" is hard to kill.

ASSESS
Answers

Before students respond, you may wish to have them write a brief objective summary of the selection. As they answer the questions below, remind them to support their answers with evidence from the text.

1. (a) He says, "Does she belong to you?" (b) It reveals that the slaveholding spirit is still alive in the streetcar conductor.

2. (a) She and her friends took down the number of each streetcar and reported the conductor to the president of the company. (b) Students may say that it was an effective and safe way for Truth to handle the problem.

3. (a) He is dismissed from his job, arrested, and tried for assault and battery. (b) Both demonstrate the struggles involved in ending segregation in stores, public places, schools, on public transportation, and in other areas of American society.

4. **Possible response:** Students may say the punishments were appropriate since both conductors lost their jobs and one was tried for assault and battery.

5. **Possible response:** Truth's account shows that getting one's <u>freedom</u> on paper is not the same as being free. A society that refuses to change presents a challenge to each individual who is discriminated against, and, to better the society, the individual must have courage to stand up for himself or herself. In this account, Truth's actions exemplify the American spirit of independence and <u>self-determination.</u>

Vocabulary
ascended (ə send´ əd) *v.* climbed up

assault (ə sôlt´) *n.* violent attack

Nell Irvin Painter
Scholar's Insight The African American journalist Ida B. Wells went to court in 1884 after being denied first-class passage despite having purchased a first-class ticket. (She won her case, then lost on appeal.)

necessities for the patients in the Freedmen's Hospital where I have been doing and advising for a number of months. I thought now I would get a ride without trouble as I was in company with another friend, Laura S. Haviland of Michigan. As I ascended the platform of the car, the conductor pushed me, saying "Go back—get off here." I told him I was not going off, then "I'll put you off" said he furiously, clenching my right arm with both hands, using such violence that he seemed about to succeed, when Mrs. Haviland told him he was not going to put me off. "Does she belong to you?" said he in a hurried angry tone. She replied, "She does not belong to me, but she belongs to humanity." The number of the car was noted, and conductor dismissed at once upon the report to the president, who advised his arrest for assault and battery as my shoulder was sprained by his effort to put me off. Accordingly I had him arrested and the case tried before Justice Thompson. My shoulder was very lame and swollen, but is better. It is hard for the old slaveholding spirit to die. But die it must. . . .

Critical Reading

Cite textual evidence to support your responses.

1. **Key Ideas and Details (a)** What does the streetcar conductor say to Laura Haviland about Sojourner Truth? **(b) Infer:** What does his question reveal about the "old slaveholding spirit"?

2. **Key Ideas and Details (a)** What action does Truth take following each incident of discrimination described in her account? **(b) Evaluate:** Do you think this is the best course of action in each situation? Explain.

3. **Key Ideas and Details (a)** What happens to the conductor who refuses service to Truth? **(b) Synthesize:** What do details of these events of 1865 have in common with the civil rights movement of the 1950s?

4. **Integration of Knowledge and Ideas Take a Position:** Do you think the conductors received appropriate punishments for their acts? Explain.

5. **Integration of Knowledge and Ideas** What does Truth's account suggest about the individual's responsibility to act with courage to promote positive social change? In your response, use at least two of these Essential Question words: *integrity, self-determination, freedom, challenge. [Connecting to the Essential Question: What makes American literature American?]*

Concept Connector

Reading Skill Graphic Organizer
Ask students to review the graphic organizers in which they have identified relevant facts and details and determined Truth's essential message. Then have students share their organizers and compare the facts and details they identified.

Activating Prior Knowledge
Have students return to their responses to the Activating Prior Knowledge activity. Ask them to explain whether their thoughts have changed and if so, how.

Writing About the Essential Question
Have students compare the responses to the prompt before they completed reading Sojourner Truth's account with their thoughts after reading it. Have them work individually or in groups, writing or discussing their thoughts, to formulate their new responses. Then lead a class discussion, probing for what students have learned that confirms or invalidates their initial thoughts. Encourage students to cite specific textual details to support their responses.

Literary Analysis

© 1. Craft and Structure (a) Truth's **general purposes** for writing this account were to inform and persuade. How would you describe her **specific purpose for writing? (b)** Do you think she achieved that purpose? Explain.

© 2. Craft and Structure (a) How would you describe Truth's **tone** in this account? **(b)** Using a chart like the one shown, note three examples that reflect this tone. Then, explain how Truth's tone suits her purpose for writing.

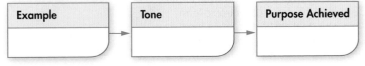

Example	Tone	Purpose Achieved

Reading Strategy

3. (a) What is the **essential message** of this account? **(b)** Cite three **relevant details** from Truth's account that support that message.

4. Well-chosen details often shed light on a situation in more than one way. Identify two details Truth includes that do so. Write a paragraph in which you *defend and clarify* your choices.

PERFORMANCE TASKS
Integrated Language Skills

© Vocabulary Acquistion and Use

True or False Determine whether each statement below is true or false. Explain your answers.

1. Someone who experiences an *assault* will have positive feelings.

2. Someone who is trying to get to a rooftop restaurant would take an elevator that *ascended.*

Writing

© Informative Text Rewrite Truth's account as a **newspaper article.** First, determine how the change of form will affect your approach. For example, a newspaper article, written by a reporter rather than a participant, should maintain a formal style and objective, or neutral, tone. As you write your article, incorporate the changes you have outlined. Your article should include

- a *headline* that summarizes the event and engages readers' interest.
- a gripping first sentence, or *lead.*
- relevant facts that identify *who, what, where, when,* and *why.*
- *quotes* from participants and eyewitnesses that shed additional light on the events described.

An Account of an Experience With Discrimination **557**

© Common Core State Standards

Writing

2. Write informative/ explanatory texts to examine and convey complex ideas, concepts, and information clearly and accurately through the effective selection, organization, and analysis of content.

2.a. Introduce a topic; organize complex ideas, concepts, and information; include formatting when useful to aiding comprehension.

2.b. Develop the topic thoroughly by selecting the most significant and relevant facts, concrete details, quotations, or other information and examples appropriate to the audience's knowledge of the topic.

2.e. Establish and maintain a formal style and objective tone while attending to the norms and conventions of the discipline in which they are writing.

Answers

1. (a) **Possible response:** Students may say that Truth wanted to inform readers about how acts of discrimination hurt individuals on a daily basis and to persuade others to work to end the injustice. (b) She makes her point clearly and supports it with details.

2. (a) Truth's tone is impersonal and factual. (b) **Sample answer:** Example: "The number of the car was noted, and conductor dismissed at once upon the report to the president, who advised his arrest"; Tone: informational; Purpose: informs the reader that an objective third person (the company president) saw that an injustice was done.
   Another sample answer can be found on the **Reading Strategy Graphic Organizer A**, page 118 in *Graphic Organizer Transparencies.*

3. (a) The essential message is that African Americans were treated harshly even after slavery ended and that such treatment should stop. (b) **Sample answer:** Truth was dragged down the street by a conductor who refused to stop; a second conductor tried to push her off a streetcar; he asked her white friend, "Does she belong to you?"

4. **Possible response:** Truth mentions how two other women witnessed the incidents, showing she is not exaggerating; she says the women tried to help her, showing they agreed Truth was mistreated.

Vocabulary Acquisition and Use

1. False. An *assault* is a violent attack, so someone who experiences an assault will probably experience fear or anger.

2. True. Someone who wants to get to the roof would take an elevator that *ascended,* or went up.

Writing

1. To guide students in writing this essay, use the Support for Writing worksheet (*Unit 3 Resources,* p. 119).

2. Evaluate students' article using the **General Writing Rubrics,** in *Professional Development Guidebook,* pages 282–283.

Assessment Resources

Unit 3 Resources

L1 L2 EL **Selection Test A, pp. 124–126.** Administer Test A to less advanced readers.

L3 L4 EL **Selection Test B, pp. 127–129.** Administer Text B to on-level or more advanced students.

L3 L4 **Open-Book Test, pp. 121–123.** As an alternative, give the Open-Book Test.

All **Customizable Test Bank**

All **Self-tests** Students may prepare for the **Selection Test** by taking the **Self-test** online.

PHLit Online! All assessment resources are available at **www.PHLitOnline.com.**

About the Texts

1. Introduce the forms, using the instruction on the student page.

2. Tell students that they will apply their knowledge of periodical abstracts and government forms as they read the two documents.

Reading Strategy

1. Introduce the strategy, using the instruction on the student page.

2. Tell students that they will apply systematic strategies to organize and record information as they read the documents.

Think Aloud: Model the Strategy

Model the strategy of organizing and recording information. Say to students:

Most of the periodical abstracts I read I discover in the library. When I am interested in a particular article, I will make a photocopy of the abstract so that I can freely mark the text. I highlight key information in the article and write notes and even questions in the margins. This anecdotal scripting helps me extract and remember the essential material in the article. Often the abstract by itself has the facts I need, but I always retain information about the original source in case I need to refer to the full article.

Content-Area Vocabulary

1. Have students say each word aloud.

2. Then, use each word in a sentence that makes its meaning clear. Repeat your sentence with the vocabulary word missing and have students "fill in the blank."

For more guidance, consult the *Classroom Strategies and Teaching Routines* card on introducing vocabulary.

Reading for Information

Analyzing Functional and Expository Texts

Periodical Abstract • Government Form

About the Texts

A **periodical abstract** is a summary of a long article from a magazine or scholarly journal. An abstract allows you to quickly evaluate the relevance of a source or gain a general overview of the subject. Abstracts can be found in both print and electronic form. In addition to a summary, most periodical abstracts contain the full article's title, author's name, and publication information; a list of the full article's key points; and photos or other elements from the original article.

A **government form** is a document that allows organizations to compile information efficiently. Forms use quick-response features and a minimal amount of extended text. Basic features include the label or logo of the relevant organization; headings for different categories of information; and checklists, short answer lists, write-on lines, and other text features that capture and organize information.

Reading Strategy

Researchers use abstracts and forms to locate information and evaluate its usefulness. They apply various strategies to assess the quality of information, connect facts and concepts, and outline key points. As you read, **apply systematic strategies to organize and record information.** The chart below highlights strategies you may use at different stages of your own research.

Content-Area Vocabulary

These words appear in the selections that follow. They may also appear in other content-area texts.

archaeology (är´ kē´ äl´ ə jē´) *n.* the study of material evidence from human life in the past

dig (dig) *n.* an archaeological excavation to explore human life from the past

site (sīt) *n.* the place or setting of an event

Note-Taking Strategy	When to Use
Anecdotal Scripting (highlighting texts and making marginal notes)	When first surveying a source (only on a personal copy or photocopy)
Outlining	When you want to extract key points or trace a line of reasoning
Making an Annotated Bibliography	When you want to keep track of information in a wide variety of sources
Concept Mapping (a diagram that uses key words and branching lines to show relationships among related ideas)	When many concepts are linked

558 Division, Reconciliation, and Expansion (1850–1914)

Teaching Resources

Reading Support

L2 L3 *Reader's Notebook*

L1 *Reader's Notebook: Adapted Version*

EL *Reader's Notebook: English Learner's Version*

Periodical Abstract

ARCHAEOLOGY

A Publication of the Archaeological Institute of America

abstracts

Volume 59 Number 6, November/December 2006

The title, date, volume, and number of the source magazine for this abstract are clearly identified.

A Community's Roots

by Samir S. Patel

With Frederick Douglass's help, the past and present come together on a Maryland plantation.

(National Portrait Gallery, Smithsonian Institution/Art Resource)

The first section of the abstract includes an element from the article.

In Talbot County, Eastern Shore, State of Maryland, near Easton, the county town, there is a small district of country, thinly populated, and remarkable for nothing that I know of more than for the worn-out, sandy, desert-like appearance of its soil, the general dilapidation of its farms and fences, the indigent and spiritless character of its inhabitants, and the prevalence of ague and fever. It was in this dull, flat, and unthrifty district or neighborhood, bordered by the Choptank river, among the laziest and muddiest of streams surrounded by a white population of the lowest order, indolent and drunken to a proverb, and among slaves who, in point of ignorance and indolence, were fully in accord with their surroundings, that I, without any fault of my own, was born, and spent the first years of my childhood.

—Frederick Douglass,
  Life and Times of Frederick Douglass (1881)

The summary of the full article begins here.

Under the boughs of a huge tulip poplar, buried among clumps of roots and piles of oyster shells, is the brick foundation of a building, a remnant of a once-thriving slave community. For 18 months in the early nineteenth century, it was home to a young Frederick Douglass, the future African-American statesman, diplomat, orator, and author. Here, at the age of seven or eight, a shoeless, pantless, precocious Douglass first saw whippings and petty cruelties. Here, he first realized he was a slave. "A lot of the horror that comes through his autobiographies is grounded in those months that he was there," says James Oakes, a historian at the City University of New York who is working on a book about Douglass's relationship with Abraham Lincoln. The modest excavation at Wye House Farm,

About Periodical Abstracts

1. If students have read the excerpt from Frederick Douglass's *My Bondage and My Freedom* in this unit, briefly review details of his life and the significance of his work. If students have not read the selection, provide background on Douglass using the biographical information on page 519.

2. Before students read the periodical abstract, point out that such publications are intended for an audience of scholars and others interested in a particular area of knowledge.

3. **Ask** students: How do periodical abstracts make a search for information more convenient and efficient?
   Possible response: Students may note that periodical abstracts present information about a wide number of articles, allowing readers to identify the articles they most need to read. This saves them the chore of obtaining and reading articles of little relevance. Students may describe a periodical abstract as a catalog, a filter, and a "sneak preview."

Differentiated Instruction   for Universal Access

Support for Special-Needs Students
Frederick Douglass's vocabulary will be challenging for many students. Read the passage twice to the class. In your first reading, pause to supply synonyms for words that students will find difficult, for example, *dilapidation* (ruin or falling apart condition), *indigent* (poor), *prevalence* (commonness), *unthrifty* (wasteful), and *indolent* (lazy). Once students grasp its general meaning, reread the passage as printed.

Support for Less Proficient Students
For some students, outlining or making an annotated bibliography may be more of an obstacle than a viable strategy. For these students, promote anecdotal scripting and concept mapping. If possible, model both strategies on the board or use an overhead projector. For text, use a recent article from the local or school newspaper.

Reading Strategy

Applying Strategies to Organize and Record Information

1. Read and analyze "A Community's Roots" as a class. If possible, display the two paragraphs of the article with an overhead projector to model anecdotal scripting. As an alternative, distribute individual copies of the article to students for their annotation.

2. **Ask:** What information in this article would you highlight? What comments or questions would you jot down?
   Possible response: Students might highlight the following: that Douglass lived at Wye House Farm in his youth; the age and location of the farm; the types of items found; the date the dig started. Among questions students might have: How old was Douglass when he was at the farm? What is social archaeology?

3. Point out that the photographs and captions do not simply echo facts from the body of the abstract; they contribute additional information. One caption, for example, identifies the site supervisor.

Archaeologist Mark Leone and site supervisor Jenn Babiarz show the site to Derek Lloyd, an engineer at Howard University who may be descended from slaves who lived on the farm. (Samir S. Patel)

a 350-year-old estate on Maryland's Eastern Shore, has yielded sherds, buttons, pipe stems, beads, and precious knowledge about everyday slave life, and is allowing the descendants of that slave community, many of whom live in the nearby rural African-American town of Unionville, to reclaim a lost cultural heritage.

A team of archaeologists and students started digging here in 2005 after archaeologist Lisa Kraus proposed the dig, on the basis of Douglass's descriptions of the site, to Mark Leone, director of the urban archaeology field school at the University of Maryland. Before beginning the excavation, Leone approached St. Stephen's African Methodist Episcopal Church, the social and religious center of Unionville, to ask what the people of the community wanted to learn from the archaeology. "You should ask the people who think it's their heritage what they want to know about it," Leone says. "The answers automatically dissolve the difference between then and now." This, he adds, is the heart of social archaeology, working with descendant communities and understanding that the past and present inform one another. The people of Unionville wanted to know about slave spirituality, what remained of African life, how the owner of the slaves did or did not support freedom, and how slaves found the strength to survive. They are questions a single dig is unlikely to answer, but they have opened an avenue of dialogue between the archaeologists and the people to whom their work matters most.

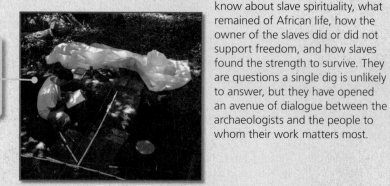

> Photographs and captions from the actual article make this a particularly useful abstract.

Pete Quantock, a University of Maryland student, profiles the site of a workshop, where slaves probably both slept and worked. (Samir S. Patel)

Samir S. Patel is an associate editor at ARCHAEOLOGY.
© 2006 by the Archaeological Institute of America

Vocabulary Development

Content-Area Vocabulary: Social Studies

Review the definitions of the content-area vocabulary with students: *archaeology, dig and, site.* Then examine each word in its context in a document. Point out, for example, that *archaeology* first appears as the title of the periodical of the Archaeological Institute of America. Note that a *dig* is the archaeological work done at a *site*, or specific location.

When you have finished with the three listed words, ask students to identify other words in the documents that fit the context of archaeological work, such as *excavation* and *sherds.* Have students look up their definitions in a dictionary and then use them in sentences about the dig at the Wye House Farm.

Virginia Department of Historic Resources

GENERAL PROPERTY INFORMATION

City/County:

Site Class: _____ Terrestrial, Open Air _____ Terrestrial, Cave/ Rockshelter _____ Submerged

Temporary Designation:

Resource Name:

Ownership Status: _____ Private

_____ Public/Local

_____ Public/State

_____ Public/Federal

Cultural Affiliation: _____ African-American

_____ Euro-American

_____ Indeterminate

Specialized Contexts:

Open to public: Y N

Gov. Modifier:

_____ Native American

_____ Other

> Checklists provide an efficient way to gather important information.

LOCATION INFORMATION

Physiographic Province:

Aspect:

Drainage:

Direction:

Landform:

Site Dimensions: _____ × _____ ft

Slope: _____ percent

Survey Description:

Elevation: _____ ft

Site Soils:

Adjacent Soils:

Distance: _____ ft

Nearest Water Source:

Acreage:

SPECIMENS AND FIELD NOTES INFORMATION

Specimens Obtained: ____ Yes ____ No Depository:

Assemblage Description:

Specimens Reported: ____ Yes ____ No

Owner Name: Owner Address:

Assemblage Description:

Field Notes: ____ Yes ____ No Depository:

> Headings define the information being collected in each section.

INDIVIDUAL/ORG AGENCY MAILING INFORMATION

Category: Informant Occupant Owner Owner of Specimens Property Mgr. Tenant

Honorific: _____ First Name: _____ Last Name: _____ Suffix: _____

Title: _____ Company: _____ Mailing Address: _____ City: _____

Zip Code: _____ Country: _____ Phone 1/Ext.: _____ Phone 2/Ext.: _____ Surveyor's Notes:

About Government Forms

1. Before going over the Virginia Department of Historic Resources form, discuss with students their own experiences with government forms. One common experience may be a learner's permit or driver's license application.
   Ask: What kinds of information are typically sought by government forms? Why do you think governments require this information?
   Possible response: Based on their experience with application forms, students may mention name, address, phone number, age, and other contact and identifying information. In the case of licensing, for example, a government that grants an individual permission to drive needs to be able to identify and contact that person.

2. Go over the Virginia Department of Historic Resources form with the class, clarifying information as necessary. Clarify that "Site Class" refers to the kind of place where the artifact was found, and *terrestrial* means "earth or land" while *submerged* means "under water."

3. **Ask:** Why do you think the state wants to collect this information?
   Possible response: Students may say that the information enables the state to gather useful information about the location of historic sites and the nature of artifacts discovered. The information also assures that the sites are managed responsibly.

Literary Analysis

1. (a) **Possible response:** The first sentences on the second page capture vital information about the project. (b) **Possible response:** The last few sentences on the second page describe the heart of the project, which is connecting the past with the present.

2. (a) **Answer:** The form captures the basic characteristics of a certain area of land. (b) **Answer:** Archaeologists or other employees at the Virginia Department of Historic Resources might use the form.

3. **Possible response:** Information about the environment might help with planning for archaeological digs or organizing preservation efforts.

4. **Possible response:** The concept map would link the past to the present by studying key details about the people and the land at different times.

5. **Possible response:** Yes, the information on the form could help the archaeologists plan a dig.

Timed Writing

1. Before students begin the assignment, guide them in analyzing key words and phrases in the prompt, using the highlighted notes.

2. Work with students to draw up guidelines for their persuasive essays based on the key words they identified.

3. Have students use the 5-Minute Planner to structure their time.

4. Allow students 40 minutes to complete the assignment. Evaluate their work using the guidelines they have developed.

After You Read
Periodical Abstract
• Government Form

Literary Analysis

1. **Key Ideas and Details (a)** If you were to use anecdotal scripting to identify the key points in the abstract, which passages would you highlight? **(b)** Which passages would you note because they contain other important details? Explain.

2. **Key Ideas and Details (a)** What information does the government form capture quickly and efficiently? **(b)** What types of workers or professionals would use this form and for what purposes?

3. **Key Ideas and Details** Why do you think the government form attempts to capture specific data about elevation, soils, and water sources?

4. **Key Ideas and Details** If you were to draw a concept map for both the abstract and the government form, what key concepts would you identify and how would you connect them?

5. **Key Ideas and Details** Do you think a government form like the one on page 561 would be useful to the researchers described in the abstract? Why or why not?

Timed Writing

Argument [40 minutes]

Format

In a **persuasive essay**, you build a well-reasoned and compelling case for a position or claim. Strengthen your argument by introducing counterclaims, or opposing opinions, and demonstrating that your position is more convincing.

Write a **persuasive essay** about the importance of archaeology and whether society has a responsibility to preserve historical sites and objects. Take and **defend** a position about the types of documents, sites, or objects that are most important and explain your reasons. Support your opinions with details from the Periodical Abstract and the Government Form.

Academic Vocabulary

When you **defend** a position, you supply varied, convincing evidence that supports your point of view. Evidence can include facts, quotations from reliable sources, and personal observation.

5-Minute Planner

Complete these steps before you begin to write.

1. Read the prompt carefully. List key words.

2. Scan the texts for details that relate to the prompt.

3. Briefly sketch an outline for your essay. **TIP** In a Timed Writing situation, an outline can be a simple numbered list of key words.

4. Reread the prompt, and draft your essay.

Common Core State Standards

Writing
1.a. Introduce precise, knowledgeable claim(s), establish the significance of the claim(s), distinguish the claim(s) from alternate or opposing claims, and create an organization that logically sequences claim(s), counterclaims, reasons, and evidence.

Extend the Lesson

Connecting to the Students' World

Invite students to create their own forms. Divide the class into small groups. Ask students to develop a form for their school or community. For example, they might develop a school form to be filled out by extracurricular groups applying to meet on school grounds. What kinds of information would the school need to know? What is the most direct and efficient way to obtain that information in a form?

Some students may create a form for the local community. For example, they might develop a form for people applying to park overnight in vacant city lots or to hold a small neighborhood parade or block party. Have students brainstorm for ideas about what information is essential for the government to know, and to design their forms accordingly. When the forms are complete, invite groups to share them with the entire class.

Forging New Frontiers

© Text Complexity: At a Glance

This chart gives a general text complexity rating for the selections in this part of the unit to help guide instruction. For additional text complexity support, see the Text Complexity Rubric at point of use.

from Life on the Mississippi	**More Accessible**
The Notorious Jumping Frog of Calaveras County	**More Complex**
To Build a Fire	**More Accessible**

Background

American Literature

The Adventures of Huckleberry Finn has been described as the quintessential American novel. It employs themes of escape from civilization, racism, coming of age, and human relationships against a setting of a raft trip on the Mississippi River. Twain picks up Huck's story where he left it at the end of his earlier novel *The Adventures of Tom Sawyer:* the orphaned Huck has been adopted by a rich widow who plans to "civilize" her new son. Civilization does not suit Huck, however, and soon he is running away across country with Jim, the widow's African slave. At first, Huck condescends to Jim because he is black and a slave, but Huck eventually learns to appreciate and respect him. Huck narrates his own story in the colorful dialect that Twain excelled at reproducing.

Critical Viewing

Possible response: Being captain or pilot of a riverboat would probably be exciting and challenging.

Literary History: Twain's World

At a time when most American writers were copying European novelists, Twain wrote about American themes.

Mark Twain: The American Bard

In the late 1800s, readers might have known him as Thomas Jefferson Snodgrass, W. Epaminandos Adrastus Blab, or simply Josh. Today, we know Samuel Langhorne Clemens as Mark Twain, his most famous literary pseudonym. Whichever name he used, Twain pulled off a rare literary feat—he created stories, novels, and essays that were both wildly popular in his own day and models of wit and skill more than a century later. Twain was so influential that fifty years after his death, Ernest Hemingway said that "all modern American literature begins" with Twain's novel *The Adventures of Huckleberry Finn.*

Life on the Mississippi Born in 1835, Samuel Clemens grew up in the small river town of Hannibal, Missouri. Steamboat men, religious revivalists, circus performers, minstrel companies, showboat actors, and every other kind of traveler imaginable made appearances in Hannibal. As a boy, Clemens met many of the characters that he would later write about.

After his father's death in 1847, Clemens was forced to leave school and became a printer's apprentice. During the 1850s, he published a few stories and traveled the country. A boat trip down the Mississippi brought back childhood memories, and he decided to become a riverboat pilot. He served as a pilot until 1861, when the Civil War closed the Mississippi to boat traffic.

Mark Twain Is Born In 1862, Clemens took a job as a reporter on a Virginia City newspaper, where he found his calling as a humorist under the byline Mark Twain. The new name, which is actually a signal yelled out by riverboat pilots, freed him to develop a new style. Before becoming "Twain," his work was typical of the low humor of the time, filled with bad puns and intentional misspellings. But in 1865, Twain published a short story entitled "The Notorious Jumping Frog of Calaveras County" (p. 576). The story won

▶ **Critical Viewing**
What do you think it would have been like to captain a Mississippi riverboat like the one shown in this photograph? **[Speculate]**

the author fame and financial success, and it marked the first appearance of his distinctive comic style.

Ordinary American Speech The targets of Twain's jokes were not new. He distrusted technology and railed against political figures, calling them swindlers and con men. What was new was Twain's feel for ordinary American people and their language. He wrote using the American English that people actually spoke. In that source, he found rich and comic poetry.

Twain's novels, such as *The Adventures of Tom Sawyer* and *The Adventures of Huckleberry Finn*, were unlike any books the world had ever seen. At a time when most American writers were copying European novelists, Twain wrote about American themes. His heroes were dirt-poor and plain-spoken, but in Twain's hands, their moral choices had as much drama as those of any tormented aristocrat in a European novel.

Not everyone appreciated Twain's humor. The author fled Virginia City when a rival journalist, offended by a story, challenged him to a pistol duel. He was chased out of San Francisco by policemen angered by critical articles. Even as his fame grew, some critics dismissed him as little more than a jokester. Yet the American public loved Twain. He made a fortune from his writings, settling with his family into a Hartford, Connecticut, mansion that was decorated to look like the inside of a steamboat.

The Old Man in a White Suit In the late 1800s, the deaths of Twain's wife and daughters left the writer bitter and cynical. Twain became so reclusive that a newspaper reported he was dead. Twain immediately wired the editors: "Reports of my death have been greatly exaggerated." History has not exaggerated Twain's legacy. He was the first, and possibly the greatest, authentically American writer.

Speaking and Listening: Oral Presentation

 Comprehension and Collaboration Like Twain, contemporary humor writers and comedians find ordinary American life a rich source of material. With a small group, research current humor on television, in movies, in periodicals, and in books. Then, using the research, write and deliver a **formal oral presentation:**

- As a group, prepare a set of focus questions, such as: What roles does comedy play today? What values does current humor transmit? Does contemporary humor challenge or perpetuate stereotypes?

- Use *systematic strategies, such as anecdotal scripting* (underlining, highlighting, and writing notes in the margins of a text) to identify key information.

Select examples to maintain a tone that is appropriate for the classroom. Work together to set goals and deadlines, organize your observations, write the text, and divide up responsibilities for the presentation.

Common Core State Standards

SL.11-12.1.a, SL.11-12.1.b, SL.11-12.1.c, SL.11-12.1.d.

[For the full wording of the standards, see the standards chart in the front of your textbook.]

Critical Thinking

Analyze

1. **Ask** students: What does the popularity of Twain's stories suggest about the American reading public?

   Answer: His popularity suggests that ordinary working people must have been buying his books, which present ordinary working people. In other words, America was a highly literate country in which people of all social classes and income levels liked to read for entertainment.

2. **Ask** students: How do you think Twain's travels and varied experiences helped his writing?

   Answer: Wherever he traveled, he could find new people and things to write about. His different job experiences helped him write knowledgeably about people who had those jobs. That is, instead of writing about what he had only read or heard reported to him, Twain was able to write from actual personal experiences

Speaking and Listening

Organize students into groups. Suggest that one student in each group record its ideas and share them with the class. Encourage students to give specific examples of their favorite aspects of American humor today. Specify the amount of time that groups will have to work together.

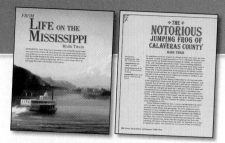

from Life on the Mississippi • The Notorious Jumping Frog of Calaveras County
Lesson Pacing Guide

DAY 1 Preteach

- Administer the Reading and Vocabulary Warm-ups (*Unit 3 Resources*, pp. 130–133) as necessary.
- Introduce the Literary Analysis concepts: Humor, Social Commentary, and Dialect.
- Introduce the Reading Strategy: Clarify and Interpret.
- Build background with the author and Background features.
- Develop thematic thinking with Connecting to the Essential Question.
- Teach the selection vocabulary.

DAYS 2–3 Preteach/Teach

- Distribute copies of the appropriate graphic organizer for the Reading Strategy (*Graphic Organizer Transparencies*, pp. 121–122).
- Distribute copies of the appropriate graphic organizer for Literary Analysis (*Graphic Organizer Transparencies*, pp. 123–124).
- Prepare students to read with the Activating Prior Knowledge activities (TE).
- Informally monitor comprehension while students read.
- Use the Reading Check questions to confirm comprehension.
- Develop students' understanding of humor, social commentary, and dialect using the Literary Analysis prompts.
- Develop students' ability to clarify and interpret using the Reading Strategy prompts.
- Reinforce vocabulary with the Vocabulary notes.
- Assess students' comprehension and mastery of the skills by having them answer the Critical Reading, Literary Analysis, and Reading Strategy questions.
- Have students complete the Vocabulary Lesson.

DAY 4 Extend/Assess

- Have students complete the Conventions and Style Lesson.
- Have students complete the Writing Lesson and write an analytical essay. (You may assign as homework.)
- Administer Selection Test A or B (Unit 3 Resources, pp. 144–146 or 147–149).

Common Core State Standards

Reading Literature 4. Determine the meaning of words and phrases as they are used in the text, including figurative and connotative meanings; analyze the impact of specific word choices on meaning and tone, including words with multiple meanings or language that is particularly fresh, engaging, or beautiful.
6. Analyze a case in which grasping a point of view requires distinguishing what is directly stated in a text from what is really meant (e.g., satire, sarcasm, irony, or understatement).
9. Demonstrate knowledge of nineteenth-century foundational works of American literature, including how two or more texts from the same period treat similar themes or topics.

Reading Informational Text 4. Determine the meaning of words and phrases as they are used in a text, including technical meanings.

Additional Standards Practice
***Common Core Companion*, pp. 41–48; 61–62; 123–130**

Daily Block Scheduling
Each day in this Lesson Pacing Guide represents a 40–50 minute period. Teachers using block scheduling may combine days to revise pacing. In addition, teachers may differentiate and support core instruction by integrating components for extended and intensive support as students require. See the Guide to Selected Leveled Resources (facing page).

Guide to Selected Leveled Resources

<table>
<tr>
<td colspan="2" style="background:#000;color:#fff">R T I   Tier 1 (students performing on level)</td>
<td style="background:#000;color:#fff">from Life on the Mississippi • The Notorious Jumping Frog of Calaveras County</td>
</tr>
<tr>
<td>Warm Up</td>
<td>Practice, model, and monitor fluency, working with the whole class or in groups.</td>
<td>Vocabulary and Reading Warm-ups B, Unit 3 Resources, pp. 130–131, 133</td>
</tr>
<tr>
<td>Comprehension/Skills</td>
<td>Support and monitor comprehension and skills development, having students complete the activities, graphic organizers, and interactive prompts independently or as a class.</td>
<td>
• Reader's Notebook, adapted instruction and full selection
EL Reader's Notebook: English Learner's Version, adapted instruction and adapted selection
• Reading Strategy Graphic Organizer B, Graphic Organizer Transparencies, p. 122
• Literary Analysis Graphic Organizer B, Graphic Organizer Transparencies, p. 124
</td>
</tr>
<tr>
<td>Monitor Progress</td>
<td>A Monitor student progress with the differentiated curriculum-based assessment in the Unit Resources.</td>
<td>
• Selection Test B, Unit 3 Resources, pp. 147–149
• Open-Book Test, Unit 3 Resources, pp. 141–143
</td>
</tr>
</table>

<table>
<tr>
<td colspan="2" style="background:#000;color:#fff">R T I   Tier 2 (students requiring intervention)</td>
<td style="background:#000;color:#fff">from Life on the Mississippi • The Notorious Jumping Frog of Calaveras County</td>
</tr>
<tr>
<td>Warm Up</td>
<td>Practice, model, and monitor fluency in groups or with individuals.</td>
<td>
• Vocabulary and Reading Warm-ups A, Unit 1 Resources, pp. 130–132
• Hear It! Audio CD
</td>
</tr>
<tr>
<td>Comprehension/Skills</td>
<td>
• Support and monitor comprehension and skills development, working in small groups or with individuals.
• As students complete the selection in the appropriate version of the Reader's Notebook, monitor comprehension frequently with group questions and individual instruction.
• Model strategies while guiding students in completing the activities and prompts in the Reader's Notebook, as well as the graphic organizers.
• Practice skills and monitor mastery with the Reading Kit worksheets.
</td>
<td>
• Reader's Notebook: Adapted Version, adapted instruction and adapted selection
EL Reader's Notebook: English Learner's Version, adapted instruction and adapted selection
• Reading Strategy Graphic Organizer A, Graphic Organizer Transparencies, p. 121
• Literary Analysis Graphic Organizer A, Graphic Organizer Transparencies, p. 123
• Reading Kit, Practice worksheets
</td>
</tr>
<tr>
<td>Monitor Progress</td>
<td>A Monitor student progress with the differentiated curriculum-based assessment in the Unit Resources and in the Reading Kit.</td>
<td>
• Selection Test A, Unit 3 Resources, pp. 144–146
• Reading Kit, Assess worksheets
</td>
</tr>
</table>

TIER 3 Tier 3 intervention may require consultation with the student's special-education or dyslexia specialist. For additional support, see the Tier 2 activities and resources listed above.

One-on-one teaching   Group work   Whole-class instruction   Independent work   Assessment

For a complete guide to selection support, including support for Advanced students, see the Overview of Resources in the frontmatter.

from Life on the Mississippi
• The Notorious Jumping Frog of Calaveras County

RESOURCES FOR:

- **L1** Special-Needs Students
- **L2** Below-Level Students (Tier 2)
- **L3** On-Level Students (Tier 1)
- **L4** Advanced Students (Tier 1)
- **EL** English Learners
- **All** All Students

Vocabulary/Fluency/Prior Knowledge

EL **L1** **L2** Vocabulary Warm-ups A and B, pp. 130–131

Also available for these selections:

EL **L1** **L2** Reading Warm-ups A and B, pp. 132–133

All Vocabulary Builder, p. 137

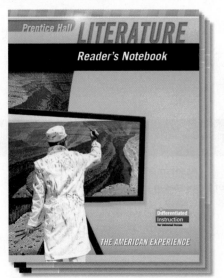

Reader's Notebooks

Pre- and postreading pages for these selections, as well as "The Notorious Jumping Frog of Calaveras County," appear in an interactive format in the *Reader's Notebooks*. Each *Notebook* is differentiated for a different group of learners. The selections in the Adapted and English Learner's versions are abridged.

- **L2** **L3** *Reader's Notebook*
- **L1** *Reader's Notebook: Adapted Version*
- **EL** *Reader's Notebook: English Learner's Version*
- **EL** *Reader's Notebook: Spanish Version*

© *Common Core Companion*

Additional instruction and practice for each Common Core State Standard

Selection Support

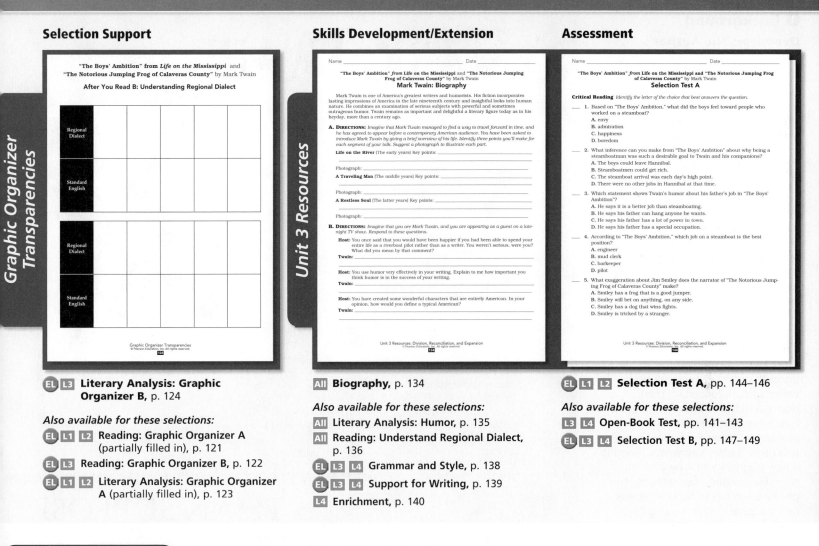

"The Boys' Ambition" from *Life on the Mississippi* and
"The Notorious Jumping Frog of Calaveras County" by Mark Twain

After You Read B: Understanding Regional Dialect

Regional Dialect					
Standard English					

Regional Dialect					
Standard English					

Graphic Organizer Transparencies
© Pearson Education, Inc. All rights reserved.
124

Graphic Organizer Transparencies

EL L3 **Literary Analysis: Graphic Organizer B,** p. 124

Also available for these selections:

EL L1 L2 **Reading: Graphic Organizer A** (partially filled in), p. 121

EL L3 **Reading: Graphic Organizer B,** p. 122

EL L1 L2 **Literary Analysis: Graphic Organizer A** (partially filled in), p. 123

Skills Development/Extension

Name ____________________ Date ____________

"The Boys' Ambition" *from* Life on the Mississippi and "The Notorious Jumping Frog of Calaveras County" by Mark Twain
Mark Twain: Biography

Mark Twain is one of America's greatest writers and humorists. His fiction incorporates lasting impressions of America in the late nineteenth century and insightful looks into human nature. He combines an examination of serious subjects with powerful and sometimes outrageous humor. Twain remains as important and delightful a literary figure today as in his heyday, more than a century ago.

A. Directions: *Imagine that Mark Twain managed to find a way to travel forward in time, and he has agreed to appear before a contemporary American audience. You have been asked to introduce Mark Twain by giving a brief overview of his life. Identify three points you'll make for each segment of your talk. Suggest a photograph to illustrate each part.*

Life on the River (The early years) Key points: ____________

Photograph: ____________

A Traveling Man (The middle years) Key points: ____________

Photograph: ____________

A Restless Soul (The latter years) Key points: ____________

Photograph: ____________

B. Directions: *Imagine that you are Mark Twain, and you are appearing as a guest on a late-night TV show. Respond to these questions.*

Host: You once said that you would have been happier if you had been able to spend your entire life as a riverboat pilot rather than as a writer. You weren't serious, were you? What did you mean by that comment?

Twain: ____________

Host: You use humor very effectively in your writing. Explain to me how important you think humor is in the success of your writing.

Twain: ____________

Host: You have created some wonderful characters that are entirely American. In your opinion, how would you define a typical American?

Twain: ____________

Unit 3 Resources: Division, Reconciliation, and Expansion
© Pearson Education, Inc. All rights reserved.
134

Unit 3 Resources

All **Biography,** p. 134

Also available for these selections:

All **Literary Analysis: Humor,** p. 135

All **Reading: Understand Regional Dialect,** p. 136

EL L3 L4 **Grammar and Style,** p. 138

EL L3 L4 **Support for Writing,** p. 139

L4 **Enrichment,** p. 140

Assessment

Name ____________________ Date ____________

"The Boys' Ambition" *from* Life on the Mississippi and "The Notorious Jumping Frog of Calaveras County" by Mark Twain
Selection Test A

Critical Reading *Identify the letter of the choice that best answers the question.*

____ 1. Based on "The Boys' Ambition," what did the boys feel toward people who worked on a steamboat?
A. envy
B. admiration
C. happiness
D. boredom

____ 2. What inference can you make from "The Boys' Ambition" about why being a steamboatman was such a desirable goal to Twain and his companions?
A. The boys could leave Hannibal.
B. Steamboatmen could get rich.
C. The steamboat arrival was each day's high point.
D. There were no other jobs in Hannibal at that time.

____ 3. Which statement shows Twain's humor about his father's job in "The Boys' Ambition"?
A. He says it is a better job than steamboating.
B. He says his father can hang anyone he wants.
C. He says his father has a lot of power in town.
D. He says his father has a special occupation.

____ 4. According to "The Boys' Ambition," which job on a steamboat is the best position?
A. engineer
B. mud clerk
C. barkeeper
D. pilot

____ 5. What exaggeration about Jim Smiley does the narrator of "The Notorious Jumping Frog of Calaveras County" make?
A. Smiley has a frog that is a good jumper.
B. Smiley will bet on anything, on any side.
C. Smiley has a dog that wins fights.
D. Smiley is tricked by a stranger.

Unit 3 Resources: Division, Reconciliation, and Expansion
© Pearson Education, Inc. All rights reserved.
144

EL L1 L2 **Selection Test A,** pp. 144–146

Also available for these selections:

L3 L4 **Open-Book Test,** pp. 141–143

EL L3 L4 **Selection Test B,** pp. 147–149

PHLit Online!
www.PHLitOnline.com

- complete narrated selection text
- a thematically related video with writing prompt
- an interactive graphic organizer
- highlighting feature
- access to all student print resources, adapted to individual student needs
- Spanish and English summaries
- adapted selection translations in Spanish

Online Resources: All print materials are also available online.

Background Video

Also available:

Get Connected! (thematic video with writing prompt)
All videos are available in Spanish.

Writer's Journal (with graphics feature)

Also available:

Vocabulary Central (tools and activities for studying vocabulary)

❶ Background

Overview: The Author's Work

They are unlikely ingredients of greatness: boyhood nostalgia; native speech; crude country humor; stray vignettes from an itinerant life. When Mark Twain is able to fuse these elements with realism and with psychological acuity, the result is literature of a unique American temper.

In a long and prolific career, Twain did not always approach the epic level he achieved in *The Adventures of Huckleberry Finn;* no writer could. But even when Twain lapses into mere regionalism, or sentimentality, or idiosyncrasy, one can still hear his voice, a storyteller's voice, indelibly American.

The Writer in His Time

Mark Twain relished his role as the uncouth outsider, the roughneck writer who disconcerted, then dominated the refined literary establishment of the East. His cheerful mockery of James Fenimore Cooper and other literary eminences brought a new pugnacity to American criticism. He enjoyed, too, satirizing the phony splendors of his time; it was he who gave the era a name that stuck, and hurt: the Gilded Age.

Over the last years of his life, Twain achieved international status as a sort of literary Uncle Sam, distinctive in his iconic white suit. Twain's final paradox is that, beneath that bright image, he hid a despair and a misanthropy that emerged only in posthumous publications.

❶ ❷ MARK TWAIN 1835–1910

Be good & you will be lonesome.
Clemens   Mark Twain
3–10–

Although Mark Twain is widely regarded as one of the greatest American writers, the world-renowned author once indicated that he would have preferred to spend his life as a Mississippi riverboat pilot. The comment was probably not entirely serious, but Twain so loved life on the river that, as a young man, he did in fact work as a riverboat pilot for several years. His childhood on the banks of the Mississippi fostered more than a love of riverboats—it also became the basis for many of his most famous works, including *The Adventures of Tom Sawyer* (1876) and *The Adventures of Huckleberry Finn* (1884).

Life on the River

Twain, whose given name was Samuel Langhorne Clemens, felt so closely tied to the Mississippi River that he even took his pen name, Mark Twain, from a river man's call meaning "two fathoms deep," indicating that the river is deep enough for a boat to pass safely. He grew up in the Mississippi River town of Hannibal, Missouri. His father died when he was eleven, and he left school to become a printer's apprentice. He worked as a printer in a number of different cities before deciding at age twenty-one to pursue a career as a riverboat pilot.

IT IS WISER TO FIND OUT THAN SUPPOSE.

566 Division, Reconciliation, and Expansion (1850–1914)

© Text Complexity Rubric

	from **Life on the Mississippi**	**The Notorious Jumping Frog of Calaveras County**
Qualitative Measures		
Context/ Knowledge Demands	Riverboat life 1 2 ③ 4 5	Tall tale; literary knowledge demands 1 2 3 ④ 5
Structure/Language Conventionality and Clarity	Some long sentences and jargon 1 2 3 ④ 5	Regional dialect; use of slang 1 2 3 ④ 5
Levels of Meaning/ Purpose/Concept Level	Accessible (ambition) 1 2 ③ 4 5	Accessible (humor) 1 2 ③ 4 5
Quantitative Measures		
Lexile/Text Length	1060L / 1,636 words	1190L / 2,539 words
Overall Complexity	**More accessible**	**More complex**

A Traveling Man

When the Civil War closed traffic on the Mississippi, Twain went west to Nevada. There, he supported himself as a journalist and lecturer, developing the entertaining writing style that made him famous. In 1865, Twain published "The Notorious Jumping Frog of Calaveras County," his version of a tall tale he had heard in a mining camp in California while he was working as a gold prospector. The story made him an international celebrity.

Following the publication of *The Innocents Abroad* (1869), a successful book of humorous travel letters, Twain moved to Hartford, Connecticut, where he was to make his home for the rest of his life. There, Twain began using his past experiences as raw material for his books. He drew on his travels in the western mining region for *Roughing It* (1872). He turned to his childhood experiences on the Mississippi for *The Adventures of Tom Sawyer, Life on the Mississippi,* and his masterpiece, *The Adventures of Huckleberry Finn.*

A Restless Soul

Twain traveled widely throughout his life, including residential stints in such major American cities as St. Louis, New York, Philadelphia, Cincinnati, and San Francisco. He made extended visits to England, Germany, Switzerland, Italy, and Palestine. His adventures, both at home and abroad, were fuel for a number of books. After living in Europe for several years, he returned home with his family. Following the death of his wife and three of their four children, Twain was unable to reproduce the balance between pessimism and humor that he had captured so brilliantly in *The Adventures of Huckleberry Finn.* In his later works, such as *A Connecticut Yankee in King Arthur's Court* (1889), *Pudd'nhead Wilson* (1894), and *The Man That Corrupted Hadleyburg* (1900), Twain's writing depicted an increasingly pessimistic view of society and human nature. However, he continued to display the same masterful command of language that had already established him as one of America's finest fiction writers.

Extended Study: Mark Twain **567**

Daily Bellringer

For each class during which you will teach these selections, have students complete one of the five activities for the appropriate week in the *Daily Bellringer Activities* booklet.

Multidraft Reading

To assist struggling readers and to enhance reading for all, assign the text in chunks as warranted by length and apply multidraft reading protocols. For each reading, have students set the purpose indicated:

- **First reading**—identifying key ideas and details and answering any Reading Checks.
- **Second reading**—analyzing craft and structure and responding to the side-column prompts.
- **Third reading**—integrating knowledge and ideas, connecting to other texts and the world, and answering the end-of-selection questions.

For more guidance, refer to the *Classroom Strategies and Teaching Routines* card, **Multidraft Reading.**

Background
❷ More About the Author

The critic Maurice LeBreton said of Mark Twain's accomplishments: "[His] work is a panorama of the West in all its vitality. He has observed everything: landscapes, environments, ways of life, customs, beliefs, superstitions. Through him we know the little Missouri town. . . . He has described for us the Mississippi. . . . We follow him into the isolated Arkansas farm. . . . The entire West files past us in a succession of precise, faithful images."

© Text Complexity: Reader and Task Suggestions

from Life on the Mississippi		The Notorious Jumping Frog of Calaveras County	
Preparing to Read the Text	**Leveled Tasks**	**Preparing to Read the Text**	**Leveled Tasks**
• Using the information on SE p. 566, discuss Twain's fascination with the Mississippi River. • Ask students, "When you were very young, what did you want to be when you grew up?" Discuss how their thinking has changed. • Guide students to use Multidraft Reading strategies (TE p. 567).	*Structure/Language* If students will have difficulty with jargon, have them look at the definitions in the footnotes before they skim the excerpt. Then, have them reread to ensure their understanding of young Twain's ambition to become a steamboatman. *Evaluating* If students will not have difficulty with the jargon, have them explain why they think readers respond to young Twain's ambition today, long after the era of steamboats.	• Using the information on TE p. 576, discuss the characterisics of a tall tale. • Ask students if they ever recognized that someone was exaggerating when recounting a "real" story. Discuss how they felt about the exaggeration. • Guide students to use Multidraft Reading strategies (TE p. 567).	*Knowledge Demands* If students will have difficulty with knowledge demands, have them skim Wheeler's story and summarize its beginning, middle, and end. As students reread, have them add notes about the exaggeration in each section. *Analyzing* If students will not have difficulty with knowledge demands, ask them how the character of Simon Wheeler also is an exaggeration—a perfect narrator for a tall tale.

❶ The Quotable Twain

1. Have students read the text on Mark Twain's quotations.

2. Point out to students that the illustration shows Twain on a lecture-hall stage, a reminder of his sideline career as a lecturer and after-dinner speaker. Since Twain was hired to be funny, he was essentially working as a nineteenth-century stand-up comedian. Many of the "one-liners" shown on the page were first delivered before live audiences.

3. Discuss with students their reactions to the quotations. Which do they find most amusing? Which contain uncomfortable truths? Which are most relevant to the present day?

4. As a live performer, Twain was aware of the importance of comic timing (see his essay on p. 575). He believed that a pause that is too brief or too long could completely destroy the effect of a joke. **Ask** students which of the quotes on this page could be delivered with a pause to increase the humorous effect.
   Possible response: Students might select quote 5, adding a pause before "except Congress"; quote 8, adding a pause before "including this one"; and quote 9, adding a pause before "and astonish the rest."

❶ THE QUOTABLE TWAIN

"CLOTHES MAKE THE MAN," Mark Twain once wrote. In his case, it was words that made the man. From novels to travel correspondence to social commentary, Twain's words were passionately celebrated and hotly criticized. As the great writer and humorist himself declared, "An author values a compliment even when it comes from a source of doubtful competency." What follows are ten more quotable quotes from Twain.

1. "When in doubt, tell the truth."

2. "Let us be thankful for the fools. But for them the rest of us could not succeed."

3. "Don't part with your illusions. When they are gone you may still exist, but you have ceased to live."

4. "It is curious—curious that physical courage should be so common in the world, and moral courage so rare."

5. "It could probably be shown by facts and figures that there is no distinctly native American criminal class except Congress."

6. "We find not much in ourselves to admire, we are always privately wanting to be like somebody else. If everybody was satisfied with himself there would be no heroes."

7. "It is better to keep your mouth shut and appear stupid than to open it and remove all doubt."

8. "All generalizations are false, including this one."

9. "Always do right. That will gratify some of the people, and astonish the rest."

10. "The only way to keep your health is to eat what you don't want, drink what you don't like, and do what you'd rather not."

568 Division, Reconciliation, and Expansion (1850–1914)

Vocabulary Development

Vocabulary Knowledge Rating
Create a **Vocabulary Knowledge Rating Chart** (*Professional Development Guidebook,* p. 33) for the vocabulary words on the student page. Give each student a copy of the chart with the words on it. Read the words aloud, and have students mark their rating in the Before Reading column. Urge students to attend to these words as they read and discuss the selection.

In order to gauge how much instruction you need to provide, tally how many students are confident in their knowledge of each word. As students read, point out the words and their context.

PHLit Online! **Vocabulary Central**, featuring student tools for recording and studying vocabulary, is available online at **www.PHLitOnline.com.**

Before You Read

from *Life on the Mississippi* •
*The Notorious Jumping
Frog of Calaveras County*

❷ Connecting to the Essential Question Mark Twain portrayed America in a way that continues to define our national character. As you read, look for images, expressions, characters, and ways of thinking that strike you as distinctly American. This will help as you consider the Essential Question: **What makes American literature American?**

❸ Literary Analysis

Humor, which may appear in all literary genres, is writing intended to amuse. Humorists use a variety of devices and techniques to achieve that goal:

- **Incongruity,** or differences in logic or degree. For example, a speaker may use a serious tone to describe ridiculous events.
- **Hyperbole,** or the exaggeration of details or embellishment of events beyond what is logical
- **Comic uses of language,** including funny names

Twain's humor is not just funny. Even his most comic works carry an undercurrent of **social commentary,** or critique of society. His social commentary is infused with Twain's keen observations *of human foibles,* or weaknesses, which he usually describes with affection. Twain is also a master of **dialect**—ways of speaking that are specific to a particular area or group of people. This, too, adds to the humor of his writing. As you read, look for these hallmarks of Twain's comic style.

❹ Reading Strategy

© **Preparing to Read Complex Texts** Twain uses *technical language* to describe steamboats and *dialect* to convey a sense of authentic speech. Both types of language may be unfamiliar to you. To **clarify** technical language, consult footnotes. To **interpret** regional dialect, read unfamiliar words aloud to find that they are simply different pronunciations of words you know. Use a chart like the one shown to translate dialect into modern Standard English.

❺ Vocabulary

transient (tran´ zē ənt) *adj.* not permanent (p. 571)

prodigious (prə dij´ əs) *adj.* of great power or size (p. 572)

eminence (em´ ə nəns) *n.* greatness; celebrity (p. 573)

garrulous (gar´ ə ləs) *adj.* talking too much (p. 576)

conjectured (kən jek´ chərd) *v.* guessed (p. 576)

monotonous (mə nät´ ən əs) *adj.* tiresome because unvarying (p. 576)

interminable (in tʉr´ mi nə bəl) *adj.* seeming to last forever (p. 576)

**Common Core
State Standards**

Reading Literature
6. Analyze a case in which grasping a point of view requires distinguishing what is directly stated in a text from what is really meant.

9. Demonstrate knowledge of nineteenth-century foundational works of American literature, including how two or more texts from the same period treat similar themes or topics.

Reading Informational Text
4. Determine the meaning of words and phrases as they are used in a text, including technical meanings.

Language
5.a. Interpret figures of speech in context and analyze their role in the text.

Regional Dialect

. . . there couldn't be no solit'ry thing mentioned but that feller'd offer to bet on it, and take ary side you please. . . .

↓

Standard English

Not one thing could be mentioned without him offering to bet on it, taking any side.

**PHLit
Online!**
www.PHLitOnline.com

from Life on the Mississippi • The Notorious Jumping Frog of Calaveras County **569**

**PHLit
Online!**
www.PHLitOnline.com

Teaching From Technology

Preparing to Read
Go to **www.PHLitOnline.com** and display the **Get Connected!** slide show for these selections. Have the class brainstorm for responses to the writing prompt, entering ideas in the interactive journal. Then have students complete their responses individually. You may also have students complete the assignment as homework.

To build background, display the Background video and More About the Author features.

Using the Interactive Student Edition
Go to **www.PHLitOnline.com** and display the **Enriched Online Student Edition.** As the class reads the selection or listens to the narration, record answers to side-column prompts using the graphic organizers accessible on the interactive page. Alternatively, have students use the online edition individually, answering the prompts as they read.

**❷ Connecting to the
Essential Question**

1. Review the assignment with the class.
2. Share an example of a writer or musician who embodies American identity. Explain how, in your view, the person's identity relates to the Essential Question.
3. Point out to students that distinctly American attitudes may be signaled by humor or regionalisms. Then discuss those topics.

❸ Literary Analysis
Introduce the strategy, using the instruction on the student page.

Think Aloud: Model the Skill
Say to students:

I laugh almost too easily at hyperbole but only when it is presented with a "straight face"—when the writer presents an outrageous exaggeration as if it were perfectly normal. I wonder what tone Twain takes with hyperbole in his "Jumping Frog" story.

❹ Reading Strategy

1. Introduce the skill, using the instruction on the student page.
2. Give students a copy of **Reading Strategy Graphic Organizer B,** page 122 in *Graphic Organizer Transparencies,* to fill out as they read.

Think Aloud: Model the Skill
Say to students:

When I find a passage of dialect hard to understand, I try reading it aloud. Often, *hearing* the expression helps me make a connection when the printed word does not. For example, I was puzzled by Twain's word *summerset.* When I read the passage out loud, I heard the connection: "Oh, he means *somersault.*"

❺ Vocabulary

1. Pronounce each word, giving its definition, and have students say it aloud.
2. For more guidance, see the *Classroom Strategies and Teaching Routines* card for introducing vocabulary.

❶ About the Selection

With charm and wit, Mark Twain draws an insightful picture of the hopes and ambitions of a boy growing up in a town along the Mississippi River. The boy dreams of becoming a steamboat man and working on one of the great riverboats on the majestic river. His desire for the opportunities and prestige the job affords, his envy of a boy who already has such a job, and the contrast he sees between the dullness of his small town and the adventures the river promises provide a rich bounty of humorous situations and descriptions.

❷ Activating Prior Knowledge

Tell students that Mark Twain was a writer who used exaggeration, embellishment, regional dialect, and boyhood recollections to make his stories humorous. Then ask students to brainstorm a list of different kinds of humor that they enjoy—such as humorous stories, jokes, or riddles—and invite students to name examples for each category. Ask them to think about the differences between spoken humor and humor meant to be read, and have them describe what it is about written humor that makes them laugh. Invite students to enjoy two selections by an eminent American writer and humorist, Mark Twain.

Concept Connector ➡

Tell students that they will return to their ideas about humor after reading the selections.

FROM
❶ ❷ LIFE ON THE MISSISSIPPI

MARK TWAIN

BACKGROUND Mark Twain was an eyewitness to the nineteenth-century expansion of the western frontier. He was a young man when wagon trains left his home state of Missouri to cross the prairies, and he later saw the transcontinental railroad built. He traveled throughout the nation, working first on the Mississippi and then in the West, before settling in Connecticut. However, as this excerpt shows, the Mississippi River held a special place in his memory.

570 Division, Reconciliation, and Expansion (1850–1914)

Enrichment: Investigating Career Connections

"Mark Twain!"
Twain's pen name comes from his days as a riverboat pilot. "Mark twain" is a phrase that indicates the river's depth is two fathoms or twelve feet—safe enough for a riverboat hull. The first time Twain piloted a boat by himself, the crew tricked him into thinking he was in shallow water. In a panic, Twain begged the engineer to reverse the paddlewheels. As the crew laughed, the pilot, Mr. Bixby, warned him never to be tricked again but to have confidence in his knowledge of the river. Twain never forgot this lesson.

Activity: Presentation Riverboats and barges still work the Mississippi River. Encourage students to find out what kinds of workers are needed on the river today. Suggest that they record information in the **Enrichment: Investigating Career Connections** work sheet, in *Professional Development Guidebook,* page 221. Students can then report their findings to the class.

THE BOYS' AMBITION

❸ When I was a boy, there was but one permanent ambition among my comrades in our village[1] on the west bank of the Mississippi River. That was, to be a steamboatman. We had transient ambitions of other sorts, but they were only transient.

When a circus came and went, it left us all burning to become clowns; the first Negro minstrel show that came to our section left us all suffering to try that kind of life; now and then we had a hope that if we lived and were good, God would permit us to be pirates. These ambitions faded out, each in its turn; but the ambition to be a steamboatman always remained.

Once a day a cheap, gaudy packet[2] arrived upward from St. Louis, and another downward from Keokuk.[3] Before these events, the day was glorious with expectancy; after them, the day was a dead and empty thing. Not only the boys, but the whole village, felt this. After all these years I can picture that old time to myself now, just as it was then: the white town drowsing in the sunshine of a summer's morning; the streets empty, or pretty nearly so; one or two clerks sitting in front of the Water Street stores, with their splint-bottomed chairs tilted back against the wall, chins on breasts, hats slouched over their faces, asleep—with shingle shavings enough around to show what broke them down; a sow and a litter of pigs loafing along the sidewalk, doing a good business in watermelon rinds and seeds; two or three lonely little freight piles scattered about the levee;[4] a pile of skids[5] on the slope of the stone-paved wharf, and the fragrant town drunkard asleep in the shadow of them; two or three wood flats[6] at the head of the wharf, but nobody to listen to the peaceful lapping of the wavelets against them; the great Mississippi, the majestic, the magnificent Mississippi, rolling its mile-wide tide along, shining in the sun; the dense forest away on the other side; the point above the town, and the point below, bounding the river-glimpse and turning it into a sort of sea, and withal a very still and brilliant and lonely one. Presently a film of dark smoke appears above one of those remote

---

1. **our village** Hannibal, Missouri.
2. **packet** *n.* boat that travels a regular route, carrying passengers, freight, and mail.
3. **Keokuk** (kē′ ə kuk′) town in southeastern Iowa.
4. **levee** (lev′ ē) *n.* landing place along the bank of a river.
5. **skids** *n.* low, movable wooden platforms.
6. **flats** *n.* small, flat-bottomed boats.

Vocabulary

transient (tran′ zē ənt) *adj.* not permanent

❹ ◀ **Critical Viewing** How does this painting convey a sense of the glamour steamboats brought to the Mississippi River? **[Analyze]**

❺ ☑ Reading Check

How did the boys' ambitions change with each new visitor to their town?

from Life on the Mississippi **571**

❸ Background

Emphasize to students the importance of riverboat trade to the economy around the river. In an age without television or radio, the boats were also an important link between river communities and the rest of the world.

❹ Critical Viewing

Answer: Students may say that the majestic portrayal of the steamboats amid the river's natural beauty conveys a sense of the excitement and glamour that accompanies the arrival of people and things from great distances.

❺ Reading Check

Answer: The boys want (for a short while) to try the kind of life lived by each glamorous visitor to their town.

6 Critical Viewing

Answer: Students may point out that the painting shows other water-craft, narrow channels, and an island in the river, all of which would challenge boat captains and pilots navigating the river.

7 Reading Strategy

Clarifying and Interpreting Language

1. Point out that Twain uses several technical terms in the bracketed text. **Ask** students to name some technical terms they hear and use in the course of their lives.
   Answer: Students may mention computer, audio, and cell-phone terms such as JPEG, IM, and MP3 or terms from science or math.

2. Tell students that many historical and technical books include footnotes and glossaries to assist readers. **Ask** the Reading Strategy question.
   Answer: Footnotes provide definitions that apply specifically to the terms' use in the passage, which makes it much easier for me to follow the author's train of thought.

6 ▶ Critical Viewing
What does this painting suggest about some of the challenges steamboat captains faced in navigating the river? **[Infer]**

Vocabulary
prodigious (prə dij´ əs) *adj.* of great power or size

Reading Strategy
Clarifying and Interpreting Language How do footnotes clarify your understanding of the technical terms in this paragraph?

7

points; instantly a Negro drayman,[7] famous for his quick eye and prodigious voice, lifts up the cry, "S-t-e-a-m-boat a-comin'!" and the scene changes! The town drunkard stirs, the clerks wake up, a furious clatter of drays follows, every house and store pours out a human contribution, and all in a twinkling the dead town is alive and moving. Drays, carts, men, boys, all go hurrying from many quarters to a common center, the wharf. Assembled there, the people fasten their eyes upon the coming boat as upon a wonder they are seeing for the first time. And the boat is rather a handsome sight, too. She is long and sharp and trim and pretty; she has two tall, fancy-topped chimneys, with a gilded device of some kind swung between them; a fanciful pilothouse, all glass and gingerbread, perched on top of the texas deck[8] behind them; the paddleboxes are gorgeous with a picture or with gilded rays above the boat's name; the boiler deck, the hurricane deck, and the texas deck are fenced and ornamented with clean white railings; there is a flag gallantly flying from the jackstaff;[9] the furnace doors are open and the fires glaring bravely; the upper decks are black with passengers; the captain stands by the big bell, calm, imposing, the envy of all; great volumes of the blackest smoke are rolling and tumbling out of the chimneys—a husbanded grandeur created with a bit of pitch pine just before arriving at a town; the crew are grouped on the forecastle;[10] the broad stage is run far out over the port bow, and an envied deckhand stands picturesquely on the end of it with a coil of rope in his hand; the pent steam is screaming through the gauge cocks; the captain lifts his hand, a bell rings, the wheels stop; then they turn back, churning the water to foam, and the steamer is at rest. Then such a scramble as there is to get aboard, and to get ashore, and to take in freight and to discharge

---

7. **drayman** (drā´ mən) *n.* driver of a dray, a low cart with detachable sides.
8. **texas deck** deck adjoining the officers' cabins, the largest cabins on the ship.
9. **jackstaff** (jak´ staf) *n.* small staff at the bow of a ship for flying flags.
10. **forecastle** (fōk´ səl) *n.* front part of the upper deck.

572 Division, Reconciliation, and Expansion (1850–1914)

Think Aloud

Vocabulary: Using Context
Point out to students the phrase "husbanded grandeur," an unusual expression they may not understand. Say to students:

I may not know the meaning of *husbanded grandeur,* but I can use details in the passage to figure out its possible meaning. Twain uses the phrase to describe the thick, black smoke rising from the steamboat's chimneys. I know this effect is produced on purpose because Twain tells us the secret: pitch pine is tossed into the boiler fires just as the steamboat is coming to a town. This tells me that the effect is probably reserved for special occasions to impress people in the towns. I think the phrase *husbanded grandeur* refers to a carefully managed grand effect.

freight, all at one and the same time; and such a yelling and curs-
ing as the mates facilitate it all with! Ten minutes later the steamer
is under way again, with no flag on the jackstaff and no black smoke
issuing from the chimneys. After ten more minutes the town is dead
again, and the town drunkard asleep by the skids once more.

My father was a justice of the peace, and I supposed he possessed
the power of life and death over all men and could hang anybody that
offended him. This was distinction enough for me as a general thing;
but the desire to be a steamboatman kept intruding, nevertheless. I
first wanted to be a cabin boy, so that I could come out with a white
apron on and shake a tablecloth over the side, where all my old comrades could see me; later I thought I would rather be the deckhand
who stood on the end of the stage plank with the coil of rope in his
hand, because he was particularly conspicuous. But these were only
daydreams—they were too heavenly to be contemplated as real possibilities. By and by one of our boys went away. He was not heard of
for a long time. At last he turned up as apprentice engineer or striker
on a steamboat. This thing shook the bottom out of all my Sunday
school teachings. That boy had been notoriously worldly, and I just
the reverse; yet he was exalted to this eminence, and I left in obscurity and misery. There was nothing generous about this fellow in his
greatness. He would always manage to have a rusty bolt to scrub
while his boat tarried at our town, and he would sit on the inside
guard and scrub it, where we could all see him and envy him and
loathe him. And whenever his boat was laid up he would come home
and swell around the town in his blackest and greasiest clothes, so
that nobody could help remembering that he was a steamboatman;
and he used all sorts of steamboat technicalities in his talk, as if
he were so used to them that he forgot common people could not
understand them. He would speak of the labboard[11] side of a horse
in an easy, natural way that would make one wish he was dead.
And he was always talking about "St. Looey" like an old citizen; he
would refer casually to occasions when he "was coming down Fourth
Street," or when he was "passing by the Planter's House," or when
there was a fire and he took a turn on the brakes of "the old Big
Missouri"; and then he would go on and lie about how many towns
the size of ours were burned down there that day. Two or three of the
boys had long been persons of consideration among us because they
had been to St. Louis once and had a vague general knowledge of its
wonders, but the day of their glory was over now. They lapsed into
a humble silence, and learned to disappear when the ruthless cub
engineer approached. This fellow had money, too, and hair oil. Also
an ignorant silver watch and a showy brass watch chain. He wore
a leather belt and used no suspenders. If ever a youth was cordially

---

11. **labboard** (lab′ ərd) larboard, the left-hand side of a ship.

Spiral Review
Tone How would you
describe the author's
tone in this paragraph?
Explain.

Vocabulary
eminence (em′ i nəns) *n.*
greatness; celebrity

Reading Strategy
**Clarifying Regional
Dialect** What does the
apprentice engineer's use of
riverboat jargon reveal about
him?

**Reading
Check**
What activities and actions
of the boy who worked on a
steamship inspired envy?

from Life on the Mississippi **573**

Spiral Review
Tone

1. **Remind** students that they
   studied the concept of tone
   in an earlier lesson.

2. **Ask** students the Spiral
   Review question.

   Possible response: By
   describing bitterness and
   envy that is out of proportion
   to the situation, Twain sets a
   humorous tone.

❽ Reading Strategy
Clarifying Regional Dialect

1. **Read** the passage aloud for
   students and urge them to note
   any examples of jargon or other
   terms that indicate a familiarity
   with the world of riverboats. If
   necessary, draw students' attention to terms such as "labboard,"
   "St. Looey," "Fourth Street,"
   "Planter's House," and "the old
   Big Missouri."

2. **Ask** students the Reading
   Strategy question.
   Answer: Some students may
   say that the apprentice uses jargon to enhance the celebrity of
   his position before his envious
   former peers. Others may say
   that it reveals that he is little different from young Twain and his
   friends—they plan to do the same
   if they get the chance.

❾ Reading Check

Answer: The boy inspired envy
merely by scrubbing a rusty bolt,
walking around town in his dirty
work clothes, or using riverboat
jargon.

**Differentiated
Instruction** for Universal Access

Background for Special-Needs Students
Encourage students to obtain and examine a
map showing the Mississippi River and the states
of Missouri, Illinois, and Iowa. You might need
to help students get more specific bearings by
locating Hannibal, Keokuk, and St. Louis for
them. Have students use the Internet to identify
which of these towns have museums or festivals
that celebrate the days of riverboats.

**EL Vocabulary for
English Learners**
Point out the jargon in the selection. Encourage
students to identify other pursuits that require
the use of specialized terms, or jargon. Examples
might include medicine, law, or their own science or social studies classes. Ask students to
share examples of specialized terms used in
their first languages. Help students see that
such terms help people communicate effectively
about specialized topics.

Humor

1. Read the bracketed passage aloud.

2. **Ask** the Literary Analysis question.
   Answer: By describing the boy as a reptile, Twain uses hyperbole, grossly exaggerating his disdain for a person he actually envies.

⑪ 🅠 Engaging the Essential Question

1. Read the bracketed passage, noting how boys took up work different from that of their fathers.

2. **Ask:** Do you think openness to taking up new kinds of work is an American characteristic? Explain.
   Possible response: Students may say that responding to new technologies and opportunities and readiness for change are typical of Americans.

ASSESS

Answers

Before students respond, you may wish to have them write a brief objective summary of the selection. As they answer the questions below, remind them to support their answers with evidence from the text.

1. (a) All want to be steamboat men. (b) Twain's ambition to travel to different places as pilot of a steamboat reflects the American desire for expansion and adventure.

2. (a) They hurry to greet the boat as it arrives and watch the boat's operations with fascination. (b) Twain's description of the town suggests that it is a sleepy place where not much happens.

3. (a) Most students will probably say that Twain's firsthand experience as a pilot was crucial to his ability to write convincingly. (b) **Possible response:** Twain's love for the Mississippi led him to describe river life so eloquently. It also led him to use regional dialect to bring characters vividly to life.

4. Some students may say that glory is an effective motivator. Others may say that life decisions based on glory might be regretted later.

574

Literary Analysis ⑩
Humor How does the use of the word *reptile* add to the humor of this passage?

⑪

admired and hated by his comrades, this one was. No girl could withstand his charms. He cut out every boy in the village. When his boat blew up at last, it diffused a tranquil contentment among us such as we had not known for months. But when he came home the next week, alive, renowned, and appeared in church all battered up and bandaged, a shining hero, stared at and wondered over by everybody, it seemed to us that the partiality of Providence for an undeserving reptile had reached a point where it was open to criticism.

This creature's career could produce but one result, and it speedily followed. Boy after boy managed to get on the river. The minister's son became an engineer. The doctor's and the postmaster's sons became mud clerks; the wholesale liquor dealer's son became a barkeeper on a boat; four sons of the chief merchant, and two sons of the county judge, became pilots. Pilot was the grandest position of all. The pilot, even in those days of trivial wages, had a princely salary— from a hundred and fifty to two hundred and fifty dollars a month, and no board to pay. Two months of his wages would pay a preacher's salary for a year. Now some of us were left disconsolate. We could not get on the river—at least our parents would not let us.

So by and by I ran away. I said I never would come home again till I was a pilot and could come in glory. But somehow I could not manage it. I went meekly aboard a few of the boats that lay packed together like sardines at the long St. Louis wharf, and very humbly inquired for the pilots, but got only a cold shoulder and short words from mates and clerks. I had to make the best of this sort of treatment for the time being, but I had comforting daydreams of a future when I should be a great and honored pilot, with plenty of money, and could kill some of these mates and clerks and pay for them.

Critical Reading ©

Cite textual evidence to support your responses.

© 1. **Key Ideas and Details (a)** What is the one permanent ambition of the narrator and his boyhood friends? **(b) Connect:** How does this childhood ambition reflect the American spirit that gave rise to the settlement of new frontiers?

© 2. **Key Ideas and Details (a)** How do the people of Hannibal respond to the arrival of the steamboat? **(b) Interpret:** What impression of the town does Twain convey by this response?

© 3. **Craft and Structure (a) Hypothesize:** Do you think Twain could have written so well about riverboat life had he not become a pilot himself? Explain. **(b) Apply:** In what ways do you think Twain's love for the Mississippi River contributed to his success as a writer?

© 4. **Integration of Knowledge and Ideas Evaluate:** The last paragraph suggests that the young Twain was driven by a desire for glory. Is a desire for glory a reasonable motivation in life? Explain.

574 Division, Reconciliation, and Expansion (1850–1914)

Enrichment: Investigating Daily Life

Steamboats

By the early nineteenth century, steamboats were regularly carrying cargo on the Mississippi and Ohio rivers. The boats were essential to the economy of towns along these rivers, linking them to each other and to the rest of the world. Until the 1850s, when railroad development grew rapidly in the West, steamboats carried more freight than trains did.

Activity: Creative Writing Have students do research to find out about daily life on the great riverboats during Twain's time. Among other things, they can research routes, jobs, onboard entertainment, the size and speed of the boats, and the cargo they carried. Suggest that students record information in the **Enrichment: Investigating Daily Life** work sheet, in *Professional Development Guidebook*, page 224. Students can then write a creative sketch of a day in the life of a steamboat worker or passenger.

Critical Commentary

⑫ from "How to Tell a Story"

An Essay by Mark Twain

I do not claim that I can tell a story as it ought to be told. I only claim to know how a story ought to be told, for I have been almost daily in the company of the most expert story-tellers for many years.

There are several kinds of stories, but only one difficult kind—the humorous. I will talk mainly about that one. The humorous story is American, the comic story is English, the witty story is French. The humorous story depends for its effect upon the *manner* of the telling; the comic story and the witty story upon the *matter*.

The humorous story may be spun out to great length, and may wander around as much as it pleases, and arrive nowhere in particular; but the comic and witty stories must be brief and end with a point. The humorous story bubbles gently along, the others burst.

The humorous story is strictly a work of art—high and delicate art—and only an artist can tell it; but no art is necessary in telling the comic and the witty story; anybody can do it. The art of telling a humorous story—understand, I mean by word of mouth, not print—was created in America, and has remained at home.

The humorous story is told gravely; the teller does his best to conceal the fact that he even dimly suspects that there is anything funny about it; but the teller of the comic story tells you beforehand that it is one of the funniest things he has ever heard, then tells it with eager delight, and is the first person to laugh when he gets through. And sometimes, if he has had good success, he is so glad and happy that he will repeat the "nub" of it and glance around from face to face, collecting applause, and then repeat it again. It is a pathetic thing to see.

Very often, of course, the rambling and disjointed humorous story finishes with a nub, point, snapper, or whatever you like to call it. Then the listener must be alert, for in many cases the teller will divert attention from that nub by dropping it in a carefully casual and indifferent way, with the pretense that he does not know it is a nub. . . .

But the teller of the comic story does not slur the nub; he shouts it at you—every time. And when he prints it, in England, France, Germany, and Italy, he italicizes it, puts some whooping exclamation-points after it, and sometimes explains it in a parenthesis. All of which is very depressing, and makes one want to renounce joking and lead a better life.

© **Key Ideas and Details** Why does Twain think Americans are skilled at telling humorous stories? What is the difference between a humorous story and a comic story?

Extended Study: Mark Twain **575**

⑫ Critical Commentary

1. Prepare to discuss this commentary by assigning it as homework. Ask students, as they read, to try to think of an example of each type of story Twain describes: the humorous story and the comic or witty story.

2. After they have read the essay, review the Check Your Comprehension questions to determine that students have grasped Twain's ideas. Then have students share examples of the two types of stories. Examples should demonstrate that students have grasped Twain's distinction between a humorous story and a joke.

3. Tell students to choose an example of humor they enjoy (whether from professional comedy or from everyday life). In small groups, have them share their examples and then discuss whether each falls more squarely in the category of "humorous storytelling" or "joke." Late-night television talk shows often display both types of humor: the host opens the show with a stand-up routine of jokes; later, guests entertain by telling funny stories.

⑬ Key Ideas and Details

Answers

• According to Twain, the humorous story is an American invention; therefore Americans are most skilled at telling them (he may, of course, be joking about that).

• A humorous story takes time to wander to a conclusion. It must be told without a hint that it is humorous; even the punch line, if there is one, must be delivered with a straight face. A comic story is short, is told with the expectation of laughter, and has a nub, or punch line.

Differentiated Instruction
for Universal Access

Culturally Responsive Instruction

Culture Focus After students have read Mark Twain's essay "How to Tell a Story," tell students that while laughter may be universal in the human race, people do not always laugh at the same things. Twain himself insists that the "humorous story is American, the comic story is English, the witty story is French."

Discuss the cultural component of humor by asking students what kinds of jokes and stories are common in their home culture. Does the humor tend to be verbal or visual? Does it depend on timing or cleverness?

After reviewing your standards of material appropriate to the classroom, ask students to collect and share with the class examples of stories, jokes, cartoons, and other forms that are characteristic of the humor in their home cultures, providing translations as necessary.

→ THE ← NOTORIOUS JUMPING FROG OF CALAVERAS COUNTY

MARK TWAIN

Vocabulary

garrulous (gar′ ə ləs) *adj.* talking too much

conjectured (kən jek′ chərd) *v.* guessed

monotonous (mə nät′ ən əs) *adj.* tiresome because unvarying

interminable (in tʉr′ mi nə bəl) *adj.* seeming to last forever

In compliance with the request of a friend of mine, who wrote me from the East, I called on good-natured, garrulous old Simon Wheeler, and inquired after my friend's friend, Leonidas W. Smiley, as requested to do, and I hereunto append the result. I have a lurking suspicion that *Leonidas W.* Smiley is a myth; that my friend never knew such a personage: and that he only conjectured that if I asked old Wheeler about him, it would remind him of his infamous *Jim* Smiley, and he would go to work and bore me to death with some exasperating reminiscence of him as long and as tedious as it should be useless to me. If that was the design, it succeeded.

I found Simon Wheeler dozing comfortably by the barroom stove of the dilapidated tavern in the decayed mining camp of Angel's, and I noticed that he was fat and baldheaded, and had an expression of winning gentleness and simplicity upon his tranquil countenance. He roused up, and gave me good day. I told him a friend of mine had commissioned me to make some inquiries about a cherished companion of his boyhood named *Leonidas W.* Smiley—*Rev. Leonidas W.* Smiley, a young minister of the Gospel, who he had heard was at one time a resident of Angel's Camp. I added that if Mr. Wheeler could tell me anything about this Rev. Leonidas W. Smiley, I would feel under many obligations to him.

Simon Wheeler backed me into a corner and blockaded me there with his chair, and then sat down and reeled off the monotonous narrative which follows this paragraph. He never smiled, he never frowned, he never changed his voice from the gentle-flowing key to which he tuned his initial sentence, he never betrayed the slightest suspicion of enthusiasm; but all through the interminable narrative there ran a vein of impressive earnestness and sincerity, which showed me plainly that, so far from his imagining that there was anything ridiculous or funny about his story, he regarded it as a really important matter, and admired its two heroes as men of transcen-

576 Division, Reconciliation, and Expansion (1850–1914)

dent genius in *finesse*. I let him go on in his own way, and never interrupted him once.

"Rev. Leonidas W. H'm, Reverend Le—well, there was a feller here once by the name of *Jim* Smiley, in the winter of '49—or maybe it was the spring of '50—I don't recollect exactly, somehow, though what makes me think it was one or the other is because I remember the big flume[1] warn't finished when he first come to the camp; but anyway, he was the curiousest man about always betting on anything that turned up you ever see, if he could get anybody to bet on the other side; and if he couldn't he'd change sides. Any way that suited the other man would suit *him*—any way just so's he got a bet, *he* was satisfied. But still he was lucky, uncommon lucky; he most always come out winner. He was always ready and laying for a chance; there couldn't be no solit'ry thing mentioned but that feller'd offer to bet on it, and take ary side you please, as I was just telling you. If there was a horse race, you'd find him flush or you'd find him busted at the end of it; if there was a dogfight, he'd bet on it; if there was a cat fight, he'd bet on it; if there was a chicken fight, he'd bet on it; why, if there was two birds setting on a fence, he would bet you which one would fly first; or if there was a camp meeting,[2] he would be there reg'lar to bet on Parson Walker, which he judged to be the best exhorter about here and so he was too, and a good man. If he even see a straddle bug[3] start to go anywheres, he would bet you how long it would take him to get to—to wherever he was going to, and if you took him up, he would foller that straddle bug to Mexico but what he would find out where he was bound for and how long he was on the road. Lots of the boys here has seen that Smiley, and can tell you about him. Why, it never made no difference to *him*—he'd bet on *any* thing—the dangdest feller. Parson Walker's wife laid very sick once, for a good while, and it seemed as if they warn't going to save her; but one morning he come in, and Smiley up and asked him how she was, and he said she was considable better—thank the Lord for his inf'nite

1. **flume** (flōōm) *n.* artificial channel for carrying water to provide power and transport objects.
2. **camp meeting** religious gathering at the mining camp.
3. **straddle bug** insect with long legs.

15

16 ▼ **Critical Viewing**
Would Twain have been amused or offended by this caricature of himself? Explain. **[Speculate]**

18 ☑ **Reading Check**
What does the narrator suspect about Leonidas W. Smiley?

16 Critical Viewing
Answer: Students may say that Twain, as a writer who knew the effectiveness of exaggeration, would have enjoyed the humor in this caricature—particularly the deadpan expression on his face.

17 Reading Strategy
Interpreting Regional Dialect
1. Invite a student volunteer to read aloud the first several sentences of Wheeler's narrative. Then have students go back and read the same sentences silently once more.
2. **Ask** students the following question: What examples of dialect can you find as Wheeler's tale begins?
   Answer: Examples include "feller," "by the name of," "recollect," "warn't," "when he first come," "curiousest," "you ever see," and "so's he got a."

▶ **Monitor Progress Ask** students to provide Standard English ways of expressing the words and phrases they have identified as dialect.
   Sample answer: "fellow," "named," "remember," "was not," "when he first arrived," "most curious," "imaginable," and "so as to get."

▶ **Reteach:** If students have difficulty with dialect language, reread the passage as a class, stopping to clarify each word that puzzles students.

18 Reading Check
Answer: The narrator suspects that he does not exist.

⑲ Literary Analysis

Humor

1. Read aloud the bracketed paragraph as students listen for examples of Twain's use of humorous techniques.

2. **Ask** students the first Literary Analysis question.
   Answer: Students might mention the nickname "the fifteen-minute nag," the idea of betting on such a slow horse, or the host of medical conditions from which the mare is said to suffer.

⑳ Reading Strategy

Interpreting Regional Dialect

1. Have two or three student volunteers read this sentence aloud slowly for their classmates. Point out potentially challenging examples of dialect, such as "warn't" ("wasn't").

2. **Ask** students the following question: How would you rephrase the sentence beginning "And he had" in Standard English?
   Sample answer: Smiley's bulldog puppy looked as though it did nothing but look bad tempered and try to sneak food.

㉑ Literary Analysis

Humor

1. Recall with students the techniques for creating humor.

2. Then read aloud the bracketed text describing Smiley's dog. **Ask** students the second Literary Analysis question.
   Sample answer: The dog's name is funny because of the incongruity of a dog being named after a man who was a war hero and an American president.

Literary Analysis
Humor What is funny about this description of the mare?

Literary Analysis
Humor Why is the dog's name—Andrew Jackson—funny?

mercy—and coming on so smart that with the blessing of Prov'dence she'd get well yet; and Smiley, before he thought, says, 'Well, I'll resk two-and-a-half she don't anyway.'

⑲ Thish-yer Smiley had a mare—the boys called her the fifteen-minute nag, but that was only in fun, you know, because of course she was faster than that—and he used to win money on that horse, for all she was so slow and always had the asthma, or the distemper, or the consumption, or something of that kind. They used to give her two or three hundred yards start, and then pass her under way; but always at the fag end[4] of the race she'd get excited and desperate like, and come cavorting and straddling up, and scattering her legs around limber, sometimes in the air, and sometimes out to one side among the fences, and kicking up m-o-r-e dust and raising m-o-r-e racket with her coughing and sneezing and blowing her nose—and *always* fetch up at the stand just about a neck ahead, as near as you could cipher it down.

⑳ And he had a little small bull-pup, that to look at him you'd think he warn't worth a cent but to set around and look ornery and lay for
㉑ a chance to steal something. But as soon as money was up on him he was a different dog; his under-jaw'd begin to stick out like the fo' castle[5] of a steamboat, and his teeth would uncover and shine like the furnaces. And a dog might tackle him and bullyrag him, and bite him, and throw him over his shoulder two or three times, and Andrew Jackson—which was the name of the pup—Andrew Jackson would never let on but what *he* was satisfied, and hadn't expected nothing else—and the bets being doubled and doubled on the other side all the time, till the money was all up; and then all of a sudden he would grab that other dog jest by the j'int of his hind leg and freeze to it—not chaw, you understand, but only just grip and hang on till they throwed up the sponge, if it was a year. Smiley always come out winner on that pup, till he harnessed a dog once that didn't have no hind legs, because they'd been sawed off in a circular saw, and when the thing had gone along far enough, and the money was all up, and he come to make a snatch for his pet holt,[6] he see in a minute how he'd been imposed on, and how the other dog had him in the door, so to speak, and he 'peared surprised, and then he looked sorter discouraged-like, and didn't try no more to win the fight, and so he got shucked out bad. He give Smiley a look, as much as to say his heart was broke, and it was his fault, for putting up a dog that hadn't no hind legs for him to take holt of, which was his main dependence in a fight, and then he limped off a piece and laid down and died. It was a good pup, was that Andrew Jackson, and would have made a name for hisself if he'd lived, for the stuff was in him and he had genius—I know it, because he hadn't no opportunities to

---

4. **fag end** last part.
5. **fo'castle** (fōk´ səl) *n.* the forward part of the upper deck.
6. **holt** hold.

Enrichment: Understanding Economics

A Forty-Dollar Bet

Explain to students that forty dollars—the amount of the bet placed on the frog's ability to jump—was a great deal of money at the time of this story, equal perhaps to a month's wages.

Activity: Pie Chart Have students do research to learn what basic necessities cost in America around the middle of the nineteenth century, as well as how much people were paid for various jobs. Suggest that they record information in the **Enrichment: Understanding Economics** work sheet, in *Professional Development Guidebook,* page 225. Students can then create a pie chart or other form of graphic organizer to show how far forty dollars would have taken a person toward the goal of paying for a month's worth of housing, food, clothing, and so on.

speak of, and it don't stand to reason that a dog could make such a fight as he could under them circumstances if he hadn't no talent. It always makes me feel sorry when I think of that last fight of his'n, and the way it turned out.

Well, thish-yer Smiley had rat terriers,[7] and chicken cocks,[8] and tomcats and all them kind of things, till you couldn't rest, and you couldn't fetch nothing for him to bet on but he'd match you. He ketched a frog one day, and took him home, and said he cal'lated to educate him; and so he never done nothing for three months but set in his back yard and learn that frog to jump. And you bet you he *did* learn him, too. He'd give him a little punch behind, and the next minute you'd see that frog whirling in the air like a doughnut—see him turn one summerset, or maybe a couple, if he got a good start, and come down flatfooted and all right, like a cat. He got him up so in the matter of ketching flies, and kep' him in practice so constant, that he'd nail a fly every time as fur as he could see him. Smiley said all a frog wanted was education, and he could do 'most anything—and I believe him. Why, I've seen him set Dan'l Webster down here on this floor—Dan'l Webster was the name of the frog—and sing out, "Flies, Dan'l, flies!" and quicker'n you could wink he'd spring straight up and snake a fly off 'n the counter there, and flop down on the floor ag'in as solid as a gob of mud, and fall to scratching the side of his head with his hind foot as indifferent as if he hadn't no idea he'd been doin' any more'n any frog might do. You never see a frog so modest and straightfor'ard as he was, for all he was so gifted. And when it come to fair and square jumping on a dead level, he could get over more ground at one straddle than any animal of his breed you ever

7. **rat terriers** dogs skilled in catching rats.
8. **chicken cocks** roosters trained to fight.

22 ▲ Critical Viewing
Which moment of the story is depicted in this illustration? **[Connect]**

Literary Analysis
Humor What exaggerations in this passage make the description funnier?

24
What was most unusual about Smiley and his betting habits?

22 Critical Viewing
Answer: Students may say that the illustration shows the defeat of Dan'l by the stranger's frog.

23 Literary Analysis
Humor
1. Invite a student volunteer to read the passage aloud as other students jot down Twain's humorous exaggerations.
2. **Ask** students the Literary Analysis question.
   Answer: Students might mention details such as "he done nothing for three months," "whirling in the air like a doughnut," "turn one summerset," "come down flatfooted," "nail a fly every time," and "all a frog wanted was education."

24 Reading Check
Answer: He would wager on anything and often won unlikely bets, such as the ones on the mare and the dog named Andrew Jackson.

Differentiated Instruction for Universal Access

Strategy for Less Proficient Readers

Humor can be the driving force of a story. It can also be subtle and coy, teasing the reader just enough to lighten the mood of the story or to break up a long narrative paragraph. Either way, humor provides added enjoyment when reading. Help students recognize the humorous elements in Twain's writing, from his creation of unique characters to his deadpan delivery of absurd statements. Entertainment is a valid purpose for reading, and many books are written primarily for this reason. Encourage students to read to be entertained, looking for the humorous elements in Twain's writing.

1. As you read this passage aloud, have students identify examples of Twain's use of dialect. If students need help focusing on the dialect, point out examples such as "git," "hopped off lively," "give a heave," "hysted up his shoulders," "warn't no use," or "couldn't no more stir."

2. **Ask** students the following question: How does the use of dialect add to the humor of this passage?
   Answer: It grounds the characters—the stranger, the frog, and especially Smiley—in time and place, and it exaggerates aspects of their personalities or behaviors.

'IT MIGHT BE A **PARROT,** OR IT MIGHT BE A **CANARY,** MAYBE, BUT IT AIN'T—IT'S ONLY JUST A **FROG.'**

see. Jumping on a dead level was his strong suit, you understand; and when it come to that, Smiley would ante up money on him as long as he had a red.[9] Smiley was monstrous proud of his frog, and well he might be, for fellers that had traveled and been everywheres all said he laid over any frog that ever *they* see.

Well, Smiley kep' the beast in a little lattice box, and he used to fetch him downtown sometimes and lay for a bet. One day a feller—a stranger in the camp, he was—come acrost him with his box, and says:

'What might it be that you've got in the box?'

And Smiley says, sorter indifferent-like, 'It might be a parrot, or it might be a canary, maybe, but it ain't—it's only just a frog.'

And the feller took it, and looked at it careful, and turned it round this way and that, and says, 'H'm—so 'tis. Well, what's *he* good for?'

'Well,' Smiley says, easy and careless, 'he's good enough for *one* thing, I should judge—he can outjump any frog in Calaveras county.'

The feller took the box again, and took another long, particular look, and give it back to Smiley, and says, very deliberate, 'Well,' he says, 'I don't see no p'ints about that frog that's any better'n any other frog.'

'Maybe you don't,' Smiley says. 'Maybe you understand frogs and maybe you don't understand 'em; maybe you've had experience, and maybe you ain't only a amature, as it were. Anyways, I've got *my* opinion, and I'll resk forty dollars that he can outjump any frog in Calaveras county.'

And the feller studied a minute, and then says, kinder sad like, 'Well, I'm only a stranger here, and I ain't got no frog; but if I had a frog, I'd bet you.'

And then Smiley says, 'That's all right—that's all right—if you'll hold my box a minute, I'll go and get you a frog.' And so the feller took the box, and put up his forty dollars along with Smiley's, and set down to wait.

So he set there a good while thinking and thinking to hisself, and then he got the frog out and prized his mouth open and took a teaspoon and filled him full of quailshot[10]—filled him pretty near up to his chin—and set him on the floor. Smiley he went to the swamp and slopped around in the mud for a long time, and finally he ketched a frog, and fetched him in, and give him to this feller, and says:

25 'Now, if you're ready, set him alongside of Dan'l, with his forepaws just even with Dan'l's, and I'll give the word.' Then he says, 'One—two—three—*git*!' and him and the feller touched up the frogs from behind, and the new frog hopped off lively, but Dan'l give a heave, and hysted up his shoulders—so—like a Frenchman, but it warn't no use—he couldn't budge; he was planted as solid as a church, and he couldn't no more stir than if he was anchored out. Smiley was a good

9. **a red** red cent; colloquial expression for "any money at all."
10. **quailshot** small lead pellets used for shooting quail.

580 Division, Reconciliation, and Expansion (1850–1914)

Vocabulary Development

Vocabulary Knowledge Rating
When students have completed reading and discussing the selections, have them take out their **Vocabulary Knowledge Rating** charts for the stories. Read the words aloud and have students rate their knowledge of words again in the After Reading column. Clarify any words that are still problematic. Have students write their own definitions and example or sentence in the appropriate column. Then have students complete the Vocabulary Lesson at the end of the selection. Encourage students to use the words in further discussion and written work about the selection. Remind them that they will be accountable for these words on the **Selection Test,** *Unit 3 Resources,* pages 144–146 or 147–149.

deal surprised, and he was disgusted too, but he didn't have no idea what the matter was, of course.

The feller took the money and started away; and when he was going out at the door, he sorter jerked his thumb over his shoulder—so—at Dan'l, and says again, very deliberate, 'Well,' he says, 'I don't see no p'ints about that frog that's any better'n any other frog.'

Smiley he stood scratching his head and looking down at Dan'l a long time, and at last he says, 'I do wonder what in the nation that frog throw'd off for—I wonder if there ain't something the matter with him—he 'pears to look mighty baggy, somehow.' And he ketched Dan'l by the nap of the neck, and hefted him, and says, 'Why blame my cats if he don't weigh five pound!' and turned him upside down and he belched out a double handful of shot. And then he see how it was, and he was the maddest man—he set the frog down and took out after that feller, but he never ketched him. And—"

Here Simon Wheeler heard his name called from the front yard, and got up to see what was wanted. And turning to me as he moved away, he said: "Just set where you are, stranger, and rest easy—I ain't going to be gone a second."

But, by your leave, I did not think that a continuation of the history of the enterprising vagabond *Jim* Smiley would be likely to afford me much information concerning the Rev. *Leonidas W.* Smiley, and so I started away.

At the door I met the sociable Wheeler returning, and he button-holed me and recommenced:

"Well, thish-yer Smiley had a yaller one-eyed cow that didn't have no tail, only just a short stump like a bannanner, and—"

However, lacking both time and inclination, I did not wait to hear about the afflicted cow, but took my leave.

Critical Reading

© 1. **Key Ideas and Details (a)** What prompts Simon Wheeler to tell the story of Jim Smiley? **(b) Infer:** Why had the narrator's friend suggested that he ask Wheeler about Leonidas Smiley?

© 2. **Key Ideas and Details (a)** What was Jim Smiley's response to any event? **(b) Infer:** Based on this behavior, what can you infer about his character?

© 3. **Integration of Knowledge and Ideas** What image of America do both the excerpt from Twain's memoir and this comic story paint? Consider the sense of place, character, and event. In your response, use at least two of these Essential Question words: *adventure, individualism, sincerity, ambition. [Connecting to the Essential Question: What makes American literature American?]*

Cite textual evidence to support your responses.

Concept Connector

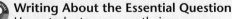

Reading Skill Graphic Organizer
Ask students to review the graphic organizers that they used to rephrase regional dialect into Standard English. Then have students share their organizers and compare their interpretations of regional dialect.

Activating Prior Knowledge
Have students return to their responses to the Activating Prior Knowledge activity. Ask them to explain whether their thoughts have changed and if so, how.

Writing About the Essential Question
Have students compare their responses to the prompt before they completed reading these selections with their thoughts after reading them. Have them work individually or in groups, writing or discussing their thoughts, to define their new responses. Then lead a class discussion, probing for what students have learned that confirms or invalidates their initial thoughts. Encourage students to cite specific textual details to support their responses.

---

26 Reading Strategy
Clarifying and Interpreting Language

1. Have a student volunteer read the bracketed paragraph. **Ask** students what sort of mood Smiley is in at this moment.
   Answer: He is perplexed and concerned about the frog's failure to perform.

2. Point out that in this state Smiley uses slang expressions that might be difficult to understand or to readily "translate." Elicit from students that one such phrase is "blame my cats." Then **ask** the Reading Strategy question.
   Sample answer: He caught Daniel by the nape of the neck and lifted him. He said, "Why, I'll be darned! He weighs five pounds!" He turned the frog upside down and Daniel belched out a double handful of shot.

ASSESS
Answers

Before students respond, you may wish to have them write a brief objective summary of the selection. As they answer the questions below, remind them to support their answers with evidence from the text.

1. (a) The narrator's friend suggests that he ask about a friend with the same last name. (b) The narrator now suspects that his friend knew that Wheeler would tell the story of Jim Smiley.

2. (a) He would bet on anything and everything. (b) **Possible response:** He is a comic, exaggerated character.

3. **Possible response:** Twain's memoir demonstrates the strong <u>ambition</u> of the young people of his time to expand their horizons by finding work that allows them to leave their homes. The characters in his comic story illustrate the <u>individualism</u> that feeds the sense of <u>adventure</u> of the American people of Twain's day.

581

Answers

1. Twain's overstated description adds humor by showing through contrast how foolish some of his childhood ambitions were.

2. (a) Twain portrays life in a small river town. (b) Humor allows him to offer a truthful and affectionate impression of life, avoiding sentimentality.

3. (a) The narrator is brisk and businesslike; Wheeler takes his time. (b) The reader senses the narrator's growing impatience.

4. **Sample answer:** Hyperbole: The bull pup's teeth shine like furnaces. What Is Exaggerated: The dog's fearsome look. Why It Is Amusing: It makes the little dog appear monstrous.

5. (a) The use of dialect underscores the exaggerated qualities Twain gives to characters and situations. (b) The story would be less effective because the dialect adds humor, particularly to those moments when Wheeler is trying to be serious and straightforward.

6. (a) Wheeler's main activity is to place improbable bets. (b) Twain might be saying that not all people are trustworthy.

7. Students may say that Twain views the characters with more sympathy in "The Boys' Ambition," since that story involves people involved in honest, interesting work.

8. The image of Uncle Sam mourning suggests that Americans experienced Twain's death as a personal loss.

9. **Sample answer:** (a) Technical term: *labboard.* (b) The term refers to the left-hand side of a ship, and I clarified that information by consulting a footnote.

10. **Sample answer:** He appeared surprised and discouraged. He gave up the fight and was badly fooled.

582

COMMON CORE • EXTENDED STUDY: MARK TWAIN

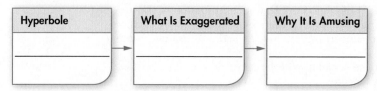

After You Read

from *Life on the Mississippi* •
The Notorious Jumping Frog of Calaveras County

Literary Analysis

C 1. Craft and Structure In the excerpt from *Life on the Mississippi*, how does Twain's use of the word *heavenly* to describe ordinary activities (shaking out a tablecloth or holding a rope) add to the **humor** of his narrative?

C 2. Craft and Structure **(a)** What place and way of life does Twain describe in the excerpt? **(b)** How does humor help Twain avoid sentimentality in dealing with this subject?

C 3. Craft and Structure **(a)** In "The Notorious Jumping Frog of Calaveras County," what basic **incongruity** exists between the narrator and Simon Wheeler? **(b)** How does this contrast add to the story's humor?

C 4. Craft and Structure Use a chart like the one shown to analyze two examples of **hyperbole** in "The Notorious Jumping Frog of Calaveras County."

Hyperbole	What Is Exaggerated	Why It Is Amusing

C 5. Craft and Structure **(a)** How does the use of **dialect** in "The Notorious Jumping Frog of Calaveras County" add to the story's humor? **(b)** Why would the story be less effective if Wheeler spoke in Standard English?

C 6. Key Ideas and Details **(a)** What is Wheeler's main activity in "The Notorious Jumping Frog…"? **(b)** What **social commentary** about this activity might Twain be making through humor?

7. **Integration of Knowledge and Ideas** In which selection does Twain view the characters' foibles, or weaknesses, with more sympathy? Explain.

8. **Analyze Visual Information** What does this drawing, made after Twain's death, show about his place in American culture?

Reading Strategy

9. In the excerpt from *Life on the Mississippi*, the narrator—the older Twain—peppers his account with steamboat terminology. **(a)** Identify two examples of this use of *technical language*. **(b)** Explain what each example means and how you **clarify** that information.

10. **Interpret** the regional dialect in this passage by "translating" it into modern Standard English: *…he 'peared surprised, and then he looked sorter discouraged-like, and didn't try no more to win the fight, and so he got shucked out bad.*

582 Division, Reconciliation, and Expansion (1850–1914)

Common Core State Standards

Language

4. Determine or clarify the meaning of unknown and multiple-meaning words and phrases based on *grades 11–12 reading and content*, choosing flexibly from a range of strategies. (p. 583)

4.b. Identify and correctly use patterns of word changes that indicate different meanings or parts of speech. (p. 583)

4.c. Consult general and specialized reference materials, both print and digital, to determine or clarify the precise meaning of a word. (p. 583)

5. Demonstrate understanding of word relationships and nuances in word meanings. (p. 583)

5.b. Analyze nuances in the meanings of words with similar denotations. (p. 583)

THERE IS A TIME TO LAUGH AN[D]
THERE IS A TIME TO WEEP

Assessment Practice

Context (For more practice, see *All-in-One Workbook*.)

Many tests require students to use contextual analysis to determine the meaning of figurative expressions. Use the following sample test item to demonstrate.

> I went meekly aboard a few of the boats that lay <u>packed together like sardines</u> at the long St. Louis wharf, and very humbly inquired for the pilots, but got only a cold shoulder and short words from mates and clerks.

In this passage, the expression "packed together like sardines" means—

A The boats were docked closely together.

B The boats had been fishing for sardines.

C The boats were made of metal like tins for sardines.

D The boats were packed with passengers.

A is the correct answer.

Integrated Language Skills

© Vocabulary Acquisition and Use

Word Analysis: Greek Prefix *mono-*

The Greek prefix *mono-* means "alone," "one," or "single." A *monotonous* storyteller, therefore, uses a single tone, without varying volume or pace. Likewise, a *monosyllabic* word is made up of one syllable, and a *monocle* is a form of eyeglass with only one lens. Add the prefix *mono-* to each word root listed below. Using your understanding of the prefix and the definition of each root, tell the meaning of each newly created word.

1. *theism* = belief in a god or gods
2. *logue* = speech; speaking
3. *lith* = stone
4. *syllable* = unit of sound

Which of the new words best describes Simon Wheeler's tale? Explain.

Using Resources to Build Vocabulary

Funny Business: Words for Overstating the Case

Twain infuses his prose with humor by using overblown words to describe common feelings, experiences, and situations. Here are a few of them:

glorious	heavenly
fragrant	tranquil
grandeur	transcendent

Return to Twain's stories to review these words in context. Then, *use a print or an electronic thesaurus* to find a less inflated synonym for each one. (For example, a milder synonym for *glorious* might be *bright*.) On your own paper, rewrite the sentence in which the word appears by replacing the word with the deflated synonym. Read over your new lines, and, in a sentence or two, explain why they are less amusing than Twain's originals.

Vocabulary: Antonyms

Antonyms are words with opposite or nearly opposite meanings. Review the words in the vocabulary list on page 569. Then, select the letter of the word in the right column that is the best antonym for each vocabulary word in the left column. Explain your answers.

1. transient	a. varied
2. prodigious	b. meager
3. eminence	c. quiet
4. garrulous	d. permanent
5. conjectured	e. verified
6. monotonous	f. obscurity
7. interminable	g. brief

Integrated Language Skills **583**

Answers

Vocabulary Acquisition and Use

1. Introduce the skill, using the instruction on the student page.
2. Have students complete the Word Analysis activity and the Vocabulary practice.

Word Analysis

1. *monotheism:* belief in a single god
2. *monologue:* a long speech made by a single speaker
3. *monolith:* a large stone that stands by itself
4. *monosyllable:* a word of one syllable

Simon Wheeler's tale is a monologue, an extended speech given by a single speaker.

Vocabulary

1. d. Something permanent remains in one place; something <u>transient</u> moves around.
2. b. A <u>prodigious</u> thing is dominant; a meager thing is not.
3. f. <u>Eminence</u> is prominence; obscurity is vagueness.
4. c. Someone who is <u>garrulous</u> is talkative, not quiet.
5. e. <u>Conjectured</u> means "guessed"; verified means "confirmed."
6. a. <u>Monotonous</u> means "without diversity"; varied means "diverse."
7. g. Something <u>interminable</u> seems to go on forever; something brief takes little time.

Using Resources to Build Vocabulary

Sample Answers

- . . . the day was <u>wonderful</u> with expectancy.
- I can picture the <u>odorous</u> town drunkard . . .
- . . . a husbanded <u>richness</u> created with a bit of pitch pine . . .
- . . .they were too <u>enjoyable</u> to be contemplated as real possibilities.
- . . . it diffused a <u>calm</u> contentment among us.
- . . . as men of <u>boundless</u> genius in *finesse.*

The milder synonyms diminish the hyperbole and incongruity.

Writing

1. To guide students in writing this essay, give them the **Support for Writing Lesson** page (*Unit 3 Resources*, p. 139).

2. Work with students to develop guidelines for their analytical essays, based on the assignment. The guidelines may include the following:

- The essay should include the Twain quotation in the proper format and with correct punctuation.

- The introduction to the quotation should explain which aspect of the definition is being illustrated.

- The essay should explain the connection between the passage and Twain's deinition.

- The essay should explain the writer's own insights about humor and an assessment of Twain's definition.

- Students should use a graphic organizer or chart to gather details and organize their thoughts.

- Students' analytical essays may be assessed using the developed guidelines. You may also use the **Rubrics for Critiques**, in *Professional Developement Guidebook*, pages 276–277.

Writing

Expository Text In the essay excerpted on page 575, Twain defines some of the elements that contribute to a humorous story:

> *The humorous story may be spun out to great length, and may wander around as much as it pleases, and arrive nowhere in particular. . . . [It] is told gravely; the teller does his best to conceal the fact that he even dimly suspects there is anything funny about it.*

Write an **essay** in which you analyze Twain's application of these techniques in his own story "The Notorious Jumping Frog of Calaveras County." Include in your analysis an evaluation of Twain's definition. Determine whether his definition is universal—true in most times and places—or true only in Twain's day and age.

Prewriting Select several humorous passages from the story to analyze according to the main ideas in Twain's definition. Use a chart like the one shown to organize your thoughts.

Model: Organizing to Show Comparison

spins out at length	arrives nowhere	is told gravely	conceals humor

Drafting Organize your essay point by point, connecting Twain's definition to passages from the story. For each passage, do the following:

- Introduce the passage by indicating which aspect of the definition it will illustrate.

- Provide the passage in the form of a quotation. Introduce shorter passages with a colon, and enclose them in quotation marks. Set longer passages off from the text. Include a parenthetical page reference after each quotation.

- Explain the connection between the passage and Twain's definition. Strengthen your analysis by adding your own insights about how and why a certain technique creates humor.

Conclude your draft with an assessment of Twain's definition. To end the essay on a lively note, consider imitating Twain's style or otherwise injecting your own variety of respectful humor.

Revising Review your essay to find ideas that you can support more effectively with additional examples, details, or quotations. Return to your notes or to the story to find additional supporting evidence.

584 Division, Reconciliation, and Expansion (1850–1914)

Common Core State Standards

Writing

2. Write explanatory texts to examine and convey complex ideas, concepts, and information clearly and accurately through the effective selection, organization, and analysis of content.

2.a. Introduce a topic; organize complex ideas, concepts, and information so that each new element builds on that which precedes it to create a unified whole.

2.b. Develop the topic thoroughly by selecting the most significant and relevant facts, extended definitions, concrete details, quotations, or other information and examples appropriate to the audience's knowledge of the topic.

2.f. Provide a concluding statement or section that follows from and supports the information or explanation presented.

Language

1. Demonstrate command of the conventions of standard English grammar and usage when writing or speaking. (*p. 585*)

Teaching Resources

The following resources can be used to enrich or extend the instruction.

Unit 3 Resources

- **L3 L4** Vocabulary Builder, p. 137
- **L3 L4** Support for Writing Lesson, p. 139.
- **L3 L4** Grammar and Style, p. 138
- **L4** Enrichment, p. 140

All Enriched Online Student Edition
Interactive Grammar Tutorial: available under After You Read for this selection
Internet Research Activity: available under After You Read for this selection

Professional Developement Guidebook
Rubrics for Critiques, pp. 276–277

PHLit Online! All resources are available at www.PHLitOnline.com.

584

Conventions and Style: Fixing Misplaced and Dangling Modifiers

A **misplaced modifier** seems to modify the wrong word in a sentence because it is too far away from the word it really modifies. A **dangling modifier** seems to modify the wrong word or no word at all because the word it *should* modify is not in the sentence. Misplaced and dangling modifiers can be single words, phrases, or clauses. Your writing will be clearer if you avoid misplaced and dangling modifiers.

Misplaced: *Disappointed*, the riverboat captain ignored the boy.
Fixed: The riverboat captain ignored the disappointed boy.

Misplaced: Twain's adventures inspired a number of books *in foreign countries*.
Fixed: Twain's adventures in foreign countries inspired a number of books.

Dangling: *Full of quailshot*, jumping was impossible.
Fixed: Full of quailshot, the frog could not jump.

Dangling: *While working as a journalist*, an entertaining writing style developed.
Fixed: While working as a journalist, Twain developed an entertaining writing style.

TIP Dangling modifiers most often appear as introductory phrases or clauses.

Practice Rewrite each sentence to fix the misplaced or dangling modifier and make the sentence clear. You may have to change the wording slightly. In items 1–5, the misplaced or dangling modifier is in italics.

1. The frog *only* lost one race.
2. The pup would grab the other dog *to win the fight* by the hind leg.
3. *Determined*, Twain's plan was to work on a steamboat.
4. *Eager to make a bet*, Smiley's frog is left with the stranger.
5. *After his wife's death*, pessimism overcame Mark Twain.
6. The young men were talking about their future jobs on steamboats yesterday.
7. Having found a second frog, the jumping contest was started.
8. Clemens met many characters that he would write about later as a boy.
9. Assembled at the wharf, their eyes were fixed on the handsome steamboat.
10. The boy would become a writer who dreamed of piloting a riverboat.

© **Writing and Speaking Conventions**

A. Writing For each numbered item, write a sentence using the phrase or clause as a modifier. Then, tell what word or words the phrase or clause modifies.

1. near the Mississippi River
2. who envied him
3. gone for a long time
4. placing his bet

Example: near the Mississippi River
Sentence: As a boy, Clemens lived near the Mississippi River.
Word Modified: lived

B. Speaking Describe an occupation you dream of having. Correctly use at least three different types of modifiers.

> **PH WRITING COACH**
> Further instruction and practice are available in *Prentice Hall Writing Coach*.

Integrated Language Skills **585**

Extend the Lesson

Sentence Modeling

Write the following sentence on the board:

> *When I was a boy, there was but one permanent ambition among my comrades in our village on the west bank of the Mississippi River.* (from *Life on the Mississippi*)

Point out that the sentence uses phrases as modifiers. Have students identify the modifiers and match each one with the word or phrase it modifies. (<u>Among my comrades</u> modifies <u>was</u>, <u>in our village</u> modifies <u>comrades</u>, <u>on the west bank</u> modifies <u>village</u>, and <u>of the Mississippi River</u> modifies <u>bank</u>.) Then, have them rewrite the sentence with the modifiers placed elsewhere and explain how these changes in position alter the meaning of the sentence. Then have students imitate the sentence in a sentence on a topic of their own choosing, matching the grammatical and stylistic feature discussed. Collect the sentences and share them with the class.

Answers

Conventions and Style

Introduce and discuss the skill, using the instruction on the student page.

Practice
Sample Answers

1. The frog lost <u>only</u> one race.
2. <u>To win the fight</u>, the pup would grab the other dog by the hind leg.
3. The <u>determined</u> Twain planned to work on a steamboat.
4. <u>Eager to make a bet</u>, Smiley left his frog with the stranger.
5. <u>After his wife's death</u>, Mark Twain was overcome by pessimism.
6. <u>Yesterday</u> the young men were talking about their future jobs on steamboats.
7. <u>Having found a second frog</u>, Smiley started the jumping contest.
8. <u>As a boy</u>, Clemens met many characters that he would write about later.
9. <u>Assembled at the wharf</u>, they fixed their eyes on the handsome steamboat.
10. The boy <u>who dreamed of piloting a riverboat</u> would become a writer.

Writing and Speaking Conventions

A. Sample Answers

1. Twain's hometown <u>near the Mississippi River</u> is now a major tourist attraction. Modifies *hometown*
2. The boy got a job on the river and was taunted by other boys <u>who envied him</u>. Modifies *boys*
3. Smiley was <u>gone for a long time</u>, so the stranger took advantage of him. Modifies *Smiley*
4. <u>Placing his bet</u>, Smiley felt lucky. Modifies *Smiley*

B. Sample Answers

<u>Ever since I was young</u> I have dreamed of being an airline pilot. <u>During a flight</u>, I always imagine what the pilot is doing. <u>Curious about this career</u>, I have started researching opportunities in aviation.

> **PH WRITING COACH** | Grade 11

Students will find additional information on modifiers in Chapter 16.

❶ **School of American Humor**

School of American Humor

1. Before students read "School of American Humor," tell them that the page simulates a student's course catalog, right down to a coffee stain and chewed pencil.

2. Tell students that all of the "professors" teaching the courses are famed for their verbal wit and humorous writing. Dorothy Parker, James Thurber, and S. J. Perelman are particularly known for their association with *The New Yorker* magazine; Erma Bombeck's humor columns were widely syndicated in American newspapers. Of the "professors" listed, Bill Bryson is the only writer still alive and working.

3. Have students read the course catalog, including the names listed near the top of the page. Invite students who are familiar with any of the writers or their works to share their knowledge with the class.

4. **Ask:** If you were starting your own school of humor, what professors—comedians, comic actors, humorous writers of the present day—would you put on your faculty?
Possible response: Students should list contemporary comic performers and writers that reflect their own tastes in humor.

"School" of American Humor

Mark Twain, President & Founder
Robert Benchley, Punster & Wordsmith
Dorothy Parker, Resident Wit
James Thurber, Fabulist
S. J. Perelman, Wry *Feuilletonist*
Russell Baker, Memoirist & Humorist
Art Buchwald, Political Satirist

Garrison Keillor, Storyteller
Bill Cosby, Comedian of Stage, Screen, and Print
Erma Bombeck, Humorous Housewife
Dave Barry, Humor Columnist
Bill Bryson, Backpacking Comic

"Semper Ridere"

COURSE CATALOGUE

Humor Writing 101
Dry Wit, Dialect, and Local Color
Prof. **Mark Twain**
Meets: M-W-F, 11:00–12:00 *4 credits*

Knowing your audience is the key to effective humor, and Prof. Twain shares his time-tested techniques in this required humor course. Learn to be an observer and develop a keen ear for speech to make your writing richer and funnier.

Humor Writing 102
Bon Mots, Biting Wit, and Blistering Sarcasm
Prof. **Dorothy Parker**
Meets: F 5:00–11:00 *4 credits*

If Oscar Wilde had an American sister, it would have been Prof. Parker. She'll teach you to write satirical fiction, brutal barbs and viciously funny poems. Wield wit as a weapon. Torpedo the double standard. Subvert the status quo. Students will emerge as seasoned professionals. "The most beautiful words in English," says Parker, "are 'check enclosed.'"

Humor Writing 103
Satire, Punch Lines, Cartoons, and Deadpan Delivery
Prof. **James Thurber**
Meets T-TH, 9:00 – 10:00 *4 credits*

Unlock the absurdity in your secret life. Prof. Thurber will show how writing about small, timid protagonists can earn you a whale of a reputation. Humor, as Prof. Thurber will demonstrate, is emotional chaos remembered in tranquility. This is his class and welcome to it.

586

Humor Writing 104
Humorous Sketches and Absurdist Screenplays
Prof. **S. J. Perelman**
Meets: W 2:00–5:00 *4 credits*

Feuilletons is a French literary term meaning "little leaves." Prof. Perelman shows how he produces his *feuilletons*—brief, amusing sketches for *The New Yorker*. On the syllabus: making wry observations, tossing up non-sequiturs, infusing everyday events with irony, and writing absurdist screenplays a la *Horsefeathers* and *Monkey Business*.

Humor Writing 105
Hyperbole and Screwball Characters
Prof. **Erma Bombeck**
Meets: M-W-F 10:00–11:00 *4 credits*

Learn how to turn mundane household chores into comic opera for a newspaper column. Master screwball characters, down-home hyperbole, and the self-deprecating voice. Prof. Bombeck will show you how to make outrageous claims—such as, "Motherhood is the second oldest profession," —without bursting your own balloon.

Humor Writing 106
Anthropology, Incongruity, and Human Foibles
Prof. **Bill Bryson**
Meets: T-TH 9:00–11:00 *4 credits*

If you look at your own backyard and see an exhibit on alien culture, you may have what it takes to become a best-selling author. After Prof. Bryson leads you on a tour of Main Street USA, it will never seem quite the same again. His tools of the trade include regional detail, hyperbole, embellishment, and comic characters. Wear your walking shoes.

Comparing Literary Works

Mark Twain's Writings • from *The Life and Times of the Thunderbolt Kid*

Common Core State Standards

- Reading Literature 9.a
- Reading Informational Text 4
- Writing 2, 2.b
- Language 4.c, 5.a

❷ Comparing American Humor Past and Present

Writing Humor American humor writing falls roughly into two categories: the refined, moral wit of figures such as Benjamin Franklin and Washington Irving; and the folk humor, or "humor of the people," of writers such as Mark Twain and contemporary writer **Bill Bryson.** While the first type of humor is characterized by a subtle, high-minded cleverness, the second makes use of more obvious humorous devices, including the following:

- **hyperbole:** the exaggeration of details or embellishment of events
- **incongruity:** elements that seem not to fit their context
- **regionalism:** language or behaviors specific to a certain part of the country
- **foibles:** a focus on human flaws

When used in conjunction with everyday subject matter, such as making a bet or cooking dinner, these elements produce snapshots of real life that are familiar, funny, and revealing of larger ideas about human nature.

Like Mark Twain, Bill Bryson began his career as a journalist; also like Twain, Bryson used his observational skills in humorous works on a wide range of subjects, including travel. Both authors deal in the humor of the everyday—the amusing aspects of regular folks trying to live in a world that is anything but "regular." Use the following chart to compare and contrast Twain's and Bryson's humor.

Humorous Device	Twain	Bryson
hyperbole	describes an apprentice engineer as an "exalted…eminence"	
regional elements	Simon Wheeler's dialect	
comic characters	the "trapped" narrator of "The Notorious Jumping Frog…"	

❸ © Gather Vocabulary Knowledge

Bryson uses related forms of the words *explode, perish,* and *recoil* to relate his early experiences with food. Use print or online glossaries and other references to explore these words.

- **Related References**: Using an etymology guide or vocabulary builder, learn more about each word's origin and meaning. Select one word and build a word map for it that includes synonyms, antonyms, and examples of use in sentences.
- **Glossaries:** Refer to the glossary of a cookbook and find three verbs that normally apply to cooking processes. Use the words in a paragraph.

www.PHLitOnline.com

Mark Twain's Writings • *from* The Life and Times of the Thunderbolt Kid **587**

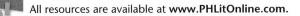

Common Core State Standards

Reading Informational Text
4. Determine the meaning of words and phrases as they are used in a text, including figurative and connotative meanings.

Language
4.c. Consult general and specialized reference materials, both print and digital, to find the pronunciation of a word or determine or clarify its precise meaning, its part of speech, its etymology, or its standard usage.

5.a. Interpret figures of speech in context and analyze their role in the text.

❷ Comparing American Humor Past and Present

1. Introduce American humor, using the instruction on the student page.

2. Encourage students to use a chart similar to the one shown to record examples of Bryson's hyperbole, regional elements, and comic characters.

Think Aloud: Model the Skill

Say to students:

When reading a good piece of humorous writing, I enjoy a writer's depiction of human foibles as much as the next person. But a part of me asks: Do I know anyone like that? Am *I* ever like that?

Asking those questions doesn't kill my enjoyment: I laugh as much as ever. These questions do make the silliest situation more real and relevant to me. I think the questions get me closer to knowing why the writer presents the foibles in the first place.

❸ Gather Vocabulary Knowledge

Have print and online resources, including a thesaurus and several cookbooks with glossaries, available for students as they build their word maps and develop their paragraphs. Demonstrate for students how to use the resources to find synonyms, antonyms, and example sentences. For example, show students how to use the index of a cookbook or find a passage of the book that uses one of their verbs in a sentence.

Teaching Resources

The following resources can be used to enrich, extend, or differentiate the instruction.

All *Unit 3 Resources,* pp. 150–152

All *Enriched Online Student Edition*

All *Common Core Companion,* pp. 75–81, 123–135, 196–207, 324–331, 332–335

All resources are available at **www.PHLitOnline.com.**

❹ Background

More About the Author

After the harrowing diet of his Des Moines boyhood, Bill Bryson has elected to live in England most of the time; perhaps it is the English cuisine that holds him. Despite his nonresident status, Bryson frequently writes about American subjects and settings. Writing about America while living in England may give Bryson an essential critical distance that sharpens his comic perspective.

❹ Bill Bryson *(b. 1951)*

Author of *The Life and Times of the Thunderbolt Kid: A Memoir*

Bill Bryson was born and raised in Des Moines, Iowa, where his father was a sports writer and his mother a home furnishings editor for the daily newspaper the *Des Moines Register*. Bryson's two older siblings had left home by the time he was a teenager, and his busy parents granted Bryson a great deal of freedom: On any given evening he might be given five dollars and told to eat out and catch a movie. This lifestyle suited Bryson, who has led what he describes as a "rootless" life ever since.

Back and Forth In 1972, Bryson abandoned his studies at Drake University in order to spend four months backpacking through Europe. The following year, he returned to England for a longer stay. While working in a psychiatric hospital near London, Bryson met his wife, a nurse. The couple returned to the United States in order for Bryson to complete his college degree. They crossed the Atlantic yet again, settled in northern England, and stayed put for almost twenty years before moving back to the United States in 1995. After eight years in New Hampshire, the couple returned to England, where they remain.

Word Wanderings During his early years in Britain, Bryson worked as a journalist. The work left him restless, though, and he retired from journalism in 1987. Bryson's first book, *The Lost Continent*, appeared two years later. True to its author's ambling spirit, the book describes a visit to the United States—38 of them, to be exact—in search of the perfect American small town. Subsequent books have ranged across the globe and across a wide spectrum of subjects, including travels in Europe, hiking the Appalachian Trail, British culture, the history of the English language, the history of science, and the life of William Shakespeare.

Looking Back Bryson's memoir, *The Life and Times of the Thunderbolt Kid*, is a portrait of his childhood that also provides insight into the stuff of Bryson's humor, which he finds in our chaotic daily lives, in our oddball habits, in those forgotten containers at the backs of our refrigerators. Bryson admits that the memoir is also a kind of lament for the loss of our collective innocence. If you were a kid in the 1950s, he reflects, "You really did expect, any day, that we'd all have jet-packs or be going on vacation to Mars. . . . And now that's completely gone."

from

The Life and Times of the Thunderbolt Kid

Bill Bryson

THE ONLY DOWNSIDE of my mother's working was that it put a little pressure on her with regard to running the home and particularly with regard to dinner, which frankly was not her strong suit anyway. My mother always ran late and was dangerously forgetful into the bargain. You soon learned to stand aside about ten to six every evening, for it was then that she would fly in the back door, throw something in the oven, and disappear into some other quarter of the house to

from The Life and Times of the Thunderbolt Kid **589**

TEACH

① About the Selection

In this excerpt from his comic memoir *The Life and Times of the Thunderbolt Kid,* Bill Bryson gives hyperbole a strenuous workout. By detailing the cooking practices and dietary preferences in his childhood home, Bryson produces hilarious insights into a specific time and place in the United States.

② Activating Prior Knowledge

Ask students to silently consider their food preferences. What kinds of food do they like, dislike, never try? After students have thought about their preferences, initiate a discussion by asking: Do you think that your tastes and preferences in food reveal something important about your personality or character? Why or why not?

After discussion, tell students to read Bryson's memoir to see how he uses food preferences to help readers understand his unusual family.

❸ Comparing American Humor

Foibles

1. Read aloud the bracketed passage describing the mother's preparation of the family dinner. You may wish to note that Bryson's mother was exceptional in the 1950s for working outside the home while also being a homemaker.

2. **Ask:** How does the Bryson family know when dinner is ready?
Answer: The sound of potatoes exploding in the oven signals that it is time to eat.

3. Remind students that a foible is a personal weakness or shortcoming that is often found amusing by others. Then **ask** students: What foibles does the mother seem to demonstrate in this passage?
Possible response: Students may say that the mother seems chronically disorganized, forgetful, and unable to prepare a meal without burning it.

❹ Critical Viewing

Answer: The tasteful, genteel, and orderly lifestyle depicted in the magazines is utterly unlike the frantic mess of the Bryson household.

Vocabulary
embark (em bärk´) v. to begin a venture, project, or activity

❹ ▲ **Critical Viewing**
How does the lifestyle presented in magazines like these compare to the realities of Bryson's household? **[Compare]**

embark on the thousand other household tasks that greeted her each evening. In consequence she nearly always forgot about dinner until a point slightly beyond way too late. As a rule you knew it was time to eat when you could hear potatoes exploding in the oven.

We didn't call it the kitchen in our house. We called it the Burns Unit.

"It's a bit burned," my mother would say apologetically at every meal, presenting you with a piece of meat that looked like something—a much-loved pet perhaps—salvaged from a tragic house fire. "But I think I scraped off most of the burned part," she would add, overlooking that this included every bit of it that had once been flesh.

Happily, all this suited my father. His palate only responded to two tastes—burned and ice cream—so everything suited him so long as it was sufficiently dark and not too startlingly flavorful.

Theirs truly was a marriage made in heaven, for no one could burn food like my mother or eat it like my dad.

As part of her job, my mother bought stacks of housekeeping magazines—*House Beautiful, House & Garden, Better Homes and Gardens, Good Housekeeping*—and I read these with a certain avidity, partly because they were always lying around and in our house all idle moments were spent reading something, and partly because they depicted lives so absorbingly at variance with our own. The housewives in my mother's magazines were so collected, so organized, so calmly on top of things, and their food was perfect—their *lives* were perfect. They dressed up to take their food out of the oven! There were no black circles on the ceiling above their stoves, no mutating goo climbing over the sides of their forgotten saucepans. Children didn't have to be ordered to stand back every time they opened *their* oven doors. And their foods—baked Alaska, lobster Newburg, chicken cacciatore—why, these were dishes we didn't even dream of, much less encounter, in Iowa.

Like most people in Iowa in the 1950s, we were more cautious eaters in our house.* On the rare occasions when we were presented with food with which we were not comfortable or familiar—on planes or trains or when invited to a meal cooked by someone who was not herself from Iowa—we tended to tilt it up carefully with a knife

---

* In fact, like most other people in America. The leading food writer of the age, Duncan Hines, author of the hugely successful *Adventures in Good Eating*, was himself a cautious eater and declared with pride that he never ate food with French names if he could possibly help it. Hines's other proud boast was that he did not venture out of America until he was seventy years old, when he made a trip to Europe. He disliked much of what he found there, especially the food.

Enrichment: Investigating Daily Life

Life in the 1950s

The 1950s in the United States has been stereotyped in the popular imagination as a bland decade in which nothing happened beyond the rearing of numerous children in idealized suburban households. Fathers wore suits and commuted to the office. Mothers remained at home to clean house in dresses and high heels. Teens went to sock hops on Friday nights, with ponytailed girls wearing poodle skirts and crew-cut boys wearing white socks with black shoes.

Activity: Multimedia Report Ask students to prepare a multimedia report on the 1950s that goes beyond the easy stereotypes. Suggest that they record information in the **Enrichment: Investigating Daily Life** worksheet, in *Professional Development Guidebook,* page 224. Budget time for students to present their reports to the class.

and examine it from every angle as if determining whether it might need to be defused. Once on a trip to San Francisco my father was taken by friends to a Chinese restaurant and he described it to us afterward in the somber tones of someone recounting a near-death experience.

"And they eat it with sticks, you know," he added knowledgeably.

"Goodness!" said my mother.

"I would rather have gas gangrene than go through that again," my father added grimly.

In our house we didn't eat

- pasta, rice, cream cheese, sour cream, garlic, mayonnaise, onions, corned beef, pastrami, salami, or foreign food of any type, except French toast
- bread that wasn't white and at least 65 percent air
- spices other than salt, pepper, and maple syrup
- fish that was any shape other than rectangular and not coated in bright orange bread crumbs, and then only on Fridays and only when my mother remembered it was Friday, which in fact was not often
- soups not blessed by Campbell's and only a very few of those
- anything with dubious regional names like "pone" or "gumbo," or foods that had at any time been an esteemed staple of slaves or peasants

All other foods of all types—curries, enchiladas, tofu, bagels, sushi, couscous, yogurt, kale, arugula, Parma ham, any cheese that was not a vivid bright yellow and shiny enough to see your reflection in—had either not yet been invented or was yet unknown to us. We really were radiantly unsophisticated. I remember being surprised to learn at quite an advanced age that a shrimp cocktail was not, as I had always imagined, a predinner alcoholic drink with a shrimp in it.

All our meals consisted of leftovers. My mother had a seemingly inexhaustible supply of foods that had already been to the table, sometimes repeatedly. Apart from a few perishable dairy products, everything in the fridge was older than I was, sometimes by many years. (Her oldest food possession of all, it more or less goes without saying, was a fruitcake that was kept in a metal tin and dated from the colonial period.) I can only assume that my mother did all of her cooking in the 1940s so that she could spend the rest of her life surprising herself with what she could find under cover at the back of the fridge. I never knew her to reject a food. The rule of thumb seemed to be that if you opened the lid and the stuff inside didn't make you actually recoil and take at least one staggered step backward, it was deemed okay to eat.

All of our meals consisted of leftovers.

Vocabulary
dubious (do͞o′ bē əs)
adj. questionable; suspicious

❼ ☑ Reading Check
Why was Bryson's parents' marriage "made in heaven"?

from The Life and Times of the Thunderbolt Kid **591**

Differentiated Instruction for Universal Access

Strategy for Less Proficient Readers
Students may have difficulty reading or recognizing some of the foods listed on this page. Read the lists of foods aloud to the class, asking students to raise their hands when they need clarification. If someone is completely unfamiliar with a particular food, ask a volunteer both what it is and, if possible, how it tastes or what more familiar food it resembles.

Enrichment for Gifted/Talented Students
It takes little effort to imagine Mark Twain writing a similar description of his family's odd dining habits, with hyperbole and incongruities and all. All that is lacking in Bryson's account is regional dialect. Ask students to rewrite a passage from Bryson's memoir as if it were being told by Simon Wheeler from Twain's "Jumping Frog" story. Suggest that students review Twain's story to renew their sense of Wheeler's style, rhythm, and word choice before they begin their rewrite.

---

❺ Comparing American Humor

Regionalism

1. Direct students to the bracketed passage. Be sure that students read the footnote about Duncan Hines as well.

2. **Ask:** What is the effect of Bryson's mention of "people in Iowa in the 1950s" and his footnoted reference to Duncan Hines?
   Possible response: Students may say that the effect is to enlarge the context of Bryson's humor, drawing Iowans and, with the Hines reference, Americans in general into his gentle mockery. Bryson is suggesting that his family's food preferences, odd as they may seem to modern readers, are not unlike those of most Iowans and most Americans in the 1950s.

❻ Comparing American Humor

Foibles

1. Review the bulleted list of foods that the Brysons never eat and the paragraph mentioning foods that are completely unknown to them.

2. Encourage students to share their own interactions with those foods. Of the foods that Bryson mentions, which do they enjoy? Which do they avoid? Can they imagine going a week without eating any of the items on Bryson's list?

3. After discussing food preferences in the Bryson household, give students three minutes to jot down lists of foods that they strongly dislike and foods they strongly prefer. Then **ask** students: If Bryson read your lists, do you think he would find them funny?
   Possible response: Students may be reluctant to concede that their personal food preferences would be amusing to others.

❼ Reading Check

Answer: The marriage was ideal because the wife always burned meals and the husband preferred burned food.

591

Hyperbole and Incongruity

1. Have students read the bracketed passage.

2. **Ask** students to find examples of hyperbole and incongruity in the passage.
   Answer: Hyperbole: a single leftover pea would be saved for another meal. Incongruity: the mother washed paper plates.

▶ **Monitor Progress: Ask** students why the claim that the family would save a single pea is hyperbole.
   Answer: A single pea is an insignificant amount of food. Claiming that the family saved even a leftover pea probably exaggerates their frugality.

▶ **Reteach:** If students have difficulty identifying or explaining hyperbole and incongruity, read the remainder of the paragraph as a class. Point out the detail of stealing sugar in packets as an example of hyperbole and the parents' "happiest moment" as an example of incongruity.

ASSESS

Answers

Before students respond, you may wish to have them write a brief objective summary of the selection. As they answer the questions below, remind them to support their answers with evidence from the text.

1. (a) The kitchen is called the Burns Unit. (b) The name shows that the family has a sense of humor about its own foibles.

2. (a) Bryson describes his family and Iowans in general as "cautious eaters" who rarely eat unfamiliar food. (b) This dietary caution suggests that life in Iowa in the 1950s was characterized by adherence to the familiar.

3. **Possible response:** Students may cite the burned meat resembling a pet salvaged from a house fire or the "mutating goo" on the sides of pans. These details are both vivid and funny.

4. (a) Bryson's tone seems both loving and amused. (b) **Sample answer:** Accept the oddness of your family; you might write a book about it.

592

My mother routinely washed and dried paper plates...

Both of my parents had grown up during the Great Depression and neither of them ever threw anything away if they could possibly avoid it. My mother routinely washed and dried paper plates, and smoothed out for reuse spare aluminum foil. If you left a pea on your plate, it became part of a future meal. All our sugar came in little packets spirited out of restaurants in deep coat pockets, as did our jams, jellies, crackers (oyster *and* saltine), tartar sauces, some of our ketchup and butter, all of our napkins, and a very occasional ashtray; anything that came with a restaurant table really. One of the happiest moments in my parents' life was when maple syrup started to be served in small disposable packets and they could add those to the household hoard.

Critical Reading

Cite textual evidence to support your responses.

© 1. **Key Ideas and Details (a)** What was the kitchen called in the Bryson house? **(b) Infer:** What does this name suggest about the family?

© 2. **Key Ideas and Details (a)** How does Bryson describe the eaters in his house—and in Iowa in the 1950s? **(b) Infer:** What does this attitude toward food tell you about other aspects of life in Iowa in the 1950s?

© 3. **Craft and Structure Evaluate:** Which word choices or descriptions do you think add most to the humor of this excerpt? Explain.

© 4. **Craft and Structure (a) Distinguish:** What tone, or attitude toward his subject, does Bryson take in this excerpt? **(b) Apply:** Keeping his attitude in mind, write a one-sentence rule for responding to exasperating situations.

After You Read

Mark Twain's Writings • from *The Life and Times of the Thunderbolt Kid*

Comparing Humor

1. Key Ideas and Details (a) What specific **regional** elements of place and time does Twain bring to light in *Life on the Mississippi*? **(b)** What specific place and time does Bryson bring to life? **(c)** What do the boys in these two different settings have in common?

2. Key Ideas and Details (a) Identify a **human foible,** or flaw, that is emphasized in Bryson's memoir. **(b)** Identify a foible Twain spotlights in one of his works. **(c)** For which foible do you have greater sympathy? Why?

3. Craft and Structure (a) Note one example each of **hyperbole** and **incongruity** in Bryson's memoir. **(b)** Identify one example of each of these devices in Twain's story "The Notorious Jumping Frog of Calaveras County." **(c)** Which examples do you find funnier? Explain.

Timed Writing

Explanatory Text: Essay

Stock characters, or character "types," are personalities that have become conventional in literature over time. The "overworked career woman" and the conniving trickster are both stock characters. Humor writers use character types to evoke laughter and sympathy and, sometimes, to critique society.

Assignment: Write a **compare-and-contrast** essay in which you examine two character "types" presented by Twain and Bryson. Prewrite by answering the questions listed below to generate ideas and focus your analysis.

- What aspects of each character suggest they are "types"?
- Why is each character funny? What makes each character sympathetic?

As you write, follow the conventions of a strong analytical essay:

- Analyze humorous nuances in the texts.
- Analyze the effects of each author's use of figurative language, such as hyperbole.

5-Minute Planner

Complete these steps before you begin to write.

1. Read the assignment carefully, noting key words and phrases.
2. Scan the selections, looking for details about your chosen characters. **TIP** Jot down details that support your interpretation in two columns, devoting one column to each character.
3. Create a rough outline for your essay.
4. Reread the prompt, and draft your essay.

Mark Twain's Writings • *from* The Life and Times of the Thunderbolt Kid **593**

Common Core State Standards

Writing

2. Write informative/explanatory texts to examine and convey complex ideas, concepts, and information clearly and accurately through the effective selection, organization, and analysis of content.

2.b. Develop the topic thoroughly by selecting the most significant and relevant facts, extended definitions, concrete details, quotations, or other information and examples appropriate to the audience's knowledge of the topic.

9.a. Apply *grades 11–12 Reading standards* to literature.

USE ACADEMIC VOCABULARY

As you write, use academic language, including the following words or their related forms:

compare
contrast
analyze
characterize

For more information about academic language, see the vocabulary charts in the introduction to this book.

Answers

Comparing Humor

1. **(a)** Twain evokes small-town life along the Mississippi River in the decades before the Civil War. **(b)** Bryson evokes family life in an Iowa household during the 1950s. **(c)** Both boys are observant of the details of their settings; both seem to have happy childhoods.

2. **Possible responses: (a)** Eccentric food preferences **(b)** Smiley's compulsion to bet on anything **(c)** Some students will have sympathy with the food foible because it may connect to their own experiences.

3. **Possible responses: (a)** The fruitcake dates to the colonial period. Incongruity: the father perfers burned food. **(b)** Twain's father can hang anyone that offends him. Incongruity: the town boys envy the boy on the boat for scrubbing a rusty bolt. **(c)** Some students may find the Bryson elements funnier because they might relate to their own experiences.

Timed Writing

1. Teach the Academic Vocabulary. Discuss the words and their related forms with students. Review with students the vocabulary they learned before reading the selection. Encourage students to use the words as appropriate in their discussion of stock characters.

2. Use these prompts to help students identify elements and qualities their compare-and-contrast essays should have:
   - A thesis statement about character types
   - Example characters that support the thesis statement
   - A discussion of the authors' use of figurative language in developing humorous character types
   - A logical organization that makes it easy to understand the similarities and differences in Twain's and Bryson's characters

Tell students they will have 40 minutes to plan and write the essay. Call students' attention to the 5-Minute Planner. Encourage students to budget their time to allow 5 minutes for outlining, 5 minutes for identifying some initial supporting text references in the works, and 10 minutes for revision and proofreading.

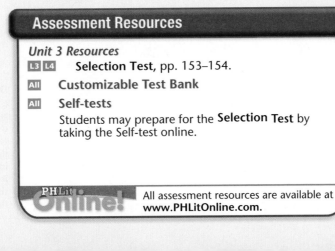

Assessment Resources

Unit 3 Resources

L3 L4 **Selection Test,** pp. 153–154.

All **Customizable Test Bank**

All **Self-tests**

Students may prepare for the **Selection Test** by taking the Self-test online.

PHLit Online! All assessment resources are available at **www.PHLitOnline.com.**

• To Build a Fire
Lesson Pacing Guide

DAY 1 Preteach

ⓒ Administer the Reading and Vocabulary Warm-ups (*Unit 3 Resources*, pp. 155–158) as necessary.

ⓒ Introduce the Literary Analysis concepts: Conflict, Setting, and Irony

• Introduce the Reading Strategy: Predict.

ⓒ Build background with the author and Background features.

• Develop thematic thinking with Connecting to the Essential Question.

ⓒ Teach the selection vocabulary.

DAYS 2–3 Preteach/Teach/Assess

• Distribute copies of the appropriate graphic organizer for the Reading Strategy (*Graphic Organizer Transparencies*, pp. 127–128).

• Distribute copies of the appropriate graphic organizer for Literary Analysis (*Graphic Organizer Transparencies*, pp. 129–130).

• Prepare students to read with the Activating Prior Knowledge activities (TE).

• Informally monitor comprehension while students read.

• Use the Reading Check question to confirm comprehension.

ⓒ Develop students' understanding of conflict, setting, and irony using the Literary Analysis prompts.

• Develop students' ability to predict using the Reading Strategy prompts.

ⓒ Reinforce vocabulary with the Vocabulary notes.

• Assess students' comprehension and mastery of the skills by having them answer the Critical Reading, Literary Analysis, and Reading Strategy questions.

ⓒ Have students complete the Vocabulary Lesson.

DAY 4 Extend/Assess

ⓒ Have students complete the Conventions and Style Lesson.

ⓒ Have students complete the Writing Lesson and write literary criticism. (You may assign as homework.)

• Administer Selection Test A or B (Unit 3 Resources, pp. 168–170 or 171–173).

ⓒ **Common Core
State Standards**

Reading Literature 3. Analyze the impact of the author's choices regarding how to develop and relate elements of a story or drama.
6. Analyze a case in which grasping a point of view requires distinguishing what is directly stated in a text from what is really meant.

Writing 1. Write arguments to support claims in an analysis of substantive topics or texts, using valid reasoning and relevant and sufficient evidence.

Language 1. Demonstrate command of the conventions of standard English grammar and usage when writing or speaking.
4.b. Identify and correctly use patterns of word changes that indicate different meanings or parts of speech.

Additional Standards Practice
***Common Core Companion**, pp. 28–35; 61–62; 185–195; 324–331*

Daily Block Scheduling
Each day in this Lesson Pacing Guide represents a 40–50 minute period. Teachers using block scheduling may combine days to revise pacing. In addition, teachers may differentiate and support core instruction by integrating components for extended and intensive support as students require. See the Guide to Selected Leveled Resources (facing page).

Guide to Selected Leveled Resources

R T I   Tier 1 (students performing on level)

To Build a Fire

Warm Up	Practice, model, and monitor fluency, working with the whole class or in groups.	Vocabulary and Reading Warm-ups B, *Unit 3 Resources,* pp. 155–156, 158
Comprehension/Skills	Support and monitor comprehension and skills development, having students complete the activities, graphic organizers, and interactive prompts independently or as a class.	• *Reader's Notebook,* adapted instruction and summary **EL** *Reader's Notebook: English Learner's Version,* adapted instruction and summary • **Reading Strategy Graphic Organizer B,** *Graphic Organizer Transparencies,* p. 128 • **Literary Analysis Graphic Organizer B,** *Graphic Organizer Transparencies,* p. 130
Monitor Progress	Monitor student progress with the differentiated curriculum-based assessment in the *Unit Resources.*	• **Selection Test B,** *Unit 3 Resources,* pp. 171–173 • **Open-Book Test,** *Unit 3 Resources,* pp. 165–167

R T I   Tier 2 (students requiring intervention)

To Build a Fire

Warm Up	Practice, model, and monitor fluency in groups or with individuals.	• **Vocabulary and Reading Warm-ups A,** *Unit 3 Resources,* pp. 168–170 • *Hear It!* Audio CD
Comprehension/Skills	• Support and monitor comprehension and skills development, working in small groups or with individuals. • As students complete the selection in the appropriate version of the *Reader's Notebook,* monitor comprehension frequently with group questions and individual instruction. • Model strategies while guiding students in completing the activities and prompts in the *Reader's Notebook,* as well as the graphic organizers. • Practice skills and monitor mastery with the *Reading Kit* worksheets.	• *Reader's Notebook: Adapted Version,* adapted instruction and summary **EL** *Reader's Notebook: English Learner's Version,* adapted instruction and summary • **Reading Strategy Graphic Organizer A,** *Graphic Organizer Transparencies,* p. 127 • **Literary Analysis Graphic Organizer A,** *Graphic Organizer Transparencies,* p. 129 • *Reading Kit,* Practice worksheets
Monitor Progress	Monitor student progress with the differentiated curriculum-based assessment in the *Unit Resources* and in the *Reading Kit.*	• **Selection Test A,** *Unit 3 Resources,* pp. 168–170 • *Reading Kit,* Assess worksheets

TIER 3 Tier 3 intervention may require consultation with the student's special-education or dyslexia specialist. For additional support, see the Tier 2 activities and resources listed above.

One-on-one teaching   Group work   Whole-class instruction   Independent work   A Assessment

For a complete guide to selection support, including support for Advanced students, see the Overview of Resources in the frontmatter.

• To Build a Fire

RESOURCES FOR:

L1 Special-Needs Students

L2 Below-Level Students (Tier 2)

L3 On-Level Students (Tier 1)

L4 Advanced Students (Tier 1)

EL English Learners

All All Students

Vocabulary/Fluency/Prior Knowledge

EL L1 L2 Reading Warm-ups A and B, pp. 157–158

Also available for these selections:

EL L1 L2 Vocabulary Warm-ups A and B, pp. 155–156

All Vocabulary Builder, p. 161

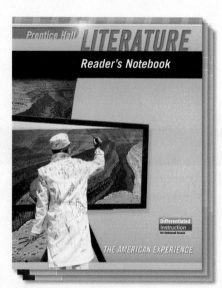

L2 L3 *Reader's Notebook*

L1 *Reader's Notebook: Adapted Version*

EL *Reader's Notebook: English Learner's Version*

EL *Reader's Notebook: Spanish Version*

Reader's Notebooks

Pre- and postreading pages for this selection appear in an interactive format in the *Reader's Notebooks.* Each *Notebook* is differentiated for a different group of learners.
The selections in the Adapted and English Learner's versions are abridged.

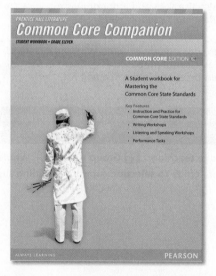

© *Common Core Companion*

Additional instruction and practice for each Common Core State Standard

Selection Support

Skills Development/Extension

Assessment

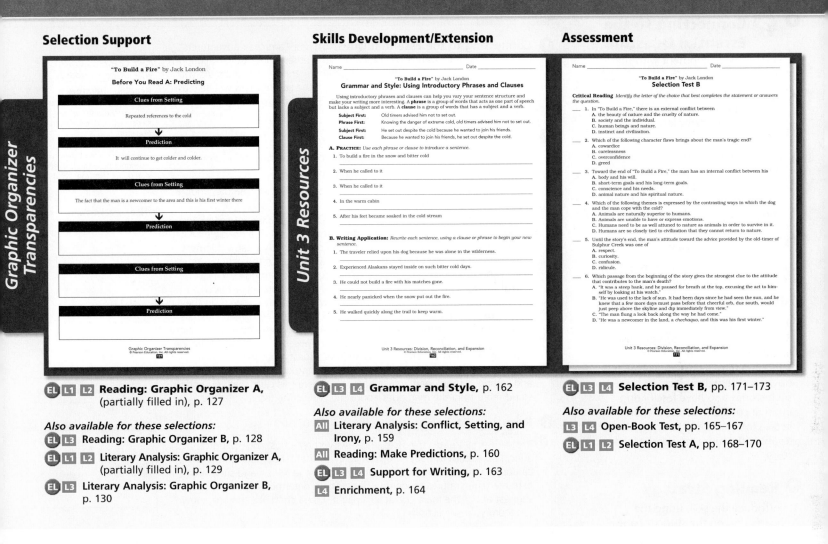

Graphic Organizer Transparencies

Unit 3 Resources

EL L1 L2 **Reading: Graphic Organizer A,** (partially filled in), p. 127

Also available for these selections:
EL L3 **Reading: Graphic Organizer B,** p. 128
EL L1 L2 **Literary Analysis: Graphic Organizer A,** (partially filled in), p. 129
EL L3 **Literary Analysis: Graphic Organizer B,** p. 130

EL L3 L4 **Grammar and Style,** p. 162

Also available for these selections:
All **Literary Analysis: Conflict, Setting, and Irony,** p. 159
All **Reading: Make Predictions,** p. 160
EL L3 L4 **Support for Writing,** p. 163
L4 **Enrichment,** p. 164

EL L3 L4 **Selection Test B,** pp. 171–173

Also available for these selections:
L3 L4 **Open-Book Test,** pp. 165–167
EL L1 L2 **Selection Test A,** pp. 168–170

PHLit Online!
www.PHLitOnline.com

Online Resources: All print materials are also available online.

- complete narrated selection text
- a thematically related video with writing prompt
- an interactive graphic organizer
- highlighting feature
- access to all student print resources, adapted to individual student needs
- Spanish and English summaries
- adapted selection translations in Spanish

Get Connected! (thematic video with writing prompt)

Also available:

Background Video
All videos are available in Spanish.

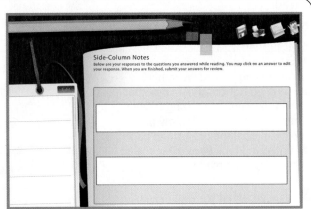

Writer's Journal (with graphics feature)

Also available:

Vocabulary Central (tools and activities for studying vocabulary)

① Connecting to the Essential Question

1. Review the assignment with the class.

2. Share an example of a job or activity that involves risks. Then have students complete the assignment.

3. Remind students that the story's protagonist faces peril in the course of making his living. This may influence the way they think about the Essential Question.

② Literary Analysis

Introduce the strategy, using the instruction on the student page.

Think Aloud: Model the Skill

Say to students:

Stories that pit characters against an impersonal opponent—the sea, a mountain, nature itself—have an obvious external conflict. To me, such stories also have fascinating internal conflicts. Often, a character's internal struggle with self-doubt is the more vital part of the story.

③ Reading Strategy

1. Introduce the skill, using the instruction on the student page.

2. Give students a copy of **Reading Strategy Graphic Organizer B,** page 128 in *Graphic Organizer Transparencies,* to fill out as they read.

Think Aloud

Say to students:

I make predictions automatically on every page I read. Whether I am proved right ("Aha! I *knew* that would happen.") or wrong ("Oops! I never expected that!"), my predictions impel me to turn the page to find out. Predictions make me an active, involved reader.

④ Vocabulary

1. Pronounce each word, giving its definition, and have students say it aloud.

2. For more guidance, see the *Classroom Strategies and Teaching Routines* card for introducing vocabulary.

Before You Read | *To Build a Fire*

① **Connecting to the Essential Question** For "armchair adventurers" at the turn of the twentieth century, this and other stories by Jack London brought to life a distant world of danger and extreme conditions. As you read, note details of extreme peril specific to the setting. This will help as you consider the Essential Question: **What is the relationship between literature and place?**

② Literary Analysis

Conflict, the struggle between opposing forces, can take two forms:

- **Internal,** occurring within the mind of a character
- **External,** occurring between a character and society, nature, another person, God, or fate

A character's efforts to resolve a conflict form the basis for the plot of a narrative. In "To Build a Fire," a man is in the throes of a deadly external conflict, struggling to survive in the bitter cold of the Alaskan wilderness. In this case, the story's **setting**—the time and place of the action—serves as the opposing force against which the protagonist struggles.

Irony involves a discrepancy between what is stated and what is meant, or between what is expected and what actually happens. In the case of **dramatic irony,** there is a contradiction between what a character thinks and what the reader knows to be true. For example, in this story the reader knows that the frigid temperature poses a much greater danger than the man realizes. The result is an ironic quality that permeates the entire story, affecting the reader's understanding of the characters, plot, and setting. As you read, notice passages where it is clear that you understand more than the man does about the conflict he faces.

③ Reading Strategy

ⓒ **Preparing to Read Complex Texts** As you read this story, **predict,** or anticipate, what will happen by noting clues that hint at later events. You can apply your *background knowledge* about the Yukon and survival at extreme temperatures to identify clues. Then, determine what the clues suggest about the main character's plight. Use a chart like the one shown to record your predictions.

④ Vocabulary

conjectural (kən jek´ chər əl) *adj.* based on guesswork (p. 597)

unwonted (un wän´ tid) *adj.* unusual; unfamiliar (p. 598)

appendage (ə pen´ dij) *n.* an external part of a plant or animal,

such as a tail or a limb (p. 599)

conflagration (kän´ flə grā´ shən) *n.* big, destructive fire (p. 605)

peremptorily (pər emp´ tə rə lē) *adv.* decisively; commandingly (p. 608)

Common Core State Standards

Reading Literature
3. Analyze the impact of the author's choices regarding how to develop and relate elements of a story or drama.
6. Analyze a case in which grasping a point of view requires distinguishing what is directly stated in a text from what is really meant.

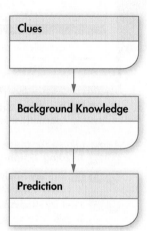

Clues

Background Knowledge

Prediction

PHLit Online!
www.PHLitOnline.com

Vocabulary Development

Vocabulary Knowledge Rating

Create a **Vocabulary Knowledge Rating Chart** (*Professional Development Guidebook,* p. 33) for the vocabulary words on the student page. Give each student a copy of the chart with the words on it. Read the words aloud, and have students mark their rating in the Before Reading column. Urge students to attend to these words as they read and discuss the selection.

In order to gauge how much instruction you need to provide, tally how many students are confident in their knowledge of each word. As students read, point out the words and their context.

Vocabulary Central, featuring student tools and activities for studying vocabulary, is available online at www.PHLitOnline.com.

⑤ JACK LONDON

Author of "To Build a Fire"

(1876–1916)

Jack London had endured more hardships by the age of twenty-one than most people experience in a lifetime. His struggles gave him a sympathy for the working class and a lasting distaste for drudgery. They also provided inspiration for novels and short stories, and became the foundation of his success as a writer.

Difficult Beginnings London grew up in San Francisco in extreme poverty. At the age of eleven, he left school and supported himself through a succession of unskilled jobs. Despite the long hours spent toiling at these jobs, London was able to read constantly, borrowing travel and adventure books from the library.

The books he read inspired London to travel, and he did so as a "tramp," using the name "Frisco Kid." After being arrested for vagrancy near Buffalo, New York, London decided to educate himself and reshape his life. He completed high school in eighteen months and enrolled at the University of California.

After only one semester, however, the lure of adventure proved irresistible. In 1897, London abandoned his studies and traveled to the Alaskan Yukon in an unsuccessful search for gold. His experiences in Alaska taught him about people's desire for wealth and power, and about our inability to control the forces of nature.

A Writing Life Once back in California, London became determined to earn a living as a writer. He rented a typewriter and worked up to fifteen hours a day, spinning his Alaskan adventures into short stories and novels. According to legend, London's stack of rejection slips from publishers grew to five feet in height. Even so, he wrote diligently every morning, setting himself a 1,000-word minimum.

In 1903, London earned national fame when he published *The Call of the Wild*. He soon became the highest-paid and most industrious writer in the country. During his career, London produced more than fifty fiction and nonfiction books, including *The Sea-Wolf* (1904) and *White Fang* (1906), which, along with *The Call of the Wild*, have become American classics.

Recognition by His Peers The well-known writer Upton Sinclair wrote that Jack London "was the true king of our storytellers." London's friend Oliver Madox Hueffer recalled that London "was the ideal yarnster . . . and one reason why I think him likely to be numbered as among the writers of real mark was that he was perfectly unconscious of it. Like Peter Pan, he never grew up, and he lived in his own stories with such intensity that he ended by believing them himself."

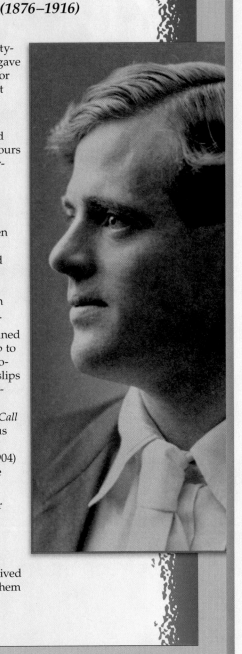

To Build a Fire **595**

📝 Daily Bellringer

For each class during which you will teach this selection, have students complete one of the five activities for the appropriate week in the *Daily Bellringer Activities* booklet.

Multidraft Reading

To assist struggling readers and to enhance reading for all, assign the text in chunks as warranted by length and apply multidraft reading protocols. For each reading, have students set the purpose indicated:

- **First reading**—identifying key ideas and details and answering any Reading Checks.
- **Second reading**—analyzing craft and structure and responding to the side-column prompts.
- **Third reading**—integrating knowledge and ideas, connecting to other texts and the world, and answering the end-of-selection questions.

For more guidance, refer to the *Classroom Strategies and Teaching Routines* card on multidraft reading.

⑤ More About the Author

Arthur Calder-Marshall, in his introduction to a collection of Jack London's works, commented: "Jack London's stories still compel the reader to read on. He learned to tell a tale, he says, when he was bumming across the United States . . . . He tells his stories like a tramp. At the end you are left with no distillation of truth, no new vision of life. But you have experienced something vicariously."

PHLit Online!
www.PHLitOnline.com
Teaching From Technology

Preparing to Read
Go to **www.PHLitOnline.com** in class or in a lab and display the **Get Connected!** slide show for this selection. Have the class brainstorm for responses to the writing prompt, entering ideas in the interactive journal. Then have students complete their responses individually. You may also have students complete the assignment as homework.

To build background, display the Background video and More About the Author features.

Using the Interactive Student Edition
Go to **www.PHLitOnline.com** and display the **Enriched Online Student Edition.** As the class reads the selection or listens to the narration, record answers to side-column prompts using the graphic organizers accessible on the interactive page. Alternatively, have students use the online edition individually, answering the prompts as they read.

① About the Selection

Along the Yukon River in the frozen northern wilderness, an inexperienced but confident prospector and his work dog make a long and dangerous journey on foot toward a camp. Though nature is the antagonist of this tale, the man's own overconfidence contributes to his downfall.

② Activating Prior Knowledge

Provide students with a visual idea of the setting of this story by showing them Alaska and the Yukon Territory on a world map or on an online satellite map. Draw them into the story by reading aloud the following description:

> Day had broken, cold and gray . . . . There was no sun nor hint of sun. . . . The Yukon lay a mile wide and hidden under three feet of ice. On top of this ice was as many feet of snow. . . . North and south, as far as his eye could see, it was unbroken white . . . . Undoubtedly it was colder than fifty degrees below [zero].

Encourage students to speculate about what might happen to a person who sets out on a daylong journey on foot in such conditions.

Concept Connector ➤

Tell students they will return to their responses after reading the selection.

① ② TO BUILD A FIRE

JACK LONDON

③ BACKGROUND The United States purchased Alaska from Russia for two cents an acre in 1867. Three decades later, thousands of prospectors, including Jack London, headed north after gold was discovered in the Yukon wilderness. London may have been searching for more than gold. He once commented: "True, the new territory was mostly barren; but its several hundred thousand square miles of frigidity at least gave breathing space to those who else would have suffocated at home."

596 Division, Reconciliation, and Expansion (1850–1914)

Ⓒ Text Complexity Rubric

To Build a Fire

Qualitative Measures	
Context/Knowledge Demands	Yukon setting 1 2 ③ 4 5
Structure/Language Conventionality and Clarity	No dialogue; much description; average vocabulary 1 2 3 ④ 5
Levels of Meaning/ Purpose/Concept Level	Accessible (survival) 1 2 ③ 4 5

Quantitative Measures			
Lexile	970L	Text Length	7,115 words
Overall Complexity	**More accessible**		

Reader and Task Suggestions

Preparing to Read the Text

- Using the Background information on TE p. 595, discuss what it means to "experience something vicariously" in a story.
- Ask students why some tales (in text or on film) involve their audience, making audience members feel that they are part of the story.
- Guide students to use Multidraft Reading strategies (TE p. 595).

Leveled Tasks

Structure/Language If students will have difficulty with the plot, have them skim and list five of the man's actions. Have them reread to see how London's descriptions involve the reader in the man's fate.

Analyzing If students will not have difficulty with the plot, discuss how the third-person point of view affects the reader's involvement.

Day had broken cold and gray, exceedingly cold and gray, when the man turned aside from the main Yukon[1] trail and climbed the high earth-bank, where a dim and little-traveled trail led eastward through the fat spruce timberland. It was a steep bank, and he paused for breath at the top, excusing the act to himself by looking at his watch. It was nine o'clock. There was no sun nor hint of sun, though there was not a cloud in the sky. It was a clear day, and yet there seemed an intangible pall over the face of things, a subtle gloom that made the day dark, and that was due to the absence of sun. This fact did not worry the man. He was used to the lack of sun. It had been days since he had seen the sun, and he knew that a few more days must pass before that cheerful orb, due south, would just peep above the skyline and dip immediately from view.

The man flung a look back along the way he had come. The Yukon lay a mile wide and hidden under three feet of ice. On top of this ice were as many feet of snow. It was all pure white, rolling in gentle undulations where the ice jams of the freeze-up had formed. North and south, as far as his eye could see, it was unbroken white, save for a dark hairline that curved and twisted from around the spruce-covered island to the south, and that curved and twisted away into the north, where it disappeared behind another spruce-covered island. This dark hairline was the trail—the main trail—that led south five hundred miles to the Chilcoot Pass, Dyea,[2] and salt water; and that led north seventy miles to Dawson, and still on to the north a thousand miles to Nulato,[3] and finally to St. Michael on Bering Sea, a thousand miles and half a thousand more.

But all this—the mysterious, far-reaching hairline trail, the absence of sun from the sky, the tremendous cold, and the strangeness and weirdness of it all—made no impression on the man. It was not because he was long used to it. He was a newcomer in the land, a *chechaquo*,[4] and this was his first winter. The trouble with him was that he was without imagination. He was quick and alert in the things of life, but only in the things, and not in the significances. Fifty degrees below zero meant eighty-odd degrees of frost. Such fact impressed him as being cold and uncomfortable, and that was all. It did not lead him to meditate upon his frailty as a creature of temperature, and upon man's frailty in general, able only to live within certain narrow limits of heat and cold; and from there on it did not lead him to the conjectural field of immortality and man's place in the universe. Fifty degrees below zero stood for a bite of frost that hurt and that must be guarded against by the use of mittens, earflaps, warm

Reading Strategy
Predicting What do you predict will happen to the "newcomer" who is "without imagination"?

Vocabulary
conjectural (kən jek´ chər əl) *adj.* based on guesswork

Reading Check
Where is the man, and what weather conditions is he experiencing?

---

1. **Yukon** (yōō´ kän) territory in northwestern Canada, east of Alaska; also, a river.
2. **Dyea** (dī´ ā) former town in Alaska at the start of the Yukon trail.
3. **Dawson . . . Nulato** former gold-mining villages in the Yukon.
4. *chechaquo* (chē chä´ kwō) slang for newcomer.

To Build a Fire **597**

❻ Literary Analysis

Conflict

1. Instruct students to create a chart identifying conflicts the man faces. Have them begin by drawing a box and writing the term "The Man" in its center.

2. Have them read the bracketed passage. Point out that London elaborates extensively on the cold.

3. Suggest that these details point out the story's central conflict. Then **ask** students the Literary Analysis question.
   Possible response: The man is in conflict with the forces of extreme weather. Students may say that he is also in conflict with the limits of his own perceptions.

4. Have students place their answers in a circle drawn onto their charts and connect the circles to "The Man."

❼ Reading Strategy

Predicting

1. Remind students that dramatic irony is created when what the reader knows about a character's circumstances contradicts what a character believes to be true. Such irony can also provide the grounds for predicting what will happen later.

2. Have students read the bracketed passage. Encourage them to pay special attention to the dog's instincts.

3. Point out to students that the dog's basic instincts tell it what the man has yet to conclude: that it is too dangerously cold to be traveling.

4. **Ask** students the Reading Strategy question.
   Possible response: The dog's instincts let the reader know just how dangerous the situation is, which leads to the prediction that the man's poor understanding of his environment will have tragic consequences.

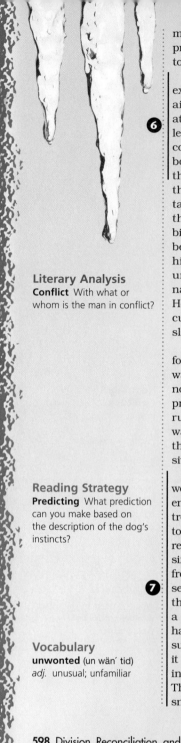

Literary Analysis
Conflict With what or whom is the man in conflict?

Reading Strategy
Predicting What prediction can you make based on the description of the dog's instincts?

Vocabulary
unwonted (un wän′ tid) *adj.* unusual; unfamiliar

moccasins, and thick socks. Fifty degrees below zero was to him just precisely fifty degrees below zero. That there should be anything more to it than that was a thought that never entered his head.

As he turned to go on, he spat speculatively. There was a sharp, explosive crackle that startled him. He spat again. And again, in the air, before it could fall to the snow, the spittle crackled. He knew that at fifty below spittle crackled on the snow, but this spittle had crackled in the air. Undoubtedly it was colder than fifty below—how much colder he did not know. But the temperature did not matter. He was bound for the old claim on the left fork of Henderson Creek, where the boys were already. They had come over across the divide from the Indian Creek country, while he had come the roundabout way to take a look at the possibilities of getting out logs in the spring from the islands in the Yukon. He would be in to camp by six o'clock; a bit after dark, it was true, but the boys would be there, a fire would be going, and a hot supper would be ready. As for lunch, he pressed his hand against the protruding bundle under his jacket. It was also under his shirt, wrapped up in a handkerchief and lying against the naked skin. It was the only way to keep the biscuits from freezing. He smiled agreeably to himself as he thought of those biscuits, each cut open and sopped in bacon grease, and each enclosing a generous slice of fried bacon.

He plunged in among the big spruce trees. The trail was faint. A foot of snow had fallen since the last sled had passed over, and he was glad he was without a sled, traveling light. In fact, he carried nothing but the lunch wrapped in the handkerchief. He was surprised, however, at the cold. It certainly was cold, he concluded, as he rubbed his numb nose and cheekbones with his mittened hand. He was a warm-whiskered man, but the hair on his face did not protect the high cheekbones and the eager nose that thrust itself aggressively into the frosty air.

At the man's heels trotted a dog, a big native husky, the proper wolf dog, gray-coated and without any visible or temperamental difference from its brother, the wild wolf. The animal was depressed by the tremendous cold. It knew that it was no time for traveling. Its instinct told it a truer tale than was told to the man by the man's judgment. In reality, it was not merely colder than fifty below zero; it was colder than sixty below, than seventy below. It was seventy-five below zero. Since the freezing point is thirty-two above zero, it meant that one hundred and seven degrees of frost obtained. The dog did not know anything about thermometers. Possibly in its brain there was no sharp consciousness of a condition of very cold such as was in the man's brain. But the brute had its instinct. It experienced a vague but menacing apprehension that subdued it and made it slink along at the man's heels, and that made it question eagerly every unwonted movement of the man as if expecting him to go into camp or to seek shelter somewhere and build a fire. The dog had learned fire, and it wanted fire, or else to burrow under the snow and cuddle its warmth away from the air.

598 Division, Reconciliation, and Expansion (1850–1914)

Enrichment: Investigating Daily Life

Dangers of Cold Weather
Discuss the dangers of exposure to extreme cold. Frostbite and hypothermia, for example, are key factors in this story. Frostbite starts for London's character with a painful loss of feeling in the extremities (the hands, feet, and face), leading to numbness, skin discoloration, and loss of function. He also suffers the effects of hypothermia: He has difficulty moving, becomes confused and drowsy, and feels warmer just before he dies.
Activity: Research The prospector is not a

native of the Yukon. Interested students can research the ways that the area's native peoples protected themselves, day to day, against extreme temperatures. As an alternative, students might research precautions that people take today in such extremes. Suggest that they record information in the **Enrichment: Investigating Daily Life** work sheet, in *Professional Development Guidebook*, page 224. Have students share their findings with the class.

The frozen moisture of its breathing had settled on its fur in a fine powder of frost, and especially were its jowls, muzzle, and eyelashes whitened by its crystalled breath. The man's red beard and mustache were likewise frosted, but more solidly, the deposit taking the form of ice and increasing with every warm, moist breath he exhaled. Also, the man was chewing tobacco, and the muzzle of ice held his lips so rigidly that he was unable to clear his chin when he expelled the juice. The result was that a crystal beard of the color and solidity of amber was increasing its length on his chin. If he fell down it would shatter itself, like glass, into brittle fragments. But he did not mind the appendage. It was the penalty all tobacco-chewers paid in that country, and he had been out before in two cold snaps. They had not been so cold as this, he knew, but by the spirit thermometer[5] at Sixty Mile he knew they had been registered at fifty below and at fifty-five.

He held on through the level stretch of woods for several miles, crossed a wide flat, and dropped down a bank to the frozen bed of a small stream. This was Henderson Creek, and he knew he was ten miles from the forks. He looked at his watch. It was ten o'clock. He was making four miles an hour, and he calculated that he would arrive at the forks at half past twelve. He decided to celebrate that event by eating his lunch there.

The dog dropped in again at his heels, with a tail drooping discouragement, as the man swung along the creek bed. The furrow of the old sled trail was plainly visible, but a dozen inches of snow covered the marks of the last runners. In a month no man had come up or down that silent creek. The man held steadily on. He was not much given to thinking, and just then particularly he had nothing to think about save that he would eat lunch at the forks and that at six o'clock he would be in camp with the boys. There was nobody to talk to; and, had there been, speech would have been impossible because of the ice-muzzle on his mouth. So he continued monotonously to chew tobacco and to increase the length of his amber beard.

Once in a while the thought reiterated itself that it was very cold and that he had never experienced such cold. As he walked along he rubbed his cheekbones and nose with the back of his mittened hand. He did this automatically, now and again changing hands. But rub as he would, the instant he stopped his cheekbones went numb, and the following instant the end of his nose went numb. He was sure to frost his cheeks; he knew that, and experienced a pang of regret that he had not devised a nose strap of the sort Bud wore in cold snaps. Such a strap passed across the cheeks, as well, and saved them. But it didn't matter much, after all. What were frosted cheeks? A bit painful, that was all: they were never serious.

Empty as the man's mind was of thoughts, he was keenly observant, and he noticed the changes in the creek, the curves and

---

5. **spirit thermometer** thermometer containing alcohol; used in extreme cold.

Vocabulary
appendage (ə pen´ dij) *n.* an external part of a plant or animal, such as a tail or a limb

Spiral Review
Point of View From what point of view is this story related? How do you know?

Reading Check
What physical effects of the cold does the man experience?

To Build a Fire **599**

---

8 Critical Thinking
Evaluate
1. Have students read the bracketed passage. Tell them to pay close attention to the man's plan.
2. **Ask** students: Does the man's plan make sense? Why or why not?
   Possible response: Students may point out that four miles an hour is a quick walking pace, one that he is unlikely to be able to keep up for very long in the snow.

9 Reading Strategy
Predicting
1. Point out that the path has not been used for a long time, as the snow indicates.
2. **Ask** students to tell whether they believe the man will reach camp as he plans, now that he is traveling on an unused trail.
   Possible response: Unlike the man, students may recognize that the trail has been unused for a reason; perhaps it is too dangerous to travel on now. They may predict he will not arrive as planned.

Spiral Review
Point of View
1. Remind students that they have studied the concept of point of view in an earlier lesson.
2. **Ask** students the Spiral Review question.
   Sample answer: The story is related from the third-person omniscient point of view. Events are told by a narrator outside the action. The narrator knows the thoughts and feelings of each character, as well as some details about the actual temperature that the dog and the man do not know.

10 Reading Check
Answer: His nose and cheekbones are numb, and his beard is frosted.

⑪ Critical Viewing

Possible response: When students have read the entire story, they may choose several descriptive words or passages from the story to describe the scene, including "intangible pall over the face of things," "subtle gloom," "gentle undulations," "spruce-covered island," "silent creek," and "arctic winter."

⑫ Reading Strategy

Predicting

1. Instruct students to construct a chart with two columns. Have them write "Clues in Passage" on the left and "You Can Predict" on the right.

2. Have students read the bracketed passage. **Ask** them to write clues they find in the left columns of their charts.
   Possible response: Students may include such details as "the changes in the creek," the springs that never freeze, the word "traps," and the fact that a person could wet himself "to the waist."

3. **Ask** students the Reading Strategy question.
   Possible response: Students will probably predict that the man might step into a spring and get soaking wet.

4. Have students write their answers on the right side of their charts.

⑪ ▲ Critical Viewing
Which words or passages from the story could be used to describe this scene? **[Analyze]**

⑫

Reading Strategy
Predicting Based on the description of the creek and hidden pools, what do you predict might happen?

bends and timber jams, and always he sharply noted where he placed his feet. Once, coming around a bend, he shied abruptly, like a startled horse, curved away from the place where he had been walking, and retreated several paces back along the trail. The creek he knew was frozen clear to the bottom—no creek could contain water in that arctic winter—but he knew also that there were springs that bubbled out from the hillsides and ran along under the snow and on top the ice of the creek. He knew that the coldest snaps never froze these springs, and he knew likewise their danger. They were traps. They hid pools of water under the snow that might be three inches deep, or three feet. Sometimes a skin of ice half an inch thick covered them, and in turn was covered by the snow. Sometimes there were alternate layers of water and ice skin, so that when one broke through he kept on breaking through for a while, sometimes wetting himself to the waist.

600 Division, Reconciliation, and Expansion (1850–1914)

That was why he had shied in such panic. He had felt the give under his feet and heard the crackle of a snow-hidden ice skin. And to get his feet wet in such a temperature meant trouble and danger. At the very least it meant delay, for he would be forced to stop and build a fire, and under its protection to bare his feet while he dried his socks and moccasins. He stood and studied the creek bed and its banks, and decided that the flow of water came from the right. He reflected awhile, rubbing his nose and cheeks, then skirted to the left, stepping gingerly and testing the footing for each step. Once clear of the danger, he took a fresh chew of tobacco and swung along at his four-mile gait.

In the course of the next two hours he came upon several similar traps. Usually the snow above the hidden pools had a sunken, candied appearance that advertised the danger. Once again, however, he had a close call; and once, suspecting danger, he compelled the dog to go on in front. The dog did not want to go. It hung back until the man shoved it forward, and then it went quickly across the white, unbroken surface. Suddenly it broke through, floundered to one side, and got away to firmer footing. It had wet its forefeet and legs, and almost immediately the water that clung to it turned to ice. It made quick efforts to lick the ice off its legs, then dropped down in the snow and began to bite out the ice that had formed between the toes. This was a matter of instinct. To permit the ice to remain would mean sore feet. It did not know this. It merely obeyed the mysterious prompting that arose from the deep crypts of its being. But the man knew, having achieved a judgment on the subject, and he removed the mitten from his right hand and helped tear out the ice particles. He did not expose his fingers more than a minute, and was astonished at the swift numbness that smote them. It certainly was cold. He pulled on the mitten hastily, and beat the hand savagely across his chest.

At twelve o'clock the day was at its brightest. Yet the sun was too far south on its winter journey to clear the horizon. The bulge of the earth intervened between it and Henderson Creek, where the man walked under a clear sky at noon and cast no shadow. At half-past twelve, to the minute, he arrived at the forks of the creek. He was pleased at the speed he had made. If he kept it up, he would certainly be with the boys by six. He unbuttoned his jacket and shirt and drew forth his lunch. The action consumed no more than a quarter of a minute, yet in that brief moment the numbness laid hold of the exposed fingers. He did not put the mitten on, but, instead, struck the fingers a dozen sharp smashes against his leg. Then he sat down on a snow-covered log to eat. The sting that followed upon the striking of his fingers against his leg ceased so quickly that he was startled. He had had no chance to take a bite of biscuit. He struck the fingers repeatedly and returned them to the mitten, baring the other hand for the purpose of eating. He tried to take a mouthful, but

...SUSPECTING **DANGER,** HE COMPELLED THE DOG TO GO ON IN FRONT.

15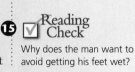
Reading Check

Why does the man want to avoid getting his feet wet?

To Build a Fire **601**

History Connection

The exact bloodline of the Alaskan husky is often debated. Some experts believe it to be a crossbreed of wolves, Siberian huskies—the genetic source of the blue eyes in many Alaskan huskies—and Irish setters or any other breed known for speed and endurance.

Connect to the Literature After discussing the information on sled dogs, ask the Connect to the Literature question: Why do you think London chooses to portray the dog's thoughts and feelings?

Possible response: The dog's thoughts and feelings emphasize to the reader the severity of the situation. They also help to show how the man has underestimated the temperature and the danger he is in.

17 **Literary Analysis**

Conflict and Irony

1. Remind students that irony involves a contrast between what a character expects to happen and what actually happens.

2. Have students read the bracketed passage. Encourage them to reflect on what the man has done to arrive here.

3. **Ask** students: In what ways is the man's thought that "one must not be too sure of things" ironic? **Possible response:** His thought is ironic because he has gotten himself into this very dangerous and frightening situation by being too sure that he knew what he was doing.

LITERATURE IN CONTEXT **16**

History Connection

Dogs and the Yukon

Dogs like the one in "To Build a Fire" have long played a key role in the Yukon. For centuries, native people in Alaska have bred dogs for a variety of purposes, including transportation. When the Klondike gold rush brought thousands of miners to the Yukon, the problem of transportation became acute. In 1910, the federal government constructed a trail more than 1,000 miles long for use by dog sled teams. That trail became known as the Iditarod.

Sled dogs are among the most powerful draft animals on earth. A team of twenty dogs can pull a ton or more. Though the man in London's story does not treat his dog with affection, for many dog sled drivers these valiant dogs provided warmth and companionship on the long, cold trail.

Connect to the Literature

Why do you think London chooses to portray the dog's thoughts and feelings?

---

the ice muzzle prevented. He had forgotten to build a fire and thaw out. He chuckled at his foolishness, and as he chuckled he noted the numbness creeping into the exposed fingers. Also, he noted that the stinging which had first come to his toes when he sat down was already passing away. He wondered whether the toes were warm or numb. He moved them inside the moccasins and decided that they were numb.

He pulled the mitten on hurriedly and stood up. He was a bit frightened. He stamped up and down until the stinging returned into the feet. It certainly was cold, was his thought. **17** That man from Sulphur Creek had spoken the truth when telling how cold it sometimes got in the country. And he had laughed at him at the time! That showed one must not be too sure of things. There was no mistake about it, it was cold. He strode up and down, stamping his feet and threshing his arms, until reassured by the returning warmth. Then he got out matches and proceeded to make a fire. From the undergrowth, where high water of the previous spring had lodged a supply of seasoned twigs, he got his firewood. Working carefully from a small beginning, he soon had a roaring fire, over which he thawed the ice from his face and in the protection of which he ate his biscuits. For the moment the cold of space was outwitted. The dog took satisfaction in the fire, stretching out close enough for warmth and far enough away to escape being singed.

When the man had finished, he filled his pipe and took his comfortable time over a smoke. Then he pulled on his mittens, settled the earflaps of his cap firmly about his ears, and took the creek trail up the left fork. The dog was disappointed and yearned back toward the fire. This man did not know cold. Possibly all the generations of his ancestry had been ignorant of cold, of real cold, of cold one hundred and seven degrees below freezing point. But the dog knew; all its ancestry knew, and it had inherited the knowledge. And it knew that it was not good to walk abroad in such fearful cold. It was the time to lie snug in a hole in the snow and wait for a curtain of cloud to be drawn across the face of outer space whence this cold came. On the other hand, there was no keen intimacy between the dog and the man. The one was the toil slave of the other, and the only caresses it had ever received were the caresses of the whiplash and of harsh and menacing throat sounds that threatened the whiplash. So the dog made no effort to communicate its apprehension to the man. It was not concerned in the welfare of the man; it was for its own sake that it yearned back toward the fire. But the man whistled, and spoke to it with the sound of whiplashes, and the dog swung in at the man's heels and followed after.

602 Division, Reconciliation, and Expansion (1850–1914)

Think Aloud

Literary Analysis: Understanding Imagery

To model the process of analyzing imagery, use the following "think aloud." Say to students:

I notice that twice on this page London refers to the cold as coming from "space." It would be more understandable to me if he had said "from the Arctic." Why is London insisting on "outer space"? As I ask that question, I think of another odd description on the previous page. The man casts no shadow because the "bulge of the earth intervened between [the sun] and Henderson Creek." Here London is suggesting that the entire planet moves to affect one man on one tiny creek. Why?

The contrast between the puny man and the vastness of earth and of space gives me my answer. London is showing through this imagery that the conflict of the story is not only one man against the cold but also human beings against an uncaring universe.

The man took a chew of tobacco and proceeded to start a new amber beard. Also, his moist breath quickly powdered with white his mustache, eyebrows, and lashes. There did not seem to be so many springs on the left fork of the Henderson, and for half an hour the man saw no signs of any. And then it happened. At a place where there were no signs, where the soft, unbroken snow seemed to advertise solidity beneath, the man broke through. It was not deep. He wet himself halfway to the knees before he floundered out to the firm crust.

He was angry, and cursed his luck aloud. He had hoped to get into camp with the boys at six o'clock, and this would delay him an hour, for he would have to build a fire and dry out his footgear. This was imperative at that low temperature—he knew that much; and he turned aside to the bank, which he climbed. On top, tangled in the underbrush about the trunks of several small spruce trees, was a high-water deposit of dry firewood—sticks and twigs, principally, but also larger portions of seasoned branches and fine, dry, last year's grasses. He threw down several large pieces on top of the snow. This served for a foundation and prevented the young flame from drowning itself in the snow it otherwise would melt. The flame he got by touching a match to a small shred of birch bark that he took from his pocket. This burned even more readily than paper. Placing it on the foundation, he fed the young flame with wisps of dry grass and with the tiniest dry twigs.

He worked slowly and carefully, keenly aware of his danger. Gradually, as the flame grew stronger, he increased the size of the twigs with which he fed it. He squatted in the snow, pulling the twigs out from their entanglement in the brush and feeding directly to the flame. He knew there must be no failure. When it is seventy-five below zero, a man must not fail in his first attempt to build a fire—that is, if his feet are wet. If his feet are dry, and he fails, he can run along the trail for half a mile and restore his circulation. But the circulation of wet and freezing feet cannot be restored by running when it is seventy-five below. No matter how fast he runs, the wet feet will freeze the harder.

All this the man knew. The old-timer on Sulphur Creek had told him about it the previous fall, and now he was appreciating the advice. Already all sensation had gone out of his feet. To build the fire he had been forced to remove his mittens, and the fingers had quickly gone numb. His pace of four miles an hour had kept his heart pumping blood to the surface of his body and to all the extremities. But the instant he stopped, the action of the pump eased down. The cold of space smote the unprotected tip of the planet, and he, being on that unprotected tip, received the full force of the blow. The blood of his body recoiled before it. The blood was alive, like the dog, and like the dog it wanted to hide away and cover itself up from the fearful cold. So long as he walked four

WHEN IT IS SEVENTY-FIVE BELOW ZERO, A MAN MUST NOT FAIL IN HIS FIRST ATTEMPT TO BUILD A FIRE—

㉑ ☑ Reading Check

What does the man do after he falls into the creek?

To Build a Fire **603**

⑱ Literary Analysis
Conflict and Irony

1. Have students read the bracketed passage. Then **ask:** What are the man's biggest concerns when he falls into the creek?
   Answer: He is angry because making a fire and drying his footgear will delay his return to the camp by an hour.

2. **Ask** students this follow-up question: Given his situation, how are his concerns ironic?
   Answer: His concerns are ironic because London has made it very clear that the man is in very grave danger and may not make it back to the camp at all.

⑲ Reading Strategy
Predicting

1. Have students read the bracketed passage. **Ask** them to identify clues in the text that suggest what will happen.
   Answer: Students should answer that "a man must not fail in his first attempt to build a fire—that is, if his feet are wet," because his feet will freeze.

2. **Ask** students: Now that he is wet, what do you predict will happen to the man?
   Possible response: Students will probably predict that he will fail to build a fire.

⑳ ⁇ Engaging the Essential Question

1. Point out to students that the narrator has previously spoken of "the cold of space" and "the face of outer space whence this cold came."

2. Reread the phrase "the unprotected tip of the planet." How does this description of the setting affect your understanding of the man's predicament?
   Possible response: London's imagery magnifies the story's predicament from one involving a foolish man out in the cold to one showing a vulnerable humanity in a pitiless universe.

㉑ Reading Check

Answer: He immediately curses his luck and begins to gather wood for a fire.

603

miles an hour, he pumped that blood, willy-nilly, to the surface; but now it ebbed away and sank down into the recesses of his body. The extremities were the first to feel its absence. His wet feet froze the faster, and his exposed fingers numbed the faster, though they had not yet begun to freeze. Nose and cheeks were already freezing, while the skin of all his body chilled as it lost its blood.

But he was safe. Toes and nose and cheeks would be only touched by the frost, for the fire was beginning to burn with strength. He was feeding it with twigs the size of his finger. In another minute he would be able to feed it with branches the size of his wrist, and then he could remove his wet foot-gear, and, while it dried, he could keep his naked feet warm by the fire, rubbing them at first, of course, with snow. The fire was a success. He was safe. He remembered the advice of the old-timer on Sulphur Creek, and smiled. The old-timer had been very serious in laying down the law that no man must travel alone in the Klondike after fifty below. Well, here he was; he had had the accident; he was alone; and he had saved himself. Those old-timers were rather womanish, some of them, he thought. All a man had to do was to keep his head, and he was all right. Any man who was a man could travel alone. But it was surprising, the rapidity with which his cheeks and nose were freezing. And he had not thought his fingers could go lifeless in so short a time. Lifeless they were, for he could scarcely make them move together to grip a twig, and they seemed remote from his body and from him. When he touched a twig, he had to look and see whether or not he had hold of it. The wires were pretty well down between him and his finger ends.

All of which counted for little. There was the fire, snapping and

Literary Analysis
Conflict and Irony What does the reader understand about the old-timer's advice that the man does not?

22

23 ▼ Critical Viewing
What aspects of the Alaskan landscape pictured here clarify the challenge the man faces in building a fire?
[Connect]

604 Division, Reconciliation, and Expansion (1850–1914)

crackling and promising life with every dancing flame. He started to untie his moccasins. They were coated with ice; the thick German socks were like sheaths of iron halfway to the knees; and the moccasin strings were like rods of steel all twisted and knotted as by some conflagration. For a moment he tugged with his numb fingers, then, realizing the folly of it, he drew his sheath-knife.

But before he could cut the strings, it happened. It was his own fault or, rather, his mistake. He should not have built the fire under the spruce tree. He should have built it in the open. But it had been easier to pull the twigs from the brush and drop them directly on the fire. Now the tree under which he had done this carried a weight of snow on its boughs. No wind had blown for weeks, and each bough was fully freighted. Each time he had pulled a twig he had communicated a slight agitation to the tree—an imperceptible agitation, so far as he was concerned, but an agitation sufficient to bring about the disaster. High up in the tree one bough capsized its load of snow. This fell on the boughs beneath, capsizing them. This process continued, spreading out and involving the whole tree. It grew like an avalanche, and it descended without warning upon the man and the fire, and the fire was blotted out! Where it had burned was a mantle of fresh and disordered snow.

The man was shocked. It was as though he had just heard his own sentence of death. For a moment he sat and stared at the spot where the fire had been. Then he grew very calm. Perhaps the old-timer on Sulphur Creek was right. If he had only had a trail mate he would have been in no danger now. The trail mate could have built the fire. Well, it was up to him to build the fire over again, and this second time there must be no failure. Even if he succeeded, he would most likely lose some toes. His feet must be badly frozen by now, and there would be some time before the second fire was ready.

Such were his thoughts, but he did not sit and think them. He was busy all the time they were passing through his mind. He made a new foundation for a fire, this time in the open, where no treacherous tree could blot it out. Next, he gathered dry grasses and tiny twigs from the high-water flotsam. He could not bring his fingers together to pull them out, but he was able to gather them by the handful. In this way he got many rotten twigs and bits of green moss that were undesirable, but it was the best he could do. He worked methodically, even collecting an armful of the larger branches to be used later when the fire gathered strength. And all the while the dog sat and watched him, a certain yearning wistfulness in its eyes, for it looked upon him as the fire provider, and the fire was slow in coming.

When all was ready, the man reached in his pocket for a second piece of birch bark. He knew the bark was there, and, though he could not feel it with his fingers, he could hear its crisp rustling as he fumbled for it. Try as he would, he could not clutch hold of it. And all the time, in his consciousness, was the knowledge that each instant his feet were freezing. This thought tended to put him in a panic, but

Vocabulary
conflagration (kän′ flə grā′ shən) *n.* big, destructive fire

☑ **Reading Check** 26
What happens to ruin the man's fire?

To Build a Fire **605**

24 Reading Strategy
Predicting

1. Before they read the bracketed passage, **ask** students to pause and consider the man's progress up to this point. Have his efforts been successful?
   Possible response: Students may observe that he remains calm after falling into the water and successfully builds a fire. Others may feel that getting wet in the first place indicates that the man is failing in his efforts.

2. Have students read the bracketed passage. Then **ask** them to tell whether they were able to predict this accident. Have them provide details to back up their predictions.
   Possible response: Students may be surprised by the specific event, but they probably expected some problem to result from the man's overconfidence.

25 Literary Analysis
Conflict

1. Remind students that the main conflict in this story comes from the man's struggle against natural forces. **Ask** them to consider what the man has done so far to resolve this conflict.

2. After students read the bracketed passage, **ask:** In what ways does the conflict intensify as the man begins to build another fire?
   Possible response: The situation becomes far more dangerous; the man feels as if "he had just heard his own sentence of death," and realizes that if he survives, he will at least lose some toes.

▶ **Monitor Progress** Encourage students to discuss the ways in which the story has built conflict. **Ask:** To what climax do they think the conflict will build?
   Possible response: At this point, students may have concluded that the man is going to freeze to death.

26 Reading Check
Answer: The snow piled on the branches of a tree falls on the fire and puts it out.

605

㉗ Literary Analysis

Conflict

1. Point out that the man is attempting to build a second fire. **Ask** students to explain what happens to his efforts in this passage.
   Answer: He has to struggle to regain feeling in his hands, which he loses immediately; his numbed fingers make him drop the matches; he cannot pick up one match, so he scoops the bunch into his lap.

2. After reviewing these details, **ask** students how this passage builds the conflict between the man and nature.
   Possible response: Students may note that the man now feels the initial pangs of panic; with each mishap, his attitude changes. Overconfident at first, he begins to laugh at his errors, then to appreciate his limitations, and, now, to experience real concern.

㉘ Reading Strategy

Predicting

1. **Ask** students to read the bracketed passage, looking closely at the details.

2. **Ask** students the Reading Strategy question.
   Possible response: Most students will predict that the man will fail to light a match and start another fire because he is so incapacitated by the extreme cold.

㉙ Literary Analysis

Conflict

1. Have students read the bracketed passage. Point out that the man's fear and pain show that he is now fully aware of how cold it actually is.

2. **Ask** students the Literary Analysis question.
   Possible response: He must now struggle with his freezing, nearly useless hands and shivering body.

---

he fought against it and kept calm. He pulled on his mittens with his teeth, and threshed his arms back and forth, beating his hands with all his might against his sides. He did this sitting down, and he stood up to do it; and all the while the dog sat in the snow, its wolf brush of a tail curled around warmly over its forefeet, its sharp wolf ears pricked forward intently as it watched the man. And the man, as he beat and threshed with his arms and hands, felt a great surge of envy as he regarded the creature that was warm and secure in its natural covering.

After a time he was aware of the first faraway signals of sensation in his beaten fingers. The faint tingling grew stronger till it evolved into a stinging ache that was excruciating, but which the man hailed with satisfaction. He stripped the mitten from his right hand and fetched forth the birch bark. The exposed fingers were quickly going numb again. Next he brought out his bunch of sulphur matches. But the tremendous cold had already driven the life out of his fingers. In his effort to separate one match from the others, the whole bunch fell in the snow. He tried to pick it out of the snow, but failed. The dead fingers could neither touch nor clutch. He was very careful. He drove the thought of his freezing feet, and nose, and cheeks, out of his mind, devoting his whole soul to the matches. He watched, using the sense of vision in place of that of touch, and when he saw his fingers on each side of the bunch, he closed them—that is, he willed to close them, for the wires were down, and the fingers did not obey. He pulled the mitten on the right hand, and beat it fiercely against his knee. Then, with both mittened hands, he scooped the bunch of matches, along with much snow, into his lap. Yet he was no better off.

After some manipulation he managed to get the bunch between the heels of his mittened hands. In this fashion he carried it to his mouth. The ice crackled and snapped when by a violent effort he opened his mouth. He drew the lower jaw in, curled the upper lip out of the way, and scraped the bunch with his upper teeth in order to separate a match. He succeeded in getting one, which he dropped on his lap. He was no better off. He could not pick it up. Then he devised a way. He picked it up in his teeth and scratched it on his leg. Twenty times he scratched before he succeeded in lighting it. As it flamed he held it with his teeth to the birch bark. But the burning brimstone went up his nostrils and into his lungs, causing him to cough spasmodically. The match fell into the snow and went out.

The old-timer on Sulphur Creek was right, he thought in the moment of controlled despair that ensued: after fifty below, a man should travel with a partner. He beat his hands, but failed in exciting any sensation. Suddenly he bared both hands, removing the mittens with his teeth. He caught the whole bunch between the heels of his hands. His arm muscles not being frozen enabled him to press the hand heels tightly against the matches. Then he scratched the bunch along his leg. It flared into flame, seventy sulphur matches at once! along his leg. It flared into flame, seventy sulphur matches at once!

Reading Strategy
Predicting As the man struggles to light the matches, what do you predict about his success? Why?

Literary Analysis
Conflict What is the conflict with which the man now struggles desperately? ㉙

Enrichment: Investigating Career Connections

Ecotourism

Relatively few people want to venture into the Arctic wilderness by themselves, like the man in this story. However, there is a growing industry that fulfills people's desire to travel into areas of unspoiled wilderness, from Alaska to the Antarctic and from the rainforests of Central America to the African savanna. This industry is called ecotourism, and within it there are many career opportunities. Cooks, naturalists, pilots, and booking agents are just a few of the people employed in ecotourism.

Activity: Presentation Encourage interested students to conduct research about this growing industry and the opportunities it provides. Suggest that they record information in the **Enrichment: Investigating Career Connections** work sheet, in *Professional Development Guidebook,* page 221, and present their findings to their classmates.

There was no wind to blow them out. He kept his head to one side to escape the strangling fumes, and held the blazing bunch to the birch bark. As he so held it, he became aware of sensation in his hand. His flesh was burning. He could smell it. Deep down below the surface he could feel it. The sensation developed into pain that grew acute. And still he endured it, holding the flame of the matches clumsily to the bark that would not light readily because his own burning hands were in the way, absorbing most of the flame.

At last, when he could endure no more, he jerked his hands apart. The blazing matches fell sizzling into the snow, but the birch bark was alight. He began laying dry grasses and the tiniest twigs on the flame. He could not pick and choose, for he had to lift the fuel between the heels of his hands. Small pieces of rotten wood and green moss clung to the twigs, and he bit them off as well as he could with his teeth. He cherished the flame carefully and awkwardly. It meant life, and it must not perish. The withdrawal of blood from the surface of his body now made him begin to shiver, and he grew more awkward. A large piece of green moss fell squarely on the little fire. He tried to poke it out with his fingers, but his shivering frame made him poke too far, and he disrupted the nucleus of the little fire, the burning grasses and tiny twigs separating and scattering. He tried to poke them together again, but in spite of the tenseness of the effort, his shivering got away with him, and the twigs were hopelessly scattered. Each twig gushed a puff of smoke and went out. The fire provider had failed. As he looked apathetically about him, his eyes chanced on the dog, sitting across the ruins of the fire from him, in the snow, making restless, hunching movements, slightly lifting one forefoot and then the other, shifting its weight back and forth on them with wistful eagerness.

The sight of the dog put a wild idea into his head. He remembered the tale of the man, caught in a blizzard, who killed a steer and crawled inside the carcass, and so was saved. He would kill the dog and bury his hands in the warm body until the numbness went out of them. Then he could build another fire. He spoke to the dog, calling it to him; but in his voice was a strange note of fear that frightened the animal, who had never known the man to speak in such way before. Something was the matter, and its suspicious nature sensed danger—it knew not what danger, but somewhere, somehow, in its brain arose an apprehension of the man. It flattened its ears down at the sound of the man's voice, and its restless, hunching movements and the liftings and shiftings of its forefeet became more pronounced; but it would not come to the man. He got on his hands and knees and crawled toward the dog. This unusual posture again excited suspicion, and the animal sidled mincingly away.

The man sat up in the snow for a moment and struggled for calmness. Then he pulled on his mittens, by means of his teeth, and got upon his feet. He glanced down at first in order to assure himself that

HIS FLESH WAS BURNING. HE COULD SMELL IT.

Literary Analysis
Conflict What conflict is intensified in the passage beginning "The sight of the dog . . ."?

Reading Check
What happens to the man's second attempt to build a fire?

To Build a Fire **607**

Culturally Responsive Instruction
With the class, review the man's treatment of the dog. Students may note that the man does not treat the dog as a companion, that he ignores the dog's instinctive reactions to the deadly cold, that he pushes the dog into danger, and that he tries to kill the dog in order to survive. Discuss with students their personal responses to the man's treatment of the dog.

Point out that cultural attitudes toward dogs vary widely. In some cultures and social groups,

dogs are regarded as beloved pets; in others, they are regarded as hunting companions; in others merely as working animals. In some societies, dogs are treated as having no value at all. Have students discuss these cultural variations, then ask them to speculate about whether London's story would have had a different outcome had the man had a different attitude toward the dog.

---

30 Literary Analysis
Conflict
1. **Ask** students to consider how the man's conflict with nature has developed up to this point in the story. Point out that his struggles with his environment have become steadily more difficult.

2. Have students read the bracketed passage. If any students find this passage upsetting, encourage them to consider how their discomfort builds their sense of the story's conflict.

3. **Ask** students the Literary Analysis question.
   Possible response: The conflict between the man and the extreme cold is intensified when killing the dog becomes his last chance to escape the cold.

▶ **Monitor Progress Ask** students what details add to the intensity of the conflict.
   Possible response: Students may cite such details as "put a wild idea into his head"; the "strange note of fear" in the man's voice; the dog's building suspicions of the man; and the dog's "restless, hunching movements."

31 Reading Check
Answer: Shivering uncontrollably, he drops a large piece of moss on the fire; when he tries to poke the moss out, he extinguishes the fire.

Predicting

1. Before they read the bracketed passage, **ask** students to compare the man's survival skills with the dog's. Remind them that the narrator indicates that the dog's instincts give it a better grasp of the cold than the man has.

2. Have students read the bracketed passage. Then **ask** them to predict whether the man will survive and whether the dog will survive. Students should support their answers with details.
   Possible response: Based on the fact that the man has no means by which to start a fire, it is unlikely he will survive. The dog, on the other hand, is likely to survive because of its protective coat and strong instinct for survival.

33 Reading Strategy

Predicting

1. If they have not done so already, instruct students to construct a "predicting chart" that includes two columns.

2. Have students read the bracketed passage. **Ask** them to write clues from the passage in the left-hand column of their charts.
   Possible response: Students may note the man's growing "fear of death" and panic, as well as his new hope that he might run all the way to the camp.

3. **Ask** students: Does the man still have a chance for survival? Explain why or why not.
   Possible response: Students might say that the man will die because his condition is so bad and the camp is so far away. His behavior and thinking at this point are symptomatic of hypothermia. Others might feel that the man's only hope is to be rescued by others.

4. Have students write their responses in the right-hand column on their charts.

Vocabulary
peremptorily (pər emp′ tə rə lē) *adv.* decisively; commandingly

32

A CERTAIN FEAR OF DEATH, DULL AND OPPRESSIVE, CAME TO HIM.

33

he was really standing up, for the absence of sensation in his feet left him unrelated to the earth. His erect position in itself started to drive the webs of suspicion from the dog's mind; and when he spoke peremptorily, with the sound of whiplashes in his voice, the dog rendered its customary allegiance and came to him. As it came within reaching distance, the man lost his control. His arms flashed out to the dog, and he experienced genuine surprise when he discovered that his hands could not clutch, that there was neither bend nor feeling in the fingers. He had forgotten for the moment that they were frozen and that they were freezing more and more. All this happened quickly, and before the animal could get away, he encircled its body with his arms. He sat down in the snow, and in this fashion held the dog, while it snarled and whined and struggled.

But it was all he could do, hold its body encircled in his arms and sit there. He realized that he could not kill the dog. There was no way to do it. With his helpless hands he could neither draw nor hold his sheath-knife nor throttle the animal. He released it, and it plunged wildly away, with tail between its legs, and still snarling. It halted forty feet away and surveyed him curiously, with ears sharply pricked forward. The man looked down at his hands in order to locate them, and found them hanging on the ends of his arms. It struck him as curious that one should have to use his eyes in order to find out where his hands were. He began threshing his arms back and forth, beating the mittened hands against his sides. He did this for five minutes, violently, and his heart pumped enough blood up to the surface to put a stop to his shivering. But no sensation was aroused in the hands. He had an impression that they hung like weights on the ends of his arms, but when he tried to run the impression down, he could not find it.

A certain fear of death, dull and oppressive, came to him. This fear quickly became poignant as he realized that it was no longer a mere matter of freezing his fingers and toes, or of losing his hands and feet, but that it was a matter of life and death with the chances against him. This threw him into a panic, and he turned and ran up the creek-bed along the old, dim trail. The dog joined in behind and kept up with him. He ran blindly, without intention, in fear such as he had never known in his life. Slowly, as he plowed and floundered through the snow, he began to see things again—the banks of the creek, the old timber jams, the leafless aspens, and the sky. The running made him feel better. He did not shiver. Maybe, if he ran on, his feet would thaw out; and, anyway, if he ran far enough, he would reach camp and the boys. Without doubt he would lose some fingers and toes and some of his face; but the boys would take care of him, and save the rest of him when he got there. And at the same time there was another thought in his mind that said he would never get to the camp and the boys; that it was too many miles away, that the freezing had too great a start on him, and that he would soon be stiff

Vocabulary Development

Vocabulary Knowledge Rating

When students have completed reading and discussing the selection, have them take out their **Vocabulary Knowledge Rating** charts for the story. Read the words aloud, and have students rate their knowledge of words again in the After Reading column. Clarify any words that are still problematic. Have students write their own definitions and example or sentence in the appropriate column. Then have students complete the Vocabulary Lesson at the end of the selection. Encourage students to use the words in further discussion and written work about the selection. Remind them that they will be accountable for these words on the **Selection Test**, *Unit 3 Resources*, pages 168–170 or 171–173.

and dead. This thought he kept in the background and refused to consider. Sometimes it pushed itself forward and demanded to be heard, but he thrust it back and strove to think of other things.

It struck him as curious that he could run at all on feet so frozen that he could not feel them when they struck the earth and took the weight of his body. He seemed to himself to skim along above the surface, and to have no connection with the earth. Somewhere he had once seen a winged Mercury,[6] and he wondered if Mercury felt as he felt when skimming over the earth.

His theory of running until he reached camp and the boys had one flaw in it: he lacked the endurance. Several times he stumbled, and finally he tottered, crumpled up, and fell. When he tried to rise, he failed. He must sit and rest, he decided, and next time he would merely walk and keep on going. As he sat and regained his breath, he noted that he was feeling quite warm and comfortable. He was not shivering, and it even seemed that a warm glow had come to his chest and trunk. And yet, when he touched his nose or cheeks, there was no sensation. Running would not thaw them out. Nor would it thaw out his hands and feet. Then the thought came to him that the frozen portions of his body must be extending. He tried to keep this thought down, to forget it, to think of something else; he was aware of the panicky feeling that it caused, and he was afraid of the panic. But the thought asserted itself, and persisted, until it produced a vision of his body totally frozen. This was too much, and he made another wild run along the trail. Once he slowed down to a walk, but the thought of the freezing extending itself made him run again.

And all the time the dog ran with him, at his heels. When he fell down a second time, it curled its tail over its forefeet and sat in front of him, facing him, curiously eager and intent. The warmth and security of the animal angered him, and he cursed it till it flattened down its ears appeasingly. This time the shivering came more quickly upon the man. He was losing in his battle with the frost. It was creeping into his body from all sides. The thought of it drove him on, but he ran no more than a hundred feet, when he staggered and pitched headlong. It was his last panic. When he had recovered his breath and control, he sat up and entertained in his mind the conception of meeting death with dignity. However, the conception did not come to him in such terms. His idea of it was that he had been making a fool of himself, running around like a chicken with its head cut off—such was the simile that occurred to him. Well, he was bound to freeze anyway, and he might as well take it decently. With this new-found peace of mind came the first glimmerings of drowsiness. A good idea, he thought, to sleep off to death. It was like taking an anaesthetic. Freezing was not so bad as people thought. There were lots worse ways to die.

6. **Mercury** from Roman mythology, the wing-footed messenger of the gods.

Literary Analysis
Conflict and Irony As the man begins to feel warm, what does the reader know that the man does not?

☑ **Reading Check**
What thought does the man refuse to consider?

To Build a Fire **609**

③④ Literary Analysis
Conflict and Irony

1. Use the Enrichment note "Dangers of Cold Weather," at the bottom of page 598 in this Teacher's Edition, to inform students about the symptoms of hypothermia.

2. **Ask** students the Literary Analysis question.
   Answer: The reader knows that the feeling of comfortable warmth is a sign that the man is dying of hypothermia.

3. Point out to students that this situation is ironic because the man believes he is now all right, while the reader knows that he is about to die.

③⑤ Literary Analysis
Conflict and Irony

1. Remind students that in literary works conflict builds up to a *climax*—a crisis or turning point in the story's plot. From the climax, the story moves to a resolution, where the conflict comes to an end.

2. Have students read the bracketed passage. Point out that the man undergoes an important change here; for the first time, he accepts the inevitability of his death.

3. **Ask** students: How does this passage suggest the story's conflict—man versus nature—will be resolved?
   Possible response: Students should recognize that the man is dying and should answer that he has lost his struggle with the extreme weather conditions and thus will lose his life.

③⑥ Reading Check
Answer: He refuses to consider the thought that the frozen parts of his body are extending.

Differentiated
Instruction *for Universal Access*

Culturally Responsive Instruction: Standard English Learners
Language Focus If you have students who habitually use nonstandard English in academic discourse, work through the first Literary Analysis question on this page. Then, ask students to write out their explanations of the irony in the bracketed text. Have volunteers share answers.

As you review answers, first affirm all correct responses, whether or not they are framed in standard English. Then, for any answer not given in standard English, provide a standard English equivalent. Explain to students that both versions have the same meaning.

Guide students in a contrastive analysis of the two versions, pointing out the similarities and differences between them. Next, ask students to explain which rules of standard English help explain the difference between the two. Finally, emphasize for students that community language—the language one speaks with family and friends—is appropriate in some contexts, but that standard English is required in academic work.

Before students respond, you may wish to have them write a brief objective summary of the selection. As they answer the questions below, remind them to support their answers with evidence from the text.

1. **Possible response:** (a) The dog's instincts tell it not to travel but to stay where there is fire. (b) The man does not have the imagination to understand the significance of the cold or the possible consequences of traveling in such weather. (c) The dog is better equipped to survive because its instincts are better than the man's decisions.

2. (a) The man tries to avoid the hidden pools of water. (b) His feet get wet, requiring him to build a fire; he builds his fire by a tree, which dumps snow on it; his hands are too frozen to build a second fire; he freezes to death.

3. **Possible response:** London suggests that it requires significant <u>resolve</u>, along with strong survival skills, for <u>vulnerable</u> human beings to conquer a harsh <u>wilderness</u>. In London's story, place assumes the role of antagonist, creating conflict with the protagonist that impels his plot.

He pictured the boys finding his body next day. Suddenly he found himself with them, coming along the trail and looking for himself. And, still with them, he came around a turn in the trail and found himself lying in the snow. He did not belong with himself any more, for even then he was out of himself; standing with the boys and looking at himself in the snow. It certainly was cold, was his thought. When he got back to the States he could tell the folks what real cold was. He drifted on from this to a vision of the old-timer on Sulphur Creek. He could see him quite clearly, warm and comfortable, and smoking a pipe.

"You were right, old hoss; you were right," the man mumbled to the old-timer of Sulphur Creek.

Then the man drowsed off into what seemed to him the most comfortable and satisfying sleep he had ever known. The dog sat facing him and waiting. The brief day drew to a close in a long, slow twilight. There were no signs of a fire to be made, and, besides, never in the dog's experience had it known a man to sit like that in the snow and make no fire. As the twilight drew on, its eager yearning for the fire mastered it, and with a great lifting and shifting of forefeet, it whined softly, then flattened its ears down in anticipation of being chidden[7] by the man. But the man remained silent. Later, the dog whined loudly. And still later it crept close to the man and caught the scent of death. This made the animal bristle and back away. A little longer it delayed, howling under the stars that leaped and danced and shone brightly in the cold sky. Then it turned and trotted up the trail in the direction of the camp it knew, where were the other food providers and fire providers.

---

7. chidden scolded.

Critical Reading

Cite textual evidence to support your responses.

1. **Key Ideas and Details** **(a)** What do the dog's instincts tell it about the cold? **(b) Compare and Contrast:** Why does the extreme cold "make no impression" on the man? **(c) Make a Judgment:** Who is better equipped to survive in the cold, the dog or the man? Explain.

2. **Key Ideas and Details** **(a)** What trap does the man unsuccessfully try to avoid? **(b) Analyze Cause and Effect:** What deadly chain of events does this begin?

3. **Integration of Knowledge and Ideas** What does London suggest about human strength in the face of nature's power? In your response, use at least two of these Essential Question words: *vulnerable, resolve, frailty, wilderness.* *[Connecting to the Essential Question: What is the relationship between literature and place?]*

Concept Connector

Reading Skill Graphic Organizer
Ask students to review the graphic organizers on which they have listed clues to help them predict events. Then have students share their organizers and compare their predictions.

Activating Prior Knowledge
Have students return to their responses to the Activating Prior Knowledge activity. Ask them to explain whether their thoughts have changed and if so, how.

Writing About the Essential Question
Have students compare the responses to the prompt before they completed reading "To Build a Fire" with their thoughts after reading it. Have them work individually or in groups, writing or discussing their thoughts, to define their new responses. Then lead a class discussion, probing for what students have learned that confirms or invalidates their initial thoughts. Encourage students to cite specific textual details to support their responses.

Literary Analysis

1. Key Ideas and Details Use a chart like the one shown to analyze the **conflict** in "To Build a Fire." **(a)** What **external conflict** drives the plot? **(b)** Identify at least three details in the **setting** that contribute to the central conflict.

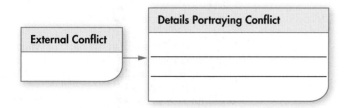

2. Key Ideas and Details In what ways does the main character's awareness of the conflict intensify as the story unfolds? Explain.

3. Key Ideas and Details What **internal conflict** develops as the plot progresses? Explain, using details from the story.

4. Key Ideas and Details What events finally resolve, or settle, the conflict?

5. Craft and Structure The man breaks through the snow and steps in the hidden spring. In what ways is this event an example of **irony?**

6. Craft and Structure What is ironic about the location in which the man builds his fire?

7. Craft and Structure In what way do London's descriptions of the dog's feelings and its instincts about survival increase the story's **dramatic irony?**

Reading Strategy

8. Early in the story, the narrator reveals that the man does not really know the temperature outside. What can you **predict** from this clue?

9. (a) What *background knowledge* about the Yukon did you bring to your reading of the story? **(b)** What predictions were you able to make based on this knowledge? **(c)** Were your predictions correct? Explain.

10. (a) What information do the man's recollections of his conversation with the old-timer provide? **(b)** What clues about the man can you draw based on his responses to the old-timer? **(c)** How do these clues help you predict what will happen at the end of the story?

11. (a) At what point did you first predict that the man would not survive his journey? **(b)** On what clues did you base your prediction?

To Build a Fire **611**

Common Core State Standards

Writing
1. Write arguments to support claims in an analysis of substantive topics or texts, using valid reasoning and relevant and sufficient evidence. *(p. 612)*

Language
1. Demonstrate command of the conventions of standard English grammar and usage when writing or speaking. *(p. 613)*
4.b. Identify and correctly use patterns of word changes that indicate different meanings or parts of speech. *(p. 612)*
4.d. Verify the preliminary determination of the meaning of a word or phrase. *(p. 612)*
5. Demonstrate understanding of word relationships. *(p. 612)*

Assessment Practice

Context (For more practice, see *All-in-One Workbook*.)

Many tests require students to use contextual analysis to determine the meanings of words and phrases. Use the following to demonstrate.

Fifty degrees below zero meant eighty-odd degrees of frost. Such fact. . . did not lead him to meditate upon his frailty as a creature of temperature, and upon man's frailty in general, able only to live within certain narrow limits of heat and cold.

In this passage, the phrase "frailty as a creature of temperature" means

A Humans can be killed by heat and cold.

B Humans are frail when they have a temperature.

C Humans can survive in the cold.

D Even frail humans can withstand extreme temperatures.

The last part of the sentence gives context clues that show **A** is the correct answer.

Answers

1. **(a)** The external conflict is between man and nature. **(b)** **Sample detail:** Students may list the presence of hidden springs.

2. **Possible response:** The forces of nature affect the man more and more as the story progresses; gradually, the man becomes aware of the danger he is in.

3. The man's lack of judgment and overconfidence conflict with his genuine fear for his own safety.

4. Falling snow puts out the man's fire; unable to start a second fire, he freezes to death.

5. It is ironic because he has been keeping a careful eye out for exactly the trap he falls into.

6. It is ironic because the success of the fire causes snow to fall from the tree above it and put it out.

7. By describing the dog's feelings and instincts, London lets the reader know what the man does not: that he is in deadly danger.

8. **Sample answer:** Temperature will be a factor in the man's fate.

9. **Possible response: (a)** The Yukon is a cold and sparsely populated area. **(b)** The extreme conditions would be difficult for the man to overcome. **(c)** My predictions were correct; it was too cold and the man was too isolated to survive.

10. **(a)** One should never travel alone in the Yukon when the temperature is less than fifty degrees below zero. **(b)** **Possible response:** Each time the man remembers the advice and laughs, it is a reminder of the fatal danger he faces. **(c)** These clues reveal the man's physical circumstances and his inner attitude, which help predict the outcome.

11. **Possible response: (a)** Students may cite the plunge into the creek or the failure of his fire. **(b)** Students should support their views with details from the text.

611

Vocabulary Acquisition and Use

1. Introduce the skill, using the instruction on the student page.

2. Have students complete the Word Analysis activity and the Vocabulary practice.

Word Analysis

1. *impending:* imminent; something impending "hangs over" those who await it

2. *pendulum:* an instrument that hangs from a fixed point

3. *suspend:* to hang from a single point

4. *perpendicular:* at a right angle; one line seems to hang on the other

5. *pendant:* a hanging ornament, perhaps on a necklace

Vocabulary

noun: conflagration

noun: appendages

adjective: unwonted

adverb: peremptorily

adjective: conjectural

Writing

1. To guide students in writing this essay, give them the **Support for Writing Lesson** worksheet (*Unit 3 Resources,* p. 163).

2. Explain to students that literary criticism digs beneath the surface of a work to present an interpretation of it. This interpretation forms the thesis, or main point, of the essay.

3. Students' essays should demonstrate a clear understanding of internal and external conflicts and how they contribute to the story's meaning. Students should use direct quotations from "To Build a Fire" to support their critiques and move them forward. Remind them to use quotations accurately.

4. Assess students' evaluations using **Rubrics for Critique**, in *Professional Development Guidebook,* pages 276–277.

ⓔ Vocabulary Acquisition and Use

Word Analysis: Latin Root -pend-

The Latin root -pend- means "to hang." Your *appendages*—your arms and legs, toes and feet—hang or extend from your torso. Likewise, if you *depend* on someone, you may be "hanging on" to him or her for help. Each of the following words contains the root -pend-. Write a definition for each word and explain how the idea of hanging or extending relates to the term. If a word is unfamiliar, use a dictionary to clarify its meaning.

1. impending
2. pendulum
3. suspend
4. perpendicular
5. pendant

Vocabulary: Word/Phrase Relationships

Scan the paragraph below. For each blank, write a sentence explaining what type of word—noun, adjective, or adverb—you would expect to find there. Then, fill in the blanks with appropriate words from the vocabulary list on page 594.

A lightning storm in the parched woodland sparked a(n) _____. The tree's dry limbs and branches fell flaming from the trees, and soon the forest floor was covered with charred _____ of the tree. This was a(n) _____ scene for the young and inexperienced fire chief. Yet, he acted _____ ordering all firefighters to work around the clock. His estimates of how long it would take to overcome the fire, however, were _____ at best.

Writing

ⓔ **Argument** Critical writing often presents and defends an interpretation of a literary work. The writer examines how elements, such as plot, setting, character, and point of view, work together to convey an insight about life. Write a work of **literary criticism** in which you present and defend your interpretation of the message expressed in "To Build a Fire."

Prewriting Review the story to identify London's message about the relationship between humanity and nature. Gather details that support your interpretation.

Drafting In your introduction, state your thesis and outline your main points. Focus each body paragraph on one main point. Cite supporting details from the story.

> **Model: Elaborating to Support an Argument**
> The dog, equipped by centuries of evolution for life in the bitter cold, serves as a symbolic foil to the man. Unlike the man, who disregards plain evidence, "... the dog knew; all its ancestry knew, and it had inherited the knowledge. And it knew that it was not good to walk abroad in such fearful cold."
>
> Providing details from the work helps to elaborate on the main point, underlined here.

Revising Review your draft, making sure your thesis is clear and your support is convincing. Look for opportunities to *elaborate ideas through supporting details.*

Assessment Resources

Unit 3 Resources   All

L1 L2 EL Selection Test A, pp. 168–170
Administer Test A to less advanced students and English learners.

L3 L4 EL Selection Test B, pp. 171–173
Administer Test B to on-level and more advanced students.

L3 L4 Open-Book Test, pp. 165–167. As an alternative, give the Open-Book Test.

All

Customizable Test Bank

Self-tests
Students may prepare for the **Selection Test** by taking the **Self-test** online.

PHLit Online! All assessment resources are available at **www.PHLitOnline.com.**

Conventions and Style: Introductory Phrases and Clauses

To keep your reader's interest, try *varying sentence structures* in your writing. For example, instead of starting every sentence with the subject, begin some sentences with phrases or clauses. A **phrase** is a group of words that acts as a single part of speech and lacks a complete subject and verb. A **clause** is a group of words that has both a subject and verb.

Using Introductory Phrases and Clauses to Vary Sentence Structure

Subject First: He stopped at the top of a steep bank to catch his breath.
Phrase First: *At the top of a steep bank,* he stopped to catch his breath. (prepositional phrase)

Subject First: The dog seemed hesitant as he slinked along behind the man.
Phrase First: *Slinking along behind the man,* the dog seemed hesitant. (participial phrase)

Subject First: He sends the dog ahead to check the thickness of the ice.
Phrase First: *To check the thickness of the ice,* he sends the dog ahead. (infinitive phrase)

Subject First: The spittle crackled and froze when he spit into the air.
Clause First: *When he spit into the air,* the spittle crackled and froze. (adverb clause)

Punctuation Tip: Place a comma after most introductory phrases and clauses.

Practice Revise each sentence by using the italicized part as an introductory phrase or clause. In some sentences, you will have to make slight changes to the original wording.

1. Huskies burrow beneath the snow *to stay warm.*
2. Thousands of prospectors *lured by visions of gold and wealth* headed to the Yukon.
3. His nose and cheekbones turned numb *even though he kept rubbing them.*
4. He could not build a third fire *in spite of all his efforts.*
5. The dog *grew suspicious* and moved away from the man.
6. He heard the crackle of ice *as he came around a bend in the creek.*
7. The dog *curled his tail around his forefeet* and sat there watching the man.
8. The man beat his hands against his sides *to restore feeling to his fingers.*
9. Jack London produced more than fifty books *during his career.*
10. London was *determined to earn a living as a writer,* so he often worked fifteen hours a day.

© **Writing and Speaking Conventions**

A. Writing Use each phrase or clause to begin a sentence.

1. in his pocket   3. numbed by the extreme cold
2. to build a fire   4. after his legs are wet

Example: If he kept the pace
Sentence: If he kept the pace, he would be at the camp by six.

B. Speaking Suppose the dog in the story could speak. Tell the story as he would relate it to the men at the camp. In your story, begin at least four sentences with an introductory phrase or clause.

> **PH WRITING COACH**
> Further instruction and practice are available in *Prentice Hall Writing Coach.*

Integrated Language Skills **613**

Extend the Lesson

Sentence Modeling
Read aloud these sentences from "To Build a Fire":

> *At the man's heals trotted a dog, a big native husky, the proper wolf dog, gray-coated and without any visible or temperamental differences from its brother, the wild wolf.*
>
> *When all was ready, the man reached in his pocket for a second piece of birch bark.*

Ask students what they notice about each sentence. Elicit from them that each sentence begins with an introductory phrase or clause.

Have them identify the introductory phrase or clause. Then have them rewrite the sentence, without an introductory clause or phrase, without altering the meaning of the sentence. Have students imitate one of the sentences in a sentence on a topic of their own choosing, matching the grammatical and stylistic feature discussed. Collect the sentences, and share them with the class.

Conventions and Style

Introduce and discuss the skill, using the instruction on the student page.

Think Aloud: Model the Skill

Model the skill of using introductory phrases and clauses. Say to students:

> When I draft, I find it very easy to fall into a monotonous subject-verb sentence pattern. To help me revise, I use highlighters on my first draft, using one color for subjects, another color for verbs. Then it is easy for me to spot places where I should vary my sentence patterns.

Practice
Sample Answers

1. <u>To stay warm,</u> huskies . . . .
2. <u>Lured by visions of gold and wealth,</u> thousands . . . .
3. <u>Even though he kept rubbing them,</u> his nose . . . .
4. <u>In spite of all his efforts,</u> he . . . .
5. <u>Growing suspicious,</u> the dog . . . .
6. <u>As he came around a bend in the creek,</u> he heard . . . .
7. <u>Curling his tail around his forefeet,</u> the dog . . . .
8. <u>To restore feeling to his fingers,</u> the man . . . .
9. <u>During his career,</u> Jack London produced . . . .
10. <u>Determined to earn a living as a writer,</u> London . . . .

Writing and Speaking Conventions

A. Sample responses:

1. <u>In his pocket</u> he kept a good supply of matches.
2. <u>To build a fire,</u> he would need to gather fuel from the sparse ground.
3. <u>Numbed by the extreme cold,</u> the man fought the urge to give up.
4. <u>After his legs are wet,</u> the man panics and loses control.

B. Sample response: <u>Although it was very cold,</u> the man gathered supplies and called me. I followed him to the trail. <u>At his pace,</u> he would reach camp by nightfall. <u>Breaking through a hidden spring,</u> he got his feet wet. His fire went out when snow fell from a tree. <u>After two more tries,</u> he gave up and lay down to die.

> **PH WRITING COACH**   Grade 11

Students will find additional information on phrases and clauses in Chapter 15.

613

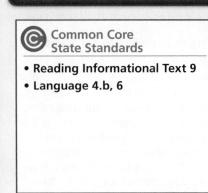

❶ About the Text Forms

1. Introduce the forms, using the instruction on the student page.

2. Tell students to think of a *personal history* as both personal and historical. It tells a person's own life and thoughts. It also describes places and events that were happening when the person wrote.

3. Remind students that a *speech* was meant to be heard. The appeals to emotions, values, and reason are more direct and simple than those in an essay.

❷ Reading Strategy

1. Introduce the strategy, using the instruction on the student page.

2. Tell students that to determine the author's unstated assumptions and beliefs, they must ask what opinion the author seems to have about a topic. They should look for pieces of information, feelings, opinions, and tone.

❸ What is the relationship between literature and place?

Tell students to look for details as they read that will help them answer the Essential Question, including the Colt family's expectations of what they would find in Kansas and Chief Joseph's final sentence.

PH WRITING COACH Grade 11

Students will find additional information about research writing in Chapter 11.

Primary Sources

Personal History   **Speech**
Heading West   **I Will Fight No More Forever**

❶ About the Text Forms

A **personal history** is a type of autobiographical nonfiction in which a writer relates his or her experiences during a particular event or era. Personal histories can take many forms, from straightforward narratives to the dated entries of a journal or diary.

A **speech** is a nonfiction work that is delivered orally to an audience. There are many types of speeches, each suited to a different kind of public gathering and setting. Speakers use a variety of strategies to express their ideas and move listeners. They may appeal to listeners' values or emotions, or to their sense of reason and logic.

❷ Reading Strategy

In addition to facts, primary-source documents written by individuals often include subjective statements, such as opinions, beliefs, prejudices, and assumptions. For later readers and researchers, these subjective statements are important for a number of reasons:

• They provide a window into history as it was truly experienced.

• They provide a sense of the principles and values that drove a society.

While authors may state these ideas explicitly, more often they will merely imply, or suggest, them. Teasing out these unstated claims, or **making inferences about an author's implicit and explicit philosophical assumptions and beliefs,** is an important part of reading primary-source documents. As you read these documents, notice references, details, opinions, and other clues to the underlying assumptions that motivate these writers.

❸ 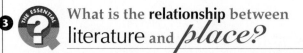 **What is the relationship between literature and *place?***

Most settlers of the American West were farmers who sought a better life for themselves and their children. This meant settling on fertile land that they could own, cultivate, and pass on to later generations. For Native Americans, however, the land was the source of all life and belonged to no one person. As you read these texts, watch for words and phrases that reflect these competing worldviews.

Teaching Resources

Unit 3 Resources
    Primary Source work sheet, p. 174
    Vocabulary Builder, p. 175
Professional Development Guidebook
    Enrichment, pp. 230, 231

❹ Note-Taking Guide

Primary-source documents are a rich source of information for researchers. As you read these documents, use a note-taking guide like the one shown to organize relevant and accurate information.

> **1** Type of Document (check one)
> ☐ Telegram   ☐ Press Release   ☐ Personal History   ☐ Letter
> ☐ Speech   ☐ Newspaper   ☐ Report   ☐ E-Mail
>
> **2** Date(s) of Document _____
>
> **3** Author of Document _____
>   Author's Position, Title, or Circumstances_____
>
> **4** Audience: For whom was the document written?_____
> _____
>
> **5** Document Information
>   **a** What is the main subject of the document? _____
> _____
>
>   **b** Find in the document a stated opinion, or belief, about the subject you listed
>   above. Write it here. _____
> _____
>
>   **c** List one additional thing the author says that you think is important.
> _____
> _____
>
>   **d** Find in the document an implied—not directly stated—opinion. Write it here.
> _____
> _____

Reading Strategy Inferring an Author's Philosophical Assumptions and Beliefs Remember that an opinion is a person's belief or judgment about something. Unlike a fact, an opinion cannot be proved. As you read, look for statements that express feelings, attitudes, or desires.

This guide was adapted from the **U.S. National Archives** document analysis worksheets.

❺ Vocabulary

shares (sherz) *n.* portions of ownership of a company or a piece of property (p. 617)

pervading (per vād´ iŋ) *v.* spreading throughout (p. 618)

levee (lev´ ē) *n.* an embankment built along the side of a river to prevent flooding (p. 618)

emigrants (em´ i grənts) *n.* people who leave one place to settle in another (p. 618)

profusion (prō fyo͞o´ zhən) *n.* abundance; rich supply (p. 619)

foothold (fo͝ot´ hōld´) *n.* a secure position from which further actions can be taken (p. 619)

prairie (prer´ ē) *n.* a treeless, grass-covered plain (p. 620)

forded (fôrd´ əd) *v.* crossed a river at a low point (p. 620)

ravine (rə vēn´) *n.* a long, deep hollow in the ground; a gully (p. 621)

---

❹ Note-Taking Guide

1. As a class, review the instruction on the student page about the note-taking guide.

2. Emphasize question 5 on the guide by having a student read the Reading Strategy note in the margin of the student page.

3. Encourage students to use a similar guide as they read the primary sources in this set. Point out that they may customize their note-taking guides to fit the particular needs of the reading assignment.

❺ Vocabulary

1. Pronounce each word, giving its definition; have students say it aloud.

2. Also see the **Classroom Strategies and Teaching Routines** card for vocabulary.

Vocabulary Development   © CCSS Language 6

Vocabulary Knowledge Rating
Create a **Vocabulary Knowledge Rating Chart** (*Professional Development Guidebook*, p. 33) for the vocabulary words on the student page. Give each student a copy of the chart with the words on it. Read the words aloud, and have students mark their rating of each in the Before Reading column. When students have completed reading and discussing the group of selections, have them take out their **Vocabulary Knowledge Rating Charts** for the selections. Read the words aloud and have students rate their knowledge again in the After Reading column. Clarify any words that are still problematic. Then have students complete the Vocabulary practice at the end of the selections.

These selections are available in an interactive format in the **Enriched Online Student Edition**, at **www. PHLitOnline.com**, which includes a thematically related video with writing prompt and an interactive graphic organizer.

615

In 1856, when Miriam Davis Colt and her family set out, Kansas was considered the far "West." It was not until later in the century that pioneers tried to reach California and Oregon in a much more treacherous journey that required them to cross the Rockies as well as the Great Plains. Settlers like Colt were farmers. They wanted individual plots to cultivate, and they considered the land they settled as their own.

Chief Joseph was born in the Wallowa Valley in what is now Oregon. In 1871 he succeeded his father as leader of the Nez Percé tribe. At that time, the United States government was trying to force the tribe to relocate to Idaho. The Nez Percé had signed a treaty in 1863 giving the government control of the tribe's land, but Chief Joseph felt that the treaty was illegal and refused to recognize it. "The earth is the mother of all people, and all people should have equal rights upon it." Chief Joseph's words express the point of view of Native Americans, who saw themselves as using land but never owning it. Because they were a culture of hunters, the Nez Percé ranged over a vast territory. These opposing viewpoints were a source of ongoing strife in frontier America.

❻ THE STORY BEHIND THE DOCUMENTS

▲ The title page of Colt's published book

▲ Chief Joseph

The history of America from its beginnings to 1900 might be summarized in two words: *westward expansion.* For more than 300 years, European explorers, colonial settlers, and American pioneers pushed west from the Atlantic Ocean toward the distant Pacific. Urged onward by curiosity, these travelers—and the ever-strengthening national government behind them—also believed that it was their right and duty to settle the continent. The consequences of this policy came to a dramatic climax during the 1800s, as unprecedented numbers of pioneers flocked westward. **Miriam Davis Colt** (1815–1900) and her family were among them. In 1856, the Colts set out on a month-long journey from upstate New York to Kansas. At the time, Kansas was in turmoil. In 1854, Congress had passed an act giving the people of the territory the freedom to decide for themselves whether to allow slavery. Both anti-slavery Northerners and pro-slavery Southerners streamed there from the East. The resulting conflicts were frequent and bloody.

Aware that their journey was history in the making, many Kansas pioneers kept a written record of their experiences. Some, like Colt, described their journeys in personal histories meant for a public audience, including relatives and future generations. Occasionally, as in Colt's case, the histories were later published as books.

Though the settlers often lived harrowing lives, the most endangered people on the western frontier were the American Indians. As the frontier advanced past the Mississippi River, tribe after tribe was driven from its ancient homeland. The cycle was always the same: As white settlers encroached upon new lands, the tribes in that region would resist. United States soldiers would be sent to secure the area, and war would ensue. Eventually, the Indians would be defeated. They would either be forced onto a reservation, or made to sign a treaty in which they were promised food or money in exchange for their lands. More often than not, these promises went unfulfilled.

One such ill-fated tribe was the Nez Percé of the Pacific northwest. When an 1863 treaty reduced the size of the tribe's lands to a small reservation in Idaho, a group of the Nez Percé continued living outside the reservation boundaries in Oregon's Wallowa Valley. They were allowed to do so until 1877, when General Oliver O. Howard issued an ultimatum. Unwilling to concede, Nez Percé leader **Chief Joseph** (1840–1904) and six hundred of his people fled northeast through the mountains of Montana, toward the Canada border. Hotly pursued by legions of soldiers and finally weakened by the onset of winter, the Nez Percé were compelled to admit defeat. The speech in which Chief Joseph surrenders contains some of the most achingly beautiful words ever spoken.

HEADING WEST

Miriam Davis Colt

BACKGROUND *Miriam Davis Colt and her family were among a group of families forming a vegetarian commune in the Kansas territory. The personal history from which this excerpt is taken was published in 1862 under the title "Went to Kansas; Being a Thrilling Account of an Ill-Fated Expedition to that Fairy Land, and its Sad Results."*

JANUARY 5TH, 1856. We are going to Kansas. The Vegetarian Company that has been forming for many months, has finally organized, formed its constitution, elected its directors, and is making all necessary preparations for the spring settlement. . . . We can have, I think, good faith to believe, that our directors will fulfill on their part; and we, as settlers of a new country, by going in a company will escape the hardships attendant on families going in singly, and at once find ourselves surrounded by improving society in a young and flourishing city. It will be better for ourselves pecuniarily,[1] and better in the future for our children.

My husband has long been a practical vegetarian, and we expect much from living in such a genial clime, where fruit is so quickly grown, and with people whose tastes and habits will coincide with our own.

JANUARY 15TH. We are making every necessary preparation for our journey, and our home in Kansas. My husband has sold his farm, purchased shares in the company, sent his money as directed by H. S. Clubb. . . . I am very busy in repairing all of our clothing, looking over bags of pieces, tearing off and reducing down, bringing everything into as small a compass as possible, so that we shall have no unnecessary baggage.

APRIL 15TH. Have been here in West Stockholm, at my brother's, since Friday last. Have visited Mother very hard, for, in all probability, it is the last visit we shall have until we meet where parting never comes—believe we have said everything we can think of to say.

❶ ▲ Primary Source: Photograph
What does this photograph suggest about the quality of life people led while on the journey west? **[Analyze]**

Vocabulary
shares (sherz) *n.* portions into which a company or a piece of property is divided

❷ ☑ Reading Check
Why do the Colts decide to travel to Kansas?

---

1. **pecuniarily** (pi kyōō′ nē er′ i lē) *adv.* financially.

Heading West **617**

---

❸ Vocabulary Builder

Latin Phrases

1. Call students' attention to the phrase *terra firma* and its definition: "firm earth" or "solid ground."

2. Explain to students that Latin phrases such as *terra firma* are often used in literature. They can often find the definitions of such Latin phrases in the dictionary.

3. **Ask:** How does Colt feel now that she is back on *terra firma*? **Answer:** She is relieved to be "safely" back where she can see where she is going and to be off the steamboat, with its unsanitary drinking water and potential for hitting snags in the river.

❹ Primary Sources

Personal History

1. Remind students that a personal history contains both personal information about the writer and general information about the time and place in which the writer lived.

2. Ask a volunteer to read the May 1st entry.

3. Then **ask** the Primary Source question: What two contrasting aspects of the pioneers' journey does Colt describe in the May 1st entry?
Answer: The first part of the entry is a description of Kansas City. Colt writes about the streets, buildings, and wagons loaded with trade goods. She also notes that the men buy the supplies for the journey in the city, and she describes the droves of cattle taken into town to sell to the settlers. The last two paragraphs are personal. In them, she thinks of her wedding anniversary, worries about the future and homesickness, and tells herself to be optimistic.

Vocabulary

pervading (per vād´ iŋ) *v.* spreading throughout

levee (lev´ ē) *n.* an embankment built along the side of a river to prevent flooding

emigrants (em´i grənts) *n.* people who leave one place to settle in another

Primary Sources

Personal History What two contrasting aspects of the pioneers' journey does Colt describe in the May 1st entry?

APRIL 16TH. Antwerp, N.Y. Bade our friends good bye, in Potsdam, this morning, at the early hour of two o'clock.

APRIL 22ND. Have been on the cars[2] again since yesterday morning. Last night was a lovely moonlit night, a night of thought, as we sped almost with lightning speed, along in the moonlight, past the rail fences.

Found ourselves in this miserable hotel before we knew it. Miserable fare—herring boiled with cabbage—miserable, dirty beds, and an odor pervading the house that is not at all agreeable. Mistress gone.

APRIL 23RD. On board steamer "Cataract," bound for Kansas City.

APRIL 24TH. A hot summer day. The men in our company are out in the city, purchasing wagons and farming implements, to take along on the steamer up to Kansas City.

APRIL 28TH. The steamer struck a "snag" last night; gave us a terrible jar; tore off a part of the kitchen; ladies much frightened. Willie is not very well; the water is bad; it affects all strangers.

❸ APRIL 30TH. Here we are, at Kansas City, all safely again on terra firma. Hasten to the hotel—find it very much crowded. Go up, up, up, and upstairs to our lodging rooms.

MAY 1ST. Take a walk out onto the levee—view the city, and see that it takes but a few buildings in this western world to make a city. The houses and shops stand along on the levee, extending back into the hillsides. The narrow street is literally filled with huge merchandise wagons bound for Santa Fe. The power attached to these wagons is seven or eight and sometimes nine pair of long-eared mules, or as many pair of oxen, with a Mexican driver who wields a whip long enough to reach the foremost pair, and who does not hesitate to use it with severity, and a noise, too.

❹ Large droves of cattle are driven into town to be sold to emigrants, who like us, are going into the Territory. Our husbands are all out today buying oxen, provisions and cooking utensils for our ox-wagon journey into the Territory.

This is the anniversary of my wedding-day, and as I review the past pleasant years as they have passed, one after another, until they now number eleven, a shadow comes over me, as I try to look away into the future and ask, "What is my destiny?"

Ah! away with all these shadowings. We shall be very busy this year in making our home comfortable, so that no time can be spared for that dreaded disease, "home-sickness," to take hold of us, and we mean to obey physical laws,[3] thereby securing to ourselves strength of body and vigor of mind.

---

2. **cars** train cars.
3. **physical laws** community's by-laws that dictated members abstain from alcohol and meat.

618 Division, Reconciliation, and Expansion (1850–1914)

Enrichment: Analyzing a Historical Event

The Kansas-Nebraska Act

Students may not be aware of the political conflicts settlers faced. The Kansas-Nebraska Act of 1854 allowed settlers to determine whether these territories would be slave or free. Hostilities between bands of proslavery and antislavery settlers erupted. Proslavery Southerners known as "border ruffians" sacked the antislavery town of Lawrence, Kansas. In response, John Brown and his sons slaughtered five proslavery settlers along Pottawatomie Creek. The violence in "bleeding Kansas" continued into 1861.

Activity: Speech Have students research the consequences of the Kansas-Nebraska Act and record information in the **Enrichment: Analyzing a Historical Event** work sheet, in *Professional Development Guidebook,* page 230. Have them prepare a short speech for a congressman of the time suggesting how to end the violence in Kansas.

MAY 2ND. A lovely day. Our husbands are loading the ox-wag-ons. . . . Women and children walk along up the hill out of this "Great City," wait under a tree—what a beautiful country is spread out before us! Will our Kansas scenery equal this . . .?

One mile from the city, and Dr. Thorn has broke his wagon tongue;[4] it must be sent back to Kansas City to be mended. Fires kindled—women cooking—supper eaten sitting round on logs, stones and wagon tongues. This I am sure is a "pic-nic." We expect "pic-nic" now all the time. We are shaded by the horse-chestnut, sweet walnut, and spreading oak; flowers blooming at our feet, and grasshoppers in profusion hopping in every direction. This is summer time.

MAY 3RD. The women and children, who slept in their wagons last night, got a good drenching from the heavy shower. It was fortu-nate for mother, sister, myself and children, that lodgings were found for us in a house. My husband said not a rain drop found him; he had the whole wagon to himself, besides all of our Indian blankets. Father, it seems, fell back a little and found a place to camp in a tav-ern (not a hotel), where he fell in with the scores of Georgians who loaded a steamer and came up the river the same time that we did. He said he had to be very shrewd indeed not to have them find out that he was a "Free States"[5] man. These Bandits have been sent in here, and will commit all sorts of depredations on the Free State set-tlers, and no doubt commit many a bloody murder.

Have passed Westport, the foothold for Border-Ruffianism. The town looks new, but the hue is dingy. Our drivers used their goads to hurry up the oxen's heavy tread, for we felt somewhat afraid, for we learned the Georgians had centered here. Here, too, came in the Santa Fe and Indian trade—so here may be seen the huge Mexican wagon, stubborn mule, swarthy driver with his goad-like whip, and the red man of the prairie on his fleet Indian pony, laden with dried meat, furs, and buffalo robes.

"What! fast in the mud, and with our wagon tongue broke?" "Why yes, to be sure." So a long time is spent before my hus-band and Dr. House can put our vehicle in moving order again. Meanwhile, we women folks and children must sit quietly in the wagon to keep out of the rain—lunch on soda biscuit, look at the deep, black mud in which our wagon is set, and inhale the sweet odor that comes from the blossoms of the crab-apple trees that are blooming in sheets of whiteness along the roadside. . . .

---

4. **wagon tongue** harnessing pole attached to the front axle of a horse-drawn vehicle.
5. **"Free States"** Free Soil movement; a group whose goal was to keep slavery out of the western territories.

Vocabulary
profusion (prō fyoo´ zhən) *n.* abundance; rich supply

foothold (foot´ hōld´) *n.* a secure position from which further actions can be taken

Reading Strategy
Inferring Philosophical Assumptions and Beliefs
What assumptions does Colt hold about the opponents of "Free States" settlers?

▼ Wagon used by Dr. Marcus and Narcissa Whitman, 19th century pioneers in the Oregon Territory

Heading West **619**

❺ Critical Thinking
Compare and Contrast

1. Ask students to consider what it would be like to travel long distances in a wagon drawn by oxen.

2. Read aloud the bracketed passage.

3. **Ask:** What are some of the dif-ficulties nineteenth-century pio-neer travelers faced that made traveling more difficult than it is today?
   Possible response: The pio-neers had to depend upon oxen and other animals for power. Such animals had to be fed and cared for. Wagons traveled slowly and often needed repairs. Roads in some areas were little more than dirt trails.

❻ Reading Strategy
Analyzing Philosophical Assumptions and Beliefs

1. Remind students to look for state-ments that express opinions, feelings, and attitudes to find a writer's philosophical assump-tions and beliefs.

2. Then have students review the bracketed passage.

3. **Ask** the Reading Strategy ques-tion: What assumptions does Colt hold about the opponents of "Free States" settlers?
   Answer: Colt holds a very poor opinion of them. She calls them "Bandits" and their behavior "Border-Ruffianism." She also says that she, her family, and the other members of their company are afraid of them.

Differentiated Instruction for Universal Access

Strategy for Less Proficient Readers
Have these students list the events of Colt's trip and construct a chain-of-events chart. Encourage them to note the different forms of transportation—train, steamboat, wagon—the Colts take to help students organize their notes. This strategy can help students comprehend the events related in "Heading West."

EL Support for English Learners
The many sentence fragments in "Heading West" may confuse students. Help them identify the missing subjects or verbs. You may guide them to restate the fragments as complete sen-tences. The description of the hotel in the April 22nd entry, for example, has sentence frag-ments.

❼ Reading Strategy
Analyzing Philosophical Assumptions and Beliefs

1. Point out that writers sometimes express their attitudes through irony.

2. Discuss what the phrases *lord of the castle* and *lord of the manor* usually bring to mind. Talk about how *lord* has connotations of wealth, power, and elegance and *castle* of luxury and great size.

3. Then read the bracketed passage. **Ask** the Reading Strategy question: What beliefs underlie Colt's ironic reference to the owner of the log cabin as the "Lord of the Castle"?
Possible response: Colt actually considers the house and living conditions quite primitive since the fireplace lacks trammels—a basic piece of equipment for hanging cooking pots—and the barefooted wife carries a sack of cornmeal over her shoulder. So the log cabin is the opposite of a castle, and the residents the opposite of refined aristocrats.

▶ **Monitor Progress** Have students reread the first paragraph of the May 11th entry and **ask:** Who are the "noble lords" in this sentence? Why does Colt refer to the men in an ironic way?
Answer: The "noble lords" are the men or husbands who are driving the wagons. She uses irony to show that she—and probably the other women—find their complaint absurd.

▶ **Reteach:** Review the paragraph and encourage students to see how Colt makes her point. Guide them to see that by listing all the items that went in the wagon, Colt shows that the settlers took very few possessions and that the small number of trunks and bags indicates there was no room for unnecessary items. In fact, the people and their food accounted for much of the weight.

Vocabulary
prairie (prer´ ē) *n.* a treeless, grass-covered plain

forded (fôrd´ əd) *v.* crossed a river at a low point

Reading Strategy
Inferring Philosophical Assumptions and Beliefs What beliefs underlie Colt's ironic reference to the owner of the log cabin as the "Lord of the Castle"?

❼

MAY 6TH. Dined on the prairie, and gathered flowers, while our tired beasts filled themselves with the fresh, green grass. . . . Have driven 18 miles to-day . . . so here we are, all huddled into this little house 12 by 16—cook supper over the fire . . . fill the one bed lengthwise and crosswise; the family of the house take to the trundle-bed,[6] while the floor is covered . . . with men, women and children, rolled in Indian blankets like silk worms in cocoons.

MAY 11TH. "Made" but a few miles yesterday. Forded the Little Osage; the last river, they say, we have to ford . . . our "noble lords" complained of the great weight of the wagons. . . . That our wagon is heavily loaded, have only to make a minute of what we have stowed away in it—eight trunks, one valise, three carpet bags, a box of soda crackers, 200 lbs. flour, 100 lbs. corn meal, a few lbs. of sugar, rice, dried apple, one washtub of little trees, utensils for cooking, and two provision boxes—say nothing of mother, a good fat sister, self, and two children, who ride through the rivers. . . .

At nightfall came to a log-cabin at the edge of the wood, and inquired of the "Lord of the Castle" if some of the women and children could take shelter under his roof for the night; the masculine number and whichever of the women that chose, couching in the wagons and under them. He said we could. His lady, who was away, presently came, with bare feet, and a white sack twisted up and thrown over her shoulder, with a few quarts of corn meal in the end that hung down her back. I said to myself—"Is that what I have got to come to?" She seemed pleased to have company—allowed us the first chance of the broad, Dutch-backed fireplace with its earthy hearth, and without pot hooks or trammels,[7] to make ready our simple evening repast. . . .

Are now [May 11th] crossing the 20 mile prairie, no roads—Think Mrs. Voorhees will get walking enough crossing this prairie. She is quite a pedestrian, surely, for she has walked every bit of the way in, so far, from Kansas City, almost 100 miles.

Arrive at Elm Creek—no house to lodge in tonight—campfire kindled—supper cooked, and partaken of with a keen relish, sitting in family groups around the "great big" fire. Some will sleep in wagons, others under the canopy of the blue vault of Heaven. The young men have built some shady little bowers of the green boughs; they are looking very cosily under them, wrapped in their white Indian blankets.

We ladies, or rather, "emigrant women," are having a chat around the camp-fire—the bright stars are looking down upon us—we wonder if we shall be neighbors to each other in the great "Octagon City. . . ."

---

6. **trundle-bed** low, portable bed that can be stored beneath a larger bed.
7. **trammels** (tram´ əlz) *n.* devices for hanging several pothooks in a fireplace.

Enrichment: Analyzing Historical Patterns, Trends, and Periods

Westward Expansion

"Manifest Destiny," a phrase used by politicians and leaders, was the belief that it was the mission of the United States to extend its borders territorially and spread the democratic ideals upon which the nation was built. Practically, Manifest Destiny allowed individuals and families to seek new opportunities on the frontier. Land was cheap and natural resources were plentiful. Politically, Manifest Destiny allowed the government the justification needed to claim new territories.

Activity: Timeline Have students gather information about the acquisition and settlement of areas farther and farther west. Suggest that they record information in the **Enrichment: Analyzing Historical Patterns, Trends, and Periods** work sheet, in *Professional Development Guidebook,* page 231. Then have them create a timeline showing when each new westward move took place.

MAY 12TH. Full of hope, as we leave the smoking embers of our camp-fire this morning. Expect tonight to arrive at our new home.

It begins to rain, rain, rain, like a shower; we move slowly on, from high prairie, around the deep ravine—are in sight of the timber that skirts the Neosho river. Have sent three men in advance to announce our coming; are looking for our Secretary, (Henry S. Clubb) with an escort to welcome us into the embryo city. If the booming of cannon is not heard at our approach, shall expect a salute from the firing of Sharp's rifles, certainly.

No escort is seen! no salute is heard! We move slowly and drippingly into town just at nightfall—feeling not a little nonplused on learning that our worthy, or unworthy Secretary was out walking in the rain with his *dear* wife. We leave our wagons and make our way to the large camp-fire. It is surrounded by men and women cooking their suppers—while others are busy close by, grinding their hominy[8] in hand mills.

Look around, and see the grounds all around the camp-fire are covered with tents, in which the families are staying. Not a house is to be seen. In the large tent here is a cook stove—they have supper prepared for us; it consists of hominy, soft Johnny cake (or corn bread, as it is called here), stewed apple, and tea. We eat what is set before us, "asking no questions for conscience' sake."

The ladies tell us they are sorry to see us come to this place; which shows us that all is not right. Are too weary to question, but with hope depressed go to our lodgings, which we find around in the tents, and in our wagons.

Vocabulary
ravine (rə vēn′) *n.* a long, deep hollow in the ground; a gully

---

8. hominy (häm′ ə nē) *n.* dry corn, usually ground and boiled for food.

Critical Reading

1. **Key Ideas and Details (a)** What financial arrangements did the Colts make as part of their preparations for heading west? **(b) Evaluate:** Do you think they were too naive and trusting? Explain.

2. **Key Ideas and Details (a)** Describe the settler woman Colt mentions in her entry of May 11. **(b) Analyze:** What does this settler woman suggest to Colt about her own future?

3. **Key Ideas and Details Compare and Contrast:** How do Colt's expectations about life at "Octagon City" compare with the reality she finds there?

4. **Integration of Knowledge and Ideas Synthesize:** Based on Colt's experiences, explain which character traits you feel were necessary to being a successful pioneer.

Answers

1. (a) Colt's husband sold their farm, invested in the Vegetarian Company, and sent money for the settlement at a company director's direction.
(b) **Possible response:** After reading that no one went to meet the Colts and that the women were "sorry" they had made the journey, students will think that the Colts were too naïve and trusting.

2. (a) The woman has bare feet and carries a white sack of cornmeal slung over her back. (b) Colt fears that she will become just as unkempt and have to do hard physical labor.

3. Colt expected a better life for herself and her family; the reality is very disappointing.

4. **Possible response:** Successful pioneers had to be courageous, hard working, flexible, adaptable, and dedicated, even in the face of enormous disappointment.

Differentiated Instruction   for Universal Access

Support for Special-Needs Students
Read the first three paragraphs of the May 12th entry with students. Tell them to note the way Colt's feelings change. Help them see that in the morning she is hopeful and optimistic but ends the day terribly disappointed. Point out how Colt's use of exclamation points and irony (in the phrases "worthy, or unworthy" and *"dear* wife") emphasizes her disappointment.

Enrichment for Gifted/Talented Students
Ask students to consider what might happen to Colt and her family after May 12, 1856. Would the family remain at the settlement? Would they begin to build a home? Would they move on to parts farther west? Have students write a new entry for Miriam Colt's journal dated two months later. They can present their entries to the class.

COMMON CORE ▪ RESEARCH PROJECT

I WILL FIGHT NO MORE FOREVER

Chief Joseph

BACKGROUND In company with fellow chiefs, Chief Joseph gave this speech on October 4, 1877, to an aide of General Oliver Howard. The aide recorded and delivered the speech to his commander.

Primary Sources
Speech Chief Joseph appeals to values and beliefs that he hopes his listeners share. What are they?

❽

Tell General Howard I know his heart. What he told me before, I have in my heart. I am tired of fighting. Our chiefs are killed. Looking Glass is dead. Toohoolhoolzote is dead. The old men are all dead. It is the young men who say yes and no. He who led on the young men is dead. It is cold and we have no blankets. The little children are freezing to death. My people, some of them, have run away to the hills and have no blankets, no food; no one knows where they are—perhaps freezing to death. I want to have time to look for my children and see how many I can find. Maybe I shall find them among the dead. Hear me, my chiefs. I am tired; my heart is sick and sad. From where the sun now stands I will fight no more forever.

Critical Reading ©

© 1. **Key Ideas and Details (a)** What has happened to many of the Nez Percé chiefs? **(b) Infer:** Who has been left to carry on the fight? **(c) Speculate:** Why do you think Chief Joseph directs part of his speech to his chiefs?

© 2. **Key Ideas and Details (a)** What reasons does Chief Joseph give for his surrender? **(b) Evaluate:** Would the speech have been more or less effective had it contained more detailed explanations?

© 3. **Integration of Knowledge and Ideas Synthesize:** Although Chief Joseph delivered this speech to confirm his tribe's surrender, his eloquent words serve another purpose for people today. What is that purpose?

Personal History • Speech

Comparing Primary Sources

Refer to your Note-Taking Guide to answer these questions.

1. (a) Note three details you learn about pioneer families from Colt's **personal history. (b)** Note two details you understand about the Native American experience based on Chief Joseph's brief **speech.**

2. (a) Use a chart like the one shown to identify one statement from each document about the subject on the left. **(b)** What **philosophical assumption,** or unstated belief, underlies each statement?

Colt		Joseph	
Statement	Assumption	Statement	Assumption
leaving home			
children			

3. Write three paragraphs in which you compare and contrast each author's understanding of nineteenth-century westward expansion. Explain the reasons for any similarities and differences.

ⒸVocabulary Acquisition and Use

Evaluating Logic Decide whether each sentence below is logical. If not, revise the sentence so that the italicized word is used in a logical way.

1. The smell of wet paint is *pervading* the art room.

2. The *levee* will cause the town to flood when the river rises.

3. A *profusion* of weeds is every gardener's dream.

4. The army established a *foothold* near the border.

5. The hikers *forded* the river by piling large rocks along its bank.

Content-Area Vocabulary Answer each question. Then, explain your answer.

6. Who is more likely to sell *shares*: a stockbroker or a musician?

7. Would *emigrants* be more likely to ask or give directions?

8. Who would have less success on a *prairie*: a lumberjack or a farmer?

9. What might a *ravine* become during heavy rains?

Etymology Study The word *mile* comes from the Latin word *mille,* for "thousand." Use a dictionary to discover how each of the following words are related to "thousand": *millennium, milligram, millimeter, million, millisecond.*

Ⓒ Common Core State Standards

Writing

7. Conduct short as well as more sustained research projects to answer a question or solve a problem; narrow or broaden the inquiry when appropriate, synthesize multiple sources on the subject, demonstrating understanding of the subject under investigation. *(p. 624)*

8. Gather relevant information from multiple authoritative print and digital sources, using advanced searches effectively; assess the strengths and weaknesses of each source in terms of the task, purpose, and audience; integrate information into the text selectively to maintain the flow of ideas, avoiding plagiarism and overreliance on any one source and following a standard format for citation. *(p. 624)*

Language

4.b. Identify and correctly use patterns of word changes that indicate different meanings or parts of speech.

Assessment Practice

Context (For more practice, see *All-in-One Workbook.*)

The reading sections of many tests require students to use context clues such as definitions and explanations to determine the meanings of unfamiliar words and phrases. Write the following passage from page 621 on the chalkboard. Then use the following exercise to help students use context clues to identify the correct definition.

In the large tent here is a cook stove—they have supper prepared for us; it consists of hominy, soft Johnny cake (or corn bread, as it is called here), stewed apple, and tea.

According to information found in this passage, what is "Johnny cake"?

A apple cake

B corn bread

C hominy

D tea cake

B is the correct answer, because it contains the explanation found in the parenthetical phrase "Johnny cake (or corn bread, as it is called here)."

Comparing Primary Sources

1. Sample answers: (a) Pioneer families were optimistic, faced hardships in their travels, and enjoyed the beauty of the places they saw. (b) Native Americans fought to keep their lands and suffered greatly.

2. Sample answers: (a) Colt: "Have visited Mother very hard, for, in all probability, it is the last visit"; "It was fortunate for mother, sister, myself and children, that lodgings were found." Chief Joseph: "My people . . . have run away to the hills"; "The little children are freezing to death." (b) Colt: They did not expect to see their family again; children stayed with the women. Chief Joseph: The people cannot take any more warfare; it is time to stop the children's suffering.

3. Possible response: Colt's diary shows that expansion gave settlers hope of a better future. Chief Joseph's speech shows that westward expansion meant the end of the Native American way of life. Both Colt and Chief Joseph face loss: Colt has lost her hopes, while Chief Joseph has lost his fight for freedom.

Vocabulary Acquisition and Use

1. logical.

2. not logical. The levee is meant to prevent the town from flooding when the river rises.

3. not logical. A profusion of weeds is every gardener's nightmare.

4. logical.

5. not logical. The hikers forded the river by piling rocks across it.

6. stockbroker. A stockbroker's job is to buy and sell shares of companies.

7. ask. Emigrants are new to an area, so they are likely to need directions.

8. lumberjack. On a prairie there are no trees to cut.

9. a stream. A ravine would probably fill with water during heavy rains.

Etymology Study *Millennium* means "one thousand years"; *milligram* is one thousandth of a gram; *millimeter* is one thousandth of a meter; *million* is one thousand thousands; and *millisecond* is one thousandth of a second.

Westward Expansion

Introduce the Assignment

1. Review the assignment. Explain that a research report of any kind should be based on different types of resources. One important type of source is books that are written for people with knowledge about the topic.

2. Using the list on the student page, students should formulate a research plan. To aid students, help them to ask open-ended research questions, such as "What was life like for settlers in Kansas?"

Guide Student Research

1. Students should explore a range of relevant sources. Point out that it is helpful to read basic works to get an overview of the topic, and accounts written by experts to get a deeper understanding of the topic.

2. Distinguish between a reliable source—information written by experts and primary source documents—and an unreliable one—information written by someone who is not an expert or a careful researcher.

Think Aloud: Model Choosing Reliable Sources

Say to students:

When I am unsure whether a source is reliable, I ask myself, "Who wrote this information?" For example, since Miriam Davis Colt wrote her own diary of moving westward, I would trust her account. However, if I found a Web site about settlers in Kansas and then realized the information was written by a young student just learning about the topic, I would look for another source.

Guide Student Writing

1. Encourage students to use parallel structure when they present related ideas.

2. Remind students to cite all sources using a standard format.

Research Task

Topic: Westward Expansion

GRAND REAL ESTATE DISTRIBUTION

Ambition, politics, principles, greed, restlessness, curiosity—all of these motives, and others, drove people West during the nineteenth century. Perhaps even more powerful than practical reasons was the image of the West created by those who wrote about it in government documents, newspaper reports, and personal histories.

Assignment: Make a **display**—a poster, a trifold poster, or a museum-style exhibit—about the Westward Expansion. In your research, investigate the reliability of early media sources that informed people about opportunities in the West. Avoid over-reliance on any one source.

▲ Advertisements such as this one from 1876 captured the imagination of adventurous Americans.

Formulate your research plan. To plan your display, make a list of relevant questions, such as the following:

- How did the government announce opportunities?
- What did people learn from pamphlets and posters?
- What did people learn from newspapers?
- How reliable was word-of-mouth news about the West?
- How reliable were the visual images of the West?

Then, choose a question or questions that will enable you to focus on a limited, manageable topic.

Gather sources. Use online and library searches to find answers to your research questions. Just like a smart American planning to go West, avoid relying too much on one source of information. Consult multiple sources, including texts written by experts in the field for scholarly audiences, as well as primary-source documents. Collect all details needed to prepare accurate citations.

Synthesize information. In deciding which information to use and which to discard, distinguish carefully between reliable and unreliable sources. A text that is awkwardly written may nevertheless be a trustworthy primary source. A source that seems dull may be accurate. A source that is entertaining may be oversimplified.

Organize and present your ideas. When you present information, use parallel structures to communicate parallel, or related, ideas. This will help viewers sift through a variety of data and clearly see your point. For example, you might organize a trifold poster with three parallel headings so that viewers can easily compare and contrast different information.

Model: Using Parallelism to Present Information

What People Learned from the Government	What People Learned from Newspapers	What People Learned from Word of Mouth

RESEARCH TIP

Set the preferences on your printer so that the full address of each Web site is included on each page you choose to print. In this way, you will have an automatic record of your Web-related sources.

Use a checklist like the one shown to create a display that is reliable, informative, and easy to understand.

Research Checklist

☐ Have I answered my research questions?

☐ Does my evidence come from experts on the topic and texts written for informed audiences in the field?

☐ Have I avoided relying too much on one source?

☐ Have I cited all sources according to a standard format?

624 Division, Reconciliation, and Expansion (1850–1914)

Assessment Resources

Unit 3 Resources

All **Selection Test,** pp. 176–177

All **Customizable Test Bank**

All **Self-tests**
Students may prepare for the **Selection Test** by taking the **Self-test** online.

All resources are available at
www.PHLitOnline.com.

Living in a Changing World

PART 3

Channel to the Mills, 1913, Edwin M. Dawes

Text Complexity: At a Glance

This chart gives a general text complexity rating for the selections in this part of the unit to help guide instruction. For additional text complexity support, see the Text Complexity Rubric at point of use.

The Story of an Hour	**More Accessible**	Richard Cory	**More Accessible**
Douglass	**More Complex**	Lucinda Matlock	**More Accessible**
We Wear the Mask	**More Complex**	Richard Bone	**More Accessible**
Luke Havergal	**More Accessible**	A Wagner Matinée	**More Complex**

Selection Planning Guide

These works examine the effects of the societal changes taking place at the turn of the twentieth century. Students will be interested to learn that Kate Chopin's dark tale "The Story of an Hour" was considered scandalous because it suggested that a woman might be happier without her husband. African Americans' struggle for acceptance and equality is reflected in the poems of Paul Laurence Dunbar. Edwin Arlington Robinson and Edgar Lee Masters paint memorable verbal portraits of four uniquely American characters who reflect the changing values of their day. Willa Cather contrasts the rigors of American frontier life with the cultural centers of the East in "A Wagner Matinée."

Humanities

Channel to the Mills, 1913, Edwin M. Dawes

Encourage students to contrast this artwork with pieces like *Indian Summer, 1855* (page 401). Help them see that the natural landscape had dominated earlier paintings. In contrast, Dawes chooses a group of mills to dominate the landscape of this painting. Use the following questions for discussion:

1. What changes in the American environment does this artwork suggest?
   Possible response: The artwork focuses on the change from a rural to an industrial society.

2. What attitude toward these changes does the artist communicate, and how?
   Possible response: The soft, shimmering colors of the artwork suggest that the artist's attitude is positive. A negative attitude is suggested by the way the buildings loom so large and blot out the horizon.

Monitoring Progress

Before students read the selections in Part 3, refer to the results for the **Vocabulary in Context** items on **Benchmark Test 2** (*Unit 1 Resources,* pp. 265–267). Use this diagnostic portion of the test to guide your choice of selections to teach, as well as the depth of pre-reading preparation you will provide, based on students' readiness for the reading and vocabulary skills.

• The Story of an Hour
Lesson Pacing Guide

DAY 1 Preteach

- Ⓒ Administer the Reading and Vocabulary Warm-ups (*Unit 3 Resources*, pp. 178–181) as necessary.
- Ⓒ Introduce the Literary Analysis concepts: Irony and Theme.
- • Introduce the Reading Strategy: Analyze the Philosophical Argument.
- Ⓒ Build background with the author and Background features.
- • Develop thematic thinking with Connecting to the Essential Question.
- Ⓒ Teach the selection vocabulary.

DAY 2 Preteach/Teach/Extend

- • Distribute copies of the appropriate graphic organizer for the Reading Strategy (*Graphic Organizer Transparencies*, pp. 133–134).
- • Distribute copies of the appropriate graphic organizer for Literary Analysis (*Graphic Organizer Transparencies*, pp. 135–136).
- • Prepare students to read with the Activating Prior Knowledge activities (TE).
- • Informally monitor comprehension while students read.
- • Use the Reading Check question to confirm comprehension.
- Ⓒ Develop students' understanding of irony and theme using the Literary Analysis prompts.
- Ⓒ Reinforce vocabulary with the Vocabulary notes.
- • Assess students' comprehension and mastery of the skills by having them answer the Critical Reading, Literary Analysis, and Reading Strategy questions.

DAY 3 Assess

- Ⓒ Have students complete the Vocabulary Lesson.
- Ⓒ Have students complete the Writing Lesson and write a reflective essay. (You may assign as homework.)
- • Administer Selection Test A or B (*Unit 3 Resources*, pp. 190–192 or 193–195).

Ⓒ Common Core State Standards

Reading Literature 6. Analyze a case in which grasping point of view requires distinguishing what is directly stated in a text from what is really meant.

Writing 3. Write narratives to develop real or imagined experiences or events using effective technique, well-chosen details, and well-structured event sequences.
3.c. Use a variety of techniques to sequence events so that they build on one another to create a coherent whole and build toward a particular tone and outcome.

Additional Standards Practice
Common Core Companion, pp. 61–62; 208–218

Daily Block Scheduling
Each day in this Lesson Pacing Guide represents a 40–50 minute period. Teachers using block scheduling may combine days to revise pacing. In addition, teachers may differentiate and support core instruction by integrating components for extended and intensive support as students require. See the Guide to Selected Leveled Resources (facing page).

Guide to Selected Leveled Resources

R T I Tier 1 (students performing on level)

The Story of an Hour

Warm Up

Practice, model, and monitor fluency, working with the whole class or in groups.

Vocabulary and Reading Warm-ups B, *Unit 3 Resources,* pp. 178–179, 181

Comprehension/Skills

Support and monitor comprehension and skills development, having students complete the activities, graphic organizers, and interactive prompts independently or as a class.

• *Reader's Notebook,* adapted instruction and summary

EL *Reader's Notebook: English Learner's Version,* adapted instruction and adapted selection

• Reading Strategy Graphic Organizer B, *Graphic Organizer Transparencies,* p. 134

• Literary Analysis Graphic Organizer B, *Graphic Organizer Transparencies,* p. 136

Monitor Progress

Monitor student progress with the differentiated curriculum-based assessment in the *Unit Resources.*

• Selection Test B, *Unit 3 Resources,* pp. 193–195
• Open-Book Test, *Unit 3 Resources,* pp. 187–189

R T I Tier 2 (students requiring intervention)

The Story of an Hour

Warm Up

Practice, model, and monitor fluency in groups or with individuals.

• Vocabulary and Reading Warm-ups A, *Unit 3 Resources,* pp. 178–180
• *Hear It!* Audio CD

Comprehension/Skills

• Support and monitor comprehension and skills development, working in small groups or with individuals.
• As students complete the selection in the appropriate version of the *Reader's Notebook,* monitor comprehension frequently with group questions and individual instruction.
• Model strategies while guiding students in completing the activities and prompts in the *Reader's Notebook,* as well as the graphic organizers.
• Practice skills and monitor mastery with the *Reading Kit* worksheets.

• *Reader's Notebook: Adapted Version,* adapted instruction and adapted selection

EL *Reader's Notebook: English Learner's Version,* adapted instruction and adapted selection

• Reading Strategy Graphic Organizer A, *Graphic Organizer Transparencies,* p. 133

• Literary Analysis Graphic Organizer A, *Graphic Organizer Transparencies,* p. 135

• *Reading Kit,* Practice worksheets

Monitor Progress

Monitor student progress with the differentiated curriculum-based assessment in the *Unit Resources* and in the *Reading Kit.*

• Selection Test A, *Unit 3 Resources,* pp. 190–192
• *Reading Kit,* Assess worksheets

TIER 3 Tier 3 intervention may require consultation with the student's special-education or dyslexia specialist. For additional support, see the Tier 2 activities and resources listed above.

One-on-one teaching   Group work   Whole-class instruction   Independent work   A Assessment

For a complete guide to selection support, including support for Advanced students, see the Overview of Resources in the frontmatter.

• The Story of an Hour

RESOURCES FOR:

- **L1** Special-Needs Students
- **L2** Below-Level Students (Tier 2)
- **L3** On-Level Students (Tier 1)
- **L4** Advanced Students (Tier 1)
- **EL** English Learners
- **All** All Students

Vocabulary/Fluency/Prior Knowledge

All **Vocabulary Builder,** p . 184

Also available for these selections:

EL **L1** **L2** **Vocabulary Warm-ups A and B,** pp. 178-179

EL **L1** **L2** **Reading Warm-ups A and B,** pp. 180-181

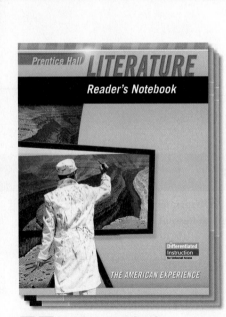

Reader's Notebooks

Pre- and postreading pages for this selection, as well as "The Story of an Hour," appear in an interactive format in the *Reader's Notebooks*. Each *Notebook* is differentiated for a different group of learners.

The selections in the Adapted and English Learner's versions are abridged.

- **L2** **L3** *Reader's Notebook*
- **L1** *Reader's Notebook: Adapted Version*
- **EL** *Reader's Notebook: English Learner's Version*
- **EL** *Reader's Notebook: Spanish Version*

© *Common Core Companion*

Additional instruction and practice for each Common Core State Standard

Selection Support

Graphic Organizer Transparencies *(left sidebar label)*

EL L3 Reading: Graphic Organizer B, p. 134

Also available for these selections:

EL L1 L2 Reading: Graphic Organizer A, (partially filled in), p. 133

EL L1 L2 Literary Analysis: Graphic Organizer A, (partially filled in), p. 135

EL L3 Literary Analysis: Graphic Organizer B, p. 136

Skills Development/Extension

Unit 3 Resources (left sidebar label)

All Reading Strategy: Relate the Work to Major Themes of the Era, p. 183

Also available for these selections:

All Literary Analysis: Irony, p. 182

EL L3 L4 Support for Writing, p. 185

L4 Enrichment, p. 186

Assessment

L1 L2 Open-Book Test, pp. 187–189

Also available for these selections:

EL L1 L2 Selection Test A, pp. 190–192

EL L3 L4 Selection Test B, pp. 193–195

PHLit Online!
www.PHLitOnline.com

Online Resources: All print materials are also available online.

- complete narrated selection text
- a thematically related video with writing prompt
- an interactive graphic organizer
- highlighting feature
- access to all student print resources, adapted to individual student needs
- Spanish and English summaries
- adapted selection translations in Spanish.

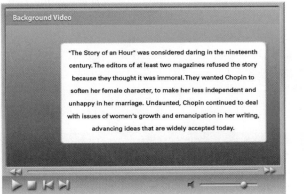

Background Video

"The Story of an Hour" was considered daring in the nineteenth century. The editors of at least two magazines refused the story because they thought it was immoral. They wanted Chopin to soften her female character, to make her less independent and unhappy in her marriage. Undaunted, Chopin continued to deal with issues of women's growth and emancipation in her writing, advancing ideas that are widely accepted today.

Background Video

Also available:

Get Connected! (thematic video with writing prompt)
All videos are available in Spanish.

Vocabulary Central (tools and activities for studying vocabulary)

Also available:

Writer's Journal (with graphics feature)

❶ Connecting to the Essential Question

1. Review the assignment.

2. Students reluctant to share observations about people may write about fictional characters.

3. As students read, have them notice details that emphasize Mrs. Mallard's independence.

❷ Literary Analysis

Introduce the skills, using the instruction on the student page.

Think Aloud: Model the Skill

Say to students:

If a story turns out different from my expectation, I consider it ironic. When I first read O. Henry's "Gift of the Magi," I thought the main characters would get satisfaction from selling their most valued possessions. By the end of the story, I saw that neither could benefit from the sacrifice each made. I concluded that the meaning, or theme, of the story was ironic.

❸ Reading Strategy

1. Introduce the strategy.

2. Give students a copy of **Reading Strategy Graphic Organizer B**, page 134 in *Graphic Organizer Transparencies,* to fill out as they read.

Think Aloud: Model the Skill

Say to students:

At the end of "The Gift of the Magi," the narrator tells us, "Let it be said that of all who give gifts [the main characters] were the wisest." Their gift giving doesn't turn out as they hoped, but by selling their treasures to buy each other the perfect gift, they learn how deep their love is. The philosophical argument underlying the story produces credible characters; we understand their motivation.

❹ Vocabulary

1. Pronounce each word, giving its definition; have students say it aloud.

2. See also the *Classroom Strategies and Teaching Routines* card for introducing vocabulary.

626

Before You Read | *The Story of an Hour*

❶ **Connecting to the Essential Question** Chopin's heroine appears to be mild and dependent, but she secretly hungers for independence. As you read, notice details that emphasize Mrs. Mallard's independence. Doing so will help as you consider the Essential Question: **How does literature shape or reflect society?**

❷ Literary Analysis

Irony is a contradiction between appearance and reality, between expectation and outcome, or between meaning and intention. In literature, readers frequently encounter three types of irony:

- **Verbal irony** occurs when someone says something that deliberately contradicts what that person actually means.
- **Situational irony** occurs when something happens that contradicts readers' expectations.
- **Dramatic irony** occurs when the reader or audience is aware of something that a character does not know.

Authors may use irony to create humor or to add an element of surprise to a story. The use of irony may also develop a story's **theme**—its central message. When irony is used in this way, the theme of the work may concern a discrepancy between surface appearances and inner truths. As you read this story, decide which type of irony Chopin primarily uses and whether it functions to create an effect or to develop the theme.

❸ Reading Strategy

© **Preparing to Read Complex Texts** Kate Chopin was among the first American authors to write with intention about women who suffer from the restrictions imposed on them by society. Her fiction is driven by a philosophy—the belief that men and women are equals but that society denies women their full humanity. As you read this story, **analyze the philosophical argument** that drives the plot. Determine how Chopin's philosophy *contributes to the credibility* of Mrs. Mallard's character. Note your ideas in a chart like the one shown.

❹ Vocabulary

forestall (fôr stôl′) *v.* prevent by acting ahead of time (p. 630)

repression (ri presh′ ən) *n.* restraint (p. 630)

elusive (ē loo′ siv) *adj.* hard to grasp (p. 630)

tumultuously (too mul′ choo əs lē) *adv.* in an agitated way (p. 630)

Common Core State Standards

Reading Literature
6. Analyze a case in which grasping point of view requires distinguishing what is directly stated in a text from what is really meant.

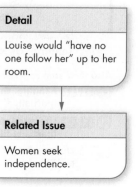

Detail
Louise would "have no one follow her" up to her room.

Related Issue
Women seek independence.

www.PHLitOnline.com

626 Division, Reconciliation, and Expansion (1850–1914)

Vocabulary Development

Vocabulary Knowledge Rating

Create a **Vocabulary Knowledge Rating Chart** (*Professional Development Guidebook,* p. 33) for the vocabulary words on the student page. Give each student a copy of the chart with the words on it. Read the words aloud, and have students mark their rating of each in the Before Reading column. When students have completed reading and discussing the selection, have them take out their **Vocabulary Knowledge Rating Charts** for the selection. Read the words aloud, and have students rate their knowledge again in the After Reading column. Clarify any words that are still problematic. Then have students complete the Vocabulary practice at the end of the selection.

Vocabulary Central, featuring tools, activities, and songs for studying vocabulary, is available online at **www.PHLitOnline.com**.

Kate Chopin (1850–1904)

Author of "The Story of an Hour"

Despite her conservative, aristocratic upbringing, Kate O'Flaherty Chopin (shō´ pan) became one of the most powerful and controversial writers of her time. In her writing, she captured the local color of Louisiana and boldly explored the role of women in society.

Family Life Kate O'Flaherty was born in St. Louis, Missouri, the daughter of a wealthy businessman who died five years later in a railroad accident. When she was twenty, Kate married Oscar Chopin, a Louisiana cotton trader. The couple settled in New Orleans, where they lived for ten years before moving to a plantation in rural Louisiana.

In 1882, Chopin's husband died, leaving her to raise their six children. Chopin carried on the work of the plantation alone until 1884, when she returned with her children to St. Louis. Then, in 1885, Chopin's mother died, leaving her in deep sorrow. Her family doctor, concerned about her emotional health, suggested that she begin to write fiction. Chopin spent the rest of her life in St. Louis, devoting much of her energy to writing.

Chopin the Writer and Rebel Chopin focused on capturing the essence of life in Louisiana in her writing. Her first novel, *At Fault* (1890), was set in a small Louisiana town inhabited by Creoles, descendants of the original French and Spanish settlers, and Cajuns, descendants of French Canadian settlers. Her charming portraits of Louisiana life often obscured the fact that she explored themes considered radical at the time: the nature of marriage, racial prejudice, and women's desire for equality.

The Awakening Chopin's finest novel, *The Awakening* (1899), is a psychological account of a woman's search for independence and fulfillment. Because the novel explored the issue of infidelity, it aroused a storm of protest. The book was eventually banned and Chopin's reputation was badly damaged. Then, in the 1950s, *The Awakening* was resurrected. Today, the book is among the five most-read American novels in colleges and universities. Chopin is now considered an early practitioner of American Realism—a literary style that seeks to avoid sentimental depictions of life. She is widely respected for her portrayal of the psychology of women and her ability to capture local color.

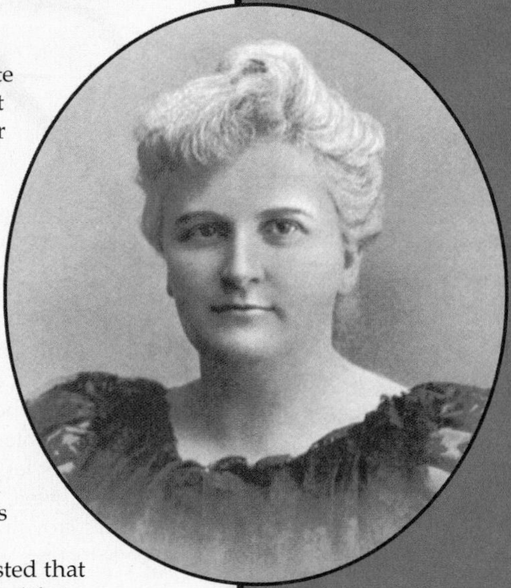

"The bird that would soar above the plain of tradition and prejudice must have strong wings."

Daily Bellringer

For each class during which you will teach this selection, have students complete one of the five activities for the appropriate week in the *Daily Bellringer Activities* booklet.

Multidraft Reading

To assist struggling readers and to enhance reading for all, assign the text in chunks as warranted by length and apply multidraft reading protocols. For each reading, have students set the purpose indicated:

- **First reading**—identifying key ideas and details and answering any Reading Checks.
- **Second reading**—analyzing craft and structure and responding to the side-column prompts.
- **Third reading**—integrating knowledge and ideas, connecting to other texts and the world, and answering the end-of-selection questions.

For more guidance, refer to the ***Classroom Strategies and Teaching Routines*** card on multidraft reading.

5 Background

More About the Author

Some commentators feel that living from an early age without a father or other strong male role models—that is, living in a household with a widowed mother, a widowed grandmother, and a widowed great-grandmother—caused Chopin as an adult to resist the prevailing cultural belief that women should submit to men in marriage.

PHLit Online! www.PHLitOnline.com — Teaching From Technology

Preparing to Read
Go to **www.PHLitOnline.com** in class or in a lab and display the **Get Connected!** slide show for this selection. Have the class brainstorm for responses to the slide show writing prompt, entering ideas in the interactive journal. Then have students complete their written responses individually in a lab or as homework.

To build background, display the Background and More About the Author features.

Using the Interactive Text
Go to **www.PHLitOnline.com** and display the **Enriched Online Student Edition.** As the class reads the selection or listens to the narration, record answers to side-column prompts using the graphic organizers accessible on the interactive page. Alternatively, have students use the online edition individually, answering the prompts as they read.

❶ About the Selection

Mrs. Mallard gets the unexpected news that her husband has been killed in an accident. She quickly recovers from the shock to discover that what she feels is relief. Though she mourns his passing, she delights in the freedom that will now be hers. Shut in her room, she relishes the opportunities ahead of her. When Mr. Mallard returns as unexpectedly as he supposedly died, Mrs. Mallard suffers a fatal heart attack. The doctors, mistakenly assuming that she had been grieving, attribute the death to "joy that kills."

❷ Activating Prior Knowledge

Ask students to reflect on the emotions a person usually demonstrates on hearing of the unexpected death of a close friend or relative. Students may cite real life, literature, or a film.

Concept Connector ➡

Tell students they will return to their responses after reading the selection.

❸ Critical Viewing

Possible response: Students may say that the light shows Mrs. Mallard's calm contentment upon recognizing the first stages of her newly found freedom. They may suggest that the light is symbolic of the new beginning of her life.

❶❷ THE STORY OF AN *Hour*

Kate Chopin

BACKGROUND "The Story of an Hour" was considered daring in the nineteenth century. The editors of at least two magazines refused the story because they thought it was immoral. They wanted Chopin to soften her female character, to make her less independent and unhappy in her marriage. Undaunted, Chopin continued to deal with issues of women's growth and emancipation in her writing, advancing ideas that are widely accepted today.

*K*nowing that Mrs. Mallard was afflicted with a heart trouble, great care was taken to break to her as gently as possible the news of her husband's death.

It was her sister Josephine who told her, in broken sentences; veiled hints that revealed in half concealing. Her husband's friend Richards was there, too, near her. It was he who had been in the newspaper office when

❸ ▶ Critical Viewing This story presents a "subtle and elusive" revelation. What connection do you see between the light shining through the window and such a discovery? **[Connect]**

628 Division, Reconciliation, and Expansion (1850–1914)

Ⓒ Text Complexity Rubric

The Story of an Hour	
Qualitative Measures	
Context/Knowledge Demands	Gender roles; life experience demands 1 2 ③ 4 5
Structure/Language Conventionality and Clarity	Formal diction; average vocabulary 1 2 ③ 4 5
Levels of Meaning/ Purpose/Concept Level	Accessible (irony in identifying the cause of a woman's death) 1 2 3 ④ 5
Quantitative Measures	

Lexile	960L	**Text Length**	1,007 words
Overall Complexity	**More accessible**		

Reader and Task Suggestions

Preparing to Read the Text
- Using the information on SE p. 627, discuss why we think of Chopin as a feminist writer.
- Ask students to comment about gender roles today—specifically, whether they believe that women today have more equality with men than their ancestors did.
- Guide students to use Multidraft Reading strategies (TE p. 627).

Leveled Tasks

Levels of Meaning If students will have difficulty with the story's irony, review the concept before the first reading. Have students reread to find ways in which irony either reinforces or overturns the gender roles of that era.

Evaluating If students will not have difficulty with the story's irony, ask them to judge how well the story speaks to readers today.

4 **Humanities**

Afternoon in Piedmont, by Xavier Martinez

Xavier Martinez was born in Guadalajara, Mexico, in 1869. He eventually moved to San Francisco, where he later taught at the California School of Fine Arts. Martinez's work has been described as poetic. His *Afternoon in Piedmont* was inspired by the famous painting by James Whistler of his mother. In his work, Martinez moved the scene to his house and used his wife as the model.

After students have read the selection, return to this painting and use these questions for discussion:

1. How would you describe the mood of this painting?
   Possible response: Students may see the yellow light entering the dark interior as the coming of dawn, bringing with it a comforting awakening.

2. What scene in the story does the painting best represent?
   Possible response: Students may say that it describes the scene in which Mrs. Mallard is looking out at the signs of early spring and is herself awakening to her true feelings and a new view of life.

This selection is available in an interactive format in the **Enriched Online Student Edition,** at **www.PHLitOnline.com,** which includes a thematically related video with writing prompt and an interactive graphic organizer.

Irony

1. Remind students that one kind of irony occurs when a story develops in a way that is opposite to what readers expect.

2. Have students read the bracketed passage. Then **ask** students the Literary Analysis question.
Answer: It is ironic that Mrs. Mallard, newly widowed, should hear the sounds and songs of life, of spring.

⑥ Reading Strategy

Analyze the Philosophical Argument

1. Before students read the three paragraphs at the bottom of the page, **ask** them to summarize Mrs. Mallard's reaction so far to hearing of her husband's death.
Answer: Mrs. Mallard fully understands the news and breaks down. Then she notices signs of spring and seems to stop thinking.

2. Now have students read the bracketed passage. Suggest that they place a relevant detail in the first box of the graphic organizer: either Mrs. Mallard's murmuring of the word "free" or her brightening eyes and quickening pulse.
Ask students to fill in the second box with the *issue* that the detail relates to.
Possible response: Mrs. Mallard sees the positive side of her husband's death.

3. Lead students to see the connection between Mrs. Mallard's new feelings and Chopin's own philosophy (as explained on p. 627) that society constrains women.

Vocabulary
forestall (fôr stôl´) v. prevent by acting ahead of time

⑤

Literary Analysis
Irony Considering the news she has just received, what is ironic about the details Mrs. Mallard notices through her window?

Vocabulary
repression (ri presh´ ən) n. restraint

elusive (ē lōō´ siv) adj. hard to grasp

tumultuously (tōō mul´ chōō əs lē) adv. in an agitated way

⑥

intelligence of the railroad disaster was received, with Brently Mallard's name leading the list of "killed." He had only taken the time to assure himself of its truth by a second telegram, and had hastened to forestall any less careful, less tender friend in bearing the sad message.

She did not hear the story as many women have heard the same, with a paralyzed inability to accept its significance. She wept at once, with sudden, wild abandonment, in her sister's arms. When the storm of grief had spent itself she went away to her room alone. She would have no one follow her.

There stood, facing the open window, a comfortable, roomy armchair. Into this she sank, pressed down by a physical exhaustion that haunted her body and seemed to reach into her soul.

She could see in the open square before her house the tops of trees that were all aquiver with the new spring life. The delicious breath of rain was in the air. In the street below a peddler was crying his wares. The notes of a distant song which someone was singing reached her faintly, and countless sparrows were twittering in the eaves.

There were patches of blue sky showing here and there through the clouds that had met and piled one above the other in the west facing her window.

She sat with her head thrown back upon the cushion of the chair, quite motionless, except when a sob came up into her throat and shook her, as a child who has cried itself to sleep continues to sob in its dreams.

She was young, with a fair, calm face, whose lines bespoke repression and even a certain strength. But now there was a dull stare in her eyes, whose gaze was fixed away off yonder on one of those patches of blue sky. It was not a glance of reflection, but rather indicated a suspension of intelligent thought.

There was something coming to her and she was waiting for it, fearfully. What was it? She did not know; it was too subtle and elusive to name. But she felt it, creeping out of the sky, reaching toward her through the sounds, the scents, the color that filled the air.

Now her bosom rose and fell tumultuously. She was beginning to recognize this thing that was approaching to possess her, and she was striving to beat it back with her will—as powerless as her two white slender hands would have been.

When she abandoned herself, a little whispered word escaped her slightly parted lips. She said it over and over under her breath: "free, free, free!" The vacant stare and the look of terror that had followed it went from her eyes. They stayed keen and bright. Her pulses beat fast, and the coursing blood warmed and relaxed every inch of her body.

630 Division, Reconciliation, and Expansion (1850–1914)

Enrichment: Investigating Technology

American Life in the 1890s

Readers will see that the telegrams mentioned above carry misinformation. Students may ask, "Why didn't someone quickly correct the message?" Although telephone companies served more than 150,000 customers in Chopin's time, telegrams were the major method of long-distance communication; telegrams required time for news to go from a source to the sending office and then from the receiving office to the addressee.
Activity: Critique Have students form a picture

of changes in communications between the 1890s and today. Suggest that they record information in the **Enrichment: Investigating Technology** work sheet, in *Professional Development Guidebook,* page 242. Ask students if they will recommend this story to peers. Is it too out-of-date, or does its datedness entertain us?

She did not stop to ask if it were or were not a monstrous joy that held her. A clear and exalted perception enabled her to dismiss the suggestion as trivial.

She knew that she would weep again when she saw the kind, tender hands folded in death; the face that had never looked save with love upon her, fixed and gray and dead. But she saw beyond that bitter moment a long procession of years to come that would belong to her absolutely. And she opened and spread her arms out to them in welcome.

There would be no one to live for her during those coming years; she would live for herself. There would be no powerful will bending hers in that blind persistence with which men and women believe they have a right to impose a private will upon a fellow creature. A kind intention or a cruel intention made the act seem no less a crime as she looked upon it in that brief moment of illumination.

And yet she had loved him—sometimes. Often she had not. What did it matter! What could love, the unsolved mystery, count for in face of this possession of self-assertion which she suddenly recognized as the strongest impulse of her being!

"Free! Body and soul free!" she kept whispering.

Josephine was kneeling before the closed door with her lips to the keyhole, imploring for admission. "Louise, open the door! I beg; open the door—you will make yourself ill. What are you doing, Louise? For heaven's sake open the door."

"Go away. I am not making myself ill." No; she was drinking in a very elixir of life[1] through that open window.

Her fancy was running riot along those days ahead of her. Spring days, and summer days, and all sorts of days that would be her own. She breathed a quick prayer that life might be long. It was only yesterday she had thought with a shudder that life might be long.

She arose at length and opened the door to her sister's importunities.[2] There was a feverish triumph in her eyes, and she carried herself unwittingly like a goddess of Victory. She clasped her sister's waist, and together they descended the stairs. Richards stood waiting for them at the bottom.

---

1. **elixir of life** (i liks′ ər) imaginary substance believed in medieval times to prolong life indefinitely.
2. **importunities** (im′ pôr tōōn′ i tēz) *n.* persistent requests or demands.

World LITERATURE CONNECTION

7

Challenging Women's Roles

Chopin was one of a growing number of writers in the late nineteenth and early twentieth centuries who challenged women's traditional social roles. A generation earlier in Britain, novelist Mary Ann Evans adopted the pen name **George Eliot** (1819–1880) to explore the theme of women's independence. In France, Amadine Dupin (1804–1876) did the same, publishing as **George Sand**. In 1929, novelist and critic **Virginia Woolf** (1882–1941), pictured below, published the essay "A Room of One's Own" in which she argued that women need community in order to realize their potential as writers. She wrote: "Masterpieces are not solitary births."

Connect to the Literature

Do you think Kate Chopin would have trouble publishing "The Story of An Hour" today? Why or why not?

9 ☑ **Reading Check**

What does Mrs. Mallard think about while alone in her room?

The Story of an Hour **631**

Concept Connector

Reading Strategy Graphic Organizer
Ask students to review the graphic organizers that show a detail and its related issue. Then have students share their organizers and compare them.

Activating Prior Knowledge
Have students return to their responses to the Activating Prior Knowledge activity. Ask them to explain whether their thoughts have changed and if so, how.

? **Connecting to the Essential Question**
Have students compare the responses they gave to the prompt before they completed reading the story with their thoughts afterward. Have them work individually or in groups, writing or discussing their thoughts, to formulate their new responses. Then lead a class discussion, probing for what students have learned that confirms or invalidates their initial thoughts. Encourage students to cite specific textual details to support their responses.

---

7 ## World Literature Connection
Challenging Women's Roles

Taking men's names for their various publications was a trick of the Brontë sisters. Emily published *Wuthering Heights* (1847) under the name of Ellis Bell, while Charlotte used Currer Bell as the author of *Jane Eyre* (1847). The fiction of Jane Austen (1775–1817) appeared initially without her name—attributed, interestingly, only to "a lady," but soon the public knew *which* female author had created them. *Frankenstein,* by Mary Wollstonecraft Shelley (1797–1851), also appeared anonymously.

Connect to the Literature
After discussing these writers' hidden identities, **ask** the connect to literature question.
Possible response: Chopin today would not meet resistance because the once-sensational topic has become mundane.

8 **?** ## Engaging the Essential Question

1. Point out to students that the bracketed passage tells, first, that Mrs. Mallard appreciated her husband and, second, of a physical action she takes.

2. **Ask** students: Which part of the paragraph illustrates Mrs. Mallard's independence?
   Answer: Her independence becomes clear when she spreads her arms to welcome the future—it is hers alone.

3. **Ask** students: What does Mrs. Mallard's action symbolize, and how does it affect readers?
   Possible response: The action symbolizes Mrs. Mallard's desire for independence. Readers are forced to reflect on the negative aspects of nineteenth-century marriages.

9 ## Reading Check

Answer: She thinks about bursting into a new life of freedom. She thinks of her positive and negative feelings toward her husband and of a more important feeling—self-assertion.

1. Read this passage aloud, and continue through the end of the story.

2. **Ask** students why Chopin included the following sentence: "He had been far from the scene of accident, and did not even know there had been one." **Possible answer:** The first detail explains how Brently Mallard managed to be alive; the second explains that he had no idea that his sudden appearance would shock Mrs. Mallard.

ASSESS

Answers

Before students respond, you may wish to have them write a brief objective summary of the selection. As they answer the questions below, remind them to support their answers with evidence from the text.

1. (a) The narrator notes that Mrs. Mallard was afflicted with "a heart trouble." (b) **Possible response:** The narrator may be referring to the dissatisfaction Mrs. Mallard feels in her marriage and her corresponding unenthusiastic outlook on life.

2. (a) She sees green trees, sparrows, and patches of blue sky—all signs of the new life of spring. (b) The spring scene conveys a sense of rebirth.

3. (a) They say she died "of heart disease—of joy that kills." (b) **Possible response:** Her death is caused by the shock and disappointment she felt at the return of her husband. (c) **Possible response:** There is nothing left for Chopin to say. She knows the reader knows what caused Mrs. Mallard's death.

4. By letting us get inside Mrs. Mallard's head, Chopin emphasizes the differences between the woman's true self and the ways in which she is perceived. We hear her thoughts that undercut the <u>perception</u> others have of Mrs. Mallard as <u>fragile</u>, needing tender care, and likely to fall ill easily.

Someone was opening the front door with a latchkey. It was Brently Mallard who entered, a little travel-stained, composedly carrying his gripsack[3] and umbrella. He had been far from the scene of accident, and did not know there had been one. He stood amazed at Josephine's piercing cry; at Richards's quick motion to screen him from the view of his wife.

But Richards was too late.

When the doctors came they said she had died of heart disease—of joy that kills.

---

3. **gripsack** (grip′ sak) *n.* small bag for holding clothes.

"Free! Body and soul free!"

Critical Reading

Cite textual evidence to support your responses.

Ⓒ 1. **Key Ideas and Details (a)** At the beginning of the story, what does the narrator call the ailment that afflicts Mrs. Mallard? **(b) Interpret:** In addition to a medical condition, what might the narrator mean by this phrase?

Ⓒ 2. **Key Ideas and Details (a)** What does Mrs. Mallard see as she gazes out her window? **(b) Connect:** How does the scene outside the window foreshadow the feelings that sweep over her as she sits in her chair?

Ⓒ 3. **Key Ideas and Details (a)** According to the doctors, what causes Mrs. Mallard's death? **(b) Draw Conclusions:** What do you believe is the actual cause of her death? **(c) Speculate:** Why do you think Chopin does not elaborate more about Mrs. Mallard's death?

Ⓒ 4. **Integration of Knowledge and Ideas** How does Chopin emphasize differences between Mrs. Mallard's true self and the ways in which she is perceived? In your response, use at least two of these Essential Question words: *perception, subservient, illusion, fragile. [Connecting to the Essential Question: How does literature shape or reflect society?]*

Assessment Practice

Context (For more practice, see *All-in-One Workbook*.)

The reading sections of many tests specify that students use the context of a targeted word or phrase to determine its meaning. Because figurative expressions are not literally true, students must try to infer the meaning of the expression from the surrounding context. Use the following sample test item to demonstrate.

Her fancy was <u>running riot</u> along those days ahead of her. Spring days, and summer days, and all sorts of days that would be her own.

In this passage, the expression <u>running riot</u> most nearly means _____.

A quietly contemplating
B causing a public disturbance
C becoming overactive
D going numb

The excitement communicated in the second sentence should lead students to recognize that **C** is correct.

Literary Analysis

1. Craft and Structure In what ways is Mrs. Mallard's reaction to her husband's death an example of **situational irony?**

2. Craft and Structure How might the diagnosis of Mrs. Mallard's cause of death be an example of **dramatic irony?**

3. Craft and Structure Use a chart like the one shown to examine elements of irony in the story's descriptive passages.

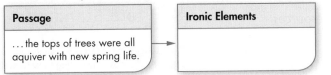

Passage		Ironic Elements
...the tops of trees were all aquiver with new spring life.	→	

4. Integration of Knowledge and Ideas How does the story's central **theme** relate to a discrepancy between perception and reality?

Reading Strategy

5. Reread the paragraph beginning, "There would be no one to live for during those coming years. . . ." **(a) Analyze the philosophical argument** about human interactions Chopin describes in that paragraph. **(b)** How does this argument illuminate Mrs. Mallard's conflict?

6. Is Mrs. Mallard a *credible* character? Explain, relating story details to Chopin's philosophy regarding women at that time period.

PERFORMANCE TASKS
Integrated Language Skills

Vocabulary Acquisition and Use

Synonyms For each item, choose the letter of the synonym, or word that most closely expresses the same meaning. Explain your reasoning.

1. forestall   **a.** intercept   **b.** facilitate   **c.** arrange

2. repression   **a.** indulgence   **b.** constraint   **c.** tolerance

3. elusive   **a.** tangible   **b.** vivid   **c.** evanescent

4. tumultuously   **a.** severely   **b.** thoughtlessly   **c.** briskly

Writing

Narrative Text In a **reflective essay,** a writer describes personal experiences and conveys his or her feelings about them. Draw upon your memory and observations to write your own "story of an hour" about a moment when your life dramatically changed. Organize precise details either chronologically or in order of importance. *Create a fresh, authentic tone* by using words and phrases that come naturally to you.

The Story of an Hour **633**

Common Core State Standards

Writing

3. Write narratives to develop real or imagined experiences or events using effective technique, well-chosen details, and well-structured event sequences.

3.c. Use a variety of techniques to sequence events so that they build on one another to create a coherent whole and build toward a particular tone and outcome.

Answers

1. The reader logically expects that Mrs. Mallard would be more saddened by her husband's death.

2. The reader knows what the doctors do not—that Mrs. Mallard has just begun to look forward to living a long life by and for herself.

3. **Possible response:** Passage: "the tops of trees were all aquiver with new spring life." Ironic Elements: We expect her observations to be about death. Passage: "she was drinking the very elixir of life through that open window." Ironic Elements: Within minutes, her heart fails and she dies.

4. **Possible response:** The theme relates to the discrepancy between what people think about Mrs. Mallard and what Mrs. Mallard actually feels about her marriage and her husband's death.

5. (a) Chopin's philosophical argument is that no one has the right to make someone else feel subservient. (b) Mrs. Mallard knows that she will feel sad on viewing the body of the man who loved her, but she is more moved by her sudden freedom from his will.

6. Many will consider Mrs. Mallard credible because she is complex: While admitting some love for her husband, she realizes how much he limited her. That recognition matches Chopin's philosophy regarding women of her time.

Vocabulary Acquisition and Use

1. a. A synonym for *forestall,* which means "prevent by acting ahead of time," is *intercept.*

2. b. A synonym for *repression,* which means "restraint," is *constraint.*

3. c. A synonym for *elusive,* which means "hard to grasp," is *evanescent.*

4. a. A synonym for *tumultuously,* which means "in an agitated way," is *severely.*

Writing

Evaluate students' reflective essays using the **Rubrics for Reflective Essay,** in *Professional Development Guidebook,* pages 293–294.

Assessment Resources

Unit 3 Resources

L1 L2 EL **Selection Test A,** pp. 190–192. Administer Test A to less advanced readers.

L3 L4 EL **Selection Test B,** pp. 193–194. Administer Test B to on-level and more advanced students.

L3 L4 **Open-Book Test,** pp. 187–189. As an alternative, give the Open-Book Test.

All **Customizable Test Bank**

All **Self-tests** Students may prepare for the **Selection Test** by taking the **Self-test** online.

All assessment resources are available at **www.PHLitOnline.com.**

Douglass • We Wear the Mask
Lesson Pacing Guide

DAY 1 Preteach

- ⓒ Administer the Reading and Vocabulary Warm-ups (*Unit 3 Resources*, pp. 196–199) as necessary.
- ⓒ Introduce the Literary Analysis concept: Formal Verse.
- Introduce the Reading Strategy: Analyze the Effect of the Historical Period.
- Build background with the author and Background features.
- Develop thematic thinking with Connecting to the Essential Question.
- ⓒ Teach the selection vocabulary.

DAY 2 Preteach/Teach/Extend

- Distribute copies of the appropriate graphic organizer for the Reading Strategy (*Graphic Organizer Transparencies*, pp. 137–138).
- Distribute copies of the appropriate graphic organizer for Literary Analysis (*Graphic Organizer Transparencies*, pp. 139–140).
- Prepare students to read with the Activating Prior Knowledge activities (TE).
- Informally monitor comprehension while students read.
- Use the Reading Check question to confirm comprehension.
- ⓒ Develop students' understanding of formal verse. using the Literary Analysis prompt.
- ⓒ Reinforce vocabulary with the Vocabulary notes.
- Assess students' comprehension and mastery of the skills by having them answer the Critical Reading, Literary Analysis, and Reading Strategy questions.

DAY 3 Assess

- ⓒ Have students complete the Vocabulary Lesson.
- ⓒ Have students complete the Writing Lesson and write a report on literary history. (You may assign as homework.)
- Administer Selection Test A or B (*Unit 3 Resources,* pp. 208–210 or 211–213).

ⓒ Common Core State Standards

Reading Literature 5. Analyze how an author's choices concerning how to structure specific parts of a text contribute to its overall structure and meaning as well as its aesthetic impact.

Writing 1. Write arguments to support claims in an analysis of substantive topics or texts, using valid reasoning and relevant and sufficient evidence.

Language 5. Demonstrate understanding of figurative language, word relationships, and nuances in word meanings.

Additional Standards Practice
Common Core Companion, *pp. 54–55; 185–195; 332–335*

Daily Block Scheduling
Each day in this Lesson Pacing Guide represents a 40–50 minute period. Teachers using block scheduling may combine days to revise pacing. In addition, teachers may differentiate and support core instruction by integrating components for extended and intensive support as students require. See the Guide to Selected Leveled Resources (facing page).

Guide to Selected Leveled Resources

R T I Tier 1 (students performing on level)

Douglass • We Wear the Mask

Warm Up	Practice, model, and monitor fluency, working with the whole class or in groups.	Vocabulary and Reading Warm-ups B, *Unit 3 Resources,* pp. 196–197, 199
Comprehension/Skills	Support and monitor comprehension and skills development, having students complete the activities, graphic organizers, and interactive prompts independently or as a class.	• *Reader's Notebook,* adapted instruction and summary **EL** *Reader's Notebook: English Learner's Version,* adapted instruction and summary • **Reading Strategy Graphic Organizer B,** *Graphic Organizer Transparencies,* p. 138 • **Literary Analysis Graphic Organizer B,** *Graphic Organizer Transparencies,* p. 140
Monitor Progress	**A** Monitor student progress with the differentiated curriculum-based assessment in the *Unit Resources.*	• **Selection Test B,** *Unit 3 Resources,* pp. 211–213 • **Open-Book Test,** *Unit 3 Resources,* pp. 205–207

R T I Tier 2 (students requiring intervention)

Douglass • We Wear the Mask

Warm Up	Practice, model, and monitor fluency in groups or with individuals.	• **Vocabulary and Reading Warm-ups A,** *Unit 3 Resources,* pp. 196–198 • *Hear It!* Audio CD
Comprehension/Skills	• Support and monitor comprehension and skills development, working in small groups or with individuals. • As students complete the selection in the appropriate version of the *Reader's Notebook,* monitor comprehension frequently with group questions and individual instruction. • Model strategies while guiding students in completing the activities and prompts in the *Reader's Notebook,* as well as the graphic organizers. • Practice skills and monitor mastery with the *Reading Kit* worksheets.	• *Reader's Notebook: Adapted Version,* adapted instruction and summary **EL** *Reader's Notebook: English Learner's Version,* adapted instruction and summary • **Reading Strategy Graphic Organizer A,** *Graphic Organizer Transparencies,* p. 137 • **Literary Analysis Graphic Organizer A,** *Graphic Organizer Transparencies,* p. 139 • *Reading Kit,* Practice worksheets
Monitor Progress	**A** Monitor student progress with the differentiated curriculum-based assessment in the *Unit Resources* and in the *Reading Kit.*	• **Selection Test A,** *Unit 3 Resources,* pp. 208–210 • *Reading Kit,* Assess worksheets

TIER 3 Tier 3 intervention may require consultation with the student's special-education or dyslexia specialist. For additional support, see the Tier 2 activities and resources listed above.

One-on-one teaching   Group work   Whole-class instruction   Independent work   **A** Assessment

For a complete guide to selection support, including support for Advanced students, see the Overview of Resources in the frontmatter.

Douglass • We Wear the Mask

Vocabulary/Fluency/Prior Knowledge

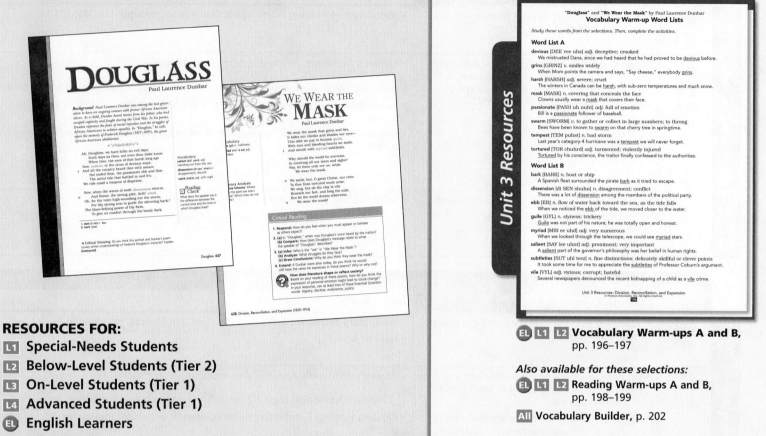

"Douglass" and "We Wear the Mask" by Paul Laurence Dunbar
Vocabulary Warm-up Word Lists

Study these words from the selections. Then, complete the activities.

Word List A

devious [DEE vee uhs] *adj.* deceptive; crooked
We mistrusted Dana, since we had heard that he had proved to be <u>devious</u> before.

grins [GRINZ] *v.* smiles widely
When Mom points the camera and says, "Say cheese," everybody <u>grins</u>.

harsh [HARSH] *adj.* severe; cruel
The winters in Canada can be <u>harsh</u>, with sub-zero temperatures and much snow.

mask [MASK] *n.* covering that conceals the face
Clowns usually wear a <u>mask</u> that covers their face.

passionate [PASH uh nuht] *adj.* full of emotion
Bill is a <u>passionate</u> follower of baseball.

swarm [SWORM] *v.* to gather or collect in large numbers; to throng
Bees have been known to <u>swarm</u> on that cherry tree in springtime.

tempest [TEM puhst] *n.* bad storm
Last year's category-4 hurricane was a <u>tempest</u> we will never forget.

tortured [TOR churhd] *adj.* tormented; violently injured
<u>Tortured</u> by his conscience, the traitor finally confessed to the authorities.

Word List B

bark [BARK] *n.* boat or ship
A Spanish fleet surrounded the pirate <u>bark</u> as it tried to escape.

dissension [di SEN shuhn] *n.* disagreement; conflict
There was a lot of <u>dissension</u> among the members of the political party.

ebb [EB] *n.* flow of water back toward the sea, as the tide falls
When we noticed the <u>ebb</u> of the tide, we moved closer to the water.

guile [GYL] *n.* slyness; trickery
<u>Guile</u> was not part of his nature; he was totally open and honest.

myriad [MIR ee uhd] *adj.* very numerous
When we looked through the telescope, we could see <u>myriad</u> stars.

salient [SAY lee uhnt] *adj.* prominent; very important
A <u>salient</u> part of the governor's philosophy was her belief in human rights.

subtleties [SUT uhl teez] *n.* fine distinctions; delicately skillful or clever points
It took some time for me to appreciate the <u>subtleties</u> of Professor Coburn's argument.

vile [VYL] *adj.* vicious; corrupt; hateful
Several newspapers denounced the recent kidnapping of a child as a <u>vile</u> crime.

Unit 3 Resources: Division, Reconciliation, and Expansion
© Pearson Education, Inc. All rights reserved.
196

EL **L1** **L2** **Vocabulary Warm-ups A and B,** pp. 196–197

Also available for these selections:

EL **L1** **L2** **Reading Warm-ups A and B,** pp. 198–199

All **Vocabulary Builder,** p. 202

RESOURCES FOR:

L1 Special-Needs Students

L2 Below-Level Students (Tier 2)

L3 On-Level Students (Tier 1)

L4 Advanced Students (Tier 1)

EL English Learners

All All Students

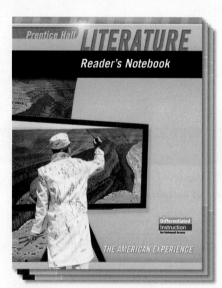

Reader's Notebooks

Pre- and postreading pages for these selections appear in an interactive format in the *Reader's Notebooks*. Each *Notebook* is differentiated for a different group of learners. The selections in the Adapted and English Learner's versions are abridged.

L2 **L3** *Reader's Notebook*

L1 *Reader's Notebook: Adapted Version*

EL *Reader's Notebook: English Learner's Version*

EL *Reader's Notebook: Spanish Version*

© *Common Core Companion*

Additional instruction and practice for each Common Core State Standard

Selection Support

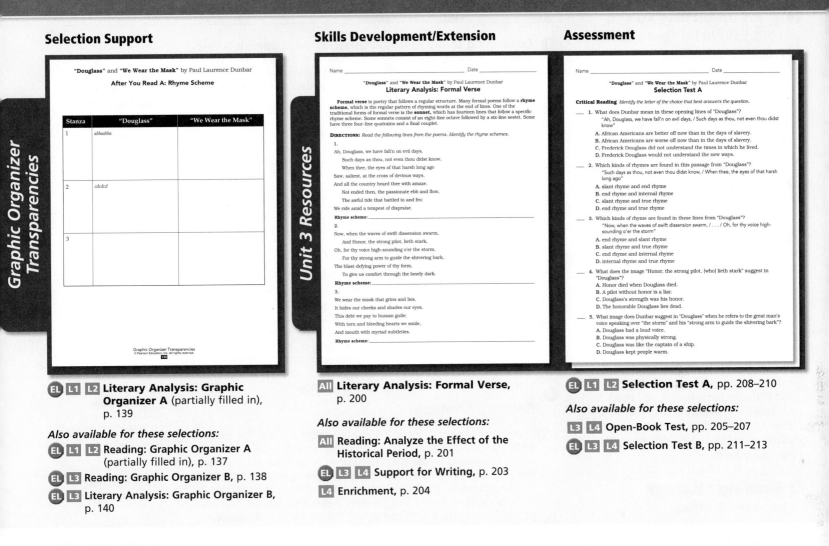

Graphic Organizer Transparencies

"Douglass" and "We Wear the Mask" by Paul Laurence Dunbar

After You Read A: Rhyme Scheme

Stanza	"Douglass"	"We Wear the Mask"
1	abbaabba	
2	cdcdcd	
3		

Graphic Organizer Transparencies
© Pearson Education, Inc. All rights reserved.
139

EL **L1** **L2** **Literary Analysis: Graphic Organizer A** (partially filled in), p. 139

Also available for these selections:

EL **L1** **L2** **Reading: Graphic Organizer A** (partially filled in), p. 137

EL **L3** **Reading: Graphic Organizer B**, p. 138

EL **L3** **Literary Analysis: Graphic Organizer B**, p. 140

Skills Development/Extension

Unit 3 Resources

Name _____ Date _____

"Douglass" and "We Wear the Mask" by Paul Laurence Dunbar
Literary Analysis: Formal Verse

Formal verse is poetry that follows a regular structure. Many formal poems follow a **rhyme scheme**, which is the regular pattern of rhyming words at the end of lines. One of the traditional forms of formal verse is the **sonnet**, which has fourteen lines that follow a specific rhyme scheme. Some sonnets consist of an eight-line octave followed by a six-line sestet. Some have three four-line quatrains and a final couplet.

DIRECTIONS: *Read the following lines from the poems. Identify the rhyme schemes.*

1.
Ah, Douglass, we have fall'n on evil days,
      Such days as thou, not even thou didst know,
      When thee, the eyes of that harsh long ago
Saw, salient, at the cross of devious ways,
And all the country heard thee with amaze.
      Not ended then, the passionate ebb and flow,
      The awful tide that battled to and fro;
We ride amid a tempest of dispraise.

Rhyme scheme: _____

2.
Now, when the waves of swift dissension swarm,
      And Honor, the strong pilot, lieth stark,
Oh, for thy voice high-sounding o'er the storm,
      For thy strong arm to guide the shivering bark,
The blast-defying power of thy form,
      To give us comfort through the lonely dark.

Rhyme scheme: _____

3.
We wear the mask that grins and lies,
It hides our cheeks and shades our eyes,
This debt we pay to human guile;
With torn and bleeding hearts we smile,
And mouth with myriad subtleties.

Rhyme scheme: _____

All **Literary Analysis: Formal Verse,** p. 200

Also available for these selections:

All **Reading: Analyze the Effect of the Historical Period,** p. 201

EL **L3** **L4** **Support for Writing,** p. 203

L4 **Enrichment,** p. 204

Assessment

Name _____ Date _____

"Douglass" and "We Wear the Mask" by Paul Laurence Dunbar
Selection Test A

Critical Reading *Identify the letter of the choice that best answers the question.*

___ 1. What does Dunbar mean in these opening lines of "Douglass"?
"Ah, Douglass, we have fall'n on evil days, / Such days as thou, not even thou didst know"
A. African Americans are better off now than in the days of slavery.
B. African Americans are worse off now than in the days of slavery.
C. Frederick Douglass did not understand the times in which he lived.
D. Frederick Douglass would not understand the new ways.

___ 2. Which kinds of rhymes are found in this passage from "Douglass"?
"Such days as thou, not even thou didst know, / When thee, the eyes of that harsh long ago"
A. slant rhyme and end rhyme
B. end rhyme and internal rhyme
C. slant rhyme and true rhyme
D. end rhyme and true rhyme

___ 3. Which kinds of rhyme are found in these lines from "Douglass"?
"Now, when the waves of swift dissension swarm, / . . . / Oh, for thy voice high-sounding o'er the storm"
A. end rhyme and slant rhyme
B. slant rhyme and true rhyme
C. end rhyme and internal rhyme
D. internal rhyme and true rhyme

___ 4. What does the image "Honor, the strong pilot, [who] lieth stark" suggest in "Douglass"?
A. Honor died when Douglass died.
B. A pilot without honor is a liar.
C. Douglass's strength was his honor.
D. The honorable Douglass lies dead.

___ 5. What image does Dunbar suggest in "Douglass" when he refers to the great man's voice speaking over "the storm" and his "strong arm to guide the shivering bark"?
A. Douglass had a loud voice.
B. Douglass was physically strong.
C. Douglass was like the captain of a ship.
D. Douglass kept people warm.

EL **L1** **L2** **Selection Test A,** pp. 208–210

Also available for these selections:

L3 **L4** **Open-Book Test,** pp. 205–207

EL **L3** **L4** **Selection Test B,** pp. 211–213

PHLit Online!
www.PHLitOnline.com

Online Resources: All print materials are also available online.

- complete narrated selection text
- a thematically related video with writing prompt
- an interactive graphic organizer
- highlighting feature
- access to all student print resources, adapted to individual student needs
- Spanish and English summaries
- adapted selection translations in Spanish

Get Connected! (thematic video with writing prompt)

Also available:

Background Video
All videos are available in Spanish.

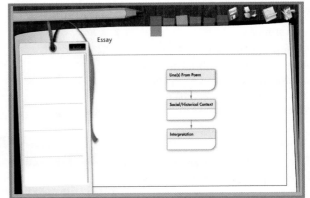

Writer's Journal (with graphics feature)

Also available:

Vocabulary Central (tools and activities for studying vocabulary)

❶ 🔎 Connecting to the Essential Question

1. Review the assignment.

2. Ask students the rules for another form of poetry—say, a haiku. Have them do the assignment.

3. As students read, have them name the emotions Dunbar conveys.

❷ Literary Analysis

Introduce the skills.

Think Aloud: Model the Skill

Say to students:

Here's a stanza by Emily Dickinson:

The Soul selects her own
Society—
Then—shuts the Door—
To her divine Majority—
Present no more—

I conclude that the rhyme scheme is *abab.* Here's why: Lines 1 and 3 end with the same sound, so I used the letter *a* to stand for that sound; lines 2 and 4 end with another identical sound, so I used the letter *b* to stand for it.

❸ Reading Strategy

1. Introduce the strategy.

2. Give students a copy of **Reading Strategy Graphic Organizer B,** page 138 in *Graphic Organizer Transparencies,* to fill out as they read.

Think Aloud: Model the Skill

Say to students:

During the 1950s and 1960s, Americans argued about the rights of African Americans. Knowing that, a song of the period makes sense. The chorus says in part:

We shall overcome
Some day.

Singers meant that they'd succeed in securing rights for all Americans.

❹ Vocabulary

1. Pronounce each word, giving its definition; have students say it aloud.

2. See also the *Classroom Strategies and Teaching Routines* card for vocabulary.

Before You Read

Douglass •
We Wear the Mask

❶ **Connecting to the Essential Question** Paul Laurence Dunbar depicts the struggles of African Americans in "Douglass" and "We Wear the Mask." As you read, take note of the issues that Dunbar raises. Doing so will help as you reflect on the Essential Question: **How does literature shape or reflect society?**

❷ ### Literary Analysis

Formal verse is poetry that follows a fixed structure. Formal structures may require a specific number of lines in a stanza, a set number of stanzas, or the use of repeated sounds. A **Petrarchan sonnet,** such as Dunbar's poem "Douglass," has fourteen lines separated into one stanza of eight lines and one of six lines. A sonnet also has a regular **rhyme scheme,** or pattern of rhyming words at the ends of lines. When notating rhyme scheme, the same sounds are indicated with lower case letters:

Ah, Douglass, we have fall'n on evil <u>days</u>, (a)
Such days as thou, not even thou didst <u>know</u>, (b)
When thee, the eyes of that harsh long <u>ago</u> (b)
Saw, salient, at the cross of devious <u>ways</u> . . . (a)

Poets also use formal structures in poems that do not use a specific fixed form. For example, "We Wear the Mask" is not written in a fixed form, but it has formal elements, including rhyme scheme. Formal elements enhance a poem's meaning and *mood,* or emotion. They also contribute to a poem's *aesthetic qualities*—the sense of art and beauty it conveys. As you read, notice how Dunbar's use of formal elements adds to the meaning, power, and beauty of these poems.

❸ ### Reading Strategy

© **Preparing to Read Complex Texts** Dunbar wrote in the decades following the Civil War. To fully appreciate his poems, consider how the period in which he wrote affected his point of view. As you read, **analyze the effect of the historical period** on the ideas, values, and themes that Dunbar expressed. A complete interpretation of the poem will account for both its *universal themes* and the ideas that reflect the poet's historical period. Use a chart like the one shown to record your interpretations.

❹ ### Vocabulary

salient (sāl′ yənt) *adj.* standing out from the rest (p. 637)

dissension (di sen′ shən) *n.* disagreement; discord (p. 637)

stark (stärk) *adj.* stiff; rigid (p. 637)

guile (gīl) *n.* craftiness (p. 638)

myriad (mir′ ē əd) *adj.* countless (p. 638)

634 Division, Reconciliation, and Expansion (1850–1914)

**Common Core
State Standards**

Reading Literature
5. Analyze how an author's choices concerning how to structure specific parts of a text contribute to its overall structure and meaning as well as its aesthetic impact.

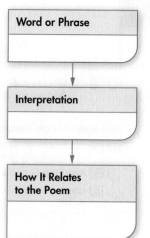

Word or Phrase

Interpretation

How It Relates to the Poem

www.PHLitOnline.com

Vocabulary Development

Vocabulary Knowledge Rating
Create a **Vocabulary Knowledge Rating Chart** (*Professional Development Guidebook,* p. 33) for the vocabulary words on the student page. Give each student a copy of the chart with the words on it. Read the words aloud, and have students mark their rating of each in the Before Reading column. When students have completed reading and discussing the selections, have them take out their **Vocabulary Knowledge Rating Charts** for the selections. Read the words aloud, and have students rate their knowledge again in the After Reading column. Clarify any words that are still problematic. Then have students complete the Vocabulary practice at the end of the selections.

 **Vocabulary Central,** featuring tools and activities for studying vocabulary, is available online at **www.PHLitOnline.com.**

Paul Laurence Dunbar (1872–1906)

Author of "Douglass" and "We Wear the Mask"

Paul Laurence Dunbar was the first African American author to attain national recognition and support himself entirely with his writing. Throughout his short career, he wrote many books of poetry, as well as four novels and four volumes of short stories.

A Literary Child Dunbar was born in Dayton, Ohio, the son of former slaves. Encouraged by his mother, he began writing poetry at an early age. The only African American student in his high school class, Dunbar served as president of the literary society, class poet, and editor of the school newspaper.

Gaining Recognition After graduation, Dunbar sought work in a newspaper or legal office, but he found it difficult because of his race. He finally took a job as an elevator operator, supporting himself while continuing to write. He first earned recognition among writers and critics in 1892, when he read his poetry during a meeting of the Western Association of Writers. A year later, he took out a loan and published his first collection of poetry, *Oak and Ivy*. In 1895, he published a second collection, *Majors and Minors*. William Dean Howells, the leading critic of the day, was so impressed with the book that he wrote an introduction for Dunbar's next collection, *Lyrics of a Lowly Life* (1896).

Characters, Themes, and Forms Dunbar's fiction often focuses on daily life in the vanished world of the southern plantation. Sometimes, however, his writing revolves around social problems facing African Americans in Midwestern towns and urban ghettoes at the turn of the century. His characters include farmers, politicians, preachers, traders, entertainers, and professionals.

Popularity at a Price Dunbar composed poems in two styles—one formal and elegant, the other informal, using a rural dialect. His gift for re-creating dialect and using it to create believable characters was profound. However, it also drew criticism from those who believed Dunbar was pandering to white readers' desire for stereotypes of prewar African Americans. In poems such as "Douglass" and "We Wear the Mask," however, Dunbar demonstrates a command of the English language that was often overlooked, capturing the struggles of African Americans in a dignified, graceful manner.

An Untimely Death By his late twenties, Dunbar was a nationally recognized poet. Sadly, his life was cut short by tuberculosis in 1906. By the end of his life, his poetry was so popular that he was able to write from Florida, "Down here one finds my poems recited everywhere."

Douglass • We Wear the Mask **635**

Daily Bellringer

For each class during which you will teach these selections, have students complete one of the five activities for the appropriate week in the *Daily Bellringer Activities* booklet.

Multidraft Reading

To assist struggling readers and to enhance reading for all, apply multidraft reading protocols. For each reading, have students set the purpose indicated:

- **First reading**—identifying key ideas and details and answering any Reading Checks.
- **Second reading**—analyzing craft and structure and responding to the side-column prompts.
- **Third reading**—integrating knowledge and ideas, connecting to other texts and the world, and answering the end-of-selection questions.

For more guidance, refer to the *Classroom Strategies and Teaching Routines* card on multidraft reading.

❺ Background
More About the Author

Dunbar long idolized Frederick Douglass, and on one occasion the two men met. The young poet appeared with Douglass in Chicago at the 1893 World's Columbian Exposition; there Dunbar recited a poem that he had written for the occasion.

Writing at a time when prejudice against African Americans was mounting in both the northern and southern regions of the United States, Dunbar created poetry that disputed the unflattering image of his people found in magazines and newspapers. He gained national prominence as a poet by the turn of the twentieth century.

PHLit Online!
www.PHLitOnline.com

Teaching From Technology

Preparing to Read
Go to **www.PHLitOnline.com** in class or in a lab and display the **Get Connected!** slide show for these selections. Have the class brainstorm for responses to the slide show writing prompt, entering ideas in the interactive journal. Then have students complete their written responses individually in a lab or as homework.

To build background, display the Background and More About the Author features.

Using the Interactive Text
Go to **www.PHLitOnline.com** and display the **Enriched Online Student Edition.** As the class reads the selections or listens to the narration, record answers to side-column prompts using the graphic organizers accessible on the interactive page. Alternatively, have students use the online edition individually, answering the prompts as they read.

❶ Humanities

Frederick Douglass, artist unknown
This portrait of the abolitionist Frederick Douglass (1817–1895) appeared on the cover of the November 24, 1883, issue of *Harper's Weekly*. **Ask** students: What qualities of Douglass does the artist capture in this portrait?
Possible answer: Students might cite the power and determination of the face and the intensity of the stare.

❷ About the Selection

In both of the poems in this lesson, the writer addresses the struggles of African Americans. In "Douglass," the speaker cries out to a hero of an earlier age. In "We Wear the Mask," the speaker describes how African Americans hide their despair from the eyes of white America.

❸ Activating Prior Knowledge

Prepare students for reading and interpreting these poems by asking them to wear a mask to class—anything from simple eye coverings to medical masks to Mardi Gras masks. Have groups discuss the difficulties of communication between two people wearing masks. Guide students to notice that masks can fool, hide, frighten, or amuse, but seldom do they encourage honesty or frankness. Then have students remove the physical masks but assume masklike facial expressions —joy, fear, boredom, and so on. How convincing can they be in maintaining the mask of an emotion when talking with friends or with strangers?

636 Division, Reconciliation, and Expansion (1850–1914)

Ⓒ Text Complexity Rubric

Douglass; We Wear the Mask			
Qualitative Measures			
Context/Knowledge Demands	Social issues; racial discrimination 1 2 ③ 4 5		
Structure/Language Conventionality and Clarity	Poetic diction; some difficult vocabulary 1 2 3 ④ 5		
Levels of Meaning/ Purpose/Concept Level	Accessible (African American struggle for equality; hiding despair) 1 2 ③ 4 5		
Quantitative Measures			
Lexile	NP	**Text Length**	111; 98 words
Overall Complexity	**More complex**		

Reader and Task Suggestions

Preparing to Read the Text
- Using the Background information on TE p. 635, discuss the focus of Dunbar's literary efforts.
- Ask students why a poet would want to share not just personal feelings but the feelings of a group of people.
- Guide students to use Multidraft Reading strategies (TE p. 635).

Leveled Tasks
Structure/Language If students will have difficulty with the poetic diction, have them first read to paraphrase unfamiliar words. Then, have them read aloud to "hear" the voice of a people.

Analyzing If students will not have difficulty with the poetic diction, discuss how Dunbar uses direct address (to Douglass and to Christ) to express a people's feelings.

2 3

DOUGLASS

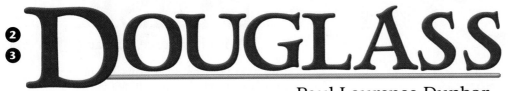

Paul Laurence Dunbar

Background *Paul Laurence Dunbar was among the last generation to have an ongoing contact with former African American slaves. As a child, Dunbar heard stories from his father, who had escaped captivity and fought during the Civil War. In his poems, Dunbar expresses the pain of racial injustice and the struggles of African Americans to achieve equality. In "Douglass," he calls upon the memory of Frederick Douglass (1817–1895), the great African-American abolitionist.*

Ah, Douglass, we have fall'n on evil days,
    Such days as thou, not even thou didst know,
    When thee, the eyes of that harsh long ago
Saw, salient, at the cross of devious ways,
And all the country heard thee with amaze.
    Not ended then, the passionate ebb and flow.
    The awful tide that battled to and fro;
We ride amid a tempest of dispraise.

4

Now, when the waves of swift dissension swarm,
    And Honor, the strong pilot, lieth[1] stark,
Oh, for thy voice high-sounding o'er the storm,
    For thy strong arm to guide the shivering bark,[2]
The blast-defying power of thy form,
    To give us comfort through the lonely dark.

1. **lieth** (lī′ eth) *v.* lies.
2. **bark** boat.

Vocabulary

salient (sāl′ yənt) *adj.* standing out from the rest

dissension (di sen′ shən) *n.* disagreement; discord

stark (stärk) *adj.* stiff; rigid

5 **Reading Check**

What does the speaker say is the difference between the current time and the time in which Douglass lived?

6 ◄ **Critical Viewing** Do you think this portrait and Dunbar's poem convey similar understandings of Frederick Douglass's character? Explain. **[Interpret]**

4 Reading Strategy

Analyze the Effect of the Historical Period

1. Remind students that the historical period in which writers live may affect their ideas, values, and themes.
2. Call students' attention to the final line of the first stanza and the first two lines of the second stanza. **Ask** students to explain in their own words what is going on around the speaker.
   Answer: Lines 8–10 tell that the speaker and his people find themselves in a tempest of disapproval and discord while humanitarian feelings are absent.
3. **Ask** students what effect that atmosphere has on the speaker.
   Answer: He responds by calling on a former leader for strength and support.

5 Reading Check

Answer: The speaker says that current conditions are even harsher than those in Douglass's time.

6 Critical Viewing

Possible response: Both the portrait and Dunbar's poem show Frederick Douglass as impressive, strong willed, and robust.

Differentiated Instruction for Universal Access

Support for Special-Needs Students
Have students complete the **Before You Read** and the **Making Connections** pages for these selections in the ***Reader's Notebook: Adapted Version.*** These pages provide abbreviated skills instruction, a selection summary, the Before You Read graphic organizer, and a **Note-taking Guide.**

Support for Less Proficient Readers
Have students complete the **Before You Read** and the **Making Connections** pages for these selections in the ***Reader's Notebook.*** These pages provide abbreviated skills instruction, a selection summary, the Before You Read graphic organizer, and a **Note-taking Guide.**

EL **Support for English Learners**
Have students complete the **Before You Read** and the **Making Connections** pages for these selections in the ***Reader's Notebook: English Learner's Version.*** These pages provide additional vocabulary, vocabulary skills, and vocabulary practice, along with a **Getting Ready to Read** activity.

PHLit Online!

These selections are available in an interactive format in the **Enriched Online Student Edition**, at **www.PHLitOnline.com**, which includes a thematically related video with writing prompt and an interactive graphic organizer.

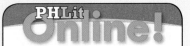

1. Have students identify the rhyme scheme in this poem; most lines are either true or slant rhymes. If necessary, help students see that the rhyme scheme is *aabba* or *aabba-slant* for the first stanza (the last word of the stanza may be pronounced with a long *i* or as a slant rhyme); *aabc* for the second stanza; and *aabbac* for the third stanza.

2. **Ask** students the Literary Analysis question.
   Answer: Lines 1, 2, 6, 7, 10, 11, and 14 are exact rhymes; line 5 may be treated as an exact rhyme or as a slant rhyme to lines 1, 2, 6, 7, 10, 11, and 14; lines 3, 4, 8, 12, and 13 are exact rhymes. Lines 9 and 15 are nonrhyming; students may observe that these two lines stand out.

ASSESS

Answers

Before students respond, you may wish to have them write a brief objective summary of the selection. As they answer the questions below, remind them to support their answers with evidence from the text.

1. (a) It was heard "long ago" in a harsh time. (b) According to the speaker, the present day needs Douglass's singleness of purpose to counter criticism and dissent.

2. (a) Dunbar speaks for African Americans. (b) They struggle against prejudice and injustice. (c) The speaker implies that showing the world their "tears and sighs" would weaken African Americans' position in society.

3. **Possible response:** Students may differ over whether relations between African Americans and other races have improved greatly.

4. **Possible response:** Each of these poems shows a writer giving voice to emotions that ordinary people—readers—may also feel. Realizing that they are not alone in their feelings, individual readers may even unite to call for social change—justice in the face of bigotry.

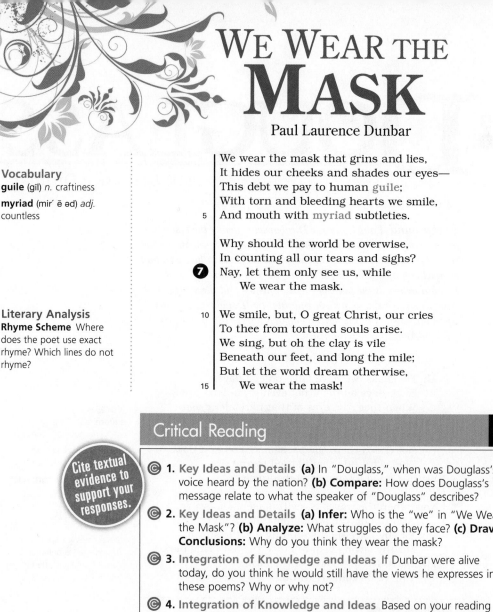

WE WEAR THE MASK

Paul Laurence Dunbar

Vocabulary
guile (gīl) *n.* craftiness
myriad (mir′ ē əd) *adj.* countless

Literary Analysis
Rhyme Scheme Where does the poet use exact rhyme? Which lines do not rhyme?

We wear the mask that grins and lies,
It hides our cheeks and shades our eyes—
This debt we pay to human guile;
With torn and bleeding hearts we smile,
5 And mouth with myriad subtleties.

Why should the world be overwise,
In counting all our tears and sighs?
⑦ Nay, let them only see us, while
        We wear the mask.

10 We smile, but, O great Christ, our cries
To thee from tortured souls arise.
We sing, but oh the clay is vile
Beneath our feet, and long the mile;
But let the world dream otherwise,
15   We wear the mask!

Critical Reading

> Cite textual evidence to support your responses.

© 1. **Key Ideas and Details** **(a)** In "Douglass," when was Douglass's voice heard by the nation? **(b) Compare:** How does Douglass's message relate to what the speaker of "Douglass" describes?

© 2. **Key Ideas and Details** **(a) Infer:** Who is the "we" in "We Wear the Mask"? **(b) Analyze:** What struggles do they face? **(c) Draw Conclusions:** Why do you think they wear the mask?

© 3. **Integration of Knowledge and Ideas** If Dunbar were alive today, do you think he would still have the views he expresses in these poems? Why or why not?

© 4. **Integration of Knowledge and Ideas** Based on your reading of these poems, how do you think the expression of personal emotion might lead to social change? In your response, use at least two of these Essential Question words: *bigotry, disclose, endurance, justice.* **[Connecting to the Essential Question: How does literature shape or reflect society?]**

Assessment Practice

Context (For more practice, see *All-in-One Workbook*.)

Some tests require students to use context to determine the meanings of unfamiliar words. Write the following passage from page 637 on the chalkboard. Then have students answer the question that follows.

We ride amid a <u>tempest</u> of dispraise.
Now, when the waves of swift dissension swarm,
    And Honor, the strong pilot, lieth stark,
Oh, for thy voice high-sounding o'er the storm.

In this passage, <u>tempest</u> means _____.
   A storm
   B sinking boat
   C discussion
   D voice

The first part of the passage says the speaker rides "amid" a tempest. That word, in combination with the references to waves and a storm, should provide the context that helps students choose **A** as the correct answer.

Literary Analysis

© 1. Craft and Structure Which words in "We Wear the Mask" rhyme with "lies"? With "guile"?

© 2. Craft and Structure Using a chart, notate the **rhyme scheme** of each poem. Use a lower-case letter to identify each rhyming sound.

Rhyme Scheme	"Douglass"	"We Wear..."
	1	1
	2	2
		3

© 3. Craft and Structure (a) What elements of **formal verse** does Dunbar use in "We Wear the Mask"? **(b)** How do these elements add to the poem's *mood* and *aesthetic qualities?* Explain.

© 4. Key Ideas and Details (a) What ideas does Dunbar introduce in the first stanza of the **sonnet** "Douglass"? **(b)** How does the second stanza build on these ideas? **(c)** What plea does he make in the final lines?

Reading Strategy

5. Analyze the effect of the historical period in "Douglass" by noting details that reveal the speaker's understanding of his times.

6. (a) What is the *theme*, or message, of "We Wear the Mask"? **(b)** How does that theme reflect problems African Americans faced during Dunbar's lifetime? Explain.

Integrated Language Skills

© Vocabulary Acquisition and Use

Antonyms For each word below, select the antonym, or word of opposite meaning, from the vocabulary list on page 634. Explain your answers.

1. inconspicuous   **3.** few   **5.** flexible
2. agreement   **4.** honesty

Writing

© Argument When it was first published, Dunbar's work received mixed reviews. Conduct research to find examples of both positive and negative responses to Dunbar's work. In a report, summarize your findings and take a position about Dunbar's legacy. Examine how ideas held during Dunbar's era—including prejudice—may have influenced critics.

Common Core State Standards

Writing
1. Write arguments to support claims in an analysis of substantive topics or texts, using valid reasoning and relevant and sufficient evidence.

Language
5. Demonstrate understanding of word relationships and nuances in word meanings.

Answers

1. Words that rhyme with "lies" are "eyes," "overwise," "sighs," "cries," "arise," and "otherwise." Some students may pronounce "subtleties" so that it also rhymes. Words that rhyme with "guile" are "smile," "while," "vile," and "mile."

2. "Douglass": *abbaabba, cdcdcd;* "We Wear the Mask": *aabba* or *aabba-slant* (the last word of the stanza may be pronounced with a long *i* or as a slant rhyme), *aabc, aabbac*

3. **(a)** All the lines except 9 and 15 have the same rhythm. Except for 9 and 15, each line ends with exact or slant rhyme. **(b)** Rhythm and rhyme give the poem a formal mood and make it memorable.

4. **(a)** In the first stanza, Dunbar introduces the idea that his times are worse than Douglass's, and he praises Douglass for his vision. **(b)** In the second stanza, Dunbar provides details about the more intense problems of his day. **(c)** He pleads for comfort from the older man.

5. Details that reveal the speaker's understanding: line 2, Douglass did not know such evil; lines 6–7, the passion and awful tide continue; line 9, no one acts honorably; lines 12 and 14 mention "shivering bark" and "lonely dark."

6. **(a)** Theme: African Americans must mask their true feelings. **(b)** It reflects the era's prejudice.

Vocabulary Acquisition and Use

1. *salient.* The antonym of *inconspicuous* is *salient,* "standing out from the rest."

2. *dissension.* The antonym of *agreement* is *dissension,* "disagreement."

3. *myriad.* The antonym of *few* is *myriad,* "countless."

4. *guile.* The antonym of *honesty* is *guile,* "craftiness."

5. *stark.* The antonym of *flexible* is *stark,* "rigid."

Writing

Evaluate students' reports using the **Rubrics for Historical Investigation Report,** in *Professional Development Guidebook,* pages 268–269.

Assessment Resources

Unit 3 Resources

L1 L2 EL **Selection Test A,** pp. 208–210. Administer Test A to less advanced readers.

L3 L4 EL **Selection Test B,** pp. 211–213. Administer Test B to on-level and more advanced students.

L3 L4 **Open-Book Test,** pp. 205–207. As an alternative, give the Open-Book Test.

All **Customizable Test Bank**

All **Self-tests**
Students may prepare for the **Selection Test** by taking the **Self-test** online.

All assessment resources are available at **www.PHLitOnline.com.**

Luke Havergal • Richard Cory • Lucinda Matlock • Richard Bone
Lesson Pacing Guide

DAY 1 Preteach

- ⓒ Administer the Reading and Vocabulary Warm-ups (*Unit 3 Resources*, pp. 214–217) as necessary.
- ⓒ Introduce the Literary Analysis concept: Narrative Poetry.
- Introduce the Reading Strategy: Comparing and Contrasting.
- Build background with the author and Background features.
- Develop thematic thinking with Connecting to the Essential Question.
- ⓒ Teach the selection vocabulary.

DAYS 2–3 Preteach/Teach/Assess

- Distribute copies of the appropriate graphic organizer for the Reading Strategy (*Graphic Organizer Transparencies*, pp. 141–142).
- Distribute copies of the appropriate graphic organizer for Literary Analysis (*Graphic Organizer Transparencies*, pp. 143–144).
- Prepare students to read with the Activating Prior Knowledge activities (TE).
- Informally monitor comprehension while students read.
- Use the Reading Check question to confirm comprehension.
- ⓒ Develop students' understanding of narrative poetry using the Literary Analysis prompts.
- ⓒ Reinforce vocabulary with the Vocabulary notes.
- Assess students' comprehension and mastery of the skills by having them answer the Critical Reading, Literary Analysis, and Reading Strategy questions.
- ⓒ Have students complete the Vocabulary Lesson.

DAY 4 Extend/Assess

- ⓒ Have students complete the Writing Lesson and write an outline for a short story. (You may assign as homework.)
- Administer Selection Test A or B (*Unit 3 Resources*, pp. 226–228 or 229–231).

ⓒ Common Core State Standards

Reading Literature 3. Analyze the impact of the author's choices regarding how to develop and relate elements of a story or drama.
9. Demonstrate knowledge of early-twentieth-century foundational works of American literature, including how two or more texts from the same period treat similar themes or topics.

Writing 3. Write narratives to develop real or imagined experiences or events using effective technique, well-chosen details, and well-structured event sequences.

Language 4.b. Identify and correctly use patterns of word changes that indicate different meanings or parts of speech.

Additional Standards Practice
Common Core Companion, pp. 28–35; 208–218; 324–331

Daily Block Scheduling
Each day in this Lesson Pacing Guide represents a 40–50 minute period. Teachers using block scheduling may combine days to revise pacing. In addition, teachers may differentiate and support core instruction by integrating components for extended and intensive support as students require. See the Guide to Selected Leveled Resources (facing page).

Guide to Selected Leveled Resources

R T I Tier 1 (students performing on level)

Luke Havergal • Richard Cory • Lucinda Matlock • Richard Bone

Warm Up	Practice, **model**, and **monitor** fluency, working **with the whole class** or **in groups**.	Vocabulary and Reading Warm-ups B, *Unit 3 Resources,* pp. 214–215, 217
Comprehension/Skills	**Support** and **monitor** comprehension and skills development, having students complete the activities, graphic organizers, and interactive prompts **independently** or **as a class**.	• *Reader's Notebook,* adapted instruction and summary EL *Reader's Notebook: English Learner's Version,* adapted instruction and summary • **Reading Strategy Graphic Organizer B,** *Graphic Organizer Transparencies,* p. 142 • **Literary Analysis Graphic Organizer B,** *Graphic Organizer Transparencies,* p. 144
Monitor Progress A	**Monitor** student progress with the differentiated curriculum-based assessment in the *Unit Resources.*	• **Selection Test B,** *Unit 3 Resources,* pp. 229–231 • **Open-Book Test,** *Unit 3 Resources,* pp. 223–225

R T I Tier 2 (students requiring intervention)

Luke Havergal • Richard Cory • Lucinda Matlock • Richard Bone

Warm Up	Practice, **model**, and **monitor** fluency **in groups** or **with individuals**.	• **Vocabulary and Reading Warm-ups A,** *Unit 3 Resources,* pp. 214–216 • *Hear It!* Audio CD
Comprehension/Skills	• **Support** and **monitor** comprehension and skills development, working **in small groups** or **with individuals**. • As students complete the selection in the appropriate version of the *Reader's Notebook,* **monitor** comprehension frequently with group questions and individual instruction. • **Model** strategies while guiding students in completing the activities and prompts in the *Reader's Notebook,* as well as the graphic organizers. • **Practice** skills and **monitor** mastery with the *Reading Kit* worksheets.	• *Reader's Notebook: Adapted Version,* adapted instruction and summary EL *Reader's Notebook: English Learner's Version,* adapted instruction and summary • **Reading Strategy Graphic Organizer A,** *Graphic Organizer Transparencies,* p. 141 • **Literary Analysis Graphic Organizer A,** *Graphic Organizer Transparencies,* p. 143 • *Reading Kit,* Practice worksheets
Monitor Progress A	**Monitor** student progress with the differentiated curriculum-based assessment in the *Unit Resources* and in the *Reading Kit.*	• **Selection Test A,** *Unit 3 Resources,* pp. 226–228 • *Reading Kit,* Assess worksheets

TIER 3 Tier 3 intervention may require consultation with the student's special-education or dyslexia specialist. For additional support, see the Tier 2 activities and resources listed above.

 One-on-one teaching   Group work   Whole-class instruction   Independent work A Assessment

For a complete guide to selection support, including support for Advanced students, see the Overview of Resources in the frontmatter.

Luke Havergal • Richard Cory • Lucinda Matlock • Richard Bone

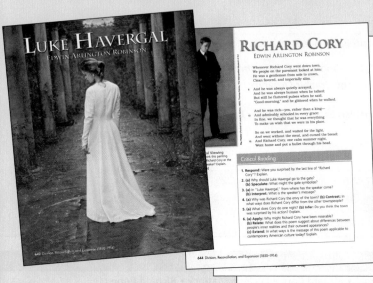

RESOURCES FOR:

L1 Special-Needs Students

L2 Below-Level Students (Tier 2)

L3 On-Level Students (Tier 1)

L4 Advanced Students (Tier 1)

EL English Learners

All All Students

Vocabulary/Fluency/Prior Knowledge

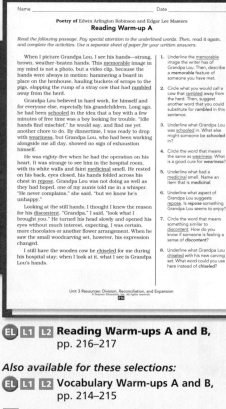

EL L1 L2 Reading Warm-ups A and B,
pp. 216–217

Also available for these selections:

EL L1 L2 Vocabulary Warm-ups A and B,
pp. 214–215

All Vocabulary Builder, p. 220

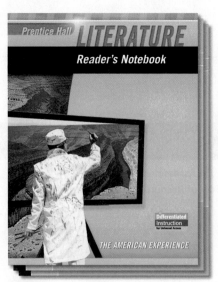

Reader's Notebooks

Pre- and postreading pages for these selections appear in an interactive format in the *Reader's Notebooks*. Each *Notebook* is differentiated for a different group of learners. The selections in the Adapted and English Learner's versions are abridged.

L2 L3 *Reader's Notebook*

L1 *Reader's Notebook: Adapted Version*

EL *Reader's Notebook: English Learner's Version*

EL *Reader's Notebook: Spanish Version*

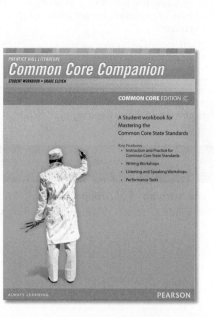

© Common Core Companion

Additional instruction and practice for each Common Core State Standard

Selection Support

Graphic Organizer Transparencies (sidebar)

EL **L3** **Literary Analysis: Graphic Organizer B,** p. 144

Also available for these selections:

EL **L1** **L2** **Reading: Graphic Organizer A** (partially filled in), p. 141

EL **L3** **Reading: Graphic Organizer B,** p. 142

EL **L1** **L2** **Literary Analysis: Graphic Organizer A** (partially filled in), p. 143

Skills Development/Extension

Unit 3 Resources (sidebar)

EL **L3** **L4** **Support for Writing,** p. 221

Also available for these selections:

All **Literary Analysis: Speaker,** p. 218

All **Reading: Comparing and Contrasting,** p. 219

L4 **Enrichment,** p. 222

Assessment

EL **L3** **L4** **Selection Test B,** pp. 229–231

Also available for these selections:

L3 **L4** **Open-Book Test,** pp. 223–225

EL **L1** **L2** **Selection Test A,** pp. 226–228

PHLit Online!
www.PHLitOnline.com

Online Resources: All print materials are also available online.

- complete narrated selection text
- a thematically related video with writing prompt
- an interactive graphic organizer
- highlighting feature
- access to all student print resources, adapted to individual student needs
- Spanish and English summaries
- adapted selection translations in Spanish

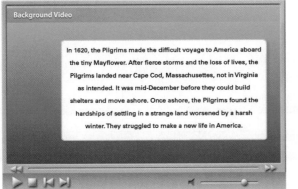

In 1620, the Pilgrims made the difficult voyage to America aboard the tiny Mayflower. After fierce storms and the loss of lives, the Pilgrims landed near Cape Cod, Massachusetts, not in Virginia as intended. It was mid-December before they could build shelters and move ashore. Once ashore, the Pilgrims found the hardships of settling in a strange land worsened by a harsh winter. They struggled to make a new life in America.

Background Video

Also available:

Get Connected! (thematic video with writing prompt)
All videos are available in Spanish.

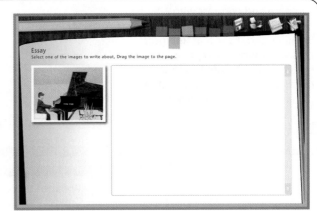

Writer's Journal (with graphics feature)

Also available:

Vocabulary Central (tools and activities for studying vocabulary)

❶ Connecting to the Essential Question

1. Review the assignment.

2. Discuss what makes a small town small. Then have students complete the assignment.

3. As students read, have them notice details of the light and dark sides of small towns.

❷ Literary Analysis

Introduce the skills, using the instruction on the student page.

Think Aloud: Model the Skill

Say to students:

The first four lines of "Richard Bone" tell me that Bone "came" to Spoon River, the *setting* of the narrative. What do the lines tell about the *character* of Bone? They may mean he didn't judge the folks whose gravestones he chiseled.

❸ Reading Strategy

1. Introduce the strategy, using the instruction on the student page.

2. Give students a copy of **Reading Strategy Graphic Organizer B**, page 142 in *Graphic Organizer Transparencies*, to fill out as they read.

Think Aloud: Model the Skill

Say to students:

To see how Robinson's poems compare and contrast with Masters's, I'll first check the rhyme. By skimming, I see that Robinson uses end rhymes here, and Masters does not. But before I work out a detailed comparison and contrast, I'll have to read more closely.

❹ Vocabulary

1. Pronounce each word, giving its definition, and have students say it aloud.

2. For more guidance, see the *Classroom Strategies and Teaching Routines* card for introducing vocabulary.

640

Before You Read

Luke Havergal • Richard Cory • Lucinda Matlock • Richard Bone

❶ **Connecting to the Essential Question** The vision of small-town America in these poems is full of contradictions. As you read, notice details that portray the light and dark sides of small-town life. This activity will help as you consider the Essential Question: **What is the relationship between literature and place?**

❷ Literary Analysis

Narrative poetry is poetry that tells a story and includes the same literary elements as narrative prose such as short stories and novels:

- **Plot:** a related sequence of events, driven by a *conflict* or problem
- **Setting:** the time and place in which a story takes place
- **Characters:** people who participate in the action

In some narrative poems, one character acts as the **speaker,** or voice that tells the story. For example, the speakers in the poems from Masters's *Spoon River Anthology* are characters buried in the cemetery of the fictional town of Spoon River: "At ninety-six I had lived enough, that is all. . . ." Instead of using a neutral speaker, Masters lets characters tell their own stories. As you read, notice how the poet's choice of speaker affects the drama and emotional power of each poem.

❸ Reading Strategy

Preparing to Read Complex Texts **Comparing and contrasting** poems in a group can give you a deeper understanding of each individual poem. It also allows you to see shared elements of works representing a certain region, time period, or literary style. As you read, use a chart like the one shown to compare and contrast the following elements:

- **Poetic Elements:** Which poems use rhyme and meter? To what effect?
- **Point of View:** How are the speakers similar and different?
- **Theme:** How are the central messages or insights about life in each poem similar and different?

❹ Vocabulary

repose (ri pōz´) *n.* state of being at rest (p. 646)

degenerate (dē jen´ ər it) *adj.* morally corrupt (p. 646)

epitaph (ep´ ə taf´) *n.* inscription on a tombstone (p. 647)

chronicles (krän´ i kəlz) *n.* stories; histories (p. 647)

Point of View	Theme

Common Core State Standards

Reading Literature
3. Analyze the impact of the author's choices regarding how to develop and relate elements of a story or drama.
9. Demonstrate knowledge of early-twentieth-century foundational works of American literature, including how two or more texts from the same period treat similar themes or topics.

PHLit Online!
www.PHLitOnline.com

Vocabulary Development

Vocabulary Knowledge Rating

Create a **Vocabulary Knowledge Rating Chart** (*Professional Development Guidebook*, p. 33) for the vocabulary words on the student page. Give each student a copy of the chart with the words on it. Read the words aloud and have students mark their rating in the Before Reading column. Urge students to attend to these words as they read and discuss the selections.

In order to gauge how much instruction you need to provide, tally how many students are confident in their knowledge of each word. As students read, point out the words and their context.

Vocabulary Central, featuring tools and activities for studying vocabulary, is available online at **www.PHLitOnline.com**.

⑤EDWIN ARLINGTON ROBINSON (1869–1935)

Author of "Luke Havergal" and "Richard Cory"

In his mid-thirties, Edwin Arlington Robinson earned twenty cents per hour as a New York City subway inspector. Yet, friends helped him arrange the private printing of three books of his poetry during these lean times, allowing Robinson to become the most successful American poet of the 1920s.

Robinson grew up in Gardiner, Maine, a small town that was the model for Tilbury Town, the fictional setting of many of his poems. He attended Harvard University for two years, but he was forced to return to Gardiner after his father's death. Upon his return, Robinson began writing poetry, depending on friends and patrons for financial support. In a letter to a friend, Robinson wrote: "Writing has been my dream ever since I was old enough to lay a plan for an air castle. Now for the first time I seem to have something like a favorable opportunity and this winter I shall make a beginning."

Four years later, Robinson returned to New York City, hoping to improve his financial situation. When President Theodore Roosevelt, an admirer of Robinson's poems, appointed him to a post at the New York Customhouse, Robinson was set free from his financial worries.

The Inner Struggle Robinson's years of poverty and struggle shaped his world view. He filled his poems with the voices and stories of the lost and the sorrowful, exploring the themes of personal defeat and unfulfilled longing. His best poems paint portraits of desperate characters who view their lives as trivial and meaningless or who long to live in another place or time. Despite his characters' pessimistic outlook, Robinson's poems possess a certain dignity that results from his traditional style, command of language, imagination, and wit.

Robinson found success when his fourth volume of verse, *The Town Down the River* (1910), sold well and received much critical praise. He went on to publish many acclaimed books and receive three Pulitzer Prizes.

▶ Multidraft Reading

To assist struggling readers and to enhance reading for all, apply multidraft reading protocols. For each reading, have students set the purpose indicated:

- **First reading**—identifying key ideas and details and answering any Reading Checks.
- **Second reading**—analyzing craft and structure and responding to the side-column prompts.
- **Third reading**—integrating knowledge and ideas, connecting to other texts and the world, and answering the end-of-selection questions.

For more guidance, refer to the *Classroom Strategies and Teaching Routines* card on multidraft reading.

---

⑤ Background

More About the Author

Among the later works of Edwin Arlington Robinson are several long, blank-verse narrative poems—such as *Merlin* (1917), *Lancelot* (1920), and *Tristram* (1927)—based on the King Arthur legends.

Teaching From Technology

Preparing to Read
Go to **www.PHLitOnline.com** in class or in a lab and display the **Get Connected!** slide show for this grouping. Have the class brainstorm for responses to the slide show writing prompt, entering ideas in the interactive journal. Then have students complete their written responses individually in a lab or as homework.

To build background, display the Background and More About the Authors features.

Using the Interactive Student Edition
Go to **www.PHLitOnline.com** and display the **Enriched Online Student Edition.** As the class reads the selections or listens to the narration, record answers to side-column prompts using the graphic organizers accessible on the interactive page. Alternatively, have students use the online edition individually, answering the prompts as they read.

LUKE HAVERGAL
EDWIN ARLINGTON ROBINSON

❶ About the Selections

These two poems by Robinson address the pain of loss. Luke Havergal grieves for his beloved and questions whether he can go on living. The speaker seems to suggest that Havergal can commune with her spirit until it is his rightful time to die and he and his beloved meet again in the next life. In contrast, "Richard Cory" reveals a whole town in shock and grief. Because ordinary townsfolk idealized the life of a wealthy, elegant man, they are unprepared for his sudden suicide.

❷ Activating Prior Knowledge

Bring in several obituaries from newspapers. (You might duplicate them for students, or you might prefer to read them aloud.) Alternately, have students visit a local cemetery to see the kinds of messages inscribed on gravestones there. Then challenge students to select a literary character and to write an obituary or epitaph for him or her in the style of the ones they have read or seen. Allow ten to fifteen minutes for this task, and then invite volunteers to share the obituaries or epitaphs. Finally, tell students that all four poems in this grouping concern people who have died, and discuss how a poem about someone who died might differ from an obituary or epitaph.

Concept Connector ➡

Tell students they will return to their responses after reading the selections.

642 Division, Reconciliation, and Expansion (1850–1914)

Text Complexity Rubric

	Luke Havergal; Richard Cory	Lucinda Matlock; Richard Bone
Qualitative Measures		
Context/ Knowledge Demands	Grief and shock 1 2 ③ 4 5	Epitaphs 1 ② 3 4 5
Structure/Language Conventionality and Clarity	Repetition; clear rhyme scheme 1 ② 3 4 5	Simple language 1 ② 3 4 5
Levels of Meaning/ Purpose/Concept Level	Accessible (loss; despair) 1 2 ③ 4 5	Accessible (attitude toward life) 1 2 ③ 4 5
Quantitative Measures		
Lexile/Text Length	NP / 252, 122 words	NP / 155, 134 words
Overall Complexity	**More accessible**	**More accessible**

Reader and Task Suggestions

Preparing to Read the Text

• Discuss with students the advantages and disadvantages of small-town life, based on their experiences or reading.

• Ask students whether a poem or an epitaph is the better form for memorializing a person's life.

• Guide students to use Multidraft Reading Strategies (TE p. 641).

Leveled Tasks

Levels of Meaning If students will have difficulty with meaning, have them summarize each stanza in their own words. Then have students reread the poem.

Evaluating If students will not have difficulty with meaning, ask them which of the four poems presents the clearest portrait of its subject.

Go to the western gate, Luke Havergal,
There where the vines cling crimson on the wall,
And in the twilight wait for what will come.
The leaves will whisper there of her, and some,
5   Like flying words, will strike you as they fall;
But go, and if you listen she will call.
Go to the western gate, Luke Havergal—
Luke Havergal.

No, there is not a dawn in eastern skies
10 To rift the fiery night that's in your eyes;
But there, where western glooms are gathering,
The dark will end the dark, if anything:
God slays Himself with every leaf that flies,
And hell is more than half of paradise.
15 No, there is not a dawn in eastern skies—
In eastern skies.

Out of a grave I come to tell you this,
Out of a grave I come to quench the kiss
❸ That flames upon your forehead with a glow
20 That blinds you to the way that you must go.
Yes, there is yet one way to where she is,
Bitter, but one that faith may never miss.
Out of a grave I come to tell you this—
To tell you this.

25 There is the western gate, Luke Havergal,
There are the crimson leaves upon the wall.
Go, for the winds are tearing them away,—
Nor think to riddle the dead words they say,
Nor any more to feel them as they fall;
30 But go, and if you trust her she will call.
There is the western gate, Luke Havergal—
Luke Havergal.

Literary Analysis
Speaker Who is the "I"
who speaks in this poem? Is
there more than one possible
interpretation?

❹ Reading
Check
What will happen at
the western gate if Luke
Havergal goes there?

Luke Havergal **643**

⑤

The Thinker (Portrait of Louis N. Kenton, 1900), Thomas Eakins, The Metropolitan Museum of Art

⑥ ▲ **Critical Viewing**
Do you think this painting suggests Richard Cory or the poem's speaker? Explain. **[Evaluate]**

RICHARD CORY
EDWIN ARLINGTON ROBINSON

Whenever Richard Cory went down town,
We people on the pavement looked at him:
He was a gentleman from sole to crown,
Clean favored, and imperially slim.

5   And he was always quietly arrayed,
And he was always human when he talked;
But still he fluttered pulses when he said,
"Good-morning," and he glittered when he walked.

And he was rich—yes, richer than a king—
10 And admirably schooled in every grace:
In fine, we thought that he was everything
To make us wish that we were in his place.

So on we worked, and waited for the light,
And went without the meat, and cursed the bread;
15 And Richard Cory, one calm summer night,
Went home and put a bullet through his head.

Critical Reading

Cite textual evidence to support your responses.

1. **Key Ideas and Details (a)** Why should Luke Havergal go to the gate? **(b) Speculate:** What might the gate symbolize?

2. **Key Ideas and Details (a)** In "Luke Havergal," from where has the speaker come? **(b) Interpret:** What is the speaker's message?

3. **Key Ideas and Details (a)** Why was Richard Cory the envy of the town? **(b) Contrast:** In what ways does Richard Cory differ from the other townspeople?

4. **Key Ideas and Details (a)** What does Cory do one night? **(b) Infer:** Do you think the town was surprised by his action? Explain.

5. **Integration of Knowledge and Ideas (a) Apply:** Why might Richard Cory have been miserable? **(b) Relate:** What does this poem suggest about differences between people's inner realities and their outward appearances? **(c) Extend:** In what ways is the message of this poem applicable to contemporary American culture today? Explain.

644 Division, Reconciliation, and Expansion (1850–1914)

❼ EDGAR LEE MASTERS (1868–1950)

Author of "Lucinda Matlock" and "Richard Bone"

For years, Edgar Lee Masters practiced criminal law by day in a successful Chicago firm and wrote poems, plays, and essays by night. In 1914, however, Masters's direction as a writer changed dramatically when a friend gave him a copy of *Selected Epitaphs From the Greek Anthology*. This collection included many concise, interconnected epitaphs that captured the essence of people's personal lives.

Spoon River Anthology Using the structure suggested by that anthology, and abandoning conventional rhyme and meter, Masters wrote a series of poems about the lives of people in rural southern Illinois. Published as *Spoon River Anthology* in 1915, the book provoked strong reactions among critics and became a bestseller. The volume was so successful that Masters quit his law career and moved to New York to earn a living as a writer.

The anthology consists of 244 epitaphs for characters buried in the mythical Spoon River cemetery. The dead themselves serve as the speakers of the poems, often revealing secrets they kept hidden during their lifetimes. Many types of people are represented, including storekeepers, housewives, and murderers. Some had happy lives, but many more had lives filled with frustration and despair. Presented together, the epitaphs paint a vivid portrait of the loneliness and isolation confronting people in small Midwestern towns around the turn of the century.

Masters went on to produce other volumes of poetry, novels, biographies, and his autobiography, *Across Spoon River*. However, he is still remembered almost exclusively for *Spoon River Anthology*.

Lucinda Matlock • Richard Bone **645**

❼ Background

More About the Author

In commenting on Edgar Lee Masters's *Spoon River Anthology*, poet May Swenson wrote that in it Masters gave "outlet to all his grudges, beliefs, indignations, insights, prophesies, discoveries of glaring injustice, revelations of life's mysteries and paradoxes—and his own eccentric philosophy. Miraculously he also created . . . a world in microcosm, new in form, timeless in space."

Differentiated Instruction   for Universal Access

Strategy for Less Proficient Readers

Help students recognize and interpret key symbols in these poems. For instance, in "Richard Cory," have them identify all the words and phrases that capture the townspeople's feeling that Cory was wealthy, kingly, and above them.

Strategy for Gifted/Talented Students

Have students complete word webs to analyze the personality of Lucinda Matlock and Richard Bone. Encourage students to identify words that express or describe emotions, opinions, attitudes, and self-image. Then have students compare and contrast the speakers and explore how, even though both poems are written in the first person, the voices of the speakers are distinct.

For more about the author, go online at www.PHLitOnline.com.

645

In the two poems by Masters, two characters in their graves speak frankly about their lives. Matlock died when she was ninety-six after a hard but fulfilling life. She dismisses the complaints of the younger generation, who she feels never developed the power to embrace life and survive its many troubles.

As a carver of tombstones, Bone came to know the people in Spoon River and to learn how closeness and affection caused relatives to ask him to carve untruths into the stone.

❾ World Literature Connection

Dramatic Monologue

Explain that in a dramatic monologue the subject the speaker talks about is not necessarily interesting. The drama lies in what the speaker unintentionally reveals about himself or herself. Tell students that to understand a dramatic monologue they should analyze the speaker's opinions about or reactions to the events described.

Connect to the Literature

After reading and discussing the information on dramatic monologues, **ask** the Connect to the Literature question.
Answer: Some students may point out that television favors flashy action over "talking heads," so dramatic monologues might not be a good format; other students may think that if the lives were acted out, they would fit the public's demand for drama and pathos.

❽ LUCINDA MATLOCK

EDGAR LEE MASTERS

I went to the dances at Chandlerville,
And played snap-out[1] at Winchester.
One time we changed partners,
Driving home in the moonlight of middle June,
5   And then I found Davis.
We were married and lived together for seventy years,
Enjoying, working, raising the twelve children,
Eight of whom we lost
Ere I had reached the age of sixty.
10   I spun, I wove, I kept the house, I nursed the sick,
I made the garden, and for holiday
Rambled over the fields where sang the larks,
And by Spoon River gathering many a shell,
And many a flower and medicinal weed—
15   Shouting to the wooded hills, singing to the green valleys.
At ninety-six I had lived enough, that is all,
And passed to a sweet repose.
What is this I hear of sorrow and weariness,
Anger, discontent and drooping hopes?
20   Degenerate sons and daughters,
Life is too strong for you—
It takes life to love Life.

Vocabulary
repose (ri pōz´) *n.* state of being at rest

degenerate (dē jen´ ər it) *adj.* morally corrupt

1. **snap-out** game in which a long line of players who are holding hands spin around in a circle, causing the players on the ends to be flung off by centrifugal force.

❾ WORLD LITERATURE CONNECTION

Dramatic Monologue

The poems from *Spoon River Anthology* are dramatic monologues, a form developed by British poets during the Victorian period. In a dramatic monologue, the speaker of the poem is a character who addresses the reader, just as a character in a play might speak directly to the audience.

The most famous writer of dramatic monologues is Robert Browning, born near London in 1812. Browning first gained celebrity with *The Ring and the Book*, a series of poems spoken by characters that describe a murder case. Today, Browning's best-known poem is "My Last Duchess," a dramatic monologue spoken by a rich Italian duke who unwittingly admits to having killed his wife: "That's my last Duchess painted on the wall, /Looking as if she were alive."

CONNECT TO THE LITERATURE

Do you think the dramatic monologues from *Spoon River Anthology* could provide the basis for an interesting television series? Why or why not?

Proserpine, 1984 Dante Gabriel Rosetti. Tate Gallery

646 Division, Reconciliation, and Expansion (1850–1914)

Vocabulary Development

Vocabulary Knowledge Rating
When students have completed reading and discussing the group of selections, have them take out the **Vocabulary Knowledge Rating Charts** for the poems. Read the words aloud and have students rate their knowledge of the words again in the After Reading column. Clarify any words that are still problematic. Have students write their own definitions and example or sentence in the appropriate column. Then have students complete the Vocabulary Lesson at the end of the selections. Encourage students to use the words in further discussion and written work about the selections. Remind them that they will be accountable for these words on the **Selection Test**, *Unit 3 Resources*, pages 226–228 or 229–231.

PHLit Online! **Vocabulary Central**, featuring tools and activities for studying vocabulary, is available online at **www.PHLitOnline.com**.

RICHARD BONE

EDGAR LEE MASTERS

When I first came to Spoon River
I did not know whether what they told me
Was true or false.
They would bring me the epitaph
5   And stand around the shop while I worked
And say "He was so kind," "He was wonderful,"
"She was the sweetest woman," "He was a consistent Christian."
And I chiseled for them whatever they wished,
All in ignorance of its truth.
10 But later, as I lived among the people here,
I knew how near to the life
Were the epitaphs that were ordered for them as they died.

But still I chiseled whatever they paid me to chisel
and made myself party to the false chronicles
15 Of the stones,
Even as the historian does who writes
Without knowing the truth,
Or because he is influenced to hide it.

Vocabulary
epitaph (ep´ ə taf´) *n.*
inscription on a tombstone
chronicles (krän´ i kəlz) *n.*
stories; histories

Critical Reading

Cite textual evidence to support your responses.

1. **Key Ideas and Details** **(a)** How old was Lucinda Matlock when she died? **(b) Infer:** Why might she have thought she "lived enough"?

2. **Key Ideas and Details** **(a)** Whom does she address at the end of the poem? **(b) Interpret:** What is the meaning of Matlock's message to those she addresses?

3. **Key Ideas and Details** **(a)** What is Richard Bone's occupation? **(b) Infer:** What does he learn after years in Spoon River?

4. **Key Ideas and Details** **(a) Interpret:** Why does Bone think the epitaphs are "false chronicles"? **(b) Speculate:** Is it likely Bone is correct in his assessment? Explain.

5. **Integration of Knowledge and Ideas** What image of life in small-town America do these poems project? In your response, use at least two of these Essential Question words: *conflict, appearance, secretive, familiar.* **[Connecting to the Essential Question: What is the relationship between literature and place?]**

Richard Bone **647**

Concept Connector

Reading Strategy Graphic Organizer
Ask students to review the graphic organizers in which they have compared and contrasted the four poems. Then have students share their organizers and compare the poetic elements, point of view, and themes they identified.

Activating Prior Knowledge
Have students return to their responses to the Activating Prior Knowledge activity. Ask them to explain whether their thoughts have changed and if so, how.

Writing About the Essential Question
Have students compare the responses to the prompt before they completed reading the poems with their thoughts after reading them. Have them work individually or in groups, writing or discussing their thoughts, to formulate their new responses. Then lead a class discussion, probing for what students have learned that confirms or invalidates their initial thoughts. Encourage students to cite specific textual details to support their responses.

Answers

1. (a) In "Richard Cory," the plot is that a man who had everything kills himself; the setting is a small town; the characters are Richard Cory and the townspeople. (b) In "Lucinda Matlock," the plot is her life story; the setting is Spoon River; the characters are Matlock, her family, and the local youth. Another sample answer can be found in the **Literary Analysis Graphic Organizer A,** page 143 in *Graphic Organizer Transparencies.*

2. (a) Havergal's conflict is that he is grieving; Cory's is a secret sadness; Matlock's is the loss of eight children; Bone's is that he lied in his epitaphs. (b) Havergal has not resolved his conflict; Matlock solved hers by living intensely. Students may say Cory resolved his problem or that suicide is not a solution. They may think Bone's conflict unresolved.

3. The speaker in "Luke Havergal" is unidentified; in "Richard Cory," a townsperson; in "Lucinda Matlock" and "Richard Bone," the title characters.

4. The speaker uses the words "We people" in line 2.

5. The speaker's admiration makes the reader think Cory's life is great.

6. (a) Another speaker might convey different views or details of Matlock's life. (b) Cory might have explained his true feelings.

7. Speakers who are "dead" have nothing to lose from their honesty.

8. (a) Robinson uses rhyme and meter; Masters uses free verse. (b) Some students may find the rhyme and meter too formal; others may find it appropriate for such serious topics.

9. (a) Bone would have described Havergal as unhappy in love, Cory as depressed, Matlock as full of life and scornful of others, and himself as complicit in others' self-deception. (b) All of the epitaphs would show the person's bad side.

10. Students may say that the poems point to the fragility or ephemeral nature of life.

648

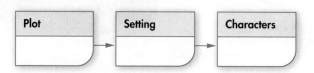

After You Read
Luke Havergal • Richard Cory • Lucinda Matlock • Richard Bone

Literary Analysis

1. **Craft and Structure (a)** Use a chart like the one shown to identify the **plot, setting,** and **characters** in the **narrative poem** "Richard Cory." **(b)** Do the same for "Lucinda Matlock."

Plot	→	Setting	→	Characters

2. **Key Ideas and Details (a)** For each poem in this grouping, identify the *conflict*—the obstacles or problems—the characters face. **(b)** Do all the characters resolve, or solve, their conflicts? Explain.

3. **Craft and Structure** Identify the **speaker** of each poem in this grouping.

4. **Key Ideas and Details** Which details suggest that the speaker of "Richard Cory" is the voice of an entire town? Explain.

5. **Craft and Structure** In what ways does the speaker's admiration for Richard Cory add to the drama and surprise of the poem?

6. **Craft and Structure (a)** In what ways might "Lucinda Matlock" be different if Masters had used a different speaker? **(b)** If "Richard Cory" spoke for himself, how might the poem be different?

7. **Integration of Knowledge and Ideas** The speakers in Masters's *Spoon River Anthology* are dead. Why might this allow them to discuss their lives more openly?

Reading Strategy

8. **(a)** Write several sentences in which you **compare and contrast** the uses of *rhyme* and *meter* in Robinson's poems and Masters's poems. **(b)** In your opinion, which type of poetic form is better suited to the topic of life in small-town America? Explain.

9. **(a)** If Richard Bone were to inscribe a true epitaph for each of the four speakers of these poems, including himself, what might each one say? **(b)** Compare and contrast those messages.

10. Taken together, is there a single *theme* all these poems express? If not, why not? If so, what is that theme?

Common Core State Standards

Writing
3. Write narratives to develop real or imagined experiences or events using effective technique, well-chosen details, and well-structured event sequences. *(p. 649)*

Language
4.b. Identify and correctly use patterns of word changes that indicate different meanings or parts of speech. *(p. 649)*

Assessment Practice

Context (For more practice, see *All-in-One Workbook.*)

The reading sections of many tests require students to use context clues to identify the appropriate meaning of a multiple-meaning word in a given passage. Use the following sample test item to demonstrate.

Whenever Richard Cory went to town,
We people on the pavement looked at him:
He was a gentleman from sole to <u>crown</u>.
Clean favored, and imperially slim.

In this passage, the word <u>crown</u> most nearly means

A symbol of royalty
B hit on the head
C top of the head
D royal government

The juxtaposition of *sole* and *crown* and the general context of describing a gentleman's appearance should lead students to recognize that **C** is the most appropriate choice.

Integrated Language Skills

Vocabulary Acquisition and Use

Word Analysis: Latin Root -genus-

The word *degenerate* combines the Latin root -genus-, meaning "birth, race, species, or kind," with the prefix *de-*, meaning "away from" or "unlike." If a person is *degenerate*, he or she has fallen away from the ancestral qualities of his or her species. Use each of the following -genus- words below to complete the sentences. If the meaning of a word is unclear, consult a dictionary.

genetic	genealogy	homogenous
ingenious	generate	general

1. Is the human race truly _____: are we really all alike?

2. We all have a nearly identical _____ makeup.

3. Most of us can _____ good solutions to everyday problems.

4. However, each of us inherits a unique _____.

5. Some of us think in _____ terms, while others dwell on the tiniest of details.

6. And while many of us can be described as "bright," only a few can be considered _____!

Vocabulary: Evaluating Logic

Indicate whether the underlined word in each sentence below is used logically. If it is, explain your answer. If it is not, explain why not and correct the sentence to restore the logic.

1. Just as I drifted off for my afternoon nap, I heard a loud yapping outside the window and was instantly wrenched into a state of annoyed <u>repose</u>.

2. Throwing up the blind, I could see that the source of the yapping was the <u>degenerate</u> beast my neighbor refers to as his pet.

3. I began to fantasize about a small gravestone bearing an <u>epitaph</u> that read *Rover, detested dog of Denton Drive*.

4. Sadly, I thought, the <u>chronicle</u> of my own life will feature a tired grump with an overactive imagination.

Writing

Narrative Text Choose the poem in this grouping that you think would make the most poignant short story. Then, create an outline that would aid you in translating the verse into a prose narrative.

Prewriting First, use a chart like the one shown to identify the beginning, middle, and end of the story. Refer back to the poem for key story events.

Beginning	Middle	End

Drafting Decide how each part of the story will unfold. Decide what new elements or events would make the beginning more engaging, the middle more suspenseful, and the end more satisfying. As you think of ways to enrich the plot, make notes in the relevant columns of your chart.

Revising Convert the contents of your chart into an outline, using Roman numerals *I, II,* and *III* for the story's beginning, middle, and end. Use the letters *A, B, C,* etc., for details within each section. Organize the story events in chronological order.

Integrated Language Skills **649**

Answers

Vocabulary Acquisition and Use

1. Introduce the skill, using the instruction on the student page.

2. Have students complete the Word Analysis activity and the Vocabulary practice.

Word Analysis

1. homogenous
2. genetic
3. generate
4. genealogy
5. general
6. ingenious

Vocabulary

1. not logical. <u>Repose</u> is rest. I was *instantly wrenched into a state of annoyed <u>wakefulness</u>.*

2. not logical. Animals are not <u>degenerate</u>, or morally corrupt. *I could see that the source of the yapping was the <u>annoying</u> beast my neighbor refers to as a pet.*

3. logical. <u>Epitaphs</u> appear on gravestones.

4. logical. A <u>chronicle</u> of one's life is one's life story.

Writing

1. To guide students in outlining their short stories, give them the **Support for Writing** worksheet (*Unit 3 Resources*, p. 221).

2. Encourage students to reveal character traits that show why the character has the conflict.

3. Remind students to use detailed descriptions of events that convey how the conflict develops and is resolved.

4. Evaluate students' outlines using the **Rubrics for Short Stories**, in *Professional Development Guidebook*, pages 252–253.

Assessment Resources

Unit 3 Resources

L1 L2 EL Selection Test A, pp. 226–228. Administer Test A to less advanced students and English learners.

L3 L4 EL Selection Test B, pp. 229–231. Administer Text B to on-level or more advanced students.

L3 L4 Open-Book Test, pp. 223–225. As an alternative, give the Open-Book Test.

All Customizable Test Bank

All Self-tests
Students may prepare for the **Selection Test** by taking the **Self-test** online.

PHLit Online! All assessment resources are available at **www.PHLitOnline.com**.

649

• A Wagner Matinée
Lesson Pacing Guide

DAY 1 Preteach

- Ⓒ Administer the Reading and Vocabulary Warm-ups (*Unit 3 Resources*, pp. 232–235) as necessary.
- Ⓒ Introduce the Literary Analysis concepts: Characterization and First–Person Point of View.
- • Introduce the Reading Strategy: Ask Questions to Clarify Meaning.
- Ⓒ Build background with the author and Background features.
- • Develop thematic thinking with Connecting to the Essential Question.
- Ⓒ Teach the selection vocabulary.

DAYS 2–3 Preteach/Teach/Extend

- • Distribute copies of the appropriate graphic organizer for the Reading Strategy (*Graphic Organizer Transparencies*, pp. 145–146).
- • Distribute copies of the appropriate graphic organizer for Literary Analysis (*Graphic Organizer Transparencies*, pp. 147–148).
- • Prepare students to read with the Activating Prior Knowledge activities (TE).
- • Informally monitor comprehension while students read.
- • Use the Reading Check question to confirm comprehension.
- Ⓒ Develop students' understanding of characterization and first–person point of view using the Literary Analysis prompts.
- • Develop students' ability to ask questions to clarify meaning using the Reading Strategy prompts.
- Ⓒ Reinforce vocabulary with the Vocabulary notes.
- • Assess students' comprehension and mastery of the skills by having them answer the Critical Reading, Literary Analysis, and Reading Strategy questions.
- Ⓒ Have students complete the Vocabulary Lesson.

DAY 4 Extend/Assess

- Ⓒ Have students complete the Writing Lesson and write an editorial. (You may assign as homework.)
- • Administer Selection Test A or B (*Unit 3 Resources*, pp. 244–246 or 247–249).

Ⓒ Common Core State Standards

Reading Literature 3. Analyze the impact of the author's choices regarding how to develop and relate elements of a story or drama.

Writing 1. Write arguments to support claims in an analysis of substantive topics or texts, using valid reasoning and relevant and sufficient evidence.
5. Develop and strengthen writing as needed by revising, focusing on addressing what is most significant for a specific purpose and audience.

Language 4. Determine or clarify the meaning of unknown and multiple-meaning words and phrases based on grades 11–12 reading and content, choosing flexibly from a range of strategies.

Additional Standards Practice
Common Core Companion, *pp. 15–22; 185–195; 226–227; 324–331*

Daily Block Scheduling
Each day in this Lesson Pacing Guide represents a 40–50 minute period. Teachers using block scheduling may combine days to revise pacing. In addition, teachers may differentiate and support core instruction by integrating components for extended and intensive support as students require. See the Guide to Selected Leveled Resources (facing page).

Guide to Selected Leveled Resources

A Wagner Matinée

Warm Up	**Practice, model,** and **monitor** fluency, working with the whole class or in groups.	Vocabulary and Reading Warm-ups B, *Unit 3 Resources,* pp. 232–233, 235
Comprehension/Skills	**Support** and **monitor** comprehension and skills development, having students complete the activities, graphic organizers, and interactive prompts **independently** or **as a class.**	• *Reader's Notebook,* adapted instruction and summary **EL** *Reader's Notebook: English Learner's Version,* adapted instruction and summary • **Reading Strategy Graphic Organizer B,** *Graphic Organizer Transparencies,* p. 146 • **Literary Analysis Graphic Organizer B,** *Graphic Organizer Transparencies,* p. 148
Monitor Progress [A]	**Monitor** student progress with the differentiated curriculum-based assessment in the *Unit Resources.*	• **Selection Test B,** *Unit 3 Resources,* pp. 247–249 • **Open-Book Test,** *Unit 3 Resources,* pp. 241–243
Assess/ Screen [A]	**Assess** student progress using Benchmark Test 5.	• **Benchmark Test 5,** *Unit 3 Resources,* pp. 255–260

A Wagner Matinée

Warm Up	**Practice, model,** and **monitor** fluency **in groups** or **with individuals.**	• **Vocabulary and Reading Warm-ups A,** *Unit 3 Resources,* pp. 232–234 • *Hear It!* Audio CD
Comprehension/Skills	• **Support** and **monitor** comprehension and skills development, working **in small groups** or **with individuals.** • As students complete the selection in the appropriate version of the *Reader's Notebook,* **monitor** comprehension frequently with group questions and individual instruction. • **Model** strategies while guiding students in completing the activities and prompts in the *Reader's Notebook,* as well as the graphic organizers. • **Practice** skills and **monitor** mastery with the *Reading Kit* worksheets.	• *Reader's Notebook: Adapted Version,* adapted instruction and summary **EL** *Reader's Notebook: English Learner's Version,* adapted instruction and summary • **Reading Strategy Graphic Organizer A,** *Graphic Organizer Transparencies,* p. 5 • **Literary Analysis Graphic Organizer A,** *Graphic Organizer Transparencies,* p. 7 • *Reading Kit,* Practice worksheets
Monitor Progress [A]	**Monitor** student progress with the differentiated curriculum-based assessment in the *Unit Resources* and in the *Reading Kit.*	• **Selection Test A,** *Unit 3 Resources,* pp. 244–246 • *Reading Kit,* Assess worksheets
Assess/ Screen [A]	**Assess** student progress using the Benchmark Test 1.	**Benchmark Test 5,** *Unit 3 Resources,* pp. 255–260

TIER 3 Tier 3 intervention may require consultation with the student's special-education or dyslexia specialist. For additional support, see the Tier 2 activities and resources listed above.

One-on-one teaching   Group work   Whole-class instruction   Independent work   [A] Assessment

For a complete guide to selection support, including support for Advanced students, see the Overview of Resources in the frontmatter.

• A Wagner Matinée

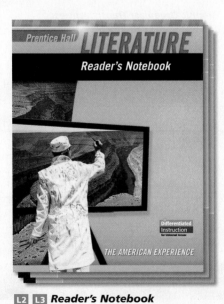

RESOURCES FOR:

L1 Special-Needs Students

L2 Below-Level Students (Tier 2)

L3 On-Level Students (Tier 1)

L4 Advanced Students (Tier 1)

EL English Learners

All All Students

Vocabulary/Fluency/Prior Knowledge

All Vocabulary Builder p. 238

Also available for these selections:

EL L1 L2 Vocabulary Warm-ups A and B, pp. 232–233

EL L1 L2 Reading Warm-ups A and B, pp. 234–235

Reader's Notebooks

Pre- and postreading pages for this selection appear in an interactive format in the *Reader's Notebooks*. Each *Notebook* is differentiated for a different group of learners.

The selections in the Adapted and English Learner's versions are abridged.

L2 L3 *Reader's Notebook*

L1 *Reader's Notebook: Adapted Version*

EL *Reader's Notebook: English Learner's Version*

EL *Reader's Notebook: Spanish Version*

© *Common Core Companion*

Additional instruction and practice for each Common Core State Standard

Selection Support

EL L1 L2 Reading: Graphic Organizer A, (partially filled in), p. 145

Also available for these selections:

EL L3 Reading: Graphic Organizer B, p. 146

EL L1 L2 Literary Analysis: Graphic Organizer A, (partially filled in), p. 147

EL All Literary Analysis: Graphic Organizer B, p. 148

Skills Development/Extension

L4 Enrichment, p. 240

Also available for these selections:

All Literary Analysis: Characterization, p. 236

All Reading: Clarify, p. 237

EL L3 L4 Support for Writing, p. 239

Assessment

L3 L4 Open-Book Test, pp. 241–243

Also available for these selections:

EL L1 L2 Selection Test A, pp. 244–246

EL L3 L4 Selection Test B, pp. 247–249

PHLit Online!
www.PHLitOnline.com

Online Resources: All print materials are also available online.

- complete narrated selection text
- a thematically related video with writing prompt
- an interactive graphic organizer
- highlighting feature
- access to all student print resources, adapted to individual student needs
- Spanish and English summaries
- adapted selection translations in Spanish

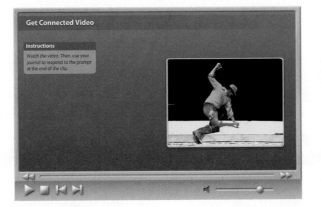

Get Connected! (thematic video with writing prompt)

Also available:

Background Video
All videos are available in Spanish.

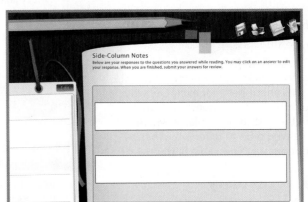

Writer's Journal (with graphics feature)

Also available:

Vocabulary Central (tools and activities for studying vocabulary)

❶ Connecting to the Essential Question

1. Review the assignment with the class.

2. Ask students whether they have ever moved and how the move affected their way of life. Then have them complete the assignment.

3. As students read, have them notice how setting affects both Georgiana and Clark.

❷ Literary Analysis

Introduce the skills, using the instruction on the student page.

Think Aloud: Model the Skill

Say to students:

When I analyze a character, I must question what the narrator says. Is the narrator sympathetic or hostile to the character? With a first-person narrator, I have to ask myself how well the narrator knows the character. Do important things happen that the narrator doesn't seem to understand?

❸ Reading Strategy

1. Introduce the strategy, using the instruction on the student page.

2. Give students a copy of **Reading Strategy Graphic Organizer B,** page 146 in *Graphic Organizer Transparencies,* to fill out as they read.

Think Aloud: Model the Skill

Say to students:

The story we're going to read concerns a pioneer. I have lots of questions about her—for example, why did she leave her home and family in the East to go to places where life would be so different? What options were available farther west?

❹ Vocabulary

1. Pronounce each word, giving its definition, and have students say it aloud.

2. For more guidance, see the *Classroom Strategies and Teaching Routines* card for introducing vocabulary.

650

Before You Read | *A Wagner Matinée*

❶ **Connecting to the Essential Question** In this story, a woman's move to a distant state changes her life and character. As you read, notice how setting affects both Aunt Georgiana and Clark. Doing so will help as you reflect on the Essential Question: **What is the relationship between literature and place?**

❷ **Literary Analysis**

Characterization is the art of revealing characters' personalities. In **direct characterization,** a writer simply states what a character is like, as in this sentence: "She was a pious woman." In **indirect characterization,** the writer uses the following methods to provide clues about the character:

- descriptions of the character's appearance, manner, and behavior
- the character's own words, inner thoughts, and actions
- comments about the character made by other characters
- the ways in which other characters react to the character

The point of view in which a story is told also affects how readers learn about characters. For example, this story uses **first-person point of view**—the narrator is part of the action and uses the pronouns *I, me,* and *we.* As a result, readers' impressions filter through the narrator's eyes. As you read, notice what characters are like and identify the clues that help you understand them.

❸ **Reading Strategy**

© **Preparing to Read Complex Texts** To fully understand a story, **ask questions to clarify meaning.** You might ask the following types of questions: What problems or obstacles do characters face? What motivates characters to think, feel, or act as they do? How do characters respond to cultural or historical influences? Then, to find answers, *reread* or *refer to footnotes and sidebars.* Use a chart like the one shown to ask questions and clarify details as you read this story.

❹ **Vocabulary**

reverential (rev′ ə ren′ shəl) *adj.* showing deep respect and love (p. 655)

tremulously (trem′ yoo ləs lē) *adv.* fearfully; timidly (p. 655)

inert (in urt′) *adj.* motionless (p. 656)

prelude (prel′ yood′) *n.* introductory section or movement of a musical work (p. 659)

jocularity (jäk′ yoo lar′ ə tē) *n.* joking good humor (p. 660)

650 Division, Reconciliation, and Expansion (1850–1914)

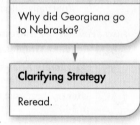

Common Core State Standards

Reading Literature
3. Analyze the impact of the author's choices regarding how to develop and relate elements of a story or drama.

Question
Why did Georgiana go to Nebraska?

↓

Clarifying Strategy
Reread.

www.PHLitOnline.com

Vocabulary Development

Vocabulary Knowledge Rating

Create a **Vocabulary Knowledge Rating Chart** (*Professional Development Guidebook,* p. 33) for the vocabulary words on the student page. Give each student a copy of the chart with the words on it. Read the words aloud, and have students mark their rating in the Before Reading column. Urge students to attend to these words as they read and discuss the selection.

In order to gauge how much instruction you need to provide, tally how many students are confident in their knowledge of each word. As students read, point out the words and their context.

 **Vocabulary Central,** featuring tools and activities for studying vocabulary, is available online at www.PHLitOnline.com.

⑤ Willa Cather (1873–1947)

Author of "A Wagner Matinée"

Although Willa Cather lived more than half her life in New York City, she turned again and again to the Nebraska prairie of her youth—at the time, a recently settled area of the American frontier—for inspiration and material for her writing. Cather captured with unflinching honesty the difficulties of life on the expanding frontier.

A Prairie Childhood Born in a small town in western Virginia, Cather moved to the Nebraska frontier when she was nine. Many of her new neighbors were immigrants struggling to build new lives while preserving their native cultures. Commenting on the diversity that surrounded her during her childhood, Cather once wrote, "On Sundays we could drive to a Norwegian church and listen to a sermon in that language, or to a Danish or Swedish church. We could go to a French Catholic settlement or into a Bohemian township and hear one in Czech, or we could go to the church with the German Lutherans."

Cather received a rich formal education, studying foreign languages, history, classical music, and opera. In 1891, she left home to study at the University of Nebraska, becoming one of the first women to receive a college education.

"Most of the basic material a writer works with is acquired before the age of fifteen."

The Making of a Literary Giant After her graduation in 1895, Cather worked as an editor at a Pittsburgh newspaper while writing poems and short stories in her spare time. Her first collection of stories, *The Troll Garden,* was published in 1905. In 1906, she moved to New York and joined the editorial staff of *McClure's Magazine.* After her first novel, *Alexander's Bridge,* was published in 1912, Cather devoted herself to writing full-time. She remained in New York for the rest of her life, but her memories of the prairie inspired her greatest work.

Over the next 35 years, Cather produced ten novels, two short-story collections, and two collections of essays. Among her outstanding works are *O Pioneers!* (1913), *My Ántonia* (1918), and *One of Ours* (1922), all of which capture the flavor of life on the Midwestern prairie. *One of Ours* won the Pulitzer Prize in 1923. Cather then shifted her attention from the Midwest to New Mexico in *Death Comes for the Archbishop* (1927) and to seventeenth-century Canada in *Shadows on the Rock* (1931).

A Wagner Matinée **651**

⟳ Daily Bellringer

For each class during which you will teach this selection, have students complete one of the five activities for the appropriate week in the *Daily Bellringer Activities* booklet.

● Multidraft Reading

To assist struggling readers and to enhance reading for all, assign the text in chunks as warranted by length and apply multidraft reading protocols. For each reading, have students set the purpose indicated:

- **First reading**—identifying key ideas and details and answering any Reading Checks.
- **Second reading**—analyzing craft and structure and responding to the side-column prompts.
- **Third reading**—integrating knowledge and ideas, connecting to other texts and the world, and answering the end-of-selection questions.

For more guidance, refer to the *Classroom Strategies and Teaching Routines* card on multidraft reading.

⑤ Background
More About the Author

In 1944, Willa Cather received the Gold Medal of the National Institute of the American Academy of Arts and Letters in recognition of the entire body of her work. Cather wrote fiction with a contemporary setting as well as stories and novels that explored the traditional values of the pioneer era. Although she continued to live in New York City after leaving *McClure's Magazine,* Cather visited her hometown of Red Cloud, Nebraska, twice a year and maintained close ties with her family.

PHLit Online!
www.PHLitOnline.com

Teaching From Technology

Preparing to Read
Go to **www.PHLitOnline.com** in class or in a lab and display the **Get Connected!** slide show for this selection. Have the class brainstorm for responses to the slide show writing prompt, entering ideas in the interactive journal. Then have students complete their written responses individually in a lab or as homework.

To build background, display the Background and More About the Author features.

Using the Interactive Student Edition
Go to **www.PHLitOnline.com** and display the **Enriched Online Student Edition.** As the class reads the selection or listens to the narration, record answers to side-column prompts using the graphic organizers accessible on the interactive page. Alternatively, have students use the online edition individually, answering the prompts as they read.

❶ Humanities

From Arkansas, 1939, by George Schreiber

Belgian-born George Schreiber came to the United States in the 1920s. Like many artists during the Great Depression, Schreiber turned his focus to farmlands. This painting records the spirit of rural America during trying times. He portrays the woman with stark realism: Her face, ragged apron, and stance reflect the hardships she has endured and the strength with which she has met them. Use this question for discussion:
What can you infer about the woman from the way she holds her arms?
Possible response: She is closed in on herself, not reaching out.

❷ About the Selection

The story explores the contrast between cultured city life and the rugged life of nineteenth-century settlers. The narrator's aunt Georgiana returns to Boston for a visit years after moving to Nebraska with her husband. A former music teacher, Georgiana has been outwardly toughened by frontier life. Yet when her nephew takes her to the opera, she cries with joy at the music and with grief at the culture she has forfeited to be with her husband. Through his aunt's pain, the narrator learns that the soul never really dies but "withers to the outward eye only."

❸ Activating Prior Knowledge

Before class, write "Wagner Matinée" on the chalkboard and the composer's name and dates of his birth and death (Richard Wagner, 1813–1883). Prepare a "program" of the pieces mentioned in the story: *Tannhäuser, Tristan and Isolde, The Flying Dutchman, The Ring of the Nibelung,* and *Siegfried.* As students enter the room, invite them to a concert. Play excerpts from the selections, and ask students to respond to the emotion of the music.

Concept Connector ➤

Tell students they will return to their responses after reading the selection.

652 Division, Reconciliation, and Expansion (1850–1914)

ⓒ Text Complexity Rubric

A Wagner Matinée	
Qualitative Measures	
Context/ Knowledge Demands	Isolation of prairie life; life experience demands 1 2 ③ 4 5
Structure/Language Conventionality and Clarity	Formal diction; challenging vocabulary 1 2 3 ④ 5
Levels of Meaning/ Purpose/Concept Level	Challenging (the soul) 1 2 3 ④ 5
Quantitative Measures	
Lexile/Text Length	1410L / 3,268 words
Overall Complexity	**More complex**

A Wagner Matinée

Willa Cather

BACKGROUND When "A Wagner Matinée" first appeared in 1904, Cather's readers would have been as familiar with Richard Wagner (väg nər) as people are today with the Beatles. Wagner, who was German, was one of the nineteenth century's great composers. His operas are characterized by adventurous harmonic language and an innovative intermarriage of music and drama. To many, Wagner represents the idea of high culture. In this story, Cather contrasts the stark realities of frontier life with life in a more cultured world.

I received one morning a letter written in pale ink, on glassy, blue-lined notepaper, and bearing the postmark of a little Nebraska village. This communication, worn and rubbed, looking as though it had been carried for some days in a coat pocket that was none too clean, was from my Uncle Howard. It informed me that his wife had been left a small legacy by a bachelor relative who had recently died, and that it had become necessary for her to come to Boston to attend to the settling of the estate. He requested me to meet her at the station, and render her whatever services might prove necessary. On examining the date indicated as that of her arrival, I found it no later than tomorrow. He had characteristically delayed writing until, had I been away from home for a day, I must have missed the good woman altogether.

The name of my Aunt Georgiana called up not alone her own figure, at once pathetic and grotesque, but opened before my feet a gulf

◄ **Critical Viewing**
What sort of life do you think the woman depicted in this painting has lived? Explain **[Interpret]**

✓ **Reading Check**
Why is Aunt Georgiana going to Boston?

◄ ***From Arkansas,*** 1939, George Schreiber, Sheldon Swope Art Museum, Terre Haute, Indiana

A Wagner Matinée **653**

---

④ **Critical Viewing**
Possible response: Students may say that the woman seems weary and worn from a life of suffering and hard work.

⑤ **Reading Check**
Answer: She needs to be present for the settling of the estate of a recently deceased relative.

ⓒ Text Complexity: Reader and Task Suggestions

A Wagner Matinée

Preparing to Read the Text
- Using the Background information on TE p. 651, discuss Cather's familiarity with prairie life and city life.
- Ask students to describe a culture clash—for example, relating to an aged relative or meeting a family from another part of the world.
- Guide students to use Multidraft Reading strategies (TE p. 651).

Leveled Tasks

Levels of Meaning If students will have difficulty distinguishing Cather's goal, have them keep lists of "Nebraska" and "Boston" details during a first read of the story. After students reread, have them summarize the clash of the prairie and city cultures.

Synthesizing If students will not have difficulty distinguishing Cather's goal, ask them to suggest ideas for a similar "culture clash" story, set in modern-day America.

This selection is available in an interactive format in the **Enriched Online Student Edition,** at **www.PHLitOnline.com,** which includes a thematically related video with writing prompt and an interactive graphic organizer.

Characterization

1. Remind students that a character's personality is revealed by means of description; by the characters' words, thoughts, and actions; and by the reactions of other characters.

2. Read aloud the bracketed passage. Ask students to listen for details about Georgiana's early life in Boston and about her subsequent life in Nebraska.

3. Then **ask** students the Literary Analysis question.
   Answer: They reveal that she was once a refined and cultured woman who, for the sake of love, exchanged a life in Boston for a life that transformed her into a figure "at once pathetic and grotesque."

❼ Engaging the Essential Question

1. Talk about the way Cather uses setting to develop both characters and Georgiana's conflict. The passage describes not only what life in Nebraska was like and the physical effects it had on Georgiana but also Clark's reactions.

2. **Ask:** How does Clark describe Georgiana's living conditions in Nebraska? How does he react to her appearance?
   Answer: He describes her living conditions as "primitive savagery." His reaction is one of "awe and respect" at her ravaged looks.

3. **Ask:** How might Georgiana's conflict be different had she and her husband stayed in Boston?
   Possible response: Had Georgiana and her husband stayed in the East, they would have had different problems. They might still have struggled financially since he was "idle and shiftless," but she might have continued teaching music. Possibly, her biggest problem would have been facing the anger and disapproval of family and friends instead of having a life of hardship and losing her health.

---

of recollections so wide and deep that, as the letter dropped from my hand, I felt suddenly a stranger to all the present conditions of my existence, wholly ill at ease and out of place amid the surroundings of my study. I became, in short, the gangling farmer boy my aunt had known, scourged with chilblains and bashfulness, my hands cracked and raw from the corn husking. I felt the knuckles of my thumb tentatively, as though they were raw again. I sat again before her parlor organ, thumbing the scales with my stiff, red hands, while she beside me made canvas mittens for the huskers.

The next morning, after preparing my landlady somewhat, I set out for the station. When the train arrived I had some difficulty in finding my aunt. She was the last of the passengers to alight, and when I got her into the carriage she looked not unlike one of those charred, smoked bodies that firemen lift from the *débris* of a burned building. She had come all the way in a day coach; her linen duster[1] had become black with soot and her black bonnet gray with dust during the journey. When we arrived at my boardinghouse the landlady put her to bed at once, and I did not see her again until the next morning.

Whatever shock Mrs. Springer experienced at my aunt's appearance she considerately concealed. Myself, I saw my aunt's misshapen figure with that feeling of awe and respect with which we behold explorers who have left their ears and fingers north of Franz Josef Land,[2] or their health somewhere along the upper Congo.[3] My Aunt Georgiana had been a music teacher at the Boston Conservatory, somewhere back in the latter sixties. One summer, which she had spent in the little village in the Green Mountains[4] where her ancestors had dwelt for generations, she had kindled the callow[5] fancy of the most idle and shiftless of all the village lads, and had conceived for this Howard Carpenter one of those absurd and extravagant passions which a handsome country boy of twenty-one sometimes inspires in a plain, angular, spectacled woman of thirty. When she returned to her duties in Boston, Howard followed her; and the upshot of this inexplicable infatuation was that she eloped with him, eluding the reproaches of her family and the criticism of her friends by going with him to the Nebraska frontier. Carpenter, who of course had no money, took a homestead in Red Willow County,[6] fifty miles from the railroad. There they measured off their eighty acres by driving across the prairie in a wagon, to the wheel of which they had tied a red cotton handkerchief, and counting its revolutions. They built a dugout in the red hillside, one of those cave dwellings whose

❻
❼

Literary Analysis
Characterization What do the contrasting details of Aunt Georgiana's life in Boston and Nebraska reveal about her character?

---

1. **duster** *n.* short, loose smock worn while traveling to protect clothing from dust.
2. **Franz Josef Land** group of islands in the Arctic Ocean.
3. **Congo** river in central Africa.
4. **Green Mountains** mountains in Vermont.
5. **callow** (kal´ ō) *adj.* immature; inexperienced.
6. **Red Willow County** county in southwestern Nebraska that borders on Kansas.

654 Division, Reconciliation, and Expansion (1850–1914)

Think Aloud

Vocabulary: Using Context

Direct students' attention to the word "physiognomy" on page 655. Use the following "think aloud" to model using context to infer the meaning of the word. Say to students:

I do not know the meaning of the word "physiognomy," but this entire paragraph describes Georgiana's appearance, so the word must have something to do with that. The sentence says that the most noticeable thing about Georgiana's "physiognomy" is her twitching mouth and eyebrows, and the previous sentence is about her false teeth. So Clark is describing her face. I think "physiognomy" means facial appearance.

7 inmates usually reverted to the conditions of primitive savagery. Their water they got from the lagoons where the buffalo drank, and their slender stock of provisions was always at the mercy of bands of roving Indians. For thirty years my aunt had not been farther than fifty miles from the homestead.

8 But Mrs. Springer knew nothing of all this, and must have been considerably shocked at what was left of my kinswoman. Beneath the soiled linen duster, which on her arrival was the most conspicuous feature of her costume, she wore a black stuff dress whose ornamentation showed that she had surrendered herself unquestioningly into the hands of a country dressmaker. My poor aunt's figure, however, would have presented astonishing difficulties to any dressmaker. Her skin was yellow from constant exposure to a pitiless wind, and to the alkaline water which transforms the most transparent cuticle into a sort of flexible leather. She wore ill-fitting false teeth. The most striking thing about her physiognomy, however, was an incessant twitching of the mouth and eyebrows, a form of nervous disorder resulting from isolation and monotony, and from frequent physical suffering.

In my boyhood this affliction had possessed a sort of horrible fascination for me, of which I was secretly very much ashamed, for in those days I owed to this woman most of the good that ever came my way, and had a *reverential* affection for her. During the three winters when I was riding herd for my uncle, my aunt, after cooking three meals for half a dozen farmhands, and putting the six children to bed, would often stand until midnight at her ironing board, hearing me at the kitchen table beside her recite Latin declensions and conjugations, and gently shaking me when my drowsy head sank down over a page of irregular verbs. It was to her, at her ironing or mending, that I read my first Shakespeare; and her old textbook of mythology was the first that ever came into my empty hands. She taught me my scales and exercises, too, on the little parlor organ which her husband had bought her after fifteen years, during which she had not so much as seen any instrument except an accordion, that belonged to one of the Norwegian farmhands. She would sit beside me by the hour, darning and counting, while I struggled with the "Harmonious Blacksmith"; but she seldom talked to me about music, and I understood why. She was a pious woman; she had the consolation of religion; and to her at least her martyrdom was not wholly sordid. Once when I had been doggedly beating out some passages from an old score of "Euryanthe" I had found among her music books, she came up to me and, putting her hands over my eyes, gently drew my head back upon her shoulder, **9** saying *tremulously*, "Don't love it so well, Clark, or it may be taken from you. Oh! dear boy, pray that whatever your sacrifice be it is not that."

Literary Analysis
Characterization In this paragraph, which details are examples of indirect characterization?

Vocabulary
reverential (rev´ ə ren´ shəl) *adj.* showing deep respect and love

Vocabulary
tremulously (trem´ yoo ləs lē) *adv.* fearfully; timidly

10  Reading Check
When Clark was a boy, what subjects did he learn from his aunt?

A Wagner Matinée **655**

---

8 Literary Analysis
Characterization

1. Remind students that in direct characterization, the narrator states what the character is like.

2. Have a volunteer read aloud the bracketed passage. Encourage students to think about the types of details given.

3. Then **ask** students the Literary Analysis question.
   Answer: The entire paragraph is indirect—a description of her appearance and the reasons for it, including her clothes, her skin, her nervous twitch.

9 Critical Thinking
Compare and Contrast

1. Direct students to the bracketed passage. Explain that in *Euryanthe,* the opera by Carl Maria von Weber (1786–1826), Euryanthe is falsely accused and then led by the man she loves into the desert to die. Elicit from students an understanding of how Euryanthe's story echoes the theme of martyrdom in the wilderness to which Cather alludes in this passage.

2. Invite students to discuss Georgiana's martyrdom and its relation to the strong feelings she has for music.

3. **Ask** students how these things influence her warning to Clark.
   Possible response: Students may say that Georgiana is a martyr because she left something she loved deeply in order to be with her husband. Recognizing the pain of her decision, she advises Clark to moderate his love for music, lest he lose it and feel pain, as she did.

10 Reading Check

Answer: He learned Latin, Shakespeare, mythology, and music.

655

⓫ Literature in Context

Music Connection

Wagner's tragic opera *Tristan and Isolde* (the prelude of which Clark and his aunt hear later in the story) tells of a tragic ending brought on by love. Isolde has been promised to the king, and Tristan must deliver her. As Tristan and Isolde declare their love for each other, a knight surprises them in the king's garden. Tristan is mortally wounded, and Isolde breathes her last breath over his body.

Connect to the Literature

Encourage students to think about a time when they had to give up something that they loved. Then **ask** the Connect to the Literature question. **Possible response:** Georgiana's response is not the result of a specific melody or lyric; her response comes from an awakening in her of something she had lost.

⓬ Vocabulary Builder

1. Read aloud the bracketed passage, and draw attention to the word "Conservatory."

2. Have students look up the origins of the word *conservatory* as a strategy for understanding its meaning. Ask them to trace the changes in the word's usage.

3. Invite some students to explain to the class how the origins of *conservatory* relate to its use in the story.

   Answer: The word derives from the Latin word *servare* ("to keep, preserve"), which comes from the Indo-European stem *ser* ("to watch over"). A *conservatory* is a school devoted to the preservation and teaching of an art form such as music as well as to the nurture of developing artists.

Music Connection

Wagnerian Opera

Aunt Georgiana has a strong reaction to the music of Richard Wagner, the composer of *The Flying Dutchman* (1843). Wagner rejected some of the traditions of opera. He usually avoided lengthy musical speeches and instead originated the *leitmotif*, a recurring musical theme used to symbolize an emotion or event. Wagner also wrote what he called "music dramas." An entire series of these works, called *The Ring of the Nibelung*, consumed twenty-six years of his life. In "A Wagner Matinée," the audience hears excerpts from *The Ring* and *Siegfried*, an opera based on the adventures of a legendary German hero.

Connect to the Literature

Does the reader need to be familiar with Wagner's operas to understand Aunt Georgiana's response? Explain.

Vocabulary
inert (in urt´) *adj.* motionless

When my aunt appeared on the morning after her arrival, she was still in a semi-somnambulant[7] state. She seemed not to realize that she was in the city where she had spent her youth, the place longed for hungrily for half a lifetime. She had been so wretchedly trainsick throughout the journey that she had no recollection of anything but her discomfort, and, to all intents and purposes, there were but a few hours of nightmare between the farm in Red Willow County and my study on Newbury Street. I had planned a little pleasure for her that afternoon, to repay her for some of the glorious moments she had given me when we used to milk together in the straw-thatched cowshed, and she, because I was more than usually tired, or because her husband had spoken sharply to me, would tell me of the splendid performance of Meyerbeer's *Les Huguenots*[8] she had seen in Paris in her youth. At two o'clock the Boston Symphony Orchestra was to give a Wagner program, and I intended to take my aunt, though as I conversed with her I grew doubtful about her enjoyment of it. Indeed, for her own sake, I could only wish her taste for such things quite dead, and the long struggle mercifully ended at last. I suggested our visiting the Conservatory and the Common[9] before lunch, but she seemed altogether too timid to wish to venture out. She questioned me absently about various changes in the city, but she was chiefly concerned that she had forgotten to leave instructions about feeding half-skimmed milk to a certain weakling calf, "Old Maggie's calf, you know, Clark," she explained, evidently having forgotten how long I had been away. She was further troubled because she had neglected to tell her daughter about the freshly opened kit of mackerel in the cellar, that would spoil if it were not used directly.

I asked her whether she had ever heard any of the Wagnerian operas, and found that she had not, though she was perfectly familiar with their respective situations and had once possessed the piano score of *The Flying Dutchman*. I began to think it would have been best to get her back to Red Willow County without waking her, and regretted having suggested the concert.

From the time we entered the concert hall, however, she was a trifle less passive and inert, and seemed to begin to perceive her

---

7. **semi-somnambulant** (se mi säm´ nam byə lənt) *adj.* resembling a sleepwalker.
8. **Les Huguenots** (lāz hyo͞o´ gə nät´) opera written in 1836 by Giacomo Meyerbeer (1791–1864).
9. **Common** Boston Common, a small park in Boston.

Enrichment: Analyzing Music

Wagnerian Operas versus Others

Although Georgiana had never heard Wagner performed, she had in the past listened to great operas by Verdi, whose *Trovatore* Clark mentions on page 660, and Mozart. Mozart's operas are known for their varied characters, wit, and engaging stories. His music expresses deep emotions and gives the voice greater importance than the orchestra.

Activity: Venn Diagram Give students synopses of Wagner's *Die Meistersinger* and Mozart's *Così Fan Tutte*. Play recordings of two love songs: the former's "Prize Song" (mentioned on p. 660) and the latter's "Per pietà, ben mio, perdona." Ask students to listen for stylistic differences and record their impressions in the **Enrichment: Analyzing Music** worksheet, in *Professional Development Guidebook,* page 236. Have students make a Venn diagram comparing and contrasting the two songs.

surroundings. I had felt some trepidation[10] lest one might become aware of the absurdities of her attire, or might experience some painful embarrassment at stepping suddenly into the world to which she had been dead for a quarter of a century. But again I found how superficially I had judged her. She sat looking about her with eyes as impersonal, almost as stony, as those with which the granite Ramses[11] in a museum watches the froth and fret that ebbs and flows about his pedestal, separated from it by the lonely stretch of centuries. I have seen this same aloofness in old miners who drift into the Brown Hotel at Denver, their pockets full of bullion, their linen soiled, their haggard faces unshorn, and who stand in the thronged corridors as solitary as though they were still in a frozen camp on the Yukon, or in the yellow blaze of the Arizona desert, conscious that certain experiences have isolated them from their fellows by a gulf no haberdasher could conceal.

The audience was made up chiefly of women. One lost the contour of faces and figures, indeed any effect of line whatever, and there was only the color contrast of bodices past counting, the shimmer and shading of fabrics soft and firm, silky and sheer, resisting and yielding: red, mauve, pink, blue, lilac, purple, ecru, rose, yellow, cream, and white, all the colors that an impressionist finds in a sunlit landscape, with here and there the dead black shadow of a frock coat. My Aunt Georgiana regarded them as though they had been so many daubs of tube paint on a palette.

When the musicians came out and took their places, she gave a little stir of anticipation, and looked with quickening interest down over the rail at that invariable grouping; perhaps the first wholly familiar thing that had greeted her eye since she had left old Maggie and her weakling calf. I could feel how all those details sank into her soul, for I had not forgotten how they had sunk into mine when I came fresh from plowing forever and forever between green aisles of corn, where, as in a treadmill, one might walk from daybreak to dusk without perceiving a shadow of change in one's environment. I reminded myself of the impression made on me by the clean profiles of the musicians, the gloss of their linen; the dull black of their coats, the beloved shapes of the instruments, the patches of yellow light thrown by the green-shaded stand-lamps on the smooth, varnished bellies of the cellos and the bass viols in the rear, the restless, wind-tossed forest of fiddle necks and bows; I recalled how, in the first orchestra I had ever heard, those long bow strokes seemed to draw the soul out of me, as a conjuror's stick reels out paper ribbon from a hat.

The first number was the Tannhäuser overture. When the violins

---

10. **trepidation** (trep´ ə dā´ shən) *n.* fearful anxiety; apprehension.
11. **Ramses** (ram´ sēz) one of the eleven Egyptian kings by that name who ruled from c. 1292 to c. 1075 B.C.

Literary Analysis
Characterization What do Clark's descriptions of his own first reactions to a concert reveal about his character?

Reading Check
What is Clark's initial feeling about being in public with Aunt Georgiana? How does that attitude change?

⓭ Literary Analysis
Characterization

1. Encourage students to summarize how Georgiana has behaved up to this point in the story. Then read the bracketed passage.

2. **Ask:** What does Georgiana's excitement about the upcoming performance reveal about her? **Answer:** It reveals that her love for music is reawakening; her hard life has not numbed her soul completely.

3. **Ask** students the Literary Analysis question. **Answer:** Clark's descriptions show that he is sensitive and shares his aunt's love of music. They also show that he empathizes with Georgiana's situation.

⓮ Reading Check

Answer: At first he feels anxious and embarrassed about how out of place and ill at ease his aunt seems. When he sees that she is absorbing details of the musicians' appearances, however, his mind wanders to memories of his own first passionate responses to the sights and sounds of an orchestra in a concert hall.

Differentiated
Instruction for Universal Access

Culturally Responsive Instruction
Culture Focus The popularity of Giuseppe Verdi and other Italian composers leads some people to think that opera belongs to Italy. Explain that opera embraces many cultures. Tell them that Richard Wagner's operas brought German mythology to life. In the Czech Republic and Russia, Antonin Dvorák and Modest Mussorgsky built their cultures' folk music into their operas. English composer Gustav Holst's *Savitri* is based on the Hindu epic *Mahabharata,* and George Gershwin dramatized African American life in *Porgy and Bess.* Spain's Enrique Granados based *Goyescas* on the paintings of Francisco de Goya. Today, composers from countries such as Japan and Chile continue writing operas based on their heritage. Encourage students to describe the musical favorites of their families and to discuss why people everywhere respond to music.

15 Visual Connection

1. Explain to students that opera houses and symphony-orchestra concert halls have traditionally been among the most elegant of theaters. Discuss how opera and symphony performances require many highly skilled artists and elaborate sets that make them expensive to stage.

2. Read the passage on page 657 describing the women's dresses. Encourage students to explore why classical music audiences in eastern cities such as Boston tended to be affluent or educated.

3. **Ask:** How does the painting illustrate the comfortable and cultured life Georgiana had given up?

   Possible response: The gold walls and columns of the balconies and the bright lights suggest the elegant surroundings she might have enjoyed from time to time. The crowded hall suggests that she also gave up the company of others who shared her love of music.

658 Division, Reconciliation, and Expansion (1850–1914)

Think Aloud

Literary Analysis: Analyzing Metaphor

Cather's story makes generous use of metaphor, which is taught on page 403. To practice the process of analyzing a metaphor, use the following "think aloud." Say to students:

On page 659, Clark says that "Wagner had been a sealed book to Americans before the sixties." When something is *sealed,* it is locked, so people can't get into it. Wagner is a composer, not a book, so what was

sealed had to be his music—or at least live or recorded performances of his music. Since there were no recordings at the time, Clark probably means that no orchestras played Wagner's music in America before the 1860s. The sentence compares Wagner's music to a "sealed book," but it doesn't use the words *like* or *as.* The omission of one of those words means the comparison is a metaphor, not a simile.

drew out the first strain of the Pilgrims' chorus, my Aunt Georgiana clutched my coat sleeve. Then it was that I first realized that for her this singing of basses and stinging frenzy of lighter strings broke a silence of thirty years, the inconceivable silence of the plains. With the battle between the two motifs, with the bitter frenzy of the Venusberg[12] theme and its ripping of strings, came to me an overwhelming sense of the waste and wear we are so powerless to combat. I saw again the tall, naked house on the prairie, black and grim as a wooden fortress; the black pond where I had learned to swim, the rain-gullied clay about the naked house; the four dwarf ash seedlings on which the dishcloths were always hung to dry before the kitchen door. The world there is the flat world of the ancients; to the east, a cornfield that stretched to daybreak; to the west, a corral that stretched to sunset; between, the sordid conquests of peace, more merciless than those of war.

The overture closed. My aunt released my coat sleeve, but she said nothing. She sat staring at the orchestra through a dullness of thirty years, through the films made, little by little, by each of the three hundred and sixty-five days in every one of them. What, I wondered, did she get from it? She had been a good pianist in her day, I knew, and her musical education had been broader than that of most music teachers of a quarter of a century ago. She had often told me of Mozart's operas and Meyerbeer's, and I could remember hearing her sing, years ago, certain melodies of Verdi. When I had fallen ill with a fever she used to sit by my cot in the evening, while the cool night wind blew in through the faded mosquito netting tacked over the window, and I lay watching a bright star that burned red above the cornfield, and sing "Home to our mountains, oh, let us return!" in a way fit to break the heart of a Vermont boy near dead of homesickness already.

I watched her closely through the prelude to *Tristan and Isolde*, trying vainly to conjecture what that warfare of motifs, that seething turmoil of strings and winds, might mean to her. Had this music any message for her? Did or did not a new planet swim into her ken? Wagner had been a sealed book to Americans before the sixties. Had she anything left with which to comprehend this glory that had flashed around the world since she had gone from it? I was in a fever of curiosity, but Aunt Georgiana sat silent upon her peak in Darien.[13] She preserved this utter immobility throughout the numbers from the *Flying Dutchman*, though her fingers worked mechanically upon her black dress, as though of themselves they were recalling the piano score they had once played. Poor old hands! They

---

12. **Venusberg** (vē′ nəs bûrg′) legendary mountain in Germany where Venus, the Roman goddess of love, held court.
13. **peak in Darien** (der′ ē ən′) mountain on the Isthmus of Panama; from "On First Looking into Chapman's Homer" by English poet John Keats (1795–1821).

Reading Strategy
Asking Questions to Clarify Meaning What questions might you ask about Clark's description of the plains?

 ◄ Critical Viewing
In what ways does this painting mirror Clark's description of the audience at the opera house? **[Connect; Compare]**

Vocabulary
prelude (prel′ yōōd) *n.* introductory section or movement of a musical work

Reading Check
Describe Aunt Georgiana's musical education.

---

16 Reading Strategy
Asking Questions to Clarify Meaning

1. Remind students that they can ask themselves questions about the characters, their conflicts, the setting, and the writer's word choice to better understand a text.
2. Have a volunteer read aloud the bracketed passage.
3. Then **ask** students the Reading Strategy question.
   Possible responses: (a) What was the "inconceivable silence of the plains"? (The silence would be the lack of music and, by extension, of culture.) (b) Why does Clark compare the plains to "the flat world of the ancients"? (The Midwest is flat, with little variation in the landscape, and the rows of corn seem to stretch to the horizon. The image also suggests going back in time to a more primitive age.)
4. Have students use a copy of **Reading Strategy Graphic Organizer B**, page 146 in *Graphic Organizer Transparencies*, to answer the questions they generated.

17 Critical Viewing

Possible response: The painting matches Clark's description on page 657 of the audience: The "contour of faces and figures" is mostly indistinct. The women's dresses look like daubs of paint of different colors, and the men's black coats sometimes blend in with the shadows.

18 Reading Check

Answer: Aunt Georgiana had been a good pianist, with a broad musical education that included familiarity with operas by Mozart and Meyerbeer.

Differentiated Instruction for Universal Access

Support for Less Proficient Readers
Have students reread the paragraph beginning "The overture closed." Help them understand that when Willa Cather wrote this story the word *films* did not mean moving pictures. Explain that, in this context, films are thin layers of grime or thin membranes that grow over aging eyes, separating Georgiana from the sights of the concert hall and the world she once knew.

Enrichment for Advanced Readers
The passage continuing at the top of page 659 contains many musical terms—"strain," "chorus," "basses," and "motifs"—and descriptions of sounds—"singing" and "ripping." Invite students to use a music dictionary to explore the meaning of these and other terms used in the story, such as "crescendo," "development," and "counterpoint." Have students explain the terms to the class.

1. **Ask:** What strategy could you use to formulate and answer questions about Georgiana's reactions to the music?
   Possible response: Reread

2. Read aloud the bracketed passage.

3. Then **ask** students the Reading Strategy question.
   Possible responses: Why did the "Prize Song" remind Georgiana of the farm hand? (The farm hand used to sing the "Prize Song" at the farm. He was Georgiana's connection to beautiful music, which she tried to foster by getting him to join her church.) Why does the memory make her cry? (He disappeared suddenly with a serious injury, ending her connection to music and possibly putting his own life in jeopardy.)

---

were stretched and pulled and twisted into mere tentacles to hold, and lift, and knead with; the palms unduly swollen, the fingers bent and knotted, on one of them a thin worn band that had once been a wedding ring. As I pressed and gently quieted one of those groping hands, I remembered, with quivering eyelids, their services for me in other days.

Soon after the tenor began the "Prize Song," I heard a quick-drawn breath, and turned to my aunt. Her eyes were closed, but the tears were glistening on her cheeks, and I think in a moment more they were in my eyes as well. It never really dies, then, the soul? It withers to the outward eye only, like that strange moss which can lie on a dusty shelf half a century and yet, if placed in water, grows green again. My aunt wept gently throughout the development and elaboration of the melody.

Reading Strategy
Asking Questions to Clarify Meaning What questions might you ask about the episode of the farm hand to clarify your understanding of its meaning to Georgiana?

⑲

During the intermission before the second half of the concert, I questioned my aunt and found that the "Prize Song" was not new to her. Some years before there had drifted to the farm in Red Willow County a young German, a tramp cow puncher who had sung in the chorus at Bayreuth,[14] when he was a boy, along with the other peasant boys and girls. On a Sunday morning he used to sit on his blue gingham-sheeted bed in the hands' bedroom, which opened off the kitchen, cleaning the leather of his boots and saddle, and singing the "Prize Song," while my aunt went about her work in the kitchen. She had hovered about him until she had prevailed upon him to join the country church, though his sole fitness for this step, so far as I could gather, lay in his boyish face and his possession of this divine melody. Shortly afterward he had gone to town on the Fourth of July, lost his money at a faro[15] table, ridden a saddled Texas steer on a bet, and disappeared with a fractured collarbone.

Vocabulary
jocularity (jäk′ yoo lar′ ə tē) *n.* joking good humor

"Well, we have come to better things than the old *Trovatore* at any rate, Aunt Georgie?" I queried, with well-meant jocularity.

Her lip quivered and she hastily put her handkerchief up to her mouth. From behind it she murmured, "And you've been hearing this ever since you left me, Clark?" Her question was the gentlest and saddest of reproaches.

"But do you get it, Aunt Georgiana, the astonishing structure of it all?" I persisted.

"Who could?" she said, absently; "why should one?"

⑳

The second half of the program consisted of four numbers from the *Ring*. This was followed by the forest music from *Siegfried*[16] and the program closed with Siegfried's funeral march. My aunt wept quietly, but almost continuously. I was perplexed as to what

---

14. Bayreuth (bī roit′) city in Germany known for its annual Wagnerian music festivals.
15. faro (fer′ ō) gambling game in which players bet on the cards to be turned up from the top of the dealer's deck.
16. Siegfried (sēg′ frēd) opera based on the adventures of Siegfried, a legendary hero in medieval German literature.

Vocabulary Development

Vocabulary Knowledge Rating

When students have completed reading and discussing the selection, have them take out the **Vocabulary Knowledge Rating Charts** for the story. Read the words aloud, and have students rate their knowledge of the words again in the After Reading column. Clarify any words that are still problematic. Have students write their own definitions and example or sentence in the appropriate column. Then have students complete the Vocabulary Lesson at the end of the selection. Encourage students to use the words in further discussion and written work about the selection. Remind them that they will be accountable for these words on the **Selection Test**, *Unit 3 Resources*, pages 244–246 or 247–249.

measure of musical comprehension was left to her, to her who had heard nothing for so many years but the singing of gospel hymns in Methodist services at the square frame schoolhouse on Section Thirteen. I was unable to gauge how much of it had been dissolved in soapsuds, or worked into bread, or milked into the bottom of a pail.

The deluge of sound poured on and on; I never knew what she found in the shining current of it; I never knew how far it bore her, or past what happy islands, or under what skies. From the trembling of her face I could well believe that the *Siegfried* march, at least, carried her out where the myriad graves are, out into the gray, burying grounds of the sea; or into some world of death vaster yet, where, from the beginning of the world, hope has lain down with hope, and dream with dream and, renouncing, slept.

The concert was over; the people filed out of the hall chattering and laughing, glad to relax and find the living level again, but my kinswoman made no effort to rise. I spoke gently to her. She burst into tears and sobbed pleadingly, "I don't want to go, Clark, I don't want to go!"

I understood. For her, just outside the door of the concert hall, lay the black pond with the cattle-tracked bluffs, the tall, unpainted house, naked as a tower, with weather-curled boards; the crook-backed ash seedlings where the dishcloths hung to dry, the gaunt, moulting turkeys picking up refuse about the kitchen door.

"I don't want to go, Clark, I don't want to go!"

Critical Reading

> **Cite textual evidence to support your responses.**

1. **Key Ideas and Details (a)** What part did Boston play in Aunt Georgiana's earlier life? **(b) Compare and Contrast:** In what ways would you compare and contrast life in Boston and life in Red Willow County?

2. **Key Ideas and Details (a)** As a boy, what did the narrator practice on the "parlor organ" in the Nebraska farmhouse? **(b) Interpret:** What does Aunt Georgiana mean when she says, "Don't love it so well, Clark, or it may be taken from you"? **(c) Connect:** Do the events of the story reinforce her statement? Explain.

3. **Integration of Knowledge and Ideas Take a Position:** Would it have been better for Aunt Georgiana if she had not come to Boston? Explain.

4. **Integration of Knowledge and Ideas** What do you think Cather would say about the importance of artistic and cultural outlets to the health of a community? Do you agree or disagree? Explain. In your response, use at least two of these Essential Question words: *expression, freedom, individualism, self-reliance.* *[Connecting to the Essential Question: What is the relationship between literature and place?]*

A Wagner Matinée **661**

Concept Connector

Reading Strategy Graphic Organizer
Ask students to review the graphic organizers in which they have asked questions and clarified details. Then have students share their organizers and compare the questions they asked.

Activating Prior Knowledge
Have students return to their responses to the Activating Prior Knowledge activity. Ask them to explain whether their thoughts have changed and if so, how.

 Writing About the Essential Question
Have students compare the responses they gave to the prompt before they completed reading the story with their thoughts after reading it. Have them work individually or in groups, writing or discussing their thoughts, to formulate their new responses. Then lead a class discussion, probing for what students have learned that confirms or invalidates their initial thoughts. Encourage students to cite specific textual details to support their responses.

1. **Possible responses:** Clark calls his aunt "pathetic and grotesque" and says she had been "a good pianist in her day."

2. **Possible responses:** Physical description: roughened, aged, twitches nervously; Clark's statements: "with that feeling of awe and respect with which we behold explorers"; Her actions/words: "Don't love it so well, Clark, or it may be taken from you."
Another sample answer can be found on **Literary Graphic Organizer A,** page 147 in *Graphic Organizer Transparencies.*

3. He is grateful and affectionate but embarrassed by her appearance, showing his superficiality at first.

4. Because of all she did for Clark, we view Georgiana with respect and sympathy through his eyes.

5. (a) Students might mention her listening to him practice Latin or telling him not to love music too much. (b) We see that despite her hard life, Georgiana loves culture.

6. (a) At the beginning, he is embarrassed by her; by the end, he recognizes her sensitivity to music. (b) His feelings encourage us to see her first as a victim but later as a person of great feeling. (c) Clark's feelings make him sympathetic.

7. The gesture after fifteen years shows his lack of thought for her, given how much she had sacrificed for him.

8. (a) How did Georgiana spend her days? (b) She cooked "three meals a day for half a dozen farmhands" and ironed until midnight. (c) They show why Aunt Georgiana would have little time to pursue musical interests.

9. (a) What was the city like? (b) Clark's mention of the symphony orchestra and his asking her whether she understood the music point to a sophisticated Boston life.

10. Students should explain how this information clarified their understanding.

11. (a) What did Wagner's music actually sound like? (b) The footnotes and sidebars gave additional information. (c) Students should explain how this information clarified their understanding.

After You Read *A Wagner Matinée*

Literary Analysis

1. **Craft and Structure** Note two examples of **direct characterization** in this story.

2. **Craft and Structure** What do you learn about Aunt Georgiana's personality through **indirect characterization?** Use a chart like the one shown to record your observations.

3. **Craft and Structure** What do Clark's thoughts and feelings about his aunt indirectly reveal about his personality? Explain.

4. **Craft and Structure** What effect does Clark's **first-person point of view** have on your perception of Aunt Georgiana?

5. **Key Ideas and Details** (a) Find two examples of events Clark recalls from living with Aunt Georgiana. (b) How do these events shape your impressions of her?

6. **Key Ideas and Details** (a) How do Clark's feelings toward his aunt change during the story? (b) How do his feelings affect your response to her? (c) How do Clark's feelings about his aunt affect your attitude toward him as a character?

7. **Craft and Structure** Aunt Georgiana's husband bought her a "little parlor organ." Explain what this small detail suggests about his character.

Reading Strategy

8. (a) What **questions** might you ask about the difficulties of Aunt Georgiana's life in Nebraska? (b) *Reread* to find two details in the story that help you understand Nebraska life at that time in history. (c) In what ways do these details **clarify the meaning** of the story for you?

9. (a) What questions might you ask about Boston life at the time of the story? (b) Which story details provide answers to your questions?

10. How do the questions you asked and answered in items 8 and 9 above help clarify your understanding of Aunt Georgiana's experiences in Boston?

11. (a) As you read this story, what questions might you ask about the composer Richard Wagner? (b) How do *footnotes or sidebars* help to answer these questions? (c) In what ways did learning about Wagner deepen your understanding of the story?

Common Core State Standards

Writing
1. Write arguments to support claims in an analysis of substantive topics or texts, using valid reasoning and relevant and sufficient evidence. *(p. 663)*
5. Develop and strengthen writing as needed by revising, focusing on addressing what is most significant for a specific purpose and audience. *(p. 663)*

Language
4. Determine or clarify the meaning of unknown and multiple-meaning words and phrases based on *grades 11–12 reading and content,* choosing flexibly from a range of strategies. *(p. 663)*
6. Acquire and use accurately general academic and domain-specific words and phrases, sufficient for reading, writing, and speaking at the college and career readiness level. *(p. 663)*

Assessment Practice

Context (For more practice, see *All-in-One Workbook.*)

Many tests require students to use context clues to choose the appropriate definition of multiple-meaning words. Use the following sample test item:

> When the train arrived I had some difficulty in finding my aunt. She was the last of the passengers to alight, and when I got her into the carriage she looked not unlike one of those charred, smoked bodies that firemen lift from the débris of a burned building.

In this passage, the word "alight" means—
  A light a fire on the platform
  B descend from the train
  C turn on the light
  D enter her compartment

The narrator is waiting for his aunt and has trouble finding her because she is the last passenger to get off the train. *B* is the correct answer.

Integrated Language Skills

Ⓔ Vocabulary Acquisition and Use

Multiple-Meaning Words from Music

Musical vocabulary often has multiple meanings. For example, a *prelude* can be the introduction to a musical work or preparation for any important matter. For each numbered item below, select the correct definition of the italicized word.

chord: (a) two or more notes played or sung simultaneously, **(b)** an emotional response

concert: (a) a performance of several short compositions, **(b)** working together

harmony: (a) a pleasing combination of musical sounds, **(b)** a peaceful situation

overture: (a) an introductory movement to an extended musical work, **(b)** any first movement

1. We put a *concerted* effort into the game.
2. The chorus sang in glorious *harmony.*
3. He made an *overture* to pay for lunch.
4. The speech struck a *chord* in the audience.

Vocabulary: Word Meanings

Answer the following questions in complete sentences. Be sure to use the underlined words in your responses.

1. If students are <u>reverential</u> toward a teacher, do they ignore or respect her?
2. Who is most likely to speak <u>tremulously</u>—a musician, a truck driver, or a child?
3. What is an example of a substance that is usually—but not always—<u>inert?</u>
4. As a <u>prelude</u> to bad news, would you expect sarcasm or seriousness?
5. Is <u>jocularity</u> more likely to be the trademark of a talk-show host or a funeral director?

Writing

Ⓔ **Argument** "A Wagner Matinée" provoked an outcry among Nebraskans who felt Cather had portrayed the state unfairly. Cather responded that the story was a tribute to pioneer strength and endurance. As the editor of a Nebraska newspaper, take a position and write an **editorial** defending your view. Structure your argument in a persuasive way, supported by precise and relevant examples.

Prewriting Review the story. Analyze the details Cather uses to portray Nebraska and Boston. Decide whether you agree with her views. Jot down ideas, observations, and facts that support your opinion.

Drafting Arrange your ideas in order of importance. Include factual evidence and emotional appeals to support your statements.

Revising Reread your work to make sure your language is specific and persuasive and that you present a sustained, unified argument. Replace irrelevant statements, and add support as needed.

Model: Using Specific Language

Cather implies that Boston offers more than Nebraska. While it may be true that Boston is a center for art,
    cultural resources   pollution and congestion
Nebraska offers many ~~things~~ without the ~~trouble~~ of a major city.

Specific references such as *cultural resources* and *pollution and congestion* make the editorial clear and persuasive.

Vocabulary Acquisition and Use

1. Introduce the skill, using the instruction on the student page.
2. Have students complete the Word Analysis activity and the Vocabulary practice.

Word Analysis

1. (b) working together
2. (a) pleasing combination of musical sounds
3. (b) any first movement
4. (b) an emotional response

Vocabulary: Word Meanings

1. If students are <u>reverential</u> toward a teacher, they respect her.
2. A child is most likely to speak <u>tremulously.</u>
3. **Sample answer:** A substance that is usually <u>inert</u> is sand.
4. I would expect seriousness as a <u>prelude</u> to bad news.
5. <u>Jocularity</u> is more likely to be the trademark of a talk-show host.

Writing

1. To guide students in writing this essay, give them the **Support for Writing** worksheet (*Unit 3 Resources,* p. 239).
2. Students' editorials should clearly express and support the editor's opinion about Cather's portrayal of Nebraska in "A Wagner Matinée."
3. If students have trouble identifying with Cather's fellow Nebraskans, as a prewriting activity you might wish to have students reflect on how an author such as Cather might portray the area in which they live. Encourage students to identify and discuss any aspects of the community or region that might be portrayed in what some might consider an unfavorable light.
4. Evaluate students' essays using the **Rubrics for Editorial,** in *Professional Development Guidebook,* pages 289–290.

Assessment Resources

Unit 3 Resources

L1 L2 EL **Selection Test A,** pp. 244–246. Administer Test A to less advanced students and English learners.

L3 L4 EL **Selection Test B,** pp. 247–249. Administer Test B to on-level or more advanced students.

L3 L4 **Open-Book Test,** pp. 241–243. As an alternative, give the Open-Book Test.

All **Customizable Test Bank**

All **Self-tests**
Students may prepare for the **Selection Test** by taking the Self-test online.

PHLit Online! All assessment resources are available at **www.PHLitOnline.com.**

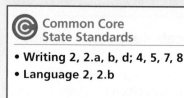

Common Core
State Standards

• Writing 2, 2.a, b, d; 4, 5, 7, 8
• Language 2, 2.b

Introducing the Writing Assignment

Review the assignment and the criteria, using the instruction on the student page.

What Do You Notice?

1. Draw class attention to the passage by Nell Irvin Painter. Have a student read the highlighted sentence aloud. **Ask** what makes the writing special.
   Possible responses: Students may cite the contrast between its content and tone; vivid verbs such as *sat* and *flourished*.

2. Then, draw students' attention to the second clause. Guide them to see how the poetic language used in the first part of the clause ("slavery flourished") subsides at the end of the clause into stark factuality ("abolition in 1862").

3. **Ask** students how this shift in tone mirrors the shift in history the clause describes.
   Possible response: The excesses of slavery gave way to the measured justice of abolition.

4. Suggest that students try shifting tone within a single sentence in their own writing.

Nell Irvin Painter on Research

Show students Segment 3 on Nell Irvin Painter on the *See It!* DVD or via the link in the **Enriched Online Student Edition**, at www. PHLitOnline.Com.

Write a Research Report

Common Core
State Standards

Writing
2. Write informative/explanatory texts to examine and convey complex ideas, concepts, and information clearly and accurately through the effective selection, organization, and analysis of content.

7. Conduct short as well as more sustained research projects to answer a question or solve a problem; narrow or broaden the inquiry when appropriate; synthesize multiple sources on the subject, demonstrating understanding of the subject under investigation.

Historical Investigation Report You can learn a great deal about a literary work by investigating the historical context in which it was written. To focus such an investigation, write a report in which you present information you have gathered, along with your own insights. An effective historical investigation report synthesizes information from multiple sources and connects ideas to form a coherent analysis. Follow the steps outlined in this workshop to write a historical investigation report.

Assignment Write a research report about the historical context in which a literary work or group of related works was written.

What to Include Your research report should have these elements:

- a clear thesis statement or main proposition
- factual support from varied sources, including primary and secondary sources found in both electronic and print texts
- direct quotations and proper citations of sources
- logical organization, including an introduction, body, and conclusion
- a formal bibliography or works-cited list

To preview the criteria on which your research report may be assessed, see the rubric on page 675.

To get a feel for historical research, read this mentor text. Notice how Painter uses clear language and logical organization to present information. For the complete text, see pages 550–551.

> *from:* Nell Irvin Painter's Introduction to "An Account of an Experience With Discrimination"
>
> *In 1791, President George Washington chose land on the border of Maryland and Virginia near his own home to serve as the nation's capital. In the 1790s, slavery existed in virtually the whole country. But during the early nineteenth century the Northern states abolished slavery, while the institution grew stronger in the South, of which Washington, D.C., was a part. The Washington slave market sat near the capitol building, and slavery flourished in the District until abolition in 1862.*

WRITE GUY
Jeff Anderson, M.Ed.

What Do You Notice?

Read the highlighted sentence several times. Then, with a partner, discuss the qualities that make it special. You might consider the following elements:

- word choice
- use of facts
- structure
- tone

Share your group's observations with the class.

Teaching Resources

The following resources can be used to enrich or extend the instruction.

Unit 3 Resources
   Writing Workshop, pp. 250–251

[All] *Professional Development Guidebook*
   Rubrics for Historical Investigation Report, pp. 268–269

[All] *Common Core Companion,*
   pp. 18–32; 40–47

[All] *Graphic Organizer Transparencies*
   Rubric for Self-Assessment: Historical Investigation Report, p. 149

[All] *See It!* DVD
   Neil Irvin Painter, Segments 3 and 4

All resources are available at **www.PHLitOnline.com.**

Prewriting and Planning

Choosing Your Topic

To find a suitable topic, use the following strategies:

- **Notebook and Textbook Review** Flip through your notebooks, literature textbooks, and writing journals, and list selections or authors you find interesting. Write down specific questions you have about the historical context in which your favorite works were written.

- **Research Preview** Once you have several possible topic choices and questions, spend 10–15 minutes researching each one on the Internet or at the library. Seek out both primary and secondary sources. A quick research preview will confirm the availability of information on each topic.

Narrowing Your Topic

Find your focus. Make sure your topic is substantial but not too ambitious for a short research paper. Narrow an overly broad topic by finding a more focused subject that fits within the larger area of interest. Use a flowchart like the one shown to do so.

Gathering Details

Organize your notes. As you gather information, use index cards to keep track of important ideas, facts, and scholarly opinions. Write down the general subject, fact or quotation, page numbers, and an identifying letter or number you will assign to the source.

Prepare to credit sources. Use another set of index cards to keep track of your sources. Use one card for each source you consult. Record the author's name, title, publisher, city, and date of publication. Label each source card with a letter or number so you can refer to sources quickly.

Fact Card
(basic principles)   p. 17
"What is the principle which underlies the anti-slavery movement? It is that slaveholding is _always_ wrong; not in this case or that case only, but in _all_ cases..."
Source Card: E

Source Card
(E)
The Anti-Slavery Reform, Its Principle and Method. by William I. Bowditch Robert F. Wallcut; Boston, 1850 Cornell University Library

---

Applying Understanding by Design Principles

Clarifying Expected Outcomes: Using Rubrics

- Before students begin work on this assignment, have them preview the **Rubric for Self-Assessment** on page 675 to learn what qualities their research reports must have. A copy of this rubric appears in the _Professional Development Guidebook_, page 268.

- Review the criteria in the rubric with the class. Before students use the rubric to assess their own writing, work with them to rate the Student Model (p. 672) using the rubric.
- If you wish to assess students' research reports with either a four-point or a six-point scoring rubric, see the _Professional Development Guidebook_, page 268–269.

Prewriting and Planning

1. Introduce the prewriting strategies, using the instruction on the student page.
2. Have students apply the strategies to choose a topic and gather details.

Teaching the Strategies

1. Emphasize the importance of crafting a well-defined, focused topic. Review topics that are too broad to deal with in a short paper, such as slavery in America or the effects of technology.
2. Remind students to keep accurate, detailed records of sources and data during research. Suggest that students use index cards, and remind them to document the author, title, publication information, referenced page numbers, direct and indirect quotations, and paraphrases for each source used.

Think Aloud: Model Gathering Details

Say to students:

Once I have focused my topic, then I have to actually do the research. The idea is to find information, not to confirm what I already think. So I read as much as I can from good sources, take notes as I go, and then review my notes. Gathering details adds new information, and I may modify my thesis to reflect what I have learned.

Six Traits Focus

✔	Ideas		Word Choice
✔	Organization		Sentence Fluency
	Voice		Conventions

PH WRITING COACH — Grade 11

Students will find additional information on historical investigation reports in Chapter 11.

Prentice Hall ESSAYScorer
A writing prompt for this mode of writing can be found on the _Prentice Hall Essay Scorer_ at www.PHLitOnline.com.

Drafting

1. Introduce the drafting strategies, using the instruction on the student page.

2. Have students apply the strategies as they draft.

Teaching the Strategies

1. Explain to students that their thesis statements should express the conclusions they have reached as a result of their research; these statements should not be taken directly from a source. Sources should supply a variety of supporting evidence.

2. Have students review each other's thesis statements. Ask students to restate each other's thesis statements. If the claim in the thesis is clear, the restatement should be easy to write.

3. Have students consider organizing their research notes under an outline format that corresponds to the headings and subheadings of their formal outlines. This strategy aligns notes, quotations, and statistics with the relevant text.

4. Remind students during drafting to incorporate their source material into passages and paraphrases, weaving the information in with their own words.

5. Have students adhere to a single format or style for citing source material.

Six Traits Focus

✔	Ideas	Word Choice
✔	Organization	Sentence Fluency
	Voice	Conventions

Drafting

Shaping Your Writing

Propose a thesis statement. Your research report should develop a coherent thesis statement or controlling idea. Review your notes and write a statement that is supported by the evidence you discovered in primary and secondary resources. Your thesis should make a claim that your report will support; it should not state a simple fact.

Weak Argument	Strong Argument
• Anti-slavery pamphlets first appeared in 1704. • Pamphlets were very influential in ending slavery.	Beginning in 1704, anti-slavery pamphlets increasingly used the tools of advertising to persuade readers that slavery was immoral.

Write a formal outline. After you have selected a controlling idea, prepare an outline. Consider points at which you might include rhetorical strategies other than exposition, or explanation. For example, use an anecdote, a form of *narration*, or include the *description* of a setting. Note ideas for a conclusion in which you attain closure by summarizing your main points and presenting a final generalization.

Providing Elaboration

Include a variety of sources. As you draft, use direct quotations, paraphrases, and visuals from sources that are reliable, valid, and varied. Do not rely on the ideas or information you find in a single source. Referencing multiple resources gives your writing more validity because it takes into account a variety of perspectives.

Analyze relationships among sources. In your research, you may have encountered differences of opinion in secondary sources or conflicting accounts of the same events in primary sources. Provide analysis and explanation about the reasons for such differences. To present a complete analysis, include answers to the questions listed in the following chart.

When Sources Agree	When Sources Disagree
• Do the writers of primary sources share similar biases that influenced their writing? • Do secondary resources confirm this perspective?	• Which primary sources do I think are more reliable and valid? Why? • Do I have a secondary resource that takes a side on this issue? Do I agree with it?

Developing Your Style

Choosing an Effective Organization

To choose the best pattern of organization for your report, consider your thesis and your findings. Then, structure your report with one of the methods listed in the chart below. You may choose an overall organizational strategy and use other methods to support it. For example, your essay might follow a chronological organization, but an individual paragraph might evaluate the causes and effects of a single important event.

Method	Description
Chronological	Discuss events in the order in which they occurred.
Cause/Effect	Analyze the causes and/or effects of an event.
Problem/Solution	Identify a specific problem and present a solution.
Parts to Whole	Relate elements of a single event or topic to a whole.
Order of Importance	Present your support from most to least important or from least to most important.
Compare and Contrast	Discuss similarities and differences between two topics.

Find It in Your Reading

Review Nell Irvin Painter's introduction to "An Account of an Experience With Discrimination" on page 664.

1. Identify the overall organizational method Painter uses.
2. Note her organization within individual paragraphs. Find examples of chronological and cause-and-effect organizations.

Apply It to Your Writing

To select an appropriate organizational method, follow these steps:

1. Review the strategies listed in the chart and consider their pros and cons. For example, chronological order can present a sequence of events clearly, but it may not establish the importance of a person or event.
2. Choose the overall organizational method that best supports your thesis statement. Draft an outline that reflects that strategy.
3. Think about the organization of information within paragraphs. Consider using cause-and-effect or problem-and-solution organization if relevant to the ideas you are presenting in that paragraph.
4. Use transitions to make your organization clear to readers.

PH | **WRITING COACH**
Further instruction and practice are available in *Prentice Hall Writing Coach*.

Writing Workshop **667**

Developing Your Style

1. Introduce patterns of organization to students, using the instruction on the student page.
2. Have students complete the Find It in Your Reading and Apply It to Your Writing activities.

Teaching the Strategies

1. Work through the chart of organizational methods with the class.
2. Most students will be familiar with these common patterns, but they may have difficulty selecting the one most appropriate to their thesis statement.
3. Point out that clues to the most effective pattern of organization may be found in their thesis or in their research notes. For example, the words *because* or *as a result* in a thesis statement point to a cause-and-effect organization pattern. If a student's research takes the form of looking at one subject in terms of another, a compare-and-contrast pattern might be best.
4. Remind students that an effective organizational pattern involves more than arranging their facts in a particular way. They should also provide pattern-specific transitions between sentences and between paragraphs in their reports. For example, a chronological pattern would be supported not simply by setting details in time order, but by using transitions such as *first, next, then, after,* and so on.

Six Traits Focus

	Ideas		Word Choice
✔	Organization	✔	Sentence Fluency
	Voice		Conventions

Strategies for Test-Taking

Some writing tests direct students to read articles, synthesize the information, and then write an essay based on this information. Students may find it helpful to approach these tests as research assignments for which a topic has already been chosen and sources already gathered. The prompt will provide a research question. Students should note how each given article addresses that question. The thesis statement should answer the prompt directly, and the essay should support the thesis with evidence from the articles.

Revising

1. Introduce the revising strategies, using the instruction on the student page.

2. Have students apply the strategies for paragraphs and word choice as they revise their research reports.

Teaching the Strategies

1. If possible, supply students with page markers and instruct them to mark each use of source material in their drafts, including paraphrased or indirectly quoted material. Have them confirm the documentation and its accuracy.

2. Explain that a transition must provide the reader with a logical bridge from one idea to another and from one paragraph to another.

3. Remind students that their word choice depends, in part, on their audience. Specialized words, such as *sampling* from contemporary music, may need explanation for a general audience.

Think Aloud: Model Revising Overall Structure

Say to students:

When I review my first draft, I want to make sure the structure is clear and coherent. Sometimes I number the paragraphs and go through each one to note its main focus. Then I decide if the order of the paragraphs makes sense or if some rearranging would improve the flow of ideas. For example, sometimes I find that my second paragraph makes a stronger opening statement than my first. I might find that one of the paragraphs breaks up the flow of ideas and that the only important piece of information it contains could be incorporated in the following paragraph.

Six Traits Focus

✔	Ideas		Word Choice
✔	Organization	✔	Sentence Fluency
	Voice		Conventions

Revising

Revising Your Paragraphs

Integrate source material smoothly. A strong research report is not a choppy collection of facts and quotations. It presents a smooth flow of ideas that are supported by valid, researched information. Review your paper, looking for points at which your source material can be integrated better. When you paraphrase another writer's ideas, include a citation that identifies the source of the idea. When you include exact quotations, follow this strategy:

- First, introduce the quotation by naming the writer or by connecting the quotation to the subject being discussed.

- Then, present the quoted material.

- Finally, explain the quotation by showing how it supports the point you are making.

Revising Your Word Choice

Define specialized vocabulary. General readers may not be familiar with specialized terms you have encountered in your research. Some words may be familiar only to experts in the field and will present obstacles to your readers' appreciation of your ideas. To aid readers' understanding, define jargon that is specific to a topic.

- Review your work and identify specialized words, such as *broadsheet* in the example shown. Add necessary definitions.

- Consider whether definitions are sufficient. If necessary, add descriptions or comparisons to more familiar concepts or objects.

- If the terms are still too challenging for your readers, consider replacing the specialized vocabulary with simpler language.

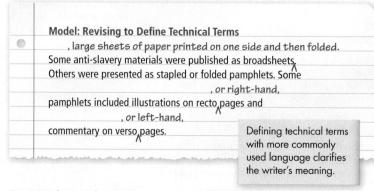

Model: Revising to Define Technical Terms

, large sheets of paper printed on one side and then folded.
Some anti-slavery materials were published as broadsheets.
Others were presented as stapled or folded pamphlets. Some
, or right-hand,
pamphlets included illustrations on recto pages and
, or left-hand,
commentary on verso pages.

Defining technical terms with more commonly used language clarifies the writer's meaning.

Peer Review: Ask a partner to review your draft and identify specialized terms. Discuss whether each term should be defined, deleted, or simplified.

Common Core State Standards

Writing
2.d. Use precise language, domain-specific vocabulary, and techniques such as metaphor, simile, and analogy to manage the complexity of the topic.
4. Produce clear and coherent writing in which the development, organization, and style are appropriate to task, purpose, and audience.
5. Develop and strengthen writing as needed by rewriting, focusing on addressing what is most significant for a specific purpose and audience.
8. Integrate information into the text selectively to maintain the flow of ideas, avoiding plagiarism and overreliance on any one source and following a standard format for citation.

Strategies for Using Technology in Writing

If students have access to word processors, encourage them to use the Insert mode rather than the Type-over mode for making corrections. By using the Insert mode in revising, students can insert proper citations and any additional information or words as needed.

In addition, many word-processing programs have features for creating Works Cited pages. Students can also use the organizing tools and revision checkers in **Writing and Grammar Interactive Textbook Online**.

Writers on Writing

Nell Irvin Painter On Using Research

Nell Irvin Painter is the author of "Defining an Era" (p. 474).

These words come from the introduction to my history of the United States between 1877 and 1919. I wanted to break down gross generalizations about Americans based on race (black/white) and ethnicity (Irish, German, Jewish) by talking about socio-economic class. Men and women experience class in different ways. In order to speak broadly, I had to research the incomes and lifestyles of many kinds of Americans, not just middle-class white people.

The broader your research, the more appealing your writing.

—Nell Irvin Painter

from *Standing at Armageddon, 1877–1919*

In both 1877 and 1919 native-born white Protestant Americans were presumed to belong to the middle (or upper) classes, even though in the South, West, and Midwest large numbers of such people belonged to the agricultural and industrial working classes. The standing of descendants of immigrants changed over time because the arrival of new groups of immigrants altered assumptions about relative class status. The Irish, who had seemed in 1877 to constitute a permanent class of casual laborers and domestic servants, had by 1919 become skilled workers and foremen, while many Irishwomen had become the teachers of eastern and southern European immigrants who early in the twentieth century formed a new industrial working class. Similarly, German Jews, many of whom in the mid-nineteenth century had been itinerant peddlers, were largely middle- and upper-class by the time of heavy Russian Jewish immigration after 1905. And the process continued. By 1920 the children of Europeans who had immigrated in the late nineteenth century had become the teachers and foremen of southern black migrants in the North and Midwest.

> I purposefully included the words *white* and *Protestant* to break up an equation that many readers take for granted: that middle-class is the same as white and Protestant. I also did research in sources that discussed the lives of many kinds of people.

> I specifically mentioned Irish immigrants, because many readers forget the history of Irish Americans as immigrants. I wanted this section to convey the sense of change over time in the status of Irish Americans in relation to later immigrants.

> I used these two particular vocations because one, teachers, is associated with women, and the other, foremen, is associated with men.

Writing Workshop **669**

Enriched Online Student Edition
Show or assign the video online at **www.PHLitOnline.com.**

Providing Appropriate Citations

Introduce the citation strategies, using the instruction on the student page or supplanting it with the procedures preferred by you or mandated by your school or district.

Teaching the Strategies

1. Point out to students that no matter what system is used, appropriate citation begins the instant they begin taking research notes. Encourage students to be meticulous in recording quotations, paraphrases, and their own notes. Carelessness is no better an excuse for plagiarism than deliberate theft.

2. Remind students that plagiarism and fakery—inventing quotations or sources—are not only wrong, they are now easy to detect through search engines and checking programs available on the Internet.

3. Emphasize to students that paraphrases must be credited as if they were direct quotations. Students may have the false impression that because they put the information "in their own words," they do not have to credit the source.

Think Aloud: Model Accurate Citing of Sources

Say to students:

I can trace almost every mistake I have made in citations back to a careless error in my notecards. As a result, I am fanatical about accurately using quotation marks to identify direct quotations. To keep me from confusing my paraphrases with my own insights, I highlight my notes. I use one color for direct quotations, another for paraphrases that must be attributed, a third for my own words.

Deciding What to Cite

Review the chart on the student page to help students distinguish common knowledge from information that needs to be credited.

Providing Appropriate Citations

You must cite the sources for the information and ideas you use in your report. In the body of your paper, include a footnote, an endnote, or a parenthetical citation, identifying the sources of facts, opinions, and quotations. At the end of your paper, provide a bibliography or a works-cited list, a list of all the sources you cite. Follow the format your teacher recommends, such as Modern Language Association (MLA) Style or American Psychological Association (APA) Style. See pages R20–R23 for more information about how to prepare citations for different kinds of sources.

If you do not credit sources accurately, you commit the serious offense of **plagiarism,** presenting someone else's work as your own. Plagiarism is stealing someone else's ideas, so it is both illegal and dishonest. Avoid this problem by fairly and thoroughly citing every source you use.

Deciding What to Cite

You do not need to cite every fact that you report. For example, facts that are considered common knowledge do not require citation. A fact that can be found in three or more sources is probably common knowledge. However, you should cite any facts and statistics that are not common knowledge. The examples in this chart reflect the difference between common knowledge and facts that should be cited.

Common Knowledge
• Slavery was abolished in the United States in 1863. • William Lloyd Garrison was a leader of the abolitionist movement. • *Uncle Tom's Cabin* was published in 1852.

Facts to Be Cited
• From the 17th to 19th centuries, about 12 million Africans were captured and sent as slaves to the Americas. Source: Ronald Segal, *The Black Diaspora: Five Centuries of the Black Experience Outside Africa* (New York: Farrar, Straus and Giroux, 1995, page 4). • Harriet Beecher Stowe's anti-slavery novel *Uncle Tom's Cabin* (1852) increased tensions between the North and the South. Source: Will Kaufman, *The Civil War in American Culture* (Edinburgh: Edinburgh University Press, 2006, page 18).

In your report, give credit for the following:

• ideas, opinions, or theories presented by other writers

• facts or statistics that are not common knowledge

• direct quotations of spoken or written words

• paraphrases of spoken or written words

Notice that you must still provide a citation even if you paraphrase someone else's ideas. It is appropriate to give credit to someone else's thoughts, whether or not you use his or her exact words. In general, it is a good idea to provide more citations rather than risk not providing enough.

Common Core State Standards

Writing
8. Integrate information into the text selectively to maintain the flow of ideas, avoiding plagiarism and overreliance on any one source and following a standard format for citation.

Works-Cited List (MLA Style)

A works-cited list must contain the following information:

- name of the author, editor, translator, or group responsible for the work
- title
- place and date of publication
- publisher

For print materials, the information required for a citation generally appears on the copyright and title pages of a work.

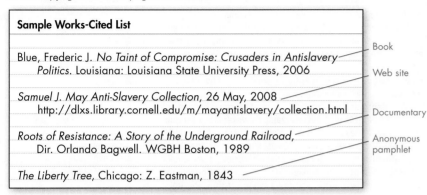

Sample Works-Cited List

Blue, Frederic J. *No Taint of Compromise: Crusaders in Antislavery Politics.* Louisiana: Louisiana State University Press, 2006 — Book

Samuel J. May Anti-Slavery Collection, 26 May, 2008 http://dlxs.library.cornell.edu/m/mayantislavery/collection.html — Web site

Roots of Resistance: A Story of the Underground Railroad, Dir. Orlando Bagwell. WGBH Boston, 1989 — Documentary

The Liberty Tree, Chicago: Z. Eastman, 1843 — Anonymous pamphlet

Parenthetical Citations (MLA Style)

A parenthetical citation appears in the body of your text and identifies the source at point of use. It refers the reader to an entry on your works-cited list. A parenthetical citation appears in parentheses. It identifies the source by the last name of the author, editor, or translator. It also gives a page reference, identifying the page of the source on which the information can be found.

Model: Parenthetical Citations

Although most of the anti-slavery pamphlets were expected to exist for only a short time, some rare examples have survived in carefully preserved collections. The founders of one large collection acknowledged the "great importance that the literature of the Anti-Slavery movement...be preserved and handed down..." (Samuel J. May Anti-Slavery Collection, "Collection Description") The variety of opinions reflected in this collection show that there were many divisions among the beliefs of abolitionists. (Blue, p. 1)

Manuscript Preparation

The final copy of your research report should be prepared according to your teacher's recommended style. Here are some common preferences:

- double-spaced lines
- 12-point type (Times New Roman or Courier is often requested.)
- italics to replace underscoring (for example, in titles of novels)
- one-inch margins on each side of the text

Student Model

Review the Student Model with the class, using the annotations to analyze the writer's successful use of the elements of a good research report.

Teaching the Strategies

1. Explain that the student model is a sample and that many research papers are longer.

2. Have students read the first paragraph. **Ask** them to identify the essay's topic and its thesis statement.
   Answer: The topic is the significance of Wheatley's poetry. Lauren's thesis is, "Although many do not consider her to be a important writer judged by today's values of originality, she persevered through the challenges of her social status to become not only a celebrated poet but also the starting point for the study of African American literature."

3. Call students' attention to Lauren's second paragraph and the note that accompanies it. **Ask** students to identify the sources she uses to support her opinions.
   Answer: She cites Miller, de Dwyer, and Wood; Mason; and Redding.

4. Point out the subheadings that Lauren uses and explain that these make her essay more organized and easier to follow.

5. Point out that in her fourth paragraph, Lauren combines factual evidence from sources and an interpretation of Wheatley's poetry, giving her opinions strong support.

Student Model: Lauren Shepherd, Tupelo, MS

The Writing Style of Phillis Wheatley

In an era when African Americans were struggling to carve an identity for themselves, Phillis Wheatley emerged as the first truly significant black poet in American literature. Although many do not consider her to be an important writer, judged by today's values of originality, she persevered through the challenges of her social status to become not only a celebrated poet, but the starting point for the study of African American literature. In this paper, I will discuss her work as a whole and present a detailed analysis of one of her most famous poems, "To His Excellency General Washington."

> Lauren clearly states her thesis in the opening paragraph.

Religious Message Wheatley was highly educated for her time and had read the classics as well as the best English poets (Miller, de Dwyer, Wood 48). She was deeply influenced by the work of the great English poet John Milton (1608–1674), who saw himself as a writer in the service of God. Like Milton, Wheatley expressed a constant awareness of "God, His Son, His beneficence and His Power." Almost every one of Wheatley's poems develops around a central theme of religious morality and sometimes has an "air of message from the pulpit" (Mason 15–17). One theme, Christian salvation, underlies nearly everything she wrote (Redding 10).

> Lauren provides thorough support for the opinions she expresses in this passage.

Wheatley's religious messages are often conveyed through embellished Bible stories. In fact, a tradition within African American literature of augmenting biblical accounts with creative license and poetic flair can be traced directly to Wheatley. Both her poems "Goliath and Gath" and "Isaiah LXIII" add creative information to a foundation of biblical narrative.

African Influences In addition to the key role of Christian religious messages in Wheatley's work, many of her writings also exhibit a subtle presence of African traditions. For example, Wheatley uses solar imagery throughout her body of poems. Her frequent use of sun imagery in such poems as "A Hymn to the Morning" and "A Hymn to the Evening" suggest that her early religious training in Africa may have consisted of some kind of hierophantic—or sun—worship (Smith, Baechler, Litz 474). Wheatley usually uses such sun imagery as a metaphor for Christian revelation, thus connecting the two essential elements of her religious life.

> Subheads add to the clarity and order of the essay.

> Lauren provides factual support for an interesting literary analysis.

Also reminiscent of Wheatley's childhood in Africa is her constant interest in panegyric—or praise—poetry. In many of the cultures of Africa, poets were instructed that political praise constituted the very core of their responsibility as writers (Smith Baechler, Litz 476). In keeping with that tradition, the majority of Wheatley's works are directed towards politically and socially prominent individuals, such as George Whitehead, a famous English clergyman, and George Washington (Johnson 29).

Racial Consciousness Although many have ventured to say that Wheatley's "unquestioning embrace of New England and white cultures" prompted her to neglect the issue of slavery (Smith, Baechler, Litz 476), a closer examination of her poetry reveals that she was quite "race conscious" (Davis 192). She refers to herself on several occasions as "Africa's muse," and even uses her skin color and presumed low social status as a reference point for her religious message of salvation (Davis 192–193).

Neoclassical Style The majority of Wheatley's poems adhere to the established patterns of the neoclassical style. Neoclassicism was a widespread movement in the visual and literary arts that began in the 1700s and lasted until the 1840s and 1850s. Classical history and mythology provided much of the subject matter of Neoclassical works. The poetry of Homer, Virgil, and Ovid, and the plays of Aeschylus, Sophocles, and Euripides provided the bulk of classical sources. Neoclassical writers, such as Alexander Pope (1688–1744), stressed order, harmony, and restraint.

Like the Neoclassicists she admired, Wheatley's work was noted for an unfaltering preoccupation with regular rhyme and rhythm (Mason 14). Breaking out of her usual form on only six occasions, Wheatley most frequently wrote using the heroic couplet—two-line stanzas written in iambic pentameter—that Alexander Pope made so effective (Mason 20). Considering that she is labeled as a spontaneous poet who would write during bouts of inspiration, the general regularity of her meter is remarkable. The influence of the Neoclassical writers also shows in Wheatley's use of elevated language (Mason 16) and in her numerous classical and mythological allusions.

"To His Excellency General Washington" The poem "To His Excellency General Washington" serves as a good example of Wheatley's style. Troubled by poor health since her arrival in America in 1761, when she was only eight years old (Perkins et al. 272), Wheatley traveled from Boston to London in 1773 in hope that the sea air would improve her well-being. Upon her return to the rebellious colonies in 1774, she found the fighting in the Boston vicinity had escalated. Wheatley composed her poem to George Washington and crossed the battle lines to deliver it in person. Two years later, Wheatley received a letter from the general himself thanking her for her adulation but insisting that she had placed him on too high a pedestal. In April 1776, Thomas Paine published her poem, its accompanying note, and Washington's reply in Pennsylvania Magazine or American Monthly Museum (Sheeler 8–10).

Although Washington's response to Wheatley's poem was modest, Wheatley gives the reader clear insight as to her opinions of the man. The entire poem is devoted to the veneration of the Continental Army and the leadership of General Washington. Wheatley adheres to her favorite poetic form of heroic couplets. She does not merely revere Washington, she portrays him as a royal figure, referring to him as "Your Excellency," and ascribing to him "a crown, a mansion and a throne that shine."

> The essay presents a variety of interpretations of the material.

> Necessary background information is essential to the readers' understanding.

> Lauren refers to other points of view regarding Wheatley's work.

> The essay makes use of a variety of historical documents, including a primary source.

6. Note that Lauren offers a variety of interpretations of Wheatley's poetry (for example, her discussion of Wheatley's "Racial Consciousness" in paragraph 6), making her essay richer and more complex.

7. Remind students of Lauren's definition of *neoclassicism* in paragraph 7. **Ask** what earlier term Lauren defined for her readers. **Answer:** *Hierophantic,* in paragraph 4, is defined as "sun worship."

8. Point out other valuable types of evidence that Lauren uses, for example, her reference to Thomas Paine's publication of Wheatley's poem. **Ask** students to explain how this information enhances the essay. **Answer:** It provides strong evidence that Wheatley's poetry was recognized as important even during her lifetime, despite her social status.

Differentiated Instruction   for Universal Access

Strategy for Special-Needs Students
Students may find the independent reading involved in doing research especially challenging. Instruct students to keep track of what they read by making notecards for each source. Monitor the students' work, periodically reviewing their cards with them to make sure that they have taken relevant notes and recorded the source information correctly. To check comprehension, have students explain the points in their own words.

Strategy for Gifted/Talented Students
Students may use visual materials among their sources. For example, reproductions of photographs and artwork, charts, graphs, or tables might be useful and interesting additions to a research paper. Explain that visual sources are intended to complement, not replace, written sources. Tell students that when they include visual materials, they should identify and refer to these items in the text as they write, using a system such as "Figure 1."

673

9. Call special attention to the first sentence of the final paragraph. Explain that Lauren has restated her thesis, in simpler terms, with the paragraph explaining her argument.

10. Call attention to Lauren's Works Cited list. Point out that each entry provides information about one of her sources, including the author's name, the title of the source, and the place and date of publication. Note that if you have format preferences for the Works Cited list other than the ones in the model, reinforce those to students at this time.

Connecting to Real-Life Writing

Tell students that research writing is not limited to school. Many useful and important documents are based on the same methods of research that students use to create their papers. Government reports, medical findings, scientific discoveries, and business studies all involve research and crediting sources. Much journalism can also be considered research writing because journalists investigate a topic and, wherever possible, cite their sources.

Wheatley resorts to a striking use of personification in the poem. In the opening lines, she mentions the sorrow of "mother earth" at the bloodshed ravaging the land. In line 15, she personifies heaven as a maiden with a "fair face." Her use of alliteration in that image adds to its effect. Wheatley also gives life to the "nations" in line 33 and describes Brittania as a defeated being who "droops the pensive head" (line 35).

Perhaps Wheatley's most notable use of personification lies in her image of the American colonies as the Goddess Columbia (line 9), who is a "native of the skies" (line 11). Wheatley created this new goddess in honor of Christopher Columbus. Later popularized by Revolutionary War poets such as Philip Freneau, the image of Columbia has its first appearance in Wheatley's poem (Jensen).

Wheatley also weaves various allusions into her poem. For example, the European countries in conflict with America are said to be "Gallic powers" (line 30). This allusion refers to the Gallic Wars at the time of Julius Caesar when France was called Gaul. Further evidence of her classical knowledge appears in the reference to "Aeolus," the God of the wind (line 15). Aeolus appeared in Homer's Odyssey (Tripp 24), which Wheatley read in Alexander Pope's famous translation. Wheatley scholars generally agree that Pope's translation of Homer greatly affected her poetry (Mason 16).

Although Phillis Wheatley never achieved a truly original poetic style, she is undoubtedly an important figure in American literature. She transcended racial and language barriers to occupy a significant position in the social and intellectual scene of both Boston and London. If one judges her work based on the impact of her poetry on her contemporaries, she is an important pioneer in the development of American literature.

> Lauren concludes by restating her thesis.

Works Cited

Davis, Arthur P. "Personal Elements in the Poetry of Phillis Wheatley." *Phylon: The Atlanta University Review of Race and Culture.* 13 vols. June 1953, pp. 191–198.

Johnson, James Weldon., ed. *The Book of American Negro Poetry.* New York: Harcourt Brace Jovanovich Inc., 1922.

Mason, Julian D., Jr., ed. *The Poems of Phillis Wheatley.* North Carolina: The University of North Carolina Press, 1989.

Miller, James E., Jr., Carlota Cárdenas de Dwyer, and Kerry M. Wood. *The United States in Literature.* Illinois: Scott Foresman and Company, 1985.

Perkins, George, et al., eds. *The American Tradition in Literature.* 1 vol. New York: McGraw-Hill Publishing Company, 1990.

Redding, J. Saunders. *To Make a Poet Black.* New York: Cornell University Press, 1988.

Sheeler, Karissa L. Phillis Wheatley. 11 February 2000. <http://www.kutztown.edu/faculty/reagan/wheat1.html>

Smith, Valerie, Lea Baechler, and A. Walton Litz, eds. *African American Writers.* New York: Charles Scribner's Sons, 1991.

Tripp, Edward. *Cromwell's Handbook of Classical Mythology.* New York: Thomas Y. Cromwell Company, 1970.

> A complete works-cited list provides information on the sources Lauren references in the report.

Editing and Proofreading

Review your historical investigation report to eliminate errors in grammar, usage, punctuation, and spelling.

Focus on accuracy. Consult your note cards to be sure you have quoted material exactly. Check all dates and statistics. You may need to return to the original source to check a specific fact.

Focus on capitalization and spelling. Make sure you have capitalized proper nouns correctly. Then, check your spelling. Follow this *spelling rule:* If an adjective ends in *-ent*, such as the word *expedient*, its parallel forms end in *-ence (expedience)* or *-ency (expediency)*.

Spiral Review: Conventions Earlier you learned that misplaced and dangling modifiers can be confusing (p. 585). Check your report to make sure you have not used any misplaced or dangling modifiers.

Publishing, Presenting, and Reflecting

Consider the following ways to share and think further about your writing.

Present an oral historical investigation report. Deliver your paper as an oral report. Incorporate visual aids and images to illustrate specific information. Provide classmates with a handout listing your sources.

Submit your paper for publication. Submit your paper to a magazine or Web site that publishes student writing or that covers your research topic.

Reflect on your writing. Jot down your thoughts on the experience of writing a historical investigation report. Begin by answering these questions: What strategies would you use again? How was conducting in-depth research on a topic different from other types of research you have done?

PH WRITING COACH

Further instruction and practice are available in *Prentice Hall Writing Coach*.

Rubric for Self-Assessment

Evaluate your research report using the following criteria and rating scale.

Criteria	Rating Scale not very → very
Focus: How clearly does your thesis statement guide your report?	1 2 3 4 5
Organization: How logical and effective is the organization?	1 2 3 4 5
Support/Elaboration: How well do you use a variety of primary and secondary sources to support your thesis?	1 2 3 4 5
Style: How well do you explain differences among your sources?	1 2 3 4 5
Conventions: According to an accepted format, how complete and accurate are your citations?	1 2 3 4 5

Common Core State Standards

Writing
5. Develop and strengthen writing as needed by editing, focusing on addressing what is most significant for a specific purpose and audience.

Language
2. Demonstrate command of the conventions of standard English capitalization, punctuation, and spelling when writing.
2.b. Spell correctly.

Editing and Proofreading

1. Introduce the editing and proofreading focuses, using the instruction on the student page.

2. Have students read their research papers carefully, marking them for line edits, including changes in word choice and corrections in grammar, spelling, and punctuation. Make sure they check for errors of the type noted in the lesson focus and the Spiral Review.

3. Once their text is corrected, have students make sure that all requirements for style and format are met. Then have students prepare their final drafts.

Six Traits Focus

✔	Ideas	✔	Word Choice
✔	Organization	✔	Sentence Fluency
	Voice	✔	Conventions

PH WRITING COACH Grade 11

Students will find further information on responding to literature in Chapter 10.

ASSESS

Publishing, Presenting, and Reflecting

1. Remind students that when they are incorporating visual aids and images in the oral presentations, they must be as careful in crediting their visual sources as they are with printed material.

2. Point out to students that they may be requested to reformat their reports somewhat to accommodate the medium in which their report will appear.

3. Ask students to discuss what they learned from researching their subjects. Have the results altered their initial perspectives?

4. Ask students to compare their experiences with this research report with those of other research papers they have done. What did they do differently this time?

Write an Analysis of a Literary Work

1. Present the guidelines for analyzing a literary work in preparation for an oral interpretation, using the instruction on the student page.

2. As students consider the literary elements in the chart, **ask** them to provide examples of each element in works they have read. **Sample answers:** Examples from "An Occurrence at Owl Creek Bridge (pp. 480–489). *Tone:* "The man who was engaged in being hanged was apparently about thirty-five years of age." Somewhat sarcastic, cynical tone. *Language and style:* "A man stood upon a railroad bridge in northern Alabama, looking down into the swift water twenty feet below." Direct, journalistic language. *Imagery:* "the brooding mists under the banks at some distance down the stream." *Theme:* Facing imminent death can lead someone to fixate on the ineffable joys of life. *Nuance and ambiguity:* The story might be viewed as Farquhar's dream, hallucination, or passage into death.

3. Remind students that when they write their analytical essays, their purpose for writing is to analyze the essential elements that they will emphasize in their oral interpretations. Explain that an effective presentation will highlight all of the significant ideas and clearly show the presenter's interpretation of any complexities in the text.

Oral Interpretation of a Literary Work

An *oral interpretation* is a performance of a literary work that highlights its most important qualities as the performer sees, or interprets, them. Generally, oral interpretations do not use scenery or other theatrical effects. Instead, they call upon a performer's ability to analyze a literary work and present it meaningfully, using *tone, vocal inflection, pacing,* and *body language.*

Prepare an Analysis of a Literary Work

Analyze the literature. To prepare a compelling oral interpretation, start by reading, analyzing, and researching a work of literature. As you read, consider the *stylistic devices* and elements shown in the chart.

Literary Element	Description	How to Identify
Tone	the author's attitude	Determine if the author is serious, playful, or critical.
Language and Style	the manner in which ideas are expressed	Study the lengths and rhythm of sentences, details, repetition, and changes to pronunciation, spelling, or grammar.
Imagery	word pictures that appeal to the senses	Analyze descriptions of places, objects, settings, or experiences.
Theme	a work's central idea, message, or insight about life	Identify the author's purpose and note images or ideas that repeat.
Nuance and Ambiguity	literary elements that can be interpreted in multiple ways	Look for significant words, figurative language, symbols, changes in characters, and the variety of meanings they may have.

Read, analyze, and research. Read your selection closely and analyze how specific literary elements help develop significant ideas and meaning. Consider both denotative, or literal, meanings and connotative meanings, or the associations or feelings that words suggest. Make sure to address any elements that are open to interpretation. Research the selection by reviewing other texts, such as critical essays, to support your ideas. Then, write a brief analytical essay detailing your findings. Incorporate *rhetorical strategies* into your writing, such as describing your first impressions of the text or recalling conversations you had with others about your selection. You will use this essay to introduce your oral interpretation.

Plan Your Interpretation

Focus on delivery techniques. Your oral interpretation should help listeners understand characters, follow shifts in plot, and hear changes in emotion. Consider how you will use the techniques shown in the graphic to add depth and drama to your interpretation.

Research other ways to enhance your performance by observing the body language and vocalization of an actor, poet, or other polished reader as he or she presents a literary work.

Mark up the selection. Make notes on your copy of the selection indicating how you will use your voice and movement to communicate your understanding of the work. Also, consider using music, images, or sound effects to enhance the artistry of your interpretation.

Practice. Plan *staging and performance details* as you rehearse in front of a mirror or record yourself. For example, consider when to move, use gestures, or include simple props. Then, practice for family or friends and apply their feedback to improve your presentation.

Appropriate Eye Contact

Look at your listeners and make eye contact with people in the back as well as the front of the room.

Vocalization

Reflect characters' speech patterns and *dialects*, and enunciate and project your voice.

Voice Register

Make characters distinct by using the high, low, and middle tones in your voice.

Gesture/Movement

Use hand gestures and move around your stage to show actions in the work.

Activities: Deliver and Analyze Oral Interpretations

© Comprehension and Collaboration For both activities, use an evaluation form like the one shown below.

A. Deliver your oral interpretation to your class. First, read your analytical essay—or a shorter, less formal version—to introduce the literary work. Then, deliver your interpretation. After your performance, apply feedback from listeners to improve your delivery.

B. With a small group, analyze a variety of interpretations of the same literary work. You may use audio or video recordings, your own interpretations, or a combination of the two. Analyze how each version interprets the source text.

Evaluation Form for Oral Interpretation

Title and Author of Literary Work: _____

How well does the speaker convey the main idea of the selection?

_____

How well does the speaker use gestures? Give examples.

_____

Comment on one effective use of voice.

_____

How well does the speaker maintain eye contact with the audience?

_____

What can the speaker improve? _____

Plan Your Interpretation

1. Present the guidelines for delivery techniques, marking up selections, and practice.

2. Ask volunteers to choose a sample sentence or passage and repeat it several times, changing their vocalization, voice register, and gestures or movements. Have listeners evaluate the effectiveness of each version.

3. Suggest that students develop a notation method that will help them mark up the selection. You might suggest these notations: underscore for vocal emphasis; circle for strong vocal emphasis; backslash for pause; up arrow for increased speed; down arrow for decreased speed.

Activities: Deliver an Oral Interpretation

1. Have students decide whether they will introduce their oral interpretations by reading their full analytical essays or presenting abbreviated versions. Point out that if they choose to read their essays, they must apply the same delivery skills they will use during the presentation in order to engage their audience. For many students, presenting a shorter, less formal introduction will allow them to emphasize the most important ideas of their analysis while maintaining contact with the audience.

2. Remind students to review the Evaluation Form before giving their oral interpretations.

3. Allow time for students to share their presentations with the class and then for students to complete the evaluation forms.

Differentiated Instruction   for Universal Access

Support for Less Proficient Readers

Students can use a word processor to prepare a large-print reader's script of their selection. Entering the text of a selection exactly as it is written can help students focus on the text on a word-by-word level. Suggest that students then set a large font size, such as twenty-four points, for their reader's script. Printing out extra copies allows students to make draft and final marked-up copies.

EL Support for English Learners

Students may wish to ask an English speaker to read the selection aloud in order to clarify specific pronunciations or conventional intonations. Point out that marked-up copies of the selection can include pronunciation reminders. To give students confidence to make bold reading choices, model two readings, one mumbled and lacking energy, the other strong and lively. Emphasize that an interested audience will respond to the speaker's energy and pay less attention to small errors.

**Common Core
State Standards**

• Language 4.a, 5, 6

Words From Mythology and Religious Traditions

1. Teach the skills, using the instruction and chart on the student page.

2. If possible, demonstrate the use of an electronic dictionary on computers in a lab or the classroom.

Think Aloud: Model the Skills

Say to students:

Learning about word origins can help me remember what a word means. It can also help me use the word correctly when I talk or write. When I look up the word *nemesis* in a dictionary, I find out that it means "a bitter enemy, especially one that cannot be beaten." The chart on this page tells me where the word comes from: Nemesis was a Greek goddess who punished humans. That origin explains why a nemesis is an enemy: people would certainly feel that someone who always punishes them was an enemy. It also explains why a nemesis is unbeatable: a human is no match for a goddess.

Practice

Answers:

1. c. If you are *jovial,* you might feel *happiness;* if you are afraid, you might feel *panic.*

2. b. A *mentor* is a teacher; a *nemesis* is an *enemy.*

....

Vocabulary Workshop

Words from Mythology and Religious Traditions

Many of the words in the English language have their origins in Greek or Roman mythology or the Bible. They entered the language during the Renaissance, a time when translations of classical and Biblical works became more readily available. Knowing the story behind the figure or event from which an English word developed will help you to infer its meaning and remember it more clearly.

For example, Hercules was an ancient Greek hero noted for his strength and his undertaking of enormous physical tasks. The word *herculean* derives from the qualities of this mythological hero, as seen in the sentence "*I was unable to face the herculean chore of cleaning my room.*" Based on the story of Hercules, you can figure out that the job of cleaning the room is huge and challenging. The chart below provides information on the mythological or Biblical origins of some common words.

**Common Core
State Standards**

Language
4.a. Use context as a clue to the meaning of a word or phrase.
5. Demonstrate understanding of word relationships in word meanings.
6. Acquire and use accurately general academic and domain-specific words and phrases, sufficient for reading, writing, speaking, and listening at the college and career readiness level.

Word	Origin	Myth
jovial	Roman	**Jove,** the chief Roman god, was believed to be the source of happiness.
mentor	Greek	In Homer's *Odyssey,* the goddess Athena disguises herself as **Mentor,** a human male, and guides Telemachus while his father is away.
nemesis	Greek	**Nemesis** was the goddess who punished mortals for their crimes against the gods.
panic	Greek	**Pan** was the god of untamed nature. His sudden appearance and the sound of his music inspired fear.
scapegoat	Biblical	An **escape goat** was sent into the wilderness to carry away the sins of the people.
tantalize	Greek	**Tantalus,** punished for murdering his son, was surrounded by food and water that moved out of reach whenever he wanted them.

Practice

Directions: Refer to the chart above to complete the **analogies.** Then, write an explanation of the word relationships for each pairing.

1. jovial : happiness :: _____ : panic

   a. dark   **b.** run   **c.** afraid   **d.** wild

2. mentor : _____ :: nemesis : enemy

   a. lead   **b.** teacher   **c.** friend   **d.** student

Directions: Make a four-column chart tracing the origins of each word below. The column heads should read: "Word," "Meaning Today," "Origin," "Sample Sentence." Use a dictionary as necessary.

   1. dire   2. spartan   3. nectar

1. Word: *dire.* Meaning Today: "dreadful, desperate." Origin: The Greek word *deinos,* meaning "terrible." Sample Sentence: The circumstances were so dire that any outcome would be terrible.

2. Word: *spartan.* Meaning Today: "spare; severe; simple." Origin: The city of Sparta was known for its strict social order and frugality. Sample Sentence: The spartan room had no decorations.

3. Word: *nectar.* Meaning Today: "liquid produced by flowering plants." Origin: In Greek mythology, nectar was the drink that maintained the gods' immortality. Sample Sentence: Flowering plants produce nectar that attracts insects and birds to assist in pollination.

Vocabulary Acquisition and Use: Context Clues

Sentence Completion questions appear in most standardized tests. They are designed to test your ability to understand what a word means from its *context*, or the way it is used in a text. In these types of questions, you are given sentences with one or more missing words. Your task is to choose the correct word or words to complete each sentence logically. Try using the following strategy: (1) Define each word in the answer options. (2) Identify clues to the meanings of words that are unfamiliar. For example, identify root words, prefixes, suffixes, or related words. (3) Test possible meanings by plugging them into the original sentence.

Practice

This exercise is modeled after the Sentence Completion exercises that appear in the Critical Reading section of the SAT.

Directions: Each of the following sentences is missing one or two words. Choose the word or set of words that best completes each sentence.

Test-Taking Tip
Later questions in this section of the test are more difficult than earlier ones.

1. The untrained soldiers, a loose _____ of men, heard a _____ and surged forward.
   A. monopoly . . . tempest
   B. aggregation . . . commotion
   C. congregation . . . spy
   D. regiment . . . bark
   E. amalgamation . . . whisper

2. The officers in the tent rose in _____ when their commander entered.
   A. insubordination
   B. alarm
   C. deference
   D. condemnation
   E. disgust

3. Many in the audience yawned as the _____ speaker droned on.
   A. intrepid
   B. prodigious
   C. compelling
   D. garrulous
   E. fervent

4. The frowning judge _____ banged the gavel to _____ the lawyer's statement.
   A. peremptorily . . . forestall
   B. aggressively . . . permit
   C. repeatedly . . . encourage
   D. happily . . . punctuate
   E. playfully . . . contradict

5. The philosopher cautioned that fame is a(n) _____ goal.
   A. transporting
   B. transparent
   C. transient
   D. transcendental
   E. transitional

6. Before dying, the miserly loner made sure to write his own _____ .
   A. epigram
   B. epitaph
   C. epigraph
   D. epitome
   E. epistle

Differentiated

Instruction   for Universal Access

EL Support for English Language Learners
In some multiple-choice items, such as items 5 and 6, the answer choices are words that appear to be closely related. Encourage students to look at the word parts that are different. For example, in item 5, all answer choices contain the prefix *trans-,* but only one answer fits logically in the sentence. Point out that sounding out each word silently may help students recognize meanings.

Practice

1. Introduce the skill, using the instruction on the student page. Be sure students understand how context clues can reveal the meaning of an unknown word.

2. You may wish to go over the first item with students, helping them use prior knowledge to define unfamiliar words. Read the first item to the class, including all of the answer choices. Emphasize that both words in the answer must fit in the sentence. As you read the list of choices a second time, ask students to raise their hands when they think a choice might work. Analyze the answer choices as a class:

   A—A group of soldiers would not be called a "monopoly." (Eliminate)

   B—Correct answer. A group of soldiers might be called a loose aggregation; if they heard a commotion they might surge forward.

   C—The entire group would not surge forward if they heard a spy. (Eliminate)

   D—A regiment would not be loose; it would not move forward if it heard a bark. (Eliminate)

   E—The group would not move forward because it heard a whisper. (Eliminate)

3. Assign the remaining items in the Practice Test. Point out that some questions require pairs of words, rather than a single word, for completion. Allow students 6 minutes to complete the questions.

Answers:
1. B
2. C
3. D
4. A
5. C
6. B

Test-Taking Practice

In this Assessment Workshop (pp. 680–683), students apply the skills in Unit 3. The practice is divided into three sections.

1. Before assigning each section, review the relevant unit skills with students. Discuss the characteristics of each type of test and specific strategies for test questions, using the instruction that precedes each practice.

2. Set a time limit for the multiple-choice items in each practice, allowing a little over 1 minute per question. Use the designated time allowance set for the Timed Writing section.

3. Administer each section. Have students write the starting time at the top of their papers. When half of the time for the multiple-choice items has run out, ask students to write the time next to the answer on which they are working. Have them make similar notes when three-quarters of the time has expired and again when time is up. Follow a similar procedure for the Timed Writing assignment.

4. Review with students the pacing reflected in their notes.

Reteaching

Have students complete each practice. Then use the Reteach charts to determine which skills require reteaching, based on the items students answer incorrectly. Reteach these skills prior to assigning **Benchmark Test 5, (Unit 3 Resources,** pp. 263–268).

Question	Pages to Reteach
1	626
2	569
3	650
4	552
5	614
6	552
7	626
8	650
9	552
10	478, 626

Test-Taking Practice

Reading Test: Humanities Passage

Humanities passages are one type of reading selection found on standardized tests. These passages may be excerpts from essays, biographies, or memoirs and address diverse topics including the arts, philosophy, and literary criticism. Questions may focus on main ideas and supporting details, the author's tone and style, or on the meanings of particular words or sentences. Some questions may require you to make generalizations or think about causes and effects.

 Common Core State Standards

RL.11-12.3, RL.11-12.5, RL.11-12.6; RI.11-12.1, RI.11-12.4, RI.11-12.6; L.11-12.1, L.11-12.2, L.11-12.3, L.11-12.4.a.
[For the full wording of the standards, see the standards chart in the front of your textbook.]

Practice

The following exercise is modeled after the ACT Reading Test, Humanities section. The full test has 40 questions.

Directions: Read the following passage from Frederick Douglass's *My Bondage and My Freedom*. Then, choose the *best* answer to each question.

Passage 1

It is easy to see, that, in entering upon the duties of a slaveholder, some little experience is needed. Nature has done almost nothing to prepare men and women to be either slaves or slaveholders. Nothing but rigid training, long persisted in, can perfect the character of the one or the
5 other. One cannot easily forget to love freedom; and it is as hard to cease to respect that natural love in our fellow creatures. On entering upon the career of slaveholding mistress, Mrs. Auld was singularly deficient; nature, which fits nobody for such an office, had done less for her than any lady I had known. It was no easy matter to induce her to
10 think and to feel that the curly-headed boy, who stood by her side, and even leaned on her lap; who was loved by little Tommy, and who loved little Tommy in turn; sustained to her only the relation of a chattel. I was *more* than that, and she felt me to be more than that. I could talk and sing; I could laugh and weep; I could reason and remember; I could
15 love and hate. I was human, and she, dear lady, knew and felt me to be so. How could she, then, treat me as a brute, without a mighty struggle with all the noble powers of her own soul. That struggle came, and the will and power of the husband was victorious. Her noble soul was overthrown; but, he that overthrew it did not, himself, escape the
20 consequences. He, not less than the other parties, was injured in his domestic peace by the fall.

Strategy

• Look for words and phrases that convey the author's attitude toward the subject. Such words may be clues to nuances in the author's intended meaning or point of view.

Strategies for Test Taking

Very often, as in the sample item on this page, the process of elimination will help students narrow down answers. Explain to students that usually one answer among the choices is blatantly wrong. In the case of reading-comprehension questions, the blatantly wrong answer might directly contradict something in the passage and so should be ruled out immediately. In addition, if the question asks about the passage as a whole, answer options that refer to only a part of the passage must also be wrong.

1. Which of the following statements best summarizes lines 1–6?
   A. Human history has a long record of slavery.
   B. Slavery is an unnatural condition for both owner and slave.
   C. Slaveholders who treat slaves kindly have been taught to do so.
   D. Slaveholders are uncaring, cruel people.

2. In the context of lines 1–9, it can reasonably be inferred that *singularly* means:
   F. alone.
   G. on one occasion.
   H. notably.
   J. lonely.

3. Which best explains what Douglass means by calling Mrs. Auld "deficient" (line 8)?
   A. She suffered from a disability.
   B. She lacked financial resources.
   C. She wasted few resources when running the home.
   D. She lacked a certain characteristic.

4. In the context of the passage, it can reasonably be inferred that "little Tommy" (lines 11 and 12) is:
   F. Mrs. Auld's favorite pet.
   G. Mrs. Auld's child.
   H. a slave like Douglass.
   J. a neighbor.

5. Which best describes Douglass's overall opinion of Mrs. Auld?
   A. She was a kindly woman with a generous nature.
   B. She was a stiff and uncompromising person.
   C. She stood up to her husband, defying him.
   D. She was difficult to live with due to wild mood swings.

6. In the context of the first part of the passage, it can reasonably be inferred that *chattel* (line 12) means:
   F. a lowly creature.
   G. a kind of house.
   H. constant talking.
   J. a piece of property.

7. The ideas expressed in lines 9 through 15 can best be described as:
   A. Douglass's view of his own situation at the time.
   B. what Douglas came to believe as an adult.
   C. Mrs. Auld's rationale for treating Douglass well.
   D. the general attitude of Southerners toward slaves.

8. In the context of lines 9–21, it can reasonably be inferred that:
   F. Mrs. Auld's treatment of Douglass changed.
   G. Mr. Auld was convinced to be kind to Douglass as well.
   H. Douglass ran away from the home.
   J. Mrs. Auld suffered a nervous breakdown.

9. In the context of lines 18–21, which best describes Mr. Auld's "injury"?
   A. He was struck in the head by a falling object.
   B. The tranquility of his home was shattered.
   C. His wife turned against him.
   D. All his slaves revolted against him.

10. Which of the following statements best describes the structure of the passage?
    F. It begins with an arresting anecdote and then draws general principles from that incident.
    G. It contains several general arguments and supporting details to substantiate each one.
    H. It opens with a generalization that helps explain the events that follow.
    J. It follows a chronological structure and ends with a surprising twist.

GO ON

Test-Taking Practice **681**

Differentiated
Instruction for Universal Access

Support for Less Proficient Readers
Read the entire passage with the class, and help students summarize the paragraph. Encourage students to break the paragraph into three parts: lines 1–6, lines 6–16, lines 16–21. Explain that breaking a long paragraph into smaller sections can help students focus on the meaning of groups of lines.

Review the ten questions, making sure that students understand "context" (items 2, 4, 6, and 8); "inferred" (items 2, 4, 6, 8, and 9); and "structure" in item 10. Allow students to ask clarifying questions about any of the question choices, being careful not to reveal correct answers.

ASSESS

Reading Test
Humanities Passage

1. Introduce the skill using the instruction on page 680. Be sure students understand the strategy set off in the boxed section.

2. You may wish to go over the first test item with students before they take the test. Have students read the paragraph silently, then, as a class, analyze each choice in the first test item.

   A—The passage does not refer to a long history of slavery. (Eliminate)

   B—Correct answer. The main idea of the lines is that "nature has done almost nothing to prepare" people to be slaves or slaveholders. Therefore, it is unnatural.

   C—These lines say nothing about slaveholders who treat slaves kindly. (Eliminate)

   D—The author argues that people must learn to be slaveholders, not that slaveholders are cruel and uncaring. (Eliminate)

3. Assign the practice exercise. Have students read the passage and answer the questions on their own. Allow 15 minutes for this process, and announce to students when they have 5 minutes and 1 minute remaining.

Answers
1. B
2. H
3. D
4. G
5. A
6. J
7. C
8. F
9. B
10. H

681

Grammar and Writing
Editing in Context

1. Introduce the skill using the instruction on the student page. Be sure students understand the strategy set off in the boxed section.

2. Read the first paragraph of the practice passage; then, go over the first test item with students, modeling the strategy of narrowing the answer options.

3. Point out that *but* is a conjunction linking two independent clauses, so some punctuation is required. Because some change is needed, students can eliminate choice A. Choice D can be eliminated because it begins a sentence with a conjunction. Students can then decide between choices B and C. They should recall that it is correct to use a comma before a conjunction that links two independent clauses, so choice B is correct.

4. Have students complete questions 2–8 on their own. Allow them 8 minutes to complete the questions.

Grammar and Writing: Editing in Context

Editing-in-context segments test your understanding of grammar and sentence structure. You may be presented with a reading passage that has numbered sentences, some of which contain errors in grammar, style, or usage. Your task is to choose the best way to correct each sentence.

Practice

The exercise is modeled after the ACT English Test, which usually has 75 questions.

Directions: For each underlined sentence or portion of a sentence, choose the best alternative. If an item asks a question about the underlined portion, choose the best answer to the question.

Strategy

Narrow the answer options.
Make your task simpler by eliminating any answers you know to be incorrect.

[1]

Lincoln begins the Second Inaugural Address <u>formally but he</u> ends with an
eloquent plea for reconciliation. <u>In the opening paragraph</u>, his use
of the passive voice and refusal even to identify himself as an actor in the
inaugural drama give the passage a stiff formality. <u>This</u> matches his
understated message, which is that he has nothing to say about the previous
four years that he <u>hasn't</u> said already.

[2]

When <u>he begins</u> discussing slavery, though, Lincoln injects a moral
seriousness into the address that is reinforced by his growing eloquence.
<u>Speculated</u> that the war might be divine retribution for decades of
suffering endured by enslaved African Americans <u>his speech</u> uses
language and rhythms that deepen the impact of his message. Then the
opening words of his final paragraph suggest a vision of reconciliation made
memorable by his cadences—<u>"With malice toward none; with charity for
all"</u>—and the contrasting absolutes of "none" and "all." Lincoln
concludes by expressing his sense of mission for the remainder of the war—
"to bind up the nation's wounds" and to "achieve a just and lasting peace,
among ourselves, and with all nations."

682 Division, Reconciliation, and Expansion (1850–1914)

Strategies for Test Taking

Point out to students that in editing-in-context tests, some editing choices are dependent on previous answers. For example, in this test, items 6 and 7 relate to changes in the same sentence. Be sure that students understand that they should choose answers for these questions that reflect the entire revised sentence. Encourage students to review their choices for both questions by silently reading the sentence with both answer choices in place.

1. **A.** NO CHANGE
   B. formally, but
   C. formally; but,
   D. formally. But

2. What is the function of this phrase?
   F. independent clause
   G. adverbial prepositional phrase
   H. adverbial dependent clause
   J. adjectival phrase

3. **A.** NO CHANGE
   B. This strategy
   C. This passive construction
   D. This formality

4. **F.** NO CHANGE
   G. has not
   H. have not
   J. hadn't

5. While reviewing Paragraph 2, the author considers deleting these two words. If the writer were to do so, the sentence would lose:
   A. the idea that the eloquence starts with the discussion of slavery.
   B. the idea that Lincoln views slavery as a moral evil.
   C. the idea that Lincoln delayed discussing slavery for much of the speech.
   D. nothing; they should be deleted.

6. **F.** NO CHANGE
   G. Speculating
   H. Lincoln speculated
   J. Asserted

7. **A.** NO CHANGE
   B. his speeches
   C. he speaks
   D. Lincoln

8. In reviewing the draft, the author considers moving this phrase to follow "his final paragraph" in the preceding line. If the writer were to do so, the effect would be:
   F. to misquote Lincoln and distort his meaning.
   G. to gain clarity about which phrases the author has in mind.
   H. to lose the author's emphasis on the rhythm of the phrases.
   J. to underscore Lincoln's moral message.

⏱ Timed Writing: Position Statement [30 minutes]

The Civil War was the first war that people were able to witness through photographs. Some might say that images of war are important because they convey much more than words alone. Others might hold that showing pain and destruction is coldhearted and disrespectful to the victims.

Write an essay in which you express and support an opinion on this question. Whichever side you take, cite specific reasons and examples to support your position. This exercise is similar to the optional ACT Writing Test.

> **Academic Vocabulary**
>
> To "express and support an opinion" you must first decide **what** you think, and then tell **why** you think it.

STOP

1. B
2. G
3. C
4. G
5. A
6. G
7. D
8. G

⏱ Timed Writing

Position Statement

1. Go over the two paragraphs of the timed writing assignment on the student page.

2. Tell students that they can quickly formulate a thesis statement for their position by completing one of the following sentence starters: "I feel that it is important to show images of war because . . . ." or "I feel that it is disrespectful to show images of war because . . . ." Students should complete the statement with a clear statement of opinion.

3. Encourage students to budget adequate time for prewriting and revising/editing. Students should spend about 8 minutes in the prewriting stage, 12 minutes drafting, and 5 minutes revising and editing. Reinforce this by announcing elapsed time at the 8-, 12-, and 20-minute marks as students respond to the assignment.

4. Use the **Rubrics for Writing for Assessment Essays,** in *Professional Development Guidebook,* pages 258–259, to evaluate students' work.

Benchmark

Reteach skills as indicated by students' performance, following the Reteach charts on pages 680 and 683. Then administer the end-of-unit **Benchmark Test 5** (*Unit 3 Resources,* pp. 255–260). Follow the **Interpretation Guide** for the test (*Unit 3 Resources,* p. 264) to assign reteaching pages as necessary in the *Reading Kit.* Use the built-in tracking software at **www.PHLitOnline.com** to automatically assign these pages.

Reteach

Question	Pages to Reteach
1	613
2	613
3	613
4	613
5	613
6	613
7	585
8	585

The **Benchmark Tests** are available online at **www.PHLitOnline.com.**

Performance Tasks

Assigning Tasks/Reteaching Skills

Use the chart below to choose appropriate Performance Tasks by identifying which tasks assess lessons in the textbook that you have taught. Use the same lessons for reteaching when students' performance indicates a failure to fully master a standard. For additional instruction and practice, assign the *Common Core Companion* pages indicated for each task.

Task	Where Taught/Pages to Reteach	Common Core Companion Pages
1	650	28–40, 196–207
2	448, 516, 552, 676	41–53, 123–135, 196–207
3	478, 516, 552	136–142, 196–207
4	594, 626	61–67, 143–155, 278–285
5	518, 527	170–176, 297–303
6	478, 650	28–40, 61–67, 297–303

Assessment Pacing

In assigning the Writing Tasks, allow a class period for the completion of a task. As an alternative, assign tasks as homework. In assigning the Speaking and Listening Tasks, consider having students do required preparation as homework. Then, allow a class period for the presentations.

Evaluating Performance Tasks

Use the rubric at the bottom of this page to evaluate students' mastery of the standards in their Performance Task responses. Review the rubric with students before they begin work so they know the criteria by which their work will be evaluated.

Performance Tasks

Follow the instructions to complete the tasks below as required by your teacher. As you work on each task, incorporate both general academic vocabulary and literary terms you learned in this unit.

© **Common Core State Standards**

RL.11-12.3, RL.11-12.6, RL.11-12.9; RI.11-12.1, RI.11-12.4, RI.11-12.6, RI.11-12.9; W.11-12.2, W.11-12.9.a, W.11-12.9.b; SL.11-12.1, SL.11-12.4, SL.11-12.6
[For the full wording of the standards, see the standards chart in the front of your textbook.]

Writing

© **Task 1: Literature [RL.11-12.3; W.11-12.2]**
Analyze Characterization in a Story

Write an essay in which you analyze the character development in a story from this unit.

- Choose a story from this unit with memorable characters.

- Describe one of the main characters. Then, provide at least two examples of indirect and at least two examples of direct characterization from the story to support your description.

- Identify the setting and point of view of the story. Analyze the role each of these choices plays in influencing the development of the main character you chose.

- Describe how the story's plot events influence the main character's development.

- Conclude by briefly restating the impression that the main character creates for the reader and evaluating which story element (setting, point of view, or plot) has the greatest influence in creating that impression.

© **Task 2: Literature/Informational Text [RL.11-12.4; RI.11-12.4; W.11-12.2]**
Analyze Word Choice

Write an essay in which you analyze the meaning and impact of the word choices in a work of fiction or nonfiction from this unit.

- Choose a work from this unit in which the writer uses a variety of interesting word choices.

- Choose particular passages in the work in order to highlight ones that you find especially effective.

- Analyze word choice by interpreting the meaning of key language in each passage and explaining why it is effective.

- Distinguish between literal meanings and figurative and connotative meanings in each passage you choose. Explain how figurative and connotative meanings add to the power of the passage and the overall work.

- Conclude by explaining how the word choice creates a tone and meaning that is appropriate to the author's audience and purpose.

© **Task 3: Informational Text [RI.11-12.5; W.11-12.2]**
Analyze and Evaluate Text Structure

Write an essay in which you analyze and evaluate the effectiveness of the structure of a work of literary nonfiction from this unit.

- Choose a work of literary nonfiction from this unit that has a clear organizational structure.

- Identify and analyze the structure of the author's argument. For example, does the author use cause and effect, comparison and contrast, or main idea and details?

- Evaluate the effectiveness of the structure for conveying the author's main argument. Assess whether the structure makes individual points clear and helps make the overall argument convincing.

- Support your analysis with examples from the work.

- Organize your ideas logically, using transitional words, phrases, and clauses to clearly show the link between ideas.

Performance Task Rubric: Standards Mastery	Rating Scale
	not very very
Critical Thinking: How clearly and consistently does the student pursue the specific mode of reasoning or discourse required by the standard, as specified in the prompt (e.g., comparing and contrasting, analyzing, explaining)?	1 2 3 4 5
Focus: How well does the student understand and apply the focus concepts of the standard, as specified in the prompt (e.g., development of theme or of complex characters, effects of structure, and so on)?	1 2 3 4 5
Support/Elaboration: How well does the student support points with textual or other evidence? How relevant, sufficient, and varied is the evidence provided?	1 2 3 4 5
Insight: How original, sophisticated, or compelling are the insights the student achieves by applying the standard to the text(s)?	1 2 3 4 5
Expression of Ideas: How well does the student organize and support ideas? How well does the student use language, including word choice and conventions, in the expression of ideas?	1 2 3 4 5

Speaking and Listening

Task 4: Literature/Informational Text [RL.11-12.6; RI.11-12.6; SL.11-12.1]

Analyze Irony

*Hold a **panel discussion** in which you analyze various authors' use of irony in works from this unit.*

- Identify all works from this unit in which irony features prominently.

- As a group, discuss why each selection you choose is ironic and identify the type of irony it represents.

- Evaluate what the author's use of irony adds to the theme or meaning of each selection.

- Finally, compare a single author's use of irony in one selection with another author's use of irony in a work from the same unit or in something else you have read or seen.

- Make sure that each person on the panel gets an opportunity to speak. Allow time for follow-up questions and debate, and try to build on each other's ideas to reach a final consensus.

Task 5: Informational Text [RI.11-12.9; SL.11-12.4]

Evaluate a Work of Nonfiction and Two Foundational Documents

*Deliver an **oral presentation** in which you assess whether the social injustices described by Frederick Douglass in the excerpt from* My Bondage and My Freedom *were addressed by the Emancipation Proclamation and the Fourteenth Amendment.*

- Review the excerpt from *My Bondage and My Freedom.* Identify the individual injustices that Douglass describes in the excerpt.

- Find the texts of the Emancipation Proclamation and the Fourteenth Amendment online or in print.

- Analyze and compare the purposes, themes, and language of the autobiographical account and the two historical documents.

- Assess the two documents to determine whether they address Douglass's grievances completely, partially, or not at all.

- Organize and present your findings logically, so your audience can easily follow your reasoning.

Task 6: Literature [RL.11-12.3, RL.11-12.6; SL.11-12.4]

Identify and Analyze Point of View

*Deliver an **oral presentation** in which you identify and analyze the point of view in a work of fiction from this unit.*

- Choose a story that effectively uses point of view.

- Identify point of view by describing whether a story is written from a first- or third-person and limited or omniscient perspective. Explain to your audience how you made this determination.

- Analyze the impact of the author's choice of point of view on the story. Do this by relating point of view to other elements in the story, such as character development or plot, and to the use of devices such as irony or understatement.

- Present your ideas in a way that makes them easy for listeners to follow.

THE ESSENTIAL ? What makes American literature American?

Primary Sources and Fiction Primary sources, such as journals and speeches, speak to readers with great immediacy, even centuries after they were written. They help us understand how people experienced life in the past. Short stories and poems also shed light on people's sense of identity and aspects of their culture at a particular time in history, but their effect is often different from that of a primary source.

Assignment Choose one primary source and one work of fiction from this unit. Write a **compare-and-contrast essay** about how the two works add to your understanding of American identity during the Civil War era.

Supporting Speaking and Listening

1. Consider having students work with partners or in groups to complete Performance Tasks involving listening and speaking. For tasks that you assign for individual work, you may still wish to have students rehearse with partners, who can provide constructive feedback.

2. As students rehearse, have them keep in mind these tips:
   - Present findings and evidence clearly and concisely.
   - Observe conventions of standard English grammar and usage.
   - Be relaxed and friendly but maintain a formal tone.
   - Make eye contact with the audience, pronounce words clearly, and vary your pace.
   - When working with a group, respond thoughtfully to others' positions, modifying your own in response to new evidence.

Linking Performance Tasks to Independent Reading

If you wish to cover the standards with students' independent reading, adapt Performance Tasks of your choice to the works they have selected. (Independent reading suggestions appear on the next page.)

THE ESSENTIAL ? What makes American literature American?

1. Remind students of the Essential Question, "What makes American literature American?"

2. Have students complete their responses to the prompt on the student page. Point out that they have read selections in this unit about the Civil War and Frontier eras and that they should draw on these selections in their responses. Remind them that they can also draw on their own experiences and what they have learned in other subject areas in formulating their answers.

Differentiated Instruction   for Universal Access

Strategy for Less Proficient Readers

Assign a Performance Task, and then have students meet in groups to review the standard assessed in that task. Remind students of the selections or independent readings to which they have previously applied the standard. Have groups summarize what they learned in applying the standard and then present their summaries. Discuss, clarifying any points of confusion. After students have completed their tasks, have groups meet again to evaluate members' work. Encourage members to revise their work based on the feedback they receive.

EL Strategy for English Learners

For each assigned Performance Task, review the instructions with students. Clarify the meaning of any unfamiliar vocabulary, emphasizing routine classroom words such as *interpretation* and *persuasiveness* and academic vocabulary such as *inference.*

Next, have students note ideas for their responses. Pair students, and have them review each other's notes, asking questions to clarify meaning and suggesting improvements. Encourage students to ask for your assistance in supplying English words or expressions they may require.

Independent Reading

Titles featured on the Independent Reading pages at the end of each unit represent a range of reading, including stories, dramas, and poetry, as well as literary nonfiction and other types of informational text. Throughout, labels indicate the works that are CCSS Exemplar Texts. Choosing from among these featured titles will help students read works at increasing levels of text complexity in the grades 11–12 text complexity band.

Using Literature Circles

A literature circle is a temporary group in which students independently discuss a book.

Use the guidance in the *Professional Development Guidebook*, pp. 47–49, as well as the teaching notes on the facing page, for additional suggestions for literature circles.

Ⓒ Meeting Unit 3 CCS Standards

Students can use books listed on this page to apply and reinforce their mastery of the CCS Standards covered in this unit.

Introducing Featured Titles

Have students choose a book or books for independent reading. Assist them by previewing the titles, noting their subject matter and level of difficulty. **Note:** Before recommending a work to students, preview it, taking into account the values of your community as well as the maturity of your students.

Featured Titles

In this unit, you have read a variety of literature of the Civil War and Frontier eras. Continue to read works related to these eras on your own. Select books that you enjoy, but challenge yourself to explore new topics, new authors, and works offering varied perspectives or approaches. The titles suggested below will help you get started.

LITERATURE

The Adventures of Huckleberry Finn
Mark Twain

Novel Set in pre-Civil War Missouri, this influential novel describes the adventures of two runaways on a raft on the Mississippi River—Huck Finn, who is escaping his abusive father, and Jim, a slave hoping to gain his freedom.

[Works by Twain begin on page 570 of this book. Build knowledge by reading a novel by this author.]

My Ántonia
Willa Cather

Novel The story of Ántonia, a self-reliant, spirited young woman growing up on the Nebraska frontier, is told by her friend and confidant, Jim Burden. *My Ántonia* chronicles their friendship and reveals both the beauty and hardship of frontier life.

[Cather's "A Wagner Matinée" appears on page 652 of this book. Build knowledge by reading a novel by this author.]

Spoon River Anthology
Edgar Lee Masters

Poetry The former residents of an Illinois town, now long dead, tell the stories of their lives from the graveyard in which they lie.

[On pages 646 and 647, you'll find "Lucinda Matlock" and "Richard Bone," two of the poems from Spoon River Anthology. *Build knowledge by reading the complete anthology.]*

INFORMATIONAL TEXTS

Historical Texts

The Classic Slave Narratives
edited by Henry Louis Gates, Jr.

Autobiographical Narrative This book presents the accounts of two men and two women who had been enslaved and describes their extraordinary experiences, ranging from surviving the dangerous Atlantic Crossing to enduring the brutal, and often short, life of a slave in the Caribbean colonies and in America.

Narrative of the Life of Frederick Douglass
Frederick Douglass

Autobiographical Narrative Born into slavery, Frederick Douglass escaped to become an abolitionist leader as well as a gifted writer and orator. This narrative describes the cruelty of slavery and gives a powerful voice to a disenfranchised people.

[An excerpt from My Bondage and My Freedom *appears on page 520 of this book. Build knowledge by reading Douglass's autobiographical narrative.]*

The American Reader: Words That Moved a Nation
edited by Diane Ravitch
HarperCollins, 1990   **EXEMPLAR TEXT** Ⓒ

Prose and Poetry This collection of prose and poetry by famous and ordinary Americans from different socioeconomic and racial backgrounds provides the reader with a rich view of American culture and history.

Contemporary Scholarship

Empire Express: Building the First Transcontinental Railroad
David Haward Bain

History On May 10, 1868, the last spike was driven to complete the transcontinental railroad. *Empire Express* describes the race to complete the railroad and presents a fresh view of the history and impact of this engineering triumph.

What They Fought For 1861–1865
James McPherson
Anchor Books, 1995   **EXEMPLAR TEXT** Ⓒ

History Scholar James McPherson investigates what motivated Civil War soldiers to fight, based on their letters and journals. Through the voices of these long-dead soldiers, McPherson gives readers a strong sense of the intense passions and ideological conflicts of the time.

686 Division, Reconciliation, and Expansion (1850–1914)

Ⓒ Text Complexity: Aligning Texts With Readers and Tasks

TEXTS	READERS AND TASKS
• *The Adventures of Huckleberry Finn* (Lexile: 980L) • *Spoon River Anthology*	**Below-Level Readers** Allow students to focus on reading for content, and challenge them to interpret multiple perspectives.
• *My Antonia* (Lexile: 1010L) • *The Classic Slave Narratives* • *Narrative of the Life of Frederick Douglass* (Lexile: 1080L) • *What They Fought For 1861–1865*	**Below-Level Readers** Challenge students as they read for content. **On-Level Readers** Allow students to focus on reading for content, and challenge them to interpret multiple perspectives. **Advanced Readers** Allow students to focus on interpreting multiple perspectives.
• *Empire Express* • *The American Reader* (Lexile: 1260L)	**On-Level Readers** Challenge students as they read for content. **Advanced Readers** Allow students to focus on reading for content, and challenge them to interpret multiple perspectives.

Preparing to Read Complex Texts

Reading for College and Career In both college and the work-place, readers must analyze texts independently, draw connections among works that offer varied perspectives, and develop their own ideas and informed opinions. The questions shown below, and others that you generate on your own, will help you more effectively read and analyze complex college-level texts.

Ⓒ Common Core State Standards

Reading Literature/Informational Text

10. By the end of grade 11, read and comprehend literature, including stories, dramas, and poems, and literary nonfiction, in the grades 11-CCR text complexity band proficiently, with scaffolding as needed at the high end of the range.

When reading analytically, ask yourself...

- What idea, experience, or story seems to have compelled the author to write? Has the author presented that idea, experience, or story in a way that I, too, find compelling?
- How might the author's era, social status, belief system, or personal experiences have affected the point of view he or she expresses in the text?
- How do my circumstances affect what I understand and feel about this text?
- What key idea does the author state explicitly? What key idea does he or she suggest or imply? Which details in the text help me to perceive implied ideas?
- Do I find multiple layers of meaning in the text? If so, what relationships do I see among these layers of meaning?
- How do details in the text connect or relate to one another? Do I find any details unconvincing, unrelated, or out of place?
- Do I find the text believable and convincing?

Ⓒ Key Ideas and Details

- What patterns of organization or sequences do I find in the text? Do these patterns help me understand the ideas better?
- What do I notice about the author's style, including his or her diction, use of imagery and figurative language, and syntax?
- Do I like the author's style? Is the author's style memorable?
- What emotional attitude does the author express toward the topic, the story, or the characters? Does this attitude seem appropriate?
- What emotional attitude does the author express toward me, the reader? Does this attitude seem appropriate?
- What do I notice about the author's voice—his or her personality on the page? Do I like this voice? Does it make me want to read on?

Ⓒ Craft and Structure

- Is the work fresh and original?
- Do I agree with the author's ideas entirely, or are there elements I find unconvincing?
- Do I disagree with the author's ideas entirely, or are there elements I can accept as true?
- Based on my knowledge of American literature, history, and culture, does this work reflect the American tradition? Why or why not?

Ⓒ Integration of Ideas

Independent Reading **687**

Ⓒ Text Complexity: Reader and Task Support Suggestions

INDEPENDENT READING

Increased Support Suggest that students choose a book that they feel comfortable reading and one that is a bit more challenging.

Pair a more proficient reader with a less proficient reader and have them work together on the more challenging text. Partners can prepare to read the book by reviewing questions on this student page. They can also read difficult passages together, sharing questions and insights. They can use the questions on the student page to guide after-reading discussion.

Increased Challenge Encourage students to inte-grate knowledge and ideas by combining the Essential Questions and the unit concepts in their approach to two or more featured titles.

For example, students might compare and contrast the ways in which the *Narrative of the Life of Frederick Douglass*—a primary source—and *The Adventures of Huckleberry Finn*—a work of fiction—help us understand how people experi-enced life in the time period they describe.

Preparing to Read Complex Texts

1. Tell students they can be attentive readers by bringing their experi-ence and imagination to the texts they read and by actively questioning those texts. Explain that the questions they see on the student page are examples of types of questions to ask about works of fiction and nonfiction.

2. Point out that, like writing, reading is a "multidraft" process, involving several readings of com-plete works or passages, revising and refining one's understanding each time.

Ⓒ Key Ideas and Details

3. Review and amplify the second bulleted point in the Key Ideas and Details box. **Ask:** What key ideas and details in the text illustrate this point of view?

   Possible response: Students may cite ideas and details that are directly related to the author's background, or details that convey a contrast with the author's background.

Ⓒ Craft and Structure

4. Focus on the first bulleted point in the Craft and Structure box. Point out that some authors out-line extensively before writing while others simply follow the story where it leads them.

   Ask: How might each approach affect the final text?

   Possible response: Following an outline could lead to a better organized text. Following the story could produce a more interesting story.

Ⓒ Integration of Ideas

5. **Ask:** How might identifying ideas as unconvincing affect your reading of a text?

   Possible response: Determining why these ideas are not persuasive can lead to a greater understanding of the entire text.

6. Finally, explain to students that they should cite key ideas and details, examples of craft and struc-ture, or instances of the integration of ideas as evidence to support their points during a discussion of works of American literature. After hearing the evidence, the group might reach a consensus or might agree to disagree.

687

Index of Authors and Titles

Note: Page numbers in *italics* refer to biographical information for authors, or commentary for titles; nonfiction and informational text appears in red.

Index of Skills

Boldface numbers indicate pages where terms are defined.

Literary Analysis

Action, rising/falling, **796**, **1026**, **1123**, 1158, **1449**

Actors, **1116**

Acts (drama), **1116**

Ad hominem, **197**, **953**

Address (speech), **96**

Advertisements, **952**

Allegory, **530**, 541, **756**, 762, **1216**, 1219, 1230, 1234, **R24**

Alliteration, **402**, 403, **1056**, 1061, **R24**

Allusion, **98**, 101, 108, 541, **706**, 709, 714, **R24**

Ambiguity, **270**, **676**, **R24**. *See also* Irony

Analogy, **196**, **376**, 390, **R24**

Analysis, **R18**

Analytic rubrics, **R44**

Anapest, **R28**

Anaphora, **96**, **425**, 430, 438

Antithesis, **96**, **97**, **1102**, 1105, 1113

APA (American Psychological Association) Style, **R23**

Aphorisms, **139**, 152

Apostrophe, **866**, 871

Appeals. *See* Persuasive techniques

Archetypal criticism, **R18**

Archetypal literary elements, **R24**

Archetype, **18**, **84**, 92

Archetype of the quest, **846**, 850, 853, 854, 857

Argument, lxiv–lxvii, lxx–lxxi, **196**, **448**, **1260**

Argument/support structure, **1102**, 1113

Assonance, **402**, **1056**, 1061, **R24**

Atmosphere. *See* Mood

Audience, **1456**

Authority, appeal to, **110**, **196**

Author's insights
   drama (Miller), **1120**, 1126, 1135, 1165, 1196
   oral tradition (Power), **32**, 35, 36, 38
   short story (O'Brien), **808**, 811, 812, 813
   See also Scholar's insights

Author's opinion, **1116**, 1117

Author's perspective, **982**, 989, 993, **1456**

Author's purpose
   essays, **1374**, 1375
   general/specific, **56**, 62, 64, 66, **552**, 557
   information texts, **242**
   information/public/private, **516**, **517**, **518**, 528
   print media, **1456**

Author's style
   analysis, **676**
   Carver's, **1324**, 1328, 1330, 1331, 1332

Cummings's, **778**, 782, 783
Dickinson's, **406**, **407**
Hemingway's, **798**, 805, 807
narrative nonfiction, **516**
Thoreau's, **376**, 380, 385, 390
Whitman's, **424**

Autobiographical essay, 165

Autobiographical narrative, **188**

Autobiographical writing, **157**

Autobiography, **139**, 141, 143, 145, 152, 165, **517**, 528, **928**, 937

Ballad, **764**, **R24**

Bandwagon, **197**, **1260**

Bias, **R20**

Biased accounts, **516**, 517

Biblical allusion, **530**, 541, **1160**, 1163, 1175, 1179, 1182

Biographical criticism, **R18**

Biography, **516**

Blank verse, **872**, 877, 880, 883, 886, **R25**

Blog, **421**, **R47**

Blogroll, **R48**

Business letter, **R38**

Camera angles, **1265**

Cartoon, **1000**

Catalogue, use of, in poetry, **424**, 438

Causality, false, **197**

Cause and effect, **667**

Central idea, **1374**

Challenging the text, 364

Character study, **357**

Characterization, direct/indirect, **R25**, **728**, 732, 734, 741, 743, 744, 748, 749, 753
   comic story, **226**, 232, 233, 237, 240
   contemporary fiction, **1310**, 1313, 1321
   drama, **1186**, 1188, 1189, 1191, 1200, 1201, 1206, 1214
   short story, **650**, 654, 655, 657, 662, **796**, **1010**, 1014, 1016, 1018, 1019, 1024

Characters, **728**, 753, **796**, **1116**, **R25**. *See also* Comic characters; Grotesque characters

Chronological order, **46**, 55, **190**, 667

Cinquain, **R25**

Citation organizer, online, **938**

Climax, **190**, **796**, **1026**, 1038, **1123**, 1158, **1449**, **R25**

College application essay, **R34**

Comedy, **R25**.

Comic characters, 587

Comic uses of language, **569**

Comments, blog, **R47**, **R48**

Commission, **242**

Comparison-and-contrast essay, **1392**, 1397

Conceit, **80**, 83

Concrete images, **449**

Conflict, internal/external, **R25**
   autobiographical narrative, **190**
   drama, **1160**, 1162, 1164, 1167, 1173, 1182
   short story, **594**, 598, 604, 606, 607, 609, 611, **814**, 819, 822, 826, 830

Connotation, **909**, **1050**, **R25**, **R54**

Consonance, **403**, **1056**, 1061, **R25**

Consumer guide, **392**

Controversial Issues, **1116**, 1117

Copyright, **R55**

Couplet, **402**, **R25**, **R32**

Cover letter, **R35**

Critical perspectives (types), **901**

Critical review, **1250**

Cultural identity, **913**

Culture, 1264

Culture-centric terms, **R20**

Dactyl, **R28**

Debate, **R55**

Deductive reasoning, **196**, **1258**

Denotation, **909**, **R25**

Description, **796**, **R26**

Descriptive essay, **1374**

Details, **516**, **764**

Development, **1026**

Dialect, **569**, 582, **858**, **928**, 937, **1310**, 1316, 1319, 1321, **R26**

Dialogue, **449**, **928**, 937, **1116**, **1450**, **R26**

Diary, **492**, **516**

Diction, **516**, **796**, **1374**, **R26**
   patriotic writing, **536**, 539, 543
   persuasive speech, **448**
   poetry, **1070**, 1077
   Safire's style, **1376**, 1381
   Whitman's style, **425**, 429, 430, 438
   Writer's Toolbox, **445**

Dimeter, **R28**

Discussion (defined), small group, **R55**

Document, **764**

Documentary, **R55**

Drama, **1116**, **R26**

Dramatic exposition, **1123**, 1127, 1129, 1138, 1146, 1147, 1151, 1158

Dramatic irony. *See* Irony

R68 Index of Skills

Index of Skills **R71**

Vocabulary

Student Edition Pages

Writing

Research and Technology

Index of Features

Student Edition Pages

Acknowledgments

Acknowledgments continued from copyright page.

William Harvey "Playing for the Fighting Sixty-Ninth" by William Harvey from *Playing for the Fighting Sixty-Ninth.* Copyright © 2001 by William Harvey. Used by permission.

Historical Museum of Southern Florida "Museum Mission/History" from *http://www.hmsf.org.* Copyright © Historical Museum of Southern Florida. Used by permission.

The Barbara Hogenson Agency, Inc. "The Night the Ghost Got In" by James Thurber. Copyright © 1933, 1961 by James Thurber, © Rosemary Thurber. Used by permission.

Henry Holt and Company, Inc. "Acquainted with the Night" by Robert Frost from *The Poetry of Robert Frost* edited by Edward Connery Latham. Copyright © 1956 by Robert Frost. Copyright 1928, © 1969 by Henry Holt and Co. "The Gift Outright" by Robert Frost from *The Poetry of Robert Frost.* Copyright 1942 by Robert Frost, © 1970 by Lesley Frost Ballantine, © 1969 by Henry Holt & Company. "Stopping By Woods on a Snowy Evening" by Robert Frost from *The Poetry of Robert Frost,* edited by Edward Connery Lathem. Copyright 1951 by Robert Frost, © 1923, 1969 by Henry Holt and Company. Used by permission of Henry Holt and Company, LLC.

Houghton Mifflin Company, Inc. "Ambush" from *The Things They Carried by Tim O'Brien.* Copyright © 1990 by Tim O'Brien. "Ars Poetica" from Collected Poems, 1917–1982 by Archibald MacLeish. Copyright © 1985 by The Estate of Archibald MacLeish. "Courage" by Anne Sexton from *The Awful Rowing Toward God* by Anne Sexton. Copyright © 1975 by Loring Conant, Jr., Executor of the Estate of Anne Sexton. Used by permission of Houghton Mifflin Company. All rights reserved.

Hyperion From *Cold Mountain: The Screenplay* by Anthony Minghella, based on a novel by Charles Frazier. Copyright © 2003 by Anthony Minghellla. Used by permission of Hyperion. All rights reserved.

International Creative Management, Inc. "One Day, Now Broken in Two" by Anna Quindlen from *Newsweek.* Copyright © 2002 by Anna Quindlen. First appeared in *Newsweek.* "Life in His Language" by Toni Morrison from *James Baldwin.* Copyright © 1989 by Toni Morrison. Published in James Baldwin: The Legacy (Quincy Troupe, ed.), Simon & Schuster, 1989. Copyright © 1989 by Simon & Schuster. Used by permission of International Creative Management, Inc.

Athena Kildegaard "untitled" poem by Athena Kildegaard used from *Rare Momentum,* Red Dragonfly Press, 2006, by permission of the author.

The Estate of Dr. Martin Luther King, Jr. c/o Writer's House LLC From "Letter from Birmingham Jail" by Dr. Martin Luther King, Jr. from *A Testament of Hope:The Essential Writings of Martin Luther King, Jr.* Used by arrangement with the Heirs to the Estate of Martin Luther King, Jr. c/o Writers House as agent for the proprietor. Copyright 1963 Martin Luther King, Jr.; renewed 1991 Coretta Scott King.

Galway Kinnell "Reckless Genius" by Galway Kinnell from *http://www.salon.com.* Used by permission.

Alfred A. Knopf, Inc. "Dream Variations" by Langston Hughes from *The Selected Poems of Langston Hughes.* Copyright © 1926 by Alfred A. Knopf, Inc. and renewed 1954 by Langston Hughes. "I, Too" by Langston Hughes from *The Selected Poems of Langston Hughes.* Copyright © 1994 by the Estate of Langston Hughes. "Refugee in America" by Langston Hughes from *The Selected Poems of Langston Hughes.* Copyright © 1943 by The Curtis Publishing Company. "The Negro Speaks of Rivers" by Langston Hughes from *Selected Poems of Langston Hughes.* Copyright © 1926 by Alfred A. Knopf, Inc. and renewed 1954 by Langston Hughes. From "The Woman Warrior" by Maxine Hong Kingston from *The Woman Warrior.* Copyright © 1975, 1976 by Maxine Hong Kingston. "Of Modern Poetry" by Wallace Stevens from *The Collected Poems of Wallace Stevens.* Copyright 1942 by Wallace Stevens and renewed 1970 by Holly Stevens from by Wallace Stevens. "Of Plymouth Plantation" by William Bradford from Of Plymouth Plantation 1620–1647 by William Bradford, edited by Samuel Eliot Morison, copyright 1952 by Samuel Eliot Morison and renewed 1980 by Emily M. Beck. From "Hiroshima" by John Hersey. Copyright 1946 and renewed 1974 by John Hersey. Used by permission of Alfred A. Knopf, a division of Random House, Inc. Excerpt from *The American Language,* 4th Edition by H.L. Mencken. Copyright © 1919, 1921, 1923, 1936 by Alfred A. Knopf, Inc. All rights reserved.

The Landmark Project "Son of Citation Machine and Landmarks Son of Citation Machine Masthead" from *http://citationmachine.net.* Copyright © 2006 by David Warlick & The Landmark Project. Used by permission of The Landmark Project.

League of Women Voters "How to Watch a Debate" from *www.lwv.org.* The material in this publication on "How to Watch a Debate" was excerpted from a League of Women Voters of the United States (LWVUS) online document of the same title, located at www.lwv.org, with express permission of the LWVUS for this one-time use in Pearson Prentice Hall Literature 8e Program. Secondary users must request permission directly from the LWVUS, the copyright owner. Copyright © 2007 League of Women Voters. All rights reserved. Used by permission.

Patricia Lee Lewis "(0)" by Patricia Lee Lewis.

Liveright Publishing Corporation "anyone lived in a pretty how town" by E. E. Cummings from *Complete Poems, 1904–1962.* Copyright 1940, © 1968, 1991 by the Trustees for the E.E. Cummings Trust. "old age sticks" by E. E. Cummings. Copyright 1958 © 1986, 1991 by the Trustees for the E. E. Cummings Trust, from *Complete Poems: 1904–1962* by E. E. Cummings, edited by George J. Firmage. "Frederick Douglass" by Robert Hayden. Copyright © 1966 by Robert Hayden, from *Collected Poems of Rober Hayden* by Robert Hayden, edited by Frederick Glaysher. "Runagate Runagate" by Robert Hayden from *The Collected Poems of Robert Hayden* by Robert Hayden, edited by Frederick Glaysher. Copyright © 1966 by Robert Hayden. "Storm Ending" by Jean Toomer from Cane. Copyright 1923 by Boni & Liveright, renewed 1951 by Jean Toomer. Used by permission of Liveright Publishing Corporation.

Los Angeles Times Syndicate "Hysteria Resides at Heart of the Frantic Crucible" by Kenneth Turan from Los Angeles Times, 12/13/96. Copyright © 1996 The Times Mirror Company, Los Angeles Times. Used by permission.

Ludlow Music c/o The Richmond Organization (TRO) "Dust Bowl Blues" Words and Music by Woody Guthrie TRO-© Copyright 1964 (Renewed) 1977 Ludlow Music, Inc., New York, NY Used by permission.

The Estate of Edgar Lee Masters "Lucinda Matlock" by Edgar Lee Masters from *The Spoon River Anthology.* Permission by Hilary Masters.

The Miami Herald "Crucible Casts a Newly Contempo rary Spell/Free from Chains of McCarthyism, Arthur Miller's Classic Soars" by Rene Rodriguez from *The Miami Herald,* 12/20/96. Copyright © 1996 The Miami Herald. Used by permission.

Milkweed Editions "Museum Indians" by Susan Power from *Roofwalker* (Minneapolis: Milkweed Editions, 2002). Copyright © 2002 by Susan Power. Used with permission from Milkweek Editions.

Navarre Scott Momaday From "The Names" by N. Scott Momaday. Copyright © by N. Scott Momaday. Used by permission.

New Directions Publishing Corporation From "A Retrospect: Few Don'ts By an Imagiste" by Ezra Pound, from *The Literary Essays of Ezra Pound,* copyright © 1935 by Ezra Pound. "Constantly Risking Absurdity" by Lawrence Ferlinghetti from *These Are My Rivers: New and Selected Poems 1955–1993.* Copyright © 1955, 1958, 1959, 1960, 1961, 1964, 1966, 1967, 1968, 1969, 1971, 1972, 1975, 1976, 1977, 1978, 1979, 1981, 1984, 1988, 1993 by Lawrence Ferlinghetti. All rights reserved. "The Great Figure" by William Carlos Williams from *Collected Poems: 1909–1939, Volume I,* copyright © 1938 by New Directions Publishing Corp. "Heat" by H. D. from *Collected Poems, 1912–1944,* copyright © 1982 by The Estate of Hilda Doolittle. "In a Station of the Metro" by Ezra Pound from *Personae,* copyright © 1926 by Ezra Pound. "Pear Tree" by H. D. from *Collected Poems, 1912–1944,* copyright © 1982 by The Estate of Hilda Doolittle. "The Red Wheelbarrow" by William Carlos Williams from *Collected Poems: 1909–1939, Volume 1,* copyright © 1938 by New Directions Publishing Corp. "The Secret" by Denise Levertov from *Poems 1960–1967.* Copyright © 1964 by Denise Levertov Goodman. "This is Just to Say" by William Carlos Williams from *Collected Poems 1909–1939, Volume I,* copyright © 1938 by New Directions Publishing Corp. Used by permission of New Directions Publishing Corp.

New York Times Agency "At the Theater/The Crucible" by Brooks Atkinson from *The New York Times,* January 23, 1953. Copyright © 1953 by the New York Times Co. "Onomatopoeia" originally titled "Zapmanship" by William Safire from *You Could Look It Up.* Copyright 1984, The New York Times. "The Nation: Backing the Attack" from *The New York Times,* September 12, 1943. Copyright © The New York Times. "Rock of the Modern Age, Arthur Miller is Everywhere" by Mel Gussow from *diversityjobmarket.com.* Used by permission and protected by the copyright Laws of the United States. The printing, copying, redistribution, or retransmission of the material without express written permission is prohibited.

Newmarket Press From "Good Night, and Good Luck: The Screenplay and History behind the Landmark Movie". Screenplay by George Clooney and Grant Heslov. Copyright © 2005 by Section Eight Production. Used by permission of Newmarket Press, 18 East 48th Street, New York, New York 10017. www.newmarketpress.com.

Naomi Shihab Nye "Streets" by Naomi Shihab Nye from *Words Under the Words: Selected Poems.* Copyright © Naomi Shihab Nye. Used by permission.

Harold Ober Associates, Inc. "A Black Man Talks of Reaping" by Arna Bontemps from *American Negro Poetry.* Copyright © 1963 by Arna Bontemps. Used by permission of Harold Ober Associates Incorporated.

Gregory K. Pincus "Fib" by Gregory K. Pincus, originally posted online at *http://gottabook.blogspot.com/2006/04/fib.html.* Used by permission of the author.

Popular Photography Magazine From "The Assignment I'll Never Forget" by Dorothea Lange from *Popular Photography,* February 1960, Vol. 46, No. 2. Copyright © Popular Photography, 1960.

Princeton University Press From "Walden" by Henry David Thoreau. Copyright © 1971 by Princeton University Press, 1999 renewed PUP, 1989 paperback edition. Used by permission of Princeton University Press.

Sean Ramsay "Urban Renewal" by Sean Ramsay. Copyright © 2001 by Sean Ramsay. Used by permission.

Random House, Inc. "A Rose for Emily" by William Faulkner from *Collected Stories of William Faulkner* copyright © 1930 and renewed © 1958 by William Faulkner. "The Unknown Citizen", copyright 1940 & copyright renewed 1968 by W.H. Auden from Collected Poems by W.H. Auden. Used by permission of Random House, Inc. "A Raisin in the Sun" by Lorraine Hansberry. Copyright © 1958 by Robert Nemiroff, as an unpublished work. Copyright © 1959, 1966, 1984, by Robert Nemiroff.

Random House, Inc. & Sterling Lord Literistic, Inc. "Man Listening to Disc" by Billy Collins from Random House Trade Paperbacks. Copyright © 2001 by Billy Collins. Used by permission.

Schomburg Center for Research in Black Culture "The Tropics in New York" by Claude McKay from *The Poems of Claude McKay.* Courtesy of the Literary Representative for the Works of Claude McKay, Schomburg Center for Research in Black Culture, The New York Public Library, Astor, Lenox and Tilden Foundations. Used by permission.

Scribner, an imprint of Simon & Schuster "In Another Country" by Ernest Hemingway from *Men Without Woman.* Copyright 1927 by Charles Scribner's Sons. Copyright renewed 1955 by Ernest Hemingway. Used by permission of Scribner, an imprint of Simon & Schuster Adult Publishing Group. "Poetry" by Marianne Moore from *The Collected Poems of Marianne Moore.* Copyright © 1935 by Marianne Moore, copyright renewed © 1963 by Marianne Moore and T.S. Eliot. Used with the permission of Scribner, an imprint of Simon & Schuster Adult Publishing Group.

Simon & Schuster, Inc. "1776" by David McCullough from Chapter 3, "Dorchester Heights." New York: Simon & Schuster, 2005. All rights reserved.

South Florida Water Management District "Kissimmee River Restoration and Upper Basin Initiatives" by Staff from *2007 South Florida Environmental Report.* Copyright © 2007 South Florida Water Management District. Courtesy of South Florida Water Management District. Used by permission.

Donald D. Stanford "Huswifery" from *The Poems of Edward Taylor* ed. by Donald E. Stanford, University of North Carolina Press, 1989. Copyright © 1960, renewed 1988 by Donald E. Stanford.

State of California—Dept. of Parks and Recreation "Archaelogical Site Record" from *http://ohp.parks.ca.gov.* Used by permission.

The Statue of Liberty-Ellis Island Foundation, Inc. "Statue of Liberty-Ellis Island Foundation Mission and Background" from *www.statueofliberty.org.* Copyright © The Statue of Liberty-Ellis Island Foundation, Inc. *www.ellisisland.org.* Used by permission.

Sterling Lord Literistic, Inc. "Mission Update blog" by Steve Squyres from *http://athena.cornell.edu/news/mubss/.* Used by permission of SLL/Sterling Lord Literistic, Inc. Copyright by Steven Squyres.

Syracuse University Press "The Iroquois Constitution" from *Arthur C. Parker on the Iroquois: Iroquois Uses of Maize and Other Food Plants, The Code of Handsome Lake; The Seneca Prophet; The Constitution of the Five Nations* by Arthur C. Parker, edited by William N. Fenton (Syracuse University Press, Syracuse, NY, 1981). Copyright © 1968 by Syracuse University Press.

Thompson and Thompson From "The Dark Tower" by Countee Cullen. Published in *Copper Sun* © 1927 Harper & Bros, NY. Renewed 1954 by Ida M. Cullen. Copyrights held by Amistad Research Center, Tulane University. Administered by Thompson and Thompson, New York, NY. Used by permission.

Anthony Thwaite "When I went to visit" by Ki no Tsurayuki translated by Geoffrey Bownas and Anthony Thwaite from *The Penguin Book of Japanese Verse*. Penguin Books copyright © 1964, revised edition 1998. Translation copyright © Geoffrey Bownas and Anthony Thwaite, 1964, 1998. Used by permission.

Charlie Todd "Surprise! Subway Birthday" by Charlie Todd and improve everywhere.com Copyright © 2002. Used by permission of Charlie Todd.

The University of Chicago Press "America's Epic" by James Miller, Jr. from Whitman: A Collection of Critical Essays. Copyright © 1957 by The University of Chicago. © 1962 by Prentice Hall, Inc.

University of Nebraska Press "Crossing the Great Divide" by Meriweather Lewis from *The Journals of the Lewis and Clark Expedition, volume 5*. Edited by Gary E. Moulton, used by permission of the University of Nebraska Press. Copyright © 1988 by the University of Nebraska Press.

University of North Carolina Press "To His Excellency, General Washington" by Phillis Wheatley from *The Poems of Phillis Wheatley*. Edited and with an introduction by Julian D. Mason Jr. Copyright © 1966 by the University of North Carolina Press, renewed 1989. Used by permission of the publisher. www.uncpress.unc.edu.

University of North Texas "Help North Texas Vote" from *http://www.eac.gov.*

Viking Penguin, Inc. "The Turtle (Chapter 3)" by John Steinbeck from The Grapes of Wrath. Copyright © 1939, renewed copyright © 1967 by John Steinbeck. "The Crucible" by Arthur Miller from *The Crucible*. Copyright 1952, 1953, 1954, renewed © 1980, 1981, 1982 by Arthur Miller. Used by permission of Viking Penguin, a division of Penguin Books USA Inc. CAUTION: Professionals and amateurs are hereby warned that "The Crucible" being fully protected under the copyright laws of the United States of America, the British Commonwealth countries, including the Dominion of Canada, and the other countries of the Universal Copyright and Berne Conventions, are subject to royalty. All rights, including professional, amateur, motion picture, recitation, lecturing, public reading, radio, television and cable broadcasting, and the rights of translation into foreign languages, are strictly reserved. Particular emphasis is laid on the question of readings, permission for which must be secured in writing. Any inquiries for The Crucible should be addressed to Viking Penguin, 375 Hudson Street, NY, NY 10014.

Virginia Department of Historic Resources "Virginia Department of Historic Resources Archaeological Site Inventory Form" from Virginia Department of Historic Resources. Used by permission.

Patricia Vogel "untitled" (Fibonacci poem) by Patricia Vogel. Used by permission of the author.

W. W. Norton & Company, Inc. "Halley's Comet" by Stanley Kunitz from *Passing Through: The Later Poems,* New and Selected. Copyright © 1995 by Stanley Kunitz. Used by permission of W.W. Norton & Company, Inc. Copyright © 1985 by Stanley Kunitz. "Who Burns for the Perfection of Paper" by Martin Espada from *City of Coughing and Dead Radiators*. Copyright © 1993 by Martin Espada. Used by permission of W. W. Norton & Company, Inc.

Wesleyan University Press "Camouflaging the Chimera" by Yusef Komunyakaa from *Neon Vernacular*. From Dien Cai Dau (Wesleyan University Press, 1988). Used by permission of Wesleyan University Press.

Wikipedia.org "Kennedy Space Center" from *http://en.wikipedia.org/wiki/Kennedy_Space_Center;* retrieved from http://en.wikpedia.org accessed on 07/06/07. "Atlanta Braves" from *http://en.wikipedia.org/wiki/Atlanta_Braves;* retrieved from http://en.wikpedia.org accessed on 07/06/07. "Mojave Desert" from *http://en.wikipedia.org/wiki/Mojave_desert;* retrieved from http://en.wikpedia.org accessed on 07/06/07.

The Wylie Agency, Inc. "Everything Stuck to Him" by Raymond Carver from *What We Talk About When We Talk About Love*. Copyright © 1981 by Tess Gallagher, used with the permission of the Wylie Agency. "Journey to the Crucible" by Arthur Miller, first published in *The New York Times*, February 8,1953 © 1953 by Arthur Miller. Copyright renewed 2008 by The Arthur Miller Estate, used with the permission of The Wylie Agency Inc.

Yale University Press From "Sinners in the Hands of an Angry God" by Jonathan Edwards from *The Sermons of Jonathan Edwards: A Reader* published by Yale University Press. Copyright © 1999 by Yale University Press. From "Mary Chesnut's Civil War" by Mary Chesnut edited by C. Vann Woodward. Copyright © 1981 by C. Vann Woodward, Sally Bland Metts, Barbara G. Carpenter, Sally Bland Johnson, and Katherine W. Herbert. All rights reserved. Used by permission of the publisher, Yale University Press.

Note: Every effort has been made to locate the copyright owner of material reproduced on this component. Omissions brought to our attention will be corrected in subsequent editions.

Credits

Photo Credits

xlvi: gallimaufry/Shutterstock; **1:** ©Imtek Imagineering/ Masterfie; **5:** © Sandra Templeton/Stock; **1:** The Art Archive / Gift of Mrs. Karl Frank / Buffalo Bill Historical Center, Cody, Wyoming / 14.86; **2:** b. Courtesy of the Library of Congress; **2:** Library of Congress; 4: l. Bettmann/CORBIS; **4:** r. Bettmann/ CORBIS; **5:** l. The Gallery Collection/CORBIS; **5:** r. Blue Lantern Studio/CORBIS; **6:** r. The Granger Collection, New York; **6:** l. Lee Snider/Photo Images/CORBIS; **7:** t. The Granger Collection, New York; **7:** bl. Bettmann/CORBIS; **7:** br. Scala/Art Resource; **8:** l. Burstein Collection/CORBIS; **8:** r. istockphoto.com; **9** br. Chris Hillier/CORBIS; **9:** t. istockphoto.com; **9:** bl. The Granger Collection, New York; **10:** l. Bettmann/CORBIS; **10:** r. Blue Lantern Studio/CORBIS; **10:** m. Bettmann/ CORBIS; **11:** r. The Granger Collection, New York; **11:** l. istockphoto.com; **12:** m. The Gallery Collection/CORBIS; **12:** r. Cynthia Hart Designer/CORBIS; **12:** l. The Granger Collection, New York; **13:** r. Francis G. Mayer/CORBIS; **13:** l. Gerrit Greve/CORBIS; **15:** r. Photo by Rebecca Dallinger; Courtesy of Susan Power; **15:** t. Michael Storrings; **16:** Smithsonian American Art Museum, Washington, DC / Art Resource, NY; **17:** Smithsonian American Art Museum, Washington, DC / Art Resource, NY; **21:** Mary Ann McDonald?CORBIS; **23:** istockphoto.com; **24:** © /Masterfile (Royalty-Free Div.); **26:** l. Yva Momatiuk/CORBIS; **26:** r. istockphoto. com; **27:** CORBIS; **30:** Julie Downing and Grahame Corbett/© Dorling Kindersley; **32:** The Granger Collection, New York; **32:** t. Photo by Rebecca Dallinger; Courtesy of Susan Power; **32:** rm. The Grass Dancer, Susan Power. Penguin Putnam, Inc. Copyright © 1994 by Susan Power; **32:** bl. The Roofwalker, Susan Power. Milkweed Editions. †Â 2002, Text by Susan Power. Cover and Interior design by Dale Cooney. Cover painting, *Migrations*, oil, 1996 by Ojibwe artist Jim Denomie; **34:** ©Brooklyn Museum/CORBIS; **35:** istockphoto.com; **37:** The Old Guitarist, 1903, Pablo Picasso, Spanish, 1881–1973, oil on panel 122.9 x 82.6 cm, Helen Birch Bartlett Memorial Collection, 1926.253. Reproduction, The Art Institute of Chicago, ©2004 Estate of Pablo Picasso/Artists Rights Society (ARS), New York; **38:** Buffalo Bill Historical Center; Cody, Wyoming; Gift of Hon. and Mrs. William Henry Harrison; NA. 202.70; **39:** DLILLC/CORBIS; **41:** John Kahionhes Fadden; **42:** CORBIS; **42:** bkgrnd. istockphoto.com; **43:** W. Perry Conway/CORBIS; **46: 50:** Courtesy Catholic Archives of Texas, Austin; **52:** © Daryl Benson/Masterfile; **53:** David Muench/CORBIS; **55:** Geoffrey Clements/CORBIS; **56:** The Granger Collection, New York; **57:** Bettmann/CORBIS; **60:** Bettmann/CORBIS; **61:** istockphoto.com; **68:** Ric Francis/epa/CORBIS; **69:** Denis Scott/CORBIS; **70 :** NASA/Handout/Getty Images; **70–71:** b. Getty Images; **71:** inset AP/Wide World Photos; **73:** Pilgrims Going to Church, George Henry Boughton, Collection of The New-York Historical Society; **75:** The Granger Collection, New York; **76:** istockphoto.com; **77:** Anne Bradstreet , The Tenth Muse Lately Sprung Up in America, Ladonna Gulley Warrick, Courtesy of the artist; **78:** m. Mimmo Jodice/CORBIS; **78:** t. The Granger Collection, New York; **78:** bl. Demetrio Carrasco © CONACULTA-INAH-MEX. Authorized by the Instituto Nacional de Antropologia e Historia; **78:** br. Dance of Apollo with the Nine Muses (tempera on panel), Peruzzi, Baldassarre (1481–1536) / Palazzo Pitti, Florence, Italy, Alinari / The Bridgeman Art Library; **85:** CORBIS; **86: 0087:** b. istockphoto.com; **87:** t. istockphoto.com; **89:** ©North Wind/North WInd Picture Archives; **90–91:** istockphoto.com; **95:** George Washington (1732–1799) (colour litho) by John Trumbull (1756–1843) (after); Private Collection/ Peter Newark American Pictures/ The Bridgeman Art Library; Nationality / copyright status: American / out of copyright;**96:** The Granger Collection, New York; **99:** National Portrait Gallery, Smithsonian Institution / Art Resource, NY; **99:** inset istockphoto.com; **100:** ©Superstock; **104:** Bettmann/CORBIS; **106:** Swim Ink 2, LLC/CORBIS; **111:** John Elk III/Getty Images; **112:** National Archives and Records Adminisitration; **112:** inset istockphoto.com; **116:** The Granger Collection, New York; **117:** The Granger Collection, New York; **118:** The Granger Collection, New York; **123:** Bettmann/CORBIS; **124:** Liberty and Washington, New York State Historical Association, Cooperstown; **129:** David Young-Wolff/PhotoEdit; **131:** David Young-Wolff/PhotoEdit; **132:** AP/Wide World Photos; **132:** b. istockphoto.com; **132:** b. istockphoto.com; **132:** t. istockphoto.com; **132:** t. istockphoto.com; **134:** The Granger Collection, New York; **135:** l. The Granger Collection, New York; **135:** m. The Granger Collection, New York; **135:** r. The Granger Collection, New York; **136:** l. Photo by Michael J. Deas/Time Magazine/Time & Life Pictures/ Getty Images; **136:** r. The Granger Collection, New York; **137:** m. The Granger Collection, New York; **137:** r. The Granger Collection, New York; **137:** l. The Granger Collection, New York; **138:** tm. The Granger Collection, New York; **138:** br. Courtesy of the Bakken Library, Minneapolis; **138:** tr. The Granger Collection, New York; **138:** tl. The Granger Collection, New York; **140:** Christieís Images/SuperStock; **146:** t. Richard Cummings/CORBIS; **146:** br. Liberty Kids is a registered trademark of DIC Entertainment Corp. Used under license. All rights reserved; **146:** bl. Accoutrements LLC; **146:** bm. istockphoto.com; **148:** The Granger Collection, New York; **149:** The Granger Collection, New York; **151:** tl. The Granger Collection, New York; **151:** bl. Seattle Art Museum, Gift of Katherine White and the Boeing Company. Photo by Paul Macapia; **151:** br. Seattle Art Museum, Gift of Katherine White and the Boeing Company. Photo by Paul Macapia; **152:** © The New Yorker Collection 1965 William Hamilton from cartoonbank.com. All Rights Reserved.; **153:** Hulton-Deutsch Collection/ CORBIS; **156: #6:** Getty Images; **156: #8:** Bassouls Sophie/CORBIS; **156: #10:** AP/ Wide World Photos; **156: #4:** The Granger Collection, New York; **156: #2:** Bettmann/CORBIS; **156: #3:** Bettmann/CORBIS; **156: #7:** Rune Hellestad/CORBIS; **156: #1:** Bettmann/ CORBIS; **156: #5:** Getty Images; **156: #9:** AP/Wide World Photos; **158:** AP/Wide World Photos; **159:** DK Limited/CORBIS; **160–161:** border Michael Storrings; **161:** Rivera, Diego (1866–1957). The grinder (La molendera). 1926. Oil on canvas, 35 7/16 x 46 1/16 in. Museo Nacional de Arte Moderno, Instituto Nacional de Bellas Artes, Mexico City, D.F., Mexico. © Banco de Mexico Diego Rivera & Frida Kahlo Museums Trust. Av. Cinco de Mayo No. 2, Col. Centro, Del. Cuauhtemoc 06059, Mexico, D.F. Reproduction authorized by the Instituto Nacional de Bellas Artes y Literatura. Courtesy of Art Resource, NY; **162:** © JUPITERIMAGES/ PHOTOS.COM / Alamy; **162–163:** border Michael Storrings; **164:** b. © Imagebroker / Alamy; **164:** t. Michael Storrings; **166:** t.

R82 Credits

Staff Credits

The people who made up the Pearson Prentice Hall Literature team—representing design, editorial, editorial services, education technology, manufacturing and inventory planning, market research, marketing services, planning and budgeting, product planning, production services, project office, publishing processes, and rights and permissions—are listed below. Boldface type denotes the core team members.

Tobey Antao, Margaret Antonini, Rosalyn Arcilla, Penny Baker, James Ryan Bannon, Stephan Barth, **Tricia Battipede,** Krista Baudo, Rachel Beckman, Julie Berger, Lawrence Berkowitz, Melissa Biezin, **Suzanne Biron,** Rick Blount, **Marcela Boos, Betsy Bostwick,** Kay Bosworth, Jeff Bradley, Andrea Brescia, Susan Brorein, Lois Brown, **Pam Carey,** Lisa Carrillo, **Geoffrey Cassar,** Patty Cavuoto, Doria Ceraso, Jennifer Ciccone, Jaime Cohen, Rebecca Cottingham, Joe Cucchiara, Jason Cuoco, **Alan Dalgleish, Karen Edmonds, Irene Ehrmann,** Stephen Eldridge, Amy Fleming, Dorothea Fox, Steve Frankel, Cindy Frederick, Philip Fried, Diane Fristachi, Phillip Gagler, **Pamela Gallo,** Husain Gatlin, **Elaine Goldman,** Elizabeth Good, John Guild, Phil Hadad, Patricia Hade, Monduane Harris, Brian Hawkes, Jennifer B. Heart, Martha Heller, John Hill, Beth Hyslip, Mary Jean Jones, Grace Kang, Nathan Kinney, Roxanne Knoll, **Kate Krimsky,** Monisha Kumar, Jill Kushner, Sue Langan, Melisa Leong, Susan Levine, Dave Liston, **Mary Luthi, George Lychock, Gregory Lynch, Joan Mazzeo, Sandra McGloster,** Eve Melnechuk, Kathleen Mercandetti, Salita Metha, Artur Mkrtchyan, Karyn Mueller, Alison Muff, Christine Mulcahy, Kenneth Myett, Elizabeth Nemeth, Stefano Nese, Carrie O'Connor, April Okano, Kim Ortell, Sonia Pap, Raymond Parenteau, Dominique Pickens, Linda Punskovsky, **Sheila Ramsay,** Maureen Raymond, Mairead Reddin, **Erin Rehill-Seker, Renee Roberts, Laura Ross,** Bryan Salacki, Sharon Schultz, Jennifer Serra, Melissa Shustyk, Rose Sievers, Christy Singer, Yvonne Stecky, **Cynthia Summers,** Steve Thomas, Merle Uuesoo, Roberta Warshaw, Patricia Williams, Daniela Velez

Additional Credits

Lydie Bemba, Victoria Blades, Denise Data, Rachel Drice, Eleanor Kostyk, Jill Little, Loraine Machlin, Evan Marx, Marilyn McCarthy, Patrick O'Keefe, Shelia M. Smith, Lucia Tirondola, Laura Vivenzio, Linda Waldman, Angel Weyant

R84 Credits